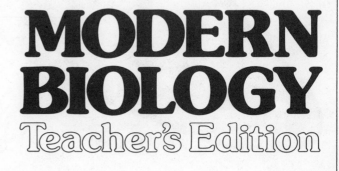

MODERN BIOLOGY
Teacher's Edition

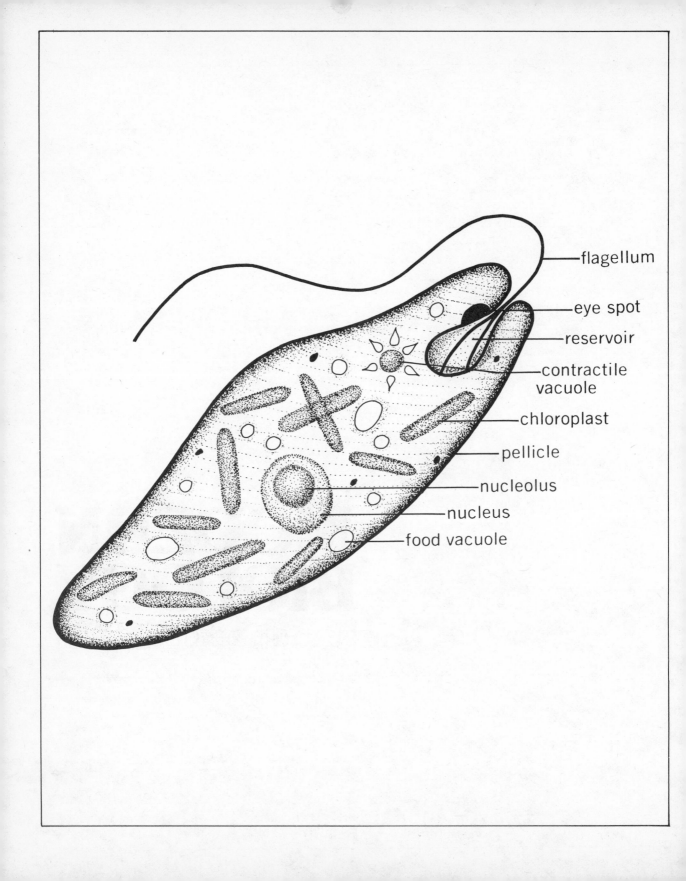

flagellum

eye spot

reservoir

contractile
vacuole

chloroplast

pellicle

nucleolus

nucleus

food vacuole

James H. Otto
Albert Towle
Myra E. Madnick

MODERN BIOLOGY

Teacher's Edition

HOLT, RINEHART AND WINSTON, PUBLISHERS

NEW YORK · LONDON · TORONTO · SYDNEY

James H. Otto

was a biology teacher and head of the Science Department at George Washington High School, Indianapolis, Indiana.

Albert Towle

is a professor of biology and supervisor of biology student teachers at California State University, San Francisco, California.

Myra E. Madnick

is a writer specializing in the biological sciences.

CONTENTS

ALTERNATIVE APPROACHES TO USING MODERN BIOLOGY

The authors have planned MODERN BIOLOGY so that units may be rearranged without loss of course continuity. The division of the subject matter of biology into these eight units allows for the greatest flexibility in approach and presentation technique. A *modular approach* to teaching MODERN BIOLOGY takes full advantage of this flexibility. Each unit can represent one "module," while each chapter represents one "minimodule" or "minicourse." Viewing the content and organization in this way, teachers have at their disposal an entire course divided into 8 modules and 53 minicourses. This modular approach lends itself to a variety of techniques including: contract teaching, team teaching, and lab inquiry.

As modules, each unit may be presented independently and in any sequence. For example, the teacher may want to present a module on *The Nature of Life* and then follow with a module on *Ecological Relationships*. Some schools prefer to shift the study of insects to the early part of the fall semester so that live specimens may be more easily obtained. Many teachers prefer to cover *Genetics* at the end of the course. This module could then be scheduled for the final weeks of school.

Each module represents a complete course in its particular subject area. The teacher may emphasize one module with one class, while spending less time or deleting that same module with another class.

Within each unit, the chapters may be treated with the same flexibility. Although the authors feel that the chapters are presented in a logical sequence, the teacher has the option of rearranging or deleting certain chapters. Each chapter is a self-contained "minicourse" with its own objectives and tests.

BIOLOGY INVESTIGATIONS is correlated with the flexible organization of MODERN BIOLOGY. The investigations are numbered according to the chapters to which they correspond. Each "minicourse" has its own laboratory investigations which relate directly to the chapter. Methods of student evaluation are included in TESTS IN BIOLOGY. Thus, the teacher is provided with a modular biology course, including laboratory and tests. These provide for a unique flexibility that is adaptable to almost any syllabus.

The following is an example of how a teacher may present a module on Ecology at any point during the school year:

MODULE: ECOLOGICAL RELATIONSHIPS (Unit 8) Approximate time: 5–6 weeks

GENERAL PURPOSE: The students should gain an understanding of the complex interactions within the living and nonliving environments and their own role in these interactions.

△**Minicourse 1** Introduction to Ecology (Chapter 48)
  Objectives: see page 635
  Ideas: refer to Teacher's Edition for Teaching Suggestions and Involvement Activities
  Laboratory: BIOLOGY INVESTIGATIONS 48-1
  Student Self-Test: see *Questions for Review* (page 646)
  Test: TESTS IN BIOLOGY (Chapter 48)

△**Minicourse 2**   The Habitat (Chapter 49)

If the social and human implications are to be stressed, then:

△**Minicourse 3**   The Land We Live In (Chapter 52)

△**Minicourse 4**   Forest and Wildlife Resources (Chapter 53)

If the straight biological ecology is stressed, then:

△**Minicourse 3**   Periodic Changes in the Environment (Chapter 50)

△**Minicourse 4**   Biogeography (Chapter 51)

For a complete module on *Ecological Relationships,* cover Unit 8 in the sequence presented in the text.

Another module that is popular with some teachers is a unit on Bioethics or The Quality of Human Life. This module demonstrates how individual chapters may be extracted from the Units and coordinated into a new module.

MODULE: BIOETHICS OR THE QUALITY OF HUMAN LIFE   Approximate time: 12 weeks

GENERAL PURPOSE: The student should gain knowledge and insight into the complex decisions that must be made when the subject of biology is applied at the social level.

△**Minicourse 1**   The Science of Life (Chapter 1)

△**Minicourse 2**   Human History (Chapter 39)

△**Minicourse 3**   Genes in Human Populations (Chapter 11)

△**Minicourse 4**   Applied Genetics (Chapter 12)

△**Minicourse 5**   Infectious Disease (Chapter 17)

△**Minicourse 6**   Tobacco, Alcohol, and Drugs (Chapter 45)

△**Minicourse 7**   Introduction to Ecology (Chapter 48)

△**Minicourse 8**   The Land We Live In (Chapter 52)

MODULE: ZOOLOGY—A SYSTEMIC APPROACH

Some teachers prefer to teach the systemic approach to zoology. This is easily done by having the student find and read the section for a particular system within each chapter in Units 5, 6, and 7. Since these chapters are in order of complexity, the student should start with Chapter 28 and proceed with each chapter through Chapter 38. Then the human system would be covered in the appropriate chapter in Unit 7. Although this method may seem tedious at first, it has the advantage of allowing the student to view each organism as a whole while comparing the systems of the various phyla in their order of complexity. As this process continues, the student finds it easier to locate the particular systems and learns how to organize this information.

MODERN BIOLOGY

Teachers using MODERN BIOLOGY have found the text to be flexible enough to meet the diverse objectives of today's students. The manner in which a high school biology course is to be presented most effectively will be determined by the background and ability of the students composing the class. As a guide in planning an individual curriculum, consideration may be given to: (1) Minimal Course; (2) Average Course; (3) Enriched Course. The following suggestions may be helpful to the teacher in individualizing the course.

	MINIMAL	AVERAGE	ENRICHED
TOPICS	The Nature of Life / Cellular Structure / Cellular Activity / Cellular Reproduction / Heredity / Natural Selection / Diversity of Life / Human Biology / Ecology / Conservation and Pollution Problems	All of the Minimal plus: Biochemistry / Photosynthesis / Respiration / Protein Synthesis / Genetics / Specific Classification and Phylogeny	All of Average plus: more emphasis on individual learning of the concepts and chemistry of photosynthesis, respiration, and protein synthesis.
APPROACH	Some class time for directed reading to help students with reading and comprehension problems. Class time may include activities and special projects.	Use of local examples selected by the teacher. Difficult concepts may be presented by directed reading, while most topics are covered in class discussion after individual reading.	Local examples include those topics in the Average course. Chapter reading assignments are given for homework.
QUESTIONS FOR REVIEW	May be discussed in class after the students have answered them in writing.	Most questions are answered by the individual student but selected topics can be discussed in class.	Students answer these on their own to check comprehension and note questions for class discussion.

PACING GUIDE

	MINIMAL (continued)	AVERAGE (continued)	ENRICHED (continued)
APPLYING PRINCIPLES AND CONCEPTS	Selected questions may be used to initiate discussion.	Used for class discussion to develop comprehension and relate contents to broader concepts.	Assigned as homework and used in class discussion.
RELATED READINGS		Some students may wish to pursue a specific area of interest by using this source.	A valuable source for beginning research on selected topics. Some may be assigned for reading and reports.
BIOLOGY INVESTI-GATIONS	Parts 1 and 2 of selected investigations.	All parts of each investigation to be done. "Investigations on Your Own" may be used for individual projects.	Student assignments and reports may be added from "Investigations on Your Own."
LABORATORY INVESTI-GATIONS	Parts 1 and 2 of selected investigations.	All parts of each investigation to be done. "Investigations on Your Own" may be used for individual projects.	Student assignments and reports may be added from "Investigations on Your Own."

HOW TO
READ BIOLOGY

The following exercises were developed to help students read biology content. These are suggested model exercises and can be applied to content in any unit. The exercises can be used either before, and, or after studying a particular unit. Students of varying ability levels can benefit from working with these exercises.

There are some other techniques which can be used by the students as they read MODERN BIOLOGY 1977. 1) The objectives, chapter, and section titles can be used as an overview guide for each chapter. 2) Recall the guide before reading chapter. 3) Read each section keeping section title in mind. The illustrations and captions should be studied. Special attention should be paid to the boldface new words, terms, and major biological principles. 4) Review the guide, study the captions, and illustrations again. 5) The end-of-chapter materials which serve as a review and as an application to the principles and concepts can help confirm the learning process.

UNIT 1

Many new words have been introduced in this unit. The following exercise in reading comprehension can be used to test understanding of some of these words. Have students fill in the blanks with the words listed under *Key Words*.

KEY WORDS
biogenesis cell theory chemical chemosynthesis control gametes homeostasis
hypothesis physical replication respiration transcription variation zygote

The process by which carbohydrates are organized without using light energy is known as _____ _____ . This process involves a _____ change. However, a _____ change takes place if particle activity and spacing are changed. _____ includes all of the reactions in which energy is released. What kind of change does it represent?

Cellular reproduction is an important aspect of ____ _____ . The process of _____ plays an important role in cell reproduction.

_____ is essential to protein synthesis. A major concept of reproduction is _____ , life coming from life. The life-giving or reproductive units are called _____ . Where these units come together, a _____ is formed. The offspring that results has a greater chance of survival because of _____ .

_____ can be defined as a state of balance in an organism. If one wanted to learn more about this state, a _____ could be suggested. Then a _____ experiment could be devised that would include all factors except the one to be tested.

Answers are given in order of appearance in sentences.

1. chemosynthesis **2.** chemical **3.** physical **4.** respiration **5.** cell theory **6.** replication **7.** transcription **8.** biogenesis **9.** gametes **10.** zygote **11.** variation **12.** homeostasis **13.** hypothesis **14.** control

UNIT 2

The crossword puzzle which follows is comprised of words learned in Unit 2. The "Across" hints are only for these words which are spelled across the page from left to right. The "Down" hints are for those words which are spelled down the page from top to bottom.

ACROSS
1. Paired genes that are identical.
2. One of a pair of genes.
3. Group within a class.
4. Unable to reproduce.
5. Branch of biology that deals with heredity.
6. Gene that is masked.

DOWN
1. Offspring from a cross.
2. Changing genetic makeup.
3. Structurally different organisms.
4. Gene that prevents expression of allele.
5. Inherited syndrome.
6. Group of four chromatids.

Answers to crossword puzzle.

ACROSS
1. homozygous
2. allele
3. order
4. sterile
5. genetics
6. recessive

DOWN
1. hybrid
2. mutation
3. species
4. dominant
5. Down's
6. tetrad

UNIT 3

Have the students circle the underlined words which are used incorrectly in the following sentences. Ask students to correct the inaccurate sentences.

1. Bacteria in milk are killed by <u>dehydration</u>.
2. <u>Spirochetes</u> are a group of organisms that seem to be between bacteria and viruses.
3. <u>Chemotherapy</u> involves the use of chemical compounds to destroy pathogenic organisms.
4. The <u>tsetse fly</u> carries malaria.
5. <u>Hemoglobin</u> is used in fighting infections.
6. <u>Saprophytes</u> feed on tissues of living hosts.
7. The mass of hyphae formed by a fungus is known as the <u>mycelium</u>.
8. A lichen is an example of <u>parasitism</u>.
9. <u>Trypanosomes</u> cause African sleeping sickness.
10. Paramecium move by means of <u>pseudopodia</u>.
11. <u>Prontosil</u> was discovered by Sir Alexander Fleming.
12. The <u>serum</u> is the part of the blood containing antibodies.
13. There are <u>four</u> basic shapes of bacteria.
14. Phages destroy bacteria in the <u>lactic cycle</u>.
15. The <u>host cell</u> is any cell attacked by a virus.

Answers

1. pasteurization
2. rickettsiae
3. correct as is
4. Anopheles mosquito
5. gamma globulin
6. parasites
7. correct as is
8. mutualism
9. correct as is
10. cilia
11. penicillin
12. correct as is
13. three
14. lytic cycle
15. correct as is

UNIT 4

The following word puzzle involves words that have been introduced in this unit. Have students fill in the missing letters for each word. Definitions according to number are given below the puzzle. The first one has been completed for the students.

1. TRACHEOPHYTE
2. R _ _ _ _ _ _ _
3. A _ _ _ _ _ _
4. C _ _ _ _ _ _
5. _ H _ _ _
6. _ _ E _ _ _ _ _ _ _ _
7. _ _ O _ _
8. P _ _ _ _ _ _ _ _ _ _
9. _ H _ _ _ _ _ _
10. _ _ Y _ _ _ _ _ _
11. _ _ T _ _ _ _
12. E _ _ _ _ _ _ _ _

1. vascular plant	7. growing region of stem
2. hairlike filaments	8. transfer of pollen
3. lives for one season	9. underground stems
4. pieces of roots	10. seed leaves
5. stem and its leaves	11. the stalk of a leaf
6. growth of a seed	12. top and bottom layer of a leaf

Answers

1. tracheophyte
2. rhyzoid
3. annual
4. cutting
5. shoot
6. germination
7. node
8. pollination
9. rhizomes
10. cotyledons
11. petiole
12. epidermis

UNIT 5

Have students read the following summary of Unit 5 and fill in the missing words from the *Key Words*.

KEY WORDS

coelom	exoskeleton	invertebrates	molting	specialization
entomology	homology	metamorphosis	sessile	symmetry

This unit discusses the _ _ _ _ _ _ _ _ _ _ _ _ _ _ , animals without backbones. Many of these animals exhibit _ _ _ _ _ _ _ _ _ _ _ _ _ _ _ _ . Certain animals in this group are _ _ _ _ _ _ _ _ . They are permanently attached by their bases. This unit has dealt with the _ _ _ _ _ _ _ _ _ or general form of an organism. The principle of _ _ _ _ _ _ _ _ is important in understanding animal evolution. One important characteristic in grouping animals is the type of _ _ _ _ _ _ _ in the adult. Characteristic of arthropods is their _ _ _ _ _ _ _ _ _ _ _ made of chitin. Growth in the size of an organism with this characteristic takes place through _ _ _ _ _ _ _ _ . Familiar arthropods include the insects. The study of insects is called _ _ _ _ _ _ _ _ _ _ _ . Many insects go through a complete _ _ _ _ _ _ _ _ _ _ _ _ _ .

Answers are given in order of appearance in sentences.

1. invertebrates
2. specialization
3. sessile
4. symmetry
5. homology
6. coelom
7. exoskeleton
8. molting
9. entomology
10. metamorphosis

UNIT 6

The crossword puzzle (opposite) is comprised of words learned in Unit 6. The "Across" hints are only for those words which are spelled across the page from left to right. The "Down" hints are for those words which are spelled down the page from top to bottom.

ACROSS
1. winter rest
2. heart wall
3. chorion plus uterine tissue
4. period of development
5. breast bone
6. poison

DOWN
1. summer rest
2. fluid containing fish sperm
3. pumping chamber of heart
4. reptile egg
5. laying fish eggs
6. food in the egg

Answers to crossword puzzle.

ACROSS
1. hibernation
2. septum
3. venom
4. gestation
5. sternum
6. placenta

DOWN
1. estivation
2. milt
3. ventricle
4. amniote
5. spawn
6. yolk

UNIT 7

Have students read the following summary of Unit 7. Ask them to circle any words in this summary that are spelled or used incorrectly. Have them insert the correct word above the one they have circled.

Unit 7 is concerned with all aspects of human biology. The branch of science concerned with human history is known as archaeology. One method of studying the age of fosils involves the use of radioactive ions. The regions of the human body include the cranial, chest, and abdominal cavities. The latter two are separated by the diafram. The elementary canal is involved in digestion. Animal starch is stored in the liver as glucagon. The red pigment in red corpusles is called hemaglobin. The two phases of a heart beat are systole and miastole. Limph is a tissue fluid that bathes the cells. The urine is pushed out of the body through the ureters. Internal respiration can be defined as the exchange of gases between the atmosphere and the blood. The building of lyctic acid causes oxygen debt. The spaces between neurons are called syntaxes. Alcohol is a strong stimulant.

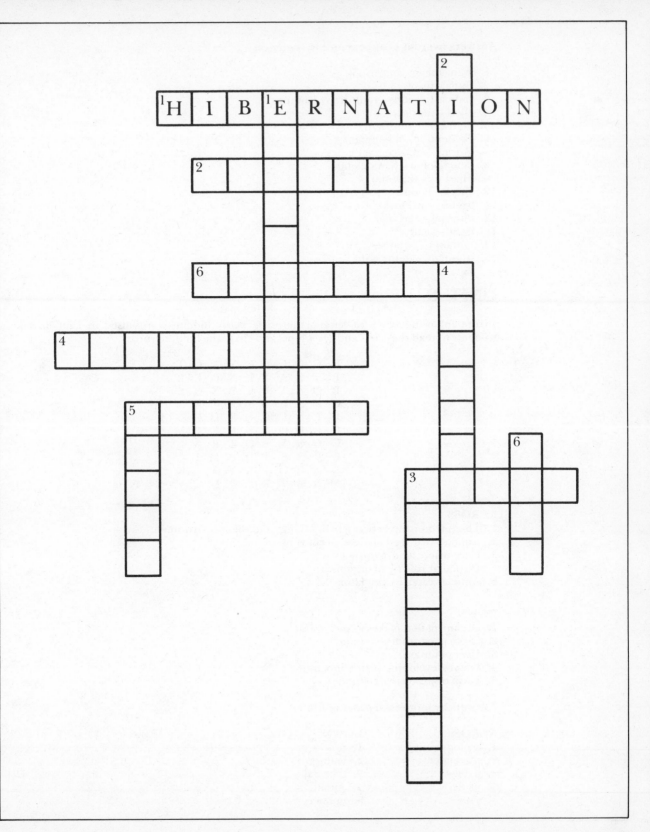

UNIT 8

In the following block of letters, there are many hidden words used in Unit 8. Ask students to read the *across* and *down* hints and circle the hidden words.

```
E  C  O  L  O  G  Y  A  O  T
P  S  C  A  V  E  N  G  E  R
R  O  A  T  J  E  B  N  R  Z
O  H  A  B  I  T  A  T  A  M
D  L  N  I  C  H  E  H  Q  I
U  R  D  O  V  K  R  E  U  M
C  C  O  M  R  O  Z  R  A  I
E  P  R  E  Y  D  P  M  T  C
R  A  R  O  J  K  U  A  I  R
M  N  A  T  R  Z  P  L  C  Y
```

ACROSS
1. The relationship between living things and their environment.
2. Animals that feed on dead organisms.
3. Place where an organism lives.
4. Particular role of an organism.
5. Animals eaten by predators.

DOWN
1. Organism that makes its own food.
2. Large geographical region.
3. Heat pollution.
4. Water-developing plants and animals.
5. Form of protective coloration.

Answers by numerical order of hints.

ACROSS	DOWN
1. ecology	1. producer
2. scavenger	2. biome
3. habitat	3. thermal
4. niche	4. aquatic
5. prey	5. mimicry

DIRECTORY OF FILM PRODUCERS AND DISTRIBUTORS

Academy Films
748 North Seward Street
Hollywood, California
90038

American Cancer Society
219 E. 42nd St.
New York, N.Y. 10017

**American Dental Association
Bureau of Audiovisual
Service**
211 E. Chicago Avenue
Chicago, Ill. 60611

American Heart Association
44 E. 23rd Street
New York, N.Y. 10010

American Lung Association
1740 Broadway
New York, N.Y. 10019

Associated Films Inc.
866 Third Avenue
New York, N.Y. 10022

Association-Sterling Films
Executive Offices
866 Third Ave.
New York, N.Y. 10022

Carousel Films
1501 Broadway
New York, N.Y. 10036

**Contemporary Films
McGraw-Hill Book Co.**
Princeton Road
Hightstown, N.J. 08520

Coronet Films
Sales Department
Coronet Building
Chicago, Illinois 60601

**duPont de Nemours and Co.,
Inc.**
Motion Picture Section
1007 Market Street
Wilmington, Delaware
19898

**Encyclopaedia Britannica
Educational Corp.**
Preview Library
1822 Pickwick Avenue
Greenview, Ill. 60025

**Environmental Protection
Agency**
National Audiovisual
Center
Station K
Atlanta, Georgia 30324

Film Associates of California
11559 Santa Monica
Boulevard
Los Angeles, California
90025

**Indiana University Audio-
Visual Center**
Bloomington, Indiana
47405

Modern Film Rentals
4 Nevada Dr.
Lake Success, N.Y. 11040

**Modern Talking Pictures
Service**
Classroom Service
Department
1212 Avenue of the
Americas
New York, N.Y. 10036

National Film Board of Canada
680 Fifth Avenue
New York, N.Y. 10019

Pyramid Films
2801 Colorado
Santa Monica, California
90404

**Scientificom (Division of
Mervin W. La Rue Films)**
708 Dearborn St.
Chicago, Ill. 60610

Shell Oil Company
Film Library
149-07 Northern Boulevard
Flushing, New York 11354

**Universal Education and Visual
Arts**
100 Universal City Plaza
Universal City, California
91608

DIRECTORY OF SUPPLY HOUSES

AMERICAN OPTICAL CO., Instrument Division, Buffalo, N.Y. 14215

BALTIMORE BIOLOGICAL LABORATORY, 1640 Gorsuch Ave., Baltimore, Md. 21218

BICO SCIENTIFIC CO., 2325 South Michigan Ave., Chicago, Ill. 60616

CALBIOCHEM, 3625 Medford St., Los Angeles, Calif. 90054

CAMBOSCO SCIENTIFIC CO., INC., 342 Western Ave., Boston, Mass. 02135

CAROLINA BIOLOGICAL SUPPLY CO., Burlington, N.C. 27215

CENTRAL SCIENTIFIC CO., 2600 South Kostner Ave., Chicago, Ill. 60623

CLINTON MISCO CORP., P.O. Box 1005, Ann Arbor, Mich. 48106

COE-PALM BIOLOGICAL SUPPLY HOUSE, 1130 Milwaukee Ave., Chicago, Ill. 60622

DALE SCIENTIFIC CO., Box 1721, Ann Arbor, Mich. 48106

DIFCO LABORATORIES, 209 Henry St., Detroit, Mich. 48104

EASTMAN ORGANIC CHEMICALS, 343 State St., Rochester, N.Y. 14650

ELGEET OPTICAL CO., 303 Child St., Rochester, N.Y. 14650

FAUST SCIENTIFIC SUPPLY CO., 5108 Gordon Ave., Madison, Wis. 53716

GENERAL BIOLOGICAL, INC. (TURTOX), 8200 South Hoyne Ave., Chicago, Ill. 60620

HARVARD APPARATUS CO., 150 Dover Road, Millis, Mass. 02054

J. R. SCHETTLE BIOLOGICALS, P.O. Box 184, Stillwater, Minn. 55082

LABORATORY EQUIPMENT CO., 532 McAllister St., San Francisco, Calif. 94102

LaPINE SCIENTIFIC CO., 6001 S. Knox Ave., Chicago, Ill. 60629

MACALASTER SCIENTIFIC CO., Route 111 and Everett Turnpike, Nashua, New Hampshire 03060

MOGUL-ED, P.O. Box 2482, Oshkosh, Wis. 54901

NASCO, Fort Atkinson, Wis. 53538 or P.O. 3837, Modesto, Calif. 95352

NORTHERN BIOLOGICAL SUPPLY, P.O. Box 222, New Richmond, Wis. 54017

OWENS-ILLINOIS SCIENTIFIC SALES, 1290 Bayshore Blvd., Burlington, Calif. 94010

SARGENT-WELCH SCIENTIFIC CO., 7300 North Linder Ave., Skokie, Ill. 60076

SCIENCE KIT INC., 2299 Military Rd., Tonawanda, N.Y. 14150

SCIENTIFIC PRODUCTS, DIVISION AMERICAN HOSPITAL SUPPLY, 1210 Leon Place, Evanston, Ill. 60201

SHERWIN SCIENTIFIC CO., N. 1112 Ruby St., Spokane, Wash. 99202

SOUTHERN BIOLOGICAL SUPPLY CO., McKenzie, Tenn. 38201

STANSI SCIENTIFIC DIVISION, FISHER SCIENTIFIC CO., 1231 North Honore St., Chicago, Ill. 60622

SWIFT INSTRUMENTS, INC., San Jose, Calif. 95106

VAN WATERS & ROGERS, 3745 Bayshore Blvd., Brisbane, Calif. 94005

WARD'S NATURAL HISTORY ESTABLISHMENT, INC., P.O. Box 1712, Rochester, N.Y. 14603

WILL SCIENTIFIC, INC., Box 1050, Rochester, N.Y. 14603

WORTHINGTON BIOCHEMICAL CORP., Freehold, N.J. 07728

The nature of life has always fascinated human beings. This unit explores the nature of life and explains some of the properties and activities of the living state. In Chapter One, the progress of science and the scientific method are documented. The second chapter of this unit explains some of the theories of life's origin. Chapter Three is devoted to the properties of matter and how energy is associated with matter. Chapter Four logically progresses to a discussion of the structural basis of life. Cellular structure is explored in great detail. The cell and its environment are discussed in Chapter Five. The permeability of cell membranes is detailed in this chapter. Matter and energy relationships are the major considerations of Chapter Six. Photosynthesis, respiration, and cell energy are explored in this chapter. Protein synthesis is the topic that is explored in Chapter Seven. The structure of DNA, replication of RNA, and the indispensable function of proteins are discussed. The final chapter of this unit is devoted to an explanation of cell growth and reproduction.

chapter one The Science of Life What is the *science of life?* This chapter gives the students an interesting historical perspective into the science of biology and related fields. The students will learn about scientific methods and how each method is utilized in scientific research. One of the most important tools of biology is the microscope. The students learn about its structure, function, and care. After studying this chapter, the student will have a greater understanding of the history of biology, scientific methods, and the tools of this science.

TEACHING SUGGESTIONS
1. Point out to students that superstition, in many areas, prevents the growth of science. Many people are unwilling to give up old ways in order to follow recent scientific findings. Ask students to give examples.
2. Stress to students some contemporary examples of the limitations of science. An excellent example of this is the side effects of drugs that may go unnoticed until many years after a drug has been in use.
3. Point out to students the important differences between a *technical method* (careful directions that will give consistent results) and the *research method* (new concepts are gained while solving a scientific problem). Stress to students that technical methods are often an integral part of the research method.
4. Ask students to give original examples of pure and applied science. Discuss the close rela-

tionship that exists between these two "sciences."
5. Students may be interested in reading *The Electron Microscope* by Aaron Klein, McGraw-Hill Book Co., 1974. This easy-to-understand book traces the development of the electron microscope, its use, and how it works.

STUDENT INVOLVEMENT ACTIVITIES
1. Ask students to write a brief report on any of the early biologists. Have some of the more interesting reports read to the class.
2. Ask students to choose an area of the biological sciences and explain how other sciences are related to this area. For example, the growing of food is related to the weather, chemical aspects of soil, insect and animal pests, and physical processes.
3. Have students bring in a magazine or newspaper article that discusses the effect of science on society.
4. Ask students to apply the research method to their daily lives. Have them briefly outline how they would go about solving an everyday problem by using the scientific method.

COMMUNITY INVOLVEMENT ACTIVITIES
1. Invite a scientist to discuss his or her area of expertise with the class. Ask this individual to discuss the use of scientific methods in that area.
2. Visit a laboratory or other facility where scientific methods

can be observed. Ask students to take notes on their observations and write a brief report about this experience.

3. Invite a technician to class to discuss the functions of his or her job. Students may have parents or siblings who are technicians.

4. If possible, have students observe an electron microscope and its use. If this is not feasible, invite an individual who uses a microscope in his or her work to speak to the class.

CAREER OPPORTUNITIES
Biochemist
Bioengineer
Biomathematician
Biophysicist
Chemist
Cytologist
Laboratory director
Medical technician
Physicist
Research scientist
Space biologist

ANSWERS TO QUESTIONS FOR REVIEW
(Page 12)

1. a. Establishing the science of anatomy by Vesalius, a Belgian; b. theory of circulation by Harvey, an Englishman; c. support of Harvey's theory by Malpighi, an Italian; d. first vaccination by Jenner, an Englishman; e. establishing bacteriology by Pasteur, a Frenchman; f. method of investigating disease and culturing bacteria by Koch, a German; g. basic principles of heredity by Mendel, an Austrian monk; h. use of arsenic compound in treating syphilis by Ehrlich, a German; i. discovery of penicillin by Fleming, a Scotsman.

2. a. Recognition and definition of a problem; b. collection of related data and information; c. forming a hypothesis; d. experimentation to prove or disprove the hypothesis; e. observation of results; f. organization and recording of data; g. drawing of conclusions; h. accurate reporting of research methods, results, and conclusions.

3. The library puts the knowledge of thousands of people and their techniques in the hands of anyone. This prevents duplication of effort so that experiments of value may continue beyond the life of the original researcher.

4. The control shows the results of an experiment minus the variable. Thus, any observed differences may be attributed to the variable being studied.

5. A hypothesis is a hunch or an idea used by the scientist as a guide in experimentation, or a tentative explanation used as a basis for drawing conclusions. A theory is a hypothesis that has been verified.

6. In pure science, research is conducted for the sake of knowledge itself; applied science makes use of the knowledge gained from pure science.

7. Magnification is the enlargement of an image; resolution involves the details that may be seen.

8. An electron microscope makes an image of the interior of an object; a scanning electron microscope makes an image of the surface of an object.

ANSWERS TO APPLYING PRINCIPLES AND CONCEPTS
(Page 12)

1. Without the microscope, only the gross structure of living things can be studied. The invention of the simple microscope allowed some structural details to be seen. As the microscope was developed, more details could be seen. Today with the electron microscope, structures at the subcellular level are revealed. Progress is made as these new discoveries give clues to cell function.

2. Answers will vary widely.

3. Magnifications reach only 1,500 to 2,000 times in the light microscope because there is a limit to which light rays may be dispersed and still produce a visible image. The electron microscope may produce magnifications up to 200,000 times because an electron beam is used instead of light.

chapter two The Living Condition What makes some things living and others nonliving? This chapter answers this question by discussing the characteristics of living things. The cell (the common unit of life) and its relationship to the total organism are explored. In addition, change in organisms is also explained. The fact that life comes from life is supported by many early experiments in this area. This chapter concludes with a discussion of biogenesis and how it is basic to our understanding of the principles of biology.

TEACHING SUGGESTIONS

1. Ask students to make a list of the characteristics of living and nonliving things. Tell them to refer back to their list as they read this chapter. At the end of the chapter, have them go over their lists and correct any discrepancies.

2. Stress to students the difference between true growth and growth by addition. Be sure that students understand that true growth involves *organization* of materials.

3. Point out to students some of the factors that affect the life span. Discuss these factors in reference to the human life span.

4. Ask students to think about how their environment affects their lives. Stress to students that different societies are affected in different ways by environment.

5. It is important that students understand that organisms *do not* change in order to survive; rather they survive because a change has taken place.

STUDENT INVOLVEMENT ACTIVITIES

1. Ask students to report on the life span of any organism. Have the student discuss each of the five stages of this organism's life span.

2. Death is an important stage in any life span. Ask students to do some research into how we can judge whether or not death has occurred. This topic can lead into an interesting discussion of medical advances that keep people alive when they might have died of natural causes.

3. Divide the class into groups and ask each group to devise a simple experiment that proves biogenesis. They may wish to modify one of the classic experiments discussed in the book.

4. Ask students to write about the modern method of pasteurization and how it is utilized in certain industries today.

COMMUNITY INVOLVEMENT ACTIVITIES

1. Visit a zoo and examine some of the adaptations that have enabled certain species to survive.

2. Invite a zoologist or botanist to class to discuss variations in certain species.

3. Visit a milk processing plant and observe the pasteurization of milk. Write a brief report on these observations.

CAREER OPPORTUNITIES

Biochemist
Botanist
Embryologist
Geneticist
Gerontologist
Laboratory assistant
Scientific illustrator
Scientific librarian
Veterinarian
Zoologist

CHALLENGES IN BIOLOGY
ORIGIN OF LIFE ON EARTH

One of the major challenges in biology is the answer to the question of how life first originated on the earth. There are many different theories. Two of the most well known are those expressed by "creationists" and "biochemists."

The creationist theory generally theorizes that life was created by God and that the fundamental teachings of the Old Testament are true in detail. The biochemist theory, on the other hand, theorizes that life originated from a "chemical soup." This "soup" contained such elements as carbon, nitrogen, oxygen, and hydrogen. These substances were thought to have come together to produce a variety of pre-life and eventually life-supporting compounds.

This controversial question remains as a challenge in biology. Although both these theories have been considered opposite, many responsible persons do not subscribe totally to either theory. Recent discoveries in science make this truly a challenge in biology.

ANSWERS TO QUESTIONS FOR REVIEW
(Pages 24–25)

1. An organism is a complete and entire protist, plant, or animal.

2. Organisms (1) organize protoplasm; (2) use energy constantly; (3) are made up of cells; (4) are capable of growth; (5) produce like organisms; (6) have a life span; (7) are affected by their environment; (8) show variation and adaptation; (9) can reproduce.

3. Protoplasm is a combination of water, certain proteins, carbohydrates, fats, and other substances organized into a system

It helps for a scientist to be well organized.

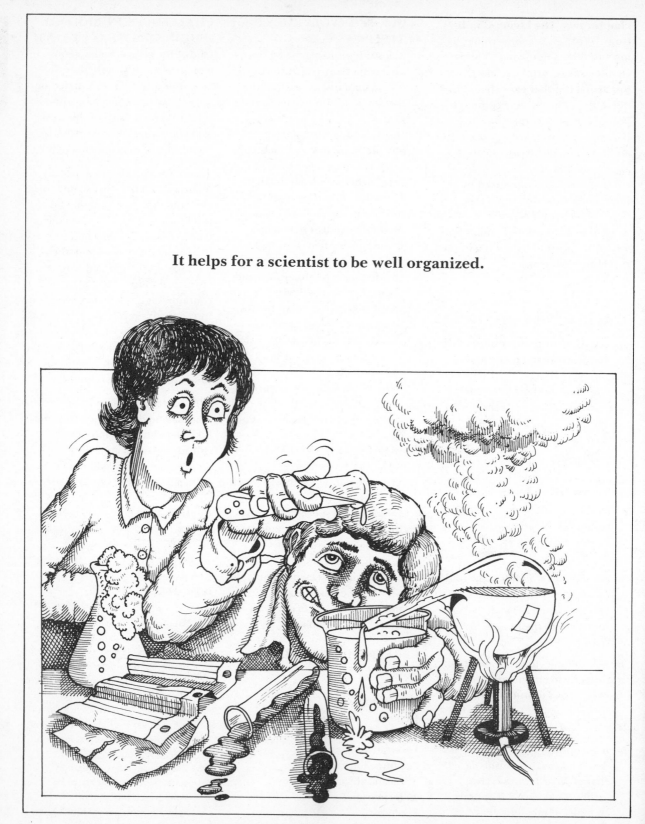

by a living organism. It is a state of chemical activity which may be called the living condition.

4. Assimilation is the reorganization of substances to form protoplasm characteristic of the organism in which it is formed. Nonliving substances, such as crystals, grow by external addition of more of the substance of which they are composed.

5. Beginning, or origin; growth; maturity, decline; death.

6. Irritability is the ability to respond to a stimulus.

7. Conditions in an environment may change rapidly or over a period of time. The variations of a species that are of survival value in allowing it to adapt to these changes will be the ones that will be perpetuated through heredity. This is called adaptation.

8. Life arises from pre-existing life.

9. Insects arising from mud; decaying meat changing into maggots; mice being produced from grain and sweat; frogs and fish being produced from clouds in a thunderstorm; geese forming from barnacles.

10. Redi placed some pieces of snake, some fish, some "eels of Arno," and a slice of milk-fed veal in each of four clean jars. He then prepared a duplicate set of four jars. One set of jars was left open. The other, which we would designate as a control, was covered and securely sealed with wax. Flies were attracted to the open jars and laid eggs which developed into maggots. The sealed jars contained no maggots. In a second experiment, he covered one set of jars with fine cloth so as to admit air but exclude flies.

11. Spallanzani conducted two experiments. The first showed that spontaneous generation did not occur in sealed flasks; the second showed that boiling did not destroy an "active principle."

12. Pasteur carried out several experiments with flasks which prevented dust from reaching the sterile broth showing that microbes entered the broth from dust in the air.

ANSWERS TO APPLYING PRINCIPLES AND CONCEPTS
(Page 25)

1. Redi used both a control and an experimental set of jars; he limited his experiment to one experimental factor.

2. Boiling had not destroyed the property of the liquid in the flask to support microorganisms, nor had the experiment excluded the "active principle" of the air thought to be necessary for spontaneous generation. Both the liquid and the air in the flask were suitable for the growth of bacteria, molds, and other organisms if they were introduced from an outside source.

3. Responses vary from the simple tropisms of plants to complex instinctive behavior such as migration.

chapter three   The Chemical Basis of Life   What makes up living things? This question is answered in Chapter Three with a review of some of the foundations of chemistry. This chapter discusses matter and energy and their interrelationships. Students learn about the differences between physical and chemical changes. They also learn about different types of energy. The elements and their structures are discussed in detail. Chemical compounds and chemical bonds are discussed and illustrated. Inorganic and organic compounds are discussed and examples are included. Having read this chapter, the student will have a better understanding of the chemical basis of life.

TEACHING SUGGESTIONS

1. Perform a simple demonstration to illustrate the solid, liquid, and gaseous states of matter.

2. Ask students to give examples of physical and chemical change. Have them point out how these changes differ.

3. Ask students to describe briefly how the human body utilizes energy. Be sure that they understand that living organisms store energy.

4. Display a model of an atom. This is often easier to understand than a picture or a description.

5. Once students understand the concept of compounds, give them some practice in writing formulas of some simple compounds.

6. Prepare a demonstration to illustrate the difference between solutions and suspensions.

7. There are many simple experiments that the students can do

to illustrate the existence of starch in a substance.

STUDENT INVOLVEMENT ACTIVITIES

1. Before beginning this chapter, ask students to define matter. Go back to their definitions after they have studied pp. 22–29. Have them compare their definitions to the correct definition.
2. Ask students to prepare a simple demonstration that illustrates one form of energy.
3. Some students may enjoy working on a model of an atom. Tell them to use materials that can be easily found at home.
4. Ask students to do a brief report on one aspect of isotopes. Isotopes are commonly used today in many areas of scientific research.
5. Ask students to write a brief report on carbohydrates, lipids, or proteins. Have them include in their report information on the use of these substances by organisms.
6. Ask a few students to write about diseases where one or more enzymes is missing in the body. These reports will enable the class to better understand the importance of enzymes in the human body.

COMMUNITY INVOLVEMENT ACTIVITIES

1. Ask a biochemist to come to class to discuss her or his job and to answer questions concerning biochemistry as a career.
2. If possible, visit a hospital or laboratory where radioisotopes are in use. Have questions prepared before going on this trip.
3. Ask a radiologist to come and speak to the class about advances in this field and career opportunities in radiology.
4. A geneticist or physician may be invited to speak on the subject of enzyme related diseases and how some of them are treated today.

CAREER OPPORTUNITIES

Biochemist
Chemist
Geneticist
Molecular biologist
Nutritionist
Organic chemist
Pharmacist
Physician
Radiologic technician
Radiologist
Research scientist

ANSWERS TO QUESTIONS FOR REVIEW
(Page 41)

1. Matter is anything that occupies space and has mass.
2. A physical change is a change from one state of matter to another; a chemical change is a change from one substance to another.
3. Answers will vary.
4. Protons have a positive charge and occupy the center of the atomic nucleus; electrons have a negative charge and revolve around the nucleus; and neutrons have no charge and are found in the nucleus of most atoms.
5. Isotopes are different forms of an element in which the number of neutrons varies.
6. A covalent bond is a force that holds two or more atoms together as a result of the sharing of pairs of electrons. An ionic bond is the force that holds two atoms together by the transfer of electrons from one atom to another.
7. The dissolving medium of a solution is the solvent; the dissolved substance is a solute.
8. Colloids are made up of particles which are larger than the molecules that form solutions yet smaller than the particles in suspensions.
9. Organic compounds contain carbon; they are not necessarily made by living organisms but may be synthetic.
10. Sugars, starches, and celluloses.
11. One glycerol molecule is joined to three fatty acid molecules in a fat molecule.
12. One protein differs from another in the kind, number, and order of the component amino acids.
13. An enzyme is an organic catalyst. All enzymes are protein molecules.
14. Nucleic acids control the synthesis of proteins; they contain the genetic message of heredity.

ANSWERS TO APPLYING PRINCIPLES AND CONCEPTS
(Page 41)

1. Student diagram.
2. Carbon tends to share the four electrons in its outer shell with those of other atoms, making possible a variety of configurations.
3. Enzymes act as catalysts in the processes essential to maintaining life. These include the building up, or synthesis, of substances, as well as the breakdown of matter. Enzymes are also indispensable in the energy-yielding processes of the cell. There is an enzyme for every chemical activity of an organism.

chapter four The Structural Basis of Life What is the structural basis of life? It is the cell, a unit that becomes more complex as we find out more about it. This chapter is concerned with the history of cell discovery and the structure and function of cells. Cell processes are examined and each part of the cell is explored in detail. The structure of plant and animal cells is discussed. This chapter concludes with a discussion of different levels of structures and explains how organisms differ in cellular complexity. After reading this chapter, the students will have a better understanding of cells and of organism complexity based on cellular organization.

TEACHING SUGGESTIONS

1. Students may be introduced to this topic by showing a number of cell slides of different organisms.

2. Have students repeat Hooke's early study of cells in cork. Ask students to write down exactly what they see. Would they have used the word "cell" to describe what they viewed?

3. Ask students to examine Fig. 4–5 carefully and to point out the structures shown in the electron micrograph.

4. Stress to students the importance of the electron microscope in enabling scientists to see structures that could not be seen under the light microscope.

5. Stress to students how division of labor relates to organisms, individuals, and societies. Ask students to discuss the effectiveness of division of labor.

STUDENT INVOLVEMENT ACTIVITIES

1. Ask students to write a brief report on one of the early scientists who contributed to our understanding of the cell theory.

2. Ask students if they can add to the list of cell processes given on p. 44. Point out to students that a *characteristic* is not a *process*.

3. Have students study animal and plant cells under a microscope. Ask them to write down the differences between these two types of cells.

4. Ask students to choose one organ and find out about the cells and tissues that make up this organ. Cytology and physiology books will be helpful to the students.

COMMUNITY INVOLVEMENT ACTIVITIES

1. If possible, visit a laboratory where different types of cells are studied under microscopes. A blood analysis laboratory or hospital laboratory would be interesting to the students.

2. Invite a cytologist (a cell specialist) to class to discuss her or his profession.

3. Invite a sociologist to class to discuss division of labor among the parts of society. This discussion will help students understand the concept of division of labor and specialization.

CAREER OPPORTUNITIES
Biochemist
Biomedical photographer
Cytologist
Embryologist
Laboratory technician
Molecular biologist
Pathologist
Pathology technician
Sociologist

CHALLENGES IN BIOLOGY
NEW METHODS OF CELL STUDY
One of the most dramatic areas of scientific research today is cellular experimentation that involves the very processes of life itself. In the past few years, researchers have been able to transplant the genetic material of one cell into cells of a different species. Other researchers have synthesized an animal gene.

The transplantation of genetic material is a biomedical breakthrough and is the subject of great controversy. While these techniques may be beneficial in understanding gene function, they may also pose certain dangers. There is the possibility of producing mutant forms through gene transplantation. Another possibility is that disease-causing bacteria will be accidentally made immune to certain antibiotics.

More will be written about the ramifications of these techniques in the *Challenges in Biology,* T. E. Chapter Seven. This issue is important from both scientific and ethical standpoints. It is a very definite challenge that must be resolved in the light of our constant quest for scientific knowledge.

ANSWERS TO QUESTIONS FOR REVIEW
(Page 52)

1. Robert Hooke observed the cell walls inside of which once were living cells.
2. a. The cell is the unit of structure and function of all living things; b. cells come from pre-existing cells, by cell reproduction.
3. Nutrition, digestion, absorption, synthesis (assimilation), respiration,

excretion, egestion, secretion, movement, response, and reproduction.

4. The light microscope shows the nuclear membrane as a barrier, but it appears as a porous structure under the electron microscope. Nuclear substances pass freely into the surrounding cell substance.

5. The plasma membrane is an interface formed on the exposed surface of the cytoplasm. The membrane consists of an inner and outer layer of protein molecules between which are two layers of fat molecules.

6. Ribosomes, mitochondria, lysosomes, Golgi apparatus, plastids.

7. The mitochondria are rod-shaped bodies in the cytoplasm. They are centers of cellular respiration, during which energy is released to support cell activities.

8. Lysosomes contain protein digesting enzymes which, if released into the cytoplasm, would allow cellular proteins to be digested, resulting in the disintegration of the cell.

9. Golgi bodies may be involved in forming new endoplasmic reticulum.

10. Because they contain the chlorophyll involved in the organization of carbohydrates from carbon dioxide and water.

11. The fluid is largely water. Ions of mineral compounds, molecules of sugars and other soluble substances, and large molecules of proteins and other organic materials in collodial suspension in the water form the content of the vacuole that is referred to as cell sap. Other vacuoles may contain food materials and waste products. Others serve as water-eliminating organelles in many one-celled organisms.

12. Cells, tissues, organs, organ systems, and organism.

ANSWERS TO APPLYING PRINCIPLES AND CONCEPTS
(Page 52)

1. The cell is the basic structural unit of all living things. It is, also, the seat of all processes involved in the living condition.

2. No, because the living condition involves more than a mere collection of chemicals. As far as we know now, all life comes from pre-existing life.

3. The cytoplasm of a cell is composed of various organelles, each associated with a specific process or activity. Ribosomes function as centers of protein synthesis; cellular respiration involves mitochondria; lysosomes are believed to store protein-splitting enzymes; Golgi bodies are believed to store glandular secretions; chloroplasts are "carbohydrate factories."

4. A unicellular organism must perform all life activities while a multicellular organism is made up of many different kinds of cells, each of which is specialized to perform a different activity.

chapter five The Cell and Its Environment Just as our environment is essential to our well-being, the environment of the cell is also essential to its life activities. This chapter explores the concept of *homeostasis,* the steady state. How does the internal environment of an organism maintain homeostasis? This question is answered by examining the cell membrane and the processes of diffusion and osmosis. Water problems in animal cells are also examined. This chapter concludes with a discussion of pinocytosis, the process by which large molecules enter the cell. Having read this chapter, the students will have a better understanding of how the cell adjusts to its environment and how homeostasis is achieved.

TEACHING SUGGESTIONS

1. The concept of homeostasis can be expanded to include examples of balance in ourselves and in society. Ask students to give some examples of homeostasis.
2. A simple example of diffusion is the antacid tablet in water. The speed of diffusion is readily observable in this experiment.
3. Ask students to bring into class stalks of celery or carrots. If these vegetables are fresh, the turgor pressure is obvious. What happens if they are left at room temperature for a few days?
4. Students may be interested in experimenting with one-celled organisms of blood cells and distilled water. They should observe their findings under the microscope.
5. If possible, show the class some slides that illustrate the interesting process of pinocytosis.

STUDENT INVOLVEMENT ACTIVITIES

1. Ask students to write a brief paragraph on how they maintain the steady state or homeostasis.
2. Ask students to design a simple experiment that will illustrate diffusion or osmosis.
3. The topic of *active transport* is being studied by many researchers. Ask students to investigate this topic and briefly report the most recent findings.
4. Ask students to briefly explain the process of pinocytosis and why it is important to the cell.

COMMUNITY INVOLVEMENT ACTIVITIES

1. Invite an industrial chemist to speak to the class concerning scientific applications of the processes of diffusion and osmosis.
2. Invite a cytologist to class to discuss the importance of these processes to his or her work.

CAREER OPPORTUNITIES

Biochemist
Chemist
Cytologist
Cytotechnician
Histologic technician
Histologist
Laboratory technician
Physicist

ANSWERS TO QUESTIONS FOR REVIEW
(Pages 60–61)

1. Homestatis is a steady state, or balance which organisms maintain by self-regulating adjustments.
2. If a substance passes through a membrane, we say that the membrane is permeable to that substance. Membranes that vary in the rate and degree of penetration of various substances are said to be selectively permeable.
3. All materials taken into the cell and all waste products which leave the cell pass through the cell, or plasma, membrane, a double layer of fat molecules embedded with protein molecules.
4. Diffusion is a gradual spreading out of molecules through random movement until they are spread evenly through any given space. This results in a state of equilibrium.
5. The higher the temperature, the greater the speed of molecular movement, and thus the faster the diffusion. The converse is true with lower temperatures. The higher the pressure, the greater the speed of molecular movement, and thus the faster the diffusion. Thus, diffusion occurs from an area of higher temperature to one of lower temperature, and from a region of higher pressure to one of lower pressure.
6. Osmosis is the diffusion of water through a selectively permeable membrane from a region of greater concentration of water to a region of lesser concentration of water.
7. If a solution outside a cell has a lower concentration of water than the cell content, the outside solution is hypertonic.
8. Passive transport is the movement of a substance across a membrane from an area of greater concentration to an area of lesser concentration. Active transport involves the movement of molecules against diffusion pressure from an area of lower concentration to one of higher concentration.
9. Large molecules cannot pass through the pores of a membrane and into a cell. It is believed that they flow into indentations of the membrane and are sealed off as the membrane closes behind them. The material is then enclosed in a membrane within the cell as a vacuole. This engulfing process is referred to as pinocytosis.

ANSWERS TO APPLYING PRINCIPLES AND CONCEPTS
(Page 61)

1. If a cell membrane were permeable to all molecules, the cell's own molecules would diffuse out into the environment and the cell would die.
2. Concentration, temperature, and pressure.
3. Cells of a fresh-water plant would lose water to the salt water. This might cause plasmolysis and, if continued, would kill the cells. Fresh water would destroy a salt-water plant by causing cytolysis due to excess water absorption by the cells.

chapter six Photosynthesis, Respiration, and Cell Energy

Is life possible without energy? This question is answered in Chapter Six which explores photosynthesis, respiration, and energy. The importance of light energy is examined in a detailed discussion of photosynthesis. Cell respiration is also examined in detail. The energy requirements of cell respiration are explored. The students will better understand the relationship between photosynthesis and respiration after reading this chapter.

TEACHING SUGGESTIONS

1. Point out to students the importance of photosynthesis to plants, animals, and human life as we know it today. Stress to students that there is a life-death dependency between plants and animals.
2. Be sure that students understand the chemical equation for photosynthesis given on p. 63. Though, this equation only establishes the general idea, if not understood now the students may have problems with the more complex equations to follow.
3. Review the structure and function of the chloroplast before going on to the more complex photosynthesis equations. A review of the plant cell may be aided by showing slides.
4. Review page 65 very carefully. Photosynthesis can only be understood if the ADP-ATP formula is thoroughly understood.
5. Review the structure of the mitochondria before discussing respiration. The equation on p. 75 (cellular respiration) should

be broken down step-by-step to help students understand what is occurring.

STUDENT INVOLVEMENT ACTIVITIES

1. Assign groups of students different experiments to perform that illustrate the effects of photosynthesis. Students can alter the amount of light in their experiments, and they can also use filtered light.
2. Certain students may want to report on plant pigments other than chlorophyll and their relationship to photosynthesis.
3. Ask a few students to report on the research that led to the understanding of photosynthesis.
4. Ask a few students to draw an original diagram that would depict what is happening in Fig. 6-6.
5. Have a few students report briefly on bacteria that do not depend on photosynthesis for life.
6. Assign some students to report on the topic of oxidation and how it affects numerous aspects of our lives.

COMMUNITY INVOLVEMENT ACTIVITIES

1. Ask a botanist to come and speak to the class about photosynthesis. Prepare questions before class begins.
2. If possible, visit an agricultural station and observe some of the experimental work being done there.
3. Invite a biochemist to class to discuss cell energy and respiration. Be sure to have questions prepared prior to the visit.

CAREER OPPORTUNITIES
Agronomist
Biochemist
Bioengineer
Biophysicist
Botanist
Chemist
Laboratory technician

CHALLENGES IN BIOLOGY
THE VITAL IMPORTANCE OF GREEN PLANTS

Try to imagine a world without green plants. It is not possible, as a world without green plants would not be able to exist as we know it today. Life is dependent on plants in many ways. Plants, through the process of photosynthesis, release oxygen into the atmosphere. Plants aid in keeping the soil fertile. They provide food for animals and humans and are an integral part of the food web where different organisms provide food for each other. Plants also provide the sources of many drugs and a variety of useful products.

The plant community is all around us, but many people overlook its contributions to other living things. It is essential that plant life, like animal life, be protected from extinction. Many species of plants are endangered today because of people's carelessness or disinterest.

The challenge remains to educate the public so that everyone will understand the vital importance of plants and protect plants from unnecessary destruction.

ANSWERS TO QUESTIONS FOR REVIEW
(Page 77)

1. All organisms depend on green plant cells for energy. These cells

produce energy by photosynthesis.

2. Photosynthesis refers to the series of chemical reactions in which glucose is organized:

$$6CO_2 + 6H_2O + \text{light energy} \rightarrow C_6H_{12}O_6 + 6O_2$$

3. Chlorophyll undergoes a change in molecular structure as it absorbs light and becomes energized. Chlorophyll serves as an organic catalyst and supplies energy in photosynthesis.

4. ATP is the energy transfer compound which traps extra energy and releases it in controlled amounts to meet cell needs.

5. Energy is required to attach a third phosphate to ADP in forming ATP. This energy is released when the phosphate is removed and ATP is converted to ADP.

6. Chlorophyll is energized; water molecules are split; energy is stored in ATP; hydrogen is trapped by NADP.

7. CO_2 is fixed by combining with RDP to produce an unstable 6-carbon sugar. This then splits to form two molecules of PGA.

8. In chemosynthesis, energy used in glucose formation is supplied from inorganic chemical reactions rather than light.

9. The energy necessary to support the processes of a cell is released during respiration.

10. Respiratory enzymes control the processes which release energy and cause them to take place at the normal temperature of the organism.

11. $C_6H_{12}O_6 + 6O_2 \rightarrow 6CO_2 + 6H_2O + \text{energy}$

12. Alcoholic fermentation: a carbon dioxide molecule is removed from pyruvic acid. The product formed is then broken down to ethyl alcohol. Lactic acid fermentation: in the absence of molecular oxygen, pyruvic acid is changed to lactic acid.

13. Energy-requiring processes of a cell include: synthesis of various carbohydrates, fats, oils, nucleic acids, and proteins; active transport; cell division; muscle contraction; and nerve impulses.

ANSWERS TO APPLYING PRINCIPLES AND CONCEPTS
(Page 77)

1. Chloroplasts reflect most green or yellow light. Since we see only this light which is not absorbed, chloroplasts appear green or yellow-green.

2. Different rays of the visible spectrum contain different amounts of energy. Different plants absorb different rays. Also, temperature affects the activity of enzymes involved in photosynthesis.

3. Cells derive their usable energy through the breakdown of glucose to ATP in cellular respiration.

4. Carbon dioxide and water are used in photosynthesis, energy is absorbed, glucose is formed, and oxygen is given off. In cellular respiration, glucose is used as a fuel molecule, energy is released, and carbon dioxide and water are formed.

chapter seven Nucleic Acids and Protein Synthesis   How are proteins synthesized? The answer to this question is examined in this chapter. The discovery and structure of DNA are examined, and the DNA molecule is discussed. The processes of transcription and replication are also explored. Students will learn about how amino acids are built into proteins and the importance of DNA to life processes. This chapter concludes with a discussion of DNA engineering which is further highlighted under *Challenges in Biology*.

TEACHING SUGGESTIONS

1. A model of the DNA molecule may help students understand its structure better. Students may be interested in making their own models out of simple materials.

2. Compare the alphabet to the triplet bases of the DNA code. Many different words can be made from our 26-letter alphabet and many code "words" can be made from the four nucleotide bases.

3. Discuss the term DNA *engineering* with students. The future of DNA engineering is very much in the news today. Such research concerns scientists because it may accidentally create drug-resistant or disease-causing germs that might escape from the laboratory.

4. Some students may be interested in reading *Genes, Dreams and Realities* by Macfarlane Burnet, Basic Books, 1971. This book discusses molecular biology in an interesting and understandable manner.

STUDENT INVOLVEMENT ACTIVITIES

1. Some students may be interested in researching the discovery of the DNA molecule.
2. Ask students to bring in a clipping concerning some aspect of DNA engineering. Students should briefly report on the material discussed in the clipping.
3. Certain students may be assigned chapters in the book *Life—The Unfinished Experiment* by S. E. Luria, Charles Scribner's Sons, 1973. This factual, easily understood book discusses the modern world of molecular biology.
4. Debate the social and scientific advantages and disadvantages posed by DNA engineering. Be sure to be thoroughly acquainted with the subject before the debate.

COMMUNITY INVOLVEMENT ACTIVITIES

1. If possible, bring together a panel of scientists that represent opposing views concerning DNA engineering. Prepare questions prior to the panel discussion.
2. Invite a geneticist to class to discuss the possible impact of DNA engineering on genetic diseases.

CAREER OPPORTUNITIES

Biochemist
Bioengineer
Biologist
Biomedical technician
Biophysicist
Geneticist
Immunologist
Laboratory technician
Molecular biologist

CHALLENGES IN BIOLOGY
THE IMPACT OF DNA ENGINEERING

Cell study which involves DNA engineering was briefly discussed in *Challenges in Biology,* T. E. Chapter Two. Genetic or DNA engineering has caused a political and ethical furor with well-known scientists and politicians taking sides.

The controversy involves the risk of such research and the ethical problems of genetic experimentation which could lead to genetic change and control of an organism.

As a result of this controversy, the National Institutes of Health appointed a committee to decide on safety precautions necessary for genetic transplant research.

Where does this leave us? The question seems to be whether or not the risk of a procedure is more important than the benefits. This is the current issue and the challenge that faces today's genetic researchers.

ANSWERS TO QUESTIONS FOR REVIEW
(Page 85)

1. Protein synthesis is important to all living things because every living cell contains proteins. Without proteins there would be no life.
2. The Watson-Crick model for DNA is a double helix, e.g., if a rope ladder with metal rungs were twisted, the result would be a double helix.
3. The triplet codes of DNA determine the order in which amino acids will be put together in building a protein.
4. In a nucleotide of RNA, ribose sugar is substituted for the deoxyribose of DNA and uracil, a nitrogen-containing base, is substituted for thymine.
5. Each strand of transfer RNA has a specific amino acid attached. The

transfer RNA delivers the amino acid to the ribosome where it is positioned correctly in a growing protein chain as the transfer RNA anticoden finds its corresponding codon in the messenger RNA template.
6. A protein molecule is composed of a large number of amino acids of different kinds bonded together in a chain. A strand of transfer RNA brings only one specific amino acid to the ribosome during protein synthesis.
7. During protein synthesis, a ribosome moves along the messenger RNA template and "reads" each codon in succession. As this is occurring, a transfer RNA unit with the proper anti-codon moves to a site on the ribosome, placing an amino acid in correct position in a growing protein chain.
8. Different sequences of amino acids give rise to different proteins.
9. Some proteins are structural, forming parts of the cell. Some proteins are intercellular enzymes; others are extracellular and serve as catalysts for reactions outside the cell. Other proteins are hormones, plant pigments, hemoglobin, and the proteins composing blood serum.

ANSWERS TO APPLYING PRINCIPLES AND CONCEPTS
(Page 85)

1. 500 triplets, or 1500 base pairs.
2. DNA in the nucleus transcribes a code for protein synthesis by determining the triplet codons in messenger RNA. These codons are the complement of corresponding triplet base codes in DNA. Messenger RNA then moves to the ribosomes where it forms a template. Anti-codons in strands of transfer RNA, with attached amino acids, find their proper places along the template and position the amino acids in proper location in a protein molecule. Thus, DNA, in determining the base codes of messenger

RNA, controls the assembly of various amino acids in the formation of a protein molecule.

3. Since DNA determines the composition of proteins, the nature of these proteins will vary with the structure of the DNA of a particular organism.
4. As cells reproduce, identical chromosomes and DNA must be contained in the resulting daughter cells. This is accomplished by the remarkable ability of DNA to duplicate its own structure, or replicate. This preserves the chemical unity of an organism in all its cells.
5. By controlling protein synthesis, DNA determines the structure of all structural proteins that form an organism as well as enzymes, hormones, and other substances that regulate its functions and chemical activities. Thus, DNA is, truly, the "key to life."

chapter eight Cell Growth and Reproduction Chapter Eight confronts the problem of how cells grow and reproduce. The process of simple cell division or fission is examined. This discussion leads to an examination of mitosis. The five phases of mitosis are explained in detail. Asexual and sexual reproduction are briefly explained in relation to mitosis and meiosis. The importance of chromosome numbers is stressed. Meiosis is explained and illustrated diagramatically. Having read this chapter, students will have a better understanding of cellular reproduction and the meiotic divisions of the sex-cells.

TEACHING SUGGESTIONS
1. Mitosis can best be appreciated by examining slides that distinctly illustrate the five phases of this process. Sufficient time should be allowed for examining each of these phases.
2. Stress to students the exactness of mitosis in that each body cell contains the same number of chromosomes. Ask them to think about the number of mitotic divisions that have taken place to produce their bodies from conception to the present.
3. Briefly discuss the advantages and disadvantages of asexual reproduction and sexual reproduction. This topic will be discussed many times during the course, but it is helpful to start the students thinking about it at this point in their work.
4. Point out to students the importance of retaining the 46 chromosome number. Persons afflicted with Down's syndrome (mental retardation and anatomical differences) have 47 chromosomes instead of 46.
5. Stress to students the im-

portance of meiotic division in the reproductive cells.

STUDENT INVOLVEMENT ACTIVITIES
1. Ask students to diagram the five phases of mitosis. This diagram will aid the students' understanding of the process.
2. Assign some students to research the question of sexual reproduction and its contribution to change in species.
3. Some students may be interested in learning more about Down's syndrome, its causes and its effects on the individual.
4. Some students may be interested in reporting on other chromosomal abnormalities. Such abnormalities include the XYY and XXY chromosomal configuration.

COMMUNITY INVOLVEMENT ACTIVITIES
1. If possible, visit a treatment center for retarded children. Children with Down's syndrome may be present.
2. Ask a special education teacher who works with Down's syndrome patients to speak to the class. Volunteers are often welcomed to work with these patients.
3. Ask a geneticist to speak to the class about the importance of sexual reproduction to change.

CAREER OPPORTUNITIES
Biochemist
Embryologist
Genetic counselor
Geneticist
Medical laboratory technician
Molecular biologist
Pediatrician

Plant geneticist
Research biologist
Special education teacher

ANSWERS TO QUESTIONS FOR REVIEW
(Page 94)

1. Binary fission is the division of a cell into two approximately equal parts.
2. Genes are believed to be active groups of nucleotide base triplets in DNA that code proteins. Chromosomes are composed of strands of DNA wound around a protein core.
3. Following the formation of a daughter cell and prior to a subsequent division, there is a period of growth and enlargement—the interphase. During this time the nucleus, in addition to directing protein synthesis, is preparing for a coming division during at least the latter part of the interphase. DNA molecules are doubling their structure and reproducing genes and chromosomes.
4. The chromosome is a rod-shaped, gene-bearing body formed in the cell nucleus during division. The chromatid is one of the parts of a double chromosome.
5. During interphase, the chromosomes are spread through the nucleus. During prophase, they grow shorter and thicker and are double along their length. Each of these parts is a chromatid. The chromatids move toward the equator. During metaphase the chromosomes, consisting of paired chromatids, mass at the equator in a random arrangement. During anaphase, the separated chromatids, now chromosomes, move to opposite poles along central spindle fibers. Shortening traction fibers attached to the centromeres of the chromosomes are believed to pull them toward the poles. After the chromosomes reach their respective poles they gradually disappear,

forming the network of chromatin material characteristic of an interphase nucleus.
6. In plant cells, a division plate forms across the spindle in the region of the equator. This becomes part of the middle lamella of the cell wall. In animal cells, a cleavage furrow forms in the region of the equator and deepens, cutting the cell in two.
7. Sexual reproduction involves the union of like or unlike gametes to form a diploid cell, the zygote. Asexual reproduction is any type of reproduction that does not involve the union of gametes.
8. In unicellular organisms, binary fission constitutes asexual reproduction. Budding and spore formation are other forms.
9. When a cell contains a full set of homologous pairs of chromosomes, we say that it has the diploid, or *2n*, chromosome number. Gametes, however, contain one chromosome of a homologous pair. Thus it is said to have the haploid, or *n*, number.
10. Meiosis occurs in two stages, with cell division taking place in each stage. It is the way haploid gametes are formed. These can then combine to form a diploid zygote.
11. Fertilization is the process by which two haploid (*n*) gametes unite to form the diploid (*2n*) zygote, hence fertilization restores the diploid chromosome number in the first cell of the new organism.

ANSWERS TO APPLYING PRINCIPLES AND CONCEPTS
(Page 94)

1. As a cell increases in size one of two things must happen. Either its rate of synthesis must slow down or it must divide its mass. Otherwise its increase in mass would bring about its death. Nutrients must pass into the cell through the plasma membrane and wastes must pass out of the cell through the same membrane. Thus, a critical relationship exists between

the volume of a cell and the surface exposure of the membrane. As a cell grows, the area of the surface does not increase proportionally with the volume.
2. Mitosis involves a single division of the nucleus, followed by a division of the cell. In the process, chromosomes split lengthwise, forming two identical chromatids joined by a centromere. The chromatids separate at the equator. A full set of chromosomes moves to each pole. Thus, the nuclei in the resulting daughter cells have identical chromosome make-up which is the same as the mother cell that produced them. Meiosis involves two successive nuclear divisions. In the first division, pairs of homologous chromosomes separate at the equator and move to opposite poles but the chromatids remain attached. This division reduces the chromosome number from diploid to haploid. In the second division, the chromatids separate. This constitutes an equal division of the haploid number of chromosomes.
3. Sexual reproduction involves the union of gametes from two different parents within a species. The zygote has a new chromosome combination which results in variations in the offspring. These variations provide for genetic change, a mechanism involved in the evolutionary theory.

unit 2 THE CONTINUITY OF LIFE

How does life go on? How do organisms maintain their distinct characteristics? How does change occur in species? These are only a few of the questions which are discussed in Unit 2. Chapter Nine is concerned with the principles of heredity and how these principles or laws function in genetics. In Chapter Ten, the essence of heredity (the genetic material) is examined. Genes, gene action, and genetic traits are discussed. Chapter Eleven is primarily concerned with human heredity. This chapter explores how genes operate in the human population. Applied genetics is the subject of Chapter Twelve. The application of genetics to agriculture and animal breeding is essential to human life. In Chapter Thirteen, the students will read about organic variation or change. These changes (evolution) have been going on for millions of years and will continue as long as there is life on earth. The final chapter in Unit 2 examines the diversity of life. The subject of classification is introduced to the students, and they will learn how plants and animals are classified under the modern classification system.

chapter nine Principles of Heredity Genetics is the branch of biology concerned with the principles of heredity. These principles are discussed in detail in Chapter Nine. The students will read about Gregor Mendel and his contributions to our understanding of heredity. Mendel's hypotheses are examined in detail and are diagrammatically illustrated. Having read this chapter, the students will have a better appreciation of Mendel's hypotheses and how they formed the basis of the science of genetics.

TEACHING SUGGESTIONS

1. Point out to students the important interrelationship between heredity and environment. Elicit comments from the students, indicating their understanding of these interrelationships and how they work in our lives.
2. Stress to students that Mendel's experiments in the 1850's were truly amazing considering the fact that there was no knowledge of genes, DNA, or chromosomes. Students may want to read Mendel's account of his painstaking experiments.
3. It is interesting to point out to students that many human traits are inherited exactly according to Mendelian laws.
4. Discuss dominant and recessive genes in relation to human traits. Students may be interested in learning that certain inherited diseases result from recessive gene combinations. PKU (phenylketonuria), Tay-Sachs disease, and Wilson's disease are transmitted by recessive genes.

STUDENT INVOLVEMENT ACTIVITIES

1. Ask students to write a brief essay on the subject of heredity versus environment. Allow them to discuss the subject in any manner that is of interest to them.
2. Ask students to write reports on one of the recessive inherited diseases. Have them include methods of screening, genetic transmission, symptoms, and treatment of these diseases.
3. Students may be interested in reading and reporting on chapters of *The New Genetics* by Margaret O. Hyde, Franklin-Watts, Inc., 1974. This informative book discusses contemporary genetics in an easily understood manner.
4. Some students may be interested in working in groups and devising their own experiments that will prove Mendel's principles of heredity.

COMMUNITY INVOLVEMENT ACTIVITIES

1. Invite a farmer or agricultural scientist to discuss how Mendel's principles are directly related to improvement in the amount and kind of crops.
2. Invite a genetic counselor to discuss screening for certain inherited diseases.
3. Have the students become involved with an educational program concerning genetic diseases.

ANSWERS TO QUESTIONS FOR REVIEW
(Page 110)

1. Genetics is the branch of biology that deals with heredity.
2. The garden peas differ consistently in seven distinct characteristics. The garden pea is easy to cross-pollinate.
3. Tall peas crossed with short peas produced an F_1 generation of tall peas. The reappearance of short peas and tall peas in the F_2 generation led Mendel to conceive of the idea of unit characters.
4. Mendel's principle of dominance states that one factor (gene) in a pair may mask the other, or prevent it from having effect.
5. Law of segregation.
6. The genotype of an organism consists of the genes that are present in the organism's body cells. The phenotype is the effect caused in the organism by these genes.
7. A homozygous black guinea pig has two genes for black. A heterozygous black guinea pig has one black gene and one white gene.
8. Alleles are different forms of genes that have contrasting effects on a trait.
9. When two parents that are hybrid for one character are crossed, the offspring will show the dominant and recessive characters in a ratio of ¾ to ¼, respectively.
10. In incomplete dominance, a pair of unlike genes exerts equal influence on the trait it determines.
11. Ratios are averages becuase many eggs and sperm are involved in the combinations. An exact ratio in a monohybrid would appear only if two eggs and two sperms were produced.

ANSWERS TO APPLYING PRINCIPLES AND CONCEPTS
(Page 110)

1. If a black guinea pig is crossed with a white one (pure recessive) and all of the offspring are black (hybrid), the black parent was pure. If both black and white appear, the black parent was hybrid. This is known as a back cross.
2. All offspring of the F_1 generation will show the three dominant traits; black, short hair, and rough coat. Two tri-hybrids crossed will produce a 27:9:9:9:3:3:3:1 ratio of possibilities.
3. A hybridizer has a much better chance of producing a dominant trait in offspring than a recessive one. Furthermore, by knowing which traits in a plant or animal are dominant and which ones are recessive, the hybridizer can plan crosses to produce the desired trait.
4. Genotype: ½ RR, ½ Rr.
   Phenotype: ½ red, ½ pink.

chapter ten The Genetic Material The principles of genetics were detailed long before scientists learned about the genetic material responsible for the principles of heredity. In this chapter, students will become acquainted with the gene hypothesis and its importance to genetics. Sex determination and sex linkage are also examined in this chapter. Students will also explore such topics as nondisjunction, gene linkage, crossing over, and mutation theory. Having read this chapter, students will have a better understanding of gene action.

TEACHING SUGGESTIONS

1. Stress to students the importance of Mendel's findings when compared to the findings of Sutton. Have students identify the parallels between the work of these two scientists.
2. Be sure that students understand Fig. 10-5, p. 114. This diagram of sex determination is as true for *Drosophila* as it is for humans.
3. This may be a good time to introduce the XYY and XXY chromosomal configurations. The XYY configuration has been associated with extreme height, severe acne, and a degree of antisocial behavior.
4. Point out to students that a team of Harvard molecular biologists recently announced that it had synthesized a mammalian gene. Stress to students the importance of such an accomplishment.
5. Point out to students that there are three distinct groups of gene related abnormalities. These groups include: (1) visible ab-

The sex of the offspring is determined by the chromosomes of the sperm cell.

normalities in form or number of chromosomes; (2) single gene abnormalities; and (3) interaction of a number of genes.

STUDENT INVOLVEMENT ACTIVITIES

1. Students may be interested in debating the question of whether or not studies of XYY children should be made. A recent study at Harvard Medical School was halted when protesters objected to the fact that XYY children could be emotionally harmed by such studies.
2. Some students may want to design a simple experiment using *Drosophila* to demonstrate genetic principles.
3. Students may be interested in reading and reporting on *Journey* by Robert and Suzanne Massie, Knopf, 1975. This is the story of a young man afflicted with the sex-linked disease, hemophilia.
4. Ask students to report on one contribution of genetics to modern medicine or agriculture.

COMMUNITY INVOLVEMENT ACTIVITIES

1. Conduct a school program to educate the public on the subject of hemophilia. Invite a physician, hemotologist, and representative of the Hemophilia Foundation to speak.
2. Invite a geneticist to speak to the class on the subject of mutations.
3. Invite a molecular biologist to discuss recent advances in this area and how they affect us medically, socially, and ethically.

CAREER OPPORTUNITIES

Criminologist
Genetic counselor
Geneticist
Hemotologist
Molecular biologist
Radiologist
Sociologist

ANSWERS TO QUESTIONS FOR REVIEW
(Page 126)

1. a. Chromosomes and genes occur in pairs in the zygote and in all somatic cells; b. chromosomes and genes segregate during meiosis, and only one member of each pair normally enters a gamete; c. chromosomes and genes maintain their individuality during segregation. Each pair of chromosomes segregates independently of all other pairs. This confirmed Mendel's law of independent assortment of the characteristics he observed in garden peas.
2. *Drosophila* are useful for genetic studies because they are easy to grow in jars, can be fed simple foods, have a short life span, and because the sexes are easy to tell apart.
3. The male and the female *Drosophila* each have three pairs of identically shaped chromosomes. The fourth pair is rod-shaped in the female, but in the male, the fourth pair is bent like a hook. These are termed the X and the Y, or the sex, chromosomes.
4. A sex-linked gene is a hereditary determiner that is carried on the X chromosome.
5. The sex chromosomes are those (the X and Y) that determine the sex of the offspring. The remaining chromosomes are called autosomes.
6. Nondisjunction is an abnormal segregation of chromosomes.
7. Segments of chromosomes, bearing many genes, may separate and exchange with a corresponding segment of the other member of a chromosome pair, resulting in new gene combinations.
8. A gene is a sequence of base triplets in a segment of DNA that functions to code a polypeptide chain.
9. If you have blue eyes, for example, every cell in your body contains the gene for blue eyes. Yet only in the cells of the iris of your eyes is this trait expressed. Here the gene for eye color produces enzymes which in turn regulate the making of blue pigment. As a result of the action of many thousands of genes, you also have many thousands of enzymes controlling the chemical activities of your cells.
10. If the skin temperature of certain areas on a Himalayan rabbit is raised or lowered the normal hair color of that area may not develop. The genetic trait has been altered. What would be curly wing *Drosophila* may develop straight wings if raised in a lower temperature.
11. Griffith found that noncapsulated organisms did not cause pneumonia, but that the capsule-forming strain did. He injected noncapsulated organisms plus capsulated organisms that he had killed with heat into the mice. Soon they developed pneumonia and died. He recovered living capsulated forms from the dead animals. Therefore, the

noncapsulated form had been transformed in some way.

12. Gene mutations may be caused by radiation and certain chemicals. Chromosome mutations may occur naturally as the result of nondisjunction during segregation in meiosis, loss of an entire chromosome or piece of a chromosome, or recombination of chromosome segments by crossing over.

13. If a mutation occurs in a body cell of a plant or animal, the variation appears in all of the tissue that descends from the original mutant cell. But the trait is not passed on to offspring, since reproductive cells are not involved. Thus, these mutations are not important to the species.

14. A gene is necessary for the synthesis of each enzyme.

ANSWERS TO APPLYING PRINCIPLES AND CONCEPTS
(Page 126)

1. He proposed that hereditary particles, or genes, are component parts of chromosomes. This was the first reference to the gene as the determiner of a genetic characteristic.

2. If nondisjunction has occurred in the formation of an egg or a sperm involved in fertilization, the resulting zygote and all cells descending from it will have abnormal chromosome content. A chromosome may be missing, or an extra chromosome may be present.

3. Transformation proves that genes are active segments of DNA and that these determiners of genetic traits can be transferred from one cell to another.

4. Each strand of DNA replicates. Each member of the replicated pair becomes part of a homologous chromosome.

chapter eleven Genes in Human Populations How do the principles of genetics operate in human populations? This is the question examined in Chapter Eleven. Students will learn about population samples and gene pools. They will also learn about twins and the difference between fraternal and identical twins. Inheritance of blood type is explored. Inherited diseases are also discussed. Having read this chapter, students will have a better understanding of human genetics.

TEACHING SUGGESTIONS

1. Point out to students that given today's increased mobility, gene pools are changing more rapidly than in the past. Ask students to give examples. An important example is that of men going to fight a war in a foreign nation. The gene pool will be affected if many children are born from mixed racial parentage.

2. Elicit responses from students who are twins or who know twins concerning likenesses and differences between them.

3. Point out to students that a recent study indicated that about 25 percent of pediatric admissions to hospitals are for problems involving a form of genetic abnormality. Major birth defects are found in two percent of all live births and chromosomal defects are found in one half of one percent of live births.

4. Stress to students that genetic screening is available for many inherited diseases. Such screening identifies whether or not a person is a carrier of a certain genetic disease.

STUDENT INVOLVEMENT ACTIVITIES

1. Do a population sampling in class for PTC or tongue rolling. Compare class results with results given on p. 128.

2. Ask students to do some research on the physical and personality traits of twins and the effect of the environment on the personalities of twins. Have them report their findings to class.

3. If possible, have students type their blood in class. Have students discuss the importance of knowing one's blood type.

4. Test in class for color blindness. Simple charts are available for screening. Have students figure out the percentage of colorblind students in the class.

5. Have students report on one inherited disease that is of interest to them. Ask them to include in their reports information on genetic screening, modern tests for presence of the condition in the fetus and child, treatment, and agencies that educate the public concerning this condition.

COMMUNITY INVOLVEMENT ACTIVITIES

1. Invite a sociologist to discuss the change in gene pools and what to expect in the future.

2. Invite a pediatrician to discuss genetic abnormalities among children.

3. Conduct a panel discussion on anniocentesis and invite the public to attend. The panel might consist of a pediatrician, obstetrician, genetic counselor, and physician.

2

19

CAREER OPPORTUNITIES

Genetic counselor
Geneticist
Hematologist
Laboratory technician
Obstetrician
Pediatrician
Sociologist

CHALLENGES IN BIOLOGY
AMNIOCENTESIS

The procedure of amniocentesis provides medicine with a tool for discovering possible genetic abnormalities prior to birth. In this procedure, a small amount of fluid is withdrawn from the uterus. This fluid contains the cells of the fetus which can then be examined for chromosomal abnormality.

What are the ethics of such a procedure? This is not a question that can be easily answered. Some people feel strongly that any interference with a fetus is wrong. Others feel that it is best to know what to expect if a genetic abnormality is a possibility.

In a case recently reported in *Today's Health,* a fetus was found to have a fatal metabolic disorder. The procedure of amniocentesis was used to diagnose the disorder. The fascinating part of this story was the treatment of the fetus *prior* to birth. Students may be interested in reading "Curing a Deadly Defect Before the Baby Is Born," by Aljean Harmetz in the December 1974 issue of *Today's Health.*

Amniocentesis is a remarkable tool of medical science. The challenge for biology is to guarantee the responsible use of this and other modern medical techniques.

ANSWERS TO QUESTIONS FOR REVIEW
(Page 139)

1. Population genetics is the study of how frequently given genes appear in a population.
2. A gene pool may be considered stable only when individuals are not entering or leaving a population.
3. Fraternal twins develop from separate eggs which are fertilized by different sperms. They are no more alike genetically than other brothers or sisters. Identical twins started life as a single cell. Early in development, two cells or groups of cells separated and continued development as separate embryos with identical genetic makeup.
4. A and B red corpuscle agglutinogens or the lack of any agglutinogen (O) are under the control of three genes. Only two genes are present in any one person. a. Genes AA or AO produce type-A corpuscles; b. genes BB or BO produce type-B corpuscles; c. genes OO produce type-O corpuscles (no agglutinogen); d. genes AB produce type-AB corpuscles (both agglutinogens).
5. Three genes control the blood type. In any one person, only two of these alleles are present. See the answer to question 4.
6. The genes associated with red-green color vision are located on the X chromosome, and the gene for normal vision is dominant. Since the female (XX) has another allele it is less likely that both the genes would be recessive for the trait. The male (XY) only has one gene for the determination of color vision, so if it is recessive, it is expressed. Therefore, this sex-linked characteristic is found more often in the male.
7. A trait produced by a gene that is dominant in males but recessive in females is said to be sex-influenced. Baldness is an example. A trait that appears in one sex or the other, but not in both, even though the genes

are carried in both sexes, is said to be sex-limited. An example is the bright plumage of the male bird as contrasted to the duller colors in the female, even though the same genes may be present in each.

8. Blue pigment is produced by a single pair of recessive genes. The genes producing brown pigment are dominant. The various shades of iris pigmentation from hazel to light brown or dark brown are apparently the result of the expression of varying numbers of genes for brown pigmentation. Other genes for pigmentation produce shades of gray ranging to green.
9. Diseases resulting from abnormal structure or function of body organs are more likely to be hereditary. An example is sugar diabetes. Other diseases that may be associated with genes are: respiratory allergies including asthma, bronchitis, nearsightedness, farsightedness, and nightblindness.
10. Sickle-cell anemia is a serious blood disease resulting from the formation of abnormal red blood cells. The abnormal shape is caused by the presence of a defect in hemoglobin.
11. The normal chromosome number in humans is 46, but the body cells of some individuals contain 47 chromosomes, while others have only 45. When the body cells of Mongolian idiots have been examined, there have always been 47 chromosomes present. Mongolian idiocy, then, seems to result from the presence of an extra 21st chromosome, resulting from nondisjunction during meiosis.
12. Four conditions caused by nondisjunction of sex chromosomes are: XO (Turner's syndrome), XXX ("super female"), XXY (Klinefelter's syndrome), and XYY (a large and overaggressive male).
13. Amniocentesis is a method of detecting genetic defects in a baby before it is born.

ANSWERS TO APPLYING PRINCIPLES AND CONCEPTS
(Page 139)

1. Although genes are determiners for such things as stature, height, shape of nose, etc., the environment also makes its mark. A person's face, for example, reflects worry, contentment, general health, emotional stress, and nutrition. Environmental influences may prevent the development of the potential inherent in genes.
2. In any quantitative study dealing with populations, the accuracy of the work depends on the selection of a representative group of people.
3. Having started life as the same cell, identical twins have identical genetic makeup. Therefore, identical twins show a marked likeness in appearance, temperament, abilities, likes and dislikes, and many other personality traits. Differences may be attributed to environmental influences. Identical twins then, provide us with valuable information regarding both genetic and environmental influences.
4. (a) Gentotype: ½ $I^A i$, ½ $I^B i$
       Phenotype: ½ type A
                  (heterozygous)
                  ½ type B
                  (heterozygous)
   (b) Genotype: ½ $X^C X^c$, ½ $X^c Y$
       Phenotype: ½ carrier females, ½ colorblind males.

---

chapter twelve Applied Genetics This chapter deals with the application of genetic principles to the improvement of plants and animals for food. The students will learn about Luther Burbank's contributions to plant breeding. They will examine some of the methods utilized in improving the plant strain and crop yield of certain food plants. Plant mutations and new plant strains are also discussed. Having read this chapter, students will have a better understanding of how genetics is used to improve and increase food supplies.

TEACHING SUGGESTIONS

1. Stress to students that without genetic applications to improve plant and animal quality and yield, the earth could not be used to feed the large population dependent on it.
2. Point out to students the amount of work required by plant and animal geneticists in order to produce an improved plant strain or animal breed.
3. Stress to students that although there is a "green revolution," many countries are still unable to feed their own people. This is expecially true in parts of Africa and Asia.
4. Point out to students that grain-fed animals consume enormous quantities of grain that could go to feed people. Discuss the ethics of this problem and the fact that some countries are beginning to do something about it.

STUDENT INVOLVEMENT ACTIVITIES

1. Have students conduct a simple hybridization experiment of their own design.
2. Ask students to examine some plant catalogs to see the numbers of different hybrid seeds that are available.
3. Ask students to report on modern methods of plant and animal breeding. New methods of rice breeding are of special interest in this period of food shortages.

COMMUNITY INVOLVEMENT ACTIVITIES

1. Invite a farmer to class to discuss some of the methods used for improving plant and animal quality and yield.
2. Invite a plant geneticist to class to discuss applications of genetic principles to improving plant quality and yield.
3. Invite a representative of the meat industry to discuss types of meat available, price, shortages, and the new grading system for meats.

CAREER OPPORTUNITIES
Agricultural scientist
Animal breeder
Botanist
Chemist
Consumer advisor
Entomologist
Farmer
Food processor
Plant geneticist
Zoologist

CHALLENGES IN BIOLOGY
THE "GREEN REVOLUTION"
The "green revolution" has never been more important than it is today. The severe food shortage suffered in many heavily populated countries makes greater food production essential.

2

The application of genetics to agriculture began with Luther Burbank (1849–1926). Since World War II, there has been a substantial increase in the quality and production of many crops. Crossbreeding, for example, has resulted in more productive strains of wheat and rice. The yield per acre of hybrid corn has increased more than three-fold in the past 40 years. The development of a new strain of rice (IR-18) has more than doubled the yield of the rice crop. It has also enabled an extra crop to be produced each year as a result of early maturation. This increase in rice production is vital to many Asian countries.

New research in gene transplantation may also improve the growth of crops. If food crops could be given the genetic ability to convert nitrogen from the air directly into growth chemicals, it would greatly reduce the need for fertilizers. Gene-transplant research could also be meaningful to agriculture in many other ways.

The "green revolution" remains as a challenge.

ANSWERS TO QUESTIONS FOR REVIEW
(Page 147)

1. Luther Burbank produced the Shasta daisy, plumcot, pitless plum, peach plum, thin-shelled walnut, and spineless cactus.
2. In mass selection, a few parent plants are chosen for breeding from a great number of individuals. In this way, the offspring are most likely to have the desired traits.
3. Hybridization is the crossing of two different but closely related strains.
4. Inbreeding is practiced to establish a pure strain of plant or animal.

5. Natural cross-pollination is avoided in producing hybrid corn by detasseling the plants and covering the developing ears with sacks. The desired pollen is dusted onto the silks artificially.
6. The mule is a true hybrid because it is the result of a cross between two different animals, the horse and the donkey.
7. Brahman cattle are excellent for crossing with domestic breeds because they endure hot, humid climates and resist insects in these climates.
8. The buffalo can survive harsh weather and eats grass instead of grain.

ANSWERS TO APPLYING PRINCIPLES AND CONCEPTS
(Page 147)

1. If offspring become weakened through continued line breeding, new and unrelated strains should be introduced. This produces hybrid vigor and prevents undesirable recessive traits from appearing.
2. Seed produced from hybrid corn will not produce other generations like the original hybrid because of its mixed parentage. The seed must be produced from known pure-line parents.
3. Pedigree and registration papers are important in breeding high quality livestock as a means of determining the exact ancestry of an animal to be used in breeding. These papers are proof of pure-line ancestry. They show the relationship of breeding animals and may, by listing all parent stock for several generations, give the livestock breeder an indication of certain characteristics he may expect in the offspring.

chapter thirteen Organic Variation How did life on earth begin? Chapter Thirteen attempts to answer this question with a discussion of some of the theories expounded on the origin of life. Evolution is defined and explored according to our present understanding of organic variation. The important contributions of Charles Darwin are examined. Darwin's theory of natural selection is explained. Students will also learn about gene mutations and how they affect populations. Changes in the environment are also examined. Students will better understand evolution and its effects on populations after reading this chapter.

TEACHING SUGGESTIONS

1. Point out to students the significance of Oparin's theory of the origin of life. More information concerning Oparin and his theory is given on T.E. p. 23, *Challenges in Biology.*
2. Theories such as that of Oparin and evolution should be discussed as theories. Other theories to explain origin of life and variation do exist.
3. Point out to students that an event may be evolutionary when the frequency of specific genes in a new generation is altered.
4. Slides of the embryonic development of different organisms may better show up the similarities at certain stages.
5. Ask students whether or not natural selection is at work in human populations today.

STUDENT INVOLVEMENT ACTIVITIES

1. Ask two groups of students to debate Oparin's theory. They

should carefully research both sides of the question.

2. Some students may be interested in following a path of evolution for a particular species.

3. Ask students to write a brief report scientifically refuting Lamarck's theories of evolution.

4. Ask students to give specific examples that correspond to each of the five steps of Darwin's theory (pp. 155–56). Examples should differ from the ones given on the pages.

5. Some students should research the question of whether or not increased exposure to radiation has affected the mutation rate of the population exposed.

COMMUNITY INVOLVEMENT ACTIVITIES

1. Invite an expert in the area of evolution to speak to the class and answer questions.

2. Invite an environmental scientist to discuss the effects that the environment has on evolution today and in recent years.

3. Visit a zoo, aquarium, or a wildlife sanctuary and observe the different species and their adaptations.

4. Invite a geologist to class to discuss the geologic timetable.

CAREER OPPORTUNITIES
Anthropologist
Archeologist
Biologist
Botanist
Environmental scientist
Geologist
Wildlife manager
Zoologist

CHALLENGES IN BIOLOGY
OPARIN'S HYPOTHESIS
The person most responsible for the heterotrophic hypothesis for the origin of life is Aleksandr Ivanovich Oparin, born in 1894 in Russia. Oparin's concept involves the possibility of organisms arising from a conglomeration of formed organic compounds.

Oparin first introduced his rather unpopular hypothesis at a 1922 meeting of the Russian Botanical Society. Oparin believed that early organisms were heterotrophic (they obtained nutrition from compounds already formed). He believed that the first organisms did not have to synthesize their own food, the way modern plants do. Oparin further hypothesized that the living state was characterized by a high degree of structural and functional organization.

In 1957 Oparin organized the first international meeting to study the origin of life. Subsequent conferences were held in 1963 and 1970.

Though many people accept Oparin's ideas, they still remain hypotheses. The challenge remains to prove or disprove these theories.

ANSWERS TO QUESTIONS FOR REVIEW
(Page 162)

1. Sedimentary rock is formed as sediment deposits in the bottom of water gradually compress and harden. It builds up in strata with the oldest at the bottom and each succeeding layer is formed during a more recent time. Thus, a sequence of geological periods in the order in which they occurred is given by this rock.

2. The biological concept of evolution encompasses all of the processes by which organisms change and new and different forms appear. Accompanying this is the decline and eventual extinction of many old forms.

3. The common ancestry of organisms is suggested by: 1) Homologous organs (such as the arms of a human, the wing of a bird and the front leg of a horse); 2) vestigial organs (such as the human appendix); 3) embryology (the resemblance of the embryos of higher animals to each other); 4) biochemistry (all organisms produce DNA and use ATP in energy transfer and the similarity of enzymes and hormones).

4. a. Theory of need—that the production of a new organ or part of a plant or animal results from a need; b. theory of use and disuse—that organs remain active and strong as long as they are used but disappear gradually with disuse; c. theory of inheritance of acquired characteristics—that all that has been acquired or changed in the structure of individuals during their life is transmitted by heredity to the next generation.

5. a. That all organisms produce more offspring than can actually survive; b. that because of overproduction, there is a constant struggle for existence among individuals; c. that the individuals of a given species vary; d. that the fittest, or the best adapted, individuals of a species survive to transmit their traits to the next generation.

6. Mutant genes are nearly always recessive. Ordinarily DNA replicates itself exactly, but occasionally an error occurs and a new genetic code results.

7. a. Migration brings new characteristics into a population; b. it provides a new environment for which an organism may have favorable adaptations that may be perpetuated in offspring.

8. A mutation occurred in the gene controlling the color of the moth. With the change in environment, the color change to black was helpful. Because of natural selection in a new environment, the moth has completely changed color.

9. Isolation prevents interbreeding from occurring so that, as muta-

2

tions occur, variations between two groups may become pronounced.

10. A species is a group of organisms that are similar in structure and that can mate and produce fertile offspring.

11. In adaptive radiation, members of a species population spread to different environments and become more and more different as variations occur and they adapt to these different environments. Convergent evolution is, virtually, the opposite. Unrelated organisms gradually become similar as they adapt, through variations, to similar environments.

ANSWERS TO APPLYING PRINCIPLES AND CONCEPTS
(Page 162)

1. Such similarities often indicate common ancestry, although structural similarities may also be the result of convergent evolution.

2. Lamarck claimed that the giraffe developed a long neck because it needed one to reach the leaves of trees and that the progress of each generation in developing such a neck was passed on to the offspring. Darwin would probably have said that some giraffes had longer necks than others and that those with longer necks had a better chance to survive than those with shorter necks. The modern theory of mutations would say that a giraffe was born with a slight difference in neck structure caused by a mutation and not present in either parent. Since this happened to be an advantage, offspring possessing this mutation had a better chance of surviving than giraffes with shorter necks. Thus, by interbreeding, the neck mutation of the giraffe became a species characteristic of the descendants.

3. The peppered moth study shows how a mutation can increase in the gene pool when it becomes favorable to the survival of a species because of a changed environment. This study

is a demonstration of the importance of natural selection in evolution.

4. Mutation: appearance of black peppered moth population. Selection: Plants with traits enabling them to survive a disease pass these traits on to the offspring. Adaptation: Llamas adapted to the mountains of South America. Convergence: Whales and seals became more alike because they share the same environment.

chapter fourteen The Diversity of Life   The relationships among living things are examined through a study of the science of classification. The contributions of Linnaeus to classification systems are discussed. Students will learn how scientific names are given and how organisms are grouped. Problems in classification are also examined. Students will have a better understanding of taxonomy, having read this chapter.

TEACHING SUGGESTIONS

1. Point out to students that species are sometimes found that have never been classified.

2. Elicit from students possible methods of classification that they would suggest to replace our present methods.

3. Discuss some of the problems of classification with students. Elicit from students their feelings about the three-kingdom system of classification.

STUDENT INVOLVEMENT ACTIVITIES

1. Ask students to report on the work of Linnaeus. There are many interesting biographies written about this man.

2. Have students become familiar with scientific naming by naming a few organisms.

3. Choose two groups of students to debate the question of the two- or three-kingdom classification. Ask the rest of the class to write a brief paragraph about how many kingdoms there should be and what organisms should be included in them.

COMMUNITY INVOLVEMENT ACTIVITIES

1. Invite a taxonomist or a person interested in classification to speak to the class.
2. Visit a botanical garden to examine different species of plant life.
3. Visit a zoo and/or aquarium to examine different species of animal life.

CAREER OPPORTUNITIES

Biologist
Botanist
Cytologist
Geneticist
Microbiologist
Taxonomist
Zoologist

ANSWERS TO QUESTIONS FOR REVIEW
(Pages 170—171)

1. Taxonomy.
2. A scientific name consists of two parts. The genus name is first, and is a capitalized noun. The species name is, usually, an adjective. In some names, a third word indicates a variety.
3. Latin is ideal for scientific classification because it is unchanging, descriptive, and a root of many modern languages.
4. Many names are used for the same organism, or one name is applied to many organisms. Common names are misleading, as "crayfish" and "starfish," which are not fish. They are, too often, based on environment, habits, and other characteristics that show no true structural relationship.
5. Scientific classification is based on structural and biochemical similarity, cellular organization, and genetic makeup.
6. Kingdom, phylum, class, order, family, genus, species, and variety.
7. In the past biologists grouped organisms into one of two kingdoms: Animalia or Plantae. Recently, however, a great amount of research has focused on simpler forms of life. These are now considered to be neither plants nor animals and are placed in the kingdom Protista.

ANSWERS TO APPLYING PRINCIPLES AND CONCEPTS
(Page 171)

1. The mouse and wren are about the same size, yet they are not related. Nor are the fish and crayfish, which share the same environment, nor the rabbit and grasshopper, which have a similar diet.
2. Answers will vary.
3. A species is a plant or animal sufficiently different from all others to justify a specific name. A breed or variety is only slightly different, but not enough to justify a new species name.

2

unit 3 MICROBIOLOGY

What is or is not a living substance is examined in this unit on microbiology. The smallest living things with the characteristics of life are discussed. In Chapter Fifteen, the students will learn about viruses. The virus is not considered alive until it is present in a living cell. In Chapter Sixteen, bacteria are discussed in detail. The students will learn about the history of the discovery of bacteria as well as about the structure and function of these abundant organisms. Infectious disease is the subject of Chapter Seventeen. The history, transmission, and types of infectious disease are discussed. Students will also learn about the different lines of defense that protect them from these pathogenic organisms. Chapter Eighteen is devoted to an examination of the protozoans. All phases of the protozoan life cycle are discussed. In Chapter Nineteen, students will learn about the fungi. Fungi are organisms that are sometimes classified as protists and sometimes classified as simple plants. This unit concludes with a discussion of the algae. Having read this unit, students will have a better understanding of the protists and their importance to our lives.

chapter fifteen The Viruses This chapter discusses a subject with which most of us are quite familiar. Students will learn about the living and nonliving properties of these organisms. They will also learn about their disease-causing properties. Viruses will provide a fascinating subject that many students may wish to examine further.

TEACHING SUGGESTIONS

1. Ask students if they have had a "virus" recently. This will be a good introduction to this chapter. Elicit from students the fact that many symptoms are blamed on a virus when people really do not know what is causing their disease.

2. If possible, show some slides of bacteriophages. These slides are most interesting to students.

3. Carefully explain the lytic cycle (see Fig. 15–7) to students. It may be helpful for students to try to draw Fig. 15–7 from memory. This will help them to understand better what is happening during this cycle.

4. Discuss with students the recent flu epidemics that have affected human populations. The most recent concern is that swine flu may become an epidemic if the population of the United States is not adequately protected. A recent outbreak of this virus in New Jersey reminded people of the 1918–19 swine flu pandemic which killed 20 million people worldwide.

5. Caution students that viral infections have been noted in cases of unhygienic ear-piercing. Caution students about making sure only a doctor or nurse pierces their ears.

STUDENT INVOLVEMENT ACTIVITIES

1. Ask students to bring in clippings about viruses from newspapers or magazines. Discuss the clippings in class.

2. Have students write a brief report on one viral disease. Have reports read to class.

3. Students may be interested in reading *Immunology: The Many Edged Sword,* Harold M. Schmeck, George Braziller Publishers, 1974. This book is based on a series by the author published in *The New York Times.* Chapter Five on viruses may be of special interest to the students.

4. Ask students to do some research on current techniques of working with viruses.

COMMUNITY INVOLVEMENT ACTIVITIES

1. Invite an epidemiologist to class to discuss the causes and control of disease epidemics.

2. Have a panel discussion that is open to the public to discuss the most effective way of seeing to it that all people are vaccinated

prior to a flu outbreak. The panel should consist of a public health administrator, physician, nurse, and interested citizens.

3. Invite a virologist to class to discuss the nature of viruses and viral diseases.

CAREER OPPORTUNITIES

Epidemiologist
Immunologist
Medical technician
Nurse
Pharmaceutical researcher
Physician
Public health administrator
Research biologist
Virologist

CHALLENGES IN BIOLOGY
MEDICAL USES OF PHAGES

Bacteriophages are very much in the forefront of medical science today. They have provided an excellent tool for the study of genetics, mutation among viruses, control of viral and bacterial diseases, and control of certain genetic diseases.

Exciting research has been done in the area of controlling genetic disease through the use of bacteriophages. Bacteriophages may pick up genetic material from the bacteria being infected. In one research experiment, a phage virus picked up the gene for the production of an enzyme that breaks down milk sugar. This virus was then used to infect the skin cells of a patient who was missing this enzyme. Several days later, it was discovered that the skin cells had the necessary enzyme to break down milk sugar.

What does this mean to us? This research and other similar research have strongly indicated that the virus had carried the bacterial gene into human DNA. Though such research is still in its early stages, it is quite possible that a virus could transmit DNA that could alter the course of certain diseases. This is one of the important challenges that face medical scientists today.

CANCER RESEARCH

Much research is being done in the search for a better understanding of the causes of cancers. The term "cancer" covers many different diseases which have one factor in common; the uncontrolled proliferation of abnormal cells. Although some research seems to point to environmental causes, there is evidence that some cancers may be caused by viruses.

It is thought that certain viruses may attack specific cells and cause changes in their genetic composition. If more research reveals the mechanism for this change, then perhaps a cure or a method to impart immunity may be found. Cancer research is one of the most familiar and well-funded areas of research today.

Cancer remains a dreaded disease despite the great advances that have been made in recent years. Research into the causes and elimination of cancer is in the forefront of our challenges in biology.

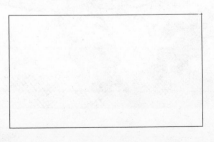

1. Viruses are subcellular, or organized below the level of the cell. A virus has no nucleus, no cytoplasm, and no surrounding membrane.

2. The name *filterable virus* refers to the fact that it passes through the extremely small pores of unglazed porcelain filters used in separating bacteria from fluids.

3. Diseased tobacco leaves.

4. The shell of a virus is composed of protein units. The core of a virus is composed of nucleic acid, either DNA or RNA.

5. *Virulence* means potency.

6. Bacterial viruses, plant viruses, and human and animal viruses.

7. A phage attaches to a bacterium with its tail down. Tiny hooks cause the phage to adhere to the bacterium as an enzyme dissolves the bacterial wall. Once the opening is made, the tail contracts, and DNA of the phage is injected into the bacterial cell. The empty protein phage shell remains outside. The phage DNA approaches the bacterial DNA and takes control of the chemical machinery of the bacterium, causing it to produce phage DNA and protein molecules. The bacterium soon contains 100 or more phage particles, which are released when the bacterial cell disintegrates. The cycle is then repeated.

8. Temperate phages are potential "seeds of destruction" because they can invade bacterial cells without causing immediate destruction.

9. Smallpox, chickenpox, influenza, rabies, the common cold, and mumps.

10. Mycoplasms can be grown in a cul-

Swine flu virus can be dangerous to humans, too.

ture without the presence of living cells; reproduction does not require the use of living cells.

ANSWERS TO APPLYING PRINCIPLES AND CONCEPTS
(Page 181)

1. The structure and virulence of a virus appears to be altered by the chemical nature and activity of the cell that produces it. The rabies virus, for example, becomes more virulent for humans and dogs when grown in the brain and spinal cord of dogs. When the virus is grown in rabbits, it becomes less virulent for humans and dogs but increases in virulence for rabbits. Mutations also may alter the virulence of a virus.

2. Free phages cannot reproduce. A phage is a nucleoprotein consisting of a shell surrounding a DNA core. Bacterial genes control the synthesis of specific enzymes and other proteins characteristic of the particular organism. Phage DNA apparently functions as a gene within the bacterial cell, and alters the chemical machinery of the bacterial cell, causing it to synthesize phage particles.

3. Viruses may be considered nonliving since they cannot reproduce on their own. Only in the presence of a living system in a cell do they show signs of life. However, the presence of nucleic acid tends to support the idea that viruses are living.

4. Viruses are not self-reproducing but are formed by alteration of the chemical processes of cells they invade. There is evidence that a particular virus requires a specific kind of cell for this close biochemical relationship. For example, the polio viruses invade and destroy only the cell bodies of motor neurons in the spinal cord of humans and certain animals.

chapter sixteen Bacteria and Related Organisms Students may be interested to learn that bacteria are the most common form of life. They will also learn that more bacteria are beneficial than harmful. The structure and function of bacteria are examined and the different forms of bacteria are discussed. Students will also learn about the economic importance of these organisms. Having read this chapter, students will have a better understanding of the fascinating world of the microorganisms.

TEACHING SUGGESTIONS

1. To introduce this chapter, read a dictionary definition of the word *pasteurization.* See how many students know what you are describing.

2. Show some slides of the different shapes of bacteria. Students will show greater interest in the subject if the slides represent specific disease-causing bacteria.

3. Stress to students the four points discussed on p. 187. These conditions are essential to bacterial viability and should be considered in any experiments with bacteria.

4. Stress to students the economic importance of bacteria. Students may be interested in reporting on a particular industry and its dependence on bacteria.

STUDENT INVOLVEMENT ACTIVITIES

1. Ask a few students to write on one of the following topics: pasteurization; ultra-pasteurization; canning and preserving techniques; and the economic importance of bacteria.

2. Have students do some research and report to class on one disease caused by bacteria.

3. Students may be interested in reading one of the following books: *How Did We Find Out About Germs?,* by Isaac Asimov, Walker & Co., 1974 (a book for the lower-level student); or *Microbes and Men* by Robert Reid, Saturday Review Press, 1974 (a book about the history of microbes for the higher-level student).

COMMUNITY INVOLVEMENT ACTIVITIES

1. Invite a microbiologist to class to discuss the functions of his or her position.

2. If possible, visit a factory (brewing, tanning, chemical, dairy) that involves the commercial use of bacteria.

3. Invite a representative of the dairy industry to discuss recent reports of high bacterial counts in ice cream and other dairy products.

4. Invite a home economist to speak to the class about proper techniques of canning and preserving foods. This discussion should be open to the public.

3

CAREER OPPORTUNITIES

Bacteriologist
Chemist
Dairy plant worker
Home economist
Microbiologist
Nutritionist
Pharmacist
Physician
Research scientist

ANSWERS TO QUESTIONS FOR REVIEW
(Page 194)

1. Discovery of bacteria in fermenting juices; germ theory.

2. Bacteria are large compared to viruses.

3. Bacteria are classified according to their shapes. Spherical forms are cocci; rod-shaped forms are bacilli; spiral or bent rod-shaped forms are spirilla.

4. Bacteria have a nuclear area, but no nuclear membrane; they have no mitochondria; they have a slime layer or capsule.

5. Various bacillus and spirillum forms of bacteria are equipped with threadlike whips, or flagella, which propel the cell through water or other fluids. There may be a single flagellum or one on both ends of a bacterial cell. In some forms, flagella may surround the cell. They are cytoplasmic extensions that project through openings in the cell wall and are composed of strands of protein molecules resembling the microscopic fibers composing muscle.

6. Brownian movement is random molecular motion. True movement of bacteria is accomplished by flagella.

7. Favorable growth of bacteria requires a suitable temperature, moisture, darkness, and source of food.

8. Crowding, competition for food, build-up of waste products.

9. Heterotrophic bacteria may be saprophytic or parasitic. Autotropic bacteria are chemosynthetic and can utilize inorganic compounds as an energy source. A few bacteria are photosynthetic.

10. Aerobic bacteria require free oxygen for respiration. Anaerobic bacteria do not require free oxygen, and many cannot grow in the presence of atmospheric oxygen.

11. Alcohol, carbon dioxide, pyruvic acid, and lactic acid are products of glucose fermentation by microorganisms.

12. Break down compounds in soil for use by plants; produce alcohol, vinegar, silage, etc.; starter bacteria used to make butter, buttermilk, cheese, etc.

13. Foods may be preserved by killing bacterial cells as in canning and pasteurization. The environment may be made unfavorable for bacterial growth by the addition of chemicals, salting, refrigeration, quick freezing, drying, and by radiation.

14. Rickettsiae are transmitted to humans by insects and their relatives, including the human body louse, ticks, and mites.

15. The best known infection caused by a spirochete is syphilis.

ANSWERS TO APPLYING PRINCIPLES AND CONCEPTS
(Page 194)

1. Studies on *E. Coli* have shown that two cells unite and the cell contents of one cell flow through a cytoplasmic bridge to the other cell. The significance may be that in recombination certain genetic variations may result in changes allowing the organism to survive in new environments or to exist in changing environments.

2. The same forces that limit the growth rate of bacteria affect all other living populations, including human beings.

3. Rickettsiae seem to be midway between the bacteria and the viruses. They are barely visible under the highest magnifications of the light microscope. They are cellular and reproduce by fission as do bacteria. However, like viruses, they can grow and reproduce only in living cells.

chapter seventeen Infectious Disease This chapter discusses a subject of great interest to all of us. Students will learn how diseases are spread, how they are caused, and about our defenses against disease. Structural, cellular, antibody, and chemical defenses against disease are examined. Students will also learn about immune therapy and other methods of treating infectious disease. Having read this chapter, students will be more familiar with infectious diseases, their nature and treatment.

TEACHING SUGGESTIONS

1. One interesting way of introducing this chapter is to elicit from students their definitions of the word *infectious*. Discuss the definitions and agree upon an acceptable one from those that are offered.

2. Stress to students the importance of health habits in the control of infectious diseases. Ask students for recommendations concerning the best way to educate the public about health habits.

3. Stress to students the importance of immunization in the eradication of certain diseases. Point out that many states are very specific in the requirement of certain immunizations at different ages throughout a person's schooling.

4. Be sure that students understand the difference between active and passive immunity. Table 17-1, p. 203, should be helpful in clarifying their understanding of this subject.

STUDENT INVOLVEMENT ACTIVITIES

1. Ask students to report on one of the venereal diseases and its symptoms and treatment.

2. Have a class discussion concerning the increase in recent years of cases of gonorrhea and syphilis.

3. Have students find out the immunity requirements of their state or local community. Compare these to the accepted immunization schedule that most doctors follow.

4. Have a class discussion on whether or not the state or federal government has the right to insist that people are immunized against certain diseases.

5. Ask some students to report on various aspects of antibiotics: types of antibiotics; resistance to antibiotics; overuse of some antibiotics; and new research in this area.

COMMUNITY INVOLVEMENT ACTIVITIES

1. Invite a physician and a public health official to school to discuss the reasons for immunization and acceptable immunization schedules.

2. Invite a member of the dog control team of your community to discuss different aspects of their job.

3. If possible, visit a pharmaceutical company and observe the production of antibiotic drugs.

4. Invite a pharmacist to class to discuss the nature and use of antibiotics today.

CAREER OPPORTUNITIES

Bacteriologist
Dog control team member
Immunologist
Laboratory technician
Nurse
Pharmacist
Physician
Public health official
Research chemist
Virologist

CHALLENGES IN BIOLOGY
ORGAN TRANSPLANTS

The first human heart transplant was performed by Dr. Christiaan Barnard on December 3, 1967. This initial heart transplant was followed by many others. However, certain problems occurred which were not easily resolved. There have been fewer and fewer transplants in recent years. The major problems are organ rejection, a shortage of donor hearts, and the difficulties of donor heart storage.

While heart transplants are considered relatively unsuccessful, kidney transplants have met with much success and wide acceptance. By 1973, more than 13,000 kidney transplants had been performed and about 5,000 of these patients had survived. In kidney transplants, the survival rate is greater for those who receive a kidney from a close relation.

Many other types of transplants are also being attempted. These trans-

3

plants have met with different degrees of success. Liver, lung, pancreas, and bone marrow transplants have been performed. Bone marrow transplants are performed in certain cases of aplastic anemia and leukemia.

The challenge to biology remains in solving the immunologic problems of rejection. This is foremost in the work of many medical researchers today. In addition, more public education is needed to alert possible donors to the needs of transplant patients.

BACTERIAL RESISTANCE

Recent newspaper articles have discussed the problem of bacterial resistance and how, in some cases, it may be linked to the overprescription of certain antibiotic drugs. With the age of antibiotics upon us, some physicians tend to prescribe an antibiotic when it may not always be necessary. Changes within bacterial cells have resulted in many bacteria becoming resistant to certain antibiotics.

Resistance to antibiotics does not occur in all organisms and with all antibiotic drugs. In some cases, bacteria are resistant to an antibiotic prior to its development. In other cases, bacteria develop a resistance to a certain drug. This happens through mutation, transduction, transformation, or conjugation.

Mutation usually involves a spontaneous change in the genetic material. Transduction involves a bacteriophage that reproduces in bacteria. The resistance to the antibiotic may be transferred by the virus to the bacterial strain. New

antibiotics are often developed that offer only a temporary solution because many bacteria will soon become resistant to them.

The challenge to biology involves research to control bacterial change which results in resistance. In addition, greater care should be taken to see that antibiotics are only given to individuals who can directly benefit from them.

1. a. Isolate the probable organisms causing the disease (Koch found them in the bloodstream of infected animals); b. grow the organisms in laboratory cultures (Koch used vitreous humor from ox eyes); c. inoculate a healthy animal with the cultured organisms (Koch inoculated mice); d. recover the causative organisms from the infected animals (Koch found the organisms had multiplied enormously in the bloodstream of mice).

2. (1) Carried in food or water, organisms may enter the digestive system through the mouth. (2) Infections can be spread through the air by sneezing or coughing. (3) Infections can be spread by direct or indirect contact with sores. (4) If the skin is broken, wound infections may occur. (5) Human immune carriers may spread infectious organisms. (6) Insects may spread disease organisms.

3. Colds, sinus infections, measles, scarlet fever, and tuberculosis.

4. Typhus fever is vectored by the human body louse, bubonic plague by the rat flea, Spotted fever by the tsetse fly, malaria by the *Anopheles* mosquito, and yellow fever by the *Aedes* mosquito.

5. An immune carrier shows no signs of disease yet carries living infectious organisms.

6. Exotoxins are chemical substances which diffuse from certain kinds of bacteria and have damaging effects when absorbed by surrounding tissue or when transported through the bloodstream. Endotoxins remain inside the bacterial cells that form them. These toxins are released with deadly effect when the bacteria die and disintegrate.

7. Food poisoning is caused by exotoxins produced by bacteria in foods, e.g., botulism.

8. Skin, mucous membranes, mucus, tears, and acid of the stomach are structural body defenses.

9. Leucocytes are phagocytic cells that pass through the walls of capillaries and move through tissue fluids to the site of an infection. They then form a wall around the infectious organisms and engulf them.

10. Fever reduces or inhibits the growth of many bacteria.

11. An antibody acts against a specific disease organism or its products.

12. Interferon causes production of an antiviral protein which prevents viruses from multiplying. Antiviral antibodies combine with viruses and make them noninfectious.

13. Natural immunity is a resistance to infection present at birth and due to inherited conditions of the human body. Acquired immunity results from recovery from an infectious disease or artificial immunization.

14. A vaccine is a biological preparation that contains dead or weakened pathogenic organisms or their products. A serum contains antibodies. A vaccine is introduced into the individual to stimulate him to form his own antibodies without having the disease. This results in an active immunity. A serum is given to the individual to give immediate, but temporary protection against an infection.

15. Antibiotics are products of living organisms.

ANSWERS TO APPLYING PRINCIPLES AND CONCEPTS
(Page 209)

1. Answers will vary.

2. Edward Jenner pioneered in immune therapy when he successfully inoculated a child with cowpox, thus making him immune to smallpox.

3. Rejection of the transplanted organ. Drugs that lower the body's natural immunity allow an organ transplant to heal without being rejected.

4. Any variant that allows a bacterium to survive antibiotic treatment would also occur in its offspring. While most bacteria are killed by the drug, the resistant strain may increase in number as its competitors are eliminated.

chapter eighteen The Protozoans   The one-celled organisms or protozoans are the subject of this chapter. Students will learn why protozoans are included in the protist kingdom. The structure and function of the ameba, paramecium, and euglena are examined. Disease-causing protozoans are also discussed. This chapter concludes with a discussion of the economic importance of these organisms. Having read this chapter, students will have a better understanding of protozoans and their effect on other organisms.

3

TEACHING SUGGESTIONS

1. Discuss with students some of the reasons for placing protozoans in the protist kingdom. As the students learn more about the characteristics of protozoans, these reasons will become clarified.

2. Have students examine living amebas under the microscope. Ask them to compare their observations to what they have read in the text.

3. Have students perform some simple experiments in order to observe the response behavior of paramecia.

4. Point out to students that, while malaria is not a danger in the United States, it is a very great danger in many parts of the world.

5. Stress to students the importance of protozoans to the food chains of many organisms. Some students may be interested in tracing a food chain that includes protozoans as well as humans.

STUDENT INVOLVEMENT ACTIVITIES

1. If possible, have students bring in samples of protozoans that they have collected.

2. Some students may wish to report on malaria. They should include present statistics on numbers of cases, countries where it is widespread, and current methods of prevention and treatment.

3. Ask students to choose a disease caused by a protozoan and report on it in some detail.

4. Have students bring to class any clippings that discuss protozoans.

5. Ask some students to draw the life cycle of certain pathogenic protozoans and their hosts. They could then explain their drawings to the class.

COMMUNITY INVOLVEMENT ACTIVITIES

1. Invite a public health official to class to discuss some of the diseases caused by protozoans.

2. Invite a physician to class to discuss some of the methods of preventing and treating amebic dysentery. This disease frequently affects Americans traveling in tropical and semi-tropical countries.

CAREER OPPORTUNITIES

Epidemiologist
Health statistician
Medical technician

Nurse
Physician
Protozoologist
Public health official
Zoologist

ANSWERS TO QUESTIONS FOR REVIEW
(Page 220)

1. Sarcodina, Mastigophora, Sporozoa, and Ciliata. Protozoans are divided into phyla on the basis of their means of locomotion. Examples of the phyla, in the order named, include: ameba, euglena, *Plasmodium,* and paramecium.

2. Flowing cytoplasm of the ameba, especially the inner endoplasm, flows against the flexible plasma membrane, causing it to bulge in the direction of movement. This type of movement is called ameboid movement.

3. The ameba extends pseudopodia around a food particle and engulfs the particle into a food vacuole.

4. The contractile vacuole serves as a hydrostatic organ in maintaining a constant or nearly constant internal water concentration in certain organisms.

5. Paramecia move by cilia. These are arranged in rows and lash back and forth like tiny oars. Since the cilia can beat forward or backward, the cell can move in either direction or turn around.

6. Paramecia multiply by fission and divide laterally. Rejuvenation is accomplished by the exchange of nuclear materials during conjugation.

7. Trichocysts are special cytoplasmic threads that lie just inside the pellicle. When a large protozoan

appears near the paramecium, the trichocysts are exploded through tiny pores. These give the cell a bristly appearance which protects it from the approaching protozoan.

8. Unlike ameba and paramecium, a euglena contains chloroplasts for photosynthesis. Light is necessary for photosynthesis. Euglenas live primarily an autotropic life but are capable of living as heterotrophs.

9. When the *Anopheles* mosquito bites a malarial patient and sucks up the blood, a few specialized individuals of *Plasmodium* are also taken in with the blood. While in the stomach of the mosquito, these mature into two entirely different kinds of cells. One is an egg cell, the other is a sperm cell. After fertilization, the egg penetrates the stomach wall of the mosquito and forms a cyst. In this condition, the parasite forms spore cells which are released when the cyst erupts. Some of the spores migrate to the salivary glands of the mosquito. If the mosquito pierces the bloodstream of an individual, some of the spores are carried with the saliva, which is injected into the puncture at the time of biting. After a period of growth and multiplication, the spores penetrate the red corpuscles and continue to multiply.

10. The ameba causing amebic dysentery lives in the large intestine where it forms cysts. These cysts containing inactive ameba are excreted in the feces of infected individuals. Therefore, when sewage is not properly disposed of or is used as fertilizer, individuals may contract amebic dysentery.

ANSWERS TO APPLYING PRINCIPLES AND CONCEPTS
(Page 220)

1. All the life processes performed in higher organisms are carried on, to

some degree, by a single protozoan cell. Since a single cell functions as an entire organism, its structures must perform these processes without dependence on any other cells. This independence results in such complicated protozoans as the paramecium which represents, probably, the maximum development of structures within a single cell.

2. The ameba lacks any definite structures for locomotion or food-getting. Cell specialization reaches a higher degree in paramecium. The organism has structures for locomotion, food getting, waste removal and protection. Euglena has a flagellum for locomotion and chloroplast with chlorophyll for photosynthesis. Since euglena can make its own food, it probably has the highest degree of specialization.

3. It is best to treat the malaria patient while the spores are in the bloodstream and before the sexual forms of the parasite are produced. Quinine is not effective against the sexual form of *Plasmodium*.

4. Protozoans are a vital part of the biological balance in a pond. They feed on organic matter and thus act as scavengers. They excrete carbon dioxide and, after death, add their substance to the organic content of the water. They are an important source of food for small animals and, thus, are a part of a food chain in an aquatic environment.

chapter nineteen   The Fungi

Fungi are organisms that never form roots, leaves, or stems and do not have chlorophyll. Students will learn about these and other characteristics of fungi as they read Chapter Nineteen. They will learn about different types of fungi molds, yeasts, plant parasites, and the best known of the fungi — the mushrooms. After reading this chapter, students will better understand how fungi can be both constructive and destructive to life.

TEACHING SUGGESTIONS

1. An interesting way of introducing this subject is to give students some of the characteristics of fungi and have them determine what group of organisms is being discussed.

2. Point out to students that fungi, like so many other organisms, can be destructive to life or can contribute in many positive ways to the lives of other living things.

3. Point out to students that a person who specializes in the study of fungi is called a *mycologist*. The field is called *mycology*. There are in excess of 250,000 varieties of fungi ranging from those that are microscopic to mushrooms that are quite large.

4. Point out to students the importance of being familiar with the poisonous varieties of mushrooms. Many poisonous types are confused with edible types. The "destroying angel" *(Amanita Phalloides)*, for example, is a poisonous mushroom that is often confused with nonpoisonous varieties.

STUDENT INVOLVEMENT ACTIVITIES

1. Ask students to bring in samples of fungi found on rotting wood. Have students identify the fungi from books on mycology.

2. Ask students to report on some aspect of the economic importance of fungi. They may want to report on growing mushrooms, molds used in drug production, yeasts, or the importance of certain molds to cheese flavoring.

3. Students may be interested in researching how mushrooms are grown for market. Some industrious students may want to grow some mushrooms on their own.

4. Ask some students to report on poisonous mushrooms. Have them include photographs of these mushrooms in their report.

COMMUNITY INVOLVEMENT ACTIVITIES

1. If possible, have a mycologist come to class and discuss his or her specialty.

2. Invite someone who grows mushrooms (either as a hobby or commercially) to speak to the class about this subject.

3. Visit a bakery and observe how the use of yeast causes bread to rise.

4. Invite a home economist to class to discuss the use of mushrooms in certain recipes. Students may want to prepare some mushroom recipes and bring them to class.

CAREER OPPORTUNITIES
Chef
Dairy industry worker
Farmer
Home economist
Mushroom grower
Mycologist
Pharmaceutical researcher
Plant disease specialist

ANSWERS TO QUESTIONS FOR REVIEW
(Page 234)

1. Fungi never form roots, stems, or leaves; they lack chlorophyll.

2. All fungi lack chlorophyll and are therefore nutritionally dependent on a host or other organic food supply.

3. Myxomycetes, Phycomycetes, Ascomycetes, Basidiomycetes, and Deutromycetes.

4. The mycelium of a fungus consists of a tangled spreading mass of colorless threads, the hyphae. They may be of various sorts, as in the bread mold (*Rhizopus*).

5. Stolons, rhizoids, sporangiophores.

6. Spores of bread mold and other molds are present in the air. If a spore settles on a piece of bread or other suitable food supply and if other growth conditions are present, the spore germinates and produces a hypha, which continues growth into the mold mycelium. A form of conjugation is involved in the sexual reproduction of bread mold. Two different hyphae referred to as plus and minus form short, specialized side branches. If the tip of a branch of a hypha of a plus strain contacts the tip of a branch of a hypha of a minus strain, conjugation occurs. Cross walls develop a short distance back of the tips of the side branches, cutting off the terminal cells that become gametes. The walls dissolve and allow the two gametes to fuse forming a zygote.

7. (1) Cause economic loss by spoiling foods; (2) agents of major plant disease; (3) parasites of animals and humans.

8. The formation of alcohol during sugar fermentation is an important industrial process. Carbon dioxide, released during fermentation, is important in the baking industry.

9. In the late spring and early summer, surface hyphae of wheat rust discharge reddish-orange, one-celled spores called uredospores. Later in the summer, these same hyphae produce a second type of spore. This is a black, two-celled spore with heavy, thick protective walls. Black spores are referred to as teliospores. Early in the spring, both cells of the teliospores germinate, producing four-celled basidia. A new spore called a basidiospore forms on each of the four cells of the basidium. If a basidiospore lodges on a leaf of the common barberry, complicated tissue changes will occur in the leaf of the barberry, and tiny cups containing rows of a fourth kind of spore will appear on the leaf. These new spores are the aeciospores.

10. The reproductive part of a mushroom develops as a bud, or button, on the mycelium, and is composed of a mass of hyphae packed tightly together. The mass grows upward and opens into the familiar mushroom above the ground. Spores form at the ends of basidia on the gill surfaces.

11. Ringworm, athlete's foot, barber's itch, and thrush are infections caused by imperfect fungi.

12. The plasmodium stage often appears as a slimy fan-shaped network of living matter. It is a mass of protoplasm containing many nuclei and lacking cell walls.

ANSWERS TO APPLYING PRINCIPLES AND CONCEPTS
(Page 234)

1. The yeast plants produce zymase, which acts on the sugars during respiration. This is an anaerobic process and can take place in an airtight container.

2. Their mycelium has exhausted the organic matter in one spot and has moved into the unused organic matter in the soil or host material. New mushrooms are produced at the outer edge of the growing ring of mycelium. The newest and most active molds grow at the outer edge of a colony so as to obtain nourishment.

3. Slime molds often resemble giant masses of amebae and might be considered protozoan-like. They resemble fungi in the production of sporangia and spores.

chapter twenty The Algae

Algae are simple organisms that lack roots, stems, and leaves. However, students will be interested to learn about the contributions of these organisms, simple as they are, as major producers of food and oxygen. Students will learn about where algae live, how they reproduce, and why they are considered as protists. Representative algae are discussed in detail. The economic value of algae is also discussed. This chapter concludes with a discussion of lichens — a fungus and alga that live together form a lichen. Having read this chapter, students will have a better understanding of an abundant organism which contributes greatly to life on this earth.

TEACHING SUGGESTIONS

1. Point out to students that algae have been considered as a possible source of oxygen for long space trips or survival on certain distant planets. Studies indicate that about two and one half kilograms of a certain type alga is sufficient to supply the oxygen requirements of one person.

2. Stress to students that too much algae growth can diminish photosynthesis by restricting it to the top layers of an aquatic environment.

3. Students may be interested in performing some simple observations of *Spirogyra* by exposing these organisms to sunlight and then removing the source of light.

4. Discuss the advantages of certain algae being able to reproduce asexually and sexually.

STUDENT INVOLVEMENT ACTIVITIES

1. Ask students to bring in algae samples for examination.

2. Some students may be interested in reporting on new research associated with the use of algae in space programs.

3. Ask some students to write brief reports on the economic importance of algae.

4. Water pollution by algae is an important problem. Ask students to research this topic and report on their findings.

COMMUNITY INVOLVEMENT ACTIVITIES

1. Invite a local water company representative to speak to the class about algae contamination of water supplies.

2. Invite a research scientist to class to discuss some of the contemporary uses of algae.

3. Visit your local water purification plant and learn about how algae is controlled in water supplies.

CAREER OPPORTUNITIES

Botanist
Food scientist
Sanitary engineer
Space scientist
Water purification worker
Zoologist

CHALLENGES IN BIOLOGY
BLUE-GREEN ALGAE AND POLLUTION

Have you ever noticed an acrid odor in your tap water? This odor may be coming from algae growth in the water source. Each year many water companies receive complaints of such odors. In most cases, the algae are not harmful in the water supply.

However, algae do indicate that a body of water may be polluted. Dissolved fertilizer or sewage that passes into a body of water may trigger the growth of a large crop of algae. This massive algae growth cuts off the sunlight at the surface of the water and limits photosynthesis to the top layer of vegetation. As the algae rate rises, the rate of oxygen production decreases (because the sunlight is blocked) and the need for oxygen increases. The result is an oxygen-deprived body of water that may "die" from such growth.

Once a body of water has "died," it is very difficult to restore it to its natural condition. The challenge to biology is in the effective treatment of sewage and fertilizers so that they do not cause such a rapid algae growth in bodies of water. Algae are marvelous contributors to oxygen and food needs; however, when their growth is uncontrolled their effects can be most harmful.

ANSWERS TO QUESTIONS FOR REVIEW
(Page 250)

1. Algae lack roots, stems, and leaves; they lack specialized tissues for carrying water and food; they are the main producers, through

3

photosynthesis, of food and oxygen in water environments.

2. Algae, unlike fungi, always contain the pigment chlorophyll and can carry on photosynthesis.

3. The cells of blue-green algae are considered primitive because they lack specialized structures such as a definite nucleus or a definite chloroplast, and they cannot reproduce sexually.

4. Cyanophyta (blue-green), Chlorophyta (green), Chrysophyta (gold-brown), Pyrrophyta (dinoflagellates), Phaeophyta (brown), and Rhodophyta (red).

   Examples of the algae in these phyla which are mentioned in the chapter are (in order as mentioned above): *Nostoc, Anabaena, Gloeocapsa,* and *Oscillatoria; Protococcus, Chlorella, Spirogyra, Ulothrix, Oedogonium,* and desmids; diatoms; *Gymnodinium; Fucus, Sargassum;* and *Chondrus, Gelidium.*

5. During conjugation of most species of *Spirogyra,* the cells of + and − filaments unite by forming conjugation tubes. The content of a − cell moves through the conjugation tube and combines with the contents of a + cell to form a zygote.

6. The occurrence of two distinct stages in the life cycle of an organism is called alternation of generations. In *Ulothrix* the vegetative cells in a filament represent the gametophyte (n) generation. Certain of these cells form gametes which fuse and form a zygote (2n) which constitutes the sporophyte generation. Meiosis occurs in spore formation in the zygote. The spores (n) give rise to new vegetative cells of a gametophyte generation.

7. A desmid cell consists of equal halves each of which contains one or two large chloroplasts. The halves are connected by a narrow isthmus in which the nucleus is situated.

8. A diatom has a valve or shell composed of two parts, one fitting over the other. The valve is composed of silicon dioxide and contains many crossline markings. They grow in open seas and the foods are stored as oils. The walls of diatoms contain pectin and silicon dioxide.

9. The alga which causes the "red tide" is the dinoflagellate, *Gymnodinium.* At periodic intervals rapid reproduction of *Gymnodinium* results in an enormous increase in their number. Release of the toxic red pigment substance from such large numbers of cells poisons millions of fish.

10. (1) Source of food for animals in their environment; (2) soil fertilizers; (3) produce agar; (4) used in dairy industry.

11. A lichen is made up of an alga and a fungus. The alga is protected and kept moist by the fungus; the fungus depends on the alga for food. This arrangement illustrates mutualism.

ANSWERS TO APPLYING PRINCIPLES AND CONCEPTS
(Page 250)

1. Each of the cells in a 50-cell alga is, in a sense, an independent organism since there is no interdependence among the cells and little, if any, cell specialization.

2. Spores are asexual bodies and are capable of forming a new organism directly. Gametes are sexual bodies and must unite during fertilization and form a zygote before cell division and formation of a new organism can occur.

3. Blue-green algae give water a foul, stagnant odor.

4. All cells in a filament of *Spirogyra* are similar in structure. In *Ulothrix,* a filament is anchored by a special holdfast cell. All cells above the holdfast are similar. *Oedogonium* filaments are anchored by a holdfast cell. In addition, modified oogonial cells form eggs and antheridial cells form sperms.

5. Algae may be found in such unusual places as at a depth of five hundred feet in the ocean, on the bark of trees, on the surface of the soil, on the underside of the blue whale, on the hair of the three-toed sloth, and within other organisms. Most species live in shallow water or float near the surface since this is where they get the most light.

unit 4 MULTICELLULAR PLANTS

The plant kingdom includes the simple mosses and liverworts and the complex seed plants. This unit will take the student on a tour past the numerous, interesting species of plants. In Chapter Twenty-One, the mosses and liverworts are discussed. The ferns are also examined. Chapter Twenty-Two is devoted to a detailed discussion of the seed plants. This is followed by an examination of leaves and their functions in Chapter Twenty-Three. Roots and stems are vital to plant absorption and are topics of discussion in Chapter Twenty-Four. Water suppply is critical to the growth and development of plants. This topic is examined in Chapter Twenty-Five. One of the most fascinating aspects of plants is their growth and responses. These topics are examined in Chapter Twenty-Six. This unit concludes with a chapter devoted to understanding plant reproduction. This unit has provided students with an introduction to the many facets of plant life. Many students may be interested in delving deeper into an area of plant life that is of special interest to them.

chapter twenty-one Mosses and Ferns   Mosses, liverworts, and ferns are the subjects of this chapter. Students will learn about the structure and life cycles of these plants. Their place in the development of plant life on earth is also examined. Having read this chapter, students will better understand plant evolution.

TEACHING SUGGESTIONS
1. Ask students to bring in and try to identify different types of mosses.
2. Point out to students that mosses and liverworts have not changed very much in more than 400 million years. Ferns, however, have evolved into seed plants.
3. Discuss with students the importance of water in the reproductive cycle of mosses. Is this an advantage or disadvantage to reproduction?
4. Discuss with students the reasons for ferns being better adapted to a land environment than are mosses or liverworts. Ferns have true roots, stems, and leaves and are generally more complex.
5. If possible, bring to class some fern leaves that have the rust-colored spots on them. These spots consist of hundreds of tiny spore cases.

STUDENT INVOLVEMENT ACTIVITIES
1. Have students bring in samples of ferns and try to identify them in a botany text.
2. Some students may be interested in reading and reporting on the evolution of plants.
3. Ask students to bring in pictures of tree ferns that exist in present-day tropical forests. These ferns will give students an idea of what the ancient ferns looked like.
4. Some students may be interested in researching the formation of different types of coal and relationship of coal to ancient mosses and ferns.

COMMUNITY INVOLVEMENT ACTIVITIES
1. Invite a botanist to class to discuss plant evolution and some of the species that lived in prehistoric times.
2. Visit a local botanical garden and observe the liverworts, mosses, and ferns.
3. Invite a member of the local horticultural society to discuss these plants with the class.

CAREER OPPORTUNITIES
Botanist
Bryologist (specialist in ferns and mosses)
Horticulturist
Paleobotanist
Phylogenist (specialist in developmental evolution)
Plant geneticist
Plant researcher

ANSWERS TO QUESTIONS FOR REVIEW
(Page 261)

1. Mosses are small and lack a root system comparable to that of higher

plants. They also lack vascular tissues for conduction.

2. Spanish moss, water moss (masses of algae) and reindeer moss are examples of plants incorrectly called mosses.

3. The gametophyte plant is the moss plant that is most often seen. It consists of a slender stem encircled by delicate leaves and is anchored in the soil by hairlike rhizoids. The egg cell is a product of the gametophyte generation, and when fertilized it forms the zygote, the first cell of the sporophyte generation. The sporophyte moss plant consists of a leafless stalk and capsule, in which spores are produced.

4. Sphagnum or peat moss forms peat which is used as fuel or as roof-building material. It is also used as mulch by gardeners.

5. Liverworts grow in wet places, for instance, near streams or springs or even in the water.

6. The gametophytes (thalli) of liverworts appear as thin, leathery leaves which lie flat on the ground. They are anchored to the soil by rhizoids growing on the underside. In *Marchantia* the thallus is often divided into many Y shaped branches.

7. Both ferns and the seed plants contain conducting or vascular tissue.

8. The gametophyte develops from a germinating spore. A filament is produced which resembles both a filamentous green alga and a moss protonema.

9. A thin film of water must be present for the antheridia to rupture, to open the neck of the mature archegonia and for the sperms to swim to any of the archegonia to fertilize an egg.

10. Club mosses and horsetails have life cycles similar to those of ferns.

ANSWERS TO APPLYING PRINCIPLES AND CONCEPTS
(Page 261)

1. Bryophytes and tracheophytes are thought to have developed along two separate lines from the algae. The bryophytes are considered to have evolved into an evolutionary blind alley since they never developed true organs for absorption and conduction (roots and stems). They are still dependent on water for their reproductive cycle. Tracheophytes have shown adaptation through continuing change in structure. They have developed true roots and stems which allow them to efficiently absorb and conduct water to their tissues. With the exception of the fern, tracheophytes have eliminated the need for water during reproduction.

2. Usually arctic and alpine regions will be quite rocky. Moss plants need only a small accumulation of soil in which to anchor their rhizoids and become established. Their small size aids them in surviving the harsh actions of wind, snow and ice that are present during the greater part of the year. Permafrost that occurs in the arctic regions will prevent the roots of higher plants from surviving or from establishing a well developed root system.

3. The fern forests that were dominant during the Carboniferous Age were probably not able to compete with the higher seed plants that had developed. Climatic and topographic changes resulted in their being reduced in numbers since they were unable to adapt to the new conditions.

4. The sporophyte of a moss plant is an inconspicuous structure dependent on the gametophyte; whereas, the sporophyte of the fern is a conspicuous plant and lives independent of the gametophyte (except in early stages). It is more advanced than the moss sporophyte because it possesses conducting tissue. Leaves are in the form of fronds.

chapter twenty-two The Seed Plants   This chapter discusses the evolutionary development of seed plants and the efficiency of seeds as a method of reproduction. Various orders and species of seed plants are examined. Structure of seed plants is explored, and woody and herbaceous plants are discussed. Students will also learn about the flowering plants. Students will have a better understanding of the success of seed plants after reading this chapter.

TEACHING SUGGESTIONS

1. Point out to students that seed plants developed more than 300,000,000 years ago. Some of these early plants outlived the dinosaurs by millions of years.

2. Point out to students the remarkable contribution of conifers to the wood supply of the United States. Such conifers as the southern pines, Douglas fir, cedar, hemlock, and spruce trees provide lumber and other products.

3. Discuss with students the importance of seeds as a method of reproduction. How are seeds both protected and nourished in the early stages?

4. Students may be interested in reading and reporting on sections of *Ingenious Kingdom,* by Henry and Rebecca Northen, Prentice-Hall, Inc., 1970. This is an excellent book on all types of plants and their relationship to the environment.

STUDENT INVOLVEMENT ACTIVITIES

1. Ask students to bring in samples of seeds and identify them.

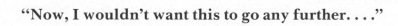

"Now, I wouldn't want this to go any further. . . ."

4

Students may be surprised to find out about the abundance of seeds.

2. Some students may want to research flowering plants and report on some of the species of this group. Ask students to bring in pictures of flowering plants.

3. Ask a few students to research the types of small greenhouses that are now available to the consumer. Many young people find a rewarding hobby in "hothouse" plant growing.

4. Arrange for students to be able to examine the different types of plant tissues under microscopes. This can be set up as a "round-robin" exercise with students going from one microscope to the next. Have them write down notes on their observations.

COMMUNITY INVOLVEMENT ACTIVITIES

1. Invite a florist to speak to the class about his or her profession. Perhaps the class can visit the greenhouse of a local florist.

2. Hold a symposium concerning flowering plants and open it to the public. Care in and timing of planting for various species should be discussed by qualified people.

3. Invite a representative of a lumber yard, paper company, or lumber manufacturer to speak to the class about his or her profession and product.

CAREER OPPORTUNITIES
Botanist
Florist
Forester
Forestry aid
Forestry technician
Horticulturist
Landscape gardener

ANSWERS TO QUESTIONS FOR REVIEW
(Page 273)

1. Gymnosperms do not produce flowers and have naked seeds borne on the upper surface of the cone scales. Angiosperms are flowering plants and bear seeds enclosed in an ovary, which develops from the pistil of the flower.

2. When all other members of its order had become extinct, the Ginkgo survived in China. It is the sole survivor of an entire order of gymnosperms, the Ginkgoales, which flourished ages ago.

3. Several well-known genera of conifers are the pines, spruces, firs, Douglas fir, cedar, cypress, yew, juniper, larches and sequoias. Conifers are the most widespread of the gymnosperms. They are the main supply source for lumber. Conifers grow larger and older than any other trees; their leaves are in the form of needles or scales.

4. Seed cones and pollen cones are the two types of cones produced by conifers.

5. The class Angiospermae is divided into two subclasses, the Dicotyledonae and the Monocotyledonae, on the basis of the seed leaves or cotyledons that are formed in the embryo plant.

6. The vegetative organs of a seed and their functions include: the root for absorption, anchorage, conduction, and storage; the stem for display of leaves, conduction, storage, and food manufacture; the leaf for food manufacture, transpiration and respiration.

7. Meristematic tissue is composed of thin-walled cells which, through repeated cell division, produce tissue which will develop into the specialized and permanent tissues (xylem and phloem) composing plant organs. It is found in the embryonic or growing regions of the plant.

8. Parenchyma tissue may be found as chlorenchyma, which is chlorophyll containing parenchyma, as found in leaves and stems. Chlorenchyma functions in photosynthesis. Parenchyma tissue may also be found as storage parenchyma where it functions in the storage of plant products such as sugars and starches.

9. Strengthening tissue may be found in the form of fibers, sclerenchyma tissue, bast fibers, or wood fibers.

10. Vascular tissue would include: 1) sieve tubes which serve as conducting channels for the downward movement of food, 2) vessels which function in the upward conduction of water and minerals, 3) tracheids which function in support as well as water and mineral conduction.

11. Both are complex tissues because they are made up of simpler tissues. Phloem is composed of sieve tubes, bast fibers, and parenchyma. Xylem is composed of vessels, tracheids, fibers, and parenchyma.

12. Herbaceous plants have soft stems containing a large amount of parenchyma tissue and little woody tissue and last, usually, a single growing season. Woody plants have stems with a large amount of woody tissue, usually increased each year by activity of the cambium.

13. The annual grows from a seed, flowers, and produces in a single growing season. The biennial usually forms the vegetative growth the first season and flowers and bears fruit the second season. The perennial grows and reproduces season after season (more than two seasons).

ANSWERS TO APPLYING PRINCIPLES AND CONCEPTS
(Page 273)

1. High development of roots allows absorption from a greater area and greater depth, storage of food and water, and anchorage of a large stem. The stem is highly developed for support of a large crown of leaves

and the conduction necessary to support such a leaf area. Leaves are ideally suited to absorption of light during food making, transpiration, respiration, and their other normal functions.

2. Since annuals are started from seeds or from young plants, an entire bed can be prepared at once. There is not the problem of wintering over. Since blooming occurs at the maturity of the plant, there is usually a large display of blossoms. The energy of the plant is directed into flower and seed production.

chapter twenty-three The Leaf and Its Functions Why are leaves so important to the plant? Without leaves, green plants would die. Leaves and their structures allow for photosynthesis to take place and provide food for the plant. The structure and function of leaves are examined in this chapter. Leaf coloration and modification are also discussed. Having read this chapter, students will have a greater appreciation of leaves and their functions.

TEACHING SUGGESTIONS

1. Point out to students that leaves are fascinating objects to examine. Ask students to take some time to examine leaves around them. They may be particularly interested in examining the leaves of house plants.
2. Prepare a leaf for examination under the microscope. Ask students to write down their observations. Ask students if they can see the stomata of the leaf.
3. Students may be interested in reading and reporting on chapters of *This Is a Leaf* by Ross E. Hutchins, Dodd, Mead and Co., 1962.
4. Have students examine a cross-section of a leaf and identify some of the structures observed.

STUDENT INVOLVEMENT ACTIVITIES

1. Ask students to bring in a number of different leaves. Have students identify the leaves, using a botany text.
2. If some students are interested in photography, ask them to take moving pictures of a leaf using time-lapse photography. The movements of the leaf will make a fascinating study.
3. Ask some students to report on modification of plants that make them cannibalistic. Some such plants include Venus's flytraps, bladderworts, butterworts, pitcher plants, and sundews.

COMMUNITY INVOLVEMENT ACTIVITIES

1. Visit a botanical garden and observe some of the exotic plants, especially those with leaves modified for feeding.
2. Invite a nursery representative or florist to discuss the care of house plants and how to prevent excessive leaf loss in plants.
3. Visit a nursery and observe the many types of leaves. Report on a plant that is of particular interest to you.
4. Invite a landscape artist to class to discuss his or her profession.

CAREER OPPORTUNITIES
Botanist
Florist
Horticulturist
Landscape artist
Nursery worker

ANSWERS TO QUESTIONS FOR REVIEW
(Pages 286–287)

1. The leaf blade, being thin and broad, allows the cells to receive the maximum amount of light. It also permits the greatest intake and discharge of gases through the stomata of the lower epidermis.
2. Veins form a supporting network for the blade and are the channels through which water and dissolved minerals and foods are conducted.

3. Dicot leaves have branching, netted veins while the veins of the monocot leaves are in parallel arrangement.

4. The cuticle functions in slowing down the movement of water vapor and other gases through the epidermal cells, thus preventing the loss of these substances from the leaf tissue.

5. The bean-shaped guard cells surround each stoma opening and unlike other epidermal cells they contain chloroplasts. The wall bordering the stoma is thickened, which is important in changing the shape of the guard cell and hence the opening and closing of the stoma.

6. Palisade mesophyll and spongy mesophyll.

7. Starch.

8. During the night, the stomata are closed due to the increase in carbon dioxide which is the result of increased respiratory activities. This raises the acidity of the guard cells and prevents the action of the starch-digesting enzyme. Thus, water leaves the guard cells causing them to close. As light increases, photosynthetic activities which use carbon dioxide resume. The acidity of the guard cells is reduced which brings about increased activity of the starch-digesting enzymes. An increase in the sugar content causes water to be taken in by osmosis. This causes the guard cells to swell and thus the stomata to open.

9. Various pigments appear in leaves in the fall when the chlorophyll, which has been masking them through the summer, breaks down and disappears on bright, cold days. Anthocyanin, a red pigment, is produced in the cell sap during cool weather.

10. The abcission layer forms across the base of the petiole. Pectin, a substance which previously had joined the parenchyma cells securely, is dissolved by an enzyme produced late in the season. The cells separate and soon the leaf is attached only through the fibrovascular bundles. The slightest jar will cause the leaf to fall.

11. Water accumulates in the tissues and supplies the plant during long periods of drought in desert and semi-desert conditions.

12. Sundew, Venus's flytrap, pitcher plants, and bladderworts are insectivorous plants.

ANSWERS TO APPLYING PRINCIPLES AND CONCEPTS
(Page 287)

1. The thin walls of leaf cells permit rapid movement of water, minerals, dissolved foods, and gases into and out of them. This is necessary in the many processes leaf cells carry on.

2. The plant uses oxygen from the air for respiration at night.

3. In photosynthesis, water and carbon dioxide are chemical raw materials, energy is absorbed, glucose is the product, and oxygen is the waste product. In respiration (oxidation), the process is reversed. Glucose and oxygen are combined chemically, energy is released, and water and carbon dioxide are released as waste products.

chapter twenty-four Roots and Stems Roots and stems are essential to the transport of water and minerals in plants. In this chapter, students will learn about the structure of roots and stems and their development. Students will also learn about the different types of roots and how to identify them. Woody, herbaceous, and modified stems are also discussed.

TEACHING SUGGESTIONS

1. Students may be interested in learning about the extensiveness of root structures. For example, it has been estimated that if the root system of even a four-month-old corn stem spread out it would be about 150 meters in length!

2. Have a variety of roots and stems available for students to examine with naked eye and by cross-section under the microscope.

3. Discuss the subject of edible roots with students. They may be surprised to discover that they are eating roots when they consume potatoes, beets, carrots, and numerous other foods. Some students may be interested in researching roots eaten in other countries and by native American Indians.

4. A fascinating book on roots may be of interest to some students. The book entitled, *Roots: Miracles Below* is authored by Charles Morrow Wilson and published by Doubleday and Co., in 1968.

STUDENT INVOLVEMENT ACTIVITIES

1. Ask students to bring in samples of roots. Some students may

want to bring in root recipes or food samples made from such recipes.

2. Taro and cassava are commonly used food roots in some parts of the world. Ask students to report on these roots and their impact on the economy of the countries where they are grown.

3. Have students bring in samples of woody stems and examine them carefully. Students always enjoy identifying the actual parts of a stem that they have read about in the text.

COMMUNITY INVOLVEMENT ACTIVITIES

1. Invite a home economist to class to discuss the nutrition of roots (especially high protein beets) and recipes made from roots. This discussion should be open to the public.

2. Invite a nursery representative to discuss the problems involved in transplanting the roots of shrubs and other plants. This discussion would be of great interest to the public.

CAREER OPPORTUNITIES
Agronomist
Botanist
Farmer
Home economist
Nursery representative

ANSWERS TO QUESTIONS FOR REVIEW
(Page 303)

1. A primary root develops from the embryo present in the seed. The secondary root grows from the pericycle of the primary root.
2. The taproot system centers around a greatly enlarged primary root.

The fibrous root system is composed of many secondary roots which spread over a large area. There is no main primary root. In many plants, the primary root ceases to grow after it forms the secondary roots.

3. Root cap, meristematic region, elongation region, and maturation region in the order named occur from the tip back. The root cap is a protective structure. The meristematic region gives rise to new cells by continuous divisions during the growing seasons. Cells, formed in the meristematic region, grow in length in the elongation region. In the maturation region, the cells mature into tissues, such as the epidermis and cortex.

4. a. Epidermis (absorption and protection); b. cortex (storage); c. endodermis (a boundary layer between the cortex and the central cylinder); d. pericycle (origin or secondary roots); e. phloem (food conduction); f. cambium (production of secondary tissues); g. xylem (conduction of water and minerals).

5. Examples of adventitious roots include the brace roots of corn and the banyan tree and climbing roots of poison ivy, English ivy, and other vines.

6. A terminal bud is found at the tip of the growing shoot. Axillary buds are also termed lateral buds. These are found along the sides of the twig and develop in the leaf axil.

7. Embryonic leaves develop from the shoot apex.

8. A stem with a strong apical dominance in the terminal bud usually grows upward as a shaft and produces an excurrent pattern of branching. When apical dominance is lacking and a terminal bud is not present, or when the lateral buds develop freely, a spreading, deliquescent branching arrangement results.

9. Bark tissues include cork for protection, cork cambium, which produces new cork each season, cortex, which manufactures food in

a young stem and becomes a place of storage later, and phloem, which serves as a food-conducting tissue as well as a bark-strengthening tissue.

10. Annual rings are formed as a result of the vascular cambium dividing to form secondary xylem on its inner side. As the woody stem increases in thickness through the years, the wood formed by cambium is arranged in layers. During the spring, larger vessels are formed than are formed during the summer. This results in a difference in texture known as annual rings.

11. The sapwood is usually light in color and has open, functioning vessels. Heartwood is darker in color, often plugged with gummy materials, and no longer functions in conduction.

12. The stems of dicotyledons have fibrovascular bundles arranged in a ring; cambium and cortex tissues are present. Monocotyledons lack these tissues and fibrovascular bundles are scattered through the stem.

13. The rhizome (iris, lily of the valley), stolon (crab grass), tuber (white potato), corm (crocus, gladiolus), and bulb (onion, lily, hyacinth, daffodil, and tulip).

ANSWERS TO APPLYING PRINCIPLES AND CONCEPTS
(Page 303)

1. The taproot system centers around a greatly enlarged primary root such as is found in the carrot and dandelion. This type of root system allows plants to grow a root directly toward a water supply. The fibrous root system is composed of many secondary roots which spread over a large area. A main primary root is missing. Fibrous root systems allow the plant to absorb water from a greater area. Better anchorage of the plant is achieved with the taproot system.

2. Growth occurs only in certain regions of roots and stems; this is

4

due to the location of meristematic tissue. Cells are added to the root by the root meristem and to the stem by the apical meristem and by the vascular cambium. Once the cells making up the plant body have specialized, they are not capable of further growth or division.

3. Each year, the wood produced by the cambium forms layers. Spring wood, which grows early in the season, contains many large vessels. Summer wood grows later and has fewer vessels. This layering of different textures forms annual rings. The annual rings, when counted, give the age of the tree.

chapter twenty-five Water Relations in Plants Water is vital to the existence of plants for many reasons. Water is necessary for transport and functioning of plants. In this chapter, students will learn about water absorption, translocation, turgidity, guttation, and other processes. Having read this chapter, students will have a great appreciation of the role of water in plant life.

TEACHING SUGGESTIONS

1. There are many simple demonstrations of water transport in plants. One of the most effective is to use colored water and watch the effect on the leaves. Students may want to devise their own experiments.
2. Experiments with different types of soils and soil water can be done in class. This will help students to see how the soil and water concentration affect the plant.
3. The health of house plants is very dependent on watering: too much is as dangerous as too little. Students may be interested in the book: *Gardening Indoors with House Plants* by Raymond P. Poincelot, Rodale Press, Inc., 1974.
4. Students may be interested in the use of water meters to determine the relative dryness of their house plants. These meters help people to water their plants properly.

STUDENT INVOLVEMENT ACTIVITIES

1. Unless an urban location makes it inappropriate, have students bring in samples of soil from their area and analyze it as being sandy, dry, moist, top soil, clay, or other. Agricultural extension agencies will analyze soil for acidity or alkalinity if there are special problems.
2. Some students may want to report on current research in the area of active transport.
3. The "grow-it-yourself" craze has increased dramatically in recent years. It is estimated that more than half the population had their own vegetable gardens in 1976. This is an excellent way of learning first-hand about water and sunlight needs of plants. Perhaps the class could plant a small plot of land and grow their own vegetables.

COMMUNITY INVOLVEMENT ACTIVITIES

1. Invite a horticulturist to speak about home vegetable gardening and methods of insuring success. If there is an agricultural station near you, this would be a good place to request a speaker.
2. Community plots are becoming very popular. In the city of Los Angeles, for example, more than 30 acres are devoted to such projects. Community plots are usually sponsored by schools, local governments, corporations, and churches. In such a plot, a number of families share the land to raise vegetable gardens. Perhaps your class could hold a public meeting to see if there is interest in such a venture.

CAREER OPPORTUNITIES
Agricultural researcher
Agricultural station employee
Agronomist

Botanist
Farmer
Home economist
Seed company distributor

ANSWERS TO QUESTIONS FOR REVIEW
(Page 311)

1. Photosynthesis, digestion, growth, and transport require water.
2. Texture is determined by the nature and size of the mineral particles. The type of particles is important in plant growth; the size of the particles determines the amount of water that passes through the soil.
3. Gravel, sand, silt, and loam. Loam is a mixture of various proportions of sand, silt, and clay.
4. Active absorption of water is due to osmotic forces operating between the root hair cells and the surrounding capillary water. It is dependent on the water and solute concentration of solutions in living root cells. Passive absorption is not dependent on the forces in the root cells. Water loss through the leaves and movement through the stem reduce the turgor pressure in the root cells and the force of the surrounding soil water creates a pressure which forces water into the root cells.
5. Root cells may lose water to the soil when the concentration of various salts and minerals in the soil is greater than the concentration in the root cells. Osmosis would then occur from the root cells to the soil.
6. In active transport cells must actively expend energy in order to absorb the minerals.
7. Root pressure, capillarity, and transpiration-cohesion are factors in translocation of water.
8. According to the transpiration-cohesion theory, water is pulled through the vessels of the stem. The loss of water through the leaves by transpiration gives a direct pull on the column of water extending through the vessels to the roots. This happens because of the molecular attraction, called cohesion, that water molecules have for each other.
9. Girdling is the complete removal of all phloem tissue of a woody stem down to the cambium. The root and stem below the girdle are deprived of food and gradually die of starvation.
10. Turgor pressure is the internal pressure that is built up in the plant cells as a result of the diffusion of water into the cytoplasm and vacuoles of the cell. Thus, a mechanical support is provided for soft herbaceous stems which are lacking in xylem-supporting tissue.
11. Temporary wilting occurs when the rate of transpiration exceeds the rate of absorption of water. Water is lost from the plant tissues, reducing the turgor pressure of the cells; hence, the herbaceous plants, being unable to support themselves, wilt.

ANSWERS TO APPLYING PRINCIPLES AND CONCEPTS
(Page 311)

1. Translocation of water apparently is dependent on the loss of water from the tissues of the leaf through transpiration and cohesion, with root pressure and capillarity playing only minor roles. Translocation of food substance is not dependent on the loss of food from the plant, but merely on food being moved to other parts of the plant. It is suggested that active transport may be involved.
2. Active absorption takes place when the stomata are closed during the night and the plant is transpiring at a slower rate. The root cells contain higher concentrations of food materials and minerals than the surrounding soil and thus osmosis takes place from soil to root cells. Passive absorption (the most common means of water absorption in land plants) occurs when root cells lose turgor pressure due to the rapid movement of water through the xylem vessels when the stomata are open. The difference between pressure in the root and that of the soil water forces water into the root cells.
3. Root pressure has been found to rarely exceed only a few pounds per square inch. This is not sufficient to force water up the majority of plant stems. Capillarity plays only a minor role in water conduction. The rise of water is dependent on the surface tension of water against the walls of the xylem vessels and tracheids. The strongest factor in the rise of water is a pull resulting from transpiration and cohesion. As water is lost from the leaves, an entire column is lifted from the roots.

4

chapter twenty-six Plant Growth and Responses This chapter is concerned with light and temperature and how they affect plant growth and responses. The students will learn about photoperiodism, the effects of temperature, plant hormones, and tropisms. After reading this chapter, students will have a better understanding of plant "behavior."

TEACHING SUGGESTIONS

1. Have students observe house plants for signs of movement toward light. Have them write down their observations and compare them to observations of other class members.
2. Students interested in plant response may enjoy reading certain chapters of *Performing Plants* by Ware T. Budlong, Simon and Schuster, 1969. This book contains some excellent experiments that involve tropisms and instructions on the best way to conduct response experiments with plants.
3. Students may be interested in conducting some simple experiments on the effect of cold on plants, especially flowers. Have students observe flowers that have been securely sealed and placed in the freezer.

STUDENT INVOLVEMENT ACTIVITIES

1. Ask students to outline an original experiment to study any aspect of plant response. Go over the outlines and point out problems in their experimental designs. Once the problems have been corrected, have students conduct their experiments and report the results to the class.
2. Students may be interested in reading and reporting on research concerning the effects of "talking" to plants. Many people assert that plants respond to the human voice. Some students may wish to report on actual experiences concerning such "conversations."
3. Students may be interested in making a plant clock. This clock is actually a circle of different flowering plants that respond differently to sunlight. The flowers chosen should open and close at different times of the day. Choices might include dwarf morning glories, dandelions, African daisies, tulips, four-o'clocks, and poppies. This is an interesting experiment to be done in a small or large plot.

COMMUNITY INVOLVEMENT ACTIVITIES

1. Invite an expert in house plant care (local nursery representative or florist) to speak to the class about whether or not plants respond to voices and music.
2. Visit a greenhouse and florist shop and observe the care taken to give plants the appropriate light and correct temperature. Also have students observe how fresh flowers are kept.
3. Hold a plant sale at your school. Students will learn a great deal about plants by running such an event. Local nurseries should be contacted for help in this matter. Proceeds may go to buy more laboratory equipment for the biology laboratory or to support a school garden.

CAREER OPPORTUNITIES

Botanist
Florist
Nursery representative
Plant researcher
Plant shop owner

ANSWERS TO QUESTIONS FOR REVIEW
(Page 319)

1. These factors include light conditions, temperature, atmospheric moisture, soil water, and mineral content of the soil.
2. The stem is pale yellow. Lack of light causes the stem to greatly elongate and thus become weak and spindly.
3. Short-day plants, such as the tulip, daffodil, crocus, forsythia, redbud, and dogwood, flower in the spring. In the fall, short-day plants including the chrysanthemums, ragweed, golden rod, poinsettias, and asters, flower. Long-day plants flowering in the late spring or early summer would include iris, hollyhock, and clover.
4. Neutral-day plants include the nasturtium, gaillardia, calendula, marigold, zinnia, snapdragon, carnation, tomato, and the garden bean. They seem to be influenced slightly, if at all, by the length of days and nights.
5. In most plants it is between 10° and 40°C.
6. Woody plants remain alive above ground with their living tissues protected by bark or the scales of winter buds. Herbaceous perennials die to the ground with only the roots or underground stems surviving through the dormant period. Annuals do not survive but the seeds produced during the growing season continue the species for the next season.
7. Hormones are produced in one part of the plant and are translocated to other parts where

they influence cell growth and elongation as well as cell division.

8. (1) Auxins—cause cells to get longer and larger; (2) gibberellins—promote elongation of cells; (3) cytokinins—influence cell division.

9. Phototropism, light; geotropism, gravity; thigmotropism, touch; hydrotropism, water; chemotropism, chemicals.

10. Nastic movements occur independently of the direction of the stimuli while tropic responses are always either positive or negative to the direction of the response.

ANSWERS TO APPLYING PRINCIPLES AND CONCEPTS
(Page 319)

1. It is the auxins which promote or inhibit cell elongation, producing positive or negative tropisms.

2. Plants that flower in the spring do so because of a short photoperiod. After vegetative growth during the summer, it is possible that they flower again in the fall when the photoperiods are comparable to those of the spring.

3. When the tip of the coleoptile is removed, elongation of the stem ceases; when the tip is replaced, cell elongation resumes. Further evidence of the translocation of auxin from the tip downward is seen when the tip is placed on an agar block. Auxin diffuses downward into the agar from the tip, and when the block is placed on the end of the decapitated coleoptile, elongation of the stem will resume.

4. When a plant is grown in a window, it bends toward the light. The bending is due to the stimulation of auxins on the cells of the shaded side. Roots, when exposed to light, grow away from the light source, indicating that greater cell elongation takes place on the lighter side. This indicates that auxin inhibits elongation of root cells. Placing a seedling on its side and observing that the

stem grows up and the root grows down shows the influence of auxins on geotropism. Auxin accumulates in the lower side of the stem and stimulates the stem cells to elongate. Auxin on the lower side of the root inhibits cell elongation, while cell elongation on the upper side causes the shoot to grow downward.

chapter twenty-seven Plant Reproduction   There are several different types of reproduction among plants. Students will learn about reproduction among flowering plants. They will explore vegetative reproduction, artificial propagation, and sexual reproduction. They will also study pollination and the formation of fruits and seeds. Having read this chapter, students will have a better understanding of how the plants around them reproduce.

TEACHING SUGGESTIONS

1. An excellent introduction to this chapter would be to show the students how to make a graft by inserting a scion from one plant into the stock of another plant. Be sure that students understand what has taken place and the fact that grafting does *not* change the characteristics of the stock or the scion.

2. Students should examine flowers first-hand in order to see the reproductive parts that are described in text. Encourage students to draw the flower and its parts from observation.

3. Have students work with beans in order to better understand the anatomy of a seed. The beans should be soaked so that the seed coats can be easily removed. Have students identify the embryo.

STUDENT INVOLVEMENT ACTIVITIES

1. Ask students to bring in samples of fruits and seeds. Each of these samples should be discussed in class.

2. Some students may wish to plant

4

bean seeds and observe their growth. A bean seed will germinate well in darkness and in light. However, once germination has taken place, some light should be present.

3. Some students may wish to report on bees and their importance as pollinators. Other students may wish to report on other insects and some birds that also act as pollinators.

COMMUNITY INVOLVEMENT ACTIVITIES

1. Invite a beekeeper to visit your class and discuss his or her job as well as the importance of bees in nature.
2. Invite a representative of a natural foods store to discuss the products that he or she sells. Some students may be very knowledgeable in this area.

CAREER OPPORTUNITIES

Agronomist
Beekeeper
Botanist
Farmer
Natural food salesperson
Organic farmer

ANSWERS TO QUESTIONS FOR REVIEW
(Page 337)

1. Strawberry plants form runners. Raspberries propagate naturally by tip layering.
2. The rooted portion is known as the stock, while the part to be joined to the stock is the scion. To be successful, the vascular cambium of the stock and the scion must be united.
3. Sepals protect the flower parts in the bud stage and help support the petals after opening. Petals are at-

tractive devices associated, for the most part, with insect pollination.

4. A stamen consists of a filament which supports a pollen-producing anther. A pistil consists of a stigma supported on slender stalk known as the style. At the base of the style is the ovary which contains the ovules.
5. Insects, wind, and water are agents of pollination.
6. The formation of the pollen tube begins when the pollen grain lodges on the stigma. This tube penetrates the stigma, lengthens and grows through the soft tissue of the style until it reaches the micropyle of the ovule. The tube nucleus remains near the tip of the pollen tube during growth, and the generative nucleus moves into the tube. The generative nucleus divides to form the two male gametes, or sperms. The pollen tube digests its way through the thin wall of the embryo sac. The tip of the tube nucleus ruptures and the two sperms are discharged into the embryo sac.
7. The zygote forms a mass of tissue which becomes the embryo plant. The endosperm nucleus forms a mass of tissue which becomes the endosperm of the seed.
8. A fruit is a ripened ovary with or without associated parts.
9. Seed pods of the bean and pea illustrate mechanical dispersal, accomplished by a sudden twisting of the walls of the pod as it dries out during the ripening process. Fleshy fruits like the cherry, raspberry, and apple may be carried by birds and other animals. The seeds may be dropped a considerable distance from the parent plant. Burrs and sticktights cling to the fur of animals and travel long distances. Dandelion fruits and milkweed seeds are dispersed by the wind. They are equipped with fine, fluffy, parachute like hairs which are easily carried away by air currents.
10. A dicotyledonous seed has only one cotyledon; a monocotyledonous seed has two.

11. Moisture, proper temperature (18 to 23 degrees C for many seeds), and oxygen.
12. The seed coat absorbs water which softens it. The hypocotyl grows out through the seed coat. The radicle (root) grows downward and forms the primary root, while the hypocotyl forms an arch and pushes its way to the surface of the soil. The hypocotyl straightens out and lifts the cotyledons upward to form the shoot. The embryonic leaves unfold and form the first true leaves. Following these germinative processes, the stem lengthens rapidly. The minute bud between the embryonic leaves develops as the terminal bud of the plant. The cotyledons wither and fall off as the plant becomes better able to make its own food.

ANSWERS TO APPLYING PRINCIPLES AND CONCEPTS
(Page 337)

1. Vegetative propagation allows commercial horticulturists and nurserymen to preserve the desired genetic qualities found in various fruit trees, ornamental trees, and shrubs. Vegetation propagation does not involve any union of gametes which would change the desired characteristics.
2. Huge quantities of pollen are necessary to guarantee fertilization of a relatively small number of ovules.
3. Insect-attracting devices include brightly colored petals, nectar, and perfume glands.
4. The seedling requires considerable moisture until its root system has become established. This moisture must be present, also, to soften the seed coats and allow germination to begin. This natural safeguard against germination under unfavorable moisture conditions.

unit 5 BIOLOGY OF THE INVERTEBRATES

Since 95 percent of all organisms in the animal kingdom are invertebrates, you can immediately see the value of studying these animals. In Chapter Twenty-Eight, the sponges and coelenterates are examined. The structure and function of these organisms are fascinating to the students. The worms are the subject of Chapter Twenty-Nine. Students may be surprised to learn about the variety of worms that exist. Many students may enjoy eating mollusks, but they may not know very much about their structure and function. In Chapter Thirty the mollusks and echinoderms are examined. Chapter Thirty-One is devoted to the study of the arthropod phylum. This phylum is especially interesting because of its diversity. Chapter Thirty-Two examines some familiar arthropods: the insects. The insects comprise the largest class of the arthropod phylum. This chapter concludes a unit that will give students a better understanding of organisms that have an important impact on our lives.

chapter twenty-eight Sponges and Coelenterates This chapter introduces the study of invertebrates and some of the characteristics of these organisms. The sponge and its particular adaptations are examined. Students will learn about the structure, function, reproduction, and economic importance of these organisms. The coelenterates are also examined in this chapter. The hydra is examined in detail. This chapter serves as an introduction to the fascinating world of the invertebrates.

TEACHING SUGGESTIONS

1. Introduce this chapter by naming a diverse group of animals and asking students to tell you what they all have in common. The answer will be that they are all invertebrates. Ask students to add to this list.

2. Discuss with students the characteristics of invertebrates. Invertebrates have been a highly successful group. Ask students how they can account for the fact that there is such a large ratio of invertebrates to vertebrates.

3. Discuss some of the ways in which sponges are adapted to their sessile lives. The methods of gas exchange and feeding allow sponges to live in this way.

4. If possible, have students observe live hydras. Regeneration and other simple experiments will be of interest to the students.

STUDENT INVOLVEMENT ACTIVITIES

1. Have students design original experiments that involve the sponges or coelenterates.

2. Have some students write a report on the economic importance of sponges. This report should include data on the impact of synthetic sponges on the natural sponge market.

3. Some students may be interested in photographing sponges and coelenterates. These photos would make an interesting exhibition.

COMMUNITY INVOLVEMENT ACTIVITIES

1. If you live near a coastal area, ask someone from the commercial fishing industry to discuss how the sponges and coelenterates affect business.

2. Invite a marine biologist to discuss sponges and coelenterates with the class.

3. If possible, invite a representative of a synthetic sponge company to discuss this product. If this is not possible, write to such a company and find out how they produce synthetic sponges.

CAREER OPPORTUNITIES
Experimental biologist
Marine biologist
Oceanographer
Sponge fisherman
Zoologist

ANSWERS TO QUESTIONS FOR REVIEW
(Page 349)

1. When a large number of cells forms an animal body, some of them can

5

become adapted to certain types of activity. These can then depend on other cells which are specialized in other ways. This arrangement is called division of labor.

2. The sponge body consists of two cellular layers supported on a framework of spicules. Coelenterates are more highly specialized, with two layers of cells forming a bag-like or bell-shaped body. They also have tentacles and stinging cells.

3. Most sponges inhabit shallow seas and tidal pools. Hydra live in freshwater streams and ponds. The size of the body has little to do with the habits of sponges and jellyfish.

4. Sponges are propagated commercially by sowing pieces of live sponges in special beds. Hydra and other coelenterates, likewise, can be cut into pieces and will regenerate the missing parts.

5. The hydra paralyzes its victim with its piercing stinging cells. The tentacles then force the prey into the gastrovasuclar cavity. An enormous amount of water moves into the sponge through its many pores. This water brings particles of food.

6. The bodies of hydra and *Aurelia* consist of two layers, and both possess stinging cells, tentacles, a mouth, and a gastrovascular cavity. The hydra is cylindrical in form; *Aurelia* is umbrella-shaped. The form of *Aurelia* is called a medusa, while that of the hydra is referred to as a polyp.

7. Tiny coral polyps secrete cases of lime around their bodies. A group of these form a coral reef. The polyps occupy tiny pores in the reef. Reefs are of three main types: the marginal type forms around an island; the barrier type forms a ring far out in the water; the atoll is a circular reef with an open center.

8. Nematocysts are stinging cells whose function is to paralyze the prey of the coelenterates.

9. The purple sails and the Portuguese man-of-war are not single animals, but are actually colonies of coelenterates. Some polyps are reproductive, some are for protection, and some are adapted for feeding. Thus each individual organism performs a special function for the benefit of the colony.

ANSWERS TO APPLYING PRINCIPLES AND CONCEPTS
(Page 349)

1. The division of labor principle is applied in modern society when people specialize in certain trades, professions, and other activities. Each specialist does a particular piece of work, but depends on the rest of society for other living requirements. The different cells of a metazoan become specialists in performing certain functions for the benefit of all the cells.

2. Jellyfish lack a circulatory system or any other means of supplying cells lying in the inner layer. Thus the animal must be hollow to allow water to contact cells of the endoderm.

3. The sponge is considered the most primitive of metazoan animals, because it has the least amount of cell specialization and the most primitive methods of reproduction—budding and regeneration from fragments.

4. Many coelenterates are mobile and are carried by currents or wind blowing over the surface of the water. Sessile coelenterates shed gametes and the young are motile. Sponges spread by pieces breaking off, and by gemmules. Warm, shallow waters are most favorable for growth of Porifera and Coelenterata.

chapter twenty-nine The Worms The students will get some idea of the diversity of worms by studying Fig. 29-1. This chapter explores the worm phyla and how the bilateral symmetry of worms differs from organisms previously studied. Students will learn about the structure and function of many different types of worms. Having read this chapter, students will have a better understanding of how worms affect us.

TEACHING SUGGESTIONS

1. Students may better be able to understand the differences between radial symmetry and bilateral symmetry by seeing diagrams of a sea anemone and a planarian. What happens when these organisms are cut in half?

2. Point out to students that planarians have a primitive brain composed of nerve cell ganglia. They also have sensory lobes that help them to find food in the water.

3. Have students discuss the excerpt from *Animals Without Backbones,* p. 357. Elicit from students whether or not they were aware of the large numbers of nematodes that exist.

4. Point out to students that earthworms are extremely important to the improvement of soil quality. Their movements and tunneling help to aerate the soil.

STUDENT INVOLVEMENT ACTIVITIES

1. Ask students to bring in samples of planaria for observation. Have students design original experiments that involve planaria.

2. Have some students do research on human worm parasites. There are a number of diseases caused by worms; one that may be of interest to students is elephantiasis.

3. Ask students to report on the economic importance of earthworms. Many individuals raise earthworms in "worm farms" for use as fishing bait.

COMMUNITY INVOLVEMENT ACTIVITIES

1. Ask a parasitologist to speak to the class about his or her work and the organisms that are studied.

2. If possible, invite a "worm farmer" to discuss this type of work with the class. Some students may be interested in becoming "worm farmers."

3. Ask a home economist to speak to the class about the correct method of cooking meat, especially pork, to eliminate worm parasites.

CAREER OPPORTUNITIES

Food processor
Home economist
Nematologist
Parasitologist
Physician
Worm farmer
Zoologist

ANSWERS TO QUESTIONS FOR REVIEW
(Page 364)

1. The types of symmetry are classified as spherical, radial, and bilateral. An animal with spherical symmetry has a body that can be divided into two equal parts by any plane passing through the diameter of the body. Radial symmetry is one in which the body has a central disc from which tentacles radiate out like spokes of a wheel. Bilateral symmetry means "two-sided shape," with the sides being symmetrical. Examples of each type in the order named are *Volvox,* sea anemone, and earthworm.

2. Planarians may be divided into several transverse sections, or cut longitudinally, and each section will regenerate the missing parts.

3. The ectoderm, mesoderm, and endoderm of the flatworm are found in all structurally more complex animals and give rise to various organs in these animals.

4. A well-developed nervous system allows the planarian to know what is happening to all the cells of its body. Its eyes perceive light and cause the animal to react.

5. Flatworms have three cell layers and greater specialization of cells than sponges and coelenterates.

6. The tapeworm has no digestive system and no means of locomotion.

7. Nematodes are found everywhere: in soil; in plants; in animals; and in lakes, rivers, and oceans.

8. Nematodes have a digestive system composed of a distinct tube, or cylinder. They take food into the mouth and eliminate the wastes through an anus.

9. The eggs of *Ascaris* are taken into the human body in contaminated food or water. The eggs hatch inside the small intestine. The larvae bore into the intestinal wall and begin a ten-day journey through the body. They finally reach the bloodstream and are carried to the lungs. Then they pass into the air passages, through the throat, and are swallowed into the digestive tube. They grow to maturity in about two and a half months. After the eggs are fertilized, they pass out of the body of the host with the feces and the cycle continues.

10. The trichina worm is eaten as a cyst in improperly cooked, contaminated pork.

11. The earthworm moves by extending its body, gripping with its setae, then shortening its body by contracting the longitudinal muscles. The posterior setae grip as the anterior end is pushed forward again.

12. Food is drawn into the pharynx, and passes through the esophagus and crop into the gizzard. After being ground up, the food passes through the intestine, where digestion and absorption occur. Indigestible matter is excreted through the anal opening.

ANSWERS TO APPLYING PRINCIPLES AND CONCEPTS
(Page 365)

1. Animals with bilateral symmetry have a definite means of locomotion; those with spherical symmetry usually float on or near the surface of the water. Animals with radial symmetry are often stationary and must obtain food and oxygen from the immediate surroundings.

2. *Ascaris* leaves the small intestine by boring into the intestinal wall, enters the bloodstream, then to the lungs. It passes into the air passages and then into the digestive tract. Symptoms of disease are most likely to be present when the larvae pass through the lungs. Inflammation occurs and generalized pneumonia may result. Adults may be so numerous in the intestine as to produce an obstruction, and nervous symptoms may appear as a result of toxic substances released by the worms. The condition is best treated in the intestinal stage.

3. Inspection and cooking of meat, especially pork, is one measure in the control of parasitic worms. Since many of these worms live in the human intestine, they may be present in intestinal waste. Thus

5

"I'd like to find out more about how your society works."

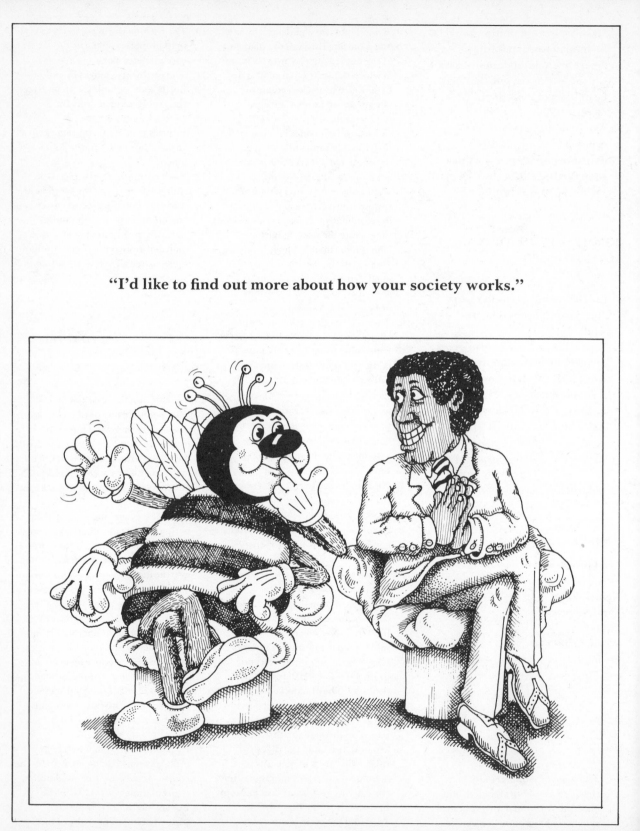

proper disposal of sewage is an important measure. Hookworm can be avoided by wearing shoes.

4. Loss of digested food in the intestine results from absorption of food by the parasite.

5. Trichina worms have penetrated the muscle tissues and formed cysts, they cannot at that stage be eliminated by the use of purgatives.

6. Tapeworms have means of attachment to the host's intestine and protection from digestive juices. They have no need for their own digestive organs. Tapeworms simply absorb nutrients and reproduce.

chapter thirty Mollusks and Echinoderms Mollusks and echinoderms are well-known organisms. Many of the mollusks serve as food. They include the clams, oysters, scallops, and mussels. Students will learn about these and other mollusks. They will study the cephalopods which include the octopus and squid. The structure and function of echinoderms conclude this chapter.

TEACHING SUGGESTIONS

1. Mollusks are specialized organisms with highly developed systems for circulation, digestion, respiration, and excretion. Point out to students the specialization of mollusks over the worms.

2. Bring into class different examples of mollusks. Have students identify them and point out how they differ from each other.

3. Point out to students that snails are often placed in aquariums. Here they help to keep the glass clean of algae by scraping it from the sides of the aquarium.

4. Bring in a collection of echinoderms or show students slides of these organisms. Some students may have collections of echinoderms that they will bring to class.

STUDENTS INVOLVEMENT ACTIVITIES

1. Ask students to bring in examples of mollusks and have them identify the class of the representative mollusk and its body parts.

2. Ask students to bring in recipes and food samples of various representatives of the mollusk phylum. Students may be surprised to learn that squid, snails, and octopus are regarded as delicacies by many people.

3. Ask students to bring in representative echinoderms. If students live near a shore area, they should be asked to collect samples along the beach. Many students may have a collection of sand dollars or starfish.

4. Students may be interested in reporting on the "ink" produced by squids and octopuses. This will make an interesting study for the students.

COMMUNITY INVOLVEMENT ACTIVITIES

1. Visit a seafood market and study the different types of mollusks offered for sale.

2. Invite a doctor to discuss the effects of hepatitis and how it is transmitted by certain mollusks.

3. Have students prepare mollusk recipes at home (in groups) and bring them to the class. Discuss the recipes and have a "tasting party."

CAREER OPPORTUNITIES
Home economist
Marine biologist
Medical researcher
Oceanographer
Seafood processor
Virologist
Zoologist

ANSWERS TO QUESTIONS FOR REVIEW
(Page 376)

1. The type of shell, if present, is the basis of dividing the mollusks into classes.

5

2. Soft body, foot, and mantle.
3. Water containing food enters the ventral siphon of the clams, enters the mantle cavity and passes over the gills. The food sticks to the thin mucous layer on the gills. Cilia beat forward and carry the mucous strands and food to the mouth. From the mouth, food enters the esophagus, passes to the stomach and then to the digestive gland.
4. Pearly layer, prismatic layer, and horny layer.
5. A pearl forms in an oyster when an encysted worm or grain of sand lodges between the mantle and the shell. Gem pearls are produced only in the pearl oyster of the Pacific and Indian Oceans.
6. Clams are *mucus feeders.* They feed on microscopic organisms which pass over the mucus on the gills.
7. In contrast to the gastropods, the cephalopods are generally without outer shells. The body is covered by a thick, toughened mantle and the foot is divided into eight or more tentacles with suction cups.
8. A hard, shell-like body which is radially symmetrical and covered with spines.
9. The starfish can grip an object with its tube feet and bend its arms to produce movement. The water-vascular system of the starfish provides the suction of the tube feet which exerts a steady pull used in opening the shells of mollusks. The starfish then extrudes its stomach between the shells and secretes digestive juices.
10. Starfish regenerate new parts.
11. A coelom is a fluid-filled cavity within the body walls of an animal.

ANSWERS TO APPLYING PRINCIPLES AND CONCEPTS
(Page 377)

1. The larvae of the mollusks and the annelids are very similar. They are called trochophores.
2. Mollusks have been used as food, for money, eating utensils, jewelry, buttons, dyes, tools, and weapons. Garden snails and slugs do great damage to plants with their rasping radulas.
3. The principal mineral substance present in mollusk shells is calcium carbonate. Other calcium compounds may be present. Marine mollusks may also contain other minerals, including iodine salts.

chapter thirty-one The Arthropods Students will be interested in learning that the arthropods are the most successful group of animals. In this chapter, students will learn about the interesting structure of arthropods and the diversity of this phylum. The differences among different classes of arthropods are discussed. Students will study representative arthropods in detail. They will be introduced to the insects which will be studied in Chapter Thirty-Two.

TEACHING SUGGESTIONS

1. This chapter may be introduced by showing slides of various arthropods and having students draw their own conclusions as to which phylum they belong. Elicit from students the characteristics of arthropods.
2. Point out to students that the organism *Peripatus* has characteristics of both the annelids and the arthropods. Discuss Table 31-1 with students using *Peripatus* as a living example.
3. Students may be interested in placing arthropods in the class to which they belong. Bring in a number of pictures of arthropods and have students identify them and place them in one of the five classes: crustacea, chilopoda, diplopoda, arachnida, and insecta.
4. Have students study the external and internal organs of the crayfish. Students may work well in groups on this exercise.

STUDENT INVOLVEMENT ACTIVITIES

1. Ask students to bring in an example of the arthropod

phylum and discuss it with the rest of the class. Some students may have interesting insect collections that can be shared with the class.

2. Have some students write a report concerning the economic importance of certain crustaceans. Shrimp, lobsters, and crabs are important as food and their cost depends upon their availability.

3. Students are usually fascinated with spiders. Ask students to choose a type of spider and report on it in detail. Point out to students that most spiders are beneficial and perform an important service by controlling many insect pests.

4. Ask students to choose a member of the arthropod phylum and design an original experiment to test a certain hypothesis about this organism. Remind them to follow the scientific method in their research.

COMMUNITY INVOLVEMENT ACTIVITIES

1. Invite a seafood restaurateur to speak to your class about the problems of acquiring and serving shrimp, lobster, and crab. He or she may be able to offer some interesting recipes to the class.

2. Invite an entomologist to discuss the insects with the class. Ask students to prepare questions in advance.

3. Invite an exterminator to discuss problems associated with certain insect pests. This discussion may be of interest to the public. Have questions prepared in advance.

CAREER OPPORTUNITIES
Conservationist
Entomologist
Food scientist
Home economist
Lobster fisherman
Marine biologist
Oceanographer
Oceanographic photographer
Seafood restaurateur

ANSWERS TO QUESTIONS FOR REVIEW
(Page 390)

1. An exoskeleton, segmented body, and jointed appendages.
2. a. Crustacea (crayfish); b. Chilopoda (centipede); c. Diplopoda (millipede); d. Archnida (spider); e. Insecta (grasshopper).
3. Both have a segmented body.
4. The exoskeleton gives excellent protection. However, its weight in proportion to the size of the body probably has limited the arthropods in size. Freedom of motion is limited in many arthropods.
5. Water enters the gill chamber at the rear edge of the cephalothorax, passes under the carapace, through the gill chambers on the sides, and out through openings at the front of the gill chamber on the lower side.
6. Crayfish respond to touch (antennae), light (compound eyes), and hearing (poorly developed ear sacs).
7. A centipede has many similar segments, each bearing a pair of legs. Many species inject poison into bites through their powerful mandibles. In contrast, the millipede has many similar segments, each bearing two pairs of very short legs. None of the millipedes inject poison when they bite.
8. The principal food of spiders is insects. All spiders inject poison into a bite. This has led many

people to believe that all spiders are dangerous, whereas only a few species are dangerous to humans.

9. Ballooning is a method by which some spiders spread to new habitats. Thus, the species has spread and their chances of survival are better than in an overcrowded limited area.

10. The spider respires through openings called book lungs. These plates expose a large surface to the air.

11. In addition to spiders, the class Arachnida includes scorpions, ticks, mites, and daddy longlegs.

ANSWERS TO APPLYING PRINCIPLES AND CONCEPTS
(Page 390)

1. The armored exoskeleton of an animal like the crayfish reduces its sense of touch on the body surface. However, sensitive antennae assume this function.

2. Crayfish living in water flowing through granite, because the exoskeleton contains a great deal of calcium, and limestone is calcium carbonate.

3. The young crayfish are protected from enemies, are provided with fresh water, and are given a proper habitat.

5

chapter thirty-two Insects—Familiar Arthropods   In this chapter, students will study insects in detail. They will learn about the general structure of insects and some of the reasons for the success of this group of organisms. The grasshopper is studied as a representative insect. They will also study insect behavior and reproduction. Having read this chapter, students will have a better understanding of a dominant group of animals.

TEACHING SUGGESTIONS

1. The best way to understand the structure of an insect is to observe one externally and internally. Grasshoppers are usually used for this purpose and make excellent examples for study. However, students should be encouraged to bring in other examples.

2. Suggest to students that they may be interested in reading and reporting on *The Bug Clan* by Ross E. Hutchins, Dodd, Mead & Company, 1973. This interesting book is easy to read and well illustrated.

3. Much research is being done in the area of controlling insect populations. Such research includes hormonal insecticides, insect viruses and bacteria, and biologically harmless toxic compounds. Another substance, pheromones, are discussed under *Challenges in Biology,* elsewhere on this page.

STUDENT INVOLVEMENT ACTIVITIES

1. Assign students to report on new methods of insect control that are being tested or used. Some of the ones mentioned in the *Teaching Suggestions* above may be interesting to students.

2. The gypsy moth has flourished in recent years and caused much destruction. This would be an excellent topic for students to report on. Some students may be interested in reading *Gypsy Moth* by Robert M. McClung, William Morrow and Co., 1974.

3. A fire-ant plague currently covers many areas of the South, including Georgia, Mississippi, and South Carolina. These insects are dangerous to both people and crops. Assign a few students to report on this plague. An interesting article on this subject appeared in the April 26, 1976, issue of *Newsweek.*

4. Some students may want to report on "killer bees." These dangerous insects have made the headlines recently and will provide an interesting topic for the students.

COMMUNITY INVOLVEMENT ACTIVITIES

1. Visit the local Mosquito Control Commission and have an employee discuss the mosquito control operation in your area.

2. Invite a representative of the country or state insect control office to discuss methods of gypsy moth control in your area.

3. Ask an entomologist to speak to your class and answer questions concerning insects.

CAREER OPPORTUNITIES
Beekeeper
Entomologist
Environmentalist
Exterminator
Mosquito control employee
Research biologist
Research chemist
Zoologist

CHALLENGES IN BIOLOGY
PHEROMONES AND INSECT CONTROL

Pheromones are used to control insect pests. A field or forest is sprayed with pheromones in order to confuse the male insect. In the confusion, the male is unable to find his female counterpart.

Pheromones are also used as bait to attract insects to other types of chemical traps. Pheromones have been used in the control of gypsy moths which are responsible for destroying hundreds of thousands of forest acres.

Pheromones are still experimental in most areas. Another area of research involves antihormones which interfere with the hormonal growth stimuli in an insect and stop reproduction. For example, a male mosquito will not develop into a reproductive adult if certain hormonal signals are disturbed.

Pheromones have also been found to exist in mammals. The research into the uses of these substances is a challenge in biology.

REPRODUCTIVE POTENTIAL IN INSECTS

Insects as a group are perhaps the best adapted animals on the earth. They flourish in great numbers in many varied environments. Because they reproduce at a very rapid rate and in great numbers, insects pose a threat to people of all nations. Insects compete with humans for food. They utilize great amounts of biological energy and thus their food requirements are high. There are many cases of reproductive booms among certain species of insects causing the mass destruction of crops.

Research has found many ways of controlling the numbers of some species of insects. For example, the population of mosquitoes is often controlled by spraying insecticides and draining breeding swamps. Other methods used to limit insect populations include insect hormones, attractants, and natural predators. However, new methods must be developed to control the reproductive potential of harmful insect pests.

Because insects still cause human suffering through starvation and disease, their control is a vital challenge in biology.

ANSWERS TO QUESTIONS FOR REVIEW
(Pages 406–407)

1. Insects outnumber all other groups of animals. They endure many unfavorable conditions in which most other animals perish. They are highly adaptable and reproduce at a rapid rate.

2. Insects have lived on the earth for nearly 300 million years. During this time insects were able to adapt to many environmental changes.

3. An insect is an arthropod that has three distinct regions, three pairs of legs, one pair of antennae, respires by tracheae, and may or may not have wings.

4. The structures of the wings and mouthparts are valuable characteristics used to separate the insects into orders.

5. The chitinous exoskeleton is a tough, flexible, and lightweight protective armor. It has a waxy coat which prevents water loss to the environment. The size-limiting effect of the exoskeleton, however, is of survival value in that the tiny creatures have a low nutritional requirement and can find shelter in small places.

6. The grasshopper has an exoskeleton, segmented body, and jointed appendages—all characteristic of the phylum Arthropoda.

7. In humans, air passes into the lungs, where the blood receives oxygen and discharges carbon dioxide. The blood contacts the tissues. In the insect, many branching trachea tubes carry air directly to the tissues.

8. The eggs of a grasshopper, laid in the fall, are deposited in a hole dug in the ground by the ovipositor of the female.

9. Pheromones are chemical substances secreted to the outside of the body. Pheromones may be used as a communication device and a sex attractant by social insects.

10. Metamorphosis is of survival value because there is no competition between the young and adult for food. Pupal stages may also allow the insect to resist unfavorable conditions.

11. The social insects exhibit division of labor. Some are adapted for gathering food, some for protection, some for tending the young, and some for reproduction. A solitary insect must perform all these functions.

12. A hive contains a queen, many workers, and drones (at certain times). The queen lays eggs. Workers perform all tasks relative to maintaining the hive and rearing the young bees. Drones have no function except mating with the new queen.

13. Bees perform a peculiar dance which communicates the location of a nectar supply.

5

ANSWERS TO APPLYING PRINCIPLES AND CONCEPTS
(Page 407)

1. First, breathing does not involve pressure changes in a body cavity, as in the human chest. Second, the insect does not maintain a constant body temperature and can remain alive at low temperatures until its protoplasm can no longer function. Third, the exoskeleton gives excellent external protection.

2. Although the answers will vary, the following will be common:
   a. Each organism could have been created to appear exactly as it does now.
   b. Individual variation might have produced an insect which somewhat resembled a thorn. If

this insect resembled a thorn, a predator might overlook it. Therefore, its resemblance would be of adaptive value and it would have had a greater chance to live to reproduce, and pass this characteristic on.

c. If variation produced a fly that somewhat resembled a bee (which has a sting), it might also be ignored by a predator and have a better chance for survival.

3. A little fly does not grow up to become a larger fly. Regardless of size, a fly is an adult stage and is beyond the period of growth, which occurred as a larva.

4. Answers will vary. Students might suggest the following as explanations for the change in the amount of juvenile hormone that a *Cecropia* moth larva might produce: the age of the larva; size of the paired structure which produces the hormone; the diet of the larva; the light intensity on the larva or the amount of light on the larva; high temperatures. Answers will also vary as to how they might go about testing a hypothesis. However, great care should be taken in running a carefully controlled experiment.

5. The students may be able to think of many experiments, some of which may involve color, scents, or varying light concentration.

6. Pheromones may be used to attract insect pests in order to trap them. Sex attractants are used to destroy the males of the species.

unit 6 BIOLOGY OF THE VERTEBRATES

This unit explores the most complex form of animal life — the chordates. What differentiates chordates from other organisms? The answer to this question is found in Chapter Thirty-Three. In this chapter, the phylum *Chordata* is introduced and the subphylum *Vertebrata* and its seven classes are discussed. Chapter Thirty-Four discusses the three classes of fish and representatives of these classes. Vertebrates that live in water as young organisms and move on to the land as mature organisms are known as amphibians. These animals and their interesting life cycle are the subject of Chapter Thirty-Five. Reptiles are discussed in Chapter Thirty-Six. Ancestors of modern reptiles, the dinosaurs, are briefly discussed. The rise of reptiles and the characteristics that set this class apart from other vertebrate classes are also examined. Representative reptiles are introduced. Chapter Thirty-Seven explores one of the most plentiful of the vertebrate classes, the birds. The characteristics of this highly successful class are examined. Adaptations for flight are discussed in detail. The structure and function of birds are also discussed. The concluding chapter of this unit is concerned with the mammals. Chapter Thirty-Eight compares mammals to other vertebrates and discusses the evolution of mammals. Characteristics of mammals and the orders of mammals are examined. Having read this unit, students will have a better understanding of all of the vertebrates. The introduction to the mammals will serve as an excellent starting point for the study of the human body in Unit 7.

chapter thirty-three Introduction to the Vertebrates How do chordates differ from other animals? This question is answered at the beginning of Chapter Thirty-Three. The students will also learn about the rise of vertebrates, characteristics of vertebrates, and specialized vertebrate systems. The development of vertebrates and their complex behavior is also examined. This chapter provides an introduction to the specific classes of vertebrates to be discussed in subsequent chapters.

TEACHING SUGGESTIONS

1. Introduce this chapter by asking students to suggest ways in which chordates differ from other animals. Have students write down their suggestions and compare them to the factors discussed on pp. 411–412.

2. Provide students with a number of pictures representing the seven classes of vertebrates. Have students work in groups and classify their pictures. Elicit from students the reasons for classifying the animals that way.

3. Discuss with students the advantages of having an endoskeleton. Elicit from students the importance of having highly specialized vertebrate systems.

4. Ask students if they think of humans as having instincts. Point out to students that many behavioral scientists do *not* think that humans possess instincts because their actions are dominated by deliberate decisions.

STUDENT INVOLVEMENT ACTIVITIES

1. Some students may want to report on embryological similarities of vertebrates. Many students do not realize the closeness of development that exists in the early stages of life.

2. Ask students to choose one specialized system of vertebrates (p. 416) and compare it with the corresponding system or function in the invertebrates. Have students draw conclusions concerning vertebrate specialization.

3. Ask students to report on the subject of instincts and how these instincts relate to animal behavior. Encourage them to use the most up-to-date sources of information.

4. Have a few students research the topic of conditioning. Ask some to report on Pavlov's experiments. Perhaps some students could design their own conditioning experiment. Have them consider whether or not they think that people can be conditioned.

COMMUNITY INVOLVEMENT ACTIVITIES

1. Invite an embryologist to speak to the class on comparative embryology. Students should read on the topic and prepare questions in advance.

2. Invite a behavioral scientist to class to discuss various aspects of animal behavior. Prepare questions in advance.

3. Invite a vertebrate zoologist to class to discuss the various species of vertebrate animals.

6

CAREER OPPORTUNITIES
Behavioral scientist
Biologist
Embryologist
Paleontologist
Psychologist
Sociologist
Vertebrate zoologist

ANSWERS TO QUESTIONS FOR REVIEW
(Page 420)

1. The presence of the notochord, a dorsal nerve cord, and the presence of gill slits sometime during their life.
2. *Amphioxus* retains its dorsal nerve cord, notochord, and gill slits throughout its life.
3. It is thought that the early ancestors of vertebrates were soft-bodied animals whose remains decayed before they could be fossilized.
4. Cyclostomata, lamprey; Chondrichthyes, sharks; Osteichthyes, bony fishes; Amphibia, frogs; Reptilia, snakes; Aves, birds; Mammalia, mammals.
5. a. Integumentary; b. muscular; c. skeletal; d. digestive; e. respiratory; f. circulatory; g. excretory; h. endocrine; i. nervous; j. reproductive.
6. The cerebrum of the brain is the center of instinct, emotions, and intelligence.
7. Innate behavior is an inborn response of an animal involving reflexes and instincts. Reflexes such as blinking, and instincts such as self-preservation and species preservation are examples.
8. Reflex actions are a form of innate behavior. An animal will respond to a certain stimulus without any control on its part. Such actions protect the organism from harm.
9. An example of a conditioned reaction would be when a dog is taught to heel at a command or shake hands at a given signal. A person's ability to

communicate by symbols, both in speaking and writing would indicate intelligent action.

ANSWERS TO APPLYING PRINCIPLES AND CONCEPTS
(Page 420)

1. Vertebrates have an endoskeleton which provides protection and flexibility; they have well-developed circulatory and nervous systems; and they have efficient digestive, excretory and reproductive systems.
2. Species preservation is a stronger instinct than self-preservation when it is present. An animal will sacrifice its life in defense of its young.
3. Instinct and intelligence are more vital to a vertebrate than to an invertebrate because, lacking the external protection of a clam, a starfish, or a crayfish, the vertebrate must face its survival problem and flee or fight.

chapter thirty-four The Fishes
This chapter opens with an interesting discussion of the sea lamprey and the way this organism has been very destructive to fishes in the Great Lakes. The different classes of fish are discussed and representative examples of each class are given. The structure and function of the "true" or bony fishes are also discussed. The spawning behavior of fishes varies greatly and is summarized in this chapter. Students will have a better understanding of some of the creatures that make up the fish world after having read this chapter.

TEACHING SUGGESTIONS

1. This chapter may be introduced by eliciting from students any experiences they have had with fishes. Some students may enjoy fishing for sport or food; others may have a tropical fish hobby. Students may be able to contribute interesting stories about this diverse group of organisms.
2. Sharks have always been fascinating organisms. The fascination may have grown with the book *Jaws* by Peter Benchley and the movie of the same name that followed. Elicit from students any personal experiences they may have had with sharks and any knowledge of these organisms. Ask students who saw the movie or read the book *Jaws,* what their reactions were.
3. Students may enjoy reading a fascinating book about sharks, *Shark Frenzy* by John Clark. This book was published by Grosset & Dunlop, Inc., in 1975. It imparts valuable information about the relationship between sharks and humans.

"Have you eaten any good PCB's lately?"

4. Point out to students that many fishes besides sharks are dangerous to humans. They include fishes that impart electric shocks such as the electric eel, electric ray, and electric catfish. Other dangerous fishes include the piranhas, moray eels, barracudas, sting rays, lionfish, stonefish, and puffers.

STUDENT INVOLVEMENT SUGGESTIONS

1. Ask students to report on a fish that is dangerous to humans. These fishes belong to groups that attack with their teeth, sting, impart electric shocks, or are poisonous to eat. Some of these fish were listed under *Teaching Suggestions.*

2. Many students are interested in tropical fish. Encourage students to begin a tropical fish club. Perhaps a small collection can be kept in a classroom aquarium.

3. Fish is an excellent food that is high in protein and low in calories. Ask students to bring in various fish recipes. Perhaps a few could be prepared at home and brought in for students to sample.

4. Fish, like other animals, have been greatly endangered by the increasing pollution of both fresh and ocean waters. Have students report on one aspect of this problem. Point out to students that the pollution affects both fish and humans because fish usually caught for food are frequently found to be contaminated and harmful for people to eat.

COMMUNITY INVOLVEMENT ACTIVITIES

1. Visit an aquarium and study the different types of fishes exhibited. Choose one type of fish of special interest to you to write about.
2. If you live near the coast, invite someone from the fishing industry to speak to your class about his or her job and some of the experiences that occur in fishing.
3. Write to one of the many fish processors for information on canning and preserving of fish.
4. Invite a home economist to speak to the class about recipes that include fish. Suggest to the home economist that the recipes should be simple so that the students could prepare them.

CAREER OPPORTUNITIES
Environmental scientist
Fish processor
Fisherperson
Home economist
Ichthyologist
Marine biologist
Marine photographer
Nutritionist
Research biologist

CHALLENGES IN BIOLOGY
SHARK ATTACKS
The media has been reporting shark attacks more frequently in recent years. In part, this may be due to the publicity given to *Jaws* and other books about sharks. This discussion will attempt to relate some of the most recent information about shark attacks.

Statistics indicate that only one out of every five people attacked by a shark is killed. The rate of survival from a shark attack is double what it was about 40 years ago. Most shark attacks take place in Australia, New Zealand, New Guinea, United States, and Pacific Ocean islands.

It should be noted that sharks do not routinely attack people for food. There are certain factors that seem to "invite" shark attacks. These factors include murkiness of the water; blood in the immediate area of the swimmer; being male; activity in the water; chemical signals of the bather; and shiny or bright colored attire.

What is being done to prevent shark attacks? Researchers are trying to perfect chemical and physical means that may be effective. Chemical shark deterrents are still in the developmental stages. Shark screens (large bags open at the top) have also been tested. These bags would prevent persons who survive ship disasters from being attacked by sharks because the screens keep the smell of blood and human chemicals within the bag.

Much more needs to be done to control the problem of off-shore attacks. This remains as one of the important challenges in biology.

ANSWERS TO QUESTIONS FOR REVIEW
(Page 436)

1. The cyclostomes lack jaws; they have a round, funnel-like mouth lined with sharp, horny teeth.

2. When the adult sea lamprey attacks a fish, it attaches its sucking mouth to the sides of the fish and chisels a hole through the scales with its rasping teeth.

3. The shark differs from a bony fish in having a cartilaginous skeleton, a mouth on the ventral side of the head, and paired gill slits.

4. Bony fishes are covered with scales which are lubricated by mucus.

5. The dorsal side of the body contains dark pigments (chromatophores) which tone down bright light striking the fish from above. The light colors on the ventral side blend with the bright light on the surface when the fish is viewed from below.

6. Paired nostrils on the top of the head lead to nasal cavities containing olfactory nerve endings associated with the sense of smell. Large eyes on the sides of the head provide clear vision for short distances. The ear mechanisms are embedded in the skull and receive vibrations by bone conduction. The immovable tongue in the floor of the mouth functions as an organ of touch. Nerve endings of the lateral line receive low-frequency vibrations and respond to water pressures.

7. The fins of the yellow perch include: the dorsals, along the top midline; the caudal, or tail fin; the anal fin, along the ventral midline and posterior to the anal opening; the pelvic fins, along the ventral side; the pectoral fins, anterior to the pelvic fins.

8. Food enters the mouth, passes into the throat cavity, or pharynx, then through a short esophagus and into the stomach, and on to the intestine. Undigested particles are eliminated through the anal opening.

9. The fish heart consists of an atrium and ventricle, with a sinus venosus above the atrium and a bulbus arteriosus at the base of the ventral aorta and joining the ventricle.

10. The air bladder is a thin, gas-filled sac lying in the dorsal region of the body cavity. It adjusts the weight and displacement of the fish at various levels in the water.

11. The regions and functions of the fish brain, named from anterior to posterior are, olfactory lobes (sense of smell), cerebrum (control of voluntary muscles and center of instincts), optic lobes (sense of sight), cerebellum (muscle coordination), medulla oblongata (nervous control of the internal organs).

12. The female lays eggs; moments later as the male swims over the eggs, he will discharge the sperm-containing fluid known as milt.

ANSWERS TO APPLYING PRINCIPLES AND CONCEPTS
(Page 436)

1. Gill filaments dry out suddenly when exposed to the air. They are adapted to absorption of oxygen from the water, but cannot absorb it from the atmosphere.

2. Many fish eggs are not fertilized during the somewhat inefficient spawning process of most fish. Many eggs are eaten before they hatch. Young fish are the food supply of countless other aquatic animals. These, and climatic conditions, prevent fish from overpopulating waters in which there is a normal natural balance.

3. Eels, having lived from five to ten years in the fresh water streams and rivers of the Atlantic and Gulf coast regions, migrate to the warm water south of Bermuda and north of the West Indies. Spawning occurs in the same spawning ground where the adults hatched. European eels will migrate a great distance from areas of Europe to their spawning grounds in the region of the Sargasso Sea. Pacific salmon show the greatest

homing instinct in that they return to the same river or branch of a river in which their parents spawned.

4. Deoxygenated blood flows through the ventral aorta to the afferent branchial arteries. These arteries carry the deoxygenated blood through the gill arches to the gill filaments. Thin-walled capillaries in the gill filaments allow diffusion to take place. The blood gives up carbon dioxide and takes in oxygen. The oxygenated blood is carried from the gill filaments by the efferent branchial arteries to the dorsal aorta.

6

chapter thirty-five The Amphibians   Amphibians are especially interesting because they live on land and in water. This chapter discusses the characteristics of amphibians and how these animals differ from all the animals that have been previously discussed. The orders of amphibia are examined and representative animals are discussed. The structure and function of the frog is explored in detail. In addition, frog behavior characterized by hibernation and estivation is discussed. Students will have a better understanding of some very familiar animals after reading this chapter.

TEACHING SUGGESTIONS

1. Elicit from students some of the reasons for the success of certain amphibians such as the frog. Would this animal be as successful if it did not live on land and in water?
2. Point out to students that the anatomy of the frog is very similar to that of humans. If possible, all students should participate in the external and internal examination of a frog. If this is not possible, demonstrate the dissection for students. The insert (following page 438) "The Anatomy of the Frog" would be particularly helpful in this demonstration.
3. Many interesting behavioral as well as anatomical observations can be accomplished with frogs. However, caution students to treat *all* animals with respect and to never torture animals.
4. Many frogs have very definite mating calls. They have a wide range of notes, most of which are audible to the human ear.

Ask students who live near water to listen to and, if possible, tape record some of the frog sounds they hear.

STUDENT INVOLVEMENT ACTIVITIES

1. Many students enjoy collecting tadpoles and frogs. Ask them to bring in specimens and identify them. Be sure to return the animals to their natural habitats.
2. Many amphibians are protected from enemies by their coloration. Ask students to write about one example or to write about the skin color changes of certain salamanders.
3. Have certain students report in detail on some aspect of the economic importance of frogs. Their chief value is as a natural insect control.
4. Have students do some research into how water pollution has affected certain species of frogs.

COMMUNITY INVOLVEMENT ACTIVITIES

1. Invite a chef to class to discuss the preparation of frog's legs. Perhaps, the chef will bring some samples of this delicacy to class.
2. A herpetologist is a specialist in the area of amphibians and reptiles. If possible, invite a herpetologist to class to discuss amphibians and answer questions about them.
3. If possible, take a field trip to a local pond and observe the amphibian life of the area. Some students may want to catch some specimens. Be sure to return them to the pond after observation.

CAREER OPPORTUNITIES

Anatomist
Chef
Ecologist
Frog "farmer"
Herpetologist
Wildlife conservationist
Zoologist

ANSWERS TO QUESTIONS FOR REVIEW
(Page 453)

1. Early lungfish had jointed, or lobed, fins somewhat resembling legs. It is believed that a fish with legs could perhaps crawl away from a dried-up pond to a pond with water. Thus it is reasoned that the primitive lungfishes, with their lobed fins, were transitional forms between true fishes and amphibians.
2. Thin, moist, flexible skin; feet often webbed; toes without claws; larval forms vegetarian, while the adults are usually carnivorous; heart two-chambered in the larval stage and becoming three-chambered in the adult; eggs directly fertilized; metamorphosis.
3. Salamanders resemble lizards in having elongated bodies, a tail and, in most species, short legs. They differ from lizards in having smooth, moist skin without scales and in lacking claws on the toes.
4. The Mexican axolotl lives in streams lacking sufficient iodine for secreting thyroid hormone which stimulates metamorphosis.
5. When an insect nears a frog's mouth, the mouth opens wide, the tongue flips out and catches the insect on its sticky surface, then flips the insect into the mouth cavity.
6. The organs of the alimentary canal of a frog are the mouth, esophagus, stomach, small intestine, colon (large intestine), and cloaca.
7. Adult frogs are able to respire through the skin while under water.

8. The frog has a three-chambered heart. It receives blood separately from the body and the lungs. Blood passes through the two-chambered heart of the fish only once in a round trip through the body.

9. Wastes are filtered from the blood by the kidneys. This urine flows through ureters to the cloaca. Urine also passes into the urinary bladder for storage.

10. External direct fertilization. The eggs are fertilized directly by the male as they pass from the female.

11. Changes occurring in the life of a tadpole include: lengthening of the body, appearance of external gills, lengthening of the tail and developing of the caudal fin, disappearance of the horny lip, growth of the fleshy gill covers, appearance of the hind legs, growth of the front legs under the operculum, appearance of the front legs, resorption of the tail, and broadening of the mouth. Many internal changes accompany these external changes.

12. Heart action and circulation are greatly reduced. Nervous activity almost ceases. Tissues are kept alive by slow oxidation of food stored in the liver and fat bodies.

ANSWERS TO APPLYING PRIN-
CIPLES AND CONCEPTS
(Page 453)

1. It is believed that the lungfish used the lobed fins to leave drying ponds in search of ponds that still had water. Thus, those that possessed these characteristics had a better chance for survival and reproduction.

2. The amphibians have never been successful on land because they cannot survive drying conditions and they are dependent on water for laying eggs and the developing of the young.

3. The frog's eyes bulge above the water when the frog floats beneath the surface. The eyes are protected by nictitating membranes. Nostrils on the head allow the frog to breathe with all but the top of the head submerged. The eardrums are on the surface of the body. The mouth is an efficient insect trap.

4. During fertilization of the eggs of a frog, sperms are spread over the eggs as they are laid. Most eggs receive a sperm. This is a more efficient method than in the fish, whose sperms are spread in the general vicinity of the eggs during spawning.

5. The tadpole has a two-chambered heart until late in the metamorphosis, gills, lateral line, operculum, tail, and caudal fin. Limbs are lacking early in its life.

chapter thirty-six The Reptiles

The earliest reptiles are well known to all of us as dinosaurs. The dinosaurs were the ancestors of our modern-day reptiles. This chapter discusses the rise of the reptiles and how this was associated with the amniote egg. The chapter examines the body characteristics of reptiles and their adaptations for life on land. Reptile classification is examined and orders and representative species are discussed. The structure and function of snakes are discussed in detail and other reptiles of special interest are also examined. Students will have a better understanding of modern reptiles and their link with the past after having read this chapter.

TEACHING SUGGESTIONS

1. Point out to students that the evolution of reptiles spans many millions of years. It is interesting to note that a single order, *Cotylosauria* gave rise to all living reptiles and many that are presently extinct.

2. Turtles are fascinating creatures because of their unique shells or "houses." Point out to students that recent information discourages individuals from keeping the miniature turtles as pets. In many cases, these turtles have been found to carry bacteria that affect humans and can cause intestinal problems.

3. Snakes are both fascinating and terrifying to many people. Students should become familiar with poisonous snakes that live in their region. They should also learn about what to do in the event of a snake bite.

4. There are certain methods of handling reptiles to ensure your

safety and theirs. Refer to literature Fig. 36-1 for ways in which to handle turtles, lizards, snakes, and crocodilians.

STUDENT INVOLVEMENT ACTIVITIES

1. There are many unusual members of the reptile family. Ask students to report on one that is of special interest to them. The Komodo "dragon" of the South Pacific is a particularly interesting and unusual reptile.
2. Have some students report from first-person observations how reptiles are kept in zoos. If there is a local zoo, students can go in a small group and observe the animals in the reptile house.
3. Certain reptiles are among the endangered species. Have students report on one of these animals and what is being done to protect them.
4. Have a class discussion on the question of whether or not all nations should forbid the catching of alligators for the use of their skins. Alligators are an endangered species in the United States but alligator hunts continue in certain states.

COMMUNITY INVOLVEMENT ACTIVITIES

1. Visit the reptile house of a local zoo and observe the exhibits.
2. Invite a herpetologist to class to discuss reptiles. Be sure to prepare questions in advance.
3. Visit a museum of natural history and have students observe dinosaur relics. Ask students to take notes on exhibits of special interest to them.

CAREER OPPORTUNITIES
Ecologist
Herpetologist
Museum curator
Paleontologist
Zoologist
Zoo worker

CHALLENGES IN BIOLOGY
THE TUATARA AND OTHER ENDANGERED REPTILES

The tuatara is regarded by some people as a living fossil. It is the only surviving animal that preserves the characteristics of the ancient reptiles. The surviving population has been greatly reduced and may number about 10,000. These animals are presently protected by the government of New Zealand and have a good chance of survival if protection is maintained and enforced.

Crocodiles and alligators are in danger of extinction in many areas where they once flourished. Some of these animals are now protected by law and some have been isolated on wildlife refuges. However, in certain states legal control is difficult and they are killed for their valuable hides. It has been estimated, for example, that more than 500,000 alligators were killed in the United States between 1968 and 1971.

Some states have made it illegal to sell products made from alligator skin. However, the problem continues because hides are frequently sold to markets abroad and are processed and made into products in these countries.

Alligators and crocodiles are endangered species and protective laws have not controlled the situation in many states. More effective means of protection and enforcement are necessary to meet this challenge in biology.

ANSWERS TO QUESTIONS FOR REVIEW
(Page 470)

1. *Brontosaurus,* the largest of the dinosaurs, was a plant-eating dinosaur. It had a very long neck, balanced by an equally long heavy tail. *Tyrannosaurus,* the tyrant lizard, was a flesh eater. It walked erect on powerful hind legs and balanced its body with its long tail. Its front legs were short and equipped with powerful claws. Its jaws were powerful and rimmed with double-edged teeth. *Pteranodon,* the largest of the flying reptiles, was the size of a turkey with a wing span of more than 9 meters. The jaws were elongated into a toothless beak. Though awkward on land it probably flew gracefully as it would swoop down over a lake to catch a fish.
2. The *shell* prevents rapid water loss and protects the interior from injury. The *chorion,* the outer layer of the amnion, lines the shell. The *amnion* encloses the embryo and secretes a protective fluid for the embryo. Many blood vessels in the *allantois* join the circulation of the embryo which allows the embryo to absorb oxygen and give off carbon dioxide and metabolic wastes. The *yolk* supplies nourishment.
3. A body covering of scales; thick, dry skin; limbs with claws on the toes; lungs for air breathing; partial or nearly complete division of the heart ventricle; a body temperature varying with that of the environment.
4. Rhynchocephalia (*Sphenodon*); Chelonia (turtles, tortoises): squamata (snakes, lizards); Crocodilia (alligators, crocodiles, gavials, and caimans).
5. Older than the dinosaurs, *Spheno-*

don is the sole surviving species of the order Rhynchocephalia. The parietal eye is a very unusual characteristic.

6. Snakes capture their prey by catching it in the mouth and swallowing it alive, by squeezing it to death, or by poisoning it.
7. The quadrate bone allows the jaws to drop downward and forward at the hinges. A ligament in the front of the lower jaw allows the halves of the jaw to be thrust forward independently. Slanting teeth hold the prey.
8. Oviparous means "egg laying." Ovoviviparous means the eggs are retained in the uterus as they develop. The young are brought forth alive.
9. Neurotoxin affects the parts of the nervous system that control breathing and heart action. Hemotoxin destroys red blood cells and breaks down the walls of small blood vessels.
10. Crocodiles are more aquatic than alligators. They are distinguished from alligators by a triangular head, a pointed snout, and on the lower jaw, a tooth that fits outside the upper jaw.
11. The turtle has been able to survive through the years because of its boxlike shell. Many can swim very efficiently. The horny, toothless beak permits the animal to eat meat or plants. Turtles can remain submerged for long periods of time.

ANSWERS TO APPLYING PRINCIPLES AND CONCEPTS
(Page 470)

1. Land dwelling vertebrates were impossible until biological limitations, laying eggs in water to prevent drying and the need for an aquatic larval stage, were overcome. The amniote egg allowed these limitations to be overcome.

2. Rare animals have survived on islands because they are free from natural enemies. Similar organisms on larger land masses were exterminated ages ago.
3. The range of these animals is confined to the tropical, subtropical, and temperate zones. They are not able to withstand extreme cold temperatures and long periods of winter.
4. Structures which indicate an advancement in structure are a body covering of scales that protect the skin surface; limbs, if present, with claws on the toes and suited for climbing, digging, or locomotion on land; well-developed lungs suited to air breathing and eliminating the need for skin or mouth respiration; partial or nearly complete division of the heart ventricle, resulting in further separation of oxygenated blood from the body tissues.

chapter thirty-seven The Birds
Why are birds often referred to as "glorified reptiles"? This question and many others concerning adaptations are discussed in this chapter. Students will read about *Archaeopteryx,* an ancient fossil bird. The characteristics of birds and structural adaptations for flight are discussed. The systems of birds are examined in some detail. The chapter concludes with an interesting discussion of embryo incubation and development and egg and parental care in birds. Students will have a better understanding of a successful and abundant class of vertebrates after reading this chapter.

TEACHING SUGGESTIONS

1. An interesting way to introduce this chapter is to play a recording of bird calls (these may be available at record stores). See how many bird calls students are able to recognize.
2. If students have pet birds at home, elicit from them information concerning the care of birds.
3. Point out to students that most wild birds are protected by law from individuals killing or possessing them. It might be interesting for a few students to find out about bird protection laws in your state.
4. Many birds are on the list of endangered species. Point out to students that ospreys, eagles, and falcons are in danger of extinction. Some students may wish to research this situation and report to the class on their findings.

6

STUDENT INVOLVEMENT ACTIVITIES

1. Ask students to observe the birds in their own neighborhood. What types of birds do they see and how do their calls sound?

2. Some birds have been found to carry diseases that are dangerous to human beings. Pigeons are the chief offenders in this regard. Ask students to report on this problem.

3. Ask students to report on fish and game hunting laws in your state. Be sure to remind them to include information about the duck hunting season.

COMMUNITY INVOLVEMENT ACTIVITIES

1. Invite an ornithologist to class to answer questions about birds.

2. Invite a veterinarian to class to discuss the care of injured birds and when to come to the aid of a bird.

3. Visit the bird house of a zoo and observe the different types of birds on exhibit.

4. Arrange for the class to take an early morning "bird-watching" tour through a park or wooded area. Encourage the students to observe the birds and listen to their calls.

CAREER OPPORTUNITIES
Ecologist
Ornithologist
Poultry farmer
Veterinarian
Zoo curator
Zoologist

ANSWERS TO QUESTIONS FOR REVIEW
(Page 487)

1. Birds have retained two conspicuous characteristics from their reptile ancestors: scales on their legs and feet, and claws on their toes.

2. Reptile characteristics of *Archaeopteryx* included teeth in the elongated jaws, three clawed fingers extending from the wings, scale covered feet with three clawed toes, and a long lizardlike tail. Bird characteristics included feathers, a long flexible neck, wings, a shortened back, support of the body on the hind limbs, and position of the toes. The *Archaeopteryx* was probably warm-blooded, another characteristic of modern birds.

3. The biological success can be measured by the number of species and individuals in the group, their adaptation to a wide variety of environmental conditions, and their distribution throughout the world.

4. Eight characteristics are: body covering of feathers; bones light, porous, and in certain cases air-filled; forelimbs developed as wings and, in most birds, used for flight—never for grasping; body supported on two hind limbs; mouth a horny, toothless beak; heart four-chambered, well-developed circulatory system with a right aortic arch only; body temperature constant (warm-blooded); amniote egg enclosed in a lime-containing shell and usually incubated in a nest.

5. The plumage of a bird includes *down feathers,* serving as insulation; *filoplumes; contour feathers,* which cover the body and give it a smooth outline and coloration; and *quill feathers,* used in flight.

6. Taste and smell are poorly developed; sight and hearing are well developed.

7. This flexibility is necessary because the bird cannot use its forelimbs for grasping; it permits the turning of the head easily so as to see in all directions; enables the use of the beak for feeding, feather preening, nest building, and other activities.

8. It serves as an attachment for muscles for flight.

9. The organs of the alimentary canal of a bird are: the mouth, esophagus, proventriculus (glandular stomach), gizzard, intestine, rectum, cloaca, and cloacal opening.

10. Air sacs increase the capacity of the lungs and function in heat elimination through the respiratory tract.

11. The bird heart consists of four chambers. The septum dividing the right and left ventricles is complete. No mixing of oxygenated and deoxygenated blood occurs in the heart, as in amphibians and reptiles.

12. The excretion of uric acid into the cloaca of a bird eliminates the urinary bladder and the storage of urine. This is considered an adaptation for weight reduction and flight.

13. Embryonic membranes in a bird egg include the yolk sac, amnion, allantois, and chorion.

14. Precocial birds usually lay 12 to 20 eggs in a nest on or close to the ground. The incubation period is relatively long (three to six weeks) and the young can walk soon after hatching. The young birds are taken to food by the parent or parents. Altricial birds usually lay six or fewer eggs. The incubation period is shortened and the young hatch in a helpless condition. They remain in the nest where they are fed by the parent bird or birds for some time (more than a week) after hatching.

ANSWERS TO APPLYING PRINCIPLES AND CONCEPTS
(Page 487)

1. Body streamlining reduces air resistance. Weight is sacrificed without reducing strength.

Enormous muscle power from large breast muscles. Bones are light and porous. Birds have no urinary bladder and females have only one ovary.

2. Several structural advances are associated with warm-bloodedness as well as the high body temperature in birds. The heart is large in proportion to the body size and is four-chambered, thus eliminating mixing of blood as in lower vertebrates. Heart action (pulse) is very rapid. Air sacs increase the lung capacity and function in heat elimination through the respiratory tract. The rate of cellular respiration is rapid. The digestive organs are well-developed. A large quantity of food is necessary to supply the high energy needs of the bird.

3. Physical barriers, such as mountains, deep canyons, and bodies of water prevent the migration of flightless birds. They are also at a disadvantage in escaping predators. For these reasons, flightless birds are limited to areas which are favorable to their survival.

4. Variations in the form of beaks and feet of birds are believed to be the result of mutations that have occurred through the ages. These variations have adapted birds for a wide variety of foods and feeding habits.

chapter thirty-eight The Mammals   How did the mammals evolve? This question is answered at the beginning of this chapter through the vivid example of the horse. This chapter also examines the diversity among mammals and the characteristics of these animals. The orders of mammals and representative examples are given. The structure and function of certain mammalian organ systems are discussed in some detail. The nervous and reproductive systems of mammals are stressed. Having read this chapter, students will better understand the class of vertebrates to which they belong. This chapter provides an excellent introduction to the next unit that is concerned with the human body.

TEACHING SUGGESTIONS

1. Point out to students that while mammals are an extremely successful class, except for the amphibians, they have the least number of species. There are about 4,300 species of mammals alive today.

2. Elicit from the class some of the reasons for mammalian success. Such reasons as warm bloodedness, ability to tolerate change, general vitality, and most importantly, the development of their brains.

3. An interesting book that students may enjoy is *The Wonderful World of Mammals* by Roger Caras, Harcourt, Brace, Jovanovich, 1973. This book, written by a well-known naturalist, uses topical stamp collections of animals as a focal point. Endangered species are pointed out and discussed.

4. Point out to students that many mammals are endangered

species. A particularly interesting book to discuss with clsss is *Vanishing Wildlife of North America* by Thomas B. Allen, National Geographic Society, 1974. This beautifully illustrated book concentrates on many aspects of endangered species.

STUDENT INVOLVEMENT ACTIVITIES

1. Numerous organizations are involved in the protection of endangered species. Some of these include the Office of Endangered Species, National Park Service, North American Association for the Preservation of Predatory Animals, and the Bureau of Sport Fisheries and Wildlife. Ask students to write to an organization of their choice and report on the information received.

2. Ask students to write about a mammal that is considered endangered. These mammals can be found in the "red book" compiled by the Office of Endangered Species and in other books on the subject.

3. Have a student debate about the pro's and con's of using the furs of animals for clothes. Have students do extensive research on this question and then open the discussion to class questions.

COMMUNITY INVOLVEMENT ACTIVITIES

1. Invite a representative of a group concerned with the preservation of wildlife to speak to your class. Prepare questions in advance.

2. Visit a local zoo and observe the

6

many animals that are exhibited. Ask students to write about one of these animals.

3. Set up a program concerning endangered species and open it to the public. A guest speaker should be invited. Students can create a photo essay to point out those species with which people may not be acquainted.

CAREER OPPORTUNITIES
Biotelemetrist
Ecologist
Endangered species consultant
Forest ranger
Mammalogist
Range manager
Veterinarian
Wildlife conservationist
Wildlife photographer
Zoologist

CHALLENGES IN BIOLOGY
COYOTES
Coyotes have been killed by sheep and cattle raisers for many years. However, many studies have shown that coyotes will feed on jack rabbits and carrion and usually prey on weak animals. However, the sheep ranchers have led the battle against the coyotes and many thousands were killed by shooting and poisoning.

In 1972, the federal government banned the use of poisons in the control of coyotes and other wildlife. Bounty hunting increased. Some states have prohibited the payment of bounties for the killing of coyotes and other species, but it continues in many areas.

The destruction of the coyote has resulted in the over-population of jack rabbits. The coyote is the

natural predator of the jack rabbit. In the absence of the coyotes, the jack rabbits have become pests and have caused extensive damage to crops.

The challenge to biology is to protect the sheep through more scientific methods of controlling the coyote population. Poisoning and bounty hunting are inhumane and these methods do not allow wildlife specialists to keep the coyote population from endangerment.

ANSWERS TO QUESTIONS FOR REVIEW
(Page 509)

1. Extinct mammals include ancestors of the modern horse, wooly rhinoceros, ancient camels, straight-horned bison, bear dogs, short-faced bear, saber-toothed cats, mastodon, and mammoth.

2. Mammalian characteristics include: body covered with hair; mostly viviparous, young nourished with milk, lung-breathing, diaphragm separating the thoracic and abdominal cavities, four-chambered heart and left aortic arch, warm-blooded, two pairs of limbs in most species, cerebrum and cerebellum highly developed.

3. Mammals are classified into orders largely on a basis of reproduction, limb and foot structure, and tooth structure. Diet and feeding habits are also considered.

4. They lay eggs, lack external ears, and have a cloaca.

5. Marsupial mammals give birth to their young in a premature stage. The young are then nourished and protected within the mother's pouch. Placental mammals give birth to young in a more advanced stage. The fetus is connected to the mother's blood supply through which it receives nourishment.

6. The members of Chiroptera have greatly lengthened fingers and membranous wings. They are the only mammals capable of true flight.

7. All are gnawing mammals with strong, chisel-shaped incisor teeth.

8. Lagomorphs have four enlarged incisor teeth in each jaw rather than two as in rodents.

9. They have streamlined bodies and forelimbs which provide locomotion. They use lungs for breathing

but can hold their breath for a long time.

10. Primates have superior brain development and well-developed arms and hands. Their fingers are used for grasping, and one or more fingers or toes are equipped with nails. Most primates can walk erect if necessary.

11. The forelimbs have been modified for digging, hanging, flying, running, defense, and capturing prey. Teeth have been modified as chisels for flesh-tearing and grinding. Antlers, horns, and protective coloration are also important adaptations.

12. The fish have two-chambered hearts; amphibians have three-chambered hearts (two atria and one ventricle); reptiles have two atria and a partially divided ventricle; birds and mammals have complete four-chambered hearts.

13. The cerebrum is most highly developed in the mammalian brain.

ANSWERS TO APPLYING PRINCIPLES AND CONCEPTS
(Page 510)

1. The continents were uplifted, and mountain ranges and high plateaus arose. Shallow seas and swamps disappeared. Water collected in great oceans. The climate changed as some areas became temperate or frigid. Seasonal temperature changes developed. To these changes the reptiles could not adjust, but these were ideal conditions for the rise of mammals in many forms.

2. The three lines of mammalian development are represented by the monotremes (the egg-laying mammals); the marsupials (the pouched mammals); and the placental mammals. The placental mammals are the most successful due to the fact that the young are born in a more advanced condition.

3. Since the protection offered by internal development increases the chances for individual survival, less eggs need be produced to ensure survival of the species.

6

unit 7 HUMAN BIOLOGY

This unit is devoted to the most successful and dominant form of life: human beings. The first chapter of this unit examines human history. Anthropology, the study of human history, is discussed. Students will learn how anthropologists put the pieces of human history together in order to have a better understanding of our prehistoric ancestors. Chapter Forty examines the framework of the body. The students will learn about the skeletal and muscular systems. Nutrition is the subject of Chapter Forty-One. The food substances and their functions in the body are discussed. The digestive system and its functions are also discussed. In Chapter Forty-Two, transport and excretion of substances is examined. Students will learn about the circulatory system and about the components of blood. The structure and function of the excretory system is also examined. This chapter concludes with a discussion of skin and its functions. Chapter Forty-Three concerns the topics of respiration and energy exchange. The two phases of respiration are discussed and all aspects of breathing are examined. Artificial respiration is also discussed. Metabolism and environmental effects on breathing conclude this chapter. The human nervous system is the subject of Chapter Forty-Four. Students will learn about the structure and function of this system in some detail. The senses are also discussed in this chapter. Chapter Forty-Five discusses the topics of alcohol, tobacco, and drugs. These substances have resulted in serious social and health problems for many individuals. The endocrine glands are the body

regulators that are discussed in detail in Chapter Forty-Six. Students will learn about the different hormones and their effects. This unit concludes with a discussion of reproduction and development in Chapter Forty-Seven. The reproductive systems of the male and female are discussed and illustrated. The menstrual cycle, fertilization, and development are examined. Through the study of this unit, students will have a better understanding of their own bodies and how they function.

chapter thirty-nine Human History What were our human ancestors like? This question and many others on this subject are answered in this chapter. The students will learn about the work of anthropologists and how the clues were put together to give us an idea of the appearance and characteristics of prehistoric human beings. Having read this chapter, students will be able to better understand the individuals who lived in prehistoric times.

TEACHING SUGGESTIONS

1. The topic evolution is very interesting to most students. However, the topic may be a sensitive one. Encourage students to have an open mind and to understand that there are a number of *theories* regarding the dawn of human beings.
2. Elicit from students the characteristics that are unique to humans. Stress the development of the human brain. Refer students to the human body insert between pages 518–519.
3. Elicit from students some of the reasons for communication being considered essential to human development. Ask them to consider the fact that without communication humans would never have accomplished the advances that we take for granted today.

STUDENT INVOLVEMENT ACTIVITIES

1. Have some students research the science of anthropology and

report about the different areas of concern to the anthropologist. Also have students find out about career possibilities in this field, amount of education, and other necessary training.

2. Ask students to read about some aspect of the subject of prehistoric humans and report about it to the class. Encourage students to write about their subjects in some detail.

3. There are still some very primitive tribes that students may be interested in reading about. Students may want to read some of the classic writings of Dr. Margaret Mead and her work with primitive people.

COMMUNITY INVOLVEMENT ACTIVITIES

1. Invite an anthropologist to class to discuss his or her work and career opportunities in the area of anthropology.

2. Visit a museum of natural history that has an exhibit about prehistoric people.

3. Prepare a picture essay of the history of human beings. Have students piece together a variety of pictures that illustrate humans in prehistoric times and in the present.

CAREER OPPORTUNITIES

Anthropologist
Archeologist
Genetecist
Historian
Museum curator

Paleontologist
Phylogenist
Research biologist
Social psychologist
Sociologist

ANSWERS TO QUESTIONS FOR REVIEW
(Page 521)

1. Humans are the only animals with truly upright posture. We have a shortened and flattened pelvis which holds the abdominal organs. Our hands are free and the action of the thumb opposes that of the fingers. The location of the eyes gives a sense of depth, and humans are intelligent.

2. True humans are distinguished from apelike primates by ability to use tools, use fire, communicate by means of symbols in written and spoken words, and by having a smaller proportion of face to brain size.

3. Charles Darwin believed that a primitive primate, perhaps back ten million years, gave rise to the various groups of primates. Thus the monkey, gorilla, chimpanzee, orangutan, and gibbon are all specialized forms. When Darwin pointed out the similarities between these forms and humans, some people interpreted his comparisons as suggesting that humans evolved from monkeys. This was not his intent.

4. The finding of an old skull links the past with the present. Archeologists can date the skull and, by careful examination, determine the age and sex of the individual, the food it consumed, and perhaps even the way it died and whether it used tools or lived in a society. It would also indicate the brain size.

5. The jaw structure indicates whether its owner had the capacity for

speech. The form of teeth indicates the diet.

6. The type of environment that existed in a given area thousands of years ago can be determined by the fossil remains of plants and animals in that area. The types of food remains around a primitive campsite indicate the climate and nature of the surroundings.

7. The diet of primitive humans has been determined by campsite remains and by the structure and wearing surfaces of the teeth.

8. The study of primitive people provides an insight into the development of modern culture, and gives clues to understanding unearthed fossils and encampments of early people.

ANSWERS TO APPLYING PRINCIPLES AND CONCEPTS
(Page 522)

1. Under usual conditions tropical forests would not provide good fossils because conditions are so ideal for a variety of living forms that a dead organism is eaten by others and decay occurs very rapidly.

2. Intelligence of primitive humans can be judged from the skull, indicating brain size, and by the tools made and used. If the same types of tools are found in several different age layers, we might believe that communication of some kind had occurred.

3. It has been theorized that once tool making began, natural selection did not favor the longer canine teeth which were used for killing animals for food.

4. Java had a slanting forehead and heavy brow ridges and the brain was only half the size of a modern human's. Neanderthal's forehead sloped backward from heavy brow

7

75

ridges and the brain was as large or larger than ours. Cro-Magnon had a high forehead and lacked the heavy brow ridges of more primitive humans. Modern humans have a high forehead with a large brain capacity.

5. Perhaps much of their communication was by way of their paintings left on the walls of their caves. The drawings represent animals living at the time and weapons used.

chapter forty The Body Framework This chapter begins with a discussion of the four types of tissues that make up our bodies. The organ-systems are introduced and the students also learn about the regions of the body. The structure and function of the skeletal system and muscular system are discussed in detail. Having read this chapter, students will better understand the physical structure and movement of their bodies.

TEACHING SUGGESTIONS

1. It might be helpful to the students if they could clearly see the relationship between cells, tissues, organs, and systems. This can be done through chalkboard diagrams using circles within circles to show the involvement of all structures.

2. Elicit from students the advantages of an internal skeleton. Why is this type of skeleton more efficient than an external skeleton? How do human beings compensate for the disadvantage of lacking external protection?

3. Point out to students that medical history was recently made when a young child received the first successful bone marrow transplant from a nonrelated donor. This child was suffering from a genetic disorder called immune deficiency disease (absence of lymphocytes). Students may want to read more about such transplants and their possible use in the treatment of leukemia and aplastic anemia.

STUDENT INVOLVEMENT ACTIVITIES

1. Students might be interested in finding out more about diseases that affect the muscular system. New information on one such disease, multiple sclerosis (MS), has indicated that MS is caused by a virus. Assign students to report on MS and other muscle-involved diseases such as polio and muscular dystrophy.

2. There have been many advances in the area of reconstructive bone surgery. One of the most recent is the two-piece artificial elbow replacement. Have students report on advances in this type of surgery.

COMMUNITY INVOLVEMENT ACTIVITIES

1. Invite an orthopedic surgeon to class to discuss the advances in the treatment of broken and diseased bones.

2. Invite a physical therapist to class to discuss his or her profession and advances in this field.

3. The students may enjoy sponsoring a physical fitness day so that both students and the public could learn about the importance of keeping physically fit.

CAREER OPPORTUNITIES

Athletic trainer
Chiropractor
Coach
Dental assistant
Dental technician
Dentist

Endodontist
Oral surgeon
Orthodontist
Orthopedic surgeon
Osteopath
Pedodontist
Periodontist
Physical educator
Physical therapist
Physician

ANSWERS TO QUESTIONS FOR REVIEW
(Page 532)

1. Tissues are groups of cells all performing the same function. They are grouped into an organ which performs a definite function. The organs that are grouped together for a certain function compose the system. For example, the muscle is a tissue in the stomach which is an organ and comprises part of the digestive system. Each part contributes to the whole and thus to division of labor.

2. The three body cavities are the abdominal, thoracic, and cranial. The abdominal cavity is enclosed by the pelvis below and the diaphragm above. It contains the stomach, intestine, liver, spleen, pancreas, kidneys, and ovaries in the female. The thoracic cavity is bounded by the diaphragm below and by the rib cage. It contains the heart and lungs. The cranial cavity is surrounded by the bones of the skull and contains the brain.

3. The functions of bones are: providing support and form for the body (the cranium, femur, tibia, pelvis, sternum); providing a place for the attachment of muscles (the femur, humerus, tibia, and fibula); protecting delicate organs (the pelvis, ribs, and bones composing the cranium).

4. The Haversian canals carry nourishment to the living cells of the bony layer by means of blood vessels that connect with those of the outer membrane.

5. Ligaments, composed of strong connecting tissue, surround many joints and keep them together as well as prevent free movement. Many joints are surrounded by a connective tissue, the synovial membrane, which maintains a fluid in the joint so that it is lubricated for ease of movement.

6. The hip and shoulder joints are ball-and-socket joints. The attachment of the ribs to the vertebrae is an example of a partially movable joint. Here only slight movement occurs during respiration. Joints of the knee and elbow are hinge joints, as they move only in one plane. Immovable joints are found in the bones of the cranium where, during growth, the bones have fused.

7. Muscles are often classified as smooth, striated, and cardiac, depending on the appearance.

8. Muscles are often found in opposing pairs in the body because when a flexing action occurs, it is necessary to have a control over the extending action.

9. When a striated muscle contracts, it shortens and becomes thicker in the middle. Electron microscopy has shown that muscle fibers consist of fine threads called myofibrils which lie parallel and run lengthwise to the fiber. The myofibrils are composed of two different protein filaments (myosin and actin) which are arranged in a definite pattern. It is believed that contraction is brought about as these protein filaments slide past one another so that the myofibrils are shortened.

ANSWERS TO APPLYING PRINCIPLES AND CONCEPTS
(Page 532)

1. An internal skeleton does not provide external protection. This protection is given by defensive behavior, made possible by a highly developed nervous system and sense organs.

2. Other factors involved in producing good teeth and healthy bones are the assimilation of the minerals provided by the diet and the obtaining of additional vitamin D required for the assimilation process.

3. The walking cast puts a broken bone under limited stress during the healing period, speeding up the repair process.

4. The heart of lower animals is much less complicated than that of higher animals. When only a small part of the heart is removed and placed in a nutrient solution, it will continue to beat. Cardiac muscle is unique and demonstrates contractility, automatism, and rhythm.

7

77

**Maybe we would be better off if we had an
exoskeleton.**

chapter forty-one Nutrition

What is food? This question introduces a chapter that explains in detail what food is and how it is utilized in the body. Students will learn about vitamins and minerals and their specific functions in the body. The process of digestion is considered thoroughly. This chapter concludes with a discussion of the absorption process and its importance to the body. This chapter will give the students a better understanding of the food they eat and how the body utilizes it.

TEACHING SUGGESTIONS

1. The title of this chapter is *Nutrition*. Elicit from students what this word means to them. You may be surprised at the variety of definitions that are offered. Have students agree on a working definition of this word.

2. What types of foods do most of your students eat? Ask the students to write down a typical daily diet that they might follow. Remind them to include the foods eaten in between meals. Have the students work in groups to determine whether or not the diets handed in are balanced.

3. Point out to students that certain experts in the field of nutrition ascribe to the "sponge" theory of weight gain. They feel that too much food early in life causes a person to produce a larger number of fat cells than the average person. These are the individuals who may have a greater tendency to be overweight in childhood and later in life.

4. An interesting syndrome that has received much attention in recent years is the Prader-Willi syndrome. This condition primarily affects 2–5 year olds and is characterized by an insatiable appetite, obesity, diabetes, and in most cases, mild retardation. Students may be interested in finding out more about this disease.

STUDENT INVOLVEMENT ACTIVITIES

1. The areas of nutrition, dieting, food additives, and vitamins are only a few of the many related topics that receive much media coverage. Ask students to bring in an article on any related subject and report on it to the class.

2. Students may also be interested in researching information about new treatments of tooth decay. A article in the March 22, 1976, *U. S. News and World Report* discussed many possibilities including a tooth decay vaccine, fluoride mouth rinses, and plastic sealants applied to the chewing surfaces of teeth.

3. There are any number of diets that people use to lose weight. Have students report on one of the "fad" diets and ask them to draw conclusions concerning its effectiveness. One of the most recent fad diet is the "fasting" diet. Some students may want to report on it.

COMMUNITY INVOLVEMENT ACTIVITIES

1. Invite the school system's dietician to class (if there is one; if not invite a hospital or industry dietician). Discuss the planning of menus and special diets. Prepare questions in advance.

2. Invite a panel consisting of representatives of weight-loss groups. Invitations could be extended to leaders of Weight Watchers, Lean Line, Overeater's Anonymous (OA), and other similar groups. Open this meeting to the public.

3. Invite a representative of a natural food store or restaurant to speak to the class and answer questions about his or her product.

CAREER OPPORTUNITIES

Chef
Chemist
Diet doctor
Diet group organizer
Dietician
Endocrinologist
Food processor
Food researcher
Home economist
Nutritionist
Pharmacist
Physician

CHALLENGES IN BIOLOGY
VITAMINS

7

Do you take vitamins every day? Have you ever thought about why you do so? Most likely you take vitamins out of habit or because of a basic misconception about them. Most experts in the area of nutrition feel that the best source of vitamins is the foods that we eat. Additional vitamins and food supplements are only needed in specific medical conditions.

There have been numerous cases that prove the point that too much of a certain vitamin can be harmful. For example, excessive amounts of vitamin D have been shown to retard mental and physical growth in children. Evidence such as this has made many people feel that the sale of vitamins should be restricted by prescription.

What about vitamin C? It is a topic of controversy in that some people have shown that it is successful in reducing the occurrence and severity of colds. Nobel prize winner, Linus Pauling is among those people who agree with this information. However, recent studies have shown no significant reduction of colds due to vitamin C.

The subject of vitamins is a controversial one and the answers to the vitamin question remain as a challenge in biology.

ANSWERS TO QUESTIONS FOR REVIEW
(Page 551)

1. Foods supply the body with energy for growth, work, repair, and for maintaining vital processes.

2. Water is vital to the maintenance of life as it is a solvent for substances and a medium for transportation in the body.

3. Generally, foods must be simplified chemically and changed to soluble substances during digestion.

4. The mouth, esophagus, stomach, small intestine, large intestine (colon), and rectum.

5. The tongue serves as an organ of speech, an organ of taste, aids in chewing, accomplishes swallowing, and keeps the inner faces of the teeth clean.

6. A tooth cut lengthwise shows the enamel layer of the crown, the cementum covering of the root, the dentine layer, and the pulp cavity, containing the nerve and blood vessels.

7. All starchy foods should be chewed thoroughly to permit the ptyalin in saliva to change the starch to maltose.

8. As the milk, butter, and ham enter the stomach, the pepsin changes the protein portion to peptones and proteoses. Rennin coagulates the casein in the milk. In the small intestine, the proteoses and peptones are changed to peptides by the trypsin of the pancreas. Erepsin from the intestinal glands further changes the peptides to amino acids. The fat globules in the milk and butter and the fat of the ham are emulsified by bile. Lipase changes the fat to fatty acids and glycerin. The bread is acted upon by the ptyalin of the saliva and the starch is changed to maltose. If all the starch is not acted upon in the mouth, the amylase from the pancreas changes it to maltose in the small intestine. The maltase of the small intestine changes the maltose to glucose.

9. A large amount of water enters the blood from the large intestine. In addition, it eliminates indigestible matter.

ANSWERS TO APPLYING PRINCIPLES AND CONCEPTS
(Page 551)

1. A deficiency can occur if the vitamin is not being assimilated properly, either because of disease or drugs that have been used.

2. Food is mixed with hydrochloric acid in the stomach. In the small intestine it becomes alkaline through enzyme action.

3. Rhythmic contractions of the walls of the large intestine should move the contents at such a rate that water absorption can take place normally. If the contents move through too rapidly, they are excreted in a watery condition, resulting in diarrhea. If the movement of the contents is delayed, too much water may be absorbed, resulting in constipation.

4. Sour milk has already undergone casein coagulation and contains acid. Both of these conditions are produced in the stomach. Thus part of the stomach function has been performed externally.

chapter forty-two Transport and Excretion The human circulatory and excretory systems are both complex and fascinating. In this chapter, students will learn about the fluid tissue, blood, and what comprises this substance. They will also examine the structure and function of the heart and blood vessels. Circulation in the body is discussed. The lymph system is also examined. The second part of this chapter is concerned with the excretory system, its structure and function. The skin as an excretory organ is also discussed. This chapter serves as an introduction to two of the body's most vital functions.

TEACHING SUGGESTIONS

1. This chapter includes a great amount of material. The students will be learning about the circulatory and excretory systems and related information. Much of the material in this chapter can be made more relevant to the students by including information about the heart, blood, and kidneys that may directly affect them or their families. Some of this information will be mentioned in the points that follow.

2. Point out to students that there are a number of conditions that contribute to heart disease. These conditions include high blood pressure; buildup of fatty deposits in the coronary arteries; smoking; genetic factors; infections; and psychological factors. Encourage students not to assume that heart disease is an adult problem as it can begin early in life if the right factors are present.

3. Point out to students that more than 2,500 Americans underwent kidney transplants in 1974. An interesting article on this subject was published in June 9, 1975, edition of *U. S. News and World Report.* It is entitled, "What It's Like to Live With a Kidney Transplant." Students might want to read and report on this article.

4. Dialysis is another important aspect of modern medical accomplishments in cases of kidney failure. Dialysis machines allow patients with severe kidney disease to stay alive by filtering the blood. An informative article on the subject entitled, "Dialysis or Death" by Alan Anderson Jr. appeared in the March 7, 1976, *The New York Times Magazine.*

STUDENT INVOLVEMENT ACTIVITIES

1. Have students choose any topic related to heart disease research. Students should summarize their reports and discuss them with the class.

2. Have students write to major organizations associated with heart and kidney disease and ask for information about these conditions. The American Heart Association and The National Kidney Foundation are two of the most well-known organizations.

3. There has been a great deal of controversy concerning the role of diet in heart disease. Have students research different aspects of this subject. They may be interested in the effects of fats, sugar, coffee, and weight on one's heart.

COMMUNITY INVOLVEMENT ACTIVITIES

1. Have the class become involved with a blood-pressure testing program at their school. The program would be for the students and the local citizens.

2. Invite a panel of experts in the area of heart disease to speak with the class on this and related subjects. Open the panel discussion to the public and have a question and answer period following the discussion.

3. Have a first-aid representative show the class how to give cardiac resuscitation in cases of heart attack. *This knowledge can often save a life.*

CAREER OPPORTUNITIES
Cardiac care nurse
Cardiologist
Dermatologist
Dietician
Genetic counselor
Geneticist
Hematologist
Medical researcher
Medical technician
Nutritionist
Vascular surgeon
Urologist

CHALLENGES IN BIOLOGY
CARDIOVASCULAR DISEASE

Cardiovascular or heart disease is considered the number one killer of Americans. More than 700,000 people die each year as a result of this disease.

Research has indicated that there are certain risk factors associated with the form of heart disease called coronary artery disease. These risk factors include sex (males are more prone to coronary disease than premenopausal women); smoking (coronary attack rate is much higher for smokers); diet (one's weight and fat intake are factors); and high blood pressure.

Progress in heart disease has been made along many fronts. Research has identified risk factors, and education has helped to identify those people who may suffer from coronary or other forms of heart disease. In addition, transplants, artificial valves, bypass operations, and pacemakers have helped many individuals live longer and healthier lives.

Despite the progress in this area, heart disease still kills hundreds of thousands of people each year. This is why heart disease remains as a challenge in biology.

ANSWERS TO QUESTIONS FOR REVIEW
(Page 568)

1. Blood is a peculiar type of connective tissue composed of cells in a fluid. It is a transporting medium for all body substances.

2. White corpuscles are produced in the bone marrow and lymph glands. Both red corpuscles and platelets are produced in the red marrow of bones.

3. A high white-cell count usually indicates some kind of infection.

4. Thromboplastin, formed from disintegrating platelets, combines with the enzyme prothrombin and calcium to form thrombin. The thrombin then combines with fibrinogen to form fibrin, which forms a network and traps blood cells, thus forming a scab.

5. Plasma does not require typing. Furthermore, it can be dehydrated and stored, then rehydrated with sterile distilled water.

6. A drop of blood entering from the vena cava passes through the right atrium to the right ventricle, then out the pulmonary artery through the lungs, returning to the left atrium through a pulmonary vein. The left atrium pumps it to the left ventricle and out the aorta to the body.

7. The artery wall, carrying blood from the heart, bulges with each contraction of the heart during systole. A vein, because it has little pressure, does not bulge with heart contractions.

8. The tissue fluid that bathes the cells is called lymph. The lymph glands filter the lymph and return it to the blood. The lymph from the right side of the head and right arm enters the right lymphatic duct, which returns it to the blood by opening into the right subclavian vein. The lymphatics from the rest of the body drain into the thoracic duct, which in turn empties into the left subclavian vein.

9. Lymph contains neither red corpuscles nor platelets. It also lacks certain of the proteins present in whole blood.

10. The kidney capsules receive much of the water and other substances that the blood contains. The content of the blood leaving the kidneys is regulated by reabsorption from the kidney tubules.

11. The glomerular fluid contains not only water and nitrogenous wastes, but foods, salts, and other necessary substances. The urine contains only a small amount of water, some of the salt, and the nitrogenous wastes.

ANSWERS TO APPLYING PRINCIPLES AND CONCEPTS
(Page 568)

1. High blood pressure, kidney disorders, and heart disease may result from hardening of the artery walls. These arterial changes have damaging effects on the general health.

2. With increased circulation in the skin, due to dilation of the blood vessels, the temperature of the body surface would be increased, while the temperature of the vital organs deeper in the body would be decreased.

3. During the first transfusion with Rh-positive blood, the Rh-negative person produced antibodies against the factor in his blood. These antibodies caused agglutination of the positive blood when it was added in the second transfusion.

4. Valuable compounds in the body are released into the bloodstream and are used to manufacture new red blood corpuscles.

5. During hot weather the flow of perspiration increases greatly, resulting in increased excretion of salt from

the blood and tissue fluid. The intake of salt should be increased to keep the salt content of the blood and tissue fluid at a normal level.

6. In a normally functioning nephron, water entering the glomerulus is re-absorbed by the tubules. The amount of water reabsorbed or ex-creted in the urine, then, maintains the water balance in the body.

chapter forty-three Respiration and Energy Exchange Without energy, living cells could not sur-vive. The human body needs oxygen for its energy requirements, and through the process of respira-tion, oxygen is taken into the body. The students will learn about the two phases of respiration and how oxygen is inhaled. Other related topics, such as artificial respiration, pollution and oxygen debt, are also discussed. The students will gain a better understanding of the func-tions of the respiratory system by studying this chapter.

TEACHING SUGGESTIONS

1. Students often confuse *external* and *internal* respiration. Point out the difference between these two phases by the use of dia-grams. However, be sure to also point out the relationship between the two phases.
2. Point out to students that air pollution and pollution asso-ciated with certain jobs (such as mining) have caused serious lung disease in the form of em-physema, "black" lung, and lung cancer. In certain areas, air pol-lution is so bad that children are not allowed to have outdoor play periods.
3. It might be helpful for students to learn the basics of artificial respiration. An up-to-date *American Red Cross* manual will contain this information. A stu-dent in the class who is knowledgeable in this area may want to demonstrate the tech-nique. Refer students to Fig. 43-5.

STUDENT INVOLVEMENT ACTIVITIES

1. Assign students to work in groups and design a model that illustrates the mechanics of breathing. Tell them to use simple materials and their imaginations.
2. Assign a few students to report on oxygen debt and its effect on athletes. Have students report to the class on their findings.
3. If possible, have students take a BMR test. The machine used to test the BMR can usually be found in a physiology labora-tory. Discuss the results of the testing.

COMMUNITY INVOLVEMENT ACTIVITIES

1. Invite a physician to class to dis-cuss some of the common ill-nesses that affect the respiratory system. These illnesses include colds, coughs, sore throats, bronchitis, and influenza.
2. Invite some athletes to class to discuss what they do to improve their respiratory function. This may be very helpful to the non-athletes in the class.
3. Invite a first-aid representative to discuss the ways to avoid car-bon monoxide poisoning and what to do if it occurs.

CAREER OPPORTUNITIES
Ear, nose, and throat specialist
Environmentalist
Medical technician
Physician
Pollution control specialist
Professional athlete
Speech therapist

CHALLENGES IN BIOLOGY
AIR POLLUTION AND LUNG DISEASE
Although cigarette smoking receives much publicity as a major

7

cause of lung disease, air pollution is also an important contributor to lung disease. The effects of air pollution on our lungs and respiratory tracts are numerous. Irritants in the air slow down the action of the cilia that prevent the mucus from lodging in the respiratory tract. Pollutants also constrict the air passages and cause an increase in the mucus of the respiratory tract.

Conditions such as chronic bronchitis, emphysema, and asthma are adversely affected by air pollution. Some people develop nonchronic coughs and respiratory infections during periods of increased air pollution.

Although much has been done to correct air pollution problems, more needs to be accomplished. Air pollution is an important contributor to diseases of the lungs and the respiratory system. The challenge in biology is the solution of the air pollution problem that will result in an improvement in our respiratory health.

ANSWERS TO QUESTIONS FOR REVIEW
(Page 578)

1. Respiration is an exchange of gases carried on by all living cells. Breathing is a mechanical process involving the lungs and air movements during external respiration.
2. Nerves from the lungs, diaphragm, and ribs lead to the respiratory control center in the base of the brain. The brain detects the amount of carbon dioxide in the blood and stimulates the diaphragm and ribs to control breathing rate to keep the carbon dioxide at a low level.
3. The properties of gases which aid the body in respiration are: increased pressure increases the solubility of a gas; gases are capable of diffusing through membranes; gases are not equally soluble in all solutions; and solubility of various gases in a solution will vary with temperature.
4. Oxygen enters the capillary surrounding the air sac, as the concentration of oxygen in the air sac is higher than that in the capillary. Here it combines with hemoglobin. In the tissues where the concentration of oxygen is lower than in the blood, hemoglobin releases its oxygen. The affinity of hemoglobin for oxygen decreases with increasing acidity. The movement of carbon dioxide and water in the lungs is the opposite of that of oxygen.
5. If the pressure within the chest cavity is reduced to below that of the atmosphere by expanding the chest, air enters the lungs to equalize the pressure. When the ribs spring back and the diaphragm rises, the pressure in the chest rises and air passes through the respiratory passages to the atmosphere.
6. Hemoglobin has such an affinity for oxygen that it enables the blood to carry nearly the same percentage of oxygen as in air. The hemoglobin molecule combines with oxygen where the concentration of oxygen is high in the lungs, but it releases the oxygen where the concentration is low in the tissues.
7. Oxygen combines with hemoglobin in the blood. When the blood reaches the tissues the oxygen diffuses into the tissue fluid.
8. Carbon dioxide is carried from the tissues to the lungs in several ways: about 20 percent is carried by hemoglobin; about 10 percent is carried dissolved in plasma; about 70 percent is carried within the erythrocyte as a bicarbonate ion.
9. Artificial respiration is necessary when normal breathing movements have ceased.
10. An oxygen debt is built up when the cells use oxygen faster than the lungs and bloodstream can supply it. Thus the blood becomes temporarily low in oxygen content and respiration becomes anaerobic. The debt is paid when the increased need for oxygen ceases and the respiratory organs can replenish the oxygen deficiency in the blood.
11. Carbon monoxide combines 250 times more readily with hemoglobin in red corpuscles than does oxygen. Furthermore, it forms a stable compound which is not changed in the tissues. Thus as carbon monoxide enters the blood, it soon combines with sufficient hemoglobin to destroy the oxygen-combining power of the blood, resulting in death from tissue suffocation.
12. Breathing is difficult on a high mountain because of reduced air pressure and oxygen content. In space, air pressure and oxygen content are so greatly reduced that astronauts must have controlled pressure and an artificial source of oxygen.

ANSWERS TO APPLYING PRINCIPLES AND CONCEPTS
(Pages 578–579)

1. During hours of darkness, photosynthesis stops and plants take oxygen from the atmosphere through leaf stomata. In daylight hours, some oxygen released during photosynthesis is used in respiration.
2. If you were to hold your breath for a period of time the carbon dioxide and acid content of your blood would increase and the oxygen content would decrease and respiration would resume. After several deep breaths, breathing stops for a time because the increase in oxygen content of the blood automatically reduces the rate of breathing.
3. Low moisture content of the air increases the rate of evaporation of perspiration from the body surface and increases heat loss. Furthermore, the dry air receives moisture from the lungs more readily and reduces the feeling of stuffiness in humid air.

4. When divers come up from great depths, they have been breathing air at pressures many times that of sea level. Their blood and tissue fluids are saturated with air under the increased pressure. As the divers come up to the surface, they rise to a given depth where the pressure is less and wait for a period of time to allow the gases to diffuse out of the body fluids slowly. Then they rise to another level and repeat the waiting process. The decompression procedure allows the removal of the dissolved gases at a slow rate and without the formation of gas bubbles. If decompression were rapid, actual bubbles of gas would form in the blood and tissue fluids. These bubbles would damage delicate tissues, such as the brain, and create hemorrhages as the capillaries rupture. This condition is called the "bends" and may lead to permanent damage or death. A complete understanding of decompression is only one of the reasons why people should not attempt diving with air tanks without adequate instruction.

5. People living at high altitudes of the Andes are breathing air at a much lower pressure than those living at sea level. Therefore, a greater volume of air is required to obtain the same amount of oxygen as at sea level even though the actual percentage of oxygen is the same. The bodies of persons living at these high altitudes accommodate for this situation by producing more red blood cells and more hemoglobin.

6. The solubility of carbon dioxide is about 30 times greater than that of oxygen. When protozoa, fish, and other aquatic organisms give off carbon dioxide, it dissolves quickly and diffuses through the water.

chapter forty-four Body Controls The human nervous system is one of the most complex systems in the human body. Students will learn some of the basics of the structure and function of the nervous system in this chapter. They will learn about the central nervous system and its functions. The autonomic nervous system is also discussed in some detail. The senses are also discussed and included is a detailed explanation of hearing and sight. A great amount of information is contained in this chapter, and it is hoped that students will derive a fundamental understanding of the nervous system and its functions.

TEACHING SUGGESTIONS

1. The nervous system is often one of the most difficult subjects to teach because of its complexity. The nervous system can be made easier to understand through the use of models. Students often relate better to something that they can pick up and examine.

2. If possible, bring an electroencephalogram to class to show students how electrical activity of the brain appears when graphed.

3. Ask students to consider Fig. 44-5 and give an original example that involves muscular coordination, sense integration, thought and memory, and emotions. Some students may want to draw their answer as done in Fig. 44-5.

4. Headaches are a common symptom associated with the nervous system. An interesting interview with Dr. David R. Codden, Director of the Headache Clinic,

Mount Sinai Medical Center, New York City appeared in September 15, 1975, *U. S. News and World Report.* The article is entitled "Why You Get Headaches and What To Do About Them." Students should report on this and other articles concerned with headaches.

STUDENT INVOLVEMENT ACTIVITIES

1. A number of conditions affect the central nervous system. One of the most common is brain damage that may occur before or after birth. Have students report on an area of brain damage that is of particular interest to them. Point out to students that frequently brain damage is very mild and results in symptoms that are barely observable.

2. How does the society we live in affect our hearing? According to an article by Dr. Wesley Bradley, "How Modern Life Can Damage Your Hearing," the effects can result in hearing loss. This article appeared in the May 3, 1976, issue of *U. S. News and World Report.* Assign students to report on this article and others that discuss society and hearing.

3. Students may be interested in reporting on new research in the area of the senses. Such research includes a form of hearing testing for infants and the use of lasers in correcting blindness due to diabetes. Ask students to bring in articles concerning new techniques in testing or treating the senses.

COMMUNITY INVOLVEMENT ACTIVITIES

1. Invite a panel of experts to speak to the school on the sub-

7

ject of learning disabilities. Many students and parents have heard this term but are not sure what it encompasses.

2. Call the local associations for retarded children and autistic children. Invite a speaker from one or both of these groups to come to the class. Find out how the students can contribute their time to these organizations.

3. Invite an audiologist to demonstrate hearing testing and to answer questions about hearing and the effects of noise on hearing.

CAREER OPPORTUNITIES
Audiologist
Ear, nose, and throat specialist
Learning disabilities specialist
Medical researcher
Medical technician
Neurologist
Neurosurgeon
Opthalmologist
Optician
Optometrist
Otolaryngologist
Psychiatric nurse
Psychiatric social worker
Psychiatrist
Psychologist
Speech therapist
Teacher of exceptional children

ANSWERS TO QUESTIONS FOR REVIEW
(Page 596)

1. The general parts of the nervous system include the *central nervous system* (brain and spinal cord), the *peripheral system,* and the *autonomic system.* The central nervous system receives sensory impressions, initiates and coordinates motor activity, and is the center of memory, intelligence, emotions, and other high-level nervous activities. The peripheral nervous system is an extension of the central nervous system to all parts of the body. The autonomic system regulates activity of the vital organs in an involuntary manner.

2. Peripheral nerves that contain axons are considered to be motor nerves because they are transmitting impulses from the brain and spinal cord to muscles or to organs of secretion.

3. A nerve impulse is electrochemical, and it brings about a change in the nerve fiber. It travels at various speeds and by means of changing charges on both sides of the membrane of the nerve fiber.

4. The motor neuron terminates at the motor end plate. An impulse causes the release of acetylcholine, which causes the contraction of the muscle. After contraction, the nerve ending releases cholinesterase, which neutralizes acetylcholine and causes the muscle fibers to relax.

5. The brain includes the cerebrum, cerebellum, and brain stem including the medulla oblongata, midbrain, and pons. The cerebrum is the center of memory, intelligence, emotion, instinct, sensory impressions, and motor control. The cerebellum coordinates motor impulses from the cerebrum. The medulla oblongata of the brain stem controls impulses to the vital organs.

6. The autonomic nervous system includes both the sympathetic and parasympathetic systems.

7. The five sensations in the skin are touch, pressure, pain, cold, and heat. The receptors are different, but any one may cause the sensation of pain. Some receptors are many-celled; some consist of only one specialized cell; and some are bare nerve endings.

8. Much of the sensation we associate with flavor is actually smell and not taste.

9. The sound waves in the air travel through the auditory canal to the eardrum. These waves cause the eardrum to vibrate, and the vibrations are transmitted and intensified by the three bones of the middle ear. The fluid of the cochlea allows the vibrations to travel to the nerve endings which transform the vibrations into nerve impulses.

10. A middle ear infection can cause temporary deafness by producing pressure on the eardrum and by causing swelling and discharge which interferes with transmission of vibrations across the bones of the middle ear.

11. The semicircular canals consist of three loop-shaped tubes, each at right angles to the other two. The head movements that stimulate each semicircular canal separately are: the movement of the head forward and backward; the turning of the head; or the raising and lowering of the head by bending and straightening the knees.

12. We see poorly at night because the fovea of the retina, the area in which we see clearly, has no rods. In contrast, the owl can see well at night because of the presence of many rods essential for night vision.

13. You can see objects out of the corner of the eye at night because rods are present in the retina in that area. Since the fovea has no rods, the image disappears when you focus.

ANSWERS TO APPLYING PRINCIPLES AND CONCEPTS
(Page 596)

1. Intelligence is a complex relationship between your impressions of past experiences and sensory impressions, your association areas of the cerebral cortex, and your ability to reason and to associate impressions of past experiences with present problems and experiences.

2. The muscle spasms and uncoordinated activities of a chicken with its head cut off result from loss of muscle control by the cerebrum and, especially, the cerebellum.

3. The sympathetic nervous system is often called "the system for fight or flight" because of its control over the heart beat and secretions of glands. When a person is angry or frightened, the glands pour their secretions into the bloodstream, and the individual has strength that is not present under normal conditions.

4. Design a pair of spectacles that inverts the image in front of the eye. The eye lenses will then re-invert the image on the retina. If these spectacles were worn continuously, the brain would soon accommodate to this abnormal condition. If the spectacles were then removed, the person would interpret his normal vision as an inverted image.

chapter forty-five Tobacco, Alcohol, and Drugs The three items discussed in this chapter have both social and health implications for students. The chapter discusses tobacco and the effects of smoking. The subject of alcohol and its effects are also discussed. Different types of drugs and sources are examined. Students will read about the addictive and "mind-expanding" drugs and some of their effects. The chapter briefly discusses some of the types of treatment presently available to drug addicts. This chapter encourages students to look at the facts and make their own decisions concerning the use and non-use of these substances.

TEACHING SUGGESTIONS

1. Point out to students that smoking, drinking, and drug taking are often the result of both peer and media pressure. Most students will be familiar with peer pressure and how it operates. However, many may not realize the pressure they are under from advertising. For example, point out to students that Americans spend approximately $60 million a year on over-the-counter drugs. These drugs include sedatives, tension relievers, and stimulants. Ask students for other examples of advertising pressure.

2. Discuss with students the relatively recent problem of alcoholism among teenagers. The National Institute of Alcohol Abuse has reported that about one third of high school students drink excessively at least once a month. The institute further reports that more than 1,300,-000 young people between the ages of 12 and 17 suffer from serious drinking problems.

3. Students may be interested in a recent report from the University of Washington School of Medicine. This report indicated that babies born to alcoholics had a five times greater mortality rate and those babies that survived tended to have small heads, stunted body size, below-normal mentality, and facial abnormalities.

4. Point out to students that alcoholism affects more than 10 million American workers. Absenteeism, poor productivity, lack of judgment, and general inefficiency may result in an economic cost in excess of 10 billion dollars a year. Business has begun to fight alcoholism through private and group counseling, medical treatment, and family aid.

STUDENT INVOLVEMENT ACTIVITIES

1. Ask students to bring in current articles that pertain to alcohol, tobacco, and drugs. Have each student briefly report the article and then discuss it with the class.

2. Have students take a poll on cigarette smoking among classmates. Find out who smokes, why they do, whether or not family members smoke, and if they are aware of the dangers of smoking. Have students draw conclusions from the findings.

3. Ask students to write a brief comment on why they think that alcoholism has increased among young people. Have some students read their papers to class.

4. Debate the question of the legalization of marijuana. Warn students to be well prepared for

7

the debate and the question and answer period.

COMMUNITY INVOLVEMENT ACTIVITIES

1. Invite representatives of Al-Anon, Alateen, and Alcoholics Anonymous to speak to the class on the functions of these organizations.
2. Invite a representative of a large company that has a program for alcoholics to speak to the class about this and similar industrial programs.
3. Invite a psychologist to discuss problems of alcohol, tobacco, and drug addiction with the class. Have questions prepared in advance.
4. Sponsor an education day to educate people about the seriousness of smoking, drinking, and taking drugs. Have guest speakers and individuals who represent interested agencies and self-help groups. Open this meeting to the public.

CAREER OPPORTUNITIES
Agency worker
Drug researcher
Health educator
Medical researcher
Pharmacist
Physician
Psychiatrist
Psychologist
Social worker

CHALLENGES IN BIOLOGY
ALCOHOLISM
What are some of the causes of alcoholism? Most experts in this area refer to the psychological causes which include emotional problems. The other causes usually include peer pressure, family drinking habits, and the stresses of modern civilization. Certainly, all of these factors may contribute to alcoholism. However, some recent research also indicates that there may be some physiological causes.

Some individuals may have a metabolic predisposition to alcoholism. This may result in an excessive craving for alcohol. If this research proves to be true, a *cure* for alcoholism could be developed based on this knowledge. This would be a great benefit to those afflicted with alcoholism and to society in general. Today, alcoholism remains as a very serious challenge in biology.

METHADONE TREATMENT
Methadone is used today as a substitute for heroin. The controversy over methadone arises from the fact that it is an addictive drug. Methadone is used, in certain cases, to *maintain* a heroin addict so that the addict can function in society.

The problem presented by opponents of methadone maintenance is that one drug has been substituted for another. In this case, methadone is a substitute for heroin. Although the addicted individual can return to society on methadone, he or she is still an addicted individual.

People in favor of methadone maintenance claim that without methadone many addicts would be unable to function and some would become antisocial due to their addiction. Heroin addiction and the solution to this problem remains as a challenge in biology.

1. There were 70 percent more deaths from all causes among smokers than among nonsmokers. The greater number of deaths from certain diseases among smokers was particularly marked. There were 1000 percent more deaths from lung cancer and 500 percent more from chronic bronchitis and emphysema.
2. Smoking is an expensive habit and gets more so every year. It also stains the teeth and fingers. It is messy and annoying to other people who do not smoke. It causes throat irritation, nervousness, and stomach discomfort due to increased gastric activity.
3. It is absorbed from the stomach rapidly and may reach the blood in two minutes. Absorption of alcohol continues in the small intestine. The blood carries it to the tissues, where oxidation in the cells occurs rapidly. Heat from this oxidation is carried to the skin. Some of the alcohol is excreted as vapor from the lungs and skin. Much of it reaches the kidney in solution with water.
4. The liver is especially affected by alcohol as it must detoxify it. Alcohol causes cirrhosis of the liver and can cause brain damage.
5. The idea that alcohol is a body stimulant is purely psychological. Actually, it is a depressant.
6. The cortex of the brain is affected first resulting in the loss of judgment and emotional control. Then, in order, vision and speech are involved; loss of coordination of muscles as the cerebellum becomes involved; unconsciousness results when the cortex ceases to function.
7. An alcoholic drink slows sensory and motor reaction time and impairs judgment and emotional control. These are the hazards in driving an automobile.
8. Narcotic drugs, according to classi-

fication by the federal government, include opium, morphine, heroin, codeine, and cocaine.

9. Both have a sedative effect and death may result as each doubles the effect of the other.

10. A person may develop a mental dependence on both amphetamines and barbiturates because they are contrasting drugs. A person may take barbiturates to relieve emotional anxiety or pain, or use these to induce sleep. During working hours, however, the person may feel the need for stimulating drugs to "pep up," then, at bedtime, be so active and awake that she or he cannot get to sleep without taking another barbiturate. Such people, therefore, become mentally dependent on both these drugs. Proper diet and the development of healthy habits which balance work and recreation may help to relieve the felt need for drugs.

11. They may produce mental depression and changed personalities which may lead to mental breakdown or suicide.

12. A person may begin misusing drugs or chemicals after a severe illness in which a narcotic drug had been used medically. Many begin taking drugs for a thrill or to "join the crowd," or because they believe a drug will help them escape problems. One alternative to drugs is to learn to face problems squarely and to deal with them in a scientific or analytical manner. Sometimes help is needed from a professional.

ANSWERS TO APPLYING PRINCIPLES AND CONCEPTS
(Page 609)

1. Inhaling smoke carries it into the bronchi and lungs.
2. Food in the stomach reduces the rate of absorption of alcohol.
3. Large amounts of heat, released from the tissues and received by the

blood, reach the skin in an increased flow of blood in the skin capillaries. The presence of this excess flow of blood in the skin causes a flush and a false feeling of body warmth, due to stimulation of heat receptor nerves in the skin.

4. Drug addiction requires that the user deal illegally with organized crime in order to get his supply. Furthermore, drugs may cost as much as forty dollars a day, and most users have to steal to obtain this much money. Drug addicts and alcoholics show character weakness by trying to cover up their problems rather than solving them.

chapter forty-six Body Regulators The ductless or endocrine glands are the subject of this chapter. The students will learn about which hormones control certain bodily functions. The thyroid gland and conditions caused by over and under secretion are discussed. Students will also study the functions of the pituitary gland, adrenals, pancreas, ovaries and testes, thymus and hypothalamus. The dynamic balance in the endocrine glands is also examined. Having read this chapter, students will have a better understanding of how their bodies are regulated.

TEACHING SUGGESTIONS

1. Stress to students the importance of the hormones or body regulators. Mention a number of bodily functions that are directly related to hormonal control.
2. Point out to students that there are cases where persons who are too short or too tall can be treated. The treatment is usually given by a pediatric endocrinologist, a medical doctor who specializes in the hormonal problems of children and young adults.
3. A recent article discussed the use of hormones in cases of chronic depression. This article was written about a study conducted at Worcester State Hospital, Worcester, Massachusetts. The study involved the use of natural estrogen to help patients with severe depression. Point out to students how hormones may have other effects than those usually associated with them.
4. Students may be interested in

7

reading an interview with Dr. George F. Cahill, President, American Diabetes Association. This article entitled, "New Hope for Diabetics," appeared in the November 24, 1975, issue of *U. S. News and World Report.*

STUDENT INVOLVEMENT ACTIVITIES

1. Many aspects of the endocrine system are frequently written about in newspapers and magazines. Have students report on a current article related to the endocrine system.
2. Have students choose one hormone and report to the class in detail about the functions of this hormone. Encourage students to refer to recent literature in their reports.
3. Write to the American Diabetes Association for information concerning childhood diabetes and summer camps for children afflicted with this disease. Report your findings to the class.

COMMUNITY INVOLVEMENT ACTIVITIES

1. Invite an endocrinologist to class to discuss his or her specialty and to answer student questions. Have students prepare questions in advance.
2. Invite a representative of the American Diabetes Association to discuss this disease with the class. This discussion should be open to the public.

CAREER OPPORTUNITIES
Drug researcher
Endocrinologist
Gynecologist
Laboratory technician
Medical researcher
Pharmacist
Physician

CHALLENGES IN BIOLOGY
DIABETES

Diabetes mellitus has been ranked fifth among the leading causes of death in the United States. However, a recent report published by the National Commission on Diabetes indicated that diabetes may have become the third-ranking cause of death following heart disease and cancer. This conclusion was based on recent statistics that indicated more than 300,000 deaths could be attributed to diabetes and its complications.

Though insulin therapy can control the condition, in most cases, it cannot cure diabetes. The disease often results in blindness, kidney problems, and heart damage. Further long-range research is essential to solve the challenge in biology presented by diabetes.

ANSWERS TO QUESTIONS FOR REVIEW
(Page 620)

1. The blood delivers the substances required by endocrine glands in producing hormones and delivers the hormones to the body tissues.
2. Thyroid hormone regulates the rate of oxidation as well as other metabolic functions of cells.
3. Hypothyroidism lowers the rate of metabolism. During infancy and early childhood, this may result in cretinism. Later in life, it may cause sluggishness and a tendency to become overweight. Hyperthyroidism may cause a rise in body temperature, increase in blood pressure and heart action, sweating, extreme nervousness, and irritability.
4. The pituitary gland produces the somatotropic hormone, which regulates the growth of the skeleton and other connective tissues. Underactivity may result in a pituitary dwarf, or midget. Overactivity may produce a giant. The thyroid gland influences growth through its effect on cell metabolism. A thyroid dwarf is a cretin.
5. The gonadotropic hormone of the anterior lobe of the pituitary gland influences the development and activity of the reproductive organs.
6. The thyroid dwarf and pituitary dwarf are similar only in that both are small. The thyroid dwarf has a stunted body, a bloated face, large lips and, in many cases, a protruding tongue. He is usually mentally retarded. The pituitary dwarf is small but proportioned normally and is of normal intelligence.
7. ACTH is a secretion of the anterior lobe of the pituitary gland. It stimulates the adrenal cortex.
8. At puberty, the reproductive organs mature and begin the secretion of estrogen or testosterone. These result in the appearance of secondary sexual characteristics as sweeping emotional changes. Sexual maturity is linked closely with the action of the gonadotropic hormone of the anterior lobe of the pituitary gland.
9. A diabetic has a deficiency in insulin, produced in the islet cells of the pancreas. Because of insulin deficiency, a diabetic cannot normally store sugar in the liver, nor can his cells utilize blood sugar. Thus, sugar appears in the blood and is excreted in the urine. Recent research indicates an enzyme may control the action of insulin.
10. The hypothalamus detects imbalances in the blood and releases factors that stimulate endocrine glands to correct the balance.

ANSWERS TO APPLYING PRINCIPLES AND CONCEPTS
(Page 621)

1. The thyroid gland, because of its influence on the metabolism of cells through thyroid hormone, may influence intelligence.
2. Emotional tension and excitement of a basketball player or other athlete before a game increases adrenal function. Increase in epinephrine in the blood increases the rate of heartbeat as well as other functions.
3. Both the endocrine and nervous systems are control systems.
4. The female hormone estrogen, injected into the bloodstream of a male rat, will produce a mothering instinct, just as its secretion normally does in the female.
5. In feedback, the accumulation of a substance in the blood automatically cuts down its production by the endocrine gland. Conversely, a shortage of the hormone triggers its increased production by the gland. In this way a state of balance is achieved.

chapter forty-seven Reproduction and Development   This chapter stresses the genetic significance of sexual reproduction. The male and female reproductive organs are both illustrated and discussed. The ovarian and uterine cycle is also discussed. Fertilization and the development of the resulting zygote is examined. The structures of the embryo are also discussed. This chapter concludes with a discussion of the birth of a child. Having read this chapter, students will have a better understanding of the reproductive process and its significance.

TEACHING SUGGESTIONS

1. This chapter may make some students uncomfortable. It may be helpful to ask students to anonymously submit questions that they may have concerning reproduction and development. It would be wise to read through the questions before discussing them in class.
2. It may be appropriate in this chapter to remind students how the sex of a child is determined. They may have forgotten some of their earlier study of genetics.
3. Boys and girls may have many misconceptions concerning the menstrual cycle. Encourage students to ask questions about myths concerning this cycle.
4. Point out to students that many babies are born prematurely and suffer from the respiratory-distress syndrome (RDS). This syndrome claims the lives of more than 10,000 infants each year. However, a new treatment technique seems to be effective in reducing deaths from this condition. The treatment involves the injection of steroid drugs prior to the delivery of the child. The drugs seem to work by speeding up the maturation of the child's lungs.

STUDENT INVOLVEMENT ACTIVITIES

1. There are a number of organizations and clinics that provide young people with information about birth control. One of the most well known is Planned Parenthood. Students may wish to visit or write to this organization for information about birth control.
2. Students may be interested in reporting on the Lamaze method of natural childbirth. Another interesting method of childbirth has received much attention in recent months. This is the Leboyer method, a gentle, quiet way of delivering children. This method was introduced by the French obstetrician, Frederick Leboyer. An interesting article on this subject entitled, "Giving Birth" by Hal Higdon appeared in the May, 1976, *Family Health*.
3. Students may be interested in learning more about such topics as miscarriage and ectopic pregnancy. Encourage students to report on any related topic of interest to them and discuss these reports in class.
4. Encourage students to bring in current articles that are related to the topic of reproduction and development. Discuss these topics with the class.

COMMUNITY INVOLVEMENT ACTIVITIES

1. Invite an obstetrician to class to discuss prenatal care and the de-

7

livery of a child. Have students prepare questions in advance.

2. If possible, visit a hospital nursery and observe the newborn babies. Have a staff member explain how the incubator is used for premature infants.

3. Invite a pediatrician to class to discuss his or her function after a baby has been delivered. Most students may not realize that the pediatrician examines the child soon after birth and checks the child during his or her stay in the hospital.

CAREER OPPORTUNITIES
Genetic counselor
Geneticist
Medical technician
Obstetrical nurse
Obstetrician
Pediatrician
Social worker

ANSWERS TO QUESTIONS FOR REVIEW
(Pages 630–631)

1. Sexual reproduction allows for genetic recombination and thus variation of individuals.

2. Sperms are produced in the testes and they pass through the seminiferous tubules, epididymis, vas deferens, seminal vesicle, past the prostate and Cowper's gland, and out the urethra.

3. Semen is the fertilizing fluid made up of sperm and fluid from the seminal vesicle, prostate gland, and Cowper's gland. It carries the sperm cells in a favorable environment.

4. There are about 130 million sperms to every ovum. The semen, containing the sperms, alters the chemical reaction and allows the sperms to travel to the ovum where one sperm will unite with the egg.

5. The ovum leaves the ovary and is swept into the Fallopian tubes by cilia. The ovum travels into the uterus and if fertilization does not occur, it is discharged through the vagina.

6. The development of the ovum and of the uterus is coordinated by hormones. The ovary forms a follicle where the ovum is developing. This cycle is controlled by FSH, produced in the anterior lobe of the pituitary. As the egg matures, the follicle produces estrogen and the follicle becomes the corpus luteum. This is controlled by another hormone, LH, also produced by the pituitary gland. The corpus luteum in turn produces progesterone, which maintains growth of the lining in the uterus. If the ovum is not fertilized, the corpus luteum degenerates, progesterone is not produced and the lining of the uterus is discharged.

7. a. Menstruation is the discharging of the uterine lining. b. The follicle stage occurs from the end of menstruation to the release of the ovum. c. Ovulation is the release of a mature ovum from the ovary. d. The corpus luteum stage lasts from ovulation to menstruation.

8. The zygote divides into two cells soon after fertilization. Then, by successive divisions, it soon forms a sphere of cells and then a hollow ball. An indentation in one area marks the beginning of the gastrula and the formation of three germ layers. Differentiation begins to become more obvious as the embryo becomes a fetus.

9. The chorion, which attaches the embryo to the uterine wall; the amnion, which forms a fluid-filled cavity and protects the developing embryo from injury and keeps it moist; the yolk sac, which is small and insignificant in the human; the allantois, which is present in humans for only a short time, but serves in respiration in birds and reptiles.

10. See the table on p. 627.

11. The umbilical cord is formed by the lengthening of the yolk sac and the allantois. It contains two umbilical arteries and one umbilical vein.

12. After birth, the ductus arteriosus closes off so that the blood must pass through the pulmonary arteries to the lungs.

ANSWERS TO APPLYING PRINCIPLES AND CONCEPTS
(Page 631)

1. Fertilization must occur in the Fallopian tube prior to the movement of the ovum into the uterus in order that the chorionic membrane has time to form the villi which will adhere to the uterine wall.

2. Since the pituitary gland produces FSH and LH, which influence the development of the ovary, anything altering the normal function of the pituitary would alter the course of events in the ovary.

3. If an egg is fertilized, the corpus luteum continues to produce progesterone, which functions to maintain the growth of the uterine lining.

4. During fetal life, the ductus arteriosus functions to carry blood from the pulmonary artery to the aorta, thus short-circuiting the lungs, which are not functioning. Shortly before or after birth, this vessel closes off and the blood passes through the pulmonary artery to the lungs. Failure of the vessel to close is one cause of a blue baby. A mixing of oxygenated and deoxygenated blood occurs.

unit 8 ECOLOGICAL RELATIONSHIPS

Organisms depend upon each other and upon the land on which they live. This principle is the basis for studying the chapters in this unit. Chapter Forty-eight serves as an introduction to ecology. Students become familiar with the language of the ecologist. They are introduced to the ecosystem and the biotic community. In this chapter, they will also learn about the physical cycles of nature and information about population and its growth. Chapter Forty-Nine discusses the habitat in detail. Factors that affect habitats are discussed. Nutritional relationships among organisms are explored. Camouflage is also examined. Chapter Fifty is concerned with periodicity and its effect on animal life. Hibernation, estivation, migration, and lunar and annual rhythms are explored. Change in biotic communities is also noted. In Chapter Fifty-One, students will learn about distribution of plants and animals. The biomes and life in these biomes are examined. Chapter Fifty-Two is devoted to the land that we live on and some of the problems encountered on this land. Erosion, water conservation, water pollution, air pollution, and the energy crisis are a few of the topics dealt with in this chapter. This unit concludes with a discussion of forest and wildlife conservation. Having read this unit, students will have a greater understanding and respect for the land they live on and the organisms that inhabit this land.

chapter forty-eight Introduction to Ecology Ecology is a commonly used and often misunderstood word. Students will learn about the true meaning of the word and the relationship between ecology, the biosphere, and the ecosystem. Physical cycles in nature are also explored. These cycles include the water cycle, carbon-oxygen cycle, and nitrogen cycle. This chapter also delves into the subject of population change. All of the topics in this chapter have a direct effect on human life. Students will have a greater understanding of ecological factors after reading this chapter.

TEACHING SUGGESTIONS

1. Ask students for their definitions of the word *ecology.* Have them discuss their definitions and compare them to the explanation in the text.
2. Point out to students that organisms in an ecosystem are interdependent upon one another. When one species has difficulty in surviving, it could affect many of the other species within that ecosystem.
3. Stress to students that ecosystems, biotic communities, and natural physical cycles existed long before human beings. However, in many cases our influence on the environment has altered the natural or "pure" condition.
4. Point out to students that overpopulation is a serious problem in many nations today. It has been estimated that, at the current birth rate, the

world's population increases by 200,000 people a day. Have students react to this staggering statistic.

STUDENT INVOLVEMENT ACTIVITIES

1. Ask students to choose an example of a biotic community and to describe the organisms that make up the populations of this community. Also, have them point out the functions of each population and how the populations interrelate.
2. Ask students to write about some aspect of the population problem that is of interest to them. Some suggestions may include: famine; overcrowding, zero population growth, overconsumption of resources, and the energy crisis.
3. Ask students to bring in and report on current articles concerned with any aspect of ecology. There are numerous articles that have been written on this subject.

COMMUNITY INVOLVEMENT ACTIVITIES

1. Invite a local ecology activist to class to discuss the functions of his or her group in dealing with ecological problems of your community.
2. Have students discuss ecological problems in their neighborhoods. Try to find solutions to these problems and, if possible, carry the solutions out to solve the problems.
3. Invite a representative of a

population group to come to class and discuss what this group represents. Ask students to do some reading on the subject of population and have questions prepared in advance.

CAREER OPPORTUNITIES
Biomathematician
Biotelemetrist
Ecologist
Environmentalist
Geologist
Geophysicist
Population researcher
Statistician

CHALLENGES IN BIOLOGY
HUMANS AND THE ENVIRONMENT
For many thousands of years, humans have altered the environment without seriously thinking about the consequences. Roads, buildings, and giant industries have come first and environmental considerations last. However, to some degree, this is beginning to change and more people are fighting for the preservation of the natural environment. Much more needs to be done and this problem is a very real challenge in biology.

HUMAN POPULATION
Human population growth is a significant problem in many parts of today's world. The Malthusian principle that food production increases arithmetically as human reproduction increases geometrically has proven to be correct. Thousands of people are starving each day because there is just not enough food to feed them. It is essential that population be

controlled and that widespread assistance be given to the efforts being made to increase food production. This is one of the most crucial problems facing us today.

ANSWERS TO QUESTIONS FOR REVIEW
(Page 646)

1. The biosphere is the area in which life on our planet is possible.
2. By counting the individual organisms of any species in a definite area that we consider representative, we can make an estimate regarding the density of the species in a larger area.
3. Populations vary from year to year, but some factors determining the population of an organism at any time are the rates at which individuals are dying, being produced, or moving into or out of the area.
4. There are interactions between the ecosystem and the physical environment as well as the biotic community. However, there are also interactions between the physical environment and the biotic community.
5. Interactions between the biotic community and the physical environment include the ways in which organisms are affected by sunlight, soil, and temperature. Organisms may in turn alter the soil or the temperature or the water content of an area.
6. Within the physical environment, interactions may be temporary, as when a cloud reduces the light intensity, or they may be permanent as when floods or earthquakes alter conditions in an area.
7. The water cycle is the movement of water from the earth to the atmosphere and back to the earth. It is very important to organisms on the earth. Water evaporates from the bodies of water and from rivers and vegetation. Later it returns to the earth in precipitation. Some water runs into rivers or lakes,

while other water sinks into the ground to raise the water table from which our wells and springs draw water. The cycle is repeated, but in the interim, water is used by many living organisms.
8. As the green plant fixes carbon dioxide in photosynthesis, oxygen is released to the atmosphere. The oxygen is used by the animals during respiration and carbon dioxide is released. When plants and animals die and decay, the carbon is released as carbon dioxide to the atmosphere.
9. Nitrogen forms proteins and makes up 78 percent of the air. However, free nitrogen cannot be used by plants or animals. The understanding of the ways in which organisms use nitrogen is important to the horticulturist and farmer as well as the biologist.
10. Density-dependent factors would include reproductive rate, death rate, parasitism, disease, and predation. These depend on the density of a particular population at any given time. Those factors not related to the density of the population—such as weather, temperature, humidity, daily and seasonal changes, and available energy—are termed density-independent factors.
11. The factors which affect plant and animal populations will enable us to better understand our own problems brought about by density. People are resourceful enough to have provided for their needs in many areas of the world.

ANSWERS TO APPLYING PRINCIPLES AND CONCEPTS
(Page 646)

1. Answers will vary depending on the locality, but most will probably describe a lake.
2. Biologists speak of a balanced aquarium or terrarium as a closed ecosystem. However, energy enters

the system in the form of light, so it is not actually a closed system.

3. Annual variations in populations may occur as the result of an increase (or a decrease) in the number of predators (or carnivores). Unusual physical factors such as a hard winter may decrease a given population. An unusually heavy rain on a desert may produce a spring of beauty not seen for many years.

4. The shore region of a lake is a wet environment, perhaps even warm in the winter. Nitrogenous wastes and decaying organisms at the water's edge allow a growth of algae and larger plants. The deep-water bottom region may remain in constant darkness so that no plants can carry on photosynthesis. However, the temperature may be constant. Organisms living there depend on food produced above and filtering down to them.

5. As population density increases, the same factors limiting populations of other organisms are in operation for people. However, temporary populations may not be the same in all areas.

chapter forty-nine   The Habitat

The habitat is defined as the place where an organism lives. This chapter explores some of the factors that affect the habitat. These factors include soil, temperature, water, light, and the atmosphere. Students will also examine the ecological food chains and food webs. Special nutritional relationships are explored. This chapter concludes with a discussion of passive protection and adaptive behavior. Students will have a better understanding of the habitat of organisms after reading this chapter.

TEACHING SUGGESTIONS

1. Elicit from students facts about the habitats of some common organisms. This will help students to understand the ecological meaning of this word.

2. Stress to students that organisms that have a great amount of *tolerance* will tend to be more successful than those who are not *tolerant.* Some organisms can overcome environmental problems if they are sufficiently hardy.

3. Discuss the food relationships of humans to other organisms. There are many aspects of this including famine, over-consumption, and vegetarianism. Discuss with students each of these points and elicit student opinion on some of these issues.

4. Encourage students to observe nature and suggest examples of passive protection. Many species of birds and insects exhibit passive protection.

STUDENT INVOLVEMENT ACTIVITIES

1. If possible, have students visit a habitat of their choice and write about their observations. Tell them to discuss the niches of the plants and animals observed.

2. Have students dig up some local soil samples and try to identify them by their composition.

3. Ask students to prepare an original example of an ecological food chain. It can be prepared in the form of a food pyramid, as in Fig. 49-8.

COMMUNITY INVOLVEMENT ACTIVITIES

1. Invite a farmer to speak to the class about the importance of limiting factors on the environment as related to agriculture.

2. Invite an animal behaviorist to speak to the class about this interesting topic.

3. If possible, take a class trip to an area where one can study natural habitats. Have students write about their observations.

CAREER OPPORTUNITIES
Biogeologist
Biomathematician
Biometeorologist
Biophysicist
Biotelemetrist
Ecologist
Environmentalist
Statistician

CHALLENGES IN BIOLOGY
AN ANSWER TO FOOD SHORTAGES
One suggestion often given as a way to solve the food problem is to obtain our food lower on the food

8

chain. The energy pyramid shows us that we would have more efficient use of food from lower on this pyramid. The grain we feed our cattle loses some energy in moving through this step. It is suggested that we would derive more energy from our food if we utilized these grains directly as our food supply. Much grain is wasted by feeding it to animals subsequently used for food instead of feeding it to people.

ANSWERS TO QUESTIONS FOR REVIEW
(Pages 658–659)

1. The habitat of an organism is the place in which it lives. The niche is the role or "occupation" the organism fills in this habitat. A lake may be the habitat of a large fish. Its niche may be as a consumer of smaller fish.
2. Plankton, composed of the floating organisms on a lake or ocean, forms the major food for many fish. Larger fish feed on the smaller herbivorous ones, so plankton has often been called the "grass of the seas."
3. An organism's ability to withstand a variety of environmental conditions is called its tolerance. The extremes of tolerance of organisms to various conditions determine where they can live.
4. Several important controlling physical factors of the environment are: soil type and chemical make-up, temperature, water, light, atmosphere, and topography.
5. "Cold-blooded," or poikilothermic animals do not maintain a constant body temperature. Their body temperatures vary with the environment. "Warm-blooded," or homoiothermic, animals maintain a relatively constant body temperature regardless of the environmental temperature.

6. There are two kinds of aquatic environments: fresh-water and salt-water, or marine. Plants living in very moist environments are hydrophytes and those of the desert or semi-deserts are xerophytes. Plants living in neither extremely wet nor dry environments are mesophytes.
7. Hydrophytes usually have large leaves and thin epidermal layers, while xerophytes have very small leaves, even reduced to spines, with thick epidermal layers to prevent loss of water by evaporation. Xerophytes usually have extensive root systems for absorbing water. The leaves of mesophytes are of a size in between.
8. Even organisms spending their entire lives in darkness are dependent on the energy from the sun that was used in photosynthesis. The herbivores yield the energy to carnivores, which may then be eaten by the dark-dwellers.
9. Oxygen may be a limiting factor in ocean depths where water exchange is at a minimum. Compact boggy soils have a low oxygen content. Deep in most soils the oxygen deficiency would inhibit organisms.
10. The food chain begins with the food producers, which are then consumed by the herbivores. The herbivores are the first food consumers of the ecosystem. Next are the first- and second-level carnivores. At death, the organisms are consumed by scavengers, after which the decomposers and transformers release minerals back into the soil.
11. Symbiosis is a nutritional relationship in which individuals live in direct association with each other. *Parasitism* occurs when one of the organisms benefits while the other is harmed. *Mutualism* is when both are benefited. *Commensalism* occurs when one is benefited while the other is not affected.
12. A fixed pattern of behavior involves a series of reflex actions which must

occur in sequence. Each action brings about a response that in turn causes another response. The behavior pattern exhibited by the stickle-back fish during the reproductive process serves as an example for a fixed pattern of behavior.

ANSWERS TO APPLYING PRINCIPLES AND CONCEPTS
(Page 659)

1. The answers to this question will vary widely.
2. A knowledge of the limiting factors of specific organisms enables us to predict the environment in which we may find them. We can also predict other areas where they may be able to live. This may be of significance to horticulturists and farmers, as well as to biologists.
3. Yes, although humans have basic water, food, and oxygen needs and a limited tolerance to temperature extremes. We have the unique advantage, however, of being able to alter conditions to suit our needs.
4. The warm-blooded animals can extend their habitats over a wide range of temperatures and can remain active through all seasons. On a cold morning they can run from their enemies or stalk and chase prey, whereas a cold-blooded animal has to warm up.
5. Plants growing in reduced light usually have larger, lighter green leaves and may grow spindly. Many plants in such areas normally have tendrils so that they climb other plants. Thick pine forests may be composed of thin, spindly trees with only a tuft of green at the very tops.
6. The answers to this question will vary widely.
7. Migration of birds, complicated courtship behavior, caring for the young, building of nests, and the spinning of webs by spiders are all fixed patterns of behavior. If the web

This habitat isn't big enough for the both of us.

of a spider or the nest of a bird is destroyed or damaged during its construction, the animal must start from the beginning to form a new one. These fixed patterns are all common to a particular species; for example, all robins will build nests of similar materials and the nests will be positioned in similar places.

chapter fifty Periodic Changes in the Environment Alternating periods of activity are referred to as *periodicity*. This periodicity is affected by a number of factors that students will read about in this chapter. In addition, movement patterns of organisms are also explored. Changing biotic communities are examined through the succession of forests and ponds. An understanding of periodic changes and their causes will give students a better understanding of the biotic communities around them.

TEACHING SUGGESTIONS

1. Point out to students that humans as well as animals are subject to daily rhythms. Students may be interested in talking about their biorhythms. Do they tend to be "day" or "night" people?

2. Elicit from students a discussion of animals in their areas that adjust to seasonal community changes. Some students may want to do some research on a particular animal.

3. Pond or lake succession is often hastened by water pollution. Stress to students that certain chemicals act as nutrients for algae and weeds and stimulates their growth. This process leads to an early death of a body of water and is termed *eutrophication.*

STUDENT INVOLVEMENT ACTIVITIES

1. Have students do research on bird migration and report to the class. Students may be amazed at the length of certain migratory flights.

2. Ask students to observe a local pond or other body of water and report on the rate of succession in this body of water. Have them discuss the factors that affect succession.

3. Have students report on any aspect of periodicity. Some students may be interested in learning more about the "biological clock" in humans.

COMMUNITY INVOLVEMENT ACTIVITIES

1. Visit a forest area and have students observe the succession that has taken place. Are they able to pick out the *climax species* in the area?

2. Invite a zoologist to discuss periodicity among animals. There are many fascinating examples of periodicity in nature.

CAREER OPPORTUNITIES
Animal behaviorist
Biotelemetrist
Ecologist
Environmentalist
Meteorologist
Ornithologist
Psychologist
Zoologist

ANSWERS TO QUESTIONS FOR REVIEW
(*Page 669*)

1. The owl and hawk do not compete with one another because they occupy similar niches but at different times.

2. When the white-footed mouse is kept in constant darkness, its waking and sleeping periods continue as if it were exposed to normal periods of daylight and darkness.

3. Animals meet seasonal changes by either adjusting or moving away. Many insects die during the first freezing nights of winter, but many find crevices or hollow trees for protection. The eastern cottontail rabbit, white-tailed deer, and cardinal find protection in the deep woods during extreme conditions. Bears hide in caves. Ground squirrels, chipmunks, woodchucks, and many reptiles and amphibians hibernate. The monarch butterfly and many birds migrate.

4. Both hibernation and estivation are terms indicating that an animal enters a period of deep sleep. The body metabolism slows, and heart rate and respiration decrease. The animal loses consciousness. Hibernation occurs in the winter and estivation occurs in the summer.

5. Migration is usually associated with birds, but some mammals also migrate. Bighorn sheep, elk, and fur seals are a few examples. The monarch butterfly also makes seasonal migrations.

6. The oceans and large bodies of water are affected by lunar rhythms, which produce tides.

7. Grunion spawn from March to August on the second, third, and fourth nights of the highest night tides. Thus the rhythm is referred to as lunar periodicity.

8. Periodicity may bring organisms together for reproduction, as in the swarming of the grunion. Male and female oysters, marine worms, sea anemones, and many others release their gametes into the water at the same time. Such periodicity is essential if these species are to continue.

9. Succession can be studied by clearing off a piece of land or a rock in the ocean and observing the passing parade of organisms inhabiting the area. Succession may be studied in a jar of water, or in the field by examining a large area, theorizing about the stages that have occurred prior to the climax.

ANSWERS TO APPLYING PRINCIPLES AND CONCEPTS
(page 669)

1. The major reason that human activities are not entirely governed by external rhythms is that we can alter our environment to suit our needs. Electric lights enable us to produce summer-blooming flowers in the winter. We can preserve goods for consumption all year.

2. Nocturnal animals have a keen sense of hearing and smell. Their eyes are adapted for seeing in dim light.

3. The desert and arctic treeless plains are similar in that they are actually biological deserts. Water is scarce. In the desert the water is not available to organisms because it is too deep and in the arctic plain, the water is all frozen, so that it is useless to plants.

4. The answers to this question will vary depending on the locality.

5. The answers to this question will vary depending on the locality.

chapter fifty-one Biogeography

How are plants and animals distributed? The study of animal and plant distribution is called biogeography. In this chapter, students will learn about barriers to dispersal, various biomes, and their inhabitants. Having read this chapter, students will be more familiar with different types of biomes and the creatures that inhabit them.

TEACHING SUGGESTIONS

1. Point out to students the positive and negative contributions of humans to the dispersal of animals and plants. Positive dispersal may be the spreading of organisms into other areas. However, negative dispersal may result from a disruption of an ecosystem due to human expansion in the area.

2. Ask students if they can think of any other barriers to dispersal. Some organisms may not be able to survive in an area inhabited by their natural enemies.

3. Ask students to describe the biome in which they live. Would they prefer to live in another biome?

4. Elicit from students any experiences they may have had traveling through different biomes. This will be of interest to students who have not been out of their area.

STUDENT INVOLVEMENT ACTIVITIES

1. Have students bring in samples of plant life that are characteristic of the biome in which they live.

2. Have students choose any biome

8

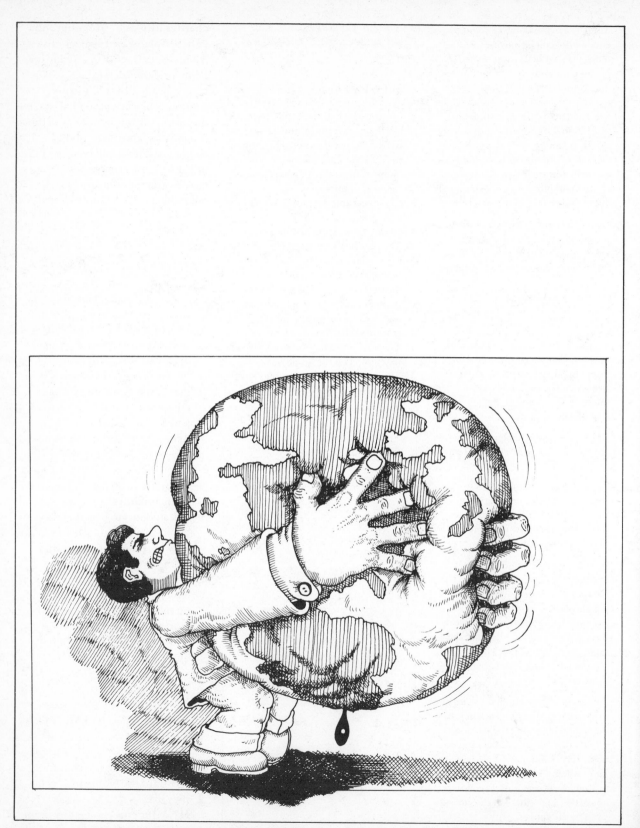

with which they are unfamiliar and ask them to write a brief report on their choice.
3. If students live near the ocean, ask them to observe the intertidal zone and write down their observations of this area. Many diverse organisms live within the intertidal zone.

COMMUNITY INVOLVEMENT ACTIVITIES
1. Take a class trip to a marine biome, if possible, and collect some of the organisms that live along the share. There are usually many examples of shells in the intertidal zone.
2. Invite an oceanographer to class to discuss the benthic and pelagic zones of the marine biome.
3. Invite a travel agent to speak about the location of certain biomes such as the rain forest. Perhaps, the agent could bring along a film or slides that may be of interest. Students may also have films or slides of biomes they have visited.

CAREER OPPORTUNITIES
Biometeorologist
Biotelemetrist
Biologist
Geologist
Geophysicist
Marine biologist
Oceanographer
Travel agent
Zoologist

CHALLENGES IN BIOLOGY
ALTERING THE ENVIRONMENT
By extending our livable areas, we alter the environment to suit our needs. Irresponsible and wasteful alterations of the environment cause harm to other living things and to ourselves. Careful planning and consideration are necessary to protect and maintain an ecological balance. This requires the attention of everyone and should not be left to a few individuals. There are many groups devoted to maintaining the environment and meeting this challenge in biology.

ANSWERS TO QUESTIONS FOR REVIEW
(Page 683)

1. Plants that spread underground stems will grow in areas where there are many of their kind. Milkweed seeds or young spiders floating on silken threads will travel farther and most likely alight in an area where there are not so many of their kind. Methods of dispersal, then, determine the distance an organism may spread.
2. Bodies of salt water are geographical barriers to many organisms such as the frog. High mountains are barriers across which many plants and animals cannot pass. Lack of food may be a biotic barrier preventing grazing animals, such as a zebra, from crossing a desert. For deer, squirrels, and other forest animals, the desert would be a climatic as well as a biotic barrier. A swift river may prevent the spread of small mammals such as mice and shrews.
3. Arctic region, including Northern Canada, part of Alaska, Greenland; temperate region, including most of Canada and the United States; semitropical region, including much of Florida; and the tropical region, including Mexico.
4. Altitude and rainfall.
5. The Antarctic is a large land mass most of which is covered with ice and snow during the entire year. Since most of the water is frozen, it is not available for organisms. Strong winds and extremely low temperatures make most of the Antarctic unsuitable for plants and animals. The surrounding oceans also provide an effective barrier.
   The Arctic, on the other hand, consists of a thin ice sheet, so the underlying water moderates the temperature. Where a land mass does protrude into the Arctic, nine-tenths of it is uncovered during the summer months and the temperatures may reach 23°C. These conditions are favorable to many animals and plants.
6. The coniferous forests in the United States are found, primarily, in the Great Lakes and the St. Lawrence River Valley and along the coastal ranges of Washington, Oregon, and California.
   The eastern United States is or once was covered with large stands of deciduous trees. Today deciduous trees cover much of the Appalachian Mountain chain.
   In the United States, the grasslands occur in the Great Plains east of the Rocky Mountains.
7. Reptiles, some insects, and birds excrete nitrogenous wastes in the form of uric acid. Uric acid can be excreted in an almost dry form, thus enabling the animal to conserve water. Most mammals of the desert burrow during the day to conserve moisture. Some rodents obtain enough water from the seeds and fruits they eat.
8. Rain forests have an abundant water supply and little seasonal variation.
9. Epiphytes have thick, porous roots adapted to catching and holding rainfall. Many have leaves arranged so that they catch water, insects, falling leaves, and other debris. The epiphytes do not take nourishment from the trees upon which they grow.
10. The intertidal zone has extremes of moisture and drying, cold and hot, and concentration of salt water.
11. Organisms living in total darkness

8

in the depths of the ocean are dependent on other organisms inhabiting the area and on organic material filtering down from above for their food.

12. Water gets heavier (more dense) as the temperature is lowered. However, as it freezes, the density decreases so that freezing water rises. Thus, the surface of lakes may freeze solid but organisms continue to live at the bottom where the water remains unfrozen.

13. Variations are found among organisms of a species occupying different environments. This illustrates adaptive radiation, a principle of evolution.

ANSWERS TO APPLYING PRINCIPLES AND CONCEPTS
(Page 683)

1. The answers to this question will vary widely. Some students will think of: pine cone, squirrel, hawk, or coyote.

2. Rats often stow away on ships and are transported across an ocean barrier. Rodents may occasionally be set adrift on a log and thus be transported over a barrier. A ballooning spider may be transported over a high mountain to the other side where it may find a suitable environment.

3. As the climatic regions of the earth vary from either the north or south poles to the equator, so do the principal kinds of living things. These broad zones of the same kinds of living things may be found on a high mountain at the equator.

4. The growing season is shorter in the coniferous forest but rainfall may average 200 centimeters per year. In the deciduous forest rainfall is around 100 centimeters per year.

5. The preponderance of life at the intertidal zone creates a space problem. Many organisms such as limpets, barnacles, and sea anemones live on shells of other animals. Many crabs

spend the major part of their lives on floating kelp. Limpets living at the high water mark clamp down tightly to prevent loss of water. Mussels and barnacles close their shells when exposed to the warm, drying sun. Epiphytic algae are found growing on kelp and on the shells of many crustaceans.

chapter fifty-two The Land We Live In This chapter stresses environmental problems and the responsibilities involved in correcting these problems. The problem of the loss of soil fertility is discussed as well as problems of soil erosion. The cycle of soil and water problems is examined. Water conservation methods are explored. Water pollution is discussed in some detail. Methods of correcting water pollution, including recycling are discussed. Air pollution is also discussed in some detail. This chapter concludes with a discussion of the energy crisis and what it means to present and future human populations. Having read this chapter, students will have a greater appreciation for the environmental problems faced by the world today.

TEACHING SUGGESTIONS

1. Point out to students that a major controversy exists over the safety of certain pesticides. The Environmental Protection Agency has made many decisions against the use of certain pesticides and these decisions have angered both farmers and the pesticide industry.

2. One source of water pollution is oil spills. Students may be interested in reading a fascinating account of the Santa Barbara oil spill. The book is *Black Tide* by Robert Easton, Delacorte Press, 1972.

3. The growing waste problem is identified and discussed in the book *Going to Waste* by James Marshall, Coward, McCann and Geohegan, Inc., 1972. This book suggests some imaginative methods of controlling and treating refuse.

8

4. Point out to students that a controversy currently exists concerning the use of nuclear energy plants. Many persons fear the possibility of a nuclear accident. Others claim that nuclear energy has a perfect record for safety and it is the answer to our current energy problem.

STUDENT INVOLVEMENT ACTIVITIES
1. Have students report on the subject of noise pollution, a topic not often thought of when referring to pollution. An interesting book on this subject is *Our Noisy World* by John Gabriel Navarra, Doubleday and Co., Inc., 1969. A discussion of the SST may also be appropriate here.
2. Water pollution has been found in many city water supplies. Have students check into the method of purifying water in your community. What are the state standards for water purity?
3. Have students bring in recent articles that are related to problems of the environment. Discuss these articles in class.
4. Have students do some research on new methods of cleaning up the environment. Have some of these reports read to the class.

COMMUNITY INVOLVEMENT ACTIVITIES
1. Sponsor a school-wide environment day that would offer workshops in the areas of air, water, thermal, environmental, and noise pollution. Guest speakers could be invited to speak on their area of expertise.
2. Visit the local waste processing plant and find out how your community disposes of garbage.

Is it recycled in any way? Is there a paper recycling program? If not, find out how to start one.
3. Invite a representative of your local water company to discuss water purification in your locality.

CAREER OPPORTUNITIES
Biochemist
Chemist
Environmental engineer
Environmentalist
Environmental health technician
Waste processing technician
Water purification specialist
Sanitary engineer

CHALLENGES IN BIOLOGY
EROSION
Both urban and agricultural development have caused the erosion of topsoil from many areas. The loss of this topsoil affects both the land from which it is lost and the area to which it is washed. Avoiding this type of damage is a challenge to urban developers and farmers.

DETERGENTS
Detergents with phosphates are an example of how we met a challenge with a workable solution. Phosphates were removed from detergents through legislation and consumer demand. This has saved many bodies of water from becoming further polluted. This challenge in biology has been resolved.

PCB's
PCB's (polychlorinated biphenyls) are toxic, nonbiodegradable compounds. PCB's are used pri-

marily as electrical insulation, but are also used in waterproofing. They are harmful to animals because PCB's build up in the food chain and are more persistant than DDT. However, a new technique has proven successful in rendering PCB's harmless. This technique was introduced by Dr. Dickson Liu, a Canadian biochemist. Hopefully, Liu's use of bacteria to devour PCB's will be the answer to this problem.

AIR POLLUTION LEGISLATION
Legislation passed by Congress has led to the regulation and control of substances emitted into the air by industries and automobiles. Although the devices which are being used have increased costs, they have been effective in reducing dangerous air pollutants. The laws that were passed require still further reduction of air pollution from automobiles. The challenge is to produce automobiles which cause a minimum of waste within a reasonable cost.

NUCLEAR POLLUTION
Many nations now have nuclear capacity. Although this source of power may provide needed energy, the testing of nuclear devices presents an environmental hazard. Some nations have agreed not to test nuclear devices in the atmosphere. Atmospheric pollution by fallout threatens all life in the biosphere.

ANSWERS TO QUESTIONS FOR REVIEW
(Page 698)

1. In past years, crops were grown over and over in the same soil. The produce was removed in the

harvest. This resulted in depletion of soil minerals. Many fields were abandoned to the ravages of erosion when the minerals were depleted to the point that further crops were unprofitable.

2. Sheet erosion is caused by seasonal floods removing a thin layer of soil. Rill erosion is caused by rain falling on hilly areas. The runoff water forms tiny channels or rills. Gully erosion occurs when rill erosion is not checked, and the rills deepen and widen.

3. Cover crops, planted between row crops in strip cropping, catch and hold water and soil running off the exposed soil in the rowcrop strips.

4. Terracing is used when a steep hillside is planted in crops.

5. Wind erosion can be controlled by planting shelterbelts or windbreaks, planting soil-binding crops, plowing the soil while it is moist and at right angles to the wind, and by irrigating fields. While these measures could be used in any region where wind erosion is a problem, they apply mostly to the Southwest and the Great Plains states.

6. A watershed is a hilly region, usually extending over a large area, that conducts surface water to streams.

7. Several sources of water pollution are: sewage, garbage, industrial waste, pesticides, detergents, and power plants. The government has passed laws regulating the pollutants that industries may release into the water. Laws regulating sewage treatment have also been passed.

8. Materials such as sewage and garbage are decomposed by natural processes and are considered biodegradable. Oil and other petroleum products from refineries are not decomposed by bacterial action and are considered to be nonbiodegradable.

9. Thermal pollution is the addition of heat to a river, lake, bay, or to an area of an ocean.

10. When sewage or other organic materials are put into water, bacterial populations increase rapidly. Thus, the dissolved oxygen is used to the point that many fish and other animals die of suffocation.

11. Recycling is making use of solid waste materials. Some materials can be reused as they are, while others must be reduced to raw materials. Recycling helps to reduce waste and conserve natural resources.

12. Pollutants in the form of liquid droplets or small particles of solid materials that are suspended in the air are called particulates.

13. Toxic gases associated with air pollution are: sulfur dioxide, nitric oxide, nitrogen dioxide, and carbon monoxide.

14. Smog is a combination of smoke and fog.

15. Two sources of pollutants that form smog are industries (such as blast furnaces, power plants, or factories) and automobile exhausts.

16. A temperature inversion may occur when a layer of cool air moves into an area below a layer of warm air.

17. Strontium-90 is a radioactive substance resulting from nuclear explosions. When it falls to the earth, it is taken up by plants and animals which may be eaten by people. Strontium-90 accumulates in bones and when a certain concentration is reached, its radiations can destroy tissues, cause cancer or even death.

18. Renewable energy sources include: solar energy, geothermal energy, water, tide, winds, and even burning garbage. Nuclear fuels may also provide future energy.

ANSWERS TO APPLYING PRINCIPLES AND CONCEPTS
(Page 698)

1. A crop rotation program might include corn, grown as a crop which exposes much of the soil and draws heavily on minerals. Corn can be followed by wheat, a cover crop which uses somewhat different minerals. The third year, oats might be planted as a second cover crop. The fourth year, the land should be planted in clover, cowpeas, or lespedeza. The legume crops restore nitrogen, due to the action of the nitrogen-fixing bacteria on their roots. Thus, the same minerals are not being removed from the soil every year.

2. In hilly agricultural areas, crops should be planted in strips laid out on the contour of hills. Contour plowing prevents water erosion which would occur if the plowing were up and down the hill. Strip cropping prevents water erosion. Crops planted in the strips may be varied year after year in a program of crop rotation.

3. Water pollution may deplete the oxygen and cause the death of many fishes and other organisms. Excessive phosphate pollution may stimulate the growth of algae in streams and lakes and upset the balance. At the end of the growing season the death and decay of the algae would, then, have the same effect as an overbalance of sewage by supporting a great mass of bacteria and thus depleting the oxygen in the water.
Chemical wastes poison aquatic plants and animals in the food chain. Pollution may spread disease and render areas unsuitable for recreation.

4. PCB's are nonbiodegradable, highly toxic chemicals. Once released into the waters by various manufacturing processes they enter the food chain. Here they present a human health hazard.

5. Air pollution can be reduced by eliminating trash burning, using efficient indoor incenerators, using antismoke devices on factory stacks, and using gas rather than coal and

8

oil. The installation of precipitators, cyclones, and filters reduces pollution. Antismog devices are being installed on automobiles, and manufacturers have reduced the compression in engines to burn low-octane gasoline with a lower lead content. Continuing research may provide us with more efficient power for the future.

chapter fifty-three   Forest and Wildlife Resources   Without our forest and wildlife resources, this country would be both barren and economically deprived. This chapter discusses the forests and the need to conserve them. Methods of conservation through forest management are discussed. Fire, a major enemy of forests, is also examined. Wildlife conservation and the problems of endangered and extinct species are explored, and the threat of insecticides to other animals is stressed. Students will gain a better understanding of these resources and the need to protect them by reading this chapter.

TEACHING SUGGESTIONS

1. Point out to students that there are many groups interested in the preservation of our wildlife. These groups helped to pass the 1973 Endangered Species Act which gives protection to any species considered endangered.

2. There is presently a search for substitutes to pesticides to replace DDT, chlordone, and heptachlor. These chemicals have been suspended from use by the EPA. New techniques involve the use of a bacteria known as BT to kill pests. Another technique is the use of a chemical growth regulator to control mosquito infestation.

3. A conservationist battle was recently won when tuna fishermen were ordered to stop using porpoises to help them find tuna schools. The porpoises are often killed when they are caught in the tuna nets.

STUDENT INVOLVEMENT ACTIVITIES

1. Students may be interested in writing to groups concerned with wildlife preservation. Some of these groups include: The National Wildlife Federation, Sierra Club, Audubon Society, Scientists' Institute for Public Information, Defenders of Wildlife, Environmental Defense Fund, and Friends of the Earth. Addresses of these and other organizations can be found in your local public library.

2. Have students choose an area of interest concerning the preservation of wildlife and report on it to class.

3. Have a few students discuss safety tips for campers. These tips will be useful in preventing forest fires.

COMMUNITY INVOLVEMENT ACTIVITIES

1. Invite a representative of a conservationist group to speak to the class about the goals of the organization.

2. Invite a firefighter to class to discuss the prevention of fires in the wilderness.

CAREER OPPORTUNITIES
Conservationist
Environmentalist
Field guide
Firefighter
Forest manager
National Park manager
Range manager
Zoologist

CHALLENGES IN BIOLOGY
EXTINCTION OF WILDLIFE
Many unique species of wildlife are nearing extinction. We have the

responsibility to preserve these species. Some countries have already started to meet this responsibility. In 1973, delegates from eighty countries met to agree upon an international pact to protect endangered species. However, much more needs to be done in this area.

Many species of whales are among the representatives of marine life which are endangered today. While some whales appear to have adequate numbers to ensure survival, others have so few that reproduction will be limited. It is essential that whale hunting be controlled and whales be allowed to increase their numbers. This is a challenge faced by all nations.

INSECTICIDES

Although insecticides are beneficial in their primary use to obtain more food, certain nonbiodegradable pesticides are causing the endangerment of many species of birds and fishes. The need for food is apparent, but we are challenged to develop insect controls that act only on their primary target.

ANSWERS TO QUESTIONS FOR REVIEW
(Page 710)

1. The two great forest belts in the United States are the East and the West. The regions are: Pacific Coastal forest, Rocky Mountain forest, Central hardwood forest, Northern forest, Southern forest, and Tropical forest.
2. Pulpwood for newsprint, book paper, stationery, packaging, and other paper products comes from the coniferous forests of the United

States and Canada. Distillation products, such as wood alcohol, oxalic acid, charcoal, and lampblack come from the hardwood forests. Pine products, including turpentine, rosin, and pine tar are derived from the Southern forests.
3. In improvement cutting, in a managed forest, trees of undesirable species, crowded trees, crooked trees, damaged trees, and diseased trees are removed. Whole sections of a forest are removed by block-cutting when the trees are mature and of the same age, as in a forest planted in a reclaimed area.
4. Block-cutting is used in planted stands of timber in which all the trees are about the same age. A complete area of trees is removed after which it is replanted with seedlings.
5. Causes of forest fires include: incendiarists, debris burners, smokers, lightning, campers, railroads, and lumbering. Incendiary fires are deliberately set. Debris burners, smokers, and campers cause fires through carelessness. Lightning is the only natural cause.
6. A fish ladder is a series of water terraces broken by projecting plates. A fish can ascend the ladder by a series of short leaps. Fish ladders are built to bypass dams which block the rivers in regions to which fish return to spawn.
7. Eight endangered bird species are the ivorybilled woodpecker, prairie chicken, California condor, American (Southern) bald eagle, Everglades kite, osprey, brown pelican, and the whooping crane.
8. The research center in Patuxent, Maryland collected eggs of the whooping crane from wild nests and incubated them for rearing. Since this bird normally lays two eggs but only rears one chick, the collection of eggs did not reduce the wild population. In 1971, the total number of birds was increased from 50 to 80. Therefore, this interesting animal may be saved from extinction.

9. DDT used in insect control washes down to rivers, streams, lakes, and the ocean. It clings to algae and is consumed by fish which are, in turn, consumed by larger fish and man. In the food chain, these chemicals are concentrated and exhibit a cumulative effect. DDT is believed to be responsible for the laying of thin-shelled eggs in many birds. Thus, the eggs break and place the population in jeopardy. Another danger in the use of DDT is that certain insects, through natural selection, become immune to its effects and this results in a need to develop other methods of control. PCB's share the same dangers in the food chain.
10. Biological control involves the conservation of such animals as the praying mantis, ladybird beetle, fish, frogs, toads, and birds which consume enormous numbers of insects.

ANSWERS TO APPLYING PRINCIPLES AND CONCEPTS
(Page 710)

1. In a forest managed on a sustained yield basis, every tree is a good timber species. Trees are properly spaced as a result of thinning out. The forest is free of damaged, crooked, and diseased trees. Trees are harvested as they mature. Block-cutting, strip cutting, and reforestation are all helpful in forest conservation.
2. Sports people are among the most ardent supporters of the wildlife

8

conservation programs. They are aware of the problems involved and, in the interest of hunting and fishing, work toward correction of the problems. The fees they pay for hunting and fishing licenses help support the conservation programs.

3. As the population increases and cities grow larger, food and nesting sites of some birds are destroyed. Other birds, such as the finch, the sparrow, and the pigeon, however, adapt to people and cities. They are able to nest and rear their young in areas which would not be suitable to some of the larger birds.

4. Our efforts to eliminate one of our most severe competitors, the insects, has been directed toward the development of effective, long lasting insecticides. However, the use of these chemicals has taught us not only that some organisms are able to become resistant to the poison, but that some of our most effective animals for biological control of insect pests have also been drastically reduced by insecticide dispersal.

6. Since whales inhabit the open seas, international cooperation is needed to protect these animals. Unfortunately, economic factors in some countries make cooperation and enforcement difficult.

The Holt
MODERN BIOLOGY
Program

MODERN BIOLOGY   Otto and Towle

SUPPLEMENTS TO MODERN BIOLOGY

Annotated Teacher's Edition to the Modern Biology Text
Biology Investigations   Otto, Towle, and Otto
Annotated Teacher's Edition to Biology Investigations
Laboratory Investigations   Otto, Towle, and Otto
Test Masters in Biology

OTHER BASIC TEXTS IN LIFE SCIENCE

Biological Science: Invitations to Discovery   BSCS
Biological Science: Patterns and Processes   BSCS
Human Physiology   Morrison, Cornett, Tether, and Gratz
Living Things   Fitzpatrick, Bain, and Teter
Modern Health   Otto, Julian, and Tether
Modern Life Science   Fitzpatrick and Hole
Modern Sex Education   Julian and Jackson

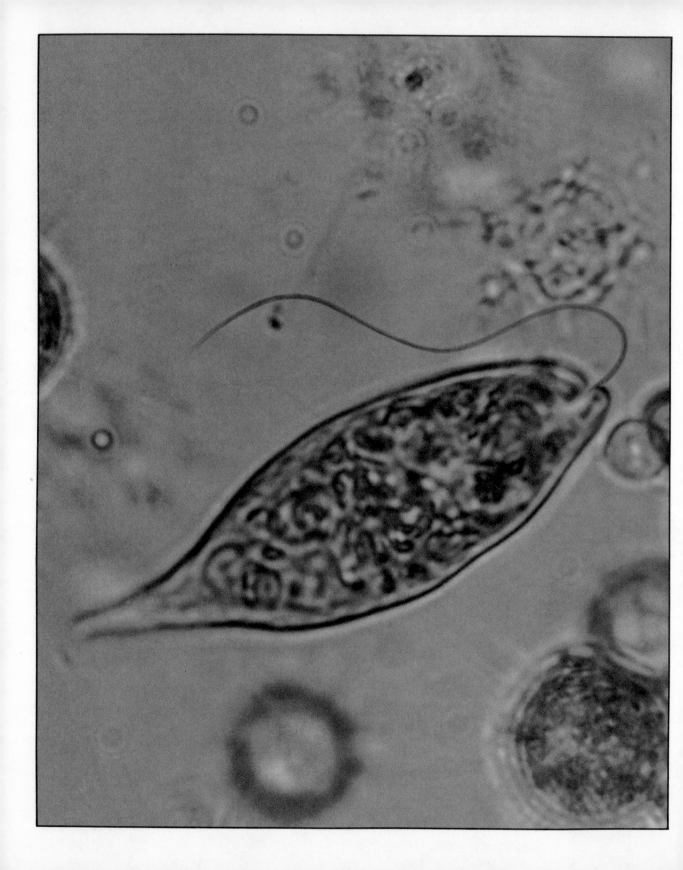

James H. Otto
Albert Towle

MODERN BIOLOGY

HOLT, RINEHART AND WINSTON, PUBLISHERS
NEW YORK · LONDON · TORONTO · SYDNEY

James H. Otto

was a biology teacher and head of the Science Department at George Washington High School, Indianapolis, Indiana.

Albert Towle

is a professor of biology and supervisor of biology student teachers at California State University, San Francisco, California.

Cover: *Euglena*

This simple, unicellular organism is of particular interest to biologists because it has some characteristics of plants and some of animals.

• Photography by Runk/Schoenberger from Grant Heilman.

Unit opening photographs

2 Lennart Nilsson
3 Manfred Kage, Peter Arnold
4 EPA—DOCUMERICA
5 H.R.W. Photo by Russell Dian
6 H. Rienhard, Bruce Coleman Inc.
7 Lennart Nilsson
8 NASA

page x—Perry Rubin/Monkmeyer backdrop center—NYPL bottom—Courtesy of General Electric *page 1*—backdrop, left—The American Museum of Natural History top, left—Ken Wittenberg bottom, left, bottom, center—Al Satterwhite/Jungle Habitat backdrop bottom, right—NYPL *page 2*—backdrop top, left—NYPL top right—H.R.W. Photo by Russell Dian backdrop center, left—Courtesy of Burndy Library center, right—Ken Wittenberg bottom, left—Ron Sherman/Nancy Palmer Photo Agency bottom, right—H.R.W. Photo by Russell Dian

All other photographs are acknowledged on the page on which they appear.

Frog Insert art by John Murphy

Human Body insert courtesy of W. B. Saunders Company

ISBN: 0-03-017751-0
67890 032 987654321

PREFACE

MODERN BIOLOGY begins with a discussion of the unique properties of living organisms that set them apart from the nonliving. The presentation of molecular and cellular biology, next, gives a background for the concepts of reproduction and genetics. Understanding the continuity of life and the transmission of characteristics to offspring by hereditary determiners gives meaning to organic variation and scientific classification. Units dealing with microbiology, multicellular plants, invertebrate animal life, the vertebrate animals, and human biology follow in logical sequence. The final unit dealing with biogeography, ecological relationships, pollution and conservation serves a fitting climax and an overview of the entire biology course.

The authors of MODERN BIOLOGY have always believed that the learning process should involve a mastery of certain fundamental concepts at the beginning of the course in biology. From these initial understandings, the progression from cell to protists, to plants and animals, and finally to the human will come naturally. In this systematic approach to the study of biology, the student discovers unity in the organisms.

The approach and methodology that have evolved successfully in thousands of secondary school classrooms and laboratories have been preserved in MODERN BIOLOGY. These features have been tested and proved effective by thousands of science teachers. The many professional biologists making significant contributions in the research laboratories who have learned from earlier editions of this text are evidence of the value of such an approach.

As in previous editions, this ninth revision of MODERN BIOLOGY has been updated in all areas in which new knowledge is significant to the high school student. The authors have attempted to maintain the readability at a level proportionate to the average student. Reorganization within the various chapters has reduced the length of the text. An *APPENDIX*, which includes the metric system of measurement and a modern system of classification with major characteristics, has been added in this edition.

In the sections of MODERN BIOLOGY dealing with evolution, scientific data have been used to present this material as theory rather than fact. The information presented allows for the widest possible interpretation that can be applied to any set of values, either religious or scientific. Every effort has been made to present this material in a nondogmatic manner.

As in previous editions of this book, the style of writing has been kept as informal as possible. Difficult words are pronounced phonetically, and all new words and terms stand out in **boldface italic** type. These words are defined the first time they are used. *Italic* type is used for emphasis. The *GLOSSARY* is a further aid for developing a "working" vocabulary. *RELATED READING* lists provided at the end of each unit have been found to be useful by many teachers and students.

The authors recognize the need to present the subject of biology to students of varied abilities. In order to present the subject in a form that allows for comprehension on various levels, certain features have been added to this edition. *Objectives* for the student are indicated at the beginning of each chapter. These objectives serve to guide the student in studying the major concepts of the chapter. The questions for review at the end of each chapter reinforce the students' understanding of the material. A **boldface** type is used to point out the major biological principles in each chapter. This aids the student in understanding and reviewing the material. Also, important topics that are currently considered as "challenges in Biology" are indicated by a symbol that reflects the cover of MODERN BIOLOGY.

A special feature of MODERN BIOLOGY are the two inserts. The *Human Body* helps students to understand the structure of their own bodies. The *Frog Anatomy* is a valuable reference tool for the study and dissection of the frog.

The present authors are indebted to the late Truman J. Moon, whose successful texts BIOLOGY FOR BEGINNERS and BIOLOGY were the predecessors for this book. The many letters and comments from students, teachers, and parents have been appreciated and further suggestions from teachers are invited. The authors have tried to maintain authority in MODERN BIOLOGY. Appreciation is hereby acknowledged to the critics who read the units in their area of specialty.

unit	reviewer
1	**Gerard A. O'Donovan** Department of Biochemistry Texas A and M
2	**Adela Baer** Professor and Chairman Department of Biology San Diego State University
3	**Philip Carpenter** Department of Microbiology University of Rhode Island
4	**Knut Norstog** Northern Illinois University
5	**Robert Barnes** Professor of Biology Gettysburg College
6	**Robert T. Orr** California Academy of Sciences
7	**Douglas Humm** Department of Zoology University of North Carolina
8	**D. A. Chant** Vice President and Provost Professor of Zoology University of Toronto

In addition, the text was reviewed by the Editorial Committee of the American Society for Environmental Education, Inc. This review was provided by: Dr. William Mayo, Executive Director of ASEE; Dr. Jonathan Wert, Environment Center, University of Tennessee; Dennis M. Wint, an environmental consultant; Dr. James J. Gallagher, Director of Education, ASEE.

MODERN BIOLOGY is a recommended publication of the American Society for Environmental Education.

CONTENTS

unit

1

THE NATURE OF LIFE

What is life? We know that living things are different from nonliving things. Each living thing appears different in some ways from all other living things. However, all living things have basic similarities. In our study of biology, we will start with an unknown—the living state—and will explore it many ways. We may never be able to explain life, but our investigations will bring us closer to an understanding of the marvelous condition that is life.

ECOLOGIST

MARINE BIOLOGIST

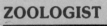

ZOOLOGIST

VETERINARIAN

MEDICAL RESEARCHER

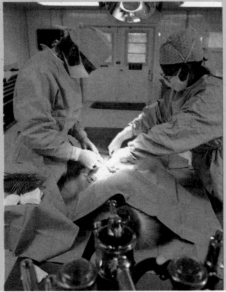

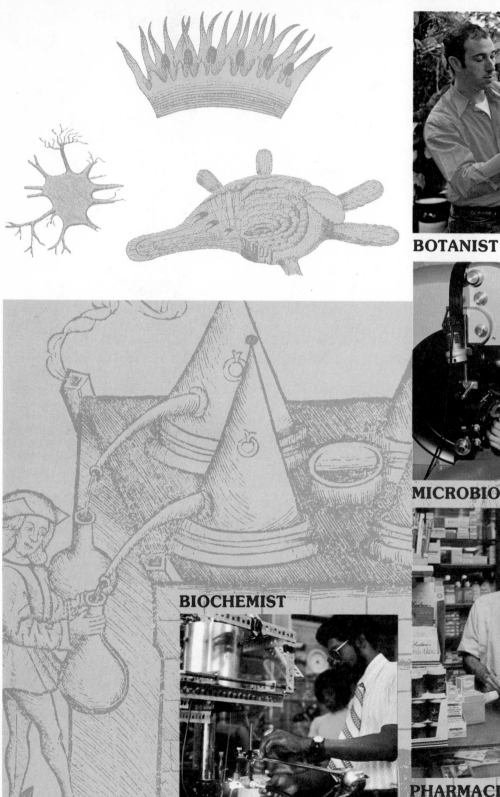

BOTANIST

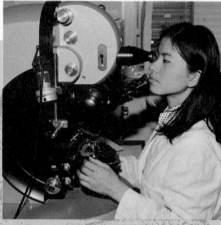

MICROBIOLOGIST

BIOCHEMIST

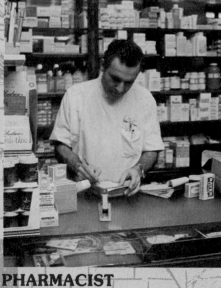

PHARMACIST

BIOLOGY AS A SCIENCE

The word *biology* comes from the Greek *bios,* meaning "life," and *logos,* meaning "thought" or "science of." **Biology, then, is the science of life.**

Any science is both a body of knowledge and a method of gaining more knowledge. Biology is all the knowledge of living things that has come to us from the past. Biology is also the logical, scientific method by which biologists today are adding to that knowledge.

Like other sciences, biology arose from the human need to understand events and solve problems. We have always tried to learn more about ourselves and other living things. What we have learned has helped us to survive and to improve our condition on the planet Earth.

Again, like other sciences, biology today is moving forward with great speed. We have gained more biological knowledge in the past quarter century than in the twenty centuries before! What brought biology, and science in general, to this golden age? Let's look at some of the answers.

SCIENCE AS A UNIVERSAL EFFORT

During the Middle Ages, walls of ignorance and superstition blocked the search for understanding. With the coming of the Renaissance, scientists began to break through these walls. Slowly at first, then faster and faster, new ideas took hold.

In the sixteenth century, Andreas Vesalius of Belgium rebelled against the methods of medieval medicine. In their place, Vesalius established a scientific study of anatomy, an important branch of biology.

In the eighteenth century, an English doctor, Edward Jenner, vaccinated a small child against smallpox. It was the first vaccination in history. In the nineteenth century, Louis Pasteur of France established the science of bacteriology. A few years later, Robert Koch (KOKE) of Germany developed methods for growing bacteria in laboratory cultures. These methods opened the way for study of bacteria-caused diseases.

We have mentioned only a few of the great moments in the history of biology. But from them you can see that **modern biology has grown from the work of many people in many different lands.**

SCIENCE OVERCOMING SUPERSTITION AND PREJUDICE

People always have tried to explain things that they did not understand. Many events were explained only by guesswork, in terms of superstition and magic. An example is the belief that a person's life is shaped by the positions of stars and planets. Did anyone ever find any evidence for this idea? Did anyone even try? People also believed that mud in ponds turned into eels, fish, and frogs. It has taken science several centuries to overcome this kind of thinking. Indeed, superstition is still with us in many ways. But a

The Science of Life

OBJECTIVES

- UNDERSTAND the universal nature of science.
- DEMONSTRATE the use of the scientific method.
- IDENTIFY the parts of a light microscope.
- EXPLAIN the limitations of the light microscope.
- EXPLAIN the advantages of the electron microscope.

The first biologist was Alcmaeon, a Greek, who did much of the original work in anatomy. He contributed to the Hippocratic Collection, a group of writings on anatomy that date from the fourth century B.C.

Students should be encouraged to report on a scientist of their choice. There are many biographies available about both early and recent biologists. Have students discuss the contributions of the biologist and how this biologist was affected by the time in which he lived.

Ask students to explain why nonscientific interests often become popular. Examples may be horoscopes, faith healing, and quackery. Students may want to report on some aspects of these and other nonscientific interests.

new system based on fact and logic is winning out. Today, the scientist is free to investigate, to prove and disprove, and to base conclusions on observed facts.

There is no end to science. The solving of one problem points to new problems for investigation. You might think of scientific knowledge as a circle of light in a sea of darkness. Through the centuries, the scientists of many nations have widened this circle greatly. But as the circle grows, so does the length of its outer edge. In other words, the more we learn, the more we realize how little we know.

A RAPIDLY GROWING SCIENCE

At one time, clear lines could be drawn between the major fields of science. Today the lines are gone. **All sciences are related.** Can we separate chemistry from biology? We cannot, as you will discover in your study of the living condition. Everything about life as biologists understand it can be thought of in terms of a complex biochemical system. Growth, response, and heredity—all result from chemical activity. Physics, too, is important to the biologist. Without a knowledge of physics, we could not hope to understand the changes in matter and energy involved in life.

Nor can we separate biology from space science, earth science, and oceanography. Satellites in orbit send back information that is changing many of our concepts about the earth. The earth is flattened at the poles and bulges at the equator. Its crust varies in thickness. Oceanographers are mapping the great currents of the seas. How do these things affect human beings and all other life on the earth? The answers will be found only through the work of many generations of biologists.

One of the most important tools of modern biology is the electronic computer. Computers are used to handle mathematical and statistical work associated with biological investigations. Computers are also used to analyze blood samples. Stress to the students the importance of the computer in many areas of science.

So-called "scientific truths" are constantly being recalled for further investigation. Modern examples of this include the thalidomide tragedy, food additive investigations, and the research concerning polyvinyl chloride and cancer. Ask students to bring in a clipping about new findings that refutes a once accepted "scientific truth."

THE LIMITS OF SCIENCE

In the Middle Ages, "scientific truths" were handed down from earlier times. These "truths" were not to be questioned, much less disproved. People who dared to disagree were ridiculed, attacked, and sometimes killed. Even a generation ago, science was believed to be much more exact than we now know it to be. **Today, we no longer think of any scientific answer as a final one. We know that we may have to change any concept in the light of new discoveries.**

SCIENCE AND SOCIETY

Two hundred years ago, angry crowds threw rocks at Edward Jenner when he vaccinated a child against smallpox. One hundred years ago, people laughed at Louis Pasteur when he said that invisible microbes caused certain diseases. Today, both of these great scientists would surely receive great honors for their work. **Our society accepts and supports modern science.**

1-1 Students attempting to solve a problem in a high school biology laboratory. (John King)

SCIENTIFIC METHODS

A scientific method is a logical, orderly way of trying to solve a problem. It is this logic and order that makes scientific methods different from ordinary, hit-or-miss approaches. Remember, though, that scientific methods are not magic. Even the best planned experiment can fail. Yet failure itself may lead to final success. By careful study of each result, the scientist may find a new direction to take. Often this new direction leads to an even more important discovery than the one first expected.

Several methods are used in science, depending on the nature of the problem. Perhaps the most important, especially for your biology course, is the **research method.**

THE RESEARCH METHOD

It is by a research method that new knowledge and new concepts are gained. You will have many chances to use a research method in your study of biology.

The steps in this research method are logical and orderly. In fact, they are simply a system of common sense:

- *Define the problem.* You can't solve a problem unless you see that one exists. Science calls for the kind of mind that recognizes problems and asks questions. For example, how does a root absorb water from the soil? Why does a plant stem bend toward the light? What controls your heartbeat? Well planned experiments can answer each of these questions. But in science, every answer raises new questions. Successful research leads to new research and new knowledge.

Paul Ehrlich is an example of the importance of "staying with" an experiment despite failure. After 605 unsuccessful attempts at finding a cure for syphilis, he was successful with attempt 606, also called salvarsan. This drug was used in treating syphilis prior to the discovery of penicillin.

Ask students to debate the question of whether or not a research method can be used to investigate everyday problems that are not necessarily of a scientific nature. Students may be surprised to find out that "scientific thinking" is used in many nonscientific ventures.

- *Collect information on the problem.* Scientists must build on the work of other scientists. Otherwise science could not advance beyond what one person could learn in one lifetime. Before beginning an experiment, the scientist studies all important information that has to do with the problem. Often it turns out that someone has already answered many of the questions involved. For this reason, a library of scientific papers, journals, and books is an important part of a research center. Your textbook and laboratory guide, along with other reading, will serve you in the same way in this course.

- *Form a hypothesis.* The available information may not fully explain the problem. The researcher must then begin to experiment. At this point, a **hypothesis** is needed. **The hypothesis is a sort of working explanation or trial answer.**

  The hypothesis gives the experimenter a point to aim at. But no matter how reasonable the hypothesis seems, it cannot be accepted until supported by a large number of tests. The research worker must be open-minded enough to change or drop a hypothesis if the evidence does not support it.

- *Experiment to test the hypothesis.* The scientist must set up an experiment that will either support or disprove the hypothesis. This means that the experiment must test *only* the condition involved in the hypothesis. All other factors must be removed or otherwise accounted for. The one factor to be tested is called the **single variable** or the **experimental factor.**

  Often, a second experiment called the **control** is done along with the first experiment. In the control experiment, all factors *except the one to be tested* are the same as in the first experiment. In this way, the control shows the importance of the missing experimental factor.

- *Observe and record data from the experiment.* Everything about the experiment should be recorded accurately. How was it planned and set up? Under what conditions was it carried out? What happened *during* the experiment? And finally, what were the results? The record may include notes, drawings, tables, graphs, or other forms of information. This information is called data. In modern research, data is often processed by computer.

- *Draw conclusions.* Data have value only when valid conclusions are drawn from them. Such conclusions must be based *entirely* on facts observed in the experiment. **If other experiments continue to support the hypothesis, it may come to be called a *theory*. A good theory explains the facts and also predicts new facts.**

A CONTROLLED EXPERIMENT USING THE RESEARCH METHOD

You can follow the steps of the research method by doing a simple controlled experiment in the laboratory. The experiment will involve the growth and development of bean seedlings. It will test the importance of one factor—light. We can define the problem as follows: *Is light necessary for the normal growth and development of bean seedlings?*

Observation is essential in any scientific investigation. However, observation can be aided by the use of certain chemicals, microscopes, and other scientific equipment.

Point out to students the importance of a controlled experiment. The limitation of one variable factor (in this case, light) reduces the uncertainty of other factors. In addition, such an experiment can be reproduced with the same results. This is important to the scientific validity of an experiment.

Having defined the problem, you should look in the library for information about the effects of light on plant growth. Much has been written on this subject. Still, you might not find an exact answer to the problem about bean seedlings.

At this point, lacking full information, you form a hypothesis. You might assume, for instance, that *light is necessary for the normal growth and development of bean seedlings.* This hypothesis must now be supported or disproved by experiment.

A logical experiment would involve growing two sets of bean seedlings, one set in darkness and the other in light. Begin by planting two beans in each of six three-inch pots filled with loose, sandy soil. Mark three of the pots *experimental* and put them in a dark closet. Mark the other three pots *control.* Place them near a window or in some other place that gets full light. The temperature should be as nearly the same as possible for both sets of plants. Water the plants regularly, making sure that all plants get the same amount of water.

The experiment will last about four weeks. As it goes on, keep an accurate daily record of the condition of each seedling. Note the date on which each seed sprouts. Also, record daily the length and width of all stems, the size and number of leaves, and the color of each plant.

It is likely that the two sets of plants will develop very differently. Those grown in the light probably will have thick stems and large, healthy green leaves. Those grown in the dark probably will have long, weak stems and small yellow leaves. These results would give strong support for the hypothesis: *Light is necessary for the normal growth and development of bean seedlings.*

Remember that any controlled experiment must account for all factors, with only a single variable. In this experiment, light was the only factor that varied for the two sets of plants. If any other factor had varied, our conclusion would not have been valid. For example, suppose that the dark set had been planted in a different kind of soil. You could not then know whether their poor growth was caused by lack of light or by poor soil.

We concluded from the experiment that light is necessary for the normal growth and development of bean seedlings. But this conclusion raises several other questions. For example, how much light is needed? Also, we know that there are different wavelengths of light, which we see as different colors. Are all colors of light needed equally? Or do plants use some colors more than others? Again, we know that plants normally undergo periods of both light *and* darkness. Is the dark period important? These are only a few of the questions that our simple experiment raises. A hypothesis that has strong support usually leads to many more experiments.

PURE AND APPLIED SCIENCE

We often say that there are two kinds of science—**pure science,** or basic research, and **applied science.** In pure science, research is

Have the students discuss what would happen if scientific experiments were not controlled. Could the findings of such experiments be considered valid?

Steps of the Research Method

Define the Problem

 Do bean seedlings need light for normal growth?

Gather Information

Form Hypothesis

I think light is necessary for normal growth of bean seedlings?

Prove or Disprove by Experimentation

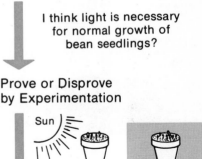

Collect Data

Date	Stem length	Dia	Number leaves	Color

Conclusion

Light was necessary for the normal growth of the bean seedlings.

1-2 Steps of the research method used in a controlled experiment.

Stress to students that in most biology laboratory investigations the *technical method* is used. In such investigations, one does not set out to prove or disprove a hypothesis, but to confirm established scientific findings.

Scientific research is often divided into two branches: the technical *(applied)* and *pure*. Technical or applied research is used to understand current and definable problems. Pure research attempts to expand the body of knowledge in a particular area.

1-3 Early microscopes. (The Bettmann Archive)

done for the sake of knowledge itself. Applied science makes practical use of this knowledge. For example, much pure-science research has been done on the effects of radiation on living matter. Applied science uses this knowledge in treating certain kinds of cancer with radiation.

THE MICROSCOPE—AN IMPORTANT TOOL

With modern tools and methods, biologists today are reaching a new and broader understanding of life. Perhaps the most important tool is the microscope. It's hard to say who actually invented the microscope. Even a single-lens magnifying glass is really a *simple microscope*. And single lenses that could magnify ten to twenty times were being used in the Middle Ages.

The first known *compound microscope* was made about 1590 by the Janssen brothers, two Dutch eyeglass-makers. Their microscope had *two* lenses, one mounted at each end of a tube-within-a-tube barrel. One lens magnified the already enlarged image of the other. The microscope was focused by sliding the tubes back and forth. Galileo used another early compound microscope to study biological materials in 1610.

Some years later, a Dutch merchant named Anton van Leeuwenhoek (LAVE-in-HOOK) began grinding lenses as a hobby. Altogether, he is said to have made about 250 different simple microscopes. Each was designed for examining a specific thing. For example, one microscope had a tube for holding a small fish in front of the lens. When van Leeuwenhoek held the lens to his eye, he saw blood surging through vessels in the fish's tail. Another of his microscopes was built for examining pond water. Through it, he saw teeming microscopic animals which he described as "cavorting beasties." Improvements allowed van Leeuwenhoek's microscopes to magnify by about three hundred times. In a very real sense, this Dutch merchant's hobby opened up one of the most important fields of modern science—microbiology.

THE MODERN COMPOUND MICROSCOPE

Compound microscopes have improved steadily since the time of the Janssen brothers. More powerful lenses and finer mechanical parts have been developed. Since modern microscopes use ordinary light, such instruments are called *light* microscopes. A light microscope may have its own light source. Or it may simply have a mirror which reflects available room light through the lenses.

A light microscope contains several lenses. One lens is the *eyepiece* at the top of the microscope. Other lens sets are contained in *objectives*. Microscopes have from one to four objectives. Different objective lenses give different magnifying powers. The microscopes used in most high schools magnify about 100 times (100×) at low power. At high power, they may magnify by 430 times (430×) or 440

General biology classes require an eyepiece of 10×. The revolving nosepiece should contain three objectives having 3.5×, 10×, and 43×. These powers are desirable for most routine high school biology investigations.

Depending on the student and the level of the course, a microscope that has a 100-500× magnification can be used. Such microscopes allow one to focus at low power and adjust the objective from 100-500× without losing focus.

1–4 A modern compound microscope being used by biology students. (H.R.W. Photo by Russell Dian)

times (440×). At these enlargements, cells and many microscopic plants and animals may be seen clearly. But smaller cell structures and very small organisms such as bacteria need more magnification. Special objectives can give enlargements of 1,000 to 1,500 times, depending on the eyepiece used.

LIMITS OF LIGHT MICROSCOPES

Lenses could be made that would give enlargements greater than 1,500×. Yet no light microscope magnifies much more than this. Why not? The answer lies not in lenses or other microscope parts, but in the nature of light itself.

There are two important factors to consider here. One is the microscope's **magnification,** how much it enlarges an image. The other factor is **resolution,** the microscope's capability to deliver a visible image with clear details. Magnification and resolution are closely related.

Each set of lenses bends the light rays in such a way that the rays are spread apart. This spreading forms the *magnified image* that reaches the eye. The more the light rays are bent and spread, the greater the magnification. On the other hand, the more the rays are spread, *the fewer rays actually reach the eye.* As fewer light rays reach the eye, the image becomes less bright and its details less clear. In other words, **higher magnification brings lower resolution.**

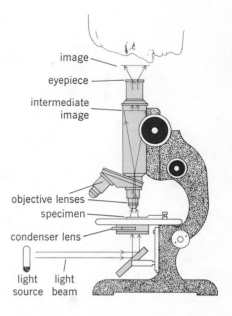

1–5 Passage of light rays through the compound microscope allows us to view the specimen clearly.

You might compare this problem with what happens when you magnify a newspaper picture. The picture itself is clear, with sharp details. If you view it through a reading glass, you see that is is made up of small dots. If you use stronger and stronger lenses, these dots appear farther and farther apart. Finally, so few dots are visible in the field that the picture is lost.

THE ELECTRON MICROSCOPE

A new and very different kind of instrument has opened up worlds that no light microscope could reach. The *electron microscope* does not use ordinary light. Instead it uses a stream of electrons. And instead of ordinary lenses, it uses electromagnets. A heated, very fine wire sends off a stream of electrons. An electromagnet called the *magnetic condenser* focuses the beam on the material to be studied. Some electrons pass through the material with little change of direction. Others strike molecules of the material and are scattered. The thicker or denser parts of the material scatter more electrons. An electromagnet now focuses the electrons that were not scattered. Finally, the electrons strike a *view plate* and produce a

Another type of microscope frequently used in certain biology courses is the binocular microscope with lower magnification. This is excellent for teacher demonstrations and for students working with specimens which are too large to be observed under monocular microscopes.

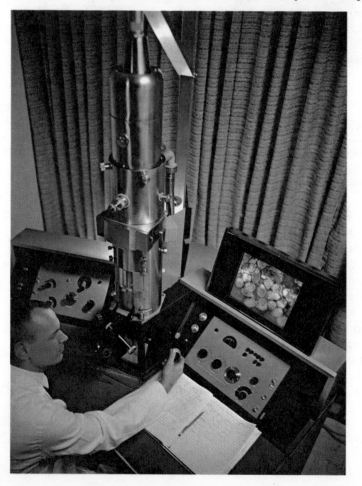

1–6 A biologist using an electron microscope. Notice that the image of the specimen appears on a television screen. (courtesy Parke, Davis & Co.)

visible image. The areas that scattered electrons in the material appear as dark areas on the view plate.

Often, a photograph of the view-plate image is made. If the photograph is then enlarged, very small details of the image become visible. Of course, only details that were present in the image in the first place can be brought out in this way.

With one set of electromagnets, an electron microscope magnifies from 1,400 to 32,000 times. By changing one electromagnet, a useful magnification of 100,000 to 200,000 times can be reached. If a photograph of this image is enlarged five times, total magnification can reach one million times actual size.

A newer model of the electron microscope makes an image of the *surface* of the object. It is capable of very high magnification. It is called a *scanning electron microscope*. This has been a useful addition to the biologists' tools.

In this chapter, we have seen some of the methods and tools that biologists use in their work. Now we can move on and consider the living condition itself.

Ask students to do research on the scanning electron microscope (SEM). They may be interested in the report on the SEM in Time-Life, *Nature-Science Annual*, 1971. Some students may want to report on other recent advances in electron microscopes.

1–7 Blood cells observed through:
a) light microscope. (Carolina Biological Supply Co.)
b) scanning electron microscope. (Manfred Kage, Peter Arnold)

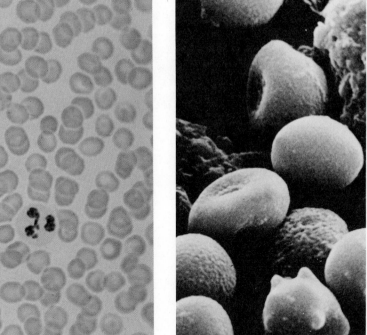
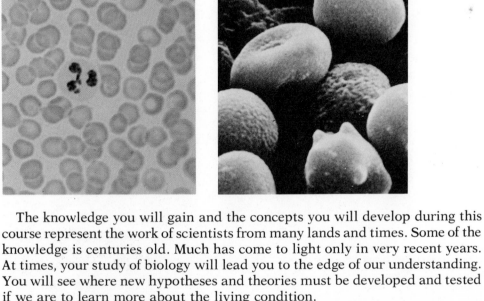

The knowledge you will gain and the concepts you will develop during this course represent the work of scientists from many lands and times. Some of the knowledge is centuries old. Much has come to light only in very recent years. At times, your study of biology will lead you to the edge of our understanding. You will see where new hypotheses and theories must be developed and tested if we are to learn more about the living condition.

You will have many chances to use the scientific methods which have led biologists to their great discoveries. How curious are you? How closely do you

SUMMARY

observe the living world around you? What is your place in the world of living things? Your study of biology can help you to find some answers.

BIOLOGICALLY SPEAKING			
research method	control	magnification
hypothesis	theory	resolution
single variable	pure science	electron microscope
experimental factor	applied science	

QUESTIONS FOR REVIEW

1. Give examples of scientific achievements that show science as a universal effort.
2. Describe the steps of the research method.
3. We often think of research as being in the laboratory. Why is the library important?
4. What is the purpose of a control in a scientific experiment?
5. Distinguish between a hypothesis and a theory.
6. What is the difference between pure and applied science?
7. Distinguish between magnification and resolution of a light microscope.
8. Describe the difference in the pictures obtained from an electron microscope and a scanning electron microscope.

APPLYING PRINCIPLES AND CONCEPTS

1. Discuss ways in which progress in biology has paralleled the perfecting of the microscope.
2. Outline a controlled experiment designed to test a single factor.
3. Discuss the advantages of an electron microscope over the limitations of the light microscope.

2-1 Mountain goats. Name the living and nonliving things in the photograph. (Bob and Ira Spring)

The Living Condition

OBJECTIVES

- DISTINGUISH between living and nonliving.
- LIST the characteristics of living things.
- NAME the five stages in the life span of an organism.
- UNDERSTAND why organisms must adapt to their environment.
- COMPARE spontaneous generation and biogenesis.
- EXPLAIN the roles of Redi and Spallanzani in the theory of spontaneous generation.
- DESCRIBE Pasteur's experiment that proved biogenesis.

Point out to students that there are living organisms in the above photograph that they cannot see with the naked eye. Refer to the study of the microscope in the previous chapter.

THE LIVING AND THE NONLIVING

What is life? Where does it come from? In order to answer these questions, we must first understand what we mean by the words *living* and *nonliving*.

Look at a nature photograph. You should have no trouble separating living things from nonliving in this scene. The plants and the animals are **organisms.** That is, they are *complete and entire living things*. **Organisms are made up of substances organized into living systems.** On the other hand, the water, rocks, and fallen log are *nonliving*. Their substances are organized very differently from the substances of the organisms.

Clearly, the living and nonliving conditions are different. Yet they are also closely related. The substances that make up organisms come, directly or indirectly, from nonliving soil, air, and water. And when an organism dies, its substances return to the nonliving state. What, then, *is* the difference between living and nonliving? What do we mean when we say that a thing is "alive"?

Characteristics of Living Things

ORGANISMS ORGANIZE PROTOPLASM

Life is a complex system of substances organized in a special state of chemical activity. We often call this system *protoplasm*. Only in living things are substances organized in this way. In other words, **only organisms organize protoplasm.**

If we were to analyze protoplasm chemically, we would find it to be about seventy percent water. Protein, fats, oil, carbohydrates, and minerals make up the remainder of the substance.

The composition of protoplasm is constantly changing. The cells are continuously manufacturing different substances and breaking down other substances. Protoplasm never remains constant.

At one time, biologists thought that protoplasm was a definite, living substance. Today we know that this is not so. In the first place, protoplasm is not a definite "substance" in the way that water, salts, sugars, and acids are "substances." Protoplasm differs from one kind of plant or animal to another. It also differs in individuals of the same kind. In fact, protoplasm even differs in different *parts* of an individual. On top of all this, the makeup of any given bit of protoplasm is changing constantly.

As for "living," protoplasm itself is not "alive." None of the proteins, carbohydrates, fats, or other substances of which protoplasm is made are living. Yet when these substances are organized into a system by an organism, the state of chemical activity we call the *living condition* is established.

It may seem that the concept of protoplasm is not very clear. Yet no matter how greatly protoplasm differs from one organism to another, all protoplasm is alike in certain basic ways. The term *protoplasm* is a helpful one if we remember that it does not refer to a definite, living substance. Instead, **protoplasm refers to the complex, constantly changing system of substances that establishes the living condition.**

ORGANISMS USE ENERGY CONSTANTLY

All chemical activities need energy. Since life is a state of constant chemical activity, it needs a constant supply of energy. Almost all of the energy used by living things comes from the sun. Much of this energy is stored in the complex chemical substances we call *foods*. Both plants and animals break down foods and release this stored energy. The energy is then used to support other life processes. **Life continues only as long as energy is supplied and put to use.**

ORGANISMS ARE MADE UP OF CELLS

All organisms are made up of cells—one cell, a few cells, or billions of cells. For this reason, cells have been called the *common unit of life*. In this course, you will study many different organisms —from bacteria to seed plants, from ameba to human beings. In every case, you will be dealing with cells. Some will be fairly simple, others more complex. But always, you will find that **cells are the basic units in which substances are organized in the living condition.**

Cells may remain for some time after an organism dies, so their presence alone does not prove a living condition. However, we know that **cells are produced only by organisms and are never organized by nonliving materials.**

At this point, we should mention the problem of viruses. Viruses are not cells. They are *subcellular*, or less complex than cells, in their makeup. Yet, they have certain chemical properties that are found only in living cells. Are viruses organisms? Are they

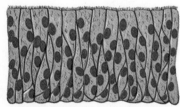

animal cells

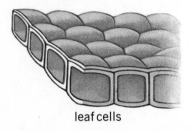

leaf cells

2–2 The basic units of all living substances are cells.
a) animal cells
b) plant cells

living? Or are they a link between the living and nonliving states? We will explore these questions when we study viruses in Chapter Fifteen.

ORGANISMS ARE CAPABLE OF GROWTH

· During at least part of their lives, all organisms grow larger. But nonliving things such as icicles and crystals can grow larger, too. What, then, do we mean when we say that growth is a characteristic of the living condition? What kind of growth are we talking about?

An icicle grows larger as more and more water freezes on its surface. A crystal grows larger in much the same way. In either case, the material "grows" only as more material of the same kind attaches to its surface.

The growth of organisms is not at all like this. A tree doesn't grow by collecting more "tree" on its surface. You don't grow by sticking food onto your skin. In fact, you don't even grow simply by taking food into your body. Your growth involves a complex series of chemical processes. During these processes, the food you take in is greatly changed. In other words, living things do not simply gather more of their own material, they organize it.

Of course, many plants and animals live long after growth seems to have stopped. But they have only stopped growing *larger*. They are still growing in another way. All organisms must constantly replace the materials of which they are made. This growth by replacement continues as long as an organism lives.

ORGANISMS PRODUCE LIKE ORGANISMS

If someone asked you to describe a tiger, you probably would have no trouble. You could tell what a tiger looks like and how large tigers usually grow. With only slight changes, your description would fit almost any full-grown tiger. What allows you to make

The majority of viruses cannot be seen under the light microscope. However, the electron microscope can magnify viruses many thousands of times.

The growth of living organisms is dependent on genetics, metabolism, and nutrition. Stress to students the importance of these three factors in determining different growth rates.

2–3 A bison with its offspring. Like produces like. (Allan Roberts)

Five Stages of Life Span

Beginning

Growth

Maturity

Decline

Death

2–4 The five stages in the life span
of a chicken.

such a description? How can you be sure that a baby tiger won't
grow up to look like a horse, or even a tree?

The answer, of course, lies in the old saying that *like produces
like*. We expect mature plants and animals to be like their parents
in both form and size. Have you ever wondered why this is so?
This is a mystery that will be discussed in our study of heredity
in Unit 2.

ORGANISMS HAVE A LIFE SPAN

A rock you pick up may be a million years old. And it may not
change much for another million years or so. The substances of the
rock are organized in a very different way from those of organisms.
Life is activity. When conditions no longer favor this activity, life
ends. **All organisms have a fairly definite period of life, which we call
the *life span*.**

We may divide the life span of any organism into five stages.
These stages are (1) beginning, (2) growth, (3) maturity, (4) decline, and (5) death. After an organism is formed, it goes through
a period of rapid growth. This growth period may last for minutes,
weeks, months, or years, depending on the organism. As the plant
or animal grows larger, the rate of growth decreases. Finally
maturity is reached. During this period, growth is reduced to repair and replacement of the organism's substances. At last the
organism reaches a point at which it can no longer repair or replace all damaged or worn-out materials. This marks the period
of decline, which ends in death.

How long can an organism live? The answer differs greatly for
different organisms. Certain insects live only a few weeks. Five
years is old for some fish. A horse may reach an age of thirty or
more. A white oak may live five hundred years. Certain kinds of
California redwood trees would be young at that age and might live
for thousands of years. For human beings, the average life span in
the United States is about seventy years. Perhaps in a few generations we can lengthen this span.

We say that a definite life span is a characteristic of all living
things. But why does life have this limit? If an organism could continue to organize and replace its substances, couldn't it go on
living forever? Perhaps it could, if certain changes could be avoided.
But we are only beginning to learn about the processes involved in
these changes.

Of course, in a way, some organisms *do* live forever. In your study
of biology, you will deal with many one-celled organisms such
as bacteria. A bacterium may be formed and reach maturity in a
half hour or less. At this point, it splits into two bacteria, which
then grow and repeat the process. In this way, a bacterium never
dies of old age. It lives as long as conditions allow growth and reproduction. The same is true for ameba and other one-celled organisms. You may already have thought that any ameba alive today
is part of the first ameba that ever lived.

ORGANISMS CAN RESPOND TO THEIR ENVIRONMENT

A living organism is able to respond to conditions outside itself. We refer to this function of living systems as *irritability*. An organism responds to a *stimulus* from the environment. The stimulus may be light, temperature, water, sound, pressure, the presence of chemical substances or food sources, or a threat to life. The organism's *response* is the way it reacts to a stimulus.

Different organisms respond in very different ways. For example, a plant may have a growth response. This happens when a root pushes toward water or a stem grows unevenly and bends toward light. Animals can react in more complex ways. Sight, hearing, taste, touch, and smell are responses to conditions in the environment. More complex responses include fleeing from or fighting an enemy, hunting for food, and seeking or building shelter.

Nonliving substances may change as conditions change. For example, water freezes or turns to steam at different temperatures. But such changes in form are not responses. Only living organisms can respond to a stimulus.

ORGANISMS ARE AFFECTED BY THEIR ENVIRONMENT

All organisms face a constant struggle for life. The environment plays a key role in this struggle. For factors in the environment both support life and threaten it.

Exactly what is the environment? **An organism's *environment* is all the conditions under which the organism lives. The environment includes physical factors such as weather, air and water supply, light, soil conditions, and so on. It also includes all of the many life forms that share the physical environment.**

The physical environment differs greatly from place to place. Consider the differences between a desert and a rainy jungle, for example. As conditions vary, so do life forms. Desert plants and animals could not survive in the jungle, nor could jungle life survive in the desert.

An organism may be well suited to its physical environment. Even so, the organism must compete with the other living things around it. Sometimes it competes for food or for other things necessary to life. For example, a young tree on the forest floor must compete with many other plants for growing room. Organisms must also compete with natural enemies. For instance, robins are a constant threat to worms and caterpillars. But hawks, crows, and cats in turn present a constant threat to robins.

VARIATION AND ADAPTATION

Conditions in an environment change from time to time. Sometimes the changes are sudden, as when there is a fire, a storm, or a long dry period. Other changes may take place over a very long time. These include such things as changes in climate, changes in

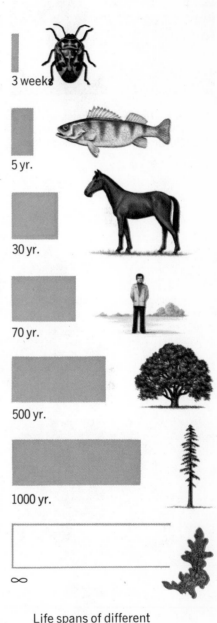

3 weeks

5 yr.

30 yr.

70 yr.

500 yr.

1000 yr.

∞

Life spans of different organisms vary greatly

2–5 Organisms differ greatly in their life spans.

2-6 This deer illustrates adaptation and natural selection. (Leonard Lee Rue III, Monkmeyer Press Photos)

Natural selection allows those organisms with a certain "advantage" to survive. This usually results in the stronger members of the species surviving.

soil, and the steady wearing down of mountains and hills.

If organisms are not suited to a new condition, they can no longer survive. In order to survive they must do one of two things. They must either move to a better environment, or change. Change does not occur in one generation but over many generations.

The characteristic that allows organisms to survive changing conditions is called **variation.** No two offspring are exactly alike, nor are they exactly like their parents. Many of the differences, or variations, have little to do with whether the offspring survives. Only rarely does a variation give an organism a better chance of surviving. But if such a variation is passed on to other offspring, they too will have a better chance of surviving. In time, all organisms of that type may have the helpful characteristic. **This process, in which a species slowly or rapidly becomes better suited to survive, is called *adaptation.***

In speaking of adaptation, people often say that an organism changes to fit its environment. This does not happen. Plants and animals do not change *in order* to survive. They survive *because* change has taken place.

The northern white-tailed deer did not develop long legs in order to run fast. Instead, deer that had long legs could run fast and so survived. In turn, they produced offspring that also had long legs and could run fast. Deer with short legs could not run as fast. Often, these deer did not survive long enough to produce offspring which would also have short legs. In the end, all northern white-tailed deer had the helpful characteristic of long legs.

Whether or not the variations are helpful, the possibility of variation remains a characteristic of the living condition.

ORGANISMS CAN REPRODUCE

We have just seen the role of reproduction in variation and adaptation. Of course, the ability to reproduce is necessary on a much more direct level. Since all organisms have a definite life span, they must reproduce if life is to continue.

Reproduction takes many forms in the living world. A cell may reproduce by splitting. In many cases, parent organisms form special reproductive cells. In still other cases, a part of the parent organism may be removed and is then able to grow on its own. (A good example of this is the cutting of a stem or root of a plant.) Yet all forms of reproduction are alike in principle. In each, either a mass divides or a small part of a mass is separated from the parent. A human being develops from a bit of living matter no larger than a pinhead. The substance of this matter comes from both parents. It can live and grow for a lifetime.

Only living things produce offspring. And with this we end our list of the characteristics of the living condition. Now we can go on to the second question asked at the beginning of this chapter: Where does life come from?

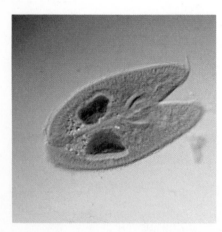

2-7 Single celled organism reproducing. (Manfred Kage, Peter Arnold)

Life Comes from Life

THE PRINCIPLE OF BIOGENESIS

As we have seen, the life of every organism comes from its parents or parent. Does life ever spring from nonliving matter? We can find no evidence of this happening. So far as we can tell, *life comes only from life.* Biologists call this the principle of **biogenesis** (BY-oh-JENN-uh-siss). Though all the evidence argues for it, biogenesis actually is a fairly new idea.

Ask students to bring in living and nonliving things and discuss the relationships that exist between them.

BELIEF IN SPONTANEOUS GENERATION

From ancient times until less than a century ago, most people believed that certain nonliving materials could change directly into living organisms. A closely related belief was that one life form could give rise to a completely different form. For example, a tree could produce a lamb or a goose. We say that people who believed these things believed in **spontaneous generation.**

Many stories of spontaneous generation had to do with smaller animals such as insects and worms. This was natural, since people in early times had little knowledge of how such animals grew and developed. One of the strangest stories came from the Belgian doctor Jean van Helmont some three centuries ago. According to van Helmont, a dirty shirt placed in a container of wheat would produce

Spontaneous generation, or abiogenesis, was widely accepted prior to the nineteenth century. Many early scientists contributed to the study of abiogenesis. Have students report on the experiments of any of the following scientists involved in disproving the concept of spontaneous generation: Francesco Redi, Hermann Boerhaave, Lazzaro Spallanzani, and Louis Pasteur.

2–8 Spontaneous generation myths: Frog and fish from mud, geese from barnacles, mice from wheat.

mice in 21 days. The mice would be formed in the fermenting wheat. The human sweat in the shirt would supply an "active principle" needed for the process.

There were many other ideas about spontaneous generation. For example, frogs and fish were thought to develop in clouds and to fall to earth with rain. Also, it was believed that flies came from the dead, decaying bodies of animals such as horses. These flies really came from maggots that hatched from eggs laid in the body. But since no one had seen the eggs being laid, the belief was not questioned for centuries.

REDI ATTACKS SPONTANEOUS GENERATION

Until the late nineteenth century, most scientists accepted the idea of spontaneous generation without question. There was no real evidence for this idea. In those times, people often drew conclusions that were not supported by facts. But a seventeenth-century Italian scientist, Francesco Redi (RAY-dee) demanded proof. Could decaying flesh change into flies? Redi said no. Flies came from eggs laid by flies. The decaying meat was nothing more than food for the maggots.

In 1668, Redi tested his hypothesis in an experiment. He placed bits of veal, snake, fish, and eel in four different clean jars. He then did the same with four other jars. One set of jars, which today we could call the *control set*, was left open. The other set,

2–9 Redi's first experiment to disprove spontaneous generation.

Experiment 1

beginning of experiment

open jars

end of experiment

beginning of experiment

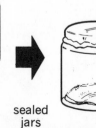

sealed jars

end of experiment

which we would call the *experimental set*, was tightly sealed. Flies soon gathered inside the open jars and laid eggs. In a short time, maggots appeared in all of the open jars. Several weeks later, Redi opened the sealed jars. He found rotten meat but no maggots. From this evidence, Redi concluded that maggots hatch from eggs laid by flies and are not produced by spontaneous generation.

If Redi had stopped there, his point would not have been proved. Those who believed in spontaneous generation would have said that air was needed as an "active principle." Air could not enter the sealed jars. So Redi's first experiment involved not one but two valuable factors: air and flies.

But Redi did a second experiment. He filled four jars with the same materials as before. But this time he covered the jars only with a fine cloth. Air could pass through the cloth but flies could not. As the meat decayed, flies laid eggs on the cloth, but no maggots appeared in the meat.

This second experiment gave strong proof that flies come only from flies and not from rotting meat. But the supporters of spontaneous generation continued in their belief. What was true of flies might not be true of such animals as worms. Though flies came only from flies, other organisms might still arise by spontaneous generation.

THE MICROSCOPE AND SPONTANEOUS GENERATION

By the eighteenth century, the microscope had become a widely used tool of science. Biologists were viewing all sorts of microscopic organisms that had not been visible before. Samples of broths and sugar solutions were seen to be swarming with bacteria, yeasts, molds, and other organisms. Where had these organisms come from? Some scientists supported spontaneous generation as the only possible answer. Another group argued that the organisms could come only from other organisms.

The English scientist John Needham supported the idea of spontaneous generation. Needham boiled a meat broth for a few minutes in loosely sealed flasks. After a few days, he viewed the broth

Review the scientific method discussed in Chapter One by using Redi's experiment as an example.

Ask some students to repeat Redi's two experiments concerning spontaneous generation. The experiments will hold much greater meaning for the students if they are reenacted in front of them.

A class demonstration of microscopic organisms in a broth infusion should be prepared. Students will be interested in studying the organisms in the hay infusion under the microscope.

2–10 Redi's second experiment. This experiment was designed to disprove his critic's argument that in his first experiment air was not admitted into the sealed jars.

Experiment 2

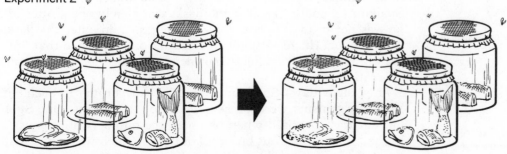

jars covered with fine netting

Stress to students the importance of having *all* the facts in an experiment. Needham's conclusion overlooked the fact that the flasks were loosely sealed.

Needham's Experiment

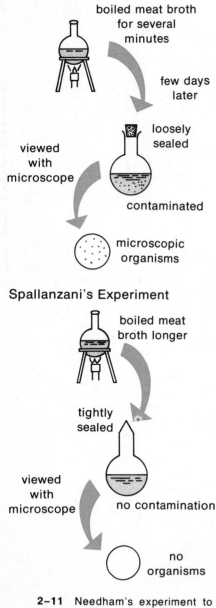

boiled meat broth
for several
minutes

few days
later

loosely
sealed

viewed
with
microscope

contaminated

microscopic
organisms

Spallanzani's Experiment

boiled meat
broth longer

tightly
sealed

viewed
with
microscope

no contamination

no
organisms

2–11 Needham's experiment to prove spontaneous generation and Spallanzani's experiment to disprove spontaneous generation.

with a microscope and found it teeming with microscopic organisms. He repeated the experiment with other meat and vegetable broths. The results were the same. Needham claimed that boiling had destroyed all life in the broths. And since the flasks were sealed, he said, the organsims present after standing must have formed in spontaneous generation.

SPALLANZANI QUESTIONS NEEDHAM'S CONCLUSIONS

About twenty-five years after Needham's experiments, Lazzaro Spallanzani of Italy led an attack against the conclusions Needham had drawn. Spallanzani felt that Needham had not boiled the broths long enough to destroy all life and had not sealed the flasks tightly enough. If so, the organisms found later in the broths could have come from organisms that survived the boiling. Or they could have come from organisms that entered the flasks from the air. In any case, Spallanzani hypothesized that the organisms had not come from spontaneous generation.

Spallanzani now did a series of experiments of his own. He boiled some seeds in water for a short time and placed the broth in glass flasks. He then completely sealed each flask by melting the glass together at the top. All the flasks were placed in boiling water for one hour and then removed. After several days, Spallanzani opened each flask and looked for evidence of life in the broth. None of the broths contained living organisms.

To Spallanzani, this experiment proved that the organisms found by Needham could not come from spontaneous generation. But this evidence did not satisfy Needham's supporters. They claimed that boiling for an hour had destroyed the "active principle" of the broth. This, they said, was why spontaneous generation had not taken place.

Spallanzani felt certain that no "active principle" was destroyed by boiling. To meet such claims, he did a second series of experiments.

Spallanzani reasoned that if boiling destroyed some "active principle," longer boiling would destroy *more* of the "principle." Thus, he boiled one set of flasks for half an hour, another for an hour, a third for an hour and a half, and a fourth for two hours. After boiling, the flasks were loosely sealed and carefully marked. Spallanzani could have left the flasks completely open. After all, he was not trying to show that organisms could enter the flasks from the air. His experiment was meant only to prove that boiling did not destroy an "active principle" needed for spontaneous generation.

After eight days, Spallanzani checked the broths in each set. Living organisms were present in all of the broths. But Spallanzani was surprised when he noted the numbers of organisms in the broths. In all but one kind of broth (which was made with corn), *the broths boiled longest contained the most organisms!* What had happened? Spallanzani concluded that, in all but the corn broth, longer boiling dissolved more seed or egg yolk. In other words, the broths boiled longest offered the richest food supply for organisms.

Clearly, heating destroyed no "active principle" in seed broths. In fact, heating made the broths better suited for the growth of microscopic organisms. Yet the supporters of spontaneous generation did not give up in the face of this evidence. The argument went on for another fifty years. Then, at last, it was settled by a young scientist just beginning his brilliant life's work.

PASTEUR DEFEATS SPONTANEOUS GENERATION

It was Louis Pasteur, the nineteenth-century French chemist, who finally laid to rest the theory of spontaneous generation. As a young man, Pasteur was studying the chemical changes that take place as sugars turn to alcohol in wine fermentation. Many yeasts and other microscopic organisms were present in fermenting fruit juices. Pasteur was sure that these organisms came from the air. If so, dust particles, grape skins, and other materials exposed to the air must carry great numbers of such organisms. In testing this hypothesis, Pasteur carried out several experiments. Though quite simple, these experiments gave evidence that clearly defeated the supporters of spontaneous generation.

In his first series of experiments, Pasteur used several liquids that would support growth by bacteria and other organisms. Each liquid was sealed in a flask and boiled long enough to kill all organisms present. Pasteur then took the flasks to several places where the air contained different amounts of dust. In flasks opened along dusty roads, great numbers of organisms grew within a few days. Flasks opened on hills and mountains showed much less growth of organisms. These results supported Pasteur's belief that bacteria and other organisms were present in the air with dust.

Pasteur set out to find support for his hypothesis under the more controlled conditions of his laboratory. He prepared a liquid containing sugar and yeast and poured it into flasks. He heated the long neck of each flask and bent it into an S-shape somewhat like a swan's neck. The liquid was then boiled for several minutes, forcing air out of the flask. As the liquid slowly cooled, air returned to the flask through the neck.

Throughout the experiment, air moved into the flasks. But water and dust particles from the air settled in the trap formed by the swan's-neck curve. Thus, no organisms appeared in the sugar liquid even though it was in constant contact with the outside air. On the other hand, a flask could be tipped so that the liquid came in contact with the trapped dust. If this was done, great numbers of organisms were present in the liquid within a few days.

No argument could stand against Pasteur's simple experiment. It was clear that boiling had not destroyed the ability of the liquid to support organisms. Nor had the flasks kept out any "active principle" that might be in the air. Both the liquid and the air

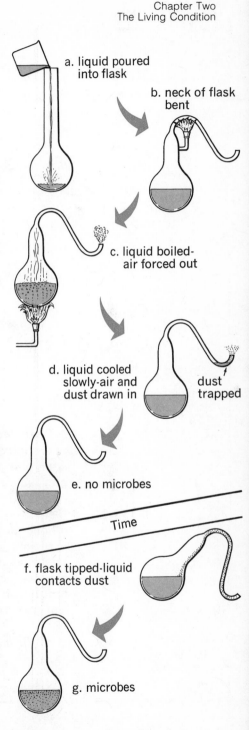

a. liquid poured into flask

b. neck of flask bent

c. liquid boiled-air forced out

d. liquid cooled slowly-air and dust drawn in

dust trapped

e. no microbes

Time

f. flask tipped-liquid contacts dust

g. microbes

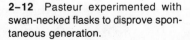

2-12 Pasteur experimented with swan-necked flasks to disprove spontaneous generation.

would support the growth of bacteria and other organisms. But these organisms had to come from outside the flask, not from spontaneous generation within it.

The theory of spontaneous generation, accepted for centuries without any real evidence, was defeated. From Pasteur's time to the present, all experiments have supported biogenesis: Life comes only from life.

A QUESTION YOU MAY HAVE ASKED

We have seen the idea of spontaneous generation defeated by the concept that life comes only from life. Yet a question remains that you yourself may have asked. *How did the first life on earth begin, if not by spontaneous generation?*

We do not know the answer to this question. We may never know. We cannot say for certain that spontaneous generation never took place. We cannot say for certain that it never will take place. Who knows? Perhaps, on some far planet, life is beginning by spontaneous generation at this very moment. Or perhaps, someday, a biologist will organize life by mixing together just the right nonliving materials. And what about the viruses? Are they living at some times, nonliving at others?

What we can say is that we have found no evidence for spontaneous generation. All the evidence that we have supports the principle of biogenesis. In the world as we know it, life comes only from life.

SUMMARY

To understand what we mean by the word *life*, it is best to compare living and nonliving things. In this chapter, you have considered several characteristics of living organisms. All living things, from the simplest to the most complex, share these characteristics. Nonliving things do not.

It is true that living things are organized from nonliving substances. But there is no magic in this. It is simply part of the orderly, complex, and wonderful chemical activity of all living organisms.

Biogenesis is a basic concept accepted by all biologists today. There is no scientific evidence to support the old idea of spontaneous generation. Yet we wonder if spontaneous generation did take place at one time, giving rise to the first life on earth. Biologists have offered several theories as to how life began. But no proof has been found for any of these theories.

BIOLOGICALLY SPEAKING

organism	irritability	adaption
protoplasm	environment	biogenesis
life span	variation	spontaneous generation

QUESTIONS FOR REVIEW

1. What is the biological concept of an organism?
2. List the main characteristics of living things.
3. Give a definition of protoplasm in line with modern biological concepts.

4. In what way is growth by living things different from nonliving things?
5. List the five stages in the life span of an organism.
6. Define irritability.
7. Explain the relationship of variations to adaptations.
8. State the theory of biogenesis.
9. Give examples of myths based on belief in spontaneous generation.
10. Describe Redi's experiments to disprove spontaneous generation.
11. How did Spallanzani refute Needham's support of spontaneous generation?
12. Describe Pasteur's contribution to the belief in biogenesis.

APPLYING PRINCIPLES AND CONCEPTS

1. Describe how Redi's experiments coincide with modern scientific practice. Why was his second experiment of special importance?
2. Explain how Pasteur accounted for all variable factors in his experiments disproving spontaneous generation of microorganisms.
3. Discuss various ways in which living organisms respond to external stimuli.

chapter three

The Chemical Basis of Life

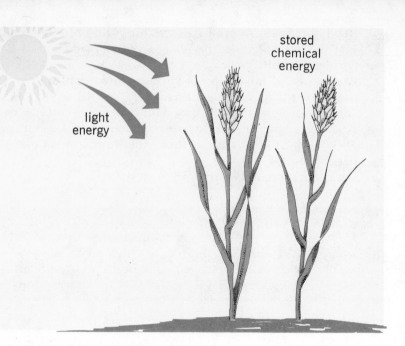
light energy

stored chemical energy

3-1 The wheat plant stores energy from the sun.

OBJECTIVES

- DEFINE the terms matter and energy.
- DESCRIBE the changes that matter can undergo.
- IDENTIFY the different forms of energy.
- DESCRIBE the structure of the atom.
- DEFINE isotopes and their use.
- EXPLAIN chemical and ionic bonding.
- DISTINGUISH between solutions and colloids.
- DISTINGUISH between inorganic compounds and organic compounds.
- EXPLAIN the functions of carbohydrates, lipids, proteins, and nucleic acids.
- EXPLAIN the role of enzymes in the living cell.

BIOLOGY, MATTER, AND ENERGY

Matter and energy make up our universe and all living things. Clearly, the study of biology must deal with matter and energy as they relate to life. As you continue to explore the living condition, your need for an understanding of matter and energy will grow.

The questions we can ask about matter, energy, and life are endless. Think of a single wheat plant, for example. What chemical substances does it take from the soil and air? How does it store energy from the sun? How do animals release this energy when they eat the wheat as food? How do the animals organize the wheat substances into living body structures?

Scientists understand many of the changes in matter and energy involved in the living condition. Other changes are not yet understood. Biology will interest you much more if you understand some basic facts about matter and energy in living things.

WHAT IS MATTER?

You probably have studied matter and changes in matter in other science courses. You may remember that **matter is anything that occupies space and has mass.** Anything you could name, except energy, would be matter. Matter includes all solids, liquids, and gases. These states of matter seem quite different, but they are all alike in certain basic ways. If we could magnify solids, gases, and liquids millions of times, we would see that all are made up of very tiny particles. Further, we would see that these particles are moving constantly.

In the *solid state*, the particles are packed closely together. Yet even in a dense solid such as lead, the particles vibrate constantly and have space between them. In the *liquid state*, the space between particles is much greater. The particles vibrate more actively and move freely through the liquid. In the *gaseous state*, the particles are much farther apart and move even more freely. In some gases, such as chlorine, the particles are close enough together for the gas to be visible. Often, though, the particles of a gas are so far apart that the gas cannot be seen. Air is made up of several gases, none of which can be seen. Yet gases are matter. Even hydrogen, the least dense gas, has mass and occupies space.

CHANGES IN MATTER

The solid, liquid, and gaseous states arise from differences in particle activity and space between particles. Thus, a substance may change from one state to another if particle activity and spacing are changed. Such **physical changes** take place often. The physical changes of water are a good example. At or below the freezing point, water molecules are close together in the solid state called ice. If the ice is heated, the molecules vibrate more rapidly and move farther apart, forming water in its liquid state. At the boiling point, liquid water changes to steam, a gas.

A **chemical change** is different. Here, matter changes *from one substance to another*, not simply to a different state. The burning of wood is an example of a chemical change. As wood burns, its substances are changed into quite different substances. These include several gases which are given off into the air. One of these gases is steam, or water in the gaseous state. It might surprise you that burning wood gives off water. But remember that wood is formed in a series of complex chemical changes in a living tree. The tree used many different substances from the soil and air. One of these substances was water.

ENERGY AND ENERGY CHANGES

Energy supports life and plays a part in all life activities. It is involved with all matter and all changes in matter. It is hard to define energy clearly. But we often say that **energy is that which is capable of doing work or causing change.**

We also speak of two general types of energy. **Kinetic energy** is energy in action—energy that actually is doing work or causing change. The *motion* of a mass, such as a moving car or running water, is one form of kinetic energy. Kinetic energy also takes the form of *radiant* energy. Such radiation included electric waves, radio waves, heat, visible light, and rays such as X rays.

The other type of energy is **potential energy.** As the name suggests, potential energy represents a *potential* for doing work or causing

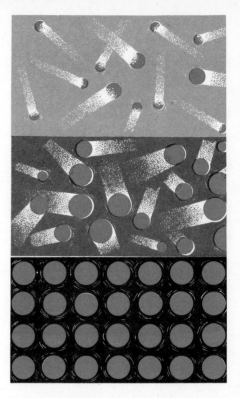

3-2 The gaseous, liquid, and solid states of matter. What characteristics of each state have been illustrated?

Ask students what happens to wood when it is cut. Is this a physical or chemical change? When a piece of cut wood is burned, what type of change occurs? Ask students for other examples of physical and chemical changes.

Stress to students the understanding of the Law of Conservation of Energy that states: energy may neither by created nor destroyed, but may pass from one form to another.

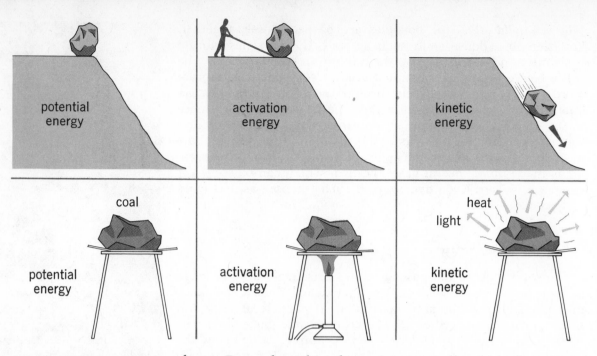

3-3 In both cases, potential energy is converted into kinetic energy by adding activation energy.

change. But such work or change is not actually taking place. **Chemical energy is one form of potential energy.**

Potential energy and kinetic energy are closely related. Each can be changed into the other. Chemical energy is stored in substances we call *compounds*. Coal is such a compound. The energy stored in coal remains potential until the coal is burned. Then the stored energy is released as heat and light, two forms of kinetic energy. The energy needed to start the coal burning is called *activation energy.*

Energy changes take place in all living organisms. For example, chemical energy is stored in food compounds called sugars, the basic fuel of life. As these foods are broken down, their stored energy is released. This energy may be changed to energy of motion or used to support other chemical changes needed for life.

ELEMENTS—THE ALPHABET OF MATTER

There are more than half a million words in the English language. Yet the spellings of these words come from the 26 letters of our alphabet. In much the same way, all the matter of our world is formed from 92 natural *chemical elements.* Like letters of the alphabet, these elements may be combined in many different ways. But most of the natural elements are quite rare. Fewer than 15 form 99 percent of the substances of the earth. So if the elements are a chemical alphabet, most of the words are "spelled" with only a few letters.

Elements are made up of very small units of matter called *atoms.* Even the largest atoms are too small to be seen with the most powerful microscope. Atoms are the basic units of matter. This means that, *in ordinary chemical changes*, substances are broken down to the atoms of which they are made. But the atoms themselves are not split. You can reduce a word to its letters, but you cannot split the letters.

We often represent an atom of an element with a *symbol*. In most cases, the symbol is the first letter or two of the element's name. For example, the symbol *C* represents one atom of the element carbon. *Ca* stands for calcium and *Cl* for chlorine. *H* represents one atom of hydrogen, while *O* stands for an oxygen atom. Some chemical symbols come from old Latin names for elements. For example, *Na* stands for sodium *(natrium)* and *Fe* for iron *(ferrum).*

Students should be given a complete list of elements. Those elements, such as carbon (C), oxygen (O), and nitrogen (N), should be pointed out as elements commonly found in living things. Such lists are readily available in high school chemistry texts. Also, refer students to p. 34, Table 3-1.

THE STRUCTURE OF ATOMS

For several centuries, scientists thought that atoms were the smallest possible form of matter. That is, an atom could not be divided into any smaller particles. Today we know that atoms *are* made up of still smaller particles. Further, all atoms are made up of the *same kinds* of particles. For example, an oxygen atom is made up of exactly the same kinds of particles as an iron atom. What makes the two atoms different is that these particles are present in different numbers and arranged in different ways. The same thing is true of the atoms of any two different elements.

Let's take a look at the structure of atoms. We can begin with the smallest and simplest atom, that of the element hydrogen. The center of an atom is called the **nucleus.** The nucleus of an ordinary hydrogen atom contains a single particle, known as a *proton.* The proton has a positive electric charge. Moving around the proton is a single, very small particle called an *electron.* Compared with the proton, the electron has almost no weight. But the electron does carry a negative electric charge. Thus, the charges of the proton and electron balance, and the atom as a whole has no charge.

The second simplest element, helium, has two protons and two electrons in its atom. Carbon, an element you will hear much about in biology, has 6 protons and 6 electrons. Oxygen has 8 protons and 8 electrons. The largest natural atom, uranium, has 92 protons and 92 electrons. The number of protons in the nucleus is called the **atomic number.** There are 92 atomic numbers in the series of natural elements.

The movement of electrons about a nucleus has been compared with bees swarming around a hive. That is, electrons do not follow clear, regular paths. But electrons do move at given distances from the nucleus. We speak of these different distances as *energy levels.* One or two electrons orbit at the first energy level, nearest the nucleus. Then there is a gap out to the second energy level, where as many as eight electrons may orbit. Up to eight electrons also may occupy the third energy level. In larger and larger atoms, the electrons are arranged in more and more complex ways.

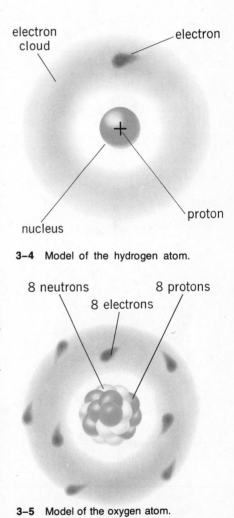

3–4 Model of the hydrogen atom.

8 neutrons   8 protons
8 electrons

3–5 Model of the oxygen atom.

3-6 Model of the chlorine atom showing the different energy levels.

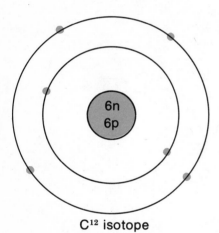

C^{12} isotope

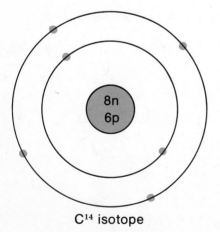

C^{14} isotope

3-7 The isotope carbon-14 has 8 neutrons while ordinary carbon-12 has 6 neutrons.

A third kind of particle found in atoms is the *neutron*. You will remember that the ordinary hydrogen nucleus contains only a single proton. The nuclei of all other atoms contain one or more neutrons as well. Neutrons have about the same mass as protons but have no electric charge. Thus, a neutron adds to the mass of an atom but does not affect its chemical activity. The **atomic mass** of an atom is the total number of protons and neutrons present. For example, ordinary carbon atoms have 6 protons and 6 neutrons. Carbon, then, has an atomic *mass* of 12, with the atomic *number* 6. An ordinary hydrogen atom, with one twelfth the mass of an ordinary carbon atom, has an atomic mass of 1. An ordinary oxygen atom, with 8 protons and 8 neutrons, has the atomic number 8 and an atomic mass of 16. If a uranium atom has an atomic mass of 238 and has 92 protons, how many neutrons are present?

WHAT ARE ISOTOPES?

We have spoken several times of "ordinary" atoms of an element. Are there atoms that are not "ordinary"? The answer is yes. Some elements have several different kinds of atoms. The difference has to do with the number of neutrons present. *All* atoms of a given element have the same number of protons. But the number of neutrons may vary. For this reason, different atoms of the same element may have different atomic masses. We refer to these different forms of the same element as **isotopes.**

The isotopes of carbon may have 5, 6, 7, or 8 neutrons. Ordinary carbon, with 6 neutrons, is known as carbon-12. Carbon-14 has 8 neutrons. This isotope has been very important in biological research, as you will see later. Oxygen, too, has several isotopes. Ordinary oxygen is oxygen-16, with 8 neutrons. Oxygen-18, with 10 neutrons, is another isotope of great importance in research.

RADIOISOTOPES

Certain isotopes of some elements send off charged particles and radiant energy from their nuclei. This kind of spontaneous change in an atom is called *radioactivity*. The isotopes are called **radioisotopes.**

The elements uranium and radium have natural radioisotopes. Several other radioisotopes have been produced by science. They are made by exposing isotopes that are not radioactive to the neutrons given off by nuclear reactors. Many of these radioisotopes are used in research. Some are also used in treating cancer and other diseases. You will explore some of the uses of radioisotopes as your study of biology continues.

COMPOUNDS

Early chemists discovered that some substances contain only one element, while others are made up of two or more elements.

A substance in which two or more elements are combined chemically is called a *compound*. If we think of elements as letters of a chemical alphabet, then compounds are the words they form. Just as a symbol stands for each element, a *formula* stands for a compound. The formula H_2O stands for water. This formula shows that a molecule of water is made up of two atoms of hydrogen and one atom of oxygen. NaCl is the formula for sodium chloride, or table salt. Cane sugar, $C_{12}H_{22}O_{11}$, is made up of carbon, hydrogen, and oxygen. There are 12 atoms of carbon, 22 of hydrogen, and 11 of oxygen in each molecule of cane sugar.

As you learn more about compounds, the following important concept will be developed:

1. Under certain conditions, *most* elements will combine with one or more other elements. We say that such elements are *chemically active*. Certain other elements show almost no chemical activity. The *inert* elements include helium, neon, argon, krypton, xenon, and radon.

2. Each element has its own *combining capacity* for joining with other elements. For example, the chemical properties of hydrogen allow it to combine with certain other elements, such as oxygen. But there are other elements with which hydrogen cannot combine.

3. In forming compounds, elements combine in *definite proportions*. In forming water, for example, two atoms of hydrogen always combine with one atom of oxygen.

4. A compound has *its own properties*. These properties are not the same as the properties of the elements making up the compound. For example, water has its own properties, and these properties are not the same as those of hydrogen and oxygen. Also, sodium chloride has none of the properties of either sodium or chlorine.

CHEMICAL BONDS

Chemical bonds are forces that hold two or more atoms together in a molecule. To understand how such bonds work, we must look more closely at electron activity. **The chemical activity of an atom depends upon the number of electrons and the way in which they are arranged. Most important are the electrons at the highest energy level, farthest from the nucleus.**

In some cases, atoms *share* electrons at the highest energy level. **The shared electrons orbit both atomic nuclei. This sharing of electrons is known as a** *covalent bond*. Certain atoms share one pair of electrons, each atom supplying one electron. The energy needed to break a covalent bond and separate the atoms is called *bond energy*.

A very different kind of bond involves a *transfer* of electrons between atoms. Some atoms tend to give up electrons. Such atoms are called *electron lenders*. Other atoms tend to gain electrons and are called *electron borrowers*. **The transfer of one or more electrons**

Point out to students that compounds are atoms that are joined together. A chemical formula represents a simple explanation of the number and kind of each atom in a compound. Ask students to write some formulas and to explain their makeup.

from one atom to another forms an *ionic bond.* Compounds involving ionic bonds are quite different from those involving covalent bonds, as you will see.

MOLECULAR AND IONIC COMPOUNDS

Atoms that share electrons in covalent bonding form units of matter called *molecules.* Some molecules are made up of two atoms of the same element. Several gaseous elements form such *diatomic molecules.* Hydrogen atoms, for example, tend very strongly to combine with other hydrogen atoms. Oxygen, nitrogen, and chlorine also form diatomic molecules. These diatomic molecules are involved in many chemical reactions in living organisms.

We represent a molecule of hydrogen as H_2. The bond in this molecule is a single bond. That is, two hydrogen atoms share one pair of electrons. Molecular chlorine, CL_2, also has a single bond. In the oxygen molecule, O_2, the two oxygen atoms share two pairs of electrons. Three pairs of electrons are shared in molecular nitrogen, N_2.

Atoms of *different* elements also combine and form molecules by covalent bonding. In a molecule of water, two hydrogen atoms form bonds with an oxygen atom. Both of these bonds are single bonds. In each, a hydrogen atom and the oxygen atom share one pair of electrons. Energy is necessary to break the bonds and release hydrogen and oxygen atoms.

A very different kind of compound is the *ionic compound.* One ionic compound is sodium chloride, or table salt, NaCl. You know that table salt is in the form of crystals. Under a hand lens, these crystals appear as small cubes. Are salt crystals made up of molecules? The answer is no because covalent bonding is not involved here.

When atoms carry positive or negative electric charges, we call them *ions.* A salt crystal is made up of great numbers of sodium and chlorine ions. Each sodium ion carries a positive charge, while each chlorine ion has a negative charge. Because of their opposite charges, sodium and chlorine ions are attracted to each other and held together in the crystal. This kind of bonding is *ionic,* not covalent.

Atoms usually are neutral. The positive charges of the protons in an atom usually exactly balance the negative charges of the electrons. Thus, the atom as a whole carries no charge. How, then, do ions and ionic bonding arise?

As we have said, the ionic bond involves an electron *transfer,* rather than a sharing. The sodium atom has 11 protons and 11 electrons, and so is neutral. The chlorine atom, with 17 protons and 17 neutrons, is also neutral. But the sodium atom is an electron lender. That is, it tends to *give up* an electron. The chlorine atom, an electron borrower, tends to *gain* an electron. The transfer of an electron from sodium to chlorine changes the electric charge on both atoms. With 11 protons and only 10

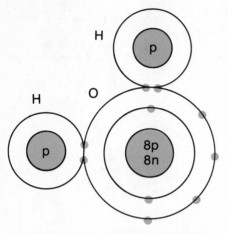

3–8 A representation of the electrons being shared in the covalent bonds of a water molecule.

Many atoms exist in a diatomic form. These atoms include hydrogen, oxygen, nitrogen, chlorine, fluorine, bromine, and iodine.

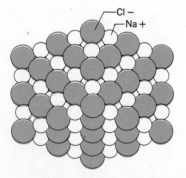

3–9 A model of some sodium chloride crystals. The sodium and chloride ions are held together in the crystals by ionic bonds.

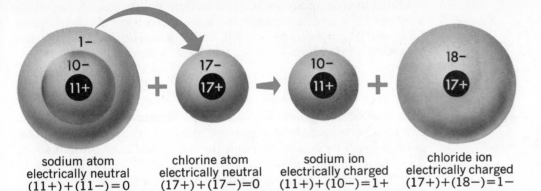

sodium atom	chlorine atom	sodium ion	chloride ion
electrically neutral	electrically neutral	electrically charged	electrically charged
(11+)+(11−)=0	(17+)+(17−)=0	(11+)+(10−)=1+	(17+)+(18−)=1−

electrons, the sodium atom becomes an ion with a charge of +1. And the chlorine ion, with 18 electrons and only 17 protons, has a charge of −1.

Ions are very important in biology. Plant roots absorb them, and we have them in our blood and tissue fluids. Ions affect the functions of muscles and nerves and, in general, are necessary to all forms of life.

MIXTURES

A *mixture* occurs when two or more elements are mixed together with no chemical change taking place. There is no bonding of atoms, and no new molecular or ionic substance is formed. We can best describe a mixture by comparing its properties with those of a compound.

1. The substances that form a mixture are placed together physically, but not joined chemically.
2. The substances in a mixture can be separated by physical means.
3. A mixture has the properties of the substances forming it.
4. When a mixture is formed, there is no chemical action involving energy changes.

SOLUTIONS AND SUSPENSIONS

There are several kinds of mixtures. For example, one substance may be dissolved in another. We call such a mixture a **solution.** The dissolved substance is called the *solute;* the substance in which it is dissolved is called the *solvent.*

A solution is formed when molecules or ions of a solute are spread evenly through molecules of a solvent. When you add sugar to water, the sugar crystals dissolve in the water. That is, sugar molecules separate from the crystals and spread evenly among the water molecules. Here, water is the solvent and sugar is the solute. At a given temperature, a given amount of water can dissolve only a given amount of sugar. When no more sugar will dissolve, we say that the solution is *saturated.*

3–10 A representation of the formation of sodium and chloride ions.

A mixture can best be defined as a *heterogeneous* as opposed to a *homogeneous* (solution) material. A mixture is not uniform and has a varying composition.

A demonstration of iron and sulfur powder may be used to demonstrate the properties of a mixture and of a compound. One may also use iron, sand, and water to make a mixture. The iron (element) and the sand (compound) will eventually settle undissolved to the bottom of the container.

Demonstrate a few simple solutions to the class. Students learn more quickly when they can see what is being discussed. This would be a good place to introduce the neutral, acid, and basic solutions and how they differ from one another.

Most ionic compounds, such as sodium chloride, dissolve easily in water. The ion pairs separate and spread through the solvent. This splitting up of ion pairs is called *dissociation*. Dissociation of sodium and chlorine ions can be represented as follows:

$$Na^+Cl^- \xrightarrow{\text{water}} Na^+ + Cl^-$$

Another kind of mixture involves particles that are much larger than ions or molecules. We call such a mixture a **suspension.** You can form a suspension by stirring starch into water. The starch particles will be spread through the water and may remain so for some time. In the end, though, the particles will settle to the bottom. They do this because the force of gravity is stronger than the force that holds them in suspension. It is the size of the particles that determines whether they will be dissolved or only suspended. In general, particles large enough to form suspensions can be seen through a light microscope.

COLLOIDAL SYSTEMS

Somewhere between solutions and suspensions lie the mixtures known as **colloids** (KAHL-oydz). Many substances, when mixed with water, break up into very large molecules or groups of smaller molecules. These particles are larger than the molecules that form solutions, yet smaller than the particles in suspensions. Because of their small size, particles in colloids remain suspended, as do molecules or ions in solutions.

In cells, large molecules or groups of molecules are suspended in water, forming colloids. The particles suspended in these systems interact with the water molecules in an interesting way. As you will see, certain properties of colloids are important to all living things.

BIOLOGICAL CHEMISTRY

We are now ready to consider chemistry only as it relates to biology. From here on, then, we will focus mainly on just 18 of the 92 natural elements. These 18 elements and their compounds are by far the most common substances in the makeup of living organisms. They supply by far the greater part of the materials needed in the chemical activities of living things.

INORGANIC COMPOUNDS—RAW MATERIALS OF LIFE

If there were no life on earth, the natural elements and many of their compounds would still exist. There still would be oxygen, nitrogen, carbon dioxide, and other gases in the air. There still would be water in lakes, rivers, and oceans, in the air, and in the great ice caps. There still would be minerals in the soil and in the salt water of the sea. In short, without life, the elements and the **inorganic compounds** of the earth would remain. Inorganic

Colloids are physical combinations of materials that are almost homogeneous in composition. For example, fog is a colloid in which water is dispersed in air. Ask students to suggest other examples of colloids.

Table 3-1 ELEMENTS ESSENTIAL TO HUMANS

ELEMENT	AMOUNT IN BODY (154-pound person)
oxygen	100.1 pounds
carbon	27.72
hydrogen	15.4
nitrogen	4.62
calcium	2.31
phosphorus	1.54
potassium	0.54
sulfur	0.35
sodium	0.23
chlorine	0.23
magnesium	0.077
iron	0.006
manganese	0.0045
iodine	0.00006
silicon fluorine copper zinc	minute traces

compounds are quite different from those formed by living organisms. Yet the natural elements and inorganic compounds of the earth are the raw materials from which life builds more life.

Oxygen, as molecular oxygen, makes up nearly 21 percent of the mixture of gases we call air. Oxygen is necessary for respiration in most living things. You will learn more about oxygen and respiration in Chapter Six.

Water is the most abundant inorganic compound. It is also the most abundant compound in organisms. Water forms about 65 to 95 percent of the substance of every living thing. Again and again in biology, you will see how important water is to the living condition. Protoplasm itself is made up of materials dissolved or suspended in water. Water is the medium in which dissolved materials are taken in from the environment. It is the medium of transport for foods, minerals, and other substances in living systems. Many organisms actually live *in* water.

Carbon dioxide is an inorganic compound that supplies carbon as well as oxygen. All chemical products or organisms contain carbon. Thus, directly or indirectly, carbon dioxide is necessary to all life.

Mineral compounds supply the other elements needed for life. Minerals may come from the soil. Or they may be dissolved in water or found as salts in sea water.

Human beings cannot directly use carbon dioxide and many of the necessary minerals. We cannot build our bodies directly from carbon dioxide, minerals, and water. Like nearly all animals, we must rely on the green plants as a link to these inorganic compounds. The plants organize such compounds into the complex foods we use as energy sources and building materials.

Because of the importance of water to life, stress to students the harmful effect that water pollution has had and will continue to have on living things. Ask students to report on what is being accomplished in this area.

Have students investigate some of the industries that are dependent upon organic compounds.

ORGANIC COMPOUNDS—PRODUCTS OF LIVING ORGANISMS

All living organisms produce *organic compounds* quite unlike the inorganic substances of the earth. Scientists once thought that *only* organisms produced organic compounds, which explains the term *organic.* Today we know that this is not so. In fact, many organic compounds used today are synthetic products of industry.

Whether synthetic or made by living organisms, all organic compounds have one thing in common. They all contain carbon. Several things about carbon help make it the key element in organic compounds. First, a carbon atom's electron structure allows it to form up to four covalent bonds with other atoms. Carbon atoms also tend to link with each other in rings or long chains. These carbon groups form a "backbone" to which atoms of other elements attach. The result is a large, complex organic molecule.

Organic chemists have learned exactly how the atoms are arranged and bonded in thousands of organic molecules. A *structural formula* is a map of the atoms and bonds in a molecule. A close look at a structural formula will give you a good idea of how organic molecules are put together. The carbon atoms may form rings in one

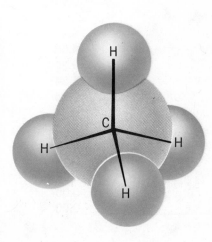

3–11 The structural formula of methane shows the arrangement of the carbon and hydrogen molecules.

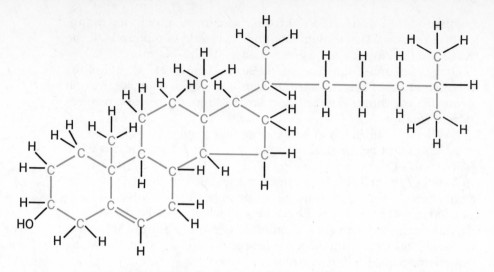

3-12 The structural formula for cholesterol shows how carbon atoms bond to each other to form rings and branching chains in the same molecule.

part of the molecule and a branching chain in another part. The lines stand for bonds. The carbon atoms form bonds with each other, with hydrogen atoms, and with OH molecules. Each carbon atom forms four single bonds, or two single bonds and one double bond.

We can also represent a molecule by an *empirical formula.* The empirical formula for cholesterol is $C_{27}H_{45}OH$. Compare this with the structural formula.

The building of organic molecules by living organisms is known as *biosynthesis.* Biochemists are greatly interested in learning how biosynthesis works. Somewhere in this complex process we may find the key to how life continues.

CARBOHYDRATES

One important group of organic compounds are the *carbohydrates.* Carbohydrates are made up of carbon, hydrogen, and oxygen. The proportion of hydrogen atoms to oxygen atoms is two to one, as in water. Examples of carbohydrates are *sugars, starches,* and *celluloses.*

Sugars are organized in plants but, as foods, they provide the basic fuel for animal life as well. There are several types of sugars. Simple sugars, or *monosaccharides* (MON-uh-SACK-uh-RIDES), may contain either five or six carbon atoms. Three simple sugars are well known and important in biology. *Glucose* is the main cell fuel in both plants and animals. *Fructose* and *galactose* are quite similar to glucose. In fact, all three have six carbon atoms and the empirical formula $C_6H_{12}O_6$. However, their structural formulas are different.

Certain plants combine two molecules of simple sugar and form one molecule of a double sugar, or *disaccharide.* One molecule of water is given off in the reaction, called *dehydration synthesis.* Disaccharides have the empirical formula $C_{12}H_{22}O_{11}$.

In a process much like this, a glucose molecule and a fructose molecule combine. The product is *sucrose,* our common table sugar

Explain the difference between monosaccharides, disaccharides, and polysaccharides. Ask students to bring in examples of different types of carbohydrates from the simple to the complex.

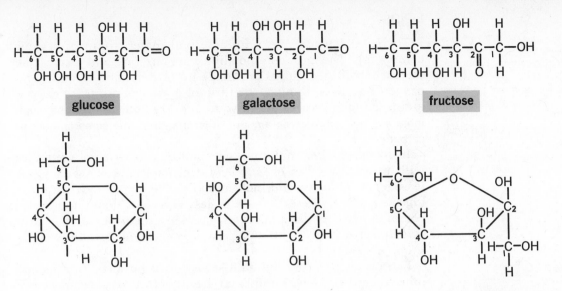

glucose   galactose   fructose

3-13 Structural formula of three different monosaccharides. All three molecules have the same numbers of carbon, hydrogen, and oxygen atoms. But all have a different arrangement of atoms.

taken from sugar cane or sugar beets. Glucose and galactose molecules combine and form lactose, or milk sugar.

Starches are complex carbohydrates made up of glucose units in chains. Starches are *polysaccharides*. Each glucose unit in a starch has six carbon atoms, but a molecule of water has been removed. There may be from dozens to many thousands of glucose units in a starch.

Corn and potato plants produce starches, as do rice, wheat, and other grains. Animal starch, or *glycogen*, is produced in the liver and stored in the liver and muscles. When extra fuel is needed, the liver breaks this starch down to glucose.

Cellulose molecules are even larger and more complex than those of starches. In cellulose, long chains of glucose units are bonded side by side. This gives cellulose fibers great strength. Cellulose is formed in the cell walls of plants, and gives them support. You are familiar with cellulose in the forms of wood, paper, cotton, and many other plant products.

Ask students to study the structural formulas of glucose, galactose, and fructose (Fig. 3-13). Have them explain the differences between these three sugars.

3-14 The dehydration synthesis of maltose from two molecules of glucose.

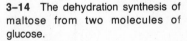

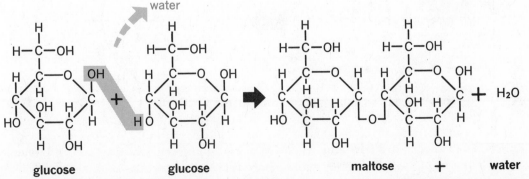

glucose   glucose   maltose   +   water

LIPIDS

The *lipids* (LIP-idz) make up a second major group of organic compounds. The most common lipids are *fats, oils,* and *waxes.* Like the carbohydrates, lipids are made up of carbon, hydrogen, and oxygen. In lipids, though, the ratio of hydrogen atoms to oxygen atoms is much greater than two to one. **The body can release much more energy from a given amount of fat than from the same amount of carbohydrate.**

In forming a *fat* molecule, one molecule of *glycerol* combines with three molecules of *fatty acid.* One molecule of water is released as each fatty acid molecule joins the glycerol. When fat is digested, this process is more or less reversed. Water molecules combine with the fat molecules, breaking them down into fatty acid and glycerol. This breaking down by addition of water is called *hydrolysis.*

Fats occur mainly in animal tissues and as butterfat in milk and other dairy products. Lipids that are liquid at room temperature are known as *oils.* You are familiar with sugar vegetable oils as corn oil, peanut oil, and soybean oil.

Waxes, such as beeswax and the waxes found on fruits and leaves, are related to fats. However, the fatty acids in waxes are joined to alcohol rather than glycerol.

PROTEINS AND AMINO ACIDS

Proteins are the most common organic compounds in living cells. Proteins are very complex and occur in very many different forms. *Structural proteins* form the cell structures you will study in Chapter Four. *Enzymes* are proteins that control all chemical activity in living organisms.

3-15 The dehydration synthesis of a fat molecule from three fatty acid molecules and a glycerol molecule.

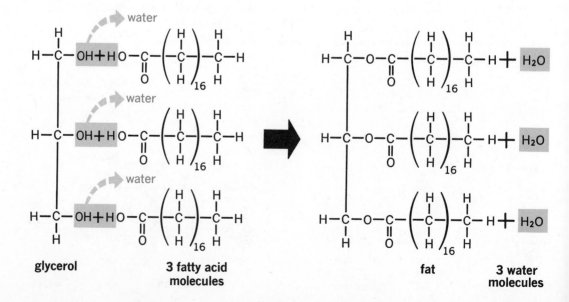

glycerol   3 fatty acid molecules   fat   3 water molecules

Protein molecules are made up mainly of carbon, hydrogen, oxygen, and nitrogen atoms. Sulfur is often present, and sometimes iron and phosphorus. The basic building blocks of protein molecules are *amino acids*. There are about 20 different amino acids, each made up of two groups of atoms.

Amino acid units are joined together by *peptide bonds*. Two joined amino acids make up a *dipeptide*. Dipeptides, in turn, may join and form chains called **polypeptides.** Many protein molecules are made up of a single long polypeptide chain. In other proteins, parallel polypeptides are joined by cross links.

A single protein molecule may contain as few as fifty or as many as three thousand amino acid units. Also, several different kinds of amino acid may be present, though no protein contains all 20 kinds. Finally, the amino acid units may be arranged in many different ways. As you can see, then, there is almost no limit to the number of different proteins possible.

Different kinds of plants and animals may contain very different proteins. Members of the same species have many kinds of proteins in common. For example, certain kinds of proteins are found in all human beings, and in no other organisms. Even within a species, though, the protein makeup varies. Every cell of your body contains as many as 2000 different proteins. And some of your proteins are unlike those of any other person. In fact, we can say that some proteins make us human, while others make us individuals.

The plant and animal proteins we take in as foods are different from our own. We cannot use them directly but must first break them down into amino acids. We then organize the amino acids into new polypeptide chains that match our own proteins. Later you will learn more about this process and its importance in making you as you are.

ENZYMES

An organism is a living chemical system in which substances are constantly changing. Molecules react with other molecules. Materials are organized and broken down. What starts these changes? What controls them? What keeps one change from interfering with another? The answer is **enzymes. Enzymes are proteins that act as catalysts.** That is, enzymes cause chemical changes to occur and affect the rate of change, but are not part of the product.

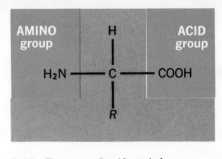

3-16 The generalized formula for an amino acid.

Proteins differ from one another because of the arrangement of amino acids. There are twenty amino acids that can be arranged in almost endless combinations. Ask students to consider the possible combinations of the letters of the alphabet. This will give them some idea of the endless combinations that exist with protein arrangements.

An enzyme is a protein that will act only under specific conditions which include temperature, degree of acidity or alkalinity (pH), and on a specific substrate.

3-17 The dehydration synthesis of a peptide. As water is removed the two amino acid molecules become linked by a peptide bond.

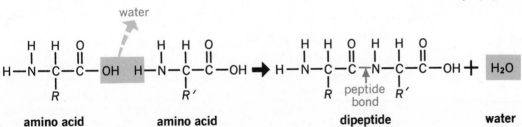

amino acid   amino acid   dipeptide   water

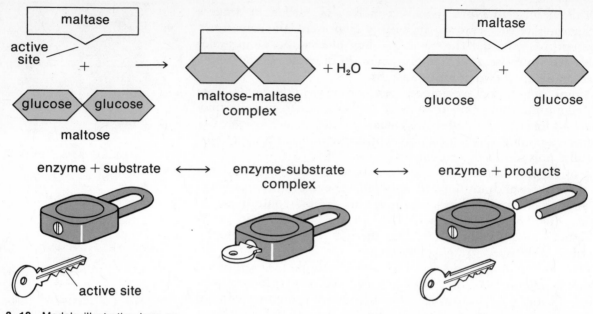

3-18 Models illustrating how enzymes work on a specific substrate.

A demonstration of the classic experiment to extract enzymes from yeast may be of interest to students. Another interesting demonstration involves the detection of enzyme action in *Paramecium*. Both of these experiments are explained in detail in the book *Experimental Biology* by William Berman, ARCO Publishing Co., New York, 1975.

Enzymes are *specific* in their action. That is, each one has a certain job. For example, an enzyme in your saliva acts on the starches you eat, changing them to maltose sugar. If you chew a starchy food such as a potato, you swallow sugar. This enzyme acts only on starch. Other enzymes cause chemical changes in fats, proteins, and other substances. Enzymes also control the chemical changes involved in growth, respiration, and so on.

Exactly how enzymes work is not yet known. Many possible models of enzyme action are hypothesized. In one model, the enzyme is seen as being something like a piece of a puzzle. At one place on the enzyme molecule is an *active site*. This site fits with a certain *substrate*—the substance which the enzyme causes to react. An *enzyme-substrate complex* is produced. This complex reacts quickly, forming products from the substrate but not changing the enzyme. The enzyme lowers the amount of activation energy needed. This speeds the reaction.

Often, one chemical reaction in an organism involves several different changes. This calls for a group, or "team," of enzymes. Such a group is called an *enzyme system*. Certain other molecules which are not proteins may take part in the enzyme activity. Such molecules are known as **coenzymes.** We'll look more closely at some of these reactions later.

NUCLEIC ACIDS

We have seen that proteins make us what we are. They control our structure and the chemical reactions of our bodies. Proteins differ from one another by the kind, number, and sequence of their amino acids. How are these amino acids put into the proper sequence in our cells?

The answer seems to lie in the functioning of organic compounds called *nucleic acids.* Two important nucleic acids are DNA and RNA. These molecules control the synthesis of proteins. They also contain the genetic message of heredity. We will take a detailed look at nucleic acids in Chapter Seven.

SUMMARY

All the matter of the earth is made up of 92 natural elements and their compounds. In physical changes, matter changes from one state into another. In chemical changes, matter is changed to different kinds of matter. Energy is involved with all matter. Energy may be either kinetic or potential.

The natural compounds of the earth are called inorganic compounds. Living organisms organize these substances into organic compounds. Among the important organic compounds are carbohydrates, lipids, proteins, and nucleic acids. Some of these compounds determine what we are and how we differ from each other.

BIOLOGICALLY SPEAKING

physical change	compound	organic compound
chemical change	covalent bond	structural formula
kinetic energy	bond energy	empirical formula
potential energy	ionic bond	biosynthesis
activation energy	molecule	carbohydrate
chemical element	diatomic molecule	monosaccharide
atom	ion	lipid
nucleus	mixture	protein
atomic number	solution	enzyme
atomic mass	suspension	amino acid
isotope	colloid	polypeptide
radioisotope	inorganic	coenzyme
		nucleic acid

QUESTIONS FOR REVIEW

1. What is matter?
2. Describe the difference between physical and chemical change.
3. Given an example of the conversion of potential energy to kinetic energy.
4. List the three particles of an atom and give their location and charge.
5. What are isotopes?
6. Distinguish between covalent and ionic bonding.
7. Explain the relationship of a solvent and a solute in a solution.
8. What is meant by a colloid?
9. How is the present-day definition of "organic compound" better than the original definition?
10. Give examples of the three forms of carbohydrates.
11. What are the molecules that compose a fat molecule?
12. How does one protein differ from another?
13. What is an enzyme?
14. What is the important function of the nucleic acids?

APPLYING PRINCIPLES AND CONCEPTS

1. A certain atom has 6 protons and 8 neutrons. How many electrons does it have? Diagram this atom.
2. Discuss the key position of carbon in the organization of organic compounds.
3. Discuss the vital role of enzymes in the chemical reactions occurring in organisms.

chapter four

The Structural Basis of Life

OBJECTIVES

- DESCRIBE the contributions of Dujardin, Schwann, Hooke, and Schleiden to studies of the cell.
- EXPLAIN the cell theory.
- LIST the processes of a living cell.
- IDENTIFY the parts of the cell.
- DESCRIBE the functions of the parts of the cell.
- EXPLAIN cell specialization.

The study of cells is known as *cytology*. The study of the tissues that are composed of cells is called *histology*. Students may be interested in learning about the work of cytologists and histologists. Interested students should be assigned this project.

There were many individuals who contributed to our knowledge of cell theory. Besides those already mentioned, there were the following scientists: Caspar Wolff (1733-94); Marie Francois Bichat (1771-1802); Johannes Purkinje (1787-1869); Hugo von Mohl (1805-72); and Karl von Siebold (1804-85). Certain students may want to report on the contributions of these scientists as well as the others discussed in the text.

4–1 Hooke's microscope, and cork cell drawings. (Bausch & Lomb; N.Y.P.L.)

THE CELL—THE BASIC UNIT OF LIFE

In Chapter Three, we talked about some of the elements and compounds important to life. But how are these materials actually put together in living things? What forms do they take? The answer is that they are organized into specific structures in cells. At this point, the materials are no longer simply chemicals. Organized into cells, they have become living matter.

The cell is the basic structural unit of life. All organisms are made up of cells, and all the substances of an organism are products of its cells. The simplest organisms have only one cell. More complex organisms may have thousands, millions, or even billions of cells. Your body, for example, probably contains about 50 thousand billion cells. An organism's size depends on the *number*, not the size, of its cells. In general, elephant cells are no larger than ant cells. The elephant simply has more cells.

A working knowledge of cells and their structures is necessary to any study of the living condition. Almost every branch of biology deals in some way with cells. Yet in many ways the cell remains a frontier, waiting to be explored. Physicists have opened up a whole new world of knowledge in studying such basic units of matter as atoms. In the same way, biologists are making important discoveries as they explore the basic unit of life, the cell.

THE DISCOVERY OF CELLS

More than three hundred years ago, the British scientist Robert Hooke observed some thin slices of cork through a microscope. In

1665, his report *Micrographia* told what he had seen. To his surprise, Hooke said, the cork was a mass of tiny cavities. Since each cavity was surrounded by walls like the cells in a honeycomb, Hooke called the cork structures "cells."

Hooke did not realize that the most important part of the cells was missing. The empty shells he saw had once held active, living materials. Yet Hooke did not follow up his discovery by studying plant or animal cells that still contained such materials. In fact, it was not until 1835 that another scientist discovered these substances. It was French biologist Dujardin (DOO-ZHAR-DAN) who viewed living cells with a microscope and found what we now call *protoplasm*. Three years later, the German botanist Matthias Schleiden proposed that *all* plants are made up of cells. The following year, Theodor Schwann, a German zoologist, stated that all animals also are made up of cells. The work of these and other nineteenth-century biologists established the **cell theory.** According to this theory:

- **The cell is the unit of structures and function of all living things.**
- **Cells come from other cells by cell reproduction.**

EXPLORING THE CELL TODAY

During the hundred years after Dujardin's discovery, other biologists added greatly to our knowledge of cells. Still, these scientists could not work beyond the limits of the light microscope. Then, suddenly, new tools and methods began to push back the limits to discovery. Most important, of course, was the electron microscope. But there were many other advances. High-speed centrifuges spin the different cell materials into separate layers. New methods allowed biochemists to learn the chemical makeup and molecular structure of these materials. With other instruments, tiny cell structures could actually be *removed* from a cell for study. Radioisotopes, serving as *tracer elements*, gave further aid. Now scientists can follow different chemical reactions through a cell and relate each change to a specific structure.

Such advances have brought us a much, much greater knowledge of cells. We have learned more in the past 25 years than had been learned in all the time since Hooke saw his dead and empty cork cells. Today we believe that we know the answers to many questions about how cells are organized and how they function. But much remains to be learned. New knowledge may force us to change our ideas many times in the years to come. But each change will bring us closer to a full understanding.

PROCESSES OF CELLS

All life processes involve energy changes. These changes take place at the level of the cell. It is often hard to separate one cell activity from other closely related activities taking place at the same time. Also, each specialized cell part may be involved in one or more reactions. Still, it will help us to understand cell activities

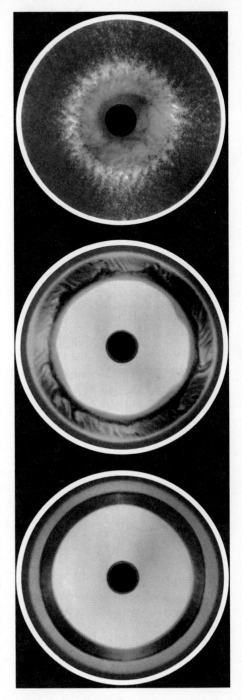

4-2 Centrifuge tubes after spinning showing separation of contents into layers. (DeLaval Separator Co.)

A cell is the basic unit of life having definite boundaries. Inside of each cell, there is constant chemical activity. If the chemical activity ceases, so does the life of that cell.

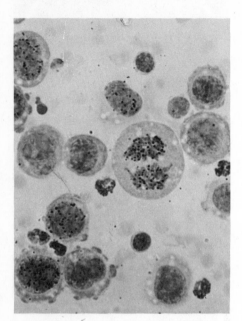

4-3 Radioautograph of cells from a mouse tumor. DNA, labeled with radioactive tritium, appears as black dots in the nuclear material. (courtesy Renato Baserga)

It is important to stress to students that each of the cell processes is carried on by the individual cell as well as many cells.

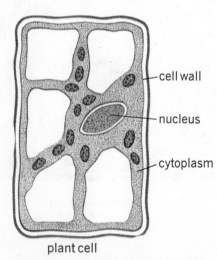

plant cell

4-4 The plant cell can be divided into three major parts: nucleus, cytoplasm, and cell wall.

if we separate them under certain general headings. The following, then, are the processes that occur in living cells:

- *Nutrition.* Food molecules are necessary to supply both energy and building materials in cells. Some cells form their own food molecules. Others take them in from the environment.
- *Digestion.* Many foods must be broken down into simpler forms in order for a cell to use them. Certain enzymes in the cell speed up these breaking-down reactions.
- *Absorption.* A cell absorbs water, food molecules, ions, and other necessary materials from the environment.
- *Biosynthesis.* Cells organize many organic substances, including fats and carbohydrates. They also form their own specific proteins. This biosynthesis is necessary for growth and for the production of enzymes to control cell activity.
- *Respiration.* Chemical energy is released when certain organic molecules, especially glucose, are split. This energy is necessary to all cell activities.
- *Excretion.* Waste materials of cell activity are passed from the cell to the environment.
- *Secretion.* Certain cells synthesize molecules of substances such as vitamins and hormones. When *secreted* (se-KREE-ted), or passed out, of the cell, these substances affect the activities of other cells.
- *Response.* Cell activities may change in response to stimuli from the environment such as heat, light, or pressure. Movement is a response to stimuli.
- *Reproduction.* Cells divide from time to time. In a complex organism, such splitting results in more cells in the organism. With one-celled organisms, splitting simply produces more organisms.

THE CELL NUCLEUS

We've mentioned cell structures, or cell parts, often. Now we are ready to take a closer look at these parts. We will begin with a very important part, the cell **nucleus. The nucleus is the control center for all cell activity. Without its nucleus, a cell will die.**

The nucleus usually is a sphere or an oval in shape, often lying near the center of the cell. It is contained within a thin, double *nuclear membrane.* This membrane separates the nuclear materials from other parts of the cell but is not really a solid barrier. The electron microscope shows openings, or pores, in the membrane. These pores may allow certain substances to pass between the nucleus and the rest of the cell.

The nucleus contains a thick colloid, rich in protein, called *nucleoplasm.* At least one **nucleolus** is also present. Spread through the nucleoplasm are fine strands of **chromatin** material. These structures are thought to be the active forms of the **chromosomes,** which control the activities of the cell. *Chromosomes* are made up of protein molecules joined with a substance known as *DNA.* You will learn more about this very important substance in Chapter Seven.

THE CYTOPLASM

Cell substances outside the nucleus make up the **cytoplasm.** Under a light microscope, cytoplasm appears as a clear semifluid filling most of the cell. It often flows about in the cell in a movement called *streaming*. The nucleus often flows with the cytoplasm, changing shape as it moves.

At its outer edge, the cytoplasm forms a **plasma membrane,** or *cell membrane*. This membrane separates the cell from other cells and from surrounding fluids. Like the nuclear membrane, it is not a solid barrier. Molecules can pass through it. However, the plasma membrane controls this traffic. **The plasma membrane acts like a "gate," allowing some molecules to pass and keeping others out.**

The plasma membrane is made up of a double layer of lipid molecules. The membrane is not smooth. Protein molecules are embedded in the lipid layers. The membrane is also folded with indentations and bulges. This increases the amount of surface through which molecules may pass. The membrane forms wherever the cytoplasm borders on another substance. If the membrane is cut, cytoplasm may ooze through the opening for a short time, but other molecules will soon plug the opening.

The main body of cytoplasm is known as the **cytoplasmic matrix.** Under a light microscope, it looks like a clear semifluid containing many tiny grains of other substances. But the electron microscope shows a much more complex structure. For one thing, cytoplasm contains a system of double membranes that tend to lie parallel to one another. The system, the **endoplasmic reticulum,** fastens to the plasma membrane and the nuclear membrane. Biologists think that the endoplasmic reticulum may act as a system of canals. Through this system, materials may pass from the plasma membrane to the nucleus. The endoplasmic reticulum also provides a surface to which enzymes and other cell structures are attached.

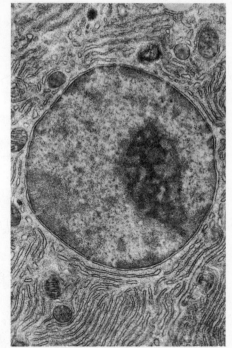

4–5 Electron micrograph of the nucleus. The nucleolus is the dark mass within the nucleus. Note the pores in the nuclear membrane. (courtesy Don W. Fawcett)

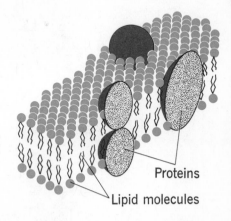

Proteins

Lipid molecules

4–6 The plasma membrane is made up of a double layer of lipid molecules embedded with protein molecules.

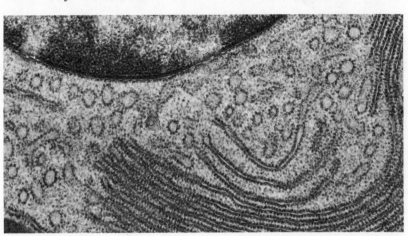

4–7 Electron micrograph of the endoplasmic reticulum lined with ribosomes. Part of the nucleus appears at the left.

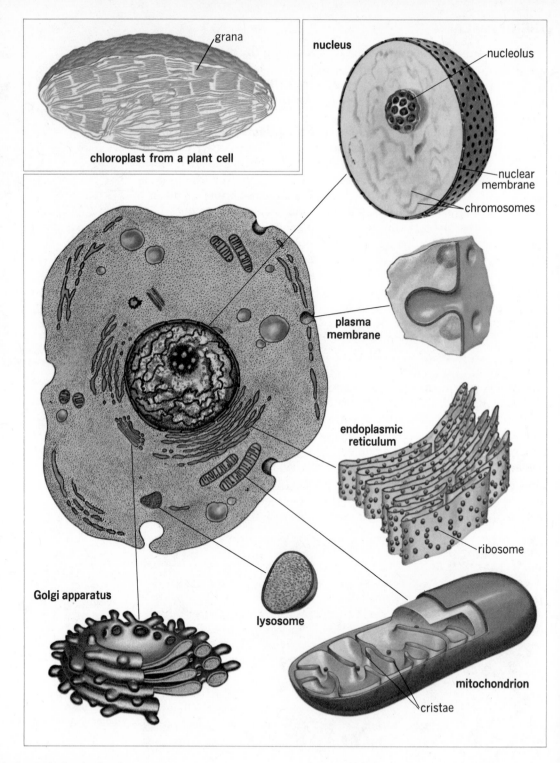

grana

chloroplast from a plant cell

nucleus

nucleolus

nuclear membrane

chromosomes

plasma membrane

endoplasmic reticulum

ribosome

Golgi apparatus

lysosome

mitochondrion

cristae

4–8 Model of a typical animal cell and its organelles.

ORGANELLES

The cytoplasm also contains several organized structures called **organelles,** which means "little organs." Some organelles can be seen through a light microscope. Others were not known until the electron microscope came into use. Each kind of organelle seems to take part in a specific chemical activity. Later, we will describe these chemical activities in detail. But for now we will deal mainly with the structure, makeup, and location of the organelles.

At high power, an electron microscope shows many tiny, grainy structures attached to the endoplasmic reticulum. These are the **ribosomes.** The ribosomes contain large amounts of RNA, a substance closely related to DNA. They also contain enzymes that contain protein synthesis. In fact, the evidence points to the ribosomes as the protein factories of the cell. Thus, though they are among the smallest cell structures, their function is one of the most important.

The electron microscope also shows details of the rod-shaped or ganelles called **mitochondria** (MY-tuh-KON-dree-uh). These are the centers of respiration in the cell. Here the energy that supports all cell activities is released. A *mitochondrion* has two membranes, each made up of a layer of protein molecules and a layer of fat molecules. The inner membrane forms long inward folds at several points. These long folds, called *cristae*, increase the surface area of the membrane. Mitochondria contain enzymes that split organic molecules and transfer energy to other compounds. From these compounds, the energy is then released in the cell.

The cytoplasm of most, if not all, cells contains rounded organelles called **lysosomes.** Lysosomes are somewhat smaller than mitochondria and have only a single membrane. Lysosomes contain enzymes that cause digestion of proteins. If a lysosome released all its enzymes, they would cause a cell to destroy itself by digesting its own proteins. For this reason, lysosomes are sometimes called "suicide sacs." Usually, the enzymes in lysosomes are used to digest bacteria and other foreign substances. These enzymes also speed up the breakdown of worn-out tissues. When a cell dies, the lysosomes burst open and their enzymes quickly break down the cell proteins.

We do not yet know the exact function of certain cell structures. Among these are the **Golgi** (GOHL-jee) **apparatus.** These structures were first seen in 1898, by the Italian scientist Camillo Golgi. The electron microscope shows much more of their detail than Golgi could see. Golgi bodies appear as small groups of parallel membranes in the cytoplasm near the nucleus. They are most common in cells of glands. This fact may indicate that the Golgi bodies serve as storehouses for the special substances secreted by such cells. There is also evidence that they are involved in synthesizing these secretions by combining carbohydrate and protein. Golgi bodies may be involved in forming new endoplasmic reticulum.

Plastids are organelles found most often in plant cells and in certain very simple organisms. Some plastids act as chemical factories, while others serve mainly to store foods.

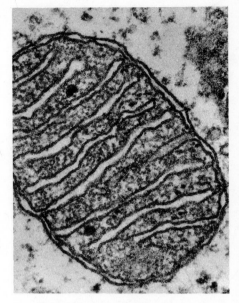

4–9 Electron micrograph of a mitochondria showing the outer and inner membranes and cristae.

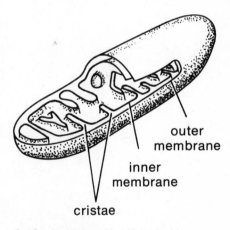

outer membrane

inner membrane

cristae

4–10 A mitochondria with its double-layered membrane.

A microprojector or prepared 35 mm slides can be used to preview the discussion of cell structure and what students should look for when they examine their own specimens under the microscope.

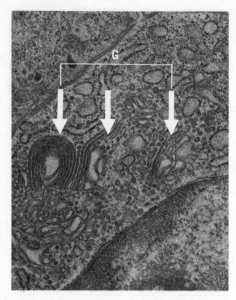

4–11 Electron micrograph of Golgi apparatus.

4–12 Electron micrograph of grana in a chloroplast. (courtesy Myron C. Ledbetter, Brookhaven National Laboratory)

The most familiar plastid is the *chloroplast*, which contains the green pigment *chlorophyll*. The chlorophyll is packed between layers of protein and lipids in bodies called *grana*. Chloroplasts vary both in size and in shape in different kinds of organisms. Their main function is in forming carbohydrates, for they contain the enzymes necessary to this process.

Besides chlorophyll, some chloroplasts contain pale-yellow pigments called *xanthophylls* (ZANTH-uh-fills) and yellow or orange pigment known as *carotenes*. Other plastids, often called *chromoplasts*, may produce red or blue pigments. These plastids are found in some flower petals and in the skins of fruits such as the tomato and cherry. In some cells, the chloroplasts lose their chlorophyll and become chromoplasts. This happens, for example, when a tomato ripens and changes from green to red.

Leucoplasts (LOO-kuh-PLASTS) are plastids that function mainly as food storehouses. They contain enzymes that cause glucose molecules to join and form starch molecules. This process sometimes occurs in chloroplasts, but leucoplasts are the main centers for storing starch. In cells, starch is stored *only* in plastids. Starch does not dissolve in water, and so is not found in the nucleus or in the cytoplasm outside plastids.

CELL VACUOLES

Plant cells often contain one or more cavities in the cytoplasm. These cavities are filled with fluid and are known as **vacuoles.** The cytoplasm forms a *vacuolar membrane*, much like the plasma membrane, around each vacuole. This membrane controls the movement

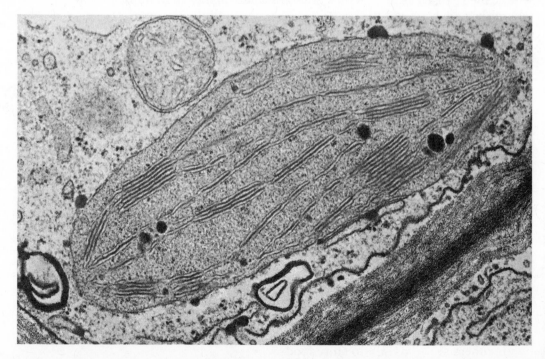

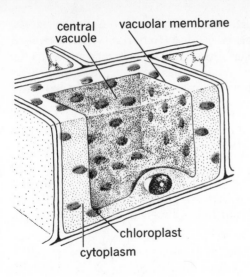

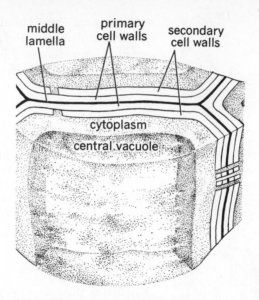

4-13 A representation of a typical plant cell. The central vacuole is completely surrounded by cytoplasm.

4-14 Structure of a plant cell wall. The cell wall is rigid, but porous.

of molecules between the vacuole and the rest of the cell. In some plant cells, the vacuole may be a large, central structure. As a plant cell grows, small vacuoles join and form a single large vacuole. Pressure from this vacuole may force the cytoplasm into a thin layer around the edge of the cell.

The fluid in plant vacuoles is mainly water. Also present are ions of mineral compounds, sugar and protein molecules, and other organic materials. Together, these substances make up the colloid we call *cell sap*. Other vacuoles may contain food materials and waste products. In many one-celled organisms, vacuoles serve as organelles in getting rid of extra water.

A cell mobile can be prepared that shows the dynamic action of a cell. By the use of simple materials such as cellophane, pipe cleaners, styrofoam, and clay, interesting models can be made. Assign this project to a few students and allow them to experiment with materials.

THE CELL WALL

Most plant cells are surrounded by a **cell wall.** This structure both protects and supports the cell. It is made up of several layers and is formed by the cell itself. Where two cells meet, each builds a part of the cell wall between them. In a way, this wall is like a plaster wall that separates two rooms. A cell wall begins with a thin layer called the *middle lamella*. This structure contains jellylike substances called *pectin* (PECK-tin). Many fruits, including apples, contain large amounts of pectin. Released during cooking, this pectin forms a jelly as it cools.

Attached to the middle lamella are thin *primary walls*, formed by the cells on either side. In the same way, a first coat of plaster is laid on a wall between rooms. The primary walls are made up of cellu-

Cell specialization can also be explained as division of labor. Many cells performing a similar function work together in a body system. Digestion and excretion are just two examples of this process. Ask students to suggest others.

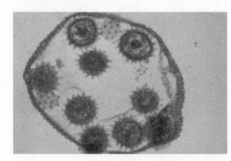

lose and pectin. In soft plant structures such as leaves, flower petals, and soft fruits, these walls are fairly thin. In harder structures such as stems, the walls are thicker. Other cellulose layers make up the *secondary walls*. These firm, rigid walls may remain long after the cells are dead. Wood, for example, has very thick secondary walls.

DIFFERENT LEVELS OF STRUCTURES

The simplest organisms are organized at only one level of structure—the cellular level. As organisms become more complex, their structures are organized in more complex ways. We will end this chapter by looking at the different levels of structure found in organisms.

THE CELLULAR LEVEL

The cell is the *first* level at which life is organized. The cell is the basic unit of structure in all living things. Thus, we can say that *every* organism is organized at the cellular level. In fact, many organisms are organized *only* at the cellular level. This is the case with one-celled, or **unicellular,** organisms such as bacteria, yeasts, and ameba. It is also the case with **colonial** organisms. These are unicellular organisms that tend to group together in colonies. Such a colony may appear to be a single, complete organism made up of many cells. But in fact, these cells are not related except by being near one another. They are not organized at any level beyond the cellular level.

TISSUES—THE SECOND LEVEL OF STRUCTURE

The more complex organisms are **multicellular,** or made up of many cells. These cells are not simply grouped in a colony. They work closely together and depend on one another. They also show **cell specialization.** That is, there are different *kinds* of cells, each kind suited for a different activity.

A *tissue* is a group of cells that are alike in structure and activity in an organism. This is the second level at which structures are organized in living things. Your body contains many different tissues—muscle tissue, nerve tissue, bone tissue, and so on. Plants also have tissues.

Each kind of tissue has a special job. Muscle tissue, for example, provides motion. The cells in muscle tissue *specialize* at this job. However, they must also continue the chemical activities that keep them alive. They must take in food and oxygen, form proteins and other organic compounds, and so on. This brings us to another characteristic of multicellular organisms—*division of labor*.

You can see how division of labor works in our own society. Doctors do not have to spend their days hunting or raising food because farmers do this job. Factory workers do not have to spend months

4–15 Levels of organization. A unicellular organism, a colonial organism (The Bergman Associates), seed plant tissue (Photo Researchers, Inc.), striated muscle tissue (William H. Amos)

building their own houses because carpenters do this job. In the same way, the different kinds of cells in complex organisms divide their labor. Muscle cells, for example, can specialize in motion because other cells help supply them with food, oxygen, and other needs.

ORGANS—THE THIRD LEVEL OF STRUCTURE

Higher plants and animals require more complex structures than tissues for their life activities. An *organ* is made up of several tissues working as a unit. The organ is the third level of structure in organisms.

A hand is an organ. It is made up of skin, bone, blood, muscle, nerves, and other tissues. Your heart, stomach, and brain are other examples of organs. A plant stem, such as a tree trunk, is an organ made up of wood, bark, and other tissues.

ORGAN SYSTEMS

In higher organisms, especially animals, several organs may work together in carrying out a certain activity. This is the fourth level of structure, the *organ system.* In your body, for example, many organs are involved in breaking down foods to molecules your cells can use. How many organs of this organ system can you name? Another organ system carries these molecules to all parts of your body. This system includes the heart, blood vessels, and lymph vessels. In higher animals, there is an organ system for almost every life activity.

We think of the organism itself as a fifth level of structure. At this level, all other structures are organized into a complete living thing.

SUMMARY

The cell is the basic unit of structure and function in all living things. Thus, a knowledge of cells is of great importance in biology. With modern tools and methods, biologists are learning a great deal about cells.

Living things may be organized according to different levels of structure. Some organisms are made up of a single cell. Others are made up of many cells organized as tissues, organs, and organ systems. At this level, cells specialize in different activities. The different kinds of cells in an organism support each other through division of labor.

Prepared slides showing simple and complex organisms will help students to understand one-celled and many-celled organisms.

BIOLOGICALLY SPEAKING

cell	endoplasmic reticulum	cell wall
cell theory	organelle	unicellular
nucleus	ribosome	colonial
nucleolus	mitochondrion	multicellular
chromatin	lysosome	tissue
chromosome	Golgi apparatus	cell specialization
cytoplasm	plastid	organ
plasma membrane	vacuole	organ system
cytoplasmic matrix		

1. In one sense Robert Hooke discovered cells; in another he did not. Explain.
2. Name the two principles of the cell theory.
3. List nine processes that characterize the living condition.
4. The nuclear membrane holds certain structures but is not a barrier. Why is this important?
5. Describe the molecular makeup of the plasma membrane.
6. List the cytoplasmic organelles of the cell.
7. Describe the structure and function of the mitochondria.
8. In what respect are the lysosomes "suicide sacs" in a cell?
9. What is the current theory about the function of the Golgi apparatus?
10. Why are chloroplasts referred to as carbohydrate factories?
11. Describe the various contents of cell vacuoles.
12. List the levels of biological organization from simple to complex.

**APPLYING
PRINCIPLES
AND CONCEPTS**

1. In what respect is the cell the basic unit of life?
2. Do you believe that the mere presence in a test tube of all the vital substances composing protoplasm would result in a living condition? Give possible reasons supporting your opinion.
3. Discuss the specialization of cell content in various organelles.
4. Discuss why a unicellular organism is usually more versatile than one cell of a multicellular organism.

5-1 The human body is an example of biological balance.

The Cell and Its Environment

OBJECTIVES

- DEFINE homeostasis.
- DISTINGUISH between a permeable and a selectively permeable membrane.
- EXPLAIN diffusion pressure.
- UNDERSTAND the principle of diffusion through a plasma membrane.
- EXPLAIN the process of osmosis as it relates to the cell.
- DEFINE turgor pressure, cytolysis, and plasmolysis.
- UNDERSTAND the behavior of cells in different solutions.
- EXPLAIN the principles of active transport.
- DESCRIBE pinocytosis.

HOMEOSTASIS—BALANCE ON A BIOLOGICAL TIGHTROPE

Imagine walking a tightrope, high above the ground. Everything depends on your sense of balance. As you cross the swaying rope, you must adjust constantly. With each careful step you lean just to the left or just to the right, keeping your balance. Lean too far, or not far enough, and you fall.

You may never walk a real tightrope. But, like every other living thing, you walk a biological tightrope all your life. All organisms face constantly changing conditions, both within themselves and in their environment. To survive, an organism must adjust constantly to these changing conditions. It must keep up a state of balance between its life activities and the conditions that affect them. We call such a state of balance **homeostasis,** or a *steady state*.

Homeostasis occurs at all levels in living things. In many cases, a whole organism adjusts to change. For example, a frog escapes the cold of winter and heat of summer by burying itself in mud beneath a pond. *You* adjust to winter and summer by wearing heavier or lighter clothing, or by staying in warm or cool places. Much of this course will deal with the ways in which organisms adjust to such changes.

Homeostasis also occurs at the level of organs and organ systems.

Homeostasis is one of the most important concepts in biology. It refers to cells as well as the entire organism. Homeostasis is that "steady-state" where fine adjustments are made in order for the entire organism to stay in balance.

The thousands of homeostatic adjustments are interdependent. If some of these adjustments are not made, the organism will have difficulty surviving. Stress to students the complexity of an organism as indicated by these adjustments.

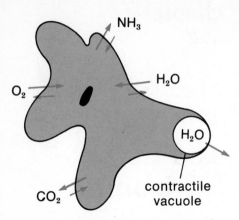

5-2 Single cells must also be in the state of balance with the environment.

In the higher animals, organs work closely together in keeping conditions inside the body at their best possible level. For example, all organs depend on heart action for their supply of oxygen-carrying blood. Heart action changes as body needs change. During exercise, the body needs more oxygen, and the heart speeds up. The increased blood supply is also needed to remove extra cell wastes produced by greater cell activity. In turn, the kidneys remove many of these wastes from the blood.

Even a single cell must be in a state of homeostasis with its environment in order to survive. For example, pond water is a perfect environment for many different one–celled organisms. But a single nerve or muscle cell from your body would die in pond water.

We have mentioned only a few examples of homeostasis. You will discover many others in your study of biology.

THE CELL MEMBRANE AND HOMEOSTASIS

At the cellular level, homeostasis depends greatly on the movement of certain materials into and out of the cell. Foods, oxygen, and other materials are taken into the cell by absorption. Waste products and other substances are removed by excretion. All of these materials must pass through the cell membrane, or plasma membrane.

In Chapter Four, we described the plasma membrane as a double layer of fat molecules embedded with protein molecules. Against this membrane, molecules and ions move in a steady stream. Some of them pass through the membrane freely, some less freely, and some not at all. Thus, the membrane has a great effect on which materials enter and leave the cell. But why is this so? Why does the membrane stop some substances while others pass? There is no single answer. Several factors are important here, including:

1. *The size of the particles.* Some large molecules cannot pass through the plasma membrane. On the other hand, some large molecules pass through in greater numbers than much smaller ions.

2. *Whether or not the particles will dissolve in water.* The fluids that bathe cells usually are solutions of molecules and ions in water. Substances which do not dissolve in water cannot pass through the plasma membrane.

3. *Conditions inside or outside the cell.* Conditions in the cell or the outside environment may affect absorption. We will be studying some of these conditions later.

4. *The structure of the plasma membrane itself.* As we noted in Chapter Four, the surface of the membrane seems to have many tiny openings, or pores. There must also be spaces between the molecules that make up the membrane. These spaces might be too small for large molecules to pass through, but large enough for smaller molecules.

The rates and degrees at which certain substances penetrate the plasma membrane varies. If a substance passes through a membrane, we say that the membrane is **permeable** to that substance. If a membrane lets some substances pass but not others, we say that it is **selectively permeable.** The plasma membrane is selectively permeable.

DIFFUSION

To understand better how substances pass through the cell membrane, we need to understand more about molecules and their motion. In any substance, the molecules are constantly moving. This motion results from kinetic energy within the molecules themselves and not from outside forces. Molecular motion is slight in solids, but much greater in liquids and gases. The movement of the molecules is *random*. That is, the molecules move in straight lines until they collide with other molecules. Then they bounce off and move in straight lines again until they collide with still other molecules. As you can imagine, this kind of movement results in a gradual spreading out of the molecules. In the end, they will be spread evenly through any given space. This gradual, even spreading out of molecules is known as **diffusion.**

As an example of diffusion, think of what happens if you open a jar of ammonia in a classroom. As soon as you open the jar, the ammonia molecules start diffusing into the air. Soon the people in the front of the room smell the ammonia. As diffusion continues, the smell of ammonia becomes stronger. The smell becomes stronger further back in the room. More and more ammonia molecules spread out in random motion among the molecules of gases in the air. Finally, a state of *equilibrium* is reached. The ammonia molecules, though still in motion, are spread evenly among the air molecules in the room.

Actually, as ammonia diffused into the air, air molecules also diffused into the ammonia jar. This fact brings us to a basic law of diffusion. According to this law, **substances diffuse from areas of greater concentration to areas of lesser concentration.** You can see that this happened with both the air molecules and the ammonia molecules. Diffusion continued until the concentration of air and ammonia molecules was equal in all parts of the room.

OTHER EXAMPLES OF DIFFUSION

In the case of ammonia diffusion, we were dealing with gas molecules. But solids and liquids, or liquids and other liquids, can also diffuse into each other. (Of course, only substances that normally mix and do not repel each other can do this.) For example, drop a cube of sugar in a glass of water. As the sugar dissolves, taste the water from time to time. The water will become sweeter as more sugar molecules diffuse into it. The sugar is diffusing from an area of greater concentration (the lump) to an area of lesser concen-

Brownian movement can be demonstrated by observation of the particles of carbon which compose India ink.

Open a container of ammonia or peppermint oil to demonstrate the random movements of molecules in diffusion.

The demonstration illustrated in Fig. 5-3 should be done in front of the class. Prepare one beaker where diffusion has already taken place. Then prepare a second beaker in front of the class. Diffusion may take several days depending on the amount of copper sulfate placed in the water.

5-3 The diffusion of a solid in a liquid. Copper sulfate diffuses into water until a state of equilibrium is reached. This is when the particles are equally distributed throughout the water.

tration (the water). Meanwhile, the water is also diffusing into the sugar. Finally, all of the sugar will be dissolved and all parts of the solution will taste equally sweet. This is the equilibrium state.

FACTORS THAT AFFECT DIFFUSION

We've seen that substances diffuse from areas of greater concentration to areas of lesser concentration. Concentration also affects the *rate* at which substances diffuse. The greater the concentration, the more rapidly diffusion takes place. *Temperature* also affects diffusion. The higher the temperature, the greater the speed of molecular motion. Thus, diffusion takes place from areas of higher temperature to areas of lower temperature. *Pressure* also speeds up molecular motion. Thus, diffusion takes place from areas of high pressure to areas of low pressure.

To sum up, differences in molecular concentration, temperature, and pressure all affect diffusion. Together, these differences result in the force we call **diffusion pressure.**

DIFFUSION THROUGH A PERMEABLE MEMBRANE

How does a membrane affect the movement of molecules in diffusion? The answer, of course, depends on the nature of the membrane and the substances being diffused.

You can do a simple experiment with a *permeable* membrane of fine muslin. The bulb of a thistle tube is filled with sugar syrup. A piece of muslin is then tied tightly over the open end of the bulb. Finally, the bulb is placed in a jar of water.

Since muslin is permeable to both water and sugar molecules, two things will happen. Water molecules will diffuse from the jar into the sugar syrup in the tube. At the same time, sugar molecules will diffuse from the tube into the water in the jar. Finally, the concentration of sugar and water molecules will be the same on both sides of the muslin. This is the equilibrium state. At this point, we could say that the *diffusion pressure* is zero.

DIFFUSION THROUGH A SELECTIVELY PERMEABLE MEMBRANE

The permeable muslin membrane had little effect on diffusion. What if the plasma membrane of a cell were as permeable as muslin? The answer is simple: the cell would die. True, molecules of water and other substances could enter the cell more easily. But at the same time, the cell's *own* molecules would diffuse out into the environment! Clearly, the plasma membrane must be only *selectively permeable* if the cell is to survive.

You can do another experiment very much like the one with the muslin membrane. Here, however, a selectively permeable membrane such as sheep bladder is used instead of muslin. Water molecules penetrate a selectively permeable membrane much more

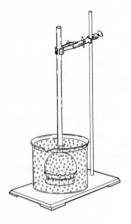

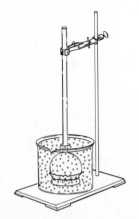

5-4 Diffusion through a permeable membrane: The bulb of a thistle tube is filled with a sugar solution. It is covered tightly with a piece of muslin then placed in a jar of water. Water molecules (blue) move through the membrane into the sugar solution as sugar molecules (red) move through the membrane into the water in the jar.

rapdily than sugar molecules do. Thus, in our experiment, water molecules from the jar diffuse freely through the sheep bladder into the tube. But the diffusion of sugar molecules from the tube to the jar takes place much more slowly. After several hours, the level of solution in the tube has risen, while the level in the jar has fallen.

As the solution rises in the tube, the force of gravity becomes important. Gravity pulls down on the solution in the tube. This, in turn, puts pressure on the inner surface of the membrane. When this pressure is equal to the diffusion pressure of the water molecules, diffusion stops. Equilibrium is reached, even though the concentration of water molecules remains greater in the jar than in the tube.

OSMOSIS—A DIFFUSION OF WATER

The experiment just described is an example of *osmosis.* **Osmosis is the diffusion of water through a selectively permeable membrane from an area of greater concentration to an area of lesser concentration.** Notice that the word *osmosis* refers only to the diffusion of *water.* Thus, in our definition, the word *concentration* refers only to the concentration of water molecules.

We are now going on to discuss the effects of osmosis and other diffusion on living cells. In doing so, remember that diffusion is a purely physical process. Usually no cell energy is involved in it. The molecules move by their own kinetic (heat) energy. For this reason, we say that diffusion is a form of *passive transport.*

OSMOSIS AND PLANT CELLS

When two different solutions are separated by a selectively permeable membrane, an *osmotic system* is formed. We set up such a system in our experiment with water, sugar syrup, and sheep bladder. In living cells, the cell content is separated from solutions outside the cell by the plasma membrane. This, too, is an osmotic system.

Osmosis plays a very important part in the lives of plants. Let's see how this process works in a plant cell. We will assume that the solution outside the cell is *hypotonic.* This means that the solution has a *greater* concentration of water molecules than does the cell content. Thus, there will be a net movement of water *into* the cell.

As water diffuses into the cell by osmosis, it builds up a pressure known as *turgor pressure.* Remember that a plant cell is surrounded by the cell wall. Thus, the cell cannot swell up as the turgor pressure grows. However, the pressure does force the cytoplasm and plasma membrane firmly against the cell wall. This causes the cell to become stiff. At some point, the turgor pressure becomes equal to the diffusion pressure of the water molecules outside the cell. A state of equilibrium is then reached, and diffusion stops.

As long as there is enough water in the cell environment, turgor

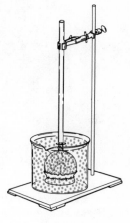

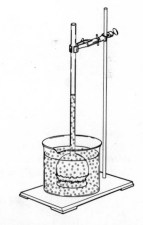

5–5 Diffusion through a selectively permeable membrane: In this experiment a selectively permeable membrane separates the sugar solution in the thistle tube from the water in the jar. The water molecules move through the membrane rapidly into the sugar solution. The sugar molecules move through the membrane at a much slower rate.

pressure will be kept up. This is especially important for soft plant tissues such as leaves, petals, and soft stems. Turgor pressure keeps such tissues stiff and firm. If the pressure drops, the plant will wilt.

WATER PROBLEMS IN ANIMAL CELLS

Animal cells do not have cell walls like plant cells. Thus, in animal cells, turgor pressure cannot build up to a point at which osmosis stops. Water simply continues to diffuse into the cells. As you can see, the cells must get rid of some of this water. Otherwise, they would swell until they burst.

Many one-celled organisms that live in fresh water have special organelles known as **contractile vacuoles.** These vacuoles work like tiny pumps, constantly pushing extra water out through the cell membrane. Without these structures, the cells would soon burst. Fish and other water animals that breathe through gills also take in large amounts of water. In these animals, extra water is removed by excretion in the form of urine. In human beings, the kidneys, sweat glands, and lungs help to remove extra water.

In nature, water contains minerals and other dissolved substances. This lowers the concentration of water molecules, resulting in lower diffusion pressure. Distilled water, on the other hand, has a 100 percent concentration of water molecules. If certain one-celled organisms are placed in distilled water, they will swell and burst. Their contractile vacuoles cannot overcome the rapid osmosis caused by the high diffusion pressure of distilled water. If you place a drop of blood in distilled water, much the same thing will happen. The cells will quickly swell and burst. This bursting of cells caused by pressure within them is called **cytolysis** (sy-TAHL-uh-sis).

PLASMOLYSIS—LOSS OF CELL TURGOR

Remember that a cell has no control over osmosis. The direction in which water diffuses depends only on the different concentration of water molecules inside and outside the cell. We've just seen what happens when the solution outside the cell is hypotonic. What if the solution outside the cell has a *lower* concentration of water than the cell content? The outside solution is then **hypertonic,** and water

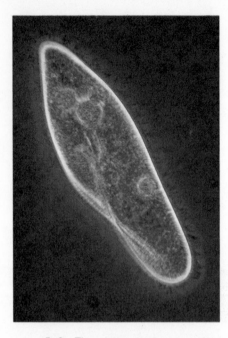

5–6 The circles in the one-celled organism are contractile vacuoles. (Photo Researchers, Eric Grave)

5–7 Normal *Anacharis* cells in isotonic solution (left); plasmolyzed. *Anacharis* cells in hypertonic solution (right). (Phillip A. Harrington)

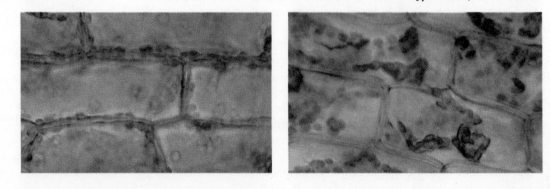

diffuses *out* from the cell into the environment. As outward diffusion continues, turgor pressure is lost and the cell content shrinks. This condition is called *plasmolysis* (plazz-MAHL-uh-siss).

You can observe this water loss in a simple experiment with two pieces of potato. Place one piece in a strong salt solution and the other in tap water. After several minutes, the piece in salt water will be limp from loss of water and cell turgor. With a microscope, you can view water loss as it occurs. In animal cells, which have no cell walls, the whole cell will shrink. Temporary loss of water can be corrected simply by adding more water. But if the condition lasts very long, the cell will die. Now you can understand why salt kills grass and shipwreck victims die from drinking salt water.

CELLS IN ISOTONIC SOLUTIONS

In some cases, the solution outside a cell has just the same concentration of water molecules as the cell content. Such a solution is said to be **isotonic.** Water molecules diffuse through the plasma membrane both into and out of the cell. But the rate of diffusion is the same in both directions, and the cell neither gains or loses water.

In the body, red blood cells are suspended in blood plasma. Under normal conditions, the water concentration of the plasma is the same as that within the cells. Thus, the cells neither gain nor lose water.

DIFFUSION OF IONS THROUGH THE CELL MEMBRANE

Many mineral salts, acids, and bases form ionic solutions in water. The charged ions in such solutions penetrate the cell membrane very slowly. We are not sure why this is so. It may be that the membrane itself has an electric charge. For example, a negative charge on the membrane would repel ions with negative charges. On the other hand, the negative charge might attract positive ions strongly enough to keep them from passing through. Still, some ions *do* pass through the membrane. Such ions play an important part in the chemical activity of the cell.

ACTIVE TRANSPORT

In many cases, certain molecules pass in or out of the cells *against* diffusion pressure. A root cell may absorb mineral ions from soil solutions with a *lower* ion concentration than that within the cell. According to the laws of diffusion, such ions should move out of the cell, not into it. Certain sea algae cells have iodine concentrations thousands of times greater than the iodine concentration of sea water. Yet these algae continue to absorb iodine from the water. Clearly, some force other than diffusion must be at work in such cases. We call this force *active transport.*

Some facts have been learned about active transport, but many

5–8 Red blood cells in three solutions. (Phillip A. Harrington)

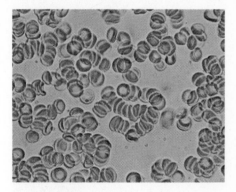

a) Normal red blood cells in isotonic solution.

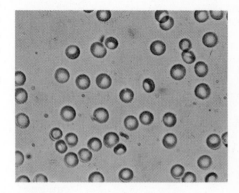

b) Swollen red blood cells in hypotonic solution. Water pressure may burst the cells.

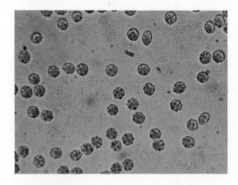

c) Shrunken red blood cells in hypertonic solution.

According to some cell researchers, certain molecules (perhaps enzymes) are involved in the active transport process.

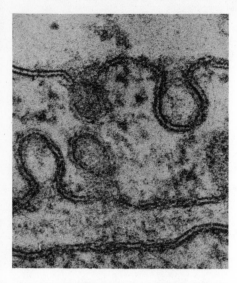

5-9 Electron micrograph showing the pouches that are formed by pinocytosis. (courtesy George E. Palade, The Rockefeller University)

questions remain. For example, we know that cell energy is used in active transport. This energy use is what makes active transport "active," rather than passive. But we do not yet know just *how* the cell energy is used. Also, we know that the cell membrane becomes more permeable or less permeable to certain substances as cell needs change. But we do not know just how the membrane does this.

HOW DO LARGE MOLECULES ENTER THE CELL?

Water molecules, ions, and other materials discussed so far are small enough to pass through pores in the cell membrane. But what about large molecules such as amino acids and lipids? These molecules cannot pass through membrane pores. Yet they and even larger particles are known to enter cells. How does this happen?

In Chapter Four, we said that the cell membrane pouches inward in places. Biologists believe that large molecules and other particles flow into these pouches. The membrane then closes behind the particles and seals them off. Surrounded by a membrane, the materials then enter the cell as a vacuole. This process is known as **pinocytosis** (PIN-oh-sy-TOSE-iss).

SUMMARY

To survive, an organism must remain in a state of balance with its environment. An important factor in this balance is the movement of materials in and out of the cell. All of this traffic must pass through the cell membrane.

The cell membrane is selectively permeable. That is, different molecules and ions pass through it at different rates. Foods, water, wastes, and other materials can pass through the membrane. But the materials of the cell structures themselves are kept within the membrane.

The forces of diffusion control the movement of molecules and other particles through the membrane. Diffusion of water is called osmosis. No cell energy is used in diffusion. For this reason, movement of molecules by diffusion is called passive transport. In some cases, cells absorb ions against the force of diffusion. Cell energy is used in this process, which is known as active transport. Large molecules cannot pass through membrane pores. Instead, they flow into pouches in the membrane and are sealed off. They then enter the cell as vacuoles.

BIOLOGICALLY SPEAKING

homeostasis	passive transport	hypertonic
permeable	hypotonic	plasmolysis
selectively permeable	turgor pressure	isotonic solution
diffusion	contractile vacuole	active transport
diffusion pressure	cytolysis	pinocytosis
osmosis		

QUESTIONS FOR REVIEW

1. What is homeostasis?
2. Distinguish between a permeable and a selectively permeable membrane.
3. What is a plasma membrane? What is its composition?

4. What is diffusion? What is the name for the balance that results from diffusion?
5. Describe the external factors that influence diffusion rates.
6. Define osmosis.
7. What is meant by a "hypertonic solution"?
8. Distinguish between active and passive transport.
9. How are some cells able to bring in materials too large to enter by active or passive transport?

1. Discuss what might happen to a cell if the membrane were permeable to all molecules.
2. What factors determine whether or not a particle will permeate a plasma membrane?
3. What might happen to the cells of a freshwater plant if it were placed in salt water? Why would fresh water destroy a salt-water plant?

APPLYING PRINCIPLES AND CONCEPTS

chapter six

Photosynthesis, Respiration, and Cell Energy

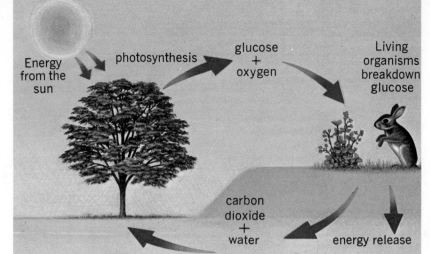

6-1 Energy and living things.

OBJECTIVES

- COMPARE photosynthesis and respiration.
- EXPLAIN how energy is held and released by ATP.
- DESCRIBE the function of chlorophyll.
- WRITE a simplified chemical equation for photosynthesis.
- DESCRIBE the light reactions and dark reactions of photosynthesis.
- LIST some of the conditions necessary for photosynthesis.
- DISTINGUISH between photosynthesis and chemosynthesis.
- LIST the stages in cellular respiration.
- DISTINGUISH between cellular respiration and fermentation.

ENERGY AND LIFE

All living cells must have a constant supply of energy. If a cell's energy supply fails, even for a moment, the cell will die. **The basic energy source for living cells is the simple sugar glucose. The energy in glucose—the energy that supports all life on earth—comes from the sun.** How is the sun's energy stored in glucose? How is it released for use by cells? To answer these questions, we must understand *photosynthesis* and *respiration*.

Photosynthesis refers to the series of chemical reactions in which glucose is organized. In this process, *light energy is changed to chemical energy and stored in glucose molecules*. **Respiration** is the process in which living cells break down glucose and release its stored energy. This process involves chemical changes.

Respiration goes on constantly in all living cells. But photosynthesis occurs *only* in certain green plant cells. We say that such cells are "self-fueling." With these basic facts in mind, we can begin our study of photosynthesis and respiration.

THE IMPORTANCE OF PHOTOSYNTHESIS

Only the "self-fueling" cells, through photosynthesis, organize glucose. With very few exceptions, *all other organisms depend on these cells for energy*. The dependence may be direct, as in the case of a cow that eats grass. Or it may be indirect, as when a human being eats beef or drinks milk from the cow. In the end, though, all life depends on photosynthesis.

To understand this dependence more fully, imagine that photosynthesis suddenly stopped. Suppose, for example, that the earth were somehow cut off from the light of the sun. Without sunlight, the "self-fueling" green plant cells would no longer form glucose.

The green plants would soon die. Other organisms might survive for a time. Animals could eat other animals. Plants such as fungi could live off rotting organic matter. But sooner or later the food would run out, and almost all life would end.

What if the sun kept shining, but all the green plants were somehow removed? The result would be the same. The remaining organisms would have light energy all around them. But they could not put it into any form that their cells could use. Sooner or later, all would die.

In the living world, matter is recycled constantly. Simple substances are organized into complex ones, and complex substances broken down to simple ones. This goes on over and over, year after year, century after century. But this process requires energy, and *energy is not recycled*. New energy must be supplied constantly. This new energy comes from the sun through photosynthesis.

This might be a good place to discuss the carbon cycle briefly. This cycle can be illustrated on the chalkboard. Its importance to photosynthesis should be stressed. The carbon cycle is discussed in detail in Chapter Forty-Eight.

THE GENERAL NATURE OF PHOTOSYNTHESIS

In a way, the word *photosynthesis* defines itself. *Photo* refers to light, while *synthesis* means the building of a complex substance from simpler substances. Here, the simple substances are carbon and water. The complex substance formed is glucose. Light energy is also required for photosynthesis, and oxygen is given off as a by-product. We can write a simple chemical equation for photosynthesis as follows:

$$6CO_2 + 6H_2O + \text{light energy} \rightarrow C_6H_{12}O_6 + 6O_2$$

carbon + water + light energy $\rightarrow$ glucose + oxygen
dioxide

This equation gives only the most general idea of what happens. It shows a single reaction, but photosynthesis is actually a complex series of reactions. What happens in these reactions? Does carbon dioxide unite *directly* with water? Does the oxygen by-product come from the carbon dioxide, the water, or both? How is light energy changed into chemical bond energy? Biologists asked these and other questions for many years. Before we learn some of their answers, let's look at a few more key facts about photosynthesis.

THE ROLE OF CHLOROPHYLL

We have said that photosynthesis occurs only in green plant cells. Actually, the plant itself does not have to be green. Photosynthesis may take place even in red or brown plants, such as certain seaweeds. What is important is not the plant's color, but the presence in its cells of the green pigment **chlorophyll. Photosynthesis takes place only in the presence of chlorophyll.**

In Chapter Four, we noted that chlorophyll is found in cell structures called *chloroplasts*. Here, the chlorophyll molecules are packed between layers of proteins and lipids in disc-shaped bodies

Review the structure of chloroplasts. Refer to the thin membranes or *lamellae* that compose the interior of the chloroplast. The chloroplasts usually thicken and darken to form the *grana*.

Review Fig. 6-2 with students to make certain
they understand the ATP-ADP cycle. Select
a few students to draw the cycle on the chalkboard and to explain it to the class.

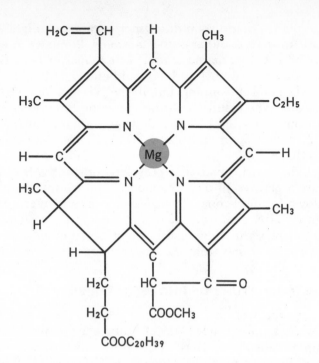

6–2 The structural formula of the chlorophyll molecule.

6–3 Plants contain color pigments other than green chlorophyll. The red maple contains the reddish-orange pigment carotene. (H.R.W. Photo by Russell Dian)

called *grana*. Some very simple plants, such as the blue-green algae, do not have chloroplasts. But they do have grana, which are spread through the cell cytoplasm. We might think of grana as the workbenches upon which glucose is built in photosynthesis.

Chlorophyll cannot develop without light. If plants such as bean seedlings sprout in total darkness, they will be yellow rather than green. If the plants are moved into the light, photosynthesis will not occur until chlorophyll develops. Chlorophyll, then, is necessary for photosynthesis. But in what way?

In photosynthesis, chlorophyll acts as a *catalyst*. Remember that a catalyst is a substance that affects a reaction but does not enter into it chemically. Several enzymes are also necessary as catalysts in photosynthesis. Other pigments, including the xanthophylls and carotenes, also can help out by transferring energy to chlorophyll.

Suppose we mixed carbon dioxide and water in a flask along with chlorophyll and other catalysts. If we placed the flask in light, would photosynthesis take place? The answer is no. Photosynthesis can still occur in whole chloroplasts that have been removed from cells. But chlorophyll alone is not enough. It seems that living cell processes or, at least, the grana, are needed for photosynthesis.

ATP—THE ENERGY TRANSFER COMPOUND

Light energy may enter a cell too rapidly for the cell to store it all in glucose by photosynthesis. On the other hand, in respiration, energy may be released too rapidly for a cell to use it all.

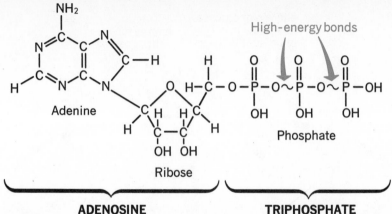

6–4 A structural formula of an ATP molecule.

There must be a way to trap the extra energy and release it in controlled amounts to meet cell needs. The substance that does this important job is the *energy transfer compound* known as **ATP,** or *adenosine triphosphate.*

ATP is organized in the cell mitochondria and released to all parts of the cell. The chemical structure of ATP can be changed quickly so as to store or release energy. In one part of the molecule, a unit of *adenine* is bonded to a unit of *ribose,* a five-carbon sugar. Together, these two substances make up *adenosine.* A short chain of smaller *phosphate* molecules is attached to the adenosine. ATP is called adenosine *tri*phosphate because it has *three* phosphates attached.

In building up ATP, one phosphate is first bonded to adenosine. At this point, the molecule is *adenosine monophosphate,* or **AMP.** A second phosphate builds up the molecule to **ADP,** or *adenosine diphosphate.* This phosphate is attached by a high-energy bond. A third phosphate, attached by a still higher-energy bond, gives us ATP.

This last high-energy bond is the key to the storing, transfer, and release of energy by ATP. The third phosphate can be rapidly removed, changing ATP to ADP, or attached, changing ADP back to ATP. It is the energy involved in these changes that is important. The bonding of a phosphate to ADP, forming ATP, requires energy. This energy is *stored* in the ATP molecule. If a phosphate is removed from ATP, forming ADP, the stored energy is *released.* The ADP molecule is then ready to store more energy by adding a phosphate again. We can represent these changes by a simple equation:

$$ADP + phosphate + energy \rightleftarrows ATP (ADP \sim P)$$

The symbol $\sim$ stands for a high-energy bond.

These changes occur over and over again in a cell. Energy is stored in ATP, moved around the cell, and released as needed. With this understanding of ATP, we are ready to approach photosynthesis itself.

As energy is utilized for work, the high-energy phosphate is changed to low-energy phosphate. When low-energy phosphate is converted to high-energy phosphate the process is called phosphorylation.

Models of the chlorophyll molecule can be constructed using styrofoam balls of different colors. Some students may be interested in constructing a mobile of the molecule using pipe cleaners and styrofoam balls or other common materials.

PHOTOSYNTHESIS IS SOLVED

The first major discovery in photosynthesis research involved

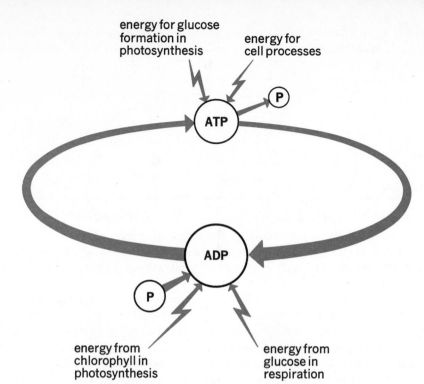

energy for glucose
formation in
photosynthesis

energy for
cell processes

ATP

P

ADP

P

energy from
chlorophyll in
photosynthesis

energy from
glucose in
respiration

6-5 ADP receives energy and attaches a phosphate molecule, changing to ATP. This energy is stored in the ATP molecule. If a phosphate is removed from ATP, forming ADP, the energy is released.

Some students may be interested in isolating the chloroplasts of a leaf. This is a fairly complicated procedure and it is explained in detail on pp. 55-57 of William Berman's book, *Experimental Biology*, ARCO Publishing Company.

Stress to the students that photosynthesis cannot be reduced to a simple reaction. Briefly discuss the dark reactions of photosynthesis. In addition, emphasize that photosynthesis is the only biological reaction which is dependent upon an outside source of energy.

water molecules. Biologists did not know whether the oxygen given off during photosynthesis came from water or from carbon dioxide. The question was answered when plant cells were grown in water that contained the radioisotope oxygen-18 (H_2O^{18}). This radioisotope could be traced through chemical reactions. The oxygen given off by the cells contained oxygen-18. But glucose taken from the cells contained *no* oxygen-18. Clearly, water molecules were geing split somewhere in the process.

This was a surprising finding. It takes a great amount of energy to split water molecules. Where could this energy be coming from? Since light was necessary for the process, light was the logical energy source. Biologists already knew that light supplied the energy stored in glucose. But the idea that light energy split water molecules was a new one. It was also found that cylorophyll plays an important part in this energy transfer. The reactions among water, light, and chlorophyll make up the first phase in photosynthesis. Since these reactions occur only in light, this phase is called the **light reactions.**

The second phase of photosynthesis involves carbon dioxide. Here, glucose finally is synthesized and water is given off as a by-product. What part does carbon dioxide play? Carbon dioxide containing carbon-14 ($C^{14}O_2$), a traceable radioisotope, gave the answer, at least in part. The carbon is fixed in a series of reactions that do not require light. The oxygen combines with hydrogen from the first phase and forms water. The change from inorganic carbon dioxide to organic glucose involves many steps. Several different products are formed along the way. During these changes, carbon atoms bond and form chains. Many other atoms can join to these chains, forming a great number of organic compounds. This second phase is called the *dark reactions.*

We can sum up these changes in the following equation:

$6CO_2$ + $12H_2O$ * + light energy $\rightarrow$ $C_6H_{12}O_6$ + $6H_2O$ + $6O_2$ *
carbon + water + light energy $\rightarrow$ glucose + water + oxygen
dioxide

The asterisk (*) stands for oxygen-18. Notice that the oxygen given off as a by-product ($6O_2$*) comes from the splitting of water molecules. The oxygen in the glucose comes from carbon dioxide. Also, notice that the water molecules that enter the first phase are not the water molecules given off in the second phase.

Our equation represents only the main facts of photosynthesis as we understand it today. Now let's look at some of the details of the light and dark reactions.

THE LIGHT REACTIONS

The first phase of photosynthesis involves reactions that occur only in light and require chlorophyll. In these light reactions, water molecules are split and energy stored for later use. On paper, this process seems long and complex. In fact, the whole series of light reactions takes place in a split second. Still, it helps to describe these reactions as a series of steps, even though they take place at almost the same time. Refer to the diagram on page 69 as you read the following description.

Explain to students that the dark reaction does not have to occur in the dark, but it occurs after the light reaction. Light is not necessary for the dark reaction to occur.

6-6 Photosynthesis: In the light reaction, energy and raw materials are used on the left; while the product is formed during the dark reaction at the right.

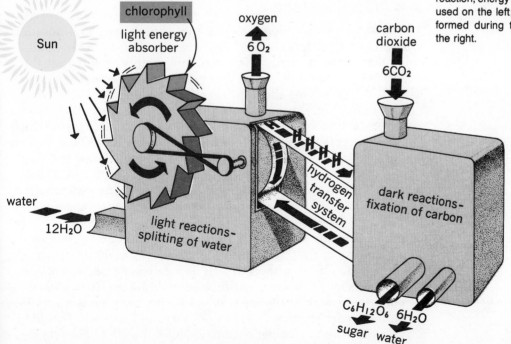

■ *Chlorophyll is energized.* Chlorophyll acts as an **energy carrier** in the light reactions phase. It is thought that light energy causes a sudden change in the atoms of chlorophyll molecules. Electrons move from lower to higher energy levels. Thus, kinetic light energy is stored as chemical potential energy in the chlorophyll. Chlorophyll molecules in this state are said to be *energized*, or excited. When the stored energy is released, the electrons drop back to lower energy levels. The chlorophyll is no longer energized, but can trap more light and become energized again.

■ *Water molecules are split.* Hydrogen atoms are joined to oxygen by very strong bonds in a water molecule. It takes a great deal of energy to break these bonds and split the molecule. We do not know just *how* water molecules are split in photosynthesis. But we do know that the energy used in the process comes from energized chlorophyll.

■ *Energy is stored in ATP.* Chloroplasts contain ADP. Some of the energy released by energized chlorophyll is not used in splitting water molecules. Instead, this energy is stored by changing ADP to ATP. Thus, ATP is a second energy carrier in photosynthesis. The energy stored in ATP will be released and used later. Meanwhile, chlorophyll may accept and store more light energy.

NADP + 2H → NADPH₂. The combined hydrogen will be used in the synthesis reactions which occur during the dark reactions.

■ *Hydrogen is trapped by NADP.* Chloroplasts contain a coenzyme known as *NADP*. NADP is a **hydrogen acceptor.** It combines readily with the hydrogen released by the splitting of water molecules, forming NADPH₂. It is important that the hydrogen be trapped so that it does not escape or combine with oxygen again. The oxygen released from the water molecules is given off as a by-product.

THE DARK REACTIONS

The name *dark reactions* does not mean that these reactions must take place in the dark. In fact, they usually occur in the light along with the light reactions. The word *dark* simply means that these reactions do not require light energy. Instead, they use the energy stored in ATP during the light reactions phase.

The most important result of the dark reactions is *the fixing of carbon in a carbohydrate.* This process involves several steps which make up a cycle. Compounds are formed, broken down, and formed again. During this activity, carbon atoms form chains. Hydrogen and oxygen atoms can bond to these chains and form carbohydrates. It is here that the whole world of organic compounds begins.

Refer to the diagram on page 70 as you follow the steps involved in the dark reactions.

■ *Carbon dioxide is fixed by RDP.* Chloroplasts contain *ribulose diphosphate*, or *RDP*. This is a 5-carbon sugar molecule, with two phosphate groups attached. RDP is a **carbon dioxide acceptor.** Almost as soon as carbon dioxide enters a chloroplast, it is fixed by combining with RDP. The product of this reaction is a very unstable 6-carbon sugar. This sugar splits quickly into two molecules of *PGA*, or *phosphoglyceric* (FAHSS-foe-gli-SEHR-ick) *acid.*

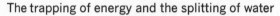

THE LIGHT REACTIONS

The trapping of energy and the splitting of water

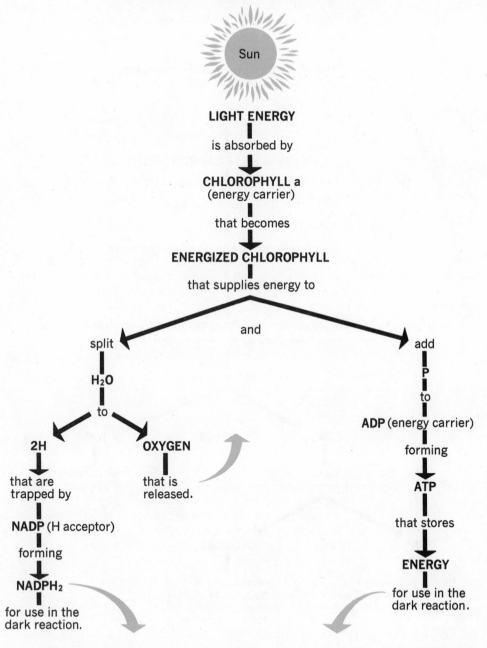

The fixing of carbon in a carbohydrate

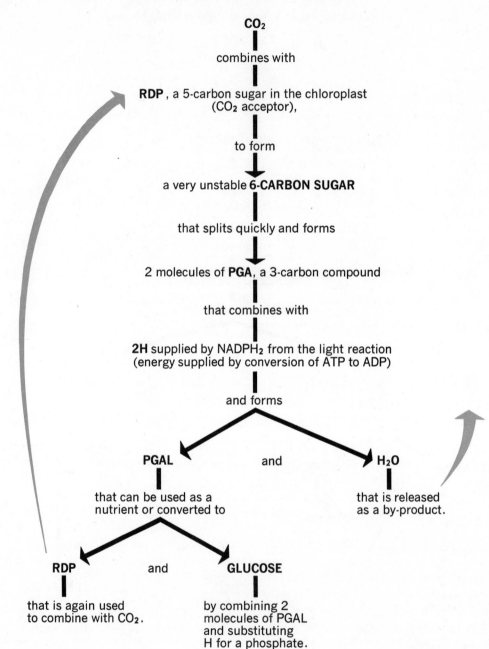

CO₂

combines with

RDP , a 5-carbon sugar in the chloroplast
(CO₂ acceptor),

to form

a very unstable **6-CARBON SUGAR**

that splits quickly and forms

2 molecules of **PGA**, a 3-carbon compound

that combines with

2H supplied by NADPH₂ from the light reaction
(energy supplied by conversion of ATP to ADP)

and forms

PGAL   and   **H₂O**

that can be used as a
nutrient or converted to

that is released
as a by-product.

RDP   and   **GLUCOSE**

that is again used
to combine with CO₂.

by combining 2
molecules of PGAL
and substituting
H for a phosphate.

6–8   The dark reaction.

■ *PGA combines with hydrogen and forms PGAL.* PGA quickly combines with hydrogen taken from $NADPH_2$. This reaction requires a large amount of energy, which is supplied by ATP. The products are water and a very important substance known as *PGAL*. PGAL can be used directly as an energy source for cell activity. In fact, plants supplied with PGAL can survive without photosynthesis or any other food source. For this reason, we might even think of PGAL as the main product of photosynthesis.

Some PGAL *is* used directly by the cell. But, in photosynthesis, a cell produces much more PGAL than it needs. Much of this PGAL is changed into other products in further chemical reactions.

■ *Other products of PGAL.* Some PGAL molecules are used in forming RDP. This RDP can then fix more carbon dioxide, starting the dark reactions cycle over again.

Other PGAL is changed to glucose. In this reaction, two PGAL molecules combine. The formula for PGAL is $C_3H_5O_3 \sim$ (P). The symbol (P) stands for an attached phosphate group. This phosphate is removed and replaced by hydrogen in each of the two PGAL molecules. This results in $C_6H_{12}O_6$, or glucose. The simple sugar fructose can also be produced from PGAL.

The simple sugars formed from PGAL may be combined in double sugars such as sucrose ($C_{12}H_{22}O_{11}$). Or the simple sugars may join in long chains and form starches and celluloses. Some plants also build PGAL molecules into oils such as corn oil, peanut oil, and so on.

CONDITIONS FOR PHOTOSYNTHESIS

Since light is the energy source for photosynthesis, light conditions have a great effect on the process. Sunlight is made up of light rays of different wavelengths and energy. We see the different rays in sunlight as red, orange, yellow, green, blue, and violet in a rainbow. Together, these rays make up the **visible spectrum.** Red rays have the longest wavelength and the least energy of the visible rays. Violet rays, at the other end of the spectrum, have the shortest wavelength and the highest energy.

Chloroplasts absorb some rays more than others. Also, different plants vary in the rays they absorb. Most land plants absorb the most energy from violet and blue rays, and somewhat less energy from red and orange rays. Some green and yellow light is absorbed, but much is reflected or passes through plant structures. We see only the rays that are not absorbed. This fact explains why chloroplasts appear green or yellow-green.

Ocean plants live under different light conditions. Seawater absorbs most of the red and violet rays. It also lowers the total intensity of the light. In shallow water, ocean plants absorb energy for photosynthesis mostly from blue, green, and yellow rays. Deep-water algae, living 20 meters or more underwater, rely mainly on blue and green rays for energy.

Temperature also affects the rate of photosynthesis, but not as

A simple experiment can be performed to illustrate the presence of sugar in plant tissues. Use two coleus plants. Place one in the dark for eight hours. Place the other in light for the same period of time. Remove an equal-sized leaf from each plant and grind each leaf separately with 20 ml of water. Filter the result of each with filter paper into a small test tube. Support each test tube in a rack. Add a clinitest tablet to each tube. Shake each test tube gently. Compare the color. Ask students to draw conclusions.

Stress to the class that the major portion of the dark reaction is concerned with the reformation of the CO_2 acceptor—RDP.

A prism will help to demonstrate what happens when white light is passed through it. Different wavelengths are separated and the visible spectrum of color can be seen. Relate this demonstration to the discussion concerning conditions for photosynthesis.

6–9 The absorption spectrum of chlorophyll in alcohol. Notice most of the green light is not absorbed. (Sol Mednick)

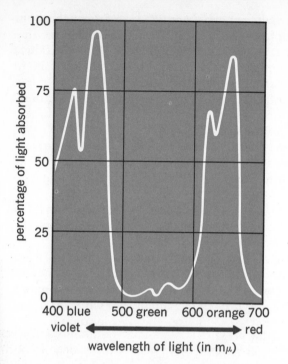

much as you might expect. Temperature probably affects the activity of enzymes involved in photosynthesis. Normal temperature changes during a plant's growing season seem to have little effect on enzyme action. However, above about 32° C (90° F), rises in temperature seem to lower the rate of photosynthesis.

CHEMOSYNTHESIS

Photosynthesis is the chemical link between the inorganic and organic worlds. We might even think of photosynthesis as a bridge. Only by crossing this bridge can carbon dioxide, water, and light energy be organized into PGAL, glucose, and other organic compounds. Without this bridge, almost all life on earth would end.

However, as we said early in this chapter, there are exceptions. Certain bacteria do *not* depend on photosynthesis. These bacteria have enzyme systems that can trap energy released during *inorganic* chemical reactions. Thus, they can organize their own carbohydrates *without using light energy*. This process is known as *chemosynthesis.*

From the carbohydrates formed in chemosynthesis, these bacteria can build all of their fats, proteins, and nucleic acids. We often think of bacteria as low forms of life. But in terms of cell chemistry, they are as well prepared for survival as any organisms on earth.

RESPIRATION—THE "FIRE" OF LIFE

Respiration includes all of the reactions in which energy is released

6–10 The rate at which bubbles of oxygen are released varies under conditions of different light. This illustrates the relationship between light intensity and the rate of photosynthesis in green water plants.

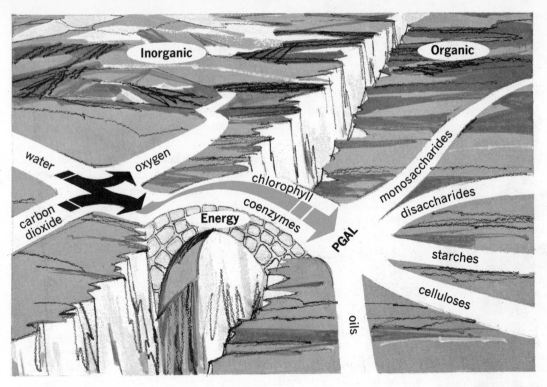

Inorganic

Organic

water

oxygen

carbon dioxide

chlorophyll

coenzymes

Energy

PGAL

monosaccharides

disaccharides

starches

celluloses

oils

6–11 Photosynthesis can be linked to a chemical bridge between the inorganic world and the organic world.

in support of cell life. These reactions include the breaking down of glucose and other foods and the transfer of energy to ATP. The exact reactions involved, products formed, and amount of energy released may vary. But respiration in some form is necessary to the life of every cell.

When we think of respiration, we tend to think of breathing. But breathing is only an exchange of gases between the body and the atmosphere. It is in the body cells—mainly in the cell mitochondria—that respiration takes place. It is here that the "fire" of life burns constantly.

At this point, it may help to consider what happens when an organic fuel such as coal or wood burns. The fuel molecules break down rapidly as oxygen is added. Chemical bond energy is changed to heat and light energy. This reaction occurs only at high temperature. Also, the burning is not *controlled*—almost all of the fuel molecules are broken down.

Respiration also involves a "burning" of organic fuels. Glucose and other organic molecules are broken down and their chemical bond energy released. But these reactions are very different from the burning of coal or wood. For one thing, high temperatures are not involved; the cell mitochondria could not withstand them. Also, **respiration is a controlled process. It occurs in small steps, each of which releases a small amount of energy. Respiratory enzymes control these processes and cause them to take place at the normal temperature of the organism.**

RESPIRATION FUELS AND OXIDATION

Any organic molecules present in a cell can be fuel for respiration. Such molecules include glucose, fatty acids and glycerol, amino acids, and even vitamins and enzymes.

In Chapter Three, we discussed the bonds that hold atoms together in molecules. Chemical energy is stored in these bonds. When the molecules break down, the bonds are broken and their energy released. The chemical bond energy in organic fuel molecules was once light energy from the sun. This light energy was stored in the molecules during photosynthesis. Thus, **the chemical bond energy released in respiration first came from the sun.**

Just how is this energy released? The answer is *oxidation.* Oxidation involves either adding oxygen or removing hydrogen from a molecule, usually glucose. In either case, energy is released. In most oxidation in cells, hydrogen is removed.

CELLULAR RESPIRATION

In *cellular respiration,* glucose is broken down in two main stages, the second of which requires molecular oxygen. These two stages involve a series of reactions and many respiratory enzymes. But we can sum them up as follows:

■ The first stage is called *anaerobic* since it does not involve molecular oxygen. This stage occurs outside the mitochondria. As

6–12 A burning Brazil nut demonstrates the large amounts of chemical bond energy that is released from food. (John King)

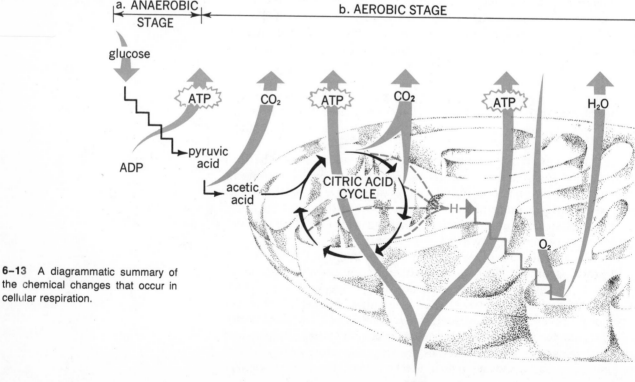

6–13 A diagrammatic summary of the chemical changes that occur in cellular respiration.

many as 12 enzymes are used in this series of reactions. The main result is that a glucose molecule is broken down to two 3-carbon molecules of *pyruvic acid*. Two ATP molecules supply the energy needed for this process. However, enough energy is released in splitting the glucose molecule to form four ATP molecules. Thus, there is a net gain of two ATP molecules. The energy released is about seven percent of the energy in the glucose molecule. The rest of its energy remains in the bonds of the pyruvic acid molecules.

■ The second stage is called the *aerobic* stage since it requires molecular oxygen. In this stage, pyruvic acid is broken down. Water and carbon dioxide are given off and energy is released. This stage involves two main series of steps.

First, two hydrogen atoms and one carbon dioxide molecule are removed from each pyruvic acid molecule. Two *acetic acid* molecules result. The carbon dioxide is released. The acetic acid enters a mitochondrion. There, each acetic acid molecule is joined to a 4-carbon acid already present. Two 6-carbon molecules of *citric acid* result. This is one of a series of reactions known as the *citric acid cycle*. As the cycle continues, one carbon atom is removed from the citric acid. A 5-carbon acid is formed and carbon dioxide given off. In another step, a second carbon atom is removed. This leaves a 4-carbon acid which combines with more acetic acid and repeats the cycle. Again, the carbon joins with molecular oxygen and is released as carbon dioxide.

Hydrogen is also released during the citric acid cycle. In the second part of the aerobic stage, this hydrogen is involved in a series of reactions called *hydrogen transport*. During these reactions, energy is stored in ATP formed from ADP. Finally, the hydrogen atoms combine with oxygen and form water.

We can sum up the stages of cellular respiration in the following equation:

$$C_6H_{12}O_6 + 6O_2 \rightarrow 6CO_2 + 6H_2O + \text{energy (38 ATP)}$$

glucose   oxygen   carbon   water
                        dioxide

The useful energy stored in both stages comes to 38 molecules of ATP. This represents between 55 and 60 percent of the total bond energy in one glucose molecule.

FERMENTATION

Another kind of respiration is *fermentation*. In this process, glucose again is broken down by enzyme action. However, molecular oxygen is not present.

Fermentation begins much as cellular respiration did. Glucose is broken down to two pyruvic acid molecules, and a small amount of energy is released. From this point, the pyruvic acid may be broken down in two different ways.

■ In yeasts and certain other organisms, a carbon dioxide mole-

Review the structure of the mitochondrian discussed in Chapter Four. Also review the functions of enzymes on pp. 39-40.

Anaerobic respiration occurs without oxygen. Aerobic respiration needs oxygen to take place. Respiration in yeast cells is anaerobic.

Stress to students that anaerobic respiration occurs outside of the mitochondrian. In all forms of anaerobic respiration glucose is split to form pyruvic acid.

Fermentation has many industrial uses particularly in brewing and baking. Students may be interested in the action of yeast cells in the expansion or rising of dough. Have students explain this process. What happens if yeast is not used in the baking process?

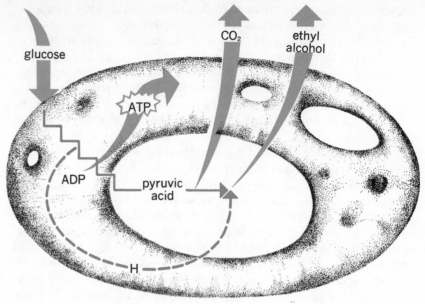

6-14 A diagrammatic summary of
the chemical changes that occur in
alcoholic fermentation.

cule is removed from pyruvic acid. The product formed is then
broken down to the end product, ethyl alcohol. This process,
known as *alcoholic fermentation,* can be represented as follows:

$$C_6H_{12}O_6 \rightarrow 2\ C_2H_5OH + 2\ CO_2 + \text{energy (2 ATP)}$$

glucose   ethyl   carbon
alcohol   dioxide

■ In animal tissues such as muscle, *lactic acid fermentation* may take
place. Here, with no molecular oxygen present, pyruvic acid is
changed to lactic acid as an end product. This process is represented by the following equation:

$$C_6H_{12}O_6 \rightarrow 2\ C_3H_6O_3 + \text{energy (2 ATP)}$$

glucose   lactic acid

Notice that much less energy is released and stored in ATP during
fermentation than during aerobic respiration. Most of the energy
of the glucose remains in the chemical bonds of the fermentation
end products.

USES OF CELL ENERGY

What happens to the energy released from glucose during respiration? Some is given off as heat. In warm-blooded animals, this
heat keeps the body temperature constant. The remaining energy,
stored in ATP, can be released for use in many cell activities. It
may be used in building starches, fats and oils, nucleic acids and
proteins, and other substances. It also may support active transport, cell division, muscle contraction, and other activities.

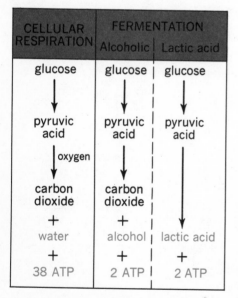

CELLULAR RESPIRATION	FERMENTATION	
	Alcoholic	Lactic acid
glucose	glucose	glucose
↓	↓	↓
pyruvic acid	pyruvic acid	pyruvic acid
↓ oxygen	↓	↓
carbon dioxide	carbon dioxide	
+	+	↓
water	alcohol	lactic acid
+	+	+
38 ATP	2 ATP	2 ATP

6-15 A comparison of the end products and energy released in cellular
respiration and alcoholic and lactic
acid fermentation.

Almost all forms of life depend on photosynthesis, which occurs only in the grana of green plants. Through this process, carbon dioxide and water are organized into organic compounds such as PGAL and glucose, the basic fuel for all cells. Light energy is necessary for photosynthesis and is stored as chemical energy in glucose. Chlorophyll and certain enzymes act as catalysts. The energy transfer compound ATP also acts as the unit of stored energy for living things.

The energy stored in glucose during photosynthesis is of no use unless it is released in cells. This is done in cellular respiration. Glucose molecules are broken down and their chemical bond energy released. Some of this energy is given off as heat. Some is stored in ATP for use in cell activities. Respiration must go on constantly, for all living cells must have a constant supply of energy.

photosynthesis	light reactions	chemosynthesis
respiration	dark reactions	oxidation
chlorophyll	energy carrier	cellular respiration
ATP	hydrogen acceptor	alcoholic fermentation
AMP	carbon dioxide acceptor	lactic acid fermentation
ADP	visible spectrum	

1. Describe the importance of photosynthesis to all life.
2. Define photosynthesis using words and the chemical formula.
3. What part does chlorophyll play in the process of photosynthesis?
4. Describe the importance of ATP to living things.
5. How does a molecule of ATP store and release energy?
6. Outline the steps of the light reactions of photosynthesis.
7. Outline the steps in the fixation of CO_2 in the dark reactions.
8. How is chemosynthesis different from photosynthesis?
9. What is the biological importance of respiration?
10. How does respiration occur without high temperature of fuel combustion?
11. Define cellular respiration with a chemical equation.
12. Describe the two types of fermentation.
13. List several processes requiring cell energy.

1. Explain why chloroplasts appear green in color.
2. Describe the conditions that affect photosynthesis.
3. How do cells derive their usable energy?
4. Why might we consider photosynthesis and respiration complementary processes?

chapter seven

Nucleic Acids and Protein Synthesis

OBJECTIVES

- RECOGNIZE the importance of protein synthesis to all life.
- DESCRIBE the replication of DNA.
- IDENTIFY the chemical structure of DNA and RNA.
- UNDERSTAND the process of transcription of the DNA code to RNA.
- STATE the importance of the triplet code of DNA.
- DESCRIBE the role of RNA in protein synthesis.
- LIST the functions of proteins in living cells.

As an introduction to this chapter, ask students to consider why humans give birth to humans, cats to cats, and birds to birds. What makes it possible for characteristics to be carried on from generation to generation? Introduce the term DNA and explain that it is the DNA found in the nucleus of cells that makes heredity possible.

7–1 Life's spiral staircase. (H.R.W. Photo by Russell Dian)

PROTEIN SYNTHESIS—ANOTHER KEY TO LIFE

In Chapter Six, we saw the importance of photosynthesis to life. **Protein synthesis** is just as important. Every living cell contains proteins. Cell membranes, organelles, and cytoplasm itself are made up largely of proteins. Enzymes, which are necessary to all cell activities, are protein molecules. We could give many other examples of proteins and their importance. But the point is clear enough: **without proteins, there would be no life.**

Photosynthesis and protein synthesis may be equally important, but they are also quite different. For one thing, photosynthesis takes place only in green plant cells. But protein synthesis takes place in *all* cells. Every cell organizes its own protein molecules. Another difference is that photosynthesis always involves the same series of reactions and the same products—PGAL and glucose. In protein synthesis, on the other hand, cells build many different proteins. Further, the proteins formed vary from species to species, individual to individual, and even within the same organism. This difference between proteins is important in organ transplants such as kidney transplants. Such transplants sometimes fail because of a reaction to the proteins of the new organ.

There are many millions of different proteins in the living world. Yet a cell must build only the proteins it needs. For years, biologists wondered how this process was controlled. They knew that the protein "factories" of cells are the ribosomes. It is on these tiny bodies, attached to the endoplasmic reticulum, that proteins actually are formed. But it was also known that the control center for all cell activities lay in the nucleus. What substance in the nucleus had this control? How did this substance code the building of proteins? How was the code delivered from the nucleus to the ribosomes? The answers to these questions came with one of the most important discoveries in the history of biology.

THE DISCOVERY OF DNA

Chromosomes are dark, rod-shaped bodies in the cell nucleus. Biologists had looked to these structures as the most likely control centers of the cell. Studies had shown that chromosomes are made up of two substances, *protein* and *nucleic acid*. One of these substances must control all cell activity, including protein synthesis. But which one?

Studies in the 1940's pointed to nucleic acid, rather than protein, as the control substance. Then research centered on the nucleic acid molecule itself. Its chemical makeup was known. But its structure, the way the atoms are actually arranged, had not been learned.

The breakthrough came in 1953. It was the work of two young scientists at Cambridge University in England. One member of the team was the American biologist James D. Watson. The other was the British biophysicist F.H.C. Crick. Together, they proposed a model of perhaps the most complex of all organic molecules. This molecule was **DNA,** or *deoxyribonucleic* (dee-OCK-see-RY-boe-NOO-KLEE-ick) *acid.*

THE STRUCTURE OF DNA

Sometimes, in working a puzzle, a key piece falls into place. Suddenly, the structure of a whole section of the puzzle becomes clear. The model of DNA offered by Watson and Crick had much the same effect. Suddenly, the answers to a great many questions about the control of protein synthesis and other activities became clear.

Watson and Crick described the DNA molecule as a *double helix*, a type of spiral. To understand this structure better, imagine a rope ladder with metal rungs. If the ladder is twisted a double helix is formed. Imagine, further, that the ladder is in two parts. Each part is made up of a length of rope to which many half-rungs are attached. The whole ladder is formed by joining the half-rungs from each part in the middle.

This "ladder" structure is similar to the DNA molecule. The "rope" parts are long strands in which *phosphate* units are joined to units of *deoxyribose*, a five-carbon sugar. Also attached to each deoxyribose unit is a nitrogen-containing *base*, forming a "half-rung" of the "ladder." Each base is joined by weak hydrogen bonds to a base from the other strand of DNA.

There were many people involved in the research leading to the structural model of DNA proposed by Watson and Crick. Students may be interested in investigating the contributions of Friedrich Miescher (1844-1895); Albrecht Kossel (1835-1927); Phoebus Aaron Levene (1869-1940); Alexander Todd (1907-   ); Oswald Avery (1877-1955); Heinz Fraenkel-Conrat (1910-   ); and Rosalind Franklin (1920-1958).

The DNA model was accepted by scientists prior to its being seen under the electron microscope. It was not until 1969 that the double helix of the DNA molecule was first seen under the electron microscope.

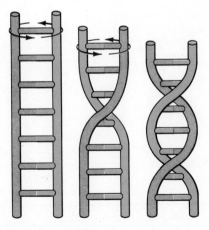

7–2 The formation of a double helix can be compared to the twisting of a flexible ladder.

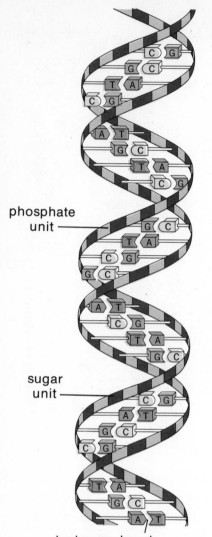

phosphate
unit

sugar
unit

hydrogen bond

7-3 Model of the double helix of DNA.

Each three-part unit of phosphate, deoxyribose, and attached base is called a *nucleotide.* Thus, you can think of a DNA molecule as a double strand of nucleotides bonded by their bases. There may be several thousand nucleotides in each strand.

There are four types of bases in DNA. Two are organic molecules known as *purines* (PURE-eens), either *adenine* (ADD-uh-NEEN) or *guanine* (GWAH-NEEN). The other two are *pyrimidines* (pie-RIM-uh-DEENS), either *thymine* (THI-MEEN) or *cytosine* (SY-tuh-SEEN). These four bases have the DNA code letters A, G, T, and C. We will look more closely at the DNA code soon. For now, simply note that **the nucleotide bases are part of a code system that controls protein synthesis.**

Take a closer look at the bonding between the four DNA bases. Notice that these substances bond in only two combinations—adenine to thymine, and guanine to cytosine. This is very important to the DNA code system.

DNA, RNA, AND PROTEIN SYNTHESIS

One amazing thing about DNA is that a DNA molecule can build an exact double of itself. This process is known as *replication.* It is very important in cell reproduction. **DNA replication allows the cell to pass its code from one generation to the next.** DNA "unzips" its two halves. Nucleotides then attach to the proper bases. In the end, two duplicate DNA molecules are formed.

A similar process, called *transcription,* is more important in protein synthesis. In transcription, a strand of DNA codes the building of a near-double of itself. This near-double is a molecule of *ribonucleic acid,* or *RNA*.

The sugar in RNA is *ribose,* which contains one more oxygen atom than the deoxyribose in DNA. RNA contains the same bases as DNA except for thymine. In RNA, thymine is replaced by another pyrimidine called *uracil.* Thus, the code letters for RNA are A, G, U, and C. RNA is usually a single strand, rather than a double strand like DNA.

The DNA code controls protein synthesis. But DNA lies in the nucleus, while the ribosomes where proteins are formed are in the cytoplasm. Somehow, the DNA code must be carried from the nucleus to the ribosomes. This is the job of *messenger RNA.* Before learning more about transcription and messenger RNA, we need to understand the DNA code itself.

THREE-LETTER CODE WORDS IN DNA

We represent the four nucleotide bases of DNA as A, G, T, and C. These bases make up the "alphabet" from which DNA code "words" are formed. There may be thousands of bases on a DNA strand, and they may occur in any order. However, it is not *single* bases that are important, but groups of three called *triplet codons.* Each base triplet is a three-letter code word. For example, CGT, ACG, and AAA stand for base triplet code words in DNA.

The four letters of the DNA code can be combined into 64 different three-letter words. How do these words affect protein synthesis? What exactly is it that they code? The answer is *amino acids*. Remember that proteins are made up of long chains of amino acid units. *Each DNA code word codes an amino acid.* Further, **the order of the words on a DNA strand codes the order in which amino acids will be put together in building a protein. Each DNA code word always codes the same amino acid. But in different organisms the code words may be arranged in very different order, giving rise to many different proteins.**

TRANSCRIPTION OF THE DNA CODE TO RNA

How is the DNA code passed on to messenger RNA? Let's set up an example. We will begin in the nucleus, where a strand of DNA is directing the synthesis of a strand of RNA. There are thousands of base triplets, or three-letter code words, on the DNA strand. The DNA molecule "unzips" and exposes its bases. Suppose that three of these triplets are CGT, ACG, and AAA. The bases on the RNA strand must fit the bases on the DNA strand. Thus, the triplet code words on the RNA will be GCA, UGC, and UUU. (Remember that RNA contains U, or uracil, instead of T, thymine.)

As in DNA, there are 64 possible three-letter code words, or *codons*, in messenger RNA. However, there are only 20 amino acids. Thus, several different codons may code the same amino acid. A few codons, though, do not code any amino acid. Instead, these **"nonsense codons"** seem to act as signals for the end of a protein chain. We might think of such a codon as the period at the end of a protein "sentence."

Table 7-1 on the following page shows the known messenger RNA codons for the 20 amino acids. The strand of messenger RNA in our example had the codons GCA, UGC, and UUU. Which amino acids do these triplets code?

BUILDING AMINO ACIDS INTO PROTEINS

After transcription, messenger RNA may be stored briefly in the nucleolus, or may move directly out through the nuclear membrane. Once in the cytoplasm, it acts as a pattern, or **template,** for the building of amino acids into proteins. Several protein molecules are organized at the same time along the messenger RNA strand. Let's take a look at this process.

First, it is thought, a ribosome attaches to the template at each point where a protein chain will begin. There are several such points on the RNA strand, each marked by special **initiator codons.**

The amino acids needed for protein synthesis are spread through the cytoplasm. Individual amino acid units must be picked up and brought to the template in the right order. This is the job of a third type of RNA, **transfer RNA.**

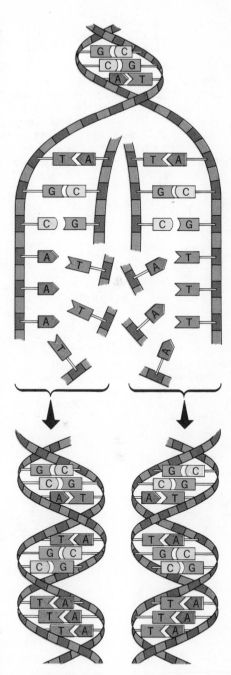

7–4 Replication of a DNA molecule. DNA "unzips", nucleotides then attach to the proper bases. Now there are two duplicated DNA molecules.

Table 7-1 MESSENGER RNA CODONS FOR THE AMINO ACIDS

AMINO ACID	TRIPLET CODE
alanine	GCA, GCG, GCC, GCU
arginine	CGA, CGG, CGC, CGU, AGA, AGG
asparagine	AAC, AAU
aspartic acid	GAC, GAU
cysteine	UGC, UGU
glutamic acid	GAA, GAG
glutamine	CAA, CAG
glycine	GGC, GGU, GGA, GGG
histidine	CAC, CAU
isoleucine	AUC, AUU, AUA
leucine	CUC, CUU, CUA, CUG, UUA, UUG
lysine	AAA, AAG
methionine	AUG
phenylalanine	UUU, UUC
proline	CCA, CCG, CCC, CCU
serine	UCA, UCG, UCC, UCU, AGU, AGC
threonine	ACA, ACG, ACC, ACU
tryptophan	UGG
tyrosine	UAC, UAU
valine	GUA, GUG, GUC, GUU

The table illustrates that there are a number of different codons that correspond to different amino acids. There are also starting and stopping codons. These codons are helpful in permitting a single messenger RNA molecule to carry instructions for several different protein molecules. When a "stop" codon is reached, the protein chain is released.

Emphasize the difference in structure that exists between DNA and RNA. RNA includes uracil instead of thymine and ribose instead of deoxyribose.

Strands of transfer RNA are much shorter than those of messenger RNA. Usually, a transfer RNA strand has only 70 to 80 nucleotides. This strand doubles back on itself and forms loops. At one end of the strand is a triplet code word. The bases in this triplet fit the bases in a specific RNA codon. For this reason, the transfer RNA triplet is called an *anti-codon*.

At the other end of the transfer RNA strand is another triplet. This triplet is always CCA. It is to this triplet that an amino acid from the cytoplasm attaches. Of the 20 amino acids, only one kind will attach to a given strand of transfer RNA. Why is this so? It is believed that an enzyme in the cytoplasm "recognizes" the transfer RNA strand by its anti-codon. Using energy from ATP, the enzyme then bonds the right amino acid to the strand. This process would require a different enzyme for each kind of amino acid.

The transfer RNA strand, with an amino acid unit attached, now goes to the template. A ribosome moves along the messenger RNA template, "reading" the codons. As each codon is "read," the transfer RNA strand with the proper anti-codon moves to a point on the ribosome. This action places the attached amino acid in the right position to be added to a protein chain.

After delivery of its amino acid, the transfer RNA strand moves off into the cytoplasm. The ribosome moves on and "reads" the next codon. Again, the transfer RNA strand with the proper anti-codon delivers its amino acid to the ribosome. This process is repeated again and again until the protein is completed. The ribo-

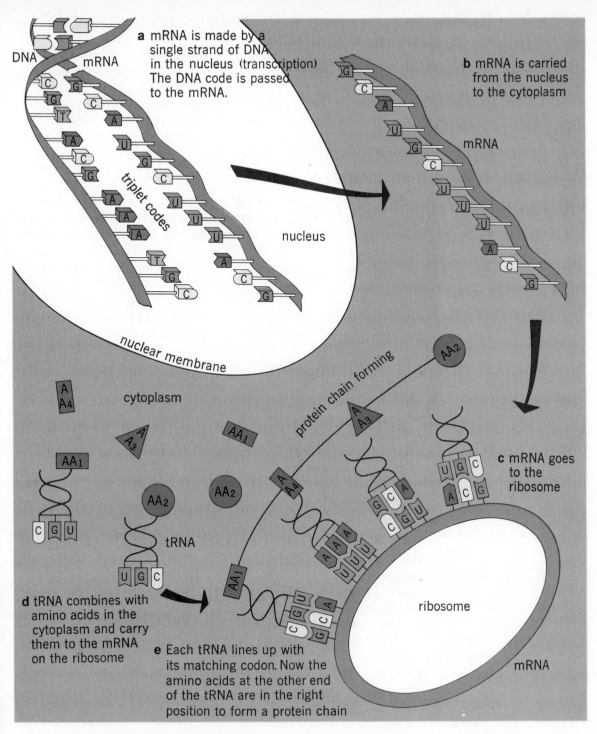

DNA **mRNA**

a mRNA is made by a single strand of DNA in the nucleus (transcription) The DNA code is passed to the mRNA.

triplet codes

nucleus

b mRNA is carried from the nucleus to the cytoplasm

mRNA

nuclear membrane

cytoplasm

protein chain forming

c mRNA goes to the ribosome

tRNA

d tRNA combines with amino acids in the cytoplasm and carry them to the mRNA on the ribosome

e Each tRNA lines up with its matching codon. Now the amino acids at the other end of the tRNA are in the right position to form a protein chain

ribosome

mRNA

7–5 The role of DNA and RNA in protein synthesis.

some then releases the protein into the cytoplasm and moves away from the messenger RNA.

A single ribosome builds only one protein molecule. However, several ribosomes may be building different protein molecules at the same time along the messenger RNA template. There is also evidence that transfer RNA units may attach amino acids more than one time. In some cells, though, they seem to function only once. Further, it is thought that a strand of messenger RNA may act as a template more than once.

THE IMPORTANCE OF DNA

DNA determines the makeup of structural proteins, enzymes, and all other proteins. In this way, DNA controls not only the physical makeup of cells, but their chemical activities as well. In fact, DNA controls the whole organism.

By working with viruses, biochemists were able to determine the structures of many of the proteins and parts of the nucleic acids that make them.

As you go on in biology, you will see the importance of DNA again and again. How do organisms grow? How does an organism keep its identity through its whole life? Why are organisms like their parents in some ways but different in others? DNA provides the answers to all these questions.

DNA ENGINEERING

In the past few years, scientists have made many interesting discoveries. One of the most exciting discoveries was the ability to transplant genetic material. Scientists developed a technique to transplant strands of DNA from one cell to another. They removed pieces of DNA from one type of bacterium. They placed these pieces of DNA into another type of bacterium found in the human intestine. In this way, scientists actually changed the genetic makeup of a cell.

Ask students to choose one type of protein and briefly report on its functions. This assignment will enable students to see why proteins are indispensable to life.

As a result of these transplants, scientists have been able to learn more about the cell's activities. Eventually, this technique could lead to a better understanding of diseases, such as cancer. However, DNA transplanting, if not used carefully, could be very dangerous. By transplanting pieces of DNA, new strains of disease-causing bacteria could be produced. There is a danger that these new bacteria could cause an uncontrolled spread of a new disease. Scientists have agreed to take steps to avoid this danger.

SUMMARY

All living cells contain protein, and protein synthesis is a key process in the living condition. DNA controls protein synthesis through a code of 64 base triplet "words." By transcription, this code is passed on to messenger RNA.

Messenger RNA carries the code out into the cytoplasm. Here, the messenger RNA strand acts as a template for the building of proteins. Units of transfer RNA bring amino acids to this template. A ribosome "reads" the codons on the template. With the help of transfer RNA, the amino acids are attached to the ribosome in the proper order for forming the correct protein molecule.

QUESTIONS FOR REVIEW

1. Explain the importance of protein synthesis to all living things.
2. Describe the Watson-Crick model for DNA.
3. What do the triplet codes of DNA determine?
4. In what two ways is RNA different in structure from DNA?
5. Explain the function of messenger RNA in protein synthesis.
6. How does transfer RNA contribute to protein synthesis?
7. What is the function of ribosomes?
8. Why is the specific sequence of amino acids important?
9. List several functions of proteins in cells.

APPLYING PRINCIPLES AND CONCEPTS

1. If a certain protein is composed of 500 amino acids, how long is the gene responsible for its synthesis?
2. Describe the chemical mechanisms by which DNA controls protein synthesis.
3. Explain why proteins are specific in individual organisms.
4. Why is replication an extremely important property of DNA?
5. Discuss why DNA is called "the key to life."

chapter eight

Cell Growth and Reproduction

OBJECTIVES

- EXPLAIN the nature of cell division.
- DISCUSS the significance of mitosis.
- NAME and DESCRIBE the phases of mitosis.
- DISTINGUISH between sexual and asexual reproduction.
- DESCRIBE the forms of asexual reproduction.
- DEFINE meiosis and its importance to sexual reproduction.
- DESCRIBE the major differences between mitosis and meiosis.

It is important to have students understand the concept of controlled growth and division of controlled growth and division among cells. Cells that divide in an uncontrolled manner are known as cancer cells. This understanding will serve as an introduction into the process of cell division.

8–1 Cells of the onion root tip in various stages of mitosis. (Manfred Kage, Peter Arnold)

LIMITS TO CELL GROWTH

One form of cell growth is the repair and replacement of worn-out cell parts through protein synthesis. But a cell normally builds more new materials than it can use in repair and replacement. The cell makes room for these materials by growing larger.

How large can a cell grow? Science fiction writers dream up huge cells that destroy whole cities or even planets. In real life, of course, no such cells exist. There are limits to cell growth. These limits have to do with the cell membrane. As you know, all materials needed to support cell life must enter through this membrane. All waste products must pass out through it. Thus, there is an important relationship between the *surface area* of the membrane and the *volume* of the cell content. There must be enough membrane surface to meet the needs of a given volume of cell content.

What would happen if a cell were to keep growing? At some point, the surface area would become too small, relative to the cell volume, to support life.

How do cells keep from reaching this limit? In most cases, the answer is *cell division*.

THE NATURE OF CELL DIVISION

Most kinds of cells grow larger for a time and then divide. This splitting of a cell is called *fission*. Most cell fission is **binary fission.** That is, the cell splits into two parts which are more or less equal in size. The cell that divides is called the *mother cell*. The cells that result from this division are called *daughter cells*.

Actually, cell fission usually involves two different kinds of division. The first is called *mitosis.* **In mitosis, the materials in the nucleus of the mother cell are duplicated and divided into two identical sets.** After this happens, the cytoplasm itself divides. Two daughter cells result, each having an identical set of nuclear materials.

MITOSIS AND ITS IMPORTANCE

The key structures in the cell nucleus are the chromosomes. Each chromosome is made up of a protein core around which strands of DNA are wound. You know that DNA controls all cell activities through a code system of base triplet "words." DNA also controls *heredity,* the passing on of traits from parents to offspring. The materials that determine these traits are *genes.* Genes are thought to be active groups of DNA base triplets on chromosomes.

DNA can duplicate itself by *replication.* This is just what happens at the beginning of mitosis. By replication, the chromosomes in the mother cell are duplicated. There are now two identical sets of chromosomes—and genes—in the mother cell. In cell division, each daughter cell receives one of these sets. Thus, **the chromosomes in each daughter cell exactly match, in kind and number, those of the mother cell.**

You can understand the importance of this process if you think about your own growth. You began as a single cell. Countless cell divisions produced the billions of cells of which your body is made today. Yet every normal body cell contains chromosomes exactly identical, in kind and number, to those of the first cell. This is why you keep your identity as an individual. If you are a tall person with brown eyes, for example, you will always be. Further cell divisions will not change you into a short person with blue eyes.

Interphase is the period of time between mitoses. It is the stage when a cell is preparing for nuclear replication. The observation of most cells under the microscope is during this stage.

At one time, interphase was referred to as the "resting stage." Ask students to discuss whether or not there is such as thing as a "resting stage."

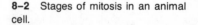

8-2 Stages of mitosis in an animal cell.

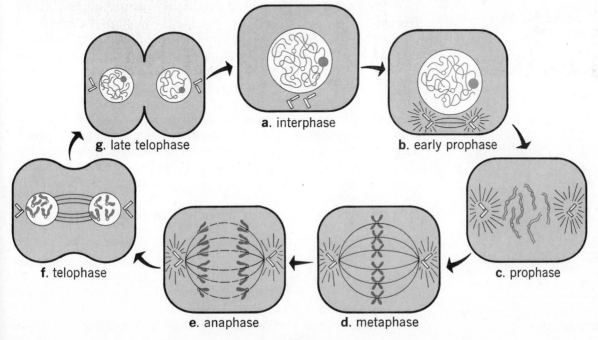

g. late telophase

a. interphase

b. early prophase

c. prophase

d. metaphase

e. anaphase

f. telophase

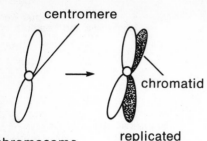

centromere

chromatid

chromosome

replicated chromosome

8–3 Chromosome replication illustrating chromatid formation.

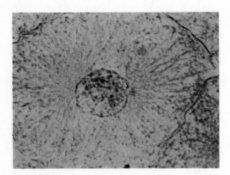

8–4 Mitosis: interphase. (Carolina Biol. Supply Co.)

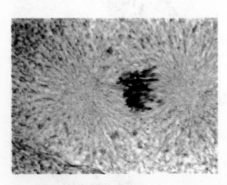

8–5 Mitosis: prophase. (Carolina Biol. Supply Co.)

With this understanding, we can go on to take a closer look at mitosis and cell division. In doing so, it will help to separate the events before and during mitosis into five phases. These phases are (1) interphase, (2) prophase, (3) metaphase, (4) anaphase, and (5) telophase. In a living cell, there is no sharp line between these phases. But each phase has certain main events that set it apart from other phases.

INTERPHASE

The *interphase* is not really part of cell division but is the period between cell divisions. Much of the cell's life span is spent in this period. It is a time of growth and other normal cell activities that do not involve reproduction.

During interphase, the chromosomes are spread through the nucleus like a fine network of very long threads. One or more nucleoli are present, and the nucleus is surrounded by a nuclear membrane. Just outside this membrane, in most animal cells, is a small, dense area of cytoplasm. This area is called a *centrosome.* Within it lies one or two *centrioles.* Through the electron microscope, the centrioles appear as clusters of tiny tubes. Centrioles play a part in mitosis, though the exact nature of this role is not known.

Near the end of interphase, the chromosomes are doubled by DNA replication. Soon after this, the centrioles divide and start to move apart. Mitosis is about to begin.

PROPHASE

In early *prophase,* there are clear signs that mitosis is starting. The centrioles move to opposite sides of the nucleus. As they do so, the cytoplasm around them changes. Protein fibers, called *astral rays* because they look like the rays of a star, form around each centriole. A centriole and its rays together are known as an *aster.*

During prophase, the chromosomes grow shorter and thicker and can be clearly seen through a light microscope. They are double all along their length except for the small point at which they are attached. This point is called a **centromere.** Each of the two identical parts of a double chromosome is called a **chromatid.** If you held two identical pieces of string between your fingers, each piece would be like a chromatid. The point where your fingers meet would be the centromere.

As prophase moves toward metaphase, more fibers form between the centrioles. Together, these fibers make up a structure shaped somewhat like a football. This structure is called the *spindle.* Each end of the spindle is called a pole, and the point halfway between the poles is called the equator. Some fibers reach from pole to pole. Other fibers reach only from one pole or the other to the equator. These are called *traction fibers.*

In late prophase, both the nuclear membrane and the nucleolus break down and disappear into the cytoplasm. The paired chromatids move toward the equator. The exact cause of this movement is not known.

METAPHASE

With the paired chromatids at the cell equator, mitosis enters the *metaphase* stage. The chromatid centromeres split, and the chromatid pairs separate into identical chromosomes. The centromere of each of these single chromosomes attaches to a traction fiber. The chromosomes in each matching pair attach to fibers leading to opposite poles.

Each phase of mitosis is directly dependent on the previous stage. It is important to stress that during metaphase each chromosome lines up on a *separate* spindle fiber. What does this tell us? Students should respond that this makes it possible for one of each kind of chromosome to be present in the new nucleus.

ANAPHASE

As soon as the chromatid centromeres split, the matching chromosomes seem to repel each other. The chromosomes in each pair begin to move toward opposite poles. This movement makes up the *anaphase* stage of mitosis.

Each chromosome moves along a fiber of the spindle. The cause of this movement is not fully understood. It may have to do with a shortening of the traction fibers attached to the centromeres. As the chromosomes move, the centromeres lead. Anaphase ends when the chromosomes reach the poles.

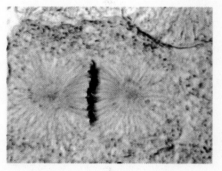

TELOPHASE

The last stage of mitosis is *telophase.* Soon after reaching the poles, the chromosomes lengthen into fine networks as in the interphase state. The spindle fibers and asters disappear. Two new nuclei are formed, with a membrane around each nucleus.

At the same time, the cytoplasm begins to divide. The cytoplasm pinches inward, forming a *cleavage furrow* near the equator. This furrow deepens until the two daughter cells separate. Both cells then enter a new interphase.

8–6 Mitosis: metaphase. (Carolina Biol. Supply Co.)

Stress to students that each daughter cell is genetically identical to the parent cell. Following mitosis, the cells enter into interphase and soon mitosis will occur once again.

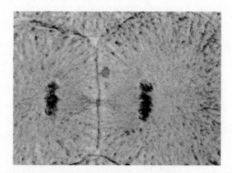

8–7 Mitosis: anaphase. (Carolina Biol. Supply Co.)

8–8 Mitosis: telophase. (Carolina Biol. Supply Co.)

The materials of the cytoplasm are not divided as exactly as those of the nucleus. One daughter cell may receive more ribosomes, plastids, and so on than the other. This does not matter much since the new cell soon organizes any structures it may need.

MITOSIS IN PLANT CELLS

Mitosis in plant cells differs in certain ways from that in animal cells. For one thing, plant cells have no centrosomes and so do not form asters.

The greatest difference, however, appears in telophase. A *division plate*, or cell plate, forms in the center of the spindle. This plate becomes wider until it reaches completely across the cell, separating the two daughter cells. By adding cellulose to the plate, the daughter cells build a new cell wall.

The major significance of mitosis is that it ensures genetic continuity. Mitosis guarantees that each daughter cell will receive the necessary genetic information that will result in normal development.

DIFFERENT RATES OF CELL DIVISION

Cell division takes place at different rates in different kinds of cells. In some cells, the process may be completed in half an hour or less. In others, it may take several hours.

Division also occurs more often in some cells than in others. For example, the tissue cells of an embryo are dividing almost constantly. But nerve tissue cells divide only rarely, if at all. **In general, the least specialized cells divide most often.**

An injury can cause increased cell division. For example, skin cells normally divide slowly. But if the skin is damaged, the cells around the wound will divide rapidly and repair the damaged tissue.

ASEXUAL REPRODUCTION

It is important to stress to students that mitosis is involved in all types of asexual reproduction.

Reproduction of an organism may be sexual or asexual. **Sexual reproduction** involves a joining together of reproductive cells. **Asexual reproduction** does not involve any such joining of cells. There are several forms of asexual reproduction.

Binary fission, which we have just studied, is asexual reproduction by cell division. In complex organisms, fission simply increases the number of cells, resulting in growth or cell replacement. In one-celled organisms, however, fission is the means of reproduction for the whole organism. Under good conditions, one-celled organisms can reproduce very rapidly. Certain bacteria, for example, can divide as often as every 20 or 30 minutes.

Budding is another type of asexual reproduction. It also involves cell division, but the cells produced are not of equal size. The bud forms as a knob on the mother cell. The nucleus divides by mitosis, with identical parts going to both the bud and the mother cell. The bud receives only a small part of the cytoplasm but can organize more on its own. Thus, the bud may grow until it is as large as the mother cell and can form buds of its own. In some cases, buds remain attached to the mother cell. In others, they break away and live as separate organisms.

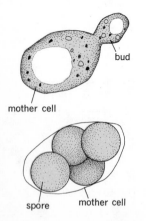

8–9 Yeast cells reproduce by budding. Under certain conditions, they also form spores.

Spore production is a very common form of asexual reproduction. Spores are formed by divisions of special mother cells and are released from the parent organism. Some spores are carried by the wind. Spores produced by organisms that live in water often have whiplike structures that allow them to swim. Many spores are protected by a thick wall that helps them to survive even very cold or very dry conditions. Though spores are reproductive cells, they do not join together. A single spore develops into a new organism.

SEXUAL REPRODUCTION

In sexual reproduction, two special reproductive cells unite. **These sex cells are called *gametes* and their joining is called *fertilization*. The body formed by the joining of two gametes is called a *zygote*.**

In some organisms, all gametes formed are alike. Thus, we cannot use the terms *male* and *female* for these gametes. In other organisms, two different kinds of gametes are formed. The differences allow us to refer to one gamete as male and the other as female. A male gamete is called a ***sperm,*** and a female gamete is called an ***egg.***

In your study of biology, you will find several different forms of gamete production. For example, the same organisms may produce both male and female gametes. Most often, however, a male parent produces sperms and a female parent produces eggs.

CHROMOSOME NUMBERS IN CELL REPRODUCTION

A very important fact of biology has to do with the *number* of chromosomes found in cells. Every body cell of a given organism has the same number of chromosomes. But we need not stop with individual organisms. In fact, **all normal members of the same species contain the same number of chromosomes in their body cells.**

We can go still further and state that *the chromosomes in body cells always occur in pairs.* The two chromosomes in each pair are identical in form and in the way their genes are arranged. For this reason, we call the chromosomes in such a pair **homologous** (huh-MAHL-uh-gus) **chromosomes.** Human body cells, for example, contain 23 pairs of homologous chromosomes—46 chromosomes in all. This number is constant in *all* normal human beings.

A cell that contains a full set of homologous chromosome pairs is said to have the **diploid** chromosome number. Thus, the diploid number for human beings is 46. Your life began as a single diploid cell. This cell contained 46 chromosomes in 23 homologous pairs. As you may have guessed, **one chromosome in each pair came from one parent, and one from the other parent.**

CHROMOSOME NUMBERS IN GAMETES

In cell reproduction, the chromosomes double before mitosis. Thus, each daughter cell receives the diploid number of chromo-

Ask students to comment on the major problem inherent in asexual reproduction. Some students may conclude that the variety of an organism is greatly limited because it is genetically identical to its parent.

8–10 Identical pairs of human female chromosomes (top) and of human male chromosomes. (Theodore T. Puck)

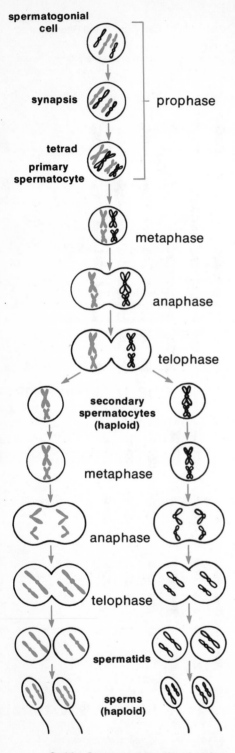

spermatogonial cell

synapsis

prophase

tetrad
primary spermatocyte

metaphase

anaphase

telophase

secondary spermatocytes (haploid)

metaphase

anaphase

telophase

spermatids

sperms (haploid)

8–11 Spermatogenesis showing the two stages of cell division in meiosis.

somes. But what if gametes were formed in the same way? If so, human gametes would each contain the diploid number, 46 chromosomes. When sperm and egg joined, the fertilized egg would contain 92 chromosomes. This, of course, does not happen. Instead, **each gamete contains only one chromosome from each homologous pair**—23 chromosomes in all. This number, which is half the diploid number, is called the **haploid** number.

Cells of the *ovaries*, which produce eggs, and of the *testes*, which produce sperm, have the diploid chromosome number. How, then, do these cells form gametes that have the haploid number? The answer lies in a special kind of cell division known as **meiosis** (my-OSE-iss).

MEIOSIS—A TWO-STAGE DIVISION

Mitosis involves a single division of the cell nucleus. Because of replication, each daughter cell has the diploid chromosome number. *Meiosis*, on the other hand, occurs in two stages, with cell division taking place in each stage. The gametes that result from this process have the haploid chromosome number.

The first stage of sperm formation by meiosis begins with *spermatogonial cells*. Such cells are formed in the testes by mitosis. Like all other body cells, they are diploid and contain pairs of homologous chromosomes.

In the prophase of the first stage of meiosis, a spermatogonial cell grows larger. The chromosomes become shorter and thicker. In middle prophase, homologous chromosomes move toward each other until they lie side by side. The causes of this event, called *synapsis*, are not yet known. Near the end of prophase, each chromosome duplicates by replication. Thus, each homologous chromosome pair becomes *two pairs of joined chromatids* lying side by side. Such a group is called a *tetrad*, because it contains four chromatids. The cell itself is now called a *primary spermatocyte*.

During this prophase activity, events much like those of mitosis have been taking place. The nucleoli and nuclear membrane have broken down, and the centrioles have moved apart. Finally, the tetrads have moved to the cell equator.

As metaphase begins, each tetrad attaches to a spindle fiber. Remember that a tetrad is made up of two separate pairs of joined chromatids. In anaphase, *the joined chromatid pairs* of each tetrad are pulled toward opposite poles. Thus, when the cell divides in telophase, each daughter cell receives one member of a homologous chromosome pair. This gives each daughter cell the haploid chromosome number. However, each chromosome is still made up of two identical joined chromatids.

The daughter cells produced in the first stage of meiosis are called *secondary spermatocytes*. These cells go quickly into another division—the second stage of meiosis. No replication of chromosomes occurs. Instead, the cells go directly into metaphase. The joined chromatid pairs attach to fibers at the equator. The centromere of each pair is split apart, and two identical chromosomes result. In anaphase, these two chromosomes are drawn to opposite poles.

You can see what happens when the secondary spermatocytes divide in telophase. Each daughter cell receives the haploid number of single chromosomes. These cells are known as *spermatids*. Each spermatid enters an interphase, grows a "tail," and develops into a mature sperm.

Eggs are also produced by meiosis. The divisions involved are much like those in which sperms are formed. Cell division is unequal, and, of the four haploid cells produced, only one survives. This is the *ootid* (OH-uh-tid), which develops into a mature egg. The other three haploid cells, called *polar bodies*, are reabsorbed.

Both sperm and egg have the haploid chromosome number. When they are joined in fertilization, the diploid number is restored. The organism that develops from a fertilized egg grows by cell division. All of these divisions involve normal mitosis.

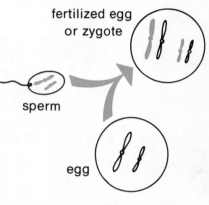

8–12 Fertilization. The combining of the chromosomes of two haploid gametes. This restores the diploid number.

Organisms grow by the cell division known as mitosis. Each daughter cell produced in mitosis has the diploid chromosome number. Further, the chrosomes of the daughter cells are identical to those of the mother cell. All body cells in all members of the same species contain the same kind and number of chromosomes.

Sperms and eggs are produced by a different kind of division, known as meiosis. Meiosis involves two stages of division. The cells that result contain the haploid chromosome number. When these cells join in fertilization, the diploid number is restored.

SUMMARY

BIOLOGICALLY SPEAKING

binary fission	anaphase	zygote
mitosis	telophase	sperm
interphase	sexual reproduction	egg
prophase	asexual reproduction	homologous chromosome
aster	budding	diploid
centromere	spore	haploid
chromatid	gamete	meiosis
metaphase	fertilization	

1. What is binary fission?
2. Distinguish between chromosomes and genes.
3. What important change occurs in nuclear DNA during interphase?
4. Distinguish between a chromosome and a chromatid.
5. Describe the movement of chromosomes during each stage of mitosis.
6. How does the division of cytoplasm differ in plant and animal cells?
7. Distinguish between sexual and asexual reproduction.
8. Describe several forms of asexual reproduction.
9. What is the difference between haploid and diploid chromosome numbers?
10. What is meiosis and why is it necessary?
11. Explain how fertilization restores the diploid chromosome number.

**APPLYING
PRINCIPLES
AND CONCEPTS**

1. Discuss the necessity of cell division in the life of the cell.
2. Compare the chromosome changes that occur in mitosis and meiosis.
3. Discuss sexual reproduction as a mechanism of change and variation.

Books

Anderson, M. D., *Through the Microscope.*
Natural History Press (distr., Doubleday and Co., Inc.), Garden City, 1965. The use of different kinds of microscopes to probe an unseen world.

Asimov, Isaac, *A Short History of Biology.*
Natural History Press (distr., Doubleday and Co., Inc.), Garden City, 1965. Discusses many of the leading biologists (chronologically arranged), explaining their ideas and the fields in which they are important.

Eckehard, Munck, *Biology of the Future.*
Franklin Watts, Inc., New York, N.Y. 1974. Reviews recent biological developments and gives insights into the vast frontiers of biology.

White, Emil H., *Chemical Background for the Biological Sciences* (2nd ed.). Prentice-Hall, Inc., Englewood Cliffs, N.J., 1970. Presents and explains the chemical nature of life.

Articles

Brachet, Jean, "The Living Cell," *Scientific American*, September, 1961. A good introduction to the study of the structure and function of the cell.

Frieden, Earl, "The Chemical Elements of Life," *Scientific American*, July, 1972. Names the elements that make up living organisms, with an explanation of their uses.

Galston, Arthur W., "The Membrane Barrier," *Natural History*, August-September 1974. A discussion of the cell membrane and the way materials move into the cell.

Gould, Stephen J., "On Heroes and Fools in Science," *Natural History*, August-September, 1974. A look at how some scientists based their discoveries on facts while others on superstition.

Levine, R. P., "The Mechanism of Photosynthesis," *Scientific American*, December, 1969. Discusses the food-making process in plants.

Mazia, Daniel, "The Cell Cycle," *Scientific American*, January, 1974. A fascinating account of cells and how they reproduce.

unit 2

THE CONTINUITY OF LIFE

When sexual reproduction occurs, both parents contribute a copy of a chemical code that controls the development of the offspring. Each new organism resembles its parents in some ways yet differs in others. What chemical code controls this influence? The answer lies in the study of cells and their chromosomes. Here we find DNA and the genetic code. This genetic material controls the development of every inherited trait in an organism.

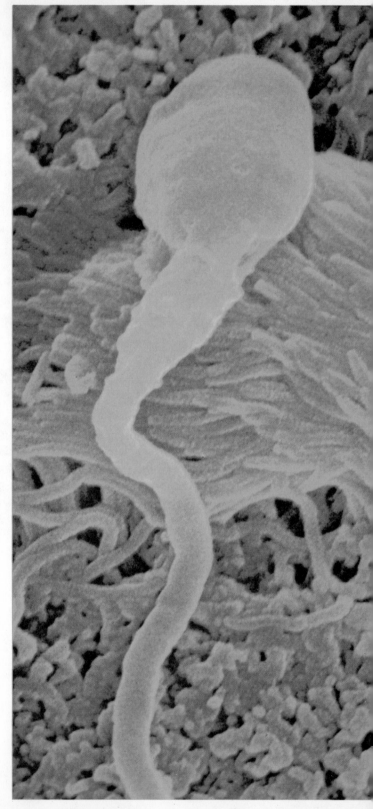

HEREDITY AND ENVIRONMENT

Two great influences, acting together all through your life, have made you what you are at this moment. These influences are *heredity* and *environment.* Heredity is the passing on of traits from parents to off-spring. Environment is all of the outside forces that act on an organism.

Sometimes it's hard to tell just where the effects of heredity end and those of environment begin. For example, heredity determines the size to which your body will grow. But factors in the environment, such as the foods you eat and the exercise you do, also affect your growth. Again, you may have received the trait of good eyesight from your parents. But if you strain your eyes or do not eat well, your eyesight may suffer. In other words, heredity controls what you *can* become. But what you *do* become often depends on environment as well.

Through most of this unit, you will be learning about heredity. We laid down the basis for this study in Chapter Eight. There, we noted that offspring receive *chromosomes* from their parents. **These chromosomes contain groups of base triplets known as *genes.*** It is genes that code the traits passed on from parents to offspring. Because genes are so important, the branch of biology that deals with heredity is called *genetics.*

WHAT KINDS OF TRAITS ARE INHERITED?

In some ways, all members of a species are alike. That is, they all carry the genes for certain traits. Such traits are celled **species traits.** For example, the ability to walk erect is a species trait of human beings. So is having a more complex brain than any

chapter nine

Principles of Heredity

OBJECTIVES

- UNDERSTAND how heredity and environment determine individual makeup.
- DESCRIBE Mendel's work with garden peas.
- EXPLAIN Mendel's three contributions to the basic principles of genetics.
- DEFINE the terms: genotype, phenotype, homozygous, heterozygous, and alleles.
- DEMONSTRATE a monohybrid cross using a Punnett square.
- DEMONSTRATE a cross involving two traits.
- UNDERSTAND Mendel's law of independent assortment.
- EXPLAIN incomplete dominance.

Ask students to discuss the age-old question of heredity versus environment in relation to the development of the individual. Responses will be interesting to students and will give the teacher an opportunity to see how much students understand about the genetic process.

9–1 People inherit certain abilities, but their environment determines whether they develop them to the full potential. (Jack Zehrt, F.P.G.)

other animal. All normal human beings carry the genes for these traits.

Besides species traits, you have inherited **individual traits** that make you different from any other person. Such traits include hair and eye color, body build, and many others. Since the genes for these traits came from your parents, you are like each parent in some ways. But since you received genes from *both* parents, you are not *exactly* like either one.

All through history, people have noted that parents seem to pass on certain traits to their offspring. Thus, the idea of heredity is not new. What *is* new is our knowledge of the *principles* of heredity. We owe an important part of this knowledge to the work of one man.

9–2 Mendel's seven pairs of contrasting traits in garden peas.

TRAIT STUDIED						
stem length	flower position	seed shape	seed color	seed coat color	pod shape	pod color
DOMINANT						
tall	axial	round	yellow	colored	inflated	green
RECESSIVE						
short	terminal	wrinkled	green	white	constricted	yellow

GREGOR MENDEL—PIONEER OF GENETICS

The roots of modern genetics reach back to a small garden in nineteenth-century Austria. The garden was kept by a monk named Gregor Mendel, who also taught high school in the town of Brünn. Mendel had an interest in heredity and used his garden for experiments with plants. These experiments, carried out over a period of years, were not the first in the field of heredity. But they were the first of any scientific value.

Mendel's most important work was done with pea plants. These plants differed in several traits. For example, some plants were short, while others grew tall. Some produced yellow seeds, others green seeds. All in all, Mendel noted seven such pairs of contrasting traits. His experiments were aimed at learning how these traits were passed on.

In 1865, Mendel published his findings and conclusions. With little change, these conclusions stand today as the basis for the science of genetics. This fact is even more surprising when we remember that Mendel himself knew nothing about genes, chromosomes, or DNA. Mendel received no credit for his great work during his lifetime. In fact, 35 years passed before his paper was found and put to use by other scientists. Yet even then Mendel's findings had the power to set off a chain reaction of genetic discoveries. We will study some of these discoveries in Chapter Ten.

Point out to students that, for many years following the publishing of Mendel's paper, his research was disregarded and went unnoticed. It was not until other researchers reached the same conclusions, years later, that Mendel's findings were recognized as valid.

Three other scientists who were involved in research into the laws of heredity were: Hugo de Vries (1848–1935); Karl Correns (1864–1933); and Erich von Seysenegg (1871–1962). Students may be interested in reading about their contributions.

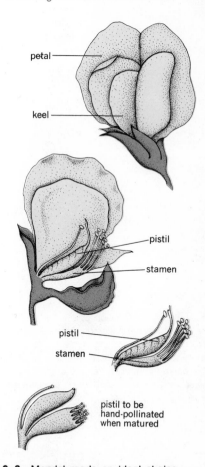

POLLINATION—A KEY TO MENDEL'S EXPERIMENTS

To understand Mendel's work, you need to have an idea of how seed plants reproduce. As you may know, the flower is the reproductive structure in such plants. Each flower of a pea plant contains several *stamens*. These structures produce pollen grains, which form sperm nuclei. Each pea plant flower also has a structure called a *pistil*, which contains egg cells at its base. The transfer of pollen from stamens to pistil results in fertilization. This process is called *pollination*.

Pea plants normally carry on *self-pollination*. That is, pollen is transferred from stamens to pistil on the same flower or on flowers of the same plant. But Mendel's experiments also involved *cross-pollination*. In this process, pollen is transferred from one plant to the flowers of a different plant. Thus, egg and sperm come from different plants. You can see why this would be important in studying how contrasting traits are passed on in heredity. Mendel made sure of cross-pollination by removing the stamens from a young pea plant flower. Later, when the pistil of this flower matured, he transferred pollen to it from another plant.

Cross-pollination of pea plants is easy to do by hand. This fact, along with the seven pairs of contrasting traits noted by Mendel, made peas a perfect subject for study.

9–3 Mendel made an ideal choice selecting the garden pea. If the stamens are removed before natural pollination occurs, the flower may be hand-pollinated when the pistil is mature.

Stress to students the scientific methods that Mendel used to arrive at his conclusions. Mendel carefully planned, executed, and recorded each of his experiments. Other scientists of his day failed to reach the correct conclusions because they lacked a scientific approach to the problem.

The Law of Segregation points out the importance of understanding meiosis and how factors or genes are segregated. It is interesting to note that though Mendel came to this correct conclusion, the cellular processes involved in production of gametes were first discovered 25 years later.

MENDEL'S EXPERIMENTS AND RESULTS

Mendel began his experiments by observing the results of self-pollination in pea plants. Generation after generation, these results were always the same. Seeds from tall plants always produced tall plants. Yellow seeds always produced plants that developed yellow seeds. The same was true for each trait in the seven contrasting pairs. The traits of the parent plant were always passed on to its offspring.

Mendel's next step was to cross plants with contrasting traits. First, he transferred pollen from tall plants to the pistils of short plants. He then planted the seeds that matured on the pistils. Would the offspring be tall, short, or somewhere in between? The seeds produced *only tall plants*. Further, the same thing happened when Mendel transferred pollen from short plants to tall ones. *All offspring were tall.*

In the same way, Mendel experimented with the other contrasting traits. In each case, he crossed plants that differed in only one trait. And in each case, *only one trait of a pair showed up in the offspring.* For example, plants with the trait of yellow seeds were crossed with plants that had the trait of green seeds. The seeds that developed were yellow, and they produced plants that also had yellow seeds. All seven crosses had the same kind of result. Only one trait of a pair would appear in the first generation of offspring. The other trait seemed to be lost.

Were the traits that did not appear really "lost"? In finding out, it will help to use some symbols used by Mendel himself. Mendel represented the parent plants used in a first cross as P_1. He referred to the offspring of such a cross as the *first filial*, or F_1, generation. For example, the tall and short plants crossed by Mendel were P_1. Their offspring, all tall, were F_1. Self-pollination of these F_1 plants would produce a *second filial*, or F_2, generation.

What would such an F_2 generation be like? Would all offspring still be tall? Mendel decided to find out. The results were striking. Three fourths of the F_2 plants were tall, *but one fourth were short*. Mendel tested the F_1 plants from his other six crosses in the same way. In each case, the "lost" trait showed up again in about one fourth of the F_2 plants.

These results were as important as they were surprising. From them, Mendel formed three great hypotheses which today stand as basic principles of genetics.

MENDEL'S HYPOTHESES

What were Mendel's three hypotheses? How did he arrive at them? We will follow his logic in terms of the traits *tall* and *short*. But the same logic would apply to the other traits as well.

■ Tall plants crossed with short plants produced an F_1 generation of tall plants. But short plants appeared again in the F_2

generation. Thus, some influence *within* the plants must control height (Mendel called such influences *factors.* Today we call them genes.) Further, since plants were either tall or short, a *pair* of factors must be involved. This reasoning led to Mendel's first hypothesis, the **concept of unit characters. This concept states that inherited traits are controlled by factors (genes), which occur in pairs.**

- The tall F_1 plants must contain a factor for their tallness. But they must also contain a factor for shortness, since short plants appeared among their F_2 offspring. Then why were no F_1 plants short? Mendel's answer was his second hypothesis, now called the **principle of dominance and recessiveness.** According to this principle, **one factor (gene) in a pair may mask the other, or prevent it from having effect.** Some traits, such as tallness, always appeared in crosses between parents with contrasting traits. Mendel called such traits *dominant.* Other traits, such as shortness, did not appear in the F_1 generation, though they appeared again in F_2 plants. Mendel called these traits *recessive.*

  Today we would say that, in Mendel's crosses, one parent plant was pure tall. This plant had both genes for tallness. The other parent was pure short, having both genes for shortness. Members of the F_1 generation were *hybrid.* This is the term we use for offspring of two parents that differ in one or more traits. The hybrid F_1 plants had one gene for tallness and one for shortness. But they appeared tall because the gene for tallness was dominant.

- Mendel's third hypothesis is now called *Mendel's first law,* or the **law of segregation.** It states that **a pair of factors (genes) is segregated, or separated, in forming gametes.** In other words, a gamete contains only one gene of a pair. The other gene goes to another gamete. Further, Mendel's hypothesis states that one gene of a pair is not changed by the presence of the other gene. For example, a recessive gene in a hybrid is not changed by the presence of a dominant gene. The recessive gene may be paired with another recessive gene in an offspring of the hybrid. In that case, the recessive trait will come out again.

  Mendel was right about the segregation of factors. But since he knew nothing of genes or chromosomes, he could not have known exactly *why* he was right. Remember that *genes are located on chromosomes.* All body cells contain the diploid number of chromosomes. These chromosomes are present in *identical pairs.* Thus, the genes on them are also present in identical pairs. Gametes, on the other hand, have the haploid chromosome number—*one chromosome from each pair.* Thus, gametes contain only one *gene* of a pair as well.

- Our knowledge of chromosomes also has allowed us to put another of Mendel's hypotheses into more exact terms. Mendel believed that factors in a pair separated and were distributed to gametes in a way completely independent of what happened to other factor pairs. Today this hypothesis is stated as the modern

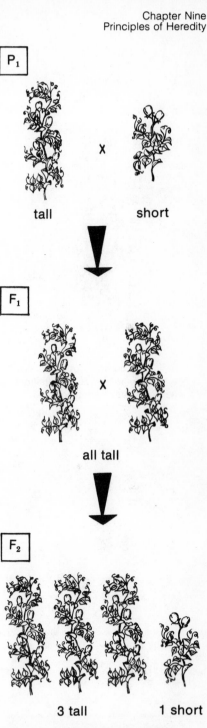

9-4 A cross between a tall pea plant and a short pea plant results in tall offspring. The short trait shows up in the next generation.

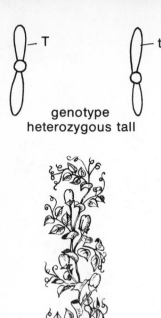

genotype
heterozygous tall

phenotype
tall

9–5 The outward appearance of an organism (phenotype) results from its gene makeup (genotype).

Ask students to draw conclusions from the diagrams on pages 104–105. What are the results of crossing a pure dominant with a hybrid and a pure recessive with a hybrid?

law of independent assortment. By this law, **when the gene pairs on a given pair of chromosomes are separated, they are distributed to gametes completely independently of the way other gene pairs on other chromosomes are distributed.** Notice that this law applies only to genes on *different chromosome pairs.* For it is chromosomes, not genes, that separate and are distributed independently.

SOME GENETIC TERMS

We can represent the genes for any trait in an organism by symbols such as letters. For example, we might let T stand for a gene for tallness. If so, we would represent the genes of a pure tall plant as TT. (The capital letter shows that this trait is dominant.) A gene for the contrasting trait, shortness, would be written as t. A pure short plant would be tt.

Such paired symbols show the **genotype** of an organism. That is, they show the genes that are present in the organism's body cells. The *effect* caused in the organism by these genes is called its **phenotype.** For example, a hybrid tall pea plant has the genotype Tt and the phenotype *tall*.

The paired genes for a trait may be identical, as with TT and tt. If so, we say that the organism is **homozygous** (HOME-oe-ZY-gus) for that trait. If the paired genes are *not* identical *(Tt)*, the organism is **heterozygous** (HET-uh-roe-ZY-gus).

The different forms of genes that have contrasting effects on a trait are called **alleles** (uh-LEELZ). In the gene pair Tt, T is an allele of t, and t is an allele of T. In the gene pair Yy, Y is an allele of y, and y is an allele of Y. But T is not an allele of Y, and so on. Some genes have three or more alleles.

PUNNETT SQUARES AND PROBABILITY

A *Punnett square* is a special chart, or grid system, named after its inventor, R. C. Punnett. You can use such squares to predict the results of crosses such as Mendel's. For example, the Punnett squares on page 104 show the possible gene pairings that can result in different crosses of peas. The alleles are T and t—tall and short.

As you can see, genes present in gametes from the female parent are given across the top of the grid. Genes from gametes from the male are shown down the left side. To work the square, simply combine the genes from both parents in the proper section of the grid. How many different possible pairings of genes does each Punnett square show?

Besides showing possible gene pairings, a Punnett square gives the probability for each pairing. That is, the square shows how often, on the average, a given pairing will occur. For example, Grid B shows a probability ratio of one TT to two Tt to one tt. Remember that such a ratio represents an *average.* Thus, a small number of offspring may not have the exact ratio of gene pairings given by the square. But the larger the sample of crosses involved,

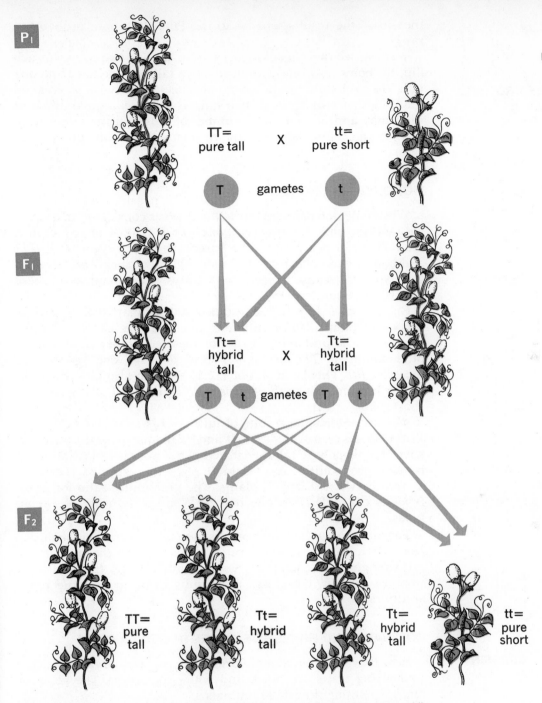

P₁

TT= pure tall X tt= pure short

T gametes t

F₁

Tt= hybrid tall X Tt= hybrid tall

T t gametes T t

F₂

TT= pure tall

Tt= hybrid tall

Tt= hybrid tall

tt= pure short

9–6 Mendel's law of segregation. The F₁ generation consists only of tall plants, while the recessive gene for shortness is again expressed in the F₂ generation. What kinds of plants would result from a cross between the two F₂ plants, shown at the bottom left?

A. RESULTS OF CROSSING TT AND tt

Female →   t   t
GENES
  Male ↓

	t	t
T	Tt	Tt
T	Tt	Tt

B. RESULTS OF CROSSING Tt AND Tt

Female →   T   t
GENES
  Male ↓

	T	t
T	TT	Tt
t	Tt	tt

C. RESULTS OF CROSSING TT AND Tt

Female →   T   t
GENES
  Male ↓

	T	t
T	TT	Tt
T	TT	Tt

D. RESULTS OF CROSSING Tt AND tt

Female →   t   t
GENES
  Male ↓

	t	t
T	Tt	Tt
t	tt	tt

the closer the results will be to the Punnett square probability ratio.

You can see this effect for yourself by flipping two coins. In each flip, the coins may land two heads, two tails, or one head and one tail. The probability of one head and one tail is twice as great as that of either two heads or two tails. *By chance*, a quite different ratio may appear in a small number of flips. But the more times you flip the coins, the closer the results will be to the probability ratio.

MONOHYBRID CROSSES

When only one pair of contrasting traits is considered in a cross, we describe the offspring as *monohybrid*. Grid A charts such a cross between pea plants. The parents are homozygous tall *(TT)* and homozygous short *(tt)*. The monohybrid offspring all have the genotype *Tt*. Because the gene for tallness is dominant, all of these offspring are tall.

Grid B shows the possible results of self-pollination of the heterozygous *Tt* plants. Three different gene pairings can result—*TT, Tt,* and *tt*. The probability ratio for these genotypes is one fourth pure dominant *(TT)*, one half hybrid *(Tt)*, and one fourth pure recessive *(tt)*. This is a ratio of 1:2:1. You can also find the probability ratio for phenotypes. This ratio is three tall plants to every short plant, or 3:1.

We can predict the results of further crosses in the same way. Grid C charts a cross between *Tt* and *TT* plants. All of the offspring have the phenotype tall. What genotypes are possible, and what is their probability ratio? Grid D gives the expected results of a cross between *tt* and *Tt* plants. The probability ratio for genotypes is one half *Tt* to one half *tt*. What is the ratio of phenotypes?

The table shows Mendel's results with two generations of garden peas. Both Mendel's actual ratio of results and the probability ratio are given for each trait. Notice that the larger the number of samples studied, the closer the results came to the true probability ratio.

DOMINANT AND RECESSIVE GENES IN GUINEA PIGS

Now let's look at a monohybrid cross between guinea pigs. The contrasting traits are black and white coat color. The gene for black is dominant in these animals.

Consider a cross between a homozygous black guinea pig and a homozygous white one. All of the F_1 offspring are heterozygous black. What happens if two of these hybrid animals are crossed? The Punnett square shows the expected results. The probability ratio for genotypes is one fourth *BB*, one half *Bb*, and one fourth *bb*. The ratio for phenotypes is three black to one white. These expected results exactly match those in Mendel's crosses of pea plants.

P₁ Cross	F₁ Generation	F₂ Generation	Actual Ratio	Probability Ratio
round X wrinkled	round	5,474 round 1,850 wrinkled	2.96:1	3:1
yellow X green	yellow	6,022 yellow 2,001 green	3.01:1	3:1
colored X white	colored	705 colored 224 white	3.15:1	3:1
inflated X constricted	inflated	882 inflated 229 constricted	2.95:1	3:1
green X yellow	green	428 green 152 yellow	2.82:1	3:1
axial X terminal	axial	651 axial 207 terminal	3.14:1	3:1
long stem X short stem	long stem	787 long 277 short	2.84:1	3:1

9–7 Results of Mendel's monohybrid crosses.

Again, remember that we are dealing with *averages.* In any given cross between hybrid guinea pigs, any combination of black and white offspring might result. But in a large number of such crosses, the expected ratio would appear.

CROSSES THAT INVOLVE TWO TRAITS

When *two* pairs of contrasting traits are involved in a cross, the offspring are **dihybrid.** The same principles apply to such a cross as to a monohybrid cross. However, the dihybrid cross is more complex because there are more possible combinations of genes.

Let's try a dihybrid cross in pea plants. One contrasting trait pair involves seed shape, while the other involves color. For shape,

RESULTS OF CROSSING Bb AND Bb

Female → GENES Male ↓	B	b
B	BB	Bb
b	Bb	bb

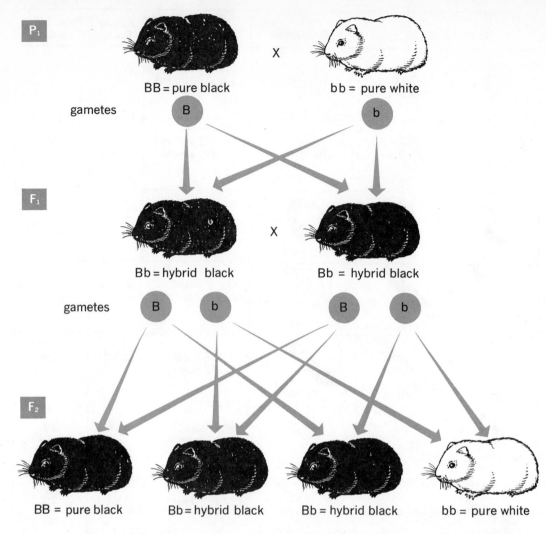

9-8 A cross between a homozygous black guinea pig and a homozygous white guinea pig.

the dominant trait is round *(R)* and the recessive trait is wrinkled *(r)*. The dominant seed color is yellow *(Y)*, while the recessive color trait is green *(y)*. One parent is pure for round, green seeds *(RRyy)*. All gametes formed by this plant contain the genes *Ry*. The other parent is pure for yellow, wrinkled seeds *(rrYY)*. All gametes formed by this plant have the genes *rY*.

When these parent plants are crossed, the F_1 seeds all have the genotype *RrYy*. All are round and yellow since these traits are dominant. If plants grown from these dihybrid seeds are crossed, the F_2 generation becomes more complex. Each *RrYy* dihybrid can produce *four* kinds of eggs or sperms. During meiosis, the *Rr* pairs are split and each gene goes into a different gamete. The same is true of the *Yy* pairs. The gametes that result may be *RY, Ry, rY,* or *ry*.

What will the F$_2$ offspring produced from these gametes be like? A Punnett square gives the possible results. This square works exactly like the ones for monohybrid crosses. The only difference is that more room must be allowed for the greater number of combinations. If you study the square, you will find the following:

$^9/_{16}$ of the seeds are round and yellow.

$^3/_{16}$ of the seeds are round and green.

$^3/_{16}$ of the seeds are wrinkled and yellow.

$^1/_{16}$ of the seeds are wrinkled and green.

Thus, there are *four* possible F$_2$ phenotypes, in an expected ratio of 9:3:3:1. How many genotypes can you find? Note that some seeds are pure round, while others are hybrid round. Some are pure yellow, while others are hybrid yellow. How many seeds are pure dominant for both traits? How many are pure recessive for both traits?

Finally, remember the law of independent assortment. It is chromosomes, not individual genes, that separate during meiosis. Thus, in our dihybrid cross, the genes for shape and color had to be *on different pairs of chromosomes.*

Ask students to diagram a Punnett square for a cross between a red four-o'clock and a white four-o'clock. Have them explain the results.

9-9 A cross involving two traits. A pea plant that produces round (R), green (y) seeds is crossed with a pea plant that produces wrinkled (r), yellow (Y) seeds.

Stress to students the need for using a large number of individuals to assure the validity of any scientific experiment. Statistics that cite a few cases are never considered valid results. Ask students to discuss the importance of using large numbers in scientific investigations.

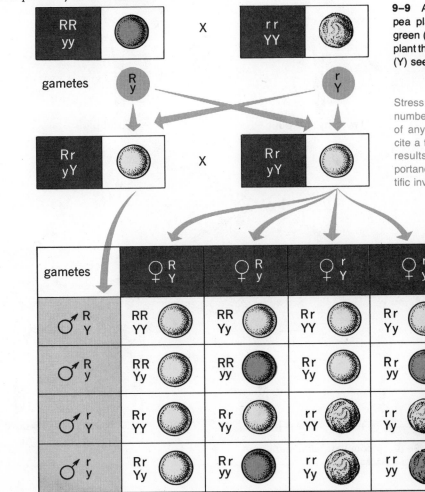

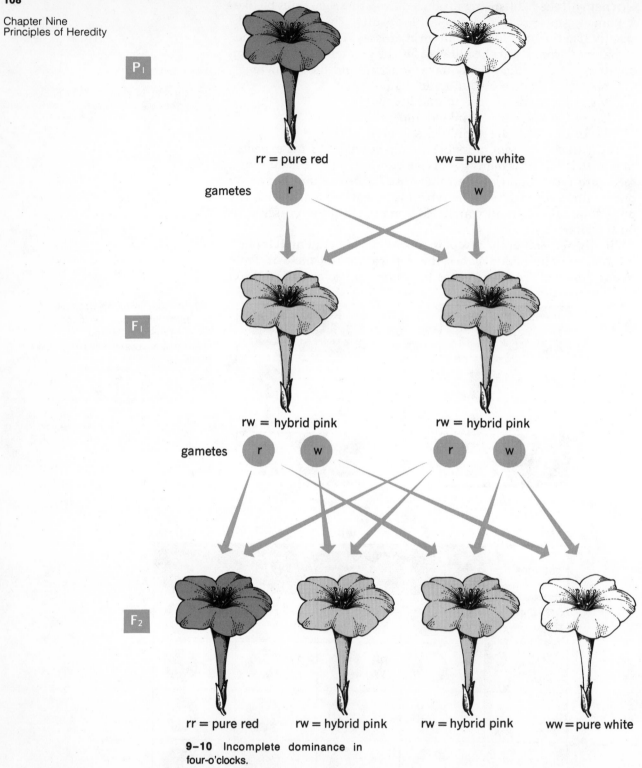

P₁

rr = pure red   ww = pure white

gametes   r   w

F₁

rw = hybrid pink   rw = hybrid pink

gametes   r   w   r   w

F₂

rr = pure red   rw = hybrid pink   rw = hybrid pink   ww = pure white

9-10 Incomplete dominance in four-o'clocks.

INCOMPLETE DOMINANCE

Genes are not always dominant or recessive. In some cases, both alleles of a pair can affect a trait. We say that such genes show *incomplete dominance.*

One case of incomplete dominance appears in the flowers known as four-o'clocks. In a cross between pure red *(rr)* and pure white *(ww)* four-o'clocks, neither color is completely dominant. Thus, the F_1 flowers appear pink *(rw)*. If these heterozygous pink flowers are crossed, the possible F_2 offspring will be as shown in the figure. One fourth are pure red, one half hybrid pink, and one fourth pure white. The fact that the pure traits show up again proves that the genes did not somehow "mix" in the F_1 flowers.

Another case of incomplete dominance involves Shorthorn cattle. A homozygous red animal mated with a homozygous white one produces a blend of white and red called *roan.* If two roan animals are mated, the probability ratio for offspring is one fourth red, one half roan, and one fourth white.

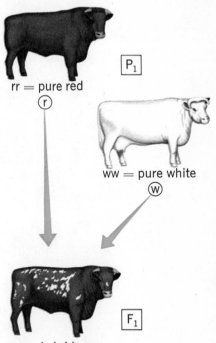

rr = pure red
(r)

ww = pure white
(w)

P_1

rw = hybrid roan

F_1

9–11 Incomplete dominance in shorthorn cattle.

SUMMARY

It was the work of Gregor Mendel with garden peas that opened up the field of heredity to science. Mendel's hypotheses about genes, which he called *factors,* have become basic principles of genetics. Among these principles are the ideas that genes control heredity, occur in pairs, and may be dominant or recessive.

Mendel also proposed that factor (gene) pairs separate and go to different gametes. He believed that they did so independently of other gene pairs. Today we understand that it is chromosomes, rather than individual genes, that are separated during meiosis. But with this one change, Mendel's conclusions still apply.

			BIOLOGICALLY
heredity	principle of dominance	homozygous	**SPEAKING**
environment	hybrid	heterozygous	
genes	law of segregation	allele	
genetics	law of independent	monohybrid	
species traits	assortment	dihybrid	
individual traits	genotype	incomplete dominance	
concept of unit	phenotype		
characters			

1. What is genetics?
2. Why did Mendel choose garden peas for his experiment?
3. What observation led Mendel to his hypothesis of unit characters?
4. State Mendel's principle of dominance.
5. Mendel reasoned that a pair of genes was separated during the formation of gametes. Which of his laws is based upon this reasoning?
6. Distinguish between the terms "genotype" and "phenotype."
7. The gene for black coat color is dominant in guinea pigs. How is homozygous black different from heterozygous black, even though the guinea pigs look alike?
8. Define the term "allele."
9. When two parents that are heterozygous for one trait are crossed, what ratios of phenotypes and genotype can be expected?
10. What is meant by incomplete dominance?
11. In breeding experiments, why do ratios obtained represent averages rather than definite numbers?

**APPLYING
PRINCIPLES AND
CONCEPTS**

1. Outline a possible cross to determine whether a black guinea pig is homozygous or heterozygous for the coat color trait.
2. In guinea pigs, black coat color is due to a dominant gene *(B)*, and white is due to its recessive allele *(b);* short hair to a dominant gene *(S)*, and long hair to its recessive allele *(s)*. The gene for rough coat *(R)*, is dominant over that for smooth *(r)*. Cross a homozygous rough, short-haired, black guinea pig with a smooth, long-haired, white one. What are the phenotypes of the F_1 and F_2 generations?
3. Why should a hybridizer know which traits in plants or animals with which he is working are dominant or recessive?
4. In four-o'clocks, the gene for red flowers *(R)* is incompletely dominant to the gene for white flowers *(r)*. The heterozygous condition results in pink flowers. A pink and a red four-o'clock are crossed. What are the expected genotypic and phenotypic ratios?

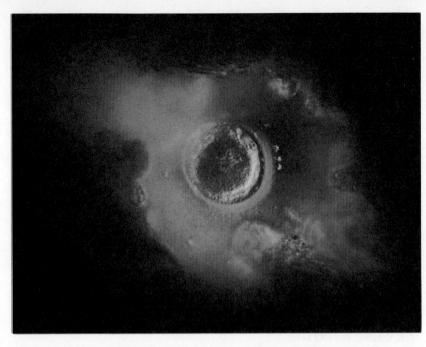

10–1 The human egg contains half the genetic material. (Lennart Nilsson)

The Genetic Material

OBJECTIVES

- DESCRIBE how Mendel's theories apply to the behavior of chromosomes and genes.
- EXPLAIN why *Drosophila* are used in genetic studies.
- EXPLAIN sex determination and sex linkage.
- UNDERSTAND the mechanism of chromosomal nondisjunction.
- DESCRIBE gene linkage and crossing over.
- DEFINE a gene in terms of DNA and RNA.
- EXPLAIN some of the causes of mutations.
- DESCRIBE the contributions of Beadle and Tatum.

THE CHROMOSOME THEORY OF INHERITANCE

Mendel's 1865 paper brilliantly described *what* happened in genetic crosses. But he knew nothing of actual genetic materials or the processes by which they worked. Mendel had never heard of chromosomes or meiosis. In fact, 20 years passed before scientists even learned where in a cell the genetic materials are stored: in the cell nucleus.

Before that discovery, biologists had been searching individual cells for genetic information. They understood the nature of sexual reproduction. That is, they knew that an egg cell and a sperm cell united in fertilization. It was clear that the offspring of sexual reproduction had traits of both parents. Obviously then, *something* in both the egg and the sperm influenced the genetic makeup of the offspring. But what was this something? Where in the cell was it hidden?

Suppose, for example, that the whole egg and the whole sperm influenced heredity. The influence of the egg should then be greater, since the egg is often much larger than the sperm. But the influence of egg and sperm seemed to be equal. What could explain this? What did egg and sperm have in common? The most obvious answer was the cell nucleus. Egg and sperm nuclei are about the same size. Did the nuclei, then, hold the genetic material?

These were important questions for biologists during the 1880's. At the same time, another problem had to be faced. It was clear that egg and sperm must each supply only *half* the genetic material. If not, the offspring would have a double genetic makeup. That is, they would have *all* the traits of *both* parents. This was impossible.

Ascaris has been used frequently by cytologists. *Ascaris* was found to have very few large chromosomes. Because of this chromosomal structure, it was easy to observe mitosis as well as meiosis.

The German biologist August Weismann suggested an answer. The genetic material is halved, Weismann said, *when egg and sperm cells are formed*. He also predicted that biologists would soon discover just how this happened. About a year later, his prediction came true: Theodore Boveri, another German, actually observed meiosis in the cells of the roundworm *Ascaris*, (AKS-uh-riss), a common parasite.

During all this time, Mendel's paper lay forgotten. But in 1900, three scientists working independently rediscovered his work. They were von Tschermak, an Austrian biologist; De Vries, a Dutch botanist; and Correns, a German botanist. Each of these men found copies of Mendel's paper in the library of the Natural History Society of Brünn, Austria.

At last, after 35 years, Mendel's findings could be put to use. Biologists had learned a great deal about chromosomes and believed that they carried genetic information. Now here were Mendel's law of segregation and the evidence for it. The way was open for a landslide of discoveries in genetics.

THE GENE HYPOTHESIS

In 1903, a young graduate student at Columbia University in New York published a very important research paper. Walter S. Sutton was the student's name. His paper suggested that **chromosomes held smaller genetic particles called genes. Each gene accounted for a single trait handed down in reproduction. This was the first time that genes were suggested as determiners of genetic traits.**

How did Sutton make this breakthrough? First, he had studied Mendel's work on garden peas. He understood Mendel's idea that genetic traits segregate when gametes are formed. Sutton himself was familiar with the segregation of chromosomes during meiosis. This behavior matched Mendel's ideas very well. Sutton concluded that chromosomes must carry the material of heredity.

Second, Sutton was aware of Mendel's reciprocal crosses in garden peas. You may remember that Mendel reversed many of his crosses. He wanted to see if it mattered whether a trait was supplied by the male (pollen) or female (seed) part of the plant. He found that it made no difference. Sutton knew that eggs and sperms are not alike in size or structure. But he found likenesses in their chromosomes. This was more evidence that chromosomes carry particles that determine heredity. Sutton also thought that these particles, or genes, must occupy matching positions on both chromosomes in a pair. Later, this was proved to be true.

Finally, Sutton reasoned that chromosome pairs keep their identity when somatic (body) cells divide. Segregation does not occur. Instead, all chromosomes split lengthwise. In this way, each daughter cell receives identical genetic material. This happens in mitosis, which you have already studied.

To sum up, Sutton found three important parallels between Mendel's genetic "factors" and the behavior of chromosomes and genes:

10-2 Walter S. Sutton was the first to propose that hereditary particles were component parts of chromosomes. (V. A. McKusick)

Chromosomes and genes occur in pairs in the zygote and in all somatic (body) cells.

Chromosomes and genes segregate during meiosis. Only one member of each pair normally enters a gamete.

Chromosomes and genes keep their identity during segregation. Each pair segregates independently of every other pair. This confirmed Mendel's law of independent assortment of the traits he had studied in garden peas.

HOW MANY GENES IN A CHROMOSOME?

Sutton had established the gene hypothesis. Now he attacked another problem. An organism might have only ten pairs of chromosomes. But it would have hundreds or even thousands of inherited traits each determined by a single gene. Clearly, each chromosome must hold many different genes. Did all of these genes segregate independently during meiosis? Sutton thought not. He believed that they must move *in sets* on a chromosome. In other words, the genes on a chromosome were linked in a certain order.

But did Sutton's theory of **gene linkage** fit with Mendel's findings? Remember that Mendel had studied seven pairs of different traits: tall stem and short stem, round seeds and wrinkled seeds, yellow seeds and green seeds, and so on. He had based his law of independent assortment on the fact that each pair of traits segregated and then recombined independently. But this could not happen if the genes for two or more of the seven traits were linked on a chromosome.

Sutton believed that the genes for each of Mendel's traits must be on different chromosome pairs. He could not prove this, but today we know that he was right. The peas Mendel used had seven pairs of chromosomes. By pure chance, each of the paired traits he studied was determined by genes on different chromosome pairs!

Sutton believed that his observation indicated cellular proof of Mendel's findings. Theodor Boveri had reached the same conclusions at about the same time. It is interesting to note that both Sutton's and Boveri's work was based on the still unproved theory that the hereditary factors (genes) were located on chromosomes.

There are many thousands of genes located on the 46 chromosomes of humans. Those genes that occur on the same chromosome are said to be linked. Ask students to discuss the effects of gene linkage in reducing variety among offspring.

DISCOVERY OF SEX CHROMOSOMES

Sutton never proved his theory of gene linkage. But a few years later, another great geneticist found strong evidence to support it. This man was Thomas Hunt Morgan, who won the Nobel Prize in medicine and physiology in 1933. Working with him at Columbia University were three younger scientists who also were to do great work in genetics. They were Calvin Bridges, A. H. Sturtevant, and H. J. Muller.

Morgan and his co-workers discovered in one tiny fly something that made genetic history. They were studying *Drosophila melanogaster* (droe-SOFF-uh-luh MELL-uh-noe-GASS-ter). This is a small fly often found around rotten fruit. Most people think of *Drosophila* as a pest, but it is very useful in research. It is easy to grow in jars and can be fed simple foods such as mashed bananas. It lives only 10 to 15 days, so many generations can be studied in a short time. Also, it is easy to tell the sexes of *Drosophila* apart.

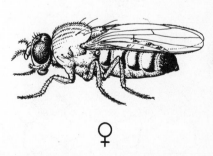

10-3 The common fruit fly, *Drosophila melanogaster*. Note that the male above is smaller than the female. The posterior end of the male is darker and blunter than that of the female.

Morgan and the others found the history-making fly one day in a large batch of *Drosophila*. Usually, *Drosophila* have red eyes. But this one, a male, had white eyes. This white-eyed male was mated with a normal red-eyed female. The offspring in the F_1 generation all had normal red eyes. By Mendel's principle of dominance, this meant that red eyes are dominant over white eyes in *Drosophila*.

Now members of the F_1 generation were mated to produce an F_2 generation. About three fourths of the F_2 flies had red eyes, while the other fourth had white eyes. Again, this matched Mendel's results with garden peas that were hybrid, or heterozygous, for one trait. But now came the surprise: All of the white-eyed flies were males!

Morgan had discovered a **sex-linked trait** in *Drosophila*. Two questions now arose:

(1) How was sex determined in *Drosophila*?

(2) How was the gene for white eyes related to sex?

SEX DETERMINATION

No one had yet examined the chromosomes in *Drosophila*. This was the next step for Morgan and his group. They found that the nuclei of somatic cells in *Drosophila* had four pairs of chromosomes. This is the diploid ($2n$) chromosome number. Female flies had four different kinds of chromosomes, each paired with an identical mate.

In the male, three chromosome pairs were like those in the female. But in the fourth pair, one chromosome was different. It did not match its mate. Instead of being rod-shaped, it was bent like a hook. The rod-shaped chromosome in both sexes are called *X chromosomes*. The hook-shaped chromosomes in the male is called the *Y chromosome*. These X and Y chromosomes are the **sex chromosomes.** The other three chromosome pairs in *Drosophila* are identical in both males and females. They care called **autosomes.**

These findings solved the problem of sex determination in *Drosophila*. **The X chromosomes (XX) produce a female. An X chromosome paired with a Y chromosome (XY) produces a male.** Later work has shown that the same thing happens in most animals, including humans, and in many plants that have sex differences. (In some organisms, however, the male has no Y chromosome. In these organisms, XX produces a female, while a single X results in a male.)

In Chapter Nine, we charted Mendel's crosses on *Punnett squares*. We can chart sex determination in the same way. When eggs are formed, the XX chromosome pair segregates. Each egg gets a single X chromosome. But when sperms are formed, the chromosome pair XY segregate to X and Y. So half of the sperms contain the X chromosome, and half contain the Y chromosome. The sex of the offspring is a matter of chance. If a sperm with an X chromosome fertilizes the egg, the offspring is female. If a sperm with a Y chromosome fertilizes the egg, the offspring is male.

Sex determination in humans happens in the same way. Each of your somatic cells contains 23 pairs of chromosomes. 22 of these pairs are autosomes. The remaining pair are sex chromosomes.

X   Y   X   X

10-4 The sex chromosomes of *Drosophila* are shown in color. The male has one X chromosome and one hook-shaped Y chromosome (left), whereas the female has two X chromosomes.

SEX DETERMINATION

Female CHROMOSOMES Male	X	X
X	XX	XX
Y	XY	XY

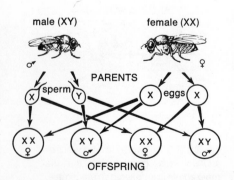

10-5 The inheritance of sex in *Drosophila*.

Now that you have seen how sex chromosomes work in determining sex, let's go back to Morgan's white-eyed male flies. We will let R stand for the gene for normal red eyes, and r for the white-eye gene. Both of these genes are on X chromosomes and so are sex-linked. The Y chromosome in *Drosophila* has *no* gene for eye color. So it plays no part in determining eye color.

Advantages of *Drosophila* in genetic studies: They are small and reproduce rapidly; they have large numbers of offspring.

10–6 Sex linkage in *Drosophila*.

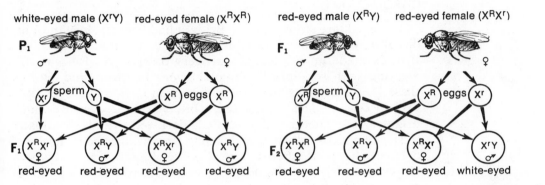

Morgan's first white-eyed male fly had a gene for white eyes on its X chromosome. We can represent this fly as X^rY. The normal red-eyed female, with genes for red eyes, would be X^RX^R. Because of segregation, the sperms formed by the white-eyed male would be half X^r and half Y. *All* eggs formed by the normal red-eyed female would be X^R.

What happens in the F_1 generation? Eggs fertilized by half of the sperms have X^RX^r chromosomes. These eggs produce females that are heterozygous for eye color. The other half of the offspring have X^RY chromosomes. These flies are males with a single gene for red eyes. Both males and females of F_1 generation are red-eyed because the red-eye gene is dominant.

Now we go to the F_2 generation. These flies are offspring of an F_1 male and female. Half of the eyes produced by an F_1 female contain X^R, and half contain X^r. Half the F_1 sperms contain X^R, and half contain Y. You can see that some offspring would be X^RX^R and some would be X^RX^r. All of these flies would be red-eyed females. Of the male offspring, some would be X^RY, with red eyes. But others would be X^rY, white-eyed. By the law of averages, about one fourth of the offspring would be of each type. So about three fourths would be red-eyed and one fourth white-eyed. And all of the white-eyed offspring would be males. This is just what Morgan found.

Could a white-eyed female appear in the next (F_3) generation? Yes, if an X^RX^r female were mated with a white-eyed X^rY male. Can you figure out what gene type this white-eyed female would have?

The discovery of **sex linkage** brought a new and important principle to genetics. Sex-linked traits are not limited to *Drosophila*. In humans, for example, men are about ten times as likely to be color-blind as women. Also, about ten times as many men as

INHERITANCE OF SEX-LINKED CHARACTERISTICS

Female SEX CHROMOSOMES Male	X^R	X^R
X^r	X^RX^r	X^RX^r
Y	X^RY	X^RY

RESULTS OF CROSSING F_1 HYBRIDS RED-EYED MALE AND RED-EYED FEMALE

Female SEX CHROMOSOMES Male	X^R	X^r
X^R	X^RX^R	X^RX^r
Y	X^RY	X^rY

Ask students to examine Fig. 10–4 and to conclude which parent determines sex in *Drosophila*. Is this pattern also true for humans?

Explain to students the necessity of adding the sex-linked gene to the sex chromosome as a superscript. This allows one to indicate the gene linkage.

The chromosome theory of heredity was further enhanced by Bridges' discovery of nondisjunction. Bridges did not actually see the genes on the chromosomes, but his findings added strength to the chromosome theory.

RESULTS OF CROSSING VERMILION-EYED FEMALE AND RED-EYED MALE

Female SEX CHROMOSOMES Male	X^r	X^r
X^R	$X^R X^r$	$X^R X^r$
Y	$X^r Y$	$X^r Y$

women have hemophilia, or "bleeder's disease." We will look at these conditions more closely in Chapter Eleven.

On the other hand, some traits that *seem* to be sex-linked really are not. For example, baldness is far more common in men than in women. But it is not a sex-linked trait. Conditions like this will also be taken up in Chapter Eleven.

NONDISJUNCTION—ABNORMAL SEGREGATION OF SEX CHROMOSOMES

As a graduate student, C. B. Bridges had helped Morgan in his discovery of sex-linked traits in *Drosophila*. About ten years later, Bridges made an important discovery of his own. He was still working with sex-linked eye color genes in *Drosophila*. But in these flies, the genes were for red eyes and vermilion eyes. Red eyes in *Drosophila* are dark red, while vermilion eyes are much brighter red. The gene for normal, dark red eyes is dominant.

These genes usually behave just like other sex-linked traits. What normally happens when a vermilion-eyed female is mated with a red-eyed male? Half the offspring are red-eyed females and half are vermilion-eyed males. But in about one case in two thousand, Bridges noticed a strange thing. A vermilion-eyed female mated with a red-eyed male and produced a vermilion-eyed female. Normally this would be impossible. Look at a Punnett square of this cross. Here, R stands for the dominant gene for red eyes. The recessive gene for vermilion eyes is r. The male fly with red eyes is $X^R Y$, while the vermilion-eyed female is $X^r X^r$.

Now look at the F_1 generation. Each female offspring must get an X^R chromosome from the male parent and an X^r chromosome from the female parent. Since R is dominant, how could a vermilion-eyed female result? This would take two X^r chromosomes. And both X^r chromosomes are in the female parent. Yet, somehow, vermilion-eyed females *were* produced. Did this mean that the whole theory of sex-linked traits was wrong? Bridges set out to find the answer. He found it in the body cells of the flies. The cells of vermilion-eyed females had *three* sex chromosomes—two X chromosomes and a Y chromosome. We can write this as $X^r X^r Y$. The extra X chromosome produced a female even with the Y chromosome present. The two recessive genes on these X chromosomes produced vermilion eyes.

A close look at this cross will show how this came about. The red-eyed male parent produced normal sperms, half containing X^R and half containing Y. But in the female parent, the $X^r X^r$ chromosome pair did not segregate when eggs were formed. So half of the eggs had $X^r X^r$ chromosomes and half had *no* sex chromosomes at all. We call this **nondisjunction.** Four kinds of offspring were produced:

¼ red-eyed females ($X^R X^r X^r$), which usually die
¼ vermilion-eyed females ($X^r X^r Y$)
¼ red-eye males (X^R), lack a chromosome and are sterile
¼ flies (Y) with no X chromosomes, and so with no eye-color genes (These always die at birth.)

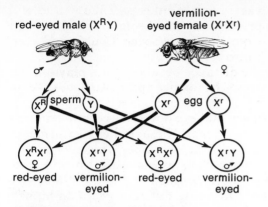

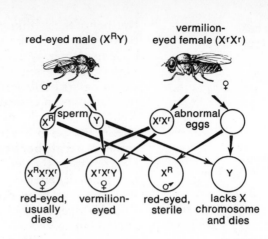

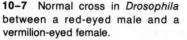

10-7 Normal cross in *Drosophila* between a red-eyed male and a vermilion-eyed female.

10-8 Nondisjunction in *Drosophila*.

Bridges' discovery of nondisjunction did not disprove the chromosome theory of heredity. In fact, it gave the theory strong support. There was now no doubt that genes are located on chromosomes. And it was also clear that the eye-color genes in *Drosophila* are on X chromosome.

Nondisjunction sometimes takes place in autosomes as well as in sex chromosomes. Studies of nondisjunction in human beings have led to an understanding of how conditions like *Down's syndrome* come about. We will go into this further in Chapter Eleven.

Crossing over may be demonstrated by using different colored pieces of wire or other material. Stress to students that crossing over may result in an entirely different inheritance by the offspring.

GENE LINKAGE AND CROSSING OVER

Keep in mind that it is chromosomes, not individual genes, that segregate during meiosis. A single chromosome contains *many* genes linked together (gene linkage). If one chromosome in a pair has 50 genes, so will the other chromosome in the pair. And the genes on each chromosome will either be alleles or will match each other.

But this linkage is not perfect. **Part of a chromosome, holding many genes, may separate. It may then switch places with the matching part of the other chromosome in the pair. This is called *crossing over.*** When do you think crossing over would be most likely to happen? When are the chromosomes in a pair closest together? In Chapter Eight, we discussed the stages in meiosis. At one point, the genes have replicated and each chromosome has formed two joined chromatids. These joined chromatids of a homologous pair lie close together in a group of four called a *tetrad*. It is now that parts of two chromatids may switch places, that is, cross over.

Let's look at how crossing over works. The letters *A, B,* and *C* stand for three of the many genes on a chromatid. The corresponding genes on a chromatid of the other homologue are *a, b,* and *c.* Now, suppose that one chromatid separates between genes A and B. The other chromatid separates between genes a and b. The separated parts then switch places. Each of the two chromatids now have a new gene linkage. These new linkages are *a, B, C* and *A, b, c.*

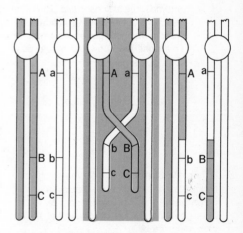

10-9 Crossing over. Following the tetrad formation (left), crossing over occurs between adjacent chromoatids (center). The final result shows a new grouping of genes on the chromosomes (right).

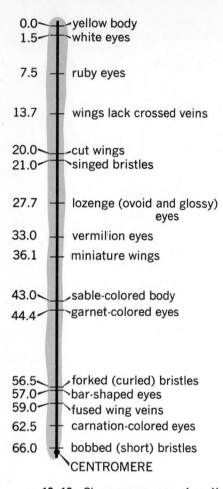

0.0	yellow body
1.5	white eyes
7.5	ruby eyes
13.7	wings lack crossed veins
20.0	cut wings
21.0	singed bristles
27.7	lozenge (ovoid and glossy) eyes
33.0	vermilion eyes
36.1	miniature wings
43.0	sable-colored body
44.4	garnet-colored eyes
56.5	forked (curled) bristles
57.0	bar-shaped eyes
59.0	fused wing veins
62.5	carnation-colored eyes
66.0	bobbed (short) bristles
	CENTROMERE

10-10 Chromosome map of an X chromosome of *Drosophila*. The numbers in the left column indicate the order in which the genes are arranged. This does not show the actual positions of the genes.

In late 1975, a team of Harvard molecular biologists announced that it had synthesized a complete mammalian gene in a test tube. This gene directs the production of hemoglobin in a rabbit.

Neither of these linkages was present in either parent. But they will be passed on to the offspring after the chromatids separate in meiosis. We have described a single crossover. Double and even triple crossovers are known to take place.

Biologists believe that the distance between genes plays an important part in crossing over. The farther apart two genes are on a chromosome, the more likely the chromosome is to separate between them. Studies have been made of how often certain chromosomes separate between certain genes. These studies give an idea of how far apart the genes are on the chromosomes. This information has helped geneticists to make **chromosome maps.** Chromosome mapping has been done for both *Drosophila* and corn. Methods like this are also being used to locate different genes on human chromsomes.

WHAT IS A GENE?

We've talked a lot so far about chromosomes and the inherited traits that genes produce. But what is a gene? And how does it work? Why does one gene produce a tall pea plant, while another produces a short plant? To find possible answers, we must go back to the DNA molecule.

In Chapter Seven, you learned that DNA *transcribes* its genetic code on messenger RNA. Messenger RNA, in turn, acts as a template in the building of amino acids into polypeptide chains. Enzymes and all other proteins are made up of these chains. In this way, DNA determines the nature of all enzymes and proteins synthesized in an organism. It is as though DNA were an architect and RNA a builder. RNA uses the "blueprint," the genetic code supplied by DNA, to put together proteins in the cell.

A closer look at the structure of DNA may help us to further define "gene." In Chapter Seven, we stated that nucleotide bases in RNA work in groups of three in coding amino acids. We call these base triplets *codons*. There are 20 different amino acids. Each is coded by from one to six codons. In Chapter Three, you learned that a single protein molecule may be made up of as many as three thousand amino acids. It would take at least 3,000 codons, 9,000 nucleotide bases, to code such a molecule. This may seem like a large number. But a *single strand* of DNA contains the genetic code for hundreds and perhaps thousands of proteins!

What does all this have to do with genes? Just this: **A gene may be simply a series of base triplets on part of a strand of DNA. This series of triplets would code a polypeptide chain, which in turn would become part of an enzyme or other protein.**

A chromosome is made up of a spiral of DNA around a protein "backbone," or core. The way in which the DNA is bonded to this protein core seems to determine which parts of the DNA strand are genetically active. It is thought that the genetically active parts, the genes, lie near the surface. There are thousands of these genetically active parts on a strand of DNA. The ends of the strand seem to be genetically inactive. So do the parts of the strand thought of as "nonsense codons."

GENE ACTION

Biologists understand fairly well how genes control protein synthesis through RNA codons. But they do not yet know how this control brings about the genetic traits themselves. That is, they do not know how a gene, by controlling protein synthesis, brings about red eyes or white eyes, tall plants or short plants. Much study is being done in this field today.

As you may know, you have 46 chromosomes in every somatic cell of your body. Your genes are present in homologous pairs on these chromosomes. A haploid sperm fertilized a haploid egg and produced a diploid zygote, your first somatic cell. From that moment on, every gene in every cell has replicated before the cell divides in mitosis. **So every cell of your body contains your complete genetic code.** If you have blue eyes, every cell contains genes for blue eyes. Yet you do not have blue skin or blue teeth. The genetic trait of blue eyes appears *only* in the cells of the irises of your eyes. In the same way, your iris cells and all other cells contain genes that determine hair color. But these genes act *only* on the cells of hair roots. The same thing is true for every genetic trait. You have genes for your blood type and for your ear shape in every cell. But the blood-type genes do not affect ear shape, and the ear-shape genes do not affect blood type.

Why does this happen? It may be that each gene becomes active only in a certain cell environment. Enzymes are thought to affect gene action. Perhaps different kinds of cells have chemical differences that make it easier to synthesize one enzyme and harder to synthesize another. Some research suggests that *hormones* may have something to do with control of gene action.

ENVIRONMENTAL INFLUENCE AND GENETIC TRAITS

Can conditions *outside* the cell affect the action of a gene? In some cases, at least, the answer is yes. One example involves hair color in the Himalayan rabbit.

Normally, this rabbit is white except for black nose, ears, tail, and feet. But biologists have found that temperature changes affect this color pattern. For example, hair may be pulled from one of the white areas such as the back. If this area is then kept cooler than normal, the hair that grows back will be black. On the other hand, hair may be taken from a normally black area such as the ears. If this area is then kept warmer than usual, the new hair will be white. It seems clear that temperature affects hair color in this rabbit. Hair is white in warm body areas and black in areas such as the ears, which are cooler. **Temperature differences may affect the gene action or enzyme action.** In either case, a genetic trait is changed by the environment.

Temperature also affects at least one trait in *Drosophila*. A gene for curly wings produces this trait if the flies are raised at 25°C. But if they are raised at 16°C, the wings are straight and normal.

a

b

c

10–11 A genetic trait altered by environmental conditions. (a) The normal color pattern of the hair of the Himalayan rabbit. (b) After the hair was removed from a portion of the rabbit's back, an ice pack was kept in position while the hair grew in. (c) New hair in this region kept at a lower-than-normal temperature was black.

Yet the gene for curly wings is still there because the next generation grows curly wings at 25° C.

TRANSFORMATION IN PNEUMOCOCCUS—PROOF OF DNA

You may have wondered why biologists are so sure that DNA is the genetic material. Some of the strongest evidence comes from studies of *pneumococcus* bacteria, which cause one kind of pneumonia. It is interesting that these studies were begun over forty years ago by a scientist who had never heard of DNA.

This scientist was Frederick Griffith of Great Britain. In 1928, Griffith was working with two different strains of pneumococcus. The cells of these two strains looked much alike. Both were tiny spheres joined in pairs or short strands. But there was one clear difference between the two. One strain had a slimy capsule around the cells. The other strain did not. Griffith found that the bacteria without capsules did not cause pneumonia. Evidently, when injected into mice or other test animals, they were destroyed by white blood cells. It seemed that the capsule kept white blood cells from destroying the bacteria.

At one point, Griffith injected mice with *both* strains of pneumococcus. In one injection, he used living bacteria without capsules. In the other, he used bacteria with capsules, but which had been killed by heat. To his surprise, the mice died of pneumonia. And their blood was found to contain *living* pneumonia bacteria with capsules! How could this be? All of the capsule-forming bacteria had been dead when injected. So the living bacteria without capsules must somehow have been changed, *transformed*, into a capsule-forming strain.

About fifteen years later, three scientists set out to find the reason for Griffith's results. These three were Oswald T. Avery and his co-workers, C. M. MacLeod and M. McCarty. Avery and his group grew Type II pneumonia bacteria. These have no capsules and their cells appear "rough." They also grew Type III pneumonia bacteria, whose cells have capsules and appear "smooth." Each strand continued to produce its own kind of cells, generation after generation.

Avery's group prepared a *cell-free extract* from heat-killed Type III-S cells. They mixed this extract with living Type II-R cells. Most of the cells that then grew were Type II-R. But *some* of them were Type III-S cells, alive and with capsules. These were taken out and grown separately. When injected into mice, they caused pneumonia.

Clearly, something in the extract had transformed harmless Type II-R cells into deadly Type III-S cells. This change was passed on to the offspring of the transformed cells. But what was the substance that caused the change? At last Avery and his co-workers found it. At first, it was thought to be a protein. But it turned out to be a nucleic acid—DNA, as you might have guessed.

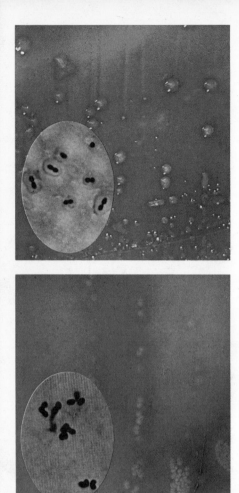

10–12 Pneumococcus. "Smooth" colonies of the capsulated, infectious Pneumococcus. (above). "Rough" colonies of the noncapsulated noninfectious Pneumococcus strains. Insets show the microscopic difference between the strains. (Louis Koster; insets: Robert Austrian and *Journal of Experimental Medicine*)

a. inject noncapsulated organisms

b. inject capsulated organisms

c. kill capsulated organisms and inject living noncapsulated
   organisms and heat-killed capsulated organisms

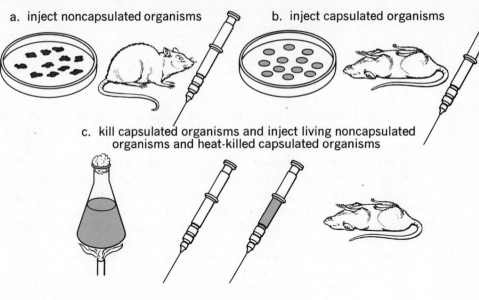

10–13 The discovery of transformation in pneumococcus.

Avery and associates' investigation with *Pneumococcus*

a. prepare suspension of
   living noncapsulated
   type II-R organisms

b. kill capsulated type III-S
   organisms and prepare
   cell-free extract

c. mix suspension of
   living noncapsulated type II-R
   organisms with cell-free extract
   from heat-killed capsulated
   type III-S organisms; then culture

d. both noncapsulated
   type II-R and capsulated
   type III-S colonies grow

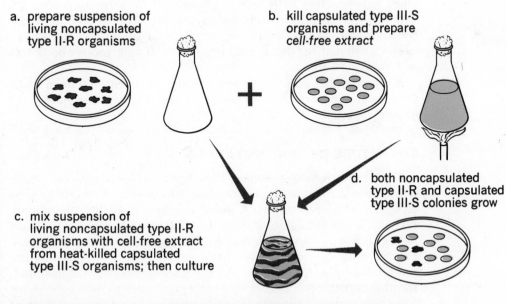

10–14 Avery and associates' discovery of the transforming substance. It was later
determined that DNA from the heat-killed capsulated type 111-S organisms had
entered some of the noncapsulated organisms and transformed them into capsulated
cells.

The discovery of transformation in pneumococcus is of great importance for two reasons. It adds evidence that DNA is the material of genes. And it shows that DNA can be moved from one organism to another and still determine genetic traits.

MUTATIONS—ERRORS IN THE GENETIC CODE

Genes replicate and chromosomes segregate during meiosis in a very regular way. They may do so millions of times without an error. The genes from both parents combine in new ways in the offspring, but the individual genes are not changed.

Still, from time to time, there is an error. An organism appears with a trait totally unlike any trait in either parent. Since this new trait is passed on to offspring, we know that it is not just a matter of environmental influence. Instead, it must result from a *genetic* change. **We call a sudden genetic change like this a *mutation*. The organism in which it appears is called a *mutant*.**

There are two types of mutation. One arises when the base code of a DNA molecule is changed in any way. Such a change naturally changes or destroys the trait produced by the gene. This type of mutation is a **gene mutation,** also called a *point mutation*. Less common than gene mutations are **chromosome mutations.** These may result from nondisjunction during meiosis, crossing over, or the loss of all or part of a chromosome.

A mutation that occurs in a body cell of a plant or animal is called a *somatic mutation*. The new trait appears in all tissue that descends from the mutant cell. But the trait is not passed on to offspring, since reproductive cells are not involved. (Traits produced by somatic mutations in some plants *can* be reproduced asexually by several different methods. Many new plant varieties have been developed by these methods. We will talk more about this in Chapter Twelve.)

A mutation that occurs in a reproductive cell is called a *germ mutation*. Germ mutations may be passed on to offspring, and have great genetic importance.

THE NATURE OF GENE MUTATIONS

Most mutations are *minor*. They may have little or no visible effect on the mutant organism. Any effects they do have may be either helpful or harmful. A *major* mutation, on the other hand, causes a great change in a trait. And this change is almost always harmful. Sometimes it is *lethal*, causing the death of the organism. For example, suppose a gene that controls chlorophyll production mutates in a plant. The plant will die since it must have chlorophyll for photosynthesis.

A mutant gene is nearly always recessive to a dominant normal gene. For this reason, a mutation in a heterozygous organism usually does not actually affect a trait. But the recessive mutant gene may be passed on to offspring. If it is then paired with a match-

Point out to students that there are relatively few mutations considering the millions of gene replications and chromosomal segregations that occur.

Some mutations can cause diseases in humans. One such disease is called *phenylketonuria* (PKU). More than 400 babies are born with this condition each year. Individuals with this condition are missing an enzyme that breaks down a compound called *phenylketone*. This inability to break down phenylketone can result in mental retardation However, if caught in time, a special diet can control this condition.

ing mutant gene from the other parent, the trait controlled by the gene probably will change.

Some mutations occur more often than others. Some genes mutate as often as once in two thousand cell divisions. Others mutate only once in millions of divisions. A gene sometimes mutates several times in a row. Or it may mutate once and then mutate back to its normal form. All these differences may occur because some genes are chemically more stable than others. Of course, it is hard to determine the rate at which some genes mutate because many mutations have no clear effect.

Mutations occur in all types of life. They are known in viruses and are common in bacteria. All plants and animals studied genetically have shown mutations. Chapter Eleven will deal with some of the mutations that occur in human beings.

CAUSES OF MUTATIONS

A major cause of mutations is high-energy radiation. Cosmic rays from outer space and radiation from radioactive elements may cause natural mutations. Radiation from artificial sources also may cause mutations. This radiation includes X rays, gamma rays, beta particles, and ultraviolet light. Biologists have raised both the number and the rate of mutations in organisms by using these types of radiation. A rise in temperature also may cause more mutations to occur. As may the use of certain chemicals.

RADIATION AS A CAUSE OF MUTATIONS

It was Hermann J. Muller who first proved that radiation causes mutations. As a graduate student, Muller had worked with Morgan and Bridges in the early studies of heredity in *Drosophila*. In 1927, at the University of Texas, he was again working with *Drosophila*. His experiments were aimed at showing that radiation can cause mutations, and that artificial radiation can raise the number of mutations.

Before this time, geneticists had tried many methods of producing mutations in *Drosophila* and other test animals. They had used different temperatures, foods, lighting, and other conditions. None of these experiments had given good results. Why not? For one thing, the experimenters may have missed the importance of a few simple facts about genes. Think about it. The two genes for a given trait lie very close together in a cell, each gene on one chromosome of a chromosome pair. Any chemical change in the cell will almost always affect both genes in the same way. So will any change in the environment, such as temperature. Suddenly, one gene in a pair mutates, while the other does not change at all. What would be most likely to cause this pinpoint effect? Muller thought that the answer was high-energy radiation. It was to prove this idea that he began his experiments. He also thought that radiation would be most likely to cause lethal mutations.

Gene mutation rate is greatly increased by overexposure to radiation. Discuss with students some of the recognized dangers of radiation exposure.

Using a Punnett square, illustrate the cross and offspring in Muller's radiation experiment. Use colored chalk to indicate the irradiated chromosome.

Neurospora was chosen to work with because the rate of mutation with *Drosophila* was too slow. *Neurospora* is well suited for this type of work because it reproduces rapidly in large numbers and the nuclei (spores) can be easily examined.

The following is a very simple account of Muller's work. First, he picked a male *Drosophila* with known sex-linked traits. He then radiated it with a strong dose of X rays. This fly was mated with a female with known sex-linked genes on the X chromosomes. In the F_1 generation, half of the flies were female and half male. The females all had a radiated X chromosome from the male parent and a normal X chromosome from the female parent. The males all had a normal X chromosome from the female parent and a radiated Y chromosome from the male parent. When two of these flies were crossed, four kinds of offspring should have resulted in the F_2 generation:

¼ females with two normal X chromosomes

¼ females with one normal X chromosome and one radiated X chromosome

¼ males with a normal X chromosome and a radiated Y chromosome

¼ males with both X and Y chromosomes radiated

These *should* have been the offspring. But the last group did not appear. The radiated X chromosome carried a lethal gene that kept these flies from developing. This did not happen in the females with a radiated X chromosome because of a dominant (normal) gene on the other X chromosome.

Discuss with students the importance of gene-enzyme research to modern medical knowledge.

It was for this work that Muller won the Nobel Prize in medicine and physiology in 1946. After his experiments, he and others produced many more mutations in *Drosophila* and other organisms. **Artificial radiation has been found to cause as many as 150 times the normal number of mutations.**

10–15 Some of the changes caused by mutations in the reproductive cells of wild-type *Drosophila*.

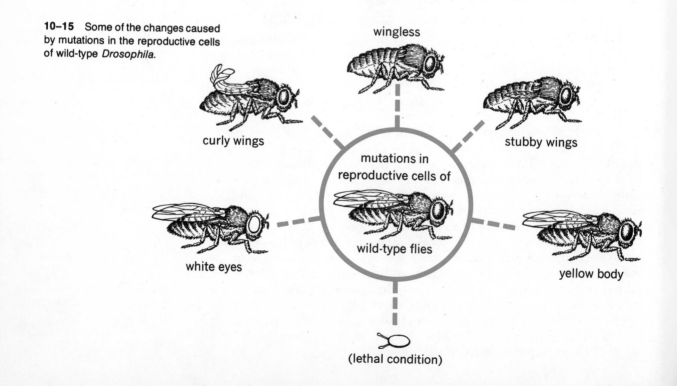

wingless

curly wings

stubby wings

mutations in reproductive cells of

white eyes

wild-type flies

yellow body

(lethal condition)

MUTANT GENES AND METABOLIC PROCESSES

Much research is being done with simple organisms such as molds and bacteria. These organisms have very short life cycles, so results can be seen quickly. Also, their metabolic processes are easy to study for evidence of gene action in cell biochemistry.

In the 1940's, George W. Beadle and Edward L. Tatum did the first important experiments with the common red mold, *Neurospora*. Beadle and Tatum produced several mutations in *Neurospora* by radiating the spores with X rays. The radiated spores were placed in a simple medium normally used to grow the mold. But some of the spores did not grow and produce new mold plants. It seemed likely that a mutation had stopped them from synthesizing one or more substances needed for growth. But which substance or substances could no longer be synthesized?

By growing the red mold on different nutrients, they found a missing enzyme. How did the damaged genes affect this change? Beadle and Tatum did more nutrition and breeding experiments with *Neurospora*. They found that each gene was necessary for the synthesis of a different enzyme. Mutations changed the genes so that they could not produce polypeptides to form the enzymes.

Beadle and Tatum worked with many other mutant strains of *Neurospora*. This work established the "one gene—one enzyme" hypothesis of gene action. It showed that a gene was necessary for the synthesis of each enzyme. Beadle and Tatum won the Nobel Prize for medicine and physiology in 1958.

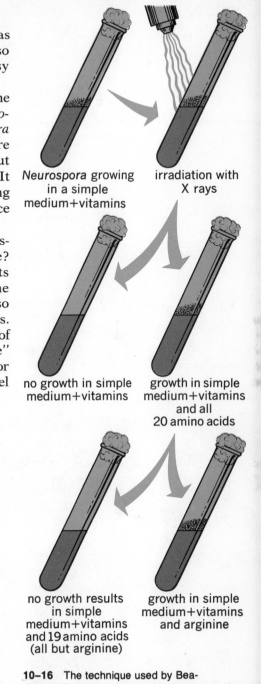

Neurospora growing in a simple medium+vitamins

irradiation with X rays

no growth in simple medium+vitamins

growth in simple medium+vitamins and all 20 amino acids

no growth results in simple medium+vitamins and 19 amino acids (all but arginine)

growth in simple medium+vitamins and arginine

10–16 The technique used by Beadle and Tatum to detect and isolate a nutritional mutant in *Neurospora*. They also identified the amino acid it could not synthesize.

SUMMARY

More than a century has passed since Gregor Mendel's experiments with garden peas opened up the science of genetics. Since 1900, scientists have probed deeper and deeper into the wonders of the living cell and its genetic material. Sutton, Morgan, Bridges, Griffith, Muller, and many others have made important contributions. Today's geneticists work with a vast knowledge of biochemistry and cell biology. They have the aid of electron microscopes, ultracentrifuges, computers, and other sophisticated equipment. No wonder the science of genetics is moving forward so rapidly!

Modern genetics is answering many questions about human heredity. Most of the traits we inherit are necessary and helpful. But some harmful traits do arise. We are finding out more and more about these genetic problems. Often, learning the cause of a problem leads to its correction. In this and other ways, genetics may be of great help to the science of medicine. This will become even clearer as you study genes in human population.

BIOLOGICALLY SPEAKING

gene linkage

sex chromosome

autosome

sex linkage

nondisjunction

crossing over

chromosome map

mutation

mutant

gene mutation

chromosome mutation

somatic mutation

germ mutation

QUESTIONS FOR REVIEW

1. List three parallels that Sutton found between Mendel's hereditary factors and the behavior of chromosomes and genes.
2. Why are *Drosophila* useful for genetic studies?
3. Describe the chromosome makeup of male and female *Drosophila*.
4. What is a sex-linked gene?
5. Distinguish between sex chromosomes and autosomes.
6. Explain chromosomal nondisjunction.
7. How does crossing over alter gene linkage?
8. Define a gene in terms of genetic activity of DNA.
9. Explain the relation of enzymes to gene action.
10. Give an example of an environmental influence on a trait.
11. What observation led to the discovery of transformation?
12. List several natural causes of mutation.
13. Why are mutations that occur in body cells not important to the entire species?
14. What did Beadle and Tatum mean when they put forward the "one gene-one enzyme" hypothesis?

APPLYING PRINCIPLES AND CONCEPTS

1. Discuss the significance of the gene hypothesis proposed by Sutton.
2. Explain why nondisjunction is lethal in many offspring.
3. Discuss two important genetic principles illustrated in transformation.
4. Trace the changes in DNA during the chromosome movements of mitosis.

11–1 Parent and child resemblance. (Paul Fusco, Magnum X)

Genes in Human Populations

OBJECTIVES

- DEFINE population genetics.
- DEFINE the term gene pool.
- DISTINGUISH fraternal twins from identical twins.
- DEFINE multiple allele.
- DESCRIBE the inheritance of blood types.
- LIST several sex-linked human characteristics.
- DESCRIBE sickle-cell anemia.
- UNDERSTAND the inheritance of mental disorders.
- EXPLAIN the genetic basis for Down's syndrome.
- NAME three syndromes that result from nondisjunction of sex chromosomes

THE NATURE OF HUMAN HEREDITY

The same laws of heredity apply to all organisms, from bacteria to garden peas to human beings. Yet biologists probably know more about passing on of traits in *Drosophila* and other "lower" organisms than in ourselves. Why? One reason is the length of human life. We can study many generations of *Drosophila* in a few months, or many generations of bacteria in a week. But we do well to see six human generations in a lifetime.

Another problem involves the number of offspring. In many plants and animals, a single cross many produce hundreds or even thousands of offspring. Human parents produce only a few offspring at most. Thus, there is a very small sample of genetic possibilities to study in a given family. Further, the two parents themselves almost always come from completely different families. Thus, each parent has a completely different genetic background.

The influence of the environment also causes problems in studying human genetics. For example, we can account for traits such as hair or eye color in terms of genes. But experience and emotion also leave their marks on human faces. What about traits like height and body build? Genes influence these traits, but so do your diet, general health, and gland activity. All of these influences, in turn, may be influenced by your emotions and other experiences.

Finally, consider how many different traits are involved in human heredity. *Drosophila*, with only four pairs of chromosomes, has hundreds of inherited traits. Human beings have 46 chromosomes, and each chromosome holds a huge number of genes. There is almost no limit to the number of possible combinations. **Unless you have an identical twin, not one of the billions of people in the world is your genetic double.**

Pose a number of questions to elicit from students their opinions on the "nature vs. nurture" question. Ask students to think about their own families before answering the question.

11-2 A true cross-section of the population must take into consideration sex, age, race, and occupation. Do the people in this photo represent a true cross-section? (Mimi Forsyth, Monkmeyer Press Photo)

POPULATION GENETICS

Mendel formed his hypotheses about heredity after observing many pea plants over several generations. But in dealing with human families, the problem of limited numbers arises. We can trace certain traits from children to parents to grandparents. We can include aunts, uncles, and other close relatives. Still, such a sampling is very small.

Trying to look farther back in time will not help much, either. Consider the fact that you had 16 great-great-grandparents and 32 great-great-great-grandparents. Could you trace any one trait back through all of these ancestors? Even if you could, you would be limited to some easily recognized trait such as eye color. You may be surprised when you realize what a large part of the population you may claim as distant relatives!

For these reasons, biologists have turned more and more to the methods of *population genetics*. Here, the unit studied is not a single family, but a whole population. **Population genetics is based on finding *gene frequencies*. That is, we want to learn how often specific genes appear in a given population. With this information, we can predict the probability that a given trait will appear in any offspring.**

POPULATION SAMPLING

It would not make sense to test every member of a large population for a single genetic trait. How, then, do we arrive at the gene frequencies used in population genetics? The answer is by *population sampling*.

Opinion polls are examples of population sampling. Such a poll can be very accurate. For example, on a major election night, television networks make early predictions of winners and losers. These predictions may be based on only two or three percent of the total vote. But they are seldom wrong.

To allow such accurate predictions, a poll must cover a true cross section of the population. Men and women of all ages, races, and occupations must be included. The use of computers has helped greatly in population sampling.

Let's look at an actual case of population sampling for a specific genetic trait. The trait involves the ability to taste a substance known as *PTC*. To some people, whom we will call *tasters*, PTC tastes very bitter. To other people, *nontasters*, PTC has no taste at all. The ability to taste PTC is dominant, so we will represent this trait as *T*. Thus, a taster may be homozygous *(TT)* or heterozygous *(Tt)*.

By population sampling, the ratio of tasters to nontasters has been found for the population of the United States. This ratio is about 65 percent tasters to 35 percent nontasters. From these figures, we can easily predict how many people are likely to be tasters in any given population. You could test for this trait in your class and see how close to the national average it comes.

Another inherited trait can be easily sampled. Some people can roll their tongues into a U shape, while others cannot. The ability to roll the tongue is dominant. Thus, people who can do so may be homozygous *(RR)* or heterozygous *(Rr)*. People who cannot roll their tongues are homozygous recessive *(rr)*. As with the ability to taste PTC, only a single pair of genes is involved in this trait. For this reason, a population sampling for the ability to roll the tongue should give results much like those for tasting PTC.

THE GENE POOL

Geneticists refer to all the genes present in a given population as the **gene pool.** We can consider any member of a population to have a random sample of the genes present in the whole population. How often will a given trait appear in the population? Only as often as the gene or genes for that trait appear.

Be sure to point out to students that there is a considerable amount of intermingling of genetic traits. Although certain characteristics are likely to be more prevalent among certain groups of people, many other traits are also present.

Let's go back to our tasters and nontasters of PTC. The fact that both traits appear is evidence that both dominant *(T)* and recessive *(t)* genes are present. Further, consider the national ratio of 65 percent tasters to 35 percent nontasters. This ratio is fairly close to the 3:1 ratio expected in a monohybrid cross with dominance. We might assume, then, that about one fourth of the population are homozygous tasters *(TT)*, one half heterozygous tasters *(Tt)*, and one fourth homozygous nontasters *(tt)*. Thus, the genes *T* and *t* would be present in about equal numbers.

Might there be parts of the world where only the dominant gene is present in a population? If so, all members of the population would be tasters. Another population might have only the recessive trait in its gene pool. All members of this population would be nontasters.

In many populations, we do see evidence of high gene frequencies for certain traits. For example, the trait of dark, straight hair is very common in American Indians. Their facial features resemble those of the Mongoloid peoples of Asia. It is believed that the American Indians migrated from Asia many thousands of years ago. They then separated into different culture areas. In each such area, a different gene pool came to be established. Thus, Eskimos came to have certain traits unlike those of Plains Indians, while Eastern Woodlands Indians had certain traits unlike those of either group.

Gene pools change as populations shift. New gene combinations occur. These new combinations may cause changes in traits such as hair, eye, or skin color, height and build, and blood type. The greater the number of people that move from one area to another, the more the gene pool changes.

11-3 The facial features of the American Indian (top) resemble those of Mongoloid peoples of Asia. It is believed that Indians migrated from Asia thousands of years ago. (A. Sirdofsky, Editorial Photocolor Archives; Monkmeyer Press Photos)

TWINS

Having discussed population genetics, let's look at the effects of genes in individuals. As we said earlier, it is sometimes hard to

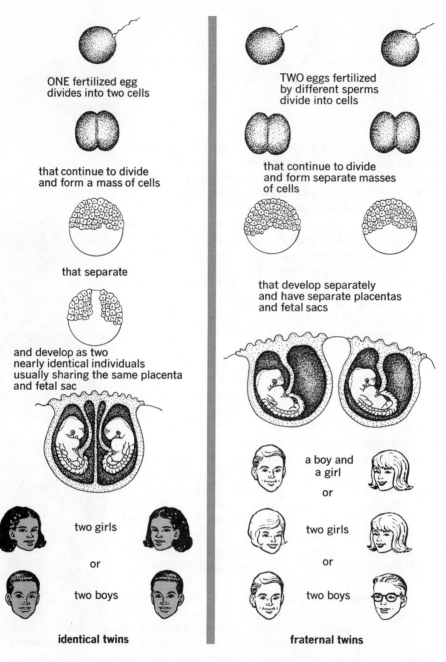

ONE fertilized egg divides into two cells

that continue to divide and form a mass of cells

that separate

and develop as two nearly identical individuals usually sharing the same placenta and fetal sac

two girls

or

two boys

identical twins

TWO eggs fertilized by different sperms divide into cells

that continue to divide and form separate masses of cells

that develop separately and have separate placentas and fetal sacs

a boy and a girl

or

two girls

or

two boys

fraternal twins

11–4 Since identical twins develop from a single egg and sperm, they have the same genetic makeup. Fraternal twins, developing from different eggs and sperm, are no more alike than other brothers and sisters.

separate the influences of heredity from those of environment. In an effort to make this separation clearer, geneticists have made studies of twins. Twins are of two types.

Fraternal twins are the more common type of twins. Such twins develop from two different eggs fertilized by different sperms. **Thus, fraternal twins are two completely different people. That is, their genes are no more alike than those of normal brothers and sisters.** Most fraternal twins are brought up in very similar environments. Yet they may be quite different in body, in personality, and in mental ability. These differences are helpful in learning which traits are inherited and which result from the influence of environment.

Identical twins, on the other hand, are nearly the same person in duplicate. They develop from a single fertilized egg. At some point early in development, the cells formed from this egg split into separate masses. Instead of growing into a single embryo, these cell masses develop into *two* embryos.

Since they developed from the same egg, identical twins have exactly the same genetic makeup. Thus, the likenesses between them indicate traits controlled by genes. For example, identical twins always have the same sex. Usually, they are mirror images of each other. They often are very much alike in mental and physical ability, likes and dislikes, and many other personality traits. However, the environment may have a strong influence on some of these traits.

Several studies have been made of identical twins who were separated early in life and brought up in different environments. In such cases, each twin experiences a different home and family life, education, friendships, and so on. All of these influences leave their marks. Yet the twins remain closely alike in looks, basic personality, and learning ability. They may differ somewhat in some ways. But these differences seem to reflect the influences of environment rather than a change in basic ability.

11–5 Identical twins have the same genetic makeup. (J. Gerard Smith/Monkmeyer)

Ask students to discuss certain behavioral characteristics of twins that they know. Do identical twins tend to act similarly? If they were to be separated, would they still act the same way?

HEREDITY AND BLOOD TYPE IN HUMAN BEINGS

In 1900, Dr. Karl Landsteiner of Vienna made an important discovery while studying human blood. He found that mixing blood from certain people resulted in clumping of red corpuscles. Later, he learned that red corpuscles from different people may vary in the presence of a protein substance. This substance, found on the corpuscle surface, is known as an **agglutinogen.** It may be of two types—type A or type B. Some corpuscles have only one type, some have both, and some have neither. **Thus, we can classify all human blood as type A, B, AB, or O.**

How is blood type inherited? There are *three* genes, rather than a single pair, that code blood type. We call such genes *multiple alleles.* However, though there are three possible genes for blood type, only two are present in any individual. We can represent these genes as *A*, *B*, and *O*. The *A* gene produces

Students are usually very interested in typing their own blood. The teacher may want to refer them to Chapter Forty-Two, where an agglutination chart appears. Some students may want to carry this exercise one step further by typing members of their families.

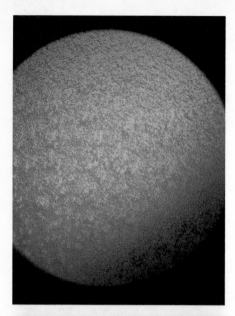

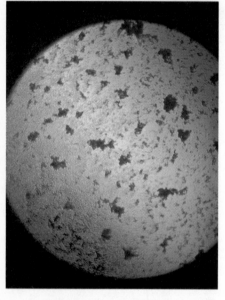

11–6 Normal red blood cells (above). Mixing of different blood types could cause agglutination of the red blood cells (bottom). (Lester V. Bergman and Associates)

type-A corpuscles and the *B* gene type-B corpuscles. The *O* gene produces neither agglutinogen on corpuscles. Different combinations of these genes in heredity produce the four blood types:

- Genes *AA* or *AO* produce type-A blood
- Genes *BB* or *BO* produce type-B blood
- Genes *OO* produce type-O blood (no agglutinogen)
- Genes *AB* produce type-AB blood (both agglutinogens)

We can represent the three alleles for blood type by writing the dominant as *I* and the recessive as *i*. The agglutinogens produced would then be I^A, I^B, and *i*. Type A may be homozygous I^AI^A or heterozygous I^Ai. Type B may be homozygous I^BI^B or heterozygous I^Bi. Type AB is always heterozygous I^AI^B, while type O is always homozygous *ii*.

You can chart a cross between parents of different blood types on a Punnett square. Consider a cross between heterozygous type A *(I^Ai)* and heterozygous type B *(I^Bi)*. All four blood types may result from such a cross. Further, the probability ratio is one fourth of each type. In fact, it would be unusual for this ratio to appear in a given family, but it could happen.

In recent years, surveys have been made to find the frequencies of the four blood types in different populations. Such populations may differ in race, geographic location, or both.

Table 11-1 BLOOD TYPE PERCENTAGES IN VARIOUS REGIONS OF THE WORLD

BLOOD TYPE	A	B	AB	O
U.S.A.—white	41.0%	10.0%	4.0%	45.0%
U.S.A.—Negro	26.0%	21.0%	3.7%	49.3%
Swedish	46.7%	10.3%	5.1%	37.9%
Japanese	38.4%	21.8%	8.6%	31.2%
Hawaiian	60.8%	2.2%	0.5%	36.5%
Chinese	25.0%	35.0%	10.0%	30.0%
Australian aborigine	44.7%	2.1%	0.0%	53.1%
North American Indian	7.7%	1.0%	0.0%	91.3%

SEX-LINKED TRAITS IN HUMAN BEINGS

One well-known sex-linked trait in human beings is **red-green color blindness.** While rare in women, this trait appears in about eight percent of the male population. People with this condition see the colors red and green as shades of gray.

The fact that this trait appears more often in males than in females indicates that it is sex-linked. The genes for red-green color vision are on the X chromosomes. The gene for normal color vision *(C)* is dominant over the recessive gene for color blindness *(c)*. Thus, the possible combinations of these genes are as follows:

X^CX^C, a normal female, homozygous for color vision

X^CX^c, a carrier female, heterozygous but with normal vision

X^cX^c, a color-blind female, homozygous for color blindness

X^CY, a normal male with a single gene for color vision

X^cY, a color-blind male with a single gene for color blindness

Look at a cross between a carrier female (X^CX^c) and a normal male (X^CY). Such a cross could produce a color-blind son (X^cY) even though both parents had normal vision. Can you figure out a cross that might produce a color-blind female?

Hemophilia (HEE-muh-FILL-ee-yuh) is another sex-linked trait passed on in much the same way as color blindness. People with hemophilia lack a substance needed for normal clotting of blood. This substance is not produced because the gene that codes for it is missing. Hemophilia is dangerous. People with it bleed badly from even the smallest wound. They may die from loss of blood.

Hemophilia tends to run in families and to appear in males. It can appear in a female only when the mother is a carrier and the father has hemophilia. Several studies have been made of families in which hemophilia is common. One such study involves the family of Queen Victoria. The family chart shows how many females were carriers and how many males had hemophilia.

SEX-INFLUENCED AND SEX-LIMITED TRAITS

Some traits that might appear to be sex-linked actually are not. Baldness, for example, is not sex-linked but **sex-influenced.** The gene for baldness is dominant in males but recessive in females. Thus, a mother can pass on baldness to her son without showing it herself. We can represent the gene for baldness as *B* and the gene for normal hair growth as *b*. If so, a *Bb* male would be bald, while a *Bb* female would not be. On the other hand, the genes *BB* would produce baldness in either a male or a female. The genes *bb*, of course, would produce normal hair growth in either sex.

Another type of trait is known as **sex-limited.** The genes for such traits are present in both male and female. However, the trait itself shows up in only one sex. It is believed that sex-limited traits appear only in the presence of sex hormones.

In human beings, sex-limited genes affect such traits as beard growth. A woman might have a gene for a beard trait, but would not show the trait since she lacks male hormones. However, the trait could be passed on and might show up in her son.

EYE AND SKIN COLOR

Eye color in human beings is coded by multiple alleles. Blue eyes are coded by a single pair of recessive genes. The genes for brown eye pigment are dominant. The different shades from hazel through light brown to dark brown seem to result from different numbers of genes for brown. Other genes produce shades from gray to green.

INHERITANCE OF COLOR BLINDNESS

Female SEX CHROMOSOMES Male	X^c	X^e
X^c	X^cX^c	X^cX^e
Y	X^cY	X^eY

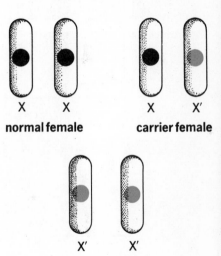

X   X
normal female

X   X′
carrier female

X′   X′
color-blind female

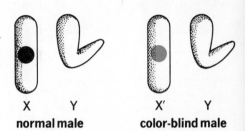

X   Y
normal male

X′   Y
color-blind male

11-7 The gene for color blindness is indicated in color. The chromosome that carries it is designated as X′. Two such chromosomes are necessary for a color-blind female while only one is necessary for a color-blind male.

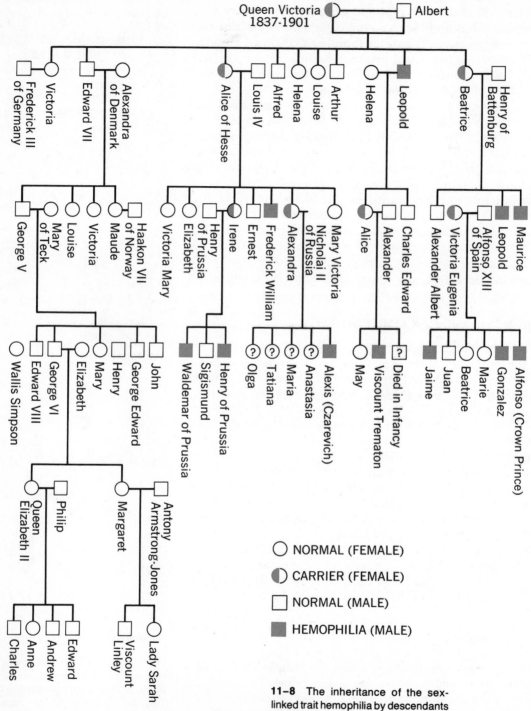

NORMAL (FEMALE)

CARRIER (FEMALE)

NORMAL (MALE)

HEMOPHILIA (MALE)

11–8 The inheritance of the sex-linked trait hemophilia by descendants of Queen Victoria. Is the mutant gene still present in the royal family of Great Britain?

Skin color is thought to be determined by several pairs of genes. Some geneticists suggest that two pairs of alleles are involved. Others think that there may be from four to as many as eight such pairs of alleles. In any case, the range of skin color from dark brown to white results from different numbers of genes that code production of skin pigments. Other genes produce pigments that give the skin colors of Orientals and of many American Indians.

ARE DISEASES INHERITED?

The question of whether or not diseases are inherited is of great importance. Some diseases appear to run in families. Geneticists have tried to learn how these diseases might be related to genes. In infections such as tuberculosis, the disease itself cannot be inherited. However, there is evidence that chemical conditions in body tissues are important in resisting such infections. Genes may affect these chemical conditions. Thus, heredity might make it more *likely* that a person would contract a disease such as tuberculosis.

On the other hand, **diseases resulting from abnormal structure or function of body organs can be inherited.** Such a disease is sugar diabetes. In this condition, the pancreas does not produce enough of a substance known as *insulin*. We will study this disease more closely in Chapter Forty-Seven. For now, we are interested mainly in how it is inherited.

Diabetes appears often in certain families. It is thought to be caused by a recessive gene. However, the disease is less serious in some people than in others. Also, control of diet and body weight may prevent or arrest diabetes even when the genes are present. There is evidence that multiple factors may be involved in diabetes. If so, the seriousness of the disease might be affected by the number of genes present.

There is evidence that genes may play a part in other conditions also. Among these are certain allergies, asthma, bronchitis, nearsightedness, farsightedness, and night blindness.

SICKLE-CELL ANEMIA

Sickle-cell anemia is a serious blood disease most common among Negroes. Figures for North American blacks vary. One survey indicates that 8½ percent of the black population carries the disease, while between 0.3 and 1.3 percent actually have it. Sickle-cell anemia is even more common among peoples of central and western Africa. There, as much as 4 percent of black Africans may have the disease.

Sickle-cell anemia results from formation of abnormal red blood cells. Their abnormal shape is caused by the presence of a defect in the blood protein called hemoglobin. Sickle shaped red blood cells cause damage to certain body organs and leave the victim

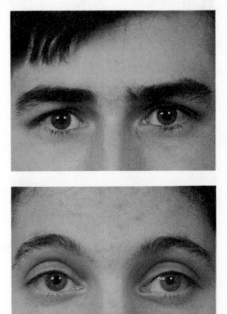

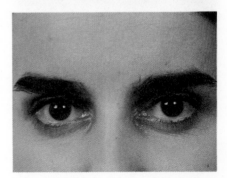

11-9 The color of your eyes is coded by multiple alleles. (H.R.W. Photos by Russell Dian)

There are a number of inherited diseases known to science today. Some of these diseases, such as sickle-cell anemia, tend to affect a majority of individuals of one group. Sickle-cell anemia is thought to be carried by about eight percent of all black Americans. There are other diseases that also affect one particular group. For example PKU and cystic fibrosis are usually diseases of white people. Tay-Sachs disease usually affects Jews, and Cooley's disease (a type of anemia) affects Greeks and Italians.

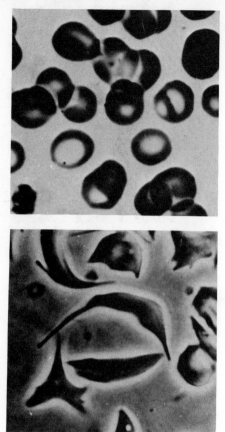

11-10 Normal red blood cells (above). Sickle shaped red blood cells from a patient with sickle-cell anemia (bottom). (Dept. of H.E.W.)

more open to infections. Normal and sickle-cell hemoglobin differ in only one amino acid out of the over 560 amino acids in each molecule. This error results from a mistake in coding of the DNA.

Sickle-cell anemia is thought to result from a recessive gene. Thus, it appears only in homozygous individuals. Heterozygous individuals, with a normal gene, do not develop the disease. However, they may pass it on to offspring.

Proper treatment can add many years to the life of a sickle-cell anemia victim. For this reason, it is important to discover the disease as early as possible. There are many testing programs aimed at doing this.

HEREDITY AND THE MIND

To what degree do genes affect intelligence? This is a hard question to answer, since intelligence itself is hard to define. Yet there is some evidence that intelligence *is* related to genes. For example, identical twins tend to have very similar scores in intelligence tests. Fraternal twins have less similar scores, and normal brothers and sisters have less similar scores. The more distant the relatives involved, the less similar the scores are likely to be.

Environment, of course, has some effect on how a person will score on such tests. But it seems clear that heredity also has an influence in determining the level of intelligence.

On the other hand, there is strong evidence that certain kinds of mental retardation have a genetic basis. Certain kinds of mental illness, too, may be related to genes. For example, manic-depressive psychosis is thought to be inherited, at least to some degree. The same is true of schizophrenia. Much remains to be learned about the effects of genes on all of these conditions. This is one of the most important fields of research in genetics today.

NONDISJUNCTION OF HUMAN CHROMOSOMES

In Chapter Ten, you studied nondisjunction in *Drosophila*. The same thing may occur during meiosis in human beings. Nondisjunction may involve either somatic chromosomes or sex chromosomes. It may take place in either the first or second division in meiosis. Often, a chromosome fails to move from the equator to a pole during anaphase. This lag produces one daughter cell with an extra chromosome and one lacking a chromosome.

Suppose that a gamete has such an extra chromosome. This chromosome will be passed on to a zygote in fertilization. The zygote will then have three chromosomes in place of a normal pair. This condition is called **trisomy.** On the other hand, if a gamete lacks a chromosome, the fertilized zygote will have only one chromosome instead of the normal pair. This condition is known as **monosomy.** If either trisomy or monosomy occurs in the fertilized egg, it will also appear in every body cell of the organism.

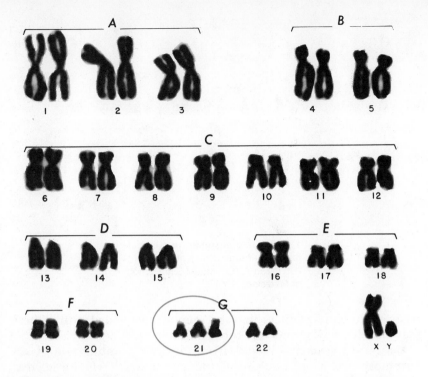

11–11 Down's Syndrome, or mongolism. Almost all individuals with this disorder have forty-seven chromosomes instead of the normal forty-six. This results from the failure of the two chromosomes of pair 21 to separate during oogenesis. (D. H. Carr & M. L. Barr)

DOWN'S SYNDROME

Down's syndrome, or mongolism, results in severe mental retardation. Abnormal physical features, such as an enlarged tongue and weak muscles, may also result. About one in 600 babies are born with Down's syndrome. However, this rate varies with the age of the mother. With mothers under 35, less than one baby in 1,000 has the syndrome. With mothers over 45, about one baby in 60 has it.

Down's syndrome is caused by the presence of an extra twenty-first chromosome in all body cells. This extra chromosome results from nondisjunction during meiosis, probably in egg formation. Because three twenty-first chromosomes are present, Down's syndrome is also known as trisomy-21. All other chromosomes are present in normal numbers.

OTHER CONDITIONS RESULTING FROM NONDISJUNCTION

Several abnormal conditions result from nondisjunction in human sex chromosomes. Some of these conditions involve trisomy, while others involve monosomy.

One such condition is **Turner's syndrome,** or monosomy X. This syndrome results from the absence of a sex chromosome. All body cells receive only 45 chromosomes. This condition results in an abnormally short female who does not develop mature sexual organs and is sterile.

Trisomy X produces females with an extra sex chromosome. The traits involved vary. Some women with trisomy X show certain

This would be an appropriate place to discuss genetic counseling and what it can do to help individuals. According to the president of the American Society for Human Genetics, Dr. Hirschhorn, every human carries from three to eight recessive genes. In addition, geneticists estimate that about five percent of all Americans need or could profit from genetic counseling.

11–12 Chromosomes in Turner's syndrome (XO) above left. (Dr. Lillian Y. Hsu, Mount Sinai School of Medicine, N.Y.)

11–13 Chromosomes in Klinefelter's syndrome (XXY) above right. (Dr. Lillian Y. Hsu, Mount Sinai School of Medicine, N.Y.)

The XYY combination has been associated with extreme height, severe acne, and criminal behavior, and it is found in approximately one in 1,000 babies.

Down's syndrome is a defect that can be diagnosed prior to a baby's birth. Through the process of *amniocentesis*, amniotic fluid containing the child's cells can be removed and examined for the presence of the extra chromosome.

basic male traits. Others may be mentally retarded. Still others may develop symptoms like those of Turner's syndrome.

Klinefelter's syndrome results from an XXY combination of sex chromosomes. This condition is thought to arise when a normal egg is fertilized by an XY sperm formed by nondisjunction. The result is a sterile male who does not develop mature sexual organs. This male is sometimes mentally retarded.

DETECTING GENETIC DISORDERS

Some of these genetic defects can be detected before a baby is born. The process involved, called **amniocentesis,** is new. A sample of fluid and loose cells are removed from the sac around the unborn baby. By studying the chromosomes of these cells, a geneticist can identify such diseases as Down's syndrome.

At this time, however, nothing can be done to cure such diseases. Perhaps future discoveries will allow cures to be made.

SUMMARY

For several reasons, it is difficult to study the effects of heredity in human beings. However, much progress has been made in this direction. The methods of population genetics and studies of twins have played an important part in this progress.

We are only beginning to learn the effects of genes on such things as intelligence, mental disorders, and physical disease. Research in these fields is of great importance today. Also important is the study of disorders caused by abnormal chromosome combinations.

population genetics	red-green color blindness	Down's syndrome
gene frequency	hemophilia	Turner's syndrome
gene pool	sex-influenced trait	trisomy X
fraternal twins	sex-limited trait	Klinefelter's syndrome
identical twins	sickle-cell anemia	amniocentesis
agglutinogen	trisomy	
multiple alleles	monosomy	

1. What is population genetics?
2. When is a gene pool considered stable?
3. Distinguish between fraternal and identical twins.
4. How do type-A and type-B agglutinogens account for four blood types?
5. In what way does the inheritance of blood type involve multiple alleles?
6. Why do more males have red-green color blindness than females?
7. Distinguish between sex-influenced and sex-limited traits. Give an example of each.
8. Explain how eye color in humans is inherited.
9. List some diseases that may be associated with genes.
10. What is sickle-cell anemia?
11. What chromosome abnormality is the cause of Down's syndrome?
12. Describe three conditions resulting from nondisjunction of sex chromosomes.
13. What is the purpose of amniocentesis?

1. Discuss environmental influences as factors in the study of human genetics.
2. How is random sampling applied to studies in population genetics?
3. How can identical twins supply valuable data in the study of human genetics?
4. What are the probable genotypes and phenotypes of the offspring resulting from the following crosses?
   a. a blood type-AB male with a type-O female
   b. a color-blind female with a normal male

chapter twelve

Applied Genetics

OBJECTIVES

- DEFINE the terms hybridization, inbreeding, and polyploidy.
- EXPLAIN the importance of mass selection.
- UNDERSTAND how people improve varieties and breeds of plants and animals by applying the principles of heredity.

12–1 Genetically manipulated squash. (Clyde H. Smith, Peter Arnold)

12–2 Luther Burbank, the genius of plant breeding. He is probably holding one of the many root crops that his work did so much to improve. (the Bettmann Archive)

PLANT AND ANIMAL BREEDING—OLD AND NEW

Since a time before recorded history, people have been raising and breeding plants such as grains, fruit trees, and flowers. The same is true of animals such as sheep, goats, fowl, cattle, and even dogs.

The **aim of breeding always has been to produce plants and animals better suited to human needs.** But until very recent times, breeding was at best a hit-or-miss process. No one had any clear idea of even the most basic laws of heredity. The development of an improved breed was mainly a matter of chance.

The rise of the science of genetics, starting with Mendel's work, changed all this. Plant and animal breeding today is largely a matter of *applied genetics*. Our modern knowledge of the laws of heredity has made breeding much more efficient. Still, the breeding of plants and animals is not an exact science. Hundreds or even thousands of different traits may be involved in a breeding experiment. Thus, the results are not always as easy to predict as they were for Mendel's seven traits in peas.

LUTHER BURBANK AND HIS FIRST SUCCESS

The name of Luther Burbank is a great one in the field of plant breeding. The new and improved plants developed by Burbank are far too many to be listed here. But the story of one of his experiments will serve as a good introduction to plant breeding.

Most of the brilliant work for which Burbank is famous was done on his farm in California. But his first great success came when he was a young man in Massachusetts. One day in 1871, Burbank was looking over a field of potatoes. He noticed a fruit growing on one of the plants. This was unusual. It is normal for potato plants to have flowers, but they seldom bear fruit. New plants are grown from pieces of potato rather than from seeds.

Burbank saved the fruit, and later planted the seeds. When plants grew from the seeds, Burbank checked the potatoes on the roots. The potatoes differed from plant to plant. Some were large, others small. Some plants produced many potatoes, others only a few. One plant had more potatoes than any other, and these potatoes were fine, large, smooth ones. Burbank sold them to a gardener for $150—his first profit from plant breeding. The new strain of potatoes was named in his honor. Burbank potatoes soon became popular all over the country.

PLANT BREEDING BY MASS SELECTION

In *mass selection,* a very few parent plants are chosen for breeding from a great number of individuals. This is how Burbank arrived at his fine potatoes. From all the plants grown from seed, he chose the one plant that had the traits he wanted. Mass selection may be the oldest form of plant breeding. Farmers who use seed from their own crops have long practiced mass selection. They always save the seeds from their best plants for the next planting. In this way, the offspring are most likely to have the desired traits.

Mass selection is also important in producing strains of plants that resist disease. For example, suppose that a cabbage disease has swept into an area. Almost all of the cabbage crop has been destroyed. Yet among the thousands of ruined plants, we find two or three that have survived and are healthy. Some unknown combination of genes has caused them to resist the disease.

Seeds from these healthy plants are grown the next year. Again, the disease strikes the crop. This time, a few more plants survive than did the year before. These plants have inherited the trait that resists the disease. Over several years, this cycle is repeated. Each year, more plants survive as the helpful trait becomes more common. Finally, a whole strain is developed in which all normal plants resist the disease.

HYBRIDIZATION, ANOTHER BREEDING METHOD

Hybridization is the crossing of two different but closely related strains. A new, hybrid strain results. The hope is that this hybrid strain will have the best traits of each parent. For example, we might choose one parent because it grows quickly or resists disease. The other parent might be chosen for the fine quality of its fruit or flowers. If all goes well, some of the hybrid offspring will have all of these traits.

Often, the new combination of genes in a hybrid brings out traits not shown in either parent. The hybrid may grow larger than either

141

Students may be surprised at the amount of research that selective breeding requires. A farmer, a plant researcher, a botanist, or a representative from a local agricultural station should be asked to speak to the class.

12–3 Hybridization. The mountain laurel (top) has decorative pink flowers. But it grows too tall to be acceptable as an ornamental plant. In contrast, the sandhill, or hairy laurel (center) grows smaller, but has somewhat less attractive, white flowers. Some of the hybrid offspring (bottom) of a cross, between the two above plants, combine the desirable traits of both. (courtesy Connecticut Agricultural Experiment Station)

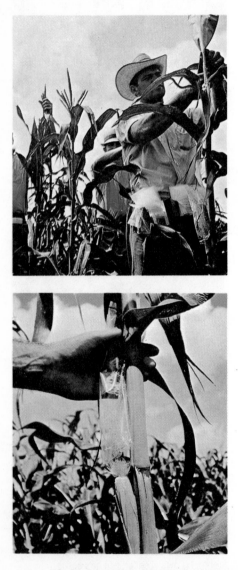

12–4 Controlled pollination of corn. Care is being taken to insure that natural pollination does not occur. As a result, the necessary inbred lines required for hybridization can be produced. (courtesy W. R. Grace & Co.)

parent, bear more fruit, or grow more quickly. It may resist disease, insects, or harsh weather better than either parent strain. Such improvements are examples of *hybrid vigor.*

INBREEDING, THE OPPOSITE OF HYBRIDIZATION

Suppose that we have been trying to develop a plant with certain traits. Finally, either by mass selection or hybridization, we produce such a plant. The next step is to grow more plants with the same traits.

This is a simple matter when asexual reproduction is involved, since the offspring have the same genes as the parent. The Burbank potato is a good example. To grow more such potatoes, we need only cut out and plant potato pieces with two or three "buds" or "eyes." The plants that grow will be exactly like the parent. Other methods of asexual reproduction are often used with fruit trees and with plants such as roses. These methods, which we will study more closely in Chapter Twenty-Seven, include grafting, cutting and budding.

With seed plants such as corn or wheat, the problem is more complex. Fertilized seeds result from the joining of two gametes in sexual reproduction. Thus, the offspring may have gene combinations quite different from those found in the parents. This is especially true of crop plants. Such plants have been crossed by human beings for centuries. They may carry genes from many different strains.

This problem can be solved by generations of *inbreeding.* **Inbreeding is the opposite of hybridization. Instead of crossing two parent plants, inbreeding involves self-pollination of a single parent.** In this way, no new genes are introduced from a different plant.

To see how inbreeding works, suppose that we have found a plant with just the traits we want. We allow this plant to produce seeds by self-pollination. When offspring grow from these seeds, we sort them carefully. Only those with the same traits as the parent are chosen to be seed plants for the next generation. We repeat this process over and over. In each generation, more plants inherit the desired traits. In the end, the strain is pure and ready for the market.

BREEDING MODERN HYBRID CORN

Years ago, farmers saved the best corn from a crop as seed for the next year. By this kind of mass selection, they hoped to produce more corn like the best of the old crop. This method was anything but sure because the corn was so mixed in its heredity. Only some of the seeds on an ear of corn might have the genes for the desired traits. Further, the farmer had no idea of the quality of the other parent plant. Some seeds might have resulted from self-fertilization. But others might have been fertilized by pollen from distant and very different corn plants.

Under these conditions, strange things happened with the new crop. Some ears might have red and white kernels mixed with the yellow ones. Often, kernels of sweet corn and popcorn were mixed with those of field corn. These problems and others like them kept the crop down to between 20 and 40 bushels per acre.

Most modern farmers no longer use their own corn for seed. Instead, they buy hybrid corn seed produced by scientific, controlled pollination. There is no guesswork about these seeds. They produce plants with good root systems, strong stalks, broad leaves, and large ears of corn. Such plants yield from 100 to 180 bushels of corn per acre.

How are these modern hybrids produced? Many result from a double cross involving four different strains of parent plants. As a

12–5 Crossing inbred corn plants, then crossing the resulting single crosses to produce double-cross hybrid seed. The four plants—A, B, C, and D—represent the products of four different inbred lines. Strain A is crossed with strain B. Strains C and D are crossed in a similar way. The F_1 generations of these two lines are then crossed to produce the hybrid corn seed that is used by farmers today.

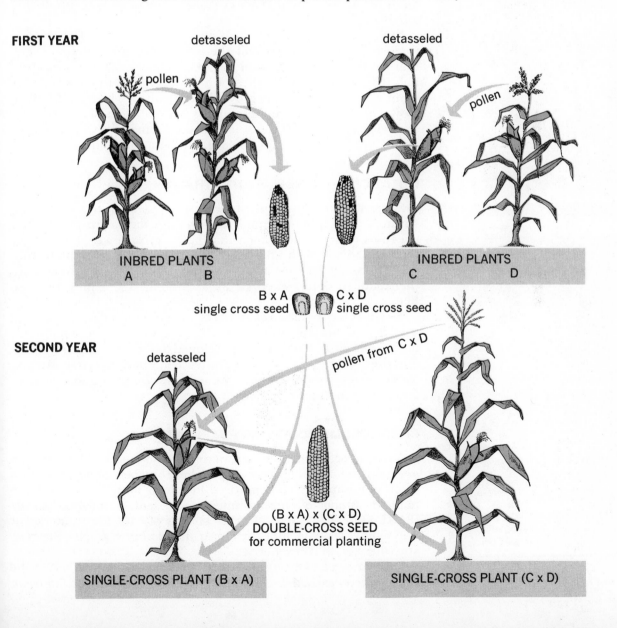

FIRST YEAR

detasseled

pollen

detasseled

pollen

INBRED PLANTS
A   B

INBRED PLANTS
C   D

B x A
single cross seed

C x D
single cross seed

SECOND YEAR

detasseled

pollen from C x D

(B x A) x (C x D)
DOUBLE-CROSS SEED
for commercial planting

SINGLE-CROSS PLANT (B x A)

SINGLE-CROSS PLANT (C x D)

result of inbreeding, each parent strain is pure. Further, each strain has been chosen for some important trait. One strain might grow quickly, another might resist disease, and so on. The hybrid offspring produced are better than any of the parent strains. One reason seems to be that many helpful traits are dominant. Thus, these traits tend to mask many harmful, recessive ones.

Let's see how such a double cross works. We will let A, B, C, and D stand for the four parent plants. During the first cross, plant A is crossed with plant B. The tassel, which produces pollen, is removed from plant B to prevent self-pollination. Further, the developing ears on plant B are covered until they are ready to receive pollen. At that time, they are dusted with pollen from plant A. The seeds that result produce a single-cross hybrid, plant AB. Plants C and D are crossed in the same way, producing a hybrid plant CD.

In the second year, plants AB and CD are crossed. The tassel is removed from plant AB and the young ears are covered. When mature, they are dusted with pollen from plant CD. The seeds produced are hybrid ABCD. These are the seeds sold to the farmer for planting. All of the plants grown from them will be hybrid ABCD. However, the corn from these plants will not be used as seed for a second generation. If it were, new gene combinations would appear, and the second crop might be quite different from the first.

MUTATIONS AND NEW PLANT STRAINS

Somatic mutations in plants sometimes give rise to a whole new strain. An example is the pink tea rose. One day, a grower of white tea roses noticed one branch that had a pink flower. The grower removed this branch and set it in a cutting bed. The plant that grew from the branch had all pink flowers. These flowers were then budded onto rooted stems to produce more pink tea rose plants.

The pink tea rose is an example of *bud mutant*. It developed when a color gene mutated in a stem cell of the white tea rose plant. All of the cells of the branch that developed had the mutant trait. Several other plant strains have resulted from bud mutation. Among these strains are California navel oranges, Delicious apples, seedless grapes, and pink grapefruit.

CHROMOSOME POLYPLOIDY IN PLANTS

Large specimens of fruit may result from ideal growing conditions and/or a polyploid condition.

At the grocery market, you may have noticed blueberries that are twice as large as ordinary ones. These blueberries have four sets of chromosomes. This condition, in which more than twice the haploid number of chromosomes are present, is called **polyploidy** (PAHL-i-ploy-dee). Several other strains of fruit are examples of polyploidy. These include certain strains of plums, grapes, cherries, strawberries, and cranberries.

Polyploidy can be caused by artificial means through use of the drug *colchicine* (KAHL-chuh-seen). If plant shoots are put in weak solutions of colchicine, the chromatids will not separate during mitosis. Thus, each cell of the plant that develops will have twice the normal chromosome number. In another form, the drug can be applied to plant buds. Colchicine has been used to develop new strains of blueberries, lilies, cabbage, and other plants.

THE "GREEN REVOLUTION"

Every living organism depends on its environment for the materials it needs for life. We must realize that some of these materials need to be replaced for future use. One such material is our food supply. With the world population increasing, the need for more food increases. Through mass selection, hybridization, and inbreeding, we have been able to produce more and better food. Geneticists and plant breeders have opened the door. New strains have been developed. Plants have been produced with larger heads of grain. This is called the "green revolution" and as a result, more people are being fed. However, the problem is far from being solved. Our present population growth is still causing a world food crisis. Therefore, we must continue improving the techniques and methods of plant breeding.

MASS SELECTION IN ANIMAL BREEDING

The same principles used in plant breeding also apply to animals. As with plants, the oldest method of breeding animals is mass selection. Over the centuries, mass selection has been used in breeding everything from racehorses to goldfish.

Several modern strains of chickens are good examples of the effects of such breeding. Some strains are not very good for eating, but lay large numbers of eggs. Other strains are known for their delicious meat, but produce few eggs. A few strains, such as the Plymouth Rock, can serve either purpose.

The turkey is another example of how much an animal can be changed by breeding. The wild turkey hunted by the Pilgrims in New England was a slender bird. It flew well and often perched high in trees. Over the years, the turkey has been bred for very different traits. The main aim, of course, has been to produce the most meat possible. The result is the large, clumsy bird we know today.

It is interesting to note here that although egg production has never been higher, consumption has dropped. This is largely due to warnings concerning the high cholesterol content of eggs. Ask students if egg consumption is high or low in their homes.

HYBRID ANIMALS

The mule is a strong, useful animal produced by crossing a female horse with a male donkey. From the horse, the mule gets its size. From the donkey, it inherits long ears, sureness of foot, endurance, and ability to live on rough food. But with all its hybrid vigor, the mule is usually *sterile.* That is, it cannot reproduce.

Several kinds of hybrid cattle have been produced by crossing domestic beef breeds with Brahman cattle. The Brahman was first

12-6 Animal hybridization. The mule is produced by crossing a female horse with a male donkey. (Grant Heilman)

Chapter Twelve
Applied Genetics

12–7 The result of a cross between a Brahman bull (left) and a Angus cow (center) is a Brangus (right). (American Brahman Breeders Association; American Angus Association; International Brangus Breeders Association)

imported from its native India in 1849. It is a large animal with a fatty shoulder hump. Colors range from gray to brown or red. The Brahman has a great ability to resist heat, insect attack, and disease. In the United States most beef cattle are raised where the summer is hot or humid or both. The Brahman is much better suited to these conditions than domestic beef cattle.

One of the most successful Brahman crosses was made at the King Ranch in Texas. The first cross involved a Brahman bull and a Shorthorn cow. Over a period of thirty years, the cross was perfected. The result was a new strain of beef cattle known as Santa Gertrudis. In this breed, the Brahman ability to survive harsh conditions is combined with the fine beef traits of the Shorthorn. Several other crosses between Brahman and domestic beef cattle have also been successful.

Another interesting cross involves the North American bison, or buffalo. In this cross, a bison bull is mated with a domestic cow. The hybrid offspring is known as a beefalo. Like the Brahman, the bison can survive very harsh weather. The bison also eats grass instead of grain. The beefalo cross is an attempt to combine this trait with the beef quality of the domestic breed.

SUMMARY

For many centuries, people have worked at breeding improved strains of plants and animals. In the last century, genetic science has given us a much better understanding of the principles involved in plant and animal breeding.

Three important methods of breeding are mass selection, hybridization, and inbreeding. Mass selection involves choosing the parents for further breeding from a large number of individuals. Hybridization is the crossing of two different strains. An example of inbreeding is self-pollination in plants. Over several generations, the offspring with the desired traits are sorted out by mass selection. In the end, a pure strain is produced.

Breeding by these methods over many years has produced a great many of the plant and animal strains most useful to us today.

| **BIOLOGICALLY** | mass selection | hybrid vigor | polyploidy |
| **SPEAKING** | hybridization | inbreeding | sterile |

1. Describe the contributions of Luther Burbank to genetics.
2. Describe the relation of "mass selection" to plant breeding.
3. What is hybridization?
4. Why is inbreeding practiced in plant and animal breeding?
5. How is natural cross-pollination prevented during the growing of hybrid corn?
6. In what way is the mule a true hybrid animal?
7. Why are Brahman cattle good parent stock for breeding purposes?
8. What favorable qualities are found in the buffalo?

1. If inbreeding is practiced too long, offspring may become weak and inbred. How could this condition be remedied?
2. A farmer does not use the seed from his hybrid corn for the next year's crop. Explain why not.
3. What is the importance of pedigrees and registration papers in breeding livestock?

chapter thirteen

Organic Variation

OBJECTIVES

- UNDERSTAND the importance of fossil study.
- DESCRIBE Oparin's hypothesis of the origin of life.
- LIST some evidences of common ancestry.
- DESCRIBE the theories in Lamarck's explanation of evolution.
- LIST the chief factors in Darwin's theory of natural selection.
- DESCRIBE how gene mutations relate to organic variation.
- EXPLAIN migration and isolation as factors in evolution.
- GIVE EXAMPLES of adaptive radiation and convergent evolution.

Some students may have difficulty in understanding the age of the earth in terms of millions of years. Time spirals, charts, or a representative time line may help students to better comprehend the age of the earth.

You may want to discuss some of the theories concerning the origin of the earth and its atmosphere. This discussion will prepare students for the discussion of evolution.

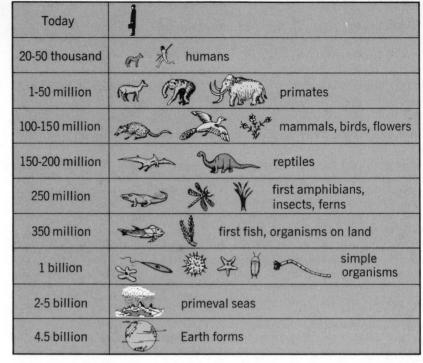

Today	
20-50 thousand	humans
1-50 million	primates
100-150 million	mammals, birds, flowers
150-200 million	reptiles
250 million	first amphibians, insects, ferns
350 million	first fish, organisms on land
1 billion	simple organisms
2-5 billion	primeval seas
4.5 billion	Earth forms

13-1 Theoretical development of life on earth.

OUR CHANGING EARTH

Scientists estimate that the earth is more than five billion years old. Try to imagine so much time. It's hard, isn't it? Most of us are used to thinking of a few months or a few years as a long time. The idea of *billions* of years is so vast that it seems to lose its meaning.

Just as vast are the changes our planet has undergone. Since its beginning, the earth has been changing constantly. Land masses have risen, then sunk below the sea. Mountains have been thrust up, only to be worn away by wind and rain. Rivers have cut deep channels in soil and rock. Long warm periods have been followed by ice ages. Deserts have spread, then disappeared, as centuries of drought gave way to centuries of heavy rain.

Changes like these are still going on. But they take place so slowly that we are not aware of them. How, then, do we know about the great changes of the past? The earth itself holds the answer.

A STORY WRITTEN IN ROCK

The rings of a tree can tell us a lot about its life. They hold the record not only of the tree's age, but of dry years and wet years, forest fires and disease. In much the same way, layers of **sedimentary rock** record millions of years of the earth's history. Such rock was formed from particles that settled to the bottom of oceans and other bodies of water. As more sediment built up over the ages, its great pressure turned the lower layers to rock. Layer after layer was formed in this way, new rock on top of old.

By studying these layers, scientists can learn a great deal. They can tell when a section of the earth was under water and when it was dry land. They can see the effects of glaciers and of erosion. On the basis of such information, the history of the earth has been divided into great **eras** many millions of years long. Eras, in turn, are divided into shorter **periods.**

How do we know the age of a given rock layer? A recent method has given us a very accurate dating key. Radioactive elements such as uranium may be found in a rock layer. Such elements decay and change to other elements at a very steady rate. A given sample of uranium, for instance, will change completely to lead in 4.5 billion years. Thus, if we measure the ratio of uranium to lead in a rock layer, we get a very good idea of the rock's age.

LIFE ON EARTH

Evidence indicates that life on the earth began more than three billion years ago. But how did life begin? We cannot be certain. Several hypotheses have been offered, but none proved. However, there does seem to be growing support for one hypothesis. This hypothesis was first put forth by the Russian scientist A. I. Oparin in 1936.

Oparin suggested that the earth was very different billions of years ago. The atmosphere was made up mainly of gases such as ammonia (NH_4), methane (CH_4), and water vapor (H_2O). Energy from lightning or radiation split up some of these molecules. The

The uranium-decay method of dating rocks does not always give accurate information. In addition, some rocks do not contain uranium. In some cases, radioactive potassium is used instead of uranium.

A person who studies fossil remains is called a *paleontologist*. Carbon-14, a radioactive form of carbon, is used to determine the age of certain fossils. By comparing the amount of carbon-14 in a fossilized piece of wood with the amount in a piece of living wood, scientists can determine the approximate age of the fossil.

13–2 Sedimentary rock in the Grand Canyon. In some places in the world, sedimentary rock is as much as ten miles thick. It took many millions of years for such layers to form. (Union Pacific Railroad color photo)

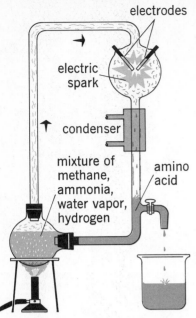

electrodes

electric spark

condenser

mixture of methane, ammonia, water vapor, hydrogen

amino acid

13–3 Miller's experiment shows that under suitable conditions inorganic molecules can combine to form organic molecules.

13–4 A fossil brittle starfish from the Devonian period in a piece of slate. The body of the starfish was gradually replaced by the mineral *pyrite*. (courtesy Ward's)

elements carbon, hydrogen, nitrogen, and oxygen then bonded in new combinations as *organic* molecules. Finally, the right organic molecules came together in the right way, and life began.

Part of this hypothesis was tested in the laboratory by Stanley Miller in 1953. Large charges of electricity were sent through gas mixtures like the one mentioned. Such tests *have* produced organic molecules, including amino acids, sugars, and even DNA. This proves that the first part of Oparin's hypothesis *could* be correct, but not that it *is* correct. Further, no experiment has produced a living organism. Thus, the question of how life began remains open.

ORGANIC VARIATION

In the billions of years since the dawn of life, countless different organisms have developed on earth. Again, it is the earth itself that provides a record. Sedimentary rock often contains **fossils** of organisms that died and sank to the sea floor. In some cases, a fossil is only an imprint. In others, the tissues of the organism have slowly been replaced by minerals. Thus, the whole organism is preserved in mineral form.

Other organisms are preserved in different ways. Small land organisms, especially insects, are found in *amber*, a fossil plant resin. Fossil skeletons of very large animals are preserved in tar pits. More complete remains of animals, some with almost no damage, have been found frozen in glacial ice.

By dating fossils and other preserved organisms, we can get a good idea of what kinds of life were on earth at a given time. Our record is not complete, of course. Many species may never have left fossils. Still, **the fossil record shows a clear pattern. Certain very simple organisms were present from very early times. Such organisms include bacteria, algae, fungi, and protozoans. More complex forms of life developed in more recent times.**

Some organisms seem to have remained almost the same for many millions of years. But the fossil record also gives much evidence of change. Organisms vary and new forms appear, while old forms decline or become extinct. This process is known as **evolution.** The differences that occur among individual organisms are called **organic variation.**

PATHS OF EVOLUTION

In Chapter Fourteen, you will see the system by which scientists classify all living things. This system begins with large groups, which are broken down into smaller and smaller subgroups. The smaller the subgroup, the more alike its members are. These likenesses are strong evidence that the subgroup members had, at some point far in the past, a common ancestor.

In most cases, of course, such a common ancestor must have become extinct long ago. So must many of the other forms that developed between the ancestor and its modern descendants. For

13–5 Rancho La Brea Tar Pits.
(American Museum of Natural History)

this reason, the paths of evolution are not clear. But let's look at some evidence that scientists use to show the existence of these paths.

First, in both plants and animals, we find **homologous organs.** These are body parts that are similar in structure and seem to have developed in the same way, though they may have very different uses in different species. The bones of a bird's wing, a horse's front leg, a whale's paddle, and a human arm are homologous organs. These bones are so similar that, for the most part, they have the same names. The *differences* seen in these bones reflect adaptation to conditions in the environment. Their *likenesses* indicate a genetic relationship through a common ancestor.

Homologous structures are used as a method of classifying organisms. Those organs that have the same function are called *analogous.* An example of an analogous structure would be the wings of birds and insects.

13–6 Homologous bones in the fore-limbs of several vertebrate animals.

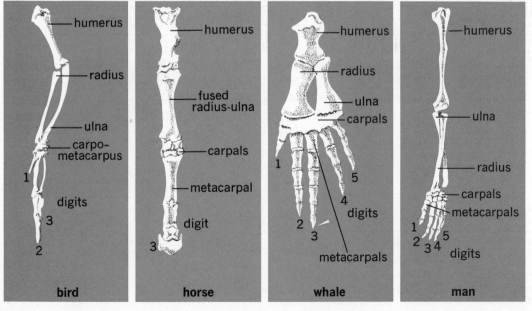

Geological Time Table

Era	Period	Epoch	Years since beginning	Years duration	Conditions and characteristics
Cenozoic	Quaternary	Recent	15,000		moderating climate; glaciers receding
		Pleistocene	1,000,000	1,000,000	warm and cold climates; periodic glaciers
	Tertiary	Pliocene	10,000,000	9,000,000	cold climate; snow building up
		Miocene	25,000,000	15,000,000	temperate climate
		Oligocene	35,000,000	10,000,000	warm climate
		Eocene	55,000,000	20,000,000	very warm climate
		Paleocene	70,000,000	15,000,000	very warm climate
Mesozoic	Cretaceous		120,000,000	50,000,000	warm climate; great swamps dry out; Rocky Mtns. rise
	Jurassic		150,000,000	30,000,000	warm climate; extensive lowlands and continental seas
	Triassic		180,000,000	30,000,000	warm, dry climate; extensive deserts
Paleozoic	Permian		240,000,000	60,000,000	variable climate; increased dryness; mountains rising
	Pennsylvanian (Late Carboniferous)		270,000,000	30,000,000	warm, humid climate; extensive swamps; coal age
	Mississippian (Early Carboniferous)		300,000,000	30,000,000	warm, humid climate; shallow inland seas; early coal age
	Devonian		350,000,000	50,000,000	land rises; shallow seas and marshes; some arid regions
	Silurian		380,000,000	30,000,000	mild climate; great inland seas
	Ordovician		440,000,000	60,000,000	mild climate; warm in Arctic; most land submerged
	Cambrian		500,000,000	60,000,000	mild climate; extensive lowlands and inland seas
(Pre-Cambrian) Proterozoic			1,500,000,000	1,000,000,000	conditions uncertain; first glaciers; first life
(Pre-Cambrian) Archeozoic			3,500,000,000	2,000,000,000	conditions uncertain; earth probably lifeless

13-7 The Earth through the ages. This geological time table shows the sequence and estimated length of the eras, periods, and epochs.

Time Scale of Life Based On Fossil Records

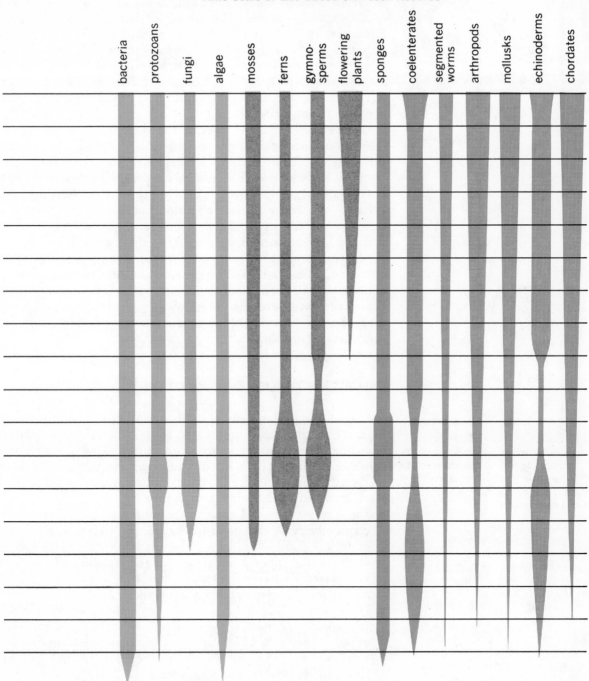

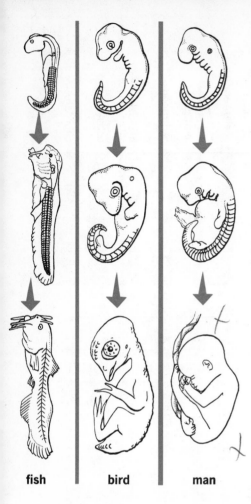

fish   **bird**   **man**

13–8 Different stages in the development of three vertebrate animals. Note their similarities in the very early stages and their differences in the later stages.

Discuss the expression "ontogeny recapitulates phylogeny." Explain how Fig. 13–8 illustrates this expression. Point out to students the existence of the "tail" in man at certain stages.

Though Lamarck's theory of inheritance of acquired characteristics has never been scientifically proved, it did open the subject of evolution to further investigation. Point out to students how errors in thinking often lead one to finding the scientific truth.

Most animals also have certain structures that seem to have no use, though similar structures are quite useful in related species. Such structures are called **vestigial organs.** The human coccyx is a familiar example. This group of bones has no known use. However, in certain mammals it is extended into a tail. It is believed that the genes for the human coccyx were inherited from some ancestor in which it was useful. These genes still cause us to grow a coccyx, though our changed environment has left us no use for it. Another human vestigial organ includes the remains of ear muscles.

Likenesses between *embryos*, the developing organisms, also seem to indicate common ancestors. For example, the embryos of different vertebrate animals are very similar during early growth. In these early stages, it would be hard to tell a fish embryo from that of a bird or mammal. It appears that all of these animals received, from some remote common ancestor, genes that control development for a time. Later, other genes take over and cause the fish, bird, and mammal to develop in different ways.

All organisms seem to be alike in some ways. For example, the evidence indicates that all organisms produce nucleic acids, especially DNA. All organisms also seem to use ATP in energy transfer. Certain enzymes are alike in many forms of life. So are hormones. Many human beings with sugar diabetes owe their lives to insulin taken from hogs and cattle.

LAMARCK'S THEORY OF EVOLUTION

One of the first scientists to theorize about evolution was the French biologist Jean Lamarck, in 1801. Lamarck believed that the environment was a key factor in evolution. This agrees with current theory. But his ideas about how organisms changed in response to the environment were far off the mark. Actually, three theories were involved in these ideas:

- *The theory of need.* Lamarck thought that plants and animals change because they *need* to change. For example, the early ancestors of snakes had legs and short bodies. But changes in the environment made it necessary for these animals to go through very narrow spaces. For this reason, they began to stretch their bodies and to crawl rather than walk.
- *The theory of use and disuse.* Organs remain active and strong when they are used. If they are not used, they weaken and disappear. The snakes of each new generation continued to stretch their bodies more and more. But they used their legs less and less. Finally, the legs disappeared.
- *The theory that acquired traits can be passed on to offspring.* Lamarck believed that a trait acquired by an individual during its life was passed on to its offspring. The old snakes that lost their legs through disuse passed this trait on. Thus, modern snakes also have no legs.

Lamarck also tried to explain other traits by his theory. For example, he said that giraffes once had short necks and legs. Then the competition for food such as grass became too great. The giraffe began to stretch its neck and legs so that it could reach the leaves of trees. Later generations inherited the longer neck and stretched it even more. Finally, the modern giraffe resulted.

Parts of Lamarck's theory seem at first to make sense. For example, we can see that a football player develops strong legs through use. If the football player breaks a leg, the muscles will become small and weak from disuse while in a cast. However, there is *no* evidence that either of these acquired traits can be passed on in heredity.

In fact, many biologists have tested the idea that acquired traits can be inherited. For example, one experimenter cut the tails off mice then allowed the mice to mate. He repeated this process through twenty generations of mice. But the mice in the twenty-first generation still grew long tails. Other experiments have produced similar evidence that acquired traits are not passed on. Thus, Lamarck's whole theory falls apart.

DARWIN'S THEORY OF NATURAL SELECTION

In 1859, the English scientist Charles Darwin published his theory of **natural selection.** This theory of how different species develop in evolution is one of the most important in the history of science. We can sum it up in the following five steps:

- *All organisms produce more offspring than can actually survive.* This effect is very clear in some organisms. For example, a fern plant may produce 50 million spores in a year. If all spores survived, fern plants would cover North America within two fern generations. In the same way, an oyster may shed more than 100 million eggs in a single spawning. If all offspring survived, oysters would soon completely fill the ocean.

- *Every organism faces a constant struggle to survive.* All species overproduce, but only a fraction of the offspring survive. Each individual must struggle constantly to get enough food, water, space, and so on. This struggle is at its worst among members of the same species because they compete for the same things. Those who win the struggle survive. The others die.

- *The individuals of a given species vary.* Except for identical twins, every individual differs in some ways from all other members of the species. We see this clearly in human beings and other complex organisms. But it is also true of even very simple organisms.

- *The individuals that are best adapted to the environment survive.* Individuals vary because they inherit different traits. Some of these traits are better suited to the environment than others. Individuals with these helpful traits tend to survive. Individuals without them tend to die out. A good example occurs when disease strikes a plant crop. A few plants may have traits that allow

13–9 Lamarck's theory of the evolution of the giraffe's long neck. The competition for food caused the giraffe to stretch its neck to reach the leaves. Later generations inherited the longer neck.

13–10 Darwin's theory of the evolution of the giraffe's long neck. Giraffes had different size necks. Those with the longer necks survived while the shorter neck giraffe died.

them to resist the disease. These plants will survive, while the others will die. Darwin called this part of his theory the **survival of the fittest.**

■ *The organisms that survive pass their traits on to offspring.* In general, offspring resemble their parents. Parents that survive because of some helpful trait pass the genes for that trait on to their offspring. Offspring in which the trait appears will also tend to survive. The same will be true in each generation, so long as the same forces are at work in the environment. In the end, all members of a species may have the helpful trait.

You can see how Darwin's theory differs from that of Lamarck. Lamarck was right about the importance of the environment. But his ideas about how evolution takes place were backwards. Organisms do not change *in order* to survive in their environment. Rather, it is the *environment,* through natural selection, that determines which organisms have a chance to survive.

In other words, organic variation has nothing to do with need. **Organisms vary whether they need to or not. Whether a variation is helpful or harmful depends on the environment.** Darwin recognized these facts. However, Darwin worked in an age in which little was known of genetics. Thus, while he knew that organisms *do* vary, he had no idea of *why* they vary. It remained for the Dutch botanist Hugo De Vries, years later, to point out the main cause of organic variation.

MUTATION THEORY OF EVOLUTION

In 1901, De Vries presented his mutation theory of evolution. He based this theory on many years of work with primrose plants. Of some 50,000 plants, at least 800 showed striking new traits not present in the parents. Yet these traits were passed on to offspring of the mutant plants. De Vries concluded that mutations must occur often in other organisms as well. This change by mutation, he believed, was the basis for evolution. These conclusions supported Darwin's theories of variation and survival of the fittest.

Today, we have a better understanding of the theory first offered by De Vries. Modern methods and discoveries have given us a much closer look at mutations and how they occur.

GENE MUTATIONS AND CHANGE

Mutations have been found in every kind of plant and animal studied by geneticists. The most common mutations are gene mutations. It is these gene mutations that are the main cause of the changes involved in evolution.

Genes tend to be stable. The DNA of which they are made replicates time after time without change. Yet mutations do occur. How often? The rate varies for different organisms. Geneticists have learned the rate of mutation for certain traits in many plants and animals. For example, the genes for seed color in corn mutate about once in 2,000 gametes. This may seem like a slow rate. But remember that there are more than 2,000 plants in a single acre of corn. Thus, the mutant trait appears more often than you might think.

Many gene mutations have such slight effects that they are hard to detect. For example, each body cell of a fruit fly contains about 40,000 genes. Thus, the effect caused by mutation of a single gene might be too small to notice. This may explain why clear changes in a population appear only over many generations.

Mutant genes are nearly always recessive. For this reason, the mutant trait will not appear in offspring in which the other allele is normal.

Gene mutation often produces a trait that leaves the organism no chance to survive. Such a **lethal gene,** like other mutant genes, is almost always recessive. Thus, the lethal trait may not appear even though many members of a population carry the gene. When the trait *does* appear in homozygous recessive offspring, they tend to die without reproducing. For this reason, the lethal gene should become less common in the population. However, if more normal genes mutate to the lethal gene, the problem will continue.

Chromosome mutations occur less often than gene mutations, but their effects are usually much greater. Changes in chromosome structure and number may cause new traits in offspring.

EFFECT OF THE ENVIRONMENT

Organisms vary because of gene and chromosome mutations and because of new gene combinations formed in reproduction. But it is the environment that determines whether a variation is helpful or harmful. Thus, the environment controls the direction that evolution will take.

Suppose that a population already is suited very well to its environment. If so, further changes are not likely to make members of the population any *better* suited. Under these conditions, the population may change very little over long periods of time.

But what if the environment itself is changed? Genetic mutation may then improve the chances of survival in the new environment. Over many generations, variation may continue until the population becomes a whole new species.

A change of environment may arise in one of two ways:
- An organism may migrate to an area with a different environment.
- The environment itself may change in a given area.

MIGRATION AND VARIATION

Migration is the movement of animals from one environment to another. Migration opens the door to change in two different ways. To see how this works, we will assume that several members of an animal population have migrated to a new area.

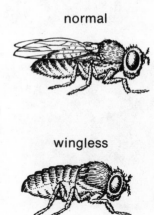

normal

wingless

13–11 An example of gene mutation in *Drosophila.*

Darwin's expedition on the *Beagle* provides interesting reading. Some students may wish to report on his complete findings. Use the five points discussed to elicit attitudes toward Darwin's theories. How do these points stand up in the light of today's knowledge?

Students may be interested in learning about Thomas Robert Malthus (1766–1834) and his book, *An Essay on the Principle of Population.* Malthus' book had a profound impact on Darwin's thinking. In his book, Malthus concluded that human population always increased faster than the food supply and that population had to be eventually controlled by starvation, disease, or war.

Refer students back to Chapter Ten where mutations were discussed in some detail. Review DNA coding and how changes in this coding result in mutations.

Students may be interested in the concept of *genetic engineering* and how it can change the genetic makeup of an organism. The present controversy concerning genetic transplantation experiments and their dangers are discussed in a fascinating article that appears in the January 12, 1976, issue of *Newsweek.* The article is entitled, "Politics and Genes."

13–12 Camel ancestor; dromeday or Arabian camel; Bactrian or Asian camel; a South American llama. (Rue, National Audubon Society; Jerry Frank; George Holton, Photo Researchers)

First, these animals all carry certain gene combinations found only in the population from which they came. Suppose these animals breed with the native animals in the new area. The native animals also have certain gene combinations found nowhere else. When these two different gene pools are mixed, new traits will result from the new gene combinations.

Remember, too, that migration has taken the animals into a new environment. New traits caused by mutations and new gene combinations may make offspring more likely to survive in this environment. In the end, all members of the population may have these traits. Thus, migration also opens the door to further change by natural selection.

A good example of the kind of change that can result from migration is seen in camels. It is thought that the first camels developed in North America. Some of these early camels migrated to Asia across a land bridge believed to have existed at that time. Others migrated to South America. Migration continued until the camel ancestors were spread around a large part of the world.

Then came a great Ice Age. The camel populations in most areas died out. Camels survived only in a few widely scattered areas. In one area, they developed into the African camel, with one hump. In another area, evolution produced the Asian camel, with two humps. Though these modern animals look somewhat different, both are well suited to life in a dry environment.

Early camels also survived in the mountains of South America. There they developed into the llama, an animal quite different from the two modern camels. The llama has no hump but is sure of foot and has a thick coat of hair. These traits are most helpful in the cold, rocky mountains where the llama lives. You can imagine how such traits must have developed over the ages. In each generation, animals with slightly thicker coats were more likely to survive the cold winter. Sure-footed animals with shorter legs were better able to escape enemies on the rugged mountain slopes. Animals with these traits tended to survive and reproduce. Animals without them tended to die out.

CHANGE IN THE ENVIRONMENT

Having seen the effects of migration, let's look at a case in which the environment itself changed in a given area. The case in point is an especially clear one. It involves the peppered moth population in the region of Manchester, a British industrial city.

Before 1845, the peppered moth was light-colored with a pattern of dark specks. It could hardly be seen when it rested on the light-gray bark of trees. Then, in 1845, an almost completely black peppered moth was found in Manchester. A gene for color had mutated.

Normally, of course, this mutation would be harmful. A black moth on light bark would be easy prey for birds. But something else was happening in Manchester. The city was becoming an industrial center. Coal smoke pouring from factory chimneys was turning gray tree bark nearly black all over the area. In this changed environment, the black mutation was very helpful. Now it was the light-colored moths that were easy prey.

What finally happened is a classic example of evolution in action. Between 1845 and 1895, the black moth population increased from *one* known individual to *99 percent of the population.* Because of natural selection in a new environment, the peppered moth has completely changed color in only 50 years! A change in coloration caused by industrial pollution is called *industrial melanism.*

ISOLATION AS A FACTOR IN EVOLUTION

Two squirrel populations in the Grand Canyon area clearly show the effects of *isolation* on evolution. On the north rim of the canyon, we find the Kaibab squirrel. This animal has long ears, a white tail, and dark underparts. On the south rim, we find the Abert squirrel. The Abert has long ears, but its tail is gray and its underparts are light. The Kaibab and the Abert are two different species, but they are thought to have developed from the same ancestor species. Why did they develop such different traits in almost the same environment?

The answer is that the Kaibab and Abert were isolated from each other by the canyon. Thus, they could not share their gene pools by breeding with each other. As mutations occurred over thousands of years, the gene pools of the two populations became quite different. This resulted in the different traits we see today.

In this case, the canyon (and the river running through it) acted as a physical *barrier* between the squirrel populations. Other such barriers include deserts, mountains, and oceans. The ocean is an especially strong barrier to breeding between populations. Thus, the plant and animal populations of islands are often striking examples of the effects of isolation.

Not all barriers to breeding between populations involve physical isolation. Other factors include different mating times, different mating habits, and differences in structure that prevent mating.

SPECIATION

In this Unit on heredity, we have often referred to different species. **A *species* is a group of organisms that are similar in structure and that can mate and produce fertile offspring. All members of a species have the same number of chromosomes, and the genes on these chromosomes are arranged in the same way.**

The development of a species is called *speciation.* Since life began, species have been disappearing and developing. This process is still going on today. We already have seen the forces involved in speciation: migration, change in environment, mutation, natural selection, and isolation. These forces work together in two basic patterns, which we will now discuss.

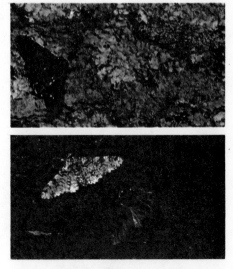

13-13 The principle of industrial melanism. In each situation, which peppered moth is likely to survive the longest? (courtesy Dr. H. B. Kettlewell)

13-14 The Kaibab squirrel (top) lives on the north side of the Grand Canyon. The Abert squirrel lives around the south side. The canyon, serving as a barrier, has isolated these two species. (Sonja Bullaty, Audubon Society; Al Lowry, Photo Researchers)

13-15 Adaptive radiation. Genetic variations produced adaptations for different environments and changes in body structure in each species: mule deer (left), elk (center), and moose. (photos by Leonard Lee Rue IV, Monkmeyer Press)

ADAPTIVE RADIATION

The pattern in which different species develop from a common ancestor is called *adaptive radiation.* In this process, a population branches out to new and different environments. As variations occur, the new environment determines whether they are helpful or harmful. Organisms with the helpful traits tend to survive and pass these traits on to their offspring. The variations may be slight at first. But they become greater over many generations. After thousands of years, two related species may be so different that it is hard to tell they had a common ancestor.

We've mentioned one case of adaptive radiation, involving camels. We can also see the results of this kind of evolution in the different members of the deer family in North America. Among these species are the mule deer and the much larger elk. Both of these deer live in mountain forests in the summer and move to sheltered valleys in the winter. The moose, the largest member of the deer family, lives in northern swamp and lake areas in the summer. It winters on higher ground in nearby forests.

These different deer are not closely related. Yet if we could trace them back, we might find that they developed from a common ancestor by adaptive radiation.

13-16 Convergent evolution. Animals are similar in many ways because of adaptations to a similar environment. The kangaroo, a marsupial, and the deer, a placental mammal are similar. The same applies to the whale and the seal. (George Leavens, Photo Researchers; Harvey A. Schwartz; Bruce Coleman; Bartlett, Bruce Coleman)

CONVERGENT EVOLUTION

In some ways, **convergent evolution** has effects opposite those of adaptive radiation. *Convergent* means "moving closer together." In convergent evolution, organisms with very different ancestors become more alike because they share the same environment.

The whale and the seal are good examples. Both mammals live in the open sea. Both have flippers and are strong swimmers. Though they breathe through lungs, both can hold their breath and stay under water for long times. Both also have a layer of fat that prevents loss of body heat in the cold water. But the seal and whale are not closely related. Their likenesses result instead from adaptation to the same environment.

Certain mammals of North America show strong likenesses to mammals in Australia. For example, the deer and the kangaroo have little relationship. But they have similar head structures and feeding habits. These traits represent adaptations to very similar environments.

Discuss the term "teleology" with students and the fact that change does not occur in a directed manner. It is not a matter of *desire* for change. An interesting discussion will probably develop among the students concerning this matter.

Point out to students that many mutations are termed as *neutral*. This simply means that these mutations are neither negative or positive.

SUMMARY

Life on earth began more than three billion years ago. In all the time since then, life has been in a constant state of change. New species develop as old ones change or disappear.

Biologists understand this process as evolution by natural selection. New traits appear in organisms as a result of mutations or new gene combinations. Whether these traits are helpful or harmful depends on the environment. All organisms face a constant struggle for survival. Those with the helpful traits are more likely to survive and pass these traits on. Organisms without these traits tend to die out. In the end, all members of a population may have the helpful traits.

BIOLOGICALLY SPEAKING

sedimentary rock	vestigial organ	isolation
geological era	natural selection	barrier
geological period	survival of the fittest	species
fossil	lethal gene	speciation
evolution	migration	adaptive radiation
organic variation	industrial melanism	convergent evolution
homologous organ		

**QUESTIONS
FOR REVIEW**

1. Explain how sedimentary rock forms a geological timetable.
2. What is the biological concept of evolution?
3. List the kinds of evidence used to establish common ancestry of organisms.
4. Describe Lamarck's idea of evolution.
5. Explain the five concepts included in Darwin's theory of evolution.
6. Explain how gene mutations cause variations in organisms.
7. List two direct evolutionary results of migration.
8. Explain the impact of environmental change on the evolution of the peppered moth.
9. Give an example of how isolation acts as a factor in evolution.
10. Define the term "species."
11. Compare adaptive radiation and convergent evolution.

**APPLYING
PRINCIPLES AND
CONCEPTS**

1. Discuss the importance of structural, physiological, and biochemical similarities in attempting to determine the paths of evolution.
2. Explain the development of the long neck of the giraffe according to Lamarck, according to Darwin and according to modern theory.
3. Discuss the genetic and social significance of the results of studies of the peppered moth in Manchester, England.
4. Give a specific example of each of the following as it relates to evolution: mutation, selection, adaptation, and convergence.

14-1 The diversity of living organisms.

The Diversity of Life

THE SCIENCE OF CLASSIFICATION

Since ancient times, biologists have recognized the need for a system of classification for living things. One of the first to offer such a system was the Greek philosopher Aristotle, more than 2,000 years ago. Aristotle divided plants into three groups: herbs, with soft stems; shrubs, with several woody stems; and trees, with a single woody trunk. Animals also were placed in three groups: land dwellers, water dwellers, and air dwellers.

If such a system seems overly simple to us today, it is because we have more information. The science of genetics has helped us to understand how evolution works. The study of evolution, in turn, has helped us to see the natural relationships that exist between living things. It is on these relationships that the modern science of classification, known as **taxonomy,** is based.

THE WORK OF LINNAEUS

Despite the importance of genetics and evolution, modern taxonomy owes much to an eighteenth-century scientist who knew nothing of either. This was the great Swedish botanist Carolus Linnaeus. Linnaeus set up his own classification system which, in some ways, is still in use today.

Linnaeus recognized the species as the basic natural grouping, and the key to his system was *structural similarity*. That is, he grouped plants and animals according to their structural likenesses. Linnaeus also avoided using the common names of organisms. Instead, he gave them scientific names made up of Latin words. There were several reasons for his choice of Latin. First, since it was no longer in use, it would not change. Second, Latin was understood by the scientists of all countries. Finally, many Latin words were very well suited for describing the traits of organisms. Many of the names given by Linnaeus are still used today.

However, Linnaeus fell into certain traps because of his belief that the main aim of science was to find order in nature. For example, he believed that there was only a fixed number of species. Further, these species did not change. For these reasons, he simply

OBJECTIVES

- DEFINE the term taxonomy.
- DESCRIBE some contributions of Carolus Linnaeus.
- EXPLAIN the "binomial nomenclature" method of scientific naming.
- DESCRIBE the bases of scientific classification.
- NAME the groupings in the system of classification.
- DEMONSTRATE the ability to classify an organism.

Elicit from students some of the reasons for needing a classification system. Point out the importance of having an internationally accepted system of classification.

There have been many books written about Linnaeus and his work. Some students might find the book *Linnaeus, A Modern Portrait of the Great Swedish Scientist* by Heinz Goerke of great interest. This book was published in 1973 by Charles Scribner's Sons, New York City.

ignored any organism that did not fit into his system. If he had understood that such organisms were in the process of change, the theory of evolution might have developed long before Darwin.

MODERN TAXONOMY

From the time of Linnaeus until recently, structural similarity has been the main basis for classifying living things. For example, the cow, bison, and deer are similar in structure. All three chew cuds, have large teeth for grinding plants, have two-toed hoofs, and so on. Thus, these animals are grouped together. In classifying organisms, we begin with very large groups and continue down through smaller groups to single species. The smaller the group, the more alike its members are.

In recent times, other traits besides structure have become important in taxonomy. One such trait is **cellular organization,** including nuclear structure, plastids, and other organelles. Another factor is **biochemical similarity.** For example, cells of closely related organisms may form the same organic compounds.

However, *all* of the above traits are coded by genes. Thus, the strongest evidence of relationship is **genetic similarity.** Suppose, for example, that two animals have the same number of chromosomes. Further, these chromosomes are identical or very similar in structure. If so, we can assume that the animals are closely related.

SCIENTIFIC NAMES

The scientific names given by Linnaeus usually described some trait of the organism. Each name was made up of two or more parts. **This system, still used today, is called *binomial nomenclature,* which means "two-word naming." The first word names a *genus* and always begins with a capital letter. The species name follows and usually begins with a small letter.** The genus name is usually a noun, and the species name an adjective. In Latin, it is not unusual for the adjective to follow the noun.

The species is still the basic group used in classifying organisms. Members of a species are similar in structure and can mate and produce fertile offspring. For example, all domestic cats are of one species, though they differ in size, color, and other traits.

The genus is a group of closely related species. For example, maple trees belong to the genus *Acer.* There are many different species in this genus. For example, *Acer saccharum* is the sugar maple, while *Acer rubrum* is the red maple.

This system avoids the confusion of using common names. The mountain lion, for example, is also called the puma, cougar, panther, and perhaps a dozen other common names. All scientists, however, can identify this animal as *Felis concolor.* The common house cat, *Felis domesticus*, belongs to the same genus, but not the same species. *Felis once* is the jaguar, while *Felis leo* is the African lion.

Students may be interested in learning how scientists give a newly-discovered species its scientific name. These rules can be found in Bergey's *Manual of Determinative Bacteriology.*

Ask students to consider the structural method of classification. Why is this method a successful one? Point out that this method takes evolutionary change into consideration.

14-2 These members of the cat family are related, as indicated by genus name.

Students may be surprised to learn that new species of wildlife are usually discovered about once in thirty years. However, scientists have recently discovered two new species. A new species of marsupial was found in South Australia and a wild pig (thought to have been extinct 10,000 years ago) was found in Paraguay.

Point out to students that any method of classification is devised to aid the scientist. It is not necessarily a natural method. Ask students to suggest ways that they use classification systems: files, record books, notations, etc.

14–3 Common names can be misleading. Although these two animals are commonly known as jellyfish and starfish, respectively, neither is a true fish. They are unlike in structure, and they are not even closely related to one another. (Systematics-Ecology Program-MBL)

Some common names are actually misleading. For example, clams and oysters are called shellfish, but are not true fish at all. Neither is the crayfish, jellyfish, or starfish. The silverfish, of course, is an insect. We will use some of these common names even in the study of biology because they are familiar. But when we need to be really accurate, we can avoid problems by using scientific names.

GROUPINGS IN THE CLASSIFICATION SYSTEM

More than a million different plants and animals are known to exist. Suppose you had a sample of each species. How would you begin to classify them? Probably you would first separate them into plants and animals, and then into smaller and smaller groups. This is exactly what biologists have done.

The largest groups are known as *kingdoms*. Each kingdom is broken down into smaller groups known as *phyla* (singular, phylum). Each phylum, in turn, is divided into *classes*. A class contains many *orders*. A division of an order is a *family*. The family is made up of *genera* (singular, genus). Finally, each genus is divided into *species*. Sometimes members of a species vary slightly, but not enough to be considered different species. We call such slightly different organisms *varieties*. The variety name is added as a third part of the scientific name.

To see how this system works, we can apply it to human beings. Since we are animals, we belong to the kingdom Animalia. Because we have backbones, we are in the subphylum Vertebrata of the phylum Chordata. In the class Mammalia are all animals with

mammary glands, including human beings. The order Primates includes only mammals that stand nearly erect. We belong to this order, as do monkeys, chimpanzees, and gorillas. Our family is Hominadae (hoe-MIN-uh-DEE). This family includes early human-like forms and separates us from other primates. The genus *Homo* includes all true human beings. The species *sapiens* (which means "wise") is the only human species that has survived on earth. Some biologists consider the different human races as varieties.

PROBLEMS IN CLASSIFICATION

Remember that any classification system is artificial. We classify organisms only for our own convenience in studying them. Different biologists may have somewhat different ideas about how organisms should be classified. Thus, the systems used by different scientists sometimes vary. What are some of the questions that give rise to these different systems?

One important question is whether certain organisms are plants, animals, or neither of these. This problem did not concern biologists much until fairly recent years. They recognized only two kingdoms, plant and animal. This system worked well for many years. Lately, however, much research has focused on very simple life forms. Are these organisms plants, or animals? Actually, they are neither. They are more closely related to each other than organisms that are clearly plant or animal.

The old system had no place for such "in-between" organisms. Thus, biologist have tried to classify them in new ways. For example, some systems now place the bacteria and blue-green algae in a kingdom called the **Monera** (muh-NEER-uh). These organisms have one striking trait in common—they lack an organized nucleus. Some biologists even place the viruses in this kingdom. Others argue that viruses aren't even living organisms.

Another kingdom, the **Protista** (proh-TIST-uh), is now included in almost every system. However, there is some question as to what phyla belong in this kingdom. Protozoans certainly belong. If we do not recognize the kingdom Monera, then the bacteria must

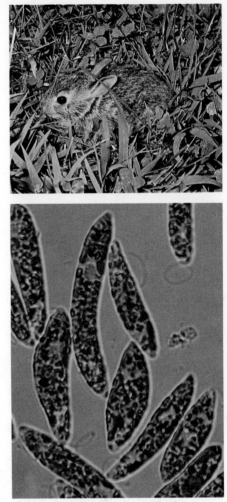

14-4 It is simple to classify the rabbit as an animal and the grass as a plant. But, it is a different story when classifying microscopic organisms, such as the euglena. Into what group does it belong? (Allan Roberts; Walter Dawn)

Table 14-1 THE CLASSIFICATION OF SIX DIFFERENT ORGANISMS

	MAN	GRASS-HOPPER	DANDELION	WHITE PINE	AMEBA	TYPHOID BACTERIUM
KINGDOM	Animalia	Animalia	Plantae	Plantae	Protista	Protista
PHYLUM	Chordata	Arthropoda	Tracheophyta	Tracheophyta	Sarcodina	Schizomycophyta
CLASS	Mammalia	Insecta	Angiospermae	Gymnospermae	Rhizopoda	Schizomycetes
ORDER	Primates	Orthoptera	Campanulales	Coniferales	Amoebida	Eubacteriales
FAMILY	Hominidae	Acridiidae	Compositae	Pinaceae	Amoebidae	Bacteriaceae
GENUS	*Homo*	*Schistocerca*	*Taraxacum*	*Pinus*	*Amoeba*	*Eberthella*
SPECIES	*sapiens*	*americana*	*officinale*	*strobus*	*proteus*	*typhosa*

Table 14-2 A MODERN CLASSIFICATION OF ORGANISMS

Kingdom — Protista

Organisms having a simple structure; many unicellular, others colonial or multicellular but lacking in specialized tissue; both heterotrophic and autotrophic; neither distinctly plant nor distinctly animal.

	PHYLUM	ORGANISMS
Algal Protists	Cyanophyta	blue-green algae
	Chlorophyta	green algae
	Chrysophyta	golden-brown algae, or diatoms
	Pyrrophyta	dinoflagellates and cryptomonads
	Phaeophyta	brown algae
	Rhodophyta	red algae
	Schizomycophyta	bacteria
Fungal Protists	Eumycophyta	fungi
	Myxomycophyta	slime fungi
Protozoan Protists	Sarcodina	amoeboid organisms
	Mastigophora	flagellates
	Ciliophora	ciliates
	Sporozoa	*Plasmodium*

Kingdom — Plantae

Multicellular plants having tissues and organs; cell walls containing cellulose; chlorophyll *a* and *b* present and localized in chloroplasts; food stored as starch; sex organs multicellular; autotrophic.

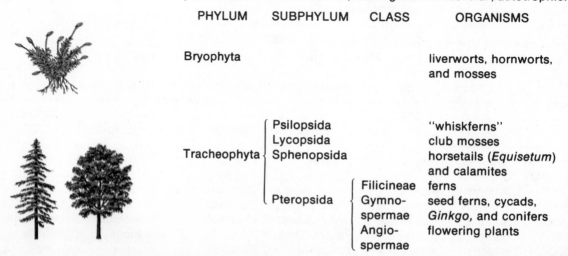

PHYLUM	SUBPHYLUM	CLASS	ORGANISMS
Bryophyta			liverworts, hornworts, and mosses
Tracheophyta	Psilopsida		"whiskferns"
	Lycopsida		club mosses
	Sphenopsida		horsetails (*Equisetum*) and calamites
	Pteropsida	Filicineae	ferns
		Gymnospermae	seed ferns, cycads, *Ginkgo*, and conifers
		Angiospermae	flowering plants

Kingdom—Animalia

Multicellular animals having tissues and, in many cases, organs and organ systems; pass through embryonic or larval stages in development; heterotrophic. (Only the major phyla are listed.)

PHYLUM	SUBPHYLUM	ORGANISMS
Porifera		sponges
Coelenterata		jellyfish, sea anemones, corals
Platyhelminthes		flatworms
Nematoda		roundworms
Trochelminthes		rotifers
Bryozoa		bryozoans, sea mosses
Brachiopoda		brachiopods, or lampshells
Mollusca		clams, snails, squids, octopi
Annelida		segmented worms (earthworm)
Arthropoda		insects, spiders, crustaceans
Echinodermata		starfishes, sea urchins
Chordata	Hemichordata	tongue worms, acorn worms
	Tunicata	tunicates
	Cephalochordata	lancelets
	Vertebrata	vertebrates

Point out to students that some scientists prefer to use the traditional two-kingdom method of classification while others use the three- or four-kingdom method. Elicit from students, thoughts on which method should be universally accepted.

Have students report on a new species that has been discovered in recent times. Some students might think that all of the species we know today were discovered hundreds of years ago.

also be classed as Protista. The real problem involves the algae and fungi. Some of the simpler members of these groups seem clearly Protista. But more complex members, such as kelp and mushrooms, seem more like true plants.

Certain factors make it seem more reasonable to place all algae and fungi in the same kingdom. **For this reason, we will use a system of three kingdoms in this book: plant, animal, and protist. The kingdom Protista will include the algae and fungi as well as the bacteria and protozoans.** Remember that this is not the only system, nor is it a perfect one. We cannot say that one system is right and another wrong. We are simply choosing one system as a convenience in order to organize our study of the living world.

A JOB THAT HAS ONLY BEGUN

The work of classification is far from over. In fact, it has only begun. Some 1.5 million animals, plants, and protists have been named and classified. But some biologists estimate that there may be as many as 5 million different kinds of organisms in the world population. If so, millions of organisms remain to be found. Many of these may be hidden deep in the seas or in remote regions of the earth.

If the number of living species seems great, remember that many times more have become extinct. These species, too, have their place in any system that attempts to classify the life of all ages.

SUMMARY

The aim of taxonomy is to classify organisms on the basis of natural relationship. Linnaeus set up a system of taxonomy on the basis of structural similarity. This concept is still important today, along with those of cellular organization, biochemical similarity, and genetic similarity. We also use the system of Latin binomial nomenclature invented by Linnaeus.

In classifying organisms, we first divide them into large kingdoms. We then go down through smaller and smaller groups: phylum, class, order, family, and genus. The smallest group is the species.

Modern systems of classification differ in some ways. We must remember that all systems are artificial, and none is perfect.

BIOLOGICALLY SPEAKING

taxonomy	kingdom	genus
structural similarity	phylum	species
cellular organization	class	variety
biochemical similarity	order	Monera
genetic similarity	family	Protista
binomial nomenclature		

QUESTIONS FOR REVIEW

1. What is the science of classification called?
2. What is meant by "binomial nomenclature"?
3. What is Latin used as the language for biological classification?
4. Discuss ways in which common names are both confusing and misleading.
5. What characteristics of an organism are used as the basis of its classification?

6. List the classification groups from the largest to the smallest.
7. What are some of the problems biologists have in classifying organisms into kingdoms?

1. Give examples to demonstrate that size, habitat, and diet similarities show no true animal relationships that could be considered in classification.
2. Make a list of plants and animals of your region that have more than one common name.
3. The fox, wolf, and coyote are different species of the dog family. On the other hand, the collie, poodle, and terrier are breeds of domestic dog. Distinguish between a species and a breed or variety.

Books

Asimov, Isaac, *The Genetic Code.*
New American Library, Inc., New York, 1962. Tells how the arrangement of the bases in the DNA molecule controls traits of living organisms.

Beadle, George and Muriel, *The Language of Life: An Introduction to the Science of Genetics.*
Doubleday and Company, Inc., Garden City, N.Y., 1966. A presentation of some of the many scientific studies in genetics.

Darwin, Charles R., *The Origin of Species.*
Doubleday and Company, Inc., Garden City, N.Y., 1960. A classical reading that explains Darwin's ideas on the way favored organisms are preserved in the struggle for life.

Hanson, Earl D., *Animal Diversity (2nd. ed.).*
Prentice-Hall Inc., Englewood Cliffs, N.J., 1964. An explanation, not just a description, of animal diversity.

Head, J. J., Ed., *Readings in Genetics and Evolution.*
Oxford University Press, New York, 1973. A series of articles on the title subjects by leading authorities.

Kuspira, John and Walker, G. W., *Genetics: Questions and Problems.*
McGraw-Hill Book Co., New York, 1973. This book is a set of questions and problems in genetics, ranging from the nuclear structure through hypotheses and theories of speciation.

Sullivan, Navin, *The Message of the Genes.*
Basic Books, Inc., Publishers, New York, 1967. A lucid account of the mechanisms of heredity showing that today's molecular biologists have arrived at a clear understanding of life itself.

Articles

McKusick, Victor A., "The Royal Hemophilia," *Scientific American*, August, 1965. An account of the gene for hemophilia and how it is found in the royal families of Europe.

Valentine, James W., and Moores, Eldridge, M., "Plate Tectonics and The History of Life in the Oceans," *Scientific American*, April, 1974. Explains how continental drift enhanced animal diversity.

unit

3

MICROBIOLOGY

In our study of microbiology, we will see the smallest of living organisms. These small organisms show the most basic properties of the living condition. In the virus, we find the lack of cellular organization. But, the virus still can reproduce under suitable conditions. As our study progresses from the primitive virus, cells increase in complexity. Among these simple organisms, we find cells grouping together to form colonies. Other organisms are organized on the multicellular level. By studying these simple organisms, we will be better able to understand higher forms of life.

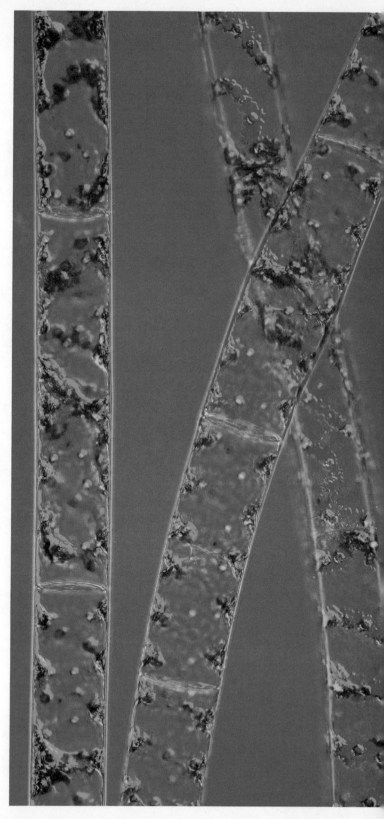

VIRUSES—LIVING OR NONLIVING?

The study of viruses is one of the newest and most interesting fields of biology. This study also raises basic questions about what we mean by the word *life*. When little was known of viruses, it was much easier to draw a line between the living and nonliving worlds. Then it was found that viruses seem to shift between these worlds, and the line became less clear.

Consider a virus alone. It is a particle unlike any other form of nonliving matter. And there are definite links to biochemical processes in the way a virus is organized. Yet the virus itself is not alive. Only in the presence of a living system in a cell does it show signs of life—and then it seems very much alive. Could viruses be living at some times and nonliving at others? It all depends on how we define *life*, and biologists have yet to agree on such a definition.

Whether viruses are living or nonliving, they belong in our Unit on microbiology. If nonliving, their effects on cells are different from those of any other nonliving material. If living, they are clearly the most basic organisms—life at the molecular level.

WHAT ARE VIRUSES LIKE?

At the mention of the word *virus*, you probably think of an agent of disease. Many viruses *do* cause diseases, including polio, small-pox, influenza, rabies, and the common cold. All in all, more than 300 viruses are known to cause diseases in certain organisms. Until recently, in fact, scientists thought that *all* viruses were **pathogenic,** or able to produce disease. However, many viruses are now known that seem to be harmless.

Virus particles are not cells. They are subcellular, or organized below the level of the cell. A virus has no nucleus, no cytoplasm, and no surrounding membrane. It is larger than a molecule but much smaller than the smallest cell. We call viruses **filterable viruses** because they pass through the very small pores of filters used to separate bacteria from fluids.

Only the very largest viruses are visible through a light microscope. Thus, little was known of the structure of viruses before the electron microscope came into use. With this instrument, even the smallest viruses have been photographed. We are now familiar with the forms and sizes of many viruses.

Viruses occur in many shapes. Some are like needles or rods, others are round. Some are shaped like cubes or like bricks. Still others have oval or many-sided heads and slender tails. As for size, we measure viruses in *millimicrons* (mμ). A millimicron is *one millionth* of a millimeter. To understand how very small this is, consider that the smallest bacteria range from 500 to 750 millimicrons. Such bacteria appear only as tiny specks through a light microscope at high power. Still these bacteria are large compared to viruses.

chapter fifteen

The Viruses

OBJECTIVES

- EXPLAIN why a virus might be considered to be living.
- DESCRIBE the chemical makeup of a virus.
- DESCRIBE how viruses are different from other cells.
- CLASSIFY the viruses according to the hosts in which they live.
- DESCRIBE the lytic cycle of a virulent phage virus.
- EXPLAIN the invasion of a cell by a temperate phage.
- LIST some better known virus diseases.
- DESCRIBE mycoplasmas.

Ask students to consider the characteristics of a virus in reference to whether or not it is living.

Point out to students that most of our knowledge about viruses has been learned through the use of the electron microscope.

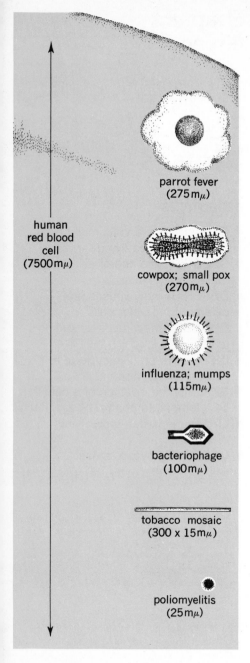

15–1 Some viruses drawn for comparison over a portion of a human red blood cell.

parrot fever
(275 mμ)

cowpox; small pox
(270 mμ)

influenza; mumps
(115 mμ)

bacteriophage
(100 mμ)

tobacco mosaic
(300 x 15mμ)

poliomyelitis
(25 mμ)

human
red blood
cell
(7500 mμ)

Some students may be interested in reading about the history of viral research. An excellent book on the subject of viruses is *The World of the Virus* by Stewart M. Brooks, published by A. S. Barnes and Co., New York City.

THE DISCOVERY OF VIRUSES

Scientists had learned to prevent certain virus diseases long before anyone knew that viruses existed. Edward Jenner gave the first vaccination for smallpox in 1796. About a century later, Louis Pasteur developed his vaccine for rabies. Yet neither of these men had ever seen or heard of viruses.

Even into the twentieth century, viruses themselves remained unknown, though many scientists were studying virus diseases. One such scientist was the Russian biologist Dmitri Iwanowski. In his work, important though it was, we can see some of the reasons viruses were not found sooner.

In 1892, Iwanowski was studying a virus disease of tobacco plants known as tobacco mosaic. The word *mosaic* refers to a pattern of light green and yellow areas that appears on the diseased tobacco leaves. Iwanowski first squeezed fluid from diseased leaves, then rubbed this fluid onto healthy plants. The healthy leaves soon showed the mosaic pattern of the disease.

Iwanowski repeated the experiment. But this time, he passed the fluid through a filter with pores small enough to remove all bacteria. The microscope showed no bacteria or other bodies that might cause disease in this fluid. But when the fluid was rubbed on healthy plants, it still caused the disease.

These results puzzled Iwanowski, and no wonder. In his day, bacteria were thought to be the smallest possible agents of disease. The viruses, of course, were far too small to be seen through his light microscope. He could only assume that some invisible poison, given off by the bacteria, had passed through the filter.

Six years later, the Dutch botanist Martinus Beijerinck repeated Iwanowski's work. He reached a different conclusion. He believed that the fluid must contain some invisible agent smaller than the smallest bacteria. He named this unknown agent **virus,** a Latin word meaning "poison."

Still, it was not until 1935 that the virus itself was found. The discoverer was Dr. Wendell Stanley. Stanley ground and removed the fluid from more than a ton of diseased tobacco leaves. From this fluid, he obtained about a teaspoonful of needlelike crystals. Stored in a bottle, these crystals seemed to have no life. Yet when they were put in water and rubbed on tobacco leaves, they produced the mosaic disease. Stanley had isolated the tobacco mosaic virus. For this work, he received the Nobel prize in chemistry in 1946.

THE CHEMISTRY OF VIRUSES

Scientists now know the chemical makeup of several viruses. The simplest ones are made up of a **protein coat,** or shell, around a **nucleic acid core.** In some viruses, this core is RNA. In others, it is DNA. Thus, we can think of a simple virus as a giant protein molecule, similar in some ways to those found in cell nuclei. More complex viruses may also contain carbohydrates, lipids, metals, and other substances.

15–2 Tobacco mosiac virus: infected leaf (left) showing mottling and healthy tobacco leaf (right). (Marvin Williams, North Carolina State University; courtesy North Carolina State University)

15–3 Tobacco mosaic virus. Compare the schematic drawing with the electron micrograph. (courtesy R. W. Horne)

The tobacco mosaic virus is a good example of a simple virus. Magnified 60,000 times or more by an electron microscope, this virus appears as a long, rod-shaped body. The protein coat, making up 95 percent of the virus, contains more than 2,000 protein units. The other 5 percent of the virus is its RNA core.

The presence of nucleic acid tends to support the idea that viruses are living. By the genetic code of DNA or RNA, the traits of the virus are passed on when new viruses are formed.

OTHER PROPERTIES OF VIRUSES

In Unit 1, we discussed the living condition as a state of constant chemical activity. This activity takes several forms—growth, respiration, and so on. These processes go on constantly in all living cells.

On its own, a virus shows no such activity. Only when in direct contact with the content of a specific host cell does a virus show any signs of life. The *host cell* is any cell attacked by a virus. Even then, its activity is limited and is made possible only by the activity of the cell itself. Removed from the cell, the virus again loses all signs of life. However, it still has the ability to infect a cell.

A virus cannot reproduce on its own. That is, it cannot divide like a cell and produce new viruses. In order to reproduce, a virus must invade a host cell and take control of the cell's activity. Biologists are not sure how this is done, and different viruses may affect cells in different ways. However, one hypothesis has received support. According to it, the virus changes the enzyme patterns that control protein synthesis in the cell. The virus

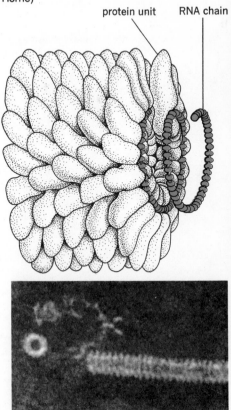

protein unit   RNA chain

does this by injecting its own DNA or RNA into the host cell. This change causes the cell to build *viruses* rather than normal cell structures.

If this hypothesis is correct, the virus acts in much the same way as a gene. Could a virus be a gene (or group of genes) that has no "home" until it invades a cell?

On the other hand, many viruses are themselves affected by the environment in which they grow. For example, the rabies virus may be grown in cells of the brain and spinal cord of a dog. If so, the strength, or **virulence** (VIR-uh-lenss), of the virus increases for dogs and human beings. If the virus is grown in rabbits, it *loses* virulence for people and dogs, but gains virulence for rabbits.

Viruses also vary by mutation. More than fifty mutant strains of the tobacco mosaic virus have been discovered. These strains differ in virulence and in the symptoms they produce in the host plant.

Such variations may explain why some epidemics of the same disease are worse than others. Perhaps the virus gains in virulence as the disease is passed from person to person. Or perhaps a mutant strain with greater virulence is involved.

CLASSIFICATION OF VIRUSES

Viruses in general invade only specific kinds of cells. For this reason, we classify viruses according to their host organisms. This system gives us the following types:

- *Bacterial viruses,* which invade the cells of bacteria.
- *Plant viruses,* which are found in the cells of seed plants.
- *Human and animal viruses,* which invade human and animal cells.

15-4 A bacterial virus, or phage. Compare the schematic drawing (left) with the electron micrograph. (courtesy T. F. Anderson)

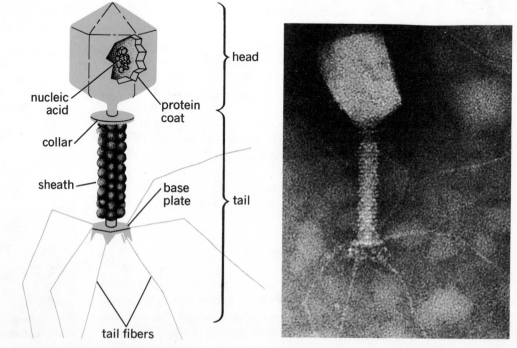

nucleic acid

protein coat

collar

sheath

base plate

tail fibers

head

tail

Actually, the relationship between virus and host is much more specific than these large groups indicate. Bacterial viruses invade only certain kinds of bacteria. A plant virus may invade only a specific plant and only specific cells, such as leaf cells, within that plant. An animal virus may become active only in certain tissue cells, such as skin cells, in a specific animal.

Some viruses are still more specific. Polio viruses attack only *one kind* of nerve cell in the brain and spinal cord. The mumps virus infects only one pair of salivary glands. It never invades the other pairs.

BACTERIOPHAGES

Much of what we know about viruses has come from study of bacterial viruses, also known as *phages* (FAH-jiz). Phages look a bit like tadpoles. They have round or many-sided heads, and slender tails with several fibers for attaching to bacteria. The coat of a phage is made up of protein. The core is usually DNA, but some phages contain RNA instead.

The first discoveries about phages were made in England in 1915. Scientists had noticed something strange that happened in cultures of a certain bacterium. Small circles appeared in which the bacteria had been killed. These circles, or **plaques,** spread until the whole colony of bacteria was destroyed. It was also found that the unknown agent that destroyed the bacteria could be transferred to other colonies with a needle.

The actual agent that killed the bacteria was not discovered for several years. But this agent was given the name we still use today —**bacteriophage,** or "bacteria eater."

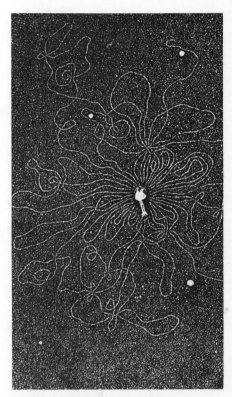

15-5 An "exploded" T$_2$ bacteriophage. Its central core of DNA is seen to be a single strand. (courtesy A. K. Kleinschmidt and *Biochimica et Biophysica Acta*)

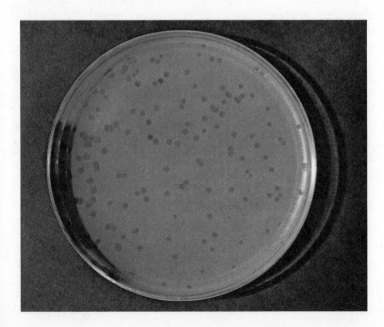

15-6 A bacteria culture spotted with plaques. (Lewis Koster)

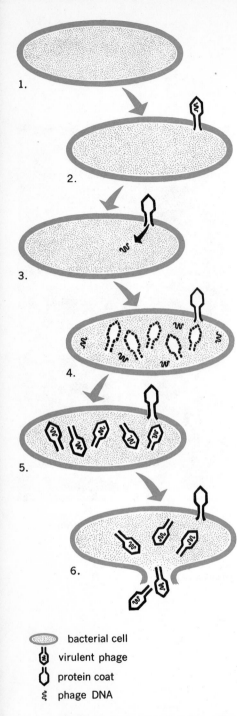

1.

2.

3.

4.

5.

6.

- bacterial cell
- virulent phage
- protein coat
- phage DNA

15–7 The lytic cycle of destruction caused by a virulent phage.

THE LYTIC CYCLE OF A VIRULENT PHAGE

Early researchers had no way of seeing phages or learning how they killed bacteria. The electron microscope changed all that. Today we have photographed not only phages, but every step in their attacks on bacteria.

Phages destroy bacteria in a cycle known as the *lytic cycle.* A phage that produces this cycle is known as a *virulent phage.* We can break down the lytic cycle into six basic steps.

1. The cycle begins with a normal bacterium, free of phages.

2. A phage attaches, tail down, to the cell wall of the bacterium. An enzyme in the tail of the phage dissolves part of the cell wall, forming an opening.

3. The tail contracts and forces the DNA of the phage core through the opening in the cell wall. The empty protein coat remains outside.

4. Within a few minutes, the phage DNA appears near the DNA of the host cell. The phage DNA destroys the cell DNA and takes control of the cell's activity. Instead of normal protein synthesis, the phage DNA codes the building of *more* phage DNA and protein. The cell becomes a virus factory.

5. Soon the bacterium may contain 300 or more virus particles.

6. The cell wall breaks open. The phages are released and can now attack other bacteria.

Biologists often use an analogy to explain this process more clearly. A tank rolls up to an automobile factory and breaks a hole through the factory wall. The tank crew enters and takes control of the factory. Machines are reset, and the materials once used to make cars are now used to build more tanks. Soon hundreds of tanks are rumbling through the factory. A wall is broken down, and the tanks spread out into the countryside to attack other factories.

Notice, in this analogy, that the tank crew needs the factory machinery in order to build more tanks. The crew cannot produce more tanks on its own. In the same way, a phage cannot reproduce on its own. It needs the "machinery" of the host cell.

The whole lytic cycle takes about 45 minutes. Since so many phages are produced in a single cycle, the phage population grows very quickly. For example, suppose that only a few phages are placed in a broth culture containing billions of bacteria. Within *three to four hours*, enough phages will have been produced to destroy the whole bacteria colony!

HOPES FOR MEDICAL USE OF PHAGES

Many diseases are caused by bacteria. Couldn't we cure these diseases by using virulent phages to destroy the bacteria? At one time, there was great hope that this could be done. But further studies have run into many problems.

For example, some diseases infect tissues deep in the body. It may be difficult to introduce a phage into such tissues. In other

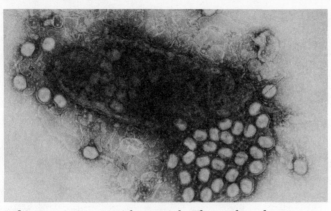

Using Figs. 15-7 and 15-9, have students compare the lytic cycle with the invasion of a bacterial cell by a temperate phage.

15-8 An electron micrograph of a T₄ bacteriophage destroying a cell of *E. coli*. (Drs. D. T. Brown & T. F. Anderson, Institute for Cancer Research, Philadelphia)

diseases, the infection is very widespread. Thus, the phages may not be able to reach enough bacteria to be helpful. Still another problem is that the human tissue environment may not be suited for phage action.

For these and other reasons, we are less hopeful today of using phages as major weapons against disease.

TEMPERATE PHAGES—BOMBS WAITING TO EXPLODE

Sometimes a phage injects its DNA into a bacterium without causing new phages to be produced. Such a phage is called a *temperate phage.* It is thought that some chemical property of the bacterial cell keeps the phage from becoming virulent.

However, the DNA of a temperate phage does not simply disappear. Biologists believe that it attaches to the bacterial chromosome. There it remains, like an extra gene. In this condition, it is called a **prophage.** When the chromosome replicates at the start of cell division, the phage DNA also replicates. Thus, each daughter cell receives the phage DNA "gene."

In this way, the phage DNA may be multiplied generation after generation with no damage done. Yet even though there are no immediate effects, the phage DNA remains dangerous. In a way, it is like a bomb that needs only some slight jolt to set it off. At any time, the temperate "gene" may mutate and become virulent. Or the cell itself may lose the trait that resists the phage. In either case, the virulent phage will take over the cell and begin the lytic cycle.

HUMAN AND ANIMAL VIRUSES

Many familiar diseases of human beings and animals are caused by viruses. In most cases, the virus invades only specific tissues. Symptoms of virus diseases are as different as the viruses that cause them. However, most virus infections interfere with normal cell activity and may damage or destroy tissue.

We have already mentioned several virus diseases that affect human beings. To this list, we could add chicken pox, measles, warts, virus pneumonia, yellow fever, cold sores, fever blisters, and many others.

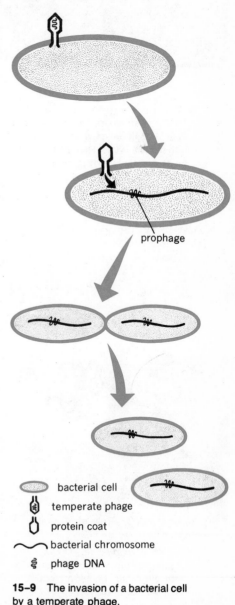

prophage

bacterial cell
temperate phage
protein coat
bacterial chromosome
phage DNA

15-9 The invasion of a bacterial cell by a temperate phage.

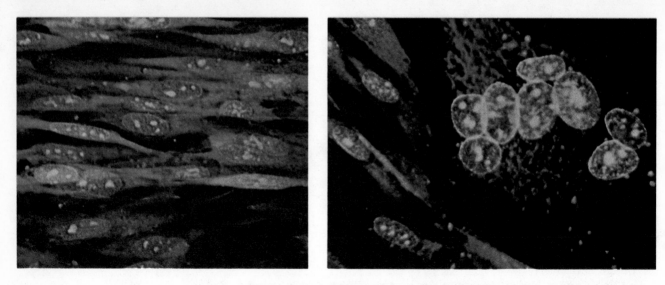

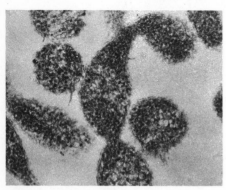

15–10 Human body cells before (left) and three days after infection with measles virus. RNA in the nucleoli and cytoplasm appears yellow-orange in color. (courtesy Chas. Pfizer & Co.)

15–11 *Mycoplasma.* These living organisms have characteristics of both virus and bacteria. (courtesy Jack Maniloff, University of Rochester)

A victim who recovers from certain virus diseases, such as chicken pox, becomes immune to the disease. In other cases, such as the common cold, the victim does not become immune.

CAN VIRUSES CAUSE CANCER?

Much recent cancer research has focused on viruses. Several viruses may be linked to certain types of human cancer. Results of experiments with animals have been encouraging. For example, a form of leukemia can be caused in mice by injecting them with a certain virus. By similar methods, more than twenty kinds of malignant tumors have been produced in mice, guinea pigs, and hamsters.

In 1975, Doctors Temin, Baltimore, and Dulbecco received the Nobel prize for their work showing that cancer viruses make an enzyme that affects human DNA. This was a major step in discovering *how* viruses might play a role in cancer.

If scientists can find viruses that *do* cause human cancers they may also find a way to prevent or cure some cancers.

MYCOPLASMAS—A POSSIBLE LINK BETWEEN VIRUSES AND CELLS

The organisms of the genus *Mycoplasma* raise important questions for biologists. The mycoplasmas are much like viruses in form and size. However, unlike viruses, mycoplasmas can be grown in a culture without the presence of living cells. Further, though their method of reproduction is not known, it does not require the use of living cells.

Mycoplasmas do not have cell walls, and so take different shapes. However, they *are* surrounded by a membrane—a definite trait of cells. Are the mycoplasmas, then, a link between viruses and the world of living cells?

Mycoplasmas have been known to live in the human mouth and nasal passages without harmful effect. However, they are also suspected of being involved in several human and animal diseases. Among these are arthritis and a form of pneumonia. Mycoplasmas have also been found in the bone marrow of the victims of certain forms of leukemia. Because of such discoveries, a good deal of attention has been given to mycoplasmas in recent years.

Stress to students that in 1975 the National Cancer Institute announced the discovery of a new virus associated with human leukemia. The action of the virus and its relation to human cancer is being studied.

SUMMARY

Viruses may be a link between the living and nonliving worlds. A virus particle is made up of protein and nucleic acid. These substances would normally be signs of a living condition. However, removed from a living cell, a virus shows no signs of life processes.

The effects of viruses on cells are clearly shown in the case of virulent phages. These phages inject their DNA into bacteria. The phage DNA takes control of the cell and causes it to build still more phages. These phages, in turn, may attack other cells.

Many diseases are caused by viruses, possibly including some forms of cancer. Much remains to be learned about viruses, and much research is being done on them today.

BIOLOGICALLY SPEAKING

pathogenic
filterable virus
virus
protein coat
nucleic acid core

host cell
virulence
plaques
bacteriophage
lytic cycle

virulent phage
temperate phage
prophage
mycoplasmas

QUESTIONS FOR REVIEW

1. What are viruses?
2. How does the term "filterable viruses" describe virus size?
3. How were viruses discovered?
4. Describe the general chemical structure of the virus.
5. What is meant by virulence of a virus?
6. Classify the viruses into three groups on the basis of the host organism.
7. Describe the lytic cycle of the virulent phage.
8. In what way is a temperate phage a potential "seed of destruction"?
9. List some better known human diseases caused by viruses.
10. How do mycoplasmas differ from viruses?

APPLYING PRINCIPLES AND CONCEPTS

1. Explain various factors that may alter the virulence of a virus.
2. Discuss several biological principles shown by the lytic cycle of a virulent phage.
3. Discuss the reasons for considering viruses living or nonliving.
4. Offer a hypothesis to account for the high degree of specificity of viruses.

chapter sixteen

Bacteria and Related Organisms

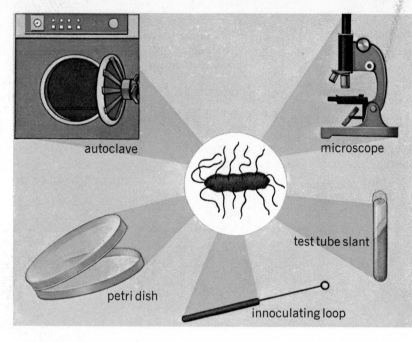

16–1 Microbiologists' tools.

OBJECTIVES

- DESCRIBE the contributions of Louis Pasteur to microbiology.
- NAME and DESCRIBE three general shapes of bacteria.
- DESCRIBE the structure and motility of a bacterium.
- LIST the condistions needed for the growth of bacteria.
- DISTINGUISH a heterotroph from an autotroph.
- DESCRIBE the various types of bacterial respiration.
- DESCRIBE three ways bacteria reproduce.
- EXPLAIN the process of pasteurization.
- LIST methods used to prevent food spoilage.
- NAME some diseases caused by rickettsiae and spirochetes.

Bacteria are very small, so small in fact that more than 500 million (of certain types) could fit on a postage stamp. Several thousand bacteria could fit on a small dot made by a pen.

BACTERIA—THE MOST COMMON FORM OF LIFE

As our study moves from viruses to bacteria and their relatives, we will see living cells at their simplest level. In fact, bacteria may have been the first form of life on earth. Many biologists believe that bacteria existed long before the first photosynthetic green plants.

These early bacteria may have taken energy from iron, sulfur, and nitrogen compounds rather than from the sun. Geologists think that the great deposits of iron ore we use today resulted from bacterial action billions of years ago.

Later, green plants arose and began building up stores of organic compounds. New kinds of bacteria developed that used these compounds as food. Still other bacteria invaded the tissues of the plants themselves. When animals came into being, bacteria developed that could live off them as well.

Bacteria have survived through the ages. Today, they are the most common life form on our planet. Too small to be seen by the naked eye, they live almost everywhere. **There are bacteria in the air, water, soil, our foods, and the bodies of all plants and animals. In fact, any environment that can support life has its population of bacteria.**

LOUIS PASTEUR AND THE BIRTH OF BACTERIOLOGY

In any science, a few names stand out above all others. In biology, one such name is that of Louis Pasteur. We have already

Era	Period		bacteria	protozoans	fungi	algae
Cenozoic	Quaternary					
	Tertiary					
Mesozoic	Cretaceous					
	Jurassic					
	Triassic					
Paleozoic	Permian					
	Pennsylvanian (Late Carboniferous)					
	Mississippian (Early Carboniferous)					
	Devonian					
	Silurian					
	Ordovician					
	Cambrian					
(Pre-Cambrian)						

mentioned Pasteur's vaccine for rabies and his defeat of the theory of spontaneous generation. Even if he had done nothing else, he would still be remembered for these works. Yet, in fact, they represent only a small part of his total achievement.

Born in France in 1822, Pasteur actually began his scientific career as a chemist. In 1854, he was appointed professor of chemistry and dean at the University of Lille. This location turned out to be quite important. The city of Lille was a center for making alcohol by fermentation of the juice of sugar beets. And it was Pasteur's studies of fermentation that opened up a whole new world to the science of biology.

Chemists at the time thought that fermentation was a purely chemical change. They had seen tiny yeast cells growing in the fermenting juices. But such cells were thought to be simply products of spontaneous generation, having nothing to do with fermentation. This was the situation when, one day, a serious problem arose. The juice in several vats began to turn sour instead of changing to alcohol. Pasteur was called in to find out what was wrong.

With his microscope, Pasteur studied the juice that was fermenting normally. He saw many yeast cells spread through the liquid. Over several hours, more yeast cells grew. As they did so, the alcohol content of the juice rose.

Were the yeasts producing the alcohol? In trying to learn the answer, Pasteur next examined the sour juice. This juice contained not alcohol but lactic acid. Further, instead of yeasts, it contained smaller, rod-shaped bodies. These bodies moved and seemed to be alive. They increased in number as the yeasts had. As these rod-shaped bodies increased, the lactic acid content of the juice also increased.

16–2 A time scale comparing the bacteria to the other protists.

Pasteur concluded from his observations that heat would destroy microorganisms. The process of Pasteurization came about in this way.

183

These discoveries led Pasteur to begin a much more complete study of fermentation. After three years, he set up a small laboratory in Paris. There he finally proved his theory. Fermentation *does* result from the action of microorganisms, and the products formed depend on the organisms involved. Yeasts produce alcohol. Lactic acid is formed by bacteria.

Pasteur did not end his studies of bacteria here. Much greater discoveries lay ahead. Perhaps the most important was his germ theory, which changed the course of modern medicine. According to this theory, bacteria could not only affect fermentation, but could cause diseases. **Modern bacteriology and microbiology both spring largely from Pasteur's work.**

WHAT ARE BACTERIA?

Since Pasteur's time, bacteria have been thought of either as plants or as animals. Recently, however, biologists have placed them in the kingdom Protista. Along with their relatives, bacteria make up the protist phylum *Schizomycophyta* (skizz-uh-my-KAH-fuh-tuh). This name means "fission fungi."

Compared with a virus, a bacterium is quite large. A single bacterium can contain as many as 300 phage viruses. But compared with the cells of most other organisms, bacteria are very small. Like viruses, bacteria are measured in millimicrons (mμ). Sphere-shaped bacteria range from about 500 mμ to 1,500 mμ in diameter. Rod-shaped bacteria may be from 200 to 2,000 mμ thick and from 500 to 10,000 mμ long. If these figures mean little to you, consider that several thousand bacteria could fit on the period at the end of this sentence.

At high power (430×), a laboratory microscope will show some bacteria and give you an idea of their shapes. However, magnification of 1,000× to 1,500× is needed to see them clearly. No light microscope is strong enough to show most cell structures of bacteria. For this, an electron microscope must be used.

Point out to students that Leeuwenhoek identified the three shapes of bacteria in his research. Call the students' attention to the common usage of "staph" infection and "strep" throat.

FORMS OF BACTERIA

While bacteria vary in size, their cells are of three basic shapes. Some bacteria tend to live as single cells. Others tend to remain attached after cell division, forming colonies. These colonies, too, have certain basic shapes. The shapes of bacteria and their colonies are as follows:

■ **coccus** (plural, *cocci*): sphere-shaped cells
   diplococcus: cells often joined in pairs or short filaments
   staphylococcus: clusters of cells
   streptococcus: filaments, or strings, of cells
   tetrad: four cells arranged in a square
   sarcina: cubes or similar groups of cells

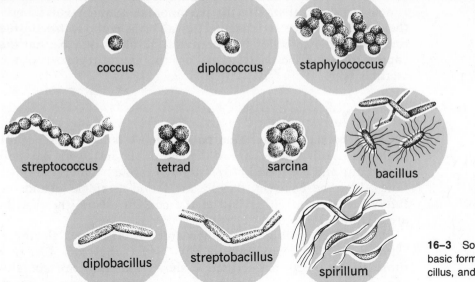

16-3 Some examples of the three basic forms of bacteria—coccus, bacillus, and spirillum.

- **bacillus** (plural, *bacilli*): rod-shaped cells
  diplobacillus: cells in pairs
  streptobacillus: cells joined end to end, forming a filament
- **spirillum** (plural, *spirilla*): cells shaped like bent rods or corkscrews

STRUCTURE OF BACTERIAL CELLS

In some ways, bacteria are much like the cells of other organisms. A bacterium has a *cell wall* that gives it its shape. Within this wall, a thin *plasma membrane* surrounds the *cytoplasm*. There is no nuclear membrane, but a *nuclear area* near the center of the cell. This area contains chromatin bodies made up of DNA in the form of genes. Some biologists think that these bodies make up a single chromosome.

Mitosis does not occur in bacteria, but the chromatin bodies do divide when the cell splits. Thus, each daughter cell receives an equal amount of DNA.

Many bacteria have granules of stored food and other substances spread through the cytoplasm. A few also contain vacuoles of water and dissolved materials. Respiratory enzymes are usually found on mitochondria in cells, but bacteria have no mitochondria. Instead, the respiratory enzymes seem to be concentrated on or near the cell membrane.

Another important difference between bacteria and other cells is the *slime layer* that surrounds a bacterium. Lying outside the cell wall, this slime may protect the bacterium and help it to stick to a food supply or host cell.

The slime layer varies in thickness in different bacteria. Some have a thick slime layer called a *capsule.* The pneumonia bacterium

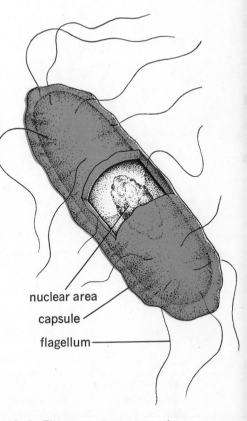

nuclear area
capsule
flagellum

16-4 The general structure of a bacterial cell.

discussed in Chapter Ten has such a capsule. In fact, the capsule is a key to the virulence of the pneumonia organism. Forms *with* the capsule produce serious infections. Forms without the capsule produce milder infections, or even none at all. It may be that the capsule protects the bacteria against the natural defenses of the victim's body.

MOVEMENT OF BACTERIA

Certain bacillus and spirillum bacteria move by means of *flagella* (fluh-JELL-uh). These threadlike whips extend from the cell membrane and are used in "swimming" through water and other fluids. In some bacteria, flagella are found as single strands or tufts of strands at either end of the cell. In others, the flagella are all around the cell.

Flagella are visible only when treated with special stains. Through a light microscope at high power, they look like tiny threads. The electron microscope shows that they are actually part of the cytoplasm, which extends through openings in the cell wall. They are made up mainly of strands of protein molecules. In some ways, these strands resemble muscle fibers. Thus, the basis for muscle contractions in animals may lie in the beating flagella of bacteria.

You can see the movement of bacteria through the microscope. True movement, **motility,** by means of flagella is a quivering, twisting motion. It should not be confused with the flowing or bouncing motion known as **Brownian movement.** Brownian movement is seen mainly in very small bacteria, especially coccus forms. It is caused by the bumping of molecules and other moving particles against the bacteria.

CONDITIONS FOR GROWTH OF BACTERIA

Bacteria do not have to remain active in order to survive. They can lie dormant, or inactive, when conditions are not right for growth and other normal activity. When conditions improve, they may be-

Students may want to demonstrate the difference between true or flagellate movement and Brownian movement. Appropriate models can be made out of commonly used materials.

Students may wish to prepare their own growth medium for bacteria. A mixture of sugar, water, gelatin, and a beef cube provides a suitable medium. Have students evaluate the function of each of these substances.

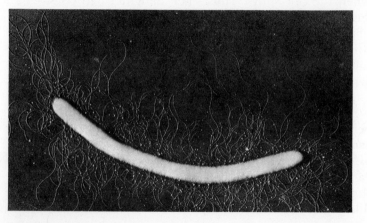

16-5 The flagella of *Proteus vulgaris* show clearly in this electron micrograph. (courtesy Houwink, Van Iterson and *Biochimica et Biophysica Acta*)

come active again, growing and reproducing very rapidly. The conditions most important to bacteria for normal activity are as follows:

■ *Temperature.* Many bacteria are most active at fairly warm temperatures, about 26° C to 38° C. Those that cause human infections grow best at 37° C—normal human body temperature. However, some bacteria grow best at temperatures as low as 0° C, the freezing point. These forms occur mainly in the far north, the ocean depths, and at very high altitudes. Still other bacteria are active at temperatures as high as 85° C. They are found in hot springs and in the hot environment of decaying organic matter such as sewage.

■ *Moisture.* Active bacteria are about 90 percent water. In dry surroundings, water loss makes the cells inactive. Dryness over a long period will kill most species.

■ *Darkness.* Most bacteria grow best in the dark. Sunlight may slow down growth. Ultraviolet rays actually kill most bacteria. This is why special lamps that give off such rays are used to sterilize hospital operating rooms.

■ *Food.* Bacteria vary greatly in terms of their food needs. Some forms require very specific foods. Most pathogenic forms, for example, need living tissues or substances much like their own in chemical makeup. Many other bacteria are less specific and can live on a wide range of foods.

NUTRITION IN BACTERIA

Some bacteria can build their own food compounds from carbon dioxide and other inorganic substances. **Organisms that are able to make their own food from inorganic matter are called *autotrophs.*** Energy is needed in this process. In some cases, energy is obtained by breaking down inorganic compounds of iron, sulfur, or nitrogen. In Chapter Six, we noted that this process is called *chemosynthesis.* Further, a few bacteria carry on a form of *photosynthesis.*

Most bacteria, however, cannot build their own foods. Instead, their nutrition must rely on organic compounds formed by other organisms. **Organisms which depend upon other living things for food are called *heterotrophs.*** For this reason, such bacteria are in direct competition for food with human beings and other animals.

Some of these bacteria are ***saprophytes*** (SAP-row-FITES). That is, they use nonliving or dead organic matter for food. Such substances include many food products intended for human use. Bacteria are a major cause of food spoilage. Other bacteria are ***parasites.*** These forms invade the bodies of plants and animals and take their food directly from living tissue. The organism invaded by a parasite is called the ***host.*** Parasitic bacteria directly harm their hosts.

There are many organisms that are saprophytic or parasitic. Certain fungi are parasites and certain mushrooms are saprophytes. Ask students to name other examples.

Bacteria secrete powerful enzymes that act as catalysts in chemical changes both inside and outside the bacterial cell. In many of these reactions, food substances are broken down to forms that can be absorbed through the cell membrane. Each enzyme acts on only one kind of food. Enzymes allow saprophytes to break down and use a wide range of substances as foods. Some of these substances, such as wood and other forms of cellulose, are of little use to other organisms.

Parasites lack many of the enzymes found in saprophytes. This explains why parasites must be in contact with living tissue, using the enzyme action of the host cells.

RESPIRATION IN BACTERIA

Atmospheric oxygen is an important factor in the growth of bacteria. Some forms require oxygen for life, while others require its absence. Still other bacteria fall somewhere between these two types.

The bacteria that require atmospheric oxygen for respiration are known as **obligate aerobes** (AIR-obes). This group includes the bacteria that cause diphtheria, tuberculosis, and cholera.

The **obligate anaerobes** (AN-uh-robes) *cannot* grow in the presence of atmospheric oxygen. Among the bacteria in this group are those that cause tetanus and botulism.

Many bacteria are **facultative anaerobes.** They grow best as aerobes but may grow, at least to some degree, as anaerobes. This group includes the common bacillus of the human intestine, *Escherichia coli* (ESH-uh-RICK-ee-uh KOE-lee), or *E. coli* for short. The bacteria that cause typhoid and scarlet fever are also facultative anaerobes.

Much less common are the **facultative aerobes.** These forms are mainly anaerobes but can keep up limited activity in the presence of oxygen.

In Chapter Six, we pointed out that fermentation is an anaerobic process. The products vary with the organisms involved. Bacteria that produce alcohol in fermentation split glucose molecules in a way that releases only a little energy. First, pyruvic acid and carbon dioxide are formed. Then hydrogen is added and the pyruvic acid is changed to ethyl alcohol. We can sum up these reactions in the following simple equation:

$$C_6H_{12}O_6 \ \rightarrow \ 2\ C_2H_5OH + 2\ CO_2 + energy$$

glucose ethyl carbon
alcohol dioxide

Other bacteria produce lactic acid by fermentation. Again, only a small amount of energy is released. Leaving out the pyruvic acid steps, we can write the following equation:

$$C_6H_{12}O_6 \ \rightarrow \ 2\ C_3H_6O_3 + energy$$

glucose lactic acid

A simple demonstration of a fermentation reaction may be accomplished by adding dry yeast pellets to a mixture of table sugar and water. Other substances that can be used for this demonstration include beef bouillon and water, apple juice, and salt and water. Have students comment on the rate of fermentation.

Another anaerobic reaction produces methane. Hydrogen and carbon dioxide are combined forming methane and water and releasing energy. We can sum up this process as follows:

$$4\ H_2 \quad + \quad CO_2 \quad \rightarrow \quad CH_4 \quad + 2\ H_2O + energy$$

hydrogen   carbon   methane   water
            dioxide

Methane is called *marsh gas* because it bubbles up from bogs, swamps, and ponds. It is formed from rotting organic matter at the bottoms of such places. Methane also makes up the main part of natural gas.

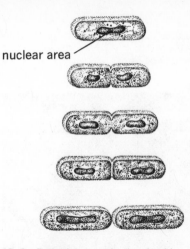

nuclear area

16–6 Bacterial reproduction by binary fission.

BACTERIAL REPRODUCTION

Bacteria reproduce by binary fission. Under good conditions, they multiply at a very rapid rate. A cell may be formed by division, mature, and begin its own division within as little as 20 minutes.

To get a clearer picture of how fast this really is, imagine an example. On a culture medium, we place a single bacterium. Within about 20 minutes, it divides. After another 20 minutes, both daughter cells divide. The cells continue to double in number every 20 minutes. At the end of three hours, there are more than 500; at the end of seven hours, more than 2 million. At the end of a full day, there would be enough bacteria to fill about 100 giant trucks!

Of course, we never find such a mass of bacteria in real life. Several forces combine and limit the growth of bacteria. As the mass grows, simple *crowding* increases. Crowding, in turn, increases the *competition for food.* Also, *waste products* begin to build up in the environment. These same forces affect all other living populations, too, including human beings. At some point, the colony can grow no larger. Bacteria continue to divide, but some of the new cells must die or become inactive. Thus, the population as a whole reaches a balance. **If a population grows without reaching a balance, conditions may become so bad that the entire population dies out.**

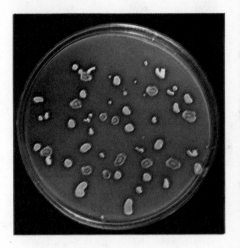

16–7 Colonies of bacteria on a Petri-dish culture. (Walter Dawn)

SPORE FORMATION

Many bacillus bacteria form **endospores.** A new mass of protoplasm develops within the cell. Still within the cell, this mass becomes covered with a hard spore coat which protects it.

In most species of bacteria, endospore formation is not a form of reproduction. Instead, it is a means for survival. If conditions would kill the cell itself, the endospore may still survive in its dormant state. When conditions again favor life, the endospore will become active and grow into a normal cell. However, a cell forms only a single endospore, which develops into only a single cell. Thus, the total number of cells does not increase.

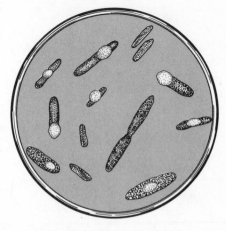

16–8 Various types of bacterial endospores.

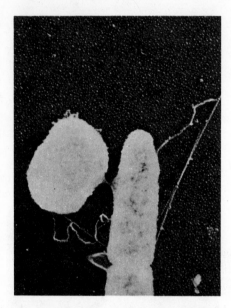

16-9 A photomicrograph of sexual reproduction in bacteria. Note the cytoplasmic bridge joining the two cells. (T. F. Anderson, E. L. Wollman, F. Jacob)

Have students carefully examine Fig. 16-9. Point out to the students the cytoplasmic bridges. It is through these bridges that DNA is transferred. The receiving cell acquires a new gene recombination.

This would be an appropriate place to introduce briefly the nitrogen cycle and the function of bacteria in this cycle. The nitrogen cycle will be discussed in detail in Chapter Forty-Eight.

Bacterial endospores have been found in deep layers of ice in the Antarctic. They had been trapped there for thousands of years. Yet when placed in a better environment, the spores became active bacillus cells! As another example, some spores can survive for an hour or more in boiling water.

The ability of certain spores to survive creates serious medical problems. For example, dormant spores of tetanus bacteria are found in the soil, on objects, and even in the air. They are not destroyed by boiling water. And when they reach an anaerobic environment, such as a closed wound, they become active tetanus bacteria.

SEXUAL REPRODUCTION IN BACTERIA

Cell division is the main form of reproduction in all bacteria. However, a form of sexual reproduction also occurs in at least some species. The *E. coli* bacteria of the human intestine are an example.

When *E. coli* are mixed in a broth suspension, two *E. coli* cells may bump together. A bridge of cytoplasm is formed between the two. One cell, called the male, has certain genetic particles that are separate from its chromatin material. The female does not have these separate particles.

The male *E. coli* injects its genetic particles and chromatin material into the female. The male then dies. However, the female now contains the separate particles. In other words, the female has become a new male.

The importance of this process is the new genetic combinations created in the new male cell. When this cell divides, each daughter cell receives these new combinations. New variations arise which may be better suited for survival. This kind of variation may have helped produce the many different types of bacteria that exist today.

HELPFUL ACTIVITIES OF BACTERIA

Not all bacteria are disease-causing, or pathogenic. In fact, most species are harmless, having no direct effect on our lives. Many bacteria are actually helpful, and there are some that we could not live without. Among these are certain bacteria that live in the soil.

As you know, green plants are the basis of the food chain upon which almost all life depends. Plants use many substances from the soil in building organic compounds. Where do these substances come from? In great part, they come from other plants and animals that have died.

It is here that soil bacteria play an important role. The compounds found in dead plants and animals are too complex for plants to use. These compounds must be broken down to simpler substances. This is exactly what the soil bacteria do. We see this breaking down as the process of decay that attacks all dead organisms. In fact, if not for bacteria, every organism that died might lie about for thousands of years with little change.

Life on earth is a system made up of many cycles of building up and breaking down. All organisms, from bacteria to human beings, have their place in this system. In Unit 8, we will look in more detail at the relationships within the living system.

USES OF BACTERIA IN INDUSTRY

Bacteria are important in making many foods and other products of industry. We have already mentioned their function in making alcohol. Vinegar is another product of bacterial action. So is *silage,* a plant food given to cattle. Because of fermentation by bacteria, silage contains lactic acid. This is of great value in the diet of milk cows.

Bacteria are very important in the dairy industry. Some forms must be guarded against carefully. For example, milk may contain bacteria that cause diseases such as tuberculosis. It also contains bacteria that tend to turn the milk sour. Bacteria in milk are killed by **pasteurization,** a heating process discovered by Louis Pasteur.

Some bacteria, however, are very helpful in making dairy products. Different types of "starter" bacteria are used in making and flavoring butter, buttermilk, and the milk curds that are the basic form of cheese. Other bacteria are used in flavoring and ripening the many hard and soft cheeses.

PRESERVING FOOD FROM BACTERIAL ACTION

Bacteria are among our chief competitors for food. We cannot even estimate the amount of food that is spoiled by the activity of bacteria.

Most foods would remain edible for years if bacteria were not present or could not reproduce. For this reason, we have developed efficient methods for preserving food. One method involves killing all bacteria present, then sealing the food in a container. *Canning* is an example of this method.

Another method involves keeping foods in conditions under which bacteria reproduce more slowly or cannot reproduce at all. This method includes such processes as *cooling* or *freezing, salt curing,* and *dehydration. Chemical preservatives* may also be used. However, their use has declined somewhat in recent years.

Radiation may be an important aid in preserving foods. The foods could be packaged and sealed, then exposed to radiation to destroy all bacteria.

Bacteria serve numerous purposes in the production of industrial and dairy products. They are used in the production of yogurt, cheese, cream, and butter. They are also used in tanning leather and curing tobacco. Students may be interested in reporting on the beneficial uses of bacteria.

Discuss with students the danger of drinking milk that is not pasteurized. Students may be interested in visiting a pasteurization plant or having a speaker from the dairy industry visit the class.

Botulism is a fatal disease that results from improperly canned foods. Students should be on the look out for "swollen" cans or canned foods that seem to have an unusual smell.

a. Dehydration
Water is removed from food to the point that bacteria cannot grow. Freeze-drying is a method of dehydration widely used today.

d. Temperature

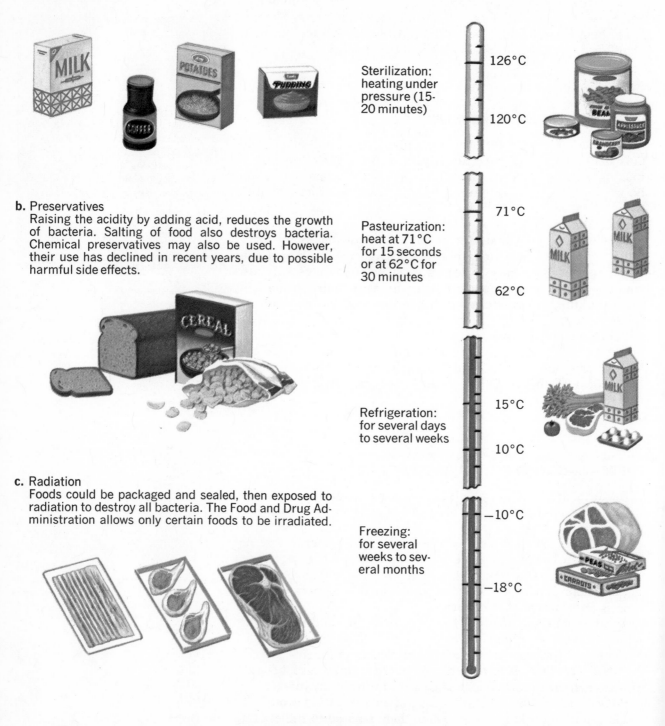

Sterilization: heating under pressure (15-20 minutes)

126°C

120°C

b. Preservatives
Raising the acidity by adding acid, reduces the growth of bacteria. Salting of food also destroys bacteria. Chemical preservatives may also be used. However, their use has declined in recent years, due to possible harmful side effects.

Pasteurization: heat at 71°C for 15 seconds or at 62°C for 30 minutes

71°C

62°C

Refrigeration: for several days to several weeks

15°C

10°C

c. Radiation
Foods could be packaged and sealed, then exposed to radiation to destroy all bacteria. The Food and Drug Administration allows only certain foods to be irradiated.

Freezing: for several weeks to several months

−10°C

−18°C

16–10 The prevention of food spoilage.

RELATIVES OF BACTERIA—THE RICKETTSIAE

The *rickettsiae* (ri-KET-see-ee) are a goup of organisms that seem to be between bacteria and viruses. Shaped like rods or spheres, they average about 300 to 500 mμ in size. They are barely visible under the highest power of a light microscope. Rickettsiae are like bacteria in that they are cellular and reproduce by fission. They are like viruses in that they can grow and reproduce only in living cells.

The rickettsiae are named for Dr. Howard Ricketts, who discovered them in 1909. Ricketts found the first rickettsiae in the blood of victims of Rocky Mountain spotted fever. Rickettsiae also cause such diseases as typhus fever, trench fever, and Q fever.

So far as we know, only insects and their relatives transmit rickettsiae to human beings. These insect carriers include certain ticks, lice, and mites. The rickettsiae live in cells of the carrier's intestine but do not cause disease in the carrier. In the human body, however, they invade cells and cause infection. Most of these infections produce fever, skin rashes, and dark blotches under the skin. The blotches result from bleeding caused by damage to small blood vessels. A victim who recovers may be immune to further damage, though the rickettsiae still remain in his or her cells.

16-11 The tiny bodies that appear blue in the photomicrograph are rickettsiae. They are smaller than bacteria and larger than viruses. (Walter Dawn)

THE SPIROCHETES

The *spirochetes* (SPY-row-KEETS) seem to lie between the bacteria and the more specialized protists called protozoans. Many of the spirochetes are in the size range of bacteria. Some, however, may be as long as 500 microns. The cells of spirochetes are long cylinders. Some have a spiral shape, while others are tight corkscrews.

So far, no spirochete is known to have an organized nucleus. Reproduction is by fission. Endospores are not produced. Spirochetes can move through fluids by a quivering action. Some have been found that have structures that look like flagella, but these are not true flagella.

We are most familiar with the spirochetes that cause human diseases. Among these is the syphilis organism, *Treponema pallidum*. This spirochete lives in the blood and may invade the nervous system.

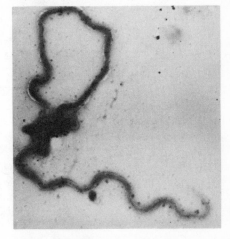

16-12 An electron micrograph of the syphilis organism, *Treponema pallidum*. (Dept. of HEW)

SUMMARY

Bacteria and their relatives are the simplest cells. They are also the most common and widespread. Any environment that supports life contains bacteria.

Under the right conditions, bacteria may grow and multiply very rapidly. Reproduction is by binary fission.

A few bacteria can build their own food substances. Most, however, must use substances already formed by other organisms.

Some bacteria are harmful to human beings. These include bacteria that cause disease and that compete with us for food. However, many bacteria are harmless, while still others are very helpful. Bacteria in the soil are necessary for the breaking down of complex organic substances to forms that green plants can use. Other bacteria are used by human beings in industry.

QUESTIONS FOR REVIEW

1. Describe the contributions of Pasteur to bacteriology.
2. How do bacteria compare to viruses in size?
3. Classify bacteria into three groups based on shape.
4. List the structural differences between a bacterium and a generalized plant cell.
5. Describe the structure and function of bacterial flagella.
6. Distinguish between true movement and Brownian movement of bacteria.
7. List four environmental conditions needed for the growth of bacteria.
8. List the three major factors that limit the rapid growth of bacteria.
9. Describe the difference between heterotrophic bacteria and autotrophic bacteria.
10. Distinguish between aerobic and anaerobic bacteria.
11. Name several products of the fermentation of glucose by microorganisms.
12. List several ways in which bacteria may be beneficial to man.
13. Describe the methods used to prevent bacteria from spoiling food.
14. How are rickettsiae transmitted to humans?
15. Give an example of an infection caused by a spirochete.

APPLYING PRINCIPLES AND CONCEPTS

1. Give evidence that supports the claim that bacteria reproduce sexually. What may be the significance of sexual reproduction in bacteria?
2. Compare the limits on the growth rate of bacteria to those that limit the human population.
3. Discuss rickettsiae in relation to bacteria and viruses.

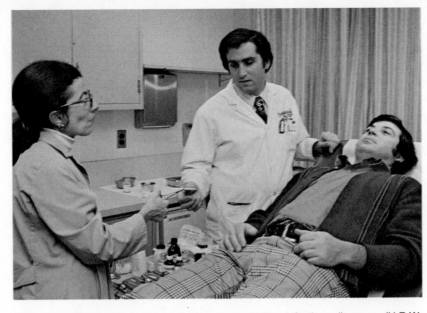

17-1 Science has made great advances in controlling infectious diseases. (H.R.W. Photo by Russell Dian)

Infectious Disease

OBJECTIVES

- DESCRIBE how Koch investigated an unknown disease.
- LIST the ways that infectious diseases can be transmitted.
- DESCRIBE how microorganisms cause disease.
- EXPLAIN the defenses the body has against disease.
- EXPLAIN the role of the interferon.
- DESCRIBE the various types of immunity.
- DESCRIBE the contributions of Edward Jenner.
- EXPLAIN immune therapy and antibiotic therapy.

KOCH AND ISOLATION OF PATHOGENIC ORGANISMS

We have already mentioned several *pathogenic,* or disease-causing, organisms. Among these were certain viruses, bacteria, rickettsiae, and spirochetes. Several yeasts, molds, protozoans, and worm parasites can also cause infectious diseases. In this chapter, however, we will deal mainly with pathogenic viruses and bacteria.

A good place to begin our story is with the work of Robert Koch. Koch, a German doctor, experimented with infectious diseases at the same time as Louis Pasteur. He was the first to isolate the bacteria that cause such major diseases as anthrax and tuberculosis. But just as important are the tools and methods he developed for the study of such organisms.

Koch's first great contribution to medicine involved the anthrax bacterium. Anthrax is an animal disease but can also infect human beings. From early times, anthrax had spread through sheep, cattle, and other herds. People often contracted the disease from infected animals or from the wool of infected sheep.

Koch began by studying animals that had died of anthrax. In their blood, he found swarms of rod-shaped bacteria. Were these the cause of anthrax? To find out, Koch inoculated a healthy mouse with some of the bacteria. The mouse soon died of anthrax. In its blood, Koch found large numbers of the same bacteria.

Koch now wanted to observe the bacteria as they multiplied. First, he took some sterile fluid. In a drop of this fluid, he placed a bit of tissue from a mouse containing anthrax bacteria. Through a microscope, he saw the bacteria multiply. Next, he transferred bacteria from one drop to another until no more mouse tissue or

Have students analyze Koch's work in terms of the scientific research method.

Point out to students the difference between an infectious disease and a chronic disease. Elicit examples from students. Point out to students that while cases of infectious diseases have decreased in recent years, there has been an increase in cases of chronic diseases. Discuss some of the reasons for this.

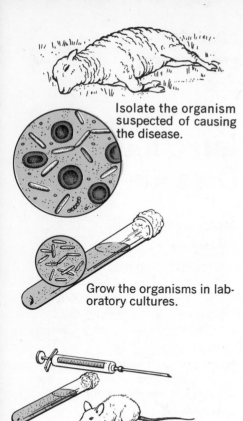

Isolate the organism suspected of causing the disease.

Grow the organisms in laboratory cultures.

Inoculate a healthy animal with the cultured organism and see if it contracts the disease.

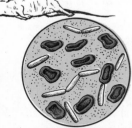

If the animal contracts the same disease, examine the diseased animal and re-isolate the organism that caused the disease.

17–2 Koch's procedure used to show that anthrax was caused by bacteria.

Some students may wish to report on some of the historical plagues caused by arthropod vectors.

blood was present. He then inoculated healthy mice with these laboratory-grown bacteria. The mice died of anthrax, and their blood was found to contain large numbers of the bacteria.

Koch concluded that anthrax was indeed caused by the bacteria. Later, he isolated tuberculosis bacteria by much the same method.

1. Isolate the organism suspected of causing the disease.

2. Grow the organism in laboratory cultures.

3. Inoculate a healthy animal with the cultured organism. See if the animal contracts the disease.

4. If the animal contracts the disease, examine the animal and re-isolate the organisms that caused the disease.

Koch developed several other important methods for the study of bacteria. He devised the technique for making bacteria smears on microscope slides, and discovered dyes for staining bacteria to make them more visible. He also developed several culture media of *gelatin* and *agar*. These act as nutrients for growing colonies of bacteria. Many of his stains, culture media, and methods for growing bacteria are still used today.

Scientists in many countries began to accept the findings and use the methods of Koch and Pasteur. The science of bacteriology developed rapidly. The battle against infectious disease is still going on. But a great many diseases have been brought under control since the days of the early giants of bacteriology.

HOW DISEASES ARE SPREAD

Pathogenic organisms enter the body in several different ways. Some, carried in *food* or *water*, enter through the mouth. Many diseases in this group center in the digestive system. Usually, the infectious organisms are present in the victim's excrement. This waste matter is highly infectious. Thus, the disease may be spread through direct contact with the victim or through contact with soiled clothing or other objects.

More often, however, such diseases are spread in food and water contaminated with waste matter. Among these diseases are typhoid fever, cholera, and dysentery. Of course, many diseases that do not center in the digestive system are also spread in contaminated food and water. **The best defense against all such diseases is the keeping up of good sanitary conditions.**

Other infections are spread through the *air*. Most of these diseases occur in the nose, throat, and lungs. They may be spread directly by sneezing or coughing, or indirectly by handling objects contaminated by infected people. Such diseases tend to spread very quickly and affect a large number of people. Colds, influenza, measles, mumps, whooping cough, and diphtheria are some of the well-known diseases spread through the air. Others are scarlet fever, tuberculosis, pneumonia, and meningitis.

Certain diseases produce sores on the skin and mucous membranes. Contact with material from these sores spreads the infection. The chicken pox and smallpox viruses are spread by such *contact infection*. The contact may be direct contact with the sores, or indirect contact with objects contaminated by matter from the sores. Syphilis and gonorrhea are other diseases spread by contact.

The skin is an effective barrier against bacteria. But if the skin is broken, *wound infections* may occur. This is why it is important to clean and properly treat even small wounds. Puncture wounds with little bleeding are especially dangerous because of the possibility of tetanus infection. Tetanus bacteria, which are anaerobic, enter the wound as spores on the objects that cause the puncture. The wound heals on the surface, leaving an airtight environment in which active tetanus cells quickly develop. Many other wound infections are dangerous and, if they spread, can even be fatal.

Human **immune carriers** present a special problem. These people show no signs of disease. Yet they carry living infectious organisms in their bodies and may transmit disease without even knowing it. In some diseases, victims who recover may remain immune carriers for weeks, months, or even years. This problem is especially great with typhoid fever, scarlet fever, diphtheria, and polio.

Arthropod carriers (insects and their relatives) also carry certain diseases. Houseflies and cockroaches carry infectious organisms on their bodies and feet. These infections may be spread by direct contact or through contaminated food or other objects. Other arthropods transmit infectious organisms through their bites. Typhus fever is transmitted by the human body louse, bubonic plague by the rat flea, and spotted fever by the tick. African sleeping sickness is transmitted by the tsetse fly. The *Anopheles* mosquito transmits the malaria parasite, and the *Aedes* mosquito the yellow fever virus.

HOW MICROORGANISMS CAUSE DISEASE

Pathogenic organisms may damage the body in several ways. One is by *destroying tissue.* In tuberculosis, for example, the main infection usually is in the lungs. As the tuberculosis organisms multiply, they destroy lung tissue cells, producing sores and bleeding. Many organisms, including streptococci, destroy blood corpuscles. In typhoid fever, the bacteria destroy cells of the intestine wall.

Many bacteria release poisonous protein substances called **exotoxins.** Exotoxins may enter the blood and reach tissues far from the site of the infection. For example, a puncture wound of the foot may result in a tetanus infection. But exotoxin given off by the tetanus bacteria may reach quite distant areas of the body, including the jaw muscles. Here, the poison causes spasms and paralysis. It is for this effect that tetanus is sometimes called *lockjaw.*

Rheumatic fever is caused by certain streptococci growing in the throat. These bacteria release exotoxins that inflame tissues in the joints and heart valves. The rash of scarlet fever is a reaction of the skin to an exotoxin. In diphtheria, exotoxins from an infection in the throat may damage tissues throughout the body.

Anopheles mosquito

Aedes mosquito

Human body louse

Rat flea

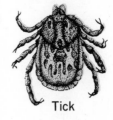

Tick

Tsetse fly

17–3 Arthropod carriers of infectious diseases. With what disease is each associated?

Ask students to find out the correct procedures for home food canning. Once the procedures are agreed upon, a list can be made up and sent home with the students.

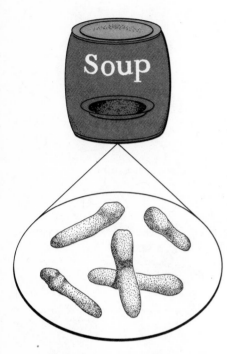

17-4 Botulism bacteria produce gases that cause cans of spoiled food to bulge.

Tears keep the surface of the eye from drying out and protect the eye from foreign objects. Ask students to suggest other functions of tears.

Infections of gamma globulin are often given when people are thought to have come in contact with certain infectious diseases. An example is hepatitis. Elicit from students the value of using gamma globulin for this purpose.

In some cases, exotoxins are formed by bacteria in foods. These **pre-formed toxins** produce *food poisoning* when the foods are eaten. The most deadly type of food poisoning is **botulism.** Like tetanus bacteria, botulism bacteria form spores. These spores may reach food before it is canned. If the food is not properly sterilized, the spores survive. When the food is sealed in an airtight container, the spores become active cells. These cells multiply and release exotoxins.

Botulism symptoms usually appear within 12 to 36 hours after the spoiled food is eaten. These symptoms include double vision, weakness, and paralysis that creeps from the neck to other body areas. Botulism is fatal in about 65 percent of the cases.

Heat destroys the botulism toxins. Thus, botulism can be prevented by boiling canned foods before tasting them. This is especially important with home-canned foods. Further, cans of spoiled food often bulge because of gas formed in them. Food from such cans should never be used.

Other organisms that form toxins in foods include certain *Salmonella* and *Staphylococcus* bacteria. These types of food poisoning are more common but less deadly than botulism.

Some bacteria form **endotoxins.** These poisons remain inside the bacteria and are released only when the bacterial cells die and break down. Endotoxins cause severe tissue reactions that may be fatal. Among the endotoxin diseases are typhoid fever, tuberculosis, cholera, bubonic plague, and bacterial dysentery.

STRUCTURAL DEFENSES AGAINST DISEASE

The human body normally hosts a huge number of bacteria and other organisms that are harmless or even helpful. At the same time, the body must defend itself against organisms that cause disease. The body's defenses work at several levels. We might think of each level as a line of defense in a battle.

The best way to avoid disease is to keep out harmful organisms in the first place. This is the job of the *first line* of defense, the *structural defenses*.

The most obvious structural defense is the *skin*. When unbroken, the skin is bacteria-proof. Further, salts and acids present in sweat are thought to destroy certain bacteria. However, the skin is not a perfect shield. Certain microorganisms may enter through natural openings such as pores or hair follicles.

The *mucous membranes* are also structural defenses. These membranes line the mouth, breathing passages, digestive tract, and genital tract. Mucous membrane cells secrete **mucus,** a slimy substance that traps bacteria on the membrane surface.

In the respiratory tract, cells that line the mucous membrane have tiny, hairlike growths. These sweep bacteria and other foreign particles up toward the throat. When such particles irritate the mucous membranes of the throat, a cough results. The particles, along with drops of fluid, are blown out into the air. Irritation of the mucous membranes in the nasal passages produces a sneeze.

Tears, secreted by tear glands, flow over the eyes constantly. Bacteria and other particles are washed into the tear ducts, which empty into the nasal passages. Both tears and mucus contain enzymes known as **lysozymes** (LICE-uh-ZIMES). These enzymes destroy the cell walls of many kinds of bacteria.

The hydrochloric *acid* secreted by glands in the stomach wall is another structural defense. Great numbers of bacteria enter the stomach in food. But few can survive the stomach's acid.

THE CELLULAR LEVEL OF DEFENSE

If bacteria somehow pass through the structural defenses of the body, they meet a second line of defense. This line operates in the body tissues themselves. The main defenders are **phagocytic** (FA-juh-SIT-ick) **cells.** These cells engulf bacteria and digest them with enzymes, including lysozymes.

Phagocytic cells are either free or fixed. Among the free ones are blood cells called **leucocytes.** These cells pass through the walls of capillaries and move through tissue fluids to the site of an infection. Here, they form a wall around the infectious organisms and begin to engulf them. As the battle goes on, a fluid of digested bacteria, broken-down leucocytes, and blood serum builds up. This is the substance known as **pus.**

Often, the tissues in the area of a local infection swell and become inflamed. The redness results from increased blood flow to the area. Lymph, a clear fluid present in the blood, also seeps into the infected region. The lymph carries bacteria and leucocytes that have engulfed bacteria away to lymph nodes, where they are filtered out.

The reactions mentioned so far occur at the main site of infection. However, invading organisms that enter the blood may be destroyed far from this site. Certain fixed phagocytic cells are found in small blood vessels in the liver, spleen, lungs, bone marrow, and other tissues. These cells capture and engulf bacteria and leucocytes that contain bacteria.

Another reaction to infection may be a rise in body temperature, or *fever.* This host reaction slows or halts the growth of many bacteria. It also sets off other body defenses and increases the general rate of chemical activity in the body. Fever is helpful unless it is too high or lasts too long. If this happens, the host's own cells may be damaged or destroyed.

ANTIBODY DEFENSES

In the third line of body defense, we come to the *antibodies.* The defenses of the first and second lines acted against any invading bacteria. But each type of antibody acts only against a specific disease organism or its products.

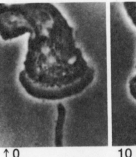

↑0   10 sec.

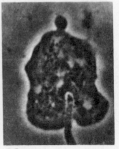

20 sec.   30 sec.

40 sec.   50 sec.

60 sec.   70 sec.

17–5 Phagocytosis. This series of photographs, taken at ten-second intervals, shows a human white blood cell engulfing a chain of *Bacillus megaterium* cells. (courtesy James G. Hirsch)

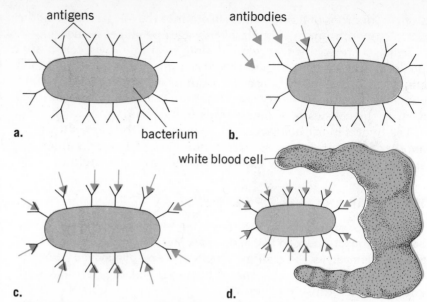

antigens   antibodies

bacterium

white blood cell

a.   b.

c.   d.

17-6 Antibodies produced by the host's body attach to the antigens on the invading bacterium. The bacterium then is easily engulfed by a white blood cell.

Invading bacteria and their toxins contain proteins that are foreign to the host organism. These foreign proteins can be "recognized" by body cells. Foreign proteins that set off a defense reaction in the host are known as *antigens.* A given antigen causes the host to produce specific antibodies. These antibodies combine with the antigens in the blood and, in the end, remove them.

Antibodies themselves are protein molecules. Found mainly in the blood serum, they are believed to come from the lymph nodes, spleen, and thymus gland. Production of specific antibodies begins within a few hours after an antigen appears in the body. Within a few days, the antibodies enter the bood. They increase in number over three or four weeks, then the rate of production slows down.

The level of a given antibody in the blood may decline very slowly. Antibodies may be produced at a relatively low rate for months or even years. If the host is again exposed to the antigen, production speeds up and the antibody level rises rapidly.

ORGAN TRANSPLANTS

Much research has been done in recent years in the field of immunology. This research has led to many advances in the field of medicine. Progress has been made in the control of infectious diseases, in cancer research, and in organ transplants.

Several kinds of organs can now be transplanted from one person to another. Probably the most common is the kidney transplant. Although the surgery may be successful, another problem often occurs. This is the problem of rejection.

As we have said, the body produced antibodies against foreign proteins. Unless the donor is an identical twin, with identical proteins, the transplant organ contains proteins that are antigens to the receiver's body. The receiver's body will produce antibodies to destroy the antigens of the new organ. Finally, the foreign organ is destroyed or rejected. The transplant is then a failure.

Medical research has developed drugs that lower the body's natural immunity protection. These drugs allow an organ transplant to heal without being rejected. But there is a danger. The patient is now defenseless against pathogenic organisms. Care must be taken to keep the transplant receiver in sterile surroundings. Despite the risk, transplant surgery has saved many lives.

CHEMICAL DEFENSES AGAINST VIRUSES

So far we have talked mainly about the body's defenses against bacteria. The chemical defenses against *viruses* are somewhat less well known. However, these defenses seem to be of two basic types.

The first type of defense has its effects *within* the cells of the host. This defense involves a protein substance called **interferon.** Interferon, discovered in 1957, was so named because it seemed to interfere with the action of viruses. Later studies indicate that the effect of interferon is less direct than at first believed.

When a virus invades a cell, its presence causes the cell to form interferon. This interferon is released from the cell and taken in to other cells. It is thought that interferon stimulates these cells to form *interferon messenger RNA*. The RNA, in turn, codes the building of an *antiviral protein*. This protein prevents invading viruses from taking control of the cells. Thus, viruses cannot multiply in cells protected by antiviral protein. The action of interferon and antiviral protein continues for about one to three weeks.

A second type of defense against viruses occurs *outside* the cell. About three days after a virus infection begins, *antiviral antibodies* appear in the blood serum. These antibodies combine with the viruses and make them noninfectious. Phagocytic white blood cells, which engulf virus particles, are also involved in this line of defense.

Antiviral antibodies are specific, acting only against specific viruses. However, they continue to be formed for long periods—sometimes for life. Thus, the interferon system and the antiviral antibodies are a double defense. Interferon acts rapidly but for a short time. Antibodies are produced more slowly but over a much longer time.

IMMUNITY

The ability of the body to resist an infectious disease is called *immunity*. Immunity may be *inborn* (present at birth), or it may be *acquired* during the lifetime of the individual.

Human beings have inborn immunity to most diseases that affect other animals and plants. Conditions in the human body simply do not support the growth of the organisms that cause these diseases. Our inherited structures, chemical makeup, body temperature, and other traits give us this immunity.

Recent studies indicate that a drug, *Propanediamine*, may be effective in curing the common cold. This drug stimulates the production of interferon.

The importance of immunization cannot be stressed too frequently. Point out to students that in 1969, for example, an outbreak of German measles was responsible for 30,000 miscarriages and the birth of 20,000 infants with congenital defects.

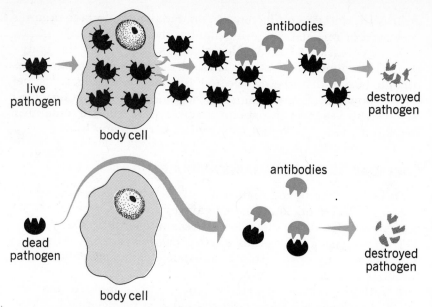

17–7 Natural immunization (top). An infectious pathogen enters the body cells. The pathogen multiplies and attacks other cells. The body responds by producing antibodies to destroy the invader. Artificial immunization (bottom). A dead or weakened pathogen is introduced into the body by vaccination. This pathogen doesn't infect the body cells. The body responds by producing antibodies to destroy the invader. These antibodies remain to destroy live pathogens, of the same type, that might enter the body later.

A schedule of immunizations should be presented and students should be urged to check on their own immunization history. Some states now require a complete immunization history to be updated yearly for entrance to school.

Ask students to find out about the regulations in their community concerning anti-rabies injections for dogs. Have them find out about what is done to an animal that has bitten someone.

Have students do some research into modern methods of treating suspected rabies.

The general immunity of one species to diseases that affect another species is called species immunity. The species immunity of human beings is not total. Several major diseases, such as tuberculosis, anthrax, and rabies, may be contracted by people from animals.

Acquired immunity may be active or passive. *Active immunity* may be acquired *naturally* as an individual recovers from certain infections. During these infections, the body produces specific antibodies against the pathogenic organisms or their products. The antibodies continue to be formed after recovery, giving permanent active immunity. Diphtheria, scarlet fever, measles, and mumps are some diseases that often result in this kind of immunity.

Active immunity may also be acquired *artificially* through the use of **vaccines.** Vaccines contain dead or weakened pathogenic organisms or their products. When introduced into the body, vaccines cause it to form antibodies just as the actual infection would. The difference is that the individual does not suffer the symptoms and dangers of the full-strength disease.

In *passive immunity*, antibodies themselves are introduced into an individual. Again, the immunity may be acquired artificially or naturally. In either case, it is only temporary.

Passive immunity is acquired naturally when an unborn infant receives antibodies from its mother's blood through the placenta. Antibodies also may be transferred to the infant in the first milk received from the immune mother. The immunity given the baby usually lasts from six months to a year.

Artificial passive immunity is acquired when an individual receives antibodies produced in other individuals or in animals. The part of the blood that contains antibodies is the **serum** (plural, *sera*). When serum containing antibodies is introduced into an individual, immediate immunity is given. In most cases, this immunity lasts from a few weeks to several months.

Table 17-1 TYPES OF IMMUNITY

TYPE		HOW ESTABLISHED	DURATION
INBORN species		through inherited anatomical, physiological, and chemical characteristics	permanent
ACQUIRED active	natural	by experiencing an infection during which contact with microorganisms or their products stimulates antibody production	usually lasting or permanent
	artificial	by injecting vaccines, toxoids, or other weakened bacterial products	usually from several years to permanent; booster shots may be necessary
passive	natural	by transfer of antibodies from mother to infant through the placenta prior to birth or in colostrum after birth	from 6 months to 1 year
	artificial	by injecting a serum containing antibodies	usually from 2 or 3 weeks to several months

EDWARD JENNER AND THE BIRTH OF IMMUNE THERAPY

Our knowledge of immunity and how to create it is an important part of medicine today. Yet this field of *immune therapy* had its beginning some two centuries ago, in the work of an English country doctor.

The doctor was Edward Jenner. Like all people of his time, Jenner was concerned about smallpox. There were terrible smallpox epidemics in those days, taking many lives. During one of the worst of these epidemics, Jenner made a discovery that changed the course of medical history.

Smallpox took its greatest toll in cities. But Jenner noticed that it seldom struck country people who worked around cattle. Further, most of these people had had cowpox, a minor disease whose main symptom was a small sore that left a scar. Had cowpox made its victims immune to smallpox? If so, why not deliberately infect people with cowpox to protect them from smallpox?

On May 14, 1796, Jenner had a chance to test his theory. Jenner made two small cuts on the arm of an eight-year-old child. Into these cuts, he placed matter taken from a cowpox sore on another person. The child developed a cowpox sore which healed and left a scar.

Was the child now immune to smallpox? Jenner inoculated the child with matter from a smallpox sore. No signs of smallpox appeared. The child was immune to smallpox!

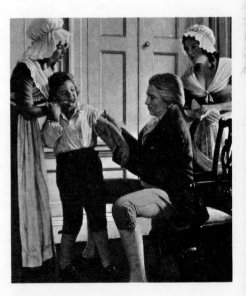

17-8 The first vaccination. Dr. Edward Jenner inoculates James Phipps with material taken from a cowpox sore. (© 1960, Parke, Davis & Co.)

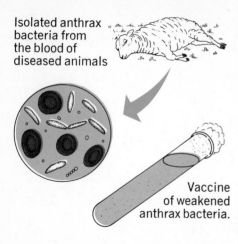

Isolated anthrax bacteria from the blood of diseased animals

Vaccine of weakened anthrax bacteria.

Two groups of animals were selected.

Experimental group   Control group

Injected the experimental group with the anthrax vaccine.

Twelve days later, the experimental group received a second injection.

After two more weeks, both groups of animals were injected with living anthrax bacteria.

Two days later . . . .

Experimental group   Control group

all animals healthy   all animals dead
and alive.   or dying

17-9 Pasteur's experiment with anthrax.

Jenner wrote a paper explaining what he had done. He called his method *vaccination*. At first, other doctors refused to listen to Jenner. Many townspeople even joined in anti-vaccination campaigns. Slowly, however, doctors and their patients accepted vaccination. In the end, smallpox epidemics were wiped out.

PASTEUR'S EXPERIMENTS WITH ANTHRAX

About 80 years after Jenner's first vaccination, Louis Pasteur did a famous series of experiments on immunity.

Pasteur made a vaccine from anthrax bacteria that were weakened after being isolated from the blood of diseased animals. He claimed that this vaccine would protect healthy animals against anthrax. Other scientists challenged him to prove this claim. Pasteur was ready for the challenge. He separated 48 healthy animals, mostly sheep, into an experimental group and a control group. He injected the animals in one group with the anthrax vaccine. Twelve days later, he gave them a second injection.

After two more weeks, Pasteur injected all 48 animals with living anthrax bacteria. Two days later, the scientists met at the pens where the animals were kept. To their surprise, all of the animals that had received vaccine were alive and healthy. All of the others were dead or dying of anthrax. This famous experiment marked an important advance in the battle against disease.

PASTEUR'S RABIES VACCINE

Late in his life, Pasteur turned his attention to one of the most feared of all diseases, rabies. In Pasteur's time, rabies was fairly common in dogs and other animals. Often, the rabies virus was transmitted to human beings by bites from these animals. The virus slowly destroyed tissue in the brain and spinal cord. After a period of a few weeks to a few months, the victim was certain to die in agony.

Pasteur found that he could cause rabies in a healthy dog by injecting it with brain tissue from a diseased one. Then came the breakthrough. Tissue from the spinal cord of a rabid animal was dried for 14 days. When this tissue was injected into a healthy animal, it did not cause rabies. It had lost its strength. Tissue dried for 13 days was only slightly stronger.

The discovery that infected tissue lost its strength with aging and drying led Pasteur to further experiments. He injected diseased brain tissue 14 days old into a healthy dog. The next day, he injected 13-day-old material. The injections of stronger and stronger material continued day by day.

On the fourteenth day, the dog received full-strength rabies virus. Yet the animal showed no ill effects. The series of injections had made it immune to rabies.

Would the same treatment work for human beings? Pasteur hardly dared try it. But in 1885, he did try this method on a child

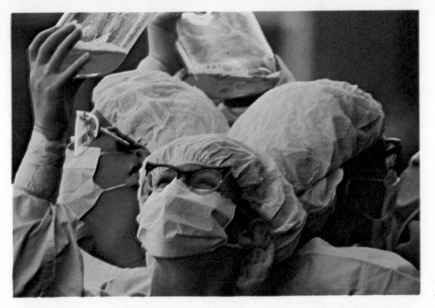

17-10 A lab technician preparing a
vaccination. (Chas. Pfizer & Co.)

who had been bitten by a rabid dog. It was the only chance to save
the child's life. Pasteur's treatment worked. After several treatments, the first human ever made immune to rabies was sent home
with no ill effects.

Since that time, the Pasteur treatment, with minor changes, has
saved the lives of a great many people bitten by rabid animals.

CREATING IMMUNITY TO DIPHTHERIA

Since earliest times, diphtheria was one of the worst epidemic
killers, especially of children. The bacteria that cause this disease grow in a thick membrane on the back wall of the throat. This
membrane may block the opening to the lungs and choke the
victim. Even more dangerous are the exotoxins given off by the
bacteria. These poisons may cause serious damage to the heart,
nervous system, and other organs.

Through the efforts of several scientists, an effective weapon
against diphtheria was found in the early part of this century. It was
noticed that laboratory animals that recovered from the disease
has immunity to it. The blood serum of these animals now containing an **antitoxin** which prevented the diphtheria toxin from
taking effect.

Serum containing antitoxin formed in sheep began to be used to
give human beings immunity. However, this immunity lasted only
a few weeks. The antitoxin, it seemed, was slowly destroyed in human blood. More work has since been done to make this procedure
safer.

OTHER EXAMPLES OF IMMUNE THERAPY

The same principles of immune therapy that we have been discussing have been used against other major diseases. An example is

the Sabin polio vaccine. This vaccine contains a weakened strain of polio virus. Taken by mouth, the vaccine stimulates the production of antibodies that work against real polio viruses.

Some vaccines contain viruses that have been killed rather than merely weakened. Examples are typhoid vaccine and Salk polio vaccine. Even though the viruses in these vaccines are dead, they cause antibody production and create immunity.

Still other vaccines contain viruses that have been made harmless by chemical treatment. Such vaccines include those for influenza and yellow fever.

For other diseases, blood *serum* containing antibodies or anti-toxins may be used instead of vaccines. Sera give immediate passive immunity and back up natural antibody production during an infection. The early treatments of diphtheria were examples of the use of a serum. Today, serum containing the blood protein *gamma globulin* is used against several infections.

CHEMOTHERAPY

Chemistry as well as biology plays a major role in modern medicine. In *chemotherapy*, specific chemical compounds are used to destroy pathogenic organisms without harming the host.

The early development of chemotherapy owes much to the brilliant German chemist Paul Ehrlich. Ehrlich spent many years trying to find a drug that would kill syphilis organisms in the blood without damaging the blood or other parts of the body. After 605 attempts had failed, he finally succeeded. The 606th drug, an arsenic compound called *salvarsan*, was used in treating syphilis long before penicillin.

Another German scientist, Gerhard Domagk (DOE-mahk), discovered in 1932 that the red dye *prontosil* was effective in killing germs. He used this drug to save the life of his own daughter, who was dying of a streptococcus infection. Later it was learned that most of the power of prontosil lay in only one part, called *sulfanila-mide* (SULL-fuh-NILL-uh-MIDE). This was the first of an important drug family known as the *sulfa drugs*. Though they are used in treating many diseases, sulfa drugs may be dangerous and should be taken only on the advice of a doctor.

ANTIBIOTICS

The chemicals called *antibiotics* are produced by living organisms, unlike the drugs used in chemotherapy. Antibiotics are used in treating many infectious diseases today.

Penicillin is the best known antibiotic, and it was also the first. It was discovered by accident in 1929 by Sir Alexander Fleming of Scotland. Fleming was working with cultures of staphylococcus bacteria. In some of the cultures, he noticed fluffy masses of mold growing. In the area around each mold colony, no bacteria would grow. It seemed that the mold gave off some substance that killed the bacteria. This probably was a helpful adaptation, since the mold and the bacteria were competing for the same food supply.

Later, the mold was identified as *Penicillium notatum*. The substance given off by it was named *penicillin*. However, penicillin was not used against infections until World War II. At that time, a great search was on for substances that would help cure wound infections. Attention turned to Fleming's work and, with his help, penicillin was developed, tested, and put to use. Penicillin may be taken in several forms, including liquid, tablets, and ointment. However, *it should never be taken in any form unless recommended by a doctor.*

Streptomycin is another antibiotic substance. It is given off by a soil organism known as *Streptomyces griseus*. Both this organism and streptomycin itself were discovered by Dr. Selman Waksman at Rutgers University. Waksman was studying the disappearance of disease organisms when the body of a diseased animal is buried. He found that this effect was caused by streptomycin in the soil.

Streptomycin is very effective against tuberculosis. It also has some effect against whooping cough, some forms of pneumonia, and several other diseases. At one time, streptomycin ranked in importance with penicillin. Today, new antibiotics have largely replaced it, though it remains valuable in treating tuberculosis.

A large number of different antibiotics have now been developed. Many of them are of a type known as *tetracycline*. The ideal antibiotic is one that works against a wide range of diseases without harming the host.

DANGERS OF ANTIBIOTICS

No antibiotic should be used unless prescribed by a doctor. There are two basic reasons for this.

17-11 The mold *Penicillium notatum* growing on a petri-dish culture. The antibiotic penicillin is obtained from this mold. (Chas. Pfizer & Co.)

17-12 Various steps in antibiotic production. (a) Testing activity against specific bacteria. (b) Culturing antibiotic organisms on agar. (c) A transfer device used to inoculate large vats with antibiotic organisms. (d) Extraction and purification of antibiotics from the producing organisms. (courtesy Eli Lilly and Co.)

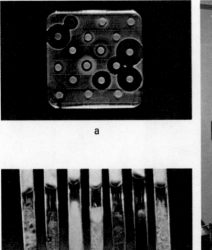

a

b

c

d

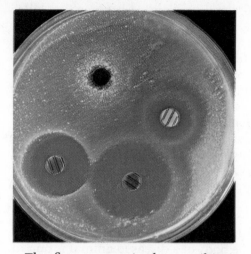

17-13 Each of the four paper disks has been soaked in a different antibiotic and then placed in a bacterial culture. The size of the zone of no growth shows the effectiveness of each antibiotic. (Walter Dawn)

The first reason is that antibiotics may produce harmful side effects. For example, quite a few people have an allergic reaction to penicillin. In some cases, this reaction is strong enough to be fatal. Certain other antibiotics destroy the normal bacteria population of the intestines. Other bacteria may then grow in the intestines and cause diarrhea or other disturbances.

A second reason for caution in using antibiotics involves adaptation in bacteria. Like all organisms, bacteria vary. Some may have traits that allow them to resist the effects of an antibiotic. These bacteria will tend to survive repeated use of the antibiotic. In the end, a whole new strain may develop in which all members resist the antibiotic. For example, penicillin was very effective against staphylococcus bacteria for many years. But several new strains of these bacteria now resist penicillin. These and other strains that resist antibiotics are becoming more and more of a problem in medicine.

17-14 Determining the effectiveness of different strengths of the same antibiotic against four microorganisms. Each culture medium contains an increasingly larger dose of the same antibiotic. The bacteria in the upper right hand corner of each dish are least affected by the antibiotic. (Society of American Bacteriologists)

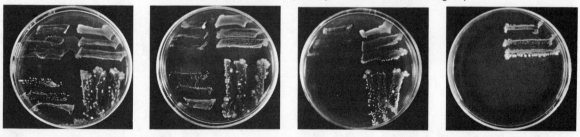

SUMMARY Throughout history, people have been plagued by a wide range of infectious diseases. Until fairly recent times, there was no real defense against most of these diseases. Then, through the work of Jenner, Koch, Pasteur, and many others, the system of immune therapy was built up. People could now be given immunity to certain diseases through the use of vaccines. In other cases, sera could be introduced with antibodies that would fight the infection.

Today, other weapons are also available for fighting disease-causing bacteria. In chemotherapy, specific chemicals such as the sulfa drugs are used against infections. Among the most important drugs used in modern medicine are the antibiotics. These are bacteria-killing substances formed by living organisms.

Immune therapy has largely wiped out the great epidemics of such diseases as smallpox that once occurred. Drugs and antibiotics easily cure many infections that once would have been fatal. Many advances remain to be made, but we have come a long way already.

BIOLOGICALLY SPEAKING

immune carriers	lysozymes	immunity
arthropod carrier	phagocytic cells	species immunity
exotoxins	leucocytes	vaccines
pre-formed toxins	pus	serum
botulism	antibodies	antitoxin
endotoxins	antigens	chemotherapy
mucus	interferon	antibiotics

QUESTIONS FOR REVIEW

1. List the four steps in Koch's investigation of anthrax disease.
2. Describe the various ways that infectious organisms are spread.
3. List several examples of air-borne infections.
4. Name several arthropod carriers of infections and the diseases with which they are associated.
5. What is meant by immune carrier?
6. Distinguish between exotoxins and endotoxins.
7. How does food poisoning occur? Give one example.
8. List the principal structural defenses of the body.
9. Describe how leucocytes help to defend against disease.
10. In what way is fever an important body defense?
11. What is an antibody?
12. Describe recent discoveries in chemical defenses against viruses.
13. Distinguish between natural and artificial immunity.
14. What is the difference between a vaccine and a serum?
15. How are antibiotics different from other drugs used in chemotherapy?

APPLYING PRINCIPLES AND CONCEPTS

1. Discuss immunity in terms of future possible uses in treatment of cancer.
2. Discuss the contributions of Edward Jenner to the rise of immune therapy.
3. What is the major problem with organ transplants? What can be done to help this problem?
4. Explain the idea that natural selection produces bacteria resistant to antibiotics.

chapter eighteen

The Protozoans

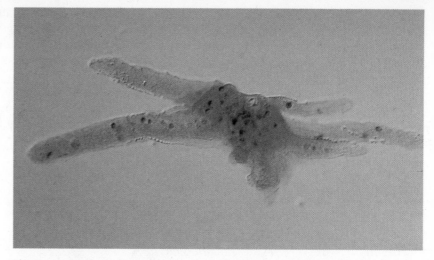

18-1 The ameba is a typical example of a protozoan. (Manfred Kage, Peter Arnold)

OBJECTIVES

- DEFINE Protozoa.
- IDENTIFY the parts of the *Ameba, Euglena, Paramecium,* and *Plasmodium.*
- DESCRIBE the various methods of locomotion in protozoans.
- DESCRIBE the methods of reproduction in protozoans.
- EXPLAIN the life cycle of *Plasmodium.*
- List some pathogenic protozoans.
- DESCRIBE the economic importance or protozoans.

WHAT ARE PROTOZOANS?

In older classification systems, the phylum *Protozoa* was included in the animal kingdom. (The word *protozoa* itself means "first animal.") The members of this phylum were a large number of related one-celled organisms. They were further divided into four classes according to their means of movement. **However, many protozoans are not clearly animal. For this reason, most biologists today place them in the kingdom Protista.** The four different classes are now thought of as four separate phyla.

Some biologists estimate that there are 15,000 protozoan species. Others believe that there may be as many as 100,000. While all protozoans are alike in certain ways, they often differ greatly from species to species. You will see some of these differences as we study members of each of the four protozoan phyla.

Phylum Sarcodina—Ameba

BITS OF "LIVING JELLY"

The genus *Amoeba* includes several interesting protozoan species. At first glance, you might mistake an ameba for something nonliving—a microscopic bit of jelly, say. Yet this tiny blob of grayish "jelly" is a complete living organism. It moves, feels, reproduces, and performs all other life functions.

Through the microscope, an ameba appears as a shapeless mass of cytoplasm surrounded by a thin plasma membrane. In an active ameba, you will see that the cytoplasm has a constant flowing motion. This streaming cytoplasm presses against the plasma membrane and pushes out projections called **pseudopodia** (soo-doe-POE-dee-uh).

Era	Period	bacteria	protozoans	fungi	algae
Cenozoic	Quaternary				
Cenozoic	Tertiary				
Mesozoic	Cretaceous				
Mesozoic	Jurassic				
Mesozoic	Triassic				
Paleozoic	Permian				
Paleozoic	Pennsylvania (Late Carboniferous)				
Paleozoic	Mississippian (Early Carboniferous)				
Paleozoic	Devonian				
Paleozoic	Silurian				
Paleozoic	Ordovician				
Paleozoic	Cambrian				
(Pre-Cambrian)					

18–2 Time scale of protozoans compared to the other protists.

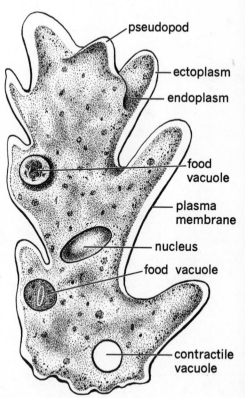

Pseudopodia (singular, *pseudopod*) means "false feet." The name is fitting, since amebas move by means of their pseudopodia. The motion is a sort of flowing, with new pseudopodia reaching out and old ones disappearing back into the cytoplasm. **On the basis of this *ameboid movement*, amebas are placed in the protist phylum Sarcodina.**

A closer look at an ameba such as *Amoeba proteus* shows that the cytoplasm is of two types. A clear, watery ***ectoplasm*** is found just inside the cell membrane. Inside the ectoplasm is the denser, grainier ***endoplasm,*** which looks like gray jelly with pepper sprinkled through it. The inner part of the endoplasm is more fluid than the outer part and flows more rapidly when the ameba moves. A disk-shaped nucleus is present which changes position as the cytoplasm flows.

Amebas live in water. They are found in slime at the bottom of streams and ponds, and on the leaves of water plants. The oxygen needed for life enters through the cell membrane by diffusion from the surrounding water. Carbon dioxide and soluble wastes such as ammonia pass out through the membrane in the same way.

Much useless water also enters the ameba cell, mainly by osmosis. If the ameba could not rid itself of this water, it would swell and burst like a balloon. This does not happen, of course. Instead, the extra water gathers in a *contractile vacuole*. When this vacuole reaches a certain size, it contracts sharply. The water is squeezed out through a temporary break in the cell membrane.

18–3 The structure of an ameba. This protist changes its shape as it moves.

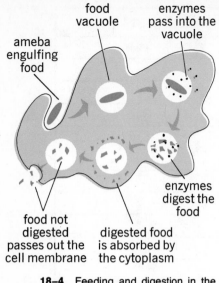

food vacuole

enzymes pass into the vacuole

ameba engulfing food

enzymes digest the food

food not digested passes out the cell membrane

digested food is absorbed by the cytoplasm

18–4 Feeding and digestion in the ameba.

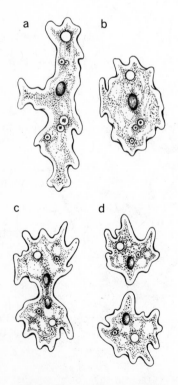

a b

c d

18–5 The ameba reproduces by simple cell division.

HOW AMEBAS GET FOOD

The food supply for amebas includes cells of algae and of certain other protists. When an ameba contacts such a cell, it simply engulfs the cell by surrounding it with pseudopodia. The food is taken into the ameba cell as a *food vacuole.* Part of the cell membrane of the ameba surrounds this vacuole. A new membrane quickly forms at the point where the food entered the ameba cell.

Digestion is carried on by enzymes formed in the cytoplasm. These enzymes pass into the food vacuole and act on the food. Digested food is absorbed by the cytoplasm. It is now ready for use as an energy source or as raw material for building more protoplasm. Particles that are not digested remain in the vacuole and may pass out at any point on the cell membrane.

RESPONSE IN THE AMEBA

Amebas respond to the conditions around them. Though they have no eyes, they are sensitive to light and seek dim or dark areas. Neither do they have nerve endings for a sense of touch. Yet they react to movement around them and move away from objects they touch.

Amebas also respond to food. When food substances are placed in an ameba culture, the amebas move toward the food. This response may be caused by chemicals given off by the foods.

Some species of ameba respond to conditions such as dryness, cold, or lack of food. Such amebas become inactive and withdraw into a round mass called a *cyst.* When conditions improve, the amebas become active again.

REPRODUCTION OF AMEBAS

Under good conditions, an ameba may double its volume in a day or two. At this point, it reproduces by simple cell division. First, the nucleus divides and the two daughter nuclei move to opposite ends of the cell. The cell then pinches in at the center, and the two halves pull apart. Each daughter cell has a nucleus and is capable of independent life and growth. The division itself takes about an hour.

Phylum Ciliophora—Paramecium

PARAMECIA—COMPLEX PROTOZOANS

Amebas are fairly simple cells with few specialized structures. In the genus *Paramecium,* we come to a much more complex form of one-celled life. Species of this genus live mainly in quiet or stagnant ponds. Great numbers of paramecia are found in the scums that form on such ponds.

The paramecium cell is shaped like a slipper. Although they are flexible enough to bend, paramecia do not change shape like amebas. Their definite shape results from a thick outer membrane, the **pellicle,** which surrounds the cell membrane.

The most striking trait of paramecia when seen through the microscope is their movement. This movement appears to be very rapid. Actually, it is no more than about seven centimeters per minute. But the microscope magnifies distance just as it magnifies size.

Paramecia move by means of hairlike threads of cytoplasm called cilia. These cilia are arranged in rows and beat back and forth like tiny oars. They cover the whole cell but are most easily seen at the edges. Cilia contain protein filaments, which biologists believe contract and cause the beating. Cilia can beat either forward or backward, moving the cell in either direction and allowing it to turn. **This kind of movement places paramecia in the protist phylum Ciliophora.**

Another striking feature of the paramecium is the **oral groove** along one side of the cell. The cell also has a definite front end, or **anterior** part, which is rounded. The rear end, or **posterior** part, is more pointed. The oral groove runs from the anterior toward the posterior end.

Cilia line the oral groove and cause the paramecium to spin around its long axis as it swims. More important, these cilia sweep food particles back toward the **mouth pore.** This pore, in turn, opens into a funnel-like **gullet** reaching into the cytoplasm. Bacteria and other foods forced into the gullet are formed into a *food vacuole.*

When a food vacuole reaches a certain size, it breaks away from the gullet. The movement of the cytoplasm carries the vacuole around the cell. During this movement, foods are digested and absorbed as in amebas. Undigested particles are passed out through the **anal pore.** This tiny opening in the pellicle is found near the posterior end. It is completely closed except when in use and is quite hard to see.

A contractile vacuole for removing extra water is found near each end of the cell. Around each vacuole are *canals* leading into the cytoplasm. These canals enlarge as they fill with water, which is then passed on to the central part of the vacuole. From there, the water is emptied out through an opening in the cell surface. Biologists estimate that in just 30 minutes a paramecium pumps out a volume of water equal to the whole cell content.

Most other waste products appear to pass out through the cell membrane by diffusion. Respiration involves diffusion of oxygen and carbon dioxide through the plasma membrane and pellicle.

RESPONSE IN PARAMECIA

Like amebas, paramecia have no specialized sense organs. Yet paramecia, too, respond to conditions around them.

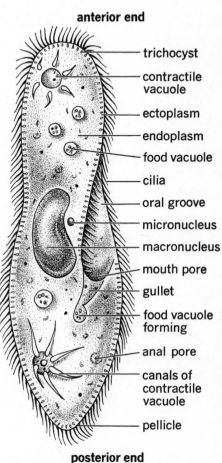

anterior end

trichocyst
contractile vacuole
ectoplasm
endoplasm
food vacuole
cilia
oral groove
micronucleus
macronucleus
mouth pore
gullet
food vacuole forming
anal pore
canals of contractile vacuole
pellicle

posterior end

18–6 The structure of the paramecium. In what ways are the paramecium and the ameba alike? In what ways are they different?

Amebas may remain in cysts for many years. Some have been known to remain in this condition for forty-nine years and then have assumed their original shapes.

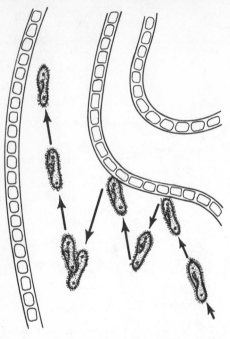

18-7 The avoiding reaction in the paramecium.

Except when feeding, the cells swim constantly. When they bump into something, they reverse, turn, and swim off in a new direction. This kind of trial-and-error response is called the **avoiding reaction.** Paramecia respond in the same way to extreme heat or cold, presence of chemicals, and lack of oxygen. They tend to move into slightly acid areas. This is a helpful trait since bacteria, a major source of food for paramecia, live in such areas.

Paramecia also have a defense response. Just inside the pellicle are the **trichocysts,** which appear as tiny lines through the microscope. When a larger protozoan approaches, the trichocysts shoot special threads of protoplasm out into the water. These threads are quite long and give the paramecium a bristly appearance. This response may be caused by chemicals given off by the larger organism. Adding acetic acid or iodine to water containing paramecia often causes their trichocysts to "fire."

REPRODUCTION IN PARAMECIA

Paramecia have two different kinds of nuclei, both found near the center of the cell. A large **macronucleus** controls normal cell activity. A much smaller **micronucleus** functions during reproduction. Some species have more than one micronucleus.

Paramecia reproduce by *cell fission*. Both the macronucleus and micronucleus divide during this process. Under good conditions, fission may occur two or three times a day.

From time to time, paramecia also reproduce by *conjugation*. After a series of nuclear divisions and other steps, two paramecia exchange micronuclei, then continue to divide by fission. This mixing of genetic material provides for more change of variation. **Variation increases the chances for the species to survive.**

a. fission

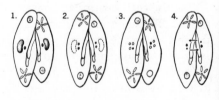

b. conjugation

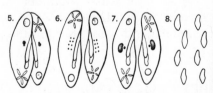

18-8 The two types of reproduction characteristic of paramecia: (a) fission, and (b) conjugation.

Phylum Mastigophora—Euglena

A PROTOZOAN THAT SEEMS PART PLANT

Several species of the genus *Euglena* live in ponds and streams. Under the microscope, euglenas have an oval or pear shape. The anterior end is rounded, while the posterior end usually is pointed.

Euglenas were classed as plants in some systems and as animals in others, since the cells have certain traits of both kingdoms. Today, they are often placed in the protist phylum Mastigophora (MASS-ti-GAH-fuh-ruh). **This classification is based on the fact that the euglena swims by means of a flagellum.** This flagellum, at the anterior end of the cell, whirls in a way that pulls the cell through the water.

Unlike any other member of its phylum, the euglena has a second method of movement. This *euglenoid* (you-GLEE-NOID) *movement* involves a gradual change in the shape of the cell. First, the cell becomes rounded as the posterior part is drawn forward. Then the anterior part is stretched forward, resulting in movement. This contraction and stretching is caused by specialized *contractile fibers* in the cell.

A typical euglena is *Euglena gracilis*. This cell is surrounded by a thin, flexible pellicle. At the anterior end, a small gullet opening leads into a larger *reservoir.* However, euglenas have never been seen to take in food through their gullets. Thus, this structure may serve only as an attachment point for the flagellum. A contractile vacuole near the reservoir pumps out extra water.

A red *eyespot* is clearly seen near the gullet. This tiny bit of specialized protoplasm is highly sensitive to light. It helps the euglena to seek out the bright areas where it thrives best. **Light is helpful because most species of euglena carry on photosynthesis.** Perhaps the most striking feature of the euglena is the presence of many oval chloroplasts spread through the cell.

Besides forming foods by photosynthesis, the euglena can absorb organic materials through the cell membrane. In fact, some species lose their chlorophyll during long periods of darkness and survive only by absorbing needed substances.

A large nucleus containing a nucleolus is near the center of the euglena cell. Reproduction is by cell fission. Under good conditions, euglenas divide about once a day. Thus, a single euglena may give rise to millions of daughter cells in less than a month. Great numbers of euglenas in ponds and streams often make the water look bright green.

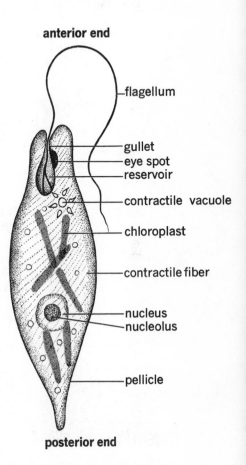

anterior end

flagellum

gullet
eye spot
reservoir

contractile vacuole

chloroplast

contractile fiber

nucleus
nucleolus

pellicle

posterior end

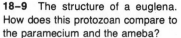

18–9 The structure of a euglena. How does this protozoan compare to the paramecium and the ameba?

Ask students to classify euglena according to its structure and other characteristics. Have them defend their position as to its classification.

Table 18-1 COMPARISON OF THREE PROTOZOANS

	AMEBA	PARAMECIUM	EUGLENA
FORM	variable	slipper-shaped	pear-shaped or oval
LOCOMOTION	pseudopodia (ameboid movement)	cilia	flagellum or euglenoid movement
SPEED	slow	rapid	rapid or slow
FOOD-GETTING	pseudopodia surrounding food	cilia in oral groove, mouth cavity, and gullet	photosynthesis or absorption
DIGESTION	in food vacuole	in food vacuole	in cytoplasm
ABSORPTION	from food vacuole by diffusion and cyclosis	from food vacuole by diffusion and cyclosis	from cytoplasm by diffusion and cyclosis
RESPIRATION	diffusion of O_2 and CO_2 through plasma membrane	diffusion of O_2 and CO_2 through plasma membrane and pellicle	diffusion of O_2 and CO_2 through plasma membrane and pellicle
EXCRETION	through plasma membrane	through plasma membrane and pellicle	through plasma membrane and pellicle
SENSITIVITY	responds to heat, light, contact, chemicals	responds to heat, light, contact, chemicals	eyespot sensitive to light; responds also to heat, contact, chemicals
REPRODUCTION	fission	fission and conjugation	fission

Phylum Sporozoa—Plasmodium

PROTOZOAN PARASITES THAT FORM SPORES

Protozoans in the protist phylum Sporozoa have no method of movement on their own. These protists are all parasites. They live by absorbing food from the cells or body fluids of a host organism. Many species live in two hosts during their life cycle.

Reproduction is by means of spores. First, the nucleus divides into many small nuclei. A small amount of cytoplasm surrounds each nucleus, forming a spore. The parent cell breaks apart and releases these spores, which can grow into mature cells. In some species, spores are protected by a thick coat. In others, there is only a plasma membrane.

A good example of this type of protozoan is *Plasmodium*. This is the organism that causes malaria in human beings and other warm-blooded animals. Malaria is transmitted by the female *Anopheles* mosquito. When this mosquito bites a person who has malaria, some of the *Plasmodium* cells are taken into the mosquito's stomach. They grow, reproduce, work their way into the insect's blood, and are carried to the salivary glands.

When the infected mosquito bites another person, the parasite is injected into the person's blood. At this point, the parasite is in a tiny, spindle-shaped form. This stage reaches the liver and develops for about two weeks. The parasites then enter the blood again and attack red corpuscles. In each corpuscle, a parasite produces 10 to 20 spores, destroying the corpuscle.

At very regular intervals, the corpuscles burst. The spores spread out through the blood and invade other corpuscles. A billion or more corpuscles may be destroyed within two weeks after the parasites enter the blood from the liver. The regular bursting of corpuscles releases waste products as well as spores into the bloodstream. These substances cause the chills, high fever, and sweating seen in malaria victims.

Another disease caused by a protozoan is African sleeping sickness. It is transmitted by the tsetse fly. The protozoan is a *trypanosome*. Review the term vector and its relationship to protozoan-caused diseases.

18–10   The life cycle of *Plasmodium*, the parasitic protozoan that causes malaria in man.

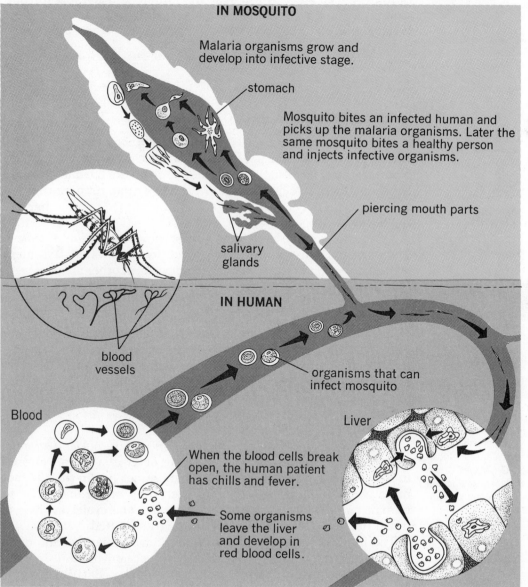

IN MOSQUITO

Malaria organisms grow and develop into infective stage.

stomach

Mosquito bites an infected human and picks up the malaria organisms. Later the same mosquito bites a healthy person and injects infective organisms.

piercing mouth parts

salivary glands

blood vessels

IN HUMAN

organisms that can infect mosquito

Blood

Liver

When the blood cells break open, the human patient has chills and fever.

Some organisms leave the liver and develop in red blood cells.

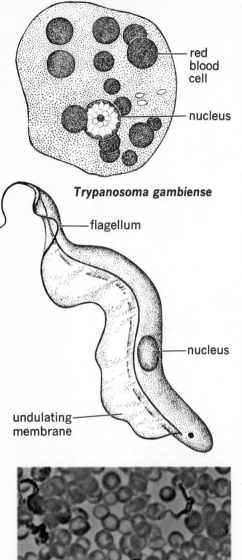

Entamoeba histolytica

red
blood
cell

nucleus

Trypanosoma gambiense

flagellum

nucleus

undulating
membrane

18–11 Two protozoans pathogenic in man—the ameba that causes amebic dysentery (top) and the flagellated protozoan that causes African sleeping sickness. Organisms of the latter type can be seen among the human blood cells in the photomicrograph. (Walter Dawn)

After several cycles of forming spores, some of the parasites enter a sexual stage and form gametes. These structures continue the cycle in the stomach of a mosquito that bites the infected person.

In fighting malaria, it is important to isolate infected people from *Anopheles* mosquitoes. This interrupts the life cycle of the parasite and prevents its spread to other people. It would be even better to destroy the *Anopheles* population itself. But this is difficult to do, especially in areas with many marshes where the mosquitos breed.

Several drugs are effective in both treating and preventing malaria. Quinine has been used for many years. Other drugs have been produced since World War II. Quinine and some of the new drugs may be prescribed for people traveling to areas where there is danger of malaria.

OTHER PATHOGENIC PROTOZOANS

Almost all people and animals are infected with some type of protozoan. The usual place for these infections is the intestine, where a great many protozoans may flourish. Some of these protists are harmless or even helpful. Others live on material in the intestine, robbing the host of food. Some may enter the blood and be carried to other parts of the host's body.

An ameba parasite causes the disease known as *amebic dysentery*. The parasite is usually transmitted in food or water. Dysentery is most common in the tropics but can occur in other areas as well. The infection centers in the large intestine. The parasites feed on the intestine wall and blood cells, causing bleeding ulcers.

Cysts containing inactive ameba cells are excreted in the feces of infected people. In many areas, sewage disposal methods are crude, and human waste may be used as fertilizer. It is in these areas that amebic dysentery is most common. Another problem is that of *human carriers.* Many people carry the parasite but have only mild symptoms, if any, of the disease. Several drugs are effective against dysentery, but proper sanitary measures are far more important.

Two protozoans known as *trypanosomes* cause *African sleeping sickness.* These oganisms move by means of flagella and are classed in the same phylum as *Euglena.* Trypanosomes live in the blood of many African mammals and insects. They are transmitted to human beings by the bite of the *tsetse fly.* The cycle involved is much like the one by which malaria is transmitted.

The infection caused by the trypanosomes is serious and often fatal in human beings. In the blood, the organisms multiply for several weeks before the first symptoms appear. Early symptoms include headache, fever, and general fatigue. As more blood cells are destroyed, the victim becomes weak and anemic. Finally, the trypanosomes attack the central nervous system. This results in a long coma, followed by almost certain death.

Several drugs are effective in destroying trypanosomes in the blood. However, treatment must begin early. There is little hope after the organisms reach the central nervous system.

As with malaria and the *Anopheles* mosquito, the best measure against sleeping sickness would be to wipe out the tsetse fly. However, the fly is found in such a vast area that this is almost impossible. Also, the process would require killing great numbers of infected animals.

ECONOMIC IMPORTANCE OF PROTOZOANS

Besides the points already discussed, protozoans are important in other ways. For one thing, protozoans are the food supply for a great many small animals. Thus, they are an important link in the food chain.

Further, certain protozoans secrete a hard wall of mineral substances. As the organisms die, their tiny skeletons sink to the sea floor. Over many years, as the earth's surface changes, these deposits dry and harden. Limestone, chalk, and flint are formed in this way.

Protozoans help to digest food in the intestines of some animals, including cattle. Protozoans in the intestines of termites help in digesting the wood that these insects eat.

Ask students to report on other protozoan-caused diseases. They should include the organism, mode of transmission, symptoms, and treatment.

Discuss with students the ecological balance of the pond community and the importance of protozoans in maintaining this balance.

SUMMARY

The protozoans are one-celled organisms that were once classed as animals. Today, they are placed in the kingdom Protista. There are four phyla of protozoans, based on methods of movement. One phylum, including amebas, moves by means of pseudopods. The paramecia and their relatives move by means of cilia. The euglena is in a phylum that swims by means of flagella. The *Sporozoa* are parasites that cannot move on their own.

Protozoans differ from one another more than you might expect. Amebas, for example, are fairly simple cells with few specialized structures. Paramecia and euglenas have much more complex systems of specialized structures.

Of the thousands of protozoan species, many are harmless or even helpful. However, some cause major diseases in human beings. Among these diseases are malaria, amebic dysentery, and African sleeping sickness.

BIOLOGICALLY SPEAKING

pseudopodia	oral groove	macronucleus
ameboid movement	anterior	micronucleus
ectoplasm	posterior	conjugation
endoplasm	mouth pore	euglenoid movement
food vacuole	gullet	contractile fibers
cyst	anal pore	reservoir
pellicle	avoiding reaction	eyespot
cilia	trichocysts	

**QUESTIONS
FOR REVIEW**

1. Name four phyla of protozoa and give an example of each.
2. Describe ameboid movement.
3. How does an ameba take in food?
4. Explain the vital function of the contractile vacuole.
5. Describe locomotion in the paramecium.
6. What types of reproduction are exhibited by paramecia?
7. How do trichocysts act as a means of defense?
8. Why do euglena seek light while ameba and paramecia avoid it?
9. Describe the life cycle of *Plasmodium*.
10. Explain the relation of amebic dysentery to unsanitary conditions.

**APPLYING
PRINCIPLES
AND CONCEPTS**

1. Biologists frequently say that understanding the life processes of single-celled protozoans helps them to understand the life processes of complicated organisms like man. Why is this probably true?
2. Compare methods of locomotion, digestion, and sensitive response in the ameba, paramecium, and euglena.
3. Once a person has become infected with the malarial parasite, at what stage in the development of the illness would you consider treatment most possible?
4. In what ways are protozoans important in a pond?

19–1 Mushrooms are typical examples of fungi. (H.R.W. Photo by Russell Dian)

The Fungi

OBJECTIVES

- LIST some general characteristics of the fungi.
- DESCRIBE the characteristics of each of the three classes of fungi.
- DEFINE the term hyphae.
- LIST some examples of true fungi.
- DESCRIBE sexual reproduction in bread mold.
- LIST some examples of the *Basidiomycetes.*
- DISTINGUISH perfect fungi from imperfect fungi.
- LIST some of the diseases caused by the imperfect fungi.
- DESCRIBE the unique life cycle of slime molds.

WHAT ARE FUNGI?

Our classification system places the fungi in the kingdom *Protista,* though some systems have classified them as simple plants called *thallophytes.* **Most species of fungi are multicellular, but fungi never form roots, stems, or leaves.** Fungi vary in size from microscopic yeasts to mushrooms weighing a half kilogram or more.

All fungi are alike in one important way: they all lack chlorophyll. Thus, like animals, fungi cannot make their own foods by photosynthesis. Further, since they cannot move about, fungi must live in close contact with their food supply. Many are *saprophytes,* living on the remains of dead plants or animals or on waste products of organisms. Others are *parasites,* feeding on the tissues of living hosts. Fungi are common wherever the food supply, moisture level, and temperature are suitable.

Fungi are a very important group in the living world. In some cases, their effects are harmful. Certain fungi cause great economic loss by spoiling foods meant for human use. Others are agents of major plant diseases. Some are parasites of animals, including human beings.

On the other hand, **certain fungi break down the organic remains of dead plants and animals. This process is necessary in keeping the soil fertile.** Several fungi species produce antibiotics that are used against bacterial disease. Fungi play key parts in making bread, cheese, alcohol, and many other products. Some fungi are important food items in themselves.

The study of fungi is called *mycology* and those who specialize in this area are called mycologists. More than 250,000 kinds of fungi have been identified. Students may be interested in learning that fungi cause ringworm, athlete's foot, and other infections.

Ask students to bring in samples of moldy food. Bread, cheese, oranges, and certain vegetables are good examples. Discuss additives in products that retard mold growth, such as calcium propionate.

Fungus diseases are common to almost every wild and cultivated plant. Late blight disease is only one example. Another fungal plant disease is cedar-apple rust which involves the cedar tree and then the apple tree. Wheat rust is another common example of a fungus disease of plants.

CLASSIFYING FUNGI

We divide the fungi into two protist phyla. The smaller of these is the phylum *Myxomycophyta* (MICK-suh-MY-KAH-fuh-tuh). This phylum includes the *slime molds*, which lack cell walls. We will discuss these organisms at the end of this chapter.

All other fungi have cell walls and are placed in the phylum *Eumycophyta* (YOO-MY-KAH-fuh-tuh). These **true fungi** are divided into four classes, largely on the basis of how they reproduce. All true fungi form spores, but in the first three classes some form of sexual reproduction is also known to occur. These three classes are:

- *Phycomycetes* (FIKE-oe-MY-SEE-teez), the *algalike fungi*. These fungi resemble green algae in some ways. They bear spores in a case known as a **sporangium.**
- *Ascomycetes* (ASK-oe-MY-SEE-teez), the *sac fungi*. These bear spores, usually eight in number, in a sac known as an **ascus.**
- *Basidiomycetes* (buh-SID-ee-oe-MY-SEE-teez), the *club fungi*. These bear spores on a club-shaped structure, a **basidium.**

All true fungi that cannot be placed in one of these classes are grouped in a fourth class:

- *Deuteromycetes* (DOO-tuh-ROE-MY-SEE-teez), the *imperfect fungi.*

Eumycophyta—The True Fungi

THE CHARACTERISTICS OF TRUE FUNGI

There are more than 75,000 different species of true fungi. These include such types as molds, mildews, blights, yeasts, mushrooms, and others.

19–2 A time scale of fungi compared to the other protists.

Era	Period	bacteria	protozoans	fungi	algae
Cenozoic	Quaternary				
	Tertiary				
Mesozoic	Cretaceous				
	Jurassic				
	Triassic				
Paleozoic	Permian				
	Pennsylvanian (Late Carboniferous)				
	Mississippian (Early Carboniferous)				
	Devonian				
	Silurian				
	Ordovician				
	Cambrian				
(Pre-Cambrian)					

The bodies of most true fungi are made up of branching filaments called *hyphae* (HIFE-ee). These are usually white or gray in color. The hyphae of many fungi are divided into cells by cross walls. In other fungi, the hyphae are not divided by walls. Each hypha is a single tube containing several nuclei. The whole mass of hyphae formed by a fungus is known as the *mycelium* (my-SEE-lee-um).

Fungi do not contain chlorophyll. However, certain fungi produce other pigments. These pigments may give the mycelium a green, yellow, orange, red, or blue color.

Fungi secrete enzymes into their food supply. The food is digested outside the fungus and then absorbed through the hyphae.

Fungi do not require light, and many grow best in darkness. Moisture and, for most species, warm temperatures are necessary for life. Nearly all true fungi are aerobes, though their oxygen requirements may be low. A few fungi, including yeasts, can live under anaerobic conditions. But even these species grow faster when oxygen is present.

As noted, all true fungi reproduce asexually by forming spores, often in great numbers. These spores may be spread by air or water currents or by contact with other moving agents. Most true fungi reproduce sexually as well.

Phycomycetes

MOLDS—SOME OF THE MOST FAMILIAR FUNGI

The *molds* include several kinds of fungi. Some molds are Phycomycetes, other Ascomycetes. In most molds, the mycelium looks a bit like cotton.

Molds grow on wood, paper, leather, cloth, and many other organic substances. They thrive best in warm, moist surroundings, but many grow at temperatures near freezing. Such molds are a serious problem in refrigerators where food is kept.

One familiar mold is *bread mold (Rhizopus nigricans)*. Moisten some bread, expose it to air, and put it in a covered culture dish in a warm, dark place. Bread mold is almost certain to appear within a few days.

Bread mold is a Phycomycete. It begins as a microscopic spore. The spore becomes active, or *germinates,* and develops into a branching mass of silver hyphae that lack cross walls. If allowed to grow, this mycelium will soon cover the bread.

The microscope shows that there actually are several different kinds of hyphae in the mold. Those that spread over the surface of the food supply are called *stolons* (STOW-lonz). At intervals along the stolons, clusters of shorter hyphae reach down into the food supply like roots. These *rhizoids* (RY-zoidz) secrete enzymes that act on sugar and starch in the bread. The digested foods, along

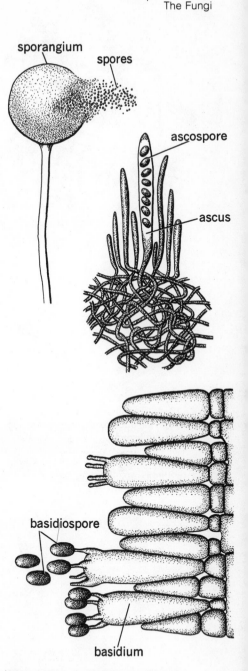

19–3 The classification of fungi is based on the type of structure associated with spore formation. A sporangium (top) is characteristic of the Phycomycetes; an ascus (center), of the Ascomycetes; and a basidium (bottom), of the Basidiomycetes.

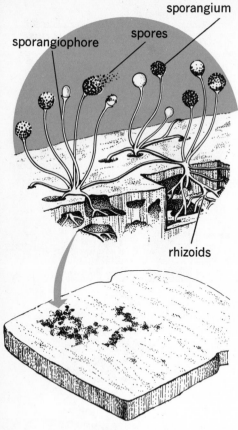

sporangium

sporangiophore   spores

rhizoids

19–4 The structure of bread mold. Note the rootlike rhizoids extending into the bread.

19–5 Sexual reproduction in bread mold requires two different mating strains.

with water, and then absorbed by the rhizoids. The flavor, odor, and color spots produced by bread mold result from the action of its enzymes.

After a few days, black knobs appear among the hyphae of bread mold. Each knob is a spore case, or sporangium. This structure grows at the tip of a special reproductive hypha, the **sporangiophore,** that reaches up into the air. More than 50,000 spores develop in each sporangium.

When a sporangium matures, it breaks open and releases its spores. The spores are carried away by air currents. If a spore lodges on a food supply in a suitable environment, it germinates. Hyphae branch out and form a new mycelium.

Bread mold also reproduces sexually by a form of *conjugation*. Although the reproductive hyphae all look alike, there actually are two different mating types. We can call these types *plus* and *minus*.

In sexual reproduction, the hyphae form short, specialized side branches. If the tip of a plus branch meets the tip of a minus branch, conjugation occurs. Cross walls form behind the end tips, leaving each tip as a gamete cell. The two gametes then fuse and form a zygote. This zygote develops a thick wall and matures into a **zygospore,** which enters a dormant period.

After from one to several months, if conditions permit, the zygospore germinates. In some cases, it produces a single sporangiophore that bears a sporangium and spores. In other cases, a short, branching hypha grows from the zygospore. A cluster of rhizoids grows from this hypha, and a sporangiophore, sporangium, and spores develop.

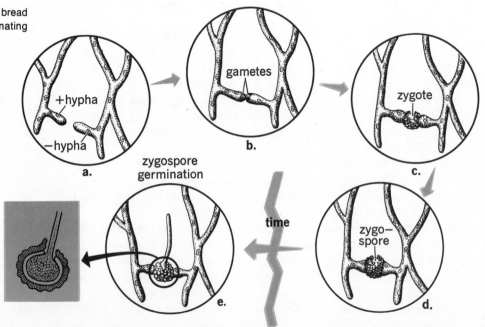

Related to bread mold are the *water molds* of the genus *Sapro-legnia* (sap-ruh-LEG-nee-uh). These Phycomycetes, like bread mold, have tubelike hyphae without cross walls.

Some water molds are saprophytes that live on the bodies of dead insects and other animals in the water. Other water molds are parasites. They invade the tissues of living fish and other water animals. Such parasites rob the host of food and usually kill it. They are a great problem in lakes, rivers, and aquariums.

LATE BLIGHT FUNGUS, A PLANT PARASITE

The Phycomycete known as *late blight fungus* causes tremendous damage in plant crops. This fungus disease caused the great famine in Ireland from 1845 to 1847 by destroying nearly the whole potato crop.

The blight fungus hyphae grow between the leaf cells of the host plant. Short branches penetrate the leaf cells and rob them of food. Some hyphae grow out through the bottom of the leaf and form sporangiophores, each of which develops a sporangium.

In some cases, the whole sporangium germinates and forms a new hypha. In other cases, the sporangium produces **zoospores.** These spores each have two flagella. They can swim across the leaf in dew or rainwater, spreading the infection rapidly.

In the end, the whole top of the plant is destroyed. Sporangia may also be washed through the soil to the potatoes themselves, causing them to rot. The late blight fungus also attacks tomatoes, causing great loss.

19-6 A cottonlike mass of a water mold, *Saprolegnia*, on a fish. (Allan Roberts)

Ascomycetes

BLUE-GREEN MOLDS AND POWDERY MILDEWS

Molds of the genus *Penicillium* often form blue-green growths on oranges, lemons, and other fruits. They also appear on bread, meat, leather, and cloth. Molds of the genus *Aspergillus* are common on foods, too, forming yellow or black rings.

19-7 Sporangium production and germination in the late blight fungus.

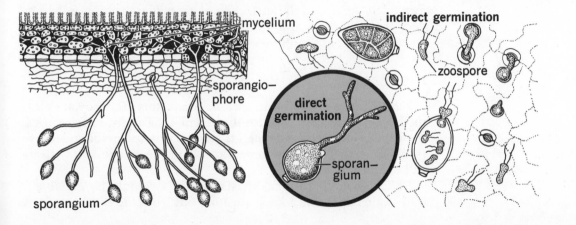

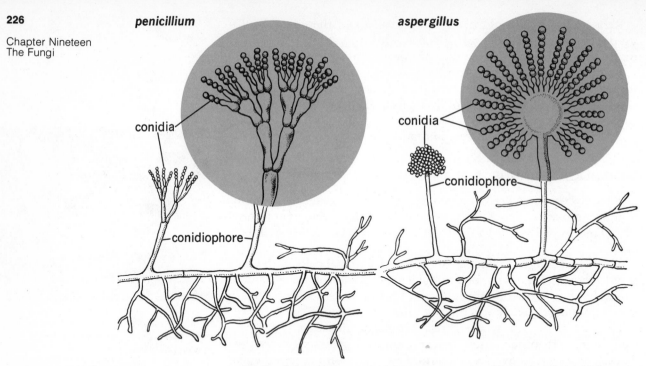

penicillium   *aspergillus*

conidia

conidiophore

conidia

conidiophore

19–8 Conidiophores and conidia of *Penicillium* and *Aspergillus*.

Many fungi are beneficial as sources of food and drugs. *Gibberellin* is a substance obtained from a fungus and used as a plant stimulant. Certain fungi, which live in the soil, trap nematodes and prevent them from injuring plant roots.

Both of these genera are Ascomycetes and have hyphae with cross walls. Some of the hyphae penetrate the food supply and absorb foods. Surface hyphae form branches known as **conidiophores.** Great numbers of spores, or **conidia,** form in rows on short branches of these structures.

Some molds of this type are very valuable. For example, several species of *Penicillium* are used in making cheeses. Added at a certain point in processing, the mold grows through the cheese during aging. Enzymes secreted by the mold give the cheese flavor. Roquefort and Camembert are two popular cheeses that contain *Penicillium* molds. Another species of Penicillium produces the antibiotic penicillin.

The *powdery mildews* are also Ascomycetes. They develop as a mass of hyphae on the surface of the host plant, usually on a leaf. Short hyphae enter the leaf tissues and absorb food. Spores are formed at the tips of the surface hyphae, giving the fungus its powdery look. Powdery mildews attack grapes, roses, clover, apples, wheat, barley, and several other plants.

THE YEASTS

Yeasts are one-celled microscopic organisms. Yet they are classified as Ascomycetes because they form an ascus at some point in their life cycle. Each yeast cell is an oval or a sphere bounded by a thin cell wall. There is a large vacuole in the cytoplasm, with the cell nucleus nearby.

Under good conditions, yeasts multiply rapidly by *budding*. A bud begins as a small knob pushing out from the mother cell. As the bud grows, the nucleus of the mother cell divides. One nucleus moves into the bud; the other stays in the mother cell. The bud remains attached and produces another bud in turn. Thus, a chain of yeast cells are formed. More buds also may form on the original mother cell.

If conditions do not favor rapid growth and budding, the yeast cell may reproduce in another way. Two nuclear divisions produce four nuclei. Each nucleus is then surrounded by cytoplasm and a cell wall. We refer to these four cells as **ascospores.** The cell that formed them is the *ascus.*

In the ascospore stage, yeasts are dormant and can survive drying and extremes of temperature. It is these dormant cells that are packaged and sold as "active yeast." Under the right conditions, the ascospores germinate and form active yeast cells.

In Chapter Six, we noted that yeasts carry on anaerobic respiration, or fermentation. In this process, the yeasts secrete the enzyme **zymase.** This enzyme splits molecules of simple sugars (glucose or fructose). A small part of the energy stored in the sugar is released for use by the yeast cells. Alcohol and carbon dioxide are by-products of the process.

Some yeasts also secrete enzymes that digest complex sugars (maltose and sucrose) to simple sugars. These simple sugars are then acted on by zymase.

You can observe yeast fermentation by adding commercial yeast to a 10 percent solution of simple sugar in water. Put this culture in a flask with a cotton stopper and keep it in a warm place. Within a few hours, the yeast cells will multiply to such numbers that the solution will become cloudy. Tiny bubbles of carbon dioxide will rise through the solution, and you can smell the alcohol in it.

Several strains of yeast are cultured for use in industry. *Baker's yeast* grows rapidly in dough, giving off carbon dioxide. Bubbles of this gas cause the dough to rise. The small amount of alcohol formed is driven off by the heat of baking. *Wine yeasts* form a much higher alcohol concentration, up to about 14 percent. This concentration can be raised by distilling after fermentation has ended.

Yeasts also produce vitamin B_2, or *riboflavin* (RY-boe-FLAY-vin). This vitamin is necessary for normal growth and for the health of the skin, mouth, and eyes. Riboflavin remains in the yeast cells. To obtain it, we must eat either yeast cells or products made from ground yeast.

Wild yeasts are common in the air and ferment sugars in natural fruit juices. A few yeasts are pathogenic.

OTHER ASCOMYCETES

The *cup fungus* and *morel* are relatives of the yeasts. These Ascomycetes are harmless saprophytes. The cup fungus lives on rotting

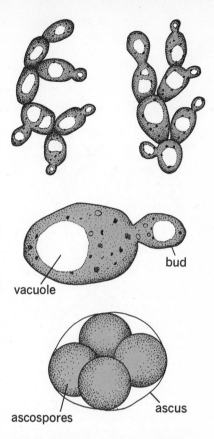

bud

vacuole

ascospores

ascus

19–9 Budding in yeast. Under ideal growth conditions, a bud develops into a mature yeast cell in about thirty minutes.

19–10 The morel, or sponge mushroom, is a highly prized edible fungus. (Alvin E. Steffan, National Audubon Society)

wood and leaves and on organic matter in rich soil. Some hyphae absorb food. Others are tightly massed in the white, orange, or red cups. Many of these hyphae end in a long ascus that contains eight spores.

The morel, of sponge mushroom, is prized for its flavor. It is one of the few mushrooms that can be safely eaten. It is not related to the true mushrooms, many of which are poisonous. We will have more to say about the true mushrooms shortly.

Some serious plant diseases are caused by Ascomycetes parasites. Among these diseases are Dutch elm disease, chestnut blight, apple scab, and ergot disease of rye.

Basidiomycetes

THE CLUB FUNGI

The Basidiomycetes, or *club fungi*, get their name from the club-shaped *basidium* found at the end of certain hyphae. Each basidium usually bears four spores on its outer surface. Four groups of fungi make up the class Basidiomycetes. These include rust fungi, smut fungi, mushrooms and bracket fungi, and puffballs.

Rust fungi cause many serious plant diseases. More than 2,000 known rusts attack flowering plants and ferns. Over 250 of these rusts are parasites on wheat, oats, barley, and other cereals. Rusts cause millions of dollars worth of crop damage each year.

Wheat rust is one of the best known plant parasites. Its complex life cycle involves two host plants, wheat and the common barberry bush.

The rust appears on wheat in late spring or early summer, when the wheat is green and growing. The rust mycelium spreads among the cells of the wheat stem and leaves. Tiny blisters appear where hyphae grow to the stem and leaf surfaces and release spores. These spores are red-orange in color and are all one-celled. Carried through the air, they spread the disease rapidly by infecting other plants.

Later in the summer, when the wheat is ripening and turning yellow, a new spore stage begins. The same hyphae that produced red spores now form black spores. These are two-celled spores protected by thick walls.

The black spores remain dormant through the winter on the wheat stubble or on the ground. In early spring, they begin a complex series of changes during which the barberry bush is infected. More spores are formed in the barberry. Released into the air, these spores infect wheat, completing the life cycle of the rust.

Both wheat and the barberry are necessary in the rust life cycle. Thus, the disease can be controlled by keeping down the barberry bush population. This works well in areas where winters are cold. In milder areas, however, red spores may survive the winter and infect the new wheat crop directly.

Certain other rusts involve two hosts. *Cedar-apple rust* involves red cedar and apple trees. *White pine blister rust* damages the white pine tree in one stage and lives in the wild currant or gooseberry in another.

SMUTS—PARASITES ON CEREAL GRAINS

The *smuts* cause great damage to corn, oats, wheat, rye, barley, and other grain plants.

One of the most familiar smuts is *corn smut*, which infects corn plants when they are young. Some weeks later a gray, slimy swell-

19–11 Life cycle of the wheat rust. The two hosts necessary for the completion of the life cycle are the common barberry bush and the wheat plant. (inset: courtesy USDA)

wheat rust

a. late summer— **wheat** (will lie dormant till spring)

b. spring— **barberry** (will infect young wheat)

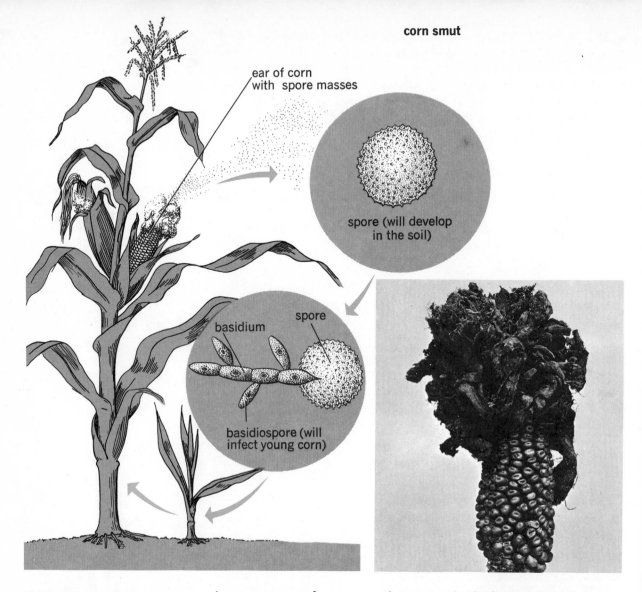

ear of corn
with spore masses

spore (will develop
in the soil)

basidium

spore

basidiospore (will
infect young corn)

19–12 Life cycle of the corn smut. Trace the life cycle from the point at which masses of hyphae develop in the corn plant until the cycle is completed. (inset: courtesy Illinois Agricultural Experiment Station)

Students usually find the study of mushrooms very interesting. Ask several students to report on types of mushrooms and their uses, poisonous mushrooms, raising mushrooms for food, and mushroom recipes. Many books and articles have been written about these subjects. Some students may want to bring in mushrooms and try to identify them.

ing appears on the ear, tassel, stem, or leaf. This swelling is a mass of hyphae. As the corn matures, the hyphae release large numbers of black, sooty spores. Carried by the wind, these spores may infect other plants or lie dormant until spring.

A dormant spore that germinates forms a basidium, which in turn produces spores. Reaching new corn plants through the air, these spores start a new smut infection. Corn smut can be controlled by burning infected plants, plowing under the corn stubble, and destroying unused stalks and leaves.

MUSHROOMS—THE BEST KNOWN FUNGI

Mushrooms seem to pop up everywhere after a warm spring or autumn rain. But what we think of as a mushroom is only the reproductive part of the whole organism. Below it, a mycelium of silvery hyphae is growing in the soil or in rotting wood. Enzymes secreted by these hyphae break down organic substances, which are then absorbed as foods. The mycelium may live for many years, slowly spreading through more and more of the wood or soil.

At certain seasons, especially fall and spring, small knobs of hyphae form on the mycelium. Pushing up through the soil, these knobs become the spore-bearing structures we call mushrooms. The mature mushroom has a stalk, or *stipe*, supporting an umbrella-shaped *cap*. At first, the cap is folded down around the stipe. After breaking through the ground surface, the cap begins to open out. A ring, or *annulus*, remains where the cap and stipe were joined.

In most cases, the cap contains many *gills* radiating out from the stipe like spokes. On each gill are thousands of basidia, each of which bears four spores. In all, a single mushroom may produce as many as 10 billion spores. These spores drop from the basidia and are carried away by air currents. If a spore lands in a suitable environment, it forms a new mycelium. If not, the spore dies.

Many mushrooms are poisonous. If eaten, they produce severe and often fatal effects. Some people use the word *toadstool* to describe a poisonous mushroom. However, only an expert can safely tell a poisonous mushroom from one that is not. In some cases, even the experts cannot easily tell the difference. For this reason, *never* eat a wild mushroom unless you know exactly what you are doing.

A puffball was given its name because when a mature one is squeezed, it releases a cloud of brown spores. These spores are usually carried away by the wind to new locations, where they germinate and produce more puffballs.

19–13 The development of a mushroom. The inset is an enlargement of a gill.

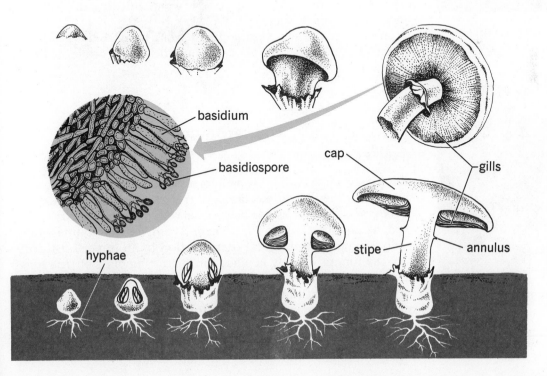

basidium

basidiospore

cap

gills

stipe

annulus

hyphae

19-14 Bracket, or shelf, fungi. (H.R.W. Photo by Russell Dian)

19-15 Puffballs. (Allan Roberts)

19-16 A fairy ring. (Walter Dawn)

Slime molds are found on the undersurface of decaying logs, especially after a heavy rain spell. Students may want to bring in slime molds and identify them.

BRACKET FUNGI AND PUFFBALLS

Bracket fungi are part of the same group of Basidiomycetes as mushrooms. These familiar fungi grow like rows of shelves on stumps or tree trunks. Some are parasites on living trees, while others live as saprophytes on dead wood.

The mycelium of a bracket fungus penetrates and breaks down the woody tissue of the host. This is very damaging to living trees. The fungus may remain attached to its host for years. As it grows older, the fungus itself becomes woody. Rings of growth can be seen where new layers of spore-bearing hyphae have formed on the underside of the shelf. The spores are released through tiny pores in this part of the fungus.

Puffballs are the fourth group of Basidiomycetes. Puffballs are round or pear-shaped growths, often white in color. They resemble mushrooms, except that the spores are released only when the reproductive structure dries and splits open. Also, most puffball species can be eaten when young, before the spores mature. No poisonous puffballs are known.

A GROWTH TRAIT OF FUNGI

Many fungi, such as fairy ring mushrooms, tend to grow in circles. The mycelium of the original growth digests the organic matter in a given spot. The mycelium then spreads out and reaches unused organic matter in the area around the original spot. This ring continues to grow. From time to time, mushrooms sprout in a circle at its outer edge.

You can see the same principle at work in a mold culture. The newest part of the mold is at the outside of the circle, with the oldest part at the center.

Deuteromycetes

IMPERFECT FUNGI

Biologists have observed some form of sexual reproduction in all members of the first three classes of true fungi. But if only asexual reproduction by spores has been observed, then the fungus is classified as *Deuteromycetes*, or *imperfect fungus*. Sometimes study produces evidence of sexual reproduction in an imperfect fungus. If so, the fungus usually is placed in the fitting class of true fungi. Most imperfect fungi are much like Ascomycetes.

Many imperfect fungi are important parasites of plants or animals. Several diseases of grains, tomatoes, citrus fruits, lettuce, cabbage, beans, and apples are caused by imperfect fungi. Ringworm fungi produce several skin infections in human beings. Among these are ringworm and athlete's foot.

Phylum—Myxomycophyta

SLIME MOLDS

The strange organisms known as *slime molds* are a problem to classify. In some ways, they are like giant masses of amebas. Thus, they might be classed as animals. However, they also form sporangia and spores, like the fungi. Some biologists have called them "slime fungi" or "fungus animals." This confusion is avoided by placing the slime molds in their own protist phylum, the Myxomycophyta.

The body of a slime mold is called a **plasmodium.** It is a mass of protoplasm with many nuclei but no cell walls. A plasmodium often appears as a slimy network of living matter. Somewhat like an ameba, it flows along on forest soil, dead leaves, or a rotting log. As it moves, it takes in bits of organic matter and digests them in food vacuoles.

After an active period, the plasmodium becomes inactive. Clusters of stalked sporangia, often delicate and beautiful, rise up. Spores are released and carried away in the air. Spores that reach wet surroundings germinate and release one or more tiny cells. Each cell has two flagella. Such cells may act as gametes and fuse in pairs. This fused pair of cells develops rapidly into a new plasmodium. In some cases, many pairs of cells unite and form the plasmodium.

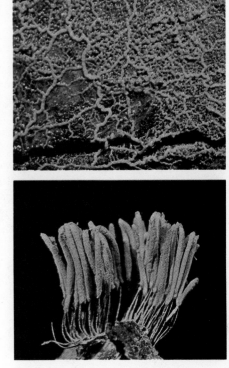

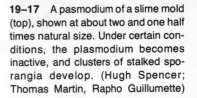

19–17 A pasmodium of a slime mold (top), shown at about two and one half times natural size. Under certain conditions, the plasmodium becomes inactive, and clusters of stalked sporangia develop. (Hugh Spencer; Thomas Martin, Rapho Guillumette)

SUMMARY

The fungi are classified as protists and divided into *true fungi* and *slime molds*. Among the true fungi are the many molds, yeasts, blights, rusts, smuts, and mildews. Also included are mushrooms, bracket fungi, and other organisms. All true fungi reproduce by forming spores, but most reproduce sexually as well. True fungi in which only asexual reproduction is known are called imperfect fungi.

All fungi lack chlorophyll and cannot build their own foods. Thus, many species compete with animals for food. Great amounts of stored food are spoiled by fungi. Fungi also cause many major diseases of living plants and animals.

On the other hand, some fungi are very helpful. Yeasts are used in making many food products and are sometimes used as food themselves. Certain molds are important in cheese-making. Molds also give us drugs such as penicillin. Many fungi, by breaking down the remains of dead organisms or other matter, help to keep the soil fertile.

BIOLOGICALLY SPEAKING

true fungi	germinate	conidiophore
sporangium	stolon	conidia
ascus	rhizoid	ascospore
basidium	sporangiophore	zymase
hyphae	zygospore	plasmodium
mycelium	zoospore	

QUESTIONS FOR REVIEW

1. Describe the general characteristics of fungi.
2. Why must all fungi live in contact with a food supply?
3. Name the classes of fungi.
4. Describe the mycelium of true fungi.
5. Name the kinds of hyphae that make up a bread mold plant.
6. Describe two methods of reproduction that occur in bread mold.
7. List several ways in which fungi may be harmful.
8. How are the products of yeast fermentation used commercially?
9. Outline the life cycle of wheat rust.
10. Describe the reproductive structure of the mushroom.
11. Name several human infections caused by imperfect fungi.
12. Describe the plasmodium stage of a slime mold.

APPLYING PRINCIPLES AND CONCEPTS

1. Sweet cider will ferment rapidly in a warm place even when it is in a tightly closed container. Explain why.
2. Explain why certain kinds of mushrooms and molds often grow in a ring.
3. In what respects could slime molds possibly represent a link between different protist phyla?

The
Algae

20-1 Algae are the dominant vegetation in the waters of the world. (Grant Heilman)

OBJECTIVES

- DESCRIBE the characteristics of the algae.
- DESCRIBE the various methods of reproduction in algae.
- LIST the six major phyla of algae.
- NAME some members of each of the six major phyla of algae.
- EXPLAIN the methods of reproduction in *Spirogyra*.
- DISTINGUISH between diatoms and dinoflagellates.
- DESCRIBE the economic importance of algae.
- EXPLAIN how lichens illustrate the concept of mutualism.

THE "GRASSES OF MANY WATERS"

If you've ever walked near a pond, lake, or ocean in the warmer months, you've seen *algae*. Water mosses, scums, seaweeds—all of these are popular terms for different kinds of algae.

Algae (singular, *alga*) have been called the "grasses of many waters." The name is fitting. For one thing, algae are as common in water as grasses are on land. For another, the algae are just as important in their environment as the grasses are in our own. **Through photosynthesis, algae are the main producers of food and oxygen in water environments. Thus, directly or indirectly, most other water organisms depend on them for life.**

There is a growing need today for new sources of food. It may not be many more years before the land is unable to support the booming world population. If that time comes, perhaps we can turn to the seas. If we could farm and harvest algae as we do plants of the land, we would have a food source almost without limit.

WHAT ARE ALGAE?

Compared with other types of plants, the algae seem very simple. They lack such usual plant organs as roots, stems, and leaves. They even lack specialized tissues for carrying water and, for the most part, food.

The algae are the simplest form of plant life, often referred to as a "low" form of life because of their lack of structural complexity. Scientists disagree about the number of types of algae but most agree that there are more than 30,000 species.

Most algae are marine; however, algal growth can be found on trees and even on snow. In fact, one type of algae thrives in the 185° F temperature of the pools and springs of Yellowstone National Park.

Yet in terms of their reproductive processes and biochemical capability, algae are quite complex. Certainly they are among the most successful life forms, having dominated water environments for more than a billion years.

Algae are found in many different forms. Some are one-celled and can be seen only with a microscope. These forms may float in the water, settle to the bottom, or swim about with flagella. Other algae, made up of great numbers of cells, may be quite large. The giant sea kelps, for example, often grow more than thirty meters long.

Whatever its size, the body of an alga lacks specialized tissues and organs. The name given such a plant body is **thallus** (plural, *thalli*).

In many species of algae, the cells group together in colonies. Often, the cells are attached in chainlike **filaments.** The filaments are branched in some species, unbranched in others. Other colonies may be shaped like sheets, plates, or spheres. In many large algae, such as the seaweeds, the thallus is a broad ribbon made up of thousands of cells. Many species form a jellylike sheath around their cells. This makes algae hard to grasp.

Almost all algae carry on photosynthesis. It is mainly this trait that separates them from the fungi. The glucose formed in photosynthesis may be built into other products in algae.

WHERE DO ALGAE LIVE?

Algae are found in nearly all bodies of water. However, different species may thrive under very different conditions. Among the factors that affect algae are water temperature, amount of light, oxygen and carbon dioxide supply, and mineral content of the water.

Algae are widely distributed. They can be found in fresh water, sea water, soil, on damp stones, on trees, and on glaciers. Ask students to bring in samples of algae for observation and identification.

20–2 A time scale of algae compared to the other protists.

Era	Period	bacteria	protozoans	fungi	algae
Cenozoic	Quaternary				
	Tertiary				
Mesozoic	Cretaceous				
	Jurassic				
	Triassic				
Paleozoic	Permian				
	Pennsylvania (Late Carboniferous)				
	Mississippian (Early Carboniferous)				
	Devonian				
	Silurian				
	Ordovician				
	Cambrian				
(Pre-Cambrian)					

Some algae grow attached to rocks in fast-flowing rapids or waterfalls. Others thrive in slow or quiet water. Most species live near the surface, where they get the most light, while others live in deeper water. Sea algae tend to live near the shore. They can be seen attached to rocks or floating in tidal pools at low tide. But some species live at depths of 150 meters or more.

Not all algae live in water. Certain species are found on tree bark or on moist soil. One unusual environment in which algae are found is on the underside of the blue whale. Another is on the hair of the three-toed sloth, a South American mammal.

Some algae live inside other organisms. One one-celled species lives inside certain paramecia. Other species live in the bodies of freshwater sponges, water snails, and other organisms. Usually, algae do not harm the organisms in which they live. In fact, they are often helpful, supplying food by photosynthesis.

METHODS OF REPRODUCTION

Many different forms of reproduction are carried on among the algae. Most species reproduce in more than one way. Often, reproductive methods are determined by conditions in the environment.

Reproduction may be either *asexual* or *sexual*. Some algae reproduce only asexually. Others reproduce by both methods during complex life cycles.

Many one-celled algae reproduce asexually by cell fission. Two new algae result. In a colony of algae, the colony grows by divisions of individual cells.

A colony itself may be broken apart by water currents, passing fish, or animals feeding on it. This purely mechanical separation of cells is called **fragmentation.** No new *cells* are produced, but the number of *colonies* is multiplied. Each fragment of the original colony can continue to grow on its own. Fragmentation occurs often and is a major factor in the spread of colonies through water environments.

Many algae reproduce asexually by forming *zoospores*, which can swim freely by means of flagella. Each spore contains at least one nucleus and some cytoplasm of the mother cell from which it was formed. Such a spore can develop directly into a new body cell of the algae. By producing zoospores, many algae spread over a wide area during a single growing season.

Sexual reproduction also occurs in many algae. As in other organisms, gametes are produced which fuse and form zygotes. In some species, all gametes are alike in size, form, and ability to move about. We call these **isogametes.** Other species form two types of gametes, male and female. These are called **heterogametes.** Male gametes, or *sperms*, usually can move on their own while female gametes, or *eggs*, cannot. Sperms are usually smaller than eggs, also.

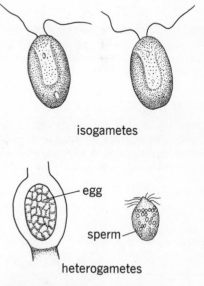

isogametes

egg

sperm

heterogametes

20–3 In some species of algae all the gametes are the same (isogametes). Other species form two types of gametes, male and female (heterogametes).

CLASSIFICATION OF ALGAE

For many years, biologists classified the algae, along with the fungi, as simple plants. More recent systems take note of the lack of specialized tissues and organs in algae. In these systems, the algae, like the fungi, are placed in the kingdom Protista.

All algae contain chlorophyll, which is green. But this color may be masked by other pigments, giving rise to different colors. These *color differences* have long been the basis upon which algae are placed in different groups. In some cases, however, even closely related species may have different pigments. Thus, factors such as *cell structure* and *forms of reproduction* must also be considered in classifying algae.

In some recent systems, the more than 30,000 species of algae are placed in six phyla:

- *Cyanophyta* (sy-uh-NAH-fuh-tuh), or *blue-green algae*
- *Chlorophyta* (kloar-AH-fuh-tuh), or *green algae*
- *Chrysophyta* (kruh-SAH-fuh-tuh), or *yellow-green algae*, golden-brown algae, and diatoms
- *Pyrrophyta* (py-RAH-fuh-tuh), mainly dinoflagellates
- *Phaeophyta* (fee-AH-fuh-tuh), or *brown algae*
- *Rhodophyta* (roe-DAH-fuh-tuh), or *red algae*

In certain systems, euglenas and related organisms are classified as forms of algae. These organisms are placed in a seventh phylum, the *Euglenophyta* (yoo-gluh-NAH-fuh-tuh).

Cyanophyta

BLUE-GREEN ALGAE

Along with bacteria, the *blue-green algae* are among the most primitive of living things. They are so simple as to be quite different from all other algae. For example, the nuclear material remains near the center of the cell, but there is no nuclear membrane. The chlorophyll is not contained in chloroplasts but spread through the outer cytoplasm. Blue-green algae usually reproduce by simple fission. None of them reproduce sexually, as do higher algae.

Most blue-green algae cells are smaller than those of other algae. Some blue-green algae form filaments. In other cases, the cells are contained in a slimy mass. You can find blue-green algae in almost any pond, stream, or ditch. Some species live on wet rocks or soil. A few live in hot springs with temperatures up to 85° C.

Blue-green algae thrive during the summer, especially in water polluted by organic matter. They are a constant problem in drinking water and swimming pools. Public water supplies are regularly checked for blue-green algae.

The phylum name *Cyanophyta* refers to the blue pigment *phyco-coyanin* (FIKE-oe-SY-uh-nin). This pigment, along with chlorophyll, gives the blue-green algae their color. Actual colors of different species range from bright blue-green to nearly black. A few species even have a red pigment. One such species sometimes appears in great numbers in the Red Sea, which may explain how that sea got its name.

FOUR BLUE-GREEN ALGAE

Four common blue-green algae will give us a good idea of the range of traits seen in this phylum.

One genus is *Nostoc* (NOSS-tock). You can find it on mud or sand near lakes or ponds, usually just where the ripples lap the shore. A *Nostoc* colony looks like a small ball of jelly, ranging in size from a pinhead to a marble. Within this jellylike sheath are many tangled filaments made up of individual cells. Each filament looks something like a string of pearl beads.

From point to point along a filament are **heterocysts.** These are empty cells with thick walls and pores at either side where they meet other cells. They may be spores that have lost their content and no longer function. Filaments of *Nostoc* usually fragment between a heterocyst and a normal cell.

The only known form of reproduction in *Nostoc* is simple fission. When a cell divides, two small cells of equal size result, and the filament grows in length.

A relative of *Nostoc* is *Anabaena* (AN-uh-BEE-nuh). The cells and filaments of these two algae are much alike. However, *Anabaena* filaments occur singly rather than in groups. Another difference is that *Anabaena* produces true spores. Each spore is a large, oval cell protected by thick walls and containing much stored food. Mature spores separate from the parent filament and may germinate in new locations.

Nostoc when dried can live for many years. In one study, *Nostoc* was found to revive and grow after being dried for eighty-seven years.

20–4 Four common blue-green algae. In what ways are they similar? How do they differ?

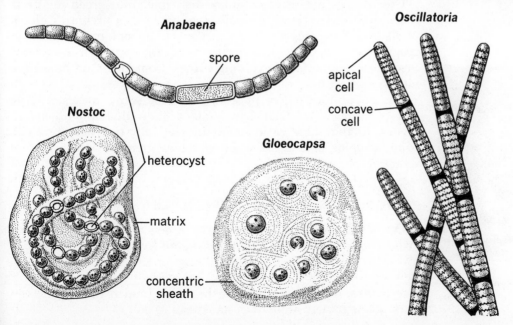

Anabaena

spore

Oscillatoria

apical cell

concave cell

Nostoc

heterocyst

matrix

Gloeocapsa

concentric sheath

One of the most primitive blue-green algae is *Gloeocapsa* (glee-oe-KAP-suh). It appears as a slimy blue-green mass, often on wet rocks or on moist flowerpots in greenhouses. The individual cells are spheres or ovals. Blue and green pigments are spread through the area close inside the cell wall.

Each *Gloeocapsa* cell secretes a slimy sheath. When a cell divides, each new cell secretes its own sheath within the old one. Thus, several layers of sheaths may result from further divisions. A colony of *Gloeocapsa* may contain hundreds of cells joined by their sheaths.

A fourth example of a blue-green alga is the *Oscillatoria* (AH-suh-luh-TOAR-ee-uh). This alga forms filaments made up of many thin, disk-shaped cells. Each filament looks somewhat like a stack of coins. The tip, or **apical** (AP-ick'l) **cell,** is round on one side in many species. When one cell in a filament dies, the cells on either side bulge into its place. The result is a *concave cell.* Such cells are weak spots at which the filaments often break into shorter pieces.

Oscillatoria thrive in ponds and streams during warm weather. Their name refers to the gentle swaying motion of the filaments in the water.

Chlorophyta

GREEN ALGAE

The *green algae* of the phylum *Chlorophyta* vary from one-celled forms to colonies made up of many cells. Most forms live in fresh water, though many live in the ocean. Some live in stranger environments, such as salt lakes or hot springs.

Green algae are more complex than their blue-green relatives. A definite nucleus with a nuclear membrane is present. Chlorophyll and other pigments are organized in chloroplasts. Some species reproduce asexually, either by fission or by forming spores. Sexual reproduction, involving either isogametes or heterogametes, also occurs.

The sugar formed by photosynthesis is sometimes stored as starch in the cells. Green algae contain chlorophyll and other pigments, in the same ratio found in seed plants. These produce colors ranging from grass green to yellow-green.

PROTOCOCCUS, A COMMON GREEN ALGA

One of the most common of the green algae is *Protococcus. Protococcus* is unusual in that it does not live in water. Rather, it grows on tree bark, unpainted buildings or fences, or damp stones. Seldom seen in dry weather, it is very evident in wet weather. On tree trunks, it usually grows on the shaded north side, where the bark has a greater amount of moisture.

Protococcus is an easily obtainable green algae because it is available throughout the year. Ask some students to bring in samples of *Protococcus.*

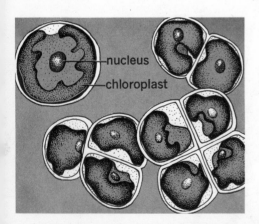

20–5 Cells of the green alga *Protococcus* occur singly or in colonies of two or more.

Protococcus cells are spheres or slightly oval-shaped. Each contains an organized nucleus and a single, large chloroplast. The cells are so small that many thousands may cover a few square centimeters of bark. They are carried from tree to tree by birds or insects, or by the wind during dry weather. Since *Protococcus* builds its own foods, it takes no food from the tree.

Protococcus reproduces by fission only. A cell may divide in any one of three planes. After division, the new cells tend to cling together in groups.

Chlorella is a one-celled green alga somewhat like *Protococcus*. It is of special interest to biologists because some species live in cells or tissues of protozoans, sponges, and jellyfish.

SPIROGYRA

During the spring or fall, almost any quiet pond will have bright green masses of threadlike *Spirogyra* (SPY-ruh-JY-ruh). The cells of this green alga form filaments from a few centimeters to a half meter long. Under a microscope, the cells appear almost transparent, joined end to end like stacked water glasses.

Each cell has one or more spiral chloroplasts winding from one end of the cell to the other. On these chloroplasts are small protein bodies, called **pyrenoids,** surrounded by layers of starch grains. The nucleus is held near the center of the cell by radiating strands of cytoplasm. Most of the cytoplasm lies near the cell wall, leaving a large central vacuole filled with water and dissolved substances. A thin sheath around each cell makes *Spirogyra* filaments slippery to the touch.

On sunny days, photosynthesis takes place at a rapid rate. Oxygen bubbles stream from the cells and collect among the filaments. If enough oxygen builds up, masses of *Spirogyra* float to the surface. At night, the oxygen dissolves in the water, and the masses sink again.

Spirogyra reproduces in two ways. The first is by asexual fission. The cells always divide crosswise, thus adding to the length of the filament.

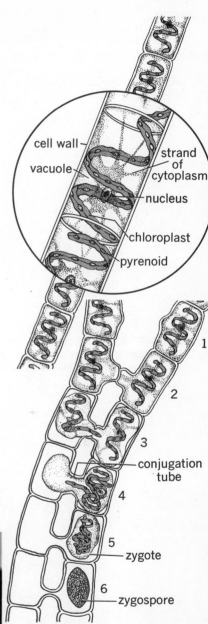

20-6 Filaments of the green alga *Spirogyra*. The structure of a single cell can be seen at the top. Conjugation is shown below. Explain what is happening in each of the numbered steps in the sequence. (Carolina Biological Supply Co.)

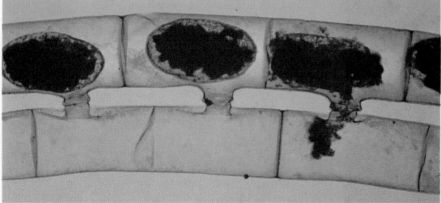

Spriogyra also reproduces sexually by conjugation. This process occurs when the weather does not favor normal growth by fission. It is most likely to be seen in late spring or early fall.

Conjugation begins with two filaments lined up next to each other. A small knob grows out from each cell until it meets the knob of the cell opposite it. The tips of the knobs dissolve, leaving a hollow tube between the two cells. The content of one cell flows through the tube and unites with the content of the other, producing a zygote.

Thick walls develop around the zygotes, after which they are known as *zygospores*. The zygospores fall from the cells and enter a dormant period. Their thick walls protect them from the cold of winter and the heat or dryness of summer. They may even be carried from one pond to another by birds or other animals. When conditions again favor growth, the zygospore becomes active and develops into a new *Spirogyra* cell. A new filament builds up by simple cell division.

An interesting note is that the cell contents move in only one direction during conjugation. The result is one filament of empty cells and one filament full of zygospores.

REPRODUCTION IN *ULOTHRIX*

A green alga that reproduces in a somewhat different way is *Ulothrix* (YOO-luh-thricks). This alga lives attached to rocks in swift, shallow water. Each short filament is anchored by a special cell called a **holdfast.** Each cell above the holdfast has a large chloroplast shaped like an open ring.

20-7 Asexual and sexual reproduction in the green agla *Ulothrix*. Sexual reproduction involves isogametes.

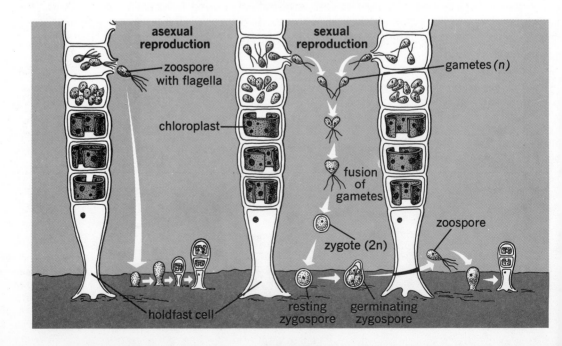

asexual reproduction — zoospore with flagella — chloroplast — holdfast cell — sexual reproduction — gametes (n) — fusion of gametes — zygote (2n) — zoospore — resting zygospore — germinating zygospore

Under ideal conditions, *Ulothrix* reproduces asexually. Each cell undergoes a series of nuclear divisions by mitosis. The cell content then splits up into zoospores, each containing a nucleus and chloroplast.

The zoospores now burst out of the parent cell. Each zoospore has four flagella, with which it propels itself through the water. When it reaches a suitable place, the zoospore grows into a holdfast cell. This cell divides, forming two new cells. The lower of these is a holdfast, while the upper is a normal *Ulothrix* cell. A new filament develops from this normal cell by further divisions.

At other times, mitosis and division of the cell content produces *isogametes* rather than zoospores. The isogametes resemble zoospores but are smaller and have only two flagella.

The isogametes leave the parent cell and swim away. If two isogametes meet, they fuse and form a zygote that becomes a zygospore. After a rest period, the zygospore undergoes meiosis. Four nuclei result, each with the haploid chromosome number. These nuclei, surrounded by some of the zygospore protoplasm, develop into zoospores. Each zoospore may produce a new holdfast and give rise to a new *Ulothrix* filament.

REPRODUCTION IN A MORE ADVANCED ALGA

Oedogonium (EE-duh-GOE-nee-um) is a common green alga that grows on rocks and other objects in quiet pools. As with *Ulothrix*, there are single filaments held in place by holdfast cells. Each cell has a single chloroplast made up of many joined strands.

Stress to students that holdfasts of marine algae are not functional roots, although they may resemble roots of land plants. Holdfasts are a means of attachment and do not provide nourishment to the algae.

Ask students to compare the reproduction of *Oedogonium* to that of *Ulothrix*. Ask students whether one type of reproduction would be more successful than the other. Elicit reasons for their answers.

20-8 Sexual and asexual reproduction in the green alga *Oedogonium*. Note that in this alga, sexual reproduction involves heterogametes.

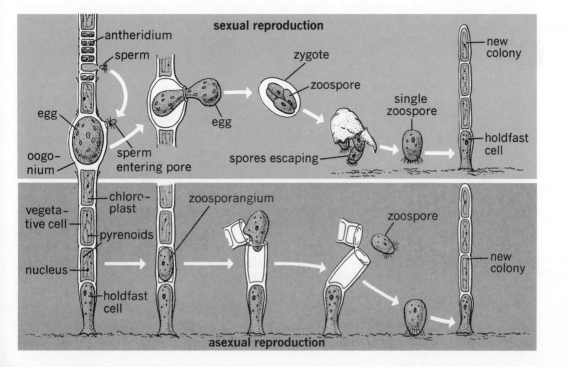

Any cell above the holdfast can change its content into a large, single zoospore. This zoospore moves through the water by means of a ring of flagella. Upon reaching a suitable spot, it becomes a holdfast and gives rise to a new filament.

Thus, asexual reproduction in *Oedogonium* is much like that in *Ulothrix*. In sexual reproduction, however, *Oedogonium* differs greatly. *Only certain cells* in a filament take part in sexual reproduction. Further, these cells form *heterogametes* that are clearly different in sexual type. For these reasons, *Oedogonium* is considered to be one of the more advanced algae.

Several cells in an *Oedogonium* filament may develop into large, single eggs. Each of these special cells is called an **oogonium** (oe-uh-GOE-nee-um). In most species, two sperms form in each of several shortened cells grouped together in the filament. Each of these cells is an **antheridium.** Eggs and sperms may develop in the same or in different filaments, depending on the species.

The sperm looks like a tiny zoospore. Soon after leaving the antheridium, it swims to the oogonium and enters through a small pore. The egg is fertilized and becomes a zygote. After a time, the oogonium wall breaks apart. The released zygote forms a thick wall and becomes a zygospore. After a dormant period, the zygospore produces four zoospores by meiosis. Each of these can begin a new strand of *Oedogonium*.

CHROMOSOME NUMBERS IN SEXUAL REPRODUCTION

We noted the beginnings of sexual reproduction in *Spirogyra*, with conjugation. In *Ulothrix*, we came to a more complex method involving isogametes. Finally, in *Oedogonium*, we saw reproduction by means of heterogametes. Each of these forms also reproduces by some asexual process.

How are chromosomes transmitted in reproduction? We can take *Ulothrix* as an example. The isogametes, like all gametes, have the haploid chromosome number. The zygote that results from the union of two gametes has the diploid number. This diploid stage in the life cycle is called the **sporophyte** generation. In *Ulothrix*, this generation is limited to the diploid zygote. In plants such as mosses, ferns, and seed plants, however, it is the main part of the plant's life.

After fertilization, the zygote undergoes meiosis. Four haploid nuclei result. These haploid nuclei become zoospores, which give rise to new haploid *Ulothrix* filaments. Each filament, besides reproducing asexually, may at times produce gametes. For this reason, the filaments are said to be in the **gametophyte** generation. This generation is the main stage in the life cycle of *Ulothrix*. The gametophyte has the haploid chromosome number, as do the gametes it forms by mitosis.

An organism that has two different stages in its life cycle is said to show *alternation of generations.* You will see alternation of generations throughout the plant kingdom.

The alternation of generations may be difficult to comprehend. A generalized diagram should be drawn on the chalkboard and explained.

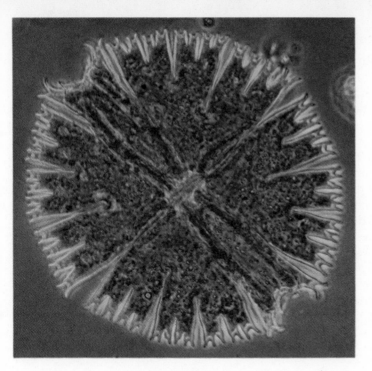

20–9 A living freshwater desmid.
(Walter Dawn)

DESMIDS

One of the most interesting forms of green algae is the *desmids*. These free-floating algae are common in the quiet waters of ponds and lakes. Some types live singly, others in colonies. Some form filaments and are called chain desmids. Along with other small, floating algae, desmids are often spoken of as **plankton.**

A desmid cell is made up of equal halves connected by a narrow isthmus in which the nucleus lies. Each half contains one or two large chloroplasts. Through the microscope, desmids often appear to be quite beautiful.

Chrysophyta

DIATOMS

Diatoms, of the phylum *Chrysophyta*, are probably the most widely distributed of all algae. More than 16,000 diatom species have been found in fresh and salt water. Next to bacteria, there are more diatoms on earth than any other life form.

Most diatoms are one-celled plankton algae that cannot move about on their own. They may live singly or in colonies. Some forms float free, while others live attached to objects or organisms. Different species vary in size and shape. They are noted for the intricate designs formed by microscopic lines on their tiny shells.

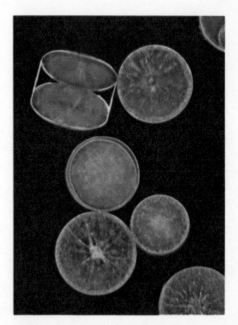

20–10 Photomicrograph of diatoms. As you can see, the shapes and sizes of the shells of living diatoms vary with the species. (D.P. Wilson)

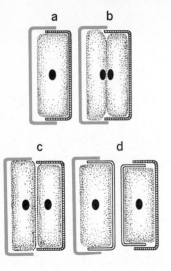

20-11 Diatoms usually reproduce asexually by cell division, as shown.

20-12 A dinoflagellate, *Peridinium*.

Nearly all diatoms contain chlorophyll in chloroplasts. Often, the green color is masked by a golden-brown pigment. Like other Chrysophyta, diatoms store foods as oils rather than carbohydrates.

The wall of a diatom has an inner layer of pectin and an outer layer of *silica*, or silicon dioxide. The wall is in two sections called *valves*. One valve overlaps the other, much as the top of a pillbox overlaps the bottom.

Cell division is the most common form of reproduction among diatoms. The nucleus divides and the cytoplasm and chloroplasts separate into two bodies around the daughter nuclei. The valves of the shell pull apart. A new inner valve forms over the open part of the two new cells.

When diatoms die, the protoplasm and inner walls decay. The clear outer walls of silica remain and settle to the bottom of the lake or sea. Over centuries, these shells build up as layers of *diatomaceous earth*. Some layers formed in ancient times are now on dry land. One such deposit in California is more than 450 meters thick.

Diatomaceous earth is mined and used in fine scouring powders and polishes, as well as in filters for refining gasoline and sugar. It is also used as insulation material and in building roads.

Pyrrophyta

DINOFLAGELLATES

The phylum *Pyrrophyta*, meaning "fire algae," is the smallest phylum of algae. Its main members are one-celled algae known as *dinoflagellates*. Most dinoflagellates live in the oceans, though a few live in fresh water. Some of the ocean species are *phosphorescent* and give off a strange light. This light can easily be seen at night if large numbers of the algae are present.

The cell walls of dinoflagellates are quite different from those of other organisms with flagella. The walls are made up of many-sided cellulose plates. There are two grooves in the wall, one lengthwise and the other circling the cell. A flagellum lies in each groove. Chloroplasts in the cell contain chlorophyll and a yellow-brown pigment that usually masks the green color.

Ocean dinoflagellates are an important source of food for other organisms. One type, however, causes terrible damage. This is *Gymnodinium*, which is responsible for the "red tide" that sometimes occurs in warm ocean waters.

At certain times, water conditions seem to favor very rapid reproduction. *Gymnodinium* cells then appear in great numbers— hundreds of millions in a few liters of water. The cells contain a red pigment that is poisonous to fish and other sea animals. Millions of fish may die in an outbreak of "red tide."

"Red tides" seem to occur at fairly regular intervals, but we do not know why. Copper compounds are known to kill the dinoflagellates but would not be practical over the wide areas affected.

Phaeophyta

THE BROWN ALGAE

The algae usually called *seaweeds* belong to two different phyla. One of these is the phylum *Phaeophyta*, containing more than a thousand species of *brown algae*. Most brown algae live in the colder ocean waters. Attached to rocks, they grow at depths of a few meters to fifteen meters or more.

All brown algae are multicellular, but they vary greatly in form and size. They range from slender filaments to flat ribbons more than thirty meters long. In some ways, many brown algae resemble the higher plants. A large, rootlike holdfast anchors the thallus. The *stipe* looks like a stem, while the *blades* may resemble leaves. Many brown algae have several air-filled bladders which serve as floats and support them in the water.

Cells of brown algae contain chlorophyll and other pigments. One of these is a golden-brown pigment that usually masks the other colors.

Fucus, or rockweed, is a common brown alga of colder waters. It can be seen in great amounts in shallow coastal waters when the tide is out. The forked thalli are up to a meter in length. They float toward the surface when covered by water. The tips of many thalli contain reproductive organs. *Fucus* is used in packing shellfish and other seafoods for shipment.

Another common brown alga is *Sargassum*. This alga floats in large masses in many areas of the Atlantic Ocean. One such area, known as the Sargasso Sea, lies between the Bahamas and the Azores. Here, floating masses of *Sargassum* and other algae cover more than one million square kilometers.

Kelps are the largest brown algae, reaching lengths over thirty meters. They are common along the western coast of North America. A kelp is made up of several flat blades attached by stalks to a holdfast. Air bladders cause kelps to float.

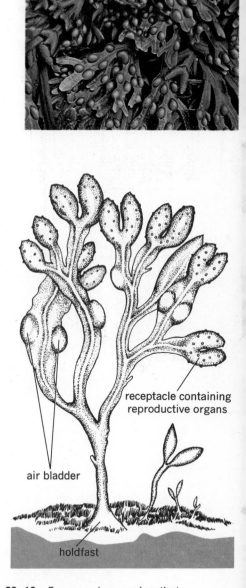

20-13 *Fucus*, a brown alga that lives along the Atlantic Coast. (D.P. Wilson)

Rhodophyta

THE RED ALGAE

Other seaweeds are among the *red algae* of the phylum *Rhodophyta*. There are more than 2,500 species in this phylum, nearly all of which live in the sea. All contain chlorophyll and carry on photosynthesis. The green color is often masked by a red pigment. Different species may be green, red, brown, or purple.

Most red algae are less than thirty centimeters in length. They may be flat and ribbonlike or finely branched and feathery. Many species live in shallow coastal waters, but some are found at depths of 150 meters or more. Red algae are most common in warm tropical areas.

More on Algae

20–14 *Chondrus crispus*, or Irish moss, a marine red alga that grows on rocks along the cold North Atlantic Coast. (Walter Dawn)

IMPORTANCE OF ALGAE

Algae are the chief source of food for much of the animal life in their environments. Many small fish eat only algae. The diet of whales, too, is made up mainly of algae.

Sea algae have long been used as soil fertilizers. They add organic matter to the soil and replace the mineral salts that growing plants have removed. Algae are very rich in iodine, which is necessary to both plant and animal life.

In some parts of the world, algae are used in making soups, gelatins, and other foods. A sodium compound taken from algae is added to ice cream to keep it smooth. The same compound added to feed for dairy cattle raises milk production.

Agar (AH-GAHR) is produced from red algae of the Indian Ocean. It is used as a gelling agent in culture media for growing bacteria. Other products of algae are used in making cosmetics, finishing leather, and many other industries.

Some algae become poisonous when they die. They pollute the water, making it dangerous for human use as well as for fish and other water life. Great care is taken to prevent this in such places as fish hatcheries.

It has been learned that algae can be mass-cultured in plastic tubes or tanks. The algae multiply if supplied with light, water, and carbon dioxide. This may be useful in long space flights. The astronauts would need a constant supply of oxygen to breathe. Algae use carbon dioxide and give off oxygen during photosynthesis. The algae could also serve as food.

LICHENS—TWO LIFE FORMS IN ONE

The *lichens* (LIKE'nz) are often grouped with the fungi but can also be classified with the algae. The reason is that both a fungus *and* an alga make up the body of a lichen.

In most lichens, the fungus is one of the Ascomycetes. The alga usually is a green or blue-green form. Cells of the alga are scattered among the hyphae of the fungus.

Lichens are of three general types. Some form a hard, grainy crust. Others look like flat, leathery leaves. Still others form a network of slender branches.

Both the alga and the fungus benefit by living together. In fact, neither could survive alone in the environments where lichens live. The fungus depends on the alga for food made by photosynthesis. The alga is protected and kept moist by the fungus hyphae. **This condition, in which two organisms benefit from their relationship, is called *mutualism.***

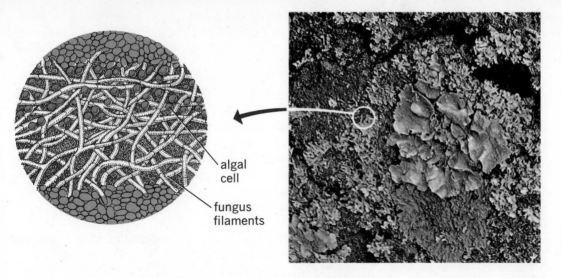

algal
cell

fungus
filaments

Lichens can live in places where few plants could survive. Some live on tree trunks. Others cling to rocks far above the timber line on high mountains. Lichens are among the most common life forms on the frozen tundra of the far north.

Mountain lichens are important pioneer organisms. Over many years, they cause rock surfaces to crumble. Their own organic remains also build up. This material is the basis for soil which can support plants.

20–15 A lichen is two kinds of organisms—an alga and a fungus—living together. This symbiotic relationship is called mutualism. (Dennis Brokaw)

SUMMARY

The algae, once thought of as simple plants, are now usually classed as protists. They are among the most common and widespread forms of life. Most live in water, though some live in other environments.

Some algae live as single cells, others in colonies made up of many cells. All contain chlorophyll and carry on photosynthesis. Many different methods of reproduction are seen among the algae. These methods range from asexual cell fission to sexual reproduction by means of heterogametes. Many forms reproduce by more than one method.

In their water environments, algae are important as sources of both food and oxygen. They are sometimes used as soil fertilizers and in other ways. Some types are harmful, such as the dinoflagellate that causes "red tides."

thallus	apical cell	gametophyte	**BIOLOGICALLY**
filament	pyrenoid	alternation of generations	**SPEAKING**
fragmentation	holdfast	plankton	
isogametes	oogonium	agar	
heterogametes	antheridium	mutualism	
heterocyst	sporophyte		

1. List the generalized characteristics of algae.
2. How are algae different from fungi?
3. In what respects are the cells of blue-green algae more primitive than those of green algae?
4. Name six phyla of algae and give some examples of each.
5. Describe conjugation in *Spirogyra*.
6. What is alternation of generations? Describe its occurance in *Ulothrix*.
7. What characteristic of desmids distinguishes them from other unicellular algae?
8. Describe several unique characteristics of diatoms.
9. What causes "red tide"? How do you account for its destruction of fish?
10. List some of the ways that algae are useful to people.
11. How does a lichen illustrate mutualism?

APPLYING PRINCIPLES AND CONCEPTS

1. A colony of 50 algae cells is not a 50-celled plant. Explain why.
2. Both spores and gametes are reproductive cells. How are they different?
3. How might blue-green algae be an indicator of water pollution?
4. Compare *Spirogyra, Ulothrix,* and *Oedogonium* in regard to specialization of cells in a filament.
5. List several unusual habitats of algae. Explain why most algae grow in shallow water or float.

RELATED READING

Books

Boettcher, Helmuth, *Wonder Drugs: A History of Antibiotics*.
J. B. Lippincott Co., Philadelphia. 1963. An entertaining history of the "wonder drugs" and the medical discoveries of the last century.

Christensen, Clyde M., *The Molds and Man (2nd ed.)*.
University of Minnesota Press, Minneapolis. 1965. A general account of the fungi and their impact on man.

Kavaler, Lucy, *The Wonders of Fungi*.
The John Day Company, Inc., New York. 1964. The story of fungi as both destroyer and saver of man, from prehistoric days to the present-day age of wonder drugs.

Lindemann, Edward, *Water Animals for Your Microscope*.
The Macmillan Company, New York. 1967. A guide to identifying and examining the variety of animals found in ponds, lakes, rivers, and at the seashore.

Schneider, Leo, *Microbes in Your Life*.
Harcourt Brace Jovanovich, Inc., New York. 1966. A good book for background information, includes a discussion of techniques used in microbiology.

Silverstein, Alvin and Virginia, *Cancer*.
The John Day Co., New York. 1972. This book explains the various forms of cancer, gives the symptoms, and explains the possible causes and treatments of cancer.

Wheeler, Margaret F., and Wesley A. Volk, *Basic Microbiology*. J. B. Lippincott Co., Philadelphia. 1964. Microbiology treated not only in terms of the categories of microorganisms but also in terms of the application of this knowledge to everyday life.

Articles

Cooper, Max D., "The Development of the Immune System," *Scientific American*, November, 1974. A detailed study about the highly diversified cells that defend the body against foreign substances.

Echlin, Robert, "The Blue-Green Algae," *Scientific American*, June, 1966. Deals with the identification and the environmental importance of the blue-green algae.

Lamb, I. M., "Lichens," *Scientific American*, October, 1969. A general account of lichens as an example of symbiotic mutualism.

Satir, Peter, "How Cilia Move," *Scientific American*, October, 1974. A detailed presentation on the hairlike appendages of living cells.

Wood, William, B., and Edgar, R. S., "Building a Bacterial Virus," *Scientific American*, July, 1967. An interesting account of the structure of a bacterial virus.

Zahl, Paul A., "Where Would We Be Without Algae," *National Geographic*, March, 1974. A dramatic article concerned with life's dependence on the algae.

unit 4

MULTICELLULAR PLANTS

Ages ago, certain aquatic plants probably changed in ways that allowed them to survive on land. Perhaps an ancestral alga growing on moist soil shot a filament into the air and pushed rootlike "fingers" into the earth. Possibly the closest living relatives to these first land plants are mosses. But they never adapted completely to a land environment. Today, *seed plants,* with their superior reproductive and productive structures, dominate the land.

THE FIRST LAND PLANTS

During the Paleozoic era, about 350 million years ago, land masses rose above the seas that had covered the earth. As the earth was uncovered, land plants began to develop, probably from green algae living in the seas. **The plants developed along two different lines: toward the phylum Bryophyta and the phylum Tracheophyta.** *Bryophytes* **are mosses and liverworts.** *Tracheophytes* **are vascular plants, such as ferns and seed plants.** A study of plants will show you that tracheophytes have evolved further than bryophytes. Tracheophytes, particularly seed plants, adapted efficiently to environmental changes through the ages. They dominate our vegetation today.

The Bryophytes

MOSSES AND LIVERWORTS

Bryophytes were among the first land plants. But they never made more than primitive adaptations to life on land. For one thing, bryophytes do not have a true root system. Thus, they cannot reach water under the soil and are unable to anchor themselves securely. They do have absorbing structures, but these are small and do not reach far. Bryophytes do not have *vascular tissue,* which conducts fluids through the plant. And, without vascular tissue, they cannot carry water very far. Because of these limitations, bryophytes have remained small.

Mosses and liverworts are limited also because they depend on water for reproduction. Their sperm cells need to swim through water to fertilize the eggs successfully.

Despite these limitations, bryophytes are widely distributed. They are most abundant in temperate and tropical climates. They do not compete with the tracheophytes, but they can live side by side with them. In fact, ferns and seed plants often provide the shade that many mosses need for survival. In such places as the windswept arctic tundra, and above the tree line in mountain areas, bryophytes are the dominant plant form.

THE STRUCTURE OF A MOSS

The word "moss" is often used incorrectly. Most of the plants people call "water mosses" are actually algae. Reindeer moss is actually a lichen. Spanish moss, which hangs from trees in the South, is actually a seed plant related to the pineapple.

You can tell real moss if you look closely. It seems to be everywhere—in the cracks of shaded sidewalks, on the ground under trees, and on rotting logs. A clump of moss is really a bunch of tiny individual plants. Each plant has a slender stem, usually less than three centimeters long, with lots of thin fragile leaves around it. These leaves are only one cell thick, except along the center. If you

Mosses and Ferns

OBJECTIVES
- EXPLAIN the development of the first land plants.
- DESCRIBE the structure of mosses.
- EXPLAIN the life cycle of the moss.
- LIST some uses for moss.
- DESCRIBE liverworts.
- DISTINGUISH bryophytes from tracheophytes.
- EXPLAIN the life cycles of the moss and the fern.
- LIST a few of the relatives of the fern.

Mosses were the dominant plants approximately 300 million years ago. At that time, giant moss plants treelike in form existed. Mosses of today are much smaller and are important to the botanist because they give clues to ancient plant life.

Prepare numerous specimens of mosses as a visual aid for the discussion of this topic.

Time Scale of Early Land Plants Based on Fossil Records

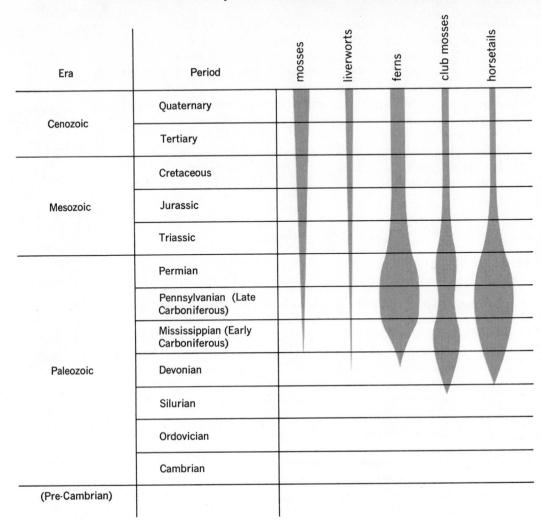

Era	Period	mosses	liverworts	ferns	club mosses	horsetails
Cenozoic	Quaternary					
	Tertiary					
Mesozoic	Cretaceous					
	Jurassic					
	Triassic					
Paleozoic	Permian					
	Pennsylvanian (Late Carboniferous)					
	Mississippian (Early Carboniferous)					
	Devonian					
	Silurian					
	Ordovician					
	Cambrian					
(Pre-Cambrian)						

21–1 A time scale of early land plants.

Mosses grow in many different localities. They often become established on cooled volcanic rocks. Ask students if they have ever seen mosses covering what was once a volcanic area.

If possible, have students observe a moss that has dried up because of hot, dry weather. Demonstrate how these "dead" looking plants will open up and become "alive" as soon as some water is poured over them. Illustrate with photographs if real plants are not available.

take a moss plant out of the ground, you will see a cluster of hair-like filaments coming out of the bottom of the stem. These are called **rhizoids. Rhizoids serve the same purpose as roots in tracheophytes. They absorb water and minerals, and anchor the plant. But, unlike roots, rhizoids are simply cellular filaments without specialized tissues.** If you examine rhizoids, you can see why mosses are limited in size.

The moss plant that we find most often is in only one stage of its life cycle. To find other stages, it is necessary to follow the moss through that life cycle.

THE LIFE CYCLE OF THE MOSS

Each moss plant goes through a set reproductive cycle. This cycle includes an asexual spore-producing stage, a sexual gamete-

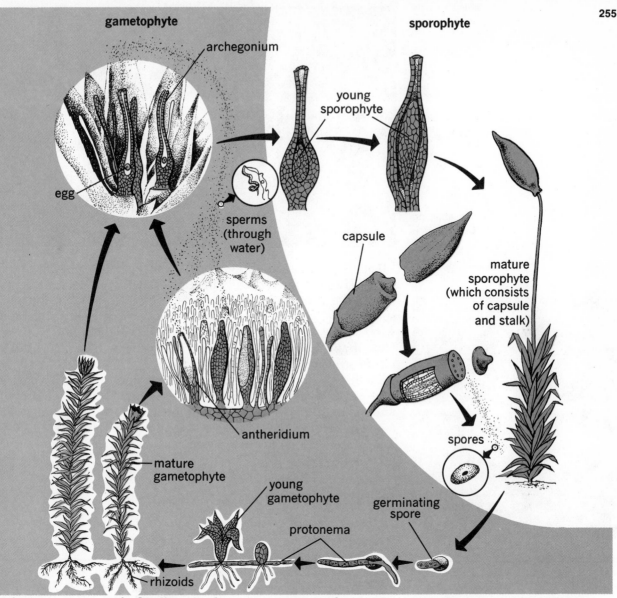

gametophyte

archegonium

egg

sperms
(through
water)

antheridium

mature
gametophyte

young
gametophyte

protonema

rhizoids

sporophyte

young
sporophyte

capsule

mature
sporophyte
(which consists
of capsule
and stalk)

spores

germinating
spore

producing stage, and, finally, another spore stage. This is an example of the "alternation of generations" discussed in Chapter Twenty.

The gamete-producing plant is the *gametophyte*. In this stage, sexual reproductive organs develop at the tips of leafy stems. Some species of moss have the male and female organs on the same plant. On other species of moss, they are found on separate plants. Sperms are formed in sac-like stalks called **antheridia**. The female organs, or **archegonia** are found on short stalks. These organs contain a single, large egg.

When the egg is ready for fertilization, the archegonium opens. If water is present, the sperms swim to the archegonium and fertilize the egg.

21–2 Life cycle of the moss. Note that alternation of generations occurs. After fertilization, a sporophyte grows out of the female gametophyte. Spores form at the top of the sporophyte and fall to the ground. These germinate and grow into a new generation of gametophytes which reproduce sexually.

21-3 A clump of moss showing stalks and capsules. (Carolina Biological Supply Co.)

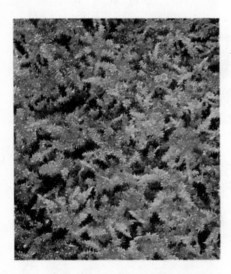

21-4 Sphagnum moss. (Carolina Biological Supply Co.)

If this unit is being studied in the spring, ask students to bring in moss spore cases. The spore cases, containing the ripening spores, appear in many shapes. Some are round while others resemble pipes or eggs. The spore cases are usually green when they first appear and later turn an orange, brown, or red color.

Explain the difference between thallus forms of liverworts and crustose forms in lichens. Students often confuse these forms.

Fertilization starts the *sporophyte* stage, or asexual part, of the cycle. The sporophyte grows into a stalk with a capsule at the top. Inside the capsule, numerous spore cells are formed. When the spores are ripe, the capsule opens. Spores are carried off by the wind. They will grow where they fall if the conditions are right. Note that the spores are spread without the help of water. But gametes still need water for fertilization.

Each spore forms a small, threadlike structure called a **protonema** (PRO-toe-NEE-muh). The cells of the protonema have chlorophyll and make their own food. The protonema resembles an alga. This once caused scientists to class mosses as a close relative of the algae. The protonema forms new stems and new rhizoids. Thus, a new moss plant is formed.

THE ECONOMIC IMPORTANCE OF MOSSES

Mosses are important in rocky areas. They create soil by growing in cracks and breaking down rocks. Enough soil gradually accumulates, giving larger plants a place to grow.

The most widely used moss is *sphagnum*, or peat moss. Peat moss grows in small lakes and bogs. There it forms thicker and thicker mats that float on the surface of the water. The older plants in the mats slowly rot and settle to the bottom where they form peat. This is a sludgy brownish-black substance that is used for fuel, or roof-building material in certain parts of the world. Sphagnum is used by gardeners as a *mulch*. They work it into the soil or put it on top. This helps make the soil loose so it holds water during dry summer months.

THE LIVERWORTS

Liverworts are less known than mosses. These small plants grow in wet places—near streams and springs, or even in the water. In their gametophyte stage, liverworts have thin leathery leaflike bodies that lie flat against the ground. These leaves are anchored to the ground by the many rhizoids on their undersides. One common liverwort, the *Marchantia*, has a plant body, called a **thallus**, that looks like a leathery green tongue. A thallus is either male or female. From a male thallus rises a projection called an antheridial stalk. The female plant forms an archegonial stalk that is 3 centimeters tall. When sperms on the antheridial stalk mature, they swim through rainwater or dew to the archegonial stalks. After fertilization, the zygote becomes a sporophyte plant. The spores then develop in a capsule that grows out of the archegonium. Eventually, the spores are discharged.

The Tracheophytes

VASCULAR PLANTS

As we have already mentioned, **plants with vascular tissues are in the phylum Tracheophyta. Early tracheophytes probably evolved from ancestral algae at about the same time that bryophytes began to evolve.** Living tracheophytes are classified into the four subphyla shown in the table in Chapter Fourteen. The fourth and largest subphylum contains the ferns and seed plants, including flowering plants. However, the discussion here is limited to ferns and other early tracheophytes.

EARLY TRACHEOPHYTES

Ferns were abundant about three hundred million years ago. In fact, during the Mississippian and Pennsylvanian periods of the Carboniferous age, they were one of the dominant plants. The damp marsh land and the warm climate were perfect for ferns and other early tracheophytes. Big mosses and horsetails grew in dense forests of tree ferns, some over ten meters high. And smaller species—like those we know today—grew beneath the big ferns, forming a thick undercover. Tree ferns still grow in Hawaii, Puerto Rico, and other tropical regions. They are reminders of their ancient relatives.

The great fern forests are gone now. But they continue to benefit people today. How is that possible? During the Carboniferous age, decomposing plants accumulated in the swampy areas where they grew. Later, shifts in the earth's crust buried and compressed this organic compost into the coal deposits that we mine today. It probably took about 100 meters of compressed vegetation to make seven meters of coal.

THE LIFE CYCLE OF THE FERN

As mentioned earlier, most mosses you see are in their gametophyte stage. On the other hand, most ferns you see growing in the woods or in a garden are in the sporophyte stage of their life cycle.

21–5 Marchantia, a common liverwort. (Carolina Biological Supply Co.)

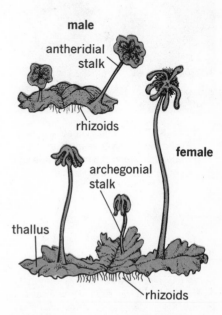

21–6 Female and male liverwort plants.

21-7 Diorama of a forest typical of the Mississippian and Pennsylvanian periods during the Carboniferous age. (American Museum of Natural History)

21-8 Tree ferns. These are small relatives of the tree ferns that were abundant some 300 million years ago. (W. H. Hodge, Peter Arnold)

Except for tree ferns, most fern stems creep horizontally just below the surface of the soil. This underground stem is called a *rhizome.* It contains fluid-carrying vascular tissue similar to that of seed plants. Clusters of roots grow out from the rhizome and burrow through the soil. These roots anchor the plant and absorb water and minerals. The leaves that rise up from the rhizome are called *fronds.* The fronds, the rhizome, and the roots of a fern sporophyte body compare to the stalk and the capsule of a moss body.

When fern fronds mature, some of them develop reproductive structures on the undersides. These structures look like small brown dots or patches. Each is called a *sorus* (plural, sori). Sori are important in identifying ferns, since they are located and shaped differently in different fern families, genera, and species. Each sorus consists of a cluster of sporangia (singular, sporangium) that are attached by slender stalks. When a sporangium is mature and has produced spores, a row of special cells along two thirds of its surface dries and starts to shrink. This stretches and then ruptures the sporangium, discharging spores.

When a spore lands on moist soil, it germinates, forming the first cell of the gametophyte generation. More cell divisions form a short filament, which soon puts out a few colorless rhizoids. The tip of the filament broadens into a sheet of cells. After several weeks of growth, this becomes the heart-shaped *prothallus.* The prothallus is the gametophyte fern plant. This stage of the fern is rarely seen. It is only one or two centimeters in width. Because all its cells contain chloroplasts, the prothallus can perform photosynthesis.

Eventually, multicellular sex organs develop on the underside of the prothallus. Archegonia, which function like those of the moss, form on the prothallus. Each archegonium usually contains one egg at its base. The base is embedded in the tissue of the prothallus. As the archegonia are developing, so are the knob-shaped antheridia. These begin to protrude from the base of the prothallus, among the rhizoids. There, the prothallus is only one cell thick. When mature, each antheridium contains several motile sperms.

When the eggs and sperm are mature, water becomes a necessity. But even the slightest film of water is enough to allow fertilization. The sperms are set free and swim along a watery path to enter the open archegonia. A single sperm fertilizes each egg, forming a zygote. This is the first cell of the sporophyte generation.

Right after fertilization, the zygote begins cell division. It grows and fills the archegonium. And soon it is an *embryo fern.* This embryo consists of a foot embedded in the tissue of the prothallus, plus

Ask students to compare the life cycles shown in Figs. 21-2 and 21-9. Be sure to point out the decrease in the gametophyte generation.

21–9 Life cycle of the fern. The gametophyte, which is so small you can hardly see it, develops on the ground.

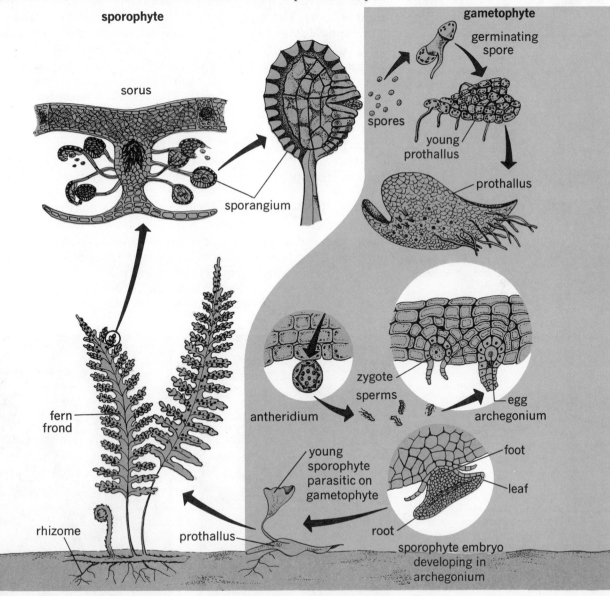

sporophyte

sorus

sporangium

gametophyte

germinating spore

spores

young prothallus

prothallus

fern frond

antheridium

zygote sperms

egg
archegonium

young sporophyte parasitic on gametophyte

foot

leaf

root

rhizome

prothallus

sporophyte embryo developing in archegonium

21-10 This club moss, *Lycopodium*, is related to the ferns because of similarity in reproduction. (Russ Kinne)

Ask students to imagine what would happen if all of the billions of fern spores survived. Ferns would then be so numerous that they would crowd out other plants. Ask students to relate this discussion to other plants and draw conclusions about the need for so many spores because most numbers will not survive.

Ask students to bring in examples of the horsetail. Field horsetails are commonly found in early spring and appear in clumps.

Discuss with the students how fossils are formed. Have the students bring in any fossils they may have found.

a root, a stem, and a leaf. After a while, the young plant becomes settled in the soil. Once this happens, the prothallus simply withers away. The young fern bears additional fronds and grows into a familiar fern clump.

Review the life cycle of a fern. You'll see that the sporophyte stage is more prominent than the gametophyte stage. The sporophyte is larger and can grow for years. The gametophyte prothallus, on the other hand, is small and lives for only a few weeks. It is clear, then, that ferns have evolved far differently than bryophytes, in which the gametophyte is the prominent stage.

CLUB MOSSES AND HORSETAILS

Club mosses, ground pines, and horsetails have life cycles like those of ferns. The sporophyte is large and prominent, while the gametophyte is inconspicuous. Despite their names, club mosses *(Selaginella)* and ground pines *(Lycopodium)* are neither mosses nor pines. Club mosses bear reproductive structures shaped like cones at the tips of some of their branches. These cone-shaped organs contain many sporangia. The leaves of these sporophyte plants are small and scalelike. Some club mosses grow flat and close to the ground. Others stand erect.

The horsetails *(Equisetum)* have rough, gritty branches. They are also called "scouring rushes" because pioneers probably used them to scour pots and pans. Horsetails are often found in ditches, lowlands, and the shallow water near lake shores. These plants have two kinds of aerial branches: vegetative and reproductive. The vegetative branches look a bit like horses' tails. They form shoots that end in tufts. The reproductive, or fertile, branches have cones at their tips. These cones contain sporangia. The horsetails represent a single genus of an ancient plant subphylum. Their ancestors were large, grew in abundance over vast areas, and were among the most important coal-forming plants of the Carboniferous age.

21-11 Horsetails or scouring rushes. The horsetail produces bushy, green vegetative shoots. A brown conelike structure contains the reproductive organs. (Carolina Biological Supply Co.; Albert Towle)

SUMMARY

Biologists consider bryophytes to be a side line in the evolutionary development of plants. The early tracheophytes are thought to be the main line of evolution leading to seed plants. Now that you are familiar with moss and fern life cycles, you can probably understand why. You saw that the structural limitations of mosses prevented them from growing larger and challenging the tracheophytes. But, despite their limitations, mosses continue to survive and increase. How? They live in tough environments that exclude most of the tracheophytes.

The ferns and their relatives, on the other hand, are plants with vascular tissues. This allows them to grow larger than mosses. Ferns and their relatives are not as dominant as they once were in the Carboniferous age. As the ferns declined, a different set of tracheophytes, the seed plants, took over. We live in the age of seed plants.

BIOLOGICALLY SPEAKING

tracheophyte	archegonia	frond
bryophyte	protonema	sorus
vascular tissue	thallus	prothallus
rhizoid	rhizome	embryo fern
antheridia		

QUESTIONS FOR REVIEW

1. Describe two characteristics of bryophytes that limit their size.
2. Name several organisms that are incorrectly called mosses.
3. Describe the life cycle of the moss.
4. What is the economic importance of sphagnum moss?
5. Where might you find liverworts growing?
6. Describe the gametophyte of a liverwort such as Marchantia.
7. What structural characteristic is common to fern and seed plants?
8. What stage of a fern develops from a germinating spore? How does this provide a link to its algal ancestry?
9. In what way are ferns, like mosses, dependent on water during sexual reproduction?
10. How are club mosses and horsetails similar to ferns?

APPLYING PRINCIPLES AND CONCEPTS

1. Discuss the lines of development from the algae to the bryophytes and tracheophytes. Point out the factors that caused one to be an evolutionary "blind alley" and the other to continue to evolve.
2. Give possible reasons for the abundance of mosses in regions with extreme climatic conditions; for example, tundra and alpine areas.
3. Give possible reasons for the disappearance of fern forests in most parts of the world.
4. Compare the sporophyte plant of a moss and a fern and explain the ways in which the fern is more advanced.

chapter twenty-two

The Seed Plants

OBJECTIVES
- DEFINE a seed plant.
- LIST the characteristics of the gymnosperms.
- LIST the characteristics of the angiosperms.
- DISTINGUISH a monocot plant from a dicot plant.
- DESCRIBE the function of each vegetative organ of a flowering plant.
- DESCRIBE the specialized tissues of a seed plant.
- DISTINGUISH a herbaceous plant from a woody plant.
- DEFINE annuals, biennials, and perennials.

Discuss with students some of the reasons seed plants have become dominant. This discussion can relate back to the previous chapter, which discussed the large numbers of spores that fail to survive.

22–1 Typical examples of deciduous trees (left) and coniferous trees. (Albert Towle; Vivian Fenster)

THE RISE OF SEED PLANTS

The first forests on earth were not made up of trees. Instead, they were made up of mosses, horsetails, and ferns. They probably developed during the Devonian period of the Paleozoic era. Among those plants were *seed ferns*, the ancestors of today's seed plants. Seed ferns have long been extinct. But they were abundant in the swamp forests of the Carboniferous age. They probably led to other forms of seed plants, including cycads and conifers, during the Permian period of the late Paleozoic era.

When the Mesozoic era dawned around 200 million years ago, the earth's climate grew warmer and drier. Biologists think this accounts for the gradual disappearance of the seed ferns during the Triassic period. At this time, other seed plants gained in number. Among these were the conifers which were predominant in the Mesozoic era. Flowering plants, the most highly evolved of the seed plants, first showed up in the Jurassic period of the Mesozoic era. And they spread rapidly throughout the Cretaceous period. Today they are the dominant form of vegetation on earth.

WHAT IS A SEED PLANT?

Seed plants have vascular tissues. This classifies them in the phylum Tracheophyta, along with the older club mosses, horsetails, and ferns. Here we are interested in the subphylum Pteropsida, which contains three classes:
- *Filicineae*—ferns
- *Gymnospermae*—cone-bearing plants, including conifers, cycads, ginkgoes, and the now extinct seed ferns
- *Angiospermae*—flowering plants

Of these classes, only the **gymnosperms** and the **angiosperms** produce seeds.

What is a seed? Why have seed plants had such a biological advantage in land environments? Why has the making of seeds helped to cover the land ever since the Carboniferous age?

In one sense, a *seed* is a packaged plant. Everything it needs to begin growing is wrapped up in one or more protecting coats. Inside the seed is a new plant or *embryo*, surrounded by stored food. Because of its coat, the seed can lie dormant for months. It may be carried with the wind, float on the water, or ride on the fur of an animal. When it lands in soil, where it gets warmth and moisture, the seed coat softens. Soon the embryo expands, sending a root into the earth and a shoot upward. **The spreading of seeds is a very efficient means of reproduction.** That is one reason seed plants have spread over so much of the land.

Seed plants have been highly successful for numerous reasons. They are so successful that there are more than 300,000 species of seed plants. In fact, one family of seed plants (Leguminosae) outnumber all of the surviving ferns.

22-2 A time scale of seed plants.

Time Scale of Seed Plants Based on Fossil Records

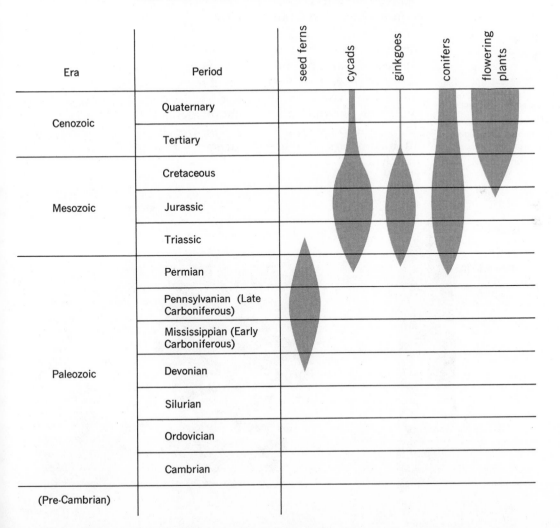

Era	Period	seed ferns	cycads	ginkgoes	conifers	flowering plants
Cenozoic	Quaternary					
	Tertiary					
Mesozoic	Cretaceous					
	Jurassic					
	Triassic					
Paleozoic	Permian					
	Pennsylvanian (Late Carboniferous)					
	Mississippian (Early Carboniferous)					
	Devonian					
	Silurian					
	Ordovician					
	Cambrian					
(Pre-Cambrian)						

The Gymnosperms

THE "NAKED SEED"

Gymnosperms are in a different class from angiosperms because of the way their seeds develop. **The name gymnosperm means "naked seed." They are called "naked" because their seeds develop exposed on the upper surfaces of cone scales. The seeds of angiosperms, on the other hand, develop within the protective wall of the ovary.**

Only about 750 different species of gymnosperm are alive today. They are the few survivors of a much larger group that once lived in earlier geological periods. Living gymnosperms are now classified in four orders. Three of these will be discussed here.

The order *Cycadales* includes about 100 kinds of ancient gymnosperms called *cycads*. They probably appeared near the end of the late Carboniferous age and spread during the Triassic and Jurassic periods of the Mesozoic era. Modern cycads look like palm trees. In fact, they are often called sago palms. They live in subtropical and tropical parts of Florida, the West Indies, and Mexico, and in certain areas of Australia and Africa.

Another order of gymnosperms, the *Ginkgoales*, has only one surviving species. It is called the ginkgo, or maidenhair tree *(Ginkgo biloba)*. The ginkgo is a large tree, sometimes as high as 30 meters or more, and one and a half meters thick. Its leaves are fan-shaped with two lobes. No other tree has leaves like it. They look something like the leaflets of the maidenhair fern. This is why the ginkgo is also called the *maidenhair tree*. Most of the leaves come out in clusters at the ends of spurs that grow out along the branches.

22–3 The bean is an example of an angiosperm, while the pine cone is an example of an gymnosperm. The bean seed is different from the pine seed in that is enclosed in a ripened ovary, or fruit. Whereas the pine seed lies exposed on a cone scale.

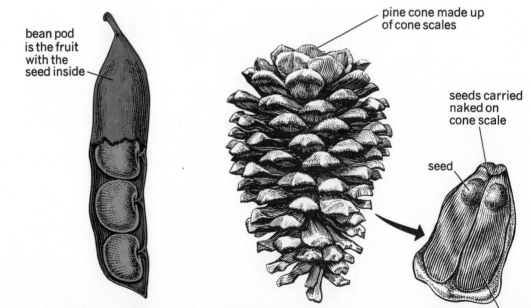

bean pod
is the fruit
with the
seed inside

pine cone made up
of cone scales

seeds carried
naked on
cone scale

seed

wing

Ginkgo trees are either male or female. Male trees produce pollen contained in short, conelike *catkins*. The female trees produce the seeds, which come in fleshy orange or yellow fruit about an inch wide. They look like plums or large cherries. Each contains a single, almond-flavored nut.

Once many species of Ginkgoales grew all over the world. But by the last glacial age, a million years ago, they could only be found in what is now China. For centuries, they were planted in Chinese temple gardens. Later, they were brought to Japan. Today, they are quite common in the United States. Even so, the ginkgo is still among the rarest of all living plants. It is the single surviving species of an order that flourished at the time of the dinosaurs.

THE CONIFERS

Familiar trees such as the pines, spruces, firs, and sequoias are put in the order *Coniferales*. **The name conifer refers to the woody cones you see on evergreens.** Although most conifers are trees, a few, like yews and junipers, are shrubs.

As a group, the conifers probably go back to the Carboniferous age. Today they are the most widespread of the gymnosperms. There are huge forests of them in North America. Some grow in rocky or sandy soils that will not support many broad-leaved trees. Others thrive in swamps and bogs and around lake edges. They flourish from Alaska to the Gulf of Mexico. They are found in all the major mountain regions, along the Great Lakes, and along the ocean coasts. These forests serve as the main source of supply for the lumber and forest products industries.

22–4 A cycad. While it resembles a palm tree in appearance, the cycad reproductive structure is like that of gymnosperms. (Albert Towle)

Point out to students the characteristics that place Ginkgo trees in the gymnosperms rather than the angiosperms.

22–5 The Ginkgo, or maidenhair tree. Its leaves resemble the leaflets of the maidenhair fern. (John H. Gerard, National Audubon Society; Walter Dawn)

22-6 A coniferous forest. (Werner H. Miller, Peter Arnold)

Point out to students the advantages of conifers and why they are the most abundant of all gymnosperms.

Ask students to bring into class examples of seed cones. Students can identify these cones from botany texts.

22-7 General Grant, a magnificent "big tree" in Kings Canyon National Park, California. (R. C. Zink)

Conifers grow larger and older than any other trees. One of the largest is a redwood *(Sequoia gigantea)* in California, 100 meters tall. It is more than 10 meters wide and probably more than 4,000 years old. An even bigger conifer is the cypress called the "Big Tree of Tule," in Mexico. This tree is fifteen meters thick and has probably been alive for more than 5,000 years.

Most conifers are evergreen. Two exceptions are the larch and the bald cypress. These trees lose their needles every fall. Conifer leaves are in the form of needles or scales.

Cones can contain either seeds or pollen. **Seed cones** are woody and take several months to develop. They produce pairs of winged seeds on the upper surfaces of shelflike *cone scales.* Seed cones come in all kinds of shapes and sizes. They are often helpful in identifying species of trees.

Pollen cones are smaller than seed cones. You find them at the tips of branches, sometimes in clusters. These cones are yellow or reddish in color. Pollen cones stay on the tree only a few days after they have shed their pollen. Most North American conifers have both seed and pollen cones, but on separate branches of the same tree.

The Angiosperms

THE FLOWERING PLANTS

The class Angiospermae includes all flowering plants. Angiosperms probably branched off from the gymnosperm line during the Jurassic period of the Mesozoic era. They developed quickly, replacing much of the vegetation during the Cretaceous period. **Today angiosperms are the dominant plant life.** They grow in most areas not occupied by coniferous forests.

There are several reasons for the success of angiosperms. Genetic variations over the ages have resulted in many forms—trees, shrubs, and herbs. They also grow in various ways. Some are upright; others climb, creep, or float. More than any other group, angiosperms can grow and reproduce rapidly in a wide variety of environments. They live in all types of soils. They survive in most extremes of temperature, rainfall, and sunshine. In one form or another, they inhabit deserts, lakes, plains, marshes, mountain slopes, and arctic regions.

The flowers, fruits, and seeds of angiosperms have all helped in their survival. Many angiosperms need water, wind, insects, and other agents for pollinating their flowers. Their fruits are carried to new places various ways, too. Their seeds contain food to keep the young plant nourished until it is rooted in its new home. Each of these advantages helps the angiosperms in competing with other land plants for survival.

MONOCOTS AND DICOTS

The class of *Angiospermae* includes about 300 families and more than 250,000 species. It is divided into two subclasses, the *Monocotyledonae* and the *Dicotyledonae*. The basic difference between the two is the number of **cotyledons,** or seed leaves, that develop in the embryo plant. The cotyledon is the first leaf of the young plant. In many species, the cotyledons act as a food supply to the seedling until it can synthesize its own food. In other species, the cotyledon carries on the first photosynthesis for the plant. As you may have guessed, **a monocot plant has a single cotyledon, while a dicot has two.** As you learn more about flowering plants, you will find other differences between these two subclasses. The arrangement of their root and stem tissues differs. They have different patterns of leaf veins and number of flower parts.

THE BODY OF A FLOWERING PLANT

Each organ of a flowering plant has a special job. And each does its job very well. The root, stem, and leaves are **vegetative organs.** They carry out all the processes necessary for life *except* reproduction. This means, of course, that they are not involved in the forming of seeds.

The **root** *anchors* the plant in the ground. It spreads through the soil to *absorb* water and soil minerals and conduct them to the stem. Many roots also *store* food for the plant until it is needed.

The stem is like a busy highway. It *conducts* water and minerals from the root up to the leaves. At the same time, it also brings foods that have been manufactured in the leaves back down to the roots. The stem is also a storage place for some of this food. In addition, it makes the leaves and displays them to the light. The green stems of many plants even carry on photosynthesis.

The **leaf** **is the center of many of the plant's activities.** In most plants, leaves are the chief organs of *photosynthesis*. Here gases are exchanged between the plant and the air by means of *respiration* and

22–8 Monterey pollen cones. (Albert Towle)

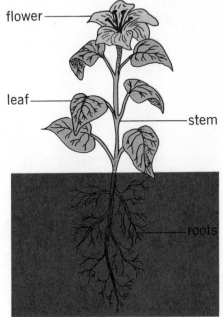

flower

leaf

stem

roots

22–9 The plant body of a flowering plant.

Table 22-1   SOME FAMILIES OF MONOCOTS AND DICOTS

FAMILY	FAMILIAR MEMBERS
Monocots	
cattail (Typhaceae)	common cattail
lily (Liliaceae)	lily, onion, tulip, hyacinth
grass (Gramineae)	cereal grains, bluegrass, sugar cane, bamboo, timothy
iris (Iridaceae)	flag, iris
palm (Palmaceae)	coconut palm, date palm, palmetto
Dicots	
beech (Fagaceae)	beech, chestnut, oak
water lily (Nymphaeaceae)	water lily, pond lily
poppy (Papaveraceae)	poppy, bloodroot
rose (Rosaceae)	rose, apple, hawthorn, strawberry, pear, peach, plum, cherry
maple (Aceraceae)	maple

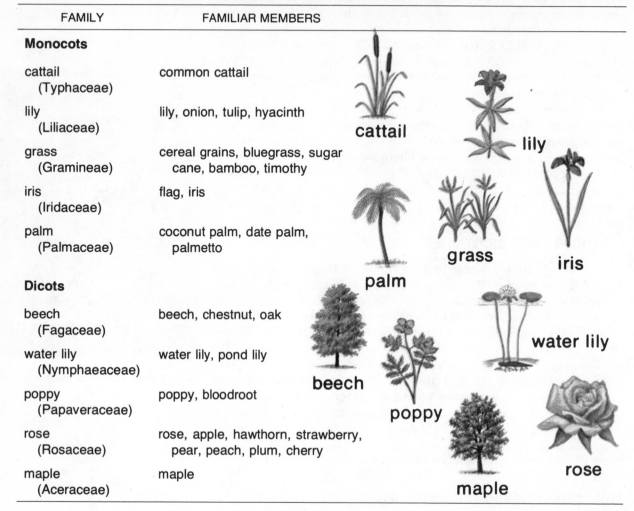

photosynthesis. A lot of the water absorbed by the root has a one-way trip through the plant to the leaves. From there, it passes into the air as water vapor. This process, called *transpiration,* will be explained in detail in Chapter Twenty-Three.

After the plant has grown for a time, it usually reproduces. **Flowers are plant organs that specialize in sexual reproduction.** Part of the flower grows into a *fruit,* which contains the seeds. The reproductive process that begins with the flower and leads to the fruit, seed, and embryo plant is the most highly evolved in the whole plant world.

SPECIALIZED TISSUE IN SEED PLANTS

The organs of seed plants perform their functions well. They are able to function because they are composed of specialized tissues. **In each tissue, the cells are slightly different. These differences help each organ carry out its special purpose better.** You will find out more about these specialized tissues later, when we discuss each plant organ. First, though, let's look at the different kinds of plant tissues and what they do.

Meristematic tissue is made up of small, thin-walled cells that can reproduce endlessly. When meristematic cells mature, they form all of the *permanent tissues* of the plant organs. During the growing season, these cells divide almost continuously to create more meristem. As you may know, animals grow all through the body. Plants, however, grow only where meristematic tissues are located. These areas are called *growing points*. They are found at the tips of roots and in the buds of stems. The **cambium** is a special layer of meristematic cells in roots and stems that makes them grow thicker.

Epidermal tissue is the covering layer on the surfaces of roots, stems, and leaves. It is usually only one cell thick. Epidermal cells protect the tissues under them from injury and lessen water loss. In young roots, the epidermis absorbs materials for food.

Cork is a covering tissue on the surfaces of woody roots and stems. Cork cells usually do not live long. But the dead cells stay on the plant. And over a period of time, they form a protective waterproof covering many cells thick.

Parenchyma tissue is made up of thin-walled cells like those of the meristem. There are parenchyma cells in flower petals, leaves, and parts of roots and stems. *Chlorenchyma* is parenchyma tissue that contains chlorophyll. It is the center of photosynthesis in leaves and young stems. The cells are loosely packed, with many intercellular spaces. These spaces are important in the exchange of gases during photosynthesis and respiration. *Storage parenchyma* also has loosely packed cells that are larger than those of the chlorenchyma. Starches, sugars, and other products are stored there.

Strengthening tissues grow in roots, stems, and the stalks and larger veins of leaves. Usually they are elongated, thick-walled *fibers*. The cells of strengthening tissues are usually short-lived, but their thick walls remain to help support the structure. *Sclerenchyma* is a strengthening tissue found in certain parts of roots, stems, and some leaves. *Bast* is a form of sclerenchyma tissue that has elongated fibers with pointed ends. *Wood fibers* look like bast but have even thicker walls.

Vascular tissues are elongated, tubular cells. They serve as passageways for plant materials to travel through. There are several different kinds of vascular tissue. *Sieve tubes* are arranged end to end, in a continuous column. Their end walls have tiny holes in them, so they look like strainers. Sieve tubes are used to conduct food, mostly downward, in leaves, stems, and roots. *Vessels* are large tubular cells with thick side walls. The end walls disappear, along with the protoplasm, leaving continuous tubes that can be almost a meter long. Vessels are channels for water and minerals moving through the roots, stems, and out into the stalks and veins of leaves. *Tracheids* are like vessels but are smaller. Their end walls are angular and perforated with little holes. They act both as

Stress to students the importance of division of labor and specialization in flowering plants. These organs have contributed to the success of flowering plants.

Point out to students that all of the plant tissues discussed here will be referred to in later chapters.

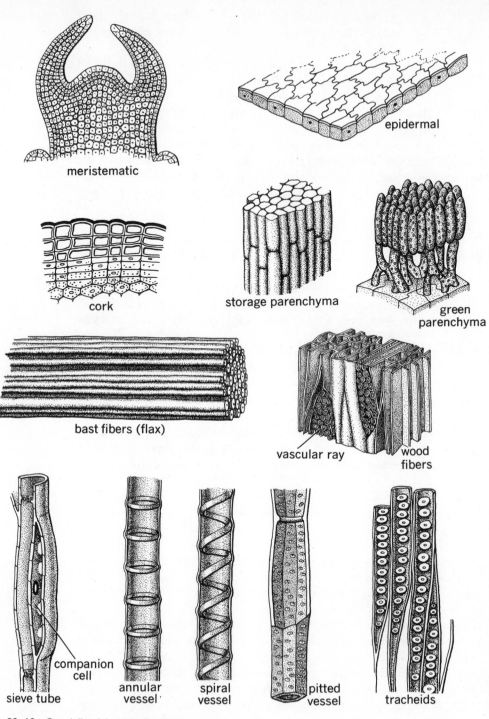

meristematic

epidermal

cork

storage parenchyma

green parenchyma

bast fibers (flax)

vascular ray

wood fibers

sieve tube

companion cell

annular vessel

spiral vessel

pitted vessel

tracheids

22–10 Specialized tissues of a seed plant.

channels for water and minerals and as support, especially in stems.

Phloem is a complex tissue made up of several simple tissues. It includes sieve tubes, bast fibers, and parenchyma. In woody stems, phloem is a part of bark tissue.

Xylem is also a complex tissue. It is made up of vessels, tracheids, fibers, and parenchyma. It is often called wood. Xylem makes up the main part of root and stems.

WOODY VS. HERBACEOUS PLANTS

Biologists often classify plants as **woody plants** or **herbaceous plants.** This depends on how long the plant normally lives and what tissues make its stem. Woody plants have a lot of strenghtening and vascular tissue. The meristematic tissue makes the stem and roots longer and bigger around every year. Long after these tissues have stopped functioning, they remain as support to the plant body. Woody plants often get to be very large because they go on adding new tissue every season. Sometimes this goes on for centuries. Trees are only one form of woody plant. Others are shrubs, and even vines, like Virginia creeper, poison ivy, and wild grape.

Herbaceous plants are nonwoody. They usually have soft stems in which the strengthening and vascular tissues are merely strands or bundles. In temperate climates, the stem or even the whole plant may only live for one season. Most garden flowers and vegetables and many wild flowers are herbaceous.

ANNUALS, BIENNIALS, AND PERENNIALS

We also group plants together on the basis of how long the plant body lives. **Plants that live for only one season are called annuals.** They grow from seed, produce flowers, then fruits and seeds, all in a single growing season. Only the seeds live until the following year.

A simple demonstration of water conduction in plants might be interesting here. Place a stalk of celery with leaves into three jars of water. Cut the stalk into three sections leaving an uncut section at the top to which the leaves are attached. Different food coloring should be added to each jar. Strongly tint the water and cut the celery stalks at a slant near the bottom. Place the celery and jars in the sun for a few hours. Have students observe the movement of colored water and the functions of the stalk.

22–11 The petunia is an example of an annual flower. (left) The foxglove is a biennial. The flower appears the second year. (center) The iris is a perennial. (right) (Dr. E. R. Degginger; Vivian Fenster; Dr. E. R. Degginger)

Relate the life cycle of the annuals, biennials, and perennials to the different climatic conditions in your area.

Using seed catalogues, students may be interested in figuring out what flowers might be used to cultivate an annual, biennial, or perennial garden.

Typical annuals are garden flowers and vegetables like the zinnia, marigold, pansy, bean and pea, as well as cereal grains.

Biennial plants have a life cycle that lasts two growing seasons. During the first year, the roots, stem, and leaves develop, often in the form of a low ring or rosette. The stem grows in the second year, bearing more leaves and the flower, fruit, and seeds. After it produces the seeds, the plant dies. Several garden vegetables are biennials, such as beets, carrots, cabbages, parsnips, and turnips.

Perennials live more than two seasons, often for many years. They usually grow roots, stems, and leaves the first year. But they do not flower until the second or third year. Every year the cells in the part of the plant that has grown above ground die. But the roots and often the underground stems live through the winter. Then they produce new stems and leaves the next spring. Once a perennial has flowered, it usually goes on for season after season as long as it has a comfortable environment. Herbaceous perennials include lilies, irises, and delphiniums. Trees, shrubs, and many vines are woody perennials.

SUMMARY

Seed plants have been developing since the close of the Carboniferous age. The gymnosperms and the angiosperms are the dominant forms of land plants today.

Seed plants, especially the angiosperms, have flourished because of their ability to live and reproduce in nearly all kinds of environments. Angiosperms, the flowering plants, are divided into two subclasses, called the monocotyledons and the dicotyledons. Some of these plants are herbaceous, and some are woody. Another means of grouping plants is by the length of their life cycle. Annuals, biennials, and perennials are grouped according to how many growing seasons the plant lives.

In later chapters, you will find out more about the organs of a flowering plant, and why seed plants have come to dominate the land environment.

BIOLOGICALLY SPEAKING

gymnosperm	root	strengthening tissue
angiosperm	stem	vascular tissue
seed	leaf	phloem
conifer	flower	xylem
seed cone	fruit	woody plant
pollen cone	meristematic tissue	herbaceous plant
cotyledon	epidermal tissue	annual
monocot	cork	biennial
dicot	parenchyma tissue	perennial
vegetative organ		

1. Distinguish the Gymnospermae from the Angiospermae.
2. Explain why we speak of the ginkgo tree as a "living fossil."
3. List several well-known conifers and the characteristics they have in common.
4. What two kinds of cones are produced by conifers?
5. Name the two large subclasses of flowering plants and explain the distinction between them.
6. List the main functions of the organs of the flowering plant.
7. In what respect is meristematic tissue different from other plant tissues?
8. Identify the function of parenchyma tissue.
9. Describe the strengthening tissues of roots, stems, and leaves.
10. Name three plant vascular tissues and indicate the functions of each.
11. In what way are xylem and phloem complex tissues?
12. Distinguish between woody and herbaceous stems.
13. How do we classify flowering plants into three groups on the basis of duration of the plant body?

1. Discuss various ways in which angiosperms have had an advantage over other kinds of plants in the struggle for existence.
2. Many of our most beautiful garden flowers are annuals. Why are they ideally suited to garden needs?

chapter
twenty-three

The Leaf and Its Function

23–1   The Norway maple has a typical dicot leaf. (Dr. E. R. Degginger)

OBJECTIVES

- DESCRIBE the external structure of the leaf.
- DISTINGUISH a compound leaf from a simple leaf.
- DESCRIBE each of the three kinds of leaf tissues.
- EXPLAIN movement of food and water through the leaf.
- DISTINGUISH photosynthesis from respiration in plants.
- DESCRIBE water loss from leaves.
- EXPLAIN how the stomata of the leaf work.
- EXPLAIN why leaves change color in the fall and drop off.
- LIST some examples of leaf modification.

Review photosynthesis with students. Refer them to Chapter Six for further review of this process.

Ask students to bring in a number of leaves in order to study their structure. Point out to students that the basic structures have different characteristics according to species.

THE LEAF—A SPECIALIZED FOOD FACTORY

The leaf is a seed plant's food factory. The most important process that takes place in the factory is photosynthesis. **For the most part, all other activities of the vegetative plant body are related to photosynthesis.**

The roots absorb water and minerals, which travel up through the stem to the leaves. The leaves absorb energy from the sunlight, causing chemical changes in the water and minerals. The foods produced by these changes are then carried back into the stem and down to the roots again. As you study the structure and tissues of the leaf, you will see why it is such a perfect organ for photosynthesis and other related activities.

A leaf usually grows and works for one season only. Even evergreens, which keep their leaves, grow new young shoots every year. That way each plant keeps its food factories up to date and working efficiently.

THE STRUCTURE OF A LEAF

A leaf is an outgrowth of the stem. Most leaves have a flattened green *blade.* Leaf blades come in many sizes and forms. The edges, or leaf margins, may be smooth, or toothed, or indented. The tips and bases of the blades also come in different shapes. These differences are often helpful clues to the plant's identity.

The blade is attached to the stem by a stalk, or *petiole.* Many leaf petioles have leaflike or scalelike *stipules* at their base. Some of these stay on all season, while others fall off soon after the leaf develops. Some leaves lack petioles entirely; these are called *sessile.*

The leaf tissue gets extra strength from a number of **veins.** Large veins look like ribs, and you can easily see them on the underside of the leaf. They have a second job, too. **While veins give support for the leaf, they also conduct water, minerals, and food back and forth to different parts of the plant.**

Large veins are arranged in patterns, or types of **venation.** These veins appear *parallel* in monocotyledons like corn, lilies, irises, and orchids. But in dicotyledons, they branch and rebranch, forming a *netted* pattern. Leaves of certain dicotyledons, like sycamores and maple trees, have large veins which start at the end of the petiole and spread out like fingers from the palm of the hand. We say they have *palmate* net venation. The leaves of other dicotyledons have one large vein called the *midrib* that runs the length of the leaf, with smaller veins branching out like feathers to the leaf edge. This pattern is called *pinnate* net venation. You can see it in elm, willow, and apple tree leaves.

A decayed leaf will illustrate the netted pattern of the remaining veins.

Have students draw and label a cross section of a leaf in order to become more familiar with the structures.

SIMPLE AND COMPOUND LEAVES

When each leaf blade is single, even if it is deeply indented, it is *simple*. In many leaves, though, the blade has several parts called **leaflets,** so it is called *compound*. Like the veins of a leaf, leaflets grow in either a palmate or a pinnate pattern. When the leaflets fan out from the base at the petiole, they are *palmately compound*. You can see these leaves on buckeye and horse-chestnut trees, and in clover, lupine, poison ivy, and Virginia creeper.

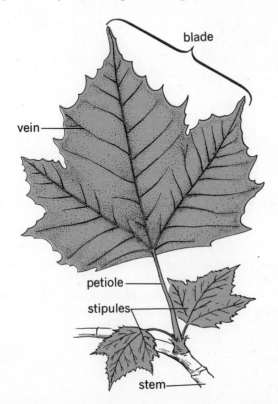

blade

vein

petiole

stipules

stem

23–2 The general structure of a leaf.

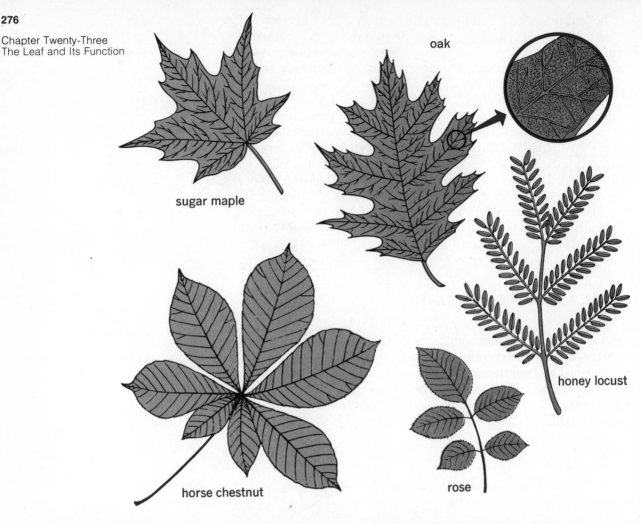

oak

sugar maple

honey locust

horse chestnut

rose

23–3 Leaves vary in form and size of the blade, venation, and compounding. They are often used as a basis for identification of plants. Identify the various types of venation and compounding shown in this drawing.

Leaflets of a *pinnately compound* leaf branch out from one central stalk. You can see this in the leaves of the pea, rose, walnut, and hickory. Sometimes the leaflets themselves are divided into little leaflets. Then they're called *bipinnately compound*. You will find them on the honey locust and the Kentucky coffee tree.

LEAF TISSUES

Cut across the blade of a leaf and look at the cross section under a microscope. You will see three different kinds of tissue. The top and bottom surfaces are covered with a single layer of cells, called **epidermis.** Between them are several layers of chlorenchyma cells, where photosynthesis takes place. These layers are known as the **mesophyll.** Veins of various sizes run through the middle of the mesophyll. All of the tissues fit together in a way that lets light in and allows gases to move in and out to the air. The tissues also serve as passageways for materials moving in and out of the mesophyll cells.

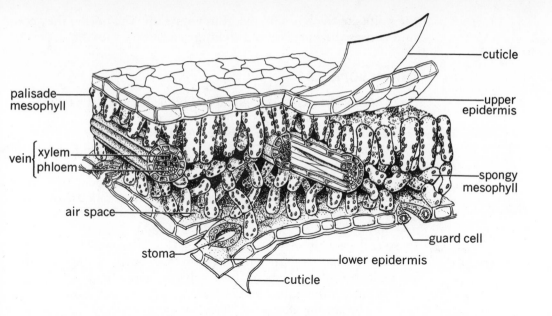

palisade mesophyll

cuticle

upper epidermis

vein { xylem / phloem }

spongy mesophyll

air space

guard cell

stoma

lower epidermis

cuticle

23–4   A cross section of a leaf.

THE LEAF EPIDERMIS

The single layers of epidermal cells on the top and bottom of the leaf are interlocking. Epidermis cells usually do not have chloroplasts. In a cross-section view, they look like cubes or bricks. From the surface, you can see how their irregular shapes fit together like pieces of a jigsaw puzzle.

Often the epidermis is covered by a thin, waxy film, the **cuticle. The cuticle slows down the escape of water vapor and other gases from the leaf tissues.** Most of the gases move in and out of the tissues through pores in the epidermis called **stomata** (singular, *stoma*). Stomata are slitlike openings into air spaces between cells of the mesophyll. Each stoma has two **guard cells** around it. The guard cells are modified epidermis cells. Unlike epidermis cells, they have chloroplasts. Their thickened walls are important factors in the stoma's opening and closing. This is important in keeping the water content in the leaf stable. How this works will be explained later on in the chapter.

Stomata can appear in both top and bottom epidermal layers. But, if the leaf is horizontal, they are usually on the underside. This is especially true of woody plants. In floating leaves, the stomata are all on top. Stomata are also found on the epidermis of herbaceous stems and young shoots of woody plants. The vertical leaves of the iris, have about equal numbers of stomata on both sides. Up to several thousand stomata may occupy four square centimeters of epidermis.

Many leaf surfaces feel velvety, fuzzy, or woolly because they have **epidermal hairs.** Actually the "hairs" are either single or multicellular outgrowths of epidermal cells. They may help reduce water loss. Many of them contain glands secreting oily or sticky substances on the leaf surface. When you touch a nettle, for instance,

Stress to students the importance of stomata in the passage of water out of the plant. More than 90 percent of the water taken in by the plant is passed out through the stomata.

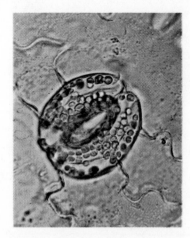

23–5   A stoma. Unlike the other cells of the epidermis, the two bean-shaped guard cells that surround each stoma, or opening, contain chloroplasts. (Hugh Spencer)

the points of the hairs break off in your skin. The poison they contain causes the burning and itching sensation.

THE MESOPHYLL

Except for the veins, the whole leaf blade between the two layers of epidermis is made up of mesophyll cells. Mesophyll cells are thin-walled chlorenchyma-type cells that stay alive and active even after they mature. They make up the main photosynthetic tissue of the leaf.

Most leaves have two kinds of mesophyll. Just under the upper epidermis lies the **palisade mesophyll.** This tissue is made up of elongated cells in upright rows that look like fence stakes. Palisade cells are well adapted to the maximum use of light. The chloroplasts of these cells stream around in a circle. The chloroplasts at the top get the most light and then move down to let others get light. In this way, all the chloroplasts in these cells get some light.

Underneath the palisades cells are the irregular, loosely packed cells of the **spongy mesophyll.** They are separated by air passages extending down from the stomata through the leaf. These cells do not have as many chloroplasts as the palisade cells. That is why the top of a leaf is usually darker green than the underside.

Vertical leaves often have a layer of palisade mesophyll just under each epidermis, with a zone of spongy mesophyll in the middle. In other leaves, the mesophyll does not separate into the two types at all.

THE STRUCTURE OF LEAF VEINS

Veins are made up of supporting and conducting tissues gathered together in **fibrovascular bundles.** One or more of these bundles enter the blade through the petiole. The large veins in a dicotyledonous leaf branch again and again, forming a network all through the mesophyll. The network is so fine that each cell is no more than a few cells removed from a vein.

A large vein has an area of *xylem vessels* on the upper side and *phloem sieve tubes* on the lower side. As veins branch out, they get smaller and have less vascular tissue. Some may only have one xylem vessel that ends in the middle of the mesophyll.

Small and medium-sized veins are enclosed in a *bundle sheath* made up of elongated parenchyma cells. Water and minerals moving from xylem cells to the mesophyll must pass through the bundle sheath. The same is true of the food that moves from the mesophyll to the phloem. The smallest veins often have no phloem sieve tubes. Then cells of the bundle sheath surrounding them carry the food along the vein to the nearest phloem tube available.

In large vascular bundles, you will often find *sclerenchyma* fibers above and below the vascular tissues going right out to the epidermis. The fibers reinforce the bundles and help strengthen the leaf.

Stress to students the advantages to photosynthesis of the vertical arrangement of palisade cells. This arrangement places more cells in contact with the surface of the leaf.

If possible, obtain an X ray of a leaf. It will give a clear picture of the veins and their minute structure.

Table 23-1   SUMMARY OF STRUCTURE AND FUNCTION OF LEAF TISSUE

REGION	TISSUE	FUNCTION
epidermis	epidermal cells	protect the upper and lower surface of the leaf
	cuticle	prevents excessive loss of water and gases
	stomata	regulate passage of air and water vapor to and from the leaf
	guard cells	regulate opening and closing of stoma
mesophyll	palisade mesophyll	active area of photosynthesis
	spongy mesophyll	active area of photosynthesis, provides air passages
fibrovascular bundle	xylem vessels	conducts water and minerals
	phloem sieve tubes	conducts dissolved food substances

PHOTOSYNTHESIS IN THE LEAF

In Chapter Six, we discussed photosynthesis as a chemical process. We talked about cells and chloroplasts, light as an energy source, raw materials, and products. Now we are interested in how the leaf's adaptations make it the main photosynthetic organ of a seed plant.

Photosynthesis happens in any green plant tissue. It even occurs in the cortex cells of herbaceous stems and young woody shoots. But it is most active in the mesophyll of the leaf. The large thin blade is ideal for exposing the most number of mesophyll cells to the light. Water gets to these food factories through xylem vessels in the many small veins throughout the mesophyll. Carbon dioxide enters through the stomata to feed the process. Later oxygen passes out by the same pores to the air.

HOW PLANTS USE SUGAR

Glucose formed from **PGAL** may be used as energy for the leaf. *Glucose serves as fuel for the leaf's respiration.* The leaf may also turn glucose into starch and store it for later use. It may become part of larger compounds like carbohydrates, fats, or proteins.

On a sunny day, a leaf may make more starch than it can easily convert to sugar. The peak of starch content usually occurs about the middle of the afternoon. Using enzymes, the plant slowly turns the insoluble starch into sugar. Sugar dissolves in water and goes into the phloem sieve tubes of the veins. Still in solution, it moves through the petiole to the stem. Here it is carried to storage places. This movement of materials goes on all night to make room in the mesophyll for the next day's work.

The presence of starch can be easily demonstrated by boiling a leaf in alcohol (using a double boiler). Iodine can be used to test for the presence of starch. If starch is present, the leaf will turn a blue-black color when iodine is added.

23-6 The leaves of the coleus are arranged so that they receive maximum sunlight. (W. H. Hodge, Peter Arnold)

LIGHT AND LEAF ARRANGEMENT

In Chapter Six, we looked at factors that limit photosynthesis. Both inside the cells and out, the important influences are light, temperature, and the supply of water and carbon dioxide. But often the vital factor is light.

How fast photosynthesis takes place depends on the brightness of the light the plants get. This is true at least until it is between one fourth and one half the brightness of full sunlight. Since a plant needs photosynthesis to survive, the leaves are usually arranged on the stem to get the maximum amount of light. Single leaves often grow in a spiral, or in pairs at right angles to each other. This growth helps leaves avoid shading each other too much. Sometimes the petiole bends to help the leaf get more light. We refer to nature's varied leaf arrangements as **mosaic.**

RESPIRATION IN GREEN PLANTS

Photosynthesis occurs during sunlight hours. But respiration goes on day and night. Respiration in plants is like that of other organisms. Glucose molecules are the main source of plant energy. Energy is released by the oxidation of glucose. This process was explained in Chapter Six.

Oxygen combines easily with hydrogen to form water, a by-product of respiration. As a glucose molecule breaks down, the carbon atoms of its skeleton combine with more oxygen to form carbon dioxide. During the day, photosynthesis produces plenty of oxygen to take care of a plant's respiration. But at night, the plant has to use oxygen from the air for its respiration. Plant respiration does not involve breathing the way it does for us. But it is just as important to them. It just takes place at a slower rate.

Plants need energy for all of their living processes. Some energy is used to get more energy. Energy is needed to synthesize organic molecules. And a constant supply of energy is necessary for plant growth.

PHOTOSYNTHESIS VS RESPIRATION

You might think that photosynthesis and respiration are opposite chemical reactions, but they are not. Each process uses different enzymes and chemical reactions. You could say instead that they are complementary, or balancing processes. Each one produces what the other needs. You can see this by comparing the matter and energy changes of both reactions. It is an important part of nature's delicate biochemical balance.

If you compare the two processes, you notice that matter is constantly being recycled. It goes from an inorganic to an organic state and back again. **But while matter can go through cycles, energy does not.** Light energy is needed for photosynthesis. Some energy is released in respiration. The rest of it is given off in the form of heat.

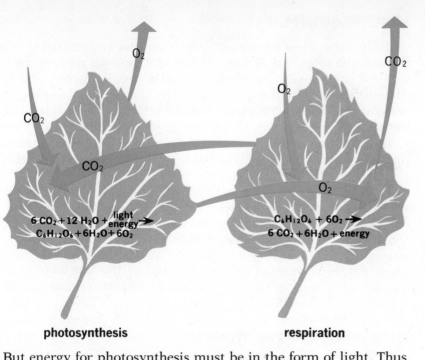

$6\,CO_2 + 12\,H_2O + \overset{\text{light}}{\underset{\text{energy}}{\longrightarrow}}$
$C_6H_{12}O_6 + 6H_2O + 6O_2$

$C_6H_{12}O_6 + 6O_2 \longrightarrow$
$6\,CO_2 + 6H_2O + \text{energy}$

photosynthesis   **respiration**

23-7 Gas exchanges due to photosynthesis and respiration. Under normal daylight conditions, five to ten times more carbon dioxide is used in photosynthesis than is produced in respiration. Also, much more oxygen is released in photosynthesis than is required in respiration.

But energy for photosynthesis must be in the form of light. Thus, **life on earth always depends on the sun for energy.**

You may be wondering how well balanced the processes of photosynthesis and respiration are in each plant. If the plant is in deep shade, they occur at about the same rate. The lack of light slows down the photosynthesis. At night, photosynthesis stops while respiration goes on. During the day, though, photosynthesis can occur ten times as fast as respiration. So, **each plant photosynthesizes much more than it respires. Thus plants supply heterotrophic plants and all animals with both food and oxygen.**

Table 23-2   COMPARISON OF PHOTOSYNTHESIS AND RESPIRATION

PHOTOSYNTHESIS	RESPIRATION
food accumulated	food broken down (oxidized)
energy from sun stored in glucose	energy of glucose released by oxidation
carbon dioxide taken in	carbon dioxide given off
oxygen given off	oxygen taken in
produces glucose from PGAL	produces CO_2 and H_2O
goes on only in light	goes on day and night
occurs only in presence of chlorophyll	occurs in all living cells

WATER LOSS IN PLANTS

During the growing season, water continuously streams up through the roots and stem to the leaves. About one percent of the water is used in photosynthesis and other processes of the plant. The rest escapes from the leaves, mostly through the stomata, as water vapor. The process in which water is lost from plants is called **transpiration.**

Transpiration is not a wasted effort, however. As a result of transpiration, leaves are cooled. The loss of water out of the leaves helps to pull water through the plant.

As water enters a leaf through the veins, it goes from the xylem vessels into the cells of the mesophyll. During transpiration, water evaporates from the wet cell surfaces. In vapor form, it diffuses into the spaces between the spongy mesophyll cells. From there, it passes out into the air through the stomata. As this happens, more water moves in through the veins to replace the lost water. The opening and closing of the stomata control the rate of transpiration.

THE FUNCTION OF THE STOMATA

In most plants, the stomata are open during the day and closed at night. They may close during the day on hot afternoons. **As turgor pressure changes, the shape of the guard cells changes. In turn, these changes cause the stomata to open and close.**

When guard cells absorb water from nearby epidermal cells, their turgor increases. The pressure from within makes the thin outer cell walls bulge. This presses them against the other epidermal cells. The thickened inner walls around the stoma are pulled into a crescent shape, opening the pore. Water evaporating through the walls of the guard cells reduces turgor pressure. This makes the guard cells shrink. As they get smaller, their inner walls straighten and the stoma closes.

HOW DO STOMATA WORK?

It may sound as though the opening and closing of the stoma are directly related to the amount of water in the leaf. But this would mean that the stomata would be open at night when the leaf tissues contain the most water. They would be closed during the day when evaporation is faster. But this is not what happens.

Obviously there must be another reason for the turgor changes. Studies show that the concentration of carbon dioxide in the guard cells may be responsible. Experiments have shown that when the concentration of carbon dioxide is more than 0.04 percent, the stomata close. When there is less than 0.04 percent of carbon dioxide in the cells, the stomata open. Other factors may be at work, too. Enzyme action, the formation of carbonic acid from carbon dioxide and oxygen, the effect of acid on the enzymes, and the water

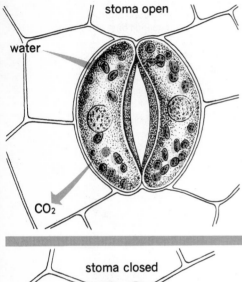

stoma open

water

CO_2

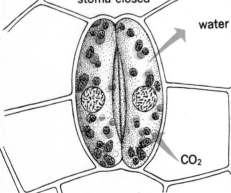

stoma closed

water

CO_2

23–8 Changes in the concentration of carbon dioxide and carbonic acid in the guard cells affect enzyme action on sugar and starch. This results in water movement and turgor change that open and close the stoma.

moving in and out of the guard cells could all be factors. All these conditions have led scientists to form a new hypothesis about why the stomata open and close.

At night, when photosynthesis has stopped, enzymes in the guard cells change sugar into starch. This chemical change occurs only in guard cells. You will remember, that in the mesophyll the reverse is happening. In mesophyll cells, starch is being changed into sugar. This sugar is dissolved in water produced by respiration. Then it is carried to the rest of the plant. In the guard cells, though, the carbon dioxide combines with water and forms carbonic acid. The enzymes that normally convert starch to sugar do not work with that much acid around. Only the enzymes that change sugar to starch can work. So the sugar content in the guard cells goes down. So the amount of water, and the turgor pressure both drop. The stomata close.

As the sun comes up, photosynthesis begins again. Now the carbon dioxide is used in photosynthesis instead of making carbonic acid. With less acid present, the starch-to-sugar enzymes get busy again. A lot of the starch that was made overnight is turned back into sugar. As the amount of sugar increases, the guard cells take in more water by osmosis to reach a balance again. The turgor increases, the guard cells swell, and the stomata open.

The *direct mechanism* in the opening and closing of the stomata is, therefore, the turgor change in the guard cells. But the *underlying cause* is the concentration of carbon dioxide. Carbon dioxide acts as a chemical regulator. It forms the carbonic acid, and affects the action of different kinds of enzymes.

LEAF COLORATION

Leaves are green during the late spring and summer because the chloroplasts contain chlorophyll. But the chloroplasts have two other pigments as well. One is a yellow pigment called *xanthophyll*. And the other is an orange pigment called *carotene*. But these are marked by the chlorophyll.

As fall arrives, the temperature gets too cold for plants to make any more chlorophyll. Light destroys whatever chlorophyll is left. So you can see the yellow and orange pigments that were hidden before.

Cool weather also causes many leaves to form the red pigment, *anthocyanin*. This pigment is made from food materials but not in the chloroplasts. Instead, it is formed in vacuoles of the leaf plants red in the cool spring and fall.

Brown leaves are caused by death of the tissues and from the formation of *tannic acid* inside the leaf.

FALLING LEAVES

At the end of the growing season, leaves fall naturally from many woody plants in temperate climates. When autumn comes, the

Have students think about the immediate and long-range effects if the stomata of all plants could not open.

Dry weather conditions tend to favor the formation of anthocyanins as the changing of leaf starch into sugar is speeded up. Maximum color is produced by cold but not freezing temperatures.

23–9 A deciduous forest in autumn. (Grant Heilman)

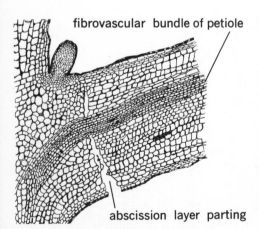

fibrovascular bundle of petiole

abscission layer parting

23–10 During autumn, the cells of the abscission layer separate.

parenchyma cells across the base of the petiole form an **abscission layer.** New enzymes develop which dissolve the pectin joining the walls of the parenchyma cells. Without the pectin, the cells separate. The petiole is left attached to the twig only by its fibrovascular bundles. The slightest jar from rain or a gust of wind can make the leaf fall. Then a thin layer of cork cells seals the scar where the leaf was attached.

Some broad-leaved trees, like oaks, never lose their leaves in fall. The leaves dry up, but they stay on the tree. They fall gradually during the winter and next spring. Evergreens, including most conifers, keep their green leaves all winter. Slowly they drop off during the next season, after they have been replaced by new shoots and leaves.

LEAF MODIFICATIONS

Most leaves are either broad and thin or needlelike (such as the conifers). But others are highly developed for special circumstances. Semidesert conditions have led to the special leaves we find on century plants, aloes, and sedums. The tissues of these thick, fleshy **succulent leaves** hold water. In this way, they can survive long dry periods. Other desert plants like the cactus have succulent stems and leaves mostly made up of protective *spines* to prevent water loss. Other plants anchor themselves with the help of **tendrils.** Tendrils are elongated leaf petioles, veins, or stipules that coil around supports. You may be familiar with those of the clematis, garden pea, or greenbrier.

INSECT-CATCHING PLANTS

Some of the most unusual leaf adaptations have developed in insectivorous plants. Leaves of the sundew, Venus's-flytrap, pitcher plants, and bladderwort are all designed to capture insects.

Sundews are small plants that grow in bogs and other wet places. The leaves grow out of long stalks in clusters. On the surfaces and edges of the rounded blades, they have several tentacles, or soft spines. A drop of sticky fluid at the tip of each tentacle makes the leaf glisten in the sun. This sticky secretion attracts insects and captures them. The tentacles bend around the insect and hold it. The secretion contains enzymes for digesting the insect right there on the leaf surface.

The Venus's-flytrap also grows in wet places, mostly in North and South Carolina. It produces a group of leaves between five and fifteen centimeters long. Each leaf has a flattened petiole and a pocketlike blade made of two hinged lobes. Each lobe has a row of stiff spines around it. On the surface of the lobes are numbers of hairs that secrete a sweet fluid to attract insects. This plant also contains digestive enzymes. When an insect lands on it, the jaws of the trap snap shut, and the marginal spines interlock to close off escape. It takes several days for the plant to partly digest the insect and absorb the food into the leaf tissues. Then the lobes open again for more prey.

Pitcher plants grow in wet soil and on mats of sphagnum moss in many parts of North America. Their leaves grow in upright clusters which are from fifteen centimeters to a meter long. They are called pitcher plants because of the vase-shaped leaves with lips that bend outward at the top. Many hairs grow downward on the inner surfaces. Glands at the base secrete digestive fluids. Often a pool of rainwater collects in the base of the leaves. Insects that crawl down into the leaf cannot get out because of the hairs. When they fall into the leaf, they are digested.

23-11 The cactus, *Cereus giganteus*, stores water in its thick, fleshy stem. The leaves are reduced to spines to prevent water loss. (Carolina Biological Supply Co.)

Students may be interested in reporting on some of the more unusual types of leaves of various species: bladderworts, butterworts, sundews, pitcher plants, and Venus's flytraps.

23-12 The Venus's flytrap (left) and the pitcher plant are insectivorous plants. These plants have special adaptations which allow them to digest insects which become trapped between their leaves. (Carolina Biological Supply Co.)

The bladderwort is an aquatic plant whose leaves grow under water. They are shaped like bladders, and trap insects and other small aquatic animals.

Insectivorous plants contain chlorophyll and synthesize their own carbohydrates. They do not need the animals as food. But they usually grow in the kind of soil where nitrates are scarce. To get the nitrogen supplement their diet requires, they must digest animals which contain nitrogen products.

SUMMARY

The leaf is important because it is the plant's main organ for making food. There are different kinds of tissues in a leaf. The epidermis is a protective tissue. The mesophyll is in the middle, where photosynthesis takes place. Veins go throughout the leaf in different kinds of networks. They carry food and food-making materials to all the cells. Leaf adaptations allow the maximum amount of light possible to hit each leaf. The photosynthesis, or food-making, process is balanced by respiration. For these processes to take place, gases must pass in and out of the leaf tissues. They go through the stomata, or pores in the epidermis, which are surrounded by guard cells. The guard cells control the opening and closing of the stomata through a series of changes in turgor pressure. This helps control the water loss, or transpiration, from the leaf.

As cold weather approaches, many leaves lose their chlorophyll, showing the red and yellow pigments they contain. At the same time, they form an abscission layer, which makes the leaf fall and protects the leaf scar. Other plants have leaves that are modified to help them catch and digest insects as part of their food.

BIOLOGICALLY SPEAKING

blade	epidermis	spongy mesophyll
petiole	mesophyll	fibrovascular bundle
stipule	cuticle	mosaic
sessile	stomata	transpiration
vein	guard cell	abscission layer
venation	epidermal hair	succulent leaf
leaflet	palisade mesophyll	tendril

QUESTIONS FOR REVIEW

1. How does the shape of most leaves adapt them for their function?
2. Name two functions of the veins of a leaf.
3. Distinguish the venation of a monocot from a dicot plant.
4. What is the function of the cuticle of a leaf?
5. Describe the structure of guard cells and their relation to a stoma.
6. Name the two layers that are the principal photosynthetic tissues of the leaf.
7. In what form is carbohydrate stored for later use by the plant?
8. Describe the changes that occur in leaf stomata during a twenty-four-hour period.
9. Explain why leaves turn yellow, orange, or red with the coming of autumn.

10. Explain what causes leaves to fall in the autumn.
11. How are succulent leaves an adaptation for life in dry environments?
12. Give several examples of insectivorous plants.

1. Cells in the mesophyll of a leaf are thin-walled and loosely arranged. Why is this important in the activities of the leaf?
2. Explain why, in most hospitals, the flowers in a patient's room may be removed at night.
3. Compare photosynthesis and respiration as they pertain to the functions of the leaf.

chapter twenty-four

Roots and Stems

OBJECTIVES

- DESCRIBE the functions of roots.
- LIST the various types of roots and root systems.
- DESCRIBE each of the four regions in a root tip.
- LIST the root tissues and their functions.
- DESCRIBE a modified root.
- DISTINGUISH primary growth from secondary growth in woody stems.
- NAME the tissues composing bark.
- DEFINE the vascular cambium.
- DISTINGUISH heartwood from sapwood.
- EXPLAIN the annual rings in wood.
- EXPLAIN the function of the pith region of a stem.
- DESCRIBE the various forms of underground stems.

A review of other "rootlike" structures would be appropriate here. Discuss root functions and compare plant roots to holdfasts and rhizoids.

Root hairs can easily be seen if allowed to germinate on a damp blotter or similar medium. Discuss with students the importance of removing sufficient soil when transplanting. This protects the roots of the plant.

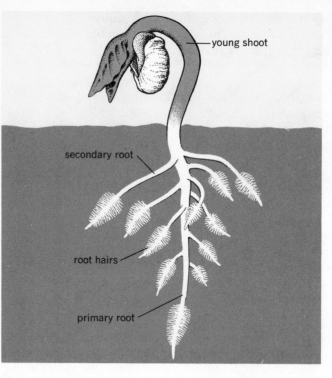

young shoot
secondary root
root hairs
primary root

24–1 Root system of a bean seedling. Note the secondary roots branching from the primary root.

Roots

THE ORIGIN OF ROOT SYSTEMS

When a seed germinates, the first root pushes downward into the soil from the lower end of the embryo plant. This is called the *primary root.* After a short growing period, *secondary roots* arise from the primary root. This goes on until the young plant develops an entire root system.

Root systems vary in form, shape, and size. Many environmental factors—type of soil, amount of moisture, temperature—affect the growth of roots. Usually, the average land plant has as much root system below ground as it has stem and branches above ground. But, the roots of most plants do not grow as deep into the earth as their stems grow high above ground. Most roots, even those of large trees, grow only about a meter below the soil surface. On the other hand, roots usually spread wider than the branches above them.

ROOTS AND ROOT SYSTEMS

In some plants, the primary root keeps growing and remains the major root of the system. In other plants, it does not. If the primary root is the major root of the system, it is called a *taproot.* Plants with taproots have many advantages. A long taproot is useful for anchorage. It can also reach water supplies that are deep in the ground. Alfalfa, for instance, stays green in the hot dry months because its taproot grows down five meters or more. Oak and hickory survive on dry hillsides because of their long tap roots.

Some plants have taproots that get thick and fleshy and serve as underground storehouses for food. Beets, radishes, carrots, turnips, and parsnips are examples. We grow many of these plants as root crops.

In plants like the grasses, secondary roots quickly outgrow the primary root. These roots are called **fibrous roots.** Fibrous root systems are usually shallow and spread through a large area of soil. They absorb water and minerals efficiently. And they are important as soil binders. They hold soil particles together. This helps prevent soil erosion by water and wind.

In some plants, such as sweet potatoes and dahlias, the secondary roots enlarge to become storage organs similar to taproots.

THE ROOT TIP

If you were to study a young root tip, you would find that it has many parts. Under the microscope, several important areas can be seen.

The **root cap** is at the very tip of the root. It covers the delicate **root apex.** As the root grows longer, it pushes the root cap through the soil. This tears away its outer surface. But new cells keep growing on its inner surface. These new cells keep the root cap in good repair. How does the delicate root tip force its way through soil without getting completely torn up? Its cells give off carbon dioxide during cellular respiration. The carbon dioxide gas reacts with water in the soil to form *carbonic acid.* This weak acid dissolves certain minerals in the soil and makes it easier for the root tip to move forward. When roots grow over limestone rocks, carbonic acid often cuts a pattern into the rock.

Right behind the root cap is the **meristematic region.** This is an area of cell division, or **apical growth.** It can be anywhere from 1.0 to 2.5 millimeters long.

Behind the meristematic region lies the **elongation region.** Here the cells stop dividing and get longer. This lengthening pushes the root tip forward. Other cells in this region mature into vascular tissues of the xylem and phloem.

In back of the elongation region is the **maturation region.** This is where elongated cells differentiate, or change, into tissues. One of the most noticeable of these changes happens in the outer cell layer. These cells become an epidermis. Tiny points spring up on the outer cell surfaces and grow into **root hairs.** You need a microscope to see the root hairs' origin in the epidermis. But you can see the fuzzy hairs themselves with a hand lens. Root hairs cover an area about 25 to 50 millimeters long. As the root grows and moves forward, new root hairs sprout continually. Older ones farther from the root tip die and fall off.

Ask students to bring in a variety of plant roots. Through dissection and use of the microscope, students will better be able to understand the structures discussed here.

24–2 Compare and contrast the fibrous root system of the grass with the taproot system of the dandelion. Which acts as the better soil binder?

24–3 Major regions of a root tip. Note the blunt, thimble-shaped root cap. This cap protects the delicate meristematic region from injury by soil particles.

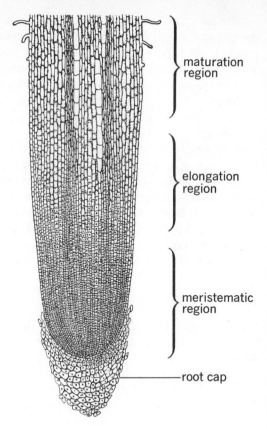

maturation region

elongation region

meristematic region

root cap

24–4 In order to locate the elongation region, the young root in *a* was marked with ink at intervals of one millimeter from the tip back. The same root is shown in *b* after 24 hours of growth. Notice the region in which elongation has occurred.

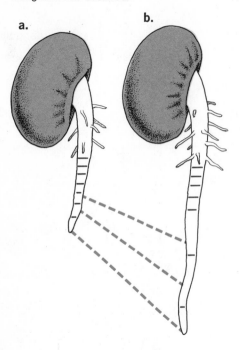

a.

b.

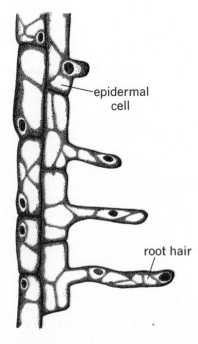

epidermal cell

root hair

24–5 Stages in the development of root hairs from epidermal cells of a young root.

The root hairs serve a very important purpose. As the root tip grows, the hairs constantly push into new soil. They greatly increase the surface area for absorption. Their thin outer membranes take in the water and minerals needed for the plant to survive.

PRIMARY TISSUES OF THE ROOT

The outer epidermal cells form the root hairs. At the same time, the cells deeper inside the root change into other specialized tissues. These tissues have definite structures and functions. They are formed in the meristematic region. And they are the first tissues that develop in a young root. For this reason, they are called ***primary tissues.*** Such tissues occupy three well-defined regions: the epidermis, the cortex, and the vascular cylinder.

The ***epidermis*** is the outermost region. It is a single layer of thin-walled cells. It absorbs water and minerals and protects the root.

Under the epidermis is the thick ***cortex region.*** This second region is made up of layers of storage parenchyma cells. These cells are rounded and loosely packed. There are many spaces between them. Water and dissolved minerals pass easily through these spaces and through the parenchyma cells. In many roots, these parenchyma cells store starch and other food substances. This food came from the leaves and the stem. The inner boundary of the cortex is formed by a single layer of cells called the *endodermis*. The walls of endodermal cells are thick and waxy. This keeps solutions from flowing between the cells.

Review the tissues that were discussed in Chapter Twenty-Two. Stress the difference between primary and secondary tissues.

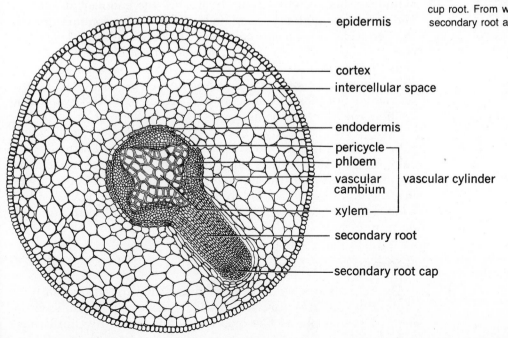

24–6 The tissues of a young buttercup root. From what tissue does the secondary root arise?

epidermis

cortex
intercellular space

endodermis
pericycle ⌐
phloem
vascular
cambium   │ vascular cylinder
xylem ⌐

secondary root

secondary root cap

The third region of the young root is its central core. This core is called the **vascular cylinder.** In this cylinder are thick-walled xylem vessels. These vessels are the channels through which water and minerals move upward through the root to the stem and leaves. In many roots, the xylem cells form a star shape. The arms of this star come out from the root core. Phloem cells lie in groups between the arms of xylem. The sieve tubes of the phloem are the channels that carry food down through the root.

At the outer edge of the vascular cylinder, next to the endodermis, there is an important ring of parenchyma cells. This is called the *pericycle.* It is one-cell thick in most roots. Unlike most plant tissues, the cells of the pericycle can grow and divide even after they mature. It is here that the secondary roots and several other tissues begin. The base of the secondary root pushes through the cortex of the root to get to the outside.

SECONDARY GROWTH IN ROOTS

In the roots of dicotyledons and conifers, primary tissues mature first. Then the **secondary tissues** begin to grow. These tissues increase the root's *diameter* rather than its length. The process is very complex. Certain parenchyma cells between the xylem and phloem become meristematic. They form a one-cell thick layer called the **vascular cambium.** Then each of the transformed cells divides into two different cells. One is still meristematic and remains a part of the cambium. The other, however, matures. Cells maturing on the inner side of the cambium become *secondary xylem.* Cells maturing on the outer side become *secondary phloem.*

These secondary tissues increase the thickness of the vascular cylinder. This growth gradually crushes the endodermis, cortex, and epidermis against the soil. In later stages of secondary growth, the pericycle forms a **cork cambium.** The cork cambium lays down cork cells around the vascular cylinder. This layer cuts off those cells that are outside of the vascular cylinder. So, after secondary thickening, a root loses one of its functions. It can no longer absorb nutrients. But it still conducts and stores food and water and anchors the plant in the ground.

Fleshy roots are mostly made up of secondary xylem and phloem. In fleshy roots, like the carrot, the secondary tissues formed by the cambium are thin-walled, rather than woody. They store food for the plant. This is why the carrot is fleshy and edible. An outer covering, the skin-like *periderm*, develops from the pericycle. Secondary roots, formed by the pericycle, run through the phloem and periderm into the soil.

There are numerous plant roots that have an economic importance as food. Taro plants, grown in the Pacific areas, are one such plant. Another is the Cassavas plant popular in tropical countries. Farina and tapioca are produced from the roots of the cassava plant. Starch and alcohol also are derived from these plants.

MODIFIED ROOTS

The root tissues we have been discussing are similar in most roots. But root structure varies widely, depending upon environment. Floating plants like duckweeds and water hyacinths have

Table 24-1 SUMMARY OF ROOT TISSUES AND THEIR SPECIAL FUNCTIONS

TISSUE	FUNCTION
epidermis	absorption and protection
root hairs	increase in absorptive area of epidermis
cortex	diffusion of water and minerals to vascular cylinder and storage of food and water
endodermis	boundary layer separating cortex from vascular cylinder
vascular cylinder	
pericycle	origin of secondary roots and formation of cork cambium and periderm of fleshy roots
phloem	conduction of food materials downward from leaves and stem
vascular cambium	formation of secondary xylem and phloem, resulting in growth in diameter
xylem	conduction of water and dissolved minerals upward to stem and leaves

aquatic roots and no root hairs. The bald cypress tree of the southern United States is another good example. It often grows in swamps. With its roots submerged in shallow water, the lateral roots produce upright growths called cypress "knees." It is thought that these may aerate the underwater roots. These "knees" do not form when the bald cypress grows in drier places.

Many plants grow *aerial roots*—especially in the tropics. Tropical orchids, for instance, live on trees. They absorb water from dew, rainwater, and the damp air. Dust, fragments of bark, and other debris collect around the tropical orchid's roots. The plant gets enough minerals from them to survive.

In some plants, *adventitious* roots develop from the stem. Sometimes, they even develop from the leaves. On corn stalks, you may see circles of roots that grow from the lower joints of the stem. These adventitious roots are called *brace roots*, or *prop roots*. They push into the ground to help the underground root system support the corn stem. If soil is piled up around the stem, more brace roots grow from the lowest joint still above the soil. Even the corn plant's soil roots are adventitious. They also grow from the stem, replacing the short-lived primary root. Another tree with brace roots is the huge banyan which grows in warm climates. This tree drops roots from its branches into the soil. These roots serve as extra trunks and help support wide-spreading limbs.

Poison ivy, English ivy, and other vines grow clusters of roots from their stems. These roots cling to trees or walls and anchor the stems. These adventitious roots are called *climbing roots*. Such plants also have ordinary soil roots to absorb water and minerals.

longitudinal section

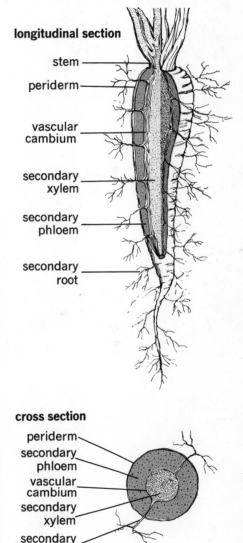

stem
periderm
vascular cambium
secondary xylem
secondary phloem
secondary root

cross section

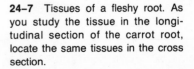

periderm
secondary phloem
vascular cambium
secondary xylem
secondary root

24-7 Tissues of a fleshy root. As you study the tissue in the longitudinal section of the carrot root, locate the same tissues in the cross section.

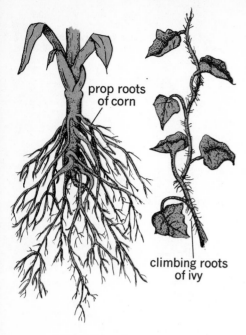

prop roots
of corn

climbing roots
of ivy

24–8 Two types of adventitious roots that develop from stem tissues.

Stems

PLANT STEMS

We have been discussing the part of the seed embryo that develops into the root. But another part develops into the stem. The stem and its leaves are called the **shoot.** In most plants, the stem and leaves rise into the air to make up the visible part.

Stems, like roots, grow in many different shapes and sizes. The trunks of monstrous forest trees that tower hundreds of feet in the air are also stems. Some stems live only a few weeks. Others grow for centuries. Stems may store food underground. Or they may creep horizontally in the upper soil layer.

The stem and roots of a plant work together. The jobs they do are different, but closely related. The tissues that make up roots and stems are also similar. However, these organs have important structural differences.

THE STRUCTURE OF A WOODY STEM

We can learn a lot about the anatomy of stems by looking at the twig of a tree. A dormant twig gives us even more information. Unlike roots, stems have little points along them where leaves develop and branches form. These spots are called **nodes.** The spaces between the nodes are called **internodes.** Leaf scars at the nodes of dormant twigs mark the spots where leaves once grew. If you put a dormant twig under a magnifying lens, you will see tiny dots on the leaf scars. These are actually closed pores called **bundle scars.** They are the ends of filaments of conducting tissue which once carried water and dissolved substances to and from a leaf. The bundle scars of different species come in different shapes, numbers, and arrangements. These can be used to identify trees.

Buds are the most noticeable structures on a dormant twig. A large *terminal bud* is usually found at the top of the twig. Smaller, *lateral buds* crop up along the sides of the twig at the nodes. They usually grow just above the leaf scars. During the growing season, lateral buds appear in the angle between the leaf stalk and the stem. This angle is called the leaf axil. A bud growing from the leaf axil is called an *axillary bud.* Overlapping *bud scales* cover the tissues inside the bud. These bud scales keep tissues from drying out and protect them from injury during the dormant season. Different species vary in the number and arrangement of bud scales.

At the beginning of the growing season, terminal buds start to swell up. Their scales drop off, leaving only a series of rings around the twig to mark where they were. These rings are called *bud-scale scars.* They show the exact location of the terminal bud at the start of the last growing season. You can tell the age of the twig by counting the sets of bud-scale scars along its length.

Along the internodes of young twigs, you can see small corky areas. These are pores called **lenticles.** Gases are exchanged between the plant's tissues and the atmosphere through the lenticles.

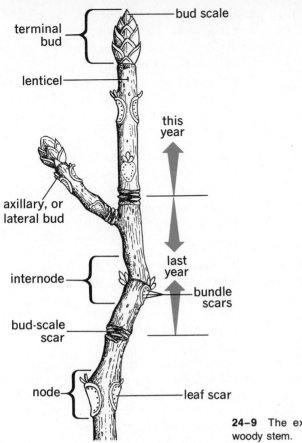

24-9 The external structure of a woody stem.

Some twigs have thorns that make the twig easy to identify. Thorns can be short and broad, long and pointed, or branching. They are located on different spots on different plants. On roses, for instance, thorns grow out of the epidermis. But in plants like the hawthorn or honey locust, the thorns are actually modified branches.

THE BUD

At the center of the terminal bud are an embryonic stem and leaves. If you cut a terminal bud lengthwise through the middle, you can see the different parts of the embryonic stem. At the tip of the stem, deep inside the bud scales, is a cone-shaped mass of meristematic tissue. This is called the **shoot apex.** It is here that young cells divide rapidly at the beginning of the growing season. They form the cells that will become the primary tissues of the stem. Other kinds of cells appear just below the shoot apex. These cells continue to divide and then quickly get longer. You may notice that these regions of the embryonic stem compare to regions of the root tip. Folded in a cluster inside the bud scales are embryonic leaves that develop from the shoot apex.

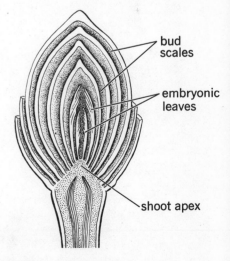

24-10 A longitudinal section through the terminal bud of a woody plant.

Not all buds are the same. Those containing a shoot apex and embryonic leaves are called *leaf buds*. These that form only embryonic flowers from the shoot apex are called *flower buds*. Another kind of bud has all three—a rudimentary shoot, leaves, and flowers. This is called a *mixed bud*.

THE GROWTH OF STEMS

As spring warms the land in temperate climates, the inner bud scales lengthen quickly. The bud opens. Cells below the shoot apex also elongate. And the shoot rapidly grows longer. Nodes compressed in the bud become separated by elongating cells in the internode. The stem grows rather like an unfolding telescope. Growth rates vary. A stem may grow many centimeters in a few weeks. As the shoot grows from the terminal bud, it makes the stem axis longer. As it grows from a lateral bud, it forms branches.

The terminal buds often grow more than lateral buds. This is called *apical dominance.* Biologists have learned that certain chemical substances, called growth hormones, can make terminal shoots grow more. At the same time, these hormones can slow down or even stop the growth of lateral buds. We will discuss how these hormones work in Chapter Twenty-Six.

Let's say a young tree has a terminal bud and strong apical dominance. The tree's main stem will grow much more than its lateral branches. A tree like this has what is called an **excurrent** growth habit. In other words, the trunk extends through the tree as the central shaft. Smaller lateral branches form at intervals along the trunk. The pine, the spruce, the hemlock, and the redwood all have this kind of growth habit. As a result, their long straight trunks are good for timber.

On the other hand, cottonwoods, willows, and elms have a different kind of branching. Some of these trees lack strong apical dominance. Others do not have terminal buds to begin with. Thus, their trunks divide into several large branches that spread outward from a common center. This type of growth is called **deliquescent.**

24–11 The spruce (left) illustrates the excurrent growth habit. In this tree, the lateral branches arise from the trunk, which acts as a central shaft. In contrast, the oak illustrates the deliquescent growth pattern, in which the trunk is divided into several large main branches. (Herbert Weihrich)

PRIMARY AND SECONDARY GROWTH

Woody stems grow in two different ways. One way is called primary growth. The other is called secondary growth. In **primary growth,** cells form in the shoot apex. These cells then grow and lengthen in the young shoot. As soon as this happens, the cells differentiate into primary tissues. They are similar to the tissues of the root. From outside to inside, primary tissue includes the *epidermis, cortex, primary phloem, primary xylem,* and *pith.* Primary growth lengthens a stem or increases its height. In most woody stems, such growth occurs rapidly. But it only lasts for a few weeks.

Secondary growth increases the diameter of the stem. It comes after primary growth and continues season after season. It involves the formation of secondary phloem and xylem by the *vascular cambium.*

The following example may help you understand these two different kinds of growth. Imagine a tree ten meters high and thirty centimeters in diameter. Its lowest branch is two meters off the ground. After ten years, the tree grows to seventeen meters high and 40 centimeters in diameter. How high above the ground is the branch? It is still two meters off the ground! Why? The twigs have lengthened at the tips. But the trunk and branches below the terminal meristematic regions have grown only in diameter.

THE PARTS OF A WOODY STEM

If you cut across a woody stem, you can see several distinct areas. The outer area is the **bark.** Inside the bark is the **wood.** During the first year of growth, the *vascular cambium* grows between the bark and the wood. This growth adds to the thickness of these regions season after season. The center region of the stem is the soft **pith.** Pith is a primary tissue. It does not increase as the stem grows in diameter. It is often hard to find the pith in an old woody stem because there is so little of it compared to the large amount of wood that is formed around it.

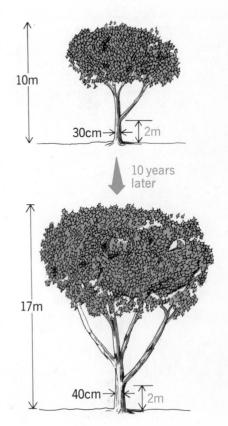

24–12 How does this tree show primary and secondary growth?

BARK TISSUES

The bark of a woody stem includes more than the hard outer covering. It has several other tissues as well. And each tissue has a specialized function.

For a while, young twigs are covered by a thin epidermis that develops as a primary tissue. But during the first growing season, the cells of the epidermis or of the outermost cortex layer produce the *cork cambium.* The meristematic cells in the cork cambium divide repeatedly. This builds up layers of cork cells on the outer side of the stem. The cork cells soon die and become air-filled pockets. These dead cells are called cork tissue. It keeps water and gases from leaving the stem tissues. Cork tissue also protects the

Students may be interested in observing cork under the microscope. Have them describe what they see and how the structure relates to the function of cork.

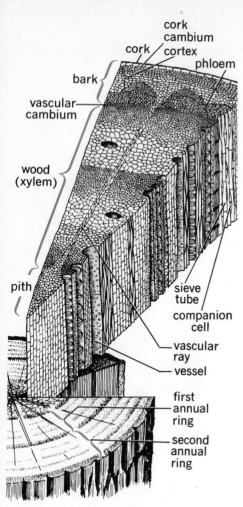

24–13 The tissues of a three-year-old dicotyledonous stem.

inner stem from insects, fungi, and other parasites. It also protects the stem from sudden temperature changes. The thick cork layers of large trees may even protect them from the heat of ground fires.

As it is weathered or destroyed on the outside, the cork cambium adds new cork on the inside. It also repairs cracks that develop as the stem increases in diameter. Cork is often called the *outer bark* to distinguish it from the deeper tissues of the *inner bark.*

Inside the cork and cork cambium is the *cortex.* It is an inner-bark region made of thin-walled parenchyma cells. While the young stem is still covered by an epidermis, these cells contain chloroplasts and carry on photosynthesis. But, as the cork forms, the cortex may even disappear as the stem ages.

The inner bark also contains vascular and structural tissues. These cells make up the phloem. Many stems have phloem cells arranged in pyramid-shaped groups. These phloem groups are separated by *phloem rays*, which may be narrow or V-shaped.

There are several kinds of phloem cells. The large *sieve tubes* are food channels. They usually carry food downward through the stem. Smaller companion cells lie beside the sieve tubes. *Phloem parenchyma* cells are scattered among the other phloem cells. They store food temporarily. Finally, areas of *sclerenchyma cells* make up the *phloem fibers.* These fibers strengthen the inner bark.

VASCULAR CAMBIUM

The *vascular cambium* is a ring of meristematic cells between the bark and the wood. It forms during the first growing season. The vascular cambium increases the diameter of the stem by forming two kinds of tissue. On the inner side, it forms secondary phloem tissues. On the outer side, it forms xylem. Xylem tissue is wood. During each season of growth, cambium forms more wood cells than phloem cells. That is why the wood area of a tree is always a lot thicker than the bark area.

WOOD TISSUES

Wood includes all of the stem tissues between the vascular cambium and the pith. It is made up of several kinds of xylem cells. These cells conduct materials and strengthen the stem. As in roots, the largest xylem elements in stems are *vessels.* These are long conduction tubes. They are made up of dead cells joined end to end. The end walls of the cells dissolve to form a continuous tube up through the stem. The xylem carries water and minerals up the stem. *Tracheids,* smaller than vessels, both conduct and support.

Year after year, the wood produced by the cambium forms layers. These layers gradually thicken the woody stem. Spring wood, which grows early in the season, usually contains many large vessels. The summer wood, which grows later, has fewer vessels. This difference in the texture of spring and summer wood results in layers called *annual rings.* These rings are easy to see when the tree is cut down. **You can tell the age of a tree by counting the annual rings.**

As a woody stem grows bigger in diameter, the older layers of wood at the center stop conducting food. Instead, they become clogged with resin, gum, tannin, and other deposits. These deposits harden and darken the wood. Such hard, dark, inactive wood is called *heartwood.* The active, functioning wood outside the heartwood is called sapwood.

THE PITH

The central core of pith takes up a large part of a young woody stem. But the pith becomes less noticeable as the stem grows in diameter. Pith is a parenchyma tissue that stores food, particularly in young stems. Because pith is not produced by the cambium, it does not increase as the stem grows in diameter.

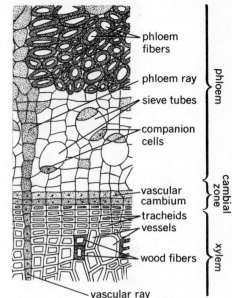

24–14 A portion of a cross section of a woody stem in the region of the vascular cambial zone. Cells formed by division of cambium cells grow and differentiate into xylem cells on one side of the cambium layer and phloem cells on the other.

Table 24-2 SUMMARY OF STRUCTURE AND ACTIVITIES OF A WOODY STEM

REGION	TISSUE OR CELL TYPE	ACTIVITY
bark	epidermis (only on young stems)	protection, reduction of water loss
	cork	protection, prevention of water loss
	cork cambium	production of cork
	cortex (only in young stems)	storage and food manufacture
	sieve tubes	conduction of food, usually downward
	companion cells	uncertain
	phloem fibers	support
vascular cambium	meristematic cells only	formation of phloem, xylem (wood), and rays
wood	xylem vessels	conduction of water and minerals upward
	tracheids	conduction and strengthening of wood
	xylem fibers	support
	vascular rays	conduction laterally
pith	parenchyma	storage

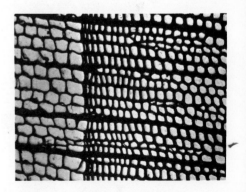

24–15 The larger tracheids (left) were formed in the spring. The smaller tracheids were formed during the summer months of the previous year. Where the spring and summer layers meet, it is possible to see each year's growth as an annual ring. (courtesy International Paper Co.)

24-17 Compare and contrast the sections of the herbaceous dicotyledonous (bean) stem and fibrovascular bundle with those of the herbaceous monocotyledonous (corn) stem and bundle.

THE HERBACEOUS DICOTYLEDONOUS STEMS

The stems of herbaceous dicotyledons, such as clover, alfalfa, buttercup, and bean, are like wood stems in many ways. They are very similar during the first growing season. They have the same general regions. And their tissues are alike in structure and function. The main difference is the length of time that the cambium functions. This leads to differences in the amounts of secondary xylem and phloem they produce.

A thin epidermis forms the outer covering. Cork is usually lacking in herbaceous stems. In many herbaceous stems, including the bean, the *cortex* region lies just below the epidermis. The cortex is made of chlorenchyma cells. These carry on photosynthesis and store food.

Herbaceous stems vary in arrangement of xylem and phloem. In some, the xylem and phloem lie in groups called fibrovascular bundles. In *dicotyledonous* stems, fibrovascular bundles usually occupy a ring-shaped zone. The phloem, made of sieve tubes and companion cells, usually lies on the outer side of a fibrovascular bundle.

Most herbaceous dicotyledonous stems develop a cambium. It usually forms between the phloem and xylem of each bundle, or in a complete ring that divides these tissues. The cambium adds layers of secondary phloem and xylem.

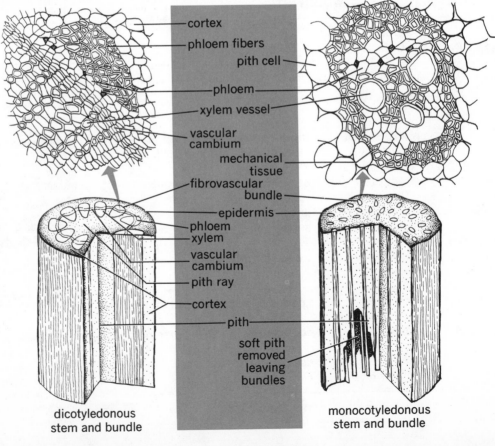

cortex
phloem fibers
pith cell
phloem
xylem vessel
vascular cambium
mechanical tissue
fibrovascular bundle
epidermis
phloem
xylem
vascular cambium
pith ray
cortex
pith
soft pith removed leaving bundles

dicotyledonous stem and bundle

monocotyledonous stem and bundle

MONOCOTYLEDONOUS STEMS

The corn stem is typical of monocotyledons. It differs from the stem of an herbaceous dicotyledon in several ways. The fibrovascular bundles are scattered throughout the stem. There is no clearly defined cortex. It also lacks cambium.

The corn stem is covered by a thick-walled epidermis. Just beneath the epidermis lies a thin layer of sclerenchyma cells. These add strength and hardness to the outer region.

In these stems, pith is the most abundant tissue. It is composed of thin-walled, loosely packed parenchyma cells. Many fibrovascular bundles are scattered throughout the pith. Most of them are near the outside of the stem. Each bundle contains both xylem and phloem. The phloem is nearer the outside of the bundle. And the xylem, including several large vessels, lies nearer the inside. A ring of thick-walled sclerenchyma cells surrounds the whole bundle. Since monocotyledonous stems do not have a vascular cambium, their growth in diameter is limited. This kind of stem usually becomes long and thin.

One of the reasons alfalfa has survived so successfully is that it can have taproots that extend 15 meters down into the ground. This enables the plant to withstand long periods of drought.

Students may want to bring in weeds with herbaceous stems in order to demonstrate the arrangement of vascular bundles.

Cut a corn stalk in several pieces so that students can observe the structure of monocot stems.

MODIFIED STEMS

Not all stems are aerial and leaf-bearing. Some plants grow underground stems. Aerial parts then spring up from the subterranean stem. Such stems often store food. They also reproduce the plant vegetatively. This form of reproduction will be discussed fully in Chapter Twenty-Seven.

The underground stems of plants like the lily of the valley and the water lily are called *rhizomes.* Most rhizomes are thick, fleshy, and grow horizontally just under the soil's surface. They produce leaf-bearing branches at their nodes. Rhizomes often contain starch and other nutrients.

A *stolon* is like a rhizome, but more slender. Stolons form branches at the bottoms of aerial stems. They shoot out sideways just under the ground. Their tips can grow up to form aerial branches. Some grasses, like crabgrass, form stolons that allow them to spread rapidly. That is why crabgrass is such a nuisance in a lawn or a garden.

In some plants, the end of the stolon swells. This swollen area is called a *tuber.* The white potato is familiar example of a tuber. The "eyes" of a potato are actually buds that develop at the nodes. A scar at one end marks the place where the potato was once attached to a stolon.

A *corm* is a short, thick underground stem enclosed in several thin scale leaves. Its fleshy tissues store food. In some plants, a corm grows a new aerial shoot every growing season. In others, such as the gladiolus, a corm grows only one aerial shoot in the plant's lifetime. During the growing season, lateral buds at the nodes produce new corms that will grow during the next season.

A variety of modified stems should be brought into class for observation. Students will enjoy studying stems that they are familiar with such as onions, potatoes, and flower corms and rhizomes.

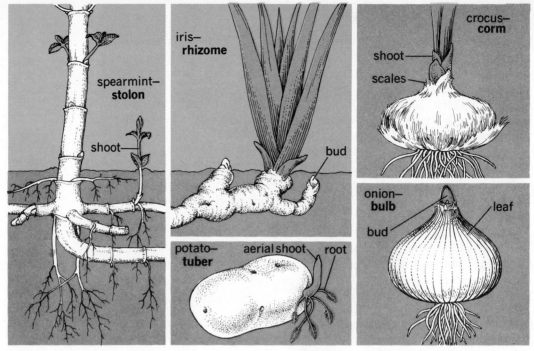

24-18 Five types of modified stems. Why are they stems rather roots?

Another kind of stem is called a *bulb.* It consists of a short basal stem that produces circular layers of thick scale leaves. In a way, a bulb is a compressed underground shoot. Food is stored in the thick leaves. The aerial stem grows through the center of the scale leaves from a bud on a short stem. Some common bulbs are onions, lilies, hyacinths, daffodils, and tulips.

SUMMARY

Imagine the inside of a tree on a summer day. In the inner bark, phloem tubes are conducting water and dissolved foods from the leaves down to the roots. In the sapwood, xylem vessels are conducting water from the roots up to the highest branches and leaves.

Some of the tissues in the roots of seed plants are similar to tissues in their stems. Others are quite different, just as the environments of the two plant organs are different. As you may have noticed, each function of these organs involves a specialized tissue. In fact, it is the development of these specialized tissues that has made seed plants the most advanced and successful of all land plants.

How can a tree suck up water and pull it higher than 30 meters? What happens to the water when it gets to the leaves? We'll talk about these questions in the next chapter.

primary root	cortex	deliquescent
secondary root	vascular cylinder	primary growth
taproot	secondary tissues	secondary growth
fibrous root	vascular cambium	bark
root cap	cork cambium	wood
root apex	shoot	pith
meristematic region	node	annual rings
elongation region	internode	heartwood
maturation region	bundle scars	rhizome
root hair	shoot apex	tuber
primary tissues	apical dominance	corm
epidermis	excurrent	bulb

1. Distinguish between primary and secondary roots.
2. Describe taproot and fibrous root systems.
3. Locate the four regions of a root tip and describe the activities that occur in each.
4. List the primary tissues of a root from outside to inside and give the function of each.
5. Give some examples of adventitious roots.
6. Distinguish between terminal and axillary buds.
7. What is the origin of the embryonic leaves inside a bud?
8. Describe two branching habits of trees related to apical dominance.
9. Name the bark tissues of a woody stem.
10. Explain the role of vascular cambium in the formation of annual rings in wood.
11. Account for the difference in appearance of heartwood and sapwood.
12. Describe three structural differences between dicotyledonous stems and monocotyledonous stems.
13. Name and describe five types of modified stems.

1. Discuss the various advantages of taproot and fibrous root systems.
2. Explain why growth occurs only in certain regions of roots and stems.
3. Explain how a cross section of a perennial dicot stem can give us clues to the age of the plant and the weather during those years.

chapter twenty-five

Water Relations in Plants

OBJECTIVES
- DESCRIBE the importance of water to plants.
- DEFINE the terms loam, topsoil, and humus.
- DESCRIBE the absorption of water and minerals by roots.
- DESCRIBE water loss from a root.
- EXPLAIN translocation of materials through a plant.
- DESCRIBE turgidity in plant cells.
- EXPLAIN loss of turgor and wilting.
- DEFINE guttation.

Stress to students the importance of water to all living things including plants. Point out that those plants that can survive in times of drought are particularly successful (the alfalfa plant is an example).

25–1 Some plants, such as the mangroove tree, grow in water. (Vivian Fenster)

PLANTS AND WATER

Water is the most important factor in a seed plant's environment. **The amount of water in an environment is critical to what types of plants an area will have.** The annual rainfall causes a particular area to be a desert, a semidesert, a short-grass plain, or a forest.

In Chapter Three, we said that water is an inorganic compound essential to living things. In this chapter, we will review some reasons why water is needed by plants.

Plants need water for almost all of their physiological processes. In photosynthesis, water supplies the hydrogen that combines with carbon dioxide to form sugar. Water also plays a key role in the structure of cells. It is the medium in which molecules of protein, fats, and other substances disperse into colloids. These substances actually make up the cell. Water is, therefore, necessary for growth.

Also, **water is the medium of transport in the plant.** Foods and soil minerals are dissolved in water inside the plant. This allows them to be carried up and down in the xylem and phloem. Finally, water pressure in the cells of nonwoody plant tissues make them firm.

SOIL AND WATER

For the most part, soil is a mixture of mineral particles and organic particles. Water and air are in the spaces between the particles. Most soil also contains a whole community of living organisms. These include: bacteria, molds and other fungi, protozoans, and a great variety of worms, bugs, and other animals.

Soil texture is determined by the nature and size of the mineral particles in the soil. These particles can be anything from large gravel, to sand, silt, or clay. Often, the different particles are mixed together to form a soil called **loam.** Good loam is valuable for growing crops. The best loam contains about 40 percent sand, 40 percent silt, and 20 percent clay.

Much of the organic matter found in soil lies in the upper region, called **topsoil.** Topsoil is made up of decaying roots and soil organisms, plus the decayed bodies of plants and animals on the soil surface. This decaying organic matter is called **humus.**

The spaces between the soil particles are important. They help make soil suitable for plants. Sandy soils have large spaces. Water passes through this soil rapidly. Clay soils are closely packed, with small spaces. Water moves very slowly through clay. Organic matter mixed with the mineral particles loosens the soil and increases the number of spaces.

When water sinks into the soil, much of it passes through the spaces between the soil particles. Eventually, it gets down to the *water table.* This is the level at which water is standing in the ground. It is usually too far down for plants to reach.

The small spaces around soil particles often hold water. This is called **capillary water.** Following a rain, capillary water moves through these spaces from higher to the lower regions in soil. As the soil dries out, the capillary water moves up again into the dried out region. Even when the surface of the soil is dry, quite a lot of capillary water remains in the spaces around soil particles. This is the water that roots can absorb.

Even when soil loses its capillary water, there is some water in it. This water is bound in a molecular film around each soil particle. It is called *hygroscopic water.* It evaporates directly from the soil particles to the air. This water is not available to plants.

Water Absorption

HOW ROOTS ABSORB WATER

A root usually takes in water through the root hairs of the epidermal cells. Capillary water runs from the spaces in the soil to the root hairs, and into the epidermal cells. Scientists do not completely understand the mechanisms involved in this water movement. Water movement seems to be affected by two factors, osmosis and transpiration. When looking at these two factors, we should consider two things. One is the movement of water through the entire plant and into the atmosphere. The other is the amount of available capillary water in the soil.

At night, the stomata are closed. So the plant transpires at a slow rate. But the soil is very moist. Scientists think that plants

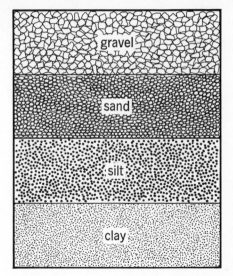

25-2 Soil is made up of many different sized particles: gravel, sand, silt, and clay.

A demonstration of the water-holding capacity of different types of plants will be most interesting to students. Have them find out what type of soil is around their homes and its water-holding capacity.

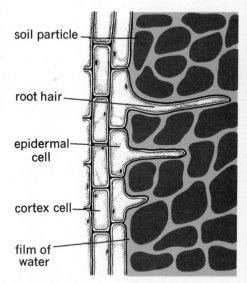

25-3 Water enters the epidermal cells of the root by active absorption. This occurs when the plant is transpiring slowly and the moisture content of the soil is high. Water enters by passive absorption when water movement through the plant is rapid and the rate of transpiration is high.

absorb water by osmosis at this time. The root hairs and epidermal cells contain minerals, foodstuffs, and other substances in solution. But the cell water contains these substances in lower concentrations than the soil water. In other words, the concentration of water molecules is greater in the soil than it is in the roots. Thus, the water moves into the root by osmosis. This kind of water movement is called **active absorption.**

Once water enters the root hair, it moves from cell to cell, through the epidermis to the cortex to the vascular cylinder. As the water moves, osmosis causes more water to be absorbed from the soil.

During the day, a different mechanism seems to be responsible for water absorption. The stomata are open. Transpiration takes place rapidly, and a large volume of water passes through the plant. The root cortex cells and the epidermis cells move water quickly to the xylem vessels. They lose their turgor pressure. So, the water pressure of the root falls below that of the soil water. This pressure difference pushes water into the root cells. This way of taking in water is called **passive absorption.** It is called *passive* because it is not caused by forces in the root cell. Instead, the absorption is caused by water loss in the leaves and water movement through the stem. This kind of absorption is responsible for most of the water intake of land plants.

WATER LOSS FROM A ROOT

Let's say there is a high concentration of soluble salts or other substances in the soil water. How does this affect the movement of water between the soil and the root? Osmotic water movement is reversed. Water goes from root to soil rather than from soil to root. This may happen if salt water or too much mineral fertilizer is poured around a plant's roots. Such a reversal of water movement can kill plant roots.

Some plants live in areas where the salt concentrations of water vary. Certain plants—called **halophytes**—are adapted to soils with a high salt content. Their root cells have a high concentration of salt. The presence of salts in the cell solutions lowers the water concentration. And thus, water diffusion pressure is below that of the soil. As a result, the root cells can absorb water from the salty soil by osmosis and maintain normal turgor.

HOW THE ROOT ABSORBS MINERALS

Soil water usually has a low concentration of soil minerals. These are in the form of dissociated ions. The essential ions include nitrate, phosphate, sulfate, calcium, potassium, and sodium. These ions reach the plasma membranes of epidermal cells in a water solution. But the entry of these minerals does not seem to depend on the intake of water.

The concentration of ions inside the root cells is usually greater than in soil water. Thus, *active transport* must be working in mineral absorption. So the cells must use energy to absorb minerals. But this active transport is not the same as *active absorption* of water by a root. Roots deprived of oxygen stop taking in ions. Since oxygen is necessary for active transport, these facts support the idea that minerals are absorbed by active transport.

Translocation

MOVEMENT OF WATER AND MINERALS IN THE PLANT

We explain the movement of water across root cells by osmosis. And we explain the entry of water into xylem vessels by pressure differences. But how does a plant move water up through its stem? In a small plant, the roots might force it up. But think of a tree over 30 meters tall. That is a long way to move water upward. For many years, scientists have been interested in how plants do this. **Translocation** is the movement of water and other materials great distances through the plant.

Once scientists thought that the cells along the xylem vessels actually pumped and squeezed water upward. But they found that this theory was wrong since they discovered that even dead stems could conduct water upward.

The whole process of translocation is *still* unclear. We do know, however, that several mechanisms are involved. One of these is root pressure. If you cut off the stem of a well-watered plant, you will see water well up from the severed xylem vessels. And if you attach a glass tube to the cut stem with a piece of rubber tubing, you will see the water rise. It will rise from several centimeters to more than one hundred centimeters. This rise is due to **root pressure.** Root pressure is caused by active absorption and turgor pressure in the cortex cells.

Scientists have found that root pressure is rarely greater than a kilogram per square centimeter. But it takes several times that much pressure to raise water fast enough to the top of very high trees. So, there must be at least one more mechanism involved in water conduction.

Capillarity is another possible factor in water conduction. **If you place a small tube in a liquid, the liquid rises in the tube higher than the water level in the container. That is because the liquid is attracted by surface forces along the sides of the tube. The smaller the tube's diameter, the higher the liquid rises. In very small capillary tubes, the liquid may go up many centimeters.** But this mechanism, like root pressure, does not explain how a big tree gets water all the way up to the top.

For the time being at least, the best theory of water translocation is the **transpiration-cohesion theory.** According to this theory, water is pulled rather than pushed through the vessels of the stem. Remember that a plant contains continuous columns of water. These columns run from the root xylem, through the stem, all the way up to the veins, and cells of the leaf mesophyll. After water

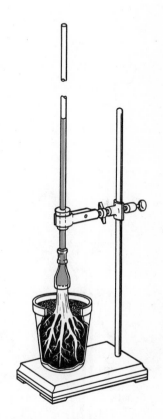

25–4 Demonstrating root pressure. Water rises a considerable distance in a glass tube attached to the stump of an actively growing plant.

Ask students why florists suggest that the stems of some flowers be placed under water while being cut.

25-5 Demonstrating capillarity. Each of the tubes has a bore of a different size. Explain the difference in heights of the liquids in the tubes.

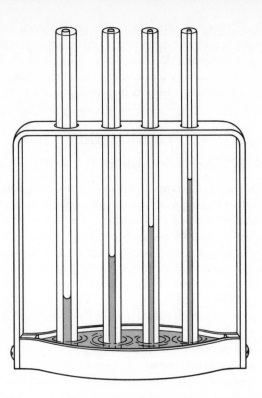

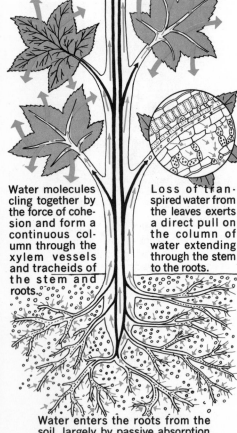

Water molecules cling together by the force of cohesion and form a continuous column through the xylem vessels and tracheids of the stem and roots.

Loss of transpired water from the leaves exerts a direct pull on the column of water extending through the stem to the roots.

Water enters the roots from the soil, largely by passive absorption as water rises through the plant.

25-6 Transpiration-cohesion theory.

enters the leaf mesophyll cells, it evaporates from the cell surfaces. This water vapor passes through the intercellular spaces and stomata during transpiration.

The loss of water from the leaves gives a direct pull on the column of water that extends through the vessels to the roots. The reason for this is that water molecules in the column have a strong attraction for each other. This molecular attraction is called **cohesion.** Cohesion explains why a cup of water can be filled just above the brim without spilling. In a plant, the transpiration pull in the leaves lifts the entire water column up slowly. The more water lost from the leaves, the faster water is pulled up from the roots. A giant Douglas fir or redwood tree lifts water more than 100 meters above the ground. So you can see that the forces must be enormous. Scientists estimate that the force needed may be as high as 100 atmospheres of pressure. **Though the transpiration-cohesion theory accounts for most of this force, root pressure must also contribute to the process.**

TRANSLOCATION OF FOODS

For many years, scientists have known that foods move from leaves to other plant parts through the phloem sieve tubes. Sap is composed of water and 10 to 25 percent dissolved materials. Most of this is sucrose. This is the major form in which carbohydrates are transported. Sap also contains smaller amounts of amino acids, mineral ions, and other substances.

Food materials usually move down through the stem and roots. But food can also go up to flowers and developing fruits. During the early spring, foods in woody perennials move up from storage spots in the stem and roots to branches and the developing buds.

There are several ways of showing that foods do move through phloem sieve tubes. *Girdling* a tree is one method. If a ring of bark is cut off down to the cambium, the phloem is destroyed. Food translocation will stop. This kills the tree because the stem and roots below the girdle will slowly die of starvation. The roots may live for months on stored food. And they will still absorb and conduct water and minerals through the xylem. But when the food reserves run out, the roots die, too. Soon after this, the whole tree dies.

Some animals, such as mice and rabbits, chew on bark. These animals girdle many trees, especially during the winter. Sometimes, farmers or gardeners girdle unwanted trees. This kills the tree and rids them of root sprouts in their gardens or fields.

Scientists do not know exactly *how* foods move through phloem sieve tubes. They do know that sap moves through the phloem under pressure. And they have also learned that the rate of flow in the sieve tubes is about 35 cm per hour. Furthermore, scientists have shown that food movement stops or slows down when there is not enough oxygen. This suggests that food translocation requires energy from respiration. In other words, active transport may play a large role in this process. But research is still being done to find out the exact mechanism.

Turgidity

WATER PRESSURE IN PLANT CELLS

When water diffuses into plant cells, the cytoplasm and vacuoles press against the cell wall. This pressure is called **turgor pressure.** The firmness of the cell when this occurs is called **turgidity.** You might say that a turgid cell is like a balloon filled with air. The pressure in a fully turgid plant can be anywhere from one to ten kilograms per square centimeter.

The turgor pressure in herbaceous plant tissues provides support for the plant. It also helps young seedlings push up through the soil. Sometimes, though, the pressure can be too much. Ripening fruits, like tomatoes, often split open because of turgor pressure.

WILTING AND THE LOSS OF TURGOR

As discussed in Chapter Twenty-Three, the stomata of leaves are usually open in the day and closed at night. So, they are open when the air warms up and dries out. This is when most transpiration occurs. If the soil is very moist, a high absorption rate will balance a high transpiration rate. But if transpiration occurs faster than absorption, a plant may be hurt by water loss.

25-7 This tree was photographed at the end of the second season of growth after girdling. You can see that the girdled region has continued to grow, while the portion below the ring has not. The roots of the tree will eventually die of starvation. (from Wilson and Loomis, *Botany*, 4th ed.)

Ask students why plants can be found growing out of paved streets or walks.

25-8 Temporary wilting. During the night, the wilted leaves (left) regain their turgor. (H. R. W. Photos by Russell Dian)

On a hot day, when the rate of transpiration is greater than that of absorption, plants may exhibit **temporary wilting.** This occurs even if the soil has enough moisture to supply the plant's needs. In the evening, the temperature goes down and the humidity rises. The rate of transpiration decreases, while water absorption increases. Thus, at night, a plant builds up its water supply again.

Temporary wilting does not really hurt a plant. But if it happens often, it can stunt the plant's growth.

Real injury to plants happens when there is not enough soil water, or when the roots are destroyed. This is called **permanent wilting.** This cannot be fixed by slowing the rate of transpiration. Permanent wilting usually occurs during droughts. But it can also happen during transplanting. Care must be taken to move enough soil to protect the roots.

GUTTATION

Most of the water lost from a plant, leaves by transpiration. But some plants lose water by a process called **guttation.** At night, closed stomata and atmospheric conditions cause a reduction in transpiration. Drops of water are forced out of the leaf through special stomata. These stomata are found along the edges of leaves or near the ends of their veins. The guard cells of these stomata are open day and night. Scientists think that high root pressure causes guttation. Grasses often force water out at the tips of their leaves. Potatoes, tomatoes, and strawberries show guttation at their leaf margins. Guttation water is not dew. Dew is condensation of water from the air onto cooler objects. Dew forms a film over the leaf. But guttation water appears only at the special stomata.

25-9 Guttation along the edge of a leaf. (Walter Dawn).

What causes water to rise great distances through a stem? Scientists do not have all of the answers to this question. Root pressure is one force involved, but only a small one. Another, more important, force is a pull from above. This involves transpiration and cohesion. As the plant loses water through its leaves, it takes in water through its roots. The entire column of water in the tube moves up the stem.

On warm days, the transpiration rate is high. So the movement of water through a plant is rapid. Water is drawn into the roots. This is called passive absorption. But, if the transpiration rate is greater than the absorption rate, temporary wilting occurs. In the evening, as transpiration slows down, the cells regain their turgor and the leaves stiffen.

The causes of food translocation are not well understood. But scientists think that active transport using cell energy is probably a major factor.

loam	translocation	girdling
topsoil	root pressure	turgor pressure
humus	capillarity	turgidity
capillary water	transpiration-cohesion	temporary wilting
active absorption	theory	permanent wilting
passive absorption	cohesion	guttation
halophytes		

1. What are some of the important plant processes that require water?
2. Explain the importance of soil texture to plant growth.
3. Name soil types on the basis of texture.
4. What forces are involved in active and passive water absorption by root hairs?
5. Under what conditions may a root lose water to the soil rather than absorb it?
6. What process is used by root cells to absorb minerals?
7. List three factors believed to be involved in translocation of water through xylem vessels of a stem.
8. Explain the transpiration-cohesion theory of water translocation.
9. How does girdling a tree demonstrate that foods are conducted through the phloem?
10. In what way is turgor pressure involved in supporting soft plant tissues?
11. Account for temporary wilting of nonwoody plant tissues.

1. Discuss the difference between the transport of sap and the transport of water.
2. Compare the conditions under which roots take in water by active and by passive absorption.
3. Compare root pressure, capillarity, and transpiration-cohesion as factors in the translocation of water through the xylem vessels and tracheids of a plant.

chapter twenty-six

Plant Growth and Responses

26–1 The flower of the night blooming cactus at night (left) and during the day. (Allen Roberts)

OBJECTIVES
- LIST some environmental factors which affect plant growth.
- DESCRIBE the effects of light on plant growth.
- EXPLAIN photoperiodism and dormancy in plants.
- DESCRIBE the roles of auxins as growth regulators.
- DEFINE gibberellins and kinins.
- DEFINE the term tropism.
- LIST various forms of tropisms.
- DISTINGUISH nastic movements from tropic responses.

There are numerous simple experiments that can be done to illustrate the influence of light and temperature on plant growth. Encourage students to design their own experiment to illustrate one of these.

Ask students to collect leaves that have been grown in light and in shade. Examine the leaves for obvious differences. Obtain diagrams which depict cross sections of leaves grown in the sun and shade. Compare the differences between the leaves.

External Factors

OUTSIDE INFLUENCES

The form and size of a plant depend a lot on heredity. Genes influence every aspect of plant structure and development. But heredity is not the only influence.

Environmental conditions are important factors in plant growth and development. The moisture in the air, the soil water and minerals, temperature, and light all play a role in the way plants develop. We shall limit our discussion here to *light* and *temperature,* two of the most important conditions affecting plant growth.

LIGHT AFFECTS PLANT GROWTH

Light has a definite effect on plant growth in several ways. Light is the energy source for photosynthesis. So light has a direct effect on the food supply. The amount of food supplied to the tissues affects the rate of cell division. This, in turn, affects the growth of all the organs of the plant. As we mentioned in earlier chapters, light is also necessary for forming chlorophyll.

The leaves and stems of plants grown in the dark are pale yellow, or **etiolated.** Lack of chlorophyll results in little or no photosynthesis, so the tissues would soon starve. The absence of light seems to make the stem grow longer. But the plant's leaves do not grow and expand normally. The stem will be weak and spindly. And the poorly developed leaves will be widely spaced.

Yet, if light is reduced instead of taken away completely, the plant may actually grow better. That is because transpiration may slow down even more than photosynthesis. The growing tissues retain more water. But they do not slow down their food-making process as much. As a result, the stem grows quickly, and produces large leaves.

A leaf exposed to bright sunlight contains more sugar and less water than a shaded leaf on the same plant. This happens because the leaf carries on respiration and photosynthesis at a faster rate.

Palisade cells may form more than one layer. The amount of conducting tissue increases. And the cuticle thickens. Although a sunlit leaf will be thicker, it is usually smaller. Shaded leaves, though, contain more water and less food. The loosely arranged cells of the spongy mesophyll increase in number. So the surface area of the shaded leaf is larger.

PHOTOPERIODISM

The *duration* of light has a specific effect on plant growth and reproduction. **The response of plants to varying periods of light and darkness is called *photoperiodism*.**

As you know, the number of hours of daylight and darkness changes with the seasons. On March 21 and September 22, day and night each last exactly twelve hours. In the Northern Hemisphere, the shortest day of the year is December 21. After that, every day has a few more minutes of light until June 21. Between June 21 and December 21, the days get shorter.

Extensive studies of plant growth have revealed a relationship between flowering and the length of days and nights. Many plants produce flowers during the spring or fall, when the days are shorter than in summer. These *short-day* plants include such familiar spring flowers as daffodils, tulips, crocuses, and dogwood. Short days in the late summer and fall are the flowering times for chrysanthemums, asters, and goldenrod. Sometimes short-day plants, like the forsythia, bloom in the spring and in the fall when the day and night, or **photoperiods,** are equal in length.

Long-day plants grow stems and leaves while the days are short. But they bloom when the days are long, in late spring and early summer. Among them are the iris, the hollyhock, and clover, and such vegetables as beets and radishes.

A third group of plants are hardly affected by the length of days and nights. First they grow, then they flower, with little response to the photoperiod. These *neutral-day* plants include tomatoes, marigolds, zinnias, snapdragons, carnations, and nasturtiums.

Commercial flower and vegetable growers make extensive use of artificial photoperiodism with lighting systems. They have found that the length of dark time may have more effect on flowering than the hours of light. This is true of many plant species. Plants can be made to bloom by controlling the photoperiod and the hours of darkness.

TEMPERATURE AFFECTS GROWTH

Temperature changes also influence plant growth and reproduction. The short days and long nights in early spring and fall are cooler on the average than the days and nights of early summer.

Every plant process tends to react to cooler and warmer temperatures. These include photosynthesis, translocation, respiration, and transpiration. If temperatures are too low or too high, plant

26–2 Compare the coleus plant on the left, grown under normal light conditions, and that on the right, grown in the dark. (H.R.W. Photo by Russell Dian)

growth will slow or stop. Somewhere between is an **optimum temperature** which is best for plant growth. Although it varies with each species, for most plants it is between 10° and 38° C. Plants may survive brief periods of temperatures above or below the optimum, but long exposure to either extreme will kill them.

DORMANCY IN PLANTS

In many parts of the world, there are seasons when the water supply, temperature, or light is wrong for growing. Many plants then become inactive, or **dormant.** Woody plants stay alive since their tissues are protected by bark or the scales on winter buds. Herbaceous perennials die above the ground, but their underground parts survive in a dormant state. Annual plants die but their seeds will live to grow in the next season.

Internal Factors

PLANT HORMONES

You know that plant growth is affected by external factors such as light and temperature. But growth is also regulated by the internal influence of hormones. Hormones are very active chemical substances secreted inside the plant. But even the production of hormones may be influenced by external conditions. This interplay of factors makes a complex growth-control mechanism.

Hormones differ from other secretions. They differ in that they are produced in certain parts of the plant and then translocated to other parts. There they influence the growth, division, and elongation of cells.

AUXINS

The most widely studied plant hormones are called **auxins.** They mostly cause cells to get longer and larger. They also act in the development of flowers and fruits. Auxins are sometimes called growth hormones. But they are really **growth regulators** since they may either increase or slow down the growth process. The main natural auxin that plants produce is called *IAA* (indoleacetic acid). Large amounts of IAA are secreted in growing parts of plant organs. These include the tips of shoots and young leaves, flowers and fruits. IAA may also be secreted in cambial cells and in the root tip. Then it is translocated from these places to other parts of the plant.

Different parts of the plant react differently to auxins. A high concentration of auxin seems to stimulate stem growth. Root tissues are affected in the opposite way. Root growth may be inhibited by high auxin concentrations.

Experiments with oat seedlings show the activity of auxins in the tip of the growing shoot. The oat's primary shoot is enclosed

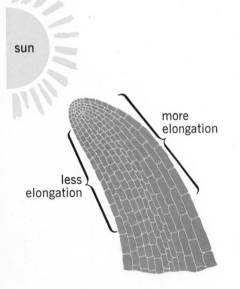

sun

more elongation

less elongation

26–3 Auxin causes cells in the stem to elongate. Can you form a hypothesis explaining why this plant grew toward the light?

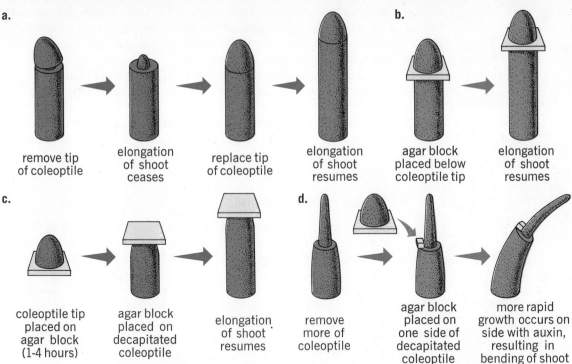

a.

remove tip of coleoptile → elongation of shoot ceases → replace tip of coleoptile → elongation of shoot resumes

b.

agar block placed below coleoptile tip → elongation of shoot resumes

c.

coleoptile tip placed on agar block (1-4 hours) → agar block placed on decapitated coleoptile → elongation of shoot resumes

d.

remove more of coleoptile → agar block placed on one side of decapitated coleoptile → more rapid growth occurs on side with auxin, resulting in bending of shoot

26-4 Demonstrating the presence and action of auxin in the tip of an oat coleoptile.

by a protective sheath called a *coleoptile.* As the seedling grows, the shoot normally pierces the tip of the coleoptile. If the tip is removed, no further growth occurs. But if the tip is replaced on the shoot, growth will begin again. Thus, auxins must be secreted by the coleoptile tip. These auxins move down into the growing cells, making them elongate.

Another experiment can be done to show this effect. The tip is placed on a block of agar. Agar will absorb the auxins from the tip. This agar block is placed on the top of the rest of the shoot. The shoot then grows as its cells elongate. It is interesting to note that this growth will occur even in the dark.

In yet another experiment, a small agar block with auxins is placed on one side of the shoot. The cells on this side of the shoot begin to grow faster. As a result of this uneven growth, the shoot bends to the side.

You can also see the power of the auxins in apical dominance. The auxins in the terminal bud move downward and inhibit the growth of lateral buds. Removal of the terminal buds causes the lateral buds to grow. Plants with terminal buds vary in amount of apical dominance. This may be caused by production of different amounts of auxins, or by other factors.

PRACTICAL USES OF AUXIN PREPARATIONS

Auxins can be used for killing weeds. The most common lawn weed-killer is a synthetic auxin known as 2,4-D. In concentrations as low as 0.1 percent, 2,4-D kills dandelions and other broad-leaved weeds without harming grass.

Auxins are involved in the growth of a plant toward light. If a box is constructed with a light source at the top and shelves blocking the light source, the plant will bend around the shelf in its growth toward the light.

Ask some students to visit a nursery or supply house and examine the ingredients listed in weed killers. Ask them to report their findings to the class.

Ask students to investigate the topic of "seedless" varieties of fruits and how they have been developed.

26–5 Effect of gibberellin on plant growth. A normal and a giant plant. (Sylvan H. Wittauer, Michigan State University)

26–6 Phototropism in a plant. The stem bends toward the light, and the leaves are at right angles to the light rays. (Walter Dawn)

Other auxin preparations prevent fruit from falling off trees. It seems the presences of the auxins keeps the tree from forming an abscission layer when the fruit is ripe. This allows the fruit-growers to harvest their crop all at once.

A very interesting use of auxins is the developing of fruit without seeds. In this case, auxins stimulate the fruit's development without pollination and fertilization. It usually takes these processes to form seeds. By using auxins, growers have produced seedless watermelons, cucumbers, and tomatoes. Some seedless fruits develop naturally without pollination, like bananas and navel oranges.

MORE GROWTH HORMONES

Another group of growth hormones are called **gibberellins.** These also promote the elongation of cells in plants. Gibberellins were discovered in Japan in 1926. Fungus-infected rice plants grew much longer than they should have. Scientists suspected that a fungus called *Gibberella* was secreting a substance which elongated the cells abnormally. In 1935, the substance was isolated and named *gibberellin* after the fungus. Later, it was discovered that other gibberellins are made in higher plants. The most important is gibberellic acid.

Experiments show that gibberellins also promote cambium activity in woody plants. They also seem to stimulate flowering and fruit development. In some effects, gibberellins may be associated with auxins.

Artificially applying gibberellins to growing plants can produce some very strange results. Cells may elongate unnaturally, producing giant plants. Plants that grow this fast may also flower early.

Cytokinins are less familiar plant regulating substances. They are usually regarded as hormones. Some biologists disagree because cytokinins are not translocated after they are produced. The best known of the cytokinins is *kinetin*.

While auxins and gibberellins causes cell enlargement and development, cytokinins influence cell division. Also cytokinins stimulate the growth of leaves and lateral buds.

TROPISMS

A growth response that is directly related to an environmental stimulus is called a *tropism* (TROPE-iz′m). External stimuli include light, gravity, contact, water, and chemicals. A tropic response may be *positive*, as when it is toward the stimulus. Or it may be *negative*, when it is away from the stimulus. While tropic responses are automatic growth reactions, they are usually an advantage to survival. They adapt the plant to environmental conditions.

A familiar tropism is the response of plants to light, which we call *phototropism* (foe-TOE-trow-PIZZ′m). You have probably seen plants on window ledges bend toward the light. This is a positive response toward light. The stem bends because of uneven cell elon-

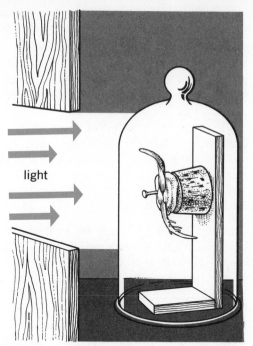

label: light

It is important the plants be "turned" often for equal growth to occur. Sunlight slows down the flow of growth-stimulating auxins. Therefore, one side of the plant stem toward the light will grow more slowly than the part toward the dark.

26–7 An explanation of the role of auxins in controlling phototropic responses. Auxin accumulates on the shaded side of the plant. Here, the auxins cause normal cell elongation in the stem but prevent normal cell elongation in the root. Because cells on the lighted side of the stem fail to elongate normally, the stem grows toward the light source.

gation. The cells on the shaded side tend to elongate more than those on the bright side. This causes the stem to grow unevenly and bend.

How does this happen? The most common explanation is that the auxin is translocated away from the light to the shady side. This causes the shady side to grow more. This uneven growth bends the stem toward light.

Roots show negative phototropism. Let's assume, again, that auxins are more concentrated on the dark side. Then in the root they must prevent cells from elongating. When the cells on the lighter side elongate normally, they bend the root away from the light, or toward the dark. From this evidence, we can say that auxins stimulate stem cell growth but limit the growth of root cells.

Gravity affects stems and roots in opposite ways, too. We call this reaction *geotropism* (jee-OW-trow-PIZZ'm). If you plant a seed upside down, the root will still grow down and the shoot, up. Why? Again, it is the effect of auxins.

Suppose you lay a seed down on its side. As auxins are secreted in the roots and the shoot, gravity makes them gather on the lower side. Thus, the underside of the stem will grow faster, making it bend upward. On the lower side of the root, though, the auxins have a reverse effect. The root cells with the auxins will not elongate as much as the cells on the upper side. This growth bends the root down. Of course, if both root and stem are growing vertically, the auxin distribution is equal.

Other tropic responses in plants are more difficult to explain. The tendrils of climbing plants curl around any object they touch. This positive reaction to contact is called *thigmotropism* (thig-MOW-trow-PIZZ'm).

26–8 An explanation of the role of auxins in controlling geotropic responses. Auxin accumulates on the lower side of the plant. Because cells on the upper side of the stem fail to elongate normally, the stem grows upward. Normal lengthening of the cells on the upper side of the root, however, causes the root to grow downward.

A new term, "skototropism," has recently been introduced. It means growing toward darkness and it describes a previously un-recognized trait of vines in tropical forests.

26–9 Nastic responses to touch in the sensitive plant: normal position of the leaves and leaflets (top), and position of the same leaves and leaflets after they had responded to a touch stimulus. (Walter Dawn)

Certain roots seem to grow toward water, so we call this ***hydro-tropism*** (hi-DROW-trow-PIZZ'm). You may notice masses of willow and cottonwood tree roots growing along riverbanks down into the water. These trees and other water-loving plants often clog drains and sewers by growing large numbers of roots between tiles or pipes. Roots do not "seek" water supplies. But it may be that they grow faster when they contact water.

The positive reaction of roots to chemicals, called ***chemotropism*** (keh-MOT-ruh-PIZZ'm), is also hard to explain. Maybe, as in the case of water, a concentration of minerals stimulates growth, with-out actually attracting the plant.

NASTIC MOVEMENTS

Other kinds of reactions to external stimuli that are seen in plants are called ***nastic movements.*** These are different from tropic responses in several ways. First, nastic movements are independent of the direction of the stimulus. Nastic movements are seen in the way flowers or leaves close up at certain times of the day. They may also occur when the temperature reaches a certain point. Morning-glories open in the morning. When dusk brings cooler temperatures, the flowers close until sunrise. The flowers of the night-blooming cereus, a cactus, do just the opposite. They stay closed all day but open to the darkness of evening.

Nastic movements are *turgor movements*. Tropic responses are *growth movements*. Tropic responses are slow, often taking days for a visible change to occur. Nastic movements happen quickly, within a few minutes or hours. Also, they are reversible; a flower that closes will open again. Tropic growth responses do not re-verse. Once the plant has grown in a certain way, those cells do not change.

A good example of an almost immediate nastic response to touch is shown by the plant *Mimosa pudica*. This sensitive plant has com-pound leaves. The leaflets are normally in the horizontal position. If a leaf is touched, a reaction occurs within three to five seconds. The stimulated leaflets will fold upward and the petiole droops. After having folded, the leaflets return to the original position as turgor returns to normal.

The mechanism is very complex. Epidermal hairs receive the touch stimulus. Sudden loss of turgor causes the petiole to droop.

Another example of this turgor change is the Venus's-flytrap. As you learned in Chapter Twenty-Three, its leaves will close suddenly to trap an insect in a nastic response. Similarly, the changes you can see in flowers like the sunflower, when it "follows the sun," are nastic and caused by turgor changes.

SUMMARY   Environmental factors have a great deal of influence on how a plant grows and adapts to its immediate surroundings. Two of the most important external conditions to the plant's development are light and temperature. The duration of the light makes a difference, too. Photoperiodism is the response of plants to differences in light duration.

Hormones are a major internal factor in regulating the way the plant grows. There are many important groups of hormones, such as the auxins, the gibberellins, and the cytokinins.

Plants respond to their surroundings by growing either toward a stimulus (positive tropism) or away from one (negative tropism). This is done according to the hormone effect on the growth of certain cells. Hormone action is affected by light and temperature changes, too. Commercial plant growers have learned to control flowering and fruit harvesting by means of artificial periods of light and darkness, as well as by hormone application.

Nastic movements are yet another indication of plants' responses to their environment. These are caused by turgor changes resulting from sudden differences in such factors as light and temperature.

			BIOLOGICALLY SPEAKING
etiolated	auxin	phototropism	
photoperiodism	growth regulator	geotropism	
photoperiod	coleoptile	thigmotropism	
optimum temperature	gibberellin	hydrotropism	
dormant	cytokinin	chemotropism	
hormone	tropism	nastic movement	

QUESTIONS FOR REVIEW

1. Name several environmental factors that influence plant growth and development.
2. Describe the appearance of a young stem grown in the dark.
3. Give examples of how flowering plants exhibit photoperiodism.
4. What are neutral-day plants?
5. What is meant by optimum temperature for plants?
6. Describe the various ways that some plants survive periods of dormancy.
7. How do hormones differ from other secretions?
8. List three groups of plant growth hormones and describe how each influences plant growth.
9. Name five tropisms and identify each with an external stimulus.
10. Distinguish a nastic movement from a tropic response.

APPLYING PRINCIPLES AND CONCEPTS

1. How do auxins relate to tropisms?
2. Explain why certain plants flower in the spring and again in the fall.
3. Discuss experimental evidence that auxin is secreted near the tip of an oat coleoptile and translocated to the tissue below the tip.
4. Cite experimental evidence that auxin causes the elongation of cells in stem tissues but inhibits elongation of root cells.

chapter twenty-seven

Plant Reproduction

OBJECTIVES

- GIVE EXAMPLES of natural vegetative reproduction.
- LIST methods of propagating plants vegetatively.
- DESCRIBE the purpose of flowers.
- DESCRIBE the function of each flower part.
- EXPLAIN how the ovule develops.
- DEFINE pollination.
- DESCRIBE fertilization in a flower.
- LIST some methods of seed dispersal.
- DISTINGUISH fruits from seeds.
- NAME some dry fruits and some fleshy fruits.
- COMPARE the structure of a bean seed and a corn seed.
- DESCRIBE the conditions needed for germination of a seed.

Stress to students that many plants are capable of reproducing without utilizing the flower. This is called vegetative reproduction.

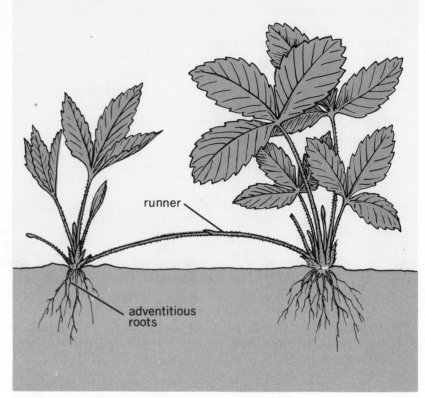

27–1 Vegetative reproduction in the strawberry.

REPRODUCTION IN FLOWERING PLANTS

There are two stages in the life cycle of a flowering plant, the vegetative and the reproductive. In the *vegetative stage,* the plant produces roots, stems, and leaves. Annual plants do all their vegetative growing in a single season. Perennials keep adding new vegetation year after year. **Many plants reproduce by producing new plants from their roots, stems, or leaves.** This type of *propagation,* or multiplication, is *asexual.* It is called **vegetative reproduction.**

The plant's vegetative growth prepares it for the *reproductive stage.* In the reproductive stage, flowers are produced and sexual reproduction occurs. The flowers produce gametes, and fertilization takes place. **The fertilized egg develops into an embryo. This embryo lies inside the protection of the seed until it germinates.** Flowers, fruits, and seeds are all products of the activities of the vegetative plant body.

First we shall look at various methods of vegetative reproduction, both natural and artificial. Then we shall continue with sexual reproduction and the flower, fruit, and seeds.

320

Vegetative Reproduction

NATURAL VEGETATIVE REPRODUCTION

Vegetative reproduction happens most in woody and herbaceous perennials. The strawberry is a good example of natural vegetative propagation. The parent plant forms *runners*, or stems that grow along the ground. The tips of the runners form shoots and adventitious roots. These give rise to new plants. A single parent plant can produce many new plants in a single season. In this way, one plant may create a whole strawberry patch by itself.

Raspberries follow a similar pattern. They grow long aerial stems. These stems arch downward, and their tips touch the ground. Adventitious roots develop and a shoot grows. The young raspberry plant soon becomes independent of its parent. The process is called *tip layering*.

Sometimes aerial shoots rise from horizontal stems growing underground near the surface. The small tree or shrub of the sumac plant does this. It produces clusters of new plants from its own roots. Trees like the osage orange, lilac, and white popular produce whole groves from their roots.

A few kinds of plants exhibit an unusual type of vegetative propagation. These plants develop new plants along their leaf edges. Such new plants form between the coarse teeth of the thick, fleshy leaves on *Kalanchoe* (bryophyllum). As they get bigger, the plantlets drop to the ground and continue to grow. Because this kind of reproduction is both unusual and interesting, bryophyllum is a popular house plant.

ARTIFICIAL PROPAGATION BY CUTTINGS

Plant growers use several ways to reproduce plants vegetatively. One easy method is by *cuttings*. Cuttings are pieces of roots, stems, or leaves from the parent plant. Most often *stem* cuttings are used. These pieces can be from several inches to a foot or more long and should have several nodes and lateral buds or leaves. The lower end of the cutting is buried in sand or loose soil. The cutting is successful if it produces adventitious roots of its own within several weeks. Then, the lateral buds should develop shoots. It is easy to propagate many woody plants like roses and pussy willows this way. You can also grow herbaceous plants like geraniums from such cuttings, or *slips*.

Newer methods have been developed to make cuttings even more reliable. Different kinds of growth-regulating hormones are used to start cell division and make roots grow. Indoleacetic acid (IAA) is a hormone often used for this purpose.

27–2 The fleshy, thickened root of the sweet potato serves naturally as a vegetative reproductive organ. For commercial production, the adventitious shoots are removed and planted in fields. (Herbert Weihrich)

Certain plants are cultivated *only* through vegetative means. These plants include the pineapple, navel oranges, varieties of grapes, and cultivated bananas. Ask students if there is any advantage to this method of reproduction.

Grafting can be fascinating to some students. Encourage a few to attempt a graft and to report on their findings.

LAYERING

Many forms of **layering** are used in artificial propagation of many plants. In one method, a rose stem is bent to the ground. All but the tip is covered with sand or soil. The buried part will grow roots, and the stem will grow up from the tip. When the new plant is strong, it is cut away from the parent rose bush and planted in another place. This process is called *simple layering.* It is useful for growing plants with strong roots, such as climbing roses.

Mound layering is used in propagating woody shrubs. The shrub is cut back to allow more growth of the lateral buds. The lower part of the shrub is covered with a mound of soil. New stems and adventitious roots grow from the buds near the base of the shrub. These can be removed and set out alone.

GRAFTING AND BUDDING

One of the most widely used methods of propagating woody plants is by **grafting.** Grafting is really splicing two stems together. The rooted part is called the *stock.* The cutting that is joined to the stock is called the *scion.* The scion is the plant the grower wants to propagate by joining it to a healthy stock.

A graft is successful only when the vascular cambiums of the stock and the scion are placed in contact with each other. Also, the graft must be made when the scion is dormant. This allows the cambiums to unite before shoots develop. For this reason, grafts are usually prepared during the winter. The area to be grafted is covered with wax and wrapped with elastic tape. This prevents the graft from drying out. It also protects it against fungi, insects, or other damaging organisms.

Budding is similar to grafting. A bud is used as the scion instead of a branch. A strong bud, together with the surrounding bark and

27–3 Grafting and budding.

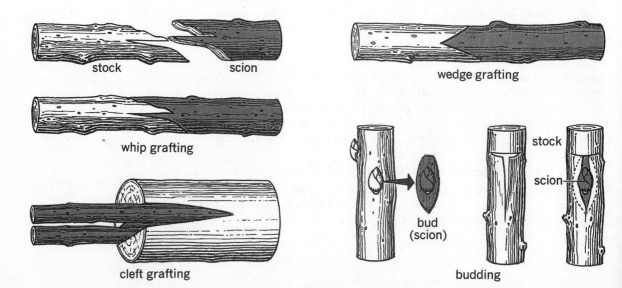

stock   scion

wedge grafting

whip grafting

cleft grafting

bud (scion)

stock

scion

budding

its active cambium, is removed. The bark of the stock is loosened by a T-shaped cut. Then the piece of bark attached to the bud is slipped under it. The vascular cambiums of scion and stock are united. Again the stock is wrapped with tape to hold the bud and prevent drying out.

Budding is usually done in the late summer or fall. When a shoot grows from the bud in the spring, the stock is cut off above where the bud was added. The rest of the plant will then grow out of the grafted bud and its shoot.

Sexual Reproduction

FLOWER PRODUCTION

Plants can propagate by vegetative means during the growing season. But, in order to survive, most of them must reproduce sexually. Sexual reproduction results in seeds. And seeds carry genetic traits into the next generation. Seeds usually have combinations of traits from different parent plants. Variations come about through the different recombinations of chromosomes and genes during the union of gametes. This occurs when the zygote is formed. **These variations, no matter how slight, may adapt a species to conditions in a changing environment.**

Flowers are the reproductive organs of higher plants. They are really branches whose leaves have modified and act as specialized *floral parts*. The nodes are very close together in flowers. Thus the floral parts are closely arranged. Flowers are specialized for the single purpose of sexual reproduction. They do not have meristematic tissue to continue the growth of the shoot. But flowers do start the development that leads to the formation of fruit and seed.

Flowers vary greatly in appearance. Some are large and colorful, like roses, orchids, lilies, and tulips. Other flowers like those of trees, grains, and grass, are not usually noticed. But they are the same reproductive organs. The essential parts of flowers are not the bright petals we admire.

FLORAL PARTS

Typical flowers, like geraniums or apple blossoms, have many parts. They all grow from a flower stalk, or *pedicel* (PED-uh-sell), whose tip is the *receptacle.* The outer ring of floral parts is formed by several green, leaflike *sepals* (SEEP'lz). The ring of sepals is called the *calyx* (KAY-licks). The sepals protect the rest of the flower in the bud stage. They also help support the other parts when the bud opens.

Inside the calyx is the *corolla* (kuh-RAH-luh), which is usually made of one or more rows of *petals.* The petals are often brightly colored. The calyx and corolla often attract insects. They also protect the inner parts. In some flowers, like the tulip, both calyx and corolla are the same color. This makes it hard to tell that both parts are there.

Ask students to bring into class a variety of flowers. This will allow them to closely examine floral parts.

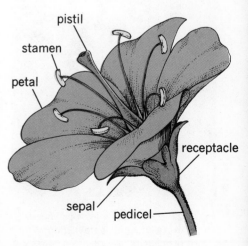

27–4   The floral parts of a complete flower.

Flowers bearing male and female parts are often described as perfect. However, flowers may be perfect and incomplete (lacking sepals or petals). It is not possible to have a complete, imperfect flower.

In the center of the flower are the two kinds of *essential* parts directly involved with reproduction. They are the stamens and the pistil. Each **stamen** (STAME'n) is a slender stalk or *filament* with a knobby sac at the end called an **anther.** The anther produces colored grains called **pollen,** which are vital to reproduction.

The **pistil** is usually shaped like a flask. It has a sticky top called a *stigma,* supported by a slender stalk or *style.* The swollen base, or *ovary,* is attached to the receptacle of the flower stalk. Inside the ovary are the **ovules,** which later become seeds. There may be from one to several hundred ovules, depending on the kind of flower. In some flowers, ovules are attached to the ovary, either at its base or along the side walls. In others, they are attached to an axis running through the center of the ovary.

VARIATIONS IN FLOWER STRUCTURE

Flowers vary greatly in colors, sizes, and shapes. But they also have variations in their reproductive structures. Many flowers have both stamens and pistil in the same flower. However, others have them in separate flowers on the same plant, such as oak trees, squash, and corn. Still other species have separate male and female plants. The female plant grows flowers bearing pistils. The male grows flowers bearing stamens. Willows and cottonwoods are familiar examples.

In your study of stems and leaves, you found that monocots and dicots differ in the arrangement of vascular tissue. They also differ in flower structure. **Monocots usually produce flower petals and essential parts in threes or multiples of three. Dicots normally have them in multiples of fours or fives.**

Some flowers that look like single flowers are really a whole cluster of flowers. The sunflower and the daisy are examples. They have dense clusters or reproductive flowers in the center. Around these are petal-like flowers that attract insects.

POLLEN FORMATION

If you look at a cross section of the developing anther on a large stamen, such as the lily's or tulip's, you can clearly see four chambers. These chambers are called **pollen sacs.** While the flower is developing, each pollen sac is filled with cells with large nuclei. As the anther grows, each of these cells goes through two meiotic divisions, forming a four-celled tetrad. These cells are called **microspores.** Eventually, each one of these microspores becomes a pollen grain. First each nucleus divides by mitosis to become two nuclei. One is a **tube nucleus.** The other is a **generative nucleus.** The wall of the cell thickens to protect the developing pollen grain. As the anther ripens, the wall between the paired pollen sacs disappears. The pollen sacs burst open, and the mature pollen grains are ready for dispersal.

27–5 Trillium, a monocot, has flowers with three petals. (top) While bunchberry, a dicot, has a flower with four petals. (Dr. E. R. Degginger; S. J. Krasemann, Peter Arnold)

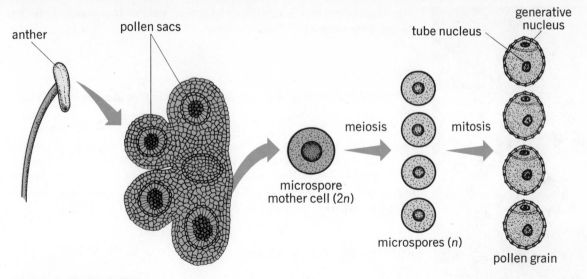

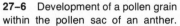

anther

pollen sacs

tube nucleus

generative nucleus

meiosis

mitosis

microspore mother cell (2*n*)

microspores (*n*)

pollen grain

OVULE FORMATION

While pollen grains are forming in the anthers, there are also changes in the ovary at the base of the pistil. Whether there are several ovules forming in the ovary, or just one, the process is basically the same.

An ovule starts as a tiny knob on the ovary wall. Each knob contains one cell. The ovule grows away from the wall on the end of a short stalk through which it is nourished. Gradually a couple of protective layers form around the ovule. It is completely enclosed except for one tiny pore called a **micropyle.**

The single ovule cell now goes through two meiotic divisions, resulting in four **megaspores.** One of these lives; the other three die. The remaining megaspore gets larger and turns into an oval **embryo sac.** More cell division occurs. And a **polar nucleus** is formed in a cell in the center of the embryo sac. This sac goes on developing until it is ready for fertilization. In order for fertilization to take

27–6 Development of a pollen grain within the pollen sac of an anther.

A flowering plant is fertilized within its ovule. Following fertilization, the ovule becomes the seed, and contains the zygote and endosperm or food source.

27–7 Development of an ovule within the ovary at the base of a pistil.

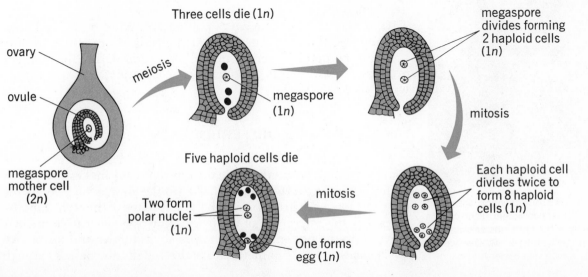

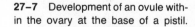

Three cells die (1*n*)

megaspore divides forming 2 haploid cells (1*n*)

ovary

ovule

meiosis

megaspore (1*n*)

mitosis

megaspore mother cell (2*n*)

Each haploid cell divides twice to form 8 haploid cells (1*n*)

Five haploid cells die

Two form polar nuclei (1*n*)

mitosis

One forms egg (1*n*)

place, a pollen grain must get to the stigma of the pistil. This can happen in several different ways.

POLLINATION

Pollination is the transfer of pollen from an anther to a stigma. In some plants, pollen goes from the anther to the stigma within the same flower. Pollen may also go to the stigma of another flower on the same plant. This is known as *self-pollination*. If flowers on two separate plants are involved, it is called *cross-pollination*. For cross-pollination, the pollen must be carried by an outside agent. Insects, wind, or water often act as these outside agents. Flowers adapt in curious ways to make cross-pollination possible.

27–8 The bee is an ideal pollinator. (H.R.W. Photo by Russell Dian)

AGENTS OF POLLINATION

The most common *insect* pollinators are the bees. But moths, butterflies, bats, birds, and some kinds of flies act as agents for cross-pollination. Insects go to flowers in search of sweet nectar secreted by glands at the base of the petals.

Bees swallow the nectar into a "honey stomach." There it is mixed with saliva and turned into honey. When the bees return to their hive, they store the honey in the honeycomb. They use it later as food. The bee's plump, hairy body makes it an ideal pollinator. As it crawls into the flower to get at the nectar, its body rubs against the anthers near the flower's opening. When it flies to the next flower, some of the pollen rubs off on the stigma. And a *new* supply of pollen brushes on from this flower.

The brightly colored petals and sweet smell of the flowers aid insects in locating them. The bright stripes on some petals may also act as guides.

At least one *bird*, the hummingbird, also acts as a pollinating agent. Its long bill and tongue reach right down into the flower as it hovers outside.

Wind may also be an agent of pollination. Wind-pollinated flowers are often found in clusters near the ends of branches. Usually there are no petals. There is rarely any nectar. Often the stamens produce large amounts of pollen. Some examples are willow, ragweed, corn, and oats.

27–9 The giant ragweed. The pollen of this wind-pollinated plant causes hay fever in people who are sensitive to it. (Georgia Extension Services in cooperation with FES)

THE POLLEN TUBE AND FERTILIZATION

What happens after a pollen grain lands on the surface of the pistil's stigma? First, a chemical from the pistil makes the pollen grain form a *pollen tube* that grows into the stigma surface. As the tube gets longer, it grows through the soft tissue of the style. Finally, it reaches the micropyle of the ovule. Now the generative nucleus moves into the pollen tube. As it does so, it divides and forms two **sperm nuclei,** or male gametes. After the pollen tube passes through

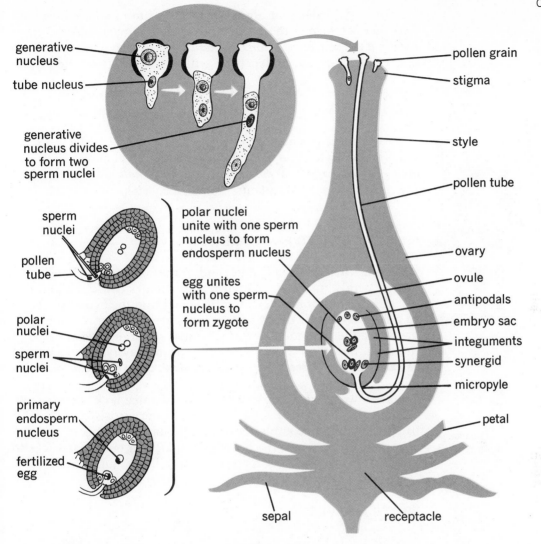

generative nucleus

tube nucleus

generative nucleus divides to form two sperm nuclei

pollen grain

stigma

style

pollen tube

sperm nuclei

pollen tube

polar nuclei unite with one sperm nucleus to form endosperm nucleus

egg unites with one sperm nucleus to form zygote

ovary

ovule

antipodals

embryo sac

integuments

synergid

micropyle

polar nuclei

sperm nuclei

primary endosperm nucleus

fertilized egg

petal

sepal

receptacle

27–10 Growth of the pollen tube and double fertilization.

the micropyle, it digests the part of the embryo sac's thin wall. The tip of the tube breaks open, and the two sperms are released into the embryo sac. At this time, the tube nucleus disintegrates.

One of the two sperms unites with the egg in fertilization. This produces the fertilized egg called a zygote. The other sperm nucleus unites with the nuclei in the embryo sac to form the *endosperm nucleus.*

At this point, auxins from the pollen grain stimulate cells within the ovule to divide. The zygote develops into an embryo plant. The endosperm nucleus grows into the seed *endosperm.* The endosperm contains food for the embryo plant. In some seeds, the embryo absorbs the food from the endosperm while the seed is developing. In others, the endosperm stays while the seed matures.

Remind students that the removal of stamens of potted plants will prolong the life of the flower. Why is this so?

Point out to students that some seeds do not have an endosperm. The seed may also provide a period of dormancy during adverse conditions for growth.

ALTERNATION OF GENERATIONS IN FLOWERING PLANTS

We noted earlier that algae, mosses, and ferns sometimes have two distinct forms, the gametophyte and the sporophyte. They produce them in *alternation of generations*. In seed plants, the male gametophyte is the pollen tube with its nuclei. And the female gametophyte is the embryo sac with the egg and the endosperm. The sporophyte is the rest of the plant, the part we see. The tissues of the sporophyte protect the vulnerable egg and sperm from drying out.

Clearly there has been an evolutionary trend toward a more obvious sporophyte. This seems to parallel the development of 1) *vascular tissue*, 2) *roots*, 3) *epidermis*, and 4) *stomata*, in evolving into the most efficient land plants, the angiosperms.

27–11 As the ovary enlarges it becomes the fruit. The fruit contains the seed that formed from the matured ovule.

FROM FLOWER TO FRUIT AND SEED

Fertilization brings a sudden end to the work of the flower. The sepals, petals, and stamens wither. Hormones cause the plant to use all its energy on developing the ovary and the ovules inside it. In a few weeks, the ovary and its contents ripen. In many plants, parts like the receptacle or the calyx get larger and become part of the fruit. **So we can define a *fruit* as a ripened ovary, with or without associated parts. A seed, though, is a matured ovule enclosed inside the fruit.**

Like flowers, fruits vary in structure. Notice how different the biological meaning of *fruit* is from the grocery store word. Not all fruits are fleshy like apples or oranges. Biologists think of a kernel of corn, a hickory nut, the beans in a pod, or a burr that sticks to your clothes, as fruit just as much as the fleshy, juicy kind.

FRUITS AND SEEDS

What would happen if seeds just fell to the ground and grew right next to the parent plant? All those seedlings would soon be competing with each other and the parent for sun, water, and minerals. Not many would survive to maturity.

Instead, many seeds are scattered some distance away from the plant that produced them. This is called **seed dispersal.** There are many means of scattering seeds. In some plants, dispersal is mechanical. In others, the dispersal is helped by agents like wind, water, or birds.

Mechanical dispersal happens in pods like the bean and pea. The pods often twist as they ripen and dry out. Eventually the strain makes them burst open, with enough force to throw the seeds some distance. When the fruits of the garden balsam, or touch-me-not, are ripe, they open at the slightest touch. They curl up violently. The seeds are often thrown several feet.

Table 27-1 CLASSIFICATION OF FRUITS

TYPE	STRUCTURE	EXAMPLES
Fleshy Fruits		
pome	outer fleshy layer developed from calyx and receptacle; ovary forms a papery core containing seeds	apple, quince, pear
drupe	ripened ovary becomes two-layered —outer layer fleshy, inner layer hard, forming stone or pit, enclosing one or more seeds	plum, cherry, peach, olive
berry	entire ovary fleshy and often juicy; thin-skinned and containing numerous seeds	tomato, grape, gooseberry
modified berry	like berry, but with tough covering	orange, lemon, cucumber
aggregate fruit	compound fruit composed of many tiny drupes clustered on single receptacle	raspberry, blackberry
accessory fruit	small and hard; scattered over surface of receptacle; edible portion formed from enlarged receptacle	strawberry
multiple fruit	compound fruit formed from several flowers in a cluster	mulberry, pineapple
Dry Fruits (open when ripe)		
pod	ovary wall thin, fruit single-chambered, containing many seeds; splits along one or two lines when ripe	bean, pea, milkweed
capsule	ovary containing several chambers and many seeds; splits open when mature	poppy, iris, cotton, lily
Dry Fruits (remain closed when ripe)		
nut	hard ovary wall enclosing a single seed	hickory nut, acorn, pecan
grain	thin ovary wall fastened firmly to single seed	corn, wheat, oats
achene	similar to grain, but with ovary wall separating from seed	sunflower, dandelion
winged fruit or samara	similar to achene but with prominent wing attached to ovary wall	maple, ash, elm

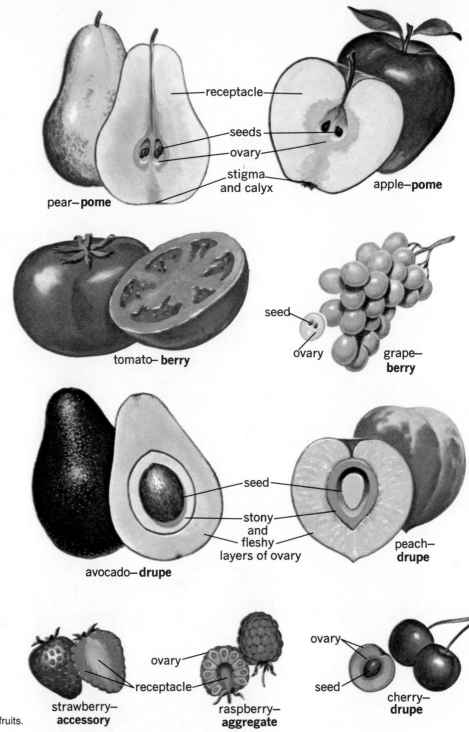

receptacle

seeds

ovary

stigma and calyx

pear–**pome**

apple–**pome**

tomato–**berry**

seed

ovary

grape–**berry**

seed

stony and fleshy layers of ovary

avocado–**drupe**

peach–**drupe**

ovary

receptacle

strawberry–**accessory**

ovary

receptacle

raspberry–**aggregate**

ovary

seed

cherry–**drupe**

27–12 Types of fleshy fruits.

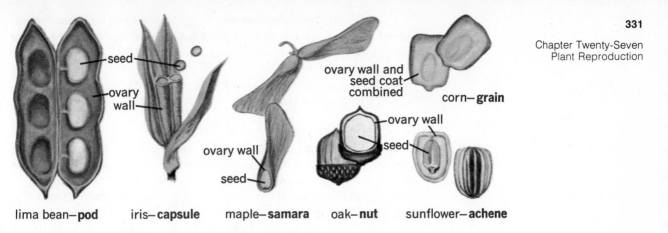

lima bean–**pod**   iris–**capsule**   maple–**samara**   oak–**nut**   sunflower–**achene**

27–13 Various types of dry fruits.

In these cases, only the seeds are dispersed. In other plants, though, the fruit plays a role. The sweetness of grapes, cherries, and other fleshy fruits acts as a sort of biological bribe. *Birds* and other *animals* eat the fruit, seeds and all. But the cellulose covers of the seeds cannot be digested. So the seeds usually pass through the digestive tracts of the animals. In this way, seeds may be dispersed to the ground.

Animals help to disperse fruit and seeds in other ways, too. Many plants produce fruit with stickers or spines that easily catch on animal fur. If you've ever found beggar-ticks or burrs on your clothes, then you probably helped disperse some seeds.

Water also serves as a dispersal agent. The shore-loving coconut palm often drops its fruit into the water, which carries it away. Other shoreline plants, like the grassy sedges, also drop their fruits into the water.

The *wind* is a familiar agent of dispersal for seeds. Some seeds have long, loose hairs or "wings" attached to them. These help the seed float to a new location. When milkweed pods split open, their seeds are carried like this. You have probably helped dandelions by blowing their fluff off. Some trees, like the maple, ash, and elm, have seeds with tiny "propellers" that whirl them away from their parent plants.

Seed dispersal methods are numerous. Water, wind, animals, mechanical means, and people are a few of the methods that aid dispersal. Ask students to discuss the advantages and disadvantages of certain methods of dispersal.

WHAT IS A SEED?

Earlier, we defined a seed as a ripe ovule, the end product of plant reproduction. A seed is made up of a tiny living embryo, stored food, and the seed coats. The young plant is nourished by the stored food from the time it starts to grow until it can produce its own food by photosynthesis. The food is stored in different areas, depending on the seed. In some, food is stored in "seed leaves" called the *cotyledons*.

When plants begin to grow, the cotyledons develop before any other leaves appear. They only last for a few days, then they wither and fall off. You may have seen the thick cotyledons on the stems of young lima bean plants shortly after they have pushed through

Point out to students that the endosperms of many plants are used for human and animal food.

the garden soil. **The classification of angiosperms into monocotyledons and dicotyledons is based on how many cotyledons there are in the seed.** Monocot plants have only one, while dicots have two cotyledons in their seeds.

Not all seeds have the same kinds of food stored in their cotyledons. In a grain of corn, the starch and protein are stored in the endosperm. The cotyledon has oils and proteins. The endosperm fills most of the corn seed. On the other hand, most of a bean seed is made up of the two cotyledons. The bean cotyledons store a large amount of starch as well as proteins and oil. Some seeds have a large endosperm. Some, like the bean, show none at all.

Seed coats develop from the wall of the ovule. They protect the seed from drying out and being damaged before it has a chance to germinate. Although some seeds have only one coat, usually there are two. The outer coat is tougher and thicker than the inner one.

A DICOT SEED

Bean seeds are usually kidney-shaped. The outer coat, or **testa,** is smooth. On the concave side, there is an oval scar called the **hilum** (HILE'm), which marks where the bean was attached to the pod wall. Near one end of the scar is a tiny pore, the *micropyle*. This was the small opening in the wall of the ovule that the pollen tube grew through just before fertilization. The inner seed coat is a thin white tissue that is hard to separate from the testa.

If you soak a dried bean, you can take off the seed coats and the cotyledons will come apart easily. The cotyledons fill the space inside the seed coats. They are also fleshy and not at all leaflike.

The other parts of the embryo plant are between the cotyledons. A finger called the **hypocotyl** fits into the protective pocket of the seed coats. It is really an embryonic stem, lying between the cotyledons and the **radicle** (embryonic root).

Part of the embryo plant lies above the point where the cotyledons are attached. That part is called the **epicotyl.** It is made of two tiny leaves folded over each other. Between these leaves lies the apical meristem tissue. This will be the terminal bud when the epicotyl develops into the shoot. As soon as the seed germinates, the hypocotyl and the epicotyl grow quickly. The cotyledons provide the food.

27–14   The structure of a bean seed.

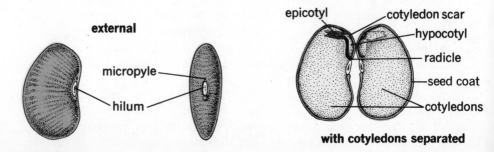

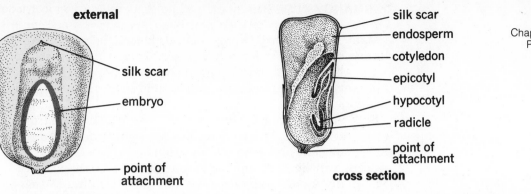

external

- silk scar
- embryo
- point of attachment

- silk scar
- endosperm
- cotyledon
- epicotyl
- hypocotyl
- radicle
- point of attachment

cross section

A MONOCOT SEED

Each kernel of corn is a complete fruit. So it can be compared to the bean pod instead of to the individual bean seed. But each grain of corn has only one seed.

The micropyle is covered by the fruit. But you can see where the corn fruit was attached to the cob. On one side of a corn grain, a light-colored oval area shows through the fruit coat. This is where the embryo is located. Near the top of the kernel is a tiny point called the *silk scar,* where the style was attached.

If you cut a grain of corn lengthwise right through the embryo, you can see the internal parts. The endosperm fills most of the seed. It contains both starch and sugar. In the sweet corn we eat, the endosperm contains both starch and sugar. But field corn stores only starch. The embryo does not have any starch, but it does contain protein.

Corn has only one cotyledon, which lies against the endosperm. It is attached to the epicotyl and to one side of the hypocotyl. During germination, the cotyledon absorbs food from the endosperm. Also, the corn grain stores most of its energy-yielding food outside the embryo. The bean, however, stores food in the cotyledon.

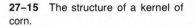

27–15 The structure of a kernel of corn.

Corn is a valuable food product used in a number of different ways. Ask students to report on corn, corn products, and the use of corn oil in margarine. What are the advantages of corn oil products?

Table 27-2 COMPARISON OF CERTAIN DICOTYLEDONOUS AND MONOCOTYLEDONOUS SEEDS

BEAN	CORN
testa with hilum and micropyle plainly visible	hilum and micropyle covered by a three-layered fruit coat; true seed coat lies inside fruit coat
two cotyledons	one cotyledon
large embryo	small embryo
no endosperm at time of dispersal	large endosperm
epicotyl fairly large	epicotyl rather small
epicotyl leaves folded	epicotyl leaves rolled
fruit a pod with several seeds	fruit a single grain with one seed

DORMANCY IN SEEDS

Many seeds go through rest periods before they germinate. This dormancy, may last for a few weeks or an entire season, or for years. Many plants produce their seeds in the fall. Their seeds lie dormant through the winter, and then germinate in the following spring or summer.

Seed and fruit coats are designed to protect the seed from cold, heat, and dryness. When conditions are right for the seed to grow, dormancy ends and *germination* begins.

Seeds can lie dormant for various lengths of time before they germinate. Again, some can live for nearly a hundred years and still germinate when conditions are right. Other seeds, like the maple, germinate almost at once after falling from the tree. As a result, in late spring you often see several maple seedlings springing up fairly near the parent tree.

It is interesting to note that some seeds will not germinate unless they undergo a cold period which corresponds to seasonal changes. Some botanists keep seeds in the refrigerator to stimulate germination.

Seeds are the only form in which annuals survive the winter months in cold climates. Their period of dormancy usually lasts from one growing season to the next. Also, the seeds of many perennials normally lie dormant through the winter months.

The ability of seeds to germinate is called **viability.** Seed viability depends on conditions during dormancy and on the amount of food stored in the cotyledons and endosperm. Ideally, seeds should rest in a cool, dry place. Warmth and moisture lower viability. Commercial seed growers run tests on the viability of different batches of seeds they sell. They find out what percent of the seeds can be expected to germinate.

WHAT IS NEEDED FOR GERMINATION?

Most seeds will germinate when they have moisture, oxygen, and the right temperature. But each species needs a certain amount of each in order to germinate.

The seeds of many water plants germinate under water. There is plenty of moisture, the temperature is even, and enough oxygen is dissolved in the water. On the other hand, the seeds of most land plants cannot germinate under water.

A simple demonstration of germination can be accomplished by filling a beaker two thirds full of corn seeds. Add water, filling the beaker one-half full. Allow germination to take place over a period of several days. What conditions are necessary for germination?

Before a seed germinates, it absorbs a lot of water. This softens the seed coats and makes the seed swell. But too much moisture encourages the growth of fungi. Fungi can decay the seed.

The best temperature for germination varies with the seed. A maple seed can germinate on a cake of ice. But it will grow slowly and may not survive. Other seeds, like corn, require higher temperatures. For most seeds, the best range is between 15° and 27° C.

During germination, the cells in a seedling divide very rapidly. This greater activity means that respiration must go on at a much faster rate than it does in an older plant. So you can see why seedlings need a lot of oxygen. This is why the soil in a garden should be loose, and why seeds should be planted near the surface.

As we have said, much of the food stored in the cotyledons or endosperm of a seed is starch. While the embryo is growing, the starch is changed into sugar by an enzyme called *amylase*. So, the new plant can use the sugar as food. This change is responsible for the sweet flavor of sprouting seeds. It also explains why sugar is extracted from sprouting grain. For this reason, soybean sprouts are used in cooking.

HOW THE SEEDLING GROWS

If you think about it, germination is an interesting process. How seeds germinate and take root varies a great deal. If a seed is lying on the ground, the root must grow down into the soil. The epicotyl can shoot straight up. But if the seed is completely buried, the epicotyl has to push through the soil in order to unfold its leaves above the ground, while the root simply grows down. Let us follow the germination process of a bean seed and a grain of corn.

After water has softened the bean's seed coats, the hypocotyl grows out through them. The root grows downward to become the primary root of the seedling. At the same time, the hypocotyl grows in an arch that pushes up toward the surface. Once above ground, the hypocotyl arch straightens out and lifts the cotyledons up to become the shoot. Then the tiny leaves unfold. They grow into the first foliage leaves of the plant. Since they are true leaves, they will stay on the plant for its lifetime.

A simple demonstration can be done to illustrate the presence of starch in the cotyledons and endosperms of plants.

Germination is dependent on environmental conditions. Certain adaptations have occurred to prevent germination of seeds until environmental conditions are favorable for development.

27–16 Germination of a bean seed.

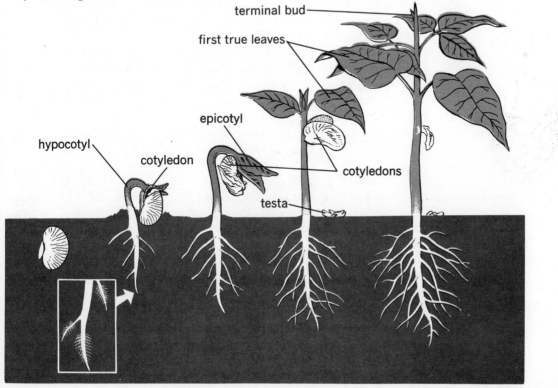

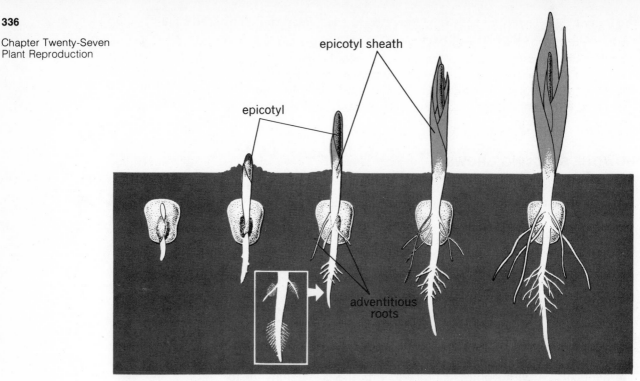

epicotyl sheath

epicotyl

adventitious roots

27–17 Germination of a kernel of corn.

The stem lengthens rapidly, developing more leaves. The apical meristematic tissue, that was between the epicotyl leaves, becomes the terminal bud. As the plant develops an ability to supply its own food, the cotyledons wither and fall off.

The corn embryo also absorbs water from the soil. Its root also pushes through the softened fruit and seed coats. But it forms a temporary primary root. Soon branch roots develop from it and eventually from the bottom of the stem, too, adding to the primary root. The leaves of the epicotyl, still tightly rolled in the coleoptile, push through the soil's surface. Once above ground, the leaves unroll and the stem continues to form the cornstalk. Unlike the bean, the corn grain's hypocotyl and cotyledon never appear above ground.

SUMMARY

Plants can reproduce themselves in two ways. When they propagate vegetatively, they send out long stems, either above or below ground. These stems eventually put down their own roots, develop independent shoots, and become separate plants. Grafting and budding are artificial means of vegetative propagation.

Sexual reproduction is the other way plants propagate their species. It is a vital means of adapting to a changing environment through variations from one generation to the next. The flower of the plant contains the parts needed for sexual reproduction. The female part is the pistil, which has a sticky stigma on top and an ovary. The ovary contains the ovule, or egg, and endosperm, at the base. The male part is the anther, which produces pollen grains. Pollen is carried to the stigma through various methods. The grain then grows a pollen tube into the stigma and down to the ovary, where the male cells fertilize the female egg. Together, they develop into the seed, surrounded by seed coats for protection. Fruits provide food and protection for the seeds and are also useful in seed dispersal.

A seed is a small living plant, packaged and ready for delivery. There are several means of dispersal. The seed comes complete with embryo, stored food, and seed coats. Most seeds lie dormant through the winter months and germinate in the spring. The bean seed and the corn kernel are good examples of different kinds of seed structure and germination processes.

BIOLOGICALLY SPEAKING

vegetative reproduction	anther	pollen tube
cutting	pollen	sperm nucleus
layering	pistil	endosperm nucleus
pedicel	ovule	endosperm
receptacle	pollen sac	fruit
sepal	microspore	seed dispersal
grafting	tube nucleus	testa
budding	generative nucleus	hilum
floral part	micropyle	hypocotyl
calyx	megaspore	radicle
corolla	embryo sac	epicotyl
petal	polar nucleus	viability
stamen	pollination	

QUESTIONS FOR REVIEW

1. Describe several methods of natural vegetative reproduction.
2. Distinguish the stock from scion in a graft. How must these be placed for the graft to be successful?
3. What purpose is served by the sepals and petals of a flower?
4. Describe the parts of the stamen and the pistil.
5. List three common agents of pollination.
6. Describe the growth of the pollen tube and double fertilization.
7. What part of the seed is produced from the zygote? from the endosperm nucleus?
8. What is the biological meaning of the term fruit?
9. Describe several ways in which seeds are dispersed.
10. How do dicotyledonous and monocotyledonous seeds differ?
11. Name three conditions necessary for seed germination.
12. List the stages in the germination of a bean.

APPLYING PRINCIPLES AND CONCEPTS

1. Discuss the importance of vegetative propagation in the commercial growing of cultivated varieties of fruit trees.
2. Plants produce much larger numbers of pollen grains than ovules. What is the survival value of this?
3. Discuss various characteristics of insect-pollinated flowers that serve as devices for attraction.
4. A seed will not germinate unless it has enough water to soften the seed coats. How is this an automatic safeguard against germination during unfavorable conditions?

RELATED READING

Books

Anderson, A. W., *How We Got Our Flowers*.
  Dover Publications, Inc., New York. 1966. A fascinating history of the common flowers of America.

Bold, Harold C., *The Plant Kingdom* (3rd ed.).
  Prentice-Hall, Inc., Englewood Cliffs, N. J. 1970. A broad presentation of the main features of structure, physiology, and reproduction in the plant kingdom.

Coulter, Merle C., *Story of the Plant Kingdom* (3rd ed., rev.).
  The University of Chicago Press, Chicago. 1964. A general survey of the plant kingdom, arranged by phyla.

Devlin, Robert M., *Plant Physiology*.
  Reinhold Publishing Corp., New York. 1966. Includes recent findings in plant physiology.

Frisch, Rose E., *Plants That Feed the World*.
  D. Van Nostrand Co., Princeton, N.J. 1967. An informative account of the flowering plants that, with few exceptions, feed the world.

Heiser, Charles B., Jr., *Seed to Civilization, the Story of Man's Food*.
  W. H. Freeman and Co., San Francisco. 1973. An interesting account of man's progress in the production of his food.

Hutchins, Ross E., *Plants Without Leaves*.
  Dodd, Mead and Co., New York. 1966. A description of these plants by a well known biologist, who explains their representative uses and odd ways of survival.

Leopold, A. C., *Auxins and Plant Growth*.
  University of California Press, Berkeley, Calif. 1965. A very useful chapter supplement.

Page, Nancy M., and Richard E. Weaver, *Wild Plants in the City*.
  Quadrangle/The New York Times Book Co., New York. 1975. An easy-to-understand handbook about plants that grow in city environments.

Salisbury, Frank B., *The Biology of Flowering*.
  Natural History Press, New York. 1971. A detailed account of the structure and physiology of plant flowering.

Wendt, Frits, and the Editors of *Life Magazine, The Plants*.
  Time-Life Books (Time, Inc.), New York. 1963. A picture-essay book that answers most of the questions biology students ask about plants.

Wilson, Carl L., and Walter E. Loomis, *Botany*.
  Holt, Rinehart and Winston, Publishers, New York. 1971. An excellent text in botany which incorporates all the newer knowledge in this field, especially molecular biology.

Articles

Epstein, Emanuel, "Roots," *Scientific American,* May, 1973. An interesting article describing the structure and function of the root.

Galston, Arthur W., "Bios: New Ways to Increase Man's Food," *Natural History,* October, 1973. The article explains how the reaction of plants to light and darkness affects crop yield.

Galston, Arthur W., "The Language of the Leaves," *Natural History,* January, 1973. Discusses the mechanisms behind leaf movement.

Spencer, Patricia W., "The Turning of the Leaves," *Natural History,* October, 1973. A clear presentation on the chemical and physical changes that cause leaves to change.

Steward, F. G., "The Control of Growth in Plant Cells," *Scientific American,* October, 1963. Describes a classic investigation in which isolated cells were stimulated to develop into adult plants.

unit

5

BIOLOGY OF THE INVERTEBRATES

More than 95 percent of all members of the animal kingdom are invertebrates. Invertebrates are organisms that do not have backbones. This unit describes many of the interesting forms and ways of life of the invertebrates. These animals vary greatly in size. A minute beetle may be only 0.2 millimeters in length. A giant squid may grow to be over 12 meters long. The study of these organisms help us to understand more about life. As we study the invertebrates, we will start with the simplest and move to the more complex. It is hoped that this will help in understanding both the unity and diversity in the living things around us.

THE ADVANTAGES OF ASSOCIATION

When cells live close together, do they have an advantage over those living alone? Yes, indeed. One person living alone on an island, for instance, can learn to gather food, make his own clothes, build his own shelter, and protect himself from enemies. But how much easier it is for ten people to do the same! One becomes an expert at hunting, another at cooking, another at carpentry, and so forth. As a group, with each member specializing in a particular skill, they function more effectively than one person performing all the tasks himself. Many-celled animals have the same advantage. Individual cells are more highly developed in specific skills. This provides for a greater efficiency than in a single-celled organism.

DIVISION OF LABOR

When cells increase in number, they can divide the labor. You know this from studying the cell in Chapter Four. In organisms with many cells, certain cells specialize in functions that benefit all the cells. The adapting of a cell for a particular use is called **specialization. As you study the animal kingdom, you will find that the more complex the structure of an animal, the more specialized are its cells.**

While division of labor allows cells to specialize, it also makes them more dependent on each other. This is called interdependence. Society works the same way. A person who makes shoes, for instance, must depend on a farmer to grow the food. A one-celled ameba can live by itself in a pond. But a cell in a muscle or bone cannot live or function without the other cells around it. The highest degree of cell specialization occurs in some of the **vertebrates,** the animals with backbones. In this unit, though, we will discuss the **invertebrates,** the animals without backbones. It may surprise you to learn that about 95 percent of the animals are invertebrates.

THE ANIMAL PHYLA

As you continue to study living things, look for similarities in characteristics. These similarities are important for understanding how animals survive and adapt to changing conditions. For example, the backbone is a characteristic used for separating animals into two groups—the vertebrates and the invertebrates.

Other characteristics are used for dividing these two groups into smaller units. **Similar characteristics among animals can indicate two things. They may point to evolutionary relationships. And they may mean that different animals have adapted in the same ways to stay alive.** As you read about the various animals, ask yourself: What are the structural features that make this animal part of its group? Where does the animal live? What are its organic needs,

chapter twenty-eight

Sponges and Coelenterates

OBJECTIVES
- UNDERSTAND the division of labor among cells.
- DESCRIBE the way of life of sponges.
- DESCRIBE the structure of sponges.
- NAME some animals in the phylum Coelenterata.
- DESCRIBE the characteristics of the Coelenterates.
- EXPLAIN the importance of regeneration.
- IDENTIFY the parts of the Hydra.
- DESCRIBE the different types of cells of Hydra.
- DISCUSS the activities of Hydra.
- EXPLAIN coral reef formation.

It might be helpful to begin this unit with a class discussion on the diagram in the appendix. Since many students may not be familiar with the terms *Porifera, Coelenterata, Protozoa,* and *Echinodermata,* have pictures available to show.

28-1 A pair of pink vase sponges.
(Dave Woodward, Peter Arnold)

and how does it satisfy them? How does the environment affect this animal? How does this animal affect other living things in the environment?

We shall study ten large animal phyla. You may want to use a classification table for reference and review. It lists the important characteristics and some typical examples of each group. You may notice that there are more than ten animal phyla. Also, there are some classes within these ten that we will not discuss. We shall be studying the largest and most important phyla, though. The first one is the sponge phylum, which includes some of the simplest animals.

Phylum—Porifera

THE SPONGES

Most sponges are marine; that is, they live in the sea. But there are a few freshwater species. Living sponges can be almost any color, from white and gray to any shade of red or yellow, even purple and black. Some sponges live singly. Others crowd together in colonies that form a crustlike layer over rock surfaces. Individual sponges can be as small as a centimeter or as big as two meters across.

When you first look at a living sponge, you may mistake it for a plant. If you had time, a good microscope, and several sponges handy, you could put a drop of India ink near a sponge and see what it does. You would see that ink particles were taken into the sponge's body through small *incurrent pores.* The ink reappears as though being forced out from the larger *excurrent pores* (also called the *osculum* (OSS-kyu-lum)). It seems the sponge does something that sets up currents in the water. Because of the many pores, the

Point out to students that most sponges used today in the home are synthetic. Have samples of synthetic and true sponges available for students to observe.

Discuss regeneration and reproduction in sponges. Also, discuss asexual and sexual reproduction. What are some of the advantages of regeneration? Why are some lower forms able to do this, while higher forms are not able to regenerate?

Era	Period	sponges	coelenterates	segmented worms	arthropods	mollusks	echinoderms
Cenozoic	Quaternary						
	Tertiary						
Mesozoic	Cretaceous						
	Jurassic						
	Triassic						
Paleozoic	Permian						
	Pennsylvanian (Late Carboniferous)						
	Mississippian (Early Carboniferous)						
	Devonian						
	Silurian						
	Ordovician						
	Cambrian						
(Pre-Cambrian)							

sponges are in a phylum called **Porifera,** which means "pore-bearing."

We tend to assume that animals actively chase, catch, and eat their food. **A sponge, though, is _sessile_** (SESS-ill). **This means that it is permanently attached by its base to something underneath.** So it must draw its food to itself. Sponges act as living filters, removing tiny food particles and oxygen from the water. They pump water in and out all day. A single sponge only one centimeter wide and ten centimeters high can pump more than 20 liters through its system in one day. This is nearly one liter an hour. The sponge is able to control the size of its osculum, or excurrent pore. This action controls the rate of flow or even stops it. Sponges feed on diatoms, small protozoans, bacteria, and organic particles drawn to them with the water. Carbon dioxide and other wastes leave through the osculum.

The sponge is very well adapted to its submerged, sessile way of life. A simple sponge has a hollow body. The body wall is formed of two layers of cells separated by a layer of jellylike substance. Loose cells, and **_spicules_** (SPI-kyoolz) are found in the jelly layer. The spicules are noncellular skeletal structures that help support the body of the animal. These spicules are secreted by living cells. Sponges are classified according to the material forming them. The spicules of some sponges are made of silicon, others of calcium carbonate (lime). A third group of sponges is supported by a fibrous network of tough, flexible material called _spongin._ Many sponges have spongin and spicules.

The outer cell layer, or **_epidermis,_** protects the sponge. The inner layer has many unusual cells with curious collars that have flagella sticking through them. The flagella of these **_collar cells_** set up the

28-2 A time scale comparing the sponges and coelenterates to the other invertebrates.

28-3 These beautiful Venus's flower basket sponges have skeletons made of silicon dioxide. (American Museum of Natural History)

currents that draw water into the sponge. As bits of food enter, they are caught by the collars. They are then digested by enzymes within the collar cells. The digested food is absorbed by special cells. These cells, called **amebocytes,** look like amebas. The amebocytes wander through the jellylike layer, carrying digested food and oxygen to the other cells. These wandering cells also carry wastes and carbon dioxide to the collar cells for disposal.

Sponges are often referred to as loose masses of cells. But you can see that their cells are interdependent enough to justify the classification of these animals as multicellular organisms.

REPRODUCTION IN SPONGES

While sponges reproduce sexually, they may also reproduce asexually in two ways. They may form **buds.** These are groups of cells that enlarge, but stay attached to the parent for a time before breaking off to live separately. Another method may occur during periods of freezing temperatures or drought. Groups of cells become surrounded by a heavy coat of organic matter. They contain little groups of amebocytes and a few spicules. These break off from the parent sponge. These are called **gemmules.** When growing conditions improve, each gemmule can develop into another sponge. Reproduction by gemmules is usually found in freshwater species.

Sponges reproduce sexually by producing eggs and sperms. The sperms are shed into the water and enter another sponge through the incurrent pores. They are taken in by the cytoplasm of the collar cells. They are then carried to the egg by wandering amebocytes. The fertilized egg develops into a flagellated larva which escapes from the sponge. After swimming around for a while, it settles down and grows into another sponge.

Sponges are able to regrow missing parts when damaged. This is called regeneration. Sponge-growers take advantage of this ability by cutting sponges in pieces and putting them in special growing beds. Sponges do not normally reproduce this way. But it is the fastest commercial means of increasing the sponge population. Sponge fishing and growing are most common in the Mediterranean and Red Seas, parts of the Gulf Coast of Florida, and throughout the West Indies.

Phylum—Coelenterata

THE COELENTERATES

If you have ever been stung by a jellyfish, you have already been introduced to one of the coelenterates. Many of these creatures bob around in the ocean, dangling long stringy tentacles under a floating, inflated sac. **Their phylum,** Coelenterata (suh-LEN-tuh-RAY-tuh), **also includes the hydroids, corals, sea fans, sea anemones, and the Portuguese man-of-war.** The size of members of this phylum range from microscopic to the largest jellyfish of the North Atlan-

28-4 Water is continually drawn into the sponge by the flagella of the collar cells. It passes through small pores into the cavity of the sponge and out through the osculum.

tic. These may be four meters across. Coelenterates live singly or united in colonies. All coelenterates live in the water, most are marine. The coelenterate cells are more highly specialized than those of the sponges.

THE HYDRA

A genus which shows characteristics typical of the coelenterate phylum is *Hydra*, a common freshwater group. Different species are white, green, and brown. They live in quiet ponds, lakes, and streams. The hydra's body has two cell layers separated by a jelly-like material called **mesoglea** (MEZ-uh-GLEE-uh). The outside cell layer is the **ectoderm;** the inner layer is the **endoderm.** The saclike body of the hydra has a single opening surrounded by **tentacles.** The tentacles have stinging cells, which contain structures called **nematocysts.** Only the coelenterates have these spearlike nematocysts.

Hydras vary in size from a centimeter, including tentacles, up to about 4 centimeters. They attach themselves to rocks or water plants with a sticky secretion from the cells of their **basal disks.** Sometimes hydras leave one place of attachment and move to another. They may secrete a bubble at their base and float upside down to the surface. They sometimes move by means of a peculiar somersaulting motion.

Hydras are sometimes hard to see because they are small and transparent. They also have a habit of contracting into little knobs when they are disturbed. But they are abundant. In fact, they are the only coelenterates which have succeeded in surviving and thriving in fresh water.

HOW THE HYDRA ACQUIRES FOOD

The hydra waits for a small animal to come into contact with one of its tentacles. At once several nematocysts explosively discharge throwing tiny hollow barbs into the victim's body. Each barb is attached to the tentacle by a thin thread. The combined strength of many threads prevents the hapless victim from escaping. At the base of each barb is a small poison sac, which releases poison through the hollow barb, and paralyzes the prey.

As soon as the animal stops moving, the tentacles bend inward. They push the victim through the hydra's circular mouth and into its hollow body. This space is lined with specialized endodermal cells. Some of the cells secrete digestive enzymes that partly break down the prey. The partly digested food is taken in by the lining cells which complete the digestion process. Because of these functions, the space is called a **gastrovascular cavity.** Digestive wastes then depart through the mouth.

The mouth and digestive cavity of the coelenterate are more complex than the feeding structures of the sponge. They allow a greater

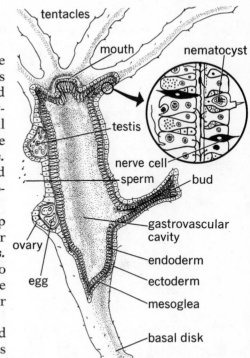

28–5 The external and internal structure of the hydra. Note the two layers of cells with a jellylike material between.

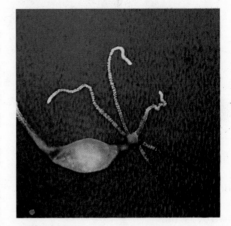

28–6 The hydra just engulfed its prey. Enzymes from the wall of the cavity will cause partial breakdown of the prey. (Ward's Natural Science Establishment, Inc.)

Discuss the apparent wastefulness of energy
in organisms that shed gametes into the
ocean.

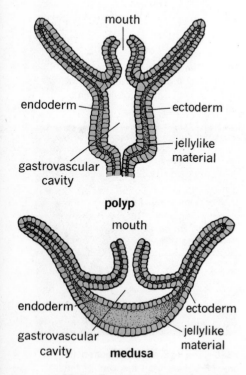

28-7 Compare the body plans of the sessile polyp and the free-swimming medusa.

range in the types and sizes of food that the animal can use. The cells discharge metabolic wastes directly into the water. Gases are also exchanged directly between the water and the cells in respiration.

HOW THE HYDRA BEHAVES

We have now seen one coelenterate reaction that shows higher specialization than the more primitive sponge. The hydra's tentacles work together to catch food and push it into its mouth. The tentacles and the entire body will contract suddenly if you touch the hydra with a needle. The stimulus applied to one tentacle will travel to cells of the other tentacles and the body through a series of nerve cells. This **nerve net** lies in the mesoglea. The contraction is caused by the shortening of thin fibers in the ectoderm. We can compare these fibers to the muscle cells of higher animals. The hydra does not have a nervous system like those in higher animals. And the hydra does not have a brain. Also, unlike higher animals, its nerve cells conduct impulses in all directions.

HOW THE HYDRA REPRODUCES

The hydra can reproduce *asexually* by forming *buds*. A bud starts as a knob growing out from the side of the adult. Later, the knob develops tentacles. After it has grown, the bud separates from the parent to live on its own. In this method of reproduction, the bud is a small outgrowth of endoderm and ectoderm, capable of becoming a new organism. The way buds form in hydra is very different from the way buds form in plants. A plant bud, you remember, is an undeveloped shoot. When it grows, it may elongate into a stem, or it may produce a leaf or a flower. But it will not become a whole new organism.

Like the sponge, the hydra is able to regenerate itself. If a hydra is cut into pieces, most of the pieces will regenerate the missing parts and become whole animals.

Sexual reproduction usually occurs in the fall. Eggs are produced along their body walls in little swellings called *ovaries*. Motile sperm cells are formed in similar swellings called *testes*.

The egg is fertilized in the ovary. The zygote divides and grows into a ball of cells with a hard, protective cover. Then it leaves the parent. It goes through a rest period before forming a new hydra.

TWO WAYS OF LIFE

Coelenterates have two different types of body forms. The hydra is a good example of the **polyp** form. Its tubular body has a basal disk at one end and tentacles at the other. The second form is bell-shaped and free-swimming, like the jellyfish. This is called a **medusa.** A medusa swims by a jerky kind of jet propulsion. It does this by taking water into the bell and then forcing it out.

Aurelia, a common jellyfish, is an interesting example of a coelenterate whose life cycle includes both medusa and polyp forms. The medusa reproduces sexually. It has protective tentacles which hang from a scalloped edge. The male medusas shed sperms into the sea. Some of the sperms enter the gastrovascular cavity of a female. Here they fertilize eggs that have been released by the female. For a short time, the zygotes are protected by folds of tissue surrounding the mouth.

The young are released in the form of small, oval-shaped, ciliated larvae called *planulae* (PLAN-yuh-lee). After a planula swims around for a time, it attaches itself to a rock or seaweed. It develops tentacles and begins feeding. At this stage, it is considered a polyp. As it grows, more polyps are formed from buds at its base. During the fall and winter, though, the polyp elongates and has several horizontal divisions, until it looks like a pile of saucers. One by one, starting from the top of the pile, the saucers break loose and swim away. On their own, they become sexually reproducing adult medusas. So you can see that the *Aurelia* is only one coelenterate, even though it has both the polyp and medusa forms, and reproduces in both phases.

OTHER COELENTERATES

Coral is the only coelenterate of economic importance. Its body is a small, flowerlike polyp. Most coral polyps live in colonies. They form skeletons from lime, which they take out of the sea water.

28–8 Compare these coelenterates with the diagrams in Figure 28–7. (Al Giddings, Bruce Coleman, Inc.; © Woodbridge Williams)

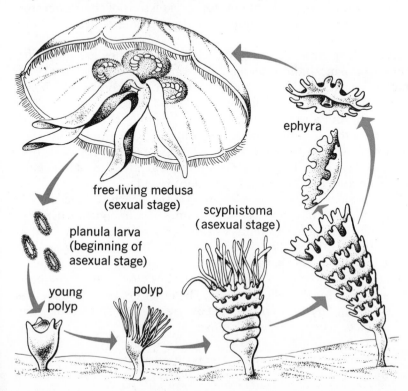

free-living medusa
(sexual stage)

planula larva
(beginning of
asexual stage)

young
polyp

polyp

scyphistoma
(asexual stage)

ephyra

28–9 Life cycle of *Aurelia*.

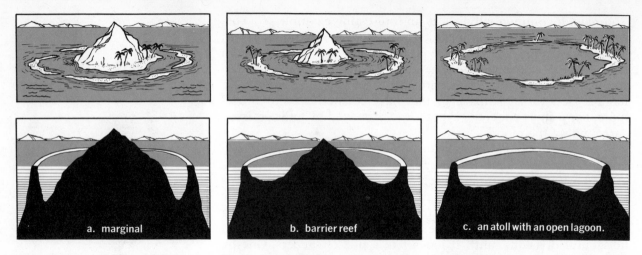

a. marginal

b. barrier reef

c. an atoll with an open lagoon.

28–10 Three different kinds of coral reefs. a. marginal; b. barrier reef widely separated from the land; c. an atoll with an open lagoon.

28–11 *Physalia*, the Portuguese man-of-war, is a colonial coelenterate. (George Lower, National Audubon Society)

They cement their own skeletons to the skeleton of the polyp next to them. When a coral animal dies, its skeleton remains. This serves as a point of attachment for another polyp. Lime skeletons of coral build up this way. A single mass may eventually support several thousand animals, all living on top of skeletons of their ancestors. Some species build solid masses. Others create delicate, complicated, fan shapes.

Over a long time, large coral reefs built up. They are most often found in warm, shallow oceans. There are three types of coral reefs. One is the *marginal type*, close to a beach. A second is the *barrier type*, which forms a ring around an island at some distance from the beach. And a third is a ring called an *atoll*, which has an open lagoon in the middle. The Great Barrier Reef off the northern coast of Australia runs for about 2,000 kilometers, parallel to the coast, and is about 80 kilometers wide. Coral is also used in jewelry, flower arrangements, and as pure decoration.

Storms on the Pacific Coast may leave beaches covered with bluish animals that look like membranes five to eight centimeters long. They belong to the genus *Velella*, and are called purple sails or by-the-wind sailors. The Portuguese man-of-war, or *Physalia*, is related to them. Both these organisms are basically colonies of polyps. Each polyp has a special job in the colony. One large polyp acts as a float for the whole colony. The other polyps are suspended from it. This large polyp float keeps the coelenterate colony near the surface, where the wind moves it through the water. Some polyps in the colony digest food caught by other polyps. Still others specialize in forming gametes. The Portuguese man-of-war is found mainly in tropical and semitropical waters. But it is also found in the Gulf Stream, which occasionally takes it all the way to the English coast. The Portuguese man-of-war may be dangerous to swimmers because of its painful sting.

SUMMARY

Division of labor in a multicellular organism is brought about by differences in cell structure and cell function. However, at the same time, one cell becomes dependent on the activities of others. The sponge is a simple multicellular organism; it has two layers of cells and a central cavity. The coelenterates are more complex than the sponges. They have, not only cell differentiation, but also coordination through a nerve net. They can eat a greater variety of food because of the gastrovascular cavity lined with specialized cells. There are two body forms of coelenterates, the polyp and the medusa. Two interesting forms of polyp colonies are the coral, whose skeletons build huge reefs in the Pacific Ocean, and the Portuguese man-of-war.

BIOLOGICALLY SPEAKING

specialization	epidermis	endoderm
vertebrate	collar cell	tentacle
invertebrate	amebocyte	nematocyst
incurrent pore	bud	basal disk
excurrent pore	gemmule	gastrovascular cavity
osculum	regeneration	nerve net
sessile	mesoglea	polyp
spicule	ectoderm	medusa

QUESTIONS FOR REVIEW

1. How does the many-celled condition permit efficient division of labor?
2. What structural features make sponges different from coelenterates?
3. In what kinds of environments would you expect to find sponges? Where would you expect to find hydra? Do you think the size of the animal body has anything to do with the particular habitats of these two groups?
4. Describe regeneration in sponges and coelenterates.
5. Compare the feeding methods of a sponge and a hydra. How are they alike, and how are they different?
6. In what ways are the *Aurelia* and hydra similar? How are they different?
7. How is a coral reef made? What are the three types of coral reefs?
8. What is the function of the nematocysts?
9. In what ways are the purple sail and the Portuguese man-of-war more highly specialized than other coelenterates you have studied so far?

APPLYING PRINCIPLES AND CONCEPTS

1. Compare the ways in which cell specialization is similar to division of labor in human societies.
2. Of what value to a jellyfish is the fact that it is hollow?
3. Is a sponge more primitive than a hydra? Give reasons for your answer.
4. How do the sponges and coelenterates spread to new habitats? What condition do you believe would be most favorable for their growth?

chapter twenty-nine

The Worms

OBJECTIVES

- DESCRIBE the types of symmetry.
- DESCRIBE the characteristics of Planaria.
- DISTINGUISH free living from parasitic forms.
- LIST the characteristics of roundworms.
- EXPLAIN regeneration in Planaria.
- DESCRIBE the adaptations of the tapeworm to the parasitic way of life.
- EXPLAIN the relationships of *Ascaris*, Trichina, and hookworm to man.
- DEMONSTRATE a knowledge of the anatomy of the earthworm.
- UNDERSTAND the physiology of the systems of the earthworm.

Symmetry is an important aspect of classification for biologists. Certain organisms, such as sponges, lack symmetry and are termed asymmetrical.

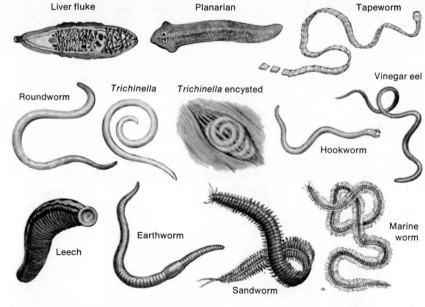

29–1 Examples of common worms.

SYMMETRY AND SIMILARITIES

By now you know why similarity of structure is so important in classification. **The general form of each organism is called its *symmetry.*** The ameba has no definite shape, so it is said to be *asymmetrical.* It orients itself to the environment by moving in any direction with its pseudopods. The radiolarians and *Volvox,* though, are protists that have *spherical symmetry.* They meet the environment on all their surfaces. You can divide them into two equal parts by passing a plane through the diameter of their bodies. A baseball is a good example of an object with spherical symmetry. Organisms with spherical symmetry often have no effective method of locomotion, and they float on or near the water's surface.

Most organisms are affected by gravity, however. The sea anemone, for example, has tentacles at one end and a basal disk for attachment at the other.

The sea anemone has *radial symmetry.* Like most other coelenterates, its tentacles radiate like spokes of a wheel from a central disk. Imagine a line drawn right through the mouth and the center of the body. This line would be the *central axis* of the sea anemone. Any plane that goes through both the basal disk and the central axis would divide the anemone exactly in half. Some sponges, most coelenterates, and most adult echinoderms, which we will study in Chapter Thirty, are radially symmetrical. Organisms which are radially symmetrical, or flat and round, are adapted to a sessile existence.

In the last chapter, you read about the nerve net in the radially symmetrical hydra. This kind of nerve network senses environmental changes on all sides of the animal. But the hydra reacts to most stimuli with an overall response. It draws in its tentacles and

Era	Period	sponges	coelenterates	segmented worms	arthropods	mollusks	echinoderms
Cenozoic	Quaternary						
	Tertiary						
Mesozoic	Cretaceous						
	Jurassic						
	Triassic						
Paleozoic	Permian						
	Pennsylvanian (Late Carboniferous)						
	Mississippian (Early Carboniferous)						
	Devonian						
	Silurian						
	Ordovician						
	Cambrian						
(Pre-Cambrian)							

shortens its entire body. It does the same thing whether it is touched on the tentacles or the basal disc. Sudden changes in the surrounding water's chemical content or temperature will cause the same reaction. These stimuli are changes in the environment of the hydra. The hydra's reaction comes from the spread of impulses over the nerve net. The nerve net is a primitive type of nervous system. Since a hydra's general reaction to strong stimulus is *withdrawal*, it is called a *negative* reaction. When it senses food, though, it has a coordinated *positive* reaction.

Actively moving organisms are better adapted for their way of life by having *bilateral symmetry*. This means "two-sided shape." Animals with this kind of symmetry are similar on two sides. They can be divided in half by a plane passing through a longitudinal axis, the center of the back, and the center of the front. The two halves of a bisymmetrical animal are a right and left side. One side is the mirror image of the other. **The upper surface of the animal is** *dorsal,* **the lower surface is** *ventral.* **It also has definite front, or anterior end, and a hind, or posterior, end. All vertebrates and many invertebrates have this kind of symmetry.**

29-2 A time scale comparing the worms to the other invertebrates.

Humans are examples of organisms that have bilateral symmetry. However, this does not mean that both sides of a human being are identical. Give some examples of how both sides of most humans are not alike (shoe size, hand size, and shape of the body). What influences affect differences in body sides?

29-3 Three types of symmetry.

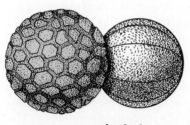

a. spherical

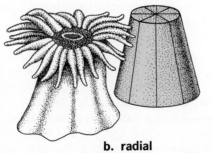

b. radial

c. bilateral

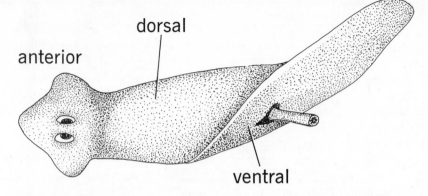

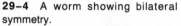

29–4 A worm showing bilateral symmetry.

Many organisms with bilateral symmetry have most of their nerves and sense organs at the anterior end. As they move forward, this is a great advantage for survival. It allows the organisms to sense and react to their environment faster.

Phylum—Platyhelminthes

THE WORM PHYLA

Worms are divided into three phyla, which include a very small number of known species of animals. But there are so many individual worms that they play an important role among living things.

The least complex worms are included in the *Platyhelminthes* (plat-ee-hel-MINTH-eez), or flatworm phylum. These flat-bodied animals have three layers of cells. They have an ectoderm and endoderm, like the coelenterates, and also a middle layer called the *mesoderm.* **Two-layered organisms form their tissues from the ectoderm and endoderm. But animals with all three cell layers have organs and organ systems.** This is true for all the other animals we will study, including human beings. The flatworm phylum is divided into three classes: *Turbellaria, Trematoda,* and *Cestoda.*

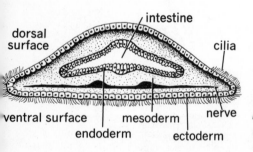

29–5 A cross section of a flatworm showing the relationship of the three layers of cells.

THE PLANARIAN

A free-living organism is one that is not a parasite. The most common examples of the free-living flatworms, or *Turbellaria,* are the *planarians.* They are aquatic. Planarians are often found under stones in freshwater ponds and streams. Planarians can be collected by tying a piece of liver to a string and lowering it into a pond. The next day, there should be planarians on the liver.

Planarians are small, usually less than a centimeter long. And their color ranges from black or brown to white. They are bilaterally symmetrical, blunt at the anterior and pointed at the posterior. The two **eyespots** at the anterior end have led to the planarian's nickname of "the cross-eyed worm." These eyespots are *photosensitive.* When light strikes the eyespots, it stimulates nerves. The animal senses the light and avoids it.

The **pharynx** is a tube on the ventral surface of the animal. When extended, this tube sucks up microscopic particles, including tiny organisms. Since they clean up the water they live in, by eating organic matter, they are called scavangers. The food is drawn into the digestive cavity and enters one of three main branches of the intestine. It then passes along to one of the side branches.

Food is digested in the cavity of the intestine and within the cells lining the intestine. Cells lining the intestine take in the food particles and digest them in food vacuoles. The digested food then diffuses to the various body tissues. Indigestible materials are eliminated through the pharynx and the mouth opening. Since the planarian has no separate circulatory system, cellular wastes are collected by tubules that branch throughout the animal. The wastes leave by the several tiny excretory pores on the surface of the worm's body.

The nervous system of the planarian is more highly developed than that of the animals we have studied so far. A mass of nerve tissue which functions as the "brain" lies just under the eyespots at the anterior end. Many nerves from this anterior region lead directly to the brain. In organisms with bilateral symmetry, this arrangement of nerves is very important. As the worm moves, its anterior end is the first part exposed to chemicals, water currents, touch, light, and heat. So the planarian can test the environment it is moving into. If the conditions are not good, it can move in a different direction. **Concentration of receptors (receivers of stimuli) and nerves at the anterior end is called *cephalization*. Cephalization is of great survival value to bilateral organisms.**

Two *longitudinal nerves* run along either side of the body near the ventral surface. They are connected by *transverse nerves*. This makes the nervous system look like a ladder. Many small nerves also run from the surface of the planarian to the longitudinal nerves. This nervous system allows the animal to be coordinated in its movements. Thus it permits the animal to respond to stimuli anywhere on its body.

If you watch planarians in a dish or an aquarium, you will see that they move in two different ways. In one, the anterior end moves from side to side. In another, the whole body moves forward in a gliding motion due to tiny muscle contractions, aided by cilia on the ventral surface.

Planarians reproduce asexually by fission, and sexually by gametes. Each animal has both the male and female reproductive organs in its body. We call this **hermaphroditic.** Cross-fertilization occurs and the eggs are shed in capsules. There are usually ten or fewer eggs per capsule. These capsules are often attached to rocks or twigs in the water. And the tiny planarians hatch in two or three weeks.

Many species of planarians have the same remarkable ability to regenerate missing parts that the sponges and coelenterates have. Some planarians will grow into complete new worms from *almost* any part. If you cut one into anterior and posterior sections, the

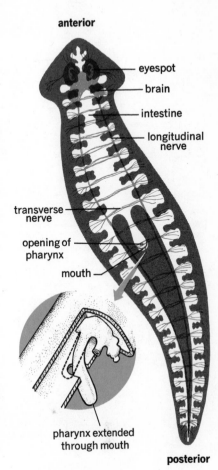

anterior
eyespot
brain
intestine
longitudinal nerve
transverse nerve
opening of pharynx
mouth

pharynx extended through mouth

posterior

29-6 The digestive and nervous systems of a planarian.

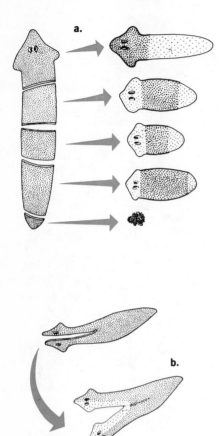

29-7 Regeneration in the planarians. a. Each section except the last will form a new head. b. Another animal is shown to form two heads. This animal will complete the separation and become two planarians.

Parasites can be extremely dangerous to one's health. They often cause a great loss of weight and a feeling of exhaustion. Contrary to public opinion, many people in the United States, today, have parasite infestations.

anterior part will grow a new tail while the posterior will grow a new head. A small section of the tail, however, does not regenerate.

A planarian can develop two heads if it is cut lengthwise halfway down the body. But soon it divides completely into two animals. We know very little about how this happens. **In general, the more complex the organism, the less it is able to regenerate lost parts.** Crabs can grow new claws, and lizards replace lost tails. Humans can grow new skin and some muscles, but not new organs.

THE PARASITE WAY OF LIFE

Most parasitic animals, including parasitic flatworms, cannot replace lost parts. When we speak of evolution, we think of forms becoming more complex as they adapt to environmental changes. But a parasite living inside the body of another animal has problems not at all like those of its free-living relatives. Its size is limited by that of its host. If it should grow too large, it would kill its host. Intestinal parasites usually have hooks or suckers so they can cling to the walls of the host's intestines. In this way, they are surrounded by digested food and they merely absorb nutrients from it. The parasite is protected from being digested by a thick **cuticle** not found in the free-living organisms.

Certain systems are reduced or lost in parasitic worms. The tapeworm, for instance, has no digestive system. We say that these worms have **degenerated.** The parasite benefits by this since they have more body room for developing eggs.

Dispersal is a problem for internal parasites. At the larval stage, they may be free living or live within another organism. The life histories of some common parasitic worms will show this.

THE FLUKES

In the class Trematoda are the *flukes.* These are parasites which live in many animals including humans. Flukes differ from planarians in that adult flukes have no external cilia. Flukes have thick *cuticles* and one or more *suckers* for clinging to the tissues of the host. An anterior sucker surrounds the mouth, which opens to a short pharynx. The fluke's nervous system is similar to the planarian's, but there are no special sense organs. Most flukes have a highly developed reproductive system and are hermaphroditic. The fluke differs from the planarians as it has a **uterus.** The uterus is a long coiled tube where the many eggs are stored. When the eggs are ready to be released, they exit through the *genital pore.*

Flukes have complicated life histories. Part of their life is spent in snails and another part in one or more other hosts. The sheepliver fluke lives as an adult in a sheep's liver and gall bladder. Its eggs pass from the gall bladder to the intestine. If the eggs fall into the water after they pass through the sheep, they hatch into young worms called **larvae** (singular, *larva*). The larvae then enter the body of a certain kind of snail. In the snail, they go through several

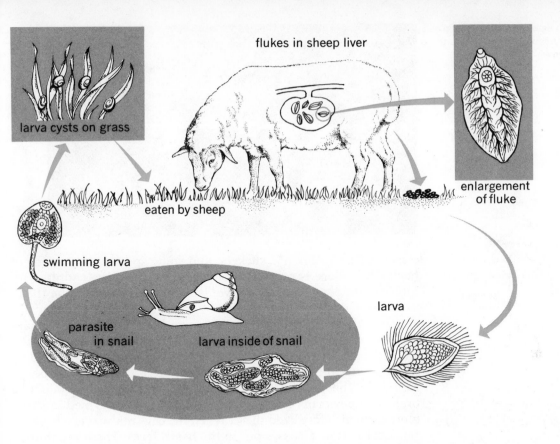

flukes in sheep liver

larva cysts on grass

enlargement of fluke

eaten by sheep

swimming larva

larva

parasite in snail

larva inside of snail

29–8 The life cycle of a sheep liver fluke.

stages and increase in number by asexual reproduction. Then they leave the snail and climb blades of grass at the water's edge. There they form **cysts.** If a sheep eats these cysts, the fluke enters its liver, and the cycle starts again.

The liver fluke makes its host sick. It causes irritability, inflammation, and swelling. Cows with liver flukes produce less milk. Any liver with flukes in it should not be eaten by humans.

Other types of flukes may live in animal blood, intestines or lungs. They are often found externally on the gills of fish and in cavities of other vertebrates which live in the water.

Although flukes in humans are most common in the Orient, they are also found in other places. Cuba has had epidemics of flukes among its residents. On our Gulf coast, farmers have suffered economic loss due to flukes infecting many cows, pigs, and sheep. The best way to control flukes is to eliminate one of the hosts in their life cycle. As a biologist, which host would you try to eliminate?

Liver flukes are more common in countries where raw fish is consumed. In Japan, vast amounts of raw fish filets called Sashimi are consumed.

TAPEWORMS

The best-known parasitic flatworms are tapeworms, members of the class Cestoda. An adult tapeworm has a flat, ribbonlike body that is grayish white. It has no cilia. The knob-shaped head is called

29–9 The tapeworm is an example of a parasitic flatworm. (Allan Roberts, Z. Leszczynski)

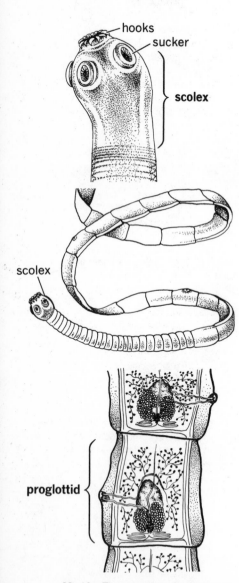

29–10 The structure of a tapeworm. The tapeworm attaches the hooks of its scolex to the intestinal wall.

a *scolex.* The scolex has suckers, and some species have a ring of hooks. But there is no mouth or digestive structures. Adults usually are attached to intestine walls, where nutrients bathe them. The digested food is absorbed through the tapeworm's body walls.

Below the slender neck, a tapeworm has many nearly square sections that extend up to ten meters. These body sections are called **proglottids** (proe-GLOT-idz). The tapeworm grows by adding new sections at the anterior end, so the oldest ones are at the posterior end. The proglottids are basically masses of reproductive organs. Tapeworms are hermaphroditic. The eggs formed in a proglottid are also fertilized there. When the eggs mature, the proglottid breaks off and passes out in the host's feces. These proglottids may be eaten by an animal such as a pig or cow. In the body of the new host, the eggs hatch into larvae that burrow into the muscles and form cysts.

Tapeworms may enter the human body as cysts. They may be in meat from infected animals that has not been cooked enough. Each cyst contains a fully developed scolex. In the human intestine, the scolex leaves the cyst, attaches itself to the intestine wall, and begins to grow.

Since tapeworms rob their hosts of nutrients, the hosts may lose weight and energy. Tapeworms are not as common in humans today because there are new ways to detect the parasites and treat people for them. Meat is also inspected more carefully for tapeworm cysts.

Phylum—Nematoda

ROUNDWORMS

The phylum *Nematoda* (nem-uh-TOE-duh) has only one class, and it is also called Nematoda. These animals are called roundworms or nematodes. They are long, slender, smooth worms, tapered at both ends. They can be as short as ¹/₅ of a millimeter or as long as 130 centimeters. **Roundworms live in soil, and in fresh or salt water. Many live as parasites in plants and animals.** The parasitic roundworms include the hookworm, trichina worm, pinworm, whip-worm, *Ascaris*, and guinea worm. In fact, there are so many of these nematodes that—

> If all the matter in the universe except the nematodes were swept away, our world would still be dimly recognizable, and if, as disembodied spirits, we could then investigate it, we should find its mountains, hills, vales, rivers, lakes, and oceans represented by a film of nematodes. The location of towns would be decipherable, since for every massing of human beings there would be a corresponding massing of certain nematodes. Trees would still stand in ghostly rows representing our streets and highways. The location of the various plants and animals would still be decipherable, and, had we sufficient knowledge, in many cases even their species could be determined by an examination of their erstwhile nematode parasites. (Ralph Buchsbaum, *Animals Without Backbones*. The University of Chicago Press, 1948.)

More than one third of the human population supports parasitic roundworms. Although this occurs mostly in the warm regions of the world, this fact makes roundworms very important. There are harmless roundworms, too, like the vinegar eel and many useful soil nematodes.

Like the flatworms, roundworms are bilaterally symmetrical with three layers of cells. But they are more complex. Their digestive system is a tube with an opening at each end. Their bodies are long and tube-shaped. The roundworm is able to take food in through the mouth and digest it. As the food moves along through the tube, the usable parts are removed from it. Undigested material is passed out through the opening in the posterior end, the *anus*. **The hydra has only one opening for both taking in food and elimination of wastes. But the roundworm's body arrangement of a tube within a tube has two openings. This allows all its material to move more easily and efficiently through the digestive tract.**

A large roundworm that may live in the intestine of pigs, horses, and sometimes people is *Ascaris*. The females, growing as long as thirty centimeters, are larger than the males. *Ascaris* eggs enter the human body in contaminated food or water. Passing through the stomach, they hatch a few hours after they reach the small intestine. The larvae then bore into the intestinal wall, beginning a ten-day trip through the body. Once in the bloodstream, they are carried to the lungs. From there, they travel through the air passages to the throat, where they are swallowed and returned to the digestive tube. Now they spend about two and a half months developing into adults. After the female has been fertilized, the eggs are surrounded by a thick, rough shell, and leave through the genital pore. The female may lay as many as 200,000 eggs a day. The eggs leave the host's body with the feces, to begin the cycle again. *Ascaris* is usually harmless to humans, except when many adult worms twist together and block the intestine with fatal results.

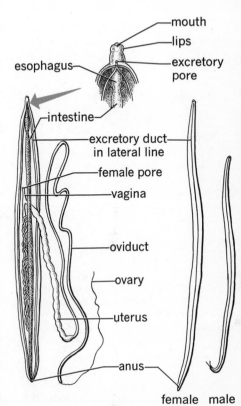

29–11 *Ascaris*, a parasitic roundworm. Side views of a male and female are shown at the right. The dissected worm is a female.

Roundworms or nematodes are responsible for many serious diseases of humans. *Ascaris* is a parasite that can cause great discomfort and can be fatal in some cases. Individuals who seem to be lazy and shiftless are often suffering from *hookworms*. Another serious disease, *elephantiasis*, is caused by filaria worms. They cause large swellings of the tissues of the legs and feet.

Trichina worms can be very serious. These worms quickly spread through the body's circulatory system and cause severe pain, weakness, fever, and even death. In some cases, steroids can alleviate the muscle pain.

29–12 The life cycle of the trichina worm. Trace the path of infection that leads to man.

The *hookworm* is a far more serious health menace. It is widespread in the southern states and all semitropical and tropical regions. Hookworm larvae develop in the soil. And they enter the body by boring through the skin of the feet. When they enter the blood vessels, they travel through the heart to the lungs. Like *Ascaris,* they pass through the air passages and the throat, then they are swallowed and pass to the intestine. They use their jaws to attach to the intestine walls. Nourished by the blood they suck, the larvae grow into adult worms.

The victim's loss of blood lowers vitality by producing anemia. A typical host may become quite sluggish. And if young enough, the host may suffer from retarded growth.

The hookworms reproduce by means of fertilized eggs which leave the host with the feces. If the eggs land in warm, moist soil, they develop into tiny larvae which begin the cycle again.

Three factors can contribute to the spread of this disease: 1) careless sewage disposal; 2) warm soil; and 3) going barefoot. Public health agencies have done a fine job in reducing the number of cases in the United States.

One of the most dangerous parasitic worms is the *trichina,* or *Trichinella.* This roundworm spends the first part of its life as a cyst in the muscles of pigs, dogs, cats, or rats. If uncooked scraps of meat from an infected animal are fed to a pig, the scraps will probably have cysts. In the pig's intestine, the larvae grow into adult worms, mate, and produce microscopic larvae. These pass into the bloodstream to muscles, where they again form cysts. The

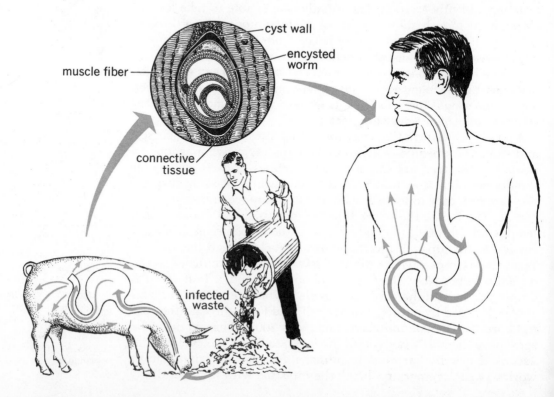

cyst wall

encysted worm

muscle fiber

connective tissue

infected waste

same thing happens when a human being eats undercooked infected meat. The cysts are released. And the larvae mature in the intestine. Each worm produces about 1,500 cyst-forming larvae. The cysts form in the muscle, causing a disease called **trichinosis.**

One way of preventing trichinosis is to feed pigs only cooked meat scraps. The best way to avoid parasitic worm infections is to cook all meat thoroughly before it is eaten.

It should now be clear that parasitic worms are important. They cause disease, multiply rapidly, and are widespread. They are spread because of poor sanitary conditions. But the eggs can be killed by proper sewage disposal. Careful inspection and thorough cooking of meat are other ways to avoid these parasites.

Phylum—Annelida

THE EARTHWORM

The segmented worms have the most complex body structures of all the worms. These typical invertebrates belong to the phylum *Annelida*, which has four classes. Most segmented worms live in salt water, although some live in fresh water. And others, including common earthworms, live in soil. Annelids are worth close study since they are more complex than the simple protists, but less so than the arthropods. Also, because segmented worms are common, biologists often study them.

If you examine an earthworm, you can easily see its segments. You can also see that the anterior end is darker and more pointed than the posterior end. It does not have a separate head, or any visible sense organs. The crescent-shaped mouth is at the anterior end, underneath a kind of upper lip called a **prostomium** (proe-STOME-ee-um). At the posterior end, the vertical *anus* opens from the intestine. Biologists often number the segments, starting with the mouth. Segments 32–37 have a distinct swelling called the **clitellum** (kli-TELL-um), involved in the worm's reproduction.

Each segment, except the first and last, has four pairs of bristles, or **setae** (SEE-tee), on the bottom and side surfaces. The earthworm uses the setae for moving and for clinging to the walls of its burrow, as any fisherman hunting for bait has found out. An earthworm moves by pushing the setae of its anterior segments into the soil, then shortening its body by using a series of muscles that stretch the length of its body. Then the worm pushes the setae of its posterior end into the soil, and withdraws the anterior setae. Next, it pushes itself forward by tightening the *circular* muscles which make its body longer.

The earthworm consists of many cells. But it also has many different kinds of specialized cells. Each group of cells has the same job, so each group makes up one kind of *tissue*. Each tissue is grouped with others in larger structures called *organs*. Each organ has a definite job to do, too. In the earthworm, a whole series of organs work together to carry on a basic body process. These are called *systems.* The earthworm has several well-developed systems: the *digestive, circulatory, excretory, nervous, muscular,* and *reproductive* systems.

THE EARTHWORM'S DIGESTIVE SYSTEM

Below the prostonium is the mouth of the earthworm. Since it has no jaws or teeth, the earthworm uses its muscular **pharynx** to suck in soil with food in it. The food particles and soil go through a long **esophagus** into a round organ called a **crop.** The crop stores the food temporarily. Then it is forced into a very muscular organ called the **gizzard.** The gizzard contracts and expands, causing grains of sand and food to rub together. In this way, the food is ground up. Food is completely digested in the **intestine,** which stretches from segment 19 to the end of the worm. Here enzymes break down the food chemically. Then the digested food is absorbed by the blood circulating through the intestine walls.

The complicated organs of the digestive system take up most of the anterior half of the earthworm's body. The earthworm ingests large amounts of soil, which has organic matter in it. The useless inorganic matter goes through the worm with no change. And this is often left on the surface of the ground in the form of *castings.* As the earthworms feed, they loosen the soil, making it easier for air and water to enter. Also its wastes add to soil fertility.

THE EARTHWORM'S CIRCULATORY SYSTEM

After the earthworm has digested the food, the blood in the circulatory system carries the products of digestion to all the cells of the body. In the lower animals we have studied, the digested food had only a short distance to go to reach all the cells. But in higher forms, the distances are greater. Also more food material is needed

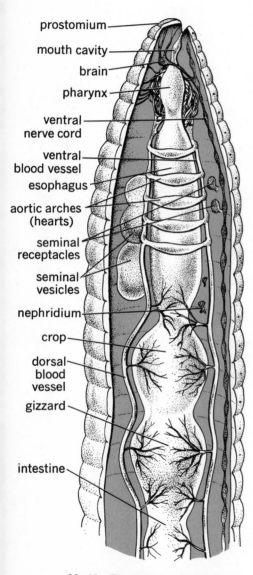

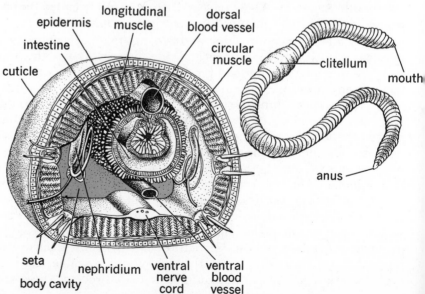

29–13 The external and internal structure of the earthworm. The anterior portion above is dissected to show the well-developed nervous and circulatory systems. One of the abdominal segments is shown in the cross section.

by the many specialized cells at work in the body. The higher forms of animals have special transportation tissue for this. It is the circulating fluid called *blood.*

The earthworm's blood moves through a closed set of tubes, or vessels. It flows forward to the anterior end inside a *dorsal blood vessel* and returns to the posterior end in a *ventral blood vessel.* Small tubes connect the dorsal and ventral vessels all through the worm. In segments 7-11, the pairs of tubes are large and muscular. They alternately contract and relax, keeping the blood flowing. Although they pump blood, they are not true hearts. So they are called **aortic arches.**

Stress to students the importance of a circulatory system in an organism as complex as an earthworm. Earthworms would be unable to distribute and remove products from their systems without a circulatory system.

RESPIRATION AND EXCRETION

A thin skin enables the earthworm to absorb oxygen and give off carbon dioxide. The skin is protected by a thin *cuticle,* which is secreted by the epidermal cells. And it is kept moist by a mucus also secreted by the epidermis. Recall that, **a moist surface is necessary for intake of oxygen and the output of carbon dioxide.** If the worm dries out in the sun, it will die because this gas exchange can no longer take place.

Cell activities produce metabolic wastes containing nitrogen. These are removed to the outside of the body by little tubes called *nephridia.* There are two nephridia in each segment except the first three and the last. Each nephridium does the same kind of work that a kidney tubule does in a human.

THE EARTHWORM'S SENSITIVITY

The nervous system coordinates the earthworm's movements. And it sends impulses received in the sense organs to certain other parts of the body. In segment 3, there is a very small nerve center. Two nerves run from the center around the pharynx, forming a connecting collar. Then they join together to become one long *ventral nerve cord.* In each segment, there are enlarged nerve centers, called *ganglia.* Three pairs of nerves branch out from each ganglion. Though the earthworm does not have eyes or ears, it is sensitive to light and sound. Certain cells in its skin are sensitive to these stimuli. And the impulses are carried to the muscles at once. That is why earthworms react so fast when you hunt them at night with a flashlight.

Earthworm sensitivity can be easily demonstrated by the use of light or by running an electric current through soil that is inhabited by earthworms.

EARTHWORM REPRODUCTION

Earthworms are hermaphroditic. Each earthworm produces both eggs and sperms. But the eggs of one worm must be fertilized by sperms from another. The sperms are produced by two pairs of testes within the testis sacs. These sperms are stored in **seminal vesicles** which extend from the sacs. Sperms received from another worm are stored in **seminal receptacles.**

Discuss some of the advantages of sexual reproduction in earthworms. Review the life cycle of the earthworm.

29-14 Reproduction in the earthworm. Even though the earthworm has the reproductive organs of both sexes, it exchanges its sperms for those of another earthworm. As shown, the sperms travel from the seminal vesicles of one worm to the seminal receptacles of the other.

Sperms travel from the seminal vesicles in one worm, out through openings in segment 15. The sperms then enter the seminal receptacles of another worm through openings in segments 9 and 10. There they are stored until eggs are laid. When the eggs mature, they leave the ovaries through openings in segment 14. They are released into a slime ring which is secreted by the clitellum. As the ring moves forward, the seminal receptacle releases the sperms it has been storing, and fertilization occurs. The slime ring eventually slips off the body and becomes the cocoon in which the young worms develop.

ANOTHER SEGMENTED WORM—THE LEECH

The leech, or bloodsucker, is an annelid found in streams and ponds. It is an external parasite on fish and other animals which live in the water. But it may also attach to your skin while you are swimming.

A leech sucks blood by attaching its posterior sucker to some vertebrate. It applies the anterior sucker to the skin and makes a wound with little jaws inside its mouth. The salivary glands of the leech secrete a substance that prevents blood from clotting while it feeds. Leeches were used medicinally in the Middle Ages and later. It was then believed that blood loss was supposed to heal the sick. The salivary substance is now extracted from the leech for use in slowing clotting after surgery.

Ask some students to review the place of leeches in early medicine. Many students will be surprised to learn the extent to which they were used in the past.

Table 29-1 SUMMARY OF CHARACTERISTICS OF THE COMMON WORMS

	PLATYHEL-MINTHES	NEMATODA	ANNELIDA
Body Types	flat, unsegmented bodies	round, unsegmented bodies	body divided into segments
Type of Life	many parasitic	some parasitic	majority *not* parasitic
Organization	3 layers, many organ systems	3 layers, many organ systems	3 layers, organs well developed
Digestive System	open at one end only	mouth and anus	mouth and anus
Reproduction	asexually by fission; sexually—hermaphroditic with cross-fertilization	sexual, definite male and female	sexually—hermaphroditic with cross-fertilization
Circulation	none	none	5 pairs of aortic arches, large dorsal vessel, small ventral vessel
Nervous System	2 longitudinal nerve cords	2 nerve cords, one dorsal, one ventral	one large ventral nerve cord with ganglia

SUMMARY

The general form of an organism is called its symmetry. Radially symmetrical animals, like the hydra, are adapted to a sessile existence. Worms are more complex than the sponges and coelenterates. Worms are bilaterally symmetrical and exhibit cephalization. This means that they have nerve tissues and sense organs concentrated at the anterior end. Thus they can sense their environment as they move. This better equips them for survival.

All worms have three layers of cells. And live in fresh and salt water, on land, and as parasites in other living animals. Certain body systems have degenerated in the parasitic worms. Roundworms are very abundant throughout the world. They include parasitic forms like the hookworm, trichina, whipworm, *Ascaris*, and pinworm. Worms belonging to the annelid phylum are segmented. Their systems are more specialized and their nervous system in particular shows more complexity than the planarians. Earthworms and leeches are the best-known examples of annelids.

BIOLOGICALLY SPEAKING

symmetry	uterus	esophagus
dorsal	larva	crop
ventral	cyst	gizzard
mesoderm	scolex	intestine
eyespot	proglottid	blood
pharnyx	trichinosis	aortic arch
cephalization	prostomium	nephridium
hermaphroditic	clitellum	ganglion
cuticle	setae	seminal vesicle
degenerate	pharynx	seminal receptacle

QUESTIONS FOR REVIEW

1. Name and define the kinds of symmetry. Give an example of each.
2. What do we mean when we say that planarians can regenerate missing parts?
3. What is the importance of the three layers of cells found in flatworms?
4. How does the planarian test its environment?
5. In what ways are the flatworms more complicated than the sponges and coelenterates?
6. In what ways does the tapeworm show degeneration?
7. Where are nematodes found?
8. In what ways are nematodes more complicated than the flatworms?
9. Describe the life cycle of *Ascaris*.
10. How does the trichina worm reach the human body?
11. Describe the way the earthworm moves.
12. Trace a bit of food through the digestive system of the earthworm, naming the organs involved.

1. Of what adaptive value is bilateral symmetry over spherical symmetry and radial symmetry?
2. Trace the path followed by *Ascaris* through the human body, naming all the structures through which it goes. At what stages are symptoms of disease most likely to be present? At what stages is treatment most likely to be effective?
3. What measures should be taken in trying to control parasitic worms?
4. Symptoms of tapeworms in an animal usually include loss of weight and general fatigue. Account for these conditions.
5. Trichinosis can become a hopeless disease. Why is it almost impossible to treat?
6. In what ways are tapeworms adapted to be efficient parasites?

chapter
thirty

Mollusks and Echinoderms

OBJECTIVES

- LIST the common characteristics of the phylum Mollusca.
- NAME some mollusks.
- DESCRIBE the mollusk's body arrangement.
- IDENTIFY the parts of a bivalve mollusk.
- DESCRIBE the characteristics of the echinoderms.
- EXPLAIN a water-vascular system.
- DESCRIBE how the starfish gets food and regenerates.

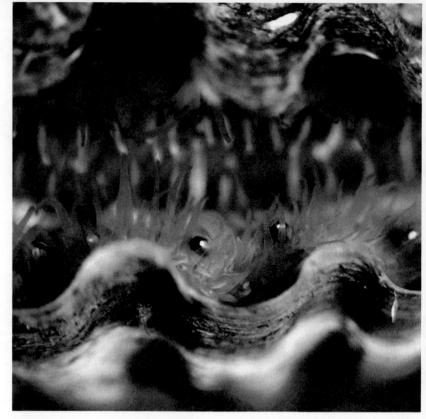

30–1 The bay scallop is an example of a mollusk. (Ward's Natural Science Establishment, Inc.)

Refer students to the blue lines in Fig. 30–3. Between these lines the esophagus, stomach, and anus of the animal can be found. The *apical organ* is the hairlike structure at the top of the larva.

Phylum—Mollusca

SOFT-BODIED INVERTEBRATES

You probably are familiar with some members of the phylum *Mollusca*. This phylum includes clams, oysters, squids, and snails. Some of these mollusks are called shellfish, but they are not fish at all. In fact, many mollusks do not have shells. Mollusks live in fresh water and marine environments. Some even live on land. Some are adapted to live buried in sand or mud, where oxygen might be too scarce for more active animals. There are more species of mollusks than any other phylum except insects.

Since earliest recorded time, mollusks have been used by human beings. They served our ancestors as food, money, dyes, tools, and weapons. Many people who know nothing about mollusk anatomy collect mollusk shells from all over the world for their beauty alone. High concentrations of shells, or their fossils, may lead engineers to oil deposits. Remember that oil is formed by compressing dead organic matter for long periods of time. Mollusk shells are often found on mountains. How do you think they got there?

Era	Period	sponges	coelenterates	segmented worms	arthropods	mollusks	echinoderms
Cenozoic	Quaternary						
	Tertiary						
Mesozoic	Cretaceous						
	Jurassic						
	Triassic						
Paleozoic	Permian						
	Pennsylvanian (Late Carboniferous)						
	Mississippian (Early Carboniferous)						
	Devonian						
	Silurian						
	Ordovician						
	Cambrian						
(Pre-Cambrian)							

THE EVOLUTIONARY LINK

You may be wondering what clams, squids, and snails have in common. Biologists compare more than the adult forms of animals. They also classify animals as being related when their larvae develop in similar ways.

Animals classified as mollusks go through a stage of larval development in which they look the same. The larval stage of the mollusk is called a *trochophore* (TROCK-uh-FORE). The trochophore has a tuft of cilia at one end and a ciliated band around its middle. In free-swimming larvae, the cilia propel through the water and bring food to their mouths. But terrestrial mollusks and many marine forms go through the trochophore stage while they are still in the egg capsule. As annelids develop, they go through a trochophore stage, too. Because of this similarity, segmented worms and mollusks are thought to be related.

30–2 A time scale comparing mollusks and echinoderms to the other invertebrates.

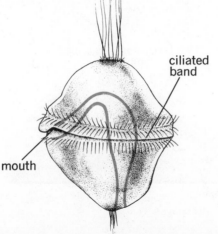

30–3 The trochopore larval form is found in the development of both mollusks and annelids. An outline of the digestive tract is shown in blue.

ciliated band

mouth

THE MOLLUSK BODY PLAN

The body of an adult mollusk has a *head*, a *foot*, and a *visceral* (VISS-uh-rul) *hump*. Inside the visceral hump are the digestive organs, excretory organs, and the heart. The visceral hump is covered by a **mantle.** The mantle is a thin skin that in most species secretes the calcium carbonate shell. The mantle hangs down over the sides and back of the body, forming a space called the **mantle cavity.** The **gills** are in this cavity. They are the respiratory organs of the aquatic mollusks. Undigested materials go from the anus into the mantle cavity before passing out of the animal.

In most mollusks, a current of water flows through the mantle cavity. The water carries in oxygen and food, and carries away carbon dioxide and other wastes. You might think that mollusks with a shell have a problem disposing of wastes. They do not. Water flows into the cavity through an opening called the **incurrent siphon.** The water circulates over the gills, where it picks up the carbon dioxide and wastes, and exits through the **excurrent siphon.**

The major means of dividing mollusks into classes is by the kind of shell or shells they have, if any. Another characteristic often used to classify mollusks is the **foot,** a muscular, ventral creeping surface.

We will be studying three of the five classes in the mollusk phylum:

- *Pelecypoda* (pell-uh-SIP-uh-duh), or hatchet-footed, two-shell mollusks
- *Gastropoda* (gas-TROP-uh-duh), or stomach-footed, single-shell mollusks
- *Cephalopoda* (sef-uh-LOP-uh-duh), or head-footed mollusks

MOLLUSKS WITH HINGED SHELLS

Mollusks like the clams, oysters, scallops, and mussels are called bivalves because their shells have two halves, called valves. A hinge connects the two valves, so they can be opened and closed by the animal. Each valve has three different layers made of materials secreted by the mantle. The smooth, shiny layer next to the mantle is the **pearly layer.** If a grain of sand or the cyst of a parasitic worm

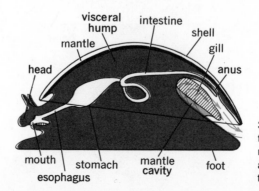

30-4 Although no mollusk living today looks like this drawing, the major characteristics of the phylum are shown. The arrows indicate direction of water flow in the mantle cavity.

gets caught in the mantle, this layer builds up around the object and forms a pearl. This middle layer is made of calcium carbonate crystals and is called the **prismatic layer.** The outer layer is called the **horny outer layer,** and it is very thin. The hinge connecting the valves is also made of this hornlike material.

The scientific name of this group is Pelecypoda. This means "hatchet-footed." This name refers to the shape of the mollusk's foot. It puts its foot into the sand, where is spreads out to form a hatchet-shaped anchor. Then the muscle of the foot contracts. The mollusk is pulled into the sand or the mud. Clams can dig into the sand very quickly this way.

A clam usually stays partly buried. Its valves are kept partly opened with the two siphons extended into the water. Water comes

30–5 Various mollusks. Giant clam. Mussel. Flame scallops. (D. Wallin, Peter Arnold; John R. McGregor, Peter Arnold; Z. Leszczynski, Animals, Animals)

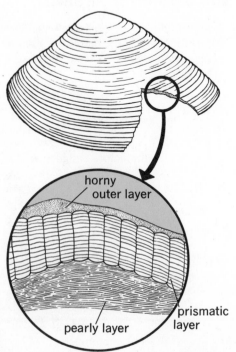

30–6 The shells of the bivalve mollusks are composed of three distinct layers.

horny outer layer

prismatic layer

pearly layer

into the mantle cavity through the incurrent siphon. The water goes through the gills and then past the anus, from which wastes are given off. The water flows out through the excurrent siphon.

As water passes over the gills, two things happen. First, oxygen is taken in, and carbon dioxide diffuses out. And second, small particles of organic matter stick to a thin layer of mucus on the gills. Cilia on the surface of the gills carry the food-bearing mucus to the dorsal surface and forward to the mouth. Animals that feed like this are called *mucus feeders*. They are scavengers, feeding on dead and decaying organic matter and the many microscopic protists living on the bottom.

If you have eaten steamed clams, you know that even after they have been cooked and have opened up, you still have to pry their two shells apart. You are tearing two large muscles, the anterior and posterior adductor muscles. These muscles can pull shells tightly shut when the clam is alive. You can recognize dead clams at the market if their shells stay open all the time. Their adductor muscles are dead and do not counter the opening action of the hinge.

Bivalves have a well-developed nervous system with several large ganglia. Sensory cells at the edge of the mantle respond to light and touch.

Clams, oysters, scallops, and mussels are all edible bivalves. However, they feed on microscopic organisms by filtering water through their bodies. Some of the organisms they eat are poisonous. When you eat raw mollusks, it is wise to be sure that they were intended to be used as food.

MOLLUSKS WITH ONE SHELL

Some mollusks are grouped in the class Gastropoda, which means "stomach-footed." Its members include land and water snails, slugs, conches, and abalones. Most of these animals have only one shell, so they are called *univalves*.

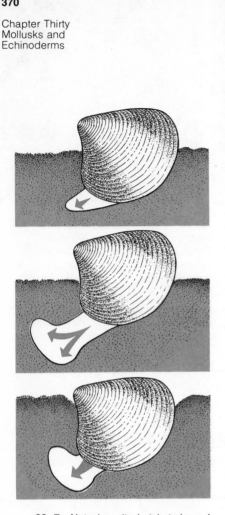

30-7 Note how its hatchet-shaped foot aids the clam in digging into sand.

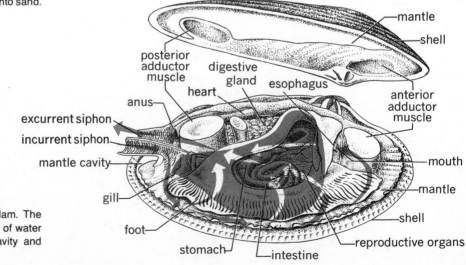

30-8 The structure of a clam. The arrows indicate the direction of water flow through the mantle cavity and the gill (gray area).

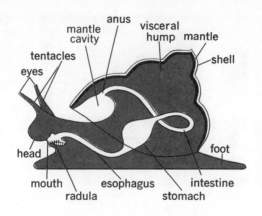

tentacles
eyes
anus
mantle
cavity
visceral
hump
mantle
shell
head
mouth
radula
esophagus
stomach
intestine
foot

30-9 Compare the structure of the land snail shown here with that of the generalized mollusk shown in Figure 30-4, and with that of the clam in Figure 30-8.

The land snail has adapted to survival outside of the water. Its mantle cavity acts as a modified lung. Oxygen diffuses through the thin membrane lining the cavity. This lining must be kept moist for gases to be exchanged. Air is most moist during the evening, night, and early morning. So it is during these times when snails are most active.

When the air is drier and cooler, snails become inactive. The snails retreat into their shells, and close themselves in with a kind of "door." If they are inactive for a time, they seal the door with a mucus secretion. This helps prevent water loss.

Land snails travel very slowly, about three meters an hour. Glands in the flat, muscular foot secrete a layer of slime on which the snail moves. Muscles in the foot contract in a wavelike rhythm, pulling the snail along. The snail's eyes are on the tops of two tentacles, which vanish upon touch by being pulled into itself much as the toes of a sock disappear when you turn it inside out.

Slugs look like snails that have lost their shells. If you look closely at a slug, you can see the opening to the mantle cavity. This is used in respiration. The animal is able to save moisture within the mantle chamber by controlling the size of the opening. Like land snails, slugs are usually active at night. They leave trails of slime wherever they go.

Many experiments have been done to find out influences on the direction of a snail's movement. In fact, in one investigation at Marine Biological Laboratory at Woods Hole, Massachusetts, 34,000 mud snails were studied. The results of this study indicated that snails seem to follow the path of the sun. After noon, however, they turn less toward the sun. They follow the moon's motion in a similar manner.

30-10 Some examples of gastropods are the land snail, garden slug, and the nudibranch. (Carolina Biological Supply Co.; Dr. E. R. Degginger; Allan Roberts)

30–11 The octopus, a mollusk with well-developed eyes, moves by pulling itself over rocks by its tentacles or by expelling a jet of water from its excurrent siphon. (D. P. Wilson; Douglas Faulkner)

Both snails and slugs can do damage by feeding on garden plants. The best way to see the feeding mechanism of a gastropod is to watch freshwater snails in an aquarium. Watch to see a snail open its mouth and scrape the glass with a tonguelike structure called a *radula* (RADJ-uh-luh). The word literally means "scraper." The snail's radula actually files algae from the glass walls of the aquarium. It is with their radulas that snails and slugs harm garden plants.

"HEAD-FOOTED" MOLLUSKS

The *cephalopods* (SEF-uh-luh-podz) include the octopus, squid, cuttlefish, and chambered nautilus. The octopus has no shell. The nautilus has an external shell. And the squid and the cuttlefish have an internal shell.

The giant squid is probably the largest invertebrate in the world. It may grow to be eighteen meters long and 1,800 kilograms. The octopus is usually rather timid, in spite of a bad reputation. A very large type of octopus lives along the Pacific Coast. Its body is about 30 centimeters long, but its slender arms can grow to five meters.

Phylum—Echinodermata

THE SPINY-SKINNED INVERTEBRATES

The phylum *Echinodermata* includes the common starfish, brittle star, sea urchin, and sand dollar. The radially symmetrical bodies of these creatures are hard and covered with spines. Some spines are long, like those of the sea urchin. Some spines, like those of the sand dollar, are very short. All the echinoderms live in the sea. Some live deep in the ocean and others live in shallow tidal pools.

The starfish is one of the most familiar echinoderms. It normally has five rays, or arms, radiating from a central disk. In a groove on the lower side of each movable ray are two rows of *tube feet*. These are part of a **water-vascular system** because they are connected to canals running through each ray. The canals in the rays lead to a circular canal in the central disk. This *ring canal* has an opening called the *sieve plate* on the dorsal surface. When the starfish presses its tube feet against an object and forces water out of its canals, the feet grip the object by means of suction. When the starfish lets water back into its canals, the feet release their grip.

The starfish uses this water-vascular system effectively to open clam and oyster shells for its food. It arches over its prey and firmly grips both sides of the valves with its tube feet. The strength of the suction exerts a steady pull. Then the starfish turns its stomach inside out through a small opening in the center of its lower side. The stomach is forced through the tiniest opening between the mollusk's valves. Some starfish can get through an opening as little as one tenth of a millimeter. Enzymes secreted by the stomach then digest the mollusk's body. The stomach absorbs the digested food and passes it into the digestive glands for more chemical change. Then the starfish pulls in its stomach and moves away leaving the empty shell of its prey.

Starfish are the natural enemies of oystermen. An adult starfish can eat eight to twelve oysters a day. But oystermen who try to destroy starfish by tearing them to pieces and throwing them back in the water are only multiplying their troubles. **A starfish ray that is still attached to part of the central disk can regenerate its missing parts to become a whole new animal.**

Starfish never fail to capture the students' curiosity. Some students may have dead starfish that they can bring into class. An aquarium containing starfish would be interesting for the students to observe.

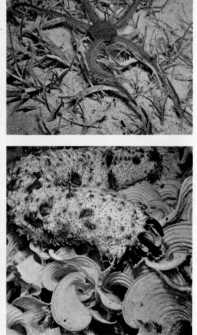

30–12 Some examples of common echinoderms are the sand dollar, common starfish, brittle starfish, sea urchin, and sea cucumber. Echinodermata is the only major phylum composed entirely of marine animals. (*Top center,* R. D. Beeman; *others,* Douglas Faulkner)

30-13 The starfish pushes its stomach out from a small opening on its lower side. Enzymes then begin the digestion of its prey. (Z. Leszczynski, Animals, Animals)

Normally, starfish reproduce sexually. They are either male or female. Starfish shed their sperms and eggs into the water during the reproductive season. Thus, **fertilization is external since it takes place outside the body.** Female starfish can produce as many as 200 million eggs in one season. These may develop into free-swimming, ciliated larvae, complete with mouths, digestive tracts, and anuses. After swimming for a while, the larvae settle to the bottom and grow into adults.

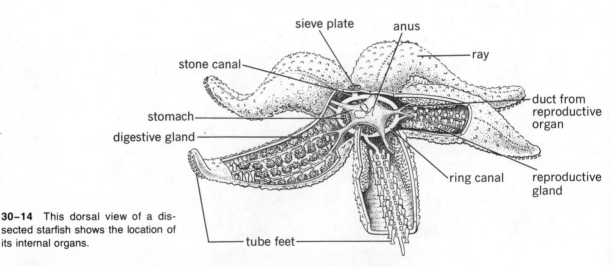

30-14 This dorsal view of a dissected starfish shows the location of its internal organs.

FURTHER CLUES TO RELATIONSHIPS

While studying invertebrates, we have seen certain similarities which can help in understanding the paths of animal evolution. One idea is that **the more similar the body plans of two groups are, the closer their relationship. This means that their common ancestor existed more recently in their history. This is the *principle of homology.***

An important characteristic in grouping animals is the type of body cavity, or **coelom** (SEEL'm), in the adult. Although flatworms are bilaterally symmetrical, they do not have a body cavity between their internal organs and the body wall. But in larger animals, a

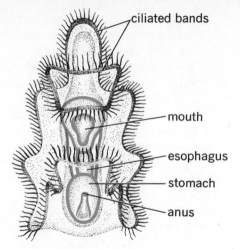

ciliated bands

mouth

esophagus

stomach

anus

30–15 A free-swimming larva of an echinoderm. Called a *bipinnaria,* it is similar to the larva of some of the lower chordates.

solid structure like that of flatworms would not be efficient. **The majority of animals have a coelom. It is a fluid-filled cavity with room for looped intestines, and aids in circulation of food and oxygen, and the removal of wastes.** The coelom has a membrane lining made of specialized cells that helps suspend the intestine within it.

Much can be learned about the phylogenetic tree from studying basic embryology. Some students may want to research this topic and report to the class on their findings.

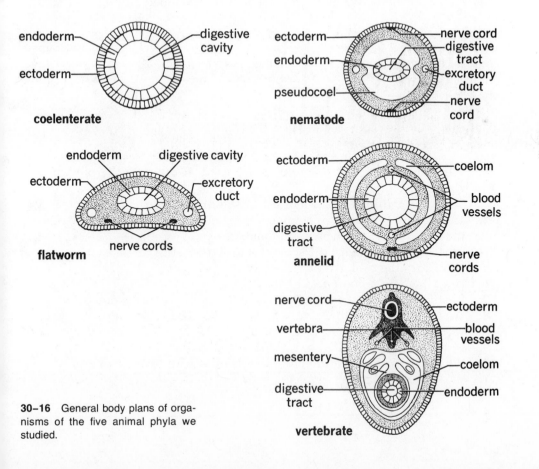

endoderm

ectoderm

digestive cavity

coelenterate

ectoderm

endoderm

pseudocoel

nerve cord

digestive tract

excretory duct

nerve cord

nematode

endoderm

ectoderm

digestive cavity

excretory duct

nerve cords

flatworm

ectoderm

endoderm

digestive tract

coelom

blood vessels

nerve cords

annelid

nerve cord

vertebra

mesentery

digestive tract

ectoderm

blood vessels

coelom

endoderm

vertebrate

30–16 General body plans of organisms of the five animal phyla we studied.

There are animals that are grouped between those with a coelom and those without one. These animals have a ***pseudocoel*** (SOO-doe-seel), or false coelom. This cavity is very different. It is not lined with the specialized cells, and the internal organs are free within the cavity instead of being suspended by a membrane.

SUMMARY

Members of the phylum *Mollusca* live on land, in fresh and in salt water. There are more species of mollusks than any other animal phylum but insects. All mollusks go through a trochophore stage, some in the egg capsule and some as larvae. Each adult has a head, a foot, and a visceral hump containing the vital organs. The hump is covered by a mantle, which in some species produces a hard shell.

There are three important classes in the mollusk phylum. The bivalves, like clams and oysters, have two halves to their shells joined by a hinge. The univalves have a single shell, like snails, or no shell, like slugs. They eat with a rough tongue and move very slowly on their foot. Cephalopods include the octopus and the squid.

The phylum *Echinodermata* includes the starfish and sea urchins. Echinoderms have hard, radially symmetrical bodies covered with spines. Their arms, or rays, have tube feet connected to a water-vascular system.

The relationships among animals can be determined from similarities in different animals. One main factor in classification is the possession of a coelom. The coelom is the body cavity in more highly developed animals.

BIOLOGICALLY SPEAKING

trochopore	gill	prismatic layer
visceral hump	incurrent siphon	horny outer layer
mantle	excurrent siphon	radula
mantle cavity	foot	coelom
water-vascular system	valve	pseudocoel
principle of homology	pearly layer	

QUESTIONS FOR REVIEW

1. What structures of the mollusks are used in dividing the phylum into classes?
2. What three things do all mollusks have in common?
3. Trace a bit of food from outside the clam to the digestive gland, naming the organs through which the food goes.
4. What layers make up the shell of a mollusk?
5. How does the oyster make a pearl?
6. Describe how a clam gets its food.
7. In what ways do the cephalopods differ from the gastropods?
8. What structures of the echinoderms make them different from other invertebrate animals?
9. Describe the movement and feeding of the starfish.
10. Why is it useless to eliminate starfish by tearing them up?
11. What is a coelom?

1. What structural similarities indicate a relationship between the mollusks and the annelids?
2. In what ways have the mollusks been of value to the human beings? In what ways have they been a pest?
3. Shells of mollusks are often ground up and used as fertilizer. What are some of the substances that these shells add to the soil?

chapter thirty-one

The Arthropods

31–1 The ghost crab is an example of an arthropod. (Albert Towle)

OBJECTIVES

- LIST the characteristics of the arthropods.
- NAME and GIVE EXAMPLES of each class of arthropod.
- DESCRIBE the tremendous variation among arthropods.
- EXPLAIN the advantages and disadvantages of an exoskeleton.
- IDENTIFY the parts of a crayfish.
- DISTINGUISH centipedes from millipedes.
- IDENTIFY the arachnids.
- DESCRIBE the parts of the spider.

Ask students to discuss some of the arthropods with which they are familiar. Many people find that members of this phylum are unattractive and/or frightening. Why is this so?

CHARACTERISTICS OF ARTHROPODS

As far as numbers are concerned, the arthropods are a most successful group of animals. The phylum *Arthropoda* includes the familiar insects, spiders, centipedes, millipedes, crayfish, crabs, and lobsters. Arthropods are found everywhere. They serve as food for humans, and they compete with us for food. Many live as parasites in or on other organisms, and some transmit disease. Arthropods are the major natural agent of flower pollination. **Arthropoda literally means "joined feet,"** and all of them share the following features:

- Jointed **appendages,** including legs and other body outgrowths.
- A hard external skeleton, or **exoskeleton,** made up of a substance called *chitin* (KITE'n). This differs from the *internal* support or skeleton in humans and other vertebrates.
- A segmented body; the exoskeleton is divided into parts.
- A dorsal heart; a heart located above the digestive system.
- A ventral nervous system; the main nerves are below the digestive system.

A RELATIONSHIP BETWEEN ANNELIDS AND ARTHROPODS

The arthropods seem to be related to the annelids. The reason is that both of their bodies are divided into segments. Biologists often refer to this relationship as the "annelid-arthropod line of development." If you compare the characteristics of the arthropods and the annelids, you can see why the arthropods have been more successful than the annelids. Their sense organs are more complex, permitting coordinated responses to their environment. Grouped

Era	Period	sponges	coelenterates	segmented worms	arthropods	mollusks	echinoderms
Cenozoic	Quaternary						
	Tertiary						
Mesozoic	Cretaceous						
	Jurassic						
	Triassic						
Paleozoic	Permian						
	Pennsylvanian (Late Carboniferous)						
	Mississippian (Early Carboniferous)						
	Devonian						
	Silurian						
	Ordovician						
	Cambrian						
(Pre-Cambrian)							

31–2 A time scale comparing the arthropods to the other invertebrates.

muscles and jointed legs contribute to better coordination when looking for food or escaping from enemies. As you see, the characteristics of arthropods permits them to be more efficient and better adapted to more environments.

The hard *exoskeleton* is more protection than the soft cuticle of the worm. It may seem odd to have a skeleton on the outside of the body. But it serves the same functions as an internal skeleton. Each gives the body a form, protects delicate internal organs, and provides an anchor for various muscles. But an exoskeleton limits the size of the animal. A large exoskeleton would need such powerful muscles to move it that it would crush the animal by its own weight. Flying insects cannot grow as large as birds because their wings would not be able to lift the weight of their exoskeletons.

Growth of an animal with an exoskeleton can only occur by *molting*, or shedding its old skeleton and forming a new one. This process will be discussed later in the chapter.

Discuss with the class some of the reasons for the "success" of this phylum. Use Table 31–1 for a comparison of arthropod and annelid characteristics.

Table 31-1 COMPARISON OF ARTHROPODS AND ANNELIDS

ARTHROPOD CHARACTERISTICS	ANNELID CHARACTERISTICS
legs divided by movable joints	no legs
hard, chitinous exoskeleton	flexible cuticle
fewer segments, more highly specialized	many similar segments
dorsal heart	dorsal heart
ventral nervous system with specialized sensory receptors such as eyes and antennae	ventral nervous system but simple sensory receptors
muscles in groups	muscles in sheets

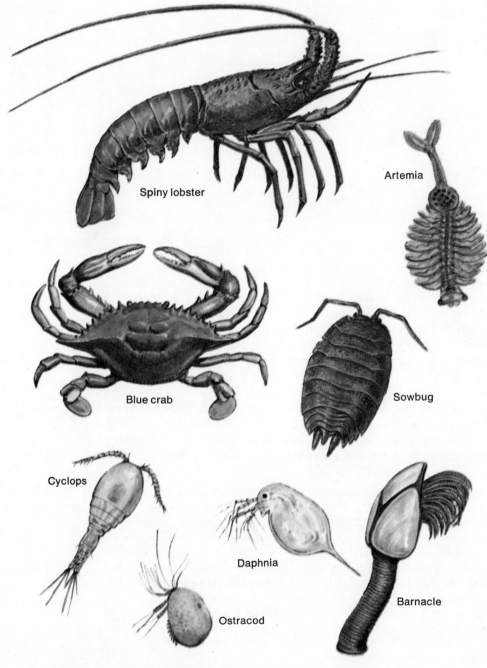

31-3 Various examples of the classes of arthropods.

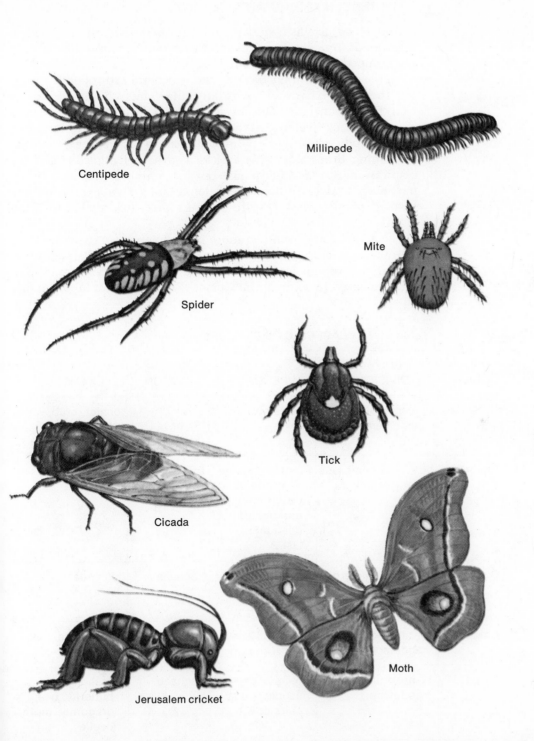

Centipede

Millipede

Mite

Spider

Tick

Cicada

Jerusalem cricket

Moth

Thus, while the exoskeleton is ideal for very small animals, it would be a disadvantage for animals of larger size.

DIFFERENCES AMONG ARTHROPODS

Butterflies, crayfish, spiders, and centipedes are all classified as arthropods. Since arthropods have such widely varied forms, they are grouped into five different classes.

All the class members have the same general arthropod features, but they also have their own particular class characteristics as well. For instance, the *Crustacea* (kruss-TAY-shuh) have two pairs of antennae, or "feelers," at the front of their bodies. They have two distinct body regions, five pairs of legs, and a chitinous exoskeleton containing lime. Most crustaceans also have featherlike **gills** for respiration. But the *Insecta* have only one pair of antennae, a three-part body, and a chitinous exoskeleton that does *not* contain lime. Instead of gills they respire through air tubes called **tracheae** (TRAY-kee-ee).

The arthropods are much more complex in their structure than the other animals we have studied. The segmented body is common to both arthropods and annelids. And the ventral nervous system first appeared in some of the worms. But division of labor among

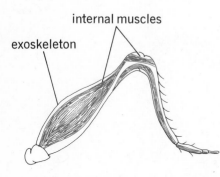

internal muscles

exoskeleton

31–4 An arthropod's leg showing the attachment of the internal muscles to the exoskeleton.

Table 31-2 CLASSES OF ARTHROPODS

CLASS	BODY DIVISIONS	APPENDAGES	RESPI-RATION	EXAMPLES
Crustacea	2 — cephalothorax, abdomen	5 pairs of legs	gills	lobster, crab, water flea, sow bug, crayfish
Chilopoda	head and numerous body segments	1 pair of legs on each segment except first one behind head and last 2	tracheae	centipede
Diplopoda	head and numerous body segments	2 pairs of legs on each body segment	tracheae	millipede
Arachnida	2 — cephalothorax, abdomen	4 pairs of legs	tracheae and book lungs	spider, mite, tick, scorpion
Insecta	3 — head, thorax, abdomen	3 pairs of legs; usually 1 or 2 pairs of wings	tracheae	grasshopper, butterfly, bee, dragonfly, moth, beetle

various organs is much more complex in arthropods than it is in earthworms. This specialization has resulted in animals that are well adapted to their present world. Since crustaceans are typical arthropods, we will look more closely at the crayfish, which is adapted to an aquatic life.

Crustaceans

THE CRAYFISH—FRESHWATER CRUSTACEAN

Crayfish make good subjects for study since they are large and easy to find. They live in nearly all bodies of fresh water that contain lime. Lime is used by the crayfish to harden its tough, chitinous exoskeleton.

The crayfish body is divided into two regions. The first part, called the **cephalothorax** (SEF-uh-loe-THORE-acks), includes the *head* and the *thorax*. The cephalothorax is protected by a shield of exoskeleton called the **carapace.** In the insects, the head and the thorax are separate.

The second part of the crayfish body is posterior to the cephalothorax and is called the **abdomen.** The abdomen has seven movable segments.

APPENDAGES OF THE CRAYFISH

The anterior pair of appendages of the crayfish are the **attenules.** These contain the hearing and the balancing, or *equilibrium*, mechanisms. The large **antennae** attach just behind the antennules. They are the organs of touch, taste, and smell. Behind them are the **mandibles,** or true jaws. They crush and chew food. They are helped by two pairs of **maxillae** (mack-SILL-ee), or little jaws. The jaws work from side to side instead of up and down. These jaws are really leg-like appendages that have adapted for chewing, and they move sideways like the other legs.

The first appendages of the thorax are three pairs of **maxillipeds** (mack-SILL-i-PEDZ). Maxillipeds, or "jaw feet," hold food while the crayfish is chewing. The next pair of appendages are the claws, or **chelipeds** (KEE-luh-PEDZ). These help to get food and to protect the crayfish. Behind the claws are the four pairs of **walking legs.** Feathery *gills*, for respiration, are attached to the appendages of the thorax. The delicate gills are protected under the carapace.

The appendages of the abdomen of the crayfish are called **swimmerets.** As you might expect, they are used for swimming. The female attaches eggs to the last three pairs of swimmerets. The sixth pair of abdominal appendages is developed into a flipper, or **uropod** (YOOH-ruh-POD). The middle of the tail is a flat, triangular structure called the **telson.** Strong muscles can whip the tail forward, causing the animal to shoot backward very rapidly.

Recall from Chapter Thirteen that organs in different animals that have similar functions are called *analogous*. The gills of a cray-

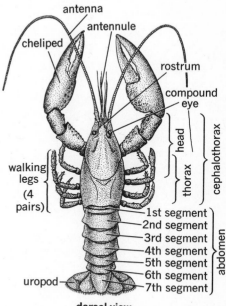

dorsal view

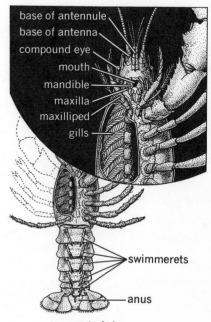

ventral view

31–5 The crayfish, a common crustacean.

fish and the lungs of a human are analogous because they are the organs for respiration. But they are not *homologous* because they each have developed in a different way from different structures. The gills have developed from legs, while lungs are outgrowths of the throat.

NUTRITION IN THE CRAYFISH

The maxillae and maxillipeds hold the food while it is torn and crushed by the mandibles. The food then goes through a short esophagus to the stomach. The stomach is lined with hard, chitinous teeth. When these have ground the food even finer, it is strained through folds of tissue in the stomach and mixed with digestive juices. Next, the digested food passes to the digestive glands and is absorbed. Undigested particles do not enter the digestive glands but pass directly to the intestine, and are eliminated through the anus. The crayfish also has excretory organs called **green glands.** These are located in front of the stomach near the base of the antennae. The green glands remove wastes from the blood.

Many biology classes dissect crayfish, but it is also interesting to observe live specimens. Raw beef can be fed to them; however, remove any leftovers after the crayfish have finished eating.

CIRCULATION IN THE CRAYFISH

The heart of the crayfish pumps blood into seven large arteries. These arteries pour the blood over all the major organs of the body. The blood bathes the cells directly by flowing through the tissue spaces. Eventually it collects in one large lower cavity, the *sternal sinus.* From there, the blood is carried through vessels to the gills, where respiration occurs. Next, the blood goes through vessels to another large sinus, the *pericardial sinus* which surrounds the heart. Blood enters the heart through three pairs of tiny pores called the *ostia.* When the heart contracts, valves close off the ostia to prevent blood from flowing back into the pericardial sinus. **This type of circulation is called an *open system*, since the blood is not contained in vessels all through the body. In a closed system, the blood stays within vessels and does not bathe the organs directly.**

31–6 The internal structure of a crayfish. The term gonad refers to the ovary in the female and the testis in the male.

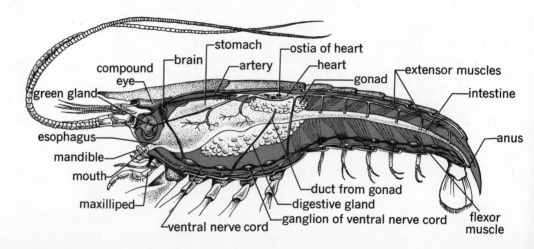

RESPIRATION IN THE CRAYFISH

Respiration, or exchange of oxygen and carbon dioxide, gets more specialized in higher forms of animals. In protists, these gases diffuse through the plasma membrane. In worms, gases diffuse through the body wall. The thin-walled gills of the crayfish have a great many blood vessels. Gases can diffuse through the thin wall between the blood and the flowing water. These gills are well adapted for the exchange of gases between the animal and its aquatic environment.

The gills are protected by the carapace. This part of the exoskeleton covers them and forms a chamber. The second maxillae keeps water flowing into the gill chamber and forward over the gills. The gill chamber can hold enough moisture to keep the crayfish alive for some time if it is taken out of the water.

Discuss the advantages of the gill chamber to the crayfish. It retains moisture and enables the crayfish to migrate to other ponds in summer and in drought.

THE NERVOUS SYSTEM AND SENSE ORGANS

The nervous system of the crayfish is similar to that in annelids, but it is more specialized. Nerves carry impulses from the eyes, antennules, and antennae to the brain. Two large nerves run from the brain to the ventral part of the crayfish's body. Here they unite to form a large double ganglion. They then continue together as the ventral nerve cord, which passes to the posterior end of the body. In each segment, the ventral nerve cord enlarges into a ganglion from which nerves run out to the appendages, muscles, and other body organs.

The antennae have receptors sensitive to smell and taste. The eyes are set on two short movable stalks. Each eye has more than 2,000 lenses. This type of eye is called a **compound eye.** The compound eye can detect movement. Many arthropods have compound eyes.

The antennae also have many sensory bristles that react to touch. These sensory bristles also grow all over the body, including the appendages. It is thought that these bristles may also react to sound waves.

A sac at the base of each antennule helps the crayfish keep its balance. The sac, called a **statocyst,** is lined with hairy receptor cells. Within each statocyst are grains of sand. If the crayfish becomes tilted, or upside down, sand grains stimulate the hairy receptor cells. This sends signals to the brain along nerve fibers. The crayfish reacts by righting itself.

When the crayfish molts, the grains of sand are shed along with the old exoskeleton. Usually the crayfish replaces it with other grains. In experiments, though, iron filings have been placed near the crayfish during molting. The crayfish often places one of these filings into the statocyst. When the new exoskeleton has hardened, the animal is put in another aquarium. If a magnet is held over this crayfish's back, the iron filing will brush the receptor hairs at the top of the statocyst. The crayfish will then turn on its back, staying upside down as long as the magnet is kept there.

The arthropods have a compound eye composed of many individual tubes. This eye has many lenses and, therefore, sees many images at the same time. Some students may want to compare the arthropod eye with that of the vertebrates.

REPRODUCTION AND GROWTH IN THE CRAYFISH

Crayfish usually mate in the fall. At this time, the sperms from the male are stored in small receptacles on the lower side of the female's body. In the spring, about one hundred eggs are laid. As they are laid, they are fertilized by the stored sperms. The fertilized eggs are covered with a sticky secretion so they will stick to the swimmerets. These eggs resemble a bunch of berries. The female carries these fertilized eggs and protects them for six to eight weeks, depending on the temperature and conditions of the water. When the tiny crayfish hatch, they look quite different from their parents.

The baby crayfish reach adult form by growing and molting several times. As the young crayfish begins to develop, the time span between moltings gets longer and longer. Most larvae molt seven times during the first year and about twice a year from then on. The average life span of a crayfish is three to four years.

While the crayfish is molting, the cuticle secretes an enzyme that actually digests the inside of the shell. This loosens the shell from the body. The lining of the stomach is also shed, including the teeth. Quickly, the crayfish absorbs water, swelling up to its new size. As the lime is replaced, the exoskeleton hardens. Because it is helpless during molting, the crayfish usually goes into hiding until its new exoskeleton has hardened. **It will not grow in size until it molts again.**

Crayfish often lose or injure appendages during molting or fighting with enemies. It casts off the injured limb. A double membrane prevents much blood loss. Gradually, a whole new appendage grows to replace the lost one. This is another example of regeneration of lost parts.

31–7 Regeneration. A crayfish growing a new claw. (Allan Roberts)

ADAPTATION TO A VARIETY OF ENVIRONMENTS

The edible, sea-living crustaceans like lobsters and crabs are relatively few in numbers. **Indeed, the vast majority of crustaceans are in minute and even microscopic forms.** These small animals can occur in such tremendous numbers that ships' sonar equipment have misread the bottom depth of the ocean.

Artemia, the brine shrimp, lives in tide pools and can survive in an environment with a high concentration of salt. Owners of tropical fish often buy its eggs and raise the shrimp for fish food. *Barnacles* are sessile crustaceans. They settle on a solid object when they are larvae. Then they produce a shell and use their feet to kick food into their mouths. Barnacles can gather on the hulls of ships in such large numbers that they slow down the ships.

Many crustaceans live in fresh water. If you have ever seen tiny brown specks zigzagging in the water, you may have been looking at *Daphnia* (water fleas) or *ostracods*. Ostracods are tiny crustaceans. They have hinged chitinous exoskeletons which contain lime. This exoskeleton looks like the shell of a clam. Another com-

Stress to students the vulnerability of a molting crayfish. Regeneration is an important aspect of survival for this organism.

Students should be exposed to the "live" varieties of many of the organisms that they consume. Many students have never observed a "live" shrimp, for example. Brine shrimp can be easily raised in the classroom.

mon tiny crustacean is the *copepod* (KOPE-uh-POD). Copepods are a very important part of the diet of many fish.

Interesting adaptations to land are found in terrestrial crustaceans such as the sow bugs and pill bugs. Since they have seven identical pairs of legs, these creatures are called *isopods*, or "same feet." Isopods have a series of platelike gills along the lower surface of the abdomen. The plates have tiny tubes to allow air to enter. These gills must stay moist for respiration to occur. So these animals usually live under stones and logs. Even if you do not live near the water where crayfish may be found, you can probably find isopods in your area. Terrestial isopods can live for weeks in jars with slices of potato or carrot for food.

Myriapoda

CENTIPEDES AND MILLIPEDES

The classification *Myriapoda* means "many feet" and is a heading for two different classes. You have probably seen these interesting arthropods racing away from you on their many pairs of feet when you have disturbed a log or stone. Maybe you have wondered how a centipede or millipede can work so many legs at the same time. They certainly have excellent coordination.

Centipedes belong to the class *Chilopoda*, and their bodies have many segments. The head has the antennae and mouth parts. The first body segment has a pair of poison claws, which aid in catching food. Every segment after that, except the last two, has one pair of walking legs. Centipedes move quickly and are difficult to catch. Some have as many as 173 pairs of legs, but 35 is average. In tropical countries, centipedes can grow 30 centimeters long, and may have very poisonous bites.

Millipedes, or "thousand legs," also have a multi-segmented body. Millipedes belong to the class *Diplopoda*, which means "double feet." Like the centipede, the head bears the antennae and mouth parts. But on each body segment, except the last two, there are *two* pairs of legs. Millipedes feed mostly on plants. They often move slowly, and are apt to roll into a spiral if they are disturbed.

Stress to students the important economic value of certain types of crustaceans. Lobsters, crabs, and shrimp are very popular as food and are becoming more and more expensive. Discuss some of the reasons these foods, especially lobster, are so high in price.

31-8 Compare the centipede (left) with the millipede. Note that the centipede just shed its exoskeleton. (Z. Leszczynski, Animals, Animals; Dr. E. R. Degginger)

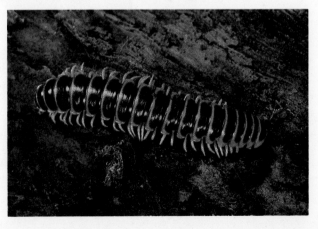

Arachnids

SPIDERS

Spiders may be very useful to humans because they destroy many harmful insects. They belong to the class *Arachnida* (uh-RACK-nid-uh). Some spiders, called *orb weavers*, spin thin silklike threads into remarkably engineered webs. When a flying insect gets trapped in the sticky web, the spider comes out from a hiding place along the edge. The spider poisons its prey with a bite. When the insect has become paralyzed, the spider wraps its meal up in more silken threads. Not all spiders spin webs, but some stalk their prey as they roam.

The spider looks like an insect but is different in several ways. It has no antennae, its eyes are simple, and it has eight legs instead of six. Like crustaceans, the head and thorax are joined in a cephalothorax. The first pair of appendages, called *chelicera* (ki-LISS-uh-ruh), act as poison fangs. They also suck the juices from the victim's body. The second pair of appendages from the head are *pedipalps.* These are sensory and are used in reproduction by the male spider.

On the tip of the abdomen of many spiders, there are three pairs of *spinnerets.* Each spinneret is composed of hundreds of microscopic tubes. The fluid silk is drawn out from the silk glands through these tubes. As it is drawn out, it hardens into a thread. The spider uses its silk to make webs, to build cocoons for eggs, and to build its nest. This thread sometimes acts as a guide to help the spider find its way back. In many species, young spiders spin long silken threads that catch the wind and carry them to other places. This method of moving is called *ballooning.*

The spider respires through slitlike openings which take in air to a pair of sacs called *book lungs.* Book lungs are located on the lower side of the abdomen. The book lungs have several leaves, or plates, to expose a large surface to the air. In addition to their book

Students will be fascinated by observing spiders. A large terrarium can be used to house them. Provide a dish of water in order to maintain proper humidity in the terrarium. Spiders are carnivorous and students may bring in other smaller insects to provide food.

31–9 A longitudinal section of a female spider.

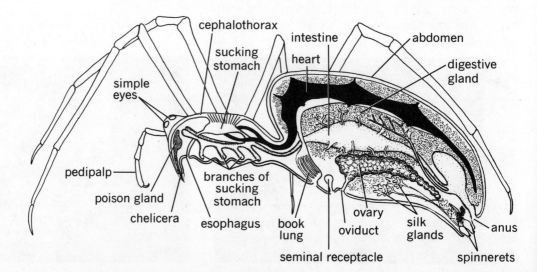

lungs, many spiders have openings in their abdomens that lead to air tubes similar to the tracheae of insects.

You can usually tell a mature male spider from the female just by size. The male is smaller. If both are the same size, the pedipalps of the male are much larger near the tips. When the male is mature, he transfers sperms to special sacs in these tips. The sperms are then placed in the *seminal receptacle* of the female by the male. In a few species, the female devours the male afterwards. When the eggs are laid, they are fertilized as they pass through the genital pore into a nest or cocoon.

Among the best known spiders are the *tarantula* (tuh-RAN-chu-luh), or banana spider, the *black widow*, and the *trapdoor spider* of the western desert.

OTHER ARACHNIDS

Spiders are related to many other forms of animal life. *Scorpions* live in the south and southwestern United States and in all tropical countries. They have long, segmented abdomens that end in poisonous stingers. But though the scorpion's sting is painful, it is seldom fatal to humans. Campers may find scorpions annoying because they often crawl into empty shoes to escape bright light. Scorpions live solitary lives except during mating. After mating, the female often devours the male. The young are hatched alive and are carried during their early life on the mother's back.

The familiar *daddy-longlegs*, or *harvestman*, is a useful arachnid since it feeds on plant lice. It, too, lives alone, traveling through fields in search of its prey.

Mites and *ticks* cause much damage to humans and other animals. Many live as parasites on the skin of chickens, dogs, cattle, humans, and others. Some forms, like the Rocky Mountain tick, carry diseases as well.

Harvest mites, or *chiggers*, are immature mites which attach themselves to the skin surface. They break the skin with beaks and draw out blood. They are almost microscopic. So the first sign of them is swelling, itching, and great discomfort. This disappears after a few days.

Point out to students that many arachnids are well camouflaged and difficult to see in their natural environments.

31-10 A female black widow spider. Note the characteristic red hourglass marking on the ventral surface of its round, black abdomen. (Allan Roberts)

SUMMARY   The arthropods are the most numerous of all the animal phyla. They have several characteristics which are more complex than those of annelids, although they are clearly related. The arthropods' jointed appendages and hard, segmented exoskeleton give them both coordination and protection in all kinds of environments—land, sea, and fresh water. Their sense organs, heart, and nervous sytem are also more highly developed. One limitation of the exoskeleton is that it must be shed, so that the animal may grow. The crayfish is an excellent example of the Crustacean class of Arthropods.

Centipedes, millipedes, and the spiders are other typical arthropods. Though many arthropods are harmful to crops and may carry diseases, some spiders are helpful to humans because they feed on harmful insects.

BIOLOGICALLY SPEAKING

appendage	antennule	uropod
exoskeleton	antenna	telson
molting	mandible	green glands
gill	maxilla	open system
trachea	maxilliped	compound eye
cephalothorax	cheliped	statocyst
carapace	walking legs	
abdomen	swimmeret	

QUESTIONS FOR REVIEW

1. List three external characteristics of an arthropod that make it different from other animals.
2. Name the five main classes of arthropods and give examples of each.
3. In what ways are the arthropods similar to the earthworm?
4. What are some advantages and disadvantages of an exoskeleton?
5. How do the gills in the crayfish carry on respiration?
6. To what stimuli is the crayfish sensitive, and what structures help in the sensitivity?
7. How does a centipede differ from a millipede?
8. Why are most spiders helpful to man? Why are many people afraid of arachnids?
9. Of what value to the spider is ballooning?
10. How does the spider carry on respiration?
11. What other animals besides the spiders are classified as arachnids?

APPLYING PRINCIPLES AND CONCEPTS

1. Why is it especially important for an animal like the crayfish to have long antennae?
2. In which area do you think the crayfish would be likely to produce weaker exoskeletons, in waters flowing through limestone rock or in waters flowing through granite? Explain.
3. Of what advantage to the young crayfish is its clinging to the adult's swimmerets until after the second molting?

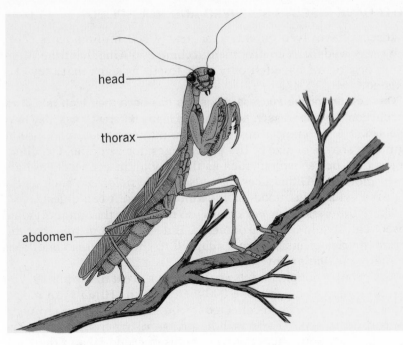

head

thorax

abdomen

32-1 How many insect characteristics can you find on this interesting animal?

Insects— Familiar Arthropods

OBJECTIVES
- DESCRIBE the characteristics of insects.
- DISTINGUISH incomplete metamorphosis from complete metamorphosis.
- IDENTIFY the parts of the grasshopper.
- STATE the function of each part of the grasshopper.
- DISCUSS the importance of insects to man.
- EXPLAIN behavior as a survival factor.
- DESCRIBE the social structure and behavior of bees.

VAST NUMBER OF SPECIES

Insects are the dominant group of animals on earth today. Insecta is, by far, the largest class of the arthropod phylum. This is the largest phylum of all classified animals. The study of insects is called *entomology.* Biologists in this field are known as *entomologists.* So far, more than 675,000 species of insects have been recorded. But entomologists think that this equals no more than half the insect species that really exist. You may have seen pictures of swarms of locusts or mayflies darkening the sky. One insect may produce thousands of offspring. But not all of them survive. As you will read later in Unit 8, many factors help control this awesome rate of reproductive potential.

WHAT IS AN INSECT?

Not all insects are "bugs." A true bug is a member of only one order among all other insects. And as you know, spiders or centipedes are not bugs; they are not even insects.

Insects are arthropods with three separate body regions. These are the *head,* the *thorax,* and the *abdomen.* The head bears one pair of antennae and the mouth parts. The thorax has three pairs of legs, and the wings, if any. The abdomen has up to eleven segments, but it never has legs. The reproductive structures are usually on the eighth, ninth, and tenth segments. Insects breathe through branched air tubes called *tracheae.*

Insects have affected and continue to affect many aspects of our lives. Products produced by insects, such as honey, are valuable economically. Insects, on the other hand, have also destroyed millions of dollars worth of crops and brought disease to millions of people.

WHY HAVE INSECTS SURVIVED AND MULTIPLIED?

Insects have lived on earth for nearly 300 million years. They have survived many environmental changes during that time. Many other organisms have left only their fossils as signs that they ever existed.

One reason for the success of insects has been their high rate of reproduction. Another reason has been the many different ways they have adapted. The differences among insects may be *structural*, as in the number, shape, or size of the appendages, for example. Or, differences may be *behavioral*, such as the way an insect reacts to light or to moisture. Differences may also be *physiological*, such as the types of cells in its blood, or the kinds of food it can digest.

These differences, or variations, do not mean that an individual insect can live in all environments. But variation means that different species of insects have adapted to the changing conditions in many particular environments.

As a group, though, insects are found in a great many places. You can find them at heights of 6,000 meters in the Himalayan mountains. Insects have been collected in the Antarctic where temperatures drop to −65°C and in hot springs rising from deep in the earth's crust. Some insects live in pools of crude oil and there are some living on the surface of the ocean.

Like other arthropods, insects are protected by a chitinous exoskeleton. This exoskeleton forms a tough, but flexible and lightweight armor. This armor is coated with wax to help retain water. Insect joints are movable. The joints have a tough, membranous covering that helps to hold their skeletal parts together. As we have said before, the exoskeleton limits the size of a land organism. So most insects are small. This small size has survival value, since it allows the insect to use small spaces and feast on tiny food particles. They can find shade beside a pebble and hide in tiny spaces.

The colors and shapes of insect exoskeletons show great variety. Many insects are a color that blends in with their environment.

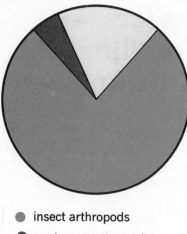

● insect arthropods

● noninsect arthropods

○ nonarthropods

32–2 Insects comprise nearly three quarters of all described species of animals.

32–3 A katydid. Can you see why camouflage is of adaptive value? (M. Vinciguerra, Monkmeyer)

32–4 Although this fly looks like a honeybee, it does not sting. Would this be of survival value to the fly? (Walter Dawn)

This helps hide the insect from its enemies. Many harmless insects look just like relatives which have a poisonous sting. Of course, those insects which *can* bite or sting are protected by the learned behavior of their enemies. An insect may also look like part of the plant in which it lives. For example, some insects look like leaves or twigs on plant stems.

Insects also survive because they can eat so many different kinds of food. They have developed specialized mouth parts. Some insects have strong jaws for chewing leaves. Some are equipped to pierce and suck plant juices. Others, like the mosquito, suck blood from animals. Some, such as butterflies, have siphoning tubes for getting nectar from flowers.

Many insects have developed wings and legs for great speed. Others, like the scale insects, have lost their legs through evolution. Some insects are adapted for an aquatic life. Others are adapted for burrowing in the ground. Some live in colonies, others live alone.

Students may be interested in starting an insect collection. The techniques of collecting, observing, classifying, and preserving are basic to this fascinating hobby.

32–5 This tree hopper resembles a thorn on a bush. (Walter Dawn)

INSECT DIVERSITY

We will not be able to study all of the insects. But we will try to look at the characteristics used to classify the orders of insects. These characteristics include type of wings, type of development, and the kind of mouth parts in the adult. Entomologists do not all agree on the grouping of insect orders. Some classify insects into twenty-nine orders. Some say there are twenty-two.

A CLOSER LOOK AT AN INSECT

It is difficult to choose an insect with characteristics typical of the entire group. But then, we cannot hope to study all the insects. There are just too many of them! We cannot say, for instance, that a grasshopper is a typical insect. But the grasshopper makes a good example since it is relatively large and it occurs in large numbers.

The grasshopper is a member of the order *Orthoptera,* which means "straight-winged." When its wings are not being used, they lie in narrow, straight folds against the body. Like that of all arthropods, the skeleton is external. But it differs from that of the crayfish since it has no lime. Instead, the grasshopper's exoskeleton is made mostly of light, tough *chitin.*

The grasshopper feeds on blades of grass. Its mouthparts are adapted for this type of food. The *labrum* is like an upper lip which keeps a blade of grass at right angles to the jaws. These rough edged jaws are called *mandibles.* Posterior to the mandibles are the *maxillae.* This second set of jaws helps to hold and cut the food. Posterior to the maxillae is the *labium,* or lower lip. This organ also holds food between the jaws. It is thought that each mouthpart contributes to the success of this insect as a grass eater.

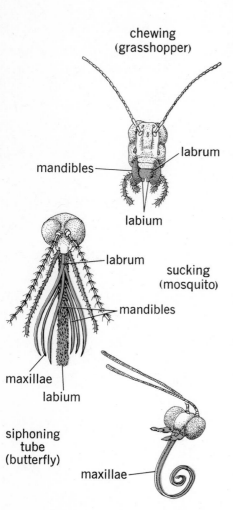

chewing
(grasshopper)

labrum

mandibles

labium

sucking
(mosquito)

labrum

mandibles

maxillae

labium

siphoning
tube
(butterfly)

maxillae

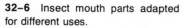

32–6 Insect mouth parts adapted for different uses.

HOW THE GRASSHOPPER MOVES

The appendages which help the grasshopper move are located on the thorax. The thorax is divided into three segments. The head and first pair of walking legs are attached to the *prothorax.* The first pair of wings and the second pair of walking legs are connected to the *mesothorax.* The third segment is the *metathorax,* which has the second pair of wings and the jumping legs.

The grasshopper uses its wings to carry it for short distances over dry fields. It also flies for many miles when swarms migrate. The long, narrow anterior fore wings are stiff. They protect the delicate underwings when the grasshopper is on the ground. But the outer wings also give lift when the grasshopper is flying or leaping. The thin underwings are posterior to the outer wings. These hind wings are like thin membranes, with many veins in them. These flying wings fold up like a fan when they are not in use.

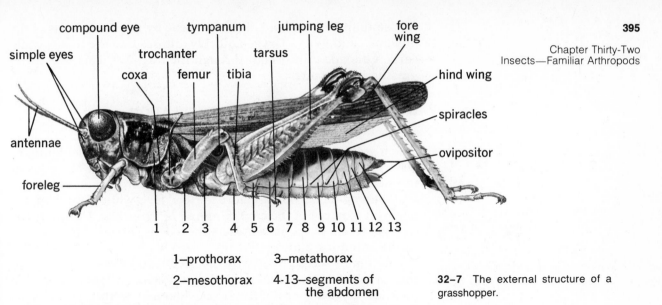

32–7 The external structure of a grasshopper.

1–prothorax   3–metathorax

2–mesothorax 4-13–segments of the abdomen

The grasshopper uses its jumping legs for short distances. It jumps to escape enemies, to search for food, and to launch into flight. It uses both jumping and walking legs to climb plants to feed on tender leaves. When it uses its legs, the spines, hooks, and pads of each foot, or *tarsus*, help it to grip. The long joint next to the tarsus is the *tibia*. The large jumping muscles are in the heaviest part of the leg, the *femur*. The leg attaches to the body like a ball-and-socket joint. This provides more freedom of motion.

Grasshoppers can be easily caught and kept alive in a container with grass. They can be observed closely in this manner.

A REMARKABLE RESPIRATORY STRUCTURE

There are ten segments to the grasshopper's abdomen. Each of these segments consists of two curved plates. The upper and lower plates are joined together by a tough but flexible membrane. This membrane allows the whole segment to expand and contract when the grasshopper breathes. The same flexible membrane also joins each segment to the ones next to it. This allows the segments to move.

The first eight segments of the abdomen have pairs of tiny openings called **spiracles.** The thorax also has spiracles on its second and third segments. These openings lead to the **tracheae,** or air tubes. The tracheae form a very complex network inside the grasshopper.

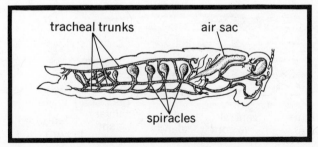

32–8 The respiratory apparatus of a grasshopper.

Air is pumped in and out of the tracheae by the movements of the abdomen and wings. Oxygen quickly diffuses into the tissue, while carbon dioxide diffuses out through the tracheae. This is how the grasshopper respires.

DIGESTION, EXCRETION, AND CIRCULATION

The grasshopper's mandibles can pinch off little pieces of grass which are then sucked into the mouth. As in many higher animals, **salivary glands** secrete juices that flow into the mouth. These juices moisten the food so that it can easily pass through an **esophagus** into the **crop.** The crop may store the food for a while. Grasshoppers may spit food out of the crop if injured or disturbed. Normally the food passes on to the **gizzard.** Here the food is shredded by plates of teeth containing chitin.

Thin plates screen the partly digested food before it passes into the large **stomach.** Outside of the stomach are several double pouches, or **gastric caeca.** The exact function of these pouches is uncertain. However, enzymes are produced and pour into the stomach. These enzymes complete the digestion in the stomach. The bloodstream absorbs the digested food through the stomach wall. The undigested material in the stomach passes into the **intestine.** The intestine is made up of the **colon** and the **rectum.** Wastes pass to the outside through the *anus.*

Cellular wastes are picked up by the blood. These wastes are collected by a series of tubes called **Malpighian** (mal-PIG-ee-un) **tubules.** The Malpighian tubules lie in the body cavity among other organs. Here, the wastes are concentrated and passed into the last part of the intestine. Wastes leave the body through the anus.

The grasshopper's circulatory system is an *open system*, like that of the crayfish. The tubular *heart* is in the dorsal part of the body. This powerful muscle forces blood out its anterior end and through the **aorta.** From there, it flows into the body cavity near the head. As blood flows from the head to the posterior of the body, it brings food to all of the organs. At the same time, the blood absorbs and carries away waste products. Finally, it returns to the heart.

It is interesting to note that insects have no red blood cells and, therefore, no hemoglobin. Their blood is clear, green or yellow colored. Students may have concluded that insects have red blood.

32-9 The internal structure of a grasshopper.

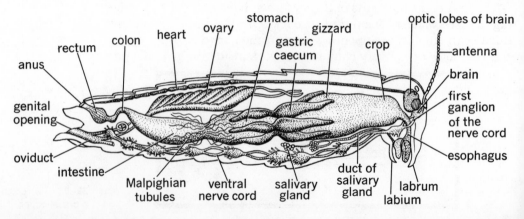

HOW THE GRASSHOPPER RESPONDS

Each side of the grasshopper's first abdominal segment has a membrane-covered cavity called the **tympanum.** These are sensory organs for hearing. The antennae are sensitive to touch and smell. The grasshopper sees through *two* sets of eyes. The three **simple eyes** are just above the base of each antenna and in the groove between them. The large **compound eyes** bulge slightly from the front and sides of the head. They are made up of hundreds of six-sided lenses. It is thought that a grasshopper can see in several directions at once from all three lenses. But focus is probably not very sharp. Entomologists consider most insects to be nearsighted. However, insects may be able to tell some colors apart. Some insects seem to be attracted to certain colors. For instance, night-flying moths seek white flowers. Flies and some other insects are attracted by red and blue.

The messages the grasshopper receives through its sense organs travel along nerves to certain parts of the body. Such parts, like muscles, then respond. Nerve centers called *ganglia* help direct the messages to the right places for coordinated reaction. The brain is actually several fused ganglia, with nerves going to the eyes, antennae, and other head organs. Other nerves go to the lower ganglia of the thorax and the abdomen. The most prominant parts of the brain are the **optic lobes.** They coordinate sight with muscle reaction through the nerves. Just move your hand toward a grasshopper and watch how fast it moves away from you! This complicated act is begun, controlled and organized by the nervous system.

32–10 The simple and compound eyes of a grasshopper. The compound eyes are made up of hundreds of six-sided lenses (inset). (Walter Dawn; inset: Hugh Spencer)

THE GRASSHOPPER'S REPRODUCTIVE ORGANS

In insects, the sexes are separate. The male produces sperm cells in the *testes.* The female produces egg cells in the *ovaries.* During mating, the male deposits his sperms into a special storage pouch in the female. This pouch is called the *seminal receptacle.* The sperms stay there until the eggs are ready to be fertilized.

The posterior segments of the female grasshopper have two pairs of hard, pointed organs called **ovipositors** (OE-VUH-POZ-it-erz). The female uses these to dig a hole and deposit the fertilized eggs. The fertilized eggs are protected by a gummy covering. One hundred or more eggs may be laid by each female in the fall. The eggs hatch the next spring.

Grasshoppers and other insects produce sound by scraping their legs against their abdominal sound organs. Some insects can detect frequencies that are 100,000 cycles per second as opposed to human ears that can detect 20,000 cycles per second.

METAMORPHOSIS

Most insects go through several distinct stages as they develop from egg to adult. This series of stages is called *metamorphosis.* Grasshoppers, bugs, aphids, and termites go through an **incomplete metamorphosis.** It occurs in three stages: the *egg,* the *nymph,* and the *adult.* The nymph hatches from the egg, resembling the adult, but smaller. The nymph has no wings or developed reproductive

Table 32-1 COMMON INSECT ORDERS WITH INCOMPLETE METAMORPHOSIS

ORDER	MOUTHPARTS IN ADULT	ECONOMIC SIGNIFICANCE	EXAMPLES
1. Thysanura ("bristle-tail") 700*	chewing	pests, feeding on starch in bindings & labels of books, clothing, paste in wallpaper	bristletails, silverfish, firebrats
2. Ephemeroptera ("for-a-day—wing") 1,500	adults do not feed	food for many fresh-water fish	mayflies
3. Odonata ("toothed") 4,870	chewing	destroy harmful insects	dragonflies, damselflies
4. Orthoptera ("straight-wing") 22,500	chewing	damage crops, act as pests	grasshoppers, crickets, katydids, locusts, cock-roaches
5. Isoptera ("equal-winged") 1,720	chewing	destroy wood in forests & buildings	termites
6. Dermaptera ("skin-winged") 1,100	chewing	damage crops and garden plants	earwigs
7. Mallophaga ("wool-eater") 2,680	chewing	most are parasitic on birds pests on poultry	chewing lice
8. Anoplura ("unarmed-tail") 250	sucking	parasitic on mammals parasitic on man transmit disease as typhus	sucking lice
9. Hemiptera ("half-winged") 23,000	sucking	damage plants, act as pests, carry disease	squash bugs, all true bugs
10. Homoptera ("like-winged") 32,000	sucking	damage crops and gardens	aphids, mealy bugs, cicada

* Numbers indicate estimated number of species known.

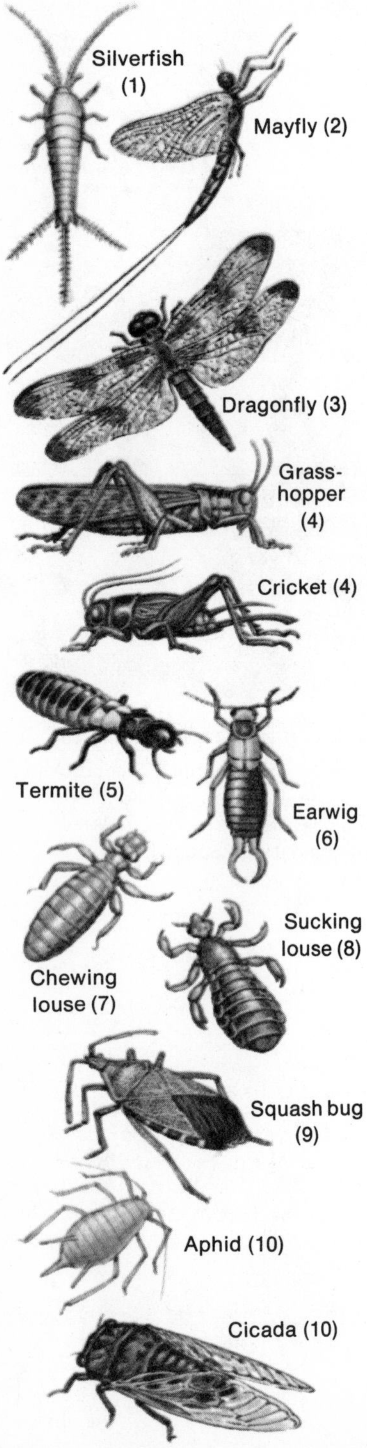

Silverfish (1)

Mayfly (2)

Dragonfly (3)

Grass-hopper (4)

Cricket (4)

Termite (5)

Earwig (6)

Chewing louse (7)

Sucking louse (8)

Squash bug (9)

Aphid (10)

Cicada (10)

32–11 Common insect orders with incomplete metamorphosis.

Table 32-2 COMMON INSECT ORDERS WITH COMPLETE METAMORPHOSIS

ORDER	MOUTHPARTS IN ADULT	ECONOMIC SIGNIFICANCE	EXAMPLES
11. Neuroptera ("nerve-winged") 4,670	chewing	destroy harmful insects	dobsonfly, lacewing
12. Coleoptera ("sheath-winged") 276,700	sucking or chewing	destroy crops, act as pests, prey on other insects	weevils, ladybugs, ground beetles
13. Lepidoptera ("scale-winged") 112,000	siphoning	pollinate flowers, produce silk damage clothing and crops	butterflies, moths
14. Diptera ("two-winged") 85,000	sucking, piercing or lapping	carry disease, act as pests	flies, mosquitoes, gnats
15. Siphonaptera ("tube-wingless") 1,100	sucking	pests, feed on blood of birds & mammals, transmit disease as bubonic plague	fleas
16. Hymenoptera ("membrane-winged") 103,000	chewing, sucking, or lapping	pollinate flowers, act as pests, parasitize other pests, make honey	bees, wasps, ants

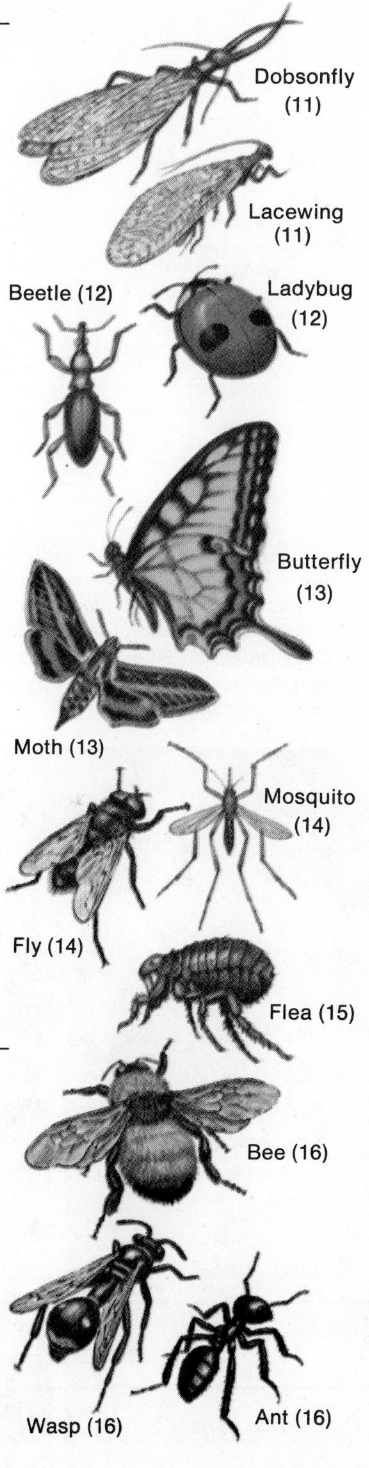

Dobsonfly (11)
Lacewing (11)
Beetle (12)
Ladybug (12)
Butterfly (13)
Moth (13)
Mosquito (14)
Fly (14)
Flea (15)
Bee (16)
Wasp (16)
Ant (16)

32–12 Common insect orders with complete metamorphosis.

organs. Most species molt five times in the nymph stage. Each time it becomes more like the adult.

Insects that go through **complete metamorphosis** include butterflies, moths, flies, and beetles. Each goes through four stages of development: *egg, larva, pupa,* and *adult.* The eggs hatch segmented larvae that look like worms. Different types of insects are called different names at this stage: they may be called caterpillars, grubs, or maggots. Larvae eat much and grow very fast for a while. Then they enter the pupal stage. The pupa are covered with a shell or case. From the outside, the pupa appears to be in a resting period. But inside the case, there is much happening. The tissues of the larva are changed into the tissues of the adult. When the shell opens again, out comes the butterfly or beetle. The change from caterpillar to butterfly or grub to beetle is a truly marvelous event in nature.

Recently, biologists have been looking at the role of hormones in insect metamorphosis. **Hormones are chemicals secreted into the blood by a gland or organ in the body.** Hormones are carried to other parts of the body, where they control chemical reactions. When scientists studied the *Cecropia* moth, they found that hormones controlled metamorphosis. Many insects which go through complete metamorphosis have their pupal stage during the winter. This is a favorable adaptation because winter conditions are not good for active insects. Perhaps the cool temperatures affect the production of a brain hormone. This hormone stimulates a gland in the prothorax to produce a second hormone. The second hormone brings about the changes from pupa to adult moth.

In experiments with *Cecropia*, the brains of the pupae were removed. Such insects never went through metamorphosis to become adult moths. But when a brain from a chilled pupa was planted in a

32–13 Complete metamorphosis. Notice that the newly hatched young of the *Cecropia* moth do not look anything like the adult. Can you think of any survival value in having two such distinct forms? (Herbert Weihrich)

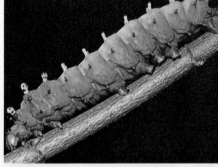

Table 32-3 NAMES OF INSECT LARVAE

THE LARVA OF THE		IS CALLED	
	beetle		grub
	fly		maggot
	mosquito		wiggler
	butterfly		caterpillar
	moth		caterpillar

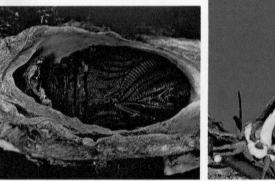

32–14 Two of the many experiments performed by Dr. Carroll Williams on metamorphosis in the *Cecropia* moth. A larva (left) is tied between the thorax and the abdomen. The anterior part continues to develop but the posterior does not. Similar results occur when a pupa is cut in two (right). Two interdependent hormone centers that control metamorphosis were pinpointed.

pupa whose brain had been removed, metamorphosis did occur. In another experiment, a pupa was cut in half, and the ends were sealed. The anterior half, where the brain was, developed into an adult. The posterior end did not. Can you locate the hormone-producing organ?

Winter brings about the formation of pupae. But a single unusual cold spell will not cause a young caterpillar to turn into a pupa. The biologists working with the *Cecropia* moth asked why. They found that when they removed a paired structure from behind the caterpillar's brain, the larva *would* form a pupa. Temperature did not seem to affect this process. It was decided that the paired structure produces a hormone in the larva. The hormone slows down or prevents metamorphosis. They called it a *juvenile hormone*, since it operates in the larval stage of the insect's development.

Encourage students to find and bring in different stages in the life cycles of certain insects. Eggs and cocoons are often easy to locate and are interesting to study in class.

ADAPTIVE VALUE OF COMPLETE METAMORPHOSIS

The process of complete metamorphosis is of value to species survival. A good example of this is the butterflies, or Lepidoptera. The sexes are separate. After mating, eggs are placed on or near material that will be food for the larva. Some eggs pass the winter in this stage. Normally, eggs are laid in the spring and developed into **caterpillars** the following summer.

Caterpillars have three pairs of jointed legs and several pairs of fleshy legs. They greedily devour plants, get large and fat, and molt several times. Since caterpillars need large amounts of food to grow so fast, they can do much damage to plants during this time.

When a caterpillar has grown large, it looks for a sheltered spot. Then it hangs with its head down, and becomes very quiet. Its body gets shorter and thicker. The exoskeleton splits down the back and falls off. Now the insect has become a pupa. While the butterfly pupa rests in a hardened brownish case, it is called a **chrysalis.** Moth larvae usually spin a strong case of silk called a **cocoon.**

Lepidoptera normally spend the winter in the pupal stage. The next spring the adult comes out as a butterfly or moth.

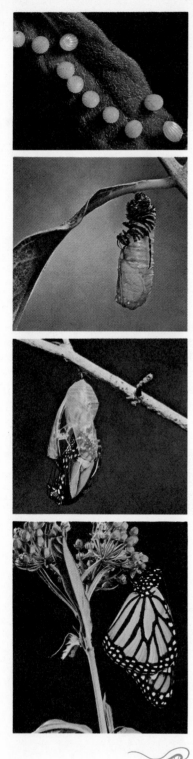

32–15 Life cycle of the Monarch butterfly. Can you name the stages shown? (*Left,* W. Clifford Healy, National Audubon Society; *right,* courtesy American Museum of Natural History)

During their life history, the Lepidoptera have two very different sets of mouth parts. Thus the larvae and the adults have completely different diets. The larvae feed on leaves, while the adults suck nectar from flowers. This means the insect has a varied diet in its lifetime. It also means there is good food supply during the time of most rapid growth. The adult serves to reproduce and disperse the species. **There is no competition for food between the young and the adult.**

Insect Behavior

ANOTHER SURVIVAL FACTOR

The success of insects is also due to their complex behavior. Such complex behavior is possible because of the development of (1) *complex sense organs,* (2) *jointed appendages,* and (3) a *brain.* The sense organs are stimulated both by the immediate environment and from a distance. These stimuli help insects escape from enemies, find food, find a mate, and find a good place for the eggs to develop. The brain is complex enough for the insects to organize information from the sense organs. They are also able to use this information to coordinate muscular responses.

Insects also communicate with each other. One interesting means of insect communication involves the secretion of hormones. We have already seen how internal hormones affect metamorphosis. But some hormones are secreted outside the body. One group of these is called *pheromones.* **Pheromones are substances that act as a chemical language between animals of the same species.**

The female gypsy moth secretes a pheromone that the male can detect with its antennae. This attracts the male to the female during mating time. Entomologists use this pheromone as bait to capture male gypsy moths. In this way, it is hoped that the gypsy moth population can be controlled.

Have you ever seen ants traveling in line along the ground? Each one follows the exact same path. These ants are following a pheromone trail laid down by the lead ants.

Pheromones are also secreted by mammals. Much study of pheromones is being done to discover new uses for these exciting chemicals.

With the development of these systems, insects can do complex, coordinated acts. They are able to change their environment by building many kinds of homes or nests. For instance, the paper wasp builds nests of chewed wood pulp. The mud dauber builds a home from mud. A large wasp called the tarantula hawk digs a burrow to store paralyzed insects as food for their larvae. Some ants construct special passages to store grain. The fungus ant builds underground gardens where it grows a certain species of fungus.

INSECT SOCIETIES

Many insects develop societies. Differences in body structure within the species allow for division of labor. Some of the insects are adapted for gathering food, some for protecting the home, some for tending the young, and some for reproduction. *Social insects* include the bees, ants, wasps, and termites. These insects do not reason, though. They do have specialized structures that are used in behavior patterns that is not taught to them. In other words, they carry out their jobs by *instinct*. As you can imagine, studies of animal behavior make very interesting research.

Students may be interested in finding out that different types of honey are produced depending on the type of flowers visited by the bees.

THE HONEYBEE, A SOCIAL INSECT

If you compare the honeybee to an airplane, you might think that the bee's wings are too small to lift its comparatively big body. But the bee has very powerful muscles in its large thorax. These muscles make the wings move so fast that the bee can actually fly with speed and endurance. The speed of these wings produces the familiar hum.

THE QUEEN BEE—MOTHER OF THE COLONY

Bees, wasps, and ants are all examples of Hymenoptera. You can notice division of labor and individual variation more clearly in this order than just about anywhere else in the animal kingdom. Variation has brought about three distinct variations: the queen, the drone, and the worker. The **queen bee** is nearly twice as large

32–16 Three distinct forms of bees: the large drone, the long slender queen, and the smaller worker.

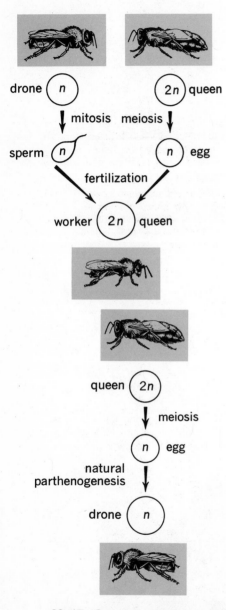

drone n $2n$ queen

↓ mitosis   meiosis ↓

sperm n n egg

fertilization

worker $2n$ queen

queen $2n$

↓ meiosis

n egg

natural
parthenogenesis ↓

drone n

32–17 Sex determination in the honey bee. Note that the drones are haploid because they develop from unfertilized eggs. In contrast, the workers and queen are diploid because they develop from fertilized eggs.

as a worker. She develops from special treatment of a fertilized egg. First, workers enlarge a wax cell where the egg is going to grow. When the grublike larva hatches, it is fed with extra helpings of *royal jelly*. This is a special high-protein food that the workers secrete. After five days, the larva becomes a pupa. Then the workers seal it into a large wax chamber. At the correct time, the old queen leaves the hive with a swarm of about half the population. She and her swarm will form a new colony, thus preventing overcrowding. After the old queen has left, the new queen emerges from her chamber.

A few days later, the young queen takes off on a special flight. During this flight, she mates with a *drone* (male bee). The queen receives several million sperms, which will fertilize all of the eggs she lays for the remaining three to five years of her life. When the queen returns to the hive, she begins laying eggs. She may lay as many as one million a year. This is her lifework. Although she is called a queen, she does not rule the hive. Instead she is its common mother.

THE DRONE, OR MALE BEE

Some of the eggs the queen lays are not fertilized. These haploid eggs develop into the males, or **drones.** The male bees are larger than the workers but smaller than the queen. They have broad, thick bodies, large eyes, and very powerful wings. Their tongues are not long enough to drink flower nectar, so they have to be fed by the workers. During the summer, a few hundred drones are tolerated in the colony. After all, one of them must function as a mate for the new queen. The rest, however, are of no use to the hive. But this easy life has a price. When autumn comes, the honey runs low. The workers will no longer support the drones. The workers starve them or sting them to death. The drones' bodies can often be found around hives in early autumn.

THE WORKER BEE

The **worker bees** form the largest part of the hive population. They are undeveloped females, smaller than drones. Their ovipositor is modified into a sting. This is a complicated organ. Two barbed darts, and strong muscles to operate them, are enclosed in a sheath. The darts are connected to a gland that secretes the painful poison delivered by the sting.

The workers carry on all the work of the hive except reproduction. They feed and care for the queen and drones. They nurse the hungry young larvae by feeding them partly digested food from their own stomachs. The workers also clear dead bees and foreign matter out of the hive. If necessary, they fan their wings to bring fresh air into the hive. Thousands of workers are constantly bringing in nectar and pollen for the use of the colony. Workers born

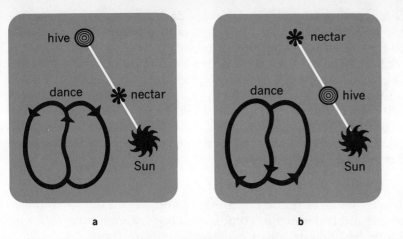

a   b   c

early in the season often work themselves to death in three or four weeks. But bees hatched in the fall may live for six months.

Worker bees are specialized in many ways for their tasks. Their mouthparts make efficient tongues for lapping up nectar. The workers last four abdominal segments have glands that secrete the wax for making the comb. Their legs have many kinds of special structures. These include an antenna cleaner, pollen packer, pollen basket, and pollen comb.

CONSTRUCTION AND PRODUCTS OF THE HIVE

The wax comb is built in six-sided cells arranged in two layers. There is no wasted space. It has the greatest amount of storage capacity for the least amount of building materials. Honey is stored in most of the comb's cells. But there is one special section, called the *brood comb*. It is here that the queen lays one egg in each cell.

The bee makes honey from the nectar that goes straight into its *crop*. There, the sugars are changed into an easily digested form. Then the bee puts them into the comb cells. The honey is left to thicken by evaporation before the cell is sealed. It does not harm the bees if people take away some of their honey, as long as there is enough for the bees to use through the winter. About 15 kilograms of honey will feed an average hive of 40,000 bees for an ordinary winter.

THE BEES' LANGUAGE

Bees seem to communicate with each other by means of a complicated set of dances. When workers return to the hive, they can tell the other bees about the nectar they have found. What kind it is, how much there is, how far away and in which direction to find it. A bee communicates this information by dancing on the vertical side of the comb. It dances in circles, going straight through the diameter of the circle every time around. The direction the bee takes on this cross-circle run shows where the honey is in relation to the sun.

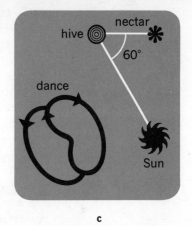

32–18 a. The dancing bee makes the diameter of the "tail-waggling dance" upward on the vertical surface of the comb. This shows the bees that a source of nectar is located in a direction toward the sun. b. This dance shows that the nectar is located in a direction away from the sun. c. What message does this dance indicate?

The person most responsible for our knowledge of bee communication is Karl von Frisch, a German zoologist. The studies of von Frisch are a model of accurate scientific observation. Students may be interested in reading more about his well-known studies.

The most interesting thing about this dancing is that the bee translates the angle between the direction of the sun and the food source into a vertical angle on the side of the comb.

The other bees watch the discoverer to find out where the food source is. They can tell how far the food is by the number of times the worker waggles its body on the way across the circle. The bees smell the kind of nectar. The more vigorous the dance, the more nectar there is.

This complex behavior allows for a coordinated society and increases the chances for species survival.

SUMMARY

Insects are by far the most numerous group of animals on the earth today. They have survived and flourished by combining a high reproductive rate with thousands of individual adaptations to different environments.

The bodies of insects have developed through variation and adaptation over millions of years. Some insect body features include the exoskeleton, coloration, small size, wings, nervous system, and sense organs. Many insects go through complete metamorphosis. This provides them with two kinds of diets and needs throughout a single lifetime. Some social insects like bees, ants, and wasps, have adapted to form efficient colonies. This is achieved by division of labor among the population. Different members of the colony work together to build the home, provide the food, raise the young, and reproduce.

Insects can have great economic impact on humans. The lives of insects are interdependent on crops and other animals.

BIOLOGICALLY SPEAKING

entomology	esophagus	incomplete metamorphosis
labrum	crop	complete metamorphosis
mandible	gizzard	caterpillar
maxilla	Malpighian tubule	chrysalis
labium	aorta	cocoon
prothorax	tympanum	pheromones
mesothorax	simple eye	social insect
metathorax	compound eye	queen bee
spiracle	optic lobe	drone
tracheae	ovipositor	worker bee
salivary glands		

QUESTIONS FOR REVIEW

1. Support the statement: Insects have evolved into a successful group.
2. Why do biologists believe insects were able to evolve with such diversity?
3. What is an insect?
4. What features separate the insect orders?
5. Of what benefit to the insect is the chitinous exoskeleton?
6. What features of the grasshopper make it similar to the crayfish?
7. What is the chief difference between the respiratory system of the grasshopper and that of the human?
8. What protection is given the eggs of the grasshopper during winter?

9. What are pheromones? How are pheromones used by social insects?
10. Of what survival value is metamorphosis?
11. What advantage do the social insects have over the solitary forms?
12. Name the different types of bees and describe the functions of each in the hive.
13. Do bees communicate with one another in the hive? Explain.

APPLYING PRINCIPLES AND CONCEPTS

1. What reasons can you give for the ability of insects to withstand unusual temperatures, pressures, and other extreme environmental conditions?
2. What theories explain why an insect might resemble a thorn on a bush or why a fly might look like a bee?
3. Can a little fly grow to be a larger fly? Explain.
4. What possible mechanisms account for the change in the amount of juvenile hormone that a *Cecropia* larva may produce? As a biologist studying the hormone balance in metamorphosis, how might you test your hypotheses?
5. What additional experiments might be performed to increase our understanding of communication among the bees?
6. How might pheromones be useful to farmers?

RELATED READINGS

Books

Buchsbaum, Ralph, and Lorus J. Milne, *The Lower Animals: Living Invertebrates of the World.*
  Doubleday and Company, Inc., Garden City, New York. 1960. A complete discussion of each animal, with accompanying photographs.

Callahan, Phillip, *Insect Behavior.*
  Four Winds Press, New York. 1970. A highly readable account of many aspects of insect behavior with a special section on possible projects and experiments.

Callahan, Phillip, *The Evolution of Insects.*
  Holiday House, New York. 1972. A readable account of insect evolution. The book is illustrated with excellent charts, diagrams, and black-and-white photographs.

Croll, W. A., *Ecology of Parasites.*
  Harvard University Press, Cambridge, Mass., 1966. The life history and economic importance of each parasite, discussed in general terms.

Farb, Peter, and the Editors of *Life Magazine, The Insects.*
  Time-Life Books (Time, Inc.), New York. 1962. A beautifully colored picture-essay type book that effectively highlights the natural history of a wide range of insects.

Gardiner, Mary S., *Biology of the Invertebrates.*
  McGraw-Hill Book Co., New York. 1972. An excellent reference for concepts in anatomy and physiology as seen in the invertebrates.

Jenkins, Marie M., *The Curious Mollusks.*
  Holiday House, New York. 1972. This volume describes the morphology, life habits, use by man, contributions to the study of neurophysiology, and the embryologic diversity of the mollusks.

Mason, Herbert M., *The Fantastic World of Ants.*
  David McKay Co., Inc., New York, N.Y. 1974. A very readable account of the ant world.

Newman, L. H., *Man and Insects.*
  Doubleday and Company, Inc., Garden City, New York. 1967. A basic book of entomology that points out man's urgent need to learn the insects' role in ecology, and stresses their role in the scheme of things.

Schisgall, Oscar, *That Remarkable Creature, The Snail.*
  Julian Messner, New York. 1970. An easy-to-read, straightforward introduction to freshwater, saltwater, and land snails.

Snow, Keith R., *The Arachnids.*
  Columbia University Press, New York. 1970. An introductory text dealing with the spiders and their relatives. This book makes a valuable reference for students interested in this arthropod type.

Articles

Cooke, John A. L., "Unveiling the Black Widow." *Natural History*, February, 1973. A very interesting article on the biology of the black widow spider.

Esch, Harold, "The Evolution of Bee Language." *Scientific American*, April 1967. An interesting presentation on the development of a complicated system of communication among bees.

Gilbert, Voss L., "Shy Monster, The Octopus." *National Geographic*, December, 1971. Discusses the natural history of the octopus, with many interesting photographs.

Herrnkind, William F., "Strange March of the Spiny Lobster." *National Geographic*, June, 1975. This article deals with the migratory habits of the spiny lobster.

Holldobler, Bert, "Communication Between Ants and Their Guests." *Scientific American*, March, 1971. A fascinating account of the ants exceptional ability to communicate and give signals.

Wellington, William G., "Tents and Tactics of Caterpillars." *Natural History*, January, 1974. This article describes the unique behavior of tent caterpillars.

unit

BIOLOGY
OF THE
VERTEBRATES

This unit introduces the most advanced of all animals—the vertebrates. All vertebrates have a spinal column made up of bones called vertebrae. Inside the spinal column is the nerve cord. This cord is joined to a highly developed brain. This system makes it possible for the vertebrate to respond to stimuli in a very effective way for its own survival. This superior nervous system is the real key to the biological supremacy of the vertebrates.

INVERTEBRATE DEVELOPMENT—A QUICK REVIEW

In our study of Unit 5, we saw several body plans for invertebrate animals. In the protozoans, for instance, the specialization of a single cell is carried to the limit. Consider the paramecium, for example. It has specialized cilia and trichocysts, a gullet and contractile vacuoles. The paramecium is an amazing single-celled organism. But it takes many cells to make a complex animal.

The sponges and coelenterates are made of large colonies of cells. In the endoderm and ectoderm of these animals, you can see the beginnings of tissue. Flatworms and roundworms have several very efficient organs. These organs function in digestion, reproduction, excretion, and response. Segmented worms have even more developed systems. They have a tubular digestive tract and an elongated and segmented body. These worms even have a well-developed circulatory system with closed vessels.

Mollusks and clams have changed very little in many millions of years. They have the best possible protection for soft-bodied animals. Their shells are both a fort and a prison.

Arthropods have exoskeletons which combine protection with free movement. But an exoskeleton would be too heavy on a big animal. Thus, the size of arthropods is limited. Still, they are important because of their great numbers.

CHORDATES—THE MOST COMPLEX FORM OF ANIMAL LIFE

The phylum *Chordata* contains the most complex animals that have ever lived on this earth. This phylum has four subphyla. The largest and most important subphylum is the *Vertebrata*. This subphylum includes fish, amphibians, reptiles, birds, and mammals.

Three factors make chordates different from all other animals.

■ **All chordate embryos have a rod of connective tissue along the length of the dorsal side of their bodies. This rod is called a *notochord.*** Primitive chordates have a notochord their entire lives. So do some lower vertebrates, such as the lamprey. But the notochord of the lamprey becomes surrounded by cartilage parts of the spinal column. In other vertebrates, the notochord appears only in the embryo. But early in life, it changes into the *vertebral column,* or backbone.

■ **All chordates have a tubular *nerve cord.*** It lies just above the notochord on the dorsal side. The anterior end of this nerve cord develops into a brain. The remaining part becomes the spinal cord. Together, the brain and the spinal cord make up the *central nervous system.*

■ **All chordates have paired *gill slits* at some time in their lives.** These gill slits form openings in the throat. Fish and the more primitive vertebrates have gill slits throughout life. The higher vertebrates, including reptiles, birds, and mammals, lose their gill slits very early in life.

chapter thirty-three

Introduction to the Vertebrates

OBJECTIVES
● LIST the chordate characteristics.
● NAME the classes of vertebrates.
● NAME animals in the various vertebrate classes.
● LIST the structural characteristics of vertebrates.
● NAME the specialized systems found in the vertebrates.
● LIST and DEFINE the types of highly developed behavior of vertebrates.

Before beginning this chapter, it might be interesting to elicit from students some of the characteristics of vertebrates. Many students may be unaware of the most common vertebrate characteristics.

Of the four chordate subphyla, we are familiar with the vertebrates. The other three subphyla are known more by biologists. These primitive chordates are all marine animals. Biologists find them interesting because they can give us an idea of what the ancestors of present-day vertebrates may have been like.

Let's look at those three chordate subphyla briefly. One subphylum is called Hemichordata. It contains two classes of wormlike animal creatures. The best known are the acorn or tongue worms. The subphylum Urochordata include the tunicates or sea squirts. The third chordate subphylum is Cephalochordata. It includes one of the best known lower chordates. This is the lancelet, or *Amphioxus*. About 5 centimeters long, this marine chordate lives in tropical and temperate coastal waters. It is often used as an example of an animal that retains the chordate characteristics throughout life.

THE RISE OF VERTEBRATES

Vertebrates are animals with backbones. When did the earliest vertebrates appear on the earth? What chordate ancestors did they develop from? There is no direct fossil evidence to answer these questions. This lack of fossil evidence may give us a small clue. This leads scientists to believe that vertebrates may have evolved from soft-bodied chordates. Soft bodies would decompose without leaving an impression in rocks. The very first vertebrates probably lived some half billion years ago, during the Ordovician period. This seems likely because many vertebrate fossils were formed during the Silurian and Devonian periods that followed.

Fossil records suggest that many vertebrate forms appeared and then disappeared during their early history. Probably only about one percent of the vertebrates alive in the Jurassic period have living descendants today. Paleontologists believe there has been a great turnover in the kinds of animals that have lived on earth.

CLASSES OF VERTEBRATES

33–1 *Amphioxus* keeps its dorsal nerve cord, notochord, and gill slits throughout its life. The notochord and gill slits disappear early in the development of higher chordates.

There are seven classes of modern vertebrates. They are listed below in order of complexity. This may also have been the order in which they evolved.

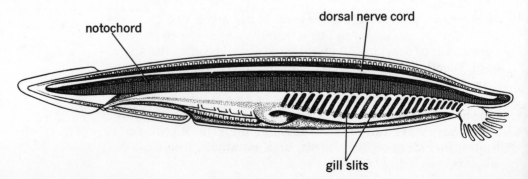

notochord

dorsal nerve cord

gill slits

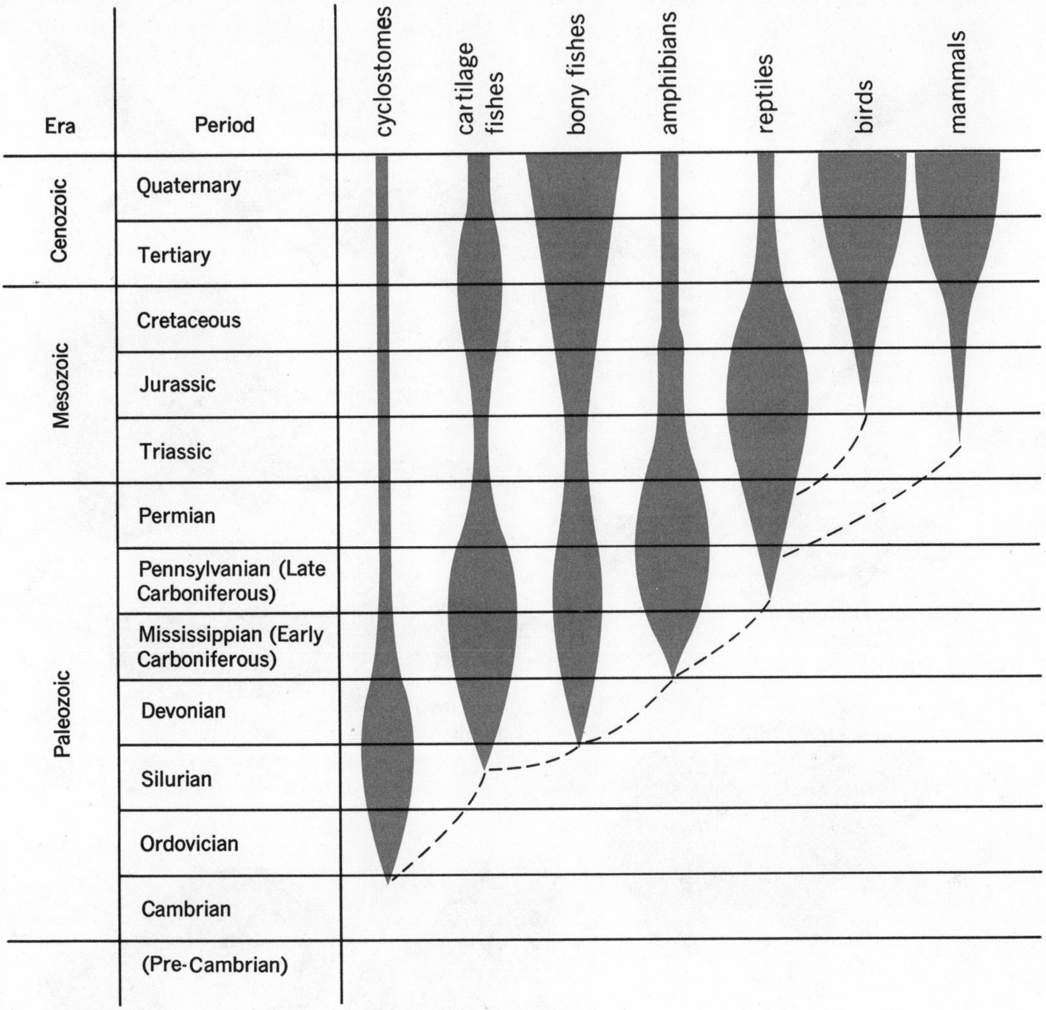

The chart shows a time scale of classes of vertebrate animals, with Era and Period on the left axis and vertebrate classes across the top.

Era	Period	cyclostomes	cartilage fishes	bony fishes	amphibians	reptiles	birds	mammals
Cenozoic	Quaternary							
	Tertiary							
Mesozoic	Cretaceous							
	Jurassic							
	Triassic							
Paleozoic	Permian							
	Pennsylvanian (Late Carboniferous)							
	Mississippian (Early Carboniferous)							
	Devonian							
	Silurian							
	Ordovician							
	Cambrian							
	(Pre-Cambrian)							

33–2 A time scale of classes of vertebrate animals.

- *Cyclostomata* (sy-kloe-STOME-uh-tuh), jawless fish, including lampreys and hagfishes.
- *Chondrichthyes* (kon-DRICKTH-ee-eez), sharks, rays, and skates.
- *Osteichthyes* (oss-tee-ICKTH-ee-eez), bony fish.
- *Amphibia* (am-FIB-ee-uh), frogs, toads, and salamanders.
- *Reptilia* (rep-TILL-yuh), snakes, lizards, turtles, and crocodilians.
- *Aves* (AH-veez), birds.
- *Mammalia* (muh-MALE-yuh), mammals.

You will study these vertebrate classes in the chapters that follow. As you do, you will notice something interesting. There is a change from animals that live in the water to those that live on land. This may have been the direction in the evolution of the vertebrates. You will also notice a movement toward more complex and efficient body organs. Finally, you will see that vertebrates can live successfully in all environments—land, water, and air.

Discuss the high degree of specialization in vertebrates as illustrated by their numerous systems. Discuss the advantages of having such specialized systems.

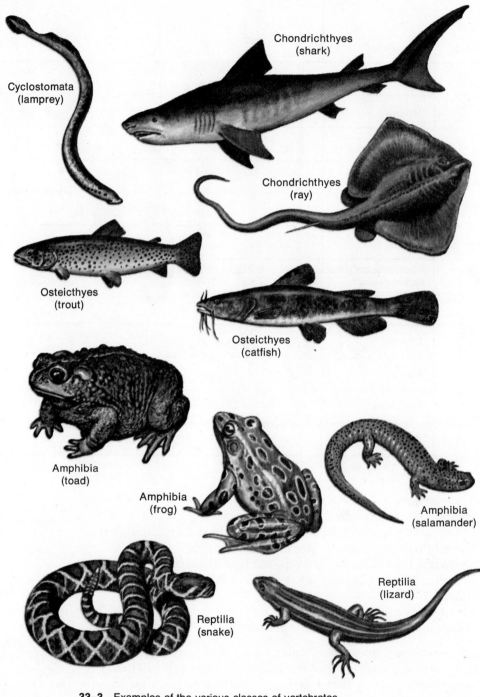

33–3 Examples of the various classes of vertebrates.

Reptilia
(alligator)

Reptilia
(turtle)

Aves
(cardinal)

Aves
(goose)

Mammalia
(horse)

Mammalia
(deer)

Mammalia
(seal)

Mammalia
(chipmunk)

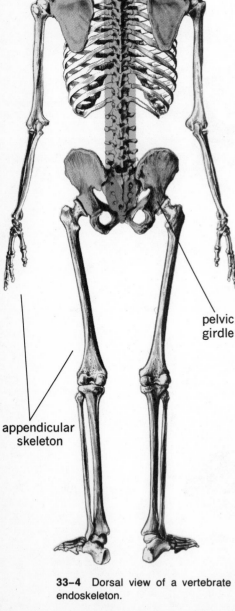

axial skeleton
(including
vertebrae)

pectoral
girdle

pelvic
girdle

appendicular
skeleton

33–4 Dorsal view of a vertebrate endoskeleton.

CHARACTERISTICS OF VERTEBRATES

Vertebrates have many unique characteristics that make them different from other animals. Vertebrates have an **endoskeleton** (internal framework). It is made up of *bone* and/or *cartilage*. And it consists of:

1. A vertebral column, or spine. This is composed of cartilage or bony parts called **vertebrae.** This backbone, along with the skull, forms the *axial skeleton.*
2. In most vertebrates, two girdles. An anterior *pectoral girdle* and a posterior *pelvic girdle* are suspended from the spinal column.
3. Limbs attached to the pectoral and pelvic girdles. They may be in the form of fins, legs, wings, or flippers. There are never more than two pairs. These form the *appendicular skeleton.*

Vertebrates have a body made up of a head and trunk. Many also have bodies with neck and tail regions. All vertebrates have an efficient closed circulatory system. This includes a ventral heart in the anterior part of the body. Their blood is partly composed of red corpuscles containing hemoglobin.

In most vertebrates, there are twelve pairs of cranial nerves that extend from the brain, as well as spinal nerves that extend from the spinal cord. They also have eyes, ears, and nostrils on the head. Vertebrates have a food tube, or alimentary canal. This tube is elongated and looped or coiled in the body. A liver and pancreas are also present.

THE SPECIALIZED SYSTEMS OF VERTEBRATE BODIES

There are several vertebrate systems. These systems have many highly developed organs. They are listed below:

- *Integumentary system*—the outer body covering and special protective outgrowths. These include scales, feathers, and hairs.
- *Muscular system*—the muscles attached to bones for body movement and the muscles forming the walls of the heart, the digestive organs, and the blood vessels.
- *Skeletal system*—the bones and cartilage that make up the body framework.
- *Digestive system*—the many specialized organs that prepare food to be used by body tissues.
- *Respiratory system*—gills or lungs and related structures used in exchanging gases between the animal and its environment.
- *Circulatory system*—the transportation system of the body. It includes the heart and blood vessels.
- *Excretory system*—organs that remove wastes from the body.
- *Endocrine system*—the glands that produce and secrete chemicals needed by other systems.
- *Nervous system*—the brain, spinal cord, nerves, and special sense organs. This is a vertebrate's most highly developed system.
- *Reproductive system*—the male or female organs of reproduction.

The skeleton shows an interesting development in the vertebrate classes. Some vertebrates have cartilage skeletons during their entire lives. These include lampreys, sharks, and rays. The fishes, amphibians, reptiles, birds, and mammals start out with a cartilage framework, too. But when these animals are still young, bone cells replace most of their cartilage. Mineral deposits in the bones make them hard and strong.

Pages 505-508 may be previewed here in order to discuss the development of vertebrate hearts and brains.

As mentioned before, vertebrate classes also show a change from life in water to life on land. Lampreys, sharks, rays, and bony fishes adapted to live in water. Their limbs take the form of fins. Their gills can absorb dissolved oxygen from the water. Water flows over the gills through gill slits in the throat. Amphibians, as you will see, represent a transition from water life to land life. During the tadpole stage, a frog is like a fish with gills and a fin. As an adult, the frog can move on land and breathe the air.

The vertebrate heart and brain are more developed than those of invertebrates. Fish hearts have two chambers. One receives blood from the body. The other pumps blood to the gills. Frogs have a three-chambered heart. They also have a more complex circulatory system. Birds and mammals have even more complex hearts with four chambers. One side of the heart receives blood from the lungs and pumps it to the body. The other side receives blood from the body and pumps it to the lungs. This type of heart is a kind of double pump. The human heart is this type of double pump.

The vertebrate brain is also highly developed. It is enclosed in a skull, or cranium. One brain region is called the **cerebrum.** The cerebrum is the center of instinct, emotion, memory, and intelligence. The more developed the vertebrate, the larger the relative size of this area of the brain. **The mammal brain has the biggest cerebrum in proportion to its body.**

THE COMPLEX BEHAVIOR OF VERTEBRATES

Behavior is the way in which an organism responds to stimuli. The vertebrates' complex behavior depends on highly developed sense organs, nerve pathways, and organs specialized for nervous control. Protists and plants, on the other hand, do not have specialized nervous tissues. Their responses are limited to simple tropisms. The nerve net of the hydra allows it to behave as a unit. Higher invertebrates have a more coordinated behavior due to their nerve cords, ganglia, and sense organs. These highly developed organs are the basis for the vertebrates' complex behavior.

In discussing animal behavior, you may want to introduce Pavlov's classic studies of conditioning. Discuss the question of human instincts.

Vertebrate behavior is often broken down into two different types. One type of behavior is *inborn.* The other type is *learned*.

Inborn behavior is called **innate behavior.** Since it is inherited, it is thought to be controlled by genes. **Reflexes** are simple innate responses. A reflex is an automatic response to a stimulus. For instance, touching the surface of the eye or eyelid will cause blinking.

Reflexes are involuntary. This means that the animal reacts to the stimulus without conscious control. Such responses usually protect the organism from harm. Humans respond by reflex to many stimuli.

Instincts are the most interesting innate responses. They are also the least understood. Instincts are often very complex. Yet they are unlearned and involuntary. **Animals act instinctively without any deliberate decision.**

Self-preservation is a very basic instinct. It can be seen in all vertebrates and many invertebrates. In times of danger, an animal will respond to the "fight-or-flight" instinct. Have you ever cornered an animal that would normally flee? A squirrel can become vicious when cornered. It will bite and claw if it cannot escape from an enemy. In such a situation, a squirrel might defend itself against a human.

A mammal's suckling instinct is another example of innate behavior related to self-preservation. The instinct to nurse is very strong during the early period of life. Baby birds show a self-preservation instinct when they peck their way through the shell at hatching time.

Scientists classify another instinct as *species preservation.* **Species preservation directs animal reproduction and the care of young.** This is what drives the Pacific salmon up the streams of the Northwest to their spawning beds. After they reproduce, the adult salmon die.

33–5 Examples of three types of behavior that are highly developed in vertebrate animals: self-preservation, species preservation, and conditioned reaction. (R. D. Estes, Photo Researchers; Walter Dawn; Ringling Brothers, Barnum and Bailey Circus)

But a new generation comes downstream to the ocean. This instinct causes the sunfish to defend its nest when it would normally flee. In responding to an instinct, an animal behaves automatically without making a choice.

Vertebrates are capable of learned behavior as well as innate behavior. This is due to their well-developed nervous systems. Learned behavior can be changed. A common form of learned behavior is called a *conditioned reaction.* **A conditioned reaction occurs when a specific behavior response always follows a particular stimulus.** If the results are pleasurable, or at least healthy, the animal will keep on responding to that same stimulus in the same way. When humans condition animals to behave in certain ways, they do it by giving rewards or punishments for certain responses. As these continue, the desired response becomes a habit to the animal. Eventually, the animal is conditioned. This is how a dog learns to sit down or roll over at a given command. Even fishes in an aquarium can be conditioned to go to one certain corner of the tank when you approach. Just be sure to always feed them in that corner.

You can see instincts in all vertebrates. Most vertebrates are even capable of some sort of conditioned behavior. But *intelligent behavior* is a more complex nervous activity. This sort of behavior involves problem-solving, judgment, and decision. Birds and mammals have a limited degree of intelligent behavior. Human beings, however, are supreme among the vertebrates in intelligence. We are unique among living things in our ability to communicate by symbols in both speaking and writing.

Discuss with students whether or not their pets show intelligent behavior. Most forms of animal behavior are conditioned rather than intelligent.

SUMMARY

With an understanding of the general characteristics of vertebrates, their systems and lines of development, you are ready to study the vertebrate classes. You will study the least developed to the most developed living vertebrates. You will notice an increase in efficiency in the heart, respiratory organs, reproductive organs, and brain.

This progression has another interesting feature. Fossil evidence seems to show that vertebrates evolved in this order.

BIOLOGICALLY SPEAKING

chordate	vertebrae	self-preservation
notochord	cerebrum	species preservation
nerve cord	innate behavior	conditioned reaction
gill slits	reflex	intelligent behavior
endoskeleton	instinct	

1. What are the three unique characteristics of chordates?
2. Why is Amphioxus considered a chordate?
3. Account for the lack of fossil evidence of vertebrate ancestry.
4. Name the seven classes of vertebrates in the order of their structural complexity.
5. Name ten organ systems composing the vertebrate body.
6. Explain why increase in the size of the cerebrum is an important evolutionary advancement.
7. What is meant by "innate behavior"? Give examples.
8. In what ways are reflex actions important in the lives of animals?
9. Give an example of (a) a conditioned reaction in a vertebrate and (b) an intelligent act.

**APPLYING
PRINCIPLES
AND CONCEPTS**

1. Discuss several structural characteristics that contribute to the success of the vertebrates.
2. Self-preservation and species preservation are instincts. Which is stronger? Given an example to support your answer.
3. Why are instinct and intelligence more vital to the survival of a vertebrate than to an invertebrate such as a clam, starfish, insect, or crayfish?

34–1 Many fish inhabit coral reefs (Wards Natural Science Establishment)

The Fishes

OBJECTIVES
- EXPLAIN the biological importance of the lamprey.
- LIST the characteristics of the class Chondrichthyes.
- DISTINGUISH sharks from bony fishes.
- DESCRIBE the external anatomy of a bony fish.
- IDENTIFY the internal systems of bony fishes.
- EXPLAIN reproduction in bony fishes.

The Lampreys

THE BLOOD SUCKERS OF THE GREAT LAKES

About forty years ago, some deadly vertebrates swam from Lake Ontario through the Welland Canal, into Lake Erie. The sea lampreys were invading new waters. Sea lampreys are very destructive predators. They attach to the sides of fish and live on their blood and other body fluids. When the host fish weakens or dies, the lamprey moves on to another victim. Lampreys have killed off most of the trout in Lake Huron and Lake Michigan, and they have seriously cut down the trout population of Lake Superior.

Much earlier, this species had migrated up the St. Lawrence River from the Atlantic coast. They became established in Lake Ontario. The lamprey could not migrate further because of the Niagara Falls. The Welland Canal was built to carry ships around the falls. But this artificial waterway also gave the lampreys a passage into Lake Erie. Ten years later, the lampreys had spread through Lake Huron. They were then able to migrate into Lake Michigan and Lake Superior.

What sort of creature is this deadly sea lamprey? Sea lampreys are in the class *Cyclostomata*. This term means "round mouthed." This small class of primitive vertebrates is also called *Agnatha* (AG-nuh-thuh), which means "jawless." Ancestors of the cyclostomes were probably the first vertebrates. They appeared about 400 million years ago in the Ordovician period. Cyclostomes and some now extinct jawless vertebrates grew in number during the Silurian pe-

The sea lamprey will make an interesting specimen for students to observe. If possible, obtain one so that the class can observe its external and internal anatomy.

Use the discussion of the sea lamprey as a lead-in to ways the balance of nature can be disturbed by organisms other than man. Stress the great economic losses suffered by the fishing industry because of the sea lamprey.

421

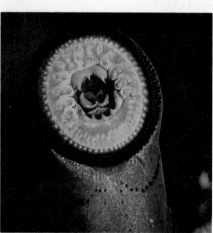

34–2 The mouth of a sea lamprey (left). Note the circular, jawless mouth and rasping teeth. The scar on the trout was caused by a sea lamprey's attack. (Russ Kinne, Photo Researchers; U.S. Fish and Wildlife Service)

riod, then declined in the Devonian. The only cyclostomes alive today are lamprey and hagfishes. The best known is the sea lamprey.

The sea lamprey has a thin body like that of an eel. The adult lamprey can be about 60 centimeters long and weigh about a half kilogram. Its skin is soft, slimy, brownish-green, and blotched. The lamprey does not have paired fins. There are two single fins along the back plus a tail fin. The lamprey uses these fins to swim in a rippling manner. The lamprey has small eyes on each side of its head. On the top of the head, between the eyes, is a nasal opening. This opening leads to a sac containing nerve endings that aid in the sense of smell. There are seven oval gill slits on each side of the head. These openings lead to spherical pouches that contain many feathery gills. Water moves in and out of the gill slits and gases are exchanged.

The lamprey's head is very different from the head of a fish. Instead of jaws, lampreys have funnel-like mouths lined with sharp, horny teeth. In the center of the mouth is a rasping tongue with teethlike projections.

The sea lamprey has caused much destruction in the Great Lakes. It uses its sucking mouth to attach to a fish. And then it tears a hole through the scales with its rasping teeth. It sucks out blood and body fluids. Sometimes the lamprey may even suck out the in-

34–3 A time scale of fish.

Era	Period	cyclostomes	cartilage fishes	bony fishes
Cenozoic	Quaternary			
	Tertiary			
Mesozoic	Cretaceous			
	Jurassic			
	Triassic			
Paleozoic	Permian			
	Pennsylvanian (Late Carboniferous)			
	Mississippian (Early Carboniferous)			
	Devonian			
	Silurian			
	Ordovician			
	Cambrian			
	(Pre-Cambrian)			

ternal organs of the fish. The injury it causes is not always fatal. Many fishes are found with scars showing where they were attacked by lampreys. Lampreys feed mainly on lake trout, an economically important fish in the Great Lakes. When there are no trout, the sea lamprey attacks whitefish, pike, and other species.

THE WAY TO BEAT THE LAMPREYS

Our understanding of the spawning habits of the lamprey is helping us to destroy this menace. In May and June, lampreys reach their sexual maturity. They swim into the fast-flowing streams that feed into the Great Lakes. There they lay their eggs in circular depressions in the gravel bottom of cold streams. An average female lays from 25,000 to 100,000 eggs. These eggs take about 20 days to hatch. The tiny, blind larvae resemble *Amphioxus*. When the larvae leave the nest, they float downstream until they reach a quiet mud bottom. Then they burrow into the mud and stay inactive for about four years. During this time, they lie in a U-shaped burrow. The larvae have cilia which produce a current to draw food into the burrow. At the end of this time, the larvae become adults and swim down to the lake. The lamprey lives for one year as an adult, feeding constantly on fish.

Using this knowledge, scientists have devised two ways to control lampreys. They can set up traps to catch the adult lampreys on their way upstream to spawn. Electrodes are set up in a row across a stream. These charge the water with electricity. This stops all aquatic animals from swimming further. This makes it easy to trap them. The lampreys are destroyed, while the fish are set free above the traps.

A more recent method involves a poison that can kill the larvae buried in the stream beds. This second method has been very successful in ridding Lake Superior of lampreys.

Cartilage Fishes

SHARKS, RAYS, AND SKATES

Sharks, rays, and skates belong to the class *Chondrichthyes*. This means "cartilage fishes." It is thought that they developed early in the Devonian period. Of the fishes that lived in the ancient seas, many cartilage fishes have survived relatively unchanged in great numbers.

Sharks are similar to true fishes in many ways. But they have certain differences which place them in a separate class. Sharks have *placoid scales* which have the same origin as the shark's teeth. The shark's body is torpedo-shaped. It has fins like those of true fishes. The long upper lobe of the tail fin is a characteristic of ancient fishes. This type of tail fin forces the head of the shark downward as it moves through the water. The mouth is a horizontal slit on the ventral side of the head. The jaws of most sharks are lined

Students may be interested in learning about the changes that took place in shark-like fish to give rise to bony fish.

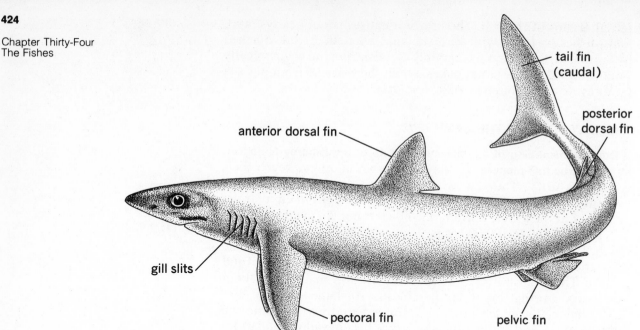

tail fin
(caudal)

anterior dorsal fin

posterior
dorsal fin

gill slits

pectoral fin

pelvic fin

34–4 External structure of a shark.

with razor-sharp, pointed teeth. They have several rows of teeth. When a tooth is lost, another one may move forward to replace it. The teeth slant backward to hold the food securely in the mouth. This, combined with great strength, make the shark a fearsome hunter.

Water enters the mouth, where it passes over the gills on either side of the head. The water is then forced out through separate pairs of gill slits. The gills are the respiratory organs of the fish. The shark has large, well-developed eyes on either side of the its head above the mouth. Paired nostrils on the ventral side of the head lead to olfactory sacs. These olfactory sacs sense odors in the water. As already mentioned, shark skeletons are made up of cartilage rather than bone.

Sharks include the largest living fishes. The whale shark may grow to be over 15 meters long and can weigh as much as 18,000 kilograms. The great white shark, a man-eater, may exceed 12 meters in length.

We do not know exactly how a shark finds its prey. It could have to do with sight or sound, or both. In experiments, sharks have had plastic shields placed over their eyes. When blinded, they take longer to find food. Thus, sight must be important in finding prey. Sharks can smell blood in the water from only 100 meters or so. But they can detect sound over some distance. Perhaps they are first attracted to a victim by splashing sounds.

Rays and skates have broad flat bodies with whiplike tails. *Rays* swim gracefully by moving their flat bodies like wings. They often lie half buried in sand on the ocean floor. Sting rays often come close to shore. The ray's tail has a sharp, barbed spike near the

tip. This causes a painful wound when it is driven into a victim. Torpedo rays have an excellent means of defense. They have modified muscle cells that produce an electric current. They can produce enough current to shock a human severely. However, this adaptation is probably used mainly to get food.

Skates have triangle-shaped bodies with long thin tails. They swim by undulating their large pectoral fins from front to rear. Two fins attached to the tail act as a steering device.

Skates are well adapted to life on the ocean bottom. They take in water through two spiracles on top of their head, just behind the eyes. Water runs over the gills and out through gill slits on the lower part of the skate's body. This way, skates avoid taking in debris when they respire half-covered in sand on the ocean floor.

Bony Fishes

THE TRUE FISHES

True fishes belong to the class *Osteichthyes*. This means "bony fishes." **Unlike the lamprey, shark, and ray, true fishes have bony skeletons.** Bony fishes first appeared in the Devonian period. This was the "Age of Fishes" because we find the greatest number and variety of fish fossils in this period. Since the time they first appeared, bony fishes have steadily increased in number. Today, they are the dominant vertebrates in both freshwater and marine environments. And they are found in many forms and sizes.

Bony fishes have *gills* for respiration. Limbs take the form of *fins*. Most fishes have an outer covering of *scales*. Fish bodies are divided into three areas—head, trunk, and tail. Many people confuse the tail of the fish with the tail fin. The tail is a solid muscular part. The tail fin is an outgrowth of this region. In most fish, the body is perfectly streamlined. It is tapered at both ends or spindle shaped. The lack of a neck is no disadvantage to a fish. It can turn its body easily in the water.

Fishes are ideally adapted to aquatic life. In some form, they live in practically every water environment.

34–6 A skate. What features do you see in the photograph that would indicate that the skate is well adapted for living on the bottom of the ocean? (Douglas Faulkner)

The coloration of many types of fish provides excellent camouflage. One such fish, the minnow, is able to adapt its color to its surroundings. Place some minnows in two jars. Put one jar on a light cloth and one on a dark cloth. Observe the colors of the fish in each jar. Then switch the jars on the cloths and continue to observe the fish coloration.

THE SCALES OF A FISH

Scales grow from pockets in the skin. They overlap like shingles on a roof. Scales grow bigger as the fish grows bigger. But they always stay the same in number. A young fish has the same number of scales as it will have when it is older. As scales grow, concentric rings form on them. These rings grow closer together in the winter than they do in the summer. So, by looking at the scale rings, you can tell the age of a fish.

Mucus, secreted by skin glands, seeps between the scales. It forms a covering that lubricates the fish body. This body slime helps fish glide through the water. It also makes the fish slippery to its enemies. Finally, this mucus forms protection against parasitic fungi, bacteria, and protozoans. If you pick up a live fish, wet your hands. Dry hands will scrape off some of this protective slime and expose the fish to parasites.

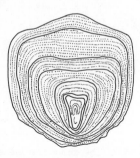

34-7 Each season, as a fish grows, a new ring forms on its scales. How old is the fish this scale came from?

Many fishes are brightly colored. These colors are often arranged in stripes or spots. Much of the coloration is caused by pigment granules. These granules are located in special skin cells called **chromatophores** (krome-AT-uh-forz). Sometimes fish even change colors. Scientists think that such color changes are an involuntary response to the environment. The color change occurs when pigment is dispersed within the chromatophores. This helps a fish hide from its enemies. The ability to change color varies with species, size, and age. So does the length of time the change takes. The flounder probably holds the "speed record" for color change. Its color can change to match a polka-dot background in just a few minutes. Most fish, however, take longer—even a couple of days—to change color. For this reason, the flounder is often used in experiments with pigmentation and color change.

The color change actually depends on the chromatophores. Scientists think that nerve impulses cause the pigment to be dispersed. This depends on what the fish sees around it.

Many fishes have a color pattern known as *countershading.* This pattern is a form of camouflage. Dark pigments on the fish's back tone down the bright light filtering through the water above. The dark colors on the dorsal side blend with the bottom of the body of water.

34-8 Flounders are able to blend into almost any environment. They automatically change dispersal or concentration of pigments in their chromatophores. (Russ Kinne, Photo Researchers)

And lighter colors on the ventral side blend with bright light on the surface when the fish is seen from below.

HEAD STRUCTURES OF FISHES

Different species of fish vary greatly in body form. But the yellow perch is a typical example. The head tapers toward the mouth, making the fish streamlined. The head is covered with plates rather than scales. Most fishes have large mouths at the anterior end. Meat-eating fishes, like the yellow perch, have many small, sharp teeth. These grow from the jaw bones and the roof of the mouth. The teeth slant backward. This makes it easy for the fish to swallow, but hard for its victim to escape. The tongue is fastened to the floor of the mouth. It cannot move. The tongue is an organ of touch rather than one of taste.

Most fish have two nostrils just under their eyes. These lead in to nasal cavities. **The nostrils of the fish function in smell only.** They do not connect to the throat for respiration. The ears are embedded in the skull bones of the fish. There are no outside openings. The fish picks up vibrations that are carried by the skull bones. Scientists think these ears also function as organs of balance.

The eyes of most fish are large. Most fish can move their eyes. There are no eyelids. The transparent cornea that covers the eye is flattened. The pupils are large compared to those of other vertebrates. They let in as much light as possible. The lens is shaped almost like a ball. It moves backward or forward as the eye focuses, just as you focus a camera.

At each side of the head is a crescent-shaped slit. This marks the back edge of the gill cover, or **operculum** (oe-PURR-kyoo-lum). This hard plate acts as a protective cover over the gills. By opening the rear edge of the operculum, you can see the gills lying in a large gill

The yellow perch provides an excellent specimen for the study of the external and internal anatomy of a bony fish.

Stress to students that the artist's drawing of the internal organs of the perch may *not* conform exactly to the specimen being dissected.

34–9 The external structure of a bony fish, the yellow perch.

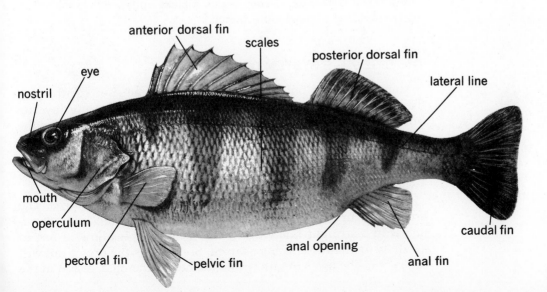

chamber. The four gills look like delicate combs. The edges of the opercula almost meet on the lower side of the fish. This marks where the head attaches to the trunk.

STRUCTURES OF THE TRUNK AND TAIL

Various kinds of fins develop from the trunk and tail. **But all fins are made up of a double membrane supported by spiny rays.** These rays are composed of cartilage. Fins serve many purposes. And they differ in form from species to species.

There are two kinds of paired fins. These are homologous to the limbs of other vertebrates. The **pectoral fins** are nearest the head. These correspond to the front legs. The **pelvic fins** are posterior to and below the pectoral fins. These correspond to the hind legs. These pelvic fins act like oars when a fish swims slowly. They also aid in steering and keeping balance when the fish is resting. They are also used when the fish moves backward.

There are several single fins. The **caudal fin** grows from the tail. It helps push the fish forward. **Dorsal fins** are found along the top of a fish's back. The anterior dorsal fin of the perch contains sharp spines. These spines act as a defense against attack. They raise toward the head, making the fish hard to swallow tail first. The posterior dorsal fin does not have spines. Both dorsal fins help the fish stay upright while swimming. Another single fin, called the **anal fin,** grows along the midline on the ventral side of the fish. Like the dorsal fins, the anal fin helps the fish keep its balance.

Powerful muscles occupy the region of the trunk above the spinal column. A thinner muscle layer lies along the body wall on the sides of the trunk. The tail region is nearly solid muscle.

Look at a fish closely. On each side, you can see a row of pitted scales in a line from the head to the tail fin. These make up the **lateral line.** Under these scales lie nerve endings and a narrow tube. **The lateral line acts as a sense organ. It picks up low-frequency underwater vibrations and pressure stimuli.**

THE DIGESTIVE SYSTEM OF FISHES

Many fishes eat only water plants and algae. But carnivorous fishes eat frogs and other fish. They also feed on many invertebrates, such as insects, worms, and crayfish. Some fishes, like the bass and the pike, swallow fish almost as big as themselves. Their mouths are large traps for catching their prey. Fish have an undeveloped "tongue" in the floor of the mouth. It does not help them swallow. Their tongues act as an organ of touch.

The *pharynx*, or throat cavity, leads to the short *esophagus*. The esophagus, in turn, joins the upper end of the *stomach*. The stomach is in a straight line with the esophagus. This allows a fish to swallow food almost as big as itself. Sometimes the prey's tail will hang from the fish's mouth, while the head is being digested in the

Students may be interested in doing some comparative anatomy and physiology of their own. Ask them to compare the digestive and circulatory systems of the fish with those of the arthropod.

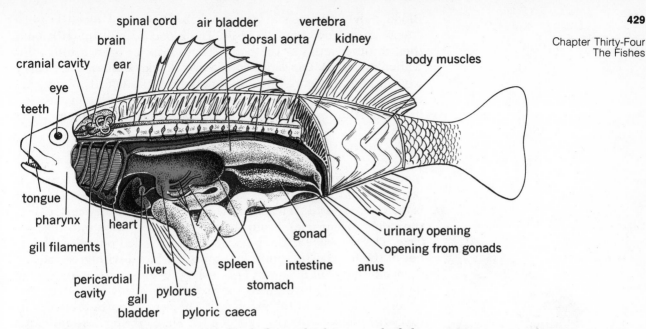

teeth
eye
cranial cavity
brain
ear
spinal cord
air bladder
dorsal aorta
vertebra
kidney
body muscles
tongue
pharynx
gill filaments
pericardial
cavity
gall
bladder
heart
liver
pylorus
pyloric caeca
spleen
stomach
intestine
gonad
anus
urinary opening
opening from gonads

34-10 The internal structure of a yellow perch.

stomach. A rather short *intestine* leads from the lower end of the stomach. At this junction, short fingerlike tubes extend from the intestine. These tubes are called *pyloric caeca* (pie-LORE-ick SEEK-uh). Close to the stomach lies a well-developed *liver*. The *pancreas* is hard to find in a fish dissection. Digestion continues as food passes along the short loops of the intestine. Digested food is absorbed through the intestine wall. Undigested material leaves through the *anus* on the lower side.

THE CIRCULATORY SYSTEM OF FISHES

The blood of fishes is similar to that of other vertebrates. It contains both red and white blood cells. **The *heart* pumps the blood.**

34-11 The circulatory system of a fish. Note that the blood flows in a single circuit—from the heart to the gills to the body and to the heart again.

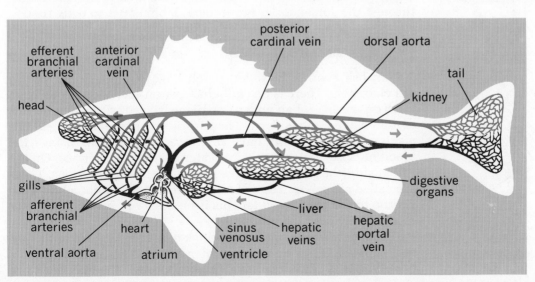

efferent
branchial
arteries
anterior
cardinal
vein
posterior
cardinal vein
dorsal aorta
tail
head
kidney
gills
afferent
branchial
arteries
digestive
organs
liver
hepatic
veins
hepatic
portal
vein
ventral aorta
heart
sinus
venosus
atrium
ventricle

Blood moves through a system of three types of blood vessels. **Arteries carry blood from the heart.** The blood goes to the gills, and then to other areas of the body. These arteries branch into thin-walled **capillaries.** **Capillaries spread into all body tissues.** They carry oxygen and nutrients into the functioning tissue cells. They also carry carbon dioxide away from tissue cells. The blood is carried by the capillaries into larger vessels called **veins.** **Veins return blood to the heart.**

The heart lies in the **pericardial cavity** on the lower side of the body behind the gills. Two large veins, the *cardinal veins*, receive blood returning from various parts of the body. Just above the heart, the cardinal veins expand into a thin-walled sac. This sac is the *sinus venosus*. It leads to the first chamber of the heart, called the **atrium** (or auricle). From the atrium, blood flows into the **ventricle.** The ventricle is the muscular, thick-walled pumping chamber of the heart. The ventricle pumps the blood with great power through the *ventral aorta*. This artery begins with a muscular bulb-shaped structure called the *bulbus arteriosius*. This structure is very noticeable in the fish heart. The ventral aorta branches to carry the blood to the two sets of gills. Then it branches again into *branchial* (BRANG-kee-uhl) *arteries* that lead to the four gills on each side of the head. From these gills, the oxygenated blood is carried off by the *dorsal aorta*. This artery has branches that supply blood to the various body parts. Blood returns to the heart through the *cardinal veins*. This completes the circulation. Some blood returns through veins from the digestive organs and the liver. Various cell wastes are filtered out as the blood goes through the kidneys.

A fish's blood flows through the heart once during a complete circulation. The heart gets deoxygenated blood from the body tissues through the cardinal vein. It then pumps the blood to the gills through the ventral aorta. In the gills, the blood picks up oxygen and gives off carbon dioxide. The oxygenated blood leaves the gills through the dorsal aorta. From there, it circulates to body tissues.

THE GILLS AND RESPIRATION

Bony fish, such as the yellow perch, have four gills in each of two gill chambers. There is one gill chamber on each side of the head. Each **gill** consists of an arch of cartilage fringed with a double row of thin-walled projections. These projections are called *gill filaments*. These filaments have many capillaries. This brings the blood in close contact with the water over a large surface. On the throat side, the gill arches have hard, fingerlike projections. These are called *gill rakers*. The gill rakers prevent food and debris from getting to the gill filaments. This is necessary to insure that water moves freely over the gills.

The *afferent branchial artery* brings blood to the base of the gill arches. Branches of this artery enter each gill filament. Here carbon dioxide is discharged from blood, through the filament wall,

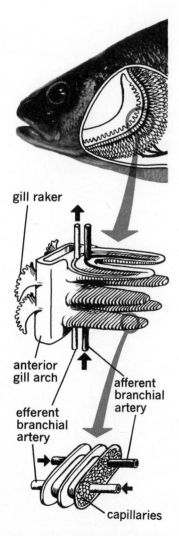

gill raker

anterior gill arch

afferent branchial artery

efferent branchial artery

capillaries

34–12 A sectioned portion of a gill filament is shown at the top of the center drawing. A portion of a single filament, much enlarged, is shown at the bottom.

and into the water. At the same time, oxygen from the water moves through the capillary walls into the blood. This oxygenated blood returns to the gill arch. From there, it flows out the top of the gill through the *efferent branchial artery*. The dorsal aorta then carries the blood to the body tissues.

Fish need a constant flow of water over their gills. Water is drawn through the open mouth as the cavity of the pharynx enlarges. The pharynx enlarges when the gill arches expand. As water is drawn in, the edge of the operculum is pressed against the body. Then the mouth closes, the gill arches contract, and the rear edge of the operculum opens. This forces water over the gill filaments, and out of the gill chamber around the raised edge of the operculum. The forward motion of a swimming fish aids in this process.

Some students may be interested in reading *The Brains of Animals and Man* by R. Friedman and J. Morriss, New York, Holiday House, Inc., 1972. This book discusses a complex subject in an easily understood manner.

THE AIR BLADDER—A PRESSURE ORGAN

A thin-walled sac, the *air bladder,* lies in the upper part of the body cavity of a fish. Some fishes swallow air. An example is the lungfish. In these fish, the air bladder is connected with the pharynx by a tube. In other fish, the bladder is inflated by gases that pass into it from the blood. These gases are oxygen, nitrogen, and carbon dioxide. The bladder acts as a float. It allows the fish to remain at any water depth without much effort. **By adjusting the amount of gas in the air bladder, the fish can move to different levels in the water.**

Fishes live at different depths at different times of year. The air bladder adjusts by losing air to the blood or receiving more air. When a fish that is adjusted to a great depth is caught and quickly brought to surface, the air bladder expands. This can push the esophagus and stomach up into the fish's mouth. Fishes called *darters* have no air bladder. They sink to the bottom whenever they stop swimming. Many shark species have no air bladder. These sharks must keep swimming to stay afloat.

THE NERVOUS SYSTEM

The fish nervous system includes the brain, spinal cord, and many nerves that lead to all parts of the body. The brain lies in a small bony cavity in the head. This is called the *cranial cavity.* The brain has five different parts. At the anterior end are the *olfactory lobes.* From here, nerves sensitive to odors extend to the nostrils. The two lobes of the *cerebrum* lie behind the olfactory lobes. The cerebrum controls the voluntary muscles. It is also the center of fish instincts. Next are the *optic lobes.* These are the largest lobes in the fish brain. Optic nerves lead from here to the eyes. The *cerebellum* is behind the optic lobes. It coordinates muscle activity. Finally, at the back of the brain, is the *medulla oblongata.* This part of the brain controls the activities of the internal organs. The *spinal cord* passes back from the medulla. The spinal cord is encased in the vertebral column. *Cranial nerves* extend

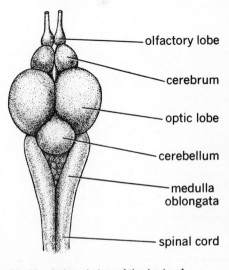

olfactory lobe

cerebrum

optic lobe

cerebellum

medulla oblongata

spinal cord

34–13 A dorsal view of the brain of a fish.

from the brain to the sense organs and head structures. **Spinal nerves** connect the spinal cord to the various areas of the body.

The fish's brain is not as well developed as those of the higher vertebrates. But the same basic regions are present. Compare the brains of other vertebrates to the fish brain. As vertebrates become more highly developed, the cerebrum is larger in proportion to the rest of the brain. With this increase comes an increase in nervous activity on higher levels. This includes emotional responses, memory, and intellectual activity.

THE SENSATIONS OF FISHES

Fish have relatively large optic lobes. This leads you to think that fish have a well-developed sense of sight. However, the amount of light is reduced underwater. This makes vision difficult. Also, fish are known to be nearsighted. They probably cannot see very clearly for much more than a half meter. Scientists were not sure whether or not fish could see colors. It was thought that fish lived in a world of black, white, and gray. Now, however, studies show that some fish may have color vision.

Unlike higher vertebrates, fish lack eardrums and middle ears. Sound vibrations are transmitted to ear structures through the skull bones.

The fish's olfactory sense is probably its keenest sense. Fish are very sensitive to substances dissolved in the water. This is similar to the sense of smell in air-breathing animals. Experiments show that fish are able to tell the difference between "smells" of different kinds of water plants. Fish can detect the odors of many animals, especially mammals. They can even detect the odor of hands washed in a stream. Scientists now believe that fish can tell where food is by odors. It is also possible that salmon use this sense to find the mouths of rivers during spawning season. They may be able to detect the odors of the plants living in fresh water.

REPRODUCTION IN FISHES

The reproductive organs of fish are called *gonads*. They lie in the posterior part of the body cavity above the digestive organs. The opening from the gonads is just behind the anal opening.

The reproductive organs of the female fish are called *ovaries*. These produce eggs over a period of several months. As the eggs grow, the ovaries swell and may bulge the sides of the fish. In many fish, including the yellow perch, paired ovaries fuse into a single ovary during embryonic growth.

In male fish, the sex organs are called *testes*. These develop sperm cells. When the female lays the eggs, or **spawns,** the male swims over them. The male discharges **milt** onto the eggs. Milt is a fluid containing the sperm. The sperms swim to the eggs and fertilize them. **This is external fertilization.**

Fertilized eggs begin to develop into embryos. This may take from a couple of days to many weeks, depending on the species and the water temperature. As the embryo develops, it is nourished by special food in the egg. This food is called **yolk.** The yolk is a large amount of nonliving material held in the egg. A *yolk sac* remains attached to a baby fish for a short time after it hatches.

In most fishes, spawning is not very efficient. Many eggs are never fertilized. Therefore, they never develop. And, many fertilized eggs are eaten before hatching by predators. Those baby fish that do hatch are in constant danger of being eaten by bigger fish and other water animals. How does a fish species continue to survive under these harsh conditions? **The species survives because of the large number of eggs that are laid.** A female fish spawns anywhere from 500 to seven million eggs depending upon the species.

Some fishes bear their young alive. The female keeps the eggs in her body. The female receives sperms from the male during mating. The young fish develop within the female's body. These kinds of fishes are called *live-bearers.* Guppies, mollies, platys, and swordtails are examples of live-bearers.

THE SPAWNING HABITS OF VARIOUS FISHES

The spawning habits of fishes vary greatly. It is important for us to know how fish behave. They are the source of much of our food. Usually, freshwater fish spawn in the waters where they normally live. But often they swim to shallower water to spawn. Shallow waters give them both greater protection and a warmer temperature. The yellow perch, for example, moves from deep lake water to spawn in shallow water near the shore. In the spring, thousands of eggs are laid in ribbonlike masses.

Some fishes make nests in which to deposit their eggs. The male stickleback, for example, builds a nest from bits of plants and other rubble. Then the male drives the female into it for spawning. Later, he drives her away from the nest. The male takes charge of the nest and eggs. Channel catfish spawn in holes in banks or channel bottoms. They may even spawn in a rusty tin can they find on the bottom.

Some fishes travel long distances to their spawning areas. They may go from lakes and rivers into small streams, from freshwater streams to the oceans, or from the ocean to freshwater streams.

The eel has an interesting spawning migration. This long, slender fish lives in the rivers and streams of the Atlantic and Gulf coast regions. A few are found further inland. Adult eels live in fresh water for five to ten years, depending on the climate and the food supply. When they are sexually mature, they go on a final journey downstream to the Atlantic Ocean. They travel to the spawning grounds where they began life. For some strange reason, they keep going until they reach the same special place just north of the West Indies and south of Bermuda. Scientists think that the eels follow warm water currents. But the exact route and depth at which they

Many fish build nests to care for the eggs and young. Encourage students to look for these nests in pond areas. Some fish that build nests include basses and sunfish. It is interesting to note that the male fish is usually responsible for nest building.

34–14 Nests of the stickleback and sunfish.

34–15 A salmon migrating upstream to the spawning areas. (Stouffer, Animals, Animals)

The effect of pollution on the spawning grounds of fish is an interesting subject. Have students report to the class on their research.

An interesting experiment can be carried out concerning the overcrowding of fish populations. Place a single pair of mature guppies into one tank (should include a gravid female). Into the other tank, place 25 assorted guppies. Keep all conditions constant. Over a two-month period, the populations will probably stabilize at 15 fish in each tank. Some researchers have concluded that this occurs because the young fish release chemicals into the water that limit the population. Have students draw conclusions concerning guppy populations from this experiment.

swim remain a mystery. Once there, each female lays a couple of million eggs. After spawning, all of the adults die.

The eel larvae hatch in the spawning grounds in the spring. By the autumn of the first year, the larvae arrive at the coast of North America. During the winter, they change into tiny adult eels. The next spring, they enter the mouths of rivers and streams in droves. Males travel only a short distance. Females go much farther, sometimes thousands of kilometers.

European eels spawn in an area near the grounds of American eels. They are farther east—near the Sargasso Sea. These eels migrate almost 5,000 kilometers through the Atlantic. But the return trip of the baby eels takes several years. American eels and European eels always go back to their own continents. Nobody knows why this happens.

Of all the migrating fish, the Pacific salmon have the strongest homing instinct. Generation after generation, the Pacific salmon leave the deep ocean waters where they live. They somehow find their way to the very same rivers in which their parents spawned three or four years earlier. Salmon migrations start in the late spring and early fall, depending on the specific species and the distance to be covered. The pink salmon travels just a few kilometers upstream from the ocean. But the king salmon goes as much as 1,600 kilometers upstream to the cold fast-flowing streams.

During the migration, salmon change color from silver to pink or even bright red. Humps develop on their backs. Their jaws become hooked. When they finally reach their spawning areas, the females lay three to five thousand eggs in a few days. The males discharge milt onto the eggs. Soon after this, the adults die. The eggs hatch after thirty or forty days, and the young salmon head to sea. There they live until they are mature. Then they return home to spawn and die.

SUMMARY

Since early geological times, fishes have ruled the seas. They are still the dominant vertebrates in most watery environments. Lampreys, hagfishes, sharks, and rays are very much like the fish that were in the ancient seas. But as time has passed, bony fishes of many types have gradually replaced most of the ancient cartilaginous fishes.

As you have seen, there are many reasons for the fishes being the dominant vertebrates in the water. Fish are very well adapted to life in the water. They have fins and a streamlined body for rapid movements. Most have air bladders that aid in swimming at different depths. Most have scales coated with mucus. This provides protection against parasites. Most fish can change color to blend into their environment. The mouths of fishes are as varied as their diets. These factors help fish to be good hunters. They also help fish to survive against other hunters.

Further, fish have efficient circulatory systems. The heart pumps blood to the gills. Here it is oxygenated and gives off its carbon dioxide. Even the limited vision of fish is not that great a disadvantage. A keen sense of smell makes up for nearsightedness. The lateral line helps them sense low frequency vibrations and pressures.

The spawning habits of fish are fascinating. Why should eels travel so far to lay their eggs? Why should salmon strain against the currents of fast-water streams to spawn and then die? And how do these creatures know how to get back to where they started? Scientists find it difficult to explain the mysteries of reproductive instinct.

BIOLOGICALLY SPEAKING

chromatophore	artery	cerebrum
countershading	capillary	optic lobe
operculum	vein	cerebellum
pectoral fin	pericardial cavity	medulla oblongata
pelvic fin	atrium	spinal cord
caudal fin	ventricle	cranial nerve
dorsal fin	gill	spinal nerve
anal fin	air bladder	spawn
lateral line	cranial cavity	milt
heart	olfactory lobe	yolk

1. What characteristic of the head of a cyclostome distinguishes it from other fish?
2. Describe how the sea lamprey attacks other fish.
3. List several characteristics that distinguish sharks from other fish.
4. Describe the body covering of bony fishes.
5. What is countershading? How does it camouflage a fish?
6. Locate and describe the sense organs of the fish.
7. Name and locate the fins of a yellow perch.
8. In the order in which food passes through them, name the parts of the fish digestive system.
9. Describe the structure of the fish heart.
10. What is the function of the air bladder in the fish?
11. Name the regions of the fish brain and state the function of each.
12. Describe external fertilization as it occurs in most fish.

APPLYING
PRINCIPLES
AND CONCEPTS

1. Why does a fish die in the air, even though the air contains more oxygen than the water?
2. Fish lay large numbers of eggs. Of what important adaptive value is this fact?
3. Discuss the homing instinct of fish using the eel and the salmon as examples.
4. Trace the path of a drop of blood from the ventral aorta through the circulatory system of the fish. Describe the changes in the blood as it passes through the gills.

35-1 It is believed that the lobe-finned fish evolved into the primitive amphibians. (American Museum of Natural History)

THE ARRIVAL OF AMPHIBIANS

Biologists believe that living things lived only in watery environments for millions of years. At the end of the Devonian period, evolutionary changes occurred that led to life on land. The fishes we discussed in the last chapter respired with gills. But remember that most fishes also had an air bladder for balancing at different depths. This bladder is similar to an adaptation of some early bony fishes. These fishes developed lunglike structures in addition to gills. This allowed them to respire in air as well as in water. These were the *lungfishes*. Some species survive even today. Lungfish are found in Australia, Africa, and South America. These are all areas of seasonal drought. When the water dries up, lungfish must be able to breathe air to survive. In times of drought, the lungfish burrows into the bottom of the pool. It curls up in an inactive state in the burrow until the rains bring water.

Early lungfishes had jointed or lobed fins that resembled legs. Until the 1930's, it was thought that lobe-finned fishes had died off in the Mesozoic era. Their fossil traces have been found in rocks of the late Paleozoic and Mesozoic eras. But there is no trace of them in the Cenozoic rocks. This led biologists to believe that they had become extinct 70 million years ago.

In 1938, however, a South African fisherman caught a strange type of fish. It was about one and a half meters long. It was covered with large bluish scales. He gave the strange fish to a local museum. It was stuffed and mounted. Finally Dr. J. L. B. Smith of Rhodes University saw it and recognized it as a lobe-finned fish called a *coelacanth*. Since then, many of these coelacanths have been

The Amphibians

OBJECTIVES

- LIST the characteristics of amphibians.
- NAME the orders of amphibians.
- DESCRIBE salamanders.
- DISTINGUISH toads from frogs.
- DEMONSTRATE a knowledge of the anatomy and physiology of the frog.
- DESCRIBE metamorphosis in frogs.
- DISTINGUISH hibernation from estivation.

Students will be interested in learning more about the coelacanth and its place in the transition from fishlike creatures to amphibians.

35-2 The coelacanth, the only known surviving lobe-finned fish. (American Museum of Natural History)

caught in the waters between Madagascar and Mozambique. In 1975, a female was dissected and found to contain four baby coelacanths. This meant that coelacanths give birth to live young. The lungs of the coelacanth are outgrowths of their throats. And their fins resemble crude legs.

The development of lungs and leglike fins were probably an adaptation for survival. There were great climatic changes in the Devonian period. Ponds and streams often dried up or became stagnant. This is what happens to the homes of modern lungfishes. Typical fishes could not survive in these conditions. But a fish that had some type of lung could survive. And a fish that could crawl on land from one pond to another would also have a chance. For these reasons, **biologists think that the primitive lungfishes were the transitional forms between true fishes and the amphibians.**

The class name *Amphibia* means "having two lives." It refers to the fact that **amphibians can live on land, but they have never become completely free of water.** Amphibians must return to water or moisture for reproduction. Otherwise their soft, jellylike eggs would dry up and die. Also, most baby amphibians must live completely in the water. Even most adult amphibians cannot travel far away from the shore. They must keep their skin moist.

In the Mississippian and Pennsylvanian periods, and into the Permian period, amphibians were the dominant vertebrates. But toward the end of the Paleozoic era, they began dying off. The last large amphibians died out in the Triassic period of the Mesozoic era. Today's amphibians include only three orders. All of them developed after that time. They represent the small handful of survivors of this once huge vertebrate class.

CHARACTERISTICS OF AMPHIBIANS

Young amphibians are similar to fish. They can only live in water. But as they mature, they move onto land to live. To become adults, amphibians go through a series of changes. They undergo a metamorphosis. They must change from a water form to a land form. Many strange combinations of gills and lungs and fins and legs occur. Gills can be found on creatures that have legs. Fins are sometimes found on animals with lungs.

Generally, amphibians differ from other vertebrate animals in the following ways:

- The skin is smooth, thin, and usually moist. There are no scales, fur, or feathers.
- The feet, if present, are often webbed.
- The toes are soft and lack claws.
- The immature or larval forms are usually vegetarian. Adults are usually carnivorous.
- Respiration is by gills, lungs, and skin.
- The heart is two-chambered in the larvae. Adults have three-chambered hearts with well-developed circulation.

35-3 Representation of early lobe-finned fishes as they may have looked when they came out onto land (top) and of early amphibians. Their skeletons have been drawn from reconstructed fossils. (courtesy of the American Museum of Natural History)

THE ANATOMY OF THE FROG
DIGESTIVE SYSTEM

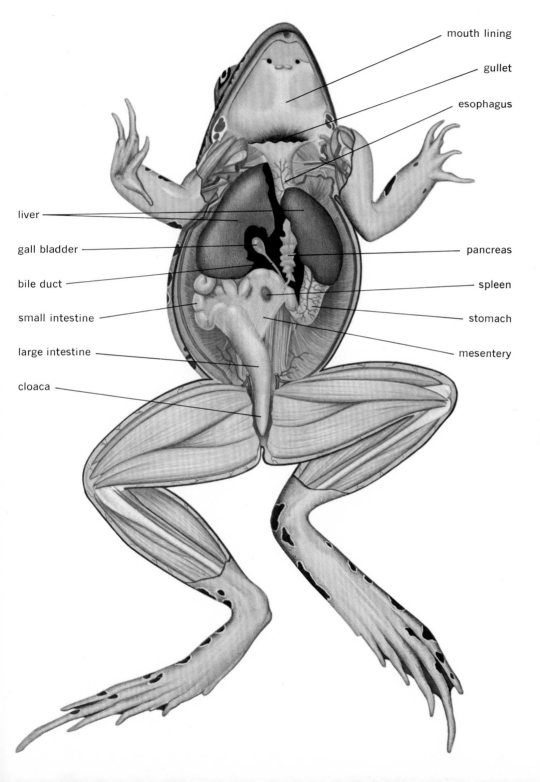

mouth lining

gullet

esophagus

liver

gall bladder

bile duct

small intestine

large intestine

cloaca

pancreas

spleen

stomach

mesentery

CIRCULATORY AND EXCRETORY SYSTEMS

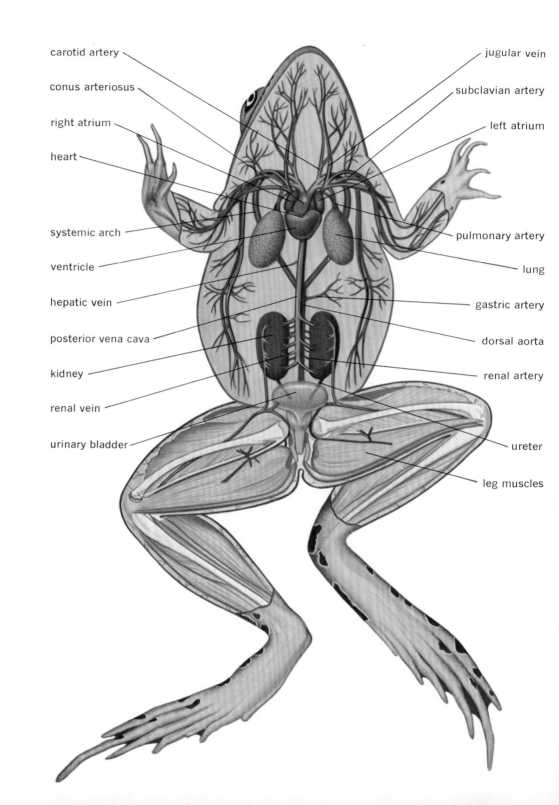

carotid artery

conus arteriosus

right atrium

heart

systemic arch

ventricle

hepatic vein

posterior vena cava

kidney

renal vein

urinary bladder

jugular vein

subclavian artery

left atrium

pulmonary artery

lung

gastric artery

dorsal aorta

renal artery

ureter

leg muscles

BACK BODY WALL AND NERVOUS SYSTEM

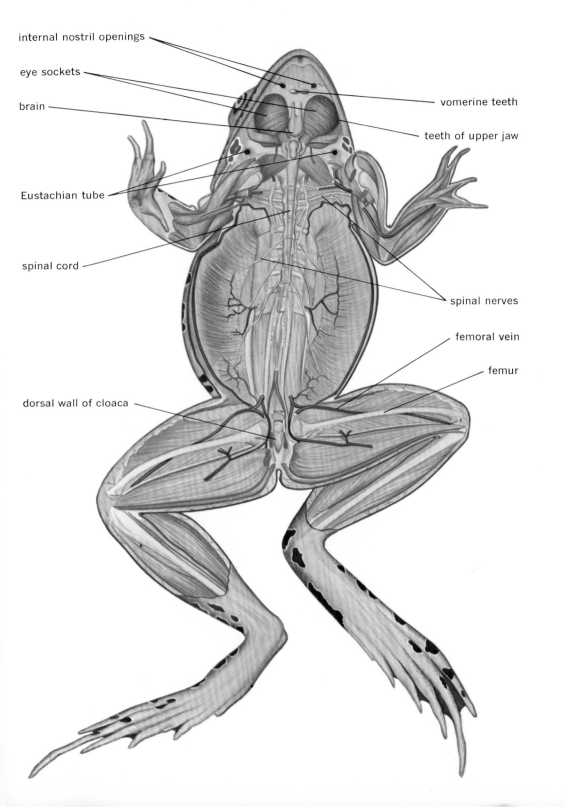

internal nostril openings

eye sockets

brain

vomerine teeth

teeth of upper jaw

Eustachian tube

spinal cord

spinal nerves

femoral vein

femur

dorsal wall of cloaca

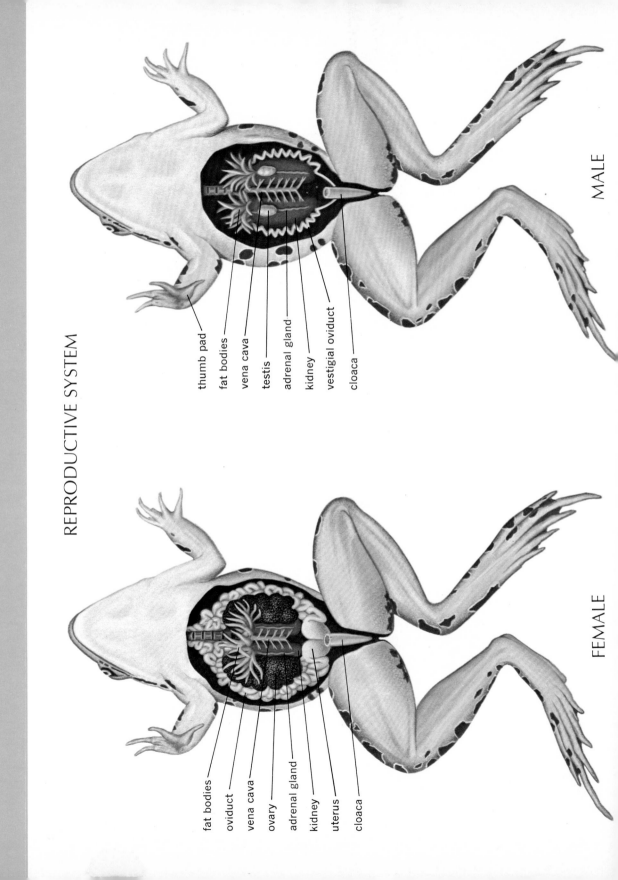

REPRODUCTIVE SYSTEM

MALE

thumb pad
fat bodies
vena cava
testis
adrenal gland
kidney
vestigial oviduct
cloaca

FEMALE

fat bodies
oviduct
vena cava
ovary
adrenal gland
kidney
uterus
cloaca

Era	Period	primitive amphibians	salamanders	frogs
Cenozoic	Quaternary			
	Tertiary			
Mesozoic	Cretaceous			
	Jurassic			
	Triassic			
Paleozoic	Permian			
	Pennsylvanian (Late Carboniferous)			
	Mississippian (Early Carboniferous)			
	Devonian			
	Silurian			
	Ordovician			
	Cambrian			
	(Pre-Cambrian)			

- The eggs are generally laid in water. Eggs are fertilized externally as soon as they are laid.
- There is a metamorphosis from an aquatic larval stage of the adult form.

35–4 A time scale of amphibians.

ORDERS OF AMPHIBIA

The order *Apoda* (AP-uh-duh) contains the few surviving legless amphibians of the tropics. These are strange wormlike creatures. A second order, *Caudata* (kaw-DA-tuh), or *Urodela*, includes amphibians that have tails throughout life. The salamanders and newts are in this order. The most familiar amphibians are the frogs and toads. These are members of the order *Salientia* (SAY-lee-EN-chuh), or *Anura*. Frogs and toads lack tails in the adult stage. This makes them different from other amphibians. These animals undergo an interesting transition. They live an aquatic life as larvae. But as adults, they live a semiaquatic or terrestrial life.

Many amphibians, including certain species of salamanders and frogs, display *aposematic* or warning coloration. These animals warn other animals to stay away through their vivid colors and markings. Ask students to mention other creatures that have this type of coloring. Certain snakes, birds, insects, and toads are included in this group.

The Salamanders

AMPHIBIANS WITH TAILS

Today's salamanders are very similar to their ancestors. The only difference seems to be the replacement of some skeletal cartilage by some bone. You are probably familiar with several of the salamanders. You might have called them lizards because they look similar. They both have long bodies, long tails, and short legs. However, salamanders have soft, moist skin and no claws. Lizards, on the other hand, have bodies covered with scales. And they have

35-5 An adult tiger salamander (top) and an axolotl. (Allan Roberts)

Some interesting habits of the spotted newt include a courtship dance, migration in large swarms, and its appearance in the woods following rain.

claws on their toes. These characteristics of reptiles are almost never found among amphibians.

Salamanders have little protection from enemies. A few have skin glands that secrete bad-tasting substances. Others have colored pigments that change in different surroundings. This helps to camouflage them. Salamanders cannot survive in dry areas. Thus, they are usually found under damp logs and stones. They may also be found swimming in the water.

Salamanders range in length from a few centimeters to about a meter. In the United States, the giant salamanders are represented by the *American hellbender*. It can grow to 60 centimeters in length. This creature has loose gray or red-brown skin. It lives in the streams of eastern United States. A Japanese relative of this salamander grows to one and a half meters in length. It is the largest living amphibian.

The *mud puppy* is another large salamander. It lives in the American Middle West. Many fishermen have been startled when they pull up one of these slimy salamanders from a mud-bottom stream. Mud puppies can grow to as long as 60 centimeters. They have flat, rectangular heads, small eyes, a flattened tail, and two pairs of short legs. But their most striking body feature is three pairs of dark red, bushy gills. These are attached at the base of the head just above the front legs. The presence of gills is a larval trait kept throughout the life of this salamander.

The tiger salamander is also found in the United States. It sometimes grows to 25 centimeters in length. The tiger salamander's colors give it its name. It has bright yellow bars and blotches on dark brown skin. The tiger salamander lives as an aquatic, gill-breathing larva for about three months. It then leaves the water and lives on land. Its lungs and thin, moist skin function in respiration during its land-living stage.

Some tiger salamanders and their close relatives remain aquatic for their whole lives. These salamanders reproduce while still in the larval stage. Larval salamanders called *axolotls* (ACK-suh-LOT'lz) are found in Mexico and the southwestern United States. Once biologists thought they were actually a separate species because they produced eggs or sperms in the larval stage. But when they were fed thyroid gland hormones, they changed into land-living adults. This showed that axolotls were larval forms of the tiger salamanders and some of their relatives. Research revealed that the waters in which axolotls live do not have enough iodine. Iodine is essential for the production of a thyroid hormone needed for metamorphosis. Thus, axolotls remain larvae because of a thyroid deficiency.

Newts are very small land-living salamanders. The *crimson-spotted newt* is particularly interesting because of its "triple life." This salamander hatches in May as a gill-breathing aquatic larva. After about two months, it changes into a land-dwelling form with lungs. At this stage, it is a coral-red color. And it is called a *red eft*. After a couple of years, its color changes to green with red spots.

The newt then moves back into the water to live. It respires through its skin while underwater. On land, it uses its lungs.

We have discussed only a few of the salamanders. You can find them in many places. Salamanders live under piles of wet leaves, under rocks in stream beds, in abandoned wells, and in other moist places. Salamanders make good pets in both their aquatic and land-dwelling stages. They can live in aquariums or in moist terrariums. With gentle urging, newts will eat mealworms and small insects from your hand.

Toads and Frogs

AMPHIBIANS WITHOUT TAILS

The toads and frogs that lived before the Jurassic period probably had long bodies and long tails. Biologists believe that this body form changed suddenly. The most obvious change was the disappearance of the tail in the adult. Other, less obvious changes made these animals better suited to life on the land. Their hind legs developed an extra joint. And their ankle bones became longer. These changes gave their legs great jumping power. Front legs stayed short. But this is suited for taking up the shock of landing from a jump. Modern frogs and toads have wide mouths. Their sticky front-hinged tongues can catch insects with lightning speed. Frogs and toads have existed for over 200 million years. They live in many places all over the world. Biologists consider them among the most successful vertebrates.

Frogs and toads are similar in structure. But frogs differ from toads in many ways in their anatomy and behavior. Of all amphibians, the toad is most able to survive on land. It leaves the water early in life. It only returns to water to lay eggs. The toad starts life as a small black **tadpole.** The tadpole soon grows legs and resorbs its tail. It hops onto land as a small, brown creature with warty skin. Adults of the common toad, *Bufo* (BOO-foe), are usually redbrown on the top and gray-yellow underneath. There is no truth to the old tale that people catch warts from toads. Warts are a viral condition that has nothing to do with toads.

Many toads are fascinating to study. Surinam toads, for example, carry their young in separate pouches on their backs. Some male toads carry strings of eggs wound around their hind legs. Students may want to report on the habits of the species of toads.

35–6 A toad (left) and a leopard frog. The skin of the toad is somewhat rough and warty, whereas that of the frog is smooth. (Walter Dawn)

Toads often live in areas with loose, moist soil. They dig in and hide from enemies and summer heat. They can dig quickly with their hind legs. If a toad is unable to bury itself when disturbed, it may crouch low to the ground and remain still. The color and texture of its skin provide good camouflage. But poison glands in the skin are a toad's best defense. These glands secrete an irritating, bad tasting substance. This causes most animals to leave the toad alone. But this defense does not keep snakes from eating the toads. Snakes are the toad's major enemy.

The toad has been called the "gardener's friend." Toads feed upon insects, worms, and other forms of food harmful to plants. Toads can easily bury themselves in moist, loose garden soil. It is probably this soil that attracts toads to gardens.

Unlike toads, frogs usually live very near water. You often see them around ponds. The most common frog in the United States is the *leopard frog*. These frogs live in almost every pond, marsh, and roadside ditch. They often travel a long way from water. Sometimes they can be seen hopping through grassy meadows. They are grayish-green with large dark spots surrounded by yellow or white rings. This coloration gives them their name. The soft underbelly of the leopard frog is creamy white. This makes it hard to see the frog when it is in the water. Its back color blends in with a grassy pond. And its belly blends with the sky when seen from below.

The *bullfrog* is named for its loud bellowing sound. It is the most aquatic of frogs. It seldom leaves the water except to sit on the bank of a lake at night. The color of bullfrogs ranges from green to nearly yellow. But most of them are greenish-brown. The underbelly is gray-white with dark splotches. Bullfrogs are excellent swimmers because of their large, webbed hind feet. Their legs are strong and well developed. Their legs can be 25 centimeters long. Bullfrogs eat insects, worms, crayfish, and small fishes. Big bullfrogs will sometimes even eat a small duckling.

The tree frogs of the genus *Hyla* are interesting amphibians. Most of them have amazing protective coloration. Several of them have the ability to change their color. Some members of the genus live in trees. These frogs have a sticky disc on each toe. This enables them to cling to vertical surfaces. The spring peeper is a member of the genus *Hyla*. This frog lives in swamps and bogs rather than in trees.

Peeper eggs are laid in early spring. The tiny tadpoles feed on algae and protozoans. But the adults help us by eating mosquitos and gnats. A swamp or bog will be filled with the noise of peepers on a spring or summer night.

The resonating chamber of spring peepers allows their songs to be heard more than a mile away. Ask students if they have ever tasted frogs' legs. Discuss some of the reasons many people are "turned off" by frogs.

THE ECONOMIC IMPORTANCE OF FROGS

A major part of a frog's diet is insects. This makes frogs valuable because they help control the insect population. Many states have laws to regulate frog hunting for this reason. These laws forbid the capture of frogs during the breeding season.

Bullfrogs' hind legs are thought to be a food delicacy. They are raised for this purpose on farms in marshy areas. Smaller frogs are often used as fish bait. Frogs are a favorite in biology labs as specimens for dissection. The frog's internal organs have the same basic arrangement as the human's. Thus, dissecting frogs is an excellent introduction to human anatomy.

Anatomy of the Frog

THE EXTERNAL STRUCTURE

The frog's body is short, broad, and angular. It lacks the stream-lined shape of fishes. For this reason, frogs do not swim as well as fish do. And the frog's hopping is not as graceful as the movement of most land animals. But the frog is able to move about in both of these environments.

Frog skin is thin, moist, and loose. It is richly supplied with blood vessels. Glands in the skin secrete mucus. This reaches the skin's surface through tiny tubes. This skin slime makes frogs hard to hold. Frog skin lacks protective growths such as the scales of fishes and reptiles.

ADAPTATIONS OF THE FROG'S LEGS

The frog's front legs are short and weak. Each foot has four in-turned toes with soft, rounded tips. These feet are not webbed and are not used for swimming. Instead, the front legs are used to prop up the body when on land. They also break the fall when the frog lands from a jump. The inner toes, or thumbs, are enlarged on male frogs. These *thumb pads* become even larger during the breeding season.

The frog's hind legs are well developed and strong. They are adapted for both swimming and jumping. The thigh and calf muscles are very powerful. The ankle area and the toes are long. This forms a foot that is longer than the lower leg. A flexible *web membrane* connects the five long toes. This webbing makes each foot a very efficient swimming organ. When a frog rests on land, its hind legs fold against its body. In this position, a frog is ready to jump very quickly.

THE HEAD

Frog eyes are very noticeable because they bulge up above the head. The colored iris surrounds an elongated black pupil opening. Muscles attached to the eyeball rotate the eye in its socket. The eyes can be pulled into the sockets and pressed against the roof of the mouth. This helps hold food in the mouth. When a frog's eyes are pulled down, the upper and lower eyelids close.

The frog can float just below the water's surface with only its bulging eyes showing. This allows the frog to see the surface when hiding in the water. The frog has a third eyelid called the **nictitating**

(NICK-tuh-TAY-ting) *membrane.* This joins the lower lid. This thin covering keeps the eyeball moist when a frog is on land. It also protects the eye when the frog is under water.

The nostrils are forward near the top of the head. This allows the frog to breathe air when all but the top of its head is under water.

Frogs have no external ears. But they do have eardrums, or *tympanic* (tim-PAN-ick) *membranes.* These are located on the body surface just behind the eyes. The cavity of the middle ear lies just below the tympanic membrane. A canal connects each middle ear with the mouth cavity. These canals are called the *Eustachian* (yoo-STAY-shun) *tubes.* The inner ears are embedded in the skull.

THE MOUTH—AN INSECT TRAP

The frog's mouth extends from ear to ear. If you watch a frog catch a fly, you will see why the mouth is so large. It is a trap for insects. The frog's thick tongue is attached to the floor of its mouth at the front. This sticky tongue has two projections at its free end.

To catch an insect, a frog opens its mouth wide and flips its tongue over and outward. If the aim is good, the insect is caught on the tongue surface and is thrown into the mouth. The mouth snaps shut quickly. Then the frog swallows the insect. This all happens so fast it is hard to see. Two teeth project from bones in the roof of the mouth. They are called *vomerine teeth*. They aid in holding the prey. Small, cone-shaped *maxillary teeth* project from

35–7 The frog's tongue is well adapted for catching insects in that it is both flexible and sticky. Note how it is attached at the front of the mouth.

35–8 The frog's mouth. Its relatively large size is an adaptation for obtaining food.

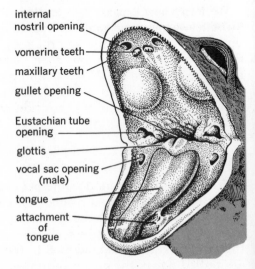

internal nostril opening

vomerine teeth

maxillary teeth

gullet opening

Eustachian tube opening

glottis

vocal sac opening (male)

tongue

attachment of tongue

the upper jaw. These also help hold on to prey. Frogs have no teeth on their lower jaws.

There are various openings inside the frog's mouth. *Internal nostril openings* are located in the roof on either side of the vomerine teeth. Far back on the sides of the roof are the openings of the *Eustachian tubes*. Openings to the *vocal sacs* are located at the back of the floor of the mouth of the male frog. When a male frog croaks, air is forced down these openings into the vocal sacs. This air forces the sacs to expand between the frog's ears and shoulders. This action makes the croak louder and more powerful. When a frog croaks under water, air is forced from the lungs, over the vocal cords, into the mouth, and then back to the lungs. The throat has two openings. The large *gullet opening* leads to the stomach. Below the gullet opening is the slitlike *glottis*. The glottis leads to the lungs.

THE DIGESTIVE SYSTEM

Adult leopard frogs usually feed on insects and worms. But they can swallow even larger meals because of their large, elastic *gullet*. The short gullet leads to a long *stomach*, an enlargement of the food tube. The upper end of the stomach is large, and it tapers at the lower end. At a point called the *pylorus*, the stomach links up with the coiled, slender small intestine. At the lower end of the stomach, there is a muscle called the *pyloric valve*. This valve controls the movement of food from the stomach into the small intestine.

The *small intestine* is looped several times. It is supported by a fanlike membrane called the **mesentery.** The anterior area of the small intestine, which curves from the pylorus, is the *duodenum*. The middle portion is the coiled *ileum*. The lower end of the small intestine leads into a short, broad *colon*. The colon is also called the *large intestine*. The colon opens into a cavity called the **cloaca** (kloe-AY-kuh). Tubes from the kidneys, the urinary bladder, and the sex organs also open into the cloaca. Waste materials and eggs or sperms pass out the cloaca through the *cloacal opening*.

Tiny *gastric glands*, in the stomach walls, secrete gastric fluid. Gastric fluid chemically digests some of the food. A large, three-lobed *liver* partially covers the stomach. **The liver stores digested food products. It also secretes bile and acts as a digestive gland.** The bile collects in the *gall bladder*, which lies between the middle and right lobes of the liver. From the gall bladder, bile runs through the *bile duct* into the upper part of the small intestine. A second digestive gland, the *pancreas*, lies inside the curve of the stomach. Pancreatic fluid and bile pass through the *common bile duct* into the small intestine. All of these fluids are necessary for digestion. *Mucous glands* in the walls of the stomach and intestine secrete *mucus*. **Mucus lubricates the passage for food.**

Basically, a frog's digestive system is like those of other vertebrates. It is a long food tube, generally called the **alimentary canal.**

After discussing the digestive system of frogs, stress to students the similarities between the frog and the human digestive system. Have students compare the frog's digestive system with that of the bony fish.

This canal has special regions for digestion and absorption of digested food. **Increased length of the alimentary canal increases the general efficiency of these processes.**

THE RESPIRATORY SYSTEM

Discuss the following question with the class: Why will frogs die if they are exposed too long to an environment lacking water?

You now know that adult frogs are air-breathers. Have you ever wondered how they can stay under water for a long time? And, during the winter, a frog will lie buried in the mud on the bottom of a pond to hibernate. The skin of the frog is thin. And the skin has a lot of blood vessels. **Thus, the frog's skin directly absorbs dissolved oxygen from the water.** It also gives off carbon dioxide. As long as a frog stays quiet, this type of respiration is enough to keep it alive. During hibernation, the frog's body processes slow down. Therefore, its oxygen need is very low. But when a frog is active and swimming, it needs more oxygen. The frog then comes to the surface and breathes air.

We inhale and exhale air by increasing and decreasing the size of our chest cavities. This is done by moving the ribs and diaphragm. The *diaphragm* is a muscular partition at the bottom of the chest cavity. **The frog has no diaphragm, and thus no chest cavity. The frog does not even have ribs.** Instead, frogs change the volume and pressure of air in their mouths. When a frog lowers the floor of its closed mouth, it causes a partial vacuum. Air rushes in through the open nostrils. Then, when the floor of the mouth springs up, air passes out through the nostrils.

The lining of the mouth is also adapted for respiration. It is thin, moist, and has many blood vessels. **Frogs can perform both mouth-breathing and lung-breathing.** They may pump air in and out of their mouths for some time without using their lungs. When the lungs are used, the nostrils are closed by skin flaps as the floor of the mouth rises. The glottis opens and air enters the windpipe, or **trachea.** This leads into the lungs. Then, with the nostrils still closed, the mouth is thrust down. This causes air to pass from the lungs into a partial vacuum. Then a sudden upthrust of the mouth forces air back into the lungs. After exchanging air between mouth and lungs a few times, the frog returns to mouth-breathing.

Frogs use their lungs only to assist mouth-breathing. As you might expect, frog lungs are small compared to lungs of higher vertebrates. Frog lungs have thin-walled sacs that lack the spongy tissue our lungs have.

THE CIRCULATORY SYSTEM

Students should find a dissection of the frog exposing the circulatory system very interesting.

The circulatory system of the frog is a step more complex than that of the fish. This represents a step toward the higher vertebrates. One of these advances is the heart. **The frog heart has three chambers.** There are two *atria (auricles)* and a muscular *ventricle.* Deoxygenated blood flows into the right atrium from various parts of the body. When the lungs are used, oxygenated blood from the lungs flows into the left atrium. Both atria contract at the same time. This forces blood into the ventricle. The ventricle then contracts and pumps blood out of the heart. The blood leaves through a large vessel that lies against the front side of the heart. This is called the *conus arteriosus*. This large vessel immediately divides into two branches, the right and left *truncus arteriosus*. Each of these again branches into three arches. The anterior pair are the *carotid arches*. These carry blood to the head. The middle pair are the *aortic arches*. They transport blood around the right and left sides of the heart. They join below the liver to form the *dorsal aorta*. This great artery carries blood to muscles, the digestive organs, and other parts of the body. The posterior pair of arches are called the *pulmocutaneous arches*. They carry blood to the lungs, skin and mouth.

The blood that returns to the frog's heart, after a trip through the body, has lost most of its oxygen. This blood is loaded with carbon dioxide and other cell wastes. Three large veins carry blood back to the heart. These are called the *venae cavae*. They join a triangle-shaped, thin-walled sac, called the *sinus venosus*, at the back of the heart. This empties into the right atrium.

Part of the blood, returning from lower parts of the body, flows through the vessels of the digestive system. There it absorbs digested food. This blood then flows through the *hepatic portal vein* which carries it to the liver. The liver picks up some of the food substances carried by this blood and screens out some of the wastes. From the liver, this blood moves on to the right atrium.

During each complete circulation, some blood passes through the kidneys. The kidneys remove some water and nitrogen-containing wastes from cell activity. *Pulmonary veins* carry blood from the lungs to the left atrium. This blood is oxygenated when the frog is using its blood in air-breathing.

Frogs have a three-chambered heart. As you may remember, the fish heart has only two chambers. Blood passes through the fish heart only once in its trip around the body. But frog hearts receive blood from both the body and the lungs. And the frog heart pumps blood to the head and the body, as well as to the various respiratory organs.

THE EXCRETORY SYSTEM OF THE FROG

Frog skin is a vital excretory organ. Most of the carbon dioxide leaving the blood passes through the frog's skin rather than through the mouth or lungs. The liver, too, removes certain wastes. The liver eliminates these wastes with bile or changes them chemically so the kidneys can remove them. The large intestine eliminates undigested food and other wastes. **But the *kidneys* are the main excretory organs.**

The kidneys are large, dark red organs. They lie on either side of the spine against the back body wall. Blood flows into the kidneys, through the *renal arteries* and out through the *renal veins*.

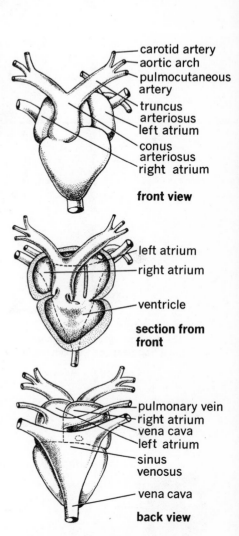

carotid artery
aortic arch
pulmocutaneous artery
truncus arteriosus
left atrium
conus arteriosus
right atrium

front view

left atrium
right atrium
ventricle

section from front

pulmonary vein
right atrium
vena cava
left atrium
sinus venosus
vena cava

back view

35–9 The frog's heart. Note that three branches of the vena cava lead to the right atrium. The pulmonary veins lead from the lungs to the left atrium. Blood from both these chambers passes through the conus arteriosus. In the back view, you can see where the venae cavae enter the sinus venosus.

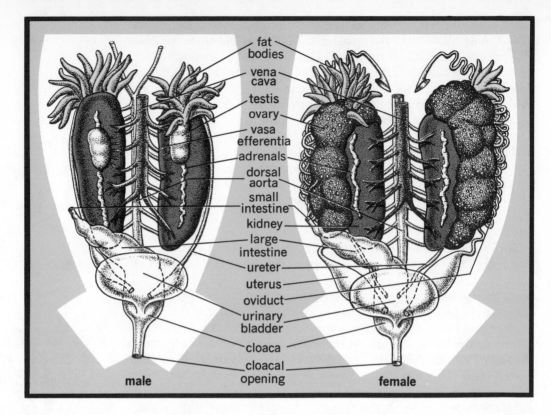

35–10 The urogenital organs of a male frog (left) and of a female frog.

The kidneys filter wastes and collect it as urine. The urine then flows to the cloaca through tiny tubes, called **ureters** (yooh-REET-erz). Urine may be excreted immediately. But frogs are also able to force urine from the cloaca through a small opening that leads to the *urinary bladder*. Here, it may be stored for a while before being excreted.

THE NERVOUS SYSTEM

The frog brain is more highly developed than the fish brain. *Olfactory lobes* lie at the anterior end of the brain. The long lobes of the *cerebrum* are proportionally larger than those of the fish. Next are the *optic lobes*. Behind the optic lobes is the *cerebellum*. This is a small band of tissue lying at right angles to the long axis of the brain. The *medulla oblongata* lies at the back of the frog brain. It joins the short, thick *spinal cord*. The spinal cord extends down the frog's back. The spinal cord is encased in bony vertebrae. As in the fish, *spinal nerves* branch from the cord to various parts of the body. In addition, ten pairs of *cranial nerves* extend from the brain.

THE REPRODUCTIVE SYSTEM

In both sexes, the frog's sex organs are internal. Thus, it is hard to tell the sexes apart, except during the breeding season. At this time, the thumbs of the males are enlarged.

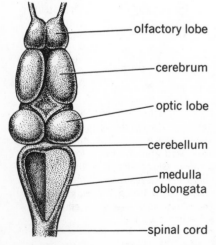

35–11 A dorsal view of the brain of a frog. Compare it with that of the fish in Chapter Thirty-Four.

35–12 Male and female frogs mating. The mass of eggs in the water indicates external fertilization. (Allan Roberts)

The male reproductive organs are two oval *testes*. The testes are a creamy-white or yellow color. They lie in the back, one on each side of the spine, in the anterior region of the kidneys. Sperm cells develop in the testes. The sperms then pass through tubes, the *vasa efferentia*, into the kidneys. When the sperms are discharged, they pass through the ureters into the cloaca. Some frog species have an enlargement, the *seminal vesicle*, at the base of each ureter.

In the female frog, the eggs develop in a pair of large lobed ovaries. The ovaries lie along the back above the kidneys. During the breeding season, the eggs enlarge and burst through the thin ovary walls. This frees the eggs into the body cavity. The abdominal muscles work the eggs toward the anterior. Here funnel-like openings to the **oviducts** gather the eggs. Oviducts are long and coiled, and are lined with ciliated cells. The cilia fan the eggs into the oviduct openings. Oviducts lead into the cloaca. Near the openings to the cloaca, the walls of the oviduct secrete a jellylike substance. This substance surrounds each egg. There is a saclike **uterus** at the base of each oviduct. The eggs are stored in the uterus until they are laid.

Stress to students the specialization of the frog's reproductive system. Compare it to that of the fish.

Frog Development

FERTILIZATION AND DEVELOPMENT OF THE EGGS

The female leopard frog lays up to 200 eggs between early April and mid-May. When the eggs are to be laid, the male clasps the female. The males uses its large thumb pads to press down on the female. This is called **amplexus.** It helps the female expel the eggs. As the eggs pass from the female's cloaca into the water, the male spreads sperm over them. The sperm cells reach most of the eggs with this *direct fertilization.*

Discuss with the class the advantages of direct fertilization. The characteristics of frog's eggs also are an advantage to survival.

The jellylike coat that surrounds each egg swells up in the water. This binds the eggs together in a round mass. In this clump, the eggs look like small beads covered by transparent jelly. **The jellylike coat protects the eggs from injury and makes it hard for fish to eat them. It also helps to keep the eggs at a constant temperature. Later, the covering serves as food for the young tadpoles.**

A frog egg is partly black and partly white. The white part is the yolk, a stored food material. This nourishes the tadpole during development. The dark part is the living protoplasm of the egg and a dark pigment. The yolk is heavier than the protoplasm. So frog eggs float with the dark side up. The dark pigment absorbs heat from the sun. The lighter lower half blends in with the light from the sky. This makes it hard to see the eggs from below. After eight to twenty days, depending on the weather and temperature, the leopard frog tadpoles hatch. They then wiggle away from the egg mass.

THE METAMORPHOSIS OF THE FROG—FROM TADPOLE TO ADULT

Point out to students the developmental pattern observed in tadpoles. Certain structures develop before others.

The hatched tadpole is a tiny, short-bodied creature. It has a little round mouth. It clings to the egg mass or to a plant. Yolk stored in the body nourishes the tadpole until it starts to feed. Soon the body grows longer and three pairs of gills develop at the outside of the head. The tail grows longer and develops a caudal fin. Then the tadpole's mouth opens. And it begins to scrape the leaves of water plants with its rough lips.

Not long after the tadpole starts to swim around, its rough lips disappear. A long, coiled digestive tract develops and the tadpole starts to eat the scum of water plants. Then a flap of skin grows over the gills, leaving only a small opening on its left side. This allows water to pass out of the gill chambers. At this stage, the tadpole is like a fish. It has a lateral line, fin, two-chambered heart, and a one-circuit circulation. It also has a relatively long intestine coiled in a spiral.

Tadpoles are fairly simple to catch in ponds. Students may want to bring one or two of them into class for further observation.

The change to an adult frog is amazing. First, hind legs appear on the tadpole's fishlike body. The front legs start to form at about the same time. But they remain hidden under the tadpole's fishlike operculum for a while. When the front legs do appear, the tadpole starts resorbing its tail. The tadpole does not shed or eat the tail.

Near the end of the metamorphosis, the mouth broadens and teeth develop. As these external changes happen, internal changes also occur. A saclike chamber, resembling the swim bladder of a fish, forms behind the tadpole's throat. This divides into two sacs, which become the lungs. The heart develops three chambers. The gill arteries change into the carotids, aortic arches, and pulmocutaneous arteries. Soon the gills stop functioning and the tadpole starts swimming to the water's surface to gulp air. At this time, the

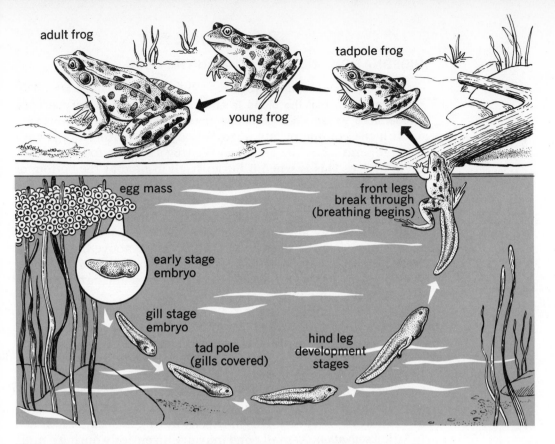

adult frog

young frog

tadpole frog

egg mass

front legs break through (breathing begins)

early stage embryo

gill stage embryo

tad pole (gills covered)

hind leg development stages

35–13 The history of the frog. The length of time for metamorphosis varies in different species of frogs.

tadpole's thin skin and broad, flat tail still play important roles in respiration.

Even before the tail is completely resorbed, the tadpole starts moving out on the land. From this point, the tadpole is considered a young frog. The young frog usually takes about a month to become a full-grown frog.

The metamorphosis of the leopard frog takes from two to three months. Adult leopard frogs usually appear around July first. Bullfrogs usually spend two winters as tadpoles. And it may be three years before the adult bullfrog is fully formed.

REGENERATION IN AMPHIBIA

Many amphibians, especially salamanders, can regrow injured or lost body parts. A foot, a part of a limb, or the tail may be lost in escaping from an enemy. Regeneration can occur rapidly. In their tadpole stages, frogs and toads also have this capability. But, as the tadpole matures, the capability disappears. No adult frogs and toads can regenerate body parts.

Frog Behavior

HIBERNATION AND ESTIVATION IN THE FROG

Like fishes and reptiles, frogs are "cold-blooded" vertebrates. This does not mean that the blood is always cold. It means that the body temperature varies with the temperature of the external environment.

With the coming of fall, a frog's body temperature drops with the temperature of the air. Soon the frog's body is too cold to remain active. This is when it buries itself in mud at the bottom of a pond. Its heart slows down and blood hardly circulates in the vessels. Because it is so inactive at this time, the frog needs very little oxygen. Enough can be supplied through the moist skin. Body tissues stay alive by the slow oxidation of stored food. The food is stored in the liver and in the **fat bodies** above the kidneys. Nervous activity stops almost completely. The frog lies in its burrow in a stupor. This is the condition of the frog during **hibernation.** Hibernation is a winter rest.

With the coming of spring, the water gradually warms. The frog's body activities speed up. And soon the frog wakes from its winter sleep. After a while, it begins the activities of a normal life again.

The hot summer months bring other problems for the frog. **Lacking a way to cool its body, the frog must escape from extreme heat.** It may lie quietly in cool, deep water. Or it may bury itself in mud at the bottom of a pond. This inactivity during the heat of summer is called **estivation.** A small pond may dry up entirely during a midsummer hot spell. Then the frog has to bury itself in the mud and estivate. Cool weather eventually returns, and the pond fills with water again. The frog comes out of estivation and continues normal activity until hibernation.

Some students may wish to refer to *Animals in Field and Laboratory* by Seymour Simon, New York, McGraw-Hill Book Co., 1968. There is an interesting experiment concerning frog hibernation in this book.

Students may be interested in learning about hibernation in certain frogs. Most frogs hibernate in the mud at the bottom of a pond. The mud keeps the frog from freezing during the winter months.

SUMMARY

The vertebrate time scale shows an interesting history for amphibians. According to our reading of fossils, the earliest amphibians date back to the close of the Devonian Period, often called the Age of Fishes. It was probably then that the early ancestors of amphibians, the lungfish and lobe-finned fishes, crawled out of the primal seas onto the edges of the land. This move offered amphibians a new environment. They no longer had to compete with fish. Thus, amphibians suddenly began to flourish in the Carboniferous and Permian periods. But during the Mesozoic Era, other vertebrates appeared who were more completely adapted to life on land. These newer creatures challenged the amphibians and greatly reduced their numbers. Today there are not many amphibians compared to other land animals, especially the mammals.

Amphibians are limited to moist areas because they need water to lay eggs and develop into adults. They represent a kind of "in-between" stage in the evolutionary process. They live in two worlds, water and land. But fish surpass them in the water. And other vertebrates surpass them on the land.

QUESTIONS FOR REVIEW

1. Why do biologists believe that the early lobe-finned lungfishes were amphibian ancestors?
2. What characteristics of amphibians distinguish them from other living vertebrates?
3. In what ways do salamanders resemble lizards? Name several ways in which they differ from lizards.
4. Explain why the axolotl does not undergo metamorphosis.
5. Describe how a frog catches a flying insect.
6. In the order in which they receive food, name the organs forming the alimentary canal of the frog.
7. How is the frog, an air-breather, able to stay under water for long periods of time?
8. In what way is the frog's heart more developed than the fish's heart?
9. Describe the structures used when the frog excretes waste from the blood.
10. Name and describe the type of fertilization exhibited by frogs.
11. List, in order of occurrance, the changes during the metamorphosis of the frog.
12. Describe the changes that occur in a frog's body during hibernation.

APPLYING PRINCIPLES AND CONCEPTS

1. Explain the statement, "The development of legs helped animals find water, not leave it."
2. Although amphibians became terrestrial, discuss why they were never successful on land.
3. Describe the structures of the frog's head that help it adapt to its life in water and on land.
4. How is the direct fertilization of the frog's eggs more efficient than spawning in fishes?
5. Explain how the frog shows a relationship to the fish in its early development.

chapter thirty-six

The Reptiles

OBJECTIVES

- LIST some reptiles of the Mesozoic era.
- EXPLAIN the evolutionary importance of the amniote egg.
- DESCRIBE the characteristics of the reptiles.
- NAME examples of each order of the reptiles.
- DESCRIBE the structural adaptations of the snake as a predator.
- COMPARE oviparous and ovoviviparous snakes.

The ancestors of the reptiles that we know today were the dinosaurs of the past. Students are usually interested in these prehistoric creatures and some may want to report on one or more to the class.

If the school is close to a museum that has dinosaur models, encourage students to visit and report on their findings.

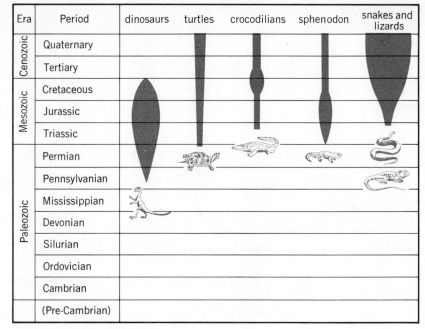

Era	Period	dinosaurs	turtles	crocodilians	sphenodon	snakes and lizards
Cenozoic	Quaternary					
Cenozoic	Tertiary					
Mesozoic	Cretaceous					
Mesozoic	Jurassic					
Mesozoic	Triassic					
Paleozoic	Permian					
Paleozoic	Pennsylvanian					
Paleozoic	Mississippian					
Paleozoic	Devonian					
Paleozoic	Silurian					
Paleozoic	Ordovician					
Paleozoic	Cambrian					
Paleozoic	(Pre-Cambrian)					

36–1 A time scale of reptiles.

THE RISE OF THE REPTILES

It is hard to say exactly when the first reptiles descended from their amphibian ancestors. Generally, only the hard body structures form fossils. This limits fossils to body parts such as bones and teeth. But many of the structures that separate early reptiles from amphibians were soft body parts. Thus, it is often impossible to tell the two apart in fossil form.

At the close of the Paleozoic era, more and more land masses rose above the ponds and swamps of earlier times. Perhaps this set the stage for the rapid rise of reptiles.

The Age of Reptiles began in the Triassic period of the Mesozoic era. The reptiles increased in numbers through the Jurassic period and into the Cretaceous period. This Age of Reptiles spanned more than 100 million years. During this time, the reptiles flourished in many forms and numbers.

There were giant plant-eating dinosaurs that weighed over 27,000 kilograms. There were also flesh-eating dinosaurs, duck-billed dinosaurs, armored dinosaurs, and flying dinosaurs. They dominated all other kinds of animals. Among them were the largest land animals that have ever lived.

Near the end of the Cretaceous period, however, reptiles declined in number. There were fewer and fewer of them, until finally the dinosaurs became extinct. Never again were the reptiles dominant over the other animals of the earth.

We can only guess why the dinosaurs became extinct. Land and weather changes must have occurred during this time. Many of the plant-eating dinosaurs lived in lakes and swamps. Many of these

454

lakes may have drained because of rising in the earth's surface. And vegetation may have changed, thus affecting the plant-eaters' food supply. As the plant-eaters disappeared, the meat-eaters lost their food supply. Changes in climate may have been another important factor. It would have been hard for a monstrous dinosaur to hibernate during cold weather. However, some of the reptiles survived these changing conditions. Many species have had little change since the Cretaceous period. Others became the ancestors of modern reptiles. These have had many changes in the past 70 million years. Before studying modern reptiles, we shall discuss some of the better-known dinosaurs.

THE DINOSAURS

Dinosaurs have been extinct for millions of years. All that remains of the once great dinosaurs are the eggs and footprints preserved in rock and fossilized bones. This evidence has been gathered in many parts of the world. Yet, it still takes great imagination for paleontologists to piece together a picture of life during the time when the dinosaurs roamed the earth.

The word dinosaur means "terrible lizard." This is a good name for these ancient reptiles. Some dinosaurs were no larger than today's large lizards. But some were giants that would dwarf an elephant.

The best-known dinosaurs were the largest. The *Brontosaurus*, or thunder lizard, was probably the largest. It was about 25 meters long, 5 meters high, and weighed over 15,000 kilograms. The *Brontosaurus* lived in shallow lakes and marshes, feeding on water plants. Its long neck was balanced by an equally long and heavy tail.

The *Stegosaurus* was one of the most heavily armored dinosaurs. It was about ten meters long. This giant lizard had a double row of plates rising almost a meter from its back. It had two pairs of sharp spikes on its tail. This was probably used as a weapon against its enemies. The *Stegosaurus* had a very small head and cranial cavity. Its brain was no larger than the brain of a small dog. This small brain was aided by a mass of nerve tissue near the spinal cord in the hip region. This second "brain" was twenty times larger than the true brain. It is thought that this second "brain" controlled the two-meter-long hind legs and large tail.

The *Tyrannosaurus*, or tyrant lizard, was the most ferocious of the dinosaurs. It walked erect on its powerful hind legs. The *Tyrannosaurus* balanced its heavy body with its long tail, much as a kangaroo does. This meat-eater was nearly 17 meters long and stood over 6 meters high. It had powerful jaws armed with double-edged teeth that were as long as 15 centimeters. These teeth could rip the hide even of an armored victim. Certainly, *Tyrannosaurus* was one of the most terrifying creatures ever to roam the earth!

During the Jurassic period, there were flying reptiles called *pterosaurs* (TEH-ruh-soarz). One of the best known was a pterodactyl, the *Pteranodon*. It had a body about the size of a turkey. But it had

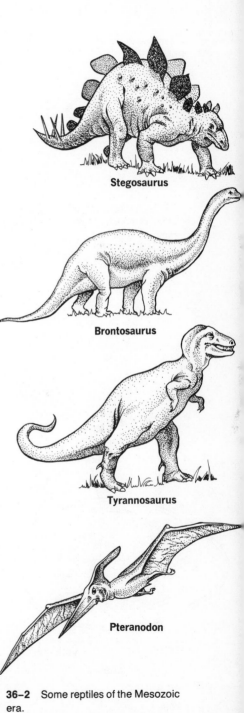

Stegosaurus

Brontosaurus

Tyrannosaurus

Pteranodon

36–2 Some reptiles of the Mesozoic era.

36–3 A reconstructed dinosaur skeleton. (American Museum of Natural History)

a wing spread of more than eight meters. Its wings were made of membranes that stretched from very long wrist bones. Its skull was almost a meter long and turned into a crest at the back. The jaws came forward into a toothless beak. The *Pteranodon* could fly and soar gracefully. But it must have been very awkward on land. Scientists believe that it fed by swooping down to catch fish swimming close to the surface of lakes.

In 1975, the fossil remains of a new species of pterosaur were found. This giant flying reptile had a wing span greater than 12 meters. Like dinosaurs, the pterosaurs died out in the late Cretaceous period. Why did they become extinct? Perhaps they could not compete with birds, which were becoming more abundant at this time.

THE AMNIOTE EGG—KEY TO THE RISE OF REPTILES

The gradual evolution of reptiles from certain amphibians was an important step forward in vertebrate development. **Reptiles were the first land vertebrates that did not depend on water for an aquatic stage or for reproduction.** What was the key to the success of reptiles on land? The answer is the ***amniote egg.*** The amniote egg is believed to have appeared first among the reptiles.

You have seen that all amphibians are bound to water. This was true of ancient amphibians and it is true of amphibians today. Even the most terrestrial forms, the frogs and toads, must live in water in their larval stage. All amphibians must lay their eggs in water or at least moisture. Their eggs lack protective structures to stop them from drying out. Reptilian eggs do not have this biological limitation.

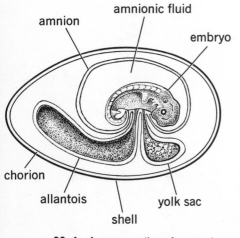

amnionic fluid

amnion

embryo

chorion

allantois

shell

yolk sac

36–4 A cross section of an amniote egg.

The amniote egg is relatively much larger than an amphibian egg. **The amniote egg is enclosed in a porous shell. This shell prevents rapid water loss and protects the internal structures.**

The egg contains three *embryonic membranes* which are very important to the survival of the embryo. One of them, the **amnion,** encloses the embryo. The cavity formed by the amnion fills with a watery, amniotic fluid. This fluid surrounds the embryo. The fluid is secreted by the amnion. Thus the reptile embryo develops in a watery environment like that of its amphibian ancestors. The embryo has its own pool within the protection of the egg. The **chorion** is the outermost embryonic membrane. The chorion lines the inside of the shell. The third embryonic membrane is the **allantois.** As the embryo develops, this double membrane thickens and actually becomes an organ of the embryo. It functions in absorption, respiration, and excretion. Many blood vessels in the allantois join blood vessels in the embryo. This allows oxygen to be absorbed and carbon dioxide to be given off.

The amniote egg contains a large **yolk.** This yolk supplies the embryo with food for a longer time than does the amphibian egg yolk. This longer period of embryonic development eliminates the larval stage. The embryo develops directly into the adult reptile.

Another reproductive advance occurred with the development of the amniote egg. This important feature is called **internal fertilization.** Internal fertilization occurs when, **during mating, sperm cells are placed into the oviducts of females.** Fertilization takes place before the development of the protective egg shell. Some reptiles lay the fertilized egg when the shell has formed. Others keep the fertilized egg in their bodies until the young reptile hatches internally and is brought forth alive.

THE BODY CHARACTERISTICS OF REPTILES

The amniote egg and internal fertilization allowed reptiles to reproduce outside of a water medium. Changes in body structure also allowed reptiles to maintain life in land environments. The reptilian characteristics are summarized below:

- A body covering of scales to protect the skin surface.
- Dry skin, lacking mucous glands and thickened to prevent water loss.
- Limbs, if present, with claws on the toes and good for climbing, digging, and moving on land.
- Well-developed air-breathing lungs, eliminating the need for skin or mouth respiration.
- A partial division of the heart ventricle. This results in further separation of oxygenated blood from the lungs and deoxygenated blood from the body tissues. The separation increases the oxygen supply to tissue.
- A body temperature that varies with that of the environment. (In this respect, reptiles are similar to amphibians and less complex vertebrates.)

Stress to students the importance of the reptile egg in the process of evolution. The egg permitted reptiles to stay on land after laying their eggs. In addition, the reptilian embryo was able to develop completely before hatching.

Ask students to compare the reproductive process of reptiles with that of amphibians.

Table 36-1 **ORDERS OF LIVING REPTILES**

NAME OF ORDER	REPRESENTATIVES
Rhynchocephalia	*Sphenodon* (tuatara)
Chelonia (Testudinata)	Turtles and tortoises
Squamata	Lizards and snakes
Crocodilia	Alligators, crocodiles, gavials, and caimans

CLASSIFICATION OF REPTILES

There are about 6,000 species in the class *Reptilia* today. This may seem like a great many. But it is only a small fraction of the number that inhabited the earth during the Age of Reptiles. Sixteen orders of reptiles once existed. But only four species of reptiles exist today. One of these orders is represented by a single species that is nearing extinction.

Some of today's reptiles are very much like their prehistoric ancestors. But others, called "modern" reptiles, have become very different. Reptiles are most numerous in the tropics. Some reptiles, however, have migrated to more temperate climates. In fact, reptiles are even found in colder parts of the earth. But there are no reptile populations in icy regions, high mountains, and the ocean depths. There are about 275 reptile species in the United States.

The Sphenodon

HOLDOVER FROM THE PAST

One of the rarest animals on the earth today is a species of reptile. This is the sole surviving species of the order *Rhynchocephalia.* This ancient reptile, even older than the dinosaurs, is *Sphenodon punctatus* or *tuatara* (тоо-ah-TAH-rah). Its closest relatives became extinct early in the Mesozoic era. They probably could not compete with more adaptable lizards. But the tuatara escaped extinction in New Zealand and its neighboring islands. Here there were no mammals with which to compete. Once English settlers brought in their rats, pigs, cats, and weasels, however, the tuatara became extinct on the mainland. Today, the last few tuatara live on a few small islands off the coast of New Zealand. The New Zealand government now protects them. Because the creatures live well in captivity, it may be possible to preserve them.

Animals very similar to the *Sphenodon* lived on the earth 170 million years ago. The order Rhynchocephalia thus seems to have had a very slow rate of evolution compared to other vertebrate groups. The tuatara reaches a length of 60 centimeters. It looks like a large lizard. The tuatara's most unusual characteristic is a third eye on the top of its head. This is called a **parietal** (puh-RY-ut'l) **eye.** This eye is not a functioning sense organ. But it still has the remains of a retina and some other normal eye structures.

36–5 *Sphenodon punctatus,* the tuatara of the islands off the coast of New Zealand, is the only surviving species of a once-flourishing order. (Allan Roberts)

Discuss some of the reasons why only 4 of the 16 reptile orders have living representatives.

The tuatara hides in a burrow during the day. It comes out at night to feed on insects, worms, and other small animals. The eggs are buried in a shallow depression in the ground. It is almost a year before they hatch. The female tuatara usually lays from twelve to fourteen eggs.

Snakes

THE MOST WIDESPREAD REPTILES

Snakes are relative newcomers among reptiles. There is no good fossil record of these creatures. But there is little doubt that they descended from reptiles with legs. In fact, pythons and boas still have vestigial hind legs. Snakes evolved rapidly during the Tertiary period. This is the same time that rodents and other small mammals were developing.

Snakes are the most numerous of today's reptiles. They are also the most widely distributed. Snakes are found in water, in the ocean, on rocks, under the ground, and in trees. They are most abundant in tropical regions. There are fewer of them in cooler climates. There are 126 species in the United States and only 22 in Canada.

Of the more than 2,000 species of snakes, only a few are poisonous. **The harm caused by the few dangerous snakes is far outweighed by the valuable service snakes render by killing insects and rodents.**

BODY STRUCTURE OF A SNAKE

Snake bodies are long and thin. A close look will show you that they have three separate areas. These areas are the head; the trunk, containing the body cavity; and the tail, which extends beyond the anus. As in all reptiles, snake bodies are covered with scales. On the back and sides, the scales are small and ovoid. But on the lower side, they form broad plates, called *scutes.*

Several times a year, snakes shed their outer layer of scales. The process is called molting. The thin outer layer loosens. Then the snake usually hooks a piece of the loose covering to a sharp object and works its way out. The newly exposed scales are brighter than the old ones.

THE STRUCTURES OF A SNAKE'S HEAD

The snake's mouth is large. On the upper jaws there is a double row of teeth. On the lower jaw is a single row. These teeth are cone-shaped and slant back toward the throat. The teeth are not used for chewing. But they are necessary to hold prey, which is swallowed whole.

Snakes have a very acute sense of smell. Olfactory nerve endings lie in the nasal cavities. These cavities open as paired nostrils near

Ask students to report on the economic importance of snakes. Elicit from students some of the reasons many people fear snakes.

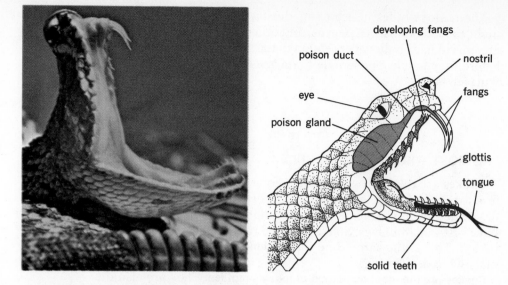

developing fangs

poison duct

nostril

eye

fangs

poison gland

glottis

tongue

solid teeth

36–6 The head of a poisonous snake is well suited for poisoning prey and swallowing it whole. (William M. Partington, National Audubon Society)

the front of the head. The sense of smell is aided by a forked tongue. This tongue rests in a sheath on the floor of the mouth. It flicks out through a small opening that is left when the jaws are closed. The tongue picks up dust and odor-bearing particles from the air. And it transfers them to tiny pits in the front of the roof of the mouth. These pits are called *Jacobson's organs.* They contain nerve endings that are very sensitive to odors.

Unlike other reptiles, snakes have no lids on their eyes. Instead, a transparent scale covers each eye. Just before molting, this scale becomes cloudy. This makes vision difficult for a time. The eyes can turn in their sockets. And a moveable lens focuses the eye sharply, especially at close range. Different snakes have different shaped pupils in their eyes. Those most active in daylight have round pupils. Those most active at night have elliptical pupils similar to those of cats.

The ears are embedded in the skull. There are no external openings. Thus, the snake cannot hear vibrations carried by air. Instead, the skull bones carry vibrations to the highly sensitive ear mechanisms.

THE FEEDING HABITS OF SNAKES

All snakes eat animals. No vegetarian snakes are known to exist. Snakes are classified into three groups according to feeding habits.

Many snakes, including most of the nonpoisonous species, simply seize an animal in their mouth and *swallow it alive.* Most of these snakes feed on insects, frogs, toads, lizards, fishes, and other small animals.

Some of the larger snakes, including the python, boa, king snake, and bull snake use a special method of food-getting. They squeeze their prey to death. These snakes seize the prey, usually by its head, and coil themselves around it. The prey is killed by *constriction.* The snake's muscular body squeezes the victim so hard that the

Students may be interested in reading about camouflage and mimicry in snakes. For example, candystick snakes are able to mimic highly poisonous coral snakes.

chest is compressed and breathing is stopped. This great pressure also cuts off the victim's circulation and stops the heart. The shock kills the prey, often without breaking a bone. If the snake feels a pulse in its victim, it will squeeze again. These snakes begin to swallow their prey as soon as it is killed. Biologists have found that warm-blooded animals are killed more quickly by constriction than cold-blooded animals.

A relatively few snakes *poison their prey*. Poisonous snakes kill their prey with toxic **venom** before swallowing the victim. They produce this venom in salivary glands at the side of their heads. The poisonous snake strikes by thrusting its head directly at the prey. It embeds its paired fangs into the prey. Venom flows from poison glands through ducts inside the fangs. The hollow fangs are like hypodermic needles. The amount of venom injected varies with the species and size of snake. But the smaller species and the young of larger species have more concentrated venom. They can be just as dangerous as the larger poisonous snakes.

Point out to students that the other internal organs of snakes are not discussed because of their similarity to frogs and higher vertebrates. Have them list such common organs.

ADAPTATIONS FOR SWALLOWING

Snakes do not eat often. They may go for weeks, sometimes even a year under some conditions, without eating. But it is amazing to watch a snake when it does eat. A snake can swallow an animal four or five times larger than its own body. This is possible because of several modifications of the snake's jaws. The lower jaws are not joined directly to the skull. They are fastened to a separate bone, called the *quadrate bone*. This acts as a hinge, allowing the jaw to drop down and forward. Also, the two halves of the lower jaw are fastened at the front by an *elastic ligament*. This allows each half to work independently of the other. As mentioned earlier, numerous slanting teeth hold the prey firmly while it is being swallowed.

During swallowing, one side of the lower jaw pulls the prey into the snake's mouth. The other side pushes forward for a new grip. With this seesaw action, the prey is slowly pulled down the snake's throat. It is similar to pulling a rope, hand over hand. The snake actually crawls-forward around its prey.

Swallowing takes quite a long time. So special adaptations for breathing are needed while the snake has a large prey in its throat. The snake's trachea extends along the floor of its mouth to a glottal opening near the front rim of the lower jaw.

HOW SNAKES MOVE

Snakes move in several different ways. When they are crawling fast or swimming in water, they use a method called *lateral undulatory movement*. The body winds from side to side in broad curving motions. And the entire body follows the same track. Little bumps and irregularities in the ground give the snake a grip.

When snakes crawl slowly in a straight line, they use a motion called *caterpillar movement*. The snake pushes its scutes forward in several body sections. The rear edge of each scute grips the ground. The body is pulled forward by wavelike muscular contractions.

The third method of snake movement is called *side-winding*. This movement is used by snakes of sandy desert areas. The snake twists its body into S-shaped loops. And except for two or three points of contact, it raises itself off the ground. The sidewinder "walks" across the sand on these loops.

Even with these special adaptations, snakes cannot move very fast. You will be relieved to learn that most travel at less than a kilometer per hour. Even the fastest snakes do not exceed five kilometers per hour. You can easily walk at this speed. And most people can run short distances at 15 to 30 kilometers per hour. Thus, you do not have to worry about being outrun by a snake!

THE INTERNAL ORGANS OF A SNAKE

A snake's spine has over 300 pairs of ribs attached to the vertebrae. These ribs are set in muscle and are flexible. This allows for movement and swallowing of large prey. Also, adaptations allow snakes to swallow their prey whole.

The right lung is well developed. But the left lung is stunted or entirely missing. Flexible ribs allow the body wall to expand for breathing. The large heart has a **septum.** This wall partially separates the ventricle into two chambers.

The snake is cold-blooded. So its rate of oxidation is much lower than that of warm-blooded animals. This means that much less heat is generated in the snake's body. While resting, a snake is often a little colder than the external environment. The little heat it does produce is soon lost, since the snake has no covering of fur or feathers. The reptile's cold-bloodedness is a disadvantage on land. In cold regions, they cannot be active during the winter. And, on hot days, reptiles must seek cool shelter. This is the only way they can cool their body temperature below the level of the outdoor temperature.

REPRODUCTION IN SNAKES

Most snakes lay eggs that resemble those of other reptiles. Each egg is enclosed in a tough white shell. This egg contains stored food to nourish the young snake during development. The female snake gives the eggs no care after she lays them. The only incubation warmth the eggs receive is from the sun. **Animals that lay eggs are called *oviparous*** (oe-VIP-uh-rus). The black snake and blue racer are oviparous.

A smaller group of snakes bring forth their young alive. The eggs are not laid. They remain in the uterus until they develop into young snakes. But the mother's body provides no food for the em-

36–7 A female pilot black snake with eggs she has just laid (left) and a mother queen snake with newly born young. Which snake is oviparous and which is ovoviviparous? (Allan Roberts)

bryos. These snakes are usually born in the late summer. **Snakes that bring forth their young already hatched are classed as** *ovoviviparous* (OE-voe-vie-VIP-uh-rus). On the other hand, **mammals which bring forth and nourish their young during development are called** *viviparous* (vie-VIP-uh-rus).

NONPOISONOUS SNAKES

Some snakes produce poison, or toxins, and others do not. You are probably familiar with the harmless *garter snake, black snake,* and *racer.* These snakes should be protected because they destroy insects, rats, and other rodents. The *king snake* is a valuable snake because it eats other snakes and rodents. The *constrictors* of South America, Africa, and Asia are also nonpoisonous snakes.

THE POISONOUS SNAKES

All poisonous snakes have specialized teeth, or fangs, for injecting venom. They are grouped into four families. The *cobras* live mostly in the tropics of Asia and Africa. Some members of the cobra family are deadly to human beings. The *king cobra* of Thailand is the largest of all poisonous snakes. Some species of cobra spit venom at their enemies in a fine spray. This spray can travel about a meter with amazing accuracy. This venom can cause temporary or permanent blindness if it enters an eye. The *coral snakes* of North America are in the same family as the cobras. They are small, but they have very beautiful coloration. Their venom is very potent. But they do not kill many humans. Their fangs are too short to get through shoes or heavy clothing.

Sea snakes are related to the cobra. But they are placed in another family. They live in the shallow waters of the East Indies. One species is often seen off the west coast of tropical South and Central America, and Mexico. These snakes seldom harm humans because they are strictly marine creatures. Fishermen, however, fear these snakes. Very rarely, one is hauled aboard a fishing vessel.

The third group of venomous snakes is made up of the *vipers.* They include all the poisonous snakes of Europe, Africa, and most of Asia that are not cobras. The most common viper is the European viper. In England, it is called the adder. But the largest number of viper species live in Africa.

The fourth family of poisonous snakes is called *pit vipers*. Pit vipers are different from true vipers in that they have heat-sensitive organs. These organs are pits located in front of their eyes. Biologists have discovered that these pits sense infrared rays. This helps pit vipers strike accurately at any prey that produces heat. Thus, pit vipers usually prey upon warm-blooded animals. Some of these snakes live in southern Asia. But most are found in North and South America. The best known are North America's *copperhead* and *cottonmouth moccasin*, South America's *fer-de-lance* and *bushmaster*, as well as the many rattlesnakes of both continents.

Rattlesnakes are the most widespread poisonous snakes in the world. They live from northern Argentina to southern Canada. Of the more than 19 species found in the United States, at least 12 live in the Southwest. The largest North American species is the *diamondback*. This snake lives in marshy areas in the Southeast. It can grow to be over two meters long. Other species include the *prairie rattlesnake, western diamondback*, and *sidewinder*. The *timber rattlesnake* is found in most of the eastern United States.

A rattlesnake has a series of dry segments, called rattles, on the end of its tail. When the snake is disturbed, it vibrates these rattles rapidly. This causes a whirring sound. This warning is the reason that few people are actually bitten by the rattlesnakes. You can step away from danger if you hear and recognize a rattlesnake's warning.

The rattlesnake's head is large and triangular. It has this shape because of the presence of poison glands. Its fangs fold upward against the roof of the mouth when the mouth is closed. This is possible because the fangs are fastened to a hinged bone on the upper jaw. Muscles pull down the fangs when the snake opens its mouth to strike. The rattlesnake can strike to a distance of more than one third the length of its body. When the rattlesnake strikes, the fangs are driven deep into the flesh of the victim. Poison flows from the glands, through the fangs, and into the wound. The rattlesnake is considered dangerous because of the length of its fangs

36–8 Three pit vipers found in the United States: the copperhead; the cottonmouth, or water moccasin; and the rattlesnake. (Allan Roberts; others: Walter Dawn)

and the large amount of poison it injects. Its bite can be especially dangerous if it happens to hit a vein.

Diamondback rattlesnakes have several economic uses. Perhaps the most important use is in making **antivenin.** Antivenin is a biological product used in treating pit viper bites.

SNAKE VENOM

The toxic part of snake venom is made up of complex protein substances. The two types of snake venom are *neurotoxins* and *hemotoxins*. **Neurotoxins affect the parts of the nervous system that control breathing and heart action.** **Hemotoxins destroy red blood cells and break down the walls of small blood vessels.** All poisonous snakes have both types, but the proportions vary with the species. The venom of cobras, coral snakes, and sea snakes contains mostly neurotoxin. That of vipers and pit vipers tends to be mostly hemotoxin.

The danger of any snakebite depends on a number of factors. The amount of venom injected and the concentration of toxins are both critical. Another important factor is where the venom enters. It can enter the main circulatory system rapidly through a blood vessel or slowly through muscle or fatty tissue.

Snakebite is a serious problem in the tropics. As many as 40,000 people die each year from snakebites. Cobra bites kill many people in India. Few people die from snakebite in temperate regions. Yet, the bite of any poisonous snake should be treated right away.

Ask students to find out about the appropriate treatment of snakebite wounds. Are all snakebite wounds fatal?

The Lizards

STRANGE AND BEAUTIFUL REPTILES

Today there are more than 2,500 species of lizards. These sprang from ancestors which developed during the Mesozoic era. Modern lizards live mostly in tropical regions, though a few live in colder areas. Because they resemble dragons and dinosaurs, they are feared by many people. But only two species of lizards are poisonous. Most lizards are shy and harmless creatures. Of all modern reptiles, lizards have developed the most adaptations for different environments.

The *iguanas* (i-GWAH-nahz) are thought to be the most primitive lizards. They look very much like typical lizards. In this family is the so-called *horned toad*. This toad has a series of horny spines on its head and back for protection. It lives in the dry plains of the western United States. The spiny skin, which conserves water, is an excellent adaptation for dry areas. This small lizard survives because its color blends with the sand and spiny cacti of its environment.

One American iguana grows to over two meters long. The best known lizard is the 12-centimeter-long *anole*. It is more commonly called the chameleon (kuh-MEEL-yun). The name chameleon is

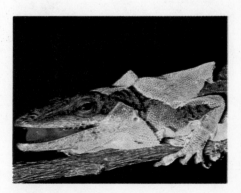

36–9 An American "chameleon" *(Anolis)* shedding its skin. Like many other lizards, the *Anolis* eats the shed skin. (Allan Roberts)

properly applied only to certain lizards. Chameleons can easily change their color. This change may be caused by light, temperature, or even their own state of excitement. The beautiful *collared lizards* are also iguanas. They are found in the southern United States and Central America.

The *geckos* are a group of highly specialized lizards. Their toes are expanded into clinging pads. They use these pads to climb up vertical surfaces and even to walk on ceilings. They are the only lizards that can make loud noises.

Skinks are known for their shiny cylindrical bodies and weak legs. They live in the forests of Africa and the East Indies, where they are the most abundant reptiles. They are also common in the United States. But they are not often seen because they are shy animals.

Gila (HEE-luh) *monsters* and their cousins, the *beaded lizards,* are the only poisonous lizards. Gilas live in the southwestern United States and Mexico. Beaded lizards live in Mexico only. A large Gila monster is less than 60 centimeters long. Poison glands are located in the rear of their lower jaws. Grooved teeth are found in both jaws. The Gila holds its victim in its mouth and shakes its head from side to side. This action releases the venom. Neurotoxins in the venom affect the nerves that control the victim's breathing. Few humans die from their bites. But Gila monsters should be treated like venomous snakes.

Monitor lizards are the largest lizards in the world. They are thought to be closely related to snakes because they have several adaptations that are also found in snakes. The largest of the monitors is the *Komodo dragon*. This monster can grow to be three meters long and sometimes weighs over 140 kilograms. It lives on Komodo Island in the East Indies. Except for their inability to breathe fire, monitor lizards look like the mythical dragons.

36–10 Examples of lizards: collared lizard (top), Gila monster, horned lizard, and Galápagos iguana. (K. Bobrowsky, Monkmeyer Press; Dr. E. R. Degginger; Stella Grafakos)

36–11 A Komodo dragon, the largest living monitor lizard. (Janet L. Stone, National Audubon Society)

The Crocodilians

CROCODILES, ALLIGATORS, AND THEIR RELATIVES

The crocodilians and their extinct relatives had their supremacy in the late Mesozoic era. They were found in many types of environments. But they thrived only in water. Crocodilians like modern alligators and crocodiles first appeared in the Cretaceous period. They have survived until today because their ancestors developed a way of breathing in the water.

They breathe through their raised nostrils. These nostrils are connected to the lungs by an air passage in the skull. At the back of the mouth is a fleshy valve that prevents water from entering the lungs when the mouth is open. With this ability, crocodilians can lie in the water, with only their nostrils and eyes above the surface. Unwary animals do not notice the crocodilian until it is too late.

Of the many crocodilian species that once lived, only a few still exist. Currently, there are 25 species of *alligators, caimans* (KAY-manz), *crocodiles,* and *gavials* in the order Crocodilia. They all live in tropical and subtropical zones. Their few differences are in length and width of snout, and arrangement of scales and teeth. The best known crocodilians are alligators and crocodiles. Crocodiles are more aquatic than alligators. Crocodiles have triangular heads and pointed snouts. On each side of the lower jaw, there is a tooth that fits into notches in the upper jaw. This distinguishes crocodiles from alligators.

Alligator hide is of great value for making fine leather. Baby alligators are in demand as pets. But the American alligator is in danger of being exterminated. The United States has outlawed the collecting and hunting of these animals. Most "alligator" hides and baby "alligators" sold in the United States are really South American caimans. Now these animals are disappearing from large areas of South America.

An interesting discussion could evolve concerning the use of alligator hide in the past and the destructive nature of such practices. This discussion can be linked to the killing of other animals for their fur or other products.

36-12 What difference do you see between the alligator (left) and the crocodile? (Stevenson, Animals, Animals; Allan Roberts)

The Turtles

REPTILES WITH SHELLS

Turtles that live on land are called **tortoises.** They have hard shells and are slow moving. They have strong feet and claws for walking on land and digging. Most tortoises are vegetarians. They live on a variety of plant foods. **Terrapins** are hard-shelled, freshwater turtles. These turtles are used as food in many parts of the country. **True turtles** are large, marine animals. Their limbs are in the form of flippers. These animals are well adapted to swimming in the ocean. **For convenience, we shall refer to all of these forms as turtles.**

Turtles have not changed much in the last 200 million years. Turtles first appeared in the Jurassic period, before lizards and dinosaurs. The turtles' armor is an unusual body structure. But it was very successful since these animals have survived for so long. However, of the over 6,000 reptile species, only 300 are turtles.

It is possible that the development of turtles may have reversed the trend of vertebrates to move from water to land. Their ancestors may have been land animals. This may explain why a few turtles still live on land. Most, however, are water dwellers. **Yet, turtles are reptiles. So they all must come to the land to lay their eggs.**

Turtles have several special adaptations that have helped them survive for so long. They have lower and upper shells that protect them like suits of armor. Many turtles can draw their heads and feet into this armor covering. **Although the shell causes turtles to move slowly, this adaptation for protection is the main key to their success.**

No one is sure just how large the shells of the first turtles were. Some modern turtles are almost completely enclosed by their shells. Others have very small shells. *Soft-shelled turtles* have a leathery skin instead of a hard, horny shell. But they have a well-developed bony shell beneath this skin. These turtles have flattened bodies. This allows them to lie hidden on the bottom of lakes or ponds. Very long necks aid these predators in capturing their prey. The upper shell of the *snapping turtle* is an excellent cover. But the lower shell is small. Still, the snapping turtle's large head and powerful jaws give it protection.

Typical *sea turtles* have large upper shells. But their lower shells are reduced in size. Sea turtles can escape their enemies because they swim well with their flippers. But sea turtles come ashore to sun themselves or lay their eggs. When on land, they are at the mercy of their enemies. If they are turned on their backs, they are helpless.

Turtles have horny, toothless beaks that enable them to eat either meat or plants. Their legs are strong and heavy. Many can stay under water for a long time. Some have even developed a substitute for gills. Sea turtles absorb oxygen from water through membranes in the cloaca and throat.

36-13 Various turtles. Galápagos tortoise, Florida box turtle, common snapping turtle, eastern soft-shelled turtle. (E. Ellingsen; John H. Gerard, L. L. Rue III, National Audubon Society)

While most turtles live in the water, tortoises are land dwellers. Some even live in dry desert conditions. Some tortoises live on islands far from any mainland. It remains a mystery how they came to be on these islands. Several species of giant tortoise inhabit the Galágpagos Islands in the eastern Pacific. They were thriving here before the arrival of explorers and their animals. Charles Darwin visited these islands during the trip around the world. His observations of these animals helped him develop his theory of evolution.

THE STRUCTURE OF THE TURTLE

Turtles are interesting creatures to observe and can be kept in an aquarium in the classroom. Be sure that the aquarium has at least three centimeters of water in it. Also, place some smooth stones in the aquarium for the turtles to climb upon. The water should be kept at about 24°C.

A turtle's upper shell is called a **carapace.** It is covered with epidermal plates called **shields.** These shields grow in a symmetrical pattern. Their number and arrangement vary from species to species. Underneath the shields are bony plates fused together to form a protective case. The shape and arrangement of these bony plates do not match those of the shields. The lower shell is called the **plastron.** Like the upper shell, it has epidermal shields that cover underlying bony plates. On the sides, the carapace and the plastron join together in a bony bridge.

Stress to students that some small turtles sold in pet stores have been found to be carriers of germs. Such germs can upset the human digestive system.

Turtle heads are usually either pointed or triangular. The mouth lacks teeth. But the sharp beak can cut through tough food. Nostrils at the top of the head make it possible for the turtle to lie covered in water with only its nose showing. The eyes are well developed. They are protected by three eyelids. In addition to the upper and lower eyelids, there is a transparent nictitating membrane. This membrane closes over the eyeball from the front corner of the eye. A smooth tympanic membrane lies just behind the angle of the upper and lower jaws.

Most turtles' legs are short. The feet usually have five clawed toes. The amount of webbing between the toes varies. The skin covering the limbs is tough and scale covered. The tails of the different species of turtles vary greatly in length.

SUMMARY

Fossils seem to show that reptiles evolved from amphibians during the Late Carboniferous Period. This was an important occurrence in the total life history of vertebrates. Amphibians have never really adapted to dry land. They are still very dependent on water. But reptiles broke this tie to the water. The development of dry skin and scales, claws, and well-developed lungs made this possible. Furthermore, the amniote egg made reptiles free of the water both for development and for an aquatic larval stage after hatching.

During the Mesozoic era, reptiles flourished and dominated animal life on the earth. Scientists call that period the Age of Reptiles. But after a few million years, at the end of the Mesozoic era, some land and weather changes occurred. The reptiles just could not adapt very well to these changes. Thus, many became extinct. Birds and mammals replaced much of the dwindling reptile population.

amniote egg   scutes   neurotoxin
shell   Jacobson's organ   hemotoxin
embryonic membrane   venom   tortoises
amnion   septum   terrapins
chorion   oviparous   true turtles
allantois   ovoviviparous   carapace
yolk   viviparous   shield
internal fertilization   antivenin   plastron
parietal eye

**QUESTIONS
FOR REVIEW**

1. Name and describe a plant-eating dinosaur, a flesh-eating dinosaur, and a flying reptile.
2. Describe the functions of the shell, chorion, amnion, allantois, and yolk of an amniote egg.
3. List six characteristics of reptiles that enabled them to live on land.
4. Give an example of each of the four orders of reptiles.
5. In what respect is *Sphenodon* a reptile of special interest to the biologist?
6. List three methods used by various snakes in capturing prey.
7. What characteristics of the snake's mouth allow it to swallow large prey?
8. Distinguish between oviparous and ovoviviparous.
9. Describe the action on the victim of each of the two types of toxin found in snake venom.
10. What are the differences between alligators and crocodiles?
11. What adaptations have enabled the turtle to survive through the ages?

**APPLYING
PRINCIPLES
AND CONCEPTS**

1. Discuss the amniote egg as the key to the development of land-dwelling vertebrates.
2. Account for the fact that many unusual and ancient animals are found today only on islands.
3. In what respect is cold-bloodedness a limiting factor in the distribution of reptiles?
4. Discuss several body structures of a reptile that represent a survival advantage over the amphibians.

37-1　Birds in flight. (Vivian Fenster)

The Birds

OBJECTIVES
- DESCRIBE the evolutionary origin of birds.
- NAME the characteristics of birds.
- EXPLAIN the structure and function of feathers.
- DEMONSTRATE an understanding of the systems of birds and their functions.
- EXPLAIN reproduction in birds.
- DESCRIBE how birds are adapted to flight.

THE ORIGIN OF BIRDS

Birds have been called "glorified reptiles." Like reptiles, modern birds have scales on their feet and claws on their toes. This may be evidence of their reptile ancestry. But birds obviously survived the changes that caused the decline of reptiles in the Late Cretaceous period. Birds were better adapted for flight than the flying reptiles, or pterosaurs. The pterosaurs disappeared more than 70 million years ago. **But today, birds are among the most plentiful vertebrates on the earth. They are abundant in number of species and individuals.**

The biological success of birds means that they were better adapted than the flying reptiles for life on land and on water. Study of the modern bird reveals some amazing adaptations. When did this "glorification" of reptiles begin? How rapidly did changes occur?

The first birds probably appeared during the Jurassic period. This was the height of the Age of Reptiles. But it was not until the late Cretaceous period and the Cenozoic era that birds gained a dominant place. This success has continued into the present.

The Archaeopteryx

A VERY IMPORTANT FOSSIL

Modern birds have none of the characteristics of the flying reptiles. Birds seemed to have developed along different, more successful lines. Still, it seems possible that birds had developed from reptilian ancestors millions of years ago. But where was the evidence of this transition from reptile to bird?

Some students may be interested in tracing the history of birds and the transitional stages between reptiles and birds. Ask these students to report their findings to the class.

471

37-2 *Archaeopteryx.* Observation of the fossils of the reptilelike bird, such as that above, led to the artist's representation at the right. (courtesy of the American Museum of Natural History)

In fact, a fossil bird that seems to be the link between birds and flying reptiles was discovered. The discovery was in Bavaria, Germany, in the late 1880's. An archeologist was digging for fossils in fine-grained rock dating to the Jurassic period. The rock seems to have formed at the bottom of a shallow lagoon. Strange reptile-like birds may have fallen into such lagoons from time to time. Gradually, they became fossilized and were preserved in stone.

Three such fossil birds of the Jurassic have been discovered. They are called *Archaeopteryx* (AHR-kee-OP-tuh-ricks), meaning "ancient bird."

The *Archaeopteryx* fossils show a skeleton. There are also clear impressions of both flight and tail feathers. Without the fossil feathers, scientists would have probably classified the bird as a reptile. Many of its characteristics were more those of a lizard than a bird. But feathers are characteristic of birds only.

The body of an *Archaeopteryx* was probably about the size of a crow or a small chicken. Its jaws and skull were elongated into a beak like a bird's. But the beak had teeth like a reptile's. Its neck was long and flexible. Its back was short and compact. This is an important characteristic for flight. Its tail, like those of lizards, was longer than its body. It had forelimbs that were modified into weak wings. And the typical bird flight feathers grew from the "hand" and lower arm. Three clawed fingers extended past the wing feathers. Biologists believe that *Archaeopteryx* used these fingers to climb up trees. From there, it could soar through the air and glide to the ground.

The bird's hind limbs were probably much like those of a modern bird. And so were the feet. They had three clawed toes pointing forward on each foot and one short toe turned backward. The development of the hind legs suggests that *Archaeopteryx* was better at running on the ground than gliding through the air. The *Archaeopteryx* was probably a weak flier at best. It probably did not have well-developed flying muscles.

The *Archaeopteryx* seems to have been a true mixture of bird and reptile. Its skeleton was mostly that of a reptile. But many of its bone modifications were those of a bird. In addition to flight feathers, *Archaeopteryx* had feathers over most of its body. For this reason, scientists believe it might have been warm-blooded. This is a definite characteristic of birds.

The *Archaeopteryx* was a product of several million years of evolution from its early reptile ancestors. It is the most ancient and primitive bird we know about today. Someday someone might find a fossil of an even more primitive bird. This would give us more clues about the evolution of birds.

During the Cretaceous period, the birds moved far along the evolutionary path that leads to modern birds. Their fingers grew together, making their wings stronger. Birds of the Cretaceous period still had teeth. But slowly these disappeared. Their mouths evolved into horny, toothless beaks or bills. By the beginning of the Cenozoic era, birds looked much like our modern birds. Most modern birds are similar in structure to one another. The various species of birds are probably a result of adaptations to different environments, diets, and types of life.

Discuss each of the characteristics of birds and how the characteristics have contributed to the survival of this class of vertebrates. Point out to students that the circulatory system of birds is very similar to that of mammals.

37–3 A time scale comparing birds with their early ancestors.

Era	Period	primitive flying reptiles	archaeopteryx	birds
Cenozoic	Quaternary			
	Tertiary			
Mesozoic	Cretaceous			
	Jurassic			
	Triassic			
Paleozoic	Permian			
	Pennsylvanian (Late Carboniferous)			
	Mississippian (Early Carboniferous)			
	Devonian			
	Silurian			
	Ordovician			
	Cambrian			
	(Pre-Cambrian)			

Gaviiformes
(loon)

Podicipediformes
(grebe)

Pelecaniformes
(pelican)

Ciconiiformes
(heron)

Anseriformes
(duck)

Falconiformes
(hawk)

Galliformes
(quail)

Gruiformes
(rail)

37-4 Some examples of common orders of North American birds.

Columbiformes
(mourning dove)

Charadriiformes
(gull)

Cuculiformes
(yellow-billed cuckoo)

Strigiformes
(owl)

Apodiformes
(hummingbird)

Caprimulgiformes
(whipporwill)

Coraciiformes
(kingfisher)

Piciformes
(sapsucker)

Passeriformes
(robin)

Modern Birds

HIGHLY SUCCESSFUL VERTEBRATES

Have students observe birds in nature for a short period of time. This observation will make them aware of the high rate of body activity common to birds.

The biological success of a group of organisms is measured by number of species and individuals, their adaptation to a variety of environments, and their distribution throughout the world. If we accept these standards for success, birds are among the most successful vertebrates. The mammals and bony fishes are also very successful. Birds range in size from tiny hummingbirds to the ostrich. Birds' diets vary to include seeds, nectar, insects, small animals, and even rotten flesh. Some birds are masters of the air. But others, like ostriches and penguins, cannot fly. Some birds never leave their home environment. Others go on migrations that span the globe. Their nests are varied. A nest can be a woven bag, a pile of sticks, a hole in a tree or in the ground.

Flying birds have an advantage over all other vertebrates. They can travel long distances and change their environment quickly. Many follow the food supply as it changes with the seasons. Ducks, geese, and other water birds are at home on the land, at sea, and in the air. This is a distinction not shared by any other vertebrates.

CHARACTERISTICS OF BIRDS

Birds differ in size, color, diet, and other adaptations. But they all have similar body structure and characteristics. The characteristics of the vertebrate class *Aves*, which includes all birds, are:

- Body covering of feathers.
- Bones that are light, porous, and sometimes filled with air.
- Forelimbs specialized as wings. These are used for flight in most birds. They are never used for grasping.
- Body supported by two hind limbs.
- Mouth in the form of a toothless, horny beak.
- A four-chambered heart; a well-developed circulatory system, with a right aortic arch only.
- A constant body temperature (warm-blooded).
- An amniote egg encased in a lime-containing shell. This is usually incubated in the nest.

Many structural adaptations are necessary for birds to fly. They need a streamlined body to reduce air resistance. Their muscle power and activity must be enormous. Weight must be sacrificed without reducing strength. Their digestive system must be efficient. Birds need large amounts of food to get the tremendous energy needed by the flight muscles.

The body temperature of a bird is higher than that of most animals. It averages from 38° to 45° C. Release of this heat energy requires a high metabolic rate. To support this cellular activity birds must have highly developed respiratory, circulatory, and excretory systems. Finally, they must have a large brain in proportion to their body to control all of this activity. Birds are vertebrate "powerhouses."

THE ORDER OF BIRDS

So far, scientists have catalogued over 8,500 species of birds. These are grouped into 27 orders. The better-known birds of North America represent 17 of these orders. Classification of this large number of species into orders, family, and genera is a difficult task for biologists.

Biologists have settled on several different bird characteristics for classifying birds in orders. Among these structures are the feet and beaks. Modifications in feet and beaks usually relate closely to the life habits and diets. Foot structure adapts some birds for diving and others for swimming, wading, perching, running, or carrying prey. Beak modifications determine if some birds are insect eaters, seed eaters, flesh eaters, mud probers, or wood borers.

Ask students to bring in bird feathers that they may have at home. Students will be interested in studying the feathers under a hand lens or three-dimensional microscope.

FEATHERS

Feathers are actually modified scales. They develop from small skin bumps called **papillae.** The bases of these feather buds sink into pits, the **follicles.** Follicles hold the feathers in the skin. Feather follicles lie in rows or tracts in certain skin areas. The feathers spread out to cover the other areas of the skin.

There are several kinds of feathers. The soft feathers on newly hatched chicks are called *down feathers.* In older birds, especially waterfowl, down feathers lie close to the skin and serve as insulation. Each down feather is made of a fluffy tuft at the end of a short quill. They reduce heat loss very efficiently. These feathers allow ducks and geese to fly through very cold air and still maintain a body temperature of over 38° C. The slender, hairlike feathers with tufts on the ends are known as filoplumes.

Ask students to think about the structure of the quill feather and how this relates to the lift and balance necessary for lift, balance, and steering in flight.

Contour feathers round out a bird's body, helping to make it streamlined. They also protect against injury and provide coloration. **Coloration is very important in the life of a bird.** Females are often less colorful than males. This allows the female to blend into the environment when nesting. *Quill feathers* are large contour feathers growing in the wing and tail. These large feathers help provide lift and balance needed for flying and steering.

The quill feather has a fairly complex structure. A broad, flat *vane* spreads from a central axis called the *rachis* (RAY-kiss). The rachis ends in a hollow *quill.* The rachis is composed of many small rays called *barbs.* If you magnify a barb, it looks like a tiny feather with many projections, called *barbules.* Tiny hooks hold the barbules together. This structure makes the vane strong. Yet it is still light and elastic. Also, the rachis is grooved. And the quill is hollow. These give the feather more strength with the least possible

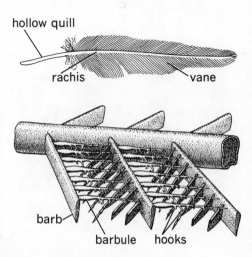

37-5 The structure of a quill feather. The enlargement shows a portion of the rachis and vane as seen with a microscope.

Students may be familiar with oil spills and their effects on birds. Why is an oil spill so disastrous to the bird population?

Birds have a poor sense of smell as compared to fishes. The olfactory lobes in the bird's brain are small. However, there are large areas of its brain that receive and process visual information. For example, an insect-eating falcon can spot a dragonfly from a distance of about 700 meters.

weight. If a vane is split, a bird can put it back together in two ways. The bird can shake itself. Or it can draw the feather through its beak. Either of these methods will rehook the barbules.

Many birds oil their feathers after they get wet. They take oil from a gland at the base of the tail. They spread this oil over the surface of their feathers. This makes them waterproof. Oil on the feathers is crucial to swimming and diving birds. It prevents water from getting through the feathers to the skin. This oil also prevents birds from chilling and helps them stay afloat. Ducks, geese, swans, loons, and grebes all need to oil their feathers.

MOLTING

A bird sheds its feathers at least once a year. This usually happens in the late summer. Thus, the bird grows new quills before its fall migration. There is often a partial molt in the spring, before the breeding season. This molt gives a bright breeding plumage to many birds. Some species have two complete molts each year. The ptarmigan of the far north is a good example of seasonal molting. An early summer molt provides plumage to blend with rocks and soil. And a fall molt gives the ptarmigan a white plumage. This allows it to blend in with winter snow.

New feathers grow from the same pits from which the old ones were shed. The wing feathers of most species are shed gradually and in pairs. This allows the bird to fly during a molt. Many water birds, including ducks, lose their flight feathers in a group. This occurs when the birds are nesting and caring for their young. They are unable to fly at this time. They grow new flight feathers as the young birds are getting their plumage.

THE HEAD AND SENSES

The bird's *skull* is made up of thin bones. These bones fuse together early in the bird's life. The *cranium* is rounded and encases the brain. The upper jaw is called the *maxilla*, and the lower jaw, the *mandible*. These project forward as the toothless beak.

37–6 Two seasonal molts occur in the ptarmigan. The early summer molt and the fall molt provide seasonal camouflage. (Krasemann, Peter Arnold)

The *tongue* is small and is used mostly as an organ of touch. Birds have a poor sense of taste. But they are known to reject bad-tasting food. Paired nostrils, or **nares,** open through the beak. The nares admit air into the mouth cavity. Birds also have a poor sense of smell.

Birds' *eyes* are large and deep set. Unlike their senses of smell and taste, **birds have a very keen sense of sight.** It is said that many birds have vision that is 8 to 10 times as keen as human vision. They can judge distance accurately both at close and at far range. Birds' eyes can shift focus rapidly. Owls and other birds active at night have excellent vision in reduced light. Eyes are protected by an upper and lower eyelid, plus a thin *nictitating membrane.* The nictitating membrane is transparent. It can be drawn across the eyeball from the front corner of the eye socket. The nictitating membrane protects the eye and keeps it moist.

Ear canals open on either side of the head just behind the eyes. These canals are covered by protective tufts of feathers. Eustachian tubes run from the middle-ear cavities to a single opening in the upper wall of the throat. Birds can hear very well. The ears are especially sensitive to high-pitched sounds.

THE NECK AND TRUNK

A bird's neck is long and flexible. It has vertebrae that slide easily on one another. This provides the freedom of movement needed to look in all directions. Birds are unable to use their forelimbs for grasping. So they need to be flexible to use their beaks to feed easily, preen, and build nests.

Tail vertebrae are also flexible. This allows a bird to move its tail feathers freely. This is needed for balance and steering during flight. The trunk bones, on the other hand, are fused together solidly. This provides needed body support during flight.

The breast bone, or **sternum,** is enlarged. It covers much of the bird's ventral side. Ribs are attached to the dorsal part of the sternum. The ventral part forms a deep ridge, called a *keel.* This provides a surface where breast muscles can attach.

THE SHOULDERS AND WINGS

The shoulder, or *pectoral girdle,* is made up of three pairs of bones. These fit together like the legs of a tripod. The *scapulae,* or shoulder blades, lie on either side of the spine above the ribs. They are embedded in the back muscles. A bone extends from each scapula to the sternum. These are called *coracoid* bones. They brace the shoulders from below. Finally, further support is provided by two *clavicles.* These run from either shoulder toward the sternum. They fuse immediately in front of the sternum. You have probably seen the clavicles of a turkey or a chicken. They make up the V-shaped wishbone.

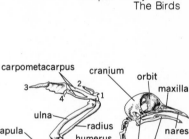
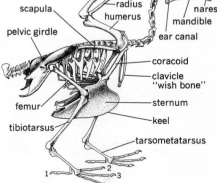

37–7 A bird's skeleton.

Stress to students the importance of the light weight of a bird's skeleton. Many bones are hollow and trussed for added strength. It is interesting to note that in some birds the weight of the feathers is greater than that of the skeleton.

There is a variety of flightless birds that students may wish to study. Assign special reports and have students discuss their findings.

The structure of a bird's wing resembles your own arm in many ways. The upper portion of a bird's wing contains a large, single bone, the *humerus.* This is similar to the human upper arm. The head of the humerus fits into a socket at the shoulder. The lower portion, as in the forearm, has two bones, the *radius* and the *ulna.* The end section of the wing is greatly modified for flight in a modern bird. Two small wrist, or *carpal,* bones are present. Other bones of the wrist and hand are fused, forming a *carpometacarpus.* The remains of three fingers, or *digits,* are also present. The first and fifth digits, found in many other vertebrates, are lacking in the bird.

The longest flight feathers, known as *primaries,* grow from the "hand" and "fingers." *Secondary* feathers grow from the "forearm." *Tertiaries* grow from the "upper arm." The quills of these feathers are covered with smaller feathers known as *coverts.* The outline of the wing as a whole is concave on the lower side. It is thick on the forward edge, and thin and flexible on the rear edge. This is a perfect design for flight.

THE WING MOTION OF FLIGHT

When a bird flies, its wings move in a horizontal figure eight. They go down and back, then up and forward. The downward stroke provides the power. The upward stroke returns the wing for the next power stroke. Each movement uses a different set of muscles. The power stroke needs stronger muscles. These are located near the surface of the breast. The return stroke uses the weaker muscles underneath the power stroke muscles. You may have noticed these muscle layers on the breast of a chicken. They separate easily.

BIRDS THAT DO NOT FLY

Some birds have lost the ability to fly. These birds inhabit many parts of the world. The best known are the ostriches of Africa, rheas of South America, kiwis of New Zealand, and cassowaries of Australia. The various penguins of the Southern Hemisphere are also flightless birds.

Many flightless birds have survived only because they live in areas free of predators. However, human beings have caused the extinction of several flightless birds. The giant elephant bird of Madagascar died off only after humans arrived with their domestic animals. The extinction of the dodo of the Mascarene Islands and the moas of New Zealand occurred only after the arrival of people to these islands.

Most flightless birds have developed interesting adaptations. The ostriches, the rheas, and the cassowaries are able to survive among predators. This is possible because of their adaptations to life on land. These birds have very strong legs and very keen vision.

37-8 The ostrich (above) and the penguins are flightless birds. (Rue III, National Audubon Society; Roger T. Peterson, Photo Researchers)

Penguins have interesting adaptations to their flightless life. Their wings are well developed. But they are used for swimming through water. Their feet are webbed. These webbed feet serve as rudders. Penguins have the keeled breast that most flightless birds lack. This serves as attachment for the muscles used in swimming.

THE PELVIC GIRDLE AND LEGS

The *pelvic girdle* is made up of three pairs of bones. These are firmly fused together, and united with the lower spine. The legs are attached at the hip joint, high on the pelvic girdle. This structure provides excellent balance. Such balance is very important to birds when they move on land. Birds must balance on only two legs when walking, running, or hopping.

The upper leg contains a large, single bone, the *femur*. The upper end of the femur joins the pelvic girdle in a ball-and-socket joint. The lower leg contains two bones. The large bone is the *tibia*, or "drumstick." A second bone, the *fibula*, is reduced to a slender spine that lies alongside the tibia. Bones of the ankle and foot are fused. They are elongated and often confused with the leg. The bird walks on its toes. In most birds, the first toe is shorter and is turned backward. The second, third, and fourth toes are directed forward. All of the toes end in claws.

Bird's feet vary greatly in structure from species to species. Feet are used in locomotion, getting food, building nests, and other activities. The feet of most ground birds are adapted for scratching the ground in search of food. Swimming and diving birds have webbed or lobed feet. The legs of these birds are set far back on the body. This position is good for paddling in the water. Wading birds have long legs and long toes. Birds of prey usually have strong feet with long, sharp claws or talons. Hawks and eagles have feet like this. Woodpeckers have two toes turned to the back and two turned forward. This helps them cling to the sides of trees. Most birds have only one backward toe.

THE DIGESTIVE SYSTEM

Birds maintain a constant, high body temperature. They use tremendous energy in flying. To meet these energy needs, birds must eat large amounts of food. But food is not always available. Thus birds must store food for use between feedings. Food is swallowed whole. This makes it difficult to digest. This is especially true of seeds. Thus, to turn the food into energy, birds need an efficient digestive system.

A bird swallows food into its long *esophagus*. At the base of the neck, the esophagus enlarges into a *crop*. The crop stores and moistens food. From the crop, the food passes into the *proventriculus*. This is the first division of the stomach. It has thick glandular walls. These walls secrete gastric fluid, which mixes with the food. Then the food passes into the second stomach area, called

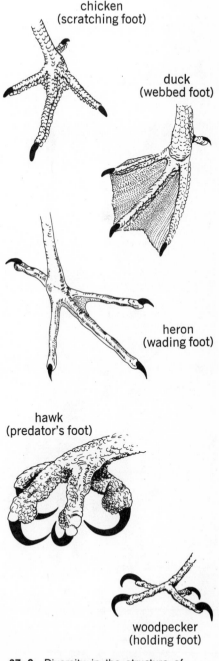

chicken
(scratching foot)

duck
(webbed foot)

heron
(wading foot)

hawk
(predator's foot)

woodpecker
(holding foot)

37–9 Diversity in the structure of birds' feet allows for adaptation.

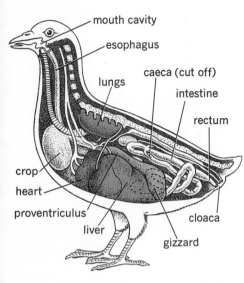

mouth cavity

esophagus

caeca (cut off)

lungs

intestine

rectum

crop

heart

proventriculus

cloaca

liver

gizzard

37-10   The internal organs of a bird.

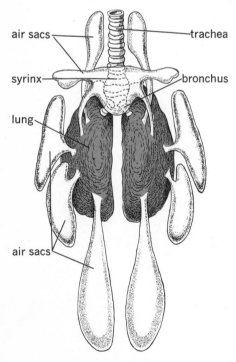

air sacs

trachea

syrinx

bronchus

lung

air sacs

37-11   The respiratory system of a bird.

the *gizzard*. This often contains small stones. With the aid of these stones, the muscular wall of the gizzard grinds up the food. This ground-up mass of food and juices then passes through the *pyloric valve* into the slender, coiled *intestine*. The lower end of the intestine joins the *rectum*. The short rectum leads to the *cloaca*. Waste products leave the body through the cloacal opening. Also opening into the cloaca are ducts from the kidneys and genital organs.

Birds have a large two-lobed liver. Some species of bird have a *gall bladder* on the lower side of the liver. Bile pours into the small intestine through two ducts. Another digestive organ, the *pancreas*, lies along the U-shaped part of the intestine. The pancreas pours its secretions into the intestine through three ducts.

RESPIRATION AND CIRCULATION

The *lungs* lie in the back of the body cavity against the ribs. **The capacity of the lungs is increased by a system of *air sacs.*** The air sacs extend from the lungs into the chest area and abdomen. They even connect with cavities in the larger bones.

Air is drawn in through the nostrils in the beak. It passes down the trachea to its lower divisions, or *bronchi*. From here, it passes to the lungs. The air is drawn in by relaxation of the thoracic and abdominal muscles. Contraction of these muscles forces air out. The lungs are quite small. So a bird must breathe rapidly to supply its body with the great amount of oxygen needed to carry on the high rate of metabolism.

The respiratory system also functions as the main temperature regulating system. **A bird has no sweat glands. It is thus unable to get rid of heat through the skin. The lungs discharge most of the bird's excess heat.** Birds actually pant on hot days. The air sacs may also help in heat elimination. At such times, the insulation of the feathers does more harm than good.

The lungs also supply air for singing. The bird's song is not produced in the throat. The song is produced in the song box, or **syrinx.** This is located at the base of the trachea, where it divides into the bronchi. The syrinx is a delicate and highly adjustable structure.

A bird's *heart* is large, powerful, and very efficient. **It has four chambers. The bird's heart is superior to any vertebrate hearts we have discussed thus far.** It consists of two thin-walled *atria* and two muscular *ventricles*. The right side of the four-chambered heart receives blood from the body and pumps it to the lungs. The left side receives blood from the lungs and pumps it to the body. The bird's heart, unlike those of amphibians and reptiles, has only a *right aortic arch*. In birds, this continues as the aorta.

A bird's heart beats at very high rates. Depending upon the bird's activity, the rate can be anywhere from 135 to 570 beats a minute for the mourning dove. The heart of the English sparrow may beat from 350 to 500. And the chickadee's heart may beat as fast as 1,000 beats per minute. Scientists think that this fast heart rate is one reason why birds have a short life-span.

THE EXCRETORY SYSTEM

A pair of dark brown, three-lobed *kidneys* lies along the back. They filter *uric acid* from the blood. **Uric acid** is a waste product of cell metabolism. The kidneys then excrete this acid through ureters into the cloaca. Here it is eliminated along with intestinal waste. Birds have no urinary bladder for the temporary storage of their urine. This is considered an adaptation that saves on weight.

THE NERVOUS SYSTEM

The brain of the bird is large and broad. It fills the cranial cavity completely. The *olfactory lobes* are relatively small, indicating a poor sense of smell. The *cerebrum*, on the other hand, is the largest of any animal we have discussed so far. The highly developed instincts of birds are centered here. Also the control of their voluntary muscles centers in this brain region. The *optic lobes* are also large, indicating excellent vision. And, the large *cerebellum* explains why birds have such good muscle coordination. The *medulla oblongata* joins the *spinal cord*. The spinal cord extends down the back. And it is encased in vertebrae.

THE REPRODUCTIVE SYSTEM

The oval *testes* of the male bird lie in its back above the kidneys. Small tubes, the *vas deferentia*, lead from the testes to openings in the cloaca. In some birds, these are enlarged at the lower ends to form sacs called *seminal vesicles*. Sperm travels from the testes through the vas deferentia. It is stored in the seminal vesicles until mating takes place. During mating, the sperm is transferred from the cloaca of the male to the cloaca of the female bird.

In most birds, the female reproductive system is greatly reduced. There is only a single left *ovary*. All of the eggs develop in this one ovary. A long coiled oviduct leads from this ovary to the cloaca. **The disappearance of the right ovary and oviduct early in life decreases the weight of the bird. Again, this is an adaptation for flight.**

An egg cell is made up of a yolk, a nucleus, and cytoplasm. The **yolk** stores food. As the egg matures, the yolk increases in size and pushes the nucleus and the cytoplasm to the egg's surface. When the yolk is full sized, the egg cell breaks loose from the ovary. It is moved into the upper end of the oviduct by waving cilia. After mating, sperm travels up the oviduct from the cloaca. Fertilization takes place at the upper end of the oviduct. Fertilization occurs before any more egg structures form around the egg cell. The egg is usually laid about forty hours after it is fertilized.

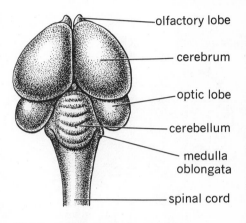

37–12 A bird's brain. Compare the size of the cerebrum to that of the fish (Fig. 34–13) and frog (Fig. 35–11). What does the size of the optic lobes indicate about the sense of sight?

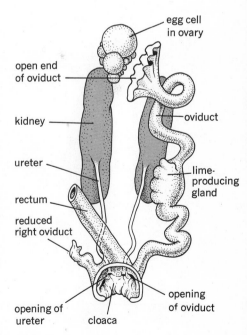

37–13 The reproductive system of a hen. Note the immature eggs in the ovary.

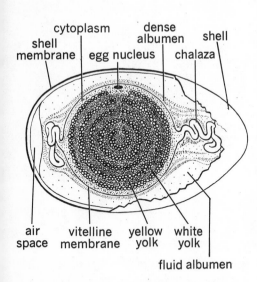

cytoplasm dense
albumen shell
shell
membrane egg nucleus chalaza

egg nucleus

air
space vitelline
membrane yellow
yolk white
yolk

fluid albumen

37–14 A chicken egg. The egg cell,
including the yolk, is held in place by
the chalaza.

Some students may be interested in dissecting and studying the internal organs of birds. The digestive system is of special interest.

Students will be fascinated in seeing slides of the development of the chick embryo at various stages.

Once fertilized, the egg begins a journey down the oviduct. It is surrounded by layers of **albumen.** Albumen is the egg white. The egg cell hangs in the albumen by strands of **chalaza.** The chalaza extends into the albumen toward the ends of the egg. Soon, a **shell membrane** forms around the albumen. Finally, these membranes are surrounded by the *shell.* The shell is secreted by *lime-producing glands* in the lower part of the oviduct. The egg is laid soon after the shell forms.

The only living part of an egg is the egg cell. This egg cell gradually develops into the young bird. The rest of the egg nourishes and protects the developing embryo. **Both the albumen and the yolk are stored food.** The albumen is mostly protein, while the yolk is protein and lipid. **The shell and shell membranes serve as protection against injury and water loss.** However, these must be porous enough to admit air for respiration. Respiration supplies energy for growth and survival during incubation. But the pores are large enough to let in bacteria. This is why eggs may rot during warm weather.

Fertilization of the egg cell is not necessary for the forming and laying of the eggs. In fact, care is taken to be sure that the eggs you buy are not fertilized.

THE EMBRYO'S INCUBATION AND DEVELOPMENT

Development of the embryo begins soon after fertilization. It continues after the egg is laid only if the egg is kept warm, or **incubated.** The female usually sits on the eggs. Although in some species her mate shares in this responsibility. The egg-incubation temperature of most birds is about 38°C. In addition to providing body warmth, the nesting bird turns the eggs with her beak at intervals. The time of incubation varies. In smaller birds, it may be 13 to 15 days. It may be as long as 40 to 50 days in larger birds. The chicken's egg is incubated for 21 days. Duck eggs require 28 days.

Once the egg is fertilized, cell division begins in the nucleus. Soon a plate of cells forms on the surface of the yolk. This embryonic bird grows gradually larger. It starts to develop various organs. As growth continues, a membrane grows out of the embryo's digestive tract. This membrane surrounds the yolk. It is called the **yolk sac.** The yolk sac contains a network of blood vessels. And it produces digestive enzymes. These enzymes transform the food in the yolk into a soluble form. This food is carried through the blood vessels of the yolk sac to the growing embryo. As the embryo gets larger, the yolk gets smaller. By hatching time, the yolk is entirely absorbed.

As with the reptiles, another membrane grows from the embryo's body wall and encloses the embryo. This is the *amnion.* It fills with amniotic fluid, which surrounds the embryo.

A third membrane, the *allantois,* grows from the embryonic digestive tract. This forms a saclike, vascular organ. The allantois

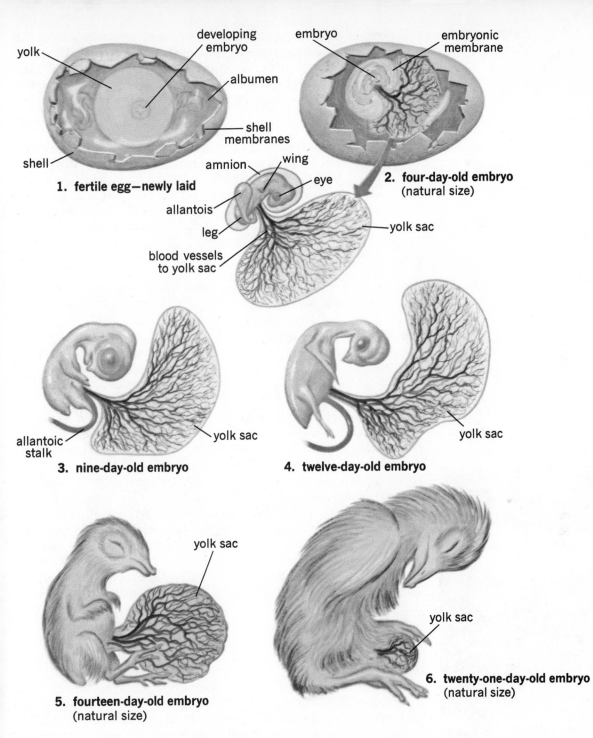

yolk

developing
embryo

albumen

shell
membranes

shell

1. fertile egg—newly laid

embryo

embryonic
membrane

2. four-day-old embryo
(natural size)

amnion

wing

eye

allantois

leg

blood vessels
to yolk sac

yolk sac

allantoic
stalk

yolk sac

3. nine-day-old embryo

yolk sac

4. twelve-day-old embryo

yolk sac

5. fourteen-day-old embryo
(natural size)

yolk sac

6. twenty-one-day-old embryo
(natural size)

37–15 A fertile hen's egg and several of the stages in the development of a chicken
embryo.

The "brood patch" is found in both males and females if they are both involved in incubation.

functions in respiration. It also receives waste products from the embryo. The allantois comes in contact with the *chorion*. The chorion is another embryonic membrane. It lies against the double shell membrane. **Thus, the development of the bird is like that of the reptile. In fact, it has been said that "the reptiles invented the amniotic egg and the birds inherited it."**

When the embryo is fully developed, hatching begins. The baby bird has a sharp structure on the tip of its bill called the **egg tooth**. The egg tooth is used to cut through the shell. The baby bird pecks a small hole in the shell. The hole is enlarged and finally cuts the shell nearly in two. The young bird pushes the halves of the shell apart and works its way out. The egg tooth is lost a few days after hatching.

EGG AND PARENTAL CARE IN BIRDS

Birds of different species lay different numbers of eggs. The young of different species are developed to different degrees when they hatch. Therefore, **the type of parental care given a young bird differs for different species.**

Precocial birds, including ducks, geese, quail, grouse, turkeys, and other fowls, lay between 10 and 20 eggs. Precocial birds, except the wood duck, nest on or near the ground. Incubation does not begin until the last egg is laid. Their incubation period is longer than that of most smaller birds. But the young are almost fully developed when they hatch. They all hatch within a few hours of one another. They are soon able to leave their nests. At this stage, they can already follow their parents and feed themselves. The young birds often cluster under the wings of the mother for warmth and protection.

Altricial birds include robins, thrushes, sparrows, and warblers. They usually lay fewer than six eggs. Again, incubation begins only when the last egg is laid. But their incubation period is shorter— usually less than two weeks. The young birds hatch at about the same time. But they are weak, helpless, and nearly featherless. Therefore, they are kept warm and fed in the nest. They remain in the nest until they are feathered and ready to fly. This means that either one or both parents is constantly busy with these tasks. But all this attention increases the chances of the young birds' survival. This protection helps to insure the survival of the smaller number of young.

Most birds defend their eggs and their young when they are threatened. But they use many different methods. Many birds that nest on the ground sit on the nest, trying to conceal it when another animal approaches. But the ground-nesting killdeer bird has a different method. It tries to lure the intruder away from its nest. The killdeer bird slowly moves away from the nest while pretending to have a broken wing. Even birds that are normally shy become brave when they are defending their offspring. Many will swoop down on an intruder, trying to divert its attention from the nest. At

37-16 The gray-checked thrush feeds its young in the nest until they are feathered and able to fly. (Dr. E. R. Degginger)

the other extreme is the cowbird. The cowbird lays its eggs in the nests of other birds. It then depends on the "foster parents" to incubate the eggs.

SUMMARY

Throughout modern history, people have dreamed of flying. But individual efforts resulted in crash landings. Compare your body with that of any bird and you will see why. Human bones are too heavy. Human muscles are too weak. The human heart could never stand the fast rate of a bird heart. And, to develop the necessary energy for flying, humans would have to spend most of their time eating.

Birds have all of the adaptations for flight. But their high metabolic rates cause them to "burn out." The life-span for most birds is a short three to five years.

BIOLOGICALLY SPEAKING

feather	bronchus	chalaza
papilla	syrinx	shell membrane
foliicle	uric acid	incubate
nare	yolk	yolk sac
sternum	albumen	egg tooth
air sacs		

QUESTIONS FOR REVIEW

1. What characteristic of modern birds shows evidence of their reptile ancestry?
2. List the characteristics of *Archaeopteryx*.
3. On what basis do biologists consider birds highly successful vertebrates?
4. List eight characteristics that distinguish birds from other vertebrates.
5. Name the different kinds of feathers forming a bird's plumage.
6. Rate the following senses of a bird as good or poor: smell, taste, sight, and hearing.
7. Why is a flexible neck important in the life of a bird?
8. Of what importance is the greatly enlarged sternum of the bird?
9. List the organs of the alimentary canal in the order in which food passes through them.
10. What is the function of the air sacs extending from the lungs of the birds?
11. What advancement can be seen in the structure of the bird heart?
12. Why is the excretion of uric acid rather than urine considered an adaptation for flight?
13. Describe the embryonic membranes of the bird egg.
14. Distinguish precocial from atricial birds.

APPLYING PRINCIPLES AND CONCEPTS

1. Discuss the structural characteristics of birds that are adaptations for flight.
2. What structural advances are associated with warm-bloodedness in birds?
3. Account for the limited distribution of flightless birds.
4. In terms of what you learned about mutation, variation, and survival, relate the various forms of beaks and feet to the diet of birds.

chapter thirty-eight

The Mammals

OBJECTIVES
- LIST the characteristics of mammals.
- DESCRIBE the various types of mammals.
- LIST several structural adaptations of mammals.
- EXPLAIN how mammals regulate their internal environment.
- DESCRIBE the development of the circulatory, respiratory, and nervous systems of mammals.
- DESCRIBE the reproduction and parental care of mammals.

This would be an appropriate place to review the time scale on page 413. Stress to students the common ancestry that both birds and mammals have with reptiles. Discuss the characteristics of mammals that have made them superior to reptiles.

Students may be interested in learning about some extinct mammals and the factors that contributed to their becoming extinct.

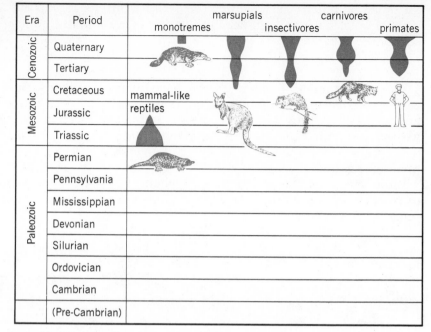

Era	Period	monotremes	marsupials / insectivores	carnivores / primates
Cenozoic	Quaternary			
Cenozoic	Tertiary			
Mesozoic	Cretaceous	mammal-like reptiles		
Mesozoic	Jurassic			
Mesozoic	Triassic			
Paleozoic	Permian			
Paleozoic	Pennsylvania			
Paleozoic	Mississippian			
Paleozoic	Devonian			
Paleozoic	Silurian			
Paleozoic	Ordovician			
Paleozoic	Cambrian			
	(Pre-Cambrian)			

38–1 A time scale of some of the mammals.

THE RISE OF MAMMALS

Mammals are a recent animal form compared to other vertebrates. Fossils show that mammals appeared during the Jurassic period. Mammals probably lived during the time of *Archaeopteryx* and other birds. Scientists believe that the ancestors of mammals were reptiles. But the evidence is very scanty. Fossils of mammal-like reptiles are limited to mostly jaws and teeth.

Biologists believe that the first mammals were small. When mammals developed, reptiles were still the dominant vertebrates. But even these small, early mammals were important in one respect. Their body characteristics enabled the mammals to dominate all other animals in a future age.

At the end of the Mesozoic era, about 70 million years ago, some changes ended the Age of Reptiles. With the end of this age came the beginning of a new one. This was the start of the Cenozoic era, or the Age of Mammals.

With the dawn of the Cenozoic era, continents were lifted up. Shallow seas and swamps disappeared. The water collected in great oceans. Mountain ranges and high plateaus arose. With changes in the land, the climate changed. The earth was no longer warm and humid all over. Climatic zones evolved in which some parts stayed warm and humid. Other areas became mild or cold. Seasonal temperature changes developed in many parts of the earth. Most reptiles could not adjust to these changes. But the mammals could. They developed in many different forms in the varied land environments. Mammals became more and more numerous

38-2 Cenozoic scene, showing early mammals.

through the seven epochs of the Cenozoic era. Eventually, mammals became the dominant land-dwelling vertebrates of the earth.

HOW MAMMALS EVOLVED

Through the early Cenozoic era, mammals increased in size. The evolution of the horse is a good example. During the Eocene period, the ancestor of the modern horse lived in the forests of North America. This horse is called *Eohippus*. It had four toes and was about the size of a fox terrier. During the Oligocene epoch, the horse developed into a three-toed mammal. It grew to the size of a sheep. During the Miocene and Pliocene epochs, horses grew to almost the size they are today. But they still had three toes on each foot. They could run rapidly over the grasslands on which they grazed. Horses developed a single-toed foot during the early Pleistocene epoch, or Ice Age. Although the horse first developed in North America, it became extinct there several thousand years ago. But by that time, the horse had migrated to Europe, Asia, and Africa. Early Spanish explorers were the first to bring horses back to North America.

Many other early mammals have also become extinct. These include the wooly rhinoceros, the ancient camel without a hump, the straight-horned bison, and the large wild pig. Flesh-eating mammals included the great bear dogs, the giant short-faced bears, and saber-toothed tigers. During the million years of the Ice Age, mastodons and mammoths migrated to Africa from North America, Europe, and Asia. These early elephants have long been extinct. But their descendants are still found in Asia and Africa.

DIVERSITY AMONG MAMMALS

Mammals, unlike birds, cannot change environments rapidly. If there is a gradual change in the environment, the mammals must either adapt or move to a new environment. In Chapter Thirteen, the basis for change in the members of a population was discussed. The changes are brought about by *adaptive radiation*. It involves natural variation and selection. We called this idea "survival of the fittest." This mechanism of change, through migration and mutations, has resulted in the many different forms of mammals that are present today.

There are four thousand or more species of mammals alive today. They are found in all parts of the world in a wide variety of forms and sizes. There are tiny mice and shrews, and huge elephants and whales. Mammals are found in the forests, grasslands, and oceans.

THE CHARACTERISTICS OF MAMMALS

Mammals differ widely in body structure. **But the following characteristics are generally true of the class *Mammalia*:**
■ Body covered with hair.

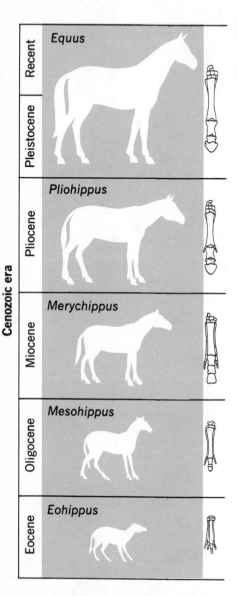

38-3 Evolution of the horse. Our knowledge of the history of horses is based on fossil records. *Eohippus*, or "dawn horse," is believed to have developed from an ancestor with five toes on each foot.

wooly mammoth

wooly rhinoceros

saber-toothed cat

giant short-faced bear

straight-horned bison

- Viviparous; young nourished during development in the uterus of the mother.
- Young nourished after birth with milk secreted by the **mammary glands** of the mother. This is the characteristic for which the class is named.
- Lung-breathing throughout life.
- A **diaphragm** (breathing muscle) separating the thoracic (chest) cavity and abdominal cavity.
- Heart four-chambered, with left aortic arch only.
- Warm-blooded.
- Seven cervical (neck) vertebrae in most species.
- Two pairs of limbs for locomotion in most species.
- Cerebrum and cerebellum of brain highly developed.

38–4 Some mammals of the Pliocene epoch that have become extinct as conditions changed.

THE ORDERS OF MAMMALS

Living mammals are classified into 18 orders. You may wonder what an elephant, a horse, a bat, and a beaver have in common. As mammals, they all have the characteristics we listed for this class.

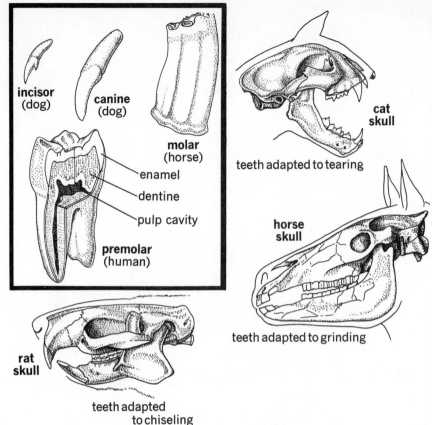

incisor
(dog)

canine
(dog)

molar
(horse)

enamel

dentine

pulp cavity

premolar
(human)

cat
skull

teeth adapted to tearing

horse
skull

teeth adapted to grinding

rat
skull

teeth adapted
to chiseling

38–5 Four types of mammalian teeth. Notice how these types are adapted for different functions in the rat, cat, and horse.

Their differences are the basis for classifying them in different orders. Their structural differences also show how these animals are adapted to various environments.

There are three lines of mammalian development based on *reproduction*. We can use this basis to separate two orders of mammals from the rest.

Difference in *teeth* also distinguish several orders. Unlike reptiles, mammals have different specialized teeth. These are related to their feeding habits. Mammalian teeth are of a definite number, depending on the species. *Incisor* teeth are for cutting or gnawing. *Canines* are for tearing flesh. *Premolars* and *molars* are for grinding, especially plant foods.

Foot structure also varies among mammals. The entire soles of the feet of some mammals rest on the ground. The human has such a foot. Many mammals walk on their toes with the heel raised. These include cats and dogs. The horse walks on one toe with the entire foot raised.

The fingers and toes of mammals also vary. Some toes and fingers have *nails* such as those of the human. Many mammals, like cats and dogs, have *claws*. Still others, like the horse, cow, and deer, have hoofs. Two orders of mammals are based upon the number of toes and the structure of the hoofs.

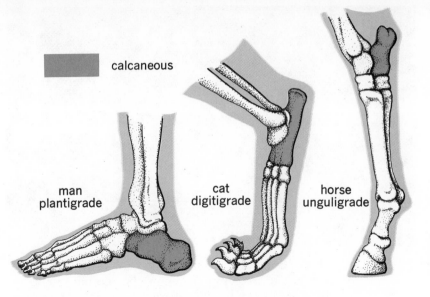

calcaneous

man
plantigrade

cat
digitigrade

horse
unguligrade

38–6 Mammalian foot modification. Note the relationship of the calcaneous in each foot.

THE THREE LINES OF DEVELOPMENT IN MAMMALS

Three different types of mammals have developed from a common ancestor. This common ancestor lived during the early Jurassic period. **Monotremes are egg-laying mammals.** There are just a few species of monotremes living today. This is a direct line of development from the common mammal ancestor.

Another line of development divided into two major branches at the end of the Jurassic period. **The marsupials are pouched mammals.** These mammals are more numerous than the monotremes.

The most important line of development led to the **placental mammals. These animals are the most highly evolved organisms on earth.** The Cenozoic era was the Age of Mammals. But the recent epoch is the Age of Placental Mammals.

Stress to students how the isolation of Australia led to the success of marsupials and monotremes on that continent. There are many books that discuss Australian wildlife that may be of interest to students.

The Monotremes

EGG-LAYING MAMMALS

The order *Monotremata* are the most primitive mammals. Like their reptilian ancestors, monotremes lay eggs. They also have a cloaca into which the intestine and urogenital system empty. Monotremes also lack external ears.

The *duckbilled platypus* and the *spiny anteater* are the only monotremes still in existence. They live in remote areas of Australia and New Guinea. Here they were isolated from large predators. If not for this isolation, monotremes would have been extinct ages ago. The platypus is about 40 centimeters long. It has waterproof fur, a ducklike bill, and feet that are modified as paddles. It burrows into stream banks and builds grass-filled nests. The platypus uses its beak to probe for worms and grubs in the mud on the bottoms of streams. The platypus usually lays two or three eggs. The

38-7 The duckbilled platypus is a monotreme. This strange looking animal is found in remote areas of Australia. (Australian Tourist Comm.)

eggs are kept in the body of the female for some time before they are laid in the nest. After laying the eggs, the mother curls herself around them to incubate them. After hatching, the young are nourished on milk secreted by sweat glands. These sweat glands are similar to the mammary glands of other mammals. The platypus has no nipples. Instead of suckling, the babies lick milk from their mother's body hair.

Spiny anteaters are found in the deep forests of Australia. They are well protected by a coat of sharp spines. Their long toothless jaws form a snout well adapted for probing into ant hills. Spiny anteaters lay two eggs at a time. These eggs are incubated in a brood pouch. This pouch is on the lower side of the mother. The eggs remain in the pouch for several weeks before hatching.

The Marsupials

POUCHED MAMMALS

38-8 Opossums. After birth, the helpless young find their way into the mother's pouch where they continue to develop. Later, they are carried on her back. (Allan Roberts)

Marsupialia is another order of primitive mammals. They are represented by a relatively small number of species. **Marsupials differ from other mammals in the way they care for their young.** The marsupial egg does not contain enough yolk to feed the fetus for the entire period of its development. Thus, marsupials are born before

their development is complete. The young are small and helpless. After they are born, the young use their front legs to pull themselves into the mother's pouch. The pouch contains mammary glands. Each baby attaches to a nipple with its mouth. Milk is pumped through the nipple from the mammary glands.

The opossum is the only marsupial found in North America. It is a common mammal. But you seldom see it because it sleeps during the day. At night, it roams the countryside in search of food. Opossums eat small birds and mammals, eggs, and insects. Two or three times a year, the opossum bears a litter of from six to twenty young. The hairless, helpless young are born after a period of development of only thirteen days. They remain in the mother's pouch for about two months. The young opossums adjust to life outside the pouch gradually. They wander out of the pouch, but later return.

During the early epochs of the Cenozoic era, marsupials lived all over the world. Biologists believe that almost every placental mammal had a marsupial counterpart. Some were bearlike, while others resembled dogs. One marsupial of the Pliocene epoch was a large flesh-eater that bore a striking resemblance to the saber-toothed cat. Other marsupials resembled modern moles, mice, and groundhogs.

During that time, marsupials competed with placental mammals and held their own. But they gradually lost the struggle for survival. **Today, marsupials abound only in those few places that were not accessible to placental mammals.** Marsupials are found mostly in Australia and New Guinea.

In Australia, the *kangaroos* and the *wallabies* live in the grasslands. They resemble the deer and antelope in head structure and grazing habits. The *koala bear* lives in the forests of Australia. It feeds only on the leaves of the eucalyptus tree. Other modern marsupials of Australia include the *wombat* and the *phalanger.* On the island of Tasmania, south of Australia, two flesh-eating marsupials are found. The *Tasmanian devil* resembles a raccoon. The *Tasmanian wolf* resembles a wild dog.

Placental Mammals

THE MOST SUCCESSFUL MAMMALS

About 95 percent of the mammals alive today are *placental mammals.* **These differ from monotremes and marsupials in the way they nourish the young before birth.** Early in its development, the embryo of a placental mammal becomes embedded in the wall of the uterus. Then the embryonic membranes begin to develop. The chorion grows from the embryo. It spreads over the wall of the uterus. The chorion plus nearby uterine tissue make up the *placenta.* The placenta receives oxygen and nutrients from the blood and passes them to the fetus. Embryonic development in placental mammals will be more fully discussed in Chapter Forty-Seven.

Placental mammals have an advantage over marsupials. **The young of placental mammals are born far more developed than those of**

Discuss the considerable advantages that placental mammals have over other animals. It is interesting to discuss here the extensive care the newborn human requires as opposed to newborns of other mammals.

38–9 The lion is an example of a placental mammal. (H. R. W. Photo by Richard Weiss)

marsupials. This is because of a longer period of development. Even the most helpless newborn placental mammals—for example, mice, rabbits, kittens, and puppies—are far more advanced than newborn marsupials. Within a week or two, these mammals are ready to move about with their parents. Hoofed mammals, including the cow, horse, deer, sheep, and pig, are born in a still more advanced condition. These mammals are able to walk within a few hours after birth. The whale is even more advanced; a newborn whale is able to swim immediately after birth.

The period of uterine development is called the *gestation period*. The length of gestation, or *pregnancy*, varies in placental mammals. Generally, the longer the gestation period, the more advanced and larger the newborn mammal is at birth.

Table 38-1 GESTATION PERIODS

MAMMAL	PERIOD	MAMMAL	PERIOD
mouse	21 days	human	40 weeks
rabbit	30 days	cow	41 weeks
cat	63 days	horse	48 weeks
dog	63 days	whale	20 months
pig	120 days	elephant	20 to 22 months

Some Typical Mammals

THE INSECT-EATING MAMMALS

Members of the order *Insectivora* were probably the first placental mammals. All of today's higher mammals probably developed from this order. These are represented today by shrews and moles. They never became very large. They have small brains and primitive teeth. The *shrew* is the smallest of all mammals. It looks like both a mole and a mouse. It has a high metabolic rate and a ravenous appetite. It eats a lot of insects, mice, and even other shrews. Shrews are hard to find because they burrow in the grass and hide under leaves. Moles are well adapted to life under the ground. They have strong claws for digging. Their small eyes are covered with flaps of skin. Their long noses are good at rooting out grubs and worms.

THE FLYING MAMMALS

Though they eat insects, the *bats* are classified in a different order from insectivores. There are more than 600 kinds of bats in the order *Chiroptera*. **Bats are the only mammals that have developed structures for flight.** Bats have lengthened finger bones covered with membranes. These modified limbs serve the same purpose as the wings of birds. Bats fly mostly at night when there are many insects in the air. They spend the days hanging in caves or hollow trees. Most are helpless on the ground because of their weak hind

Bats are fascinating creatures to study. Students may be interested in the fact that bats can "see" in the dark. Actually they do not see at all but find their way by a series of high-pitched squeaks that echo back from objects and enable bats to avoid obstacles and find food.

legs and their long wings. Bats are able to find their way in the
dark because of their highly developed hearing. In fact, they usually find their way by listening to the bouncing echoes of their
own squeaks.

Vampire bats live in tropical America. They live on the blood of
of other mammals, including horses and cattle. The front teeth of
vampire bats cut the skin and the bat laps up the oozing blood.

THE GNAWING MAMMALS

The order *Rodentia* outnumbers all other orders of mammals
combined. They are found in almost every area of the world. Most
are terrestrial, tree-living, or burrowing. But the *beaver* and the
muskrat live a semiaquatic life. The flying squirrel can even glide
from tree to tree. Rats and mice are the most common rodents.
Some others are squirrels, woodchucks, prairie dogs, chipmunks,
and gophers. The beaver is the largest North American rodent.

Why have rodents been successful? Most of them are small. This
allows them to live in environments not suitable to larger animals.
They have a rapid rate of reproduction. There is very little specialization in the body build. All have strong, chisel-shaped teeth. These
teeth have sharp edges that become even sharper with use. The
front edge is harder than the back edge, causing the biting surface
to wear at an angle. The forelimbs of rodents are adapted for running, climbing, and getting food.

38–10 The mole is an example of
an insect-eating mammal. The bat is
a flying mammal. The beaver is a
gnawing mammal. (left and right:
Leonard Lee Rue III, Monkmeyer
Press Photos; MacGregor, Peter
Arnold)

THE RODENTLIKE MAMMALS

Like rodents, the *Lagomorphs*—rabbits, hares, and pikas—have
sharp, chisel-like teeth. But instead of having two teeth in each
jaw, lagomorphs have four. They grind plants with a sideways motion of the lower jaw.

The *cottontail rabbit* is the most widely hunted mammal of the
United States. But even though preyed upon by man, predatory
birds, and other animals, these rabbits have been able to hold their
own in most localities. The *jack rabbit* is common in the broad ex-

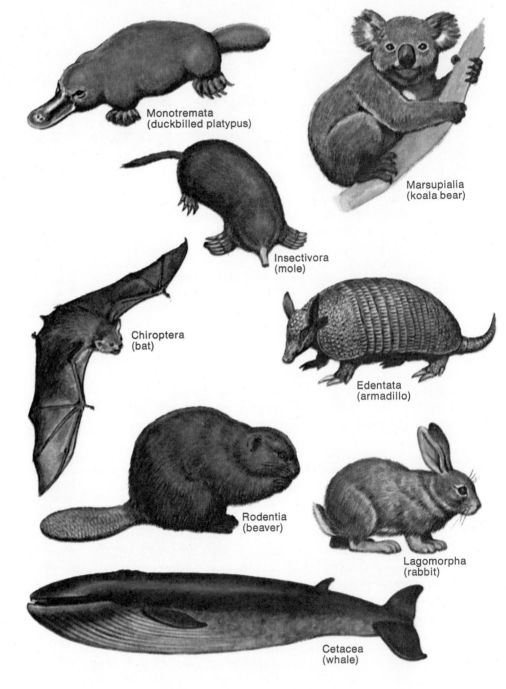

38–11 Examples of some of the better known orders of mammals.

Sirenia
(sea cow)

Proboscidea
(elephant)

Carnivora
(mountain lion)

Perissodactyla
(horse)

Artiodactyla
(bison)

Primates
(monkey)

panses of the western prairies and plains. It reaches a length of nearly 75 centimeters and has characteristic long ears and large, powerful hind legs. Both its sight and hearing are especially keen, enabling it to escape from its enemies.

THE TOOTHLESS MAMMALS

The mammals of the order *Edentata* are mostly toothless. The order is composed of armadillos, sloths, and great anteaters. They have small brains. Some have nine cervical vertebrae instead of the usual seven found in mammals. They have large claws. Armadillos have survived since the Tertiary period because of their protective armor. They eat bugs, dead flesh, bird eggs, grubs, birds, and small animals. Various species live in the Southwest, Mexico, and South America. The North American armadillo hides in a burrow during the day and digs for food at night.

Tree sloths live in the jungles of Central and South America. They spend most of their time hanging upside down from tree branches. They hang by their long limbs with two or three hooked claws. They eat leaves from the trees. The hair of some sloth species is green from the algae that live in it.

Anteaters probably evolved from the same ancestors as tree sloths. Anteater skulls are long, ending in thin, long snouts. Inside the snout is a sticky tongue that can catch termites. The feet have large, curved claws for digging up termite nests. These claws make walking and running difficult. Anteaters walk mostly on the knuckles of their front feet.

THE AQUATIC MAMMALS

The order *Cetacea* includes whales, dolphins, and porpoises. They probably evolved from some land mammal during the Tertiary period. They are well adapted to life in the ocean. They have torpedo-shaped bodies, and fishlike tails and flippers. They breathe

Ask students to tell the class about any aquatic shows where dolphins or porpoises were featured. Some students may be interested in reporting on the intelligence of these mammals and how they are trained to do the feats they perform.

38-12 The armadillo is a toothless mammal. (Leonard Lee Rue III, Monkmeyer Press Photos)

air. But they are able to hold their breath for a long time. The young of these animals can swim at birth. Just after birth, the mother pushes them to the surface for their first breath of air.

The *blue whale* is the largest animal alive today. It may be the largest animal that ever lived. Blue whales may grow longer than 30 meters and weigh as much as 130 metric tons.

Dolphins are actually small whales. They are usually under 4.2 meters long. Dolphins are found in seas throughout the world. They are very intelligent. Scientists are trying to figure out how these marine mammals communicate. Nevertheless, some fishermen slaughter them for commercial gain. *Porpoises* are closely related to dolphins. But porpoises are from a different family. They are usually smaller than dolphins and have a blunt rounded head. They travel in herds. They catch fish with their tooth-lined jaws.

Sirenia is another order of aquatic mammal. This order includes the *sea cow*. This creature is also called a manatee. These mammals resemble the walrus. The body is streamlined and the hind limbs are lacking. The forelimbs are modified to form flippers. They are found along the Atlantic coast of Africa, the Gulf of Mexico, and the east coast of South America. They inhabit rivers where they feed on aquatic plants.

THE TRUNK-NOSED MAMMALS

There are only two species of elephants still alive to represent the order *Proboscidea*. But during glacial and preglacial times there were over 30 species of elephantlike mammals. They lived in Asia, Europe, Africa, and North America. No one knows why most of these elephants became extinct.

Elephants are the largest land dwellers alive today. They can weigh more than six metric tons. The *Asiatic elephant* is the one you usually see in the circus. It is used as a beast of burden in many parts of the world. The *African elephant* is taller and more slender with larger ears. African elephants are not as easily domesticated as their Asian relatives.

38–13 The porpoise is an aquatic mammal. (Jungle Habitat)

38–14 The elephant is an example of a trunked-nosed mammal. (Leonard Lee Rue III, Monkmeyer Press Photos)

THE FLESH-EATING MAMMALS

Mammals of the order *Carnivora* probably evolved from insectivores during the Tertiary period. **Carnivores are flesh-eating mammals.** They all have strong jaws and enlarged canine teeth. All of their major characteristics help them prey on other animals. Carnivores have intelligence, keen sight and smell, strong bodies, and limbs with claws.

There are many families of carnivores, most of which are probably familiar to you. There are several members of the dog and cat families. The *mountain lion* was found over most of North America at one time. But civilization has driven it to the remote regions of the Southwest. The chief harm it does is the killing of livestock, especially young horses. Both the *bay lynx* (links), or bobcat, and the *Canadian lynx* live in deep forests and are seldom seen. The *jaguars* of South America, the *lions* of Africa, and the *tigers* of Asia are all members of the cat family.

The *gray wolf*, or timber wolf, is most frequently found in the northern forests. And it may be dangerous during the winter, when it runs in packs. The *coyote* (KY-ote), a prairie wolf, has been more successful than its larger cousin in surviving the effects of civilization. It is still abundant on the western plains. However, in some regions, too many have been destroyed. Their natural prey, including rodents and jack rabbits, have become pests. It has, therefore, been necessary to import coyotes into these regions.

The *raccoon* has a black mask and long, ringed tail. If it is captured young, it makes a nice pet. The raccoon prefers fish and clams

Many carnivores are kept in zoos or in the new "ride-through" zoological parks. Ask students to comment on these animal parks and report on any that they have visited.

Frequently we do not know enough about wildlife and destruction of certain species can be catastrophic. For example, when villagers in communities in Brazil and Argentina destroyed jungle cats and owls, their homes were invaded by disease-carrying rats. The jungle cats and owls were natural enemies of the rats. Have students draw conclusions from this discussion.

38–15 The raccoon is a carnivorous mammal. (Charles E. Summers, Jr. AMWEST)

as its food. But it will eat other things if these are unavailable. It has a habit of "washing" its food before eating. But this is probably to moisten the food rather than to clean it.

The weasel family includes some of the most bloodthirsty carnivores. It also includes some of the most valuable fur-bearing mammals. The *mink* especially is prized for its fur. These long-bodied, short-legged animals live along streams. The *ermine* is an Arctic weasel that grows a coat of white fur (except for a black-tipped tail) in winter. It is brown in summer.

The *bears* were the last carnivores to evolve. But they have changed little since Pleistocene times. Bears have teeth that are specialized for eating plant substances as well as meat. Bears are widely distributed, but are not found in Africa or Australia.

Sea lions, *walruses*, and *seals* are water-living carnivores. Their bodies are streamlined for swimming. But they have never developed the finlike appendages of whales. They have webbed feet. The front ones serve for balance and stability. And the rear ones provide an efficient means of propulsion. Walruses probably evolved from sea-lion ancestors. Their canine teeth have become long tusks. They have developed broad molars to facilitate crushing and grinding the oysters and other mollusks on which they feed.

Students may be interested in reading a fascinating article about the problems facing wildlife today. "Wildlife in Danger" appeared in the January 6, 1975, *Newsweek* magazine.

THE HOOFED MAMMALS

People have depended on hoofed mammals since prehistoric times. Hoofed mammals are called *ungulates*. **We use the ungulates as beasts of burden and as food.** The ungulates include *goats*, *horses*, *camels*, *oxen*, *llamas*, *cows*, *pigs*, *sheep*, *deer*, *elk*, *caribou*, *moose*, and *antelopes*. In all, there are about 16 families. How do we use each of the hoofed mammals listed here?

Ungulates are all herbivores, or plant-eaters. Their teeth are adapted to cropping and grinding grasses. Some of the hoofed animals have long limbs and feet that help them run rapidly over hard ground. They walk on the tips of their toes. Hoofs are modified toenails. They help to absorb the shock of running.

Some ungulates, including *cows*, *sheep*, and *antelopes*, have specialized digestive systems. Their stomachs have four chambers. While grazing, they eat large amounts of food. They store it in the first stomach division, the **rumen.** Later the food is forced back up into their mouths. It is then chewed as a cud. After it is thoroughly chewed, the cud is swallowed into the second stomach where digestion begins. The *bison*, *goat*, *camel*, *llama*, *giraffe*, *deer*, *elk*, *caribou*, and *moose* are all **ruminants** (ROO-muh-nants).

Stress both the similarities and differences between humans and other primates.

THE ERECT MAMMALS

Primates, or erect mammals, have the most highly developed brains of all living organisms. They also have well-developed hands and arms. Their fingers are used for grasping. Some of their fingers or toes are equipped with nails. Most primates can walk erect if neces-

Students may be interested in reporting on protective coloration in mammals. Be sure that students choose different animals for their research.

38-16 Jane Goodall spent many years studying chimpanzees in Africa. The chimpanzee is an example of an erect mammal. (Photo by Hugo von Lawick © National Geographic Society)

sary. Most primates tend to live in trees. Only human beings live exclusively on the ground. The teeth of primates are less specialized than any other group of mammals. Primates feed on both plants and flesh. Their sight is well developed, but their sense of smell is not.

The following animals and groups of animals are primates:

■ The *gorilla*. This is the largest of the apes. *Apes* are larger than monkeys and lack a tail. The gorilla lives in Africa. It walks on two feet.

■ The *chimpanzee*. It lives in Africa and is very intelligent. It is smaller than the gorilla.

■ The *orangutan*. This ape lives in the East Indies. It has red hair.

■ The *gibbon*. This is a long-armed ape. It lives in Asia.

■ The *Old World monkeys*. These have long tails but do not use them for climbing. They sit erect. They store food in their cheek pouches. The baboon, an Old World monkey, has a doglike nose.

■ The *New World monkeys*. These have long, flat tails that they use for climbing and hanging. They have wide noses. They have no cheek pouches.

■ The *Marmosets*. These are small squirrel-like creatures. They live in Central and South America.

■ The *Lemurs*. These animals live in Madagascar.

The apes are most like humans in body structure. Apes have no tails. Their arms are longer than their legs. These primates respond to a very high degree of training. This is especially true of the chimpanzee.

Mammalian Adaptations

HOW MAMMALS REGULATE THEIR INTERNAL ENVIRONMENT

We have now reviewed the various types of mammals. Let's look at the mammal's internal development. Here we find more complex tissue and organ specialization than in any other form of life. With this specialization comes more cell interdependence. This high degree of development needs a controlled inner environment.

Mammals, as well as birds, are warm-blooded animals. Except for periods of inactivity, a mammal's body temperature stays about the same. Many organs and organ systems help maintain this constant body temperature.

Heat is released in the tissues during respiration. The rate of cell metabolism in warm-blooded vertebrates is much higher than that of the cold-blooded vertebrates. Remember that the body temperature of cold-blooded animals changes with that of the environment. Increase in the metabolic rate requires an increase in the supply of nutrients and oxygen to the cells. Highly efficient digestive organs and well-developed lungs are necessary to supply these needs. The increased rate of metabolism results in more metabolic wastes. These wastes must be removed from the cells constantly. These require an extensive transport system and a powerful heart to force blood through its many vessels. Very efficient kidneys remove the waste products of cell metabolism. These kidneys are a complicated system of blood filters.

We find the basis for mammalian structure and function in the lower vertebrates you have studied. In fact, we can trace the development of each organ system through stages represented in these lower forms. In the following sections, we will examine some of these systems.

The circulation of blood is most efficient in mammals. This is so because in mammals all the blood travels through the heart twice during each circulation. In this way, complete separation of oxygenated and deoxygenated blood is ensured.

THE HEART AND LUNGS OF A MAMMAL

The efficiency of the blood transport system is very important for the regulation of the inner environment. However, in considering the heart and circulatory system of the mammal, we must also include the organs of respiration. These two systems are closely related.

Let us think back to the *fish*. Here a heart composed of two chambers is strong enough to force blood through the circulatory system. One ventricle gives enough pressure to force blood through the gills and to the vessels of the body. The blood does not return to the heart between the two circulations. Gills are fairly simple organs of respiration that function well in a water environment. The metabolic rate of a fish is much below that of the higher vertebrates. And it varies with the water temperature. Thus, a two-chambered heart is adequate. **However, neither gills nor two-chambered hearts are suitable for life on land.**

Ask students to prepare charts listing the comparative structures of different classes of vertebrate hearts. Have them report their findings to the class.

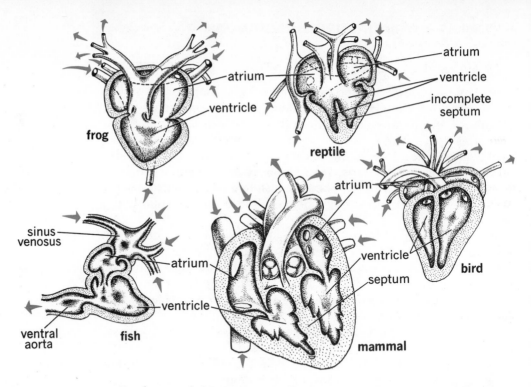

38-17 Heart structures characteristic of the vertebrate classes. Trace the increasing complexity and number of chambers, from the two-chambered heart of the fish to the human four-chambered heart.

In the *amphibians*, especially in the adult stages, the heart has had a structural change that permits life on land. Here we find the upper heart chambers separated into two atria. The presence of these two chambers separates deoxygenated blood from the body from oxygenated blood from the lungs. However, mixing occurs in the single ventricle. This ventricle forces blood both to the body tissues and to the lungs. Such a heart could not fill the needs of a bird or a mammal. For one thing, the pumping of mixed blood to the body tissue could not supply the oxygen needed by the mammal. Furthermore, the lungs of amphibians could not supply the needs of a bird or a mammal. Remember that amphibians use skin respiration. This function of the skin has been lost in the bird and mammal. Birds and mammals have thicker skin and a body covering.

The *reptile* heart is more efficient than that of the amphibian. The ventricle is partially divided by a wall, or septum. **The *mammalian* heart, like that of a bird, prevents mixing of blood. Their hearts have a complete septum forming two separate ventricles.** Thus, it is really a double pump. The right side receives the deoxygenated blood from the body and pumps it to the lungs. And the left side receives oxygenated blood from the lungs and forces it throughout the entire body.

THE MAMMALIAN NERVOUS SYSTEM

The high degree of development and specialization of their nervous systems places mammals above all other forms of life.

Mammals have brains that are larger in proportion to body weight than any other animal.

We can learn a great deal about the behavior and intelligence of the vertebrates from their brain structures. The brains of most primitive vertebrates consist of three main regions: 1) a *forebrain* composed of the olfactory lobes, or bulbs, and the two hemispheres of the cerebrum; 2) the *midbrain* containing the optic lobes; 3) the *hindbrain* composed of the cerebellum and medulla. All vertebrates have these brain regions. But the relative sizes of these regions vary. **When we compare the brain structures of the various vertebrates, we see a pattern in which the relative size of the cerebrum increases. The cerebrum reaches its highest development in the mammal.** You will recall from your studies of the brain of the fish that the cerebral hemispheres are relatively small. In the amphibian, the cerebral hemispheres are proportionally larger. This increase in the relative size of the cerebrum continues in the reptiles and also in the birds.

In the mammalian brain, the cerebral hemisphere fills most of the cranial cavity. The *olfactory area* consists of two lobes on the

The brains of fish, amphibians, reptiles, birds, and mammals increase in both size and complexity. Have the students make diagrams of the various vertebrate brains.

38–18 Compare the size of the cerebrum in the mammalian brain with that of the brains characteristic of the other vertebrate classes.

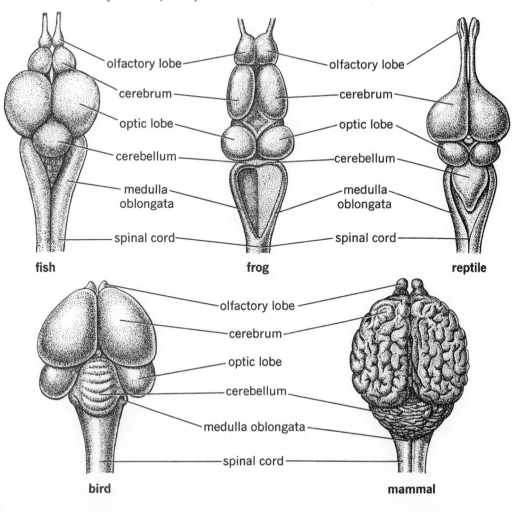

olfactory lobe
cerebrum
optic lobe
cerebellum
medulla oblongata
spinal cord

fish

olfactory lobe
cerebrum
optic lobe
cerebellum
medulla oblongata
spinal cord

frog

olfactory lobe
cerebrum
optic lobe
cerebellum
medulla oblongata
spinal cord

reptile

olfactory lobe
cerebrum
optic lobe
cerebellum
medulla oblongata
spinal cord

bird

mammal

lower side of the cerebrum. The *optic region* lies in the posterior of the cerebral hemisphere. The *cerebellum* lies below and posterior to the cerebrum. The high development of this brain region accounts for the excellent muscle coordination of the mammal. The short *medulla oblongata* controls vital body processes. It lies below the cerebrum and extends to the spinal cord. Cranial nerves extend from the brain to the sense organs and other head structures. The spinal nerves extend from the spinal cord to and from all body regions.

Ask students to compare the different methods of vertebrate reproduction. Discuss why lower forms produce large numbers of eggs while higher forms have fewer offspring. This discussion can be related to humans and their survival rate at birth. Students will be interested in finding out that birth survival rates vary widely and the United States does *not* have the highest survival rate.

MAMMALIAN REPRODUCTION AND PARENTAL CARE

Another line of vertebrate development has occurred in vertebrate reproduction. **As vertebrates become more complex, there is generally an increase in the efficiency of reproduction.** There is also a decrease in the number of young. Let us return to the fish for a moment. Fertilization is external. The male swims over the eggs and discharges sperm over them. This is inefficient. Many eggs are never fertilized. And many are eaten before they hatch. In most fishes, there is little or no parental care. But fish have beaten these odds by producing a huge number of eggs.

Amphibians lay a smaller number of eggs. These are fertilized directly as they are laid. This insures fertilization and the development of a greater proportion of the eggs. But, like fish, amphibians must lays their eggs in water. These eggs have no protection against drying out.

Reptiles were the first vertebrates to lay eggs on land. This was a big step forward. It required internal fertilization. It also required the enclosure of the egg in a protective shell. Similar eggs are produced by birds. With this greater protection, reptiles and birds need not produce as many eggs to insure survival of the young. Parental care, especially in birds, also reduces the loss of many young.

The young of all mammals but monotremes develop inside the mother. Marsupial babies are born prematurely. But the mother's pouch provides a safe "incubator" for development to continue in until the babies are stronger.

Students may be interested in finding out about various gestation periods and care needed following birth.

Placental mammals have the most highly developed system of reproduction. Uterine attachment permits a longer period of fetal development. At birth, the advanced development of a placental mammal baby increases its chances of survival.

After birth, all young mammals depend upon their mother's milk for nutrition. This requires a period of *parental care*. In most mammals, this parental care is provided by the female. Parental care requires a reduction in the number of offspring. Mice, rabbits, and other small mammals mature rapidly. Several litters of at least 10 babies per litter are born each season. On the other hand, black bears have only one or two cubs during the winter. And the mother

Students may be interested in discussing human parental care. Does this care extend for too long a period of time? What are some of the economic reasons for the long period of care and education among humans?

takes care of the cubs for a good while. Hoofed animals usually bear one or two young at a time. These animals usually care for their young for six months or more.

Of all mammals, the human being is the most developed. We are also the most helpless at birth. Thus, humans require the greatest parental care for the longest time. The period between birth and reproductive maturity averages 12 years for females and 14 years for males. This is the longest of any mammal.

SUMMARY

Mammals are the most successful land-dwelling vertebrates. Much of this success is due to their highly developed organ systems. These complex systems allow mammals to maintain a constant body temperature. This, along with their protective hair coverings, has allowed them to live in both cold and hot regions of the world. Placental mammals bear smaller numbers of young. But these young are more developed than other animals. Mammals provide milk as nourishment for their young. In most cases, they care for their young after birth. But probably the biggest reason for mammals' success is their complex brains and sense organs. These allow mammals to make all sorts of adjustments to changing environmental conditions.

BIOLOGICALLY SPEAKING

mammary glands	placenta	ruminant
diaphragm	gestation period	forebrain
monotreme	carnivore	midbrain
marsupial	ungulate	hindbrain
placental mammal	rumen	

QUESTIONS FOR REVIEW

1. Name several extinct mammals.
2. List ten characteristics of mammals that distinguish them from other vertebrates.
3. Describe several characteristics used to classify mammals into different orders.
4. What evidence of reptilian ancestry is shown in the monotremes?
5. Distinguish a marsupial mammal from a placental mammal. Give an example of each.
6. In what way is the order Chiroptera unique among the mammals?
7. Rodents vary greatly in size. What characteristics do they have in common?
8. Why are rabbits placed in a separate order from the rodents?
9. Describe how cetaceans are adapted for life in the water.
10. On what basis might we consider primates the most highly developed mammals?
11. List several structural adaptations of mammals that make them well suited for life in diverse environments.
12. Trace the increasing number of heart chambers of vertebrates from the fish to mammal.
13. Describe how the mammalian brain is more developed than the brains of other animals.

1. Discuss several environmental changes during the Cenozoic era that probably favored the survival of mammals and caused the decline of reptiles.
2. Discuss three lines of mammalian development and account for the supremacy of placental mammals today.
3. Organisms which undergo internal development usually produce and fertilize fewer eggs than organisms which undergo external development. Explain.

**RELATED
READING**

Books

Bellairs, Angus, *The Life of the Reptiles*.
Universe Books, New York. 1970. A two-volume treatise on all aspects of the reptiles, an excellent reference.

Boorer, Michael, *Mammals of the World*.
Grosset and Dunlap, Inc., New York. 1967. Presents a concise survey of evolution, overall structure and classification of mammals. Mammals are then dealt with in a systematic sequence.

Burgess, Robert F., *The Sharks*.
Doubleday & Co., Inc., Garden City, N.Y. 1970. Relates the history of man's fear of sharks and the myths invented about these fish, and how these fears are gradually being overcome.

Cousteau, Jacques Yves, *The Shark: Splendid Savage of the Sea*.
Doubleday & Co., Inc., Garden City, N.Y. 1970. A fascinating book dealing with the adventures and discoveries made by Jacques Cousteau and his crew, while studying sharks in many parts of the world.

Ewer, R. F., *The Carnivores*.
Cornell University Press, Ithaca, N.Y. 1973. Selected observations on the systematics, anatomy, behavior, reproduction, and fossil relatives of the carnivores.

Flanagan, Geraldine Lux, *Window into an Egg*.
William R. Scott, Inc., New York. 1969. Using excellent photographs, this book probes the day-by-day development of a chicken.

Minton, Sherman A., *Giant Reptiles*.
Charles Scribner's Sons, New York. 1973. An informative source on both the factual and mythical areas of reptile evolution and behavior.

Morris, Ramona, and Desmond Morris, *Men and Snakes*.
McGraw-Hill Book Co., New York. 1965. The full, illustrated story of man's relationship with the snake from the dawn of civilization to the present.

Pritchard, Peter, C. H., *Living Turtles of the World*.
T. F. H. Publications, Inc., Jersey City, N.J. 1967. A thorough, well-illustrated guide covering the natural history of turtles.

Riedman, Sarah R., and Elton T. Gustafson, *Home Is the Sea for Whales*.
Rand McNally and Co., Chicago. 1966. An excellent scientifically accurate study of Cretaceans; traces the evolution of the whales.

Seely, H. G., *Dragons of the Air: An Account of Extinct Flying Reptiles.*
Dover Publications, Inc., New York. 1967. The anatomy and evolutionary adaptations of the reptiles 60 million years before the first birds.

Van Gelder, Richard G., *Biology of Mammals.*
Charles Scribner's Sons, New York. 1969. A clear description of how mammals are born, develop, how they find shelter, food, water, and how they defend and protect themselves.

Articles

Alekswik, Michael, "Manitoba's Fantastic Snake Pits," *National Geographic,* November, 1975. An interesting account of the migration of the garter snake to its place of hibernation.

Bertram, Brian C. R., "The Social System of Lions," *Scientific American,* May, 1975. A fascinating account of the organization of the social system of lions, and how the behavior of the animals in it reflects the lion's adaptation to its environment.

Keast, Allen, "Fish Are What They Eat," *Natural History,* January, 1974. The article explains how the shape and position of a fish's mouth reveals a lot about his life in the deep.

Nicolai, Jürgen, "Mimicry in Parasitic Birds," *Scientific American,* October, 1974. Describes how the African widow bird lays its eggs in other birds' nests.

Thomson, Keith S., "Secrets of the Coelacanth," *Natural History,* February, 1973. An interesting study on the natural history of the little-known coelacanth.

Zahl, Paul A., "Nature's Living Jumping Jewels," *National Geographic,* July, 1973. A look at some of the beautiful frogs that inhabit a tropical jungle.

Zahl, Paul A., "Shadowy World of Salamanders," *National Geographic,* July, 1972. A close-up look at some of our more interesting salamanders.

unit 7

HUMAN BIOLOGY

Human beings are not as skilled in climbing, running, and flying as many other vertebrates. However, human beings have intelligence, and they stand upright. These characteristics give humans the ability to use tools. With this ability, we have achieved many wonders. People have developed spoken and written languages. We can control fire. Our machines carry us to the ocean's depth or through the air. We have landed on the moon to satisfy our curiosity about the universe. Our highly developed brain makes us more advanced than any other living organism. This brain allows us to think out and solve problems, and to develop skills by practice. We have even built computers to help us with memory and speed greater than our own. It is no wonder that we should wonder and hypothesize about our own history on earth.

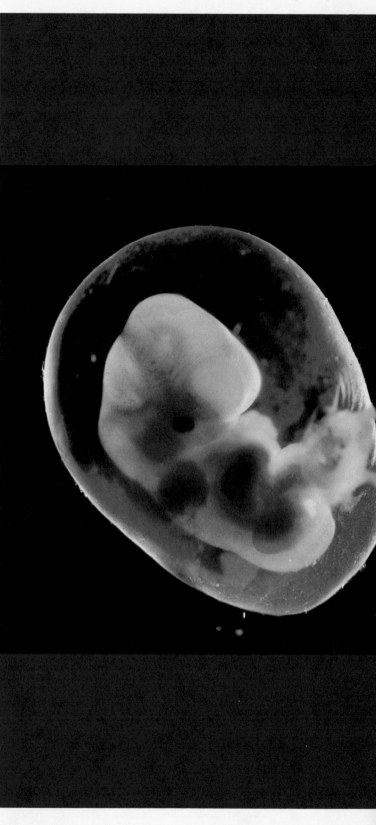

A SEARCH FOR CLUES

Human beings have both intelligence and curiosity. It is natural, therefore, that we wonder about our own history. We know that there have been changes in the earth over the ages. And we are aware of changes in the inhabitants of the earth. But what was life like for prehistoric humans? People have been asking this question for centuries. Today, there is a special branch of science that studies this very question. It is called *anthropology*. Anthropologists face an important problem as they study human history: What distinguishes early human beings from humanlike apes? **There are four characteristics used to identify early humans: 1) upright posture, 2) use of tools, 3) a larger brain than that of an ape, and 4) teeth like those humans have today.**

UPRIGHT POSTURE

The bone structure of the human pelvis makes it possible for us to walk erect. Here you can see that the human pelvis is broader than that of the gorilla. This wider pelvis can better support the internal organs in a standing position. The human pelvis has a large posterior section. This section makes the pelvis strong and acts as a place where the large muscles used in walking are attached.

A study of the environment of primitive people also gives us clues to human development. Anthropologists look for animal fossils when they find a place where early humans lived. These animals may have been used for food. If there are charred bones in the area, it may be a good clue that the humans living there knew how to use fire for cooking meat. The kind of food early people ate also tells us something about the climate in which they lived. And it gives us some idea of their natural surroundings.

Humans are the only animals that use a variety of tools to a great degree. So we can tell much about how highly developed early people were by looking at their tools. Evidence of simple stone tools would show that the people were primitive. Evidence of com-

chapter thirty-nine

Human History

OBJECTIVES
- LIST the characteristics that separate humans from other mammals.
- EXPLAIN how fossils are dated.
- DESCRIBE some of the early forms of the genus *Homo*.

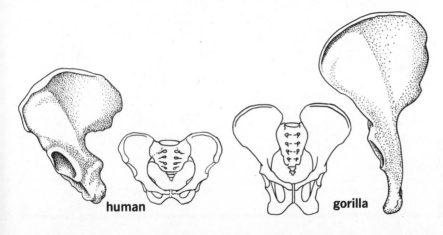

human **gorilla**

39–1 Compare the human pelvis to that of the gorilla. Structural differences allow the human to walk upright.

39-2 Human hands are well adapted for a firm grip. But they are also more suitable for manipulation of tools than those of the ape. (H.R.W. Photo by Russell Dian; Al Satterwhite, Jungle Habitat)

plicated tools made from metal usually means that the early peoples were more developed. Sometimes, similar tools are found over a large area. This suggests that the people who used them probably had some way of communicating with each other.

Humans have the ability to use tools because of unique characteristics. The fact that we have thumbs that oppose our fingers allows us to grasp objects. Also, our upright posture frees our hands for uses other than walking. Finally, the human hand is very sensitive to touch because of its many nerve endings. And it has grooves so it can grip smooth objects.

Humans are also helped in the use of tools by the structure and location of their eyes. Unlike fish, for example, both of our eyes see the same vision from slightly different angles. This give us a sense of depth.

Anthropologists have two ways of finding out about the develop-

39-3 Comparison of the skulls of a human and a chimpanzee.

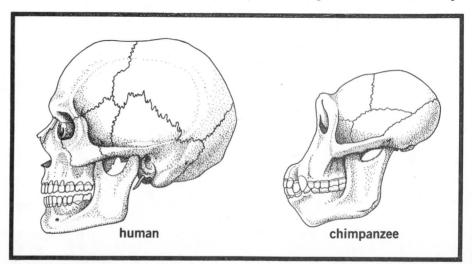

human   chimpanzee

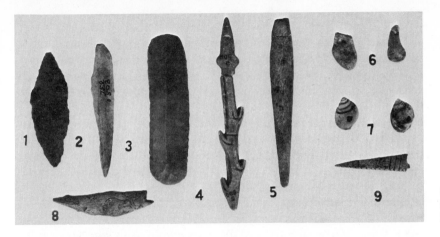

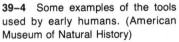

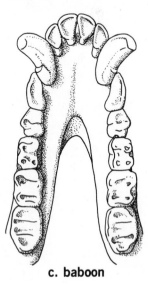

39-4 Some examples of the tools used by early humans. (American Museum of Natural History)

ment of the human brain. They have looked at fossils from the skulls of early humans. And they have compared the skulls of modern humans with those of apes. Among other things, they discovered that the front part of the human brain is highly developed. This part of the brain controls many thought processes that make human beings unique. The ape has a much smaller brain capacity with hardly any frontal bulge. These characteristics are clues that help anthropologists decide if a skull is human or ape.

Anthropologists also look at teeth when they are trying to decide if a fossil is human. There are major differences in size and arrangement between human teeth and those of the ape and the chimpanzee. All have the same number of teeth. But the shape of their jaws and teeth is different. The spacing between the teeth is also different.

The ability to communicate with each other by symbols is probably the most important difference in human development. Because we can communicate to each other by symbols, we can pass learning from generation to generation. This allows us to have a rapid cultural evolution not possible in other species.

39-5 The difference in the teeth of a chimpanzee, a human, and a baboon.

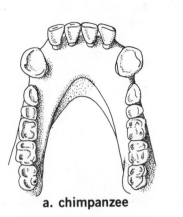

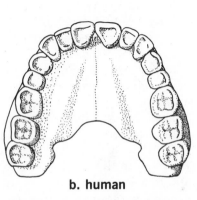

a. chimpanzee   **b. human**   **c. baboon**

HUMANS AND OTHER MAMMALS

As you can see, humans differ from other mammals in some important ways. But all mammals have many things in common. The organs and systems of their bodies are very similar. This is particularly true of the anatomy of humans and primates. You can easily see this similarity if you compare skeletons, muscles, tooth structure, eye structure and position, and the structure of hands and feet. Even facial expressions are similar! This is also true of most internal organs. The heart and blood vessels, the digestive and excretory organs, the lungs and the glands are all quite similar in humans and the other primates.

Even the chemicals of humans and other mammals are similar. Fortunately, this fact has been very useful for humans. For example, the insulin that we use to save the lives of diabetics can be obtained from the pancreas of a cow or pig. Many important discoveries in medicine have come from experiments on other mammals.

THOUGHTS ABOUT THE HISTORY OF HUMAN DEVELOPMENT

On December 27, 1831, the ship *HMS Beagle* left Plymouth, England. It was on a voyage to study the plants, animals, geography, geology, and cultures of the world. Charles Darwin, a young naturalist, was on board. The five-year trip carried Darwin to Brazil, Argentina, Terra del Fuego, Chile, Peru, the Galápagos Islands, Tahiti, New Zealand, and Australia. From these places, Darwin collected and classified many unusual organisms. He also developed some very important scientific ideas based on what he saw. In 1871, he published these ideas in his famous book, *The Descent of Man*.

Darwin pointed out the structural similarities between humans and the other primates—the monkey, gorilla, chimpanzee, orangutan, and gibbon. Some people thought Darwin was saying that human beings evolved from apes. But this is not what he meant at all. **Instead, Darwin was suggesting that all of the primates might have evolved from some very early common ancestor.**

This idea may become clearer if you think about the evolution from general to specialized forms. As you recall, biologists believe that the less specialized primitive forms can move most easily into new environments. Therefore, they are most likely to evolve into new species. The apes of today are highly specialized forms. Most likely, they evolved from less specialized primitive forms. Human beings are also a highly specialized form. Darwin was suggesting that humans may also have evolved from less specialized ancestors.

What would we find if we could trace the history of primates back ten million years? We might find that both modern humans and modern apes have evolved from the *same* early primate. However, most biologists think that the two lines of evolution separated a very long time ago. Today they are specialized in quite different ways.

When Darwin was alive, no remains of early humans had been found. Today, hundreds of bones have been found, dated, and studied. But this evidence still does not give us a complete picture of the history of human development. However, these fossils can help anthropologists hypothesize. For example, a fossil skull can show us the size of the brain, the shape of the head, and the age at death. Also, the structure of the jaw helps us determine if a primitive human was able to speak. Of course, it does not tell us if that human actually *did* speak. Still, you can see that certain bone fossils can tell us much about what our early ancestors were like.

DATING FOSSILS

In Chapter Thirteen, you learned that fossils were dated by finding out the age of the layer of earth where they were found. Another way of dating fossils is called the **radiocarbon method.** This method is very good for dating materials as old as 50,000 years.

In 1930, an isotope of carbon, with an atomic weight of 14 instead of 12, was discovered. In living organisms, there is about one carbon-14 atom to one trillion carbon-12 atoms.

Radioactive isotopes give off radiations at a steady rate. This eventually changes to a stable element. The time it takes for half a sample of a radioactive isotope to decay to a stable form is called the **half-life.** The half-life of carbon-14 is 5,568 years.

As long as an organism is alive, it adds carbon compounds to its body. But at death the addition of carbon stops. Say, for example, that a piece of bone has half the amount of carbon-14 as living organisms have today. Its age would be about 5,568 years.

Even more recent is the *potassium-argon method*. With this method, we can date materials that are millions of years old. This method also depends on a slow but constant change in certain atoms. Potassium-40 breaks down into calcium-40 and argon-40 at this very slow, constant rate. There are problems with this method, however,

The amount of argon-40 in a rock sample determines its age. So, when this method is used, it is necessary to find a rock about the same age as the organism being dated. Then the amount of argon-40 in the rock will give us the age of the organism. This method has given us some very valuable information about primitive people.

Stress the importance of radioactive dating techniques in determining the age of fossils and artifacts. Carbon-14 and potassium-argon dating have proved to be accurate dating methods. Another method of isotope dating uses uranium-238 to determine the age of cores of silt taken from the sea beds.

Zinjanthropus was discovered embedded in a living floor sited near part of an ancient lake. Near the specimen, a number of mammalian bones and the remains of small amphibians and fish were found.

PUTTING THE PIECES TOGETHER

In the last fifty years or so, there have been many exciting discoveries of human fossils. In 1924, a small fossilized skull was found in a South African quarry. It was given to a South African medical school. There, Professor Raymond Dart noticed that it looked like a human skull. He named it **Australopithecus** (aw-STRAY-lope-ith-EE-kuss) **africanus.** That means "southern ape from Africa." Since then, other bones of this primate have been found.

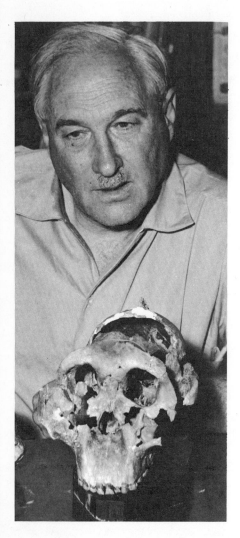

The famous anthropologist family, the Leakeys, had been digging up fossils and studying them for about 35 years. They had worked in Olduvai Gorge in Tanganyika. In 1959 they began digging in an area believed to be the campsite of some ancient humans. There the Leakeys found bones from skulls, a foot, fingers, and a lower jaw. These fragments give us many clues about the structure of a primate called *Zinjanthropus* (zin-JAN-thrup-uss). Using the potassium-argon method, scientists say it is 1,750,000 years old.

The bones of *Zinjanthropus* and *Australopithecus* are similar. They look like the bones of modern apes. But they do not have the ape's fanglike teeth. Also, the shape of the pelvis and opening for the spinal cord in the skull makes scientists think that both stood upright. Some anthropologists think they should be included in the ape family. Others think they should be put in the family that includes humans.

In 1964, Dr. Leakey discovered the bones of another primitive human form. He named it *Homo habilis.* Scientists think it is about the same age as *Zinjanthropus.* But *Homo habilis* is more like the modern human being. It probably walked and ran upright. It seems to have had a well-opposed thumb. And, like modern humans, *Homo habilis* seems to have eaten both meat and plants. Dr. Leakey believed *Homo habilis* was the ancestor of modern man. He claimed that *Zinjanthropus* and *Australopithecus* were evolutionary dead ends. If he was right, then the genus *Homo* has been on the earth for 3,750,000 years.

EARLY HUMAN FORMS

In 1891, part of a skull, a piece of jaw, and an upper leg bone were discovered on the island of Java. Similar bones were also found there in 1937. These bones belonged to what was called Java man. It is now called **Pithecanthropus erectus.** It is believed to have walked erect. *Pithecanthropus* probably lived 500,000 years ago. It had a slanting forehead and heavy brow ridges. The size of its skull shows that its brain was only about half the size of the modern

39–6 Dr. L. S. B. Leakey, the British anthropologist who unearthed the remains of the earth's earliest known humanlike creatures in East Africa. (Camera Pix, Rapho Guillumette)

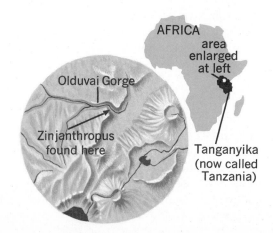

39–7 The site in Africa where *Zinjanthropus* was found.

THE HUMAN BODY

SKELETAL SYSTEM

BONES

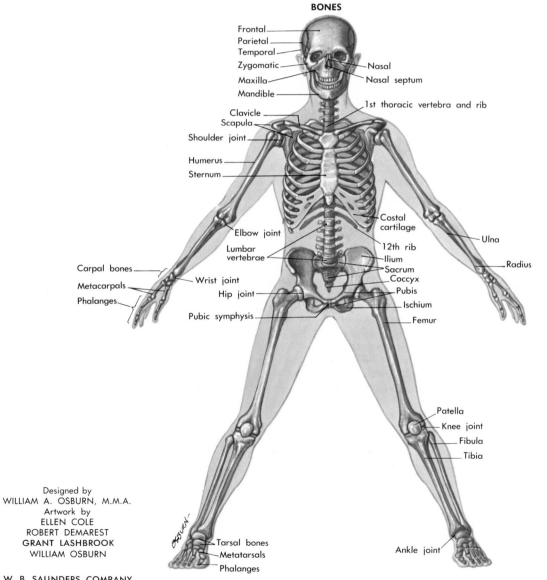

Frontal
Parietal
Temporal
Zygomatic
Maxilla
Mandible
Nasal
Nasal septum
1st thoracic vertebra and rib
Clavicle
Scapula
Shoulder joint
Humerus
Sternum
Costal cartilage
Elbow joint
12th rib
Lumbar vertebrae
Ilium
Sacrum
Ulna
Carpal bones
Coccyx
Radius
Metacarpals
Wrist joint
Pubis
Phalanges
Hip joint
Ischium
Pubic symphysis
Femur
Patella
Knee joint
Fibula
Tibia
Tarsal bones
Metatarsals
Phalanges
Ankle joint

Designed by
WILLIAM A. OSBURN, M.M.A.
Artwork by
ELLEN COLE
ROBERT DEMAREST
GRANT LASHBROOK
WILLIAM OSBURN

W. B. SAUNDERS COMPANY
Philadelphia — London — Toronto

SKELETAL MUSCLES

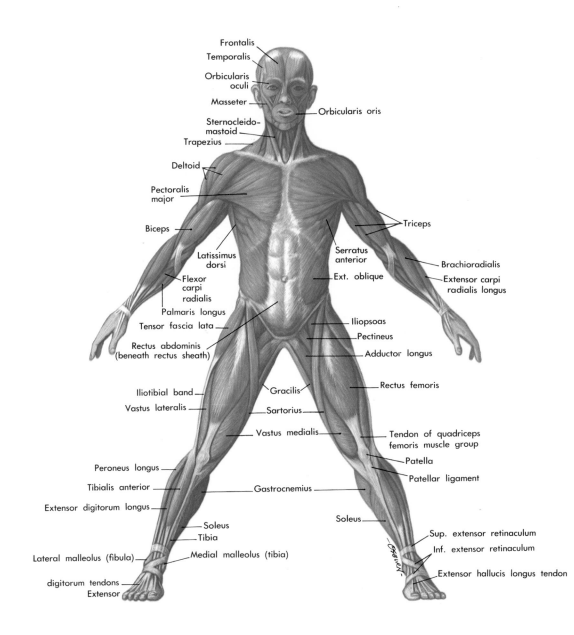

Frontalis
Temporalis
Orbicularis oculi
Masseter
Orbicularis oris
Sternocleido-mastoid
Trapezius
Deltoid
Pectoralis major
Biceps
Triceps
Latissimus dorsi
Serratus anterior
Brachioradialis
Flexor carpi radialis
Ext. oblique
Extensor carpi radialis longus
Palmaris longus
Tensor fascia lata
Iliopsoas
Pectineus
Rectus abdominis (beneath rectus sheath)
Adductor longus
Iliotibial band
Gracilis
Rectus femoris
Vastus lateralis
Sartorius
Vastus medialis
Tendon of quadriceps femoris muscle group
Patella
Patellar ligament
Peroneus longus
Tibialis anterior
Gastrocnemius
Extensor digitorum longus
Soleus
Soleus
Tibia
Sup. extensor retinaculum
Inf. extensor retinaculum
Lateral malleolus (fibula)
Medial malleolus (tibia)
Extensor hallucis longus tendon
digitorum tendons
Extensor

RESPIRATION AND THE HEART

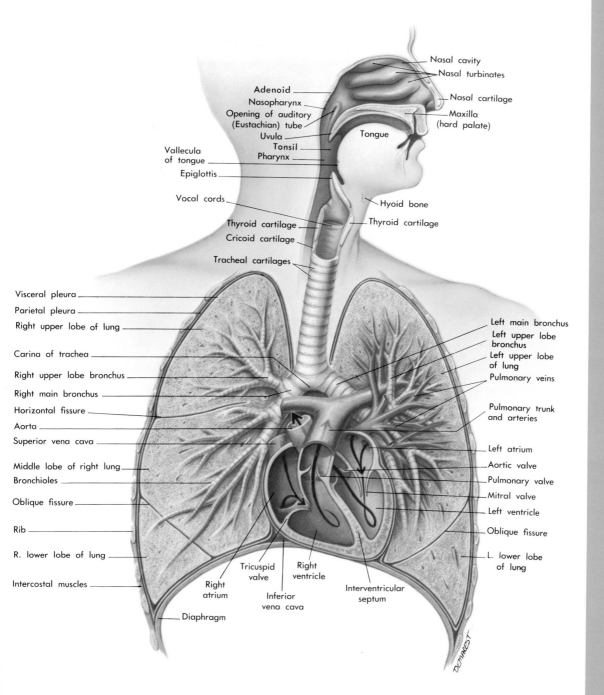

Nasal cavity

Nasal turbinates

Adenoid

Nasopharynx

Nasal cartilage

Opening of auditory
(Eustachian) tube

Maxilla
(hard palate)

Uvula

Tongue

Tonsil

Vallecula
of tongue

Pharynx

Epiglottis

Vocal cords

Hyoid bone

Thyroid cartilage

Thyroid cartilage

Cricoid cartilage

Tracheal cartilages

Visceral pleura

Parietal pleura

Right upper lobe of lung

Left main bronchus

Left upper lobe
bronchus

Carina of trachea

Left upper lobe
of lung

Right upper lobe bronchus

Pulmonary veins

Right main bronchus

Horizontal fissure

Pulmonary trunk
and arteries

Aorta

Superior vena cava

Left atrium

Middle lobe of right lung

Aortic valve

Bronchioles

Pulmonary valve

Mitral valve

Oblique fissure

Left ventricle

Rib

Oblique fissure

R. lower lobe of lung

L. lower lobe
of lung

Intercostal muscles

Tricuspid
valve

Right
ventricle

Right
atrium

Interventricular
septum

Inferior
vena cava

Diaphragm

DEMAREST

BLOOD VASCULAR SYSTEM

VEINS

STRUCTURE

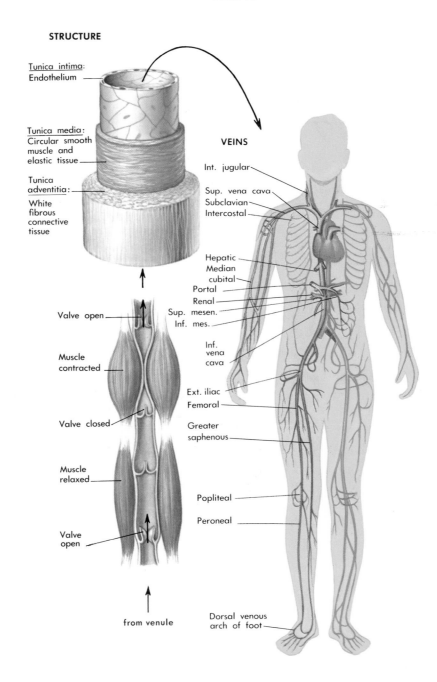

Tunica intima:
Endothelium

Tunica media:
Circular smooth
muscle and
elastic tissue

Tunica
adventitia:

White
fibrous
connective
tissue

VEINS

Int. jugular

Sup. vena cava
Subclavian
Intercostal

Hepatic
Median
cubital
Portal
Renal
Sup. mesen.
Inf. mes.

Inf.
vena
cava

Ext. iliac
Femoral

Greater
saphenous

Valve open

Muscle
contracted

Valve closed

Muscle
relaxed

Valve
open

Popliteal

Peroneal

from venule

Dorsal venous
arch of foot

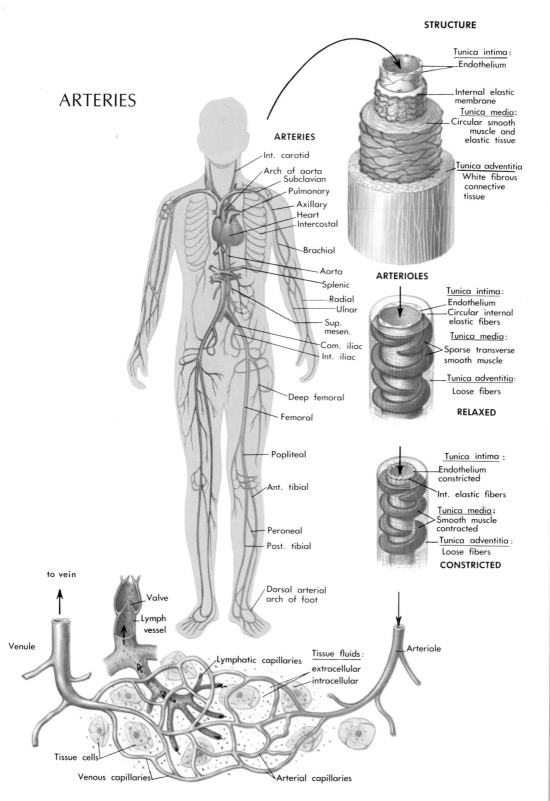

ARTERIES

STRUCTURE

Tunica intima:
Endothelium

Internal elastic membrane
Tunica media:
Circular smooth muscle and elastic tissue

Tunica adventitia
White fibrous connective tissue

ARTERIES

Int. carotid
Arch of aorta
Subclavian
Pulmonary
Axillary
Heart
Intercostal
Brachial
Aorta
Splenic
Radial
Ulnar
Sup. mesen.
Com. iliac
Int. iliac
Deep femoral
Femoral
Popliteal
Ant. tibial
Peroneal
Post. tibial
Dorsal arterial arch of foot

ARTERIOLES

Tunica intima:
Endothelium
Circular internal elastic fibers
Tunica media:
Sparse transverse smooth muscle
Tunica adventitia:
Loose fibers

RELAXED

Tunica intima :
Endothelium constricted
Int. elastic fibers
Tunica media:
Smooth muscle contracted
Tunica adventitia :
Loose fibers

CONSTRICTED

to vein
Venule
Valve
Lymph vessel
Lymphatic capillaries
Tissue fluids:
extracellular
intracellular
Arteriole
Tissue cells
Venous capillaries
Arterial capillaries

A CAPILLARY BED

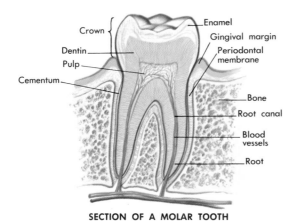

Crown {

Enamel

Gingival margin

Dentin

Periodontal membrane

Pulp

Cementum

Bone

Root canal

Blood vessels

Root

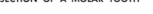

SECTION OF A MOLAR TOOTH

DIGESTIVE SYSTEM

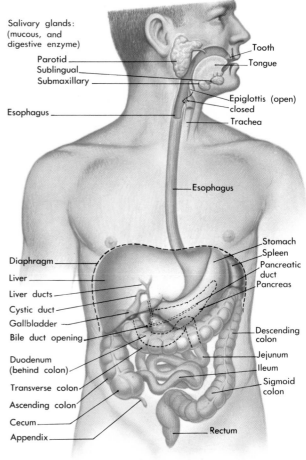

Salivary glands:
(mucous, and
digestive enzyme)

Parotid

Sublingual

Submaxillary

Esophagus

Tooth

Tongue

Epiglottis (open)
closed

Trachea

Esophagus

Diaphragm

Liver

Liver ducts

Cystic duct

Gallbladder

Bile duct opening

Duodenum
(behind colon)

Transverse colon

Ascending colon

Cecum

Appendix

Stomach

Spleen

Pancreatic duct

Pancreas

Descending colon

Jejunum

Ileum

Sigmoid colon

Rectum

DEMAREST

BRAIN AND SPINAL NERVES

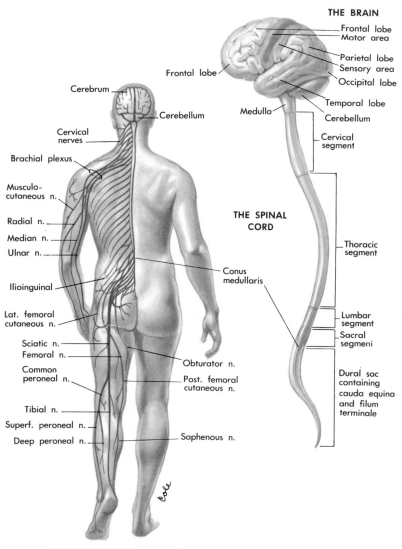

THE BRAIN

Frontal lobe
Motor area
Parietal lobe
Sensory area
Occipital lobe
Temporal lobe
Cerebellum

Frontal lobe

Medulla

Cervical segment

THE SPINAL CORD

Thoracic segment

Lumbar segment

Sacral segmeni

Dural sac containing cauda equina and filum terminale

Cerebrum

Cerebellum

Cervical nerves

Brachial plexus

Musculo-cutaneous n.

Radial n.

Median n.

Ulnar n.

Ilioinguinal

Lat. femoral cutaneous n.

Sciatic n.

Femoral n.

Common peroneal n.

Tibial n.

Superf. peroneal n.

Deep peroneal n.

Conus medullaris

Obturator n.

Post. femoral cutaneous n.

Saphenous n.

THE MAJOR SPINAL NERVES

ORGANS OF SPECIAL SENSE

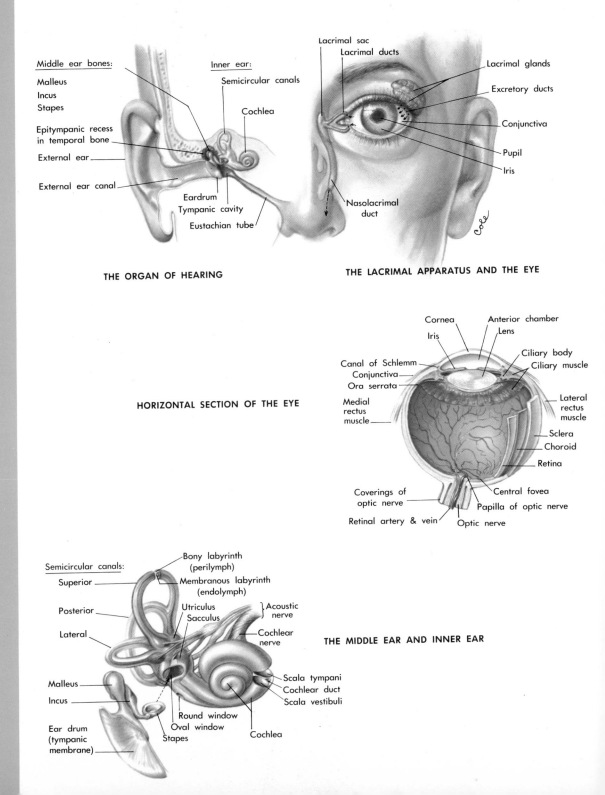

Middle ear bones:

Malleus
Incus
Stapes

Epitympanic recess
in temporal bone

External ear

External ear canal

Inner ear:

Semicircular canals

Cochlea

Eardrum
Tympanic cavity

Eustachian tube

THE ORGAN OF HEARING

Lacrimal sac
Lacrimal ducts

Lacrimal glands

Excretory ducts

Conjunctiva

Pupil

Iris

Nasolacrimal
duct

THE LACRIMAL APPARATUS AND THE EYE

HORIZONTAL SECTION OF THE EYE

Cornea
Iris
Anterior chamber
Lens

Canal of Schlemm
Conjunctiva
Ora serrata
Medial
rectus
muscle

Ciliary body
Ciliary muscle

Lateral
rectus
muscle

Sclera
Choroid
Retina

Coverings of
optic nerve

Retinal artery & vein

Central fovea
Papilla of optic nerve
Optic nerve

Semicircular canals:

Superior

Posterior

Lateral

Malleus

Incus

Ear drum
(tympanic
membrane)

Bony labyrinth
(perilymph)
Membranous labyrinth
(endolymph)

Utriculus
Sacculus

Acoustic
nerve

Cochlear
nerve

Round window
Oval window
Stapes

Scala tympani
Cochlear duct
Scala vestibuli

Cochlea

THE MIDDLE EAR AND INNER EAR

human brain. But the brain of *Pithecanthropus* was more than a third larger than that of the present-day gorilla. Anthropologists think *Pithecanthropus* knew how to use fire and stone weapons. Similar forms have been found in caves near Peking. Many of these skulls were broken near the base. This suggests that these primitive humans were headhunters.

THE NEANDERTHAL

More is known about the **Neanderthal** (nee-AN-der-thawl) form. Their remains have been found in Europe, Asia Minor, Siberia, and North Africa. Scientists think Neanderthal disappeared about 25,000 years ago. Almost one hundred Neanderthal skeletons have been found and studied. The average Neanderthal was probably about one and a half meters tall. Their bone structure shows that they were powerful. Their facial features were similar to *Pithecanthropus*. The forehead sloped backward from heavy brow ridges. The mouth was large, with a small chin.

The Neanderthal lived in caves. They were hunters of the hairy mammoth, saber-toothed cat, and woolly rhinoceros. Their brains were as large or larger than the modern human brain. The Neanderthal had stone tools and weapons. They used fire, buried their dead, and lived in family groups.

THE CRO-MAGNON

Anthropologists put the **Cro-Magnon** in the same species as the modern human, **Homo sapiens** (HOE-moe SAPE-ee-enz). The Cro-Magnon lived in Europe about 50,000 years ago. These primitive humans had high foreheads and well-developed chins. They did not have heavy brow ridges like most of the other primitive humans. Cro-Magnon skeletons have been found in caves along the coast of southern France along with their weapons of stone and bone. The walls of these caves have beautiful drawings of animals. These drawings are useful in dating the period.

Anthropologists think that the Cro-Magnon lived at the same time as the Neanderthal. The Cro-Magnon seem to have been more intelligent, though. And Cro-Magnon may have killed off the Neanderthal. It is also possible that the two groups mixed and Neanderthal lost their identity.

MODERN HUMANS

All people living today belong to the species Homo sapiens. Anthropologists sometimes divide this species into racial groups. These divisions are made according to certain physical features common to all members of a particular race. But there are many variations within each race. And, for the most part, all of us are much more alike than we are different.

The Java man was discovered by the Dutch anatomist Dubois. He found a primitive skull cap and a "modern" thigh bone. This combination was called the *Pithecanthropus erectus* and was later changed to *Homo erectus*.

Discuss Fig. 39–9 and why some of the "branches" are not connected.

39-8 Prehistoric humanlike primates and a modern human. In what ways do their skulls differ? In what ways are they similar?

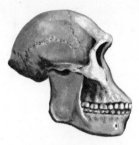

Australopithecus

Pithecanthropus

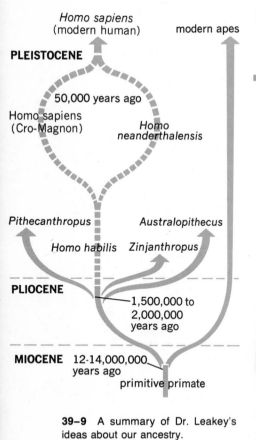

Homo sapiens
(modern human)   modern apes

PLEISTOCENE

50,000 years ago

Homo sapiens
(Cro-Magnon)   *Homo
neanderthalensis*

Pithecanthropus   *Australopithecus*

Homo habilis   *Zinjanthropus*

PLIOCENE

1,500,000 to
2,000,000
years ago

MIOCENE 12-14,000,000
years ago
primitive primate

39-9 A summary of Dr. Leakey's ideas about our ancestry.

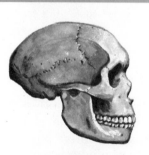

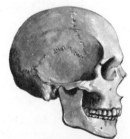

Homo neanderthalensis

Homo sapiens (modern human)

Human beings dominate today's biological world. We are not as strong physically as our primitive ancestors. And we probably could not survive the hardships of the life they had to live. But we have shown the triumph of "brain over brawn." Modern humans live three to four times longer than primitive humans did. Our greater ability for learning and for making things with our hands has given us many advantages. We are much more able to control our environment than our ancestors.

But, even today, some modern humans live in quite primitive ways. Civilization is slowly forcing these people to change their life styles. As the contacts with civilization occur more often, the areas for a primitive existence become smaller. Anthropologists study these primitive cultures in the hope of better understanding the ways of early humans.

Much of our advancement has been detailed in art work through cave and rock paintings. Many students may be interested in finding out more about these paintings.

SUMMARY

Anthropologists do not know when the "humans" first inhabited the earth. It is believed that humanlike creatures were here almost four million years ago. Careful study of fossils and sites where they lived show whether the early forms of the human walked upright and were able to use tools. Bone and teeth structure also show us much about the life of the primitive human.

The human and all mammals are alike in many ways. But the human and other primates are even more similar. Even the chemicals they make are alike.

The brain, upright posture, use of tools, and language have combined to make the human the most intelligent and curious of the animals. All people living today are of the species *Homo sapiens*. A study of primitive cultures may give us clues about early human life.

BIOLOGICALLY SPEAKING

anthropology
Australopithecus africanus
Zinjanthropus
Pithecanthropus erectus
Cro-Magnon
Homo sapiens
Neanderthal

QUESTIONS FOR REVIEW

1. What features separate the human from other animals?
2. What features are used to distinguish true humans from apelike primates?
3. What did Charles Darwin believe about the human's development, and what was the misunderstanding about his theory?
4. Why is the finding of an old skull important?
5. What can be learned from a study of the lower jaw and teeth?
6. How can we determine the type of environment of a given area thousands of years ago?
7. How can we determine the diet of primitive man?
8. Why do anthropologists study the primitive human in a modern world?

1. Do you think that tropical forests would yield good fossils? Explain your answer.
2. How can the intelligence of the primitive human be judged from fossil evidence?
3. Explain the theory that reduction of the canine teeth is related to tool-making.
4. Compare the skull of the modern human with the skulls of the Java, Neanderthal, and Cro-Magnon.
5. Did Cro-Magnon have any methods of communication? Explain.

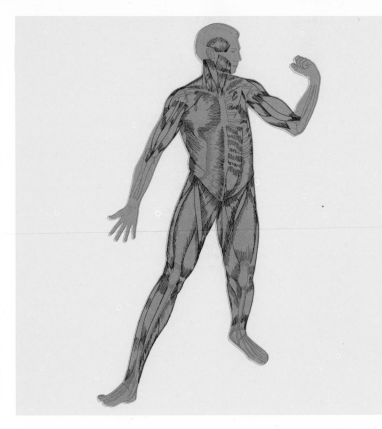

40-1 Muscles and bones act as levers for movement.

The Body Framework

OBJECTIVES
- NAME the systems of the body.
- NAME the body cavities.
- DESCRIBE the structure and function of bone.
- NAME the kinds of joints.
- EXPLAIN the theory of how muscles contract.
- DESCRIBE the three types of muscles.
- EXPLAIN the origin and insertion of muscles.

GROUPS OF CELLS

The human body is like other multicellular organisms. It is made up of cells and cell products. Groups of cells with similar structures and functions make up the different tissues of our bodies. These body tissues can be divided into four groups:

- *Connective tissues* lie between groups of nerve and muscle cells. They fill up the spaces where there are no specialized cells. And they form protective layers. Connective tissue also binds together many softer tissues. It gives them strength and firmness. Fibers in the organ walls, muscle tendons, ligaments binding bones, and the bones themselves are all forms of connective tissue.
- *Muscle tissues* function in movement. They will be discussed later in this chapter.
- *Nervous tissues* coordinate the moving parts of our bodies. They also inform us about our environment. Nervous tissues are covered in Chapter Forty-Four.
- *Epithelial tissues* cover the body surfaces, inside and out. For example, one type covers the blood vessels and the heart. Another type lines the stomach. Some cells of this lining are modified to secrete mucus and other stomach secretions. The skin is another epithelial tissue, as is the ciliated lining of the trachea.

Refer students to the human body insert. It will be a helpful aid in studying the chapters concerned with the human body.

Table 40-1 TISSUES IN THE HUMAN BODY

TISSUE	OCCURRENCE	FUNCTION
I. CONNECTIVE TISSUES		
A. bone	skeleton	composes framework for movement, support, and protection; serves as a storehouse for minerals; manufactures blood cells
B. cartilage	outer ears, ends of long bones, larynx, tip of nose, between vertebrae, juncture of ribs and breastbone, trachea	acts as cushion, lends rigidity to structures that lack bones, provides slippery surface to some joints
C. dense fibrous connective tissue		
1. regularly arranged	tendons, ligaments	joins muscles to bones or bone to bone to aid in movement
2. irregularly arranged	membrane around bone (periosteum), one of the membranes around spinal cord and brain (dura mater), inner layer of skin	provides protection and carries blood supply
D. loose fibrous connective tissue		
1. fibroelastic (elastic—strong, closely woven)	capsules of organs	holds organ together
2. fibroareolar (areolar—loosely woven)	facial area beneath skin	acts as filler tissue
3. reticular	surrounding individual cells and muscle fibers	acts as filler tissue
4. adipose	around organs, beneath skin	cushions and insulates, stores fat
E. liquid tissue		
1. blood	in heart and vessels (arteries and veins)	has essential part in respiration, nutrition, excretion, regulation of body temperature, protection from disease
2. lymph	fluid in tissue spaces between cells, cerebrospinal fluid	bathes the cells, has part in nutrition and protection from disease
II. MUSCLE TISSUES		
A. smooth	in internal organs	produces either voluntary or involuntary movement
B. skeletal	attached to bones, tendons, and other muscles	
C. cardiac	in heart	
III. NERVOUS TISSUES	brain, spinal cord, nerves	carries impulses that cause muscles to contract, carries messages to brain to inform individual about the environment
IV. EPITHELIAL TISSUES	covering surface of body (skin), lining nose, throat, and windpipe, lining all of digestive tract, many glands	provides protection, produces secretions

You are familiar with some organs of the human body. These include the arms, legs, ears, eyes, heart, liver, lungs, etc. Each of these organs is specialized. Each has its own job or group of related jobs to keep the body going. And each organ has several different tissues. For example, the arms are made up of all four kinds of tissues. These tissues work together to help us do such acts as writing, sewing, throwing a ball, or playing the drums.

Organs working together to do a specific job make up a system. Even the simplest body function involves more than one system. When you move, for example, you use bones, nerves, muscles, and blood vessels. But to make things easier, we will divide the body into the following ten systems:

- *skeletal*—bone and cartilage
- *muscular*—muscles
- *digestive*—teeth, mouth, esophagus, stomach, intestines, liver, pancreas
- *circulatory*—heart, arteries, veins, capillaries
- *excretory*—kidneys and bladder
- *integumentary*—skin and hair
- *respiratory*—nasal passages, trachea, bronchi, lungs
- *nervous*—brain, spinal cord, nerves, eyes, ears
- *endocrine*—ductless glands
- *reproductive*—testes, ovaries, uterus, oviducts

Discuss the body regions in relation to the relative advantages of the general form of the human body. Point out to students the effectiveness of the cranial cavity and the fact that the cavity is not completely closed at birth.

REGIONS OF THE HUMAN BODY

Our body form is similar to that of other vertebrates. We have limbs (arms and legs), a head, neck, and trunk. The head includes the *cranial cavity.* This cavity is formed by the bones of the skull and encloses the brain. The head also contains many of our sense organs. These are near the brain and send impulses to it.

The *thoracic cavity* is formed by our ribs, breastbone, and spine. It holds the lungs, trachea, heart, and esophagus. A dome-shaped partition, called the *diaphragm,* separates the thoracic cavity from the *abdominal cavity* in the lower trunk. The abdominal cavity holds the stomach, liver, pancreas, intestines, spleen, and kidneys. The abdominal cavity of the female also contains the ovaries.

Skeletal System

THE BODY FRAMEWORK

If you build a model airplane, you usually begin with the body framework. Then you add covering and paint. Finally, you add the motor, wheels, and other parts. But the strength of the entire structure depends on the basic framework. Like the model plane, vertebrates have a strong supporting structure. This is their internal skeleton, or **endoskeleton.** You may remember that arthropods have external skeletons, or exoskeletons.

Our bony framework is very efficient. It gives us the greatest support with the least weight. It also lets us move freely. Exoskeletons cause clumsy movement. But there is one great disadvantage to having an internal skeleton. It does not offer the protection against injury from outside that the exoskeleton does. Many soft body parts are exposed. **Thus, an organism with an endoskeleton must rely on its nervous system and sense organs for protection.**

THE FUNCTIONS OF THE SKELETON

The bones in your body serve the following functions: 1) They provide support and form. 2) They provide a surface to which the muscles attach. 3) They protect delicate organs. 4) They store minerals. 5) They manufacture red blood cells and certain white blood cells. Many of our bones have more than one function. For example, the vertebral column, the shoulder and hip girdles, and the arm and leg bones support the body. But they also give it form. And some of these bones have muscles attached to them as well. This allows us to move in a great many ways. Several special bones protect delicate organs. For instance, the cranial bones enclose the brain, the sternum covers the heart, and the ribs protect the lungs.

HOW BONE DEVELOPS

You have heard the expression "dry as a bone." Well, living bone is not like a dried-out dead bone. In fact, living bone is not dry at all. Actually it is moist and active. And it requires food just like other organs. It is true, however, that part of what we call bone is nonliving. **Bone tissue is a combination of living cells and their products and mineral deposits.**

The skeletons of some lower vertebrates are made up entirely of **cartilage.** This cartilage skeleton lasts all through their lives. And it is tough and flexible. In the early development of the human embryo, the skeleton is also made almost entirely of cartilage. But after about two months of development, certain cartilage cells disappear. They are replaced by bone cells. These cells remove calcium phosphate and calcium carbonate from the blood. These substances are used to form the bone structure. This process is called **ossification** (oss-i-fi-KAY-shun). It occurs throughout childhood. Not all cartilage undergoes ossification. You have permanent cartilage in the end of your nose. Cartilage is also found in the external ear and the walls of the voice box and trachea.

Not all bones come from cartilage. Flat bones, like those of the skull and sternum, are formed from membrane layers that later undergo ossification. The skull bones of a newborn baby are not fused together. The cranium is not solid. As babies develop, the edges of the bones come together and form irregular seams. These seams are called *sutures.*

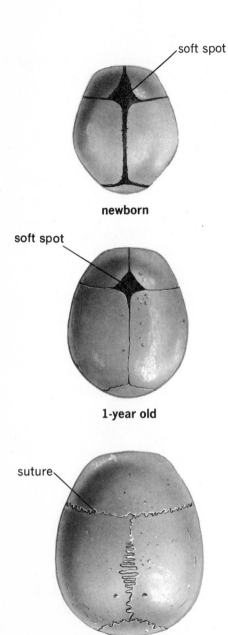

soft spot

newborn

soft spot

1-year old

suture

adult

40-2 The skull develops from a membrane that forms separate plates of bone. By the time adulthood is reached, the margins of these bony plates have joined.

As we have said, ossification involves the deposit of calcium compounds between bone cells. This makes the bone stronger. But these deposits can not be made without the proper minerals. Calcium compounds must enter the body with food and be carried to the bone tissues by the blood. So you can see that diet can make a big difference in forming your bones. This is especially true of growing children.

Milk is the natural food of all young mammals. It is an excellent source of calcium compounds. Developing bone tissue must be able to use the minerals once they have been supplied by the proper diet. Certain vitamins, especially vitamin D, are needed for the normal growth of bone. We shall study vitamins in Chapter Forty-One.

Bones grow along lines of stress. This means that they become heaviest and strongest where the strain is greatest. Physicians must think about this when they set broken bones. Some casts protect bones in such a way that they are never used while they heal. Because there is no stress, the bones take longer to heal. Walking casts are made to allow for a little stress on the healing bone. This stress speeds up the healing of the bone. But if a limb is paralyzed or made useless, the minerals are absorbed into the blood and carried elsewhere.

THE STRUCTURE OF A BONE

Let's look at the structure of a long bone, such as the thighbone. If a thighbone is cut lengthwise, several different parts can be seen. The bone is covered by a tough membrane called the *periosteum.* This membrane helps nourish the bone with a rich blood supply. It also works at repairing injuries. And it provides a surface for the attachment of muscles. Beneath the periosteum is a *bony layer.* This layer contains mineral deposits and varies in hardness. The middle region is made of extremely hard material. The material at

The most efficient and meaningful way of teaching the major bones is by using a skeleton. A large wall chart can be substituted if a skeleton is not available.

40–3 The structure of the human femur shown at increasingly greater magnification.

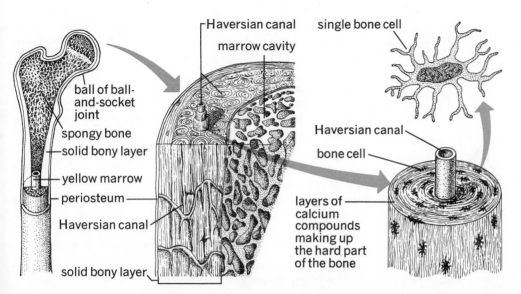

Haversian canal
marrow cavity
single bone cell
ball of ball-and-socket joint
spongy bone
solid bony layer
yellow marrow
periosteum
Haversian canal
solid bony layer
Haversian canal
bone cell
layers of calcium compounds making up the hard part of the bone

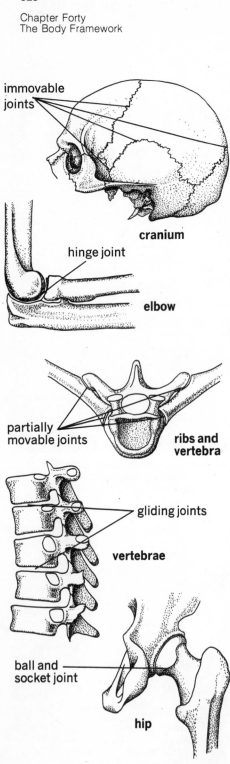

immovable
joints

cranium

hinge joint

elbow

partially
movable joints

ribs and
vertebra

gliding joints

vertebrae

ball and
socket joint

hip

40–4 Five types of joints.

the ends is porous and spongy. There are many channels forming a network running throughout the bony layer. These channels, called **Haversian canals,** carry food to the living cells of the bony layer through blood vessels. These blood vessels are connected to the blood vessels of the outer membrane.

Many bones are hollow inside. These hollows contain a soft tissue called marrow. Marrow is rich in nerves and blood vessels. There are two types of marrow. **Red marrow** is found in flat bones like the ribs and sternum. It is also found in the ends of long bones and vertebrae. Red marrow forms the red corpuscles and most of the white corpuscles of the blood. **Yellow marrow** fills the central cavity of long bones. It extends into the Haversian canals of the bony layer. Yellow marrow is made up mostly of fat cells. Normally, it is not active. However, yellow marrow may produce corpuscles in an emergency. This may happen if you lose a great deal of blood or have certain blood diseases.

Smaller bones are solid rather than hollow. And some have much more spongy bone tissue than others. Even though they are solid, these small bones have blood vessels running through them.

THE JOINTS OF THE BODY

The point at which two bones meet is called a joint. The bones in the human body are connected by several different kinds of joints. Your elbow is an example of a *hinge joint*. This kind of joint can move in one plane only. But it can give great power because there is little danger of twisting it. When the biceps muscle of the upper arms contracts, the lower arm is pulled upward only. The knee is another example of a hinge joint. You have *ball-and-socket joints* at your hips and shoulders. Here a ball on the end of the thighbone, or *femur*, fits into a socket in the hipbone, the *pelvis*. This kind of joint can move in any direction the muscles around it allow. The upper arm bone fits into the shoulder in a similar way. Tough strands of connective tissue, called **ligaments,** hold ball-and-socket and hinge joints in place. You can stretch these ligaments by exercising. This loosens the joints and lets you move more easily.

Joints attach your ribs to the vertebrae in your backbone. These joints are only *partially movable*. Long strands of cartilage attach some ribs to the breastbone in front. This allows your chest to expand when you breathe. The sacroiliac is a partially movable joint. It connects your spine with your pelvis. Many people injure the sacroiliac in sudden falls. Some joints are *immovable*. Among them are the joints in the adult skull bone. Your wrists and ankles have *angular joints*. A *pivot joint* connects your head to your spine. And the vertebrae are connected by *gliding joints*.

The inside surfaces of your joints are covered with layers of cartilage. A secretion called **synovial** (suh-NOVE-ee-uhl) **fluid** lubricates the joints. In your knee and shoulder, a sac called the *bursa* acts as a cushion between bones.

Muscle Systems

HOW MUSCLES PRODUCE MOVEMENT

Bones do not have the ability to move by themselves. **But muscle cells are specialists in motion because they are able to contract.** Every movement you make is caused by the contraction of bundles of muscle cells. You use muscles to walk, breathe, and pick up things. Even your heartbeat and the movement of your digestive system is caused by the contraction of muscle cells. There are about 400 different muscles in your body. They make up about half of your body weight.

Human muscle tissues are composed of long, slender cells often called muscle *fibers.* Each fiber contains many fine threads called *myofibrils.* Myofibrils lie parallel and run lengthwise in the fiber. Myofibrils, in turn, are bundles of two kinds of even smaller protein filaments. These are thick *myosin* filaments, and thin *actin* filaments. They are arranged in a definite pattern.

Muscle cells contract when they are supplied with energy from ATP and activated by a nerve impulse. The precise action that causes muscles to contract is still not clear. But many scientists think that the thick and thin protein filaments slide over each other. In this way, the myofibrils shorten. Several theories have been formed to explain how the filaments slide over each other.

Each nerve cell that carries impulses to a muscle branches out. Each of these branches stimulates a few muscle fibers. This combination of nerve cell and muscle fibers is called a *motor unit.* When stimulated, each fiber contracts as tight as it can. The strength of each fiber contraction is always the same. **The strength of the movement depends on how many motor units are called into action.** The more units that contract, the greater the movement. In this way, we are able to control very precise movements and very forceful ones. Muscle fibers may also be stimulated by heat, light, chemicals, pressure, and electricity.

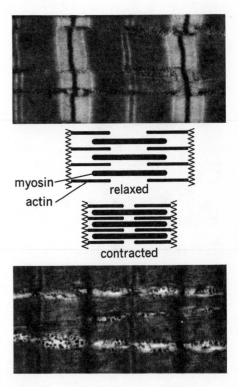

40-5 A representation of the current concept of muscle contraction. Compare the relaxed muscle tissue (top) with the contracted muscle tissue (bottom). (Lewis Koster)

TYPES OF MUSCLE CELLS

There are three types of vertebrate muscle cells: 1) smooth muscle, 2) skeletal muscle, 3) cardiac muscle. Each **smooth muscle** cell is a long spindle with one nucleus, usually near its center. The stomach and intestinal walls are layered with smooth muscles. They contract in waves to churn food or to pass it along the digestive tract. Artery walls are also layered with smooth muscle. Impulses from the nervous system can make these walls tighten. This raises your blood pressure during times of danger or emotional upset. **All smooth muscle action is controlled by parts of the nervous system over which we have no conscious control.** Smooth muscle is, therefore, *involuntary muscle.*

The *skeletal muscles* are voluntary muscles. We can control them at will. Each fiber is a long cylinder with tapering ends. Each

40-6 A motor unit. (courtesy of General Biological Supply House, Inc.)

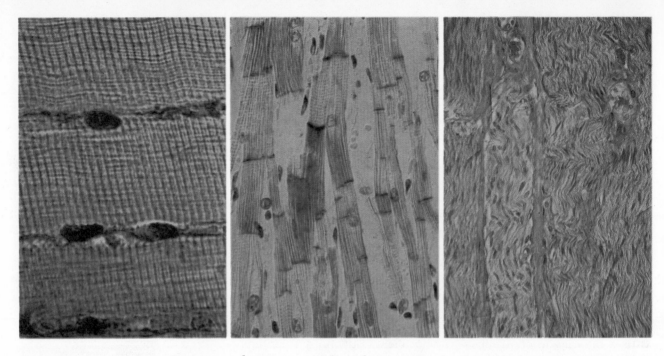

40–7 Three types of vertebrate muscle cells: smooth (left), cardiac (center), and skeletal (right). (Manfred Kage, Peter Arnold; Carolina Biological Supply Co.)

has many nuclei. These nuclei are located along the inside edges throughout the length of the cells. Most skeletal muscle fibers do not stretch from one end of a muscle to the other. Instead, they are bound together in small bundles by strips of connective tissue. These bundles are held together by heavier strips that cover the entire muscle. This structure gives most voluntary muscles a spindle shape.

Some skeletal muscles attach directly to bones. Some attach to other muscles. And some attach to bones by **tendons** that extend

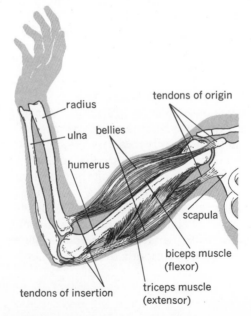

radius
ulna
humerus
bellies
tendons of origin
scapula
biceps muscle (flexor)
triceps muscle (extensor)
tendons of insertion

40–8 The biceps and the triceps, two opposing muscles.

from the tapered end. These tendons are thick bands of connective tissue that are not elastic. In order to cause movement, muscles must attach at two points. The attachment to the stationary part is called the **origin.** The attachment to the movable part is called the **insertion.** This will become clearer if you look at a drawing of the *biceps* in the arm. The *origin* of the biceps is on the shoulder and back bones. The *insertion* is on the movable forearm.

The skeletal muscles that move trunk and limb are always in pairs. The muscles of these pairs oppose each other. Muscles that bend joints are called *flexors.* Those that straighten them are called *extensors.* To see how they work, bend your elbow joint. Notice how the tendon to the contracted biceps raises the radius bone of your forearm. The other end of this muscle is attached securely to your shoulder. When you contract the biceps, you can feel it swell on the front side of your upper arm.

Now, lower your arm. The extensor muscle you are using is called the *triceps.* It is on the back side of your upper arm. Notice how the triceps contracts and the biceps relaxes. Straighten your arm completely. Can you feel the triceps muscle contract?

Even when you are not moving your joints, flexor and extensor muscles are slightly contracted. This is called **tone.** The more you use your muscles, the larger they get and the more tone they have. When you do not use them at all, muscles become weak and flabby. They get smaller and lose their tone. This is called *disuse atrophy.*

Cardiac muscle is the involuntary muscle found in the heart. It is made up of a third kind of contracting cell. It was once thought that cardiac muscle cells contained many nuclei. However, the electron microscope shows us that this is not true. These cells are separated by plasma membranes. The cells form a branching, woven network. Thus, when cardiac muscle fibers contract, the chambers of the heart are squeezed. This action forces blood out through the vessels.

Heart muscle does not act like any other muscle. The heartbeat begins in a small mass of tissue called the **sinoatrial** (SIE-noe-AY-tree-uhl) **node.** This tissue is located in the wall of the right atrium of the heart. From this *pacemaker,* the beat is carried through the muscle of the upper chambers to another node, the **atrioventricular** (AY-tree-oe-ven-TRICK-yoo-ler) **node.** From there it is relayed through the muscles of the lower chambers. The beat is conducted from cell to cell through the heart muscle. This results in the rhythmic wave of contraction that we know as the heartbeat.

Ask students to bring in tendons from fresh meat. A fresh chicken leg would help the students understand how tendons work.

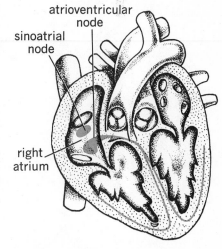

atrioventricular node

sinoatrial node

right atrium

40-9 The conducting pathways in the heart. The impulse for the heartbeat originates in the sinoatrial node. It is carried through the muscle to the atrioventricular node. It is then relayed through the muscles of the lower chambers.

SUMMARY

Our bodies are very similar to those of other vertebrates. Our organs are made up of tissues. These tissues are formed by cells and their products. Tissue cells vary, depending on their function.

Unlike some of the lower vertebrates, most of the cartilage in the human embryo is turned into bone by the time we become adults. Our internal skeleton has several functions. It gives our bodies form, provides levers for muscles, and it protects delicate organs.

Muscles produce movement. Striated muscles are attached to bones by tendons. They are voluntary muscles. Smooth muscles form layers in the walls of organs like the stomach, intestine, and arteries. They are involuntary. Special muscles which control the action of the heart are also involuntary.

BIOLOGICALLY SPEAKING

connective tissues	cartilage	motor unit
epithelial tissues	ossification	smooth muscle
muscle tissues	periosteum	skeletal muscle
nervous tissues	bony layer	tendon
cranial cavity	Haversian canal	origin
thoracic cavity	red marrow	insertion
diaphragm	yellow marrow	tone
abdominal cavity	joint	disuse atrophy
endoskeleton	ligament	sinoatrial node
		atrioventricular node

QUESTIONS FOR REVIEW

1. How do the tissues, organs, and systems of the human body show division of labor?
2. What are the three body cavities? By what structures are they enclosed? Name some of the organs found in each.
3. What are the main functions of bones? Give an example of a bone serving each purpose.
4. What are some important functions of the Haversian canals?
5. Describe some of the tissues surrounding a joint. What are their functions?
6. Describe the kinds of joints found in the body.
7. What are the three types of muscle tissues?
8. Why are muscles often found in opposing pairs in the body?
9. Describe the modern concept of muscle contraction.

APPLYING PRINCIPLES AND CONCEPTS

1. Explain the importance of a highly developed nervous system in an organism with an internal skeleton.
2. Proper diet alone does not insure good teeth and healthy bones. What other factors are involved?
3. How does a walking cast speed up the repair of a bone fracture?
4. Why is it possible that hearts removed from some lower animals and placed in nutrient solutions keep beating?

41-1 Eating nutritious food is vital to our health. (H.R.W. Photo by Russell Dian)

Nutrition

OBJECTIVES
- DEFINE food.
- EXPLAIN the body's use of water.
- LIST the food substances, their functions, and their sources.
- NAME and DESCRIBE the organic nutrients.
- EXPLAIN the importance of carbohydrates.
- DESCRIBE the anatomy and physiology of the various digestive organs.

Food

WHAT IS FOOD?

What happens to the sandwich and glass of milk you eat for lunch? In a short while, they are in your body tissues. The process of preparing the foods to enter the body occurs in a nine-meter tube. This tube is called the *alimentary canal*. Enzymes break the bread, meat, milk, and butter into smaller molecules of sugar, amino acids, and fatty acids. These can then pass into the bloodstream. **Food is nutritive substance taken into an organism for growth, work, or repair, and maintaining life processes.** In other words, you eat for several reasons: to take in energy, to grow, and to maintain your body. By this definition, water, minerals, and vitamins are food, as well as carbohydrates, fats, and proteins. Before reading on, you may want to review Chapter Three. Chapter Three outlined the chemical structure and importance of carbohydrates, fats, and proteins to living organisms.

Ask students to think about what makes this a nourishing lunch. What food substances are included in this meal?

THE MANY USES OF WATER

Water is inorganic. It does not give energy to body tissues. Nevertheless, it is essential to life. We can do without any other food longer than we can do without water.

If you weigh 50 kilograms, your body contains between 30 and 35 kilograms of water. Much of this water is in your body protoplasm and in the spaces between cells. The fluid part of blood is

Table 41-1 FOOD SUBSTANCES

SUBSTANCE	ESSENTIAL FOR	SOURCE
A. Inorganic compound		
Water	composition of protoplasm, tissue fluid, and blood; dissolving substances	all foods (released during oxidation)
B. Mineral salts		
sodium compounds	blood and other body tissues	table salt, vegetables
calcium compounds	deposition in bones and teeth, heart and nerve action, clotting of blood	milk, whole-grain cereals, vegetables, meats
phosphorus compounds	deposition in bones and teeth; formation of ATP, nucleic acids	milk, whole-grain cereals, vegetables, meats
magnesium	muscle and nerve action	vegetables
potassium compounds	blood and cell activities growth	vegetables
iron compounds	formation of red blood corpuscles	leafy vegetables, liver, meats, raisins, prunes
iodine	secretion by thyroid gland	seafoods, water, iodized salt
C. Complex organic substances		
Vitamins	regulation of body processes, prevention of deficiency diseases	various foods, especially milk, butter, lean meats, fruits, leafy vegetables; also made synthetically
D. Organic nutrients		
carbohydrates	energy (stored as fat or glycogen) bulk in diet	cereals, bread, pastries, tapioca, fruits, vegetables
fats	energy (stored as fat or glycogen)	butter, cream, lard, oils, cheese, oleomargarine, nuts, meats
proteins	growth, maintenance, and repair of protoplasm	lean meats, eggs, milk, wheat, beans, peas, cheese

called *plasma*. Plasma is 91 to 92 percent water. Water is essential in the plasma. Water dissolves the food and waste that are transported to and from body tissues. It is also a solvent in the movement of dissolved foods from the digestive tract to the blood. Tissue wastes from the skin and kidneys are dissolved in water. In fact, one to two and a half liters of water pass through the kidneys daily.

The loss of water by sweat also helps in regulating heat loss from our bodies. *Evaporation,* or the change from liquid to gas, requires heat. So when perspiration evaporates from your skin, heat from internal oxidation is lost.

In these ways, we lose water from our bodies. This loss must be balanced by the amount of water we take in. **We take in this needed water in three ways:** 1) We get some water from the food we eat. 2) We get some water as a by-product of oxidation reactions and dehydration synthesis in our cells. 3) And, of course, we get some as drinking water.

What happens if you do not drink enough water? First, you lose water from the intercellular spaces. Then you lose it from the cells themselves. When this happens, the protoplasm becomes more solid. Finally, the cell cannot function and it dies. This water loss is part of the process called *dehydration*.

Ask students to find out about the mineral content of the foods they eat regularly. What minerals are frequently missing from their diets?

MINERAL SALTS IN THE BODY

We get table salt, or *sodium chloride*, directly from our food. There are also other mineral salts in our food. We lose salts when we perspire. People exposed to considerable heat for a long time must use extra salt in their food, or take salt tablets.

Animals need *calcium* and *phosphorus* in greater amounts than other minerals. Calcium is needed for proper functioning of plasma membranes. Calcium is also needed for proper clotting of blood. And, together with *magnesium*, calcium is essential to nerve and muscle action. Phosphorus is important since it is a component in ATP, DNA, and RNA. Calcium phosphate is needed to form bones and teeth. In fact, calcium and phosphorus make up about 5 percent of animal tissue when they combine with the other elements in proteins. Milk is a good source of these two elements. You can also get them from whole-grain cereals, meat, and fish.

Potassium compounds are needed for growth. In order to form red blood corpuscles, you must have *iron compounds*. You can get this iron from meat, green vegetables, and fruits such as plums, prunes, and raisins. *Iodine salts* are needed to form the thyroid gland's secretion. You can get iodine from drinking water or by eating seafoods.

Minerals are vital to the body in many ways. But our bodies can only use them in compound form. Eating chemically pure elements, such as sodium or chlorine, would kill you. In compound form, however, sodium chloride is harmless. In fact, your body must have it.

VITAMINS—ESSENTIAL TO PROPER BODY FUNCTION

In 1911, Dr. Casimir Funk discovered some substances in very small amounts in food. They were not ordinary nutrients. But these substances seemed to be necessary to body growth and activity. They were also needed to prevent certain **deficiency diseases.** Deficiency diseases result when the body does not have enough of some important substance. These substances are called **vitamins.** At first each vitamin discovered was identified by a letter—A, B, C, and so on. The scientists discovered that some of them were made up of many different things. The vitamin-B complex is a good example.

The subject of adding vitamins to one's diet is a controversial one. Recent estimates of the vitamin business in this country are in excess of $500 million a year. Most experts in this field feel that a balanced diet requires no additional vitamins or food supplements.

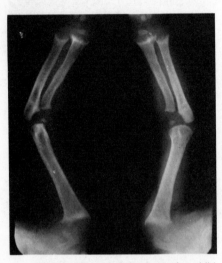

41–2 X rays of the legs of a child
with rickets. Lack of vitamin D in the
diet causes poor development of
bones. (Henry Ford Hospital, Detroit)

When its different parts were discovered, they were labeled B_1, B_2, and so on. Today, vitamins have names that describe the chemicals in them. But we still use the letters for easy identification. **Vitamins are organic substances essential to life but not required as energy sources.** They are catalysts. In this way they are like digestive enzymes. Look at Table 41-2 for more information on the better known vitamins.

Many years ago, when sailors went on long voyages, they had to live for months on preserved food. Many became ill with scurvy and died from bleeding of the gums and internal organs. Then it was discovered that eating citrus fruits prevented scurvy. British sailors began carrying barrels of limes on board ship. Thus the sailors earned the name "limeys." What was it in citrus fruits that prevented this disease? It was found to be vitamin C. The human body cannot make its own vitamin C. So we must get the needed vitamin C from our food. Some animals, like rats and hamsters, can synthesize ascorbic acid (vitamin C).

Your body can store some vitamins. But others must be supplied constantly because the excess is excreted in the urine. Vitamin D can be produced in the skin. Other vitamins must be obtained from the food you eat or from extracts, like vitamin pills. But the best way to get your vitamins is a balanced diet.

SYNTHETIC VITAMINS

You can get most vitamins in synthetic form. Vitamin pills can be taken in addition to the natural vitamins in your diet if you need them. Your doctor can tell you if you have a vitamin deficiency. He can prescribe concentrated vitamins if he thinks you need them. But if you eat properly, these additional vitamins are probably unnecessary for the average person.

WHAT ARE ORGANIC NUTRIENTS?

We call carbohydrates, fats, and proteins *organic nutrients*. This is because they are formed by living cells and contain the element carbon. Carbohydrates and fats supply energy. The tissue-building value of foods can only be measured by observing growth of animals when they are fed. But the energy value of foods can be measured in heat units. These are called **food Calories.** One food Calorie is the amount of heat needed to raise the temperature of 1 kilogram of water 1 centigrade degree. One food Calorie equals one *kilocalorie* (1 kcal).

If you are dieting, you may be "counting calories." In fact, however, you are counting kilocalories. For example, a piece of pie that is said to have 310 "calories" really has 310 food Calories or kilocalories. This is a lot of energy. It is about as much as the energy in 500 grams of coal or one sixth cup of gasoline.

The average person needs about 2,500 to 3,500 food Calories a day. But this will vary from person to person. It depends on your size and build, your age, and what you do.

Table 41-2 FUNCTIONS AND IMPORTANT SOURCES OF VITAMINS   537

VITAMINS	BEST SOURCES	ESSENTIAL FOR	DEFICIENCY SYMPTOMS

vitamin A (oil soluble)	fish-liver oils
	liver and kidney
	green and yellow
	    vegetables
	yellow fruit
	tomatoes
	butter
	egg yolk
		growth
		health of the eyes
		structure and functions
		    of the cells of the skin
		    and mucous membranes
			retarded growth
			night blindness
			susceptibility to infections
			changes in skin and
			    membranes
			defective tooth formation

thiamin (B_1) (water soluble)	seafood
	meat
	soybeans
	milk
	whole grain
	green vegetables
	fowl
		growth
		carbohydrate metabolism
		
		functioning of the heart,
		    nerves, and muscles
			retarded growth
			loss of appetite and
			    weight
			nerve disorders
			less resistance to fatigue
			faulty digestion
			    (beriberi)

riboflavin (B_2 or G) (water soluble)	meat
	soybeans
	milk
	green vegetables
	eggs
	fowl
	yeast
		growth
		health of the skin and
		    mouth
		carbohydrate metabolism
		functioning of the eyes
			retarded growth
			dimness of vision
			inflammation of the
			    tongue
			premature aging
			intolerance to light

niacin (water soluble)	meat
	fowl
	fish
	peanut butter
	potatoes
	whole grain
	tomatoes
	leafy vegetables
		growth
		carbohydrate metabolism
		functioning of the
		    stomach and intestines
		functioning of the
		    nervous system
			smoothness of the tongue
			skin eruptions
			digestive disturbances
			mental disorders
			    (pellagra)

vitamin B_{12} (water soluble)	green vegetables
	liver
		preventing pernicious
		    anemia
			a reduction in number of
			    red blood cells

ascorbic acid (C) (water soluble)	citrus fruit
	other fruit
	tomatoes
	leafy vegetables
		growth
		maintaining strength of
		    the blood vessels
		development of teeth
		gum health
			sore gums
			hemorrhages around the
			    bones
			tendency to bruise easily
			    (scurvy)

vitamin D (oil soluble)	fish-liver oil
	liver
	fortified milk
	eggs
	irradiated foods
		growth
		regulating calcium and
		    phosphorus metabolism
		building and maintaining
		    bones, teeth
			soft bones
			poor development of teeth
			dental decay
			    (rickets)

tocopherol (E) (oil soluble)	wheat-germ oil leafy vegetables milk butter	normal reproduction	(undetermined)
vitamin K (oil soluble)	green vegetables soybean oil tomatoes	normal clotting of the blood normal liver functions	hemorrhages

More than half of what you eat is carbohydrate food. But stored carbohydrates never make up more than one percent of your body weight. Why? Because carbohydrates are primarily fuel foods. They are oxidized very rapidly to supply the energy your body needs.

WHY ARE CARBOHYDRATES IMPORTANT?

You eat many different kinds and forms of *carbohydrate* foods. Some digest easily. They travel to the tissues with little chemical change. Others have to be broken down before your tissues can use them. Some carbohydrates are not digested at all. We need these in our diets for bulk, or roughage. All digestible carbohydrates reach body tissues as *glucose,* or *dextrose.* But carbohydrates need not be reduced to glucose to be absorbed into the intestines.

There are many simple sugars in your food. These include glucose, fructose, and galactose. As you learned in Chapter Three, these sugars are called *monosaccharides.* They are made up of single hexose molecules with the chemical formula $C_6H_{12}O_6$. These sugars are quick-energy sources. They require almost no chemical change before the blood can absorb them from the digestive organs.

Disaccharides are made up of two hexose units. Disaccharides include *sucrose* (cane sugar), *lactose* (milk sugar), and *maltose* (malt sugar). These double sugars undergo hydrolysis. As you learned in Chapter Three, this process breaks them into simple sugar molecules.

Starches, or polysaccharides, make up a large part of the carbohydrates in most diets. There is much starch in potatoes and cereal grains—wheat, corn, rye, oats, barley, and rice.

Starches are made up of large chains of glucose units. Each unit has the formula $C_6H_{10}O_5$. Digestion occurs when a water molecule (H_2O) is added to a glucose unit. In this process, starch is first reduced to maltose. This double sugar is then broken down into glucose. Glucose is absorbed by the blood and carried to the body tissues.

Much of the glucose that goes through the blood to the liver is turned temporarily into animal starch, or *glycogen.* As glucose oxidizes in the tissues, glycogen changes back to glucose (dextrose). This glucose is released into the bloodstream. In this way, you are able to maintain the level of blood sugar. If the liver did not do this, we would constantly have to eat small amounts of carbohydrates.

Celluloses are complex carbohydrates. They are found in the cell walls of vegetables. **Humans cannot digest celluloses.** But they are important to the digestive system. Because they are bulky, celluloses expand the intestines as they move through them. This roughage also stimulates muscle contractions in the intestine walls causing movement of the food. This muscular activity is necessary for normal digestion to take place.

41-3 Examples of the three organic nutrients. (H.R.W. Photos by Russell Dian)

FATS—HIGHLY CONCENTRATED ENERGY FOODS

Fats and oils give more than twice as much energy as carbohydrates. Common sources of fats or oils include butter, cream, cheese, margarine, shortening, vegetable oils, and meats.

During digestion, enzymes slowly hydrolyze fats. This happens in a series of three chemical reactions. The enzymes cause three water molecules to combine with each fat molecule. The result is one molecule of *glycerin* (glycerol) and three molecules of *fatty acids*.

Excess carbohydrates are converted into body fats. Most body fat is stored in tissue spaces under the skin, and around the kidneys and liver. Too much body fat is not good for you. For this reason, you should control how much carbohydrate and fat you eat.

PROTEINS AND THEIR USES

As you learned in Chapter Three, *proteins* are complex organic molecules. Proteins occur in many different chemical structures. They are made up of many units called *amino acids*. The proteins you eat are foreign to your body. They cannot be used by your body tissues as they are. But proteins are reduced to amino acids during digestion. The amino acids are the units your cells need to synthesize your own protein molecules. **Protein is very important in your diet for both the growth and repair of your body.**

Not all of the amino acid molecules absorbed by the blood are used in protein synthesis. Some are broken into two parts by a chemical action of the liver, called *deamination*. One part contains carbon and is sent to the tissues as glucose. The other part contains nitrogen. It is synthesized as urea, a waste product. Urea is transported by the blood to the kidneys. There it is excreted in the urine.

Some of the best sources of protein include lean meat, eggs, milk, cheese, whole wheat, beans, and corn. These are body-building foods. **Proteins are essential to the growth of children and teenagers. And proteins are needed to maintain and repair protoplasm in adults.**

THE PHASES OF DIGESTION

Why can't your body tissues use most foods in the forms in which you eat them? There are two reasons. First, many foods will not dissolve in water. This means that they could not get through cell membranes even if they reached them. Second, the foods you eat are chemically complex. Tissues cannot use them either in oxidation or in protein synthesis. Digestion solves both these problems. **In digestion, complex foods are broken down into small water soluble molecules.** These molecules can be absorbed and used by your cells.

Digestion occurs in two phases. The first is *mechanical*. You chew the food. Then the muscular movement of the wall of the digestive system churns and mixes it with various juices. All of this aids

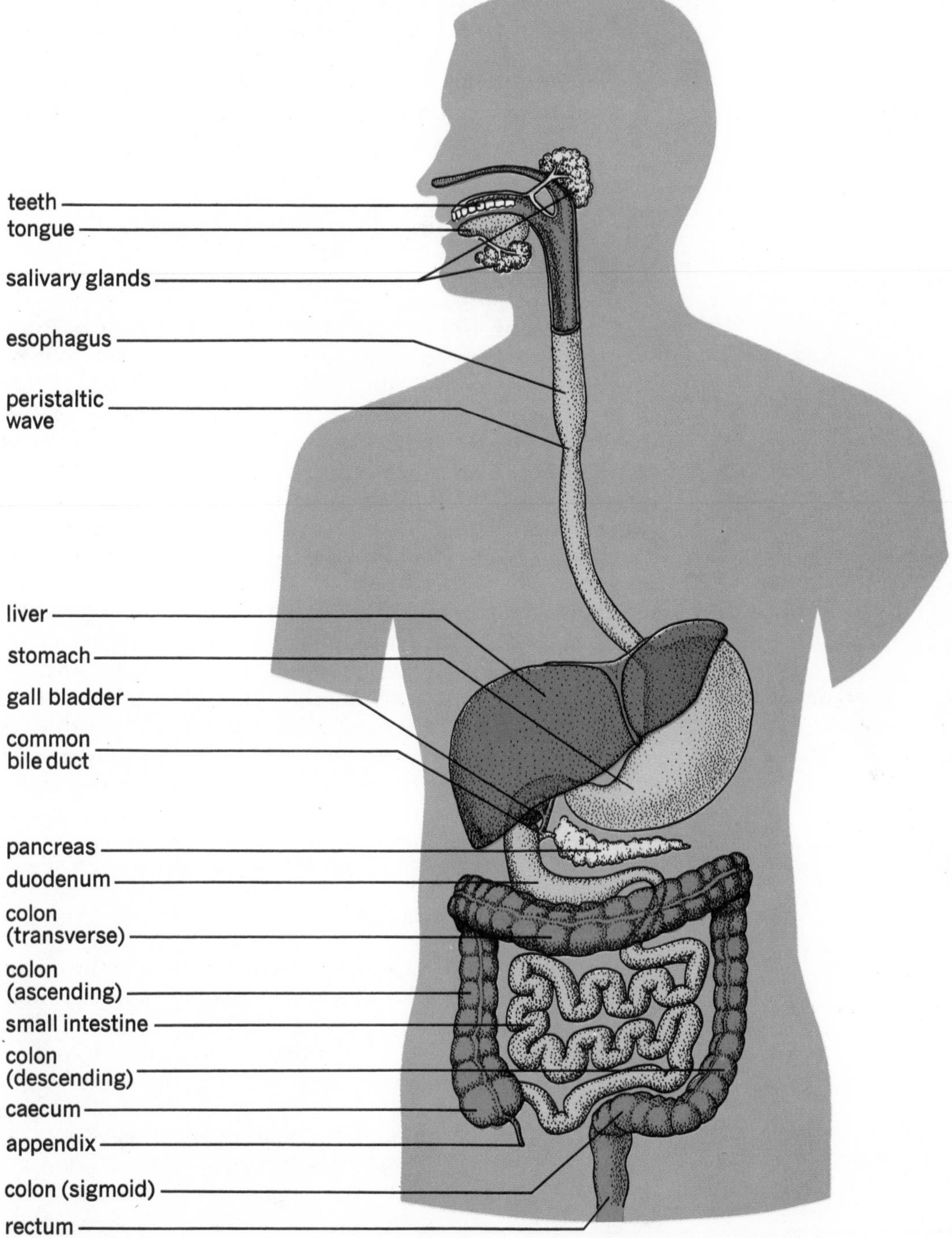

teeth
tongue
salivary glands
esophagus
peristaltic wave
liver
stomach
gall bladder
common bile duct
pancreas
duodenum
colon (transverse)
colon (ascending)
small intestine
colon (descending)
caecum
appendix
colon (sigmoid)
rectum

41–4 The organs of digestion in the human body.

the second phase of digestion, which is *chemical*. In this phase, digestive enzymes, secreted by the digestive glands, complete the job.

The digestive system includes the organs that form the **alimentary canal,** or food tube. But other organs in the digestive system do not actually receive undigested food. Instead, they deliver secretions into the alimentary canal through *ducts*. **Ducts** are tubes that go from certain glands into the organs where food is being digested.

The Digestive System

THE MOUTH—THE BEGINNING OF DIGESTION

Your mouth is an organ of sensation and speech. But its chief job is to get food ready for digestion. The roof of your mouth in the chewing area is called the **hard palate.** The hard palate is a bony structure covered with membranes. The **soft palate** is just behind the hard palate. This part of the mouth is made of folded membranes. These membranes extend from the rear of the hard palate to the top of the throat. These membranes fasten along the sides of the tongue. The knob at the end of the soft palate is called the *uvula* (YOO-vyuh-luh). The uvula can be seen in a wide open mouth.

The back of the mouth opens into a muscular cavity. This muscular cavity is called the **pharynx** (FA-ringks). The pharynx also opens into the nasal cavity. The soft palate extends into the pharynx and partly separates the mouth cavity from the nasal cavity. The inside of the cheeks are the side walls of the mouth cavity. The cheek linings are mucous membranes. They contain many mucous glands. **Mucus,** a lubricating secretion, mixes with food in the mouth. It softens the food and helps you to chew and swallow. The front of the cheek lining turns outward to form the lips.

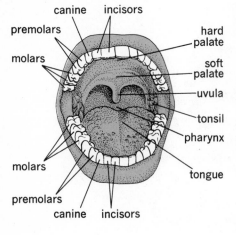

41–5 Digestion begins in the mouth.

THE SALIVARY GLANDS

In addition to the mucous glands in the cheek linings, your mouth also has pairs of **salivary glands.** The *parotid glands* are the largest of the salivary glands. There is one on each side of the face, in front of the ears. These glands secrete saliva into the mouth through ducts. These ducts are located opposite your second upper molars. The disease called mumps infects the parotid glands and causes them to swell painfully. The *submaxillary glands* are in the angles of the lower jaws. The *sublingual glands* are located in the floor of your mouth under the tongue. Ducts from these two glands open in the floor of the mouth, under the tongue. When your mouth "waters" these glands are secreting saliva. This happens when you taste and chew food. But the salivary glands may also be stimulated simply by the smell or sight of food.

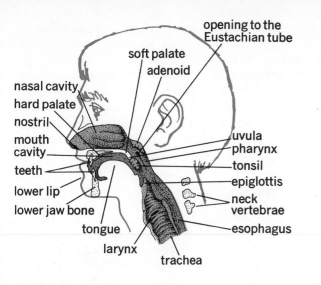

41–6 A section of the head showing structures of the mouth and throat.

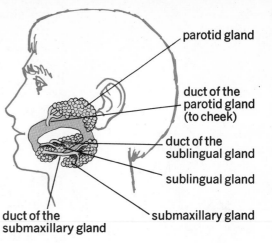

41–7 A section of the head showing the location of the three pairs of salivary glands.

THE TONGUE AND ITS FUNCTIONS

The tongue lies along the floor of the mouth. But it begins in the throat. This muscular organ has several important functions:

- It acts as an organ of taste. Notice that the surface of your tongue is covered with tiny bumps. These bumps hold **taste buds,** which have nerve endings at their bases. When you eat, the food in your mouth touches these bumps. This stimulates the nerve endings to send "taste" messages to your brain.
- It helps you chew. The movement of your tongue keeps food between your teeth.
- Your tongue helps you swallow. As you swallow, your tongue moves food toward the back of your mouth. The tongue is then jerked downward. This lodges the food in the pharynx and passes it into the esophagus opening. While this is happening, the pressure of your tongue closes off the trachea. Each time you swallow your breathing stops for a moment.
- Your tongue keeps the inner surface of your teeth clean. This happens because—though you may not be aware of it—you often roll your tongue around the inside of your mouth.
- The tongue is essential to speech. Your tongue works with your lips, teeth, and hard palate to form sounds into words. Without this interaction, sounds could not be formed into words.

Students may have overlooked the importance of the tongue in language. Have students speak in front of a mirror, and they will see how the tongue functions in speaking.

This is an appropriate place to discuss the importance of caring for one's teeth and the best way to do this. Discuss such problems as cavities, malocclusion, and extractions, and how these dental problems can be helped by trained dental professionals.

Discuss products that are used to aid digestion. Many of these products are not helpful and people can become psychologically addicted to them.

THE TYPES OF TEETH

The permanent teeth are arranged the same top and bottom. The two flat front teeth are called *incisors*. They have sharp edges for cutting food. Next to the incisors, at the corner of your lips on

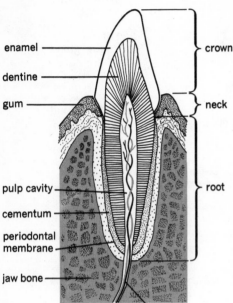

enamel

dentine

gum

crown

neck

pulp cavity

cementum

periodontal
membrane

jaw bone

root

blood vessels and nerve
fibers to pulp cavity

41-8 The structure of a canine tooth.

Constipation is a problem that many people have. However, in many cases laxatives become psychologically addictive and can result in harm to the functioning of the digestive tract.

either side, is a large cone-shaped tooth. This tooth is called the *canine*, or cuspid. Behind the canine tooth are the *premolars*, or bicuspids. There are two on either side. Next are the *molars*. You have three molars on either side if you have cut your wisdom teeth, if not, you have two. Premolars and molars have flat surfaces which are good for grinding and crushing. Many jaws are too small to hold the third molars, or wisdom teeth. In these jaws, wisdom teeth often grow in crooked or grow into the second molars. Sometimes, the wisdom teeth remain impacted.

THE STRUCTURE OF THE TEETH

A tooth has three general areas. The part above the gum is called the *crown*. A narrow part at the gum line is called the *neck*. The *root* is the part beneath the surface. The root is held in a socket in the jaw bone. A fibrous *periodontal membrane* anchors it firmly in the jaw socket. Different kinds of teeth have different shaped roots. Some are long and single. Some have two, three, or four projections. The covering of the root is called *cementum*. It holds the tooth firmly together. The crown has a hard white covering called *enamel*.

If you cut a tooth lengthwise, you can see the *dentine* beneath the enamel and cementum. Dentine is softer than these protective layers. It forms the bulk of the tooth. The *pulp cavity* lies inside the dentine area. The pulp cavity contains blood vessels and nerve fibers.

THE ESOPHAGUS AND STOMACH

As we have already noted, swallowed food passes into the **esophagus.** The esophagus is a tube about 30 centimeters long. It connects the mouth to the stomach. Layers of smooth muscle line the wall of the esophagus. They help move the food to the stomach. One layer is circular and squeezes in. The other layer runs lengthwise. It contracts in a wave that travels downward. The food is pushed ahead of the contraction.

The **stomach** is in the upper part of the abdominal cavity. It lies just below the diaphragm. The stomach walls have three layers of smooth muscle. One layer is circular. One layer runs the length of the stomach. And the third layer is arranged on an angle. The muscle fibers of these layers contract in different directions. This causes the stomach to twist, squeeze, and churn.

The stomach lining is a thick, wrinkled membrane. It contains many *gastric glands*. Each gland is a tiny tube that opens into the stomach. The gland walls are lined with secretory cells. There are three kinds of gastric glands. One kind secretes an enzyme. Another secretes hydrochloric acid. And a third secretes mucus. The mixture of these secretions is called **gastric fluid.**

Food usually stays in the stomach two to three hours. Rhythmic muscle contractions churn the food back and forth in a circular path. This churning separates food particles and mixes them thoroughly with the gastric fluid. When the stomach finishes its digesting, a valve at its intestinal end opens and closes several times. This is the **pyloric valve.** Each time the pyloric valve opens, food moves into the small intestine. When the stomach is finally empty, it rests for a while. But after several hours without food, the stomach starts contracting again. These contractions are what make you feel hungry.

Students may be interested in finding out about the different types of ulcers and the effect of gastric fluid on ulcers.

THE SMALL INTESTINE

Food moves from the stomach to the **small intestine.** This is a tube about three centimeters in diameter and seven meters long. The small intestine is a very important part of the alimentary canal. The first 25 centimeters of the small intestine are called the *duodenum* (DOO-uh-DEE-num). The duodenum curves upward, then backward to the right, beneath the liver. Beyond the duodenum is a much longer region, the *jejunum* (ji-JOO-num). The jejunum, about two meters long, is less coiled than the other parts. The lower portion of the small intestine is called the *ileum.* The ileum is about five meters long and coils through the abdominal cavity. The end of the ileum joins the large intestine.

The mucous lining of the small intestine has many tiny *intestinal glands*. These glands secrete *intestinal fluid* into the small intestine. This fluid contains enzymes used in digestion.

Cirrhosis of the liver causes destruction of liver cells and replacement of these cells with scar tissue. Cirrhosis is a serious disease associated with excessive alcoholic consumption and malnutrition. Students may want to report on aspects of cirrhosis to the class.

THE LIVER—YOUR BODY'S LARGEST GLAND

The **liver** weighs about one and one-half kilograms. It is a dark chocolate color. The liver lies in the upper right area of your abdomen. **The liver secretes bile,** a brownish-green fluid. Bile passes from the liver through a series of *bile ducts*. The bile ducts join in a Y-shape. The secreted bile travels down one branch of the Y and up the other to the **gall bladder.** Bile is stored in the gall bladder. Here bile is concentrated as part of the water in it is removed. The base of the Y is the *common bile duct.* It carries bile from the gall bladder to the duodenum. Sometimes the common bile duct becomes clogged by a gallstone or a plug of mucus. This makes the bile enter the bloodstream and causes *jaundice.* Jaundice turns the eyes and skin a yellowish color.

THE PANCREAS AND PANCREATIC FLUID

The **pancreas** looks similar to a salivary gland. The pancreas is long and white and has many lobes. It lies behind the stomach and the upper end of the small intestine against the back wall of the abdominal cavity. The pancreas performs two very different functions. It passes a digestive secretion called *pancreatic fluid* into the small intestine. Pancreatic fluid passes through the pancreatic duct. This duct leads to a common opening with the bile duct. This open-

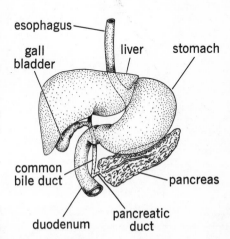

41–9 The liver and the pancreas produce substances necessary for digestion. Both of these substances empty into the small intestine through small ducts.

ing is located in the wall of the duodenum. The pancreas also produces *insulin*. This will be discussed in Chapter Forty-Six.

THE LARGE INTESTINE, OR COLON

The lower end of the small intestine connects with the large intestine, or **colon.** They join in the lower right part of the abdominal cavity. The *caecum* is located right underneath where they meet. The caecum is a blind end of the large intestine. The *vermiform appendix* is like a small finger projecting from the *caecum.* The appendix sometimes becomes painfully inflamed from infection. You have probably heard of this condition. It is called *appendicitis.* The colon is shorter and wider than the small intestine. The colon is usually about seven centimeters in diameter and one and a half meters long. It forms an upside-down U in the abdominal cavity. The right side of the colon runs upward and is called the *ascending colon.* The curved part at the top is called the *transverse colon.* The transverse colon crosses the upper region of the abdominal cavity. The left side of the colon going down is the *descending colon.* The lower end of the descending colon becomes the *sigmoid colon.* It is called the sigmoid colon because of its S shape. At the end of the large intestine is the **rectum.** The rectum is a muscular cavity. Its lower end forms the *anal opening.* A valve-like muscle in the lower end of the rectum controls the elimination of intestinal waste.

Digestion

THE CHEMICAL PHASES OF DIGESTION

Students may be interested in reviewing the digestive process by summarizing all the stages of digestion that occurred following their lunch today.

As foods move along the alimentary canal, they go through a series of chemical changes. This is a step-by-step process of simplification. At each stage, a specific enzyme is secreted. Digestive enzymes are hydrolytic enzymes. Each causes a chemical change in which water molecules interact with food molecules. Each enzyme splits specific kinds of molecules. Enzymatic action in the alimentary canal takes place *outside* the cells. This *extracellular digestion* differs from some other kinds of enzymatic action.

DIGESTION IN THE MOUTH

Chemical action on food begins in the mouth. Here a salivary enzyme begins the hydrolysis of starch. As you know, saliva is secreted by the salivary glands. Saliva is more than 95 percent water. It also contains mineral salts, lubricating mucus, and the enzyme *ptyalin* (TIE-uh-lin). This enzyme is also called *salivary amylase* (AM-i-LACE). Ptyalin changes cooked starch into the disaccharide maltose. Starchy foods, like potatoes, should be cooked before eating. This bursts their cellulose cell walls, and this allows the ptyalin to reach the starch grains. Food is only in the mouth for a short time. So starch digestion is seldom finished when food is swallowed. However, ptyalin also continues to act in the stomach.

GASTRIC FLUID AT WORK

The main enzyme in gastric fluid is *pepsin*. Pepsin is sometimes called *gastric protease*. This enzyme works on protein. It splits the complex molecules into simpler groups of amino acids. These are known as *peptones* and *proteoses*. **This splitting is the first in a series of chemical changes involved in protein digestion.**

Hydrochloric acid helps pepsin. This acid also dissolves insoluble minerals and kills many of the bacteria that enter the stomach with food. In addition, it regulates the action of the pyloric valve. You will remember that this valve opens at the end of digestion and lets the food into the small intestine.

What does the food that passes from the stomach to the small intestine contain? It contains 1) fats, unchanged; 2) sugars, unchanged; 3) maltose, formed by ptyalin acting on starch; 4) any

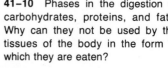

41–10 Phases in the digestion of carbohydrates, proteins, and fats. Why can they not be used by the tissues of the body in the form in which they are eaten?

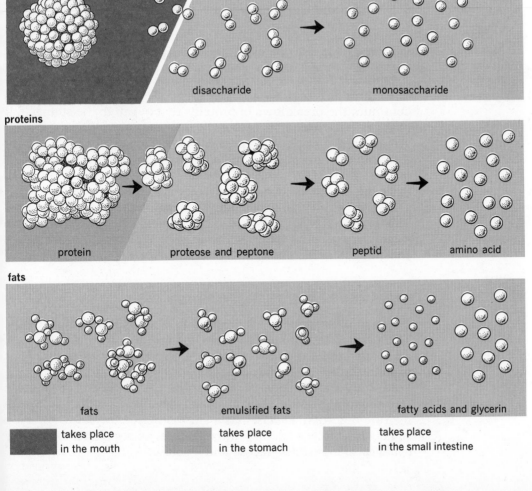

carbohydrates

disaccharide   monosaccharide

proteins

protein   proteose and peptone   peptid   amino acid

fats

fats   emulsified fats   fatty acids and glycerin

takes place in the mouth   takes place in the stomach   takes place in the small intestine starches not changed by ptyalin; 5) coagulated milk casein; 6) peptones and proteoses formed by pepsin acting on protein; and 7) any proteins not changed by pepsin.

THE LIVER AND BILE

The liver has several vital functions. It gets glucose from the blood and changes it to glycogen. Thus, it acts as a chemical factory. The liver is also a storehouse. It holds reserve carbohydrates as glycogen. And it acts on amino acids to form urea. So the liver is also an organ of excretion.

As a digestive gland, the liver secretes bile. Bile acts on the food in the small intestine. **Bile has many important characteristics.**

- In part, it is a waste substance. It contains material from dead red blood corpuscles filtered from the bloodstream by the liver.
- Bile increases the digestive action of *lipase*. This is a pancreatic enzyme that acts on fat. **Bile is not a digestive secretion. It merely breaks globules of fat into smaller droplets.** This produces a milky colloid called an *emulsion*. Pancreatic fluid can act on fats more easily in this form.
- Bile also activates lipase.

THE ROLE OF THE PANCREAS IN DIGESTION

Pancreatic fluid acts on all three kinds of organic nutrients. It contains three enzymes: *trypsin, amylase,* and *lipase* (LIP-ace). Trypsin continues the breakdown of proteins that began in the stomach. It changes peptones and proteoses into still simpler amino acid groups called *peptides*. Trypsin can also act on proteins that were not simplified during stomach digestion. Peptides are not the final product of protein digestion. An additional step is necessary to form the amino acids used in protein synthesis by the cells.

Like the ptyalin in saliva, amylase changes starch into maltose. This is how the potatoes you do not chew well get changed into sugar. Lipase splits fat into fatty acids and glycerin. Both of these substances can be absorbed by your body cells.

DIGESTION IN THE SMALL INTESTINE

The fluid secreted by the intestinal glands is highly alkaline. This neutralizes the stomach acid. It contains four main enzymes. They are erepsin, maltase, lactase, and sucrase. *Erepsin* completes protein digestion. It changes the peptides, formed by pancreatic fluid, into amino acids. *Maltase* splits the disaccharide maltose into monosaccharide glucose. This is the final product of carbohydrate digestion. *Lactase* has a similar action on *lactose,* or milk sugar. It changes lactose into glucose and galactose. *Sucrase* changes sucrose into glucose and fructose.

Table 41-3 SUMMARY OF DIGESTION

PLACE OF DIGESTION	GLANDS	SECRETION	ENZYMES	DIGESTIVE ACTIVITY
mouth	salivary	saliva	ptyalin	changes starch to maltose, lubricates
	mucous	mucus		lubricates
esophagus	mucous	mucus		lubricates
stomach	gastric	gastric fluid	pepsin	changes proteins to peptones and proteoses
		hydrochloric acid		activates pepsin; dissolves minerals; kills bacteria
	mucous	mucus		lubricates
small intestine	liver	bile		emulsifies fats; activates lipase
	pancreas	pancreatic fluid	trypsin	changes proteins, peptones, and proteoses to peptides
			amylase	changes starch to maltose
			lipase	changes fats to fatty acids and glycerin
	intestinal glands	intestinal fluid	erepsin	changes peptides to amino acids
			maltase	changes maltose to glucose
			lactase	changes lactose to glucose and galactose
			sucrase	changes sucrose to glucose and fructose
	mucous	mucus		lubricates
large intestine (colon)	mucous	mucus		lubricates

Bile, pancreatic fluid, and intestinal fluid together complete the digestion of all three classes of food. Carbohydrates, fats, and proteins become soluble substances. They leave the digestive system in the form of simple sugars, fatty acids, glycerin, and amino acids. And they enter the blood and lymph.

Absorption

ABSORPTION IN THE SMALL INTESTINE

The small intestine has many fingerlike projections in its irregular lining. These projections are called *villi*. There are so many villi that they give the intestinal wall a velvety appearance. There are *blood vessels* and branching lymph vessels inside the villi. These lymph vessels are called **lacteals.** The villi bring blood and lymph close to the digested food. Because of their form, they enor-

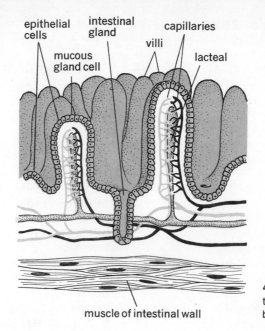

epithelial
cells

mucous
gland cell

intestinal
gland

villi

capillaries

lacteal

muscle of intestinal wall

41–11 The absorption surface of the small intestine is greatly increased by the villi.

mously increase the absorption surface of the intestine. Absorption is also increased by a constant swaying motion of the villi through the intestinal content.

Glycerin and fatty acids enter the villi and are carried away by the lymph. Eventually, they reach the general circulation and travel to the tissues. Monosaccharides and amino acids enter the blood vessels of the villi. From there, they are carried directly to the liver through the portal vein.

WATER ABSORPTION IN THE LARGE INTESTINE

The large intestine receives watery masses of undigestible food bulk from the small intestine. **As these masses move through the colon, much of the water is absorbed.** It is taken into the tissues. The remaining intestinal content is called *feces* (FEE-seez). It becomes more solid as the water is absorbed. The feces pass into the rectum. From there, they are eventually eliminated through the anal opening.

SUMMARY

Our bodies need a variety of complex organic nutrients. They also need water, minerals, and vitamins. There are three kinds of organic nutrients: carbohydrates, fats, and proteins.

The digestive system is a tube divided into various regions. This tube is called the alimentary canal. Each region is a specialized organ. Each organ is adapted for performing certain phases of the digestive process. Both our teeth and the muscles in the alimentary canal break down the food we eat mechanically. Many glands pour enzymes into the digestive tract. These enzymes break down food chemically. These mechanical and chemical changes must take place before food can be absorbed into our body cells.

BIOLOGICALLY SPEAKING

food
plasma
deficiency disease
vitamin
organic nutrients
food Calorie
digestion
alimentary canal
hard palate
soft palate
pharynx
mucus
salivary glands
taste buds
esophagus
stomach
gastric fluid
pyloric valve
small intestine
liver
bile
gall bladder
pancreas
pancreatic fluid
colon
villi
lacteals
feces

QUESTIONS FOR REVIEW

1. What are the functions of foods?
2. Why must the body have water?
3. In what two general ways must food be changed during digestion?
4. List, in order, the divisions of the alimentary canal. What digestive processes occur in each?
5. How is the tongue used?
6. Name the parts of a tooth.
7. Why is it especially important that you chew bread and potatoes thoroughly?
8. Suppose that you had a glass of milk and a sandwich made of bread, butter, and ham. Tell what would happen to each of these foods as it was digested.
9. Name two important functions of the large intestine.

APPLYING PRINCIPLES AND CONCEPTS

1. Explain how a vitamin deficiency is possible even if an adequate amount of all the vitamins is taken daily.
2. Why is food acid in the stomach and alkaline in the small intestine?
3. Explain how interference with the rhythmic waves of the walls of the large intestine may cause either constipation or diarrhea.
4. Why is it easier to digest sour milk than fresh milk?

chapter forty-two

Transport and Excretion

OBJECTIVES
- DEFINE blood.
- LIST the plasma components and the solid components of blood.
- DESCRIBE the function of each part of the blood.
- EXPLAIN how the blood clots.
- DISCUSS how Rh factor may affect childbirth.
- TRACE the circulation of blood through the parts of the heart.
- NAME and DESCRIBE the types of blood vessels.
- DEFINE lymph.
- IDENTIFY the parts and function of the kidney.

Students may be interested in learning more about hemophilia. An interesting book on this subject is *Journey* by Robert and Suzanne Massie, New York, Knopf, 1975.

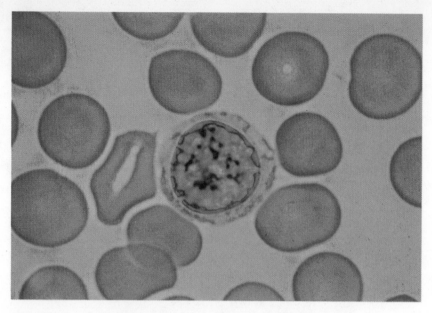

42–1   Blood cells. (1000X magnification) (Manfred Kage, Peter Arnold)

THE TRANSPORT SYSTEM

Nutritive fluids, waste materials, and water flow through living organisms. Their movement through the organism is called **circulation.** And the system can be called the *circulatory system*, or *transport system*.

Many lower organisms transport fluids in very simple ways. Sponges, for example, literally pump the ocean into their bodies! Seawater supplies each cell with the oxygen it needs. The seawater also washes away wastes. Actually, the solution that bathes human cells has a salt content very much like seawater. This solution is called *tissue fluid*.

But humans have a more complex circulatory system than that of invertebrates. We produce our own "seawater." We also add other vital substances to it. This fluid is piped through our bodies and circulated with a pump. The pump is, of course, the human heart. If your heart stops working, you are in the same trouble as a sponge that gets thrown up on the beach.

Blood

A FLUID TISSUE

The fluid that carries all of your body substances is called *blood.* The average person has about six liters of blood. This makes up about 9 percent of your body weight. Blood is a rather peculiar type of connective tissue. **Blood is made up of two different parts.** There is a nonliving fluid part, called *plasma*. And there are *solid* *components*, or blood cells. The blood cells are scattered through the plasma.

Plasma is a sticky, straw-colored liquid. Plasma is 90 percent water. Proteins in the plasma are what make it sticky. One of the plasma proteins is *fibrinogen* (fy-BRIN-uh-jin). Fibrinogen is necessary in blood clotting. *Serum albumin* is another plasma protein. It is necessary to the normal blood tissue relationships during absorption. The third is *serum globulin*. This protein gives rise to the antibodies that make you immune to various diseases. Plasma also contains an enzyme called *prothrombin*. Prothrombin is produced in the liver in the presence of vitamin K. It is usually inactive. But it functions during clotting.

The proteins in blood are important for another reason. They give your blood thickness, or *viscosity*. This helps to keep up the proper pressure in the blood vessels.

Three other materials are also in plasma:

■ *Inorganic minerals*, dissolved in water. These compounds give plasma a salt content of about 1 percent. The salt content of seawater is about 3 percent. These compounds include carbonates, chlorides, and phosphates of the elements calcium, sodium, magnesium, and potassium. They are necessary to your blood and for normal functioning of your body tissues. Without calcium compounds, for example, your blood would not clot in a wound.

■ *Digested foods* in the form of glucose, fatty acids, glycerin, and amino acids. These are transported to body tissues. They are also carried to the liver and other storage places.

■ *Nitrogenous* (ny-TROJ-uh-nus) *wastes*, from protein metabolism in the tissues. One of these wastes, *urea*, is produced largely in the liver during the breakdown of amino acids. These nitrogenous wastes travel in the plasma to the organs of excretion.

THE SOLID COMPONENTS OF BLOOD

There are three solid components of blood. They are *red corpuscles* (red blood cells, or erythrocytes), *white corpuscles* (white blood cells, or leucocytes), and *platelets* (thrombocytes). The **red corpuscles** are shaped like disks. Both sides of these disks are concave, or curved inward. Sometimes they travel in the blood in rows that look like stacks of coins. But they may also separate and float alone. Red cells are very small. Ten million of them can be spread out in about 6 square centimeters. And you have many of them in your body. A normal person has about twenty-five trillion red blood cells. If you laid the cells side by side, that is enough to go around the earth four times at the equator. **The red pigment in red corpuscles is called hemoglobin.** Hemoglobin is a protein substance essential to life.

Red corpuscles, or erythrocytes, are produced in red marrow. Red marrow is found at the ends of such bones as the ribs, vertebrae, and skull. In children, even the ends of long bones can make these

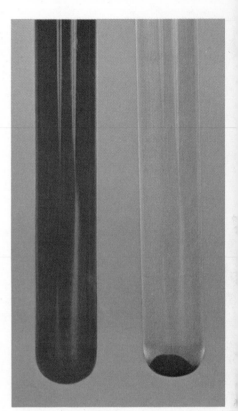

42–2 Fresh blood in a test tube and blood in a test tube after settling and centrifugation. (Percy W. Brooks)

A study of various types of blood banks, hospital and Red Cross programs would be interesting here. Have students report on methods of getting blood donations and how individuals can ensure their family's blood needs through donations.

cells. Developing erythrocytes are large, colorless, and have big nuclei. Usually, they have lost the nuclei by the time they enter the bloodstream. They have also built up hemoglobin by this time. **Red corpuscles live from 20 to 120 days.** When they die, they are removed by the liver or the spleen. At this time, these organs release certain valuable compounds into the bloodstream. These compounds are used to help manufacture new red blood cells.

WHAT DO THE ERYTHROCYTES DO?

The pigment hemoglobin is a complex protein containing iron. It lies within the membrane of a red blood cell. **Hemoglobin can carry oxygen because it contains the chemical element iron.** You have probably seen iron turn red with rust. Rust is produced when iron is oxidized. This means that the iron has combined with oxygen in the air. The iron in hemoglobin combines with oxygen in your lungs. Rusty iron does not give up its oxygen easily. But the iron of hemoglobin does. In fact, hemoglobin releases oxygen at just the right time and place in the body. The erythrocytes are bright red when their pigment is combined with oxygen. The oxygen is given up in the tissues. Then part of the carbon dioxide formed in the tissues combines with hemoglobin. In this way, much of the carbon dioxide is carried to your lungs where it is released. The cycle is then repeated.

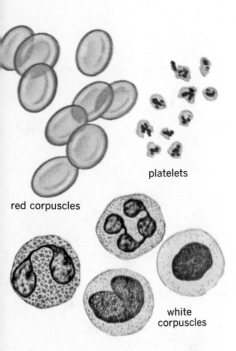

platelets

red corpuscles

white corpuscles

42–3 The solid components of blood include red corpuscles, white corpuscles, and platelets.

THE WHITE BLOOD CELLS

Most **white corpuscles** are larger than red corpuscles. And they differ from them in three ways:
- White corpuscles have nuclei.
- White corpuscles have no hemoglobin. They are nearly colorless.
- Some white corpuscles are capable of ameboid movement.

There are fewer white blood cells than there are red blood cells. The ratio is about one white cell to every six hundred red cells. White corpuscles are formed in red bone marrow and in the lymph glands. Normally, you have about eight thousand white corpuscles in a cubic millimeter of blood. There are about four and a half to five *million* red corpuscles in the same amount of blood.

Some white blood cells move about on their own. They can ooze through capillary walls into the tissue spaces. Here, they engulf solid materials, including bacteria. **Thus, white blood cells are important in defending your body against infection.** Whenever you develop an infection, your white-cell count goes way up. It may rise from 8,000 to more than 25,000 per cubic millimeter. These corpuscles collect in the infected area. Then they ingest and destroy bacteria. You have seen the pus that sometimes forms on infections. The remains of dead bacteria, white corpuscles, and tissue fluid is known as *pus*.

THE PLATELETS

Platelets are much smaller than red corpuscles. Platelets are irregularly shaped and colorless. They are probably formed in the red bone marrow. Platelets are not able to move on their own. They float along in the bloodstream. **Platelets are important for forming blood clots.**

Table 42-1 SUMMARY OF COMPOSITION OF BLOOD

PLASMA	SOLID COMPONENTS
water	red corpuscles
proteins	white corpuscles
fibrinogen	platelets
serum albumin,	
globulin	
digested foods	
mineral salts	
organic nutrients	
cell wastes	

Much has been written recently about blood transfusions that are not screened carefully resulting in hepatitis to the recipient of the transfusion. Estimates have indicated that transfused blood is the cause of more than 30,000 cases of hepatitis each year.

HOW BLOOD CLOTS

When you cut small blood vessels in a minor wound, blood oozes out. Most of us are not alarmed by such cuts. We know a clot will form and the blood flow will stop. But what would happen if the flow did not stop? What is it that forms a blood clot?

Clotting results from chemical and physical changes in the blood. When a blood vessel is cut, platelets disintegrate in the blood leaving the vessel. Platelets are probably destroyed by tissue fluids at the wound site. In the process, they release *thromboplastin*. This reacts with *prothrombin* in the presence of *calcium* to form

Ask students to trace a drop of blood through the chambers of the heart and through the major attached blood vessels.

Table 42-2 BLOOD AS A TRANSPORTING MEDIUM

TRANSPORTA-TION OF	FROM	TO	FOR THE PURPOSE OF
digested food	digestive organs and liver	tissues	growth and repair of cells, supplying energy, and regulating life processes
cell wastes	active tissues	lungs, kidneys, and skin	excretion
water	digestive organs	kidneys, skin, and lungs	excretion and equalization of body fluids
oxygen	lungs	tissues	oxidation
heat	tissues	skin	equalization of the body temperature
secretions	ductless glands	various organs, glands	regulation of body activities

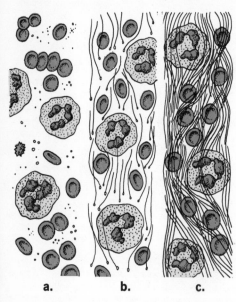

42–4 The microscopic changes that occur during the clotting of blood: a. before clotting begins, b. formation of threads of fibrin, c. shortening of the fibrin threads and trapping of blood cells.

42–5 Blood can be typed by using test serum from type A and type B bloods. (Fundamental Photos, Community Blood Council)

thrombin. Thrombin changes *fibrinogen,* a blood protein, to *fibrin.* Fibrin is made of tiny threads. These threads form a network that traps blood cells. When this happens, a clot is formed that stops any more blood from escaping. These trapped corpuscles dry out. This forms a scab. Then the edges of the wound grow toward the center until it is healed. Clotting can be summarized as:

1. thromboplastin + calcium + prothrombin → thrombin
2. thrombin + fibrinogen → fibrin

If any of these substances is missing, blood will not clot.

Sometimes blood vessels are broken under the skin. When this happens, clotting results. The discolored area is known as a *bruise.* The clotted blood is gradually absorbed as the bruise heals. As this happens, the color of the bruise changes, and finally disappears.

BLOOD TRANSFUSIONS

Certain conditions in the body require a blood transfusion. These include hemorrhage, wound shock, severe burns, and a variety of illnesses. If whole blood is used, patients get both plasma and blood cells. But the donor's blood type must match the patient's. So the blood of each must be typed. Blood type can be A, B, AB, and O. To type blood, you add a drop of a test serum to a drop of the donor's blood. If the red blood cells *agglutinate,* or clump together, the bloods are incompatible. If the red blood cells stay in suspension, then the donor's blood can be used. Can you see why using the wrong type might be dangerous? Giving the wrong blood type can result in clotting and the death of the patient. This might be a good time for you to review the inheritance of blood types in Chapter Eleven.

Often patients need only a fast increase in the *amount* of liquid in the bloodstream. They do not really need red blood cells. The red corpuscles form quickly if blood volume is high enough. This

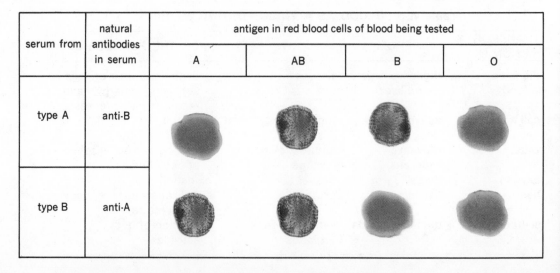

serum from	natural antibodies in serum	antigen in red blood cells of blood being tested			
		A	AB	B	O
type A	anti-B				
type B	anti-A				

condition is called *shock*. If you are in shock, plasma may be transfused instead of whole blood. Because there are no cells, typing is not necessary when only plasma is used.

THE RH FACTOR IN BLOOD

The A, B, AB, and O blood types are one factor in blood. The **Rh factor** is another factor. Rh is named for the *rhesus* (REE-sus) *monkey*. This factor was discovered from tests done on these monkeys. About 85 percent of the people in the United States have the Rh factor in their blood. Their blood is called *Rh positive*. The other 15 percent without the factor are *Rh negative*. Like blood types, the Rh factor is inherited. It is actually any one of six proteins called **antigens.**

If Rh-negative patients receive Rh-positive blood, they produce antibodies against this factor. These antibodies cause the corpuscles of the Rh-positive blood to agglutinate and dissolve. There is little danger during the first transfusion. This is because the antibody is not present when the Rh-positive blood is added.

However, a second transfusion can be serious, even fatal. Why? Because the patient has already formed antibodies against the Rh-positive blood.

THE RH FACTOR AND CHILDBIRTH

The Rh factor may cause a problem in childbearing. This problem occurs to about one in three or four hundred mothers. It may happen when the mother is Rh negative and the father is Rh positive. The child may inherit the Rh-positive factor from the father. Dur-

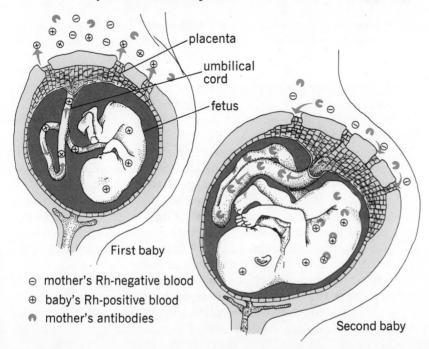

placenta

umbilical cord

fetus

First baby

⊖ mother's Rh-negative blood
⊕ baby's Rh-positive blood
⋒ mother's antibodies

Second baby

42–6 If an Rh-negative mother produces Rh-positive antibodies as a result of an earlier Rh-positive fetus, a problem may arise in a future Rh-positive fetus.

ing pre-birth development, Rh-positive blood may seep from the child into the mother's circulation. It can go through tiny ruptures in the membranes that normally keep the two circulations apart. The mother's blood can also seep into the child in the same way. The seepage usually occurs from a few days before birth to a few days after birth.

This seepage does not happen very often. So, many Rh-negative mothers bear normal Rh-positive children. Usually the situation only becomes serious if seepage occurs again with a second Rh-positive child. In that case, the mother has already produced antibodies from her first pregnancy. When the mother's blood seeps into the second child's circulation, these antibodies cause serious damage. Sometimes the child dies before birth. But sometimes the damage is not so serious. A transfusion immediately after birth may save the child's life. The child's blood may be almost entirely replaced by transfused Rh-negative blood. This blood does not contain the antibody.

A method is now used to avoid the Rh problem in future pregnancies. The Rh-negative mother is given an injection around the time of the child's birth. This injection contains Rh antibodies. These antibodies circulate in the mother's blood for several weeks. They destroy all the Rh-positive factor from the baby. Thus, the mother's system does not develop its own antibodies against Rh factor. This is a form of passive immunity. The mother should not have Rh problems with future babies.

The Circulatory System

THE HEART

The heart is a cone-shaped, muscular organ. It is located under your breastbone and between your lungs. The heart is enclosed in a sac called the *pericardium* (PER-RI-KAHR-dee-um). The heart is usually a little left of the midline of your chest cavity. The tip of the heart points downward and to the left between the fifth and sixth ribs. Your heartbeat is strongest near this tip. So many people have the mistaken idea that their hearts are entirely on the left side.

Your heart is made up of two sides, right and left. These two halves are separated by a wall called the *septum.* Each half has two chambers. There is a thin-walled chamber called the **atrium.** And there is a thick, muscular **ventricle.** The two atria are reservoirs for the blood that enters the heart. They contract at the same time. This contraction forces blood into the two ventricles rapidly. Next, the muscular walls of the ventricles contract. This forces the blood out through the great arteries.

The heart has two sets of one-way valves. They control the flow of blood from the ventricles under pressure. They also maintain pressure in the arteries between heart beats. The valves between the atria and ventricles are called the *atrioventricular valves,*

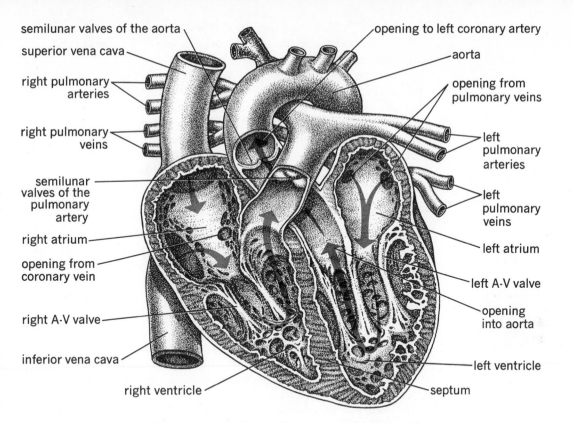

semilunar valves of the aorta

superior vena cava

right pulmonary arteries

right pulmonary veins

semilunar valves of the pulmonary artery

right atrium

opening from coronary vein

right A-V valve

inferior vena cava

right ventricle

opening to left coronary artery

aorta

opening from pulmonary veins

left pulmonary arteries

left pulmonary veins

left atrium

left A-V valve

opening into aorta

left ventricle

septum

or *a-v valves*. These valves are like flaps. They are anchored to the floor of the ventricles by tendonlike strands. Blood passes freely through a-v valves into the ventricles. But the a-v valves cannot be opened from the lower side because the tendons anchor them. The result is that blood cannot flow backward into the atria when the ventricles contract. The other set of valves are called *semilunar valves*, or s-l valves. These cuplike valves are located at the openings of the arteries. The force of blood passing from the ventricles into the arteries opens the s-l valves. The semilunar valves then prevent blood from backing up into the ventricles.

CIRCULATION THROUGH THE HEART

One of the best ways to study the parts of the heart is to trace the path of blood through it. The blood first enters the right atrium of the heart from two different directions. Blood enters through the *superior vena cava* (vay-nuh KAH-vuh) and the *inferior vena cava*. The superior vena cava carries blood from the head and upper parts of the body. The inferior vena cava returns blood from the lower parts. From the right atrium, blood goes through the right a-v valve into the right ventricle. Then the right ventricle contracts. This forces blood through a set of s-l valves into the *pulmonary artery*. This artery carries the blood to the lungs. The blood passes through the lung and into the right and left *pulmonary veins*. These vessels return blood to the heart and open into the

42–7 The human heart. Note the location of the valves to the heart chambers and blood vessels. The arrows indicate the direction of blood flow.

Students will be interested in hearing the beat of their own hearts. They should compare heartbeat rates at rest and during exercise. Ask them to think of other ways in which to use the stethoscope in learning about heart function.

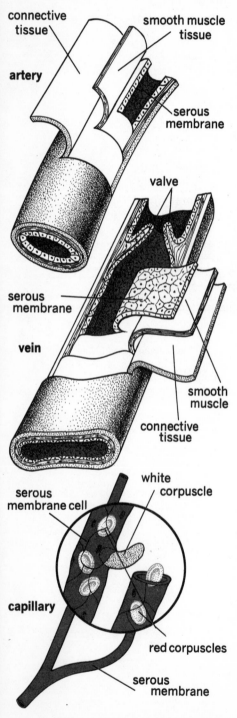

connective tissue

smooth muscle tissue

artery

serous membrane

valve

serous membrane

vein

smooth muscle

connective tissue

serous membrane cell

white corpuscle

capillary

red corpuscles

serous membrane

42–8 Three types of blood vessels.

left atrium. From there, the blood passes through the left a-v valve into the left ventricle. Finally, blood passes out the **aorta** (ay-OAR-tuh) and goes to all parts of the body.

Of course, the heart is filled with blood. But its muscle layers are too thick to be nourished by this blood. Instead, the heart muscle cells are nourished by special arteries called *coronary arteries.* The aorta is largest just as it leaves the heart. This is called the *aortic sinus.* The right and left coronary arteries branch off from here. They curve downward around each side of the heart. Each sends off smaller vessels that penetrate the heart muscle.

THE HEART, A HIGHLY EFFECTIVE PUMP

A complete cycle of heart activity is called a beat. A beat has two phases. In the first phase, or **systole,** the ventricles contract and force blood into the arteries. In the second phase, or **diastole,** the ventricles relax and receive blood from the atria.

Have you ever listened to your heart in a stethoscope? A normal heart sounds like the syllables "lub" and "dup" repeated over and over. They are in perfect rhythm. The "lub" is the systole phase. It is the sound of the contraction of the ventricle muscles and the closing of the a-v valve. The "dup" is the diastole. This is the sound of the closing of the semilunar valves at the base of the arteries.

The heart of an average adult beats about 70 times per minute. This is when the person is resting. During hard work or exercise, the heart rate may be as high as 180 beats per minute.

THE BLOOD VESSELS

Blood moves in a system of tubes or vessels of different sizes. *Arteries* and *arterioles* carry blood away from the heart. *Veins* and *venules* carry blood toward the heart. *Capillaries* are very small thin-walled vessels.

The aorta branches into several large arteries. These arteries further branch and become arterioles. The arterioles branch into capillaries. The tiny capillaries pass through tissues and organs. Then the capillaries come together to form venules. The venules join to become veins. The veins take blood toward either the inferior or superior vena cava. These large veins lead into the right atrium of the heart.

Arteries have muscular walls with smooth linings. These walls are elastic. This allows arteries to expand and absorb great pressure. This great pressure is created by the contracting ventricles at systole. The *pulse* you feel in your wrist, for example, is caused by *systolic pressure* in an artery. The pulse has the same rhythm as your heartbeat. The elastic walls also maintain the pressure in the arteries when the ventricles relax. This is called *diastolic pressure.* The pressure in the aorta leading from the left ventricle is greater than that in the pulmonary artery pumped by the smaller right ventricle. If the aorta were cut, blood would would spurt out in a stream of two meters or more.

WHAT ARE CAPILLARIES?

Arterioles penetrate the tissues. In the tissues, the arterioles branch into capillaries. The walls of capillaries are thinner than the walls of other vessels. **Capillary walls are only one-cell thick.** Also, capillaries are only a little larger in diameter than red corpuscles. So these red corpuscles must pass through the capillaries in single file. Sometimes the red corpuscles are even pressed out of shape by the capillary walls.

Veins and arteries are important for carrying blood through our bodies. **But all the vital relationships between blood and tissues occur in the capillaries.** Dissolved foods, waste products, and gases pass freely through their thin walls and in and out of the tissue spaces. White corpuscles go through tiny openings in the walls. This is how white corpuscles leave the bloodstream and enter the tissue spaces. Also, some of the plasma diffuses from the blood through the capillary walls. This filtered plasma becomes tissue fluid.

Many students have probably heard about varicose veins but may not understand what they are. Ask students to report on this subject and what can be done to relieve this problem.

VEIN STRUCTURE AND FUNCTION

As we have said, arterioles branch into capillaries upon entering organ tissues. As capillaries leave an organ, they unite to form veins. Most veins carry dark red blood. This blood has given up some of its oxygen to the tissues. You can see some veins through your skin. But the veins appear to be blue. A yellow pigment in the skin makes the dark red blood in them look bluish.

The walls of veins are much thinner and less muscular than those of arteries. So the *internal* diameter of a vein is greater. Many of the larger veins have cuplike valves. These valves keep blood from flowing backwards.

CIRCULATION IN THE BODY

Our four-chambered heart is really a double pump. Its two sides work in unison. Each side pumps blood through a major division of our circulatory system. The right side pumps blood through the *pulmonary circulation*. This is the circulation of blood through the lungs. The left side pumps to the *systemic circulation*. This is the circulation of blood through the body tissues. Systemic circulation includes several shorter circulations. Each supplies or drains a special organ of the body.

The right side of your heart receives deoxygenated blood from the body. It pumps this dark red blood through the arteries of the *pulmonary circulation*. The great pulmonary artery extends from the right ventricle. It then branches into the two smaller arteries. One goes to each lung. Within the lungs, each branches into a great

Swollen and painful lymph glands should not be overlooked. It is important that these glands be checked to rule out any serious condition.

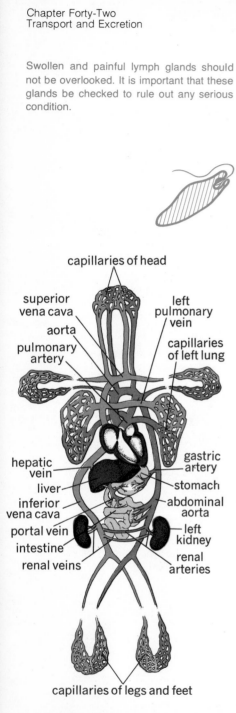

capillaries of head

superior vena cava

left pulmonary vein

aorta

pulmonary artery

capillaries of left lung

hepatic vein

gastric artery

liver

stomach

inferior vena cava

abdominal aorta

portal vein

left kidney

intestine

renal arteries

renal veins

capillaries of legs and feet

42-9 A diagrammatic representation of the various circulations in the human body. Trace the pulmonary, systemic, coronary, renal, and portal circulations.

number of arterioles and then into capillaries. In the lungs, the blood gives up carbon dioxide and water and also receives oxygen. The oxygenated blood is bright scarlet in color. It leaves the lungs and enters the pulmonary veins. The pulmonary veins carry blood to the left atrium.

Oxygenated blood passes through the left chambers of the heart and out the aorta. The blood now moves under great pressure. It is now in the **systemic circulation.** As we have said, this circulation supplies blood to the body tissues. The systemic circulation is much longer and more complicated than the pulmonary circulation. It includes all of the arteries that branch from the aorta. It also includes the capillaries that extend through your body tissues, and the many veins that lead to the venae cavae. Finally, it includes the three special circulations—coronary, renal, and portal.

The **coronary circulation** supplies blood to the heart itself. We mentioned this circulation when we talked about the heart muscle. The coronary circulation begins at the aorta. And it ends where the coronary veins empty into the right atrium. Every heartbeat depends on the free flow of blood through these vessels. A blood clot in the coronary artery may stop the flow of blood to part of the heart muscle. This damages the heart muscle. This is called a "heart attack."

The **renal circulation** starts with two renal arteries branching from the aorta. One artery goes to each kidney. Within the kidneys the arteries branch into capillaries. These capillaries extend through the kidney tissues. The *renal veins* return blood from the kidneys to the inferior vena cava. Blood in the renal circulation nourishes the kidneys. It also gets rid of water, salts, and nitrogenous cell wastes. In fact, blood in the renal veins is the purest blood in your body.

The **portal circulation** is an extensive system of veins. These veins lead from the digestive organs—stomach, pancreas, small intestines, and colon and the spleen. The large veins of the portal circulation unite to form the *portal vein.* The portal vein enters the liver. Blood coming from these digestive organs transports digested food and water. This enters the liver which acts upon the digested food. Blood carrying food to body tissues flows from the liver in the hepatic veins. The hepatic vein empties into the inferior vena cava. This ends this vital branch of the systemic circulation.

THE LYMPH

The tissue fluid that bathes your cells also collects in tubes. Here, the fluid is called lymph (limf). Tiny lymph vessels come together and form larger ones. This is similar to the way capillaries join to form venules. *Lymph nodes* are enlargements in the lymph vessels. They appear along the vessels like beads on a string. In the lymph nodes, the lymph tubes branch into many fine vessels. Certain white corpuscles collect here and destroy bacteria in the lymph. **Thus, these nodes, or lymph glands, purify lymph before returning it to the blood.** Your neck, armpits, inner elbow, and groin have the largest number of lymph nodes. If you have an infection in your hand or arm, the lymph nodes in your armpit often swell. This can be very painful. The *tonsils* and *adenoids* in your throat are masses of lymphatic tissue. They often become infected and swollen in childhood. The surgical removal of the tonsils is called a *tonsillectomy*.

The lymph in your right arm and the right side of your head and neck enters a large vessel. This large vessel is the *right lymphatic duct*. This vessel opens into the *right subclavian vein*. The lymph is thus returned to the blood. The lymph in the rest of your body drains into the *thoracic duct*. The thoracic duct empties into the *left subclavian vein*.

The larger lymph vessels have valves in their walls. These valves control the flow of lymph. They are similar to the valves found in veins. In inactive tissues, lymph flows very slowly or stops completely. When activity increases, the fluid flows faster.

The Excretory System

REMOVAL OF METABOLIC WASTES

When the body oxidizes foods involved in metabolism, it produces waste products as well. **You get rid of these metabolic wastes in a process called *excretion*.** Some waste products come from protein metabolism. The carbon and nitrogen parts in amino acids separate before the carbon is oxidized. The nitrogen part is given off as waste. Other wastes come from protein synthesis during growth processes. These nonprotein nitrogenous wastes include *urea* and *uric acid*.

A buildup of wastes in the tissues is dangerous. It causes rapid tissue poisoning, starvation, and finally suffocation. This is especially true of nonprotein nitrogen wastes. **Tissues filled with wastes cannot absorb food or oxygen.** If these tissues are not emptied, the person suffers fever, convulsions, coma, and death.

One-celled organisms empty their wastes directly into a water environment. Animals like the sponge and jellyfish also do this. But the process is not as simple for organisms made of millions of cells. In these organisms, each cell discharges its waste materials into the tissue fluid. This fluid flows to the bloodstream. Then the blood carries cells wastes to excretory organs. These organs, such as the kidneys and skin, eliminate the wastes.

KIDNEYS—THE MAIN EXCRETORY ORGANS

The **kidneys** are bean-shaped organs. They are about the size of your clenched fist. The kidneys lie on either side of the spine, in the small of your back. Deep layers of fat cover and protect each kidney. If you cut a kidney lengthwise, you can see several different regions. The firm outer part is called the *cortex*. The cortex

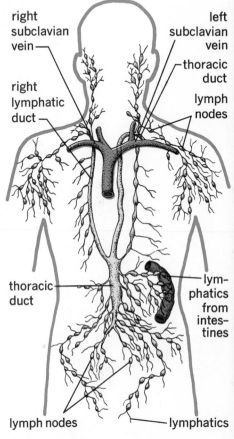

right subclavian vein

left subclavian vein

thoracic duct

right lymphatic duct

lymph nodes

thoracic duct

lymphatics from intestines

lymph nodes

lymphatics

42-10 The lymphatic system returns tissue fluid to the bloodstream.

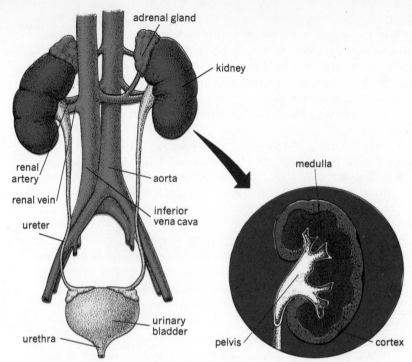

adrenal gland

kidney

renal artery

renal vein

aorta

inferior vena cava

ureter

medulla

urethra

urinary bladder

pelvis

cortex

42-11 The kidney is an efficient filtering organ.

Renal dialysis is a subject that is as controversial as it is life-saving. Discuss kidney transplants and renal dialysis as methods of aiding individuals with defective kidney function.

makes up about one third of the kidney tissue. The inner two thirds is called the *medulla*. The medulla is filled with cone-shaped projections called *pyramids*. The pyramids point into a saclike cavity. This cavity is the *pelvis* of the kidney. The pelvis leads into a long, narrow tube, the **ureter.** Two ureters, one from each kidney, empty into the **urinary bladder.**

Each kidney has about 1,250,000 tiny filters. These filters are called **nephrons. Nephrons control the chemical makeup of blood.** Each nephron has a small cup-shaped structure called a *Bowman's capsule.* A tiny, winding *tubule* comes from each capsule. This tubule becomes very narrow as it straightens and goes toward the renal pelvis. The tubule widens again and forms a loop, called *Henle's loop.* Then the tubule goes back into the cortex. In the cortex, the tubule becomes very crooked again. Then it enters a larger *collecting tubule.* The collecting tubule is a straight tube that receives the tubules of many nephrons. It carries fluid to the renal pelvis. If all these tubules were put end to end, they would reach more than 280 kilometers.

HOW DOES THE NEPHRON WORK?

Blood enters each kidney through a large *renal artery*. The renal arteries branch directly from the aorta. In the kidneys, each artery branches and rebranches. This fills all areas of the cortex with tiny arterioles.

Each arteriole ends in a coiled knob of capillaries. This knob is called the *glomerulus* (glom-ERR-yuh-lus). Each glomerulus fills the cuplike part of a Bowman's capsule. **There are two stages to** removing waste from the blood: 1) filtration and 2) reabsorption. Filtration takes place in the glomeruli. The pressure of the blood is very high here. Remember, the heart pumps blood through the aorta directly into the renal arteries. Water, nitrogenous wastes, glucose, and mineral salts are forced by this pressure through the capillary walls of the glomerulus. These filtered materials move into the surrounding Bowman's capsule. This process is called *filtration*. This solution is like blood plasma without blood proteins. But too much of the blood content is filtered out of the blood. This is corrected in the second stage of the process.

After the fluid leaves the capsule through the tubules, it passes through a network of capillaries. This network reabsorbs many of the substances into the blood by active transport. Much water is reabsorbed by osmosis. Some recent studies indicate that for every 100 milliliters of fluid that pass from the blood into the capsules, 99 milliliters are reabsorbed. What is left passes through the tubules of the pelvis of the kidney as *urine*. **Urine is made up of nitrogenous wastes, excess water, and excess mineral salts.**

The urine passes from the pelvis of the kidney to the ureters. The ureters carry the urine to the urinary bladder. The now cleansed blood leaves the kidneys through the renal veins. The blood returns to the general circulation by way of the inferior vena cava. As we said earlier, this blood is the purest in the body.

The urinary bladder is muscular. At intervals, these muscles contract. This pushes the urine out of the body through the **urethra** (yooh-REETH-ruh). Your kidneys have tremendous reserve power. If one is removed, the other will grow bigger and take over the job of both.

ANOTHER ROLE OF THE KIDNEYS

Kidneys do more than eliminate urea and wastes of protein metabolism from the body. They also excrete other substances. Sometimes your body builds up excess sugars, acids or bases, and water. The kidneys eliminate the excess of these from the blood. Kidneys also maintain just the right amount of salts in the body fluid. **If the kidneys are working properly, they keep the environment of your cells constant.** Do you remember studying the effect of changes in osmotic concentration in cells? If so, you know the importance of this constant environment, or *homeostasis*.

THE SKIN—ANOTHER EXCRETORY ORGAN

The skin also excretes some water, salts, and some urea. This excretion is in the form of *perspiration*. However, this fluid has a more important role than excretion. **Perspiration helps regulate your body temperature.**

The skin is made of two general layers. They are the epidermis, and the dermis. The *epidermis* is the outer portion of your skin. It is made up of many epithelial cells. The outer cells form the *horny*

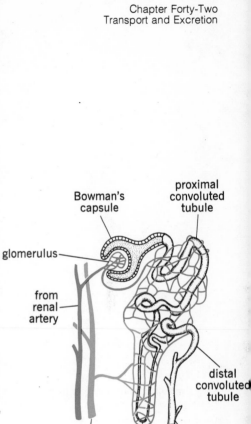

42–12 The structure of a nephron. Note the close relationship of the tubules and blood vessels by which materials are reabsorbed into the blood.

Students will probably have many questions concerning skin and hair care. Discuss many of these questions and ask students to do additional research on these topics.

layer. These outer cells are flattened, dead, and scalelike. The inner cells form the *germinative layer.* These cells are larger and more active. The epidermis protects the more active tissues beneath. Epidermal cells are rubbed off constantly. But active cells in the lower layers replace epidermal cells as fast as they are lost. Friction and pressure on the epidermis stimulate cell division. This may produce a thickening of more than a hundred cells. This thickening of the epidermis is called a *callus.*

The **dermis** lies under the epidermis. It is a thick, active layer, made up of tough, fibrous connective tissue. This tissue is filled with blood and lymph vessels, nerves, sweat glands, and oil glands.

Beneath the skin is a fatty layer of *subcutaneous tissue.*

FUNCTIONS OF THE SKIN

Here are some of the major functions of the skin:
- It protects your body from mechanical injury and invasion by bacteria.
- It keeps the inner tissues from drying out. Aided by oil glands, it is nearly waterproof. Little water passes through it, except out through the pores.
- It holds the *receptors* that respond to touch pressure, pain, and temperature.
- It excretes some wastes in the form of perspiration.
- It controls the loss of body heat. This happens when perspiration evaporates on the surface of your skin.

42-13 The structure of a highly magnified, thin section of skin.

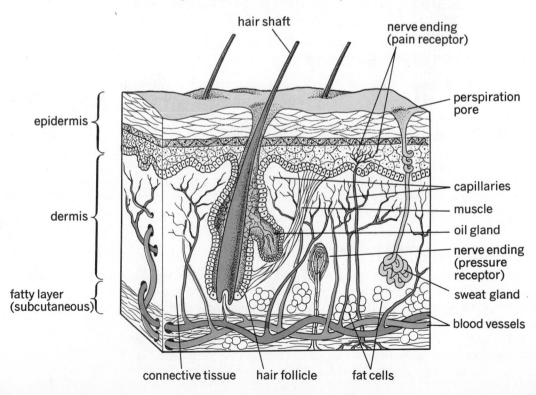

hair shaft

nerve ending (pain receptor)

perspiration pore

epidermis

dermis

fatty layer (subcutaneous)

capillaries

muscle

oil gland

nerve ending (pressure receptor)

sweat gland

blood vessels

connective tissue   hair follicle   fat cells

Earlier we mentioned that heat is used during the change of liquid water to water vapor. Thus, as sweat evaporates from the body surface, heat is withdrawn from the outer tissues. **The skin is literally an automatic radiator.** It is richly supplied with blood containing body heat. As the body temperature rises, the skin becomes more flushed with blood. Heat is thus conducted to the surface. At the same time, secretion of sweat increases and bathes the skin. This increases the rate of evaporation and the amount of heat loss.

OTHER ORGANS OF EXCRETION

During expiration, your *lungs* excrete carbon dioxide and water vapor. You will remember that the *liver* also has an excretory function. It forms urea. The bile stored in your *gall bladder* also contains waste.

The large intestine removes undigested food from your body. Of course, this is not really cell excretion. The food waste collected here was never absorbed into tissue cells.

The skin has an additional function that many of us overlook. It tells of one's emotions at a particular time. Discuss flushing and blushing and what they indicate. Ask students to think about other things that the skin may indicate: moods, age, and general health.

SUMMARY

Your circulatory system transports blood through your body. Blood is a fluid tissue. It is made up of liquid plasma and solid components. Plasma contains water, blood proteins, prothrombin, inorganic substances, digested foods, and cell wastes. Blood has three solid parts: red corpuscles, white corpuscles, and platelets. Red corpuscles transport oxygen to the body cells. They also transport carbon dioxide away from the cells as a waste product. White corpuscles help fight disease bacteria. Platelets are important in the process of blood clotting.

The heart is a pump that sends blood to all parts of your circulatory system. It has two atria and two ventricles. The atria receive blood from the veins. The ventricles force blood through the arteries by contracting. Arteries carry blood from the heart to the body tissues. Veins return it to the heart. The arterial and venous systems are connected by networks of tiny capillaries. The real interaction of blood and tissue cells takes place in these capillaries.

Part of the blood plasma seeps into tissue spaces. From there, it is collected in special tubes as lymph. The fluid is filtered by the lymph nodes and returned to the bloodstream.

Various wastes result from protein metabolism and digestion. They are removed from the body through the kidneys, skin, lungs, liver, and large intestine. The kidneys are the body's most important excretory organs. They filter practically all the nitrogenous wastes from your blood. The skin also excretes wastes. It gets rid of water, salts, and some urea in perspiration. In addition, perspiration helps control your body temperature. Of course, the skin also serves as a protective covering for your body.

QUESTIONS FOR REVIEW

1. What is blood?
2. Where are the various blood cells made in the body?
3. What conditions might cause the white-blood cell count to go up?
4. What are the steps in the clotting of blood?
5. Why is plasma more quickly and easily used in a transfusion than whole blood?
6. Trace the path of a drop of blood from the right atrium to the aorta.
7. Why can you feel the pulse in an artery and not a vein?
8. What is tissue fluid? How does it get back to the bloodstream?
9. How does lymph differ from blood?
10. How do the kidneys regulate blood content?
11. What are the differences between the glomerular fluid and urine?

APPLYING PRINCIPLES AND CONCEPTS

1. What is the reason for the saying that "we are as young as our arteries"?
2. Alcohol dilates the arteries in the skin. What would be its effect, then, on the temperature control of the body?
3. In an Rh-negative patient, why might a second transfusion with Rh-positive blood be fatal, even though the first transfusion with Rh-positive blood caused no complications?
4. How is conservation of resources by the body shown in the manufacture of red blood cells?
5. Why is increased salt intake recommended in hot weather?
6. How do the kidneys aid in maintaining water balance of the body?

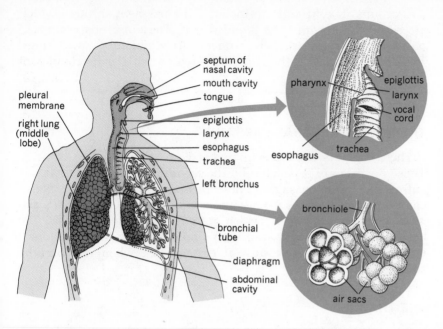

Labels for the main diagram:
septum of nasal cavity
mouth cavity
tongue
pleural membrane
epiglottis
right lung (middle lobe)
larynx
esophagus
trachea
left bronchus
bronchial tube
diaphragm
abdominal cavity

Labels for upper inset:
pharynx
epiglottis
larynx
vocal cord
esophagus
trachea

Labels for lower inset:
bronchiole
air sacs

43–1 The organs concerned with breathing and external respiration in a human.

Respiration and Energy Exchange

OBJECTIVES
- COMPARE respiration and breathing.
- DESCRIBE the functions of the parts of the respiratory system.
- EXPLAIN gas exchange in the lungs.
- DEFINE oxygen debt.
- DEFINE basal metabolism.
- EXPLAIN the external influences on breathing and respiration.
- DESCRIBE carbon monoxide poisoning.

Stress to students the importance of both external and internal respiration. If respiratory function is normal, individuals tend to be unaware of it. However, what happens when one has a respiratory ailment that results in difficulty in breathing?

RESPIRATION IS COMMON TO ALL LIVING THINGS

All living cells need a constant supply of energy. Some anaerobic cells can live without oxygen. But most would die without it. We discussed cellular respiration in Chapter Six. **We can define *respiration* as the intake of oxygen and the elimination of carbon dioxide, resulting from energy release in living cells.** In simple organisms, like protists and sponges, the cells are in direct contact with the environment. So the gas exchange between the cells and the environment occurs directly. But as organisms become more complex, all of their cells are no longer in contact with the external environment.

The environment of the cells in your body is much more stable than that of a protozoan in a pond. The fluid which bathes the cells provides a constant supply of oxygen and nutrients. In turn, these tissue fluids remove the cellular wastes.

THE TWO PHASES OF RESPIRATION

External respiration is the exchange of gases between the atmosphere and the blood. This process occurs in the lungs. **Internal respiration** is the exchange of gases between the blood or tissue fluid and the cells themselves. **Breathing** is the mechanical process that gets air (containing oxygen) into the lungs and air (containing carbon dioxide) out of the lungs.

The organs involved in external respiration can be divided into two groups. The first group includes the passages through which air travels to get into the bloodstream. These are nostrils, nasal passages, pharynx, trachea, bronchi, bronchial tubes, and lungs. The second includes those organs involved in the mechanics of breathing. This group includes the ribs, rib muscles, diaphragm, and abdominal muscles.

THE NOSE AND NASAL PASSAGES

The air enters the nose in two streams through two nostrils. These nostrils are separated by the *septum.* From the nostrils, air enters the nasal passages. These passages lie above the mouth cavity. **Before air enters the nasal passages, however, nostril hairs and moist mucous membranes screen out dirt and foreign particles. The length of nasal passages also warms and moistens the air before it enters the trachea.** These advantages are lost when you breathe through your mouth.

THE TRACHEA

From the nasal passages, air goes through the **pharynx** and down the windpipe, or **trachea.** The upper end of the trachea is protected by a flap of cartilage. This flap is called the **epiglottis.** When you swallow, the epiglottis closes over the trachea. This prevents food from getting into the lungs. The upper end of the trachea holds the voice box, or **larynx.** This forms a lump on the outside of the neck called the Adam's apple. **Vocal cords** are located inside the larynx. We use our vocal cords to make sounds.

Rings of cartilage surround the walls of the trachea. They support the trachea to keep it open for the passage of air.

The trachea and its branches are lined with tiny hairs called cilia. The cilia are constantly moving. They carry the dirt and foreign particles that we inhale upward toward the mouth. This dirt is removed when you cough, sneeze, or clear your throat.

As we all know, pollution has an effect on our respiratory systems. The lungs of a person from the country look different from those of a person who lives in an industrial area. White blood cells are able to destroy some of the particles breathed into the lungs. But other particles become embedded in the lung tissue. Some particles are coughed up. **Air pollution in the form of smoke is one of the great problems of our industrial society.**

THE BRONCHI AND AIR SACS

The trachea divides at its lower end. It forms two branches called **bronchi.** One bronchus extends to each lung. Each bronchus divides and forms many small **bronchial tubes.** These divide again into even smaller **bronchioles.** The bronchioles end in **air sacs.** And each air sac is made up of clusters of tiny sacs called **alveoli.** Lung tissue

Some people have had to have their larynxes removed because of cancer. Many of these people have learned to speak by a special method of "burping" air. Some students may want to find out more about this technique.

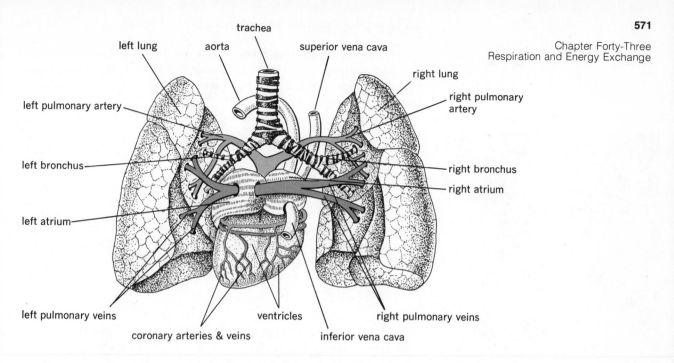

left lung   aorta   trachea   superior vena cava

left pulmonary artery

right lung

right pulmonary
artery

left bronchus

right bronchus

right atrium

left atrium

left pulmonary veins

ventricles

right pulmonary veins

coronary arteries & veins

inferior vena cava

is made up mostly of alveoli. The walls of the alveoli are very thin and elastic. Gases are exchanged through these thin walls and the air sacs. Capillaries carry the blood which unloads carbon dioxide and picks up oxygen. **All the tiny alveoli provide the great amount of surface area needed for this exchange of gases.** Thus, the lungs supply air by way of the blood for the needs of millions of body cells that are not in direct contact with air.

The lungs fill the body cavity from under the shoulders down to the diaphragm—except for the space occupied by the heart, trachea, esophagus, and blood vessels. This cavity is called the *thoracic cavity.* Lungs are composed primarily of the bronchioles, the alveoli, and many blood vessels and capillaries. These are all held together by connective tissue. This structure makes the lungs spongy. Surrounding the lungs is a double cover called the **pleural membrane.** One part sticks to the surface of the lungs. The other part covers the inside of the thoracic cavity. These membranes secrete mucus. The mucus lubricates the lungs. This lets them move freely in the chest during breathing.

THE MECHANICS OF BREATHING

When you inhale, your chest usually bulges. Many people think that this is because your lungs draw in air and expand. Actually, this is the opposite of what happens. The lungs have no muscle. They cannot expand or contract on their own. They are spongy, air-filled sacs in the chest cavity. **The power for breathing comes from rib, diaphragm, and abdominal muscles.** These muscles control the size and air pressure in the chest cavity.

43–2 This posterior view of the lungs and heart shows the branches of the pulmonary arteries and the pulmonary veins.

If possible, obtain spareribs that show the attachment of muscles and animal lungs. These can often be obtained from butchers.

THE MOVEMENTS OF BREATHING

The intake of air, or *inspiration*, occurs when the chest cavity expands. When this happens, air pressure inside the sealed cavity decreases. Air rushes into the lungs to equalize this pressure. The following movements are involved in expanding the chest cavity:

1. The rib muscles contract, pulling the ribs up and out.
2. The muscles of the dome-shaped diaphragm contract. This straightens and lowers the diaphragm. This action enlarges the chest cavity from below.
3. The abdominal muscles relax. This allows compression of the abdominal muscles when the diaphragm lowers.

Expiration, or forcing air from the lungs, occurs when the chest cavity is reduced in size. This increases the air pressure inside the cavity. In order to equalize internal and external air pressure, air is forced out of the lungs. The following movements are involved in reducing chest cavity size:

1. The rib muscles relax. This allows the ribs to spring back.
2. The diaphragm relaxes, rising to its original position.
3. The abdominal muscles contract. This pushes the abdominal organs up against the diaphragm.
4. The elastic lung tissues were stretched when the lungs were full. These shrink and force air out of the lungs.

THE CONTROL OF BREATHING

Both nerves and chemicals control your breathing and the rate of breathing. Nerves from the lungs, diaphragm, and rib muscles lead to a respiratory control center. This center is located at the base of the brain. It controls the regular rhythm of breathing. The amount of carbon dioxide in the blood is detected directly by the breathing control center. If the carbon dioxide concentration is high, the brain signals the diaphragm and rib muscles. They increase the breathing rate. This increased rate forces more carbon dioxide out through the lungs. This lowers the carbon dioxide concentration in the blood. Breathing settles back to a normal rate. In humans, inspiration and expiration occur from 16 to 24 times a minute. The exact rate depends on physical activity, position, mood, and age.

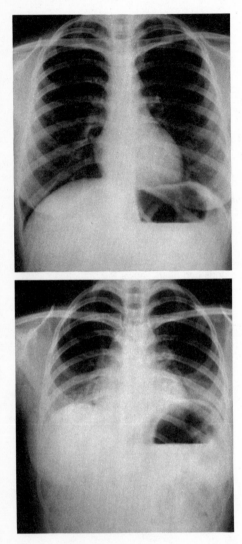

43–3 These X rays show the chest during exaggerated breathing: inhalation (top); exhalation (bottom).

THE AIR CAPACITY OF THE LUNGS

Only about 500 milliliters of air are involved each time we inhale and exhale. The air involved in normal, relaxed breathing is called *tidal air*. Forced breathing increases the amount of air movement.

You can demonstrate the effects of forced breathing. Inhale normally without forcing. Your lungs now contain about 2,800 milliliters of air. Now exhale normally. You have moved 500 milliliters of tidal air from the lungs. Now, without inhaling again, force out

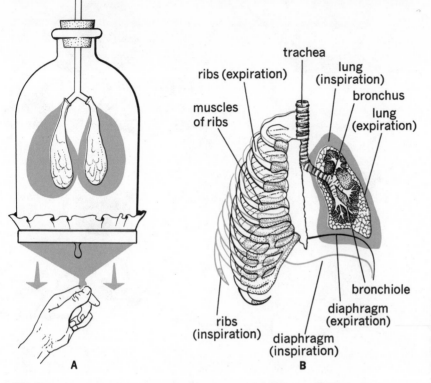

ribs (expiration)

muscles
of ribs

trachea

lung
(inspiration)

bronchus

lung
(expiration)

bronchiole

diaphragm
(expiration)

ribs
(inspiration)

diaphragm
(inspiration)

A

B

43-4 Breathing—a mechanical process. When the rubber sheet (left) is pulled downward, the pressure is decreased. Air enters through the Y-tube and inflates the balloons. Note the similarity between the model and the representation of the thorax.

all the air you can. You have now exhaled an additional 1,100 milliliters of *supplemental air*. The lungs now contain about 1,200 milliliters of *residual air,* which you cannot force out.

When you inhale normally again, you replace the supplemental and the tidal air. If you inhale with force, you can add about 3,000 milliliters of *complemental air*.

The maximum amount of air that you can move through your lungs is called the *vital capacity*. This is the total amount of air that moves through your lungs when you inhale and exhale as hard as you can. The vital capacity of the normal person is about 4,500 milliliters. A well-trained athlete may have a vital capacity of 6,500 milliliters.

ARTIFICIAL RESPIRATION—A POTENTIAL LIFE SAVER

Soon after a person stops breathing, the blood oxygen level drops below that needed for normal cell activity. If it is not raised quickly, cells cannot function. And they start to die. *Artificial respiration* is simply a way of *forcing* air into and out of the lungs. The mouth-to-mouth method of artificial respiration is the method recommended by the Red Cross.

AIR—OUR NORMAL SOURCE OF OXYGEN

The major gases that make up air are nitrogen, oxygen, and carbon dioxide. These gases have properties that are vital for life. These

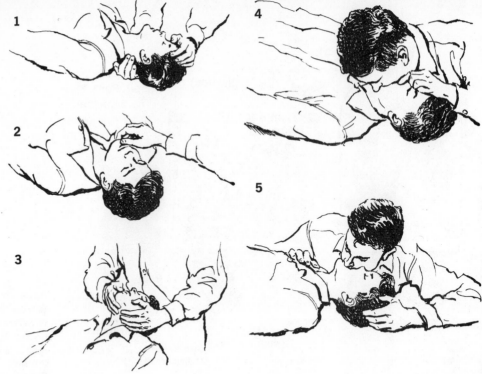

43-5 Mouth-to-mouth respiration. First, tilt the head back so the chin is pointing upward (1). Pull the jaw into a jutting-out position (2 and 3). Second, open your mouth wide and place it tightly over the victim's mouth. At the same time, pinch the victim's nostril's shut (4 and 5). Third, remove your mouth, turn your head to the side, and listen for the return rush of air that indicates air exchange. Fourth, if you are not getting air exchange, recheck the head and jaw position. If you still do not get air exchange, turn the victim on his side and administer several sharp blows between the shoulder blades to dislodge any foreign matter. (redrawn from American Red Cross diagram).

gases can diffuse through membranes. For instance, if there are different concentrations of oxygen on either side of a membrane, oxygen molecules will pass through the membrane until the oxygen concentration is the same on both sides. This property of gases is important to all forms of life.

Gases can also dissolve in liquids. This is why oxygen and carbon dioxide can be transported by the blood. The solubility of oxygen, carbon dioxide, and nitrogen varies. Temperature changes will also affect the amount of a gas that can be dissolved in a liquid. Warm water will hold less dissolved gas than will cold water. Perhaps you have seen tiny bubbles in a glass of water left on the sink. At a certain temperature, the water contained all the dissolved gases it could hold. As it warms up, gases come out of solution as bubbles.

TABLE 43-1   COMPOSITION OF NORMAL ATMOSPHERE

	Percentage of volume
Nitrogen	78.03
Oxygen	20.99
Argon	0.94
Carbon dioxide	0.03
Hydrogen, neon, helium	0.01

GAS EXCHANGE IN THE LUNGS

The *pulmonary artery* carries deoxygenated, dark red blood to the lungs. There it branches into an extensive network of small capillaries. These capillaries completely surround each alveolus. The air in the alveolus and the blood in the capillaries contain gases in different concentrations. Therefore, diffusion occurs through the thin, moist membranes of both the alveolus and the capillaries. **Oxygen diffuses from the air into the blood. And carbon dioxide diffuses from the blood into the air.**

THE TRANSPORT OF OXYGEN

Oxygen is not very soluble in the plasma of blood. It is even less soluble at our body temperature of 37° C. Oxygen would be more soluble at lower temperatures. But the erythrocytes contain a substance called hemoglobin. Hemoglobin has a chemical attraction for oxygen. This is why blood can carry such a high concentration of oxygen. At sea level, blood leaving the lungs is about 97 percent saturated with oxygen.

When the blood reaches tissues with low concentrations of oxygen, the hemoglobin releases its oxygen. The oxygen diffuses into the tissue fluid. And from there it reaches the cells. **The attraction of hemoglobin for oxygen decreases with increasing acidity.** This is an important characteristic. During exercise, lactic acid is produced by the active muscle cells. This increases the acidity of the blood. And this causes the hemoglobin to release more of its oxygen than it would normally.

THE TRANSPORT OF CARBON DIOXIDE

Carbon dioxide is much more soluble than oxygen. It passes through membranes quickly and goes into the bloodstream. In the blood, only about 10 percent of the carbon dioxide is dissolved in the plasma. Hemoglobin joins with about 20 percent. How is the remaining 70 percent of the carbon dioxide carried to the lungs? It passes into the red blood cells, and an important enzyme joins it to water to form *carbonic acid*. This weak acid stays inside the erythrocyte for a while. When the blood reaches the lungs, the opposite occurs, and carbon dioxide diffuses out of the erythrocyte. Then, it passes through the membranes of the capillaries and into the alveoli. From here, it leaves your body in the expired air.

OXYGEN DEBT

During times of great muscular activity, the cells need more oxygen than the body can supply. The lungs cannot take in oxygen fast enough. Nor can the blood deliver it fast enough. When this happens, the cells switch to anaerobic respiration. This means that oxygen is not used. Instead, pyruvic acid becomes the hydrogen

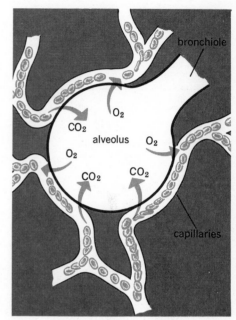

43–6 The relationship between alveoli and capillaries. A cluster of alveoli make up each air sac at the end of a bronchiole.

Ask students to discuss any time they have experienced oxygen debt. How did they overcome it?

A demonstration of a BMR test would be interesting to the students. If possible, try to arrange for students to see a test being done either in the classroom or a laboratory.

acceptor in the process of energy exchange. For a short period, the cells have enough energy to function and survive. But the anaerobic process produces *lactic acid*. This collects in the tissues, causing a feeling of fatigue. A buildup of lactic acid signals the brain's respiratory center to increase the breathing rate. Thus, breathing and heart rates speed up. This supplies the tissues with more oxygen.

If the heavy exercise continues, lactic acid keeps building up. This is called a state of *oxygen debt*. It continues until the heavy exercise ends. Then, during a half-hour rest, some of the lactic acid is oxidized. Some is converted to glycogen. Carbon dioxide and excess water are excreted. The oxygen debt is paid. The body is ready for more exercise.

THE BODY'S METABOLISM

The sum of all the processes occurring in a cell or an organism is called *metabolism*. **Metabolism has two distinct phases. These are the constructive phase and the destructive phase.** The constructive phase involves carbohydrate and protein synthesis. The destructive phase involves oxidation and energy release. The metabolic rate increases with an increase in the body's activity. Such activity may be either muscular, such as walking or running. It may also be mental. Temperature and digestive activity also affect the rate of metabolism.

Even when the body seems completely inactive, as in sleep, metabolism continues. But, in sleep, because there is less muscular and nervous activity, the metabolic rate is decreased. **The energy required to maintain basic life processes is called *basal metabolism*.** The rate at which such energy is used is called the *basal metabolic rate*, or BMR. The BMR may be calculated by measuring the amount of oxygen used up over a definite period of time. Another way is to measure the amount of heat given off from the body surface.

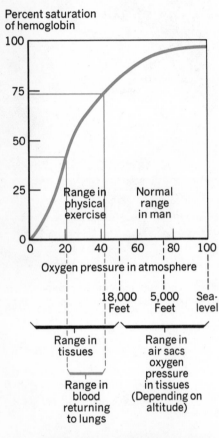

Percent saturation of hemoglobin

43–7 When hemoglobin reaches equilibrium with the atmospheric oxygen in the air sacs, it is about 97 percent saturated. When blood reaches the tissues where the amount of oxygen is low, diffusion occurs and the hemoglobin gives up its oxygen.

ENVIRONMENTAL AFFECTS ON BREATHING AND RESPIRATION

The air's temperature, moisture, oxygen, and carbon dioxide content all influence the rate of breathing and respiration. Certain of these factors involve *ventilation*. If the air in a room is stuffy, it is likely to be too warm and moist. Very rarely is it caused by build up of carbon dioxide and lack of oxygen. A ventilating system can correct these problems by moving the air. Air conditioners circulate air and remove moisture. In many houses, the air becomes too dry during the winter. This drys out mucous membranes, lowering their resistance to infection. This is why the moisture content of air should be kept as high as possible.

Temperature, humidity, and poor ventilation are all factors in respiratory difficulties. Air that is too dry is harmful to one's health. Some heating systems require additional humidifiers to add enough moisture to the air.

CARBON-MONOXIDE POISONING

Far too often, we read of people who have died in a closed garage where an automobile engine was running. The cause of death is given as *carbon-monoxide poisoning*. Actually, the death is not caused by poisoning but by *tissue suffocation*. Carbon monoxide will not support life. Yet it combines with the hemoglobin of the blood 250 times more readily than oxygen does. As a result, the blood becomes loaded with carbon monoxide. Its oxygen-combining power decreases. The tissues suffer from oxygen starvation. The victim becomes light-headed. Soon paralysis sets in. Death follows from tissue suffocation.

In areas where smog and pollution are high, people tend to have more respiratory problems. One of the gases that is harmful to the respiratory system is carbon monoxide—a common component of polluted air.

RESPIRATION AND PROBLEMS AT HIGH ALTITUDES

We live at the bottom of a large ocean of air. As we move higher in it, perhaps climbing up the Matterhorn, the air pressure becomes less. Most of us have experienced our ears "popping" during an altitude change. This means that there is not as much air pressure. Our middle ear must equalize the air pressure.

You have read about the importance of pressure in determining how the oxygen combines with the hemoglobin in the blood. This is why mountain climbers and airplane pilots have more difficulty in breathing the higher they get. At altitudes near 3,500 meters, many people get tired easily.

When an airplane approaches an altitude of 6,000 meters, the pressure becomes so low that the pilot has difficulty in seeing and hearing. This condition, called *hypoxia*, is the result of oxygen starvation of the tissues. It causes death if not corrected within a short time. Hypoxia can be avoided by wearing an oxygen mask.

Passengers in modern airliners can fly at high altitudes in the safety and comfort of pressurized cabins.

Discuss with students why athletic teams used to playing at sea level altitude are at a disadvantage when playing at higher altitudes. In what way can they adjust to the change in altitude?

RESPIRATION—A VITAL PROBLEM IN SPACE TRAVEL

At 25 kilometers above the earth, air density is only 4 percent of that at sea level. At 110 kilometers high, there is practically no atmosphere at all. Thus, astronauts must wear pressure suits. These suits support the astronauts' life systems. In studying the problems of respiration at high altitudes, scientists observed a tribe of Peruvian Indians. These Indians could carry on normal activities at altitudes at which most people would simply become exhausted. Scientists found that the Indians had greater than average lung capacity. In addition, these Indians had an extra-high red blood cell count. They had adapted to the high altitude. Then, the scientists learned that similar adaptations can take place in anybody who spends time at high altitudes. These men can exist in an atmosphere that has half the oxygen content than exists at sea level. They can carry out normal tasks in such an environment.

Discuss the necessity of pressurized suits and oxygen in the explorations of space and the moon missions.

SUMMARY

Respiration involves the exchange of gases between cells and their environment. The exchange of gases between the lungs and the blood is called external respiration. The exchange between the blood or tissue fluid and the cells is called internal respiration. Breathing is a mechanical process that moves air in and out of the lungs. It consists of inspiration and expiration.

During oxidation, foods break down, and energy is released. In lower animal forms, individual cells are in direct contact with the environment. But in higher animals, blood is the transporting medium. Atmospheric pressure and the concentration of gases in the air both play important roles in the diffusion of gases through membranes. Another vital property of gases is the ability to dissolve in water.

Metabolism involves respiration, oxidation, and the growth processes. The rate at which it occurs during rest is called the basal metabolic rate.

BIOLOGICALLY SPEAKING

respiration
external respiration
internal respiration
breathing
pharynx
trachea
epiglottis

larynx
vocal cords
bronchi
bronchial tubes
bronchioles
air sacs

alveoli
pleural membrane
inspiration
expiration
artificial respiration
basal metabolism

QUESTIONS FOR REVIEW

1. What are the differences between respiration and breathing?
2. Describe the mechanism that controls breathing rate.
3. What properties of gases aid the body in respiration?
4. Describe gas exchange in the lungs. Name the structures involved and explain why the exchange occurs.
5. How do pressure changes within the chest cavity cause inspiration and expiration?
6. Why is hemoglobin vital to the respiratory processes of the cells in our bodies?
7. How is oxygen carried from the lungs to the tissues?
8. How is carbon dioxide carried in the blood from the tissues to the lungs?
9. What is the purpose of artificial respiration?
10. How do you build up an oxygen debt? How is it repaid?
11. Explain carbon-monoxide poisoning.
12. Compare respiration problems encountered on a high mountain to those in space travel.

APPLYING PRINCIPLES AND CONCEPTS

1. If plants produce oxygen in photosynthesis, how do you explain the fact that they also respire?
2. What changes do you think would occur in the blood if you were to hold your breath for a period of time? if you were to breathe rapidly and deeply for a period of time?
3. People who live in dry climates, such as the southwestern parts of our country, report that high temperatures there are easier to tolerate than the same temperatures in more humid areas. Why?

4. Explain the decompression procedure used when divers come up from great depths.
5. What differences would you find in the blood of a person living at high altitudes compared to a person living at sea-level?
6. Why is the fact that carbon dioxide is so soluble in water of vital importance to unicellular organisms and multicellular organisms alike?

chapter forty-four

Body Controls

OBJECTIVES

- LIST the parts of the nervous system.
- DESCRIBE the structure of the nerve cell.
- EXPLAIN nerve impulses.
- NAME the parts of the brain.
- DESCRIBE the functions of each part of the brain.
- IDENTIFY the parts of the spinal cord.
- COMPARE the two parts of the autonomic nervous system.
- DESCRIBE each of the body senses.
- DEMONSTRATE a knowledge of the anatomy of the eye and the ear.

The cerebellum and cerebrum give us the control that is needed in most sports activities.

44–1 What is the difference in the acts of these two primates? (H.R.W. Photo by Russell Dian; Courtesy of Ringling Brothers, Barnum & Bailey Combined Circus)

ACTIONS AND THEIR COMPLEXITY

The two photos above illustrate coordination and complex behavior patterns in action. The chimps and the people are both riding motorcycles. But there are differences. The chimps are conditioned to sit quietly on their machine. Once the trainer starts it, the chimps balance, riding in circle after circle. They will do this until the trainer stops the motor. People on motorcycles, on the other hand, do many things besides ride in circles. They decide when to stop and start the machine. They decide where and when to turn. They try to stay out of the way of other drivers. At the end of the ride, they can tell their friends or family about their adventures. In other words, the human makes many more complex decisions than the chimpanzee. Can you imagine the results if a chimp were placed on a motorcycle and sent down a city street?

As we've discussed, the ability to perform certain functions can be determined by structure. A bear can walk erect for a while. But its bone and muscle structure makes it impossible for the bear to do this for long. Similarly, bears have vocal cords. But the structure does not make it possible to form words. Even if the vocal cords had the right structure, the bear's brain structure would prohibit complex speech. Thus, the structure of the brain may also determine the way in which an organism reacts to its environment.

The Nervous System

THE HUMAN NERVOUS SYSTEM

The nervous system is divided into three parts. The brain and the spinal cord make up the *central nervous system.* (CNS). From the central nervous system, nerves go to all parts of the body through the *peripheral nervous system* (PNS). The third part of the nervous system regulates certain vital functions. This part is called the *autonomic nervous system.* Nerve cells are called **neurons.** Each neuron acts as a link in the nervous system because of its structure. The neuron has a star-shaped cell body. This contains cytoplasm and a nucleus. Threadlike projections, called *nerve fibers*, extend from the cell body. Messages, called *impulses*, travel along the nerve fibers. In some lower animals, impulses can travel in either direction. But in human nerve fibers, impulses travel in one direction. **Fibers called *dendrites* carry impulses toward the cell body. Fibers called *axons* carry impulses away from the cell body.** As many as 200 dendrites can carry impulses toward a single cell body. But there is only one axon leaving each cell body.

We observe our environment through our senses. It is the dendrites that carry sensory impulses to the central nervous system. When you stub your toe, the impulse of the feeling of pain travels through a dendrite to the nerve cell body in the central nervous system. You probably wiggle your toe to be sure that it is all right. Before this happens, impulses travel from a nerve cell body, through the axon, to a muscle in your toe. This impulse to the muscle travels on an axon.

Nerve cell fibers run together in bundles. These bundles are called *nerves.* Nerves are like an electrical cable, made up of smaller wires bound together. In the peripheral nervous system,

Some students may be interested in making string models of a motor neuron. These models are easy to construct using a piece of rope. Tie a knot at one end of the rope and unravel both ends of the rope. The knot is the cell body and the threads near the knot are the dendrites of the model. The axon extends from the knot and ends in terminal branches.

44–2 The structure of a typical motor neuron.

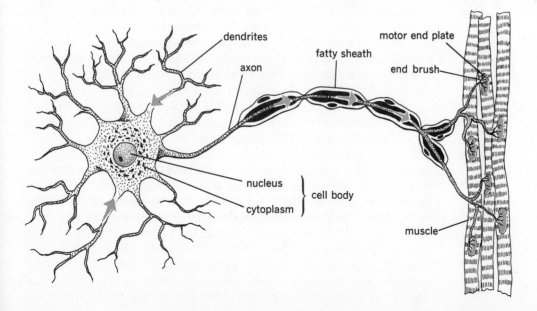

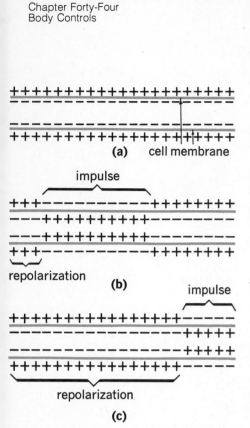

44–3 The impulse travels along the neuron and can be measured as a change in electrical charge: (a) resting neuron; (b) impulse conducted as reverse of polarity; (c) original polarity restored.

Compare nerve impulses to messages carried over phone wires. Students often enjoy elaborating on this comparison.

any neuron that carries impulses that activate muscles is called a *motor neuron.* Motor nerves are composed of the fibers of motor neurons only. Nerves that carry impulses of feeling or sensation are called sensory neurons. Sensory nerves are made up of the fibers of sensory neurons only. Many nerves of the peripheral nervous system contain both motor and sensory neurons. Such nerves are called *mixed nerves.*

Most axons are wrapped in a sheath of fatty cells. This sheath seems to protect the axon. It appears to act as an insulator. The connections between neurons are made in the central nervous system, or in ganglia. But the fibers of one neuron never really touch those of another. A space lies between them. These spaces are called **synapses** (SIN-ap-suz). Impulses must cross the synapses as they travel from one nerve to another. Furthermore, an impulse never travels from one motor neuron to another. Nor do impulses travel from one sensory neuron to another. **Impulses are able to bridge the synapse with the help of fast-acting chemical reactions.**

THE NERVE IMPULSE

Biologists have learned that an impulse travels along a nerve by a complex combination of chemicals and electricity. **A nerve impulse is not a flow of electricity.** Nerve impulses move much slower than electricity. They move at about 90 meters per second. Electricity moves at about 285,000 kilometers a second. Also, an impulse gives off carbon dioxide as it travels along a nerve. This indicates that some chemical reaction is involved in its movement. This is why we say that a *nerve impulse* is an electrochemical charge moving along a neuron.

A neuron that is not carrying an impulse has an electrical potential. The outside of the cell membrane has a positive charge. The inside of the cell membrane has a negative charge. This resting neuron is said to be *polarized.* But all this changes when an impulse moves along the neuron. The polarity reverses. The outer membrane surface becomes negative, and the inner surface becomes positive. This change in polarity sweeps along the neuron like a wave, carrying the impulse. After the impulse passes a given spot, the original polarity returns. The balance of sodium and potassium ions along the cell membrane affects this polarity change.

Biologists have also learned something about how a nerve impulse causes a muscle to contract. **As with the travel of an impulse, muscle contraction is caused by an electrochemical reaction.** The impulse reaches to the end of a motor neuron. At the tip of the motor neuron are many *motor end plates.* Here, the impulse causes the release of a minute amount of a chemical called *acetylcholine* (uh-SEET'l-KOE-leen). This substance transmits the impulse to the muscle fibers. Then the process of contraction begins. After a brief period of contraction, the nerve releases another substance, *cholinesterase* (KOLE-in-ESS-tuh-RACE). Cholinesterase neutralizes the acetylcholine, and the muscle fibers relax. This whole process takes less than 0.1 second.

As mentioned, chemical reactions at the ends of axons also transmit impulses across the synapses. Axon endings produce either acetylcholine or an adrenalin compound. These stimulate the dendrite of the next neuron to begin the impulse and carry it along. Neutralization of these chemicals prepares the synapse for the transmission of another impulse.

The Central Nervous System

THE MEMBRANES OF THE BRAIN

The brain is one of the most specialized organs in the human body. It weighs about 1.4 kilograms. And it fills the cranial cavity. **The brain is made up of soft nervous tissue. This is covered by three membranes. These are called the** *meninges* (muh-NIN-jeez). The inner membrane is called the *pia mater*. It is well supplied with blood vessels that carry food and oxygen to the brain cells. The *pia mater* is very delicate. It closely adheres to the surface of the brain. It dips down into the many folds of the brain.

The middle membrane is called the *arachnoid* (uh-RACK-noid) *mater*. It consists of fibrous and elastic tissue. This membrane does not follow the many grooves of the brain surface and the pia mater. The space between the pia mater and the arachnoid mater is filled with a clear liquid called *cerebrospinal fluid*. This fluid is also found around the spinal cord.

The outermost protective membrane is called the *dura mater*. This is a thick, strong, fibrous lining. It lines the inside of the cranium. All three meninges extend down the spinal column to protect the spinal cord.

Together, all these meninges act as a cushion to protect the brain from bumps and bruises. But sometimes a bump on the head is so hard that it does damage the brain in spite of this protection. Such a bruise is called a *concussion*.

CAVITIES OF THE BRAIN

There are four spaces inside the brain. These spaces are called *ventricles.* There are two *lateral ventricles*. These open into the *third ventricle*. The third ventricle leads to the *fourth ventricle*. The fourth ventricle connects with the space between the arachnoid mater and the spinal cord. These cavities and the central canal are all filled with cerebrospinal fluid. They are lined with ciliated epithelium to keep the fluid constantly moving.

THE CEREBRUM—LARGEST REGION OF THE BRAIN

The brain section called the **cerebrum** is proportionally larger in humans than in any other animals. It consists of two halves, or

Areas of the brain have been mapped according to the function or functions they control. Students may be interested in studying more about this and what it meant to modern medicine and the correction of certain disorders.

It is interesting to note that right-handed people have their speech area located in the left hemisphere of the brain. The opposite is true for many left-handed people.

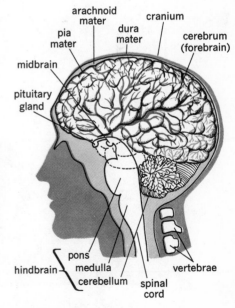

44–4 A longitudinal section of the brain, showing the regions and the meninges.

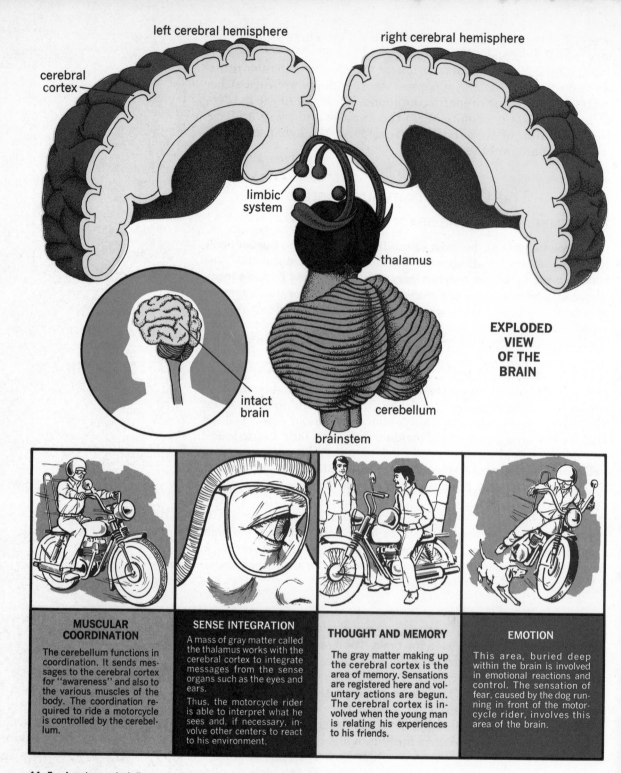

left cerebral hemisphere

right cerebral hemisphere

cerebral cortex

limbic system

thalamus

intact brain

EXPLODED VIEW OF THE BRAIN

cerebellum

brainstem

MUSCULAR COORDINATION

The cerebellum functions in coordination. It sends messages to the cerebral cortex for "awareness" and also to the various muscles of the body. The coordination required to ride a motorcycle is controlled by the cerebellum.

SENSE INTEGRATION

A mass of gray matter called the thalamus works with the cerebral cortex to integrate messages from the sense organs such as the eyes and ears.

Thus, the motorcycle rider is able to interpret what he sees and, if necessary, involve other centers to react to his environment.

THOUGHT AND MEMORY

The gray matter making up the cerebral cortex is the area of memory. Sensations are registered here and voluntary actions are begun. The cerebral cortex is involved when the young man is relating his experiences to his friends.

EMOTION

This area, buried deep within the brain is involved in emotional reactions and control. The sensation of fear, caused by the dog running in front of the motorcycle rider, involves this area of the brain.

44–5 A color-coded diagram of the brain and some of its functions.

hemispheres. These hemispheres are joined by tough fibers and by nerve tracts. The outer surface of the cerebrum is called the *cortex.* It is deeply folded in irregular wrinkles and furrows, the *convolutions.* The convolutions greatly increase the surface area of the cerebrum. And, the deeper grooves divide the cortex into lobes.

Countless numbers of neurons make up the cerebral cortex. This tissue is frequently called *gray matter* because of the color of the cells. The cerebrum below the cortex is called the *white matter.* It is formed by masses of fibers covered by sheaths. These fibers extend from the neurons of the cortex to other parts of the body.

THE FUNCTIONS OF THE CEREBRUM

Specific regions of the cerebrum control specific activites. Some areas of the cerebral cortex are called *motor areas.* Motor areas are the centers that control voluntary movement. Different motor areas of the *frontal lobe* control movements in particular body areas. Also, some areas of the cerebral cortex are *sensory areas.* This means that they interpret sensations. Different areas of the *parietal lobe* interpret sensations from particular body areas.

The sense of vision is interpreted in the *occipital lobes.* What do you think would happen if these lobes were destroyed? You would not be able to see, even if your eyes are perfect. The same is true for areas of the temporal lobes. These lobes interpret hearing, taste, and smell. The two frontal lobes are also centers of emotion, judgment, will power, and self-control. These functions are also shared by other areas of the cerebral cortex.

THE FUNCTIONS OF THE CEREBELLUM

The **cerebellum** lies below the back of the cerebrum. Like the cerebrum, it has two hemispheres. But the cerebellum has shallower and more regular convolutions. The surface of the cerebellum is made up of gray matter. Its inner part is mostly white matter. Bundles of nerve fibers connect the cerebellum with the rest of the nervous system.

In a sense, the cerebellum assists the cerebrum in controlling muscular activity. Nerve impulses do not originate in the cerebellum. You cannot control its activities. But the cerebellum *coordinates* the motor impulses sent from the cerebrum. Without the help of the cerebellum, the cerebrum's impulses would produce uncoordinated motions. The cerebellum also strengthens impulses sent to the muscles.

Another function of the cerebellum involves the maintenance of balance. Impulses from the eyes and inner ears inform the cerebellum of your position in your surroundings. Then the cerebellum produces the muscular contractions necessary to maintain balance.

The cerebellum maintains tone in muscles. It causes muscles to remain in a state of partial contraction. You are not aware of this constant function. The cerebellum works below the level of consciousness.

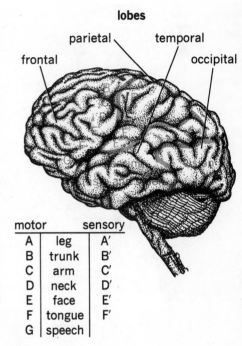

lobes

frontal — parietal — temporal — occipital

motor		sensory
A	leg	A'
B	trunk	B'
C	arm	C'
D	neck	D'
E	face	E'
F	tongue	F'
G	speech	

44–6 The control areas of the cerebrum.

What results if something happens to the dominant hemisphere of the brain? This has happened to many stroke patients and individuals with brain tumors. The other hemisphere (the nondominant one) can take over the brain functions in many activities, including speech and movement control.

white matter   posterior horn
gray matter   posterior
nerve root
anterior
horn
anterior
nerve root
spinal
nerve
spinal cord
spinal nerve
vertebra

44–7 The structures of the spinal cord and their relationship to the vertebral column. The white matter is located in the outer region of the spinal cord.

44–8 Automatic reflex action. Trace the path of the impulse from the receptor to the effector.

THE BRAIN STEM

The brain stem is an enlargement at the base of the brain. This is where nerve fibers from the cerebrum and the cerebellum collect before leaving the brain. The lowest portion of the stem is the *medulla oblongata* (muh-DULL-uh oB-long-GAH-tuh). It is located at the base of the skull. It protrudes from the skull and attaches to the spinal cord. The *pons* is another part of the brain stem. It receives stimuli from the facial area.

The medulla oblongata controls the activity of the internal organs. The respiratory control center, discussed in the last chapter, is located here. The medulla oblongata also controls heart action, muscular action in the digestive organs, glandular secretion, and other automatic activities.

There are twelve pairs of *cranial nerves* connected to the brain. These are part of the peripheral nervous system. The cranial nerves act as direct connections with certain important organs of the body. One pair, for example, connects the eyes with the brain. Another cranial nerve connects the brain with the lungs, heart, and abdominal organs.

THE SPINAL CORD AND THE SPINAL NERVES

The *spinal cord* extends down from the medulla oblongata. It passes through the bony protective arch of each vertebra, almost the whole length of the spine. The outer region of the spinal cord is white matter. It is composed of many nerve fibers covered by sheaths. The inner part of the spinal cord is gray matter. This is in a shape like that of a butterfly with outspread wings. The pointed tips of the wings of gray matter are called *horns*. The posterior pair of horns point toward the back of the cord. The anterior pair point to the front of the cord.

Thirty-one pairs of *spinal nerves* branch off the cord. These pass out between the bones of the spine. Along with the cranial nerves,

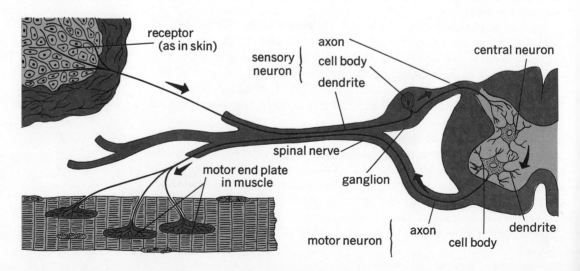

receptor
(as in skin)

sensory
neuron

axon
cell body
dendrite

central neuron

spinal nerve

ganglion

motor end plate
in muscle

axon

dendrite

cell body

motor neuron

these spinal nerves and their branches make up the peripheral nervous system.

Each spinal nerve divides just outside the cord. The sensory fibers that carry impulses from the body to the cord go to the posterior horns of the gray matter. This branch of each spinal nerve has a ganglion located near the point where it enters the cord. The sensory nerve cell bodies are found in the ganglia. The other branch at this junction comes from the anterior horns of the gray matter. It is in the gray matter that the motor cell bodies are located. The motor fibers of this branch carry impulses from the spinal cord to the body.

If your spinal cord were cut, serious problems would result. All the parts of your body controlled by the nerves that leave the cord *below* the point of the cut would be totally paralyzed. In addition, you would lose all sense of feeling in many areas below the damaged spinal cord.

REFLEX REACTIONS

There are several different kinds of nervous reactions. The simplest is called a *reflex action.* This is an automatic reaction involving the spinal cord or the brain. The knee jerk is a good example of a simple reflex action. Sit on the edge of a table and let your knee swing freely. Then tap just below the kneecap with a narrow object. Your lower leg will jerk upward. The tap stimulates a sensory neuron in the lower leg. An impulse travels along the dendrite to the spinal cord. Here the impulse travels to a central neuron. This, in turn, stimulates a motor neuron which extends to the leg muscles, causing a jerk. The entire reflex takes only a split second.

These reflex actions serve a protective function. When you touch a hot object, your hand jerks away almost instantly. The reflex is complete even before your brain registers the pain. If the muscle response were delayed until the pain impulse was complete and interpreted, the burn would be much greater. Some other reflex actions are sneezing, coughing, blinking, laughing when tickled, and jumping when frightened.

The Autonomic Nervous System

CONTROL OF AUTOMATIC RESPONSES

The *autonomic nervous system* is entirely involuntary and automatic. It is composed of two parts: the *sympathetic system* and the *parasympathetic system.* The **sympathetic system** includes two rows of nerve cords which lie on either side of the spinal column. Each cord has ganglia. These contain the cell bodies of the neurons. The largest sympathetic ganglion is located just below the diaphragm. It is called the *solar plexus.* Other sympathetic ganglia are located near the heart, the lower abdomen, and the neck. The sympathetic nervous system has a number of functions. It helps regulate the

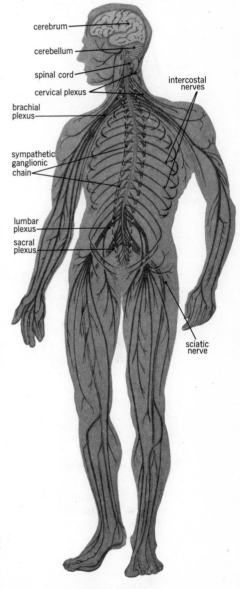

44–9 The central nervous system and the major nerve trunks of the peripheral nervous system. Only a few of the branches from the major nerve trunks are included.

action of the heart, the secretion of the endocrine glands, the arterial blood supply, the action of the smooth muscles of the stomach and the intestines, and the activity of other internal organs.

The **parasympathetic system** opposes the action of the sympathetic system. The major nerve of the parasympathetic system is the *vagus nerve*. This cranial nerve extends from the medulla oblongata down through the neck to the chest and abdomen.

The whole autonomic nervous system serves as a system of checks and balances. For instance, the sympathetic system acts to speed up heart action. But stimulation by the vagus nerve slows down the heart rate.

The Senses

THE SENSES OF THE SKIN

Special sense organs called receptors are located in the skin. *Receptors* are at the terminal branches of the dendrites of sensory neurons. Some receptors are composed of many cells. Others have one specialized cell. Some receptors are simply bare nerve endings. Each receptor is suited to receive only one type of stimulus. When a receptor is stimulated, it starts an impulse along the dendrite to the central nervous system.

There are five distinct kinds of receptors. They are specialized to receive response to stimuli of either *touch, pressure, pain, heat* or *cold.*

The *pain* receptor, for example, is a bare dendrite. If the stimulus is strong enough, a pain receptor will react to mechanical, thermal, electrical, or chemical stimuli. The sensation of pain is a protective device. It signals a threat of injury to the body. Pain receptors are located throughout the skin.

The sensory nerves of the skin are distributed unevenly over the skin area and lie at different depths in the skin. For instance, if you move the point of your pencil over your skin very lightly, you stimulate only the nerves of *touch*. The receptors for touch are close to the surface of the skin. The fingertips, the forehead, and the tip of the tongue contain many receptors that respond to touch.

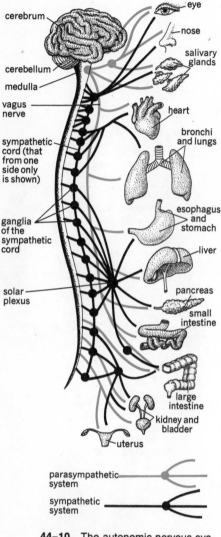

44–10 The autonomic nervous system regulates the internal organs of the body. What are the functions of its two divisions?

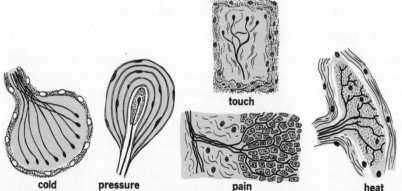

touch

cold   pressure   pain   heat

44–11 The five types of receptors found in the skin.

Receptors that respond to *pressure* lie deeper in the skin. If you press the pencil point against the skin, you feel both pressure and touch. Since the nerves are deeper, a pressure stimulus must be stronger than a touch stimulus. You may think that there is no difference between touch and pressure. But you can distinguish the mere touching of an object from a firm grip on it.

Heat and *cold* stimulate different receptors. This is an interesting protective adaptation of the body. Actually, cold is not an active condition. Cold results from a lowering in heat energy. If both great heat and intense cold stimulated a single receptor, we would be unable to tell the difference between the two. In turn, we would be unable to react to either. However, since some receptors are stimulated by heat and others by the absence of it, we can react to both conditions.

THE SENSE OF TASTE

Nearly all animals prefer some food substances to others. So they must be able to distinguish different chemical substances. **Like other senses, taste results from the stimulation of certain nerve endings.** In this case, the stimulation is chemical. In humans, the nerve endings for taste are located in *taste buds* on the tongue. Taste buds are shaped like little flasks. They lie on the front of the tongue, along its sides, and near the back. Bits of food, mixed with saliva, enter the taste buds through little pores at the tops. Once inside, they stimulate hairlike nerve endings. The message carried to the brain from these nerve endings is interpreted as a sense of taste.

Our sense of taste is not very well developed. **We can taste only four common flavors:** *sour, sweet, salty,* and *bitter.* The buds for each of these flavors are located in different areas of the tongue. Those sensitive to sweetness are on the tip of the tongue. That is why candy tastes sweeter when you lick it than when you chew it. Salt-sensitive buds are also on the tongue's tip. Those for sour flavors lie along the sides of the tongue. And those for bitterness lie on the back of the tongue. That is why, if you eat something both sweet and bitter, you taste the sweetness before the bitterness. Some foodstuffs, like pepper and other spices, have no distinct flavor. They taste the way they do because they irritate the entire tongue, causing a burning sensation.

Much of the sensation we call taste is really smell. When you chew up a bit of onion or apple, the vapors enter the inner openings of the nose. There, they reach the nerve endings for smell, and you can tell them apart. You may have noticed the loss of what you thought was taste when you had a cold. When your nose is plugged up with a cold, few food vapors can get to the nerve endings for smell. That is why food does not taste very good when you have a head cold. In fact, under these conditions, the apple and the onion may even have the same sweet flavor.

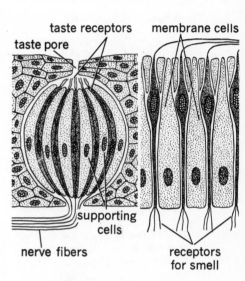

44–12 The receptor of taste (left) and smell (right), as they appear under a microscope.

Students may be interested in seeing for themselves the closeness of the senses of taste and smell. Simple demonstrations can be done to block smell through the use of nose plugs and see if students can taste various foods.

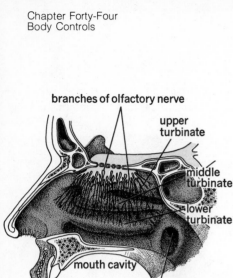

branches of olfactory nerve

upper
turbinate

middle
turbinate

lower
turbinate

mouth cavity

opening of Eustachian tube

44-13 The surface of the inner wall of the nose. What function does the Eustachian tube perform?

Hearing defects result from a variety of conditions. Some children are born completely deaf as a result of a congenital defect. There are some successful operations that can restore hearing to some people and research is continuing in this area.

THE SENSE OF SMELL

Like taste, smell results from chemical stimulation of certain nerve endings. The difference is that, in smell, the chemical stimulator is in the form of gases. The nasal passages are arranged in three layers of cavities. These are separated by bony layers called *turbinates*. The upper cavity, or turbinate, contains the branched endings of a cranial nerve called the **olfactory nerve.**

Gases entering the nasal cavity dissolve in mucus. Then, they stimulate these nerve endings. This causes impulses to go to the central nervous system. These impulses are interpreted as smell. But if smell receptors are exposed to a particular odor for a long time, they stop reacting to it. But they will still respond to other odors. If you ever go into a hospital, the iodoform odor will be obvious. But the nurses who work there are not usually aware of the odor.

HEARING—THE STRUCTURE OF THE EAR

Like all mammalians ears, human **ears** are very complex organs. The outer ear opens into the *auditory canal*. This canal is embedded in the bones of the skull. It is closed at its inner end by the *eardrum*, or *tympanic membrane*. The eardrum separates the auditory canal from the middle ear.

The *Eustachian* (yoo-STAY-shun) *tube* connects the middle ear with the throat. This connection equalizes pressure in the middle ear with that of the outer atmosphere. When the Eustachian tube becomes blocked by a cold, the inner and outer pressures do not equalize. If the pressure difference becomes great enough, the eardrum may burst.

For this reason, divers and fliers do not work when they have colds. The outside pressure increases during a dive. But with a blocked Eustachian tube, the middle-ear pressure would not be equalized. The difference might burst the eardrum. With the flier, the situation would be the reverse. The pressure would be less outside the middle ear than inside.

In the middle ear, there are three tiny bones: the *hammer*, the *anvil*, and the *stirrup*. They form a chain across the middle ear. This chain extends inward from the inner face of the eardrum. At the inner end of the middle ear, the stirrup links up with a membrane called the *oval window*. The oval window covers the opening to the inner ear.

The inner ear is composed of two general parts: the *cochlea* (KOCK-lee-uh) and the *semicircular canals*. The cochlea is a spiral passage that looks like a tiny snail shell. It is filled with fluid and its inner surface is lined with nerve endings. These nerve endings are highly sensitive to vibrations of the fluid. All these nerve endings join the **auditory nerve.** This nerve leads from the cochlea to the brain. The semicircular canals consist of three loop-shaped tubes. These tubes lie at right angles to one another. They function in keeping a sense of balance.

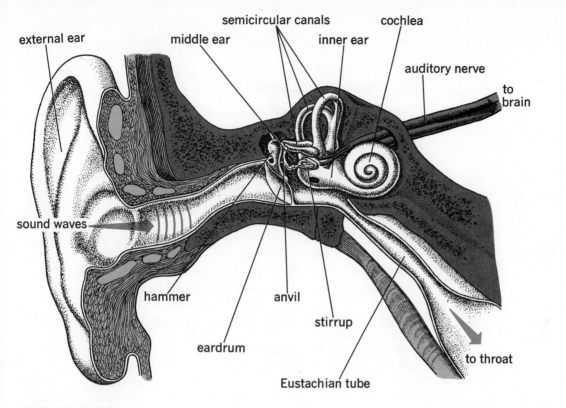

external ear

semicircular canals

middle ear

cochlea

inner ear

auditory nerve

to brain

sound waves

hammer

anvil

stirrup

eardrum

to throat

Eustachian tube

44–14 Structure of the human ear.

HOW WE HEAR

All noise is actually vibrations. When an object vibrates in the air, it mechanically moves the air molecules. Some molecules are squeezed together, or compressed. Others are spread apart, or rarefied. The regular pattern that is produced by any vibrating object in the air, or any other medium, is called a *sound wave*. When sound waves reach the ear, they pass through the outer ear, down the auditory canal and to the eardrum. The sound waves start the eardrum vibrating in the same pattern as the particular wave. The vibrating eardrum then starts the hammer, the anvil, and the stirrup to vibrate. These, in turn, cause the oval window to vibrate. And this sets up vibration in the fluid inside the cochlea. The vibrations of the fluid stimulate the nerve endings that line the cochlea. The nerve endings transmit impulses up the auditory nerve to the cerebrum. The specific pattern of the impulses is determined by the pattern of the sound wave that started the whole chain. The cerebrum picks up the impulses and translates them into a perception of sound. The whole process is a very sensitive chain reaction.

All the links in the chain are crucial to the process. If any link is destroyed, a person will either hear poorly—or not at all. Vibrations are carried mechanically to nerve endings. These endings translate the vibrations into an electrochemical impulse. This is transmitted to the cerebrum which transmutes the impulse into the perception that humans call sound. If the auditory region of

Students will have a better understanding of sound conduction if a tuning fork is used to demonstrate this.

the cerebrum does not function, the person cannot hear. This is true even if all the ear mechanisms receive vibrations normally.

THE SENSE OF BALANCE

The semicircular canals are the structures necessary to our sense of balance, or equilibrium. The canals lie at right angles to each other on three different planes. These canals contain many receptors. They also contain a fluid similar to the fluid inside the cochlea. When your head changes position, this fluid rocks and stimulates the receptors. With this stimulation, the receptors start impulses that go through a branch of the auditory nerve to the cerebellum. The brain is then made aware of changes in head position. The canals lie in three different planes so that *any* change in the head's position will rock the fluid in one or more directions.

People get dizzy when they spin around and then suddenly stop. The spinning forces the fluid to the ends of the canals. When the spinning stops, the fluid rushes back, causing the sensation of spinning in the opposite direction. This sensory conflict causes a sensation of dizziness.

In some people, regular rhythmic motions produce unpleasant sensations that involve the whole body. When this occurs in a train, a car, or other vehicle, it is called *motion sickness*. If the semicircular canals become diseased, temporary or even permanent dizziness may result.

VISION—THE STRUCTURE OF THE EYE

The normal eye is spherical, though slightly flattened from front to back. The wall of the eyeball is made of three distinct layers. The *sclerotic* (skluh-ROT-ick) *layer* is on the outside surface. It is tough and white and is normally called the "white of the eye." At its front, it bulges and is transparent. This section of the sclerotic layer is called the *cornea*.

The middle layer of the wall of the eye is called the *choroid layer*. This layer is richly supplied with blood vessels. It surrounds the eye except for the very front. The small opening at the front is called the *pupil*. The pupil lies directly behind the center of the cornea. The choroid layer contains pigmented cells around the pupil. These may be colored blue, brown, hazel, green, or combinations of these. This pigmented area is called the *iris*.

The pupil changes in size, depending on the intensity of light entering it. This adjustment is an automatic reflex. It is accomplished by muscles in the iris. In bright light, the pupil shrinks, or constricts. In dim light, it enlarges, or dilates.

Behind the pupil opening, there is a convex, *crystalline lens*. The lens is held in place by muscles that are attached to the choroid layer. These muscles are called *ciliary muscles*. When they contract, they change the shape of the lens. This allows you to focus on ob-

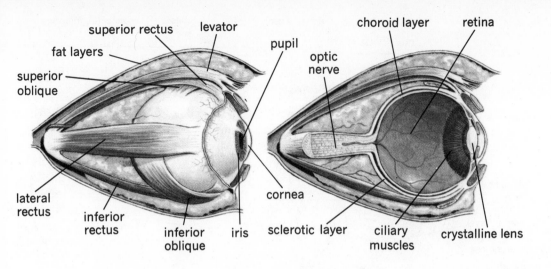

Diagram labels (left figure): superior rectus, levator, fat layers, superior oblique, pupil, lateral rectus, inferior rectus, inferior oblique, iris, cornea

Diagram labels (right figure): choroid layer, retina, optic nerve, sclerotic layer, ciliary muscles, crystalline lens

jects either close or far away. The space between the lens and the cornea is filled with a thin watery liquid called *aqueous humor*. Inside the eyeball, there is a thicker, transparent substance that keeps the eyeball firm. This fluid is called *vitreous humor*.

44–15 The human eye. The muscle and sockets are shown at the left; the various internal structures can be seen in the cutaway diagram at the right.

THE STRUCTURE OF THE RETINA

The innermost layer of the eye is the most complicated and delicate one. It is called the **retina.** Less than a millimeter thick, it is composed of several layers of cells: receptors, ganglia, and nerve fibers.

The function of all the structures of the eye is to focus light on the retina. The retina contains the receptors that are stimulated by light. These receptors are called **photoreceptors.** They are of two types: *cones* and *rods*. They lie deep in the retina. When they are stimulated, they start impulses, through a series of short nerves, to ganglia near the front of the retina. From these ganglia, more than half a million nerve fibers lead to a large cranial nerve called the **optic nerve.** There are no rods or cones at the spot where the optic nerve joins the retina. Thus, there can be no vision at this point. This spot is called the *blind spot*.

From the back of each eyeball, an optic nerve extends to the occipital lobe of the cerebrum. That is the vision center of the brain. Some of the fibers cross as they lead to the cerebrum. This means that some of the impulses from your right eye to go to the left occipital lobe. Some from the left eye go to the right occipital lobe. Thus, what you see with each eye is interpreted in both lobes.

Students should be encouraged to have frequent eye examinations. This would be an appropriate time to review the functions of the opthalmologist, optometrist, and optician.

HOW WE SEE

Light rays pass through the cornea, aqueous humor, pupil, lens, and vitreous humor, and then strike the retina. The rays stimulate photoreceptors to transmit impulses to the optic nerve. The lens

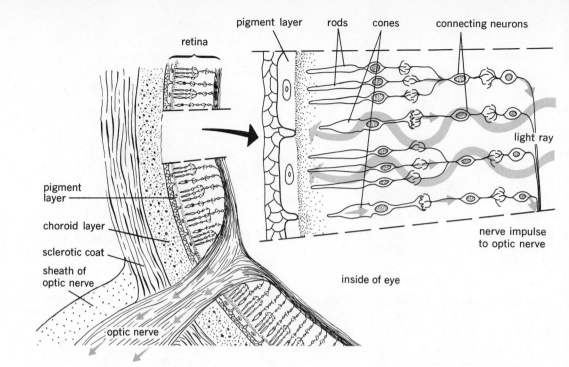

44-16 The structure of the back of the eye. The shapes and arrangement of the rods and cones are shown in greater detail in the enlargement.

44-17 How are the parts of a camera similar to those of the eye? How are the parts different? Why is the image reversed and inverted on the retina?

focuses the rays mostly on a small portion of the retina called the *fovea*. The fovea has more cones than other parts of the retina. **Cones are more sensitive to bright light than are rods. Cones are responsible for color vision.** When light is focused on the fovea, we see an object clearly. Outside of the fovea, there are not as many cones. An image focused here is less distinct. Thus, if you focus your eyes directly on an object, you see it clearly, while surrounding objects tend to lack detail.

At night, there is not enough light to stimulate the cones. But there is enough to stimulate the rods. However, rods cannot distinguish colors. Therefore, you do not see much color in dim light.

Rods produce a substance called *visual purple*. The rods do not interfere with cones in bright light because bright light fades visual purple. This makes the rods insensitive to more light. But, at night,

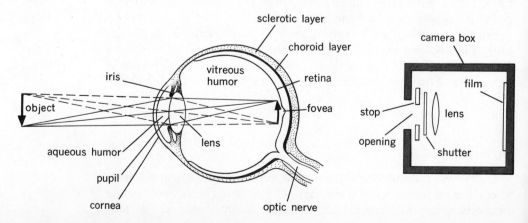

visual purple does not fade as fast. The rods are able to make it as needed. This explains why it takes you a while to see when you suddenly leave a bright room and walk into the dark night. The visual purple must be restored for you to see in dim light.

If you were to sit in a dark room, and look directly at an object, you probably won't be able to see it very well. Then look at the same thing out of the corner of your eye. You will probably be able to see it more clearly. When you look straight at something, the incoming light is focused on the fovea. **The fovea contains many cones, but no rods.** The areas outside the fovea have more rods. Thus, you can see things more clearly at night "out of the corner of your eye."

The human eye contains fewer rods than many animal eyes. So our night vision is relatively poor. The cat, deer, and owl see well at night because they have many rods. The owl, however, lacks cones in its eyes and therefore is day-blind.

EYE MOVEMENT AND PROTECTION

In its socket, the eyeball rests against protective cushions of fat. Pairs of muscles extend from the inside of the socket to the eyeball. These muscles move the eye. The sclerotic layer has pain receptors. So the brain is aware when a foreign object touches the eyeball. The eyeball is further protected by its recessed position in the socket, and by the eyelids. Tear glands keep its surface moist. Tears wash over the eye and then drain into tear ducts in the lower corners of the sockets. These ducts lead to the nasal cavity. Tears clear dirt from the eye. They also kill germs and bacteria because they contain an antibacterial enzyme.

If an optometrist could come to class, she or he could give some simple visual tests and talk to students about eye care and eye disorders.

There are a number of serious eye disorders that students may wish to research. Cataracts, glaucoma, corneal scarring, and detached retina should be included as topics for study.

SUMMARY

Humans have the most fully developed brains and nervous systems of any animal. The central nervous system is composed of the brain and the spinal cord. They communicate with all parts of the body via the nerves. The cerebrum controls most conscious activities. It is the center of the intelligence. It contains both sensory and motor areas. Impulses from cerebral motor areas pass through the cerebellum. This coordinates the impulses. The medulla oblongata controls the activity of internal organs, including the organs of respiration.

Sensory nerves carry impulses from their receptors to the central nervous system. The five different types of skin receptors respond to touch, pressure, pain, heat, and cold. Smell receptors respond to gaseous stimuli. They lie in the upper turbinate region of the nasal passages. Hearing receptors are located in the cochlea of the inner ear. They respond to vibrations called sound waves, which are transmitted mechanically to the receptors by other parts of the ear. Information on head position and balance is picked up by receptors in the semicircular canals of the inner ear.

The human eye is the most specialized of our sense organs. It receives light rays through the pupil and focuses them on the retina by means of the lens. Photoreceptors called rods and cones are stimulated by light rays and send impulses up along the optic nerve. This leads to the visual center, which is located in the brain's occipital lobes.

QUESTIONS FOR REVIEW

1. Name the three main divisions of the nervous system and state the functions of each.
2. Why are peripheral nerves that contain only axons considered to be motor nerves?
3. What is a nerve impulse?
4. What occurs at the endings of a motor neuron that causes a muscle fiber to contract? What causes it to relax?
5. Name the parts of the brain and state the functions of each.
6. In what way is the autonomic nervous system really two systems?
7. Name the five sensations of the skin. In what ways are the receptors different?
8. Account for the fact that we think we distinguish more than the four tastes the tongue can perceive.
9. Describe how a sound wave in the air stimulates the receptors in the cochlea.
10. How can an infection in the middle ear produce temporary deafness?
11. Describe the movements of the head that would be necessary to stimulate each semicircular canal separately.
12. Why is our night vision relatively poor compared to the night vision of an owl?
13. Why is it that you can see an object out of the corner of your eye at night, but when you focus on it, it disappears?

APPLYING PRINCIPLES AND CONCEPTS

1. What is intelligence?
2. Explain the activity that occurs after a chicken's head has been cut off.
3. Explain the fact that the sympathetic nervous system is sometimes called "the system for fight or flight"?
4. How would you go about designing an experiment to prove or disprove that the eye receives an image upside down and that the brain interprets it oppositely?

45-1 All of these may lead to complicated problems. (H.R.W. Photo by John King; H.R.W. Photo by Russell Dian; Carolina Biological Supply Co.)

Tobacco, Alcohol, and Drugs

OBJECTIVES
- DESCRIBE the effects of smoking on the body.
- DESCRIBE the effects of alcohol on the body.
- DISCUSS alcoholism as a disease.
- DESCRIBE the effects of alcohol on the driver of an automobile.
- DEFINE a narcotic drug.
- NAME the narcotic drugs.
- COMPARE amphetamines and barbiturates.
- DEFINE psychedelic drugs.
- UNDERSTAND some of the causes of drug addiction.

THREE SOCIAL AND HEALTH PROBLEMS

The problems resulting from the use of alcohol, drugs, and tobacco are not new. They have always caused social and health problems. We shall consider tobacco, alcohol, and drugs together. **They are all harmful substances when improperly used.** In this chapter, you will learn about some of the effects these substances have on the body. You will then have to form your own opinions and make your own decisions about their use.

TOBACCO—THE NATION'S LEADING HABIT

More than seventy million people in the United States use tobacco in some form. Most smoke cigarettes. Smokers have both a smoking habit and a tobacco habit. The first involves going through the motions of smoking. For example, many smokers automatically reach for a cigarette at regular intervals. Heavy smokers may even light a second cigarette before finishing the first one. Smokers also develop a physical desire for the nicotine in tobacco. This is the tobacco habit.

Many young people who smoke feel it makes them seem more mature. Yet, if they asked people who have smoked for several years, their advice would be not to start. Certainly, several things should be considered before deliberately starting the practice of smoking. **Smoking is habit-forming and dangerous to our health.**

Point out to students that a recent survey indicated that 75 percent of current smokers accept the fact that there are health risks in smoking.

597

Can one "save" nicotine by smoking low-nicotine cigarettes? The answer seems to be "no" because low-nicotine cigarette smokers inhale more smoke and, therefore, negate any reduction of nicotine in the cigarette.

THE EFFECTS OF SMOKING

In 1964, the Public Health Service published a report on the effects of smoking. This report was based on experiments with animals, clinical and autopsy studies in humans, and studies on the occurrence of disease. Here are some of the findings:

- *Tissue damage.* Lung tissue secretions from thousands of smokers were examined after the smokers' deaths. Abnormal cells were found in their lungs. This was true even of the individuals who did not die from cancer. Researchers also observed enlarged and ruptured aveoli and thickened arterioles. In the trachea and bronchii, the cilia and the protective cells of the mucosa were destroyed. These structures normally clean and lubricate the respiratory tract. They also help prevent infection.

- *Higher death rate.* Researchers compared the number of deaths among a large sample of nonsmokers with the number of deaths among a similar sample of smokers. These deaths were from many causes. But certain diseases stood out. There were 1,000 percent more deaths from lung cancer among the smokers. And there were 500 percent more from chronic bronchitis and emphysema. (Emphysema is a degenerative lung disease.) The death rate was also much higher for cancer of the tongue, larynx, and esophagus, and for peptic ulcer and circulatory diseases.

- *The greater the amount of smoking, the higher the death rate.* In the sample population, the death rate is about 40 percent higher for people who smoke less than ten cigarettes a day than it is for nonsmokers. The death rate is 120 percent higher for people who smoke forty cigarettes or more. The death rate also rises the same way with the number of years of smoking.

Obviously, smoking is a health hazard. Ninety-five percent of lung cancer victims are heavy smokers. One half of one percent are nonsmokers. Heart and circulatory diseases are the number one cause of death in the United States. The death rate from these diseases is 200 percent higher among smokers than nonsmokers.

45–2 Compare the lung tissue of a nonsmoker to that of a smoker. (Manfred P. Kage, Peter Arnold)

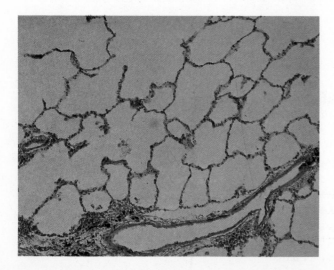
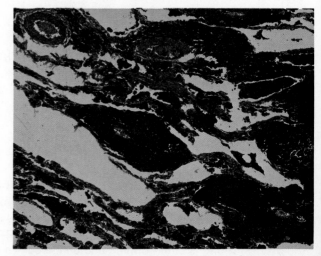

After this 1964 report, many Americans cut down on the number of cigarettes they smoked each day. Others stopped smoking altogether. And many switched to cigars or pipes. However, even with knowledge of the health hazard of smoking, tobacco sales have risen lately. Unfortunately, more young people are smoking. Among the more informed people, though, smoking has dropped noticeably.

Smoke irritates the eyes and throats of nonsmokers as well as smokers. In small rooms and closed spaces, smoke can be especially annoying. For these reasons, legislation has been passed in many places to provide for nonsmoking spaces in public areas. Many cities have ordinances prohibiting smoking in elevators and buses.

In 1971, a law became effective which prohibited cigarette advertising on radio and television. This law was passed by Congress in 1970. The same law requires each cigarette package to have a warning: "The Surgeon General has determined that cigarette smoking is dangerous to your health."

Alcohol consumption has increased among teenagers. More and more teenagers are drinking on a daily basis. Ask the class to draw some conclusions about this increase in drinking.

ALCOHOL IN THE BODY

The alcohol in beverages is *ethyl alcohol,* or ethanol. It is produced by the action of yeast on sugars. Most alcoholic drinks are made from the sugars in fruits or grains.

Alcohol can be absorbed into your system without changing its form. It starts entering the blood within two minutes after it is swallowed. Then it is rapidly carried to the tissues. Here it is absorbed by the cells. Absorption is even faster when the stomach is empty.

In the cells, alcohol oxidation begins immediately. Alcohol is oxidized at the rate of approximately one ounce in three hours. Large amounts of heat are released. The excess heat produced raises the temperature of the blood. This, in turn, stimulates the heat-control center in the brain. The brain responds by causing increased circulation to the skin. There the heat is given off by the body. The increased circulation to the skin causes a rosy skin tone. The receptors of heat are in the skin. Thus, the rush of blood to the skin gives a false impression of warmth. Actually, the internal organs are not receiving an adequate supply of blood.

Alcoholism is a serious disease that affects the entire family and how they relate to each other and to society. Groups such as Alcoholics Anonymous, Al-Anon, And Alateen can be helpful to the alcoholic and family members.

SOME EFFECTS OF ALCOHOL ON THE BODY ORGANS

Not all the alcohol in the body is oxidized. Part is released into the lungs as vapor. This causes an alcoholic breath odor. Some goes to the skin and is added to perspiration. Some passes into the kidneys. From the kidneys, it leaves the body in the urine.

Alcohol is absorbed by all the body organs. And they are all affected by its presence. But some organs seem to be affected more than others. Alcohol oxidation produces water. This water is excreted in large quantities by the skin to control body temperature. This

Alcoholism has become so prevalent that many corporations as well as the United States Government offer rehabilitation programs to alcoholics. Students may be interested in finding out more about these programs.

loss of water dries out the tissues. It also causes nitrogenous wastes to concentrate in the kidneys. This build up interferes with normal elimination of waste.

Vitamin-deficiency diseases are common among alcoholics. This is because they often eat very little during long periods of heavy use of alcohol. Also these fasts cause the liver to give up its stored food. The liver begins to swell as the carbohydrates are replaced by fats. This conditions is known as *fatty liver.* It occurs in 75 percent of alcoholics. Over a long period of time, alcohol use can lead to a serious liver disease called *cirrhosis* (si-ROE-siss). In this disease, the fatty liver shrinks and hardens as the fats are used. Heavy use of alcohol is not the only cause of cirrhosis. But it occurs eight times more frequently in alcoholics than in other people.

Excessive use of alcohol can also affect the stomach. It causes an increase in stomach secretions. This can lead to *gastritis,* a painful swelling of the stomach lining.

THE EFFECTS OF ALCOHOL ON THE NERVOUS SYSTEM

Alcohol is a *depressant.* It has an anesthetic, or numbing effect on the nervous system. Some people mistake it for a stimulant. This is because its numbing effect on the nerves makes some people less concerned about their behavior. Nonetheless, its overall effect is the opposite of a stimulant.

The brain cortex shows the first effects of alcohol. Loss of judgment, will power, and self-control occur. Alcohol influences on the frontal lobe changes emotional control. This may lead to a feeling of joy. This is often shown by laughter. Others may feel sadness and weep. When alcohol reaches the vision and speech areas of the cerebrum, drinkers may experience blurred or double vision. Their speech may become slurred. And they will have difficulty judging distance.

Muscle coordination is affected when alcohol reaches the cerebellum. Drinkers become dizzy. They may stagger or may not be able to stand at all.

In the final stage of drunkeness, the brain cortex stops working. This leaves the drinker unconscious. Heart action and digestive action slow down. So does respiration. The drinker becomes completely helpless.

ALCOHOLISM—A DISEASE

Alcoholism is a disease. People who have this disease depend on alcohol continually. It may start with occasional social drinking. But alcoholics use drinking as an escape from unpleasant problems. Heavy drinking causes loss of judgment and will power. So the possibility of solving problems really becomes less likely. The need for escape becomes greater, so the alcoholic begins to drink when alone.

About one out of ten alcoholics reaches the stage of **alcohol psychosis.** This is a form of mental illness requiring hospitalization. The cause of alcohol psychosis is not fully understood. Part of the condition may be caused by the effect of alcohol on the brain. Another cause is a deficiency in the B-complex vitamins. These vitamins are necessary for normal nervous activity.

Alcohol psychotics become very confused. They may not be able to recognize members of their family. They may not even know who they are. They also have terrifying hallucinations. These usually involve visual horror and uncontrollable trembling. That is why this state is called **delirium tremens,** or the D.T.'s. Some alcohol psychotics suffer loss of memory of recent events. Alcohol psychosis is treated with psychotherapy, a controlled diet, and vitamin supplement.

Alcohol is the tool of alcoholism. It does not appear to be the cause. People who have studied the problem of alcoholism generally agree that some other problem underlies the alcoholic's drinking. This problem must be uncovered first. Then the drinker must try to solve the problem. If it can be solved, he or she may no longer have to use alcohol as an escape. Understanding and cooperation from family and friends helps in overcoming the problem.

Most states have special agencies to deal with alcoholism. They carry on studies and research. They also give information to people who want to learn more about the disease. These agencies see the alcoholic as someone who needs help. We also see this view in the changing attitudes of our courts. Many judges now recommend medical treatment or psychiatric counsel for the alcoholic lawbreakers, rather than punishment.

45–3 An alcometer is used to determine the alcoholic content of the breath. (H.R.W. Photo by Russell Dian)

There are many private organizations working on this problem. Perhaps the best known is Alcoholics Anonymous, or AA. This voluntary organization began in 1935. Since then, about 350,000 alcoholics have stopped drinking with the help of AA.

A POSSIBLE CAUSE OF ALCOHOLISM

Perhaps there is a biochemical reason why some people are alcoholics. Several researchers have suggested that a substance in the blood causes a person to tend toward alcoholism. This substance is called *acetaldehyde*. Acetaldehyde is known to affect brain tissue. Alcoholics have higher levels of acetaldehyde in their blood than nonalcoholics. However, scientists are not sure if these levels are caused by the drinking of alcohol itself.

When alcohol is oxidized, one of the side products is acetaldehyde. So maybe the drinking of alcohol leads to higher levels of this substance in the blood. There is some evidence though, that some people naturally have more acetaldehyde in their blood. In this case, acetaldehyde may cause the person to "need" alcoholic beverage.

The alcohol then may be the victim of a vicious circle. The high level of acetaldehyde would lead the person to drink alcohol. The use of alcohol raises this person's acetaldehyde level even more.

ALCOHOL AND THE LENGTH OF LIFE

It is not certain whether limited or moderate use of alcohol shortens life. However, even moderate drinking of alcoholic beverages increases the possibility of accidental death. Alcohol also lowers body resistance. This increases the possibility of death from infectious disease. There is no question that heavy drinking shortens life considerably.

ALCOHOL AND DRIVING

Recent experiments in Pennsylvania have thoroughly tested the relationship between drinking and driving a car. These tests were carried out under actual road conditions. Motorists were given measured amounts of alcohol. But they were not given enough to make them drunk. All but one passed the police sobriety tests. All the drivers made many errors that could lead to accidents. Most had a slower breaking reaction time. They were also inaccurate in performance. Yet all of the drivers thought they were doing well. *Their judgment was found to be impaired after only one or two drinks.* This was graphically proved by psychological tests.

Therefore, it is not surprising that alcohol is a factor in a large proportion of all fatal traffic accidents. In one-vehicle accidents, 70 percent of the drivers killed had been drinking. There is a drinking driver killed in 50 percent of all multi-vehicle accidents. Alcohol was found to be partly responsible in more than 50 percent of pedestrian traffic deaths.

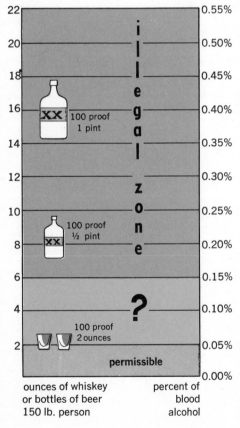

45-4 Drinking limits for drivers in the United States. Alcohol and driving do not mix. Most states have set a blood alcohol content of 0.15 percent as the legal limit for drivers. A higher percentage is proof of drunkeness.

What are the effects of alcohol on the motorist?

- It increases reaction time. The driver takes longer to brake or to swerve to avoid collision.
- It impairs vision and distance judgment.
- It takes the driver's attention away from driving.
- It makes it more difficult to associate danger signals with danger. The driver pays less attention to stop lights, stop signs, and railroad flashers.
- It gives the driver a false sense of security. Most drunk drivers think they are good drivers.
- It makes the driver hostile.

DRUGS

When anything interferes with the normal functioning of your body's cells, you become ill. Your body has some remarkable ways of defending itself against pathogenic organisms and for healing wounds. Sometimes, however, a body's recovery may be aided with *drugs*. **A *drug* is any substance used as a medicine for internal or external use.** Some drugs kill pathogenic organisms. Some speed up healing. Others treat symptoms to make you feel better. When medical doctors prescribe a drug, they are familiar with its effects on the various tissues of your body. This is important because many drugs can have harmful effects. This is especially true if they are taken for a long time or in large doses.

Medications that can be bought without a prescription are called *over-the-counter* drugs. Their labels give dosage and information on proper and improper use. It is a good idea to read these labels. You may think, for example, that common aspirin is harmless.

Discuss with students some of the reasons we are a "drugged" society. Many people tend to overmedicate themselves with over-the-counter drugs, prescription drugs are often given unnecessarily, and illegal drugs are easy to obtain. Ask students to also discuss emotional and psychological reasons for taking drugs.

45–5 Many drugs can be purchased without a prescription. These are called over-the-counter drugs.

Taken improperly, it can make you very ill, or even cause death. More than 100 children die each year from aspirin overdoses. Aspirin can also cause other problems. These include headaches, ringing in the ears, dizziness, difficulty in hearing, dim vision, mental confusion, sweating, thirst, nausea, vomiting, and diarrhea. The amount needed to cause these effects varies from person to person.

SOURCES OF DRUGS

Some drugs come from plants and are called *natural drugs.* Other drugs are made in laboratories and are called *synthetic drugs.* Sulfanilamide, and some vitamins, are examples of synthetic drugs.

There are natural drugs in coffee, tea, cocoa, and the *Kola* nut, from which cola drinks are made. The drugs in these drinks prevent sleep and cause emotional excitement. Because of this, these drugs are classified among the **stimulating drugs.**

ADDICTION

People who take a drug for a longtime may come to depend on it. This is called addiction. There are two kinds of addiction. *Psychological addiction* is an emotional dependence on a drug. *Physical addiction* is a physiological dependence on a drug. This means that the *body* requires a continuing supply. Often, the two types of addiction go together. If the supply of an addictive drug is cut off, the addict will show *withdrawal symptoms.* These symptoms may be serious. The addict may be unable to sleep and may have difficulty breathing. Other symptoms include irregular heartbeat and severe suffering. Mental symptoms include depression and derangement. Withdrawal sickness may even cause death. The longer an addicting drug is used, the more of the drug it takes to avoid withdrawal symptoms. Thus, the body develops a tolerance for the drug.

NARCOTICS

Narcotics are potentially addictive drugs. They produce sleep or stupor and relieve pain. Opium, cocaine, and the drugs that are made from them are all narcotics. So are several synthetic compounds. Nonprescription sale of narcotics is illegal in the United States.

Opium comes from the juice of the white poppy. *Morphine* and *codeine* are both made from opium. *Heroin* is a synthetic compound made from morphine. Both morphine and codeine are used as pain killers. Codeine is also an ingredient in special kinds of medicine.

Cocaine comes from the leaves of the South American coca plants (not connected with the beverage cocoa). Cocaine deadens skin and mucous membranes. Doctors sometimes use it to deaden the area around a wound. This makes the wound less painful to clean and stitch. Taken internally, cocaine stimulates the nervous system temporarily. It also causes a feeling of pleasure. However, users may later be overcome with feelings of fear. They may even become violent.

CHEMICAL AND DRUG MISUSE

Like alcoholism, drug misuse often seems to come from a desire to escape problems. People who take heroin may feel better about their problems at first. They go into a dream world. But soon the effects wear off. Another shot is needed to get that feeling back. Eventually, a craving builds up. The user has to take more and more to get the same effect. His body develops a tolerance for the drug. Four to ten times the original dose may be needed. The user becomes physically addicted. Now when the effects of the heroin begin to wear off, reaction is more serious. The user feels irritable, has watery eyes, and begins to feel withdrawal symptoms. Temperature and blood pressure increase. There is sweating, vomiting, and diarrhea. The addict's resistance to disease is lowered. His body cells now need the drug. The addict becomes desperate to get rid of these terrible feelings and pain. Thus, he takes another shot.

Possession of heroin in the United States, even for medical purposes, is illegal. Therefore, its price is high. And an addict may require up to a hundred dollars' worth of heroin a day. The need for this kind of money often turns the addict to crime. Some become "pushers" in order to get the drug for themselves.

Point out to students that many over-the-counter and prescription drugs used as sleeping pills and tension relievers are harmful. Americans take enough barbiturates, amphetamines, and tranquilizers each year to give 65 doses of each of these drugs to every person in the United States.

VOLATILE CHEMICALS

Some people get pleasure from inhaling volatile chemicals. These include kerosene, paint thinner, model glue, gasoline, lighter fluid, and other solvents. They are not actually drugs. But inhalation of these volatile chemicals causes them to diffuse into the bloodstream. This reduces the amount of oxygen in the bloodstream. The user feels dizzy and loses coordination. Other reactions are slurred speech, blurred vision, loss of color vision, ringing in the ears, and nausea. Breathing these volatiles is very dangerous. It can cause unconsciousness and even death. When the fumes are inhaled, many times the results can be permanent damage to the brain, nerves, liver, kidneys, and bones.

Many deaths are reported each year (especially among young people) from inhaling volatile chemicals. A recent news story reported numerous deaths from inhaling the fumes of aerosol cooking products.

MARIJUANA

Marijuana comes from the flowers, leaves, and seeds of *Cannabis savita*. (This is the scientific name for Indian hemp.) This plant grows wild in many parts of the world. It is also a weed in many of our midwestern states. Marijuana may be eaten. But it is usually smoked. It is not physically addictive. However, some people find it is psychologically addictive. Its effects vary from person to person. Many users cannot judge long distances. They are, of

This would be an appropriate place to discuss new findings concerning marijuana and whether or not marijuana should be legalized.

45-6 Although marijuana may be eaten, users usually smoke it. (Carolina Biological Supply Co.)

Discuss such drugs as amphetamines (often used in weight-control programs) and valium (prescribed as a relaxing agent). Both of these drugs have been under attack because they are overprescribed and can be harmful to health.

course, dangerous on the highways. Often, users develop personality changes and lose motivation to do any activity. Some marijuana users go on to use and become dependent upon narcotics. Long-term effects of marijuana on the body are still unknown. Continuing research on its use may give us some answers.

BARBITURATES

Barbiturates are synthetic drugs. They act as tranquilizers or sedatives. A **sedative** is a drug that makes you sleep. It can also reduce emotional anxiety and relieve pain. Barbiturates are used habitually by hundreds of thousands of people in this country. Barbiturates are not addictive in the same way narcotics are. But people can come to depend on them psychologically. If a heavy user is suddenly taken off barbiturates, withdrawal symptoms may occur.

Barbiturates are often used for suicide. And they can be deadly when combined with alcohol. **When alcohol and barbiturates are taken together, each one doubles the effect of the other.**

STIMULANTS

Amphetamines (am-FET-uh-MEENZ) are stimulant drugs. They are used in *pep pills*. People often take them to stay awake. But they impair judgment and vision. And they may even produce hallucinations. This is why they are dangerous to people who work machinery or must drive. Other side effects include nervousness and confusion. Most users feel a big letdown when the drug wears off.

Physicians often give dexedrine, a kind of amphetamine, to overweight patients. In excess, it causes people to be jumpy, restless, and talkative. Users may also become argumentative. Their pupils dilate and their blood pressure increases. They may even develop delusions. Amphetamines are not physically addictive. And they do not produce withdrawal symptoms. However, habitual users may become emotionally dependent on them. Some people feel the "need" for a pep pill to get through the day. This may keep them awake at night. So they try to relax with barbiturates. When this happens, a serious problem has begun.

PSYCHEDELIC, OR "MIND-EXPANDING," DRUGS

Psychedelic drugs are chemical compounds that affect the mind. They change sensory perception, reaction to time and space, and the rate and content of thought. People using them often describe visions or hallucinations. The three most common psychedelic drugs are *LSD, mescaline,* and *psilocybin.* Mescaline has been used to treat mental illness. It comes from the tops of the mescal, or peyote, cactus. Psilocybin is prepared from certain mushrooms.

LSD is d-lysergic acid diethylamide. It is so powerful that a single ounce provides 300,000 doses. It is usually taken orally. But it may be sniffed as a powder or injected as a solution. Once absorbed into the bloodstream, LSD diffuses easily into the brain. If taken during pregnancy, it diffuses through the placenta and into the fetus. The emotional effects of LSD are unpredictable. And they can change quickly. Feelings of joy may suddenly change to depression. Some people hallucinate. Others relive past experiences. Many have strong feelings of instability.

Physical reactions seem to vary the user's emotions. Heart rate and blood pressure may increase. The pupils may dilate. The user

Discuss some of the reasons people take hallucinogenic drugs. Some people report looking for a deeper meaning to life or an attempt to know themselves better. Can answers be found to these questions without taking drugs? Students may be interested in reporting on hallucinogenic drugs.

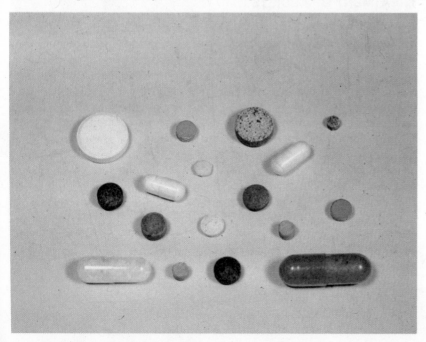

45–7 Various forms of LSD. (Carolina Biological Supply Co.)

may feel alternating periods of chill and fever. Trembling and nausea can also occur.

LSD has several obvious dangers. It is obtained illegally. So you can never be sure of its purity. Also small amounts of this drug bring about the changes mentioned above. Thus overdoses are common. Perhaps more important, however, is the fact that we do not know what LSD does to the brain cells. Each user seems to react to LSD somewhat differently. People have "flashbacks" of their LSD experiences weeks or months later. Some have become permanently deranged after taking the drug only once. Suicides and mental breakdowns have also been attributed to this drug. Several researchers believe that children born to LSD users may risk a higher chance of birth defects. Chromosomal changes resulting from LSD are well known in plants and animals. Medical investigators are continuously studying the effects of LSD on the human body.

WHY DO PEOPLE BECOME ADDICTS?

People may become addicted to narcotics in several ways. Some people become addicted to narcotics that were used to relieve pain medically. This usually happens only when the illness is a long one. Doctors may prescribe narcotics for highly nervous people. Some of these people continue to buy and use the drugs illegally after treatment has ended. As we have already mentioned, some people take drugs to forget their problems. Sometimes young people try drugs out of curiosity. They often do not realize the danger involved.

TREATMENT OF ADDICTS

The controversial topic of methadone might be discussed here. Debate the question of whether or not methadone is a helpful drug. Many individuals feel that the substitution of methadone for heroin is not rehabilitating addicts.

Discuss the treatment of drug addicts in England. Do the students feel that heroin should be given to addicts and controlled by the government? How does methadone maintenance differ from this?

We have no way of knowing the exact number of drug addicts in the United States. But the number of heroin addicts alone has been estimated at 56,000! Many of these people must turn to crime in order to pay the enormous illegal narcotics prices. Few addicts treated in hospitals can avoid drugs when they are released. Many of these addicts are teenagers. Some are as young as thirteen and fourteen.

Methadone maintenance is a new approach to the treatment of the heroin addiction problem. Patients in this program must first agree to stop taking heroin. Then they are given methadone mixed with fruit juice. This is given to them regularly in prescribed doses. It prevents withdrawal symptoms. It also reduces the craving for heroin. Over a period of several weeks or even months, the methadone dose is reduced. The person can overcome the physical dependence in this way. It takes longer to overcome the psychological dependence.

Many people are against methadone treatment, however. This is because methadone is itself addicting. Its advantage over heroin is that people addicted to it can function in society. Scientists are still searching for a nonaddictive substitute for heroin.

Tobacco is not addicting in the sense that narcotic drugs are. It does pose serious health problems, however. It tends to shorten life and seems to contribute to many diseases.

Alcohol is a depressant. Used excessively, it is the tool of an alcoholic. Alcohol can produce organic diseases, and even death. It is also socially dangerous when used by people who drive.

Misuse of drugs can be harmful to the users and may even cause death. Drug addiction can be psychological, physical, or both. Narcotic drugs may be physically addicting. People who take them habitually often do so in order to escape from problems. This is psychological addiction. But the body builds up a drug tolerance. So addicts must take more and more to escape. And physically they need more to avoid painful withdrawal symptoms. Narcotics are illegal except by prescription. So buying them is expensive. Because of this, many addicts spend most of their time looking for ways to get the drug they need. They often must turn to crime. This, of course, creates more problems for them and for society as a whole.

fatty liver	alcohol psychosis	sedative
cirrhosis	delirium tremens	stimulating drugs
gastritis	drug	barbiturates
depressant	addiction	amphetamines
alcoholism	narcotic	psychedelic drugs

1. What are some findings concerning the death rate among smokers?
2. What are some short-term disadvantages of smoking?
3. What happens when alcohol enters the body?
4. What organs of the body are especially affected by alcohol?
5. Why is alcohol not considered a stimulant?
6. Explain the progressive effects of alcohol on the nervous system.
7. Why is it dangerous for a person who has had an alcoholic drink to drive an automobile?
8. Name several drugs that fit the definition of a narcotic drug.
9. Why is it dangerous for a person who has consumed alcoholic beverages to take sleeping pills?
10. How could a person develop a mental dependence on both amphetamines and barbiturates? Can you suggest any alternatives to such a dependency?
11. In what ways might the psychedelic drugs be harmful?
12. What factors may induce a person to begin misusing drugs or chemicals which are harmful when taken into the body? Can you suggest any alternatives?

1. Why is inhaling smoke from a cigarette injurious to your health?
2. Why is drinking alcohol on an empty stomach more injurious than drinking after eating?
3. Why does the presence of alcohol in the body give a person a feeling of warmth?
4. Explain the possible relationship between drug addiction and juvenile delinquency. How do drug addicts and alcoholics show weakness?

chapter forty-six

Body Regulators

OBJECTIVES

- IDENTIFY the endocrine glands.
- DESCRIBE the anatomy of the endocrine glands.
- EXPLAIN the function of each of the endocrine glands.
- EXPLAIN the dynamic balance of the endocrine glands.

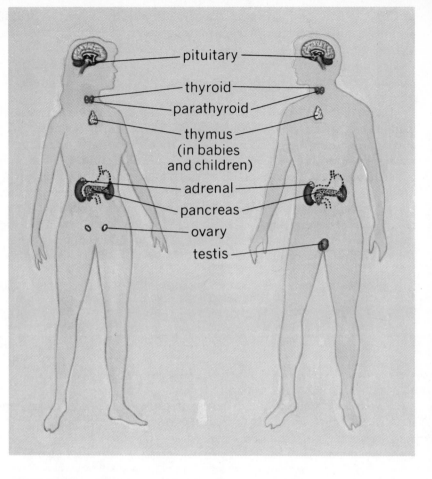

46–1 The locations of the endocrine glands in the body. Why are endocrine glands called ductless glands?

WHAT ARE THE DUCTLESS GLANDS?

You already know about some glands, like the salivary glands of the mouth and the gastric glands of the stomach. They all pour secretions into the digestive tract through ducts. We call these glands *exocrine* (EKS-oh-krin) *glands*. In this chapter, though, we will study the ductless glands. They are quite different from the digestive glands. The term *ductless* indicates that they have no ducts. Instead their secretions go directly into the bloodstream. The blood transports these secretions to all parts of the body. And they influence all of the organs. **Ductless glands are called** *endocrine* **(EN-doe-krin)** *glands.*

The secretions of ductless glands are called **hormones.** These secretions are formed from substances the glands take from the blood. **Hormones regulate the activities of all the body processes.** The circulatory system is vital to the endocrine system. It supplies the raw materials and transports the finished product. Most endocrine glands are small, but their effect on the body is great.

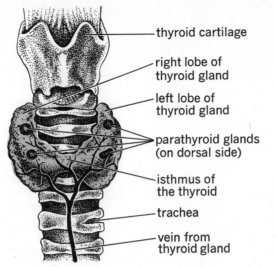

thyroid cartilage

right lobe of
thyroid gland

left lobe of
thyroid gland

parathyroid glands
(on dorsal side)

isthmus of
the thyroid

trachea

vein from
thyroid gland

46–2 The lobes of the thyroid gland lie on either side of the trachea. Note also the positions of the four parathyroid glands, embedded in the back of the thyroid gland.

THE THYROID GLAND

You have probably heard of the **thyroid** gland. This gland is relatively large. And it lies close to the body surface. The thyroid gland is in the neck, near the lower part of the larynx where it meets the trachea. The thyroid consists of two lobes connected by a narrow bridge, or isthmus. The lobes lie on each side of the trachea, extending along the sides of the larynx. The isthmus crosses the front of the trachea. The complete thyroid gland looks somewhat like a butterfly with spread wings.

The hormone produced by the thyroid gland is called *thyroxine.* This substance has the highest concentration of iodine found in any substance in the body. *Thyroid extract* is used for treating thyroid disturbances in humans. It is a purified form of the thyroid hormone that is extracted from the thyroid glands of sheep. Thyroid extract is the least expensive of all commercial endocrine preparations.

THE THYROID AND METABOLIC PROCESSES

Your body must have a normal level of thyroid hormone to function properly. The thyroid hormone regulates certain metabolic processes, especially the ones related to growth and oxidation.

If the thyroid gland is overactive, it produces a condition called *hyperthyroidism.* The rate of oxidation increases. And thus the body temperature goes up. The heart also beats faster. And blood pressure goes up. Perspiring when the body should be cool is a common symptom. And the person gets very nervous and irritable. Some people's eyes bulge slightly, and they develop a staring expression.

Surgery used to be the only treatment for hyperthyroidism. However, an effective drug called *thiouracil* (thie-oe-YOOHR-uh-sill) has been developed. Another treatment for hyperthyroidism con-

46–3 Thyroid hormones may have noticeable effects on the body. (Courtesy Ringling Brothers Barnum and Bailey Combined Circus)

Table 46-1 DUCTLESS GLANDS AND THEIR SECRETIONS

GLAND	LOCATION	HORMONE	FUNCTION OF HORMONE
thyroid	neck, below larynx	thyroid hormone	accelerates the rate of metabolism
parathyroids	back surface of thyroid lobes	parathyroid hormone	controls the use of calcium in the tissues
pituitary anterior lobe	base of brain	growth hormone	regulates growth of the skeleton
		gonadotropic hormone	influences development of sex organs and hormone secretion of the ovaries and testes
		ACTH	stimulates secretion of hormones by the cortex of the adrenals
		lactogenic hormone	stimulates secretion of milk by mammary glands
		thyrotrophic hormone	stimulates activity of the thyroid
posterior lobe		oxytocin	regulates blood pressure and stimulates smooth muscles
		vasopressin	controls water resorption in the kidneys
adrenal cortex	above kidneys	cortin (a hormone complex)	regulates metabolism, salt, and water balance controls production of certain white corpuscles and structure of connective tissue
medulla		epinephrine, or adrenalin	causes constriction of blood vessels, increase in heart action and output; stimulates liver and nervous system
pancreas	below and behind stomach		
islets of Langerhans		insulin	enables liver to store sugar and regulates sugar oxidation in tissues
ovaries follicular cells	pelvis	estrogen	produces female secondary sex characteristics; influences adult female body functions
		progesterone	maintains growth of the mucous lining of the uterus
testes interstitial cells	below pelvis	testosterone	produces male secondary sex characteristics

sists of doses of radioactive iodine. This is absorbed by the thyroid gland as though it were ordinary iodine. But the gland is bombarded by radioactivity. This destroys some of the gland tissue the way surgery does.

If the thyroid gland is underactive, the condition is called *hypothyroidism.* The symptoms are the opposite of those for hyperthyroidism. The rate of oxidation is too slow. The nervous system is not active enough. People with this condition are characteristically physically or mentally retarded. Their heartbeat slows down and often their heart enlarges. Hypothyroidism can be treated with the thyroid extract we mentioned above. Both overactivity and underactivity of the thyroid can be detected by measuring the rate of basal metabolism.

Sometimes the thyroid does not function properly during infancy. This results in *cretinism.* This condition causes stunted growth, both physically or mentally. The face usually gets bloated, the lips enlarge, and the tongue gets thick and sticks out of the mouth. If a cretin grows into childhood without being treated with thyroid extract, the dwarfism and mental retardation can never be corrected. Treatment must occur during critical stages of development.

Occasionally the thyroid slows down in adulthood. This condition is called *myxedema* (mick-suh-DEE-muh). Facial features become coarse, and the eyelids swell. Mental ability is often affected. Like cretinism, myxedema can be corrected with thyroid extract if the person is treated early.

Sometimes the thyroid gland enlarges. The major cause of this is iodine deficiency. This enlargement is called *simple goiter.* People who live near the seacoast and eat seafood rarely have this condition. Seafood contains iodine. This condition occurs more often in residents of the mountains and near the Great Lakes. In these areas, there is

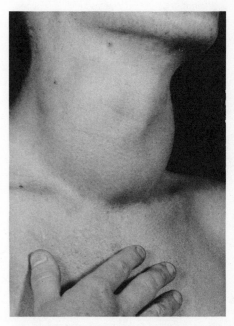

46–4 Simple goiter can be prevented by the addition of iodine to the diet. (Percy W. Brooks)

Symptoms of hyperthyroidism often include weakness, nervousness, weight loss, muscle wasting, and protrusion of the eyeballs. This condition can be treated successfully.

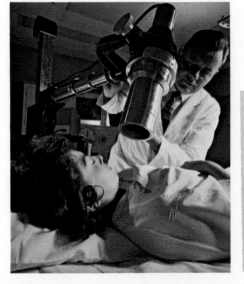

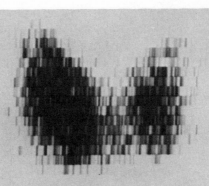

46–5 Measurement of uptake of radioactive iodine in the thyroid gland of a patient. The detector records the areas of concentration of iodine in the gland. A photograph of the record is shown (right). (Brookhaven National Lab.; Percy W. Brooks)

Violent muscle contractions or *tetany* can occur if there is too little parathyroid hormone secreted.

not much iodine in the soil. Iodine can be added to the diet in iodine compounds in table salt and in the water supply. These measures have lowered the occurrence of goiter in the Midwest.

A doctor may want to measure the activity of a patient's thyroid gland. Metabolism and oxygen consumption indicate the thyroid activity. Thus, the doctor can measure the basal metabolic rate of the patient. Even more accurate tests measure the rate at which iodine is taken in the gland. A doctor can measure the amount of iodine in your blood to find this out. But many medical centers also use radioactive iodine. The patient takes a small amount of it by mouth. A certain amount of time later, a counter is placed over the thyroid gland. The counter shows the rate at which the radioactive iodine concentrates in the thyroid tissue. This rate indicates the activity of the gland.

THE PARATHYROID GLANDS

There are four **parathyroid glands** embedded in the back of the thyroid, two in each lobe. The parathyroids secrete *parathyroid hormone*. **This hormone controls the body's use of calcium.** A constant, stable balance of calcium is vital to the body. Bone growth, muscle tone, and normal nervous activity depend on calcium balance.

THE PITUITARY GLAND

The **pituitary** is a small gland, about the size of an acorn. It is located at the base of the brain. **The pituitary used to be called the "master gland" because its secretions affect the activity of all other glands.** It is now known that other glands in turn affect the pituitary.

Two lobes make up the pituitary gland, anterior and posterior. The *anterior lobe* secretes several different hormones. One of these is the *somatotrophic hormone,* or *growth hormone*. Growth hormone controls the growth of your skeleton—your whole body framework. Other secretions of this anterior lobe are called *gonadotropic* (goe-NAD-uh-TROP-ick) *hormones*. They influence the development of your reproductive organs. They also affect the hormone secretion of the ovaries in the female and the testes in the male. The gonadotropic hormones work together with the sex hormones to produce the changes in your body during adolescence. These are the changes that cause you to become an adult.

The anterior lobe of the pituitary gland secretes still other hormones. Some stimulate the secretion of milk in the mammary glands *(lactogenic hormone)*. Others stimulate other endocrine glands such as the thyroid *(thyrotropic hormone)* and the cortex of the adrenal glands *(adrenocorticotropic hormone,* or *ACTH)*.

ACTH has been used in some interesting clinical ways. It has been tried in the treatment of leukemia and arthritis. Some success

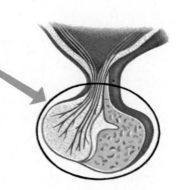

46-6 The pituitary gland is connected by a stalk to the hypothalamus. The hypothalamus regulates the anterior pituitary through blood vessels. The posterior pituitary is connected by nerves to the hypothalamus.

has been reported with certain types of arthritis. Good results in the treatment of asthma and other allergies with ACTH have also been reported. Even if ACTH does not cure these diseases, it may lead to the discovery of their actual causes.

The *posterior lobe* of the pituitary gland releases two hormones. One is *oxytocin*, which helps regulate your blood pressure and stimulates your smooth muscles. During childbirth, oxytocin is secreted in large amounts. Sometimes it is given to help make the uterus contract. The other hormone is *vasopressin*, which controls water resorption in your kidneys. Vasopressin is also called antidiuretic hormone (ADH).

Vasopressin deficiency causes a condition called *diabetes insipidus* (in-SIP-uh-dus). In this condition, large quantities of water are eliminated through the kidneys. This disease should not be confused with true diabetes, which we shall discuss in connection with the pancreas.

There are presently 52 centers in the United States that are conducting growth research. Some individuals can be treated with growth hormones. The National Pituitary Agency collects and distributes these hormones to the growth centers.

WHEN THE PITUITARY GLAND MALFUNCTIONS

The most common disorder of the pituitary gland involves the growth hormone. If the pituitary secretes too much of this hormone while a child is growing, the bones and tissue grow too fast. A *giant* may result. Some giants have been known to grow over 2.5 meters tall and wear size 30 shoes. Sometimes too much growth hormone is secreted in an adult. The bones of the face and hands become thick.

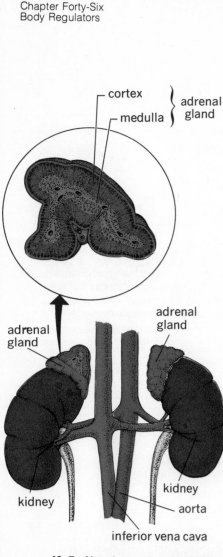

46–7 Note the position of the adrenal glands on the kidneys. What two important hormones do these glands secrete?

The adrenal gland produces hormones that can treat certain conditions. For example, adrenaline is frequently used as a heart stimulant and in the treatment of respiratory problems such as asthma.

But they cannot grow longer because the bones are fully formed in an adult. Organs and soft tissues also enlarge a great deal. This condition is called *acromegaly* (ack-roe-MEG-uh-lee). Victims of this disorder have greatly enlarged jaw bones, noses, and hands and fingers.

Deficiency of the growth hormone slows down the person's growth. These people are pituitary dwarfs called *midgets*. They are perfectly proportioned people, but very tiny. Their minds are not affected so they have normal intelligence. This is quite different from a thyroid dwarf.

THE GLANDS OF EMERGENCY

On top of each kidney are your **adrenal glands,** also called *suprarenals*. These glands have an outer layer called the *cortex*, and an inner part called the *medulla*. Unlike the adrenal medulla, the adrenal cortex is essential for life. The adrenal cortex secretes a complex of hormones called *corticoids*. These hormones control certain phases of carbohydrate, fat, and protein metabolism. They also affect balance of salt and water in your body. The adrenal cortex releases other hormones that control production of some types of white corpuscles and the structure of connective tissue.

If the adrenal cortex is damaged or destroyed, a person develops *Addison's disease*. This also occurs as a result of tuberculosis. Such people get tired easily, feel nauseous, and lose weight. Their circulation fails and their skin color changes. They can be helped by treatment with a corticoid called *cortisone*.

The medulla secretes a hormone called **epinephrine** (ep-uh-NEFF-reen), or *adrenalin*. This hormone can cause sudden body changes during anger or fright that give people startling strength. Because the adrenal glands have this effect, they are called the glands of emergency. **When a great deal of extra epinephrine, or adrenalin, suddenly pours into your blood, this is what happens:**

- You get pale, because the blood vessels in your skin constrict. If you have a surface wound, you will lose less blood because of its movement from the body surface. At the same time, more blood is supplied to your muscles, brain, heart, and other vital organs.
- Your blood pressure goes up, because the blood vessels in your skin have constricted.
- Your heart beats faster.
- Your liver releases some of its stored sugar. This provides material for increased body activity and oxidation.

THE PANCREAS

You know that the **pancreas** produces pancreatic fluid to help digestion. But this is only one function of the pancreas. There are also special groups of cells in the pancreas called **islets of Langerhans.** The islets of Langerhans secrete the hormone **insulin. Insulin** enables the liver to store sugar in the form of glycogen. This hormone also controls the oxidation of sugar.

A person who does not have insulin is unable to store or oxidize sugar properly. So the tissues are deprived of food. And sugar collects in the blood. Some of the extra sugar in the blood is excreted in the urine. Doctors call this condition *diabetes mellitus* (MELL-uh-tuss). Diabetes mellitus is probably caused by a combination of factors. It is not just the failure of the islet cells of the pancreas to make insulin. The disease is also affected by the activity of the pituitary, thyroid, and adrenal glands, as well as the liver. **People who are overweight are more likely to develop this problem. Diabetes mellitus is hereditary.** If it is in your family, your doctor should check the level of your blood sugar regularly. Once this condition is discovered, though, it can usually be controlled. If the disease is in an early stage, and properly treated, the person can lead a perfectly normal life.

Although advances in diabetes research have been made in recent years, more needs to be done. Diabetes can shorten a person's life-span. There are about 10 million diabetics in the United States today. About half of these are unaware that they have the disease.

If too much insulin is produced, the result is a condition called *hypoglycemia*. Literally, this means "low blood sugar." Excess insulin makes the liver store sugar that should be delivered to cells. Hypoglycemia makes a person tire easily. It can be controlled by a low carbohydrate diet.

THE OVARIES AND THE TESTES

The *ovaries* of the female and the *testes* of the male have dual functions. We usually think of these as the organs for producing eggs and sperms. However, **certain cells of both the ovaries and the testes do the work of ductless glands.** The ovary cells secrete female hormones called *estrogen* (ES-truh-jin) and *progesterone* (proe-JES-tuh-rone). Cells in the testes manufacture the male hormone called *testosterone* (tes-TOSS-tuh-rone). This particular hormone can now be made artificially. It is used to help disturbances of sex hormones in both males and females. Male sex hormones are not just produced by the testes. They are also secreted by the cortex of the adrenal glands in both males and females. A female's ovaries normally secrete enough estrogen to neutralize the effects of the male sex hormones from the adrenal glands. But if estrogen secretion in the ovaries is reduced, the female may become mannish. In the same way, low testosterone production in the male testes may result in feminine tendencies. **As you can see, people develop within a wide range of maleness and femaleness.**

Sex hormones affect the development of secondary sex characteristics. These changes appear at the time of the change from child to adult. They begin with the maturation of the ovaries and testes during the stage of life called *puberty.* Among animals, the changes may appear as the large comb of the rooster, the bright feathers of most

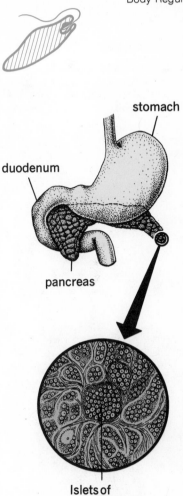

Islets of Langerhans

46-8 The pancreas is both an endocrine gland and a digestive gland located in the curvature of the duodenum.

Diabetes is presently listed as the third largest killer in the United States. It follows heart disease and cancer. In 1975, 38,000 persons died directly from diabetes, and there is evidence that as many as 300,000 deaths could be attributed to the disease and its complications.

The relationship of estrogen therapy to cancer might be discussed here. This is still under investigation and some students may want to update present research.

male birds, and the antlers of deers. Many secondary characteristics are appearing or have appeared in your own body. As a boy approaches puberty, his voice cracks and gets deeper. His beard appears, with a general increase in body hair. The chest broadens and deepens. Rapid growth of the long bones add to his height.

As a girl matures, her breasts develop and her hips get broader. Fat deposits form under the skin in those areas. Around the same time, menstruation begins. These physical changes cause both boys and girls to go through major mental and emotional changes as well. Compare your personality with that of a ten-year-old child.

Testosterone is also responsible for the normal sex drive in males. If the testes of an animal are removed by *castration*, its behavior changes. It becomes more docile and easy to manage. Of course, castration causes the animal to be sterile. If the male animal is young when this operation is performed, it will not develop into a typical male. Its behavior changes, and its body stores more fat. Domestic animals have been treated this way for thousands of years. Today, livestock breeders use castration to increase the weight of their livestock.

THE THYMUS

The *thymus* may also be a ductless gland, but it is not clear if it secretes a hormone. It grows under the breastbone, just above your heart. When you are born, your thymus weighs less than 14 grams. It doubles in size by the time you enter your teens. From then on, it gradually becomes smaller. Cells called *lymphocytes* are produced in the thymus. These may be the parents of the cells that produce antibodies in the lymph nodes and the spleen. **More research may prove that the thymus is important in helping the body defend itself against disease.**

THE HYPOTHALAMUS

The **hypothalamus** is located at the base of the brain, just above the pituitary gland. Research has shown that the hypothalamus plays a vital role in the control of many life functions. The hypothalamus controls many functions that maintain homeostasis in the body. **Body temperature, ion and water balance, and release of pituitary hormones are some of the functions regulated by the hypothalamus.**

You will recall that the pituitary was called the "master gland." Thus, its control by the hypothalamus is important. The hypothalamus detects the imbalances in the body. This is done mostly by detecting imbalances in the blood passing through the hypothalamus. The hypothalamus then directs the pituitary to release the proper amount of the needed hormone.

The *posterior pituitary* is regulated by direct nerve connections from the hypothalamus. For example, if the level of water in the blood is low, it is detected by the hypothalamus. The hypothalamus then directs the posterior pituitary to secrete more vasopressin. This causes the kidneys to resorb more water. The water balance is thus restored.

The connection between the hypothalamus and the anterior pituitary is more indirect. When needed, the hypothalamus secretes substances into the blood that affect the anterior pituitary. These substances are called *releasing factors.* There is a releasing factor for each anterior pituitary hormone. For example, there is a thyrotropin releasing factor (TRF). TRF causes the anterior pituitary to release thyrotropin or thyroid stimulating hormone (TSH). Thyrotropin (TSH) stimulates the release of thyroid hormone from the thyroid gland.

DYNAMIC BALANCE IN THE ENDOCRINE GLANDS

Endocrine glands usually maintain a careful balance among the different hormones secreted in the body. Too much or too little of any hormone can upset that balance. Each gland can affect the work of the other glands, too. While the glands influence each other, there are two more factors that contribute to the checks and balances within your body chemistry.

One of these factors is called *feedback.* **When a substance builds up in the blood, production of the substance is cut down by the endocrine gland.** For instance, you know that the parathyroid hormone regulates the level of calcium in the body. In turn, the concentration of calcium regulates the production of the parathyroid hormone.

Ask students to bring in a recent periodical or newspaper article concerned with some aspect of the endocrine system. Have them make reports to the class.

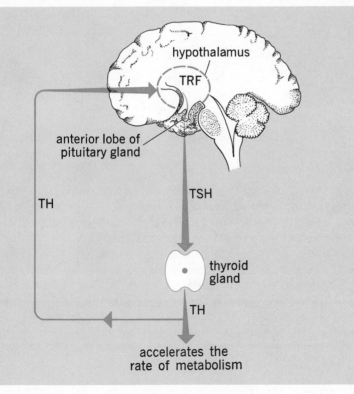

46–9 The diagram shows the feedback relationship between the central nervous system and the thyroid gland.

When the calcium level drops, more parathyroid hormone is secreted to maintain the normal balance. When the proper level of calcium is reached, the parathyroid glands slow down its secretion. This kind of feedback operates in the other glands, and between different glands. In this way, the body maintains a balanced state.

The other factor assisting the checks and balances is the effect of the nervous system on the endocrine glands. The nervous system monitors both internal and external conditions. If needed, the sympathetic nervous system signals the adrenal medulla, for instance. Your adrenal glands then produce extra adrenalin. **Nervous control and feedback are both helpful homeostatic mechanisms in your body. They work to maintain the steady state of the body in constantly changing conditions.**

SUMMARY

Ductless glands are known as endocrine glands. They secrete hormones directly into the bloodstream. Many important hormones are produced by the thyroid, parathyroid, pituitary, and adrenal glands. The pancreas, ovaries, and testes also secrete hormones essential for normal body functions. Together these hormones influence body metabolism, growth, mental ability, and chemical balance in the body fluids. Glands are controlled by their influence on each other, by feedback and by the nervous system. Their delicate balance is maintained by homeostatic mechanisms. If any one of the endocrine glands slows down or becomes overactive, chemical balance is upset and the body reacts by becoming ill.

BIOLOGICALLY SPEAKING

endocrine gland	adrenal gland	progesterone
hormone	epinephrine	testosterone
thyroid	pancreas	puberty
hyperthyroidism	islets of Langerhans	pineal body
hypothyroidism	insulin	thymus gland
parathyroid gland	diabetes mellitus	hypothalamus
pituitary	estrogen	feedback

QUESTIONS FOR REVIEW

1. How does the blood help in the work of the endocrine glands?
2. How does the thyroid gland control the rate of metabolism?
3. Explain hyperthyroidism and hypothyroidism.
4. In what ways do the pituitary and thyroid glands affect growth?
5. How does the pituitary gland affect the sex glands?
6. Compare the body characteristics of a thyroid dwarf and a pituitary dwarf. How do they differ, and in what ways are they similar?
7. What is ACTH? What is its function?
8. In what ways are puberty and adolescence a result of glandular activity?
9. Why does sugar appear in the urine of a person with diabetes mellitus?
10. Explain the role of the hypothalamus in maintaining a balanced condition.

1. Which gland has a hormone that may influence intelligence?
2. How do you account for the fact that the heartbeat of a basketball player increases a great deal before the game as well as during the game?
3. Why is a study of the endocrine glands often carried on at the same time as a study of the nervous system?
4. What hormone injected into the bloodstream of a male rat will often result in a mothering instinct? Why?
5. Discuss dynamic balance in the endocrine system that results from feedback.

chapter forty-seven

Reproduction and Development

OBJECTIVES
- EXPLAIN the significance of sexual reproduction.
- LIST the structures of the male reproductive system.
- DESCRIBE the sperm cell.
- LIST the structures of the female reproductive system.
- EXPLAIN the stages of the menstrual cycle.
- DESCRIBE the development of the human embryo.
- LIST the events of the birth process.

The concept of genetic counseling might be interesting to discuss here. This has become more common in recent years and can help individuals who may need testing or counseling concerning genetic conditions.

47–1 Offspring generally resemble their parents. (Barbara Pfeffer)

SIGNIFICANCE OF SEXUAL REPRODUCTION

Basically, sexual reproduction is the union of two gametes to form a zygote. The zygote is capable of growing into a mature form that resembles its parents. Organisms that reproduce asexually, in a one-parent system, cannot develop much variety. But the combination of unlike genes from two different parents can produce almost endless variety.

As you learned when you studied sexual reproduction in Unit 1, the gonads produce gametes. The gametes form through meiotic division. As the cells divide, the chromosome pairs separate into the haploid cells. The chromosome pairs separate in such a way that gene combinations will be varied. The genes contained in the gametes are always different.

When the zygote is formed by fertilization, the number of chromosomes becomes diploid again. Each parent has contributed one homologous chromosome to each pair of chromosomes. Now the genes function to influence characteristics in the new organism. Of course, all zygotes of a species have the broad characteristics of the particular species. But the combination of genes for unlike characteristics is acquired from the two different parents. So the offspring will vary from both parents.

These variations may also include small but favorable adaptations. These may improve the species from one generation to the next. Even asexually reproducing organisms may sometimes produce favorable mutations. But the species as a group is not as likely to adapt within a one-parent system.

622

In summary, sexual reproduction produces greater chance of variation than asexual reproduction. This variation improves the chances that a species will adapt and survive.

The Male

THE REPRODUCTIVE SYSTEM

The male gonads are the *testes*. They are located outside the body in a pouch of skin called the *scrotum*. As you learned in Chapter Forty-Six, the testes produce the male hormone that controls the development of secondary sex characteristics. **But another important function of the testes is to produce sperms.**

Within the testes are tightly coiled tubes called the *seminiferous* (sem-i-NIFF-a-russ) *tubules*. The cells in the testes divide by meiosis into haploid sperms. The action of the ciliated cells of the seminiferous tubules then move the sperms to the *epididymis* (ep-uh-DID-uh-miss). The epididymis is a storage area. Eventually, the sperms go out of the epididymis through a duct called the **vas deferens** (VASS DEF-uh-renz). This duct carries the sperms past the *seminal vesicles*. A short tube connects the seminal vesicle to the urethra by passing through the **prostate gland.** And a small organ called *Cowper's gland* also leads into the urethra. All three of these organs add their secretions to the sperms as the sperms pass by.

The fertilizing fluid called *semen* is made up of sperms and fluids from the seminal vesicle, prostate gland, and Cowper's gland. The male's urethra is the duct for the passage of semen through the penis. The urethra also carries urine from the urinary bladder to the outside of the body for excretion.

Many students may not be familiar with the internal and external anatomy of the sexes. Large diagrams and/or models can be used.

47–2   The male reproductive system.

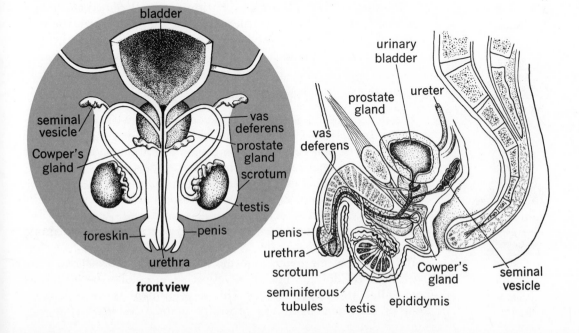

front view

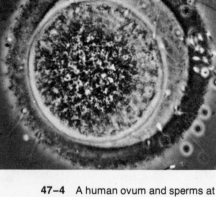

head

nucleus

middle section

mitochondria

tail

end of tail

47–3 The structure of a sperm cell.

47–4 A human ovum and sperms at fertilization. (American Museum of Natural History)

THE SPERM CELL

The human sperm cell is very small compared to the human ovum. The head of a sperm is flattened and oval shaped. It contains the nucleus with the haploid number of chromosomes. The tail acts like a flagellum or whip to move the sperm. The short middle part contains many mitochondria. Cellular respiration occurs in the mitochondria to provide energy for sperm cells. (You may remember the discussion of mitochondria in Chapter Four). The male gamete is a small, active cell. Its energy is obtained from the semen which has a high concentration of the simple sugar fructose. It takes as many as 130 million motile sperms to insure fertilization of one ovum. The sperm fertilizes the ovum by penetrating it. At that point, the tail separates from the rest of the sperm. The head and the connecting middle part enter the ovum. **The nuclei of the sperm and the ovum unite. And the zygote is formed.**

The Female

THE REPRODUCTIVE SYSTEM

The female has a pair of *ovaries* in the abdominal cavity, one on each side. They are about three and a half centimeters long and one and a half centimeters wide. The two ovaries are not connected directly to the oviducts, or **Fallopian tubes.** Instead, when an ovum is released from one of the ovaries, it is drawn into the tubes. These tubes are lined with ciliated cells, which move gently and draw the ovum into the tubes. The ovum moves down the Fallopian tube to the *uterus*, or womb.

The uterus is a hollow, muscular organ with thick walls. It is lined with a mucous membrane containing small glands and many capillaries. If the ovum is not fertilized, it passes through the narrow neck of the uterus, called the *cervix*. The cervix opens into the *vagina*. The unfertilized ovum is discharged from the vagina.

OVARIAN AND UTERINE CYCLE

The development of the ovum is coordinated with the development of the uterus. This is controlled by hormones. **Human ovaries usually produce only one egg in the course of a twenty-eight day cycle of activity.** The cycle is begun by a hormone called the *follicle-stimulating hormone*, or **FSH.** FSH is produced in the anterior lobe of the pituitary gland. This hormone causes a mass of ovarian cells to form a *follicle* in which the ovum is produced. As the egg becomes mature, the follicle fills with fluid containing the hormone **estrogen.**

The release of the ovum from the follicle is called ovulation. After ovulation, the follicle becomes yellowish in color. The follicle is now called the **corpus luteum.** This development is controlled by another hormone from the pituitary gland, the *luteinizing hor-*

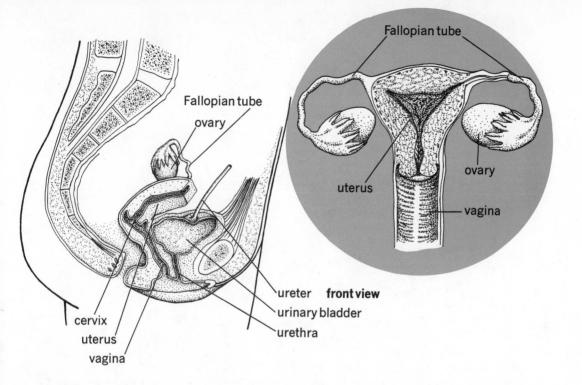

front view

ureter
urinary bladder
urethra

Fallopian tube
ovary

cervix
uterus
vagina

mone, or **LH.** The corpus luteum now produces a hormone, **pro-gesterone.**

Progesterone maintains the growth of the mucous lining of the uterus. If the ovum is not fertilized, the corpus luteum degenerates. So, no more progesterone is produced. The inside lining of the uterus detaches and sloughs off. **The breakdown and discharge of the soft uterine tissues and the unfertilized egg is called** *menstruation.*

The uterine cycle has four distinct stages:

1. *menstruation*, averaging about five days
2. the *follicle stage,* from the end of menstruation to the release of the ovum, between ten and fourteen days
3. *ovulation*, the release of a mature ovum or egg from the ovary
4. *the corpus luteum stage,* from ovulation to menstruation, about ten to fourteen days

The stages of ovum production are coordinated with the changes in the mucous membranes of the uterus.

Fertilization and Development

THE UTERINE LINING PREPARES

When a sperm enters the ovum, a membrane immediately forms around the resulting *zygote*. This is called the *fertilization membrane.* Other sperms cannot get into the ovum after this membrane forms. Fertilization usually takes place in one of the Fallopian

47–5 The female reproductive system.

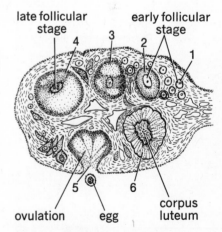

47–6 A representation of a section through the human ovary. In stages 1-4 the ovum is shown maturing. In stage 5, ovulation is shown taking place. In stage 6, the corpus luteum is shown forming.

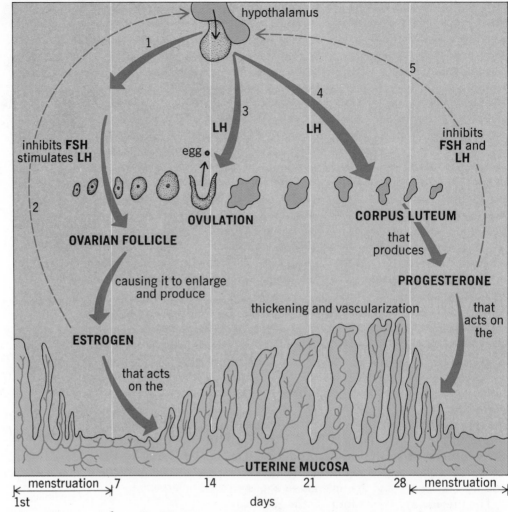

hypothalamus

1

5

3

LH   LH

4

inhibits **FSH**
stimulates **LH**

egg •

inhibits
FSH and
LH

2

OVULATION

CORPUS LUTEUM

OVARIAN FOLLICLE

that
produces

causing it to enlarge
and produce

PROGESTERONE

thickening and vascularization

that
acts on
the

ESTROGEN

that acts
on the

UTERINE MUCOSA

|← menstruation →|7   14   21   28 |← menstruation →|
1st   days

47–7 The relationship of the pituitary
gland to the uterine cycle.

The menstrual cycle is a complex process.
Fig. 47-7 should be gone over slowly and in
detail. Discuss some "menstrual myths" and
how they came about.

tubes. **Fertilization causes several important changes in the female's
body.** The corpus luteum, instead of degenerating, continues to
produce progesterone. Progesterone acts on the uterus. **Progesterone causes the membrane of the uterus to continue to thicken.** Many
additional small glands and capillaries form within the uterine
tissue. This build up prepares the uterus for the zygote.

The zygote reaches the uterus in three to five days. During this
time, the zygote continues to grow. The diploid number of chromosomes has been restored. The zygote goes through a series of mitotic
divisions. In a few days, it has become a mass of cells. During the
early stages of its development, the zygote's energy comes from
the nutrients stored in the large ovum.

THE ZYGOTE'S DEVELOPMENT

After the fertilized ovum has repeatedly divided, it gradually
becomes a sphere of cells. This sphere has a large, fluid-filled cavity.
A mass of cells develop inside one pole of the sphere. Some of these

cells will become the embryo. **An *embryo* is an organism in a very early stage of development.** It does not yet look like a member of a particular species of animal. In the human species, this stage lasts from six to eight weeks after fertilization takes place. At the end of this period. the embryo is about two centimeters long. Its growth rate increases rapidly from then on. And it starts to take on human characteristics. From this point until birth, it is called a *fetus.*

The sphere of cells that forms from the fertilized ovum is called a *blastocyst*. The blastocyst has still not attached itself to the uterine wall. Cells from the inner mass will later form the **primary germ layers.** These cell layers are the *ectoderm*, the *mesoderm*, and the *endoderm*. **These three germ layers will form the various tissues and organs of the body.** Each of these germ layers produce different body structures.

ATTACHMENT OF THE EMBRYO

As the embryo passes down the Fallopian tube to the uterus, a membrane forms around the mass of dividing cells. This is one of several membranes that will form. But since it will not become part of the embryo itself, it is called an **extraembryonic membrane.** This membrane is called the *chorion* (KORE-ee-on). The chorion forms several small, fingerlike projections known as the *chorionic villi.* Enzymes produced by the villi allow them to sink into the uterine

Table 47-1   STRUCTURES FORMED FROM SPECIFIC PRIMITIVE GERM LAYERS

ECTODERM
  skin and skin glands
  hair
  most cartilage
  nervous system
  pituitary gland
  lining of mouth to the pharynx
  part of the lining of rectum
  adrenal medulla

MESODERM
  connective tissue
  bone
  most muscles
  kidneys and ducts
  gonads and ducts
  blood, blood vessels, heart, and lymphatics

ENDODERM
  lining of alimentary canal from pharynx to rectum
  thyroid and parathyroids
  trachea and lungs
  bladder

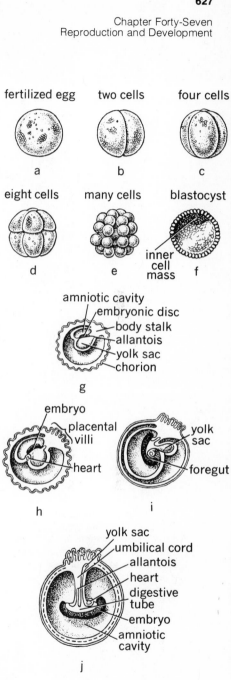

47–8 Immediately following fertilization, the cells of the zygote divide and form the blastocyst. This resembles a hollow ball with a mass of cells located at one end. g, h, i, and j show the development of the extraembryonic membranes that accompany the development of the human embryo.

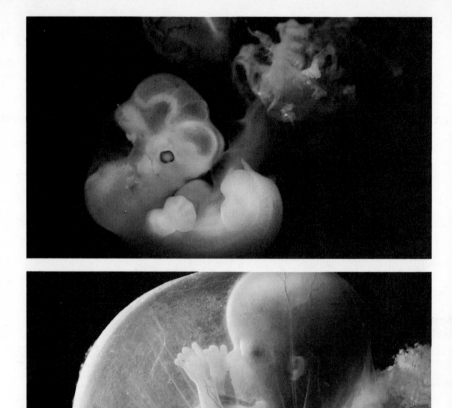

47-9 Development of the human embryo and fetus. The embryo at five weeks and a fetus of four months. (Lennart Nilsson)

membrane. This puts the villi in close contact with the capillaries in the uterine lining. Thus, nourishment is provided for the embryo.

Soon another extraembryonic membrane, the *amnion*, develops. The amnion forms a cavity around the developing embryo. This cavity is filled with fluid. This amniotic fluid protects the embryo from injury and keeps it moist. The third extraembryonic membrane is the *yolk sac*. The human yolk sac is small and not significant. But for animals that hatch from eggs, the yolk provides the food for the embryo. The *allantois* (uh-LAN-toe-iss) is the fourth extraembryonic membrane. In humans, it is present for only a short time. In birds and reptiles, though, this membrane acts as an embryonic lung.

When the chorionic villi lodge in the uterine wall, the capillaries break down and form blood sinuses around the villi. Food and waste exchange occurs between the mother and the embryo. This exchange results from diffusion through the thin membrane of the chorionic villi. **But there is no direct connection between the blood of**

the mother and embryo. The area where the chorionic villi meet maternal blood supply within the uterus is called the *placenta.*

With growth, the area that attached the embryo to the yolk sac and allantois lengthens into the *umbilical cord.* The developing embryo is connected to the placenta by two umbilical arteries, one umbilical vein, and the allantoic duct.

BIRTH OF THE CHILD

The period of fetal development ends when the child is born. **Birth occurs about forty weeks after the egg is fertilized.** The smooth muscles of the uterus begin to contract. The membrane of the amnion breaks. And the amniotic fluid passes out through the vagina. Muscles in the cervix of the uterus and the vagina relax. The size of the opening gets larger. More uterine contractions force the child from the uterus, usually head first. But the baby is still attached to the placenta by the umbilical cord. Right after birth, the cord is tied and cut. This is done so that the child will not lose blood through the umbilical vessels. Your *navel* is the scar on your abdomen where your umbilical cord attached you to the placenta. After the child is born, the placenta and the remains of the amnion are expelled. This is called the afterbirth.

Until the baby is born, it receives both oxygen and nourishment through the placenta. As the fetus grows, the movement of its thoracic muscles draws fluid into its lungs. The lungs expand because of the fluid. The first cries of the baby remove the fluid and fill its lungs with air.

Another important change takes place at birth. **In the fetus, the blood did not circulate through its lungs.** Instead, the blood would leave the right ventricle and go through a vessel called the *ductus arteriosus.* This vessel took the blood to the aorta. So the lungs were bypassed while the fetus developed. At birth, though, the ductus arteriosus closes off. Now the blood must flow through the pul-

Students may be interested in the natural or Lamaze method of birth. Ask some students to report on this method and how it differs from other birth methods.

47–10 Some forty weeks after fertilization of an ovum, uterine contractions begin, and a baby is born. (Maternity Center Assoc. of New York)

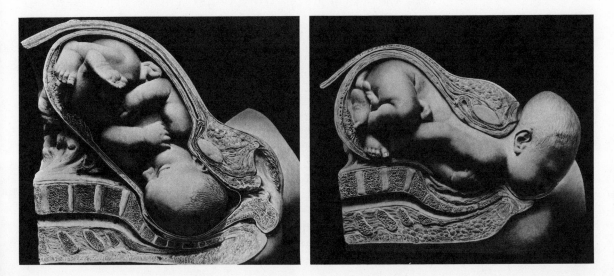

monary arteries to the lungs. The new supply of blood helps the lungs expand as the baby begins to breathe air.

Occasionally, the ductus arteriosus fails to close off completely. When this happens, not all the blood gets to the lungs. The oxygen content of the blood then falls below normal. In severe cases, the baby's skin will appear to have a bluish color. Such infants are called *blue babies*. Often the vessel will close off naturally in time. But surgery is sometimes required to tie off the vessel.

While the blood is circulating through the fetus, there is an opening between the atria of the heart. This opening is called the *foramen ovale*. A membrane grows over this opening, normally closing it completely soon after birth. If the opening does not close, the blood from the atria mix. Thus oxygenated blood mixes with deoxygenated blood. This also causes a "blue baby."

SUMMARY

Sexual reproduction combines the genetic material from two different parents. This results in greater variation. Fertilization takes place internally. The testes of the male produce gametes called sperms. The sperms are motile when they are released. Sperm cells are released in a nutritive fluid called semen. The ovum is very large compared to the sperms. It contains the food for the early life stages of the zygote. The production of several hormones by the female coordinates the development of the ovum and the uterine wall. If fertilization does not occur, the body sheds the soft uterine lining materials. This process is called menstruation. The entire cycle takes about 28 days. If fertilization does occur, the zygote travels down the Fallopian tube to the uterus. It becomes a many-celled sphere surrounded by the first of four extraembryonic membranes. The embryo then becomes attached to the uterine lining. The fetus is totally dependent on the mother for oxygen and nourishment. These materials are transferred by diffusion through thin membranes. The blood of the mother and fetus do not mix. At the time the baby is born, changes in its circulatory and respiratory systems allow it to breathe and become physically independent.

BIOLOGICALLY SPEAKING

vas deferens	LH	embryo
prostate gland	estrogen	fetus
semen	ovulation	primary germ layers
Fallopian tube	corpus luteum	extraembryonic membranes
cervix	progesterone	placenta
vagina	menstruation	umbilical cord
FSH		

QUESTIONS FOR REVIEW

1. Of what advantage to a species is sexual reproduction?
2. List the organs that sperms pass through in the male reproductive system.
3. What is semen? What is its function?
4. How does the number of sperms in the human compare to the number of ova? Explain the significance of this difference.
5. Describe the path of the ovum in the female reproductive system.

6. Describe the effect of the sex hormones on the reproductive cycle in the female.
7. Name and define the four stages in the uterine cycle.
8. Describe the changes in the formation of the embryo from the zygote.
9. Name the four extraembryonic membranes and explain what each one does.
10. Name several structures produced from each primary germ layer.
11. Name the parts of the umbilical cord.
12. Describe the important changes that take place in the circulatory system after birth.

1. Why must fertilization occur in a Fallopian tube before the ovum moves into the uterus?
2. Explain why a hormone imbalance that affects the pituitary gland might result in problems with ovarian function.
3. If an egg is fertilized, menstruation does not occur, and the lining of the uterus is prepared for implanting of the embryo. How do hormones cause this?
4. Discuss the importance of the ductus arteriosus as a bypass from the pulmonary circulation to the systemic circulation in a fetal heart.

Books

Alder, Irving, and Ruth Adler, *Taste, Touch, and Smell*.
The John Day Company, Inc., New York. 1967. A survey of the three main senses of man.

Asimov, Isaac, *How Did We Find Out About Vitamins?*
Walker and Co., New York, N.Y. 1974. An excellent case study of several vitamin deficiency diseases.

Begbie, G. Hugh, *Seeing and the Eye*.
Natural History Press, Garden City, New York. 1969. Takes the reader through the entire complex relating to vision, including the physics of light, anatomy of the eye, and the function of the brain.

Cohen, Daniel, *Human Nature–Animal Nature: The Biology of Human Behavior*.
McGraw-Hill Book Co., New York, N.Y. 1975. A very interesting book that examines the phylogenetic parallels between human and animal behavior.

Deaton, John G., M.D., *New Parts for Old: The Age of Organ Transplants*.
Franklin Publishing Company, Inc., Palisade, N.J. 1974. Relates the case histories of surgeons, patients, and scientists who participated in organ transplants.

Edwards, Gabrielle I., *The Student Biologist Explores Drug Abuse*.
Richard Rosen Press, Inc., New York, N.Y. 1975. An excellent presentation of the biological facts of drug abuse: its effect on the body, the chemistry of each drug, and where it is obtained.

Girdano, Dorothy Dusek, and Daniel A. Girdano, *Drugs—A Factual Account*.
  Addison-Wesley Publishing Co., Inc., Reading, MA. 1973. Presents a wide
  variety of information concerning such drugs as: alcohol, marijuana, LSD,
  amphetamines, barbiturates, sedatives, opiates, and nonprescription drugs.

Howell, F. Clark, and the Editors of *Life Magazine, Early Man*.
  Time-Life Books (Time, Inc.), New York. 1965. A picture-essay book covering
  the day-to-day problems and general conditions of life in the ancient times.

Jenkins, Marie M., *Embryos and How They Develop*.
  Holiday House, New York, N.Y. 1975. An easily understood survey of embryology, covering developmental processes from initial life stages to adult
  in animals.

Julian, Cloyd J., and Elizabeth Noland Jackson, *Modern Sex Education* (paper-
  back).
  Holt, Rinehart and Winston, Publishers, New York. 1972. A presentation of
  the biological facts in relation to behavioral and psychological problems of
  young people.

Luria, S. E., *Life: The Unfinished Experiment*.
  Charles Scribner's Sons, New York, 1973. The author predicts the future with
  respect to: evolution, heredity, complexity, and controls.

McMinn, R. M. H., *The Human Gut*, Oxford Biology Reader.
  Oxford University Press, London, 1974. A basic understanding of the human
  digestive system.

Muir, A. R., *The Mammalian Heart*, Oxford Biology Reader.
  Oxford University Press, London, 1971. Describes the anatomy and physiology of the Mammalian heart.

Ochsner, Alton, *Smoking: Your Choice Between Life and Death*.
  Simon and Schuster, New York. 1970. A comprehensive presentation of all
  the ramifications of smoking. Includes latest information on smoking and
  health.

Riedman, Sarah R., *Hormones: How They Work*.
  Abelard-Schuman Ltd., New York. 1973. A description of the hormones and
  a description of the effects they have on various parts of the body.

Schmidt-Nielsen, Knut, *Animal Physiology* (3rd ed.).
  Prentice-Hall, Inc., Englewood Cliffs, N.J. 1970. An excellent account of the
  physical processes involved in body functions.

Simeons, A. J. W., MD., *Food: Facts, Foibles, and Fables*.
  Funk and Wagnalls, New York. 1968. An unusual account of the development
  of food from prehistoric times to present day.

Weart, Edith L., *The Story of Your Respiratory System*.
  Coward-McCann, Inc., New York. 1964. Diagrammatic explanation of the
  respiratory system and the functions of its different parts.

Articles

Adolph, E. F., "The Heart's Pacemaker." *Scientific American*, March, 1967. An interesting article that describes the pacemaker as the source of the impulses that establish the basic rhythm of the heart.

Clarke, C. A., "The Prevention of 'Rhesus' Babies." *Scientific American*, November, 1968. An excellent presentation on the effects of Rh factor.

Davenport, Horace W., "Why the Stomach Does Not Digest Itself." *Scientific American*, January, 1972. A fascinating article on how the stomach protects itself from protein digesting enzymes.

Dempsey, David, "Transplants Are Common; Now It's the Organs That Have Become Rare." *The New York Times Magazine*, October 13, 1974. An interesting account of the need for organs that must meet the demands of transplantation.

Grimspoon, Lester, "Marijuana." *Scientific American*, March, 1969. Myths and facts about marijuana use are explored.

Heimer, Lennart, "Pathways in the Brain." *Scientific American*, July, 1971. Considers the intricate pathways of the brains impulses.

Levine, Seymour, "Stress and Behavior." *Scientific American*, January, 1971. A study on stress and its effect on the behavior of mammals.

Payne, Melvin, "The Leakeys of Africa: In Search of Prehistoric Man." *National Geographic*, February, 1965. Tells how the remains of early humans were found in the Olduvai Gorge in Tanganyika, Africa.

Segal, Sheldon J., "The Physiology of Human Reproduction." *Scientific American*, September, 1974. A somewhat advanced discussion of the physiology of the human reproductive system.

unit 8

ECOLOGICAL RELATIONSHIPS

We have looked closely at all types of organisms. We have studied their food needs, their organs, their systems, and the makeup of their cells. But no organism can live completely on its own. Each is dependent on other organisms and on the physical environment. This unit will treat the living world. We will look at its forests, grasslands, deserts, lakes, and oceans. Each of these forms a community for living things. Studying these communities is a fascinating part of biology.

People have a great influence on all aspects of the environment. Unfortunately, this influence is not always a good one. But humans have special advantages. We can learn from our mistakes. And we can discover solutions to the many environmental problems that face us.

THE SCIENCE OF THE ENVIRONMENT

All organisms depend on their surroundings for carrying on the activities of life. Biologists study the relationships of these organisms to their environment and to each other. This study is called *ecology*. The word means "the study of homes." When we look at the field or pond or forest where a plant or animal lives, we are looking at its "home."

Ecologists work everywhere in the world. They look closely at the "homes" of all forms of life. Any forest, field, pond, lake, or ocean where life exists can be a laboratory to the ecologist.

THE BIOSPHERE—LAYER OF LIFE

Our planet, Earth, and its surrounding atmosphere are immense. But the places in them where life can exist are limited. There is life in the lower atmosphere surrounding our planet. And there is life in our oceans and other bodies of water. Finally, there is life on the land and a few feet beneath its surface. **This thin layer where life exists is called the *biosphere.***

The biosphere is affected by many factors. Radiation from the sun is the most important factor.

Why? As you know, green plants need solar energy to make food. Also, some of the sun's energy is turned into heat when it reaches the earth. Many organisms need this heat to survive. Heat serves other purposes, too. For example, heat creates winds and causes water to evaporate. This water later returns to the earth's surface as rain or snow. We may think of the whole biosphere as one big biological system. In our discussion of ecology, however, we will also think of it as made up of many smaller parts, or units.

ECOSYSTEMS AS UNITS OF THE BIOSPHERE

What is an *ecosystem?* **An ecosystem is an environment in which living and nonliving things affect one another. In an ecosystem, materials are used over and over again.** An ecosystem may be a bowl containing a fish, a snail, water plants, water, and sand. It may be a person in a space ship. Or it may be larger, such as a forest, river, or pond.

A lake is a good example of an ecosystem. Many different kinds of organisms live in a lake. **The organisms that live together in an ecosystem form a biotic community.** They provide food for each other, and help keep each other alive. A group of organisms of the same kind within a community is called a ***population.*** In a lake, there are many species of fish that make up the fish population. An even greater number of insect species make up the insect population of a lake. **Each population has a special function in the ecosystem.**

chapter forty-eight

Introduction to Ecology

OBJECTIVES
- DEFINE ecology, ecosystem, and biosphere.
- EXPLAIN interactions in the biotic community.
- DISCUSS the interaction between the biotic community and the physical environment.
- DESCRIBE the water cycle.
- DESCRIBE the carbon-oxygen cycle.
- EXPLAIN the nitrogen cycle.
- LIST the environmental factors that control the changes in a population.
- DISCUSS human population growth.

Ecosystems are communities of living things that offer mutual support to each other. The survival of each member of the system directly relates to the survival of the entire ecosystem.

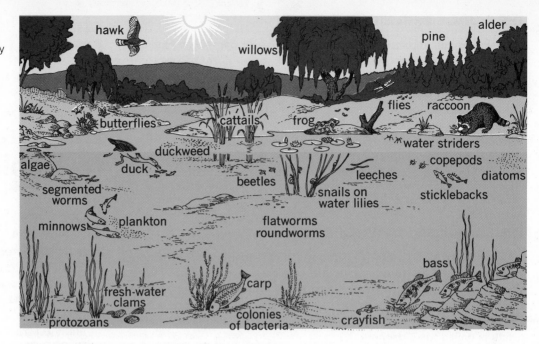

48–1 A freshwater lake is an example of an ecosystem.

An ecosystem also has a nonliving part. This is called the *physical environment.* It has an important influence on the living part. The ecosystem can be thought of in the following way:

Point out to students that an ecosystem that includes a variety of species is more stable than one with fewer varieties. Discuss some of the reasons for this.

ecosystem

biotic   physical
community ←——→ environment

Three kinds of relationships occur in an ecosystem. 1) Interactions take place among members of the biotic community. 2) Interactions take place between the biotic community and the physical environment. 3) Also, there are interactions among the physical factors.

THE BIOTIC COMMUNITY

Let's look at the lake ecosystem again. As we have said, the organisms in this ecosystem depend on each other. They also compete for food, light, oxygen, and growing space. Organisms in the same population usually compete with each other more than they compete with organisms of other populations. This is because like organisms have the same needs. For example, cattails growing near the shore need the same soil and soil depth for growing. So they must all compete for the same living space. However, cattails do not compete very strongly with duckweed. This is because duckweed does not need the same living space. It grows on the surface of the water.

THE BIOTIC COMMUNITY AND THE PHYSICAL ENVIRONMENT

Three aspects of the physical environment are extremely important to the biotic community. These are sunlight, soil, and temperature. All green plants need sunlight for photosynthesis. Even green plants that grow in a lake need the sun. This means that they must grow close enough to the water's surface to get the sun's rays. How deep the sunlight will pass through the water depends on how clear the water is. A heavy growth of algae or stirred up mud, for example, makes the water cloudy. In the clearest lakes, light can pass as deep as twenty-five meters.

The remains of dead plants and animals build up on lake bottoms. Over the years, the size of the lake may be reduced as dead plants build up at the shoreline. Decaying plants give off organic acids and pigments. These substances often change the chemical makeup and color of the water.

Water temperature is important to many organisms living in a lake ecosystem. This is especially true of temperature changes from day to day and season to season. The effects of temperature will be discussed in the next chapter.

Humans are also important in many ecosystems. People do not live in lakes, of course. But they sometimes pollute them. And water pollution by industrial waste or sewage can affect an ecosystem. It can change the balance and distribution of organisms. Water pollution can also change the water's chemical makeup. People also cause ecological problems by changing the courses of rivers or building dams. When such changes are not well planned, they can throw ecosystems out of balance.

48–2 This crater lake was created by a volcanic eruption. It represents a permanent change in the physical environment. (Wards Natural Science Establishment)

CHANGES IN THE PHYSICAL ENVIRONMENT

Some changes in the physical environment of an ecosystem are temporary. For example, a cloudy day will reduce sunlight. Other changes last longer. The shape and makeup of a lake can be changed when a flood carries many different materials into it. There are some changes in the physical environment that are permanent. An earthquake can change the course of a stream so it no longer runs into a lake. New springs may carry chemicals into a lake's water. Such changes always have their effect on the lake's ecosystem.

Physical Cycles

CHANGING ECOSYSTEMS

As you see, the ecosystem is constantly changing. You also know that water, oxygen, carbon, and nitrogen are very important to all life. But did you know that they exist in limited amounts? Organisms have been using the same water, oxygen, carbon, and nitrogen over and over again since the beginning of life. The reuse of a substance is called a *physical cycle*.

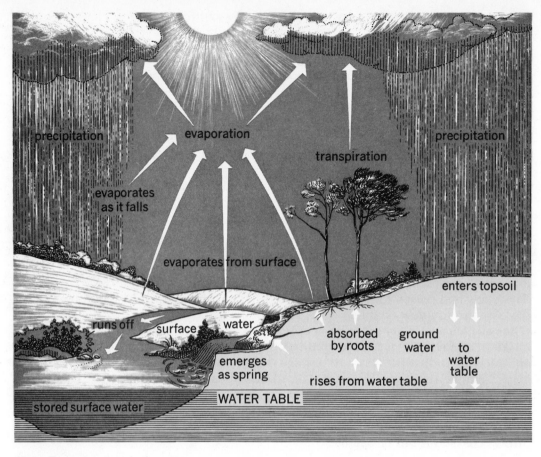

48–3 Trace the steps in the water cycle shown above.

THE WATER CYCLE

Point out to students that food chains, the water cycle, carbon-oxygen cycle, and nitrogen cycle are all intricately involved in the success or failure of the biotic community and the various organisms in it.

Water moves continuously from the atmosphere to the earth and back again. This is the *water cycle.* Water moving from the atmosphere to earth is called ***precipitation.*** Water moving from the earth to atmosphere is called ***evaporation.*** Rain is one kind of precipitation. When it rains, some of the water evaporates as it falls. And some evaporates from the surface of the ground. Much of the rainwater runs along the surface of the ground. This *runoff* water moves from rivulet to stream to river. Eventually it reaches a pond, lake, or the ocean. Water evaporates constantly from the surfaces of these bodies of water. Rainwater also soaks into the ground. This is called ***groundwater.*** Some groundwater flows through springs or underground streams. This water, like the runoff water, may reach a pond, lake, or the ocean. During dry periods, it may move upward through the soil. Then it will evaporate again into the atmosphere. Warm air carries this water vapor upward. As the air rises,

Students may be interested in examining their own communities for ways in which man has influenced the natural water flow.

it cools. The water vapor then condenses into water droplets. We see these droplets as clouds. When enough droplets collect, they form drops which fall from the clouds as rain. Snow is made in the same way. But low temperature freezes the vapor.

LIVING THINGS AND THE WATER CYCLE

Both plants and animals are involved in the water cycle. Plants absorb water through their roots. They give off water vapor from their leaves. All animals drink water. They also give off some water when they exhale. Some animals give off water when they sweat or excrete. On the whole, however, plants and animals do not play a big part in the water cycle.

THE CARBON-OXYGEN CYCLE

Two basic life processes are involved in the *carbon-oxygen cycle.* These processes are respiration and photosynthesis. Land organisms take oxygen from the atmosphere. Water organisms use the oxygen that is dissolved in water.

During respiration, compounds containing carbon are oxydized. As a result, carbon dioxide is released into the environment. During photosynthesis, green plants take water and carbon dioxide from the environment. In this process, water molecules are broken down. These hydrogen atoms from the water molecules combine

A visit to the local water source and purification plant will be interesting to students. Some students may not know where their water originates, and how it is purified and brought to their homes.

Stress to students the vital nature of the carbon-oxygen cycle. Without plants, animals could not survive and of course, the opposite is also true.

48–4 The carbon-oxygen cycle.

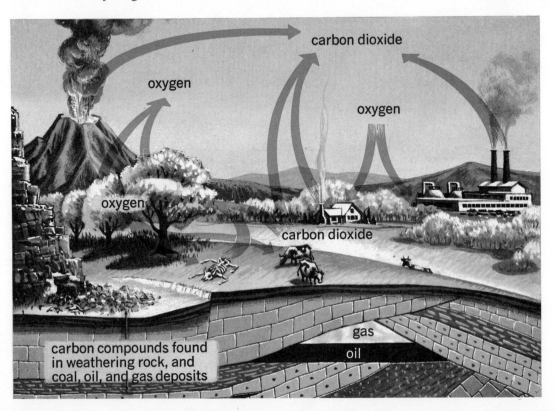

carbon dioxide

oxygen

oxygen

oxygen

carbon dioxide

gas

oil

carbon compounds found in weathering rock, and coal, oil, and gas deposits

Discuss how we have polluted the natural
oxygen-carbon cycle. This pollution has
endangered both plants and animals.

with carbon dioxide. Then green plants use these to form carbohydrates. When this happens, oxygen from the water molecules is given off into the atmosphere. The atmosphere normally contains about 21 percent oxygen and 0.04 percent carbon dioxide.

Another part of the carbon-oxygen cycle involves the making of organic compounds. Plants use carbon dioxide to make carbohydrates during photosynthesis. The other organic compounds are made from these carbohydrates. Plant-eating animals use these organic compounds to make their own protoplasm. They, in turn, are eaten by other animals. These animals also use these compounds. All organic compounds contain carbon. When plants and animals die, the organic compounds in them break down. The carbon leaves their decaying bodies as carbon dioxide.

Rocks and mineral fuels play a small part in this cycle, too. For example, when coal and petroleum form or decompose, oxygen and carbon are involved. Carbon dioxide is also released when something burns.

THE NIGROGEN CYCLE

48–5   The nitrogen cycle.

The nitrogen cycle involves green plants, animals, and several kinds of bacteria. Let's begin with green plants. The plant's roots absorb

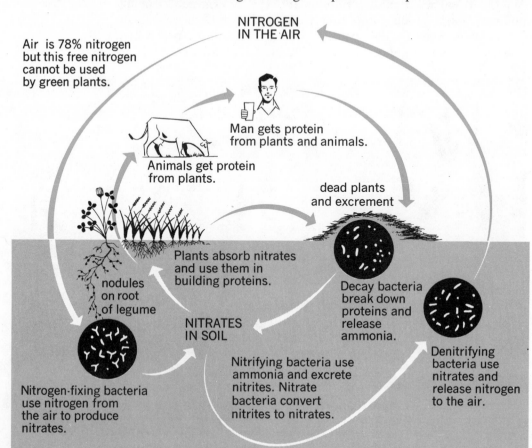

NITROGEN
IN THE AIR

Air is 78% nitrogen
but this free nitrogen
cannot be used
by green plants.

Man gets protein
from plants and animals.

Animals get protein
from plants.

dead plants
and excrement

nodules
on root
of legume

Plants absorb nitrates
and use them in
building proteins.

Decay bacteria
break down
proteins and
release
ammonia.

NITRATES
IN SOIL

Nitrifying bacteria use
ammonia and excrete
nitrites. Nitrate
bacteria convert
nitrites to nitrates.

Denitrifying
bacteria use
nitrates and
release nitrogen
to the air.

Nitrogen-fixing bacteria
use nitrogen from
the air to produce
nitrates.

nitrates from the soil. These compounds contain nitrogen combined with oxygen and usually sodium and potassium. Green plants add this nitrogen to the carbon, hydrogen, and oxygen which had been combined during photosynthesis. Sulfur and phosphorus may also be added. This forms proteins.

Animals get protein by eating plants or other animals. Digestion separates this protein into amino acids. These amino acids then combine to form another protein. Proteins are used in forming protoplasm. These proteins are specific to the animal in which they form.

But animals do not turn all of the protein into protoplasm. Some is broken down and releases energy. When this happens, the animal excretes nitrogen wastes. Then bacteria in soil or water break down these compounds even more.

Bacteria also break down dead organisms. Nitrogen from the decaying organism's protein combines with hydrogen. This combination forms *ammonia.* This part of the nitrogen cycle is called **ammonification.** Other bacteria in soil oxidize ammonia to form *nitrites.* Nitrites cannot be absorbed by plant roots. Still other bacteria oxidize nitrites to form *nitrates.* This process is called **nitrification.** These nitrates can be absorbed by plant roots. And the nitrogen cycle begins again.

About 78 percent of our atmosphere is nitrogen. But this nitrogen cannot be used by green plants. However, two groups of bacteria can change atmospheric nitrogen into nitrates and nitrites. One group lives in the soil. The other lives in the roots of legumes. Legumes are plants such as clover and alfalfa. The bacteria get sugar from the legumes and supply them with nitrates in return. This process is called **nitrogen fixation.**

Review the importance of bacteria and refer students to Chapter Sixteen. Nitrogen-fixing bacteria are essential to the nitrogen cycle.

Samples of legumes—seeds, fresh or dried plants, and roots—should be brought in to class to show nodules.

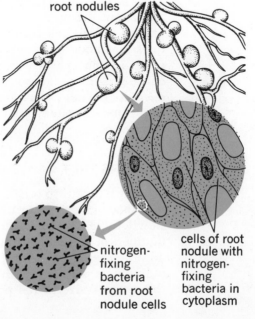

root nodules

nitrogen-fixing bacteria from root nodule cells

cells of root nodule with nitrogen-fixing bacteria in cytoplasm

48–6 Nitrogen-fixing bacteria are found in the root nodules of legumes as shown in the photograph and the diagram. (Hugh Spencer)

Legumes receive more nitrates than they need. The extra nitrates collect in the soil. So when farmers plant clover or alfalfa, they are building up the nitrates from atmospheric nitrogen in the soil. This makes the soil good for growing crops.

One part of the nitrogen cycle is not good for agriculture. Some bacteria free nitrogen by breaking down ammonia, nitrites, and nitrates. This process is called *denitrification.* Soil can lose nitrogen this way. However, the bacteria that free nitrogen from the soil are anaerobic. That is, they do not thrive in oxygen. They are most abundant in tightly packed, waterlogged soil. Farmers with well-drained, cultivated fields do not have much trouble with denitrification.

POPULATION CHANGES

As mentioned earlier, a group of organisms of the same kind is called a population. **The number of organisms in a population can change from season to season and year to year.** Ecologists can measure these changes. They count the number of individuals in a large area at different times. The number that they find in a certain area at any given time is called *population density.*

Why is knowing the population density important? It provides valuable information. For example, it may help us understand why the numbers and kinds of grasses in a field change at different times of the year. With this information, people who graze cattle can use natural pastures without destroying them. Also, game laws are based on population studies. Careful management of commercial fisheries and pest control depends a great deal on population studies.

How are density studies made? Obviously, ecologists cannot count all of the clover plants in a field. Instead, they select several areas large enough to give a representative sample. Then they actually count the number of plants in that area. Usually, organisms are not distributed evenly. Density studies help answer important questions about this uneven distribution. What factors cause uneven distribution? Why do populations vary from year to year? Will cattle grazing at one time of the year make the clover population decrease the next year? Answers to questions like these can help us to restore ecosystems that have been damaged. And they can help us prevent future damage.

FACTORS THAT CAUSE CHANGES IN POPULATION DENSITY

What happens to organisms when they are placed in an ecosystem more favorable to their development? First, the population slowly increases. Next, the reproductive rate increases. Then, the numbers of individuals multiply very fast. Finally, the rate of population increase levels off. In a balanced ecosystem, the number of individuals will vary within a definite range. This range is called the average size of the population, represented by an S-shaped curve.

The leveling off at the top of this curve is interesting to biologists. The factors that keep the population at this level come from two places. They come from within the population itself and from the outside. Here is an example of how leveling off occurs. If you were to begin a paramecium culture, you could make density counts regularly. The first result would be an S-shaped curve. But after a while, the population density would begin to drop quickly. Why? When you first started the culture, there was plenty of food. As the population size increased, the reproduction rate increased because more individuals were dividing. Soon the density could get no greater because there was not enough food and oxygen. Overpopulation turned the curve in the opposite direction. The buildup of metabolic wastes also began to change the environment. The death rate soon became higher than the birth rate. The end result in the culture would be zero population.

Just about the same things happen in larger ecosystems. But they generally work to limit the population rather than to destroy it completely. What happens, for example, when the birth rate of trout in a lake is higher than the death rate? The trout population increases. This means greater competition for food. Many trout starve to death or become weakened from the lack of food. The weakened trout are more likely to die from other causes, such as parasites or disease. It is also harder for them to protect themselves from predators. When enough trout die, the rest of the population again has enough food. And the process maintains a balance.

Factors like reproductive and death rates, parasitism, disease, and predation depend on population density. Ecologists call these *density-dependent factors.*

Some factors affect populations no matter what their density is. These are called *density-independent* factors. They include changes in weather, temperature, humidity, daily and seasonal light, and available energy. In some areas, for example, the first frosts of fall reduce the insect population, no matter how dense it may be.

POPULATION LEVELS

In the paramecium culture, we have seen some of the disadvantages of a large group of organisms living together. But sometimes there are advantages as well. A large band of monkeys, for example, has more individuals to look out for danger. A large flock of birds may present a confusing picture·to a hawk looking for food. A large herd of deer gives each member more protection than a small group does. On a warm day, a large swarm of honey bees may keep their hive from melting by fanning it. A few bees could not do this. A high population level makes it easier for the organisms to find mates. This means that the rate of reproduction will probably be greater. Some populations, like bees, ants, and termites, are very social. Their efficiency depends on large numbers of organisms living together. **We see that a large population can sometimes change the environment to benefit the organism.**

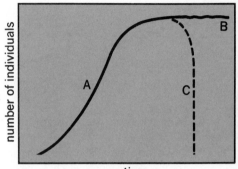

48–7 The S-shaped curve (A) represents the growth of a population in a new habitat. Once the organism is established in the ecosystem, the population density remains fairly stable. It is marked by only minor changes (B). If a population is kept in a limited environment, it will rapidly die out (C).

48–8 The hawk is a natural enemy of the rabbit, upon which it preys. (Joe Branney, AMWEST)

Point out to students that there is a tendency toward overpopulation in nature and this results in competition for both food and shelter.

It is interesting to see how different populations help to keep an ecosystem in balance. Consider this situation in an open field. A meadow mouse runs through the grasses searching for seeds. You might think that this seed-eater will reduce the population of next generation of grasses. But plants produce many more seeds than are needed to keep their population the same. It would take many mice eating seeds to change the grass population density the next season. But what keeps down the mouse population? An owl may swoop down and catch the mice. The owl is one of the **natural enemies** of mice and other small mammals. It is called a *predator* (PRED-uh-ter) because it preys on (or catches and eats) other animals. The animals eaten are called the *prey*. Without predators, mice might take over this field. If they did, two things would happen. First, they would reduce the number of grasses. Second, more mice would be competing for less food. Then, lack of food would eventually reduce the mouse population as well. This often happens when predators are removed from an ecosystem. **Wherever life is found, natural enemies play an important part in maintaining the density of populations.** Ecologists have introduced predators into ecosystems. By doing so, they have been able to control the population of certain pests.

UNDERCROWDING AND OVERCROWDING

A decline in the population density of an organism may lead to undercrowding. This may be harmful to the species involved. For example, whales have been over-hunted for centuries. The decrease in their numbers makes it harder for them to find mates. As a result, the rate of reproduction decreases. And the population density is lowered even further.

An expanding population could very easily lead to overcrowding. The environment of the organism would eventually be unable to support such growth. If this happens, there would be greater competition for available food, oxygen, and space. Scientists have studied the effects of overcrowding in many organisms. It was observed that overcrowding in rats led to aggression, disease, decline in births, and many abnormal behavior problems.

HUMAN POPULATION GROWTH

The density factors we have been discussing affect human populations, too. We can determine the rate of human population increase by looking at daily births and deaths. An estimated 270,000 babies are born into the world every day. There are an estimated 142,000 daily deaths. If you subtract deaths from births, you get the estimated daily rate of population increase. It is believed that the human population increases by about 128,000 individuals each day. Of course, common sense tells us that this rate will probably increase under natural conditions. The more people there are, the more babies there are likely to be produced. In forty-five years, the world population probably will be more than 50 billion people. If our present rate of food production stays the same, there will not be enough food to feed everyone. Already, more than 10,000 people die from starvation or malnutrition every day. So you can see that some of the same factors that control the density of other organisms also play a part in human population density.

645

Chapter Forty-Eight
Introduction to Ecology

Discuss overcrowding among human populations and what can be done about this problem. The concept of Zero Population Growth (ZPG) may be discussed here.

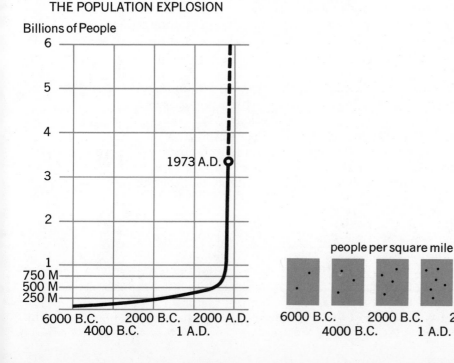

THE POPULATION EXPLOSION

SUMMARY   All organisms depend on their surroundings to stay alive. The study of the relationships of these organisms to their environment and to each other is called *ecology*.

There is a thin layer of life starting a few feet below ground and extending through the lower atmosphere of our planet. It is called the *biosphere*. It may be considered one huge *ecosystem*. Or, it may be divided into many small ecosystems. An ecosystem is an environment in which living and nonliving affect one another. It is also a system in which materials are used over and over again. Organisms that live together in an ecosystem form a *biotic community*. Groups of the same kind of organisms are called *populations*.

The nonliving part of the ecosystem is called the *physical environment*. It has much influence on the biotic community. Water, oxygen, carbon, and nitrogen are all important to life. They exist in a limited amount and are used over and over again by organisms. The processes of reuse are called *physical cycles*.

A stable population density is important to a balanced ecosystem. Many factors can change population density. Lack of food, for example, will cause a population to decrease. Removal of natural enemies will usually make it temporarily increase. These same factors influence human population density.

BIOLOGICALLY SPEAKING

biosphere	runoff water	nitrogen fixation
ecosystem	groundwater	denitrification
biotic community	carbon-oxygen cycle	population density
population	nitrogen cycle	natural enemies
water cycle	ammonification	predator
precipitation	nitrification	prey
evaporation		

QUESTIONS FOR REVIEW

1. What is the biosphere?
2. How would you make a density study?
3. What determines the size of the population of an organism at any time?
4. What does an ecologist mean when he speaks of the ecosystem?
5. How do the biotic community and the physical environment affect each other?
6. What changes take place in the physical environment?
7. Describe the water cycle and tell why it is important.
8. Summarize the carbon-oxygen cycle and its value to living things.
9. Why is the nitrogen cycle so important?
10. Generally, how do density-dependent factors differ from density-independent factors?
11. In what ways can a knowledge of ecology be useful to us?

APPLYING PRINCIPLES AND CONCEPTS

1. Describe an ecosystem near your home.
2. Biologists sometimes speak of a "closed ecosystem." Explain why this might not be an accurate term.
3. Discuss possible reasons for annual variations of any specific population.
4. Discuss the differences between the environment of the shore region of a lake and that of the deep-water bottom region.
5. Discuss the factors controlling human populations throughout the world.

49-1 What is the habitat of these animals? What is their niche? (F. Allan, Animals, Animals)

chapter
forty-nine

The Habitat

OBJECTIVES
- DEFINE habitat and niche.
- DESCRIBE the limiting factors in a habitat.
- DESCRIBE food chains in an ecosystem.
- DIAGRAM an ecological pyramid.
- DESCRIBE each of the nutritional relationships.
- DESCRIBE passive protection.
- EXPLAIN adaptive behavior.

THE ADDRESS AND OCCUPATION OF AN ORGANISM

The "address" of an organism is its *habitat.* **It is the place in which the organism lives.** Remember the ecosystem of the lake we studied in the last chapter? A lake ecosystem has many habitats. There is the habitat of the bullfrog, for example. It is quite different from the habitat of the bass. Yet both contribute to the ecosystem. Bass and bullfrog habitats may overlap. When they overlap, the bullfrog may find itself being eaten by a bass. But, generally, you do not look for bullfrogs in the middle of a lake. And you do not fish for bass in the shallows near the shore.

The "occupation" of an organism is its *niche.* There are many ways to "earn a living" in a biotic community. Consider the many species of *plankton* in a lake, for example. Plankton are tiny organisms suspended in the water. The niche of many small fish is to feed on the plankton. These small fish may share their habitat with larger fish. But the large fish have a different niche. Their niche is to feed on the small fish. When different organisms have the same habitat and the same niche, they compete. For example, wolves and mountain lions have similar diets. When they share the same habitat, they compete for the same prey.

LIMITING FACTORS IN THE HABITAT

All organisms must be able to obtain the materials they need for growth and reproduction. These materials they must obtain from their habitat. Sometimes an organism has to compete for one of these essentials. Such an essential is then called a **limiting factor.** The example of cattails growing along a lake shore will make this clearer. Cattails need a marshy area where the water is not too

Ask students to discuss different types of habitats and the influence of particular habitats on the organisms that live there.

Some habitats can "die" as a result of environmental conditions. For example, phosphates in certain lakes and rivers have resulted in the death of bodies of water. This process is called *eutrophication.*

647

Examples of rock weathering can be seen in many areas. Students should be encouraged to take photographs of areas where seasonal temperature variations have resulted in damage to rocks, driveways, sidewalks, or buildings.

49-2 In this redwood forest, fallen trees are broken down into substances that can be reused. What natural processes return minerals to the soil?

deep. Therefore, the area of the lake where the bottom is soft and the water is shallow is a limiting factor for cattails. They compete within that area and cannot live beyond it.

There are many factors that must be present in an organism's habitat. If the habitat does not have enough of something the organism needs, the organism may not survive. But too much of some things can also cause problems. How well an organism can stand a variety of environmental conditions is called its **tolerance. Understanding how little and how much of something an organism can tolerate helps us understand why it lives where it does.** For example, many organisms live in estuaries where rivers carry freshwater into the salty ocean. The amount of salt in these estuaries varies. Storms can cause a change in the salt concentration by the addition of freshwater. The rise and fall of the tides also varies the salt concentration of water. The organisms that live in these conditions have a wide tolerance for changes in salt concentration. They include many types of worms, fishes, clams, oysters, and barnacles. Other marine species have a much lower tolerance for such changes. Corals, sponges, sea urchins, and deep sea fish would die in these estuaries.

Where an organism lives depends on its tolerance. Most organisms are found in habitats where the conditions are suitable for them to carry on their life activities. Let's examine some of the important physical factors that limit the habitats of plants and animals.

SOIL—A PHYSICAL FACTOR IN THE ENVIRONMENT

Soil is the thin outer layer of the earth. It is one of the most important factors of an environment. Soil varies greatly from place to place. So does the plant and animal life it supports. Soils containing large amounts of *clay* are tightly packed. This is because clay is made of very tiny particles. *Sand* is made up of larger particles. So sandy soil is loose. *Silt* is looser than clay and more compact than sand. *Loam* is a mixture of clay, sand, and organic matter.

Different types of trees grow well in different soils. Sandy soils can support pine forests in Michigan, New Jersey, Georgia, and eastern Texas. Heavy loam is good for beech and maple forests in Ohio, Indiana, Ontario, and Quebec. Bogs and swamps have waterlogged soils good for larch, white cedar, and cypress forests in southeastern United States. Certain mountain slopes have rocky, shallow soils. These soils produce the forests of redwood, yellow pine, and spruce found in the western United States and Canada.

Soil is always changing. In some places, rocks are breaking down to form more soil. This can be caused by many factors. The action of weather breaks down rock. So can chemical disintegrations and plants growing on rocks. Some soils are losing minerals. This occurs when plants remove salts from the soil through their roots. Some soils are enriched by layers of decaying vegetation. Other soils are losing their richness. This can happen when many crops are grown in the soil and the lost minerals are not replaced. **When soils change, habitats change. This, of course, affects the plants and animals that live in these habitats.**

TEMPERATURE—AN IMPORTANT ENVIRONMENTAL FACTOR

Many animals do not have a constant body temperature. These animals are "cold-blooded," or **poikilothermic** (poy-KILL-uh-THURM-ick). They include fish, amphibians, and reptiles. Their body temperatures change with the temperature of the environment. Birds and mammals are "warm-blooded," or **homoiothermic** (huh-MOY-uh-THURM-ick). Their body temperatures remain fairly constant, even when the temperature of the environment changes. Obviously, warm-blooded animals can live in habitats with a wider range of temperatures.

On a cold morning, a snake may crawl slowly onto a flat rock in the sun. The sun raises its body temperature. As the snake warms up, it becomes more active. A butterfly also has to adjust to low temperatures. It may fan its wings for a few minutes to warm up before flying. However, a meadow mouse living in the same area can wake up on a cold morning and move about immediately.

All organisms can adjust to small temperature changes from day to night. But changes between summer and winter temperatures are a bigger problem. Most trees and shrubs in temperate climates grow in spring, summer, and fall. In these seasons, the weather is fairly warm. But in the cold winter months, many enter a **dormant period.** The life activities of dormant plants slow down. Leaves may fall, and sap may move to others parts of the plant. Life picks up again in the spring and they grow new leaves. The leaves of the pine, spruce, and other evergreen trees remain, even though most activity in the plant has stopped. Parts of nonwoody plants may die; then grow again in spring from dormant roots, stems, or seeds.

Many birds have another way of dealing with winter temperatures. They fly to warmer places. Some Arctic birds fly south to the northern United States for the winter. Birds that live in the northern United States in the summer, however, may find winter temperatures too cold. So they fly even further south. Some even go as far as the South American tropics.

Other animals burrow under the ground or live in protected caves during the winter. Their life activities slow down and they become inactive or sleep. Some desert animals stay in their burrows on hot days. Further discussion on how animals adjust to temperature changes will be covered in Chapter Fifty.

WATER—ESSENTIAL TO LIFE

Probably nothing in the environment is more important to living things than water. Plant and animal habitats vary in how much water they contain. Some, such as the ocean, are all water. Others, like the desert, have very little. Organisms in different environments meet their water needs in various ways.

The acidity and alkalinity of soil are very important factors in the growth of certain types of plants. Agricultural extension agencies will often perform soil tests for local residents to determine whether or not the soil can support the growth of certain plants. Substances can be added to the soil to correct certain conditions.

Some of the migration patterns of birds are fascinating. Ask students to report on one of these patterns.

Students may be interested in taking a few soil samples and examining the soil for the different types of organisms that live there.

Water-dwelling plants and animals are called **aquatic.** Those that can only live in salt water are called **marine.** The bodies of these organisms are adapted to water living. They cannot live in even the wettest land environments. Land-living, or **terrestrial,** plants need less water than aquatic or marine forms. Rainfall is a major factor in controlling growth and reproduction of terrestrial plants.

Plants that grow entirely or partly covered with water are called *hydrophytes.* These include pond lilies, cattails, bulrushes, eelgrass, and cranberries. Plants that grow where it's neither very wet nor very dry are called *mesophytes* (MEZ-uh-FITES). These include hardwood trees like maples and oak. They also include most of the flowers and vegetables we grow in our gardens. Most mesophytes have well-developed roots and a large leaf area.

The driest environments are deserts and semideserts. The plants that live in them are called *xerophytes* (ZEAR-uh-FITES). These plants have very well-developed root systems for absorbing water. They also have very small leaf areas. This cuts down evaporation. The leaves of cacti, for example, are reduced to spines. Their thick stems are specially adapted for water storage.

LIGHT—ANOTHER CRITICAL ENVIRONMENTAL FACTOR

All green plants need light to make food. But certain other plants and animals live in total darkness. Some fish with undeveloped eyes live in underground streams, rivers, and other dark places. Other fish live so deep in the ocean that light never reaches them. Many bacteria live without light. In fact, long exposure to direct sunlight kills many bacteria. However, all of these organisms but a few species of bacteria depend on sunlight *indirectly* for life. They all require food and its stored energy. This food can be traced back to green plants which depend on light to make the food.

49–3 Xerophytes, such as this cactus, are well suited for living in a desert habitat. (H.R.W. Photo by Richard Weiss)

49-4 Compare the cave salamander to the red salamander. (Raymond A. Mendez, Animals, Animals; Dr. E. R. Degginger)

Light conditions vary from place to place. Deep valleys, forest floors, and the north sides of hills do not receive much light. These are the places where we find plants and animals with low light needs. Here we find snails, toads, and salamanders, as well as ferns and mosses. Open fields, southern slopes, and deserts are exposed to full sunlight. Plants and animals living here are adapted to a sunny environment.

THE ATMOSPHERE—A CHEMICAL STOREHOUSE

The air around us has a direct effect on living things. Almost all organisms need free oxygen for life. It may be taken directly from the atmosphere. Or it may be dissolved in water.

Deep-sea organisms have a greater oxygen problem than those living near the surface. Water gets oxygen from the air. In some places currents may carry oxygen-rich water to depths. But, in general, the deeper the water, the less oxygen in it. However, these deep-sea organisms have managed to adapt. Most deep-sea fishes live in the ocean only down to one and a half kilometers below the surface. But many organisms have been found as deep as 11 kilometers below the water's surface!

Plants and animals do not live very far beneath the surface of the soil. One reason is the lack of food. Another is that oxygen is limited. Most plants and animals that live in the soil are found close to the surface.

Air movement is caused by changes in atmospheric pressure. This movement directly influences living things. Storms can destroy plants, and drive animals to shelter. Wind greatly increases water evaporation. This water loss affects plants and animals. High winds on mountains affect the shape of trees. These trees are forced to grow close to the ground. They usually form branches on their protected side only. Leaf size becomes smaller. And roots become longer in order to hold the trees in the ground.

49-5 Note that the branches on this cypress tree extend in only one direction. What factor is responsible for this? (Albert Towle)

NUTRITIONAL RELATIONSHIPS—IMPORTANT BIOTIC FACTORS

The ways in which living things affect one another is very important. Many of the biotic relationships involve food. Some organisms need only inorganic nutrients to synthesize organic compounds. These are the autotrophs. Because these organisms make their own food, we call them *food-producers.* There are several types of food-producers in a lake.

Among them are the rooted plants like cattails growing near the shore. Submerged plants like eelgrass grow on the bottom. Also there are the suspended algae that form the *phytoplankton.* The examination of a few drops of pond water through a microscope reveals hundreds of one-celled algae.

Phytoplankton provides food for small crustaceans like the ostracods and copepods. Because they feed on plants, these organisms are called *herbivores* (HUR-bi-voarz). Since they cannot make their own food they are heterotrophs. They are the first *food-consumers* of the lake ecosystem. Herbivores make protoplasm using the energy synthesized and stored in the phytoplankton. The next link in this food-consuming chain is the *carnivores* (KAHR-ni-voarz). They are flesh-eating animals. We can divide them in two groups. The *first-level carnivores* feed on the herbivores and use their energy. The *second-level carnivores* feed on first-level carnivores. Minnows are an example of first-level carnivores. They feed on the small crustaceans. Young fishes feed on both the herbivores and minnows. So they can be either first- or second-level carnivores.

Scavengers feed on dead organisms. They are important in the cycling of chemicals. They also transfer energy to the animals in

49–6 A lake provides an interesting example of nutritional relationships.

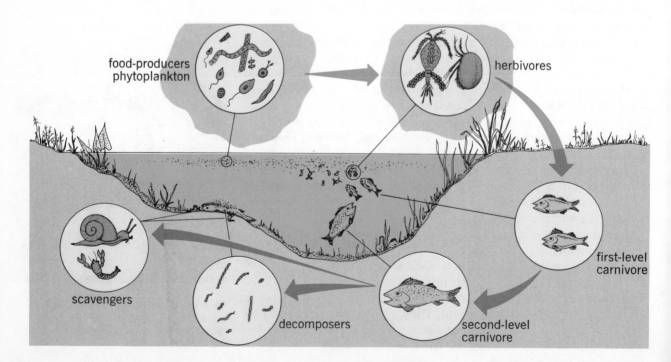

food-producers phytoplankton

herbivores

first-level carnivore

scavengers

decomposers

second-level carnivore

the ecosystem that feed on them. In lakes, these "garbage collectors" include crayfish and some snails. Many fishes are part scavenger.

Bacteria and yeasts are a lake's *decomposers.* They break down the tissues and excretions of other organisms into simpler substances. We call this the process of decay. The simpler substances are broken down even more by other bacteria. These are the *transformers.* They live in the mud bottom of the lake and in the soil. Transformers change decayed matter into nitrogen compounds. Together, the decomposers and transformers return nitrogen, phosphates, and other substances to the soil or water. Plants can then use them to begin the cycle again. Without these bacteria, matter could not be reused in the ecosystem.

FOOD CHAINS IN AN ECOSYSTEM

Green plants change energy from the sun's radiation into stored energy. Much of this stored energy is released when plants are eaten. But some of it is stored in the bodies of herbivores. When a carnivore feeds on a herbivore, the process is repeated. Some energy is used and some is stored in the carnivore. Energy passes in this way from carnivores to scavengers, decomposers, and transformers. **But not all the energy stored by a herbivore is stored by the carnivore that feeds on it. Much is used in vital processes like metabolism, movement, and reproduction.** Only the leftover energy is converted or stored.

Let's look at a lake again for examples of energy transfer. Energy goes from the algae to the copepod to the minnow to the sunfish to the bass. There is no predator to eat the bass in this ecosystem so it is the top carnivore. When it dies, it will probably be food for the crayfish. This transfer of the sun's energy through many organisms is called a *food chain.*

Of course, this food chain could be extended further. A bullfrog might eat the crayfish, and so on. Also, a lake may have more than one food chain. Food chains might even overlap.

In fact, you could list every organism in the lake and draw arrows to show which organisms were used for food by others. This diagram would show all the biotic relationships involving energy transfer. There are many possibilities. Your diagram would look more like a web than a chain. For this reason, food chains are sometimes called *food webs.*

ECOLOGICAL PYRAMIDS

The food chains in an ecosystem are often shown as pyramids. Food producers form the base. The top carnivore forms the tip. A *food pyramid* can be made to show an actual food chain. To do this, you count the numbers of individuals involved in each link of the chain. A count like this was made of a bluegrass field. There was an average of 5,842,424 food producers in an acre. The next link aver-

Point out to students the interdependence of all members of a food chain. When one member of the chain is destroyed, the other members are affected and the environment will be changed.

Ask students to research a food chain that involves a local organism. Students will find this type of exercise more interesting than the text examples.

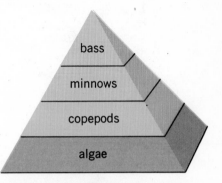

pond water and dissolved minerals

49–7 A pyramid based on the number of individuals in a pond.

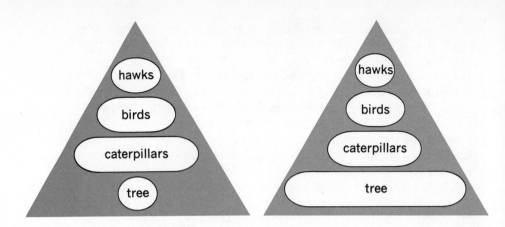

49-8 A pyramid based on numbers (left) and a pyramid based on mass.

aged 707,624 herbivorous invertebrates. These provided food for an average of 354,904 ants, spiders, and predatory beetles. An average of three birds and three moles formed the top of the pyramid. Population-density studies like this help us understand the energy relationships in ecosystems. They even help us predict future changes.

Another way of studying food chains is to determine the mass in each link. Let's consider the difference between a food pyramid based on number and one based on mass. In a food pyramid based on number, the number of trees is much less than the number of caterpillars. Obviously, one tree can support many caterpillars. Consider a pyramid based on the mass of the organisms. The mass of the tree is greater than the mass of the caterpillars. The pyramid of mass is more like an actual pyramid. Such a study might give a clearer picture of the biotic relationships.

Both of these pyramids show a condition found in an ecosystem at any given moment. But conditions in an ecosystem are always changing. The number and mass of a group of organisms depends only in part on food supply. It really depends more on how quickly that supply can be renewed.

Understanding food pyramids may help us solve a human social problem. This is the problem of the population explosion. Remember that each level of a food chain uses up some of the energy that first came from the sun. About 85 percent of the energy moving from one level of the food pyramid to the next is lost. Move of the energy is lost to respiration, excretion, heat, and movement. There is always more food energy at the base of the food pyramid. If we can find ways to get ourselves closer to the base, there will be more food energy for us. That way a larger population could be fed from the same amount of original sun-energy.

SPECIAL NUTRITIONAL RELATIONSHIPS

Most animals, including humans, are **bulk-feeders.** This means that they eat the whole organisms or parts of the organism. The **saprophytes** are another group of heterotrophs. They absorb nu-

49–9 A hermit crab with sea anemones living attached to its shell. What do biologists call such a relationship? (Walter Dawn)

trients from dead tissues or products of organisms. These include the bacteria that decompose plant and animal bodies. They also include the molds that live on bread, fruit, and other organic materials. And they include the yeasts that ferment sugars and the fungi that live on dead trees. Some of these organisms are destructive. But others are very useful.

Symbiosis is another kind of nutritional relationship. It means "living together." And that's just what symbiotic organisms do. There are three different kinds of symbiosis: parasitism, mutualism, and commensalism. In **parasitism,** the parsite lives in or on another organism, called a host. The parasite gets its food and a place to live from this situation. But the host suffers. Tapeworms and lampreys are parasites. Other parasites include certain insects, disease-causing bacteria, mildews, rusts, and smuts.

Parasites do not usually kill their hosts. If the host dies, the parasite loses its habitat and its food supply. A successful parasite takes just enough food from the host to grow and reproduce. This is true of ticks, fleas, mosquitoes, and the fungus that causes athlete's foot.

Every free-living organism seems to have its parasites. Many parasites have parasites of their own. In fact, in terms of numbers, there are more parasites than there are free-living organisms.

In **mutualism,** two different kinds of organisms benefit from living together. In some cases, they cannot live without each other. Termites, for example, can chew and swallow the cellulose in wood. But they cannot digest it. Protists living in their digestive tract digest the cellulose for them. The termite is provided a means of digestion. In return, the protist is given a place to live. There are many other examples of mutualism. The association of an alga and fungus in lichens is one. The fungus provides moisture and a place to live for the alga. The alga makes food for itself and the fungus. Insects that pollinate flowers as they take nectar from them is another example of mutualism.

Mutualism also exists in human beings. Bacteria in the feces synthesize vitamin B_{12}. In this case, the bacteria and the host benefit each other.

49–10 The wrasse feeds on scraps of food left by the moray eel. (Animals, Animals)

There are many examples of camouflage in nature including protective coloration, countershading, protective resemblance, and mimicry. Films and pictures will be helpful to illustrate this section. Perhaps some students will want to take their own photographs illustrating these passive methods of protection.

In **commensalism,** one partner benefits and the other neither benefits nor is harmed. A good example is the relationship between the remora and the shark. The remora is a small fish with a suction pad on its head. It attaches this pad to the lower side of a shark, and feeds on scraps of the shark's food. The remora thus benefits and the shark is not harmed.

PASSIVE PROTECTION

Most animals have developed some kind of protection from predators. They may defend themselves with claws, teeth, spines, stingers, or pincers. Even the ability to run fast is a defense. Other animals have a passive protection. They survive by blending into their surroundings. This way they cannot be seen by their enemies. Even predators have this kind of camouflage. It keeps them hidden from their prey. Many animals could not survive outside their usual environments that hide them. A green katydid is a good example of this. It is almost impossible to find it among the green leaves of a tree. But if it should fall from the tree, it would most likely be eaten by one of its predators, such as a bird.

There are several kinds of animal camouflage. Some animals are colored or marked the same as their surroundings. This is called **protective coloration.** For example, the tiger's orange and black stripes blend almost perfectly with the grasses and shadows of its environment. This kind of camouflage is a very common adaptation for survival.

You may remember from Chapter Thirty-Four that fishes were darker on top and lighter underneath. Such a color pattern allows fish to blend with their surroundings. This is an example of **countershading.**

Another kind of camouflage is called **protective resemblance.** This is when an animal looks like something in its environment. Several kinds of butterflies look like brown leaves when their wings are folded. The walking stick is another example. It looks very much like a twig.

Mimicry is another type of protective resemblance. In mimicry, one animals looks like another animal. Several types of defenseless flies look like stinging insects. This keeps many predators away. The viceroy and monarch butterflies are another example of mimicry. The monarch is bad tasting. Because of this, most birds will not eat it. The viceroy does not taste bad, but it looks very much like the monarch. So birds tend to avoid it, too.

It is important to remember that animals do not camouflage themselves in order to live. Rather, they survive because they blend with their surroundings. Their protection is simply the result of centuries of survival by animals best adapted to their surroundings. None of these organisms *chose* to blend with their surroundings. Over thousands of years, the animals that survived happened to look more like their surroundings.

ADAPTIVE BEHAVIOR

Behavior patterns that help an animal survive are called **adaptive behavior.** Activities that are natural, or untaught, are called *instinctive.* Bird migration, courtship behavior, caring for young, building nests, and spinning webs are all instincts. Biologists are gradually replacing the term *instinct* with the term *behavior patterns. Ethology* is the study of these patterns.

Behavior patterns are interesting to observe. The feeding behavior of a young frigate bird is a good example. The mother's arrival at the nest is a signal to the young bird. It first lowers its head and starts peeping. The parent bird looks down at the baby. Next, the baby prods the mother's breast with its bill. In response, the adult frigate lowers its bill. Then, the baby prods the base of the parent's bill. This brings about another response and the mother opens her mouth. At the same time, the young bird puts its bill down into the throat of the mother. She begins to bring up a

49–11 Mimicry. Note the resemblance between the viceroy butterfly and the monarch butterfly. (Walter Dawn)

There are many excellent books and articles written about animal behavior. Ask students to report on a particularly interesting pattern of behavior of special interest to them.

49–12 The feeding behavior of the frigate bird. (Albert Towle)

fish from her stomach. The young bird, then, puts its head completely into the mother's throat and finds its food.

This complicated chain of events is a fixed pattern, As each event occurs, it brings about a response. This, in turn, is a signal for another response. For example, if the baby bird just kept on peeping when the mother looked down, the feeding reaction would stop. Perhaps you can observe some behavior patterns by making careful observations.

SUMMARY

An organism's *habitat* is the place in which it lives. The organism's "occupation" in the ecosystem is called its *niche*. When different organisms have the same habitat and the same niche, they compete.

Organisms must live in a habitat that provides the materials necessary for growth and reproduction. Several things affect the survival of an organism in a certain habitat. These include physical factors such as type of soil, temperature, presence of water, light, and oxygen. They also include biotic factors. Nutritional relationships among organisms are the most important biotic factors. Different organisms of an ecosystem play different nutritional roles. There are *producers, consumers, scavengers, decomposers,* and *transformers.* Each organism is important in the energy transfer and cycling of inorganic compounds in a biotic community. The food chain represents this energy transfer from one type of organism to another. These chains may be shown as food pyramids. Depending on the way they get organic nutrients, heterotrophic organisms can be classified as *symbionts, saprophytes,* or *bulk-feeders.*

Many animals protect themselves from predators by using camouflage. Some predators hide from their prey in this way also. The four types of camouflage are *protective coloration, countershading, protective resemblance* and *mimicry.*

BIOLOGICALLY SPEAKING

habitat	terrestrial	parasitism
niche	producer	mutualism
limiting factor	scavenger	commensalism
tolerance	decomposer	saprophyte
poikilothermic	transformer	protective coloration
homoiothermic	food chain	countershading
dormant period	food web	protective resemblance
aquatic	bulk-feeder	mimicry
marine	symbiosis	

QUESTIONS FOR REVIEW

1. Distinguish habitat from niche. Give an example.
2. Explain the importance of plankton.
3. How does the tolerance of an organism for an environmental factor limit its distribution?
4. Name several important controlling physical factors of the environment.
5. What is meant by the terms "cold-blooded" and "warm-blooded"?
6. How are environments classified according to the available water?
7. In what ways are plants adapted to live in environments of varying water content?

8. Although some organisms can live in total darkness, most are dependent on light. Explain.
9. In what environments is oxygen a limiting factor for organisms?
10. Starting with the food-producers, name and define the various types of organisms in a food chain.
11. What is meant by symbiosis? Describe each of the three symbiotic relationships.
12. What is meant by a fixed pattern of behavior? Give an example.

APPLYING PRINCIPLES AND CONCEPTS

1. Choose some common organisms in your environment and discuss possible limiting factors for each.
2. Discuss the importance for researching the limiting factors of specific organisms.
3. Does man's tolerance to a wide variety of conditions enable him to extend his habitat? What other factors are involved?
4. Discuss the survival value of the constant internal temperature condition found in some animals.
5. Discuss the adaptations of plants growing in areas of reduced light.
6. Make a diagram of a food web that exists in your local area.
7. Cite evidence of fixed patterns of behavior in the animals in your region. How can you be sure that these are fixed patterns?

chapter fifty

Periodic Changes in the Environment

OBJECTIVES
- UNDERSTAND alternating periods of activity in organisms.
- EXPLAIN daily rhythms and seasonal community changes.
- DESCRIBE migration.
- DEMONSTRATE an understanding of lunar and annual rhythms.
- EXPLAIN natural succession of forests, ponds, and lakes.

Ask students to report on one animal that either hibernates or estivates. Students may be surprised at the number of organisms that adapt to seasonal changes.

Stress to students that plants as well as animals are subject to periodicity.

50-1 The hawk is a diurnal predator, while the owl is a nocturnal predator. (Allan Roberts)

ALTERNATING PERIODS OF ACTIVITY

In the springtime, you may waken to the sounds of hundreds of birds announcing the new day. At the same time, creatures like snails, slugs, and sowbugs are seeking protected spots where they will remain throughout the day. Somewhere a hawk is soaring in the morning sky. It spots a mouse on the ground and dives after it. At night, the attacker would have been a barn owl.

An organism that is active during the day is called *diurnal* **(die-URN'l).** *Nocturnal* **(nock-TURN'l) animals are active at night.** Diurnal and nocturnal organisms may occupy the same niche. For example, the owl occupies the diurnal hawk's predatory niche at night.

Alternating periods of activity are called *periodicity.* **When an organism's periodicity is regular, it is called** *rhythmic.* An early bird getting its worm every morning shows rhythmic behavior. Biologists have studied rhythmic behavior in organisms for many years. But many of their questions about this behavior are still unanswered. What, for example, causes certain insects, birds, or mammals to migrate? Or what causes hibernating animals to wake up in the spring? Some animals have been described as having "internal clocks."

Light seems to be important to these rhythms. Many rhythms are based on daily, seasonal, and annual light variations. Some rhythms are also based on changes in the phases of the moon. But, as you will see, factors other than light will affect rhythms of plants and animals. Animals and plants appear to "remember" their rhythms. Biologists have raised plants in a darkened room under a constant temperature. These plants had the same responses they would have had in normal periods of daylight and darkness. This "memory" of a rhythm has also been shown in chickens, lizards, and *Drosophila*. Different species may show slight differences in the length of their active and resting periods. But most seem to have a twenty-two- to twenty-six-hour cycle.

DAILY RHYTHMS

All forests have similar environmental conditions. The tall trees provide areas of shade under which the shrub layer of the forest floor grows. In sunny spaces, grasses grow in meadows. Ferns cover the banks of streams. A summer morning finds birds, chipmunks, and ground squirrels searching for food. Deer browse in the meadows. By noon, however, this activity slows down.

As evening approaches, many of these diurnal animals become active again for a short time. Dragonflies and bats dart over streams and ponds. Here they search for both diurnal and nocturnal insects. This is a period of time between day and night. The sounds of cicadas and birds gradually fade. Now crickets begin chirping. Foxes, raccoons, skunks, owls, and mountain lions begin the nocturnal search for food.

When plants bloom, their flowers may open and close at regular times of the day. The petals of the poppy, for example, open in the morning and close at night. Many cacti bloom only at night. They depend on nocturnal insects for pollination.

The desert environment has extreme temperature changes from night to day. As a result, day and night activities are different. In the early morning, birds feed on insects and seeds. Jack rabbits come out of their burrows to look for food. Snakes, hawks, vultures, and ground squirrels are also active. By noontime, most desert creatures have found a shady spot at the base of cacti, sagebrush, or creosote bushes. This is understandable. Temperature on desert surfaces can rise as high as 76°C. Many animals return to their cooler burrows. Here the moisture in the air may be twice that of

50–2 The flowers of the night-blooming cactus open only in the evening or at night. (Fritz Henle, Photo Researchers)

the sunbaked atmosphere. In early evening, many creatures come out again for a short time. The Gila monster and rattlesnake come out at night. They prey on the many small nocturnal desert mammals. The bobcat, coyote, fox, and owl are some of the larger nocturnal desert carnivores.

In contrast to the desert are the tundra and polar regions. Here very little activity takes place during the cold nights. During the short summer, most organisms are active throughout the day.

Day-night rhythms are also found in the oceans. Many copepods and shrimp move close to the surface at night. Here they can feed on plankton. These herbivores sink to a lower level during the day. Some may be found as far down as one hundred meters. Small carnivorous fish follow the daily movements of these plankton-feeders.

SEASONAL COMMUNITY CHANGES

Animals can meet the problems of seasonal change in many ways. When they are exposed to snow and freezing temperatures, they must be able to adjust or to move away. Most adult insects have completed their life cycles before the beginning of autumn. Many of these insects are killed by the first frosts. How does the species survive? That depends on the insect. Many moths spend the winter as pupae in silk-insulated cocoons. Grasshoppers, crickets, and cicadas lay eggs in the ground or in the bark of trees. Stoneflies, mayflies, and dragonflies spend the winter as nymphs in the water. Here they are sheltered beneath the water's frozen surface.

Honeybees find winter protection in numbers. They feed on the honey stored during the spring and summer. This gives them energy to keep active in their hives all winter. This activity produces heat. On a very cold day, the temperature in a hive can be as much as 24°C higher than that outside.

Some mammals and birds live in the same region all year. Among these are the eastern cottontail rabbit, the white-tailed deer, the cardinal, and the bluejay. During very cold weather, they find protection in woods and thickets. Their biggest problem is finding food when snow covers the area.

Some animals go into *hibernation* during cold weather. These include squirrels, chipmunks, woodchucks, and many reptiles and amphibians. The hibernating animal finds a protected place and remains inactive for the winter. Its body metabolic rate slows down. So does its heartbeat and respiration. Eventually, the animal loses consciousness. The decrease in activity reduces its energy needs. This drop in activity is important since the animal is living off stored fat. Hibernating animals do not wake up until the temperature rises again in the spring. Only then do their body processes speed up enough for normal activity.

Some animals such as the bear enter a period of dormancy during the winter. Dormancy is similar to hibernation. Body activities slow down and the animal lives on stored fat during its *winter sleep*.

50-3 The cardinal is a permanent resident in the midwest, eastern, and southeastern states. (Thase Daniel, Bruce Coleman, Inc.)

However, the animal's body temperature remains normal. Unlike the hibernating animal, it may be awakened during the dormancy period. The bear, for example, may leave its shelter on a mild winter day. Skunks, raccoons, and opossums have similar winter sleeps.

Many animals become dormant during hot weather. This is sometimes called *summer hibernation*. The biological term for this is *estivation*. A frog may estivate in the cool mud at the bottom of a pond. The box turtle often buries itself in leaves to escape the heat. Estivation can last for several days or several weeks.

Many animals migrate to warmer regions in winter. When we think of *migration,* we usually think of birds. But some mammals also migrate. These seasonal journeys may cover thousands of kilometers. Some mammals migrate to find food. Others migrate to a better climate. Still others make seasonal journeys to regions where they can produce their young under the best conditions.

MAMMAL MIGRATION

The bighorn sheep is a mammal that migrates. It spends summers in high meadows near the summits of the Rocky Mountains. When winter comes, it moves down into the protection of the forests on the mountain slopes. The caribou of North America migrate between 600 and 800 kilometers on seasonal journeys. During the summer, the caribou live in the tundra region north of the timber line. In July, they begin a southward migration along the same routes they follow year after year. It is on this journey that breeding takes place. The caribou remains in their winter quarters until the spring. Then, they go north giving birth to young on the way.

The fur seal also migrates. During winter, the females, young males, and pups swim the waters of the Pacific Ocean. The older males spend the winter in the cold waters near Alaska and the Aleutian Islands. The breeding season is in the spring. Then, the males migrate to the Pribilof Islands, north of the Aleutians. They arrive several weeks before the females, and then battle for a territory. Also, in the spring, the females and young seals start their long journey to the Pribilof Islands. They travel more than 4800 kilometers and arrive in June. A herd of 50 or more females gathers around each male. Pups from the past year's breeding are born in June. Then, within a week, breeding takes place again. Now, the seals migrate southward.

AN INSECT MIGRATION

The monarch is often called the milkweed butterfly. It is a very strong flier and makes a remarkable migration. At the end of summer, thousands of them gather in Canada and begin to fly south. Some travel to the Gulf states and spend the winter. Others travel along the Pacific Coast. Between mid October and November, most of them arrive in Mexico and on the Monterey Peninsula. They seek shelter in a specific grove of pine trees. Here, they hang from the

50-4 Hibernation. Many animals, such as the jumping mouse, pass the winter in underground nests in a dormant state. (Allan Roberts)

50-5 These monarch butterflies spend the winter in a pine grove in California after migrating from Canada. (Dr. E. R. Degginger)

Discuss the importance of international agreements concerning the migration of animals between countries. What problems could occur if these agreements were not reached?

branches and needles in such large numbers that the trees appear to be solid brown. On warm sunny days throughout the fall and winter, they may fly around gardens gathering nectar.

In March, the monarchs begin their northward journey. They lay eggs on milkweed plants as they travel north. Most of the monarchs die after their eggs are laid. After the eggs hatch, the larvae feed and then form pupae. The butterflies that emerge from the pupae continue the flight north. These butterflies also lay eggs on milkweed as they travel north.

By late summer, the butterflies begin to gather for another migration south. We do not know how these insects find their way to the same trees in which their ancestors spent the winter before.

BIRD MIGRATION

Many birds migrate long distances in the spring. Then they nest and raise their young in a new home. In the fall, they return to warmer climates. It is hard to understand why some birds leave food and warmth in the tropics to breed in the Far North. It is much easier to explain why insect-eating birds fly south when cold weather kills their prey. We can also see why water birds fly south before northern ponds and lakes freeze over. And the fact that fruit- and seed-eaters follow their food supply also makes sense.

Some species of birds migrate at night. Some migrate by day. Perhaps you have heard flocks of geese overhead on spring and autumn nights. Sometimes they get confused by city lights and

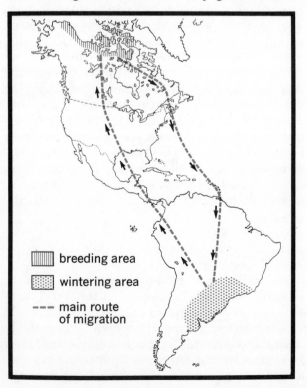

50–6 The migratory route of the golden plover. Flying more than 13,000 kilometers each way, it breeds in northern Canada during the summer, and flies to South America to spend the winter.

breeding area

wintering area

- - - main route of migration

circle about, honking noisily. You may have seen great flocks of red-winged blackbirds or grackles. These daylight-flying birds also migrate in spring and fall.

Many birds migrate slowly. They feed along the way and average only thirty to fifty kilometers a day. Others are marvels of speed and endurance. For example, the ruddy turnstone travels from Alaska to Hawaii in a single flight. The golden plover travels more than thirteen thousand kilometers from Canada to South America.

50-7 A tidal pool at low tide (left) and later the same area partly submerged by the incoming tide. (Walter Dawn)

Migratory birds have resulted in many problems. Birds have crashed into skyscrapers, and birds have been involved in some airplane crashes.

LUNAR RHYTHMS

There are many stories about the effect of the moon on planting certain crops. Even though these are interesting stories, they are not based on scientific fact. **The greatest effect of the moon is seen along the sea coasts. The moon is mainly responsible for ocean tides.** Many marine organisms live along the coastline. The rhythmic rise and fall of tidal water affects the lives of these organisms. They must continuously adjust to the changing tides. The greatest problem is the danger of drying out at low tide. Small fishes and crustaceans find protection in tidepools. These are small areas of water left behind when the tide goes out. Many limpets and snails keep from drying out by clamping down tightly to rocks. Mussels and barnacles close their shells tightly. This keeps moisture in. Some sessile sponges and tunicates live under rock ledges covered by seaweed. The seaweed covering protects them during low tide.

Organisms living in tidal areas have other problems. Summer and winter tides cause wide variations in temperature. Freshwater from rains changes the salt content of tidepools. You can see that intertidal organisms must be able to adjust to a great variety of changes.

Grunions are fish that breed along the California coast between March and August. Their breeding habits provide a good example of lunar periodicity. Grunions swim ashore exactly at the turning of the tide on the second, third, and fourth nights of the highest tides.

50-8 The rhythm of the tides means survival of the species for the grunion. (Walter E. Harvey, National Audubon Society)

Some students may be amateur ornithologists and familiar with the different types of birds that reside in their locality during various seasons. Ask them to discuss this with the class.

Students may be interested in researching information about biological clocks in humans. How are we regulated by this internal clock?

They come onto the beach in pairs. The female digs a hole in the sand. In the hole, she deposits eggs about seven centimeters below the surface. The male then fertilizes the eggs. On the next wave, the pair slips back into the ocean. The eggs remain in the sand until the next unusually high tide. This is about ten days later. The tide washes them out of the sand. As soon as the water covers the eggs, they hatch. Then the tiny fish swim into the ocean.

ANNUAL RHYTHMS

Many reproductive cycles of plants and animals are associated with seasonal changes. They also have a yearly rhythm. The female bear gives birth during winter in the protection of her den. Birds nest and lay eggs in spring. By the time winter comes, their young are fully grown. Wildflowers bloom and produce seeds in the spring. This enables the next generation of wildflowers to develop. Deciduous trees lose their leaves in the fall. These are just a few of the annual cycles of nature. You can probably think of many more.

WHAT IS THE VALUE OF PERIODICITY?

To survive, organisms must be able to adjust to environmental changes. We have seen many of the ways organisms adjust to these changes. Various populations have synchronized rhythms of behavior. Such rhythms allow members of a species to coordinate certain behavior patterns. These behavior patterns help the species survive. The behavior of swarming grunion we discussed earlier is an example. This behavior insures the coming together of males and females necessary for fertilization of the eggs. This behavior pattern also occurs in oysters. The male and female release gametes into the surrounding water at the same time. A female oyster may produce as many as 114 million eggs at one time. This would be of no use unless a neighboring male oyster releases sperms at the same time. Many biologists are looking for the causes of synchronized behavior in populations.

CHANGING BIOTIC COMMUNITIES

We have seen some of the daily and seasonal changes in biotic communities. Plants and animals are always on the move. The changes in the plant populations of an area usually happen slowly. That is why these changes are not always easy to identify. **As plant populations change, animals find new homes. This changing of communities is called** *succession.*

Winds, fires, volcanic activity, and other natural events may destroy the organisms living in an area. This also happens when humans clear land. If the area is then left alone, succession starts. Eventually, a permanent community will take over again. This process may take longer than one hundred years.

Whenever a tree falls in a forest, succession begins. This type of succession takes many years. Succession can also begin when humans change the makeup of an ecosystem. Putting rocks in a bay for a breakwater or sinking piles for a pier begins the process of succession.

Let's see how the process of succession occurs. We will begin with a section of bare soil in an open area. This area might have been cleared by fire. Perhaps it was cut for trees and not reseeded. Or it might be an abandoned agricultural field. It is located in a broad-leaved forest in the eastern United States. Here, beech and sugar-maple forests once grew over much of the land.

The first organisms to appear are grasses and other open-field plants. These plants may come from seeds that are dormant in the soil. Or they may be carried in by animals or winds. The first organisms to dominate an area are called pioneers. A meadow is produced by these pioneers. The meadow may dominate the region for several years. Next, the seeds of elms, cottonwoods, and shrubs find their way into the meadow. This marks the beginning of a forest. The larger plants shade the shorter grasses and field plants. Thus, the environment is changing from an open field to open, low woods. These woods soon become too shady even for the seedlings of the trees and shrubs. So the area slowly continues to change.

The third stage of this succession may begin with the arrival of seeds from trees such as oak and ash. These seedlings grow well in a shady environment. Gradually, the oaks and ashes begin to take over from the elms and cottonwoods. Finally, a dense forest forms. The ground becomes moist and fertile. Beech and maple seedlings win the competition for forest space. Eventually, they crowd out most of the other trees. Since the beech and maple trees are now dominant, we call them the **climax species.** If this succession had happened on a ridge, the climax species might have been an oak and hickory forest. Short grasses are the climax plants in the Great Plains.

SUCCESSION IN PONDS AND LAKES

As we learned earlier, the cattails and waterlilies around a lake or pond edge hold soil around their roots. More soil continues to build up over the years. As a result, the pond gradually grows smaller. Eventually, the pond will be completely filled in with the same types of plants that grew around its edge. We can predict the succession of plants and animals that will gradually fill in a pond. We must closely observe the organisms that grow from the pond's edge outward to the climax plants of the region. Other factors help determine how much of the pond will be filled in. These are pond size, location, and water source. These factors also determine when and how long the succession will take.

50–9 Succession in a pond (top to bottom): pioneer, open-pond stage; submerged vegetation stage; cattail stage; sedge meadow stage; climax forest stage.

A demonstration of succession should be started in class and examined over a long period of time.

In August, 1959, an earthquake occurred in the Madison River Canyon in Montana. A new lake was formed. A large portion of the land on the mountainside was cleared when tons of soil, rocks, and trees fell into the canyon. Biologists are studying the changes occurring in the new lake and clearings. A knowledge of ecological succession helps us to predict changes. But an earthquake such as this gives us the opportunity to prove our thories.

The drama in nature goes on endlessly. Conditions in any given area are never permanent. Each population of plants that occupies the area changes the environment. This often makes it unsuitable for other plants of the same type. However, it may be favorable for other types of plants that move in. Over a period of time, these changes in plant population prepare the way for the climax vegetation. The animal population depends on the plant population. Therefore, the types and numbers of animals change as plant succession occurs.

SUMMARY

There are many kinds of periodic changes in biotic communities. These changes are caused by many factors, such as light, temperature, and climatic conditions. The activity of organisms in an area change from day to night. Organisms that are active during the day are called *diurnal*. Those that are active at night are called *nocturnal*. Light seems to be an important factor in determining the daily rhythms of certain organisms.

Seasonal changes in a biotic community have much to do with changes in temperature. In areas where the winters are cold, most organisms change their activities. Some adaptations to cold weather include hibernation, dormancy, and migration. Migration may also occur for reasons of food supply and reproduction.

Lunar rhythms affect organisms that live in tidal areas. These organisms must adapt to the changes caused by the movement of the tides. Many reproductive cycles are influenced by seasonal changes and occur in yearly rhythms.

The gradual changes that take place in a given biotic community are called *succession*. Each plant population that lives in a given area changes its environment. Sometimes one type of plant will make the environment unsuitable for another. But new plants may come into the area and find the conditions favorable. Gradually, these changes in plant population prepare the way for the climax vegetation. The animal population depends on plant population. So the types and numbers of animals change as plant succession occurs.

BIOLOGICALLY SPEAKING			
diurnal	rhythmic	migration
nocturnal	hibernation	succession
periodicity	estivation	climax species

1. The owl and the hawk are both predators. Do they compete with one another? Explain.
2. What evidence is available to indicate that daily rhythms are not just influenced by light and dark?
3. In what ways do animals adjust to seasonal changes?
4. In what ways are hibernation and estivation similar? How are they different?
5. Give examples of animal migrations.
6. What environments are directly affected by lunar rhythms?
7. How does the grunion's behavior demonstrate lunar periodicity?
8. Of what value is periodicity to survival of some species?
9. By what methods can succession be studied?

1. Why are human activities not entirely governed by external rhythms?
2. Discuss the senses that are well developed in nocturnal animals.
3. Review and discuss possible causes for migration in birds.
4. Name and identify the permanent residents, winter residents, and summer residents of the bird population in your area.
5. What climax communities exist in the area in which you live? Identify any stages leading toward this climax.

chapter fifty-one

Biogeography

OBJECTIVES
- DEFINE biogeography.
- EXPLAIN dispersal barriers.
- DESCRIBE climatic zones.
- NAME the major climatic zones of North America.
- NAME and DESCRIBE the biomes.

Forest
Farmland & Prairie
Arctic Tundra
Desert & Wasteland

51–1 This map of the world shows the distribution of vegetation and use of the land.

Discuss with students the biogeography of the area in which they live. Is it primarily forest, farm, tundra, or desert land? Is it a combination of these regions? Discuss the vegetation and animal life common to the area.

Seed dispersal should be reviewed here. Refer students to Chapter Twenty-Seven.

THE DISTRIBUTION OF PLANTS AND ANIMALS

Have you ever seen or felt cobwebs floating in the breeze on a spring or fall day? These silken threads are spun by young spiders. When the webs are caught in air currents, they can support the weight of the tiny creatures. Sailors have seen tiny spiders floating more than 300 kilometers from land. They have also been found as high as three kilometers in the air. Why do spiders travel like this? Where are they going?

Most of us have picked burrs and stickers from our socks after a hike. The seeds and fruits of plants are often carried by animals in this way. This is just one of many ways fruits and seeds have of getting from one place to another, A milkweed seed, for example, may travel through the air for kilometers on its fluffy parachute. These are a few of the many methods of dispersal.

Dispersal is valuable to a species. It allows members of a species to go to new environments. The young spider and milkweed seed may float to areas where there is less competition from their own kind. Of course, if the spider lands in the ocean, it will die. So will the milkweed seed if it lands in a lake or on a granite cliff. However, the advantages of dispersal are great. It has much to do with the process of succession we studied in the last chapter.

Biologists study the distribution of plants and animals throughout the various regions of the earth. This study is called *biogeography*. Species can spread naturally. Or they can be carried by human beings deliberately or accidentally.

Some people think of Hawaii when they think of pineapples. Actually the pineapple originally came from South America. From there, it was imported to the Hawaiian Islands. **Humans have dis-**

persed many other organisms. European starlings, English sparrows, and Japanese beetles are not native to North America. They were brought here by people.

Dispersal of plant seeds is a passive process. This means that the plants do not move themselves. They must ride on currents of water or air. Sometimes spores, seeds, or fruits stick to the fur of animals. Or they may be picked up on birds' feet. The seeds within some berries are indigestible. When a bird or mammal eats them, the seeds pass through the digestive tract unchanged. After they leave the animal, the seeds can germinate.

Some animals are also dispersed passively. Eggs and larvae may float in water or air. Driftwood may carry mussels or shipworms to new places. Logs may carry rodents. Drifting ice may carry a polar bear hundreds of kilometers. Many animals, however, actively seek new habitats by swimming, flying, walking, running, or hopping.

Humans actively extend their living area. They fill in tidelands with rocks and soil. Entire communities, airports, shopping centers, and industrial sites are then built on these areas. New designs and construction materials make it possible to build on hillsides. With irrigation, it is now possible to live in deserts. Humans are inhabiting many other areas that were once considered unsuitable for human life. In this effort to extend their living area, people have destroyed the ecosystems of many organisms. However, careful planning in the future is necessary to help maintain a balance in these ecosystems.

Elicit from students the different types of barriers to dispersal. Discuss how the barriers affect the organisms involved.

BARRIERS TO DISPERSAL

A frog could easily be carried across a large lake on a log. It could jump into the water now and then to keep its skin moist. But if the log were floating in the ocean, the saltwater would kill the frog. Saltwater acts as a geographical barrier to frog dispersal. There are many different kinds of geographical barriers. Many plants and animals cannot pass across high mountains, deserts, or rivers. Even soil conditions can be barriers to dispersal. Continents are barriers to marine organisms. Deep water is a barrier to shallow-water marine organisms.

Lack of food can keep animals from moving into new areas. This is a *biotic barrier.* The Middle East might be a good habitat for an African zebra. But the zebra would have to cross the Sahara Desert to get there. It would starve in the process.

***Climatic barriers* also prevent the spread of many organisms.** Many mammals are physically able to climb over mountain ranges. But the weather conditions might keep them from doing so. The extreme temperatures of the desert are a barrier to many organisms. For deer, squirrels, and other forest animals, a desert would be both a climatic and a biotic barrier.

MAJOR CLIMATIC ZONES OF NORTH AMERICA

North America is divided into **climatic zones** according to temperature ranges. The area of the polar climate is usually called the *arctic region*. It includes northern Canada, part of Alaska, Greenland and other land masses near the North Pole. Similar climatic conditions are found above the timber line on high mountains. Most of Canada and most of the United States lie in the mid-latitude climate. This is known as the *temperate region*. Florida is in a *semitropical region*. As you move southward through Mexico, you enter the *tropical region*.

Climatic regions vary between the North or South Poles and the equator. So do the many types of living organisms. In general, a trip from the Far North begins with a region of ice and snow. This gives way to low herbaceous plants. Still farther south, we find large coniferous forests. The division between the low herbaceous plants and the conifers is called the **tree line.** Next comes the deciduous forests. Depending on the rainfall of the area, the deciduous forest may give way to prairie grassland. Then there would be a desert or a tropical forest.

Sometimes, all of the climatic zones can be found within one small area. These zones from polar to tropical can be found as one climbs a high mountain at the equator. Thus, climatic barriers can be created by the shape of the land as well as by the change in latitude.

Biomes

REGIONS WITH CLIMAX VEGETATION

Climax species are found in the coniferous, deciduous, and tropical forests of various climatic zones. **Any large geographical region identified by its climax vegetation is called a *biome*.**

THE POLES

Many people think of the North and South Poles as large frozen wastelands, with extremes of light or darkness during the day. This is only partly correct. In fact, there are a number of differences between the two Poles. The continent of Antarctica is very large indeed. It is almost as large as the United States and Canada combined. The Antarctic land is covered by ice. Its average depth is more than a kilometer. Over 90 percent of the world's ice is found here. Antarctic winds have been measured at more than 300 kilometers per hour. In no month does the mean temperature go above freezing. Because of this, the water is always frozen. So, in a strange way, Antarctica is as dry as a desert. It is believed that this continent was not always like this. Scientists have found fossil leaves and coal deposits in the Antarctic. This suggests that it once had a tropical climate. Only three types of flowering plants exist here, and they are on the very tip of the Antarctic peninsula. Even lichens

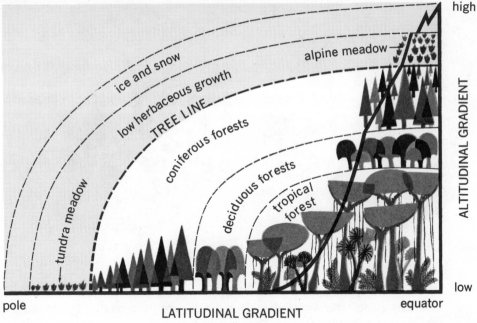

Why is there a great abundance of life at the North Pole? What is the significance of the Antarctic convergence?

51–2 Vertical climatic regions of the earth are similar to horizontal climatic regions. Life zones on a high mountain can be compared to those found from the equator to either pole.

and mosses are rare. No land mammals live in the Antarctic today. The animals of the Antarctic are the penguins, a few visiting birds, mites, a wingless fly, and a rare insect that lives at the tip of the peninsula. About 50 percent of these small invertebrates are parasites.

The Arctic is surprisingly different from the Antarctic. More than 100 species of flowering plants have been identified there. There are also many types of mosses, lichens, insects, birds, and mammals. About a million people also live within the Arctic. They are mostly American Eskimos and reindeer herders from northern Europe and Siberia.

There are several differences between the polar regions. The Arctic has less land mass than the Antarctic. The ice-sheet that covers most of the Arctic is seldom more than 5 meters thick. Stored heat from the ocean below the ice keeps the temperature within a certain range. The Arctic averages 17° C warmer than the Antarctic. Ninety percent of the Arctic's land loses its ice covering in the summer. Temperatures may rise higher than 25° C. As the upper layers of tundra thaw, the many flowering plants are supplied with water.

51–3 Mt. Erebus is the only active volcano on the Antarctic continent. (Albert Towle)

THE TUNDRA

The *tundra* is another of the earth's biomes. This large area encircles the Arctic Ocean of the Northern Hemisphere. There is no similar large land mass at this latitude in the Southern Hemisphere. The area of southern tundra is very small compared to the northern tundra. The tundra has a very cold and dry climate. About a meter below the surface, the ground is permanently frozen.

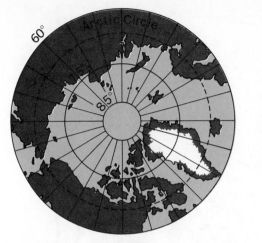

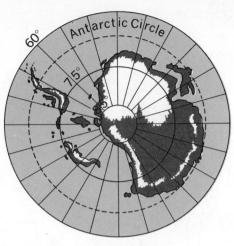

North Pole

South Pole

51–4 The North Pole is located on a sheet of ice overlying the Arctic Ocean. The South Pole is covered by the large Antarctic continent.

Ask students who have visited various biomes to discuss the characteristics of those areas. Reports can be assigned to students who have not had the opportunities to travel.

It is called the *permafrost*. During the continuous daylight of summer the surface thaws. As a result many bogs, streams, and ponds are formed.

Mosses and lichens are the main year-round vegetation. There are also a few dwarf birches, alders, willows, and conifers. Annual plants have a rapid growing season. Many of these plants produce large, bright flowers, even though there are periods of freezing temperatures. The birds are mostly summer migrants. The ptarmigan, however, is a permanent resident. Many mammals of the tundra have protective coloration. White coats are found in the Arctic hares, collared lemmings, Arctic foxes, and polar bears. Insects are numerous in the summer. Most lay eggs that resist freezing. Herds of caribou graze on tundra moss and lichens.

51–5 Annual plants of the tundra grow and reproduce during the brief growing season. (Dr. William Steere; Walter Dawn)

674

THE CONIFEROUS FOREST

Just south of the tundra in Europe, Asia, and North America is another biome. It is a large coniferous forest sometimes called the *taiga* (TIE-guh). This region's growing season may be as long as six months. Winter temperatures, however, may get as low as they do in the tundra. A noticeable tree line usually marks the change from the tundra to the taiga. The most obvious tree is the spruce. Taiga soil is shallow because of glacial scraping thousands of years ago. The Southern Hemisphere has no large taiga.

Farther south in North America, the broad coniferous belt covers much of Canada. Forests of alders, birch, and juniper are found in this region. In some areas, fire has destroyed the forest. Where succession has begun, the pioneer grasses are followed by aspens and birches. These are eventually replaced by a climax community of spruces, pines, and firs. Stands of pine, spruce, and redwoods grow along the coastal ranges of Washington, Oregon, and California. These giant trees may reach a height of 60 meters or more. Rainfall may be as heavy as 20 centimeters per year. Fog often covers the area providing additional moisture.

The coniferous forests of United States and Canada supply the lumber industry with an enormous amount of wood. The wood and its products have many important uses. Just as important, the coniferous forest is the home of many plants and animals. In order to meet our needs and the needs of its inhabitants, the coniferous forests must be used wisely.

Coniferous forests have many full-time residents. Moose live in areas where they are protected. Or where they have not been over hunted. Black bears roam the forests. So do martins, wolverines, and lynxes. The bobcat, fox, and wolf prey upon squirrels, chipmunks, rabbits, and mice. Beavers and porcupines are found in many of the coniferous forests. Many birds breed in these forests

51-6 A scene in a coniferous forest of the Northwest. (Albert Towle)

during the summer. In the fall, however, some migrate south. Many insects and other invertebrates live in the coniferous biome during the summer. They lie dormant during the cold winter months.

THE DECIDUOUS FOREST

Areas of the temperate zone have a long growing season. It may last for six months or more. Rainfall averages about 100 centimeters per year. Where the soil is suitable, there are large **deciduous forests.** These forests can be found in the eastern United States, England, central Europe, and parts of China and Siberia. A similar zone is found in South America. But it is limited in size by lack of rain.

There are a variety of different deciduous climax communities. These depend on local conditions of soil, drainage, and climate variation. Let's look at the variety of communities in the United States. Beech-maple forests are found in the north central regions. Oak-hickory forests are common in the western and southern regions. Oak-chestnut forests were once common in the Appalachian Mountains. They are now almost destroyed by blight. Other deciduous trees of the temperate zone are the sycamore, elm, poplar, willow, and cottonwood. Each of these specific forests has its typical animal species. Several animals are found in all deciduous forests. Deer are the common herbivores. Other familiar mammals are foxes, raccoons, and squirrels. Wolves wander between taiga and deciduous forests. There are many tree-nesting birds, such as the woodpecker.

Deciduous forests change from season to season. Trees are green in late spring and summer. Shrubs growing in the shelter of these trees produce beautiful blooms. During the fall, the leaves of many trees turn brilliant shades of red and yellow. In the winter, their bare branches stand out against the snow.

51–7 Deciduous forests undergo seasonal change. During what season was each photograph taken? (Russ Kinne; Herbert Weihrich; John King)

THE GRASSLANDS

Grasslands are found in vast areas where yearly rainfall is between 25 and 75 centimeters. This amount is not enough to support large trees. But it is sufficient for many species of grass. Grasslands are natural pastures. They have been used for years by huge herds of grazing animals. However, humans have allowed many of these lands to be overgrazed. Without the grass covering, the land's essential topsoil is worn away by water and wind. This erosion makes the land useless.

North American grasslands include the Great Plains and tall-grass prairies. Great herds of bison and antelope once grazed on these grassy plains. Burrowing mammals such as hares, prairie dogs, ground squirrels, and gophers are still abundant. These mammals form an important link in the food chain. They are eaten by weasels, snakes, and hawks. Locusts and grasshoppers are important members of the insect population.

The tropical grasslands of Africa are known for a variety of animal populations. These animals include the giraffe, zebra, antelope, ostrich, and lion.

A **savannah** is a grassland with scattered trees. The oak-grass savannahs are found in the western United States. In Australia, the grasslands and savannahs are used by cattle, sheep, and kangaroos. South America also has large areas of savannah.

51–8 When scattered trees are present, a grassland area, such as this one in Africa, is called a savannah. (Louise Boker, National Audubon Society)

THE DESERT

Did you know that there are both hot and cold **deserts?** Death Valley is a typical hot desert. Its climax vegetation is the creosote bush. There are several cold deserts in the northwestern United States. Sagebush is the dominant shrub in cold deserts. The plants in both hot and cold deserts are xerophytic. That is, they can live in areas with only 25 centimeters of rain per year. Their leaves are small, with thick, leathery outer layers. This helps them to conserve their water. Some desert plants have no typical leaves at all. The cactus, for example, has spines.

Desert animals also have special adaptations. Some excrete nitrogenous wastes in the form of uric acid. Uric acid may be excreted in an almost dry form. This helps animals such as reptiles, birds, and some insects conserve body water. Mammals cannot do this. Their nitrogenous wastes are urea dissolved in water. To keep them from losing too much water, most desert mammals burrow during the day. Some rodents obtain enough water from the seeds and fruit they eat. Others get water from cacti and other water-storing plants.

Desert herbs, grasses, and flowering plants come up very soon after a rain. Some of these plants, go through a complete cycle of growth, flowering, and seed production in just a few weeks. Some of the large perennial plants have very long taproots. Most desert plants have special ways to store water.

51–9 The cold desert occurs in northern latitudes. Note the sagebrush, characteristic of these areas. (Inez and George Hollis, Photo Researchers)

Specimens of Spanish moss are easy to keep in class and are interesting for study. Compare a temperate rain forest such as Olympic National Park with a tropical rain forest.

THE RAIN FOREST

Life flourishes in a *rain forest.* The conditions and ecological niches are similar in all rain forests. These areas have an abundant water supply and a long growing season. *Temperate rain forests* are found on the northwest Pacific Coast. There are *tropical rain forests* on and near the equator all around the earth. In these forests, seasonal temperatures vary less than the temperature changes between day and night.

Rain forests are rich with plant life. Short trees grow beneath tall trees. Together, they produce a thick canopy. Because of the shade, few plants can grow on the ground. Many smaller plants have adapted to this environment. Some have long vines. These vines allow them to grow roots in the moist ground and have leaves high up toward daylight. Most tropical rain forest plants have very large leaves. Conservation of water is not a problem for them. The critical problem is to find a place to grow with enough light for photosynthesis.

Epiphytes (EP-ee-FITES) are plants that attach themselves to trees. Sometimes they grow 30 meters or more above the ground. They have thick, porous roots adapted to catch and hold rainfall. The leaves of many epiphytes are arranged to catch water, insects, falling leaves, and other debris. They get essential minerals from the decomposing insects. Many species of orchids, bromeliads, mosses, ferns, and lichens are epiphytes. These plants do not get their food from the plants on which they grow. But, they can harm these plants by shading their leaves. Also, the weight of the epiphyte can break supporting limbs.

Animal life is plentiful in a rain forest. Most of the animals live high in the trees. The rain forest is quiet in the daytime. But toward

51–10 A tropical rain forest (Shostal)

evening, everything seems to come alive. Ants, beetles, termites, and other insects are numerous. They supply many other animals with food. Crickets and tree frogs begin singing. Birds make noise as they search for food. Tree-dwelling monkeys chatter and howl before settling down for the night. Nocturnal carnivorous cats begin to hunt for monkeys, deer, and other animals. These cats include the jaguar in South America, the leopard in Africa, and the tiger in Asia.

A rain forest is not a jungle. A rain forest is usually climax vegetation. A jungle is not. It is very dense ground growth found along river banks. It also occurs on land once cleared by humans or by some natural event like a flood or fire. Left alone, most jungles usually become rain forests through succession. A jungle, then, is a kind of immature rain forest.

Ask students how plants can live despite the insufficient light in many areas of a rain forest. Remind students of the skototropic trait evidenced by some tropical vines that grow toward darkness.

THE MARINE BIOME

Oceans cover more than 65 percent of the earth's surface. They support many organisms. As you learned, the changing tides produce a rhythmic rise and fall of water. The shore area covered and uncovered by this water is called the *intertidal zone.* It is exposed at low tide and covered at high tide. At the end of the shoreline is the continental shelf. Around large land masses, the continental shelf slopes down gradually to about 180 meters. Then it drops sharply to 1,800 meters or more. In some areas, there are trenches more than nine thousand meters deep.

The *marine biome* can be divided into two zones. There is the bottom, or *benthic zone,* and the ocean, or *pelagic zone.* The benthic

51–11 The ocean may be divided into several zones. Each zone has characteristics that determine the types of organisms it can support.

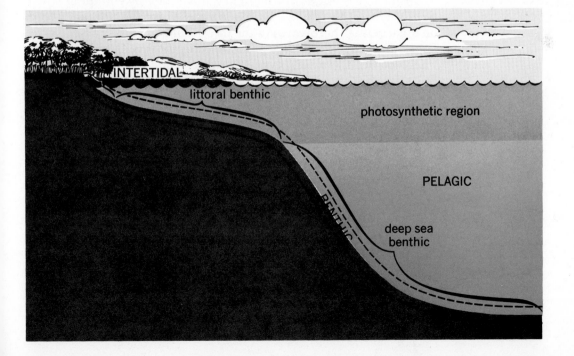

Why are there so many organisms found in the intertidal zone? If students live near an ocean, they can be asked to collect specimens found near shore as examples of intertidal life.

zone is divided by the continental shelf into the *littoral benthic zone* and the *deep sea benthic zone*. Some light passes through the waters above the continental shelf and the pelagic zone. The light passes down about 180 meters. This is the most productive region of the marine biome. Here photosynthesis occurs in the microscopic suspended algae and in the large drifting algae. These ocean plants are important in energy production. But they do not influence the environment as land plants do.

The basic food of the pelagic zone is plankton. Plankton includes diatoms, dinoflagellates, unicellular algae, protozoans, and the larval forms of many animals. Many copepods, small shrimp, small jellyfish, and worms are also plankton. The copepods feed on the microscopic diatoms and algae. In turn, the copepods are the major food of the whale. Ocean food chains involve many carnivorous fish, squids, and sharks.

What do animals beneath the photosynthetic zone eat? They depend on sinking plankton, dead animals, and the swimming organisms that pass between the two levels. Many animals have recently been discovered living on the deep-sea bottom. For food, these scavengers depend on dead animals falling from above. Bacteria live in the soft ooze on the ocean bottom. The bacteria break up complex organic molecules of the dead organisms that have settled there.

Life is abundant in the intertidal zone. It is like the tropical rain forest on land. Growing space is limited. Algae and tiny colonial animals attach themselves to rocks and to the shells of other animals. Epiphytic algae are found on most kelps. Snails, periwinkles, and barnacles can be found high on rocks. Here they are exposed to air for long periods of time. They stay moist by clamping down tightly when the tide is out. When covered by the tide, they feed on algae. Other herbivores in the intertidal zone are shrimp, small fishes, and copepods. Clams, mussels, oysters, and sponges filter microscopic organisms from the water. The carnivores include the starfish, sea anemone, larger fishes, octopus, and squid. Sea urchins "graze" on algae. Familiar scavengers of the intertidal zone include worms, crabs, and hermit crabs. Other worms and bacteria break down waste materials and dead organisms for the recycling of essential elements.

As on land, mineral exchange occurs in the ocean. Currents cause upwellings of deeper waters. This brings minerals and essential compounds to the surface. Here they can be used by phytoplankton and larger algae to make organic compounds. The upwelling also brings colder waters to the surface. In areas of upwelling, there is much phytoplankton. Also, there are many fish. These important fishing areas are near the coasts of Morocco, southwest Africa, California, and Peru.

THE FRESHWATER BIOME

The **freshwater biome** includes bodies of relatively still water such as lakes, ponds, and swamps. It also includes bodies of moving water, such as springs, streams, and rivers. Many plankton organisms found in lakes and ponds do not survive in running water. What determines the types of life that can inhabit a stream? The strength of its current and type of bottom are two factors. A stream bottom of shifting, sandy soil limits life greatly. Streams with sluggish current and a sandy bottom offer more possibilities for life. Here, many organisms burrow among the rooted vegetation. Stony streams are the habitat of actively swimming or clinging animals. The trout is one of the active swimmers. It feeds on the larvae of caddis flies, mayflies, dragonflies, and dobsonflies. All are common inhabitants of stony brooks and streams. Algae grow attached to rocks, stumps, or stones.

Water temperature is important to aquatic organisms. It takes a large amount of heat to raise the temperature of water. Also, when water evaporates, heat is absorbed from both the water and the atmosphere. This is what happens when you come out of the water on a hot summer day. Even a warm breeze can chill you as the water evaporates from your skin.

Water becomes lighter, or less dense, as it freezes. So, when water freezes, it floats. This is very important to lake organisms. A layer of ice on a lake's surface keeps the water from freezing solid. But it also keeps out some light and makes it difficult for oxygen to dissolve in the water. Because of this, lake organisms sometimes suffocate during the winter.

ANOTHER ASPECT OF THE DISTRIBUTION OF ORGANISMS

We have been studying a basic question in this chapter: Why is an organism suited for living where it does? Biologists carry their questions further. They also ask: How did this organism get here? Why are these organisms similar to another organism living thousands of kilometers away? These were some of the questions that Darwin asked when he visited the Galápagos Islands in 1835. The answers he came up with played an important role in evolution.

Darwin noticed similarities between the finches on the Galápagos Islands and those in Ecuador, almost 1,000 kilometers away. He also noticed major differences. These differences were in the shapes of their beaks and in the specialized methods for getting food.

The Galápagos Islands were never connected to any mainland. They were simply thrust up from the ocean floor. When they first arose, they were naturally completely unpopulated. So they offered a new environment for any organism reaching their shores. A thousand kilometers of ocean was a successful barrier against land organisms and most land birds. However, tropical storms may have carried other organisms to the Galápagos. These may have included some flying organisms, seeds, spores, small arthropods, and drought-resistant eggs. Small mammals may have floated to the island on uprooted trees and debris washed out to sea from tropical rivers. Most of these organisms must have died on the way from exposure, lack of food, or injury.

Students may be interested in learning more about oceanography. With the growing interest in deriving food and resources from oceans, this has become a popular course of study. High school and college courses are taught in marine biology.

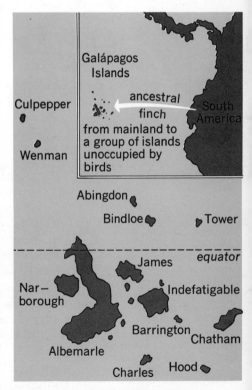

51–12 The Galápagos Islands were pushed up from the ocean floor and have never been connected to the mainland. They offered a new environment for any organism that reached them.

Once plants started growing, the arriving animals could find many niches. Perhaps the first finches to survive on the islands were groundfeeders. They would have found plenty of grass seeds to feed on. Some of these finches may have then emigrated to surrounding islands. The islands are separated by large areas of water. So cross-breeding of island populations was probably not common.

All the small land birds on the Galápagos are believed to have descended from one type of small finch. This bird must have originally been from the mainland. Today there are several distinct species. Some are still ground finches. Some feed primarily on cactus. Many live in trees. One even fills the role of a woodpecker. But it lacks the woodpecker's long tongue. Instead it uses a cactus spine to drive insects out of cracks and holes. Another finch pecks at the tail feathers of larger birds and then drinks the blood that flows.

Each type of Galápagos finch has developed a specialized bill. Some have thin bills like the warbler's. Others have heavy bills, well suited for seed-cracking. How might these different species of birds have all arisen from a common ancestor?

51–13 The finches Darwin found on the Galápagos Islands offered an excellent example of variation and adaptive radiation. Six of the species found by Darwin, are shown below: (a) *vegetarian tree finch*, a plant eater; (b) *large ground finch*, a seed eater; (c) *tool-using finch*, an insect eater; (d) *large cactus ground finch*, a plant eater; (e) *warbler finch*, an insect eater; (f) *small ground finch*, a plant and insect eater.

SUMMARY

Biogeography is the study of the distribution of plants and animals throughout the various regions of the earth. This distribution of plants and animals depends on many factors. These factors are organic, climatic, and geographical. Successful dispersal requires two things. There must be a method of travel. And the environment of the new location must be favorable.

Biomes are large geographical areas characterized by climax vegetation. The major biomes are: the poles, tundra, coniferous forest, deciduous forest, grassland, desert, rain forest, marine, and freshwater. Although both are polar biomes, the Arctic and Antarctic have very different life forms. The Antarctic is a large isolated continent. Its temperature is frigid. Its short summer months never expose much of its land or melt its ice into water. The Arctic is located on an ice sheet. The warmer ocean waters below the ice keeps the climate warmer. The Arctic is warmer by an average of 17° C. The land masses of the Arctic support many living organisms. More than a million people live in the Arctic.

Darwin studied the distribution of finches on the Galápagos Islands. The finches he found offered an excellent example of variation and adaptive radiation.

biogeography   biome   intertidal zone

geographical barrier   deciduous forest   marine biome

biotic barrier   grassland   benthic zone

climatic barrier   savannah   pelagic zone

climatic zone   desert   freshwater biome

tree line   rain forest

1. How do methods of dispersal limit the distribution of plants and animals?
2. Name the major barriers to dispersal and give an example of each.
3. Name and define the major climatic zones of North America.
4. What factors affect the types of flora and fauna within a climatic zone?
5. What reasons can you give for the great differences in the abundance of plants and animals in the Arctic and Antarctic?
6. Where are the coniferous forests, deciduous forests, and grasslands in the United States?
7. What adaptations to desert climates are found in mammals? in birds? in reptiles?
8. What environmental factors are found in a rain forest?
9. In the rain forests, the plants compete with one another for growing space. How are the epiphytes adapted for living in such forests?
10. What extremes of environmental conditions occur in the intertidal zone?
11. What furnishes the food for organisms living in total darkness in the depths of the ocean?
12. What prevents the organisms in a lake from being frozen solid in the water?
13. How has the study of the distribution of animals been used to support current evolutionary theory?

1. What are some food chains found in coniferous forests?
2. Give some examples of organisms finding their way to a favorable new environment in spite of barriers.
3. Give evidence in support of the following statement: The same climatic regions are observed as one moves up a high mountain on the equator or as one observes as he moves from the equator to either of the poles.
4. What environmental factors differ in a coniferous and a deciduous forest?
5. Discuss the adaptations of organisms in the intertidal zone.

chapter fifty-two

The Land We Live In

OBJECTIVES

- EXPLAIN possible solutions to soil and mineral depletion.
- DESCRIBE water conservation.
- DEMONSTRATE a knowledge of the causes of water pollution.
- LIST the effects of water pollution.
- DISCUSS recycling as a solution to solid waste disposal.
- NAME the sources of air pollution.
- DEFINE smog.
- DESCRIBE temperature inversion.
- DISCUSS methods used to reduce air pollution.
- DEFINE fallout.
- LIST possible sources of energy.

52–1 The clearing of trees and plowing of grasses provided fields for farming. (H.R.W. Photo by Russell Dian)

ENVIRONMENTAL PROBLEMS AND RESPONSIBILITIES

When pioneers pushed westward through the North American wilderness, they found a land rich in natural resources. Stands of hardwood trees extended from the Eastern coast to the Middle West. This was the largest deciduous forest in the world. Beyond the forest were prairies and plains. Native grasses had grown on these lands for thousands of years. The land was rich and fertile. Its topsoil had been building up for centuries. All the pioneers had to do was clear the trees and plow grasses to have rich agricultural fields.

There was wildlife everywhere. Inland waters were filled with fish, waterfowl, and aquatic mammals. Large and small game roamed the forests and grasslands. Early settlers probably thought that there was no end to these natural resources.

For more than a century, people used these resources with no thought to the future. The natural environment was wasted and destroyed. Finally, only a few decades ago, people began to realize what was happening. Much of the soil was gone. It had been washed or blown away. Wildlife was rapidly disappearing. A wealth of natural resources had been used up. Continued waste and destruction could only lead to disaster. None too soon, an effort was begun to improve these conditions.

New environmental problems have arisen in recent years. They are not directly related to nature. They have to do with human life in crowded cities. They involve the artificial environment created by science, technology, and industry. This environment includes office buildings, high-rise apartments, housing projects, apartment complexes, and residential communities. It includes shopping centers, power plants, refineries, sprawling industries, jammed streets and highways, and dense populations. The environmental

Discuss with students some of the reasons environmental problems and responsibilities were overlooked for many years. Could some of these problems have been avoided had they been tackled sooner?

problems of a city can be measured in terms of the pollution of rivers, lakes, oceans, and the air. At the same time many people depend on this artificial environment for their survival.

We are faced with many environmental problems. And we must continue to work out their solutions. Let's begin by looking at some of these problems.

THE LOSS OF SOIL FERTILITY

A century ago, our soil contained a rich store of minerals. These minerals were built up over many centuries from the growth and decay of native vegetation. Then people settled on the land. Fields were planted year after year. No thought was given to **depletion** of soil minerals. This loss of soil fertility began to show in reduced crop yields. But farmers still did not put minerals back into their fields. They just moved on to new fields.

Continuous farming and removal of plants from a field leads to another kind of soil loss. This is the **loss of organic matter.** In a natural environment, plants die and decay each season. This adds humus to the topsoil. But almost no organic matter is left in the soil after the crop plants are harvested. Soil organisms die out. Many of the processes that keep the soil fertile stop.

There are ways to prevent the loss of minerals from the soil. Scientific farmers add *fertilizers* to the soil. These fertilizers contain nitrates, phosphates, and potash (potassium compounds). Farmers can also practice **crop rotation.** Many crops are rotated in a three-year cycle. This first crop may be corn. The next may be wheat or oats. Then grass or clover is planted. Clover, alfalfa, cowpeas, lespedeza, and other legumes are important in the rotation cycle. Legumes support nitrogen-fixing bacteria on their roots. These bacteria form nitrates from atmospheric nitrogen. Valuable organic matter is added when these legume crops are plowed into the soil.

Discuss the economic and social implications of soil depletion.

52–2 Notice the difference in corn growth that can result from soil treatment. The plot on the right was treated with a fertilizer containing a high nitrogen content; the other was not. (A. L. Lang)

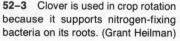
52–3 Clover is used in crop rotation because it supports nitrogen-fixing bacteria on its roots. (Grant Heilman)

52-4 This hillside shows serious rill erosion. (Grant Heilman)

52-5 Soil conservation methods. Strip cropping, terracing, and gully control. (Top, bottom right, Grant Heilman; bottom left, courtesy of Pan Am)

PROBLEMS OF SOIL EROSION

Erosion **is the most destructive form of soil loss.** It occurs when water and wind carry the soil away. Precious topsoil from millions of acres of our most productive land has been lost by erosion. This soil now lies in riverbeds and ocean bottoms. Some has blown thousands of kilometers by violent dust storms.

Erosion has always occurred. Before any land was cultivated, however, erosion was not as destructive. Soil formation generally kept up with erosion. But farming stripped the land of its natural vegetation. And poor farming methods exposed it to the forces of water and wind. The result was a far more serious and fast-moving erosion. Still today, the nation is losing 3.5 billion tons of soil each year because of erosion.

EROSION CAUSED BY WATER

Many farmers have been anxious to make every acre of land pay off. So they have cultivated river bottoms, hillsides, and all other available locations.

During seasonal floods, surface water covers the exposed soil. When this happens, a thin layer of soil is dissolved. Then, when the water drains, it removes the soil. This is known as *sheet erosion.* Sometimes sheet erosion can be prevented by draining fields. Natural vegetation should be returned to bottomlands that flood often. This is important to soil conservation and flood control.

Another kind of erosion results from rain falling on the exposed soil of rolling hills. Flowing water dissolves soil and forms tiny channels, or rills. This is the beginning of *rill erosion.* Each time water flows down the slopes it follows the same rills. These rills get wider and deeper. This finally leads to *gully erosion.* If this erosion is not stopped, gullies can become gulchs or even canyons.

Erosion occurs in cities as well as in the country. Building and construction activities can cause destruction of city lands. The stripping of ground cover is a common practice in the construction of

highways and buildings. The trees and other plant life are removed. This then leads to a heavy soil runoff. One solution would be to return trees and grasses to the exposed areas. Imagine what our roadways would look like if the plant life was not returned to their sides.

There is an agricultural solution to water erosion on a slope. It is called **contour farming.** The land is plowed across the slope of a hill rather than up and down. The trench made is called a furrow. Each furrow acts as a small dam in stopping the water from flowing downhill.

Strip cropping combines two soil conservation measures. Broad strips of land are cultivated on the contour of a slope. They are then planted with *row crops* such as corn, cotton, potatoes, or beans. These strips are alternated with strips of *cover crops*. Cover crops include wheat, oats, alfalfa, clover, and grass. These crops cover the surface of the soil completely and hold it in place. Water running from a strip of row crop is stopped as it enters a strip of cover crop. Crop rotation is often practiced in planting the strips, so that the soil remains fertile.

Terracing stops water flow on steeply sloping land. A series of banks are built on a long slope. This breaks the long slope into a series of short slopes. Flat strips are formed on the contour of the slope. Each strip is divided from another by a bank. Soil on the banks is held by plantings or rocks. There is a drainage ditch at the base of each bank. This carries the water around the slope.

Gully control requires other measures. One way to prevent gully erosion is to plant trees, grasses, or other vegetation on the slopes. They act as soil binders and prevent gullies widening. Deepening can also be stopped by building a series of dams across the gully. The dams slow the flow of water. Now, the settling soil will gradually fill in the gully.

THE PROBLEM OF EROSION CAUSED BY WIND

Wind erosion is a serious form of soil loss. This is especially true in prairie and plain regions. There, strong winds often sweep across the treeless land. At one time, the prairie soil was anchored by the spreading root systems of native grasses. However, much of this land is very fertile. And the climate is ideal for growing cereal crops. As a result most of the land has been plowed for agriculture.

In the 1930's, several late summer and early fall droughts hit the western plains. During this time, strong, hot winds blew much of the exposed topsoil away. Fine particles of soil from these great dust storms filled the atmosphere. Dust particles were in the air as far away as the East Coast. They were even found several hundred kilometers over the Atlantic Ocean.

How can dust storms be prevented? Windbreaks or **shelterbelts** are of some help. They can be planted along the edges of fields. In addition, furrows should be *plowed at right angles to the prevailing*

One can write to the United States Department of Agriculture, State University Agricultural Schools, and State Agriculture Extension Agencies for further information on water erosion and its control.

52–6 A dust storm. What harm can result from storms of this type? (Grant Heilman)

52–7 Planting rows of trees as wind-breaks helps prevent serious erosion of the soil caused by unchecked wind. (Walter Dawn)

Grasses can be planted to restrain shifting dunes. In addition, a technique of spraying the sand with a thin film of oil has proved to be advantageous. It keeps the sand from shifting and allows plants to gain a foothold for growth.

wind. The wind will blow across the furrows instead of down them. Thus each furrow will help to stop the movement of soil. In some places **irrigation** is possible. This is the running of water into the fields during the dry periods. This will check wind erosion, because moist soil does not blow away. Every centimeter of soil not cultivated regularly should be anchored firmly. This can be done by planting grasses and other *soil-binding plants.*

It is important that dust storms be prevented in the future. Scientists have warned of possible dangerous consequences. Atmospheric dust absorbs or reflects sunlight. As a result, less sunlight would reach the earth. This loss of sunlight could eventually lower the temperature of the earth's surface. Both the loss of sunlight and lowering temperatures could upset the environmental balance.

SOIL PROBLEMS AND WATER PROBLEMS—A VICIOUS CIRCLE

The two extremes in the water problem are floods and droughts. Both are the results of the misuse of soil and its plant cover. Rains that should soak into the ground run off the surface. This erodes the land. Streams flood with muddy water from the nearby land. Later in the season, there may be a water shortage. During floods, water washes soil away. During droughts, the wind blows the soil away. Soil erosion, floods, and droughts form a vicious circle.

The loss of runoff water causes the lowering of the water table. Increased demands for ground water in large cities is another cause. Wells supply much of the water for domestic use. Industries also obtain large amounts of water from these wells. More and more, cities are using the cold ground water for their air-conditioning systems.

WATER CONSERVATION METHODS

We cannot solve America's water problem until we have reduced the amount of runoff water during heavy rains. Water conservation must begin in hilly and mountainous regions. These regions are called **watersheds.** Forests and other plant cover must be returned to these areas. Vegetation breaks the fall of rain. Built up humus and leaf litter soak up water like a sponge. Water stored in watersheds flows into springs and rivulets. These, in turn, feed rivers and streams.

Rainfall is uneven and seasonal in most parts of the country. Therefore, rivers will always have high and low water stages. But a high water stage does not have to be a disastrous flood. Waters from rising rivers should spread into flood plains, sloughs, and breakwaters. As the high waters go down, these natural reservoirs should feed water back into the river. Ground and natural surface reservoirs receive excess water during rainy periods. Thus they maintain the water supply during dry periods.

Dams are another means of conserving water and preventing floods. Large dams have been built in many parts of the country.

These dams form large reservoirs. The reservoirs supply water to many large cities. Hydroelectric plants are often built next to dams. These plants use water power to make electricity. This electricity supplies large areas of the nation. Dams have also raised water levels. The result is that more rivers are now navigable for long distances. In the West, water from reservoirs is used for irrigation. Because of this, crops can now be cultivated on deserts. The deep, clear lakes formed by dams are used for water recreation.

WATER POLLUTION

One of our biggest water problems is pollution. Pollution is the adding of impurities to the environment. Many of our streams, lakes, and rivers are polluted. Some are dangerously polluted. We have even polluted the oceans. Water pollution is a matter of great national concern. How have some of our waterways become flowing sewers and death traps for aquatic life?

There are many sources of water pollution. We can discuss only a few of the major causes. **Sewage and garbage disposal is one of the major problems.** Early settlers often built towns and villages on the shores of large rivers and lakes. One reason for this was navigation. Another was waste disposal. Communities have been pouring untreated sewage, garbage, and other refuse into nearby waters for years. This was not a serious problem when towns were small and far apart. Bacteria were able to decompose organic refuse in the water. This kept pollution levels down. **Such polluting materials that can be decomposed by natural processes are said to be *biodegradable.*** Today, it is a different story. Towns have become large cities. These cities have large populations. Natural decomposition cannot possibly keep up with the rate at which sewage and refuse is poured into the waterways.

The pollution problem is complicated further by home disposal appliances. These appliances grind garbage and wash it into sewers. This method of getting rid of garbage seems both efficient and sanitary. But it adds to the problem of sewage disposal. Wastes from the food canning process add even more organic matter to our water.

Detergents also add to the pollution problems. This is especially true of detergents containing a large amount of phosphates. Phosphates stimulate the growth of algae in streams and lakes. Algal overpopulation upsets the natural balance of aquatic environments. A serious pollution problem results when these algae decompose at the end of the season. Government regulations now restrict the content of detergents.

Industrial wastes are a special pollution problem. Many industrial plants pour chemical wastes directly into streams. These wastes include toxic compounds such as cyanide, acids, alkalis, mercury compounds, salts and solvents. **Industrial wastes are *non-biodegradable.* That is, they are not decomposed by bacterial action.** Industries that pollute in this way include power plants, steel mills, paper mills, refineries, and automobile factories.

52–8 A flood may cause great damage in a residential area. (UPI)

52–9 These fish died as a result of water pollution in this stream. (A. Devaney, Inc.)

Pollution problems are also created by oil and other petroleum products. These products come from refineries, drilling and pumping operations, ship yards, and oil spills. They have destroyed wildlife and made water unfit for use in many areas. Often this oil soaks into feathers of ducks and other swimming birds. Many of these birds die of exposure or drown when their oil-soaked feathers cause them to lose buoyancy. Oil slicks often wash to the shore. These slicks foul the beach and kill many of the shore and tidepool organisms.

Thermal pollution **is the addition of heat to a body of water.** Power plants and other industries use water to cool their machinery. Then they pipe the returning hot water into a stream or lake. This changes the temperature of the nearby water environment and may kill many of the aquatic plants and animals.

EFFECTS OF WATER POLLUTION

Water pollution kills many organisms living in or near the body of water. This is its most immediate and obvious result.

Water pollution slows down the rate of photosynthesis in aquatic plants. Thus the amount of oxygen produced by these plants decreases. **Much of the world's oxygen supply is replaced through photosynthesis in aquatic plants.** Organic waste in the water increases the bacteria population tremendously. Bacterial decomposition of organic matter consumes oxygen. As a result of the lower levels of oxygen, many aquatic organisms may die of suffocation. **Preventing water pollution is essential if there is going to be a continued supply of oxygen.**

Chemical wastes poison aquatic plants and animals. Many of our major rivers once had large populations of fishes. Most of these rivers are now little more than giant drains. The Great Lakes are an example of large-scale water pollution. All the lakes are polluted with sewage, garbage, and industrial wastes. These wastes come from the many large cities along their shores.

In a recent year, it was thought that the Hudson River and the Great Lakes areas had greatly improved the water quality. Then, it was discovered that a non-biodegradable substance called PCB (polychlorinated biphenyls) was at a dangerous level. PCB's are highly toxic chemicals. They are used in the manufacture of paint and electrical equipment. There is no method known for taking them out of the water. And, once they get into the food chain, they stay.

Water pollution is also a human health hazard. Water polluted with sewages may contain bacteria and viruses. These organisms can cause typhoid, dysentery, hepatitis, cholera, and other infectious diseases. It is difficult to purify polluted water for our use. Because of pollution, many cities obtain their water from distant water supplies.

It is dangerous to eat aquatic and marine animals that come from polluted waters. Cases of typhoid, hepatitis, and other infectious

52–10 Industrial waste is a major source of pollution in our environment. (A. Devaney, Inc.)

Thermal pollution has been an increasing problem with the building of more nuclear power plants. Water returned to a river following use is often 15°C warmer than the usual temperature of the river. This disrupts spawning habits of fish, plant growth, and oxygen supplies in the water.

diseases have been traced to this cause. Certain freshwater and saltwater food fish consume and absorb harmful chemicals. These chemicals become concentrated in the fishes' bodies. Such chemicals include mercury compounds and radioactive materials. In some areas people have been warned not to eat striped bass or salmon. Some of these fish contain PCB. This health hazard is particularly serious in areas where local populations depend on fish for their food supply. Many recreational areas have been spoiled by pollution. For example, a few years ago, you could swim in the Great Lakes. Today, many of the beaches are closed because of pollution. Many resort areas have also closed because of polluted waters.

CLEANING UP OUR WATERS

The problem of water pollution is serious. But it is not hopeless. The public is now aware of the problem and willing to support corrective measures. But what should be done? We must first remove the sources of pollution as rapidly as possible. When this is done, waters will slowly begin to clean themselves. And plant and animal populations will begin to occupy these waters again.

The Clean Waters Act authorizes $4 billion over a four-year period as the Federal Government's share of matching funds for the construction of municipal waste treatment plants. However, these monies have been slow in getting to the cities. During 1975, more than 5,300 municipal sewage treatment projects were begun. But this is still not enough. The result is that pollution continues. The first stage deadline for sewage cleanup was 1977. It is expected that 9,000 communities serving 60 percent of the United States population cannot meet these standards.

Large industries are spending vast amounts of money to fight water pollution. Many of these plants, however, cannot meet the deadline. Some plants have been given permits to allow them to dump a certain amount of wastes. In all, 26,000 permits have been issued. Two plants alone have permits to discharge 30 pounds of PCB's into the Hudson River every day. This is still too much. Federal control has, however, caused a lowering of the bacteria and organic wastes that had been pouring into our water. With public support and cooperation, we can continue to improve the quality of our water.

SOLID WASTES—A MAJOR ENVIRONMENTAL PROBLEM

Almost everywhere humans go, they leave a trail of wastes. There is litter in the streets, on the beaches, and along the roadsides. Automobiles, refrigerators, and other useless trash are left in vacant lots. Littering is a costly and serious aspect of our solid waste problem.

In 1975, about 5 billion tons of solid wastes were produced in the United States. Most of these wastes were produced by agricul-

52–11 The oil polluting this beach destroys its beauty and wildlife. (Josef Muench)

Studies of purified water in some large American cities have revealed the presence of some potentially carcinogenic substances. Have students make reports on this subject.

52–12 Is there a better way to dispose of our trash? Recycling may be a solution. (H.R.W. Photo by Alan Mercer)

tural activities. Wastes from homes, businesses, and institutions make up a small part of this waste. However, these wastes are dangerous to our health. They build up in areas where many people are living. In 1970, the average American produced over two kilograms of solid waste per day. It is predicted that by 1980, we will be producing about three and a half kilograms of solid waste per day. Considering our entire population, this amount of waste would be staggering.

Did you ever wonder what happens to your household garbage after it is collected? These solid wastes include such items as food scraps, old newspapers, wood, lawn trimmings, glass, cans, furnace ashes, old appliances, tires, furniture, and many other items too numerous to mention. There are several ways these solid wastes are disposed of. The wastes are dumped, several miles out into the ocean. They are burned in open dumps. Solid wastes are also used as land fill. These means of disposal lead to additional environmental problems. The oceans, atmosphere, and ground water become contaminated. Wherever we turn, we are faced with the problems of solid waste disposal. How can we efficiently dispose of all these solid wastes?

RECYCLING—MAY BE THE ANSWER

One solution to the problem of solid waste disposal is to use it over again. This process is called *recycling*. Recycling reduces the production of waste materials that are a source of pollution. It also helps save our valuable natural resources.

It is possible to recycle paper, glass, tires, manure, food scraps, and certain metals. Many solid wastes can be neither reused nor repaired. Thus they must be reduced to raw materials. These raw materials are then remanufactured. Melting, revulcanizing, pulping, composting, and fermentation are several techniques used in this type of recycling.

In the past, cost and the abundance of natural resources limited the development of recycling technology. Also an efficient method of separating reusable wastes from the remaining wastes was needed. Today with the reduction of natural resources, we are forced to turn to recycling. However, recycling is still far from being accepted. Lack of public interest, recycling centers, funding for research, recyclable goods, and government incentive have slowed the process.

Environmental groups have been active in setting up collection centers. But it is up to the public to bring the bottles, cans, and old newspapers to be recycled. It is also up to industry to start recycling programs. And it is up to the government to propose legislation to help meet the problem. Unless we all work quickly, our environment will lose most of its natural resources. And in their place we will find our solid waste.

AIR POLLUTION

It has been estimated that more than 70 billion tons of airborne wastes are poured into our atmosphere each year. This is a staggering figure. **Atmospheric pollution is an enormous problem.** It comes from the smokestacks of industry and the chimneys of homes and apartments. It pours from the exhausts of automobiles, incinerators, and jet planes. It is all around us.

Have you ever heard the weatherman say that the air is "unacceptable" today? Did you ever wonder how to react? That's just the problem. We cannot escape atmospheric pollution. This is the only air we have. And we must breathe it. We measure the effects of air pollution in terms of human health and discomfort. But remember that plants and animals use the same air. We have no way of knowing how much wildlife has been destroyed by our careless pollution of the atmosphere.

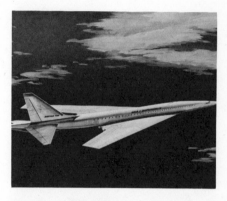

52-13 The supersonic transport (SST). (The Boeing Company)

SOURCES OF AIR POLLUTANTS

All foreign materials introduced into the atmosphere are *pollutants.* Some of these pollutants are droplets of liquids or small particles of solid materials. These are called *particulates.* We see them as smoke, dust, or haze. *Aerosols* are tiny suspended droplets of pollutants. Fine particles of carbon in the air are often called *soot.*

Various *gases* cause major air pollution problems. Most of them are products of combustion. Of these, *sulfur dioxide* (SO_2) is one of the most deadly. The main source of sulfur dioxide is electric and industrial plants. Their most abundant fuels are coal and oil. And these fuels contain sulfur. About 65 percent of the nation's sulfur dioxide is produced in urban areas. Sulfur dioxide is a heavy gas with a choking odor. It combines with water to form sulfuric acid (H_2SO_4). You can see how this would injure the moist surfaces of

52-14 Factories such as these are sources of air pollution. (Robert Perron)

your lungs when you breathe in air containing sulfur dioxide. Rain also combines with the sulfur dioxide in the atmosphere. These acid rains may be harmful to plants.

Automobile exhausts release another pollutant, nitric oxide (NO). When this combines with oxygen in the air, it forms nitrogen dioxide (NO_2). This is also a deadly gas. It combines with water (or the moisture in your lungs) to form *nitric acid* (HNO_3). Sunlight speeds up the combination of oxygen with nitric oxide. This is a **photochemical reaction.** Nitrogen dioxide is irritating to the lungs. In high concentrations, it can be fatal. It combines with water to form nitric acid (HNO_3). This acid can be damaging to humans as well as to plants and animals.

Carbon monoxide (CO) is a gas that is given off when coal, charcoal, wood, oil, and gasoline do not completely burn. Automobile exhausts are the major source of this air pollutant. More carbon monoxide is released into the atmosphere of a city than any other air pollutant. It combines with the hemoglobin in your blood faster than does oxygen. Then, since it is only slowly released, it causes suffocation.

WHAT IS SMOG?

Smog is just what the name implies. It is a combination of smoke and fog. When you think of air pollution, smog probably comes to mind.

There are several kinds of smog. The smog in industrial cities is usually a combination of fog and smoke containing sulfur dioxide. This smog often comes from blast furnaces, power plants, and factories.

Another type of smog comes from automobile exhaust pipes. This smog contains nitrogen dioxide, hydrocarbons, carbon monoxide, and other harmful gases. Smog has toxic substances that irritate the eyes and damage the lungs. They also damage plants and animals.

WHAT IS A TEMPERATURE INVERSION?

Under normal atmospheric conditions, warm air close to the earth rises and cools. Air pollutants rise with it. Then they are dispersed through the upper atmosphere. The air is cleansed each time it rains. The rain dissolves gases and they fall to the earth. This is what normally happens.

Once in a while, there is a **temperature inversion.** A layer of cool air moves into an area below a layer of still warm air. The warm air acts as a lid on the atmosphere. It prevents the cool air from moving, warming, and rising. Temperature inversions are most common in the fall. This is due to atmospheric conditions.

Temperature inversion can be disastrous in high pollution areas. Harmful gases become trapped in the lower atmosphere. These gases may remain in one place for hours, days, or even weeks. This

52-15 Smog over the Los Angeles Civic Center. (UPI)

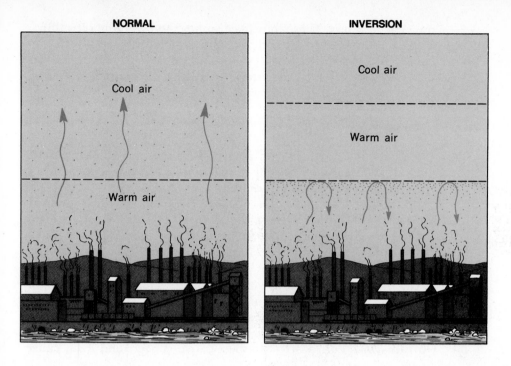

NORMAL

Cool air

Warm air

INVERSION

Cool air

Warm air

condition can cause serious illness or even death. We have no way of knowing the harm such a crisis does to wildlife.

REDUCING AIR POLLUTION

It is impossible to eliminate air pollution entirely from an industrial nation such as ours. But we can and must reduce it well below the danger point. How? Let's start at home. Do you burn trash in outdoor incinerators or open piles? Indoor incinerators are more efficient. It is even better to have your trash picked up. Do you burn your leaves in the fall? Make a compost pile out of them. Or put them in bags for collection.

Industry must do its part also. Some industries are making an effort. They are installing anti-smoke devices. Some power plants are installing devices to reduce pollution. These include precipitators, cyclones, and filters.

Laws have been passed regarding almost all phases of air pollution. Sulfur dioxide has been lowered about 75 percent of what it was in 1970. Carbon monoxide has dropped more than 50 percent. Suspended particles have lowered about 14 percent. Industry also has been making headway in the reduction of air pollution. Even with these improvements, we still have much to do to clean up our polluted atmosphere.

Automobile manufacturers have been forced to reduce compression in engines. This enables cars to burn low test gasoline. The lead and other products of combustion have been reduced in higher octane gas. Research is being done on smaller internal combustion engines. Also, manufacturers have built catalytic converters into

52–16 Cities with large quantities of pollutants in the atmosphere are often affected by a temperature inversion.

new car mufflers. These, however, appear to be giving off sulfuric acid. Scientists are still studying this problem to see if a danger exists. The possibility of steam or electric power for automobiles is also being explored. The public could also further reduce air pollution by wisely using their cars.

POLLUTION BY RADIATION

Radioactive particles can also pollute the air. These particles are carried great distances by air currents in the atmosphere. They may settle to the earth as *fallout.*

We do not know how long radioactive particles can remain in the upper atmosphere before they return to earth. Certain nuclear explosions in the atmosphere produce *strontium-90*. This radioactive material eventually settles on the earth. It is then taken up from the soil by plants. These plants may then be eaten by animals. If this happens, strontium-90 may be deposited in flesh, milk, or bones of these animals. Humans may then eat the contaminated animals. As a result of this, strontium-90 is deposited in human bones. Once a certain level of concentration is reached, strontium-90 radiations can destroy tissues, cause cancer, and even cause death.

Radioactive materials have been closely supervised over the last few years. Nations have agreed not to test atomic devices in the atmosphere. But if there is atomic warfare in any part of the world, radioactive pollution could be a major disaster.

ENERGY CRISIS—THE NEED FOR FUEL

In a natural ecosystem, the sun's energy is trapped by living plants. This energy is stored in the plant's tissue. The energy then moves through the food web. Eventually, all of the energy is released as heat. Thus, in a natural ecosystem the inflow of energy from the sun limits activities. **Also, such a natural ecosystem cannot use more energy than it receives.** An ecosystem must remain in these limitations in order to survive.

Human technology has taken us out of this natural energy flow. We need far more energy than can be supplied by this system. Today, the average American uses several thousand times as much energy as did his early ancestors of the 19th century. About 6 percent of the world's population live in the United States. And the United States uses about 35 percent of the energy consumed in the world.

In 1970, about 95 percent of the total energy used in the United States came from fossil fuel. Fossil fuels includes coal, oil, and natural gas. The remaining energy used was from a renewable supply. This was mostly power from falling water, and solar energy. A very small percent of our energy was from nuclear fuels.

Why is there an energy shortage throughout the world? One reason is that cities and surrounding areas are becoming heavily populated. As a result, fuel needs rise. The production, mining, and transportation of fuels becomes a problem. Power industries cannot respond quickly enough to these changes. Fossil-fuel generators cannot be built fast enough. A coal mine takes four years to open. Oil fields may take up to ten years to reach production. The power being used rose faster than was predicted. Therefore, the amount of fuel demanded could not be supplied. Thus, there is an energy shortage.

It is interesting to note that there is a controversy concerning the safety of nuclear power plants. Students should be asked to bring in articles that relate to this controversy.

Because of such energy shortages, more people are concerned with future energy needs. **We are beginning to realize that our supply of natural fossil fuels is dwindling.** It is believed that world energy needs are doubling every 10 years. Obviously, we need other sources of energy. One solution is to explore the various renewable energy sources. These might include energy from the sun, the heat of the earth's crust, running water, tides, wind, and even burning garbage. Nuclear fuels might also allow for an increase in energy production. Public awareness of the consumption and waste of energy is also necessary if we are going to conserve energy.

SUMMARY

When the people first settled in North America, they thought that the natural resources would never end. We now know that people have wasted many of these resources. Without knowing the widespread effects of their activities, people have caused thousands of kilometers of land to become useless.

As science, technology, and industry developed, the same wasting and destruction of our environment took place. Huge cities were built. Rapid methods of transportation made it possible for us to go to all places quickly. The population increased. With the demand for more food, the farmer began to look at what had been happening to his fields. He wanted to increase his crop yield. Today, the farmer is doing things differently. Fertilizers are now used to replace organic matter and minerals. Crop rotation is found to be of value in putting nitrogen back into the soil. Erosion, caused by wind and water, is prevented by contour farming, strip cropping, and terracing.

Water, also, has been wasted. We now know the value of storing it behind dams. Watersheds are protected and planted to keep water from making channels as it runs over the land on its way to the rivers.

The mere numbers of people, as well as industry, cause pollution problems. Biodegradable substances are broken down by bacteria. This releases minerals for recycling. But, there is a limit as to how much can be taken care of in this way. Non-biodegradable substances are not broken down. In fact, they may be toxic to organisms in the environment.

Even our air is being polluted with many kinds of chemicals. Many of these chemicals are poisonous to plants and animals. Some have caused people to die. Radioactive particles can also pollute the atmosphere. They can be carried to all parts of the earth and can cause tissue damage and death.

Realizing that the human is affected by the biotic and physical factors of the environment is important. Realizing the effects of human actions is also important. But, more important yet, is doing something about the pollution problems. Legislation has helped to provide money and direction for solving pollution problems. Every person needs to take part in restoring the soil, cleaning the water, and purifying the air.

QUESTIONS FOR REVIEW

1. How does overproduction lead to mineral depletion?
2. Describe three types of erosion caused by water.
3. Why are cover crops and row crops alternated in strip cropping?
4. In what kind of situation would terracing be practiced?
5. Outline several methods of preventing erosion caused by wind.
6. What is a watershed?
7. List several sources of water pollution. What steps is the government taking to clear up this problem?
8. What is the difference between biodegradable and non-biodegradable water pollutants? Give an example of each.
9. What is thermal pollution?
10. Explain how the decomposition of sewage and other organic materials in water kills fish and other aquatic animals.
11. How is recycling a solution to solid waste disposal?
12. What are particulates in the atmosphere?
13. List several toxic gases associated with air pollution.
14. What is smog?
15. Identify two sources of pollutants that form smog.
16. Describe the atmospheric conditions that cause a temperature inversion.
17. In what respect is strontium-90 a hazardous form of radioactive fallout?
18. What source of energy will help us meet future energy needs?

APPLYING PRINCIPLES AND CONCEPTS

1. Discuss the principle of crop rotation as a soil conservation measure.
2. Discuss the combination of strip cropping, contour farming, and crop rotation as a conservation measure in a hilly agriculture area.
3. Discuss several damaging results of water pollution.
4. Why are PCB's considered to be dangerous?
5. Discuss various methods for reducing air pollution.

53-1 We must all be concerned with protecting our natural resources. (USDA)

Forest and Wildlife Resources

OBJECTIVES

- DESCRIBE how forests are used and abused.
- DISCUSS forest management methods.
- NAME the causes of forest fires.
- DESCRIBE fish conservation.
- LIST endangered bird species.
- EXPLAIN the insecticide dilemma.
- EXPLAIN why DDT is a special problem.
- NAME the wildlife conservation programs.

FOREST AND WILDLIFE CONSERVATION

Today's environmental problems are not limited to the soil, water, and air. For many years, we have wasted our forests. And we have destroyed much of our wildlife. Part of this destruction probably could not be avoided. Agricultural development requires that we change the natural environment. So does the growth of cities. However, much of this destruction was the result of greed, carelessness, and indifference. What we need today is a *total* conservation program. It must include improvement of the physical environment. It also must provide for restoring our forests and wildlife.

SOME FOREST FACTS

Our nation's original forests covered nearly half the land. This was more than 822 million acres. Most of the eastern and western areas of our country were once forests. The large central and southwestern areas were mostly prairies, plains, and arid lands.

The two great forest belts of the East and West are divided into different types of forests. The type of forest was determined by factors such as temperature, rainfall, soil, and shape of the land.

The *central hardwood forest* covers much of the eastern and central United States. It extends all the way to the prairies in the Midwest. The timber trees of this forest are valuable. They include beech, maples, oaks, hickories, ashes, and black walnut. The *northern forest* lies in the Great Lakes and northern states regions. It extends west to Minnesota. It extends down the Appalachian Mountains to Tennessee and North Carolina. This forest also covers much of Canada. It includes species of pine, spruce, and balsam fir. These trees are mingled with birch, aspen, maples, linden, and other northern hardwoods. The *southern forest* covers the Southeastern

Forests and their products are essential to our way of life. Ask students to research articles pertaining to forest conservation and the use of forestry products. Some of the major lumber companies may be of help in this project.

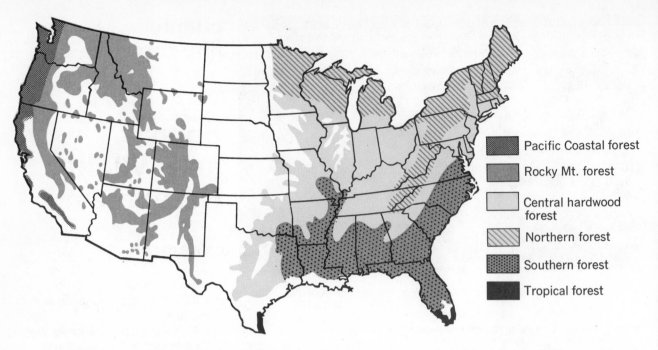

▨	Pacific Coastal forest
▩	Rocky Mt. forest
▨	Central hardwood forest
▨	Northern forest
▨	Southern forest
■	Tropical forest

53-2 The principal forest regions of the United States. They occupy nearly one third of our land.

and Gulf Coastal states. It is a mixed forest of conifers and hardwood trees.

The *Rocky Mountain forest* covers the mountain slopes to the timberline. It is made up of species of pine, spruce, fir, and larch. The *Pacific Coastal forest* is perhaps the most magnificent of all. It extends from California to Washington and far into Canada and Alaska. It forms dense and valuable stands of timber. These forests include the towering Douglas fir, coast redwood, sugar pine, white fir, and western cedar.

FORESTS—THEIR USE AND MISUSE

In the past, the clearing of land for agriculture and housing destroyed many forests. Also, the demand for lumber has been draining our forests for more than a century. Hardwood has long been used for construction. More recently, conifers have taken its place. The wood of conifers is ideal for construction. It is soft and easily worked.

Forests supply an enormous amount of *pulpwood*. It is used in making many paper products. Among them are newsprint, high quality book paper, stationery, and packaging paper. Pulpwood comes from United States and Canadian coniferous forests. Valuable *distillation products* come from hardwoods, such as beech, maple, and birch. Some of these products are alcohol, oxalic acid, charcoal, and lampblack. Most *pine products* come from the Southern states. These include turpentine, rosin, and pine tar. Maple sugar and *tannic acid* are also forest products. Tannic acid comes from the bark of hemlock, chestnut oak, and tan-bark oak.

53-3 Pulpwood is used in the manufacturing of a variety of paper products. (Vivian Fenster)

Forest products are only a part of the value of forests. Forests are important in *regulating the water supply* and preventing floods. They also *prevent soil loss* by serving as soil binders. Trees absorb large amounts of water from the ground. Eventually, most of the water transpires from its leaves to the atmosphere. Thus, it is understandable how forests can *affect the climate*.

As was mentioned, it was necessary that large areas of our original forests be cleared for agriculture. This was especially true of the central hardwood forest. The soil of this forest was deep and fertile. However, this is only part of the story of forest destruction. Much of the destruction was useless waste. At one time, entire forests were cut down in lumbering operations. Nothing was left but stumps and brush. Often, more than half of the removed timber was wasted. Forests were cut down in hilly regions. These areas were not suitable for farming. Thus, the land was left bare and easily eroded. Wise use could have supplied our timber needs and prevented the useless destruction of the forests.

There are many careers that may be of interest to students who enjoy the outdoors. Ask students to report on such careers as a forest ranger, wildlife manager, and fish and game specialist. What other careers are open in these areas?

FOREST MANAGEMENT

As early as 1905, officials in Washington became concerned about the condition of our forests. As a result, Congress created the United States Forest Service under the Department of Agriculture. Large areas of timber land were set aside as national forests. Many of these areas are in the West. There are about 500 million acres of commercial forestland in the United States today. Of this, 92 million acres are owned and managed by the Federal Government. During 1975, Congress allowed $51 million to be used to replant 400,000 acres of forest. National forests are used for camping, hunting, fishing, grazing, water use, and timbering. Projections for future use of our forests indicate that timber production will have top priority.

How can we continue this use of our forests without making the same mistakes of the past? A staff of foresters and biologists are studying this very question. They are looking for better methods of conservation. These include control of forest diseases and insect enemies, more efficient lumbering practices, and new uses for timber products. Owners and managers of private forest lands work closely with state and federal agencies.

In national, state, and many privately owned forests, trees are being managed. In managed forests, trees are grown as crops. These trees are then harvested regularly. All of these trees are valuable timber species. *Improvement cutting* removes all the trees that are crowded, crooked, damaged, or diseased. Trees with no timber value are also removed. As timber trees mature, they are removed. This is called *selective cutting*. The forest is a constant source of timber. Timber is never cut unnecessarily. Some mature trees are always left. These provide seeds for the future forest. Every meter of space produces good timber. Every tree is in good condition.

53-4 Block-cutting removes an entire stand of timber at once. Stands of timber remaining protect the land and the new seedlings. (courtesy of Weyerhaeuser)

Forest fires are both dangerous and tragic. Review with students the correct way to build a fire in the forest and how to be sure it has been completely extinguished. With the advent of camping as a national pastime, it is essential that students understand their responsibilities when camping.

Block-cutting is another kind of lumbering. It is used to cut stands of trees that are all about the same age. In this process, a complete block of trees is cut, Then the block is replanted or reseeded. Trees left around the block protect the exposed land. They also supply natural reseeding. When small trees are established, another block can be cut. This method is used in stands of Douglas fir. A similar method is used to harvest spruce. It's called **strip cutting.**

Reforestation takes a long time. And it is expensive. **But reforestation is a very important part of the conservation program.** Large forest areas have been cleared unwisely in the past. Many are useless for agriculture. These regions should be returned to forests as quickly as possible. So should areas that are heavily lumbered or burned out.

Nature also helps in the reforestation process. The Douglas fir is the main tree in the Northwest. But its seedlings will not grow in the shade of other trees. In nature's succession, the climax trees are hemlocks and cedars. These grow well in the shade of the Douglas fir. Sometimes fire may destroy a large area. When this happens, Douglas fir seeds fall on open ground. Then, they grow and produce a new stand of trees. So you see, a knowledge of ecology and succession helps us in our conservation programs. In some areas, controlled fires or clear-cutting may actually be helpful.

Seedlings of many timber species are grown in large nurseries. These nurseries are kept by forest states, the United States Forest Service, and a number of private lumber and paper companies. Trees are being grown as a crop on nearly 48 million acres of forest land in 45 states. Many hardwood forest regions are being reforested with pine. This is because pine matures rapidly. It also makes valuable construction lumber.

FIRE—A MAJOR ENEMY OF FORESTS

Fire is a major tragedy in forests. It is not only a threat to human life. A forest fire destroys standing timber. It also destroys the seeds and young trees of the future forest. A large fire can even burn into the rich humus of the forest floor. It is impossible to say how much animal life is lost in such a fire. The problems do not end when the fire is out. Rains pour over the blackened earth and debris. Because the remaining humus is not protected by vegetation, much of it is washed into streams. More than 50 years may pass before the scars of a fire are hidden in a new forest.

The causes of forest fires are shocking. The United States Forest Service recently put out a report on forest fires. The following are causes listed in order of frequency:

1. Incendiarists (people who set fires on purpose)
2. Debris burners (people who let brush fires get out of control)
3. Smokers (people who throw lighted cigarettes, cigars, and matches from automobiles)
4. Lightning
5. Campers (people who leave live coals in campfires)

6. Railroads
7. Lumbering
8. Miscellaneous

53–5 Fire, whether caused by lightning or the carelessness of people, destroys plant and animal life. (Sally Kaicher; Sonja Bullaty; both National Audubon Society)

Notice the first three causes of forest fires. All three are the result of deliberate destruction or carelessness. All these fires could have been avoided. The only natural cause listed is lightning. And it is fourth in frequency.

National and state forests are carefully watched by rangers during the danger season. These rangers are positioned in towers that overlook the forests. Firefighters are always standing ready to take action as soon as a fire is reported. They are well equipped with trucks, water tanks, chemical extinguishers, and specially equipped airplanes. However, public cooperation is important in fighting this major enemy of the forest.

WILDLIFE CONSERVATION

The term **wildlife** includes all native animals and plants. However, we will only cover the conservation problems concerning the fish, bird, and mammal populations.

Wildlife conservation problems are directly related to other environmental problems. There has been a decline in many of our wildlife populations. This is the direct result of destruction of habitats. Cities and farms can continue to develop without the wholesale destruction of wildlife. This we have witnessed in the past few years.

53–6 This fire tower permits observation of many square miles of forest for signs of fire. (L.A. Forestry Commission, AFI)

VANISHING WILDLIFE

Today, many species of animal and plant life are in danger of extinction. And people will be the major reason for their extinction.

Students should find out about the game laws in their state including the needs for hunting and fishing licenses and the seasons for these activities.

Perhaps the greatest single cause for the decline of a species is the destruction of the natural ecosystem. The increasing demand for living space and the use of chemical poisons have destroyed many habitats. There are many other reasons for our vanishing wildlife. These include hunting for sport or fashion, and the introduction of foreign species. Also the collection of animals for the pet trade has reduced the numbers of many animals.

We should be concerned about our vanishing wildlife. The loss of a single species indicates that something is wrong with our environment. This loss could drastically effect the balance of an ecosystem. With every loss of a species, we lose a genetic stock forever. Nature allows for extinction but not for our thoughtless acts that cause extinction.

FISH CONSERVATION

There is no way we can restore fish to polluted waters. We must first remove the sewage, garbage, and chemical wastes from rivers and lakes. Then we must restore healthy aquatic environments. Only after these steps are taken can fish thrive and multiply.

Dams across rivers interfere with fish migration. The solution to this problem is the use of *fish ladders.* A fish ladder is a channel built around a dam. It is designed to let fish travel upstream. The fast flow of water is broken by a series of staggered plates. These plates extend into the water from the sides. Another type of fish ladder is made of a long slope broken into a series of steps. A fish traveling upstream can leap from one step to the next. Fish ladders are very important in salmon streams.

53–7 Fish ladders are built to enable fish to travel upstream during their spawning season. (U.S. Department of Interior)

The fish populations in many of our natural waters have declined over the years. But many artificial lakes and ponds have been stocked with game fish. One type is called a *farm pond.* These ponds are built with earthen dams in the low corners of fields. Much soil, sand, and gravel is needed to build upgrades and overpasses for super highways. Small lakes have been made from the holes left where this earth has been removed. Many of these lakes are stocked with bass, crappies, bluegills, and other game fish. Artificial lakes have also been formed behind dams. These lakes are ideal for fishing.

Artificial bodies of water may satisfy fishermen. But they can never replace rivers, streams, and natural lakes as environments for fish and other aquatic life.

CONSERVATION OF OUR VALUABLE ALLIES—THE BIRDS

Humans have cut forests, cleared underbrush, and burned fields for their own needs. More than 2,000 acres of rural land each day is changed for urban use. In the process, many bird habitats have been destroyed. People have unnecessarily drained marshes and lowered the water in ponds. As a result, water birds and wading birds can no longer find a source of food and nesting sites.

In the past, many thousands of birds were slaughtered for food or feathers. State and federal laws now forbid this type of hunting. But conservation measures came too late for some species. And birds that were once common are now extinct.

The extinction of the carrier pigeon is a familiar example. In the early 1800's, the naturalist John Audubon described flocks of passenger pigeons. These flocks were so large that they darkened the sky. For many years, these birds were slaughtered in their roosting areas. Then they were gathered in sacks and sold for a few cents, or fed to hogs. An epidemic disease probably killed the last survivors. It never occurred to anyone to conserve this species until it was too late. It is estimated that there were over two billion carrier pigeons at one time. The last survivor died in the Cincinnati Zoo in 1914.

ENDANGERED BIRD SPECIES

What do birds need to survive in a changing environment? Their survival depends on several factors. Reproductive habits are important. So is the ability to adjust to new food supplies. Some bird species have actually increased with civilization. Others are holding their own. Several species are endangered. These species may soon become extinct unless rigid conservation measures to save them are successful. The ivory-billed woodpecker is one of these species. In fact, it may be extinct even now. The California condor numbers only about 60. There are less than 1,500 American (Southern) bald eagles. Only about 60 Everglades kites remain. Other endangered birds include the prairie chicken, the osprey, the brown pelican, and the whooping crane.

Of course, many plant and animal species have flourished and died out through the ages. Maybe it is normal that some species are becoming extinct today. Yet biologists hate to see this happen. It seems so unnecessary—especially if we are partially responsible and if something can be done about it. Something *is* being done to save the whooping crane.

The number of native whooping cranes has not increased for many years. Close watching and protection by humans does not seem to have helped. In 1966, there were only 43 wild whooping cranes. In addition, there were seven birds in captivity. In 1964, an artificial propagation program was started. The Bureau of Sport Fisheries and Wildlife and the Canadian Wildlife Service agreed to let researchers collect eggs from several wild nests. These eggs were incubated at a research center in Patuxent, Maryland. The hatched young were then reared at the center.

The whooping crane normally lays two eggs. But it often rears only one of the hatched chicks. Researchers found that taking one egg from several nests did not reduce the wild population. The collected eggs were shipped to the research center by jet. They were packed in rubber-lined cases, that were warmed with hot water bottles. After hatching in incubators, the chicks were given spe-

53–8 The California condor, ivory-billed woodpecker, American bald eagle, and the whooping crane are some of our endangered birds. (William Finely, Allan Cruickhank, National Audubon Society; George H. Harrison from Grant Heilman)

53–9 The American bison is an example of direct extermination through hunting. The brown pelican is an example of indirect extermination through the use of pesticides. (Z. Leszcynski, Animals, Animals; Allan Roberts)

cially prepared diets. The captive birds were returned to the wild flocks. By 1971, the total number of whooping cranes had increased. There were 21 in captivity and 59 in the wild. This is a total of 80 birds, or an increase of 60 percent. These figures are very encouraging. The same research center at Patuxent, Maryland, is now using the same methods with eggs of the bald eagle.

THE INSECTICIDE DILEMMA

Chemical poisons are a new threat to wildlife. They are particularly poisonous to fishes and birds. It is almost impossible to grow many crops without using chemical poisons to protect them from insect attack. These poisons are used for fruit, garden vegetables, flowers, and lawns. We also use chemicals to kill household pests. You have probably killed mosquitos, flies, or roaches with a spray. In our war on insects, we have filled the environment with sprays, dusts, and aerosols. Such chemical poisons are called *insecticides.* Unfortunately, we tend to destroy valuable insects at the same time we are killing off the harmful ones. Insecticides also soak into the soil and wash into streams with ground water. There, they poison fish and other aquatic animals.

Many insecticides contain mercury, lead, and other heavy metals. Insect-eating animals absorb these chemicals into their systems. When this happens, these metals remain in the animals' tissues. **The concentration builds up from animal to animal in a food chain. This buildup is called *biological magnification.*** A top carnivore may have high concentrations of these deadly metals. Many insect-eating animals are undoubtedly poisoned in this manner. They include birds, frogs, and snakes. Several species of predatory fish have been found to contain dangerous concentrations of mercury compounds, PCB's, and other poisons in their tissues. Dieldrin is another insecticide that has been used to spray fields. It also builds up in the food chain. In 1974, this chemical was banned from use in the United States. Recent laws also prohibit the sale of other dangerous insecticides.

DDT—A SPECIAL PROBLEM

DDT (dichloro-diphenyl-trichloroethane) was developed near the end of World War II. It was very effective in killing body lice and controlling a typhus epidemic in Italy. This insecticide became popular immediately. People used it to kill mosquitoes, household pests, garden pests, and agricultural pests.

DDT has a rapid paralyzing effect on insects. Insects absorb the DDT and it remains in their exoskeletons. DDT breaks down very slowly. So its effects are long lasting. This was once thought to be beneficial. But it is now a cause for great concern. When DDT is sprayed into the atmosphere, it settles on the ground. From there, it washes into streams and is carried to the oceans. Traces of DDT have been found in ocean water as far away as the Antarctic. In an aquatic environment, DDT clings to algae and other aquatic plants. These plants are consumed by herbivorous animals. **Like other insecticides, DDT concentrations increase from one animal to another in the food chain.** They may reach deadly concentrations in a top level carnivore.

Birds also suffer from the effects of DDT. When DDT concentrations build up, it affects the reproductive system and lime-producing glands. This causes the birds to lay thin-shelled eggs that are easily broken in the nest. This is particularly true of insect-eating and predatory birds. Thin-shelled eggs have been found in the nest of eagles and of the California brown pelican.

ARE CONTROL MEASURES EFFECTIVE?

Dieldrin and DDT are now banned from sale in the United States. As a result, the environmental pollution by these chemicals has

There are many birds and animals that are considered endangered today. The Red Data Book of the International Union for Conservation of Nature and Natural Resources lists more than 1,000 species threatened with extinction. More than 100 of these species are native to the United States. Some of these creatures include the whooping crane, Southern bald eagle, California condor, the bighorn sheep, the Eastern timber wolf, and the blue whale.

53–10 Biological magnification of DDT as it passes through the food chain. DDT is measured in parts per million.

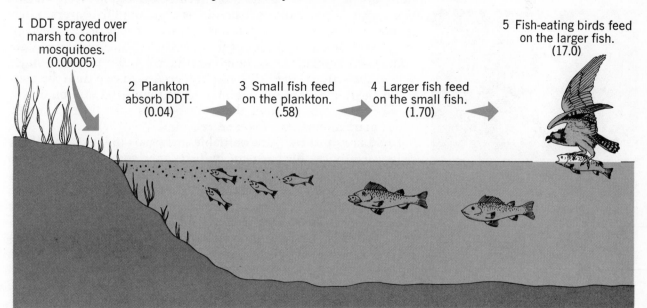

1 DDT sprayed over marsh to control mosquitoes. (0.00005)

2 Plankton absorb DDT. (0.04)

3 Small fish feed on the plankton. (.58)

4 Larger fish feed on the small fish. (1.70)

5 Fish-eating birds feed on the larger fish. (17.0)

In 1974, vinyl chloride pesticides were banned from use in homes, food-handling establishments, hospitals, and all areas that are enclosed. This substance has been associated with a rare form of liver cancer.

gone down. DDT in migratory songbirds has decreased nearly 90 percent since 1969. In the bald eagle, however, this is not true. DDT, dieldrin, other chlorinated hydrocarbons, and PCB levels were about the same in 1974 as they were in 1971. Perhaps the reason is that bald eagles are a top predator. Also they live longer than songbirds. And, they take their prey from highly polluted tidal waters.

But how do we continue to control insect pests? Clearly, some insecticides must be used. But they must be used carefully. And they must not be of a type to endanger wildlife.

The ideal answer to the insect problem is *biological control*. This is a natural method of controlling insect populations. The larvae of the lacewing explore plants for aphids and scale insects. Ladybird beetles, both adult and larvae, destroy tremendous numbers of aphids. Praying mantises wait motionless and suddenly grasp harmful plant-eating insects. In addition to these predatory insects, there are parasitic insects. These insects lay their eggs in the bodies of other living insects. For example, a certain wasp lays its eggs in a gypsy moth pupa. When the eggs hatch, the wasp larvae feed on the pupa. By conserving such insects, we use insects to fight insects. Fish, frogs, toads, snakes, and other small animals are also valuable in insect control. But birds are our best allies. Yet we are killing these animals with chemical poisons. This is the insecticide dilemma.

CONSERVATION OF SMALLER MAMMALS

At one time, our lands were rich in small mammals. But great numbers of them were killed off even before the pioneers started west. This is particularly true of the valuable fur-bearers. Early trappers set out to make their fortunes in furs. The prize catch was the beaver. It was very plentiful in the Pacific Northwest and Canada. It was known as the "empire builder." And it played a major role in the settlement of this vast wilderness. At one time the pelts of fur-bearing animals brought in more than $100 million a year to early trappers. Among these fur-bearers were beaver, mink, otter, martin, muskrat, fox, and raccoon.

Rigid laws protect these valuable mammals today. Many of the pelts used by the fur garment industry now come from fur farms and ranches. This reduces the demand for natural skins.

Protected areas have surprisingly large mammal populations. These areas include parks and residential communities. In these areas, you can find many squirrels, raccoons, opossums, groundhogs, and chipmunks. People often do not even know these mammals are around. This is because many of them are active at night. But there is evidence of their numbers. They are often found dead on city streets and highways. There seems to be no solution to the problem of animal deaths on the highways.

53-11 The beaver is a valuable fur-bearing mammal. (Leonard Lee Rue IV Monkmeyer Press Photos)

PROTECTION OF LARGER MAMMALS

A century ago, many thousands of buffalo grazed on our Great Plains. Then came the buffalo hunters. Whole herds were slaughtered. They were killed for sport and to feed the work crews building the western railroads. At one time, there were only a few hundred left. It appeared that the bison might disappear entirely.

White-tailed deer vanished from many of the eastern and central states many years ago. So did the black bear. Other large mammals began to decline in the West. These included elk, mule deer, and antelope.

Today, due to conservation measures, the situation has improved. White-tailed deer populations are again inhabiting many forest areas of the eastern and central states. Herds of bison, elk, mule deer, and antelope are increasing in the West. The problem now is reversed. How do we limit the large-mammal population? This requires scientific game management. Other large mammals are listed as endangered by the Department of the Interior. These include eight species of whales. Conservation measures are difficult to enforce. They require international cooperation.

Ask students to do some research on different wildlife conservation groups. Newspaper stories and articles should be brought into class.

NATIONAL PARKS AND NATIONAL FORESTS

There are twenty-nine national parks in the United States. Their six million acres are to be preserved forever. In addition, there are 149 national forests. These forests cover more than 181 million acres. About 92 million acres are forests that supply timber for forest products. They provide homes for wildlife. And they provide ranges for herds of big game mammals. Sometimes the national forests are opened for supervised cattle and sheep grazing. This happens when drought strikes the Great Plains in the summer months. They also provide recreational areas for camping, hunting, and fishing.

SUMMARY

Forests once covered nearly half our land. There are two great forest belts. One is in the East. The other is in the West. Each contains several different kinds of trees, depending on the temperature, rainfall, soil, and shape of the land. Many of our forests were carelessly destroyed in the past. Today, conservation measures are allowing them to build up again.

Wildlife conservation problems are directly related to other environmental problems. The destruction of habitats has also destroyed much of our wildlife population. Before we can restore our fish population, we must clean up our polluted waters. Many laws now protect nearly extinct birds. But the insecticides we use in agriculture pose a new threat to them. Insecticides also threaten our mammal population. In the past, fur trappers and hunters also threatened the mammal population. Today, we protect them in special wildlife preserves.

BIOLOGICALLY SPEAKING

block cutting	wildlife	insecticide
strip cutting	fish ladder	biological magnification
reforestation	farm pond	biological control

QUESTIONS FOR REVIEW

1. List the major forest belts and regions in the United States.
2. List various forest products and identify each with a forest region.
3. What is the difference between improvement cutting and selective cutting in forest management?
4. What is block cutting?
5. List seven causes of forest fires and indicate whether each cause is deliberate, the result of carlessness, accidental, or natural.
6. Explain the purpose of a fish ladder.
7. List eight endangered bird species.
8. Describe the work at the research center at Patuxent, Maryland, to increase the population of whooping cranes.
9. Describe several far-reaching effects of pollution by DDT, dieldrin, and PCB's.
10. What is meant by biological control of insects?

APPLYING PRINCIPLES AND CONCEPTS

1. Discuss the different methods of forest management.
2. Discuss the role of sports people in a wildlife conservation program.
3. Discuss possible reasons some bird species are now endangered while others are maintaining their numbers or even increasing.
4. In what respect are many insecticides a biological dilemma?
5. Discuss various management problems in the restoration of populations of large mammals, such as deer, elk, and bison.
6. What special problems are involved in the restoration of populations of the whales?

RELATED READING

Books

Aylesworth, Thomas G., *This Vital Air, This Vital Water.*
Rand McNally and Company, Chicago. 1968. Presents the facts about air, water, and noise pollution throughout the world in clear, straightforward language.

Hahn, James and Lynn, *Recycling: Reusing Our World's Solid Wastes.*
Franklin Watts, Inc., New York. 1973. An excellent book concerning the recycling of materials, the economic values of recycling of materials, and the value of recycling to the community.

Horwood, R. H., *Inquiry into Environmental Pollution.*
Macmillan Company, Toronto, Canada. 1973. An information and activities approach to the pollution problem.

Lauwerys, J. A., *Man's Impact on Nature.*
Natural History Press, Garden City, N.Y., 1969. An interesting account of the relation people have with their environment.

Leen, Nina, *And Then There Were None: America's Vanishing Wildlife*.
Holt, Rinehart and Winston, Publishers, New York, 1973. Describes the long list of threatened animals, why they are endangered, and what is being done to save them.

Marine, Gene, and Judith Van Allen, *Food Pollution—The Violation of Our Ecology*.
Holt, Rinehart and Winston, Publishers, New York, 1972. States the problems created by the addition of additives, preservatives, fungicides, bacteriocides, and dyes to our food.

McCombs, Lawrence G., and Nicholas Rosa, *What's Ecology?*
Addison-Wesley Publishing Co., Calif., 1973. A brief explanation of the basic concepts of ecology and related environmental problems.

McCoy, J. J., *Saving Our Wildlife*.
Crowell-Collier Press, New York. 1970. Tells of the destruction of much of North America's wildlife and describes the attempts that have been made to save the wildlife resources we have now.

Michelsohn, David R., and editors of Science Book Associates, *The Oceans In Tomorrow's World: How Can We Use and Protect Them?*
Julian Messner Publishing Co., New York, 1972. Explains the use of the oceans as a source of food, minerals, power, and living space.

Odum, Eugene P., *Ecology*.
Holt, Rinehart, and Winston, Publishers, 1971. A complete account of the principles of ecology.

Park, Charles F., *Earthbound: Minerals, Energy, and Man's Future*.
Freeman, Cooper and Co., San Francisco, Calif., 1975. Discussion of the facts of mineral and energy resources, relating these to economics, politics, and the environmental crisis.

Scheffer, Victor B., *A Voice for Wildlife*.
Charles Scribner's Sons, New York, 1974. A clear description of the relationship between humans and wildlife.

Szulc, Tad, *The Energy Crisis*.
Franklin Watts, Inc., New York, 1974. An explanation of why we are in a energy crisis and why it will continue.

van den Bosch, Robert, and P. S. Messenger, *Biological Control*.
Intext Educational Publishers, New York, 1973. An excellent introduction to the principles, methods, and philosophies of biological control.

Woodburn, John H., *The Whole Earth Energy Crisis—Our Dwindling Source of Energy*.
G. P. Putnam's Sons, New York, 1973. A careful and accurate presentation of today's energy situation.

Articles

"Our Ecological Crisis," *National Geographic*, December, 1970. The entire issue is a collection of interesting articles concerned with the problems of our environment.

Bormann, F. Herbert, and Gene E. Likens, "The Nutrient Cycles of an Ecosystem," *Scientific American*, October, 1970. A thorough and well-written description of the nutrient cycles of an ecosystem.

Clark, John R., "Thermal Pollution and Aquatic Life," *Scientific American*, March, 1969. An interesting presentation on the problem of thermal pollution and its effects on the surrounding aquatic community.

Gates, David M., "The Flow of Energy in the Biosphere," *Scientific American*, September, 1971. Deals with the pathways of energy transfer in an ecosystem.

Horn, Henry S., "Forest Succession," *Scientific American*, May, 1975. Explains the principles of how a community of trees comes to replace another.

Isaacs, John D., "The Nature of Oceanic Life," *Scientific American*, September, 1969. A fascinating account of the natural history of the living ocean.

Leydet, François, and Fanell Grehan, "America's Wilderness: How much can we save," *National Geographic*, February, 1974. A look at what is happening to our wilderness and what we can do to save it.

Palmer, John D. "Biological Clocks of the Tidal Zone," *Scientific American*, February, 1975, An interesting description of the mechanisms that control certain time-related activities of animals of the tidal zone.

Peakall, David B., "Pesticides and the Reproduction of Birds," *Scientific American*, April, 1970. A dramatic account of the effects of pesticides on reproduction and development of birds.

Wynne-Edwards, V. C., "Population Control in Animals," *Scientific American*, August, 1964. A detailed study on the natural methods animals use to control their population.

APPENDIX

I. The Metric System

Most scientists work all over the world use the **metric system** of measurement. Most other people of the world also use the metric system in their daily lives. In the United States, use of the metric system is rapidly growing. You should become familiar with it.

The units of the metric system of measurement are the **meter** (for length), the **gram** (for weight), and the **liter** (for volume). Prefixes placed before the units of *meter, gram,* or *liter,* will tell you the multiple of the unit. Therefore, once you have an understanding of each basic unit, this system is easy to use.

PREFIXES OF THE METRIC SYSTEM		
Prefix	Scientific Notation	Decimal
KILO-	10^3	or 1000 times the unit
HECTO-	10^2	or 100 times the unit
DECA-	10	or 10 times the unit
the UNIT		
DECI-	10^{-1}	or 1/10 the unit
CENTI-	10^{-2}	or 1/100 the unit
MILLI-	10^{-3}	or 1/1000 the unit

LINEAR MEASURES

The unit of length in the metric system is the *meter* (abbreviation *m*), which is equal to 39.37 inches.

KILOmeter (km)	=	1000 meters
HECTOmeter	=	100 meters
DECAmeter	=	10 meters
meter		
DECImeter	=	1/10 meter
CENTImeter	=	1/100 meter
MILLImeter (mm)	=	1/1000 meter
MICRON (μ)—unit of measurement used in microscopic work	=	1/1,000,000 meter (10^{-6} m)
MILLImicron (mμ)	=	1/1,000,000,000 meter (10^{-9} m)
Angstrom (Å)	=	1/10,000,000,000 meter (10^{-10} m)

Note: The mμ and the Å are used as measures of the wavelengths of light. The micron, millimicron, and Angstrom units are not consistent with the system of metric prefixes.

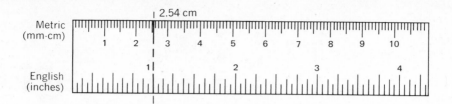

WEIGHT MEASURES

The unit of weight in the metric system is the *gram* (abbreviation *g*). One gram is the weight of one cubic centimeter of distilled water at 4° C.

KILOgram (kilo or kg)	=	1000 grams
HECTOgram	=	100 grams
DECAgram	=	10 grams
gram		
DECIgram	=	1/10 gram
CENTIgram (cg)	=	1/100 gram
MILLIgram (mg)	=	1/1,000 gram
MICROgram or gamma (γ)	=	1/1,000,000 gram (10^{-6} g)

VOLUME MEASURES

The unit of volume in the metric system is the *liter* (abbreviation ℓ). One *liter* of distilled water weighs one kilogram. The most commonly used division is:

MILLIliter (ml)   =   1/1000 liter

II. Metric-English Equivalents

1 meter = 39.37 inches
1 millimeter = approximately 1/25 inch
1 micron = approximately 1/25,000 inch
2.54 centimeters = 1 inch
1 kilogram = approximately 2.2 pounds
1 liter = approximately 1.06 quarts

III. Celsius and Fahrenheit Temperature Scales

Zero on the Celsius (also called centigrade) scale marks the freezing temperature of water. The equivalent on the Fahrenheit scale is 32°. Zero on the Fahrenheit scale is an arbitrary point: it marks the lowest temperature observed by the German scientist Fahrenheit during the winter of 1709. Zero degrees F corresponds to −17.77° C.

The temperature of boiling water, at sea level, is marked 100° on the Celsius scale. This is 212° on the Fahrenheit scale. There are 100 degrees between the melting point of ice and the boiling point of water on the Celsius scale. But there are 180 degrees between these two temperatures on the Fahrenheit scale. Therefore, one Fahrenheit degree is equal to 5/9 (100/180) of one Celsius degree.

The following procedure may be used to convert the temperatures of one scale to those of the other:

°F to °C: subtract 32, multiply by 5, divide by 9.
°C to °F: multiply by 9, divide by 5, add 32.
Expressed as formulae:

$$°C = \tfrac{5}{9} \times (°F - 32°)$$
$$°F = (\tfrac{9}{5} \times C°) + 32°$$

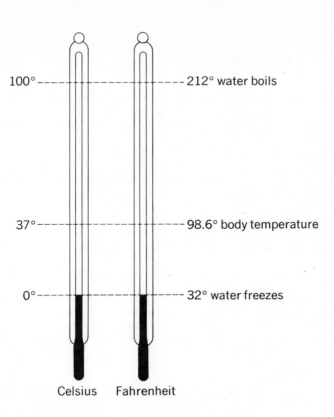

100° ---------------------- 212° water boils

37° ---------------------- 98.6° body temperature

0° ---------------------- 32° water freezes

Celsius   Fahrenheit

IV. Modern Classification of Organisms

KINGDOM PROTISTA

Organisms having structure; many unicellular, others colonial or multicellular, but lacking in specialized tissue; both heterotrophic and autotrophic; neither distinctly plant nor animal.

PHYLUM SCHIZOMYCOPHYTA (SCHIZOPHYTA) Mostly parasitic or saprophytic organisms; cells lacking an organized nucleus, with nucleoproteins in contact with cytoplasm; reproduction by fission, certain forms producing endospores: bacteria, Rickettsiae, actinomycetes, spirochetes [placed in Kingdom Monera in certain classifications].

PHYLUM CYANOPHYTA Cells containing chlorophyll and other pigments not localized in plastids; cells lacking an organized nucleus, with nucleoproteins in contact with cytoplasm; reproduction by fission and spores; blue-green algae (*Nostoc, Anabaena, Gloeocapsa, Oscillatoria)* [placed in Kingdom Monera in certain classifications].

PHYLUM CHLOROPHYTA Cells containing chlorophyll and other pigments localized in plastids; food stored as starch; cells with organized nucleus; unicellular, colonial, and filamentous forms; motile, free-floating, and sessile: green algae (*Spirogyra, Protococcus, Chlorella,* desmids, *Ulothrix, Oedogonium*).

PHYLUM CHRYSOPHYTA Cells containing chlorophyll and other pigments localized in plastids; cells often yellow-green, golden-brown, or brown in color; food stored as oil and complex carbohydrates; cell walls often containing silicon; unicellular, colonial, and filamentous forms; motile and free-floating: yellow-green algae, diatoms.

PHYLUM PYRROPHYTA Cells containing chlorophyll and other pigments localized in plastids; cells often yellow-green or golden-brown; food stored as starch or oil; unicellular flagellates with two flagella, one lateral and one longitudinal; mostly marine organisms: dinoflagellates, cryptomonads.

PHYLUM PHAEOPHYTA   Cells containing chlorophyll usually masked by a brown pigment, localized in plastids; food stored as oil and complex carbohydrates; multi-cellular; nonmotile; plant body usually large, complex, and sessile; mostly marine organisms living in shallow water: brown algae (*Fucus, Sargassum, Nereocystis, Laminaria, Macrocystis*).

PHYLUM RHODOPHYTA   Cells containing chlorophyll usually masked by a red pigment, localized in plastids; food stored as a carbohydrate related to starch; multicellular; nonmotile; plant body complex, usually sessile; mostly marine, deep-water organisms: red algae (*Chondrus, Gelidium, Polysiphonia*).

PHYLUM MYCOPHYTA (EUMYCOPHYTA)   Organisms lacking chlorophyll; parasitic and saprophytic: true fungi.

   CLASS PHYCOMYCETES: Algalike fungi: black molds (*Rhizopus*), water mold (*Saprolegnia*), white "rust," downy mildews.

   CLASS ASCOMYCETES: Sac fungi, usually producing eight ascospores in an ascus; many forms producing conidiospores: blue and green molds (*Penicillium, Aspergillus*), morels, yeasts, cup fungi, powdery mildews.

   CLASS BASIDIOMYCETES: Basidium (club) fungi: rusts, smuts, mushrooms, puffballs, bracket fungi.

   CLASS DEUTEROMYCETES: Imperfect fungi; ringworm fungi: thrush (*Candida*), athlete's foot fungus.

PHYLUM MYXOMYCOPHYTA   Amorphous slimy growths consisting of a naked proto-plasmic mass creeping slowly by a flowing, amoeboid motion; mostly saprophytes; spores produced in sporangia: slime fungi (slime molds).

PHYLUM SARCODINA   Organisms forming pseudopodia; pellicle at cell surface lacking; reproduction principally by fission; fresh-water and marine: amoeboid organisms (*Ameba, Endameba, Arcella*), foraminifers, radiolarians.

PHYLUM MASTIGOPHORA   Organisms that propel themselves with one or more flagella; pellicle usually present; fission longitudinal: flagellates (*Euglena, Trypanosoma, Volvox, Leishmania*).

PHYLUM CILIOPHORA (CILIATA)   Locomotion by means of cilia; pellicle present; many forms with macronucleus and micronucleus: ciliates (*Paramecium, Vorticella, Stentor, Stylonychia*).

PHYLUM SPOROZOA   No structures for locomotion; spore-forming; all parasitic: sporo-zoans (*Plasmodium*).

KINGDOM PLANTAE

Multicellular plants having tissues and organs; cell walls containing cellulose; chlorophyll *a* and *b* present and localized in plastids; food stored as starch; cell walls containing cellulose; sex organs multicellular; autotrophic.

PHYLUM BRYOPHYTA   Multicellular green plants living on land, usually in moist situations; alternation of generations with the gametophyte the conspicuous generation; vascular tissues lacking; reproduction by spores and gametes.

   CLASS HEPATICAE: Gametophyte leafy or thalluslike, usually prostrate: liverworts (*Marcantia, Riccia, Lunularia*).

   CLASS ANTHOCEROTAE: Gametophyte thalluslike, sporophyte elongated and cylindrical: hornworts.

   CLASS MUSCI: Gametophyte usually an erect leafy shoot, sporophyte inconspicuous and parasitic on the gametophyte: true mosses (*Polytrichium, Sphagnum*).

PHYLUM TRACHEOPHYTA   Plants with vascular tissues: sporophyte plant body prominent; highly specialized roots, stems, leaves, and reproductive organs in most forms.

   Subphylum Psilopsida: Leaves usually absent, if present small and simple; roots absent; mostly fossils (only four living species): *Psilotum, Tmesipteria.*

   Subphylum Lycopsida: Leaves simple and usually small, spirally arranged on stem: club mosses (*Lycopodium, Selaginella*).

Subphylum Sphenopsida: Leaves small and simple and arranged in whorls; mostly fossils: horsetails (*Equisetum*).
Subphylum Pteropsida: Leaves usually large and complex; plant body often large.
CLASS FILICINEAE: Sporophyte producing a leafy frond, usually bearing sporangia; rhizome usually creeping; gametophyte plant body a small prothallium: ferns and tree ferns.
CLASS GYMNOSPERMAE: Seeds not enclosed in an ovary; mostly large, woody plants; many evergreen.
Order Cycadales: Primitive fernlike gymnosperms: cycads or sago palms (*Cycas, Dioon, Zamia*).
Order Ginkgoales: Large trees with two kinds of branches, one bearing most of the wedge-shaped leaves in clusters; mostly fossils (one genus and species remaining): *Ginkgo biloba.*
Order Coniferales: Cone-bearing gymnosperms, mostly evergreen; leaves in the form of needles or scales: pines, cedars, spruces, firs, larches, yews.
Order Gnetales: Possible forerunners of the flowering plants; two seed leaves on the embryo; wood containing vessels; mostly fossils (only three remaining genera): *Ephedra, Welwitschia, Gnetum.*
CLASS ANGIOSPERMAE: Flowering plants; seeds enclosed in an ovary which ripens into the fruit.
Subclass Monocotyledonae: Embryo with one cotyledon; fibrovascular tissues scattered through the stem tissues; flower parts in 3's and 6's; leaves parallel-veined: grasses, sedges, lilies, irises, orchids, palms (including about nine orders).
Subclass Dicotyledonae: Embryo with two cotyledons; fibrovascular tissues in a zone around a central pith tissue in the stem; flower parts in 4's or 5's; leaves with netted veins: buttercups, roses, apples, elms (including about 35 orders).

KINGDOM ANIMALIA

Multicellular animals having tissues and, in many, organs and organ systems; pass through embryonic or larval stages in development; heterotrophic.
PHYLUM PORIFERA Body in two cell layers, penetrated by numerous pores; "skeleton" formed by silicious or calcareous spicules or horny spongin; marine and fresh-water animals: sponges.
CLASS CALCISPONGIAE: Simple sponges of shallow waters; calcareous spicules forming "skeleton": ascon and sycon sponges (*Grantia*).
CLASS HYLOSPONGIAE: Deep-water sponges; "skeleton" composed of silicious spicules in open framework: Venus's flower basket.
CLASS DEMOSPONGIAE: Large sponges; often brilliantly colored; "skeleton" of spongin or a combination of spongin and silicious material; fresh-water and marine: bath sponge, finger sponge, crumb-of-bread sponge.
PHYLUM COELENTERATA Usually free-swimming animals with a baglike body of two cell layers with a noncellular substance between them; gastrovascular cavity with one opening leading to the outside; many with tentacles and all with stinging capsules; solitary or colonial forms; marine and fresh-water: hydroids, jellyfish, corals.
CLASS HYDROZOA: Solitary or colonial; fresh-water and marine; reproduction by asexual buds and gametes; alternation of generations in many forms: *Hydra, Obelia, Gonionemus, Physalia.*
CLASS SCYPHOZOA: Exclusively marine; most have mesenteries; polyp stage usually absent: *Aurelia, Cyanea.*
CLASS ANTHOZOA: Marine forms; solitary or colonial; without alternation of generations; body cavity with mesenteries; numerous tentacles: sea anemones, corals, sea fans.
PHYLUM CTENOPHORA Marine animals resembling jellyfish; hermaphroditic; definite digestive system with anal pore; biradially symmetrical: comb jellies.

PHYLUM PLATYHELMINTHES   Body flat and ribbonlike, without true segments; no body cavity, skeletal, circulatory, or respiratory systems; head provided with sense organs; nervous system composed of two longitudinal nerve cords: flatworms.

CLASS TURBELLARIA: Mostly free-living aquatic or terrestrial forms; many with cilia on the epidermis: *Planaria*.

CLASS TREMATODA: Parasitic forms with mouth at anterior end; intestine present; no cilia on adults: human liver fluke, sheep liver fluke.

CLASS CESTODA: Parasitic forms; body a series of proglottids; intestine lacking; hooked scolex adapted for attachment to intestinal wall of host: tapeworms.

PHYLUM NEMERTEA   Body elongated and flattened; long proboscis extending through mouth opening at anterior end; circulatory system present; bilaterally symmetrical; mostly marine: proboscis worms.

PHYLUM NEMATODA   Body slender and elongated; unsegmented; body wall in three layers; body cavity present; bilaterally symmetrical; free-living and parasitic forms: round-worms (*Ascaris, Trichinella,* pinworm, hookworm, vinegar eel).

PHYLUM NEMATOMORPHA   Body slender and elongated, resembling a hair; larvae parasitic in insects, adults free-living in fresh water; mouth often lacking in adults: horse-hair worms ("horsehair snakes").

PHYLUM ACANTHOCEPHALA   Body elongated; digestive tract lacking; anterior probos-cis armed with many recurved hooks; parasitic in vertebrates: spiny-headed worms.

PHYLUM TROCEHLMINTHES (ROTIFERA)   "Wheel animals" with rows of cilia (around the mouth) which beat with a motion suggesting the rotation of a wheel; chitinlike jaws and a well-developed digestive system; body usually cylindrical, ending in a forked grasping foot: rotifers.

PHYLUM BRYOZOA   Microscopic organisms forming branching colonies; row of ciliated tentacles at anterior end; usually marine: bryozoans (sea mosses).

PHYLUM BRACHIOPODA   Body enclosed in dorsal and ventral shells resembling those of a clam; two spirally coiled arms within shell bearing a row of ciliated tentacles; simple circulatory system; marine animals; mostly fossil forms: brachiopods, lampshells.

PHYLUM PHORONIDA   Wormlike animals; sedentary and tube-dwelling; spirally coiled arm with ciliated tentacles at anterior end; marine: Phoronis.

PHYLUM CHAETOGNATHA   Free-swimming, transparent, slender animals resembling arrows; mouth lined with curved bristles; body divided into head, trunk, and tail with finlike projections; marine: arrow worms.

PHYLUM MOLLUSCA   Soft-bodied animals without segments or jointed appendages; most forms secrete a valve, or calcareous shell, from a mantle; muscular foot usually present; terrestrial, fresh-water, and marine animals: chitons, clams, snails, octopus.

CLASS AMPHINEURA: Elongated body and reduced head, without tentacles; many forms with a shell composed of eight plates: chiton.

CLASS PELECYPODA: Axe-footed with bivalve shell; gills in mantle cavity; head, eyes, and tentacles lacking: clam, oyster, scallop.

CLASS GASTROPODA: Flat-footed, with or without coiled shell; head, distinct eyes, and tentacles present: snail, slug, whelk.

CLASS SCAPHOPODA: Body elongated and enclosed in a tubular shell, open at both ends; gills lacking; marine animals: tooth shells.

CLASS CEPHALOPODA: Head large; foot modified into grasping tentacles; marine animals: squid, octopus, chambered nautilus, cuttlefish.

PHYLUM ANNELIDA   Segmented worms with the body cavity separated from the diges-tive tube; brain dorsal and nerve cord ventral; body wall containing circular and longi-tudinal muscles: segmented worms.

CLASS POLYCHAETA: Fleshy outgrowths, or parapodia, extending from segments; marine animals: sandworm (*Nereis*).

CLASS ARCHIANNELIDA: Similar to Polychaeta but without parapodia and with two rows of cilia: *Polygordius.*

CLASS OLIGOCHAETA: Head not well developed; setae on body wall; terrestrial and fresh-water forms: earthworm, *Tubifex, Chaetogaster.*

CLASS HIRUDINEA: Body flattened from top to bottom; no setae on body; suckers at both ends; mostly fresh-water forms, but may occur as terrestrial or marine organisms: leeches.

PHYLUM ARTHROPODA Animals with segmented bodies, the segments bearing jointed appendages; chitinous exoskeleton; aerial, terrestrial, and aquatic forms: arthropods.

CLASS CRUSTACEA: Head and thorax joined in a cephalothorax, usually five pairs of legs, two pairs of antennae; mostly aquatic; gills for respiration; many with calcareous deposits in exoskeleton: crayfish, lobster, crab, shrimp, water flea, sowbug, barnacle.

CLASS CHILOPODA: Body flattened and consisting of 15 to 170 or more segments; one pair of legs attached to each segment; maxillipeds developed into poison claws: centipedes.

CLASS DIPLOPODA: Body more or less cylindrical and composed of 25 to 100 or more segments; most segments bearing two pairs of legs: millipedes.

CLASS ARACHNIDA: Head and thorax usually fused into a cephalothorax; antennae lacking; four pairs of legs; book lungs and tracheae for respiration: spiders, scorpions, ticks, mites.

CLASS INSECTA: Head, thorax, and abdomen separate; three pairs of legs; one pair of antennae; usually two pairs of wings; tracheae for respiration: insects. The numbers in parentheses following the order names indicate an approximation of the number of species in that order.

Order Thysanura (700): Wingless; chewing mouthparts; no metamorphosis; primitive insects: silverfish.

Order Ephemeroptera (1,500): Two pairs of membranous wings, the forepair larger than the hindpair; mouthparts nonfunctioning in adults; metamorphosis incomplete; adults short-lived: Mayfly.

Order Odonata (4,870): Two pairs of strong, membranous wings, the hindpair as large as or larger than the forepair; chewing mouthparts; incomplete metamorphosis; very large compound eyes; larvae aquatic: dragonflies, damsel flies.

Order Orthoptera (22,500): Two pairs of wings, the outer pair straight and leathery; chewing mouthparts; incomplete metamorphosis: grasshoppers, cockroaches, walking stick, mantis, crickets.

Order Isoptera (1,720): Some forms wingless, others with two pairs of long, narrow wings lying flat on back; chewing mouthparts; incomplete metamorphosis; social insects: termites.

Order Dermaptera (1,100): Two pairs of wings, forewings are short and do not cover the abdomen; chewing mouthparts; incomplete metamorphosis; cerci forming forceplike tail appendages: earwigs.

Order Mallophaga (2,680): Wings absent; chewing mouthparts; incomplete metamorphosis: chicken lice.

Order Anoplura (250): Wingless; piercing and sucking mouthparts; no metamorphosis; external parasites on mammals: human body louse.

Order Hemiptera (23,000): Wingless, or with forewings leathery at the base and folded over the hindwings; piercing and sucking mouthparts; incomplete metamorphosis: true bugs, water bug, water strider, water boatman, back swimmer, bedbug, squash bug, stink bug.

Order Homoptera (32,000): Wingless, or with two pairs of wings held in a sloping position like the sides of a roof; piercing and sucking mouthparts; incomplete metamorphosis: cicada, aphids, leaf hopper, tree hopper, scale insects.

Order Neuroptera (4,670): Four membranous wings of equal size, netted with many veins; chewing mouthparts; complete metamorphosis; larvae of some forms aquatic: dobson fly (hellgrammite), aphis lion, lacewing.

Order Coleoptera (276,000): Four wings, the forepair hard and shell-like, the hindpair folded and membranous; chewing mouthparts; complete metamorphosis: beetles, ladybugs, firefly, boll weevil.

Order Lepidoptera (112,000): Four wings covered with colored scales; mouthparts modified into a coiled, sucking proboscis; complete metamorphosis: butterflies, moths, skippers.

Order Diptera (85,000): Forewings membranous, hindwings reduced to knobbed threads; mouthparts for piercing, rasping, and sucking; complete metamorphosis: housefly, bot fly, blowfly, midge, mosquitoes, crane fly, gall gnat.

Order Siphonaptera (1,100): Wingless; piercing and sucking mouthparts; complete metamorphosis; legs adapted for leaping; external parasites on mammals: fleas.

Order Hymenoptera (103,000): Wingless or with two pairs of membranous wings, the forewings larger; forewings and hindwings hooked together; chewing and sucking mouthparts; complete metamorphosis; many members living in social colonies: bees, ants, wasps, hornets, ichneumon fly.

PHYLUM ECHINODERMATA Radially symmetrical; spiny exoskeleton composed, in some cases, of calcareous plates; most forms with tube feet for locomotion; marine animals: echinoderms.

CLASS CRINOIDEA: Five branches rays and pinnules; tube feet without suckers; most forms with stalk for attachment; many fossil forms: sea lily.

CLASS ASTEROIDEA: Body usually with five rays and double rows of tube feet in each ray; eyespots: starfish.

CLASS OPHIUROIDEA: Usually with five slender arms or rays: brittle stars.

CLASS ECHINOIDEA: Body spherical, oval, or disk-shaped; rays lacking; tube feet with suckers: sea urchin, sand dollar.

CLASS HOLOTHUROIDEA: Elongated, thickened body with tentacles around the mouth; no rays or spines: sea cucumber.

PHYLUM CHORDATA Notochord present at some time, disappearing early in many forms; paired gill slits temporary or permanent; dorsal nerve cord.

Subphylum Hemichordata: Wormlike chordates; body in three regions with a proboscis, collar, and trunk: acorn worm (tongue worm).

Subphylum Tunicata (Urochordata): Marine animals with saclike body in adult; free-swimming or attached: sea squirts and other tunicates.

Subphylum Cephalochordata: Fishlike animals with a permanent notochord: lancelet (*Amphioxus*).

Subphylum Vertebrata: Chordates in which most of the notochord is replaced by a spinal column composed of vertebrae and encasing the dorsal nerve cord: vertebrates.

CLASS CYCLOSTOMATA (AGNATHA): Fresh-water or marine eellike forms without true jaws, scales, or fins; cartilaginous skeleton: lamprey, hagfish.

CLASS CHONDRICHTHYES (ELASMOBRANCHII): Fishlike forms with true jaws and fins; gills present but not free and opening through gill slits; no air bladder; cartilaginous skeleton: sharks, rays, skates.

CLASS OSTEICHTHYES (PISCES): Fresh-water and marine fishes with gills free and attached to gill arch; one gill opening on each side of body; true jaws and fins; bony skeleton: bony fishes.

Subclass Ganoidei: Mostly extinct forms with armored body; heterocercal tail; air bladder with duct: amia.

Subclass Teleostomi: Tail rarely heterocercal; air bladder present or absent: trout, eel, perch.

Subclass Dipnoi: Air bladder connected with throat and used as a rudimentary lung: lungfish.

CLASS AMPHIBIA: Fresh-water or terrestrial forms; gills present at some stage; skin slimy and lacking protective outgrowths; limbs without claws; numerous eggs, usually laid in water; metamorphosis: amphibians.

Order Apoda: Wormlike amphibians; tail short or lacking; no limbs or limb girdles: caecilians.

Order Caudata: Body elongated and with a tail throughout life; scales lacking; most forms with two pairs of limbs: salamanders, newts, sirens.

Order Salientia: Body short and tailless in adult stage; two pairs of limbs, the hindlimbs adapted for leaping; gills in larval stage, lungs in adult stage: frogs, toads, tree frogs.

CLASS REPTILIA: Terrestrial or semiaquatic vertebrates; breathing by lungs at all stages; body scale-covered; eggs provided with a leathery, protective shell; fertilization internal: reptiles.

Order Testudinata (Chelonia): Body enclosed between two bony shells, covered with scales: turtles.

Order Rhynchocephalia: Skeletal characteristics of the oldest fossil reptiles; lizard-like in form; parietal eye in roof of cranium: tuatara (*Sphenodon*).

Order Squamata: Body elongated; with or without limbs (vestigial in snakes); body covered with scales.

Order Crocodilia: Large, heavy, scaled body; muscular tail; heart approaching four chambers: alligators.

CLASS AVES: Body covered with feathers; forelimbs modified into wings; four-chambered heart: birds.

Order Gaviiformes: Loons: common loon.

Order Pelecaniformes: Tropical birds: white pelican, brown pelican, cormorant.

Order Ciconiiformes: Long-legged wading birds: heron, bittern, ibis, spoonbill, flamingo.

Order Anseriformes: Short-legged gooselike birds: duck, goose, swan.

Order Falconiformes: Large birds of prey: hawk, falcon, eagle, kite, vulture, buzzard, condor.

Order Galliformes: Fowllike birds: pheasant, turkey, quail, partridge, grouse, ptarmigan.

Order Gruiformes: Cranelike birds: crane, coot, gallinule, rail, limpkin.

Order Charadriiformes: Shore birds: snipe, sandpiper, plover, gull, tern, auk, puffin.

Order Columbiformes: Pigeons and doves: mourning dove, white-winged dove.

Order Psittaciformes: Parrots and parrotlike birds: parrots, parakeet, macaws.

Order Cuculiformes: Cuckoos: cuckoo, roadrunner.

Order Strigiformes: Nocturnal birds of prey: owls.

Order Caprimulgiformes: Goatsuckers: whippoorwill, chuck-will's widow, nighthawk.

Order Apodiformes: Swifts: chimney swift, hummingbird.

Order Coraciiformes: Fishing birds: kingfisher.

Order Piciformes: Woodpeckers: woodpecker, sapsucker, flicker.

Order Passeriformes: Perching birds: robin, bluebirds, sparrow, warbler, thrush.

CLASS MAMMALIA: Body covered with hair; warm blooded; four-chambered heart; mammary glands.

Order Monotremata: Egg-laying mammals: duckbilled platypus, spiny anteater.

Order Marsupialia: Pouched mammals: opossum, kangaroo, Koala bear.

Order Insectivora: Insect-eating mammals: mole, shrew.

Order Chiroptera: Flying, or hand-winged mammals: bat vampire.

Order Edentata: Toothless mammals: armadillo, sloth, great anteater.

Order Rodentia: Gnawing mammals: squirrel, woodchuck, prairie dog, chipmunk, mouse, rat, muskrat.

Order Lagomorpha: Rodentlike mammals: rabbits, hare, pika.

Order Cetacea: Marine mammals: whale, propoise, dolphin.

Order Sirenia: Aquatic mammals: sea cow.

Order Proboscidea: Trunk-nosed mammals: elephant, fossil mammoth, fossil mastodon.

Order Carnivora: Flesh-eating mammals: bear, raccoon, ring-tailed cat, weasel, mink, otter, skunk, lion.

Order Ungulata: Hoofed mammals: odd-toed—horse, tapir; even-toed—bison, cow, goat.

Order Primates: Erect mammals: monkey, lemur, marmoset, gibbon, orangutan, gorilla, human.

GLOSSARY OF BIOLOGICAL TERMS

A

abdomen in arthropods, the body region posterior to the thorax; in mammals, the area of the body between the thorax and the pelvis.

abiogenesis (or *spontaneous generation*), a disproved belief that certain nonliving or dead materials can be transformed into living organisms.

abscission layer the two rows of cells near the base of a leaf petiole that are involved in the natural falling of the leaf.

acetylcholine a chemical substance released at the motor end plate, causing muscle contraction.

actin slender filaments arranged in bundles in the composition of myofibrils of muscles.

active transport the passage of a substance through a cell membrane requiring the using of energy.

adaptation the process in which a species becomes better suited to survive in an environment.

adaptative behavior a set of behavior patterns that tends to insure the well-being of an animal.

adaptive radiation a branching out of a population through variation and adaptation to occupy many environments.

addiction the body's need for a drug that results from the use of the drug.

adductor muscles those in bivalves that control the opening and closing of the valves.

adenoid a mass of lymph tissue that grows from the back wall of the nasopharynx.

ADP (adenosine diphosphate) a low-energy compound found in cells that functions in energy storage and transfer.

adrenal glands two ductless glands located one above each kidney.

adventitious root one that develops from the node of a stem or from a leaf.

aerobic requiring free atmospheric oxygen for normal activity.

aerosols tiny suspended droplets of pollutants in the air.

agglutinin an immune substance in the blood that causes specific substances, including bacteria, to clump.

agglutinogen a protein substance on a blood cell's surface that is responsible for blood types.

air bladder a thin-walled sac found in fish that allows the animal to maintain a level in the water.

air sacs in insects, the enlarged spaces in which the tracheae end; in birds, cavities extending from the lungs; in the human, thin-walled divisions of the lungs.

alimentary canal those organs that compose the food tube in animals.

allantois an extraembryonic membrane that in birds and reptiles aids in respiration and excretion.

allele one of a pair of genes responsible for contrasting traits.

alternation of generations a type of life cycle in which the asexual reproductive stage alternates with the sexual reproductive stage.

altricial birds usually laying fewer than 6 eggs.

alveoli microscopic sacs in the lungs in which the exchange of gases takes place.

amebocytes amebalike cells in sponges that function in circulation and excretion.

amino acids substances from which organisms build protein; the end products of protein digestion.

ammonification the release of ammonia from decaying protein by means of bacterial action.

amniocentesis procedure to remove some amniotic fluid to determine the genetic makeup of the fetus.

amnion the innermost fetal membrane, forming the sac that encloses the fetus.

amnionic fluid secreted by the amion and filling the cavity in which the embryo lies.

amniote egg an egg laid on land by a reptile or bird, having an amnion, other membranes, and a shell.

anaerobic deriving energy for life activity from chemical changes other than that involving oxygen. In some organisms, being unable to live actively in free oxygen.

analogous organs those that are similar in function.

anaphase a stage of mitosis during which chromosomes migrate to opposite poles.

annual a plant that lives for one season only.

annulus   the ring on the stipe of a mushroom that marks the point where the rim of the cap and the stipe were joined.

antenna   a large "feeler" in insects and certain other animals.

antennule   a small "feeler" in the crayfish and certain other animals.

anther   that part of the stamen which bears pollen grains.

antheridium   a sperm-producing structure found in some plants.

anthocyanin   a red, blue or purple pigment dissolved in cell sap.

antibiotic   a germ-killing substance produced by a bacterium, mold, or other fungus.

antibody   an immune substance in the blood and body fluids.

anti-codon   the triplet nucleotide base code in transfer RNA which is the opposite of the messenger RNA codon.

antigen   a substance, usually a protein, which when introduced into the body stimulates the formation of antibodies.

antipodals   three nuclei found in the embryo sac at the end farthest from the micropyle.

antitoxin   a substance in the blood that counteracts a specific toxin.

antivenin   a serum used against snakebite.

anus   the opening at the posterior end of the digestive tube or alimentary canal.

aorta   the great artery leading from the heart to the body.

apical cell   the terminal, or tip, cell of a growing plant.

appendage   an outgrowth of the body of an animal, such as a leg, fin, or antenna.

appendicular skeleton   skeletal members forming the limbs of a vertebrate.

aquatic   living in water.

aqueous humor   the watery fluid filling the cavity between the cornea and lens of the eye.

arachnoid mater   the middle of the three membranes of the brain and spinal cord.

archegonium   an egg-producing structure found in some plants.

arteriole   a tiny artery that eventually branches to become capillaries.

artery   a large, muscular vessel that carries blood away from the heart.

ascus   in Ascomycetes, the saclike structure that contains the spores.

asexual reproduction   reproduction without the joining together of two cells.

assimilate   to incorporate digested and absorbed molecules into the makeup of an organism.

association fibers   nerve processes connecting different parts of the cerebral cortex.

asters   the fibrils that form and radiate from the centriole like rays from a star during cell division.

ATP (adenosine triphosphate)   a high-energy compound found in cells that functions in energy storage and transfer.

atrioventricular node   the structure in the heart that relays the beat to the muscles of the lower heart.

atrioventricular valves   the heart valves located between the atria and ventricles.

atrium   a thin-walled upper chamber of the heart that receives venous blood.

auditory nerve   the nerve leading from the inner ear to the brain.

autonomic nervous system   a division of the nervous system that regulates the vital internal organs. It is involuntary.

autosome   any paired chromosome other than the sex chromosomes.

autotrophs   organisms capable of organizing organic molecules from inorganic molecules.

auxin   a plant hormone that regulates growth.

axil   the angle between a leaf stalk and a stem.

axon   a nerve process that carries an impulse away from the nerve body.

B

bacillus   a rod-shaped bacterium.

bacteria   a group of microscopic, one-celled protists.

bacteriolysin   an antibody found in the blood that causes a specific kind of bacteria to dissolve.

bacteriophage   one of several kinds of viruses that can destroy bacteria.

barrier   anything that prevents the spread of organisms to a new environment.

basidium   a club-shaped structure found in the club fungus which bears the spores.

benthic zone   bottom part of the marine biome.

biennial   a plant that lives two seasons.

bile   a brownish-green emulsifying fluid secreted by the liver and stored in the gall bladder.

binary fission   the division of cells into two approximately equal parts.

binomial nomenclature   the system that gives an organism a name composed of two parts.

biodegradable   polluting materials decomposed by natural processes.

biogenesis   the biological principle that life arises from life.

biogeography   the study of the distribution of plants and animals throughout the earth.

biome   a large geographical region identified mainly by its climax vegetation.

biosphere   the area in which life is possible on our planet.

biosynthesis   the building of organic molecules by living organisms.

biotic community   all the living organisms in an ecosystem.

bivalve   a mollusk possessing a shell of two valves hinged together.

blade   the thin, green portion of a leaf, usually strengthened by veins.

blastocoel   the space between the ectoderm and endoderm in the early stages of development.

blastula   an early stage in the development of an embryo, in which cells have divided to produce an hollow sphere.

bony layer   the hard region of a bone between the periosteum and the marrow.

book lungs   air-filled respiratory sacs in spiders.

Bowman's capsule   the cup-shaped structure forming one end of the tubule and surrounding a glomerulus in the nephron of a kidney.

brain stem   an enlargement at the base of the brain where it connects with the spinal cord.

branchial arteries   those that lead to and from the gills of the fish.

breathing   the mechanical process of getting air into and out of the body.

bronchial tube   a subdivision of a bronchus within a lung.

bronchiole   one of numerous subdivisions of the bronchial tubes within a lung.

bronchus   a division of the lower end of the trachea, leading to a lung.

Brownian movement   an oscillating or bouncing movement seen in colloids or bacteria and due to random movement of molecules.

bud   an undeveloped shoot of a plant, often covered by scales; developing young forming at the bases of some coelenterates.

bud scale   a small, leaflike structure covering the growing point of a twig.

budding   the uniting of a bud with a stock; also, a form of asexual reproduction in yeast and hydra.

bulb   a form of underground stem composed largely of thick scale leaves.

bulbus arteriosus   a muscular, bulblike structure attached to the ventricle of the fish heart.

bulk feeders   animals that consume food as whole or parts of organisms.

bursa   a fluid-filled sac forming a cushion in the knee and shoulder joints.

C

Calorie (food)   used to measure food energy, the amount of heat required to raise the temperature of 1,000 grams (1 kilogram), or 1 liter, of water one centigrade degree.

calyx   the sepals, collectively.

cambium   a ring of meristematic cells in roots and stems that forms secondary xylem and phloem.

canine   (or *cuspid*) teeth for tearing, enlarged in certain mammals.

capillarity   a force causing water to move upward through a tube with a small diameter.

capillary   small, thin-walled vessel through which exchanges occur between blood and tissue fluid.

capsule   a thick slime layer surrounding some bacteria; also, the spore case of mosses.

carapace   the hard-shield covering on the back of an animal such as a crab, lobster, and turtle.

cardiac muscle   muscle composing the heart wall.

carnivore   a meat-eating organism.

carotid arch   anterior branch of the truncus arteriosus in the frog.

cartilage   a strong, pliable supporting tissue in vertebrates.

catalyst   a substance that accelerates a chemical reaction without itself being altered chemically.

cell   a unit of structure and function of an organism.

cell theory   a belief that the cell is the unit of structure and function of life and that cells come only from preexisting cells by reproduction.

cell wall   the outer, nonliving cellulose wall secreted around plant cells.

cementum   the covering of the root of a tooth.

central nervous system   the brain and spinal cord and the nerves arising from each.

central neuron   a nerve cell in the brain or spinal cord that connects a motor and a sensory nerve.

centriole   a cytoplasmic body lying just outside the nucleus in animal cells.

centromere   a single granule that, during cell division, attaches a pair of chromatids after replication.

centrosome   a small, dense area of cytoplasm appearing outside the nucleus during division of animal cells.

cephalization   concentration of nervous tissue at the anterior end of an organism.

cephalothorax   a body region in crustaceans and certain other animals, consisting of the fused head and the thorax.

cerebellum   the brain region between the cerebrum and medulla, concerned with equilibrium and muscular coordination.

cerebrospinal fluid   a clear fluid in the brain ventricles and surrounding the spinal cord.

cerebrum   the largest region of the human brain, considered to be the seat of emotions, intelligence, and voluntary nervous activities; also present in all other vertebrates.

cervix   the neck of the uterus.

chelicera   first appendages of the spider, serving as poison fangs.

cheliped   a claw foot used in food-getting and for protection in some arthropods.

chemosynthesis   the organization of organic compounds by organisms by means of energy from inorganic chemical reactions instead of energy from light.

chemotropism   the response of an organ or an organism to chemicals.

chitin a material present in the exoskeleton of insects and other arthropods.

chlorenchyma chlorophyll-containing parenchyma cells.

chlorophyll green pigments essential to food manufacture in plants.

chloroplast a cell plastid containing chlorophyll.

cholinesterase a chemical substance released at the motor end plate that neutralizes acetylcholine.

chordate animal having a notochord, nerve cord, and gill slits at some time in its development.

chorion a membrane that forms early during development and attaches, in mammals, to the uterine wall. In birds and reptiles, this membrane is found under the shell.

choroid layer the second and innermost layer of the eyeball.

chromatid during cell division, each part of a double-stranded chromosome, joined by a centromere, after replication.

chromatin material fine strands in the nucleoplasm believed to be forms of the chromosomes.

chromatophores structures containing pigments in the skin of fishes, frogs, and other animals.

chromoplasts pigment-containing bodies, other than chloroplasts, in certain plant cells.

chromosomal aberration an alteration in the structure or number of a chromosome.

chromosome a rod-shaped gene-bearing body in the cell nucleus, composed of DNA joined to protein molecules.

chrysalis the hard covering of the pupa of a butterfly.

chyme partly digested, acidic food as it leaves the stomach.

cilia tiny, hairlike projections of cytoplasm.

ciliary muscles those that control the shape of the lens in the eye.

cleavage the rapid series of divisions that the fertilized egg undergoes.

cleavage furrow an indentation that appears during the telophase of dividing animal cells.

climax species a group of plants that assume final prominence in a region.

clitellum a swelling on the earthworm when involved in reproduction.

cloaca a chamber below the large intestine in certain vertebrates into which waste is emptied.

coccus a sphere-shaped bacterium.

cochlea the hearing apparatus of the inner ear.

cocoon a silken case containing the pupa of a moth.

codon one or more groups of base triplets of messenger RNA that code a specific amino acid.

coelom the space between the mesodermal layers that forms the body cavity of an animal.

coenzyme a nonprotein molecule that works with an enzyme in catalyzing a reaction.

cohesion the clinging together of molecules, as in a column of liquid.

coleoptile a protective sheath encasing the primary leaf of the oat and other grasses.

collar cells flagellated cells in sponges that set up water currents.

colloid a gelatinous substance, such as protoplasm or egg albumen, in which one or more solids are dispersed through a liquid.

colon the large intestine.

commensalism one organism living in or on another, with only one of the two benefiting.

companion cells long, narrow, nucleated cells bordering sieve tubes in phloem tissue.

compound eye an eye composed of numerous lenses and containing separate nerve endings.

conditioned reaction an acquired behavior pattern in which a particular response regularly follows a specific stimulus.

conidia a name given to spores of molds.

conifer a cone-bearing gymnosperm.

conjugation a primitive form of sexual reproduction in *Spirogyra* and certain other algae and fungi in which the content of two cells unites; also, an exchange of nuclear substance in the paramecium.

connective tissue a type of tissue that lies between groups of nerve, gland, and muscle cells.

conservation the preservation and wise use of natural resources.

consumers the heterotrophs in an environment.

contractile vacuole a large cavity in protozoans associated with the discharge of water from the cell and the regulation of osmotic pressure.

contraction (muscle) the shortening of muscle fibers.

control in testing a hypothesis, experiments are usually conducted in duplicate, since the control lacks the experimental variable.

conus arteriosus a large vessel lying against the front side of the frog's heart.

convergent evolution the type in which organisms of entirely different origin evolve in a manner that results in certain similarities.

convolution one of man irregular, rounded ridges on the surface of the brain.

cork a tissue formed by the cork cambium that replaces the epidermis in woody stems and roots.

cork cambium a layer of cells in the outer bark of a woody stem that produces cork tissue.

corm a shortened underground stem in which the leaves are reduced to thin scales.

cornea a transparent bulge of the sclerotic layer of the eye in front of the iris, through which light rays pass.

corolla the petals of a flower, collectively.

coronary pertaining to the heart

corpus luteum refers to the follicle after the ovum is discharged.

cortex   in roots and stems, a storage tissue; in organs such as the kidney and brain, the outer region.

cotyledon   a seed leaf present in the embryo plant that serves as a food reservoir.

countershading   a form of protective coloration in which darker colors on the upper side of the animal fade into lighter colors on the lower side.

Cowper's gland   located near the upper end of the male urethra. It secretes a fluid which is added to the sperms.

cranial nerves   the twelve pairs of nerves communicating directly with the human brain.

cristae   membranous infolded paritions in mitochondria.

crop   an organ of the alimentary canal of the earthworm, bird, and certain other animals that serves for food storage.

crossing over   the exchange of segments of two chromosomes, and the genes in the segments, when the two chromosomes twist around each other during synapse in meiosis.

cuticle   a waxy, transparent layer covering the upper epidermis of certain leaves; also, the outer covering of an earthworm and some parasitic worms.

cyclosis   flowing, or streaming, of cell cytoplasm.

cyst   in lower animals and plants, a spore with a capsule covering constituting a resting stage in some algae; a resting stage of a protozoan or lower animal, enclosed by a protective wall.

cytokinins   plant hormones that influence cell division and stimulate growth of leaves and lateral buds.

cytolysis   the swelling and bursting of cells when put into a hypotonic medium.

cytoplasm   the protoplasmic materials lying outside the nucleus and inside the cell membrane.

cytoplasmic matrix   clear-appearing portion of the cytoplasm that suspends various visible bodies.

D

daughter cells   newly formed cells resulting from the division of a previously existing cell, called a mother cell. The two daughter cells receive identical nuclear materials.

decay   the reduction of the substances of a plant or animal body to simple compounds.

deciduous   woody plants that shed their leaves seasonally.

decomposers   organisms that break down the tissues and excretions of other organisms into simpler substances through the process of decay.

deficiency disease   a condition resulting from the lack of one or more vitamins.

dehydration   loss of water from body tissues.

dendrite   a branching nerve process that carries an impulse toward the nerve cell body.

denitrification   the process carried on by denitrifying bacteria in breaking down ammonia, nitrites, and nitrates and liberating free nitrogen.

dentine   a substance that is relatively softer than enamel, forming the bulk of a tooth.

deoxygenation   the process during which oxygen is removed from the blood or tissues.

depressant   a drug having an anesthetic effect on the nervous system.

dermis   the thick, active layer of tissue lying beneath the epidermis.

desert   a geographical area that has less than ten inches of rainfall each year.

diaphragm   a muscular partition separating the thoracic cavity from the abdominal cavity.

diastole   part of the cycle of the heart during which the ventricles relax and receive blood from the atria.

dicotyledon   a seed plant with two seed leaves, or cotyledons.

diffusion   the spreading out of molecules in a given space from a region of greater concentration to one of lesser concentration.

digestion   the process during which foods are chemically simplified and made soluble for use.

dioecious   having the male reproductive organs in one individual and the female reproductive organs in another.

dihybrid   an offspring having genes for two contrasting traits.

diploid   term used to indicate a cell that contains (or an organism whose cells contain) a full set of homologous pairs of chromosomes.

diurnal   active during the day.

division of labor   specialization of cell functions resulting in interdependence.

division plate   a wall of cellulose that forms across the dividing plant cell, forming a common boundary between daughter cells.

DNA (deoxyribonucleic acid)   a supermolecule consisting of alternating units of nucleotides, composed of deoxyribose sugar, phosphates, and nitrogen bases.

dominance   principle first observed by Mendel, that one gene may prevent the expression of an allele.

dormancy   a period of inactivity.

double cross   genetic process in which four pureline parents are mixed in two crosses.

double fertilization   in a spermatophyte one sperm fertilizes the egg and one units with the polar nuclei to form the endosperm nucleus.

ductus arteriosus   a connection between the pulmonary artery and the aorta during fetal life.

duodenum   the region of the small intestine immediately following the stomach.

dura mater   the outer of the three membranes of the brain and spinal cord.

E

ecology the study of the relationship of living things to their surroundings.

ecosystem a unit of the biosphere in which living and nonliving things interact, and in which materials are used over and over again.

ectoderm the outer layer of cells of a simple animal body; in vertebrates, the layer of cells from which the skin and nervous system develop.

ectoplasm the outer layer of thin clear cytoplasm, as in the ameba.

egestion elimination of insoluble, nondigested particles from a cell.

egg a female reproductive cell.

elongation region the area behind the embryonic region of a root or stem in which cells grow in length.

embryo an early stage in a developing organism.

emigration movement of organisms from one environment to another.

embryo sac the tissue in a plant ovule that contains the egg, the antipodals, the polar nuclei, and the synergids.

embryonic membrane one of the delicate coverings of a developing organism.

embryonic region the area near the tip of a root or stem in which cells are formed by division.

enamel the hard covering of the crown of a tooth.

endocrine gland a ductless gland that secretes hormones directly into the blood.

endoderm the inner layer of cells of a simple animal body; in vertebrates, the layer of cells from which the linings of the digestive system, liver, lungs, and so on develop.

endodermis a single layer of cells located at the inner edge of the cortex of a root.

endoplasm the inner portion of cytoplasm, as in the ameba.

endoplasmic reticulum a complex system of parallel membranes that extend from the plasma membrane to the nuclear membrane of a cell and that function as a system of canals.

endoskeleton internal framework of vertebrates composed of bone and/or cartilage.

endosperm the tissue in some seeds containing stored food.

endosperm nucleus the body formed by the fusion of a sperm with the polar nuclei during the double fertilization of a spermatophyte.

endospore a resting stage of some bacteria that is resistant to adverse environmental conditions.

endotoxins insoluble poisons formed by certain bacteria within the cells.

environment surroundings of an organism; all the external forces that influence the expression of an organism's heredity.

enzyme a protein that acts as a catalyst.

epicotyl in a seed, the part of the embryo plant that lies above the attachment of the cotyledons and from which the stem and leaves will develop.

epidermis the outer tissue of a young root or stem, a leaf, and other plant parts; the outside layer of cells in animals.

epiphyte a plant that grows on a tree or other plant.

epithelial tissue that composing the covering of various body organs and covering the body surface.

epiglottis a cartilaginous flap at the upper end of the trachea.

erosion the loss of soil by the action of water or wind.

erythrocytes red blood cells.

esophagus the food tube, or gullet, that connects the mouth and the stomach.

estivation a period of summer inactivity in certain animals.

ethology the study of behavior patterns in animals.

etiolated a condition of pale yellow leaves and stems of plants when they are grown in the dark.

Eustachian tube a tube connecting the pharynx with the middle ear.

evaporation movement of water in the form of water vapor from the earth to the atmosphere.

evolution the slow process of change by which organisms have acquired their distinguishing characteristics.

excretion the process by which metabolic waste materials are removed from living cells or from the body.

excurrent pore in sponges, the osculum.

excurrent siphon the structure in a mollusk through which water passes out of the body.

exoskeleton the hard outer covering or skeleton of certain animals, especially arthropods.

exotoxin a soluble toxin excreted by a certain bacteria and absorbed by the tissues of the host.

experimental factor (also called *single variable*) the one condition involved in testing a hypothesis, and differing from the control in an experiment.

expiration the discharge of air from the lungs.

extensor a muscle that straightens a joint.

extraembryonic membrane one that functions during development of reptiles, birds, and mammals, but that does not become part of the embryo.

eyespot the sensory structure in the euglena and planarian that is believed to perceive light and dark.

F

Fallopian tube oviduct in the mammal.

fallout radioactive particles that settle on the earth from the atmosphere.

fang   a hollow tooth of a poisonous snake, through which venom is ejected.

feces   intestinal solid waste material.

feedback   an operating mechanism in the body that produces a delicate check-and-balance system.

fermentation   glucose oxidation that is anaerobic and in which lactic acid or alcohol is formed.

fertilization   the union of two gametes.

fetus   mammalian embryo after the main body features are apparent.

fibrin   a substance formed during blood clotting by the union of thrombin and fibrinogen.

fibrinogen   a blood protein present in the plasma, involved in clotting.

fibrous root   secondary roots that quickly outgrow the primary root and spread out widely; are found in grasses.

fibrovascular bundle   in higher plants, a strand containing xylem and phloem.

filament   a stalk of a stamen, bearing the anther at its tip; in algae, a threadlike group of cells.

fission   asexual reproduction of unicellular organisms by division into two equal daughter cells.

flaccid   limp, due to loss of turgor pressure.

flagellate   an organism bearing one or more whiplike appendages, or flagella.

flagellum   a whiplike projection of cytoplasm used in locomotion by certain simple organisms and by the sperms of many multicellular organisms.

flexor   a muscle that bends a joint.

follicle   an indentation in the skin from which hair grows; also, a mass of ovarian cells that produces an ovum.

food   any substance absorbed into the cells·of the body that yields material for energy, growth, and repair of tissue and regulation of the life processes, without harming the organism.

food chain   the transfer of the sun's energy from producers to consumers as organisms feed on one another.

food pyramid   a quantitative representation of a food chain, with the food producers forming the base and the top carnivore at the apex.

food web   complex food chains existing within an ecosystem.

forebrain   that part of the brain composed of the cerebrum.

fossil   the imprint or preserved remains of an organism that once lived.

fovea   a small, sensitive spot on the retina of the eye where cones are specially abundant.

fragmentation   a process whereby pieces of an organism may break off and regenerate into whole organisms; an asexual method of reproduction.

fresh-water biome   a body of standing water or a river or stream in which life can exist.

fungus   a protist lacking chlorophyll and therefore deriving nourishment from an organic source.

G

gall bladder   a sac in which bile from the liver is stored and concentrated.

gamete   a male or female reproductive cell.

gametophyte   the stage that produces gametes in an organism having alternation of generations.

gamma globulin   a blood protein sometimes used to give temporary immunity to diseases.

ganglion   a mass of nerve cells lying outside the central nervous system.

gastric caecum   a pouchlike extension from the stomach of a grasshopper.

gastric fluid   glandular secretions of the stomach.

gastrovascular cavity   the central cavity of Coelenterata.

gastrula   a stage in embryonic development during which the primary germ layers are formed.

gemmule   a coated cell mass produced by the parent sponge and capable of growing into an adult sponge.

gene   that portion of a DNA molecule that is capable of replication and mutation and passes on a trait from parent to offspring.

gene frequency   the extent to which a gene occurs in a population.

gene linkage   the assemblage of genes in a linear arrangement on a chromosome.

gene pool   all the genes present in a given population.

generative nucleus   the nucleus in a pollen grain that divides to form two sperm nuclei.

genetic code   the sequential arrangement of the bases in the DNA molecule, which controls traits of an organism.

genetics   the science of heredity.

genotype   the hereditary makeup of an organism.

geotropism   the response of plants to gravity.

germination   growth of a seed when favorable conditions occur.

gestation period   the period between fertilization and the birth of a mammal.

gibberellins   growth regulating substances promoting cell elongation in plants.

gill   an organ modified for absorbing dissolved oxygen from water; in mushrooms, a platelike structure bearing the reproductive hyphae and spores.

gill arch   a cartilaginous structure in fishes to which the gill filaments are attached.

gill filament   one of many threadlike projections forming the gills in fishes.

gill raker   fingerlike projections of the gill arches in fishes.

gill slits   in chondricthyes, openings to the gills; in chordates, openings in the throat that appear during embryological development.

girdling   removal of a ring of bark down to the cambium layer and thus causing death of the tree.

gizzard   an organ in the digestive system of the earthworm and birds modified for grinding food.

glomerulus   the knob of capillaries within a Bowman's capsule of a nephron in a kidney.

glottis   the upper opening of the trachea in land vertebrates.

glycolysis (lactic acid fermentation)   the conversion of pyruvic acid to lactic acid by an organism when ample oxygen is not available; that is, under anaerobic conditions.

Golgi apparatus   small groups of parallel membranes in the cytoplasm near the nucleus.

gonads   the male and female reproductive organs in which the gametes are produced.

grafting   the union of the cambium layers of two woody stems, one of the stock and the other of the scion.

grana   disklike bodies in chloroplasts.

green gland   an excretory organ of crustaceans.

guard cell   one of the two epidermal cells surrounding a stoma.

gullet   the passageway to a food vacuole in paramecia; the food tube or esophagus.

guttation   the forcing of water from the leaves of plants, usually when the stomata are closed.

H

habitat   place where an organism lives.

halophyte   a plant living in soil with a high salt content, often above that of seawater.

haploid   a term used to indicate a cell, such as a gamete, that contains only one chromosome of each homologous pair; also, an organism having cells of this type.

hard palate   forms the roof of the mouth in the chewing area.

Haversian canals   numerous channels penetrating the bony layer of a bone.

hemoglobin   an iron-containing protein compound giving red corpuscles their color.

hemotoxin   a poison that destroys red blood cells and breaks down the walls of small blood vessels.

Henle's loop   a widened loop of a kidney tubule that enters the cortex.

hepatic portal vein   a vessel carrying blood to the liver before the blood returns to the heart.

herbaceous   an annual stem with little woody tissue.

herbivores   plant eating animals.

heredity   the transmission of traits from parents to offspring.

hermaphroditic   having the organs of both sexes.

heterocysts   in *Nostoc,* empty cells with thick walls that enable the filaments to break into pieces.

heterogametes   male and female gametes that are unlike in appearance and structure.

heterotrophs   organisms that are unable to synthesize organic molecules from inorganic molecules; that is, nutritionally dependent on other organisms or their products.

heterozygous   refers to an organism in which the paired genes for a particular trait are different.

hibernation   a period of winter inactivity in certain animals.

hilum   the scar on a seed where it was attached to the ovary wall.

hindbrain   that part of the brain that is composed of the cerebellum, the pons, and the medulla.

holdfast   the special cells at the bases of certain algae that anchor them to the substrate.

homeostasis   a steady state that an organism maintains by self-regulating adjustments.

homoiothermic   warm-blooded, as applied to birds and mammals.

homologous chromosomes   a pair of chromosomes which are identical in form and in the way the genes are arranged.

homologous organs   those similar in origin and structure but not necessarily in function.

homozygous   refers to an organism in which the paired genes for a particular trait are identical.

hormone   the chemical secretion of a ductless gland producing a definite physiological effect.

host   in a parasitic relationship, the organism from which the parasite derives its food supply.

humus   organic matter in the soil formed by the decomposition of plant and animal remains.

hybrid   an offspring from a cross between parents differing in one or more traits.

hybridization (or *outbreeding*)   the crossing of different strains, varieties, or species to establish new genetic characteristics.

hydrolysis   the chemical breakdown of a substance by combination with water.

hydrophytes   plants that grow in water or partially submerged in water in very wet surroundings.

hydrotropism   the response of roots to water.

hypertonic solution   a solution containing a higher concentration of solutes and a lower concentration of water molecules than another solution.

hypha   a threadlike filament of the vegetative body of a fungus.

hypocotyl   that part of a plant embryo from whose lower end the root develops.

hypothalamus   part of the brain that controls the pituitary by feedback.

hypothesis   a working explanation or trial answer to a question.

hypotonic solution   a solution containing a lower concentration of solutes and a higher concentration of water molecules than another solution.

I

ileum   the third and longest region of the small intestine.

immune therapy   the assistance and stimulation of the natural body defenses in preventing disease.

immunity   the ability of the body to resist a disease by natural or artificial means.

incisor   one of the cutting teeth in the front of both jaws in mammals.

incomplete dominance   a blend of two traits, resulting from a cross of these characteristics.

incubation   the providing of ideal conditions for growth and development.

incurrent pore   one of many holes in the sponge through which water passes into the animal.

incurrent siphon   the structure in a mollusk through which water passes into the body.

indehiscent   one of a class of dry fruits that do not open to discharge seeds at maturity.

independent assortment   a law based on Mendel's hypothesis that the separation of gene pairs on a given pair of chromosomes, and the distribution of the genes to gametes during meiosis, are entirely independent of the distribution of other gene pairs on other pairs of chromosomes.

individual characteristics   traits that are inherited but that make an organism different from others of the same species.

innate behavior   inborn behavior.

inoculation   the voluntary addition of bacteria, viruses, or other microorganisms to a culture medium.

insecticide   a chemical used to kill insects.

insertion   the attachment of a muscle at its movable part.

inspiration   the intake of air into the lungs.

instinct   a natural urge, or drive, not depending on experience or intelligence.

intelligent behavior   activities of an organism involving problem-solving, judgment, and decision.

interdependence   the dependence of cells on other cells for complete functioning, or of organisms on the activities of other organisms.

interface   the molecular boundary of a colloid, such as a cytoplasm.

interferon   a cellular chemical defense against a virus.

internode   the space between two nodes.

interphase   the period of growth of a cell that occurs between cell divisions.

intertidal zone   the area of the shore in the marine biome that is periodically covered and uncovered by water.

invertebrate   an animal without a backbone.

involuntary muscle   one that cannot be controlled at will, like smooth muscle.

iris   the muscular, colored portion of the eye, behind the cornea and surrounding the pupil.

irritability   the ability to respond to a stimulus.

islets of Langerhans   groups of cells in the pancreas that secrete insulin.

isogametes   male and female gametes that are structurally similar.

isolation   the confinement of a population to a certain location because of barriers.

isotonic solution   a solution containing the same concentration of solutes and the same concentration of water molecules as another solution.

isotopes   different forms of an element resulting from varying numbers of neutrons.

J K

Jacobson's organs   tiny pits containing nerve endings sensitive to odors and located close to the front of the roof of the mouth of a snake.

jejunum   a section of the small intestine lying between the duodenum and the ileum.

joint   the place at which two bones meet.

kidney   an excretory organ that filters urine from the blood.

kinetic energy   power that is actually doing work or causing change.

kinin (also *cytokinin*)   a plant hormone, but one not transported out of the cell.

L

labium   the lower mouthpart, or "lip," of an insect.

labrum   the two-lobed upper mouthpart of an insect.

lacteal   a lymph vessel that absorbs the end products of fat digestion from the intestinal wall.

larva   an immature stage in the life of an animal.

larynx   the voice box; also called the "Adam's apple."

lateral bud   a bud that develops at a point other than at the end of a stem.

lateral line   a row of pitted scales along each side of the fish, functioning as a sense organ.

layering   propagation by stimulating the growth of roots on a stem, as in burying a stem in the ground and then cutting it when roots form.

leaf scar   a mark on a twig left at the point of attachment of a leaf stalk in a previous season.

leaf trace the continuous passageway formed from bundles of conducting tissues branching from the vascular region of the stem, then passing through the petiole and into the leaf.

leaflet a division of a compound leaf.

leafy stem a term used to denote one of the stages of a moss plant.

lenticel a small pore in the epidermis or bark of a young stem through which gases are exchanged.

lethal gene one that bears a characteristic that is usually fatal to the organism.

leucocytes white blood cells.

leucoplast a colorless plastid serving as a food reservoir in certain plant cells.

ligament a tough strand of connective tissue that holds bones together at a joint.

limiting factor any factor that is essential to organisms and for which there is competition.

line breeding (or *inbreeding*) the crossing of closely related strains of plants or animals to preserve certain genetic traits.

liver the largest gland in the human body, associated with digestion and sugar metabolism.

lung an organ for air breathing and external respiration in higher animals.

lymph the clear, liquid part of blood that enters the tissue spaces and lymph vessels.

lysis the dissolution or destruction of cells.

lysogenic phage a virus that invades a bacterial cell without causing immediate destruction. It is passed along to daughter bacteria and becomes destructive at a later time.

lysosome a spherical body within the cytoplasm of most cells. It contains protein digesting enzymes.

lysozyme an enzyme that dissolves the cell walls of many bacteria.

lytic cycle the stage of a virulent phage resulting in destruction of a bacterial cell.

M

macronucleus the large nucleus of the paramecium and certain other protozoans.

Malpighian tubules long excretory tubules attached to the junction of the stomach and intestine of the grasshopper, and that collect nitrogenous wastes from the blood; small ducts in the vertebrate kidney.

mammary glands those found in female mammals that secrete milk.

mandible a strong, cutting mouthpart of arthropods; a jaw, as in the beak of a bird or the jawbone structure of other vertebrates.

mantle a thin membrane covering the visceral hump of a mollusk; in some, it secretes a shell.

marine pertaining to salt water.

marsupial a pouched mammal.

mass selection the picking of ideal plants or animals from a large number to serve as parents for further breeding.

maturation region the area of a root or stem where embryonic cells differentiate into tissues.

maxilla a mouthpart of an arthropod; the upper jaw of vertebrates.

maxilliped a "jaw foot," or first thoracic appendage of the crayfish and other arthropods.

medulla in the kidney, the inner portion composed of pyramids that, in turn, contain numerous tubules; in the adrenal gland, the inner portion that secretes epinephrine.

medulla oblongata the enlargement at the base of the brain. It controls the activity of internal organs.

medusa the bell-shaped, free-swimming stage in the life cycle of coelenterates.

megaspore mother cells diploid cells in the plant ovary that divide twice, forming four haploid megaspores.

megaspores four cells formed from the megaspore mother cell, three of which disintegrate and one of which develops into the embryo sac.

meiosis the type of cell division in which during oogenesis and spermatogenesis there is reduction of chromosomes to the haploid number.

meninges the three membranes covering the brain and spinal cord.

menstruation the periodic breakdown and discharge of uterine tissues that occur in the absence of fertilization.

meristematic tissue small, actively dividing cells that produce growth in plants.

mesentery a folded membrane that connects to the intestines and the dorsal body wall.

mesoderm the middle layer of cells in an embryo.

mesoglea a jellylike material between the two cell layers composing the body of a coelenterate.

mesophyll photosynthetic tissue composed of chlorenchyma cells and located between the upper and lower epidermis of a leaf.

mesophytes plants that occupy neither extremely wet nor extremely dry surroundings.

mesothorax the middle portion of the thorax of an insect, bearing the second pair of legs and the first pair of wings.

messenger RNA the type of RNA that is thought to receive a code for a specific protein from the DNA in the nucleus and to act as a template for protein synthesis on the ribosome.

metabolism the sum of the chemical processes of the body.

metamorphosis a marked change in structure of an animal during its growth.

metaphase the stage of mitosis in which the chromatids line up at the equator.

metathorax the posterior portion of the thorax of an insect, bearing the third pair of legs and the second pair of wings.

micronucleus   a small nucleus found in the paramecium and certain other protozoans.

micropyle   the opening in the ovule wall through which the pollen tube enters.

microspore mother cells   diploid cells in the anther that divide twice, forming four haploid microspores.

microspores   four cells, formed from the microspore mother cell, that develop into pollen grains.

midbrain   that part of the brain composed of nerve fibers connecting the forebrain to the hindbrain.

middle lamella   a thin plate composed largely of pectin, forming the middle portion of a wall between two adjacent plant cells.

midrib   the large central vein of a pinnately veined leaf.

migration   seasonal movement of animals from one place to another.

milt   sperm-containing fluid of fishes.

mimicry   a form of protective coloration in which an animal closely resembles another kind of animal or an object in its environment.

mitochondria   rod-shaped bodies in the cytoplasm known to be centers of cellular respiration.

mitosis   the division of chromosomes preceding the division of cytoplasm.

molar   a large tooth for grinding, highly developed in herbivores.

molting   shedding of the outer layer of exoskeleton of arthropods, or of a scale layer of reptiles.

monocotyledon   a flowering plant that develops a single seed leaf, or cotyledon.

monoecious   bearing staminate and pistillate flowers on different parts of the same plant; an individual with both male and female reproductive organs.

monohybrid   an offspring from a cross between parents differing in one trait.

monosomy   the presence of a single homologous chromosome in all body cells.

monotreme   an egg-laying mammal.

mosaic   a pattern of leaf arrangement for greatest light exposure.

mother cell   a cell that has undergone growth and is ready to divide.

motor end plate   the terminus of the axon of a motor nerve in a muscle.

motor neuron   one that carries impulses from the brain or spinal cord to a muscle or gland.

motor unit   the nerve cell and the individual muscle fibers it stimulates to contract.

mucous membrane   a form of epithelial tissue that lines the body openings and digestive tract and secretes mucus.

mucus   a slimy lubricating and cleansing secretion of mucous glands.

mutliple alleles   one of two or more pairs of genes that act together to produce a specific trait.

muscle tissue   cells that are specialized to contract and cause movement.

mutation   a change in genetic makeup resulting in a new characteristic that can be inherited.

mutualism   a form of symbiosis in which two organisms live together to the advantage of both.

mycelium   the vegetative body of molds and other fungi, composed of hyphae.

mycoplasmas   a group of viruslike organisms.

mycorrhiza   a fungus that lives in a symbiotic relationship with the roots of trees and other plants.

myofibrils   fine, parallel threads arranged in groups to form a muscle fiber.

myosin   a form of thick filament that together with actin filaments composes a myofibril.

N

narcotics   a group of drugs that have a pronounced effect on the nervous system and that are addictive with continued use.

nare   nostril.

nastic movement   turgor movement in plants, such as the daily opening and closing of flowers.

natural selection   the result of survival in the struggle for existence among organisms possessing those characteristics that give them an advantage.

nematocyst   a stinging cell in coelenterates.

nephridia   the excretory structures in worms, mollusks, and certain arthropods.

nephron   one of the numerous excretory structures in the kidney, including Bowman's capsule, the glomerulus, and the tubules.

nerve cord   part of the central nervous system in chordates, lying above the notochord and extending down the dorsal side of the body.

nerve impulse   an electrochemical stimulus causing change in a nerve fiber.

nervous tissue   specialized cells for transmitting impulses for coordination, perception, or automatic body functions.

neuron   a nerve cell body and its processes.

neurotoxin   a poison that affects the parts of the nervous system that control breathing and heart action.

niche   the particular role played by organisms of a species in relation to those of other species in a community.

nictitating membrane   a thin, transparent covering, or lid, associated with the eyes of certain vertebrates, such as frogs and birds; a third eyelid.

nitrification the action of a group of soil bacteria on ammonia, producing nitrates.

nitrogen cycle a series of chemical reactions in which nitrogen compounds change form.

nitrogen fixation the process by which certain bacteria in soil or on the roots of leguminous plants convert free nitrogen into nitrogen compounds that the plants can use.

nocturnal active during the night.

node a growing region of a stem from which leaves, branches, or flowers develop.

nonbiodegradable polluting materials that are not decomposed by natural processes, or if so, only very slowly.

nondisjunction the failure of homologous chromosomes to segregate during meiosis.

"nonsense" codon genetically inactive nucleotide bases at the end of a strand of DNA.

notochord a rod of cartilage running longitudinally along the dorsal side of lower chordates and always present in the early embryological stages of vertebrates.

nuclear membrane a thin layer of living material surrounding the nucleus.

nucleolus a small, spherical body within the nucleus.

nucleoplasm the dense, gelatinous living content of the nucleus.

nucleotide a unit composed of a ribose or deoxyribose sugar, a phosphate, and an organic base. Many such units make up an RNA or DNA molecule.

nucleus the part of the cell that contains chromosomes; also, the central mass of an atom, containing protons and neutrons.

O

olfactory lobe the region of the brain that registers smell.

olfactory nerve the nerve leading from the olfactory receptor endings to the olfactory lobe.

oogenesis the process of the development of female reproductive cells whereby the diploid chromosome number is reduced to the haploid.

oogonium an egg-producing cell in certain thallophytes.

ootid a cell that matures into an egg.

operculum the gill cover in fishes.

opsonins antibodies that prepare bacteria for ingestion by phagocytic cells.

optic lobe the region of the brain that registers sight.

optic nerve the nerve leading from the retina of the eye to the optic lobe of the brain.

oral groove a deep cavity along one side of the paramecium and similar protozoans.

organ different tissues grouped together to perform a function or functions as a unit.

organelles specialized structures present in the cell.

organic variation differences that occur among individual organisms within a species.

organism a complete and entire living thing.

origin the attachment of a muscle at its non-moving part.

osculum an opening in the central cavity of sponges through which water leaves the animal.

osmosis the diffusion of water through a semi-permeable membrane from a region of greater concentration of water to a region of lesser concentration of water.

ossification the process by which cartilage cells are replaced by bone cells, resulting in a hardening of the body framework as the vertebrate grows.

ovary the basal part of the pistil containing the ovules; a female reproductive organ.

oviduct a tube in a female through which eggs travel from an ovary.

oviparous producing offspring from eggs hatched outside the body, as, birds and most fish.

ovipositor an egg-laying organ in insects.

ovoviviparous bringing forth the young alive after they have developed without placental connection.

ovule a structure in the ovary of a flower that can become a seed when the egg is fertilized.

P

palisade mesophyll leaf tissue composed of elongated cells in upright rows.

pancreas a gland located near the stomach and duodenum that is both endocrine and digestive.

pancreatic fluid a digestive secretion of the pancreas.

papilla a small elevation on the skin of an animal; projections on the tongue containing taste buds.

parasite an organism that lives in or on the body of another for a period of time and gets nourishment from the other organism, called a host.

parasympathetic nervous system a division of the autonomic nervous system.

parathyroid one of the four small ductless glands embedded in the thyroid.

parenchyma the thin-walled, soft tissue in plants forming cortex and pith.

parotid gland one of the salivary glands in the side of the fact in front of and below the ear.

parthogenesis the development of an egg without fertilization.

passive absorption water intake through a root by the forces of transpiration and cohesion.

passive transport the movement of molecules by their own energy during diffusion.

pasteurization   the process of killing and/or retarding the growth of bacteria in milk and alcoholic beverages by heating to a selected temperature so that the flavor is retained.

pathogenic   disease-causing.

pectoral girdle   the framework of bones by which the forelimbs of vertebrates are supported.

pedicel   the stalk that supports a single flower.

pedipalps   the second pair of head appendages in spiders.

pelagic zone   the open ocean part of the marine biome.

pellicle   a thickened membrane surrounding the cell of some protozoans.

pelvic girdle   the framework of bones by which the hind limbs of vertebrates are supported.

pelvis   the hip girdle; in the human, consisting of the ilium, ischium, and pubis bones; also, the central portion of a kidney.

perennial   a plant that grows through more than two growing seasons.

pericardium   the membrane around the heart.

pericycle   the tissue in roots from which secondary roots arise.

periderm   the corky layer forming the outer edge of a root after secondary thickening.

periodicity   alternating periods of activity.

periodontal membrane   the fibrous structure that anchors the root of the tooth in the jaw socket.

periosteum   the tough membrane covering the outside of a bone.

peripheral nervous system   the nerves communicating with the central nervous system and other parts of the body.

permeable membrane   one that allows substances to pass through it.

petal   one of the colored parts of the flower. (In some flowers the sepals are also colored.)

petiole   the stalk of a leaf.

phage   a bacteriophage, or virus, that reproduces in a bacterium.

phagocytic cells   those that engulf bacteria and digest them by means of enzymes.

pharynx   the muscular throat cavity, extending up over the soft palate and to the nasal cavity of vertebrates; the food tube on the ventral surface of a planarian.

phenotype   the outward appearance of an organism as the result of gene action.

phloem   the tissue in leaves, stems, and roots that conducts dissolved food substances.

pheromones   secretions that act as a chemical language among animals of the same species.

photochemical reaction   a chemical reaction accelerated by sunlight.

photolysis   the splitting of water molecules by light energy in a phase of photosynthesis.

photoperiodism   the dependence of some plants on the relation between the length of light and the length of darkness in a given day.

photoreceptor   an organ that is sensitive to light.

photosynthesis   the process by which certain living plant cells combine carbon dioxide and water in the presence of chlorophyll and light energy, to form carbohydrates and release oxygen.

phototropism   the response of plants to light.

phycocyanin   the bluish pigment found in blue-green algae.

phycoerythrin   a red pigment dissolved in the cell sap of certain red algae.

pia mater   the inner of the three membranes of the brain and spinal cord.

pinocytosis   the engulfing of large particles in pockets in a cell membrane.

pistil   the part of a flower bearing the ovary at its base.

pith   a storage tissue of roots and stems consisting of thin-walled parenchyma cells.

pituitary gland   a ductless gland composed of two lobes, located beneath the cerebrum.

placenta   a large, thin membrane in the uterus, in the area of the chorionic villi, that transports substances between the mother and developing young by means of the umbilical cord.

plankton   minute floating organism suspended near the surface in a body of water that serve as food for larger animals.

planula   a ciliated swimming larva of a jellyfish.

plaques   holes in a colony of bacteria resulting from destruction of cells by a bacteriophage.

plasma   the liquid portion of blood tissue.

plasma membrane   a thin, living membrane located at the outer edge of the cytoplasm.

plasmodium   name given to the vegetative body of a typical slime mold.

plasmolysis   the shrinking of a cell due to loss of water when placed in a hypertonic solution.

plastids   organelles in the cytoplasm of plant cells.

plastron   the lower shell of the turtle.

platelet   the smallest of the solid components in the blood, releasing thromboplastin in clotting.

pleural membrane   one of two membranes surrounding each lung.

plexus   a mass of nerve cell bodies.

poikilothermic   cold-blooded, in reference to certain animals.

polar nuclei   the two nuclei in the embryo sac in flowers that fuse with one of the sperm nuclei to form the endosperm nucleus.

pollen   the microgametophyte produced in the anther of a spermatophyte.

pollen sacs   structures in the anther containing pollen grains.

pollen tube   the tube formed by a pollen grain when it grows down the style of a pistil.

pollination the transfer of pollen from anther to stigma.

pollution the addition of impurities.

polyp the sessile stage in the life cycle of coelenterates.

polyploidy the condition in which cells contain more than twice the haploid number of chromosomes.

pons a part of the hindbrain located in the brain stem.

population a group of individuals of any one kind of organism in a given ecosystem.

portal circulation an extensive system of veins that lead from the stomach, pancreas, small intestine, and colon, then unite and enter the liver.

potential energy power that has not been actively release; it has the ability for doing work or causing a change.

precipitin a blood antibody that causes bacteria to settle out in lymph nodes and other body filters.

precocial birds laying many eggs, other 12–20, and starting incubation when the last egg is laid.

predator any animal that preys on other animals.

premolars large teeth for grinding.

primary germ layers the ectoderm, endoderm, and mesoderm.

primary oocyte the structure in the female gonads that divides to form the secondary oocyte and first polar body.

primary root the first root of the plant to issue from the seed.

primary tissues the first tissues developing from the meristematic region.

proboscis a tubular mouthpart in certain insects; also, the trunk of an elephant.

proglottid a segment of a tapeworm's body.

prolegs in caterpillars, the extra pairs of fleshy legs at the end of the abdomen.

propagation the multiplication of plants by vegetative parts.

prophage the DNA of a temperate phage which attaches to a bacterial chromosome and remains as an extra gene.

prophase the stage of mitosis in which chromosomes shorten and appear distinctly double and the nuclear membrane disappears.

prostate a gland located near the upper end of the urethra in the male.

prostomium a kind of upper lip in the earthworm.

protein synthesis a universal phase of cell anabolism whereby protein molecules are built up from amino acid molecules.

prothallus the tiny, heart-shaped gametophyte that develops from the spore of the fern.

prothorax the first segment of an insect's thorax, to which are attached the head and first pair of legs.

protonema a filamentous gametophyte structure produced by a spore in mosses.

protoplasm refers to the complex, constantly changing system of substances that establishes the living condition.

proventriculus first portion of the stomach of a bird.

pseudocoel a cavity or false coelom that is not lined with specialized covering cells.

pseudopodium a "false foot" of the ameba or amebalike cells.

psychedelic drugs a class of drugs, including LSD, that affect the mind by changing the perception of all the senses, the interpretation of space and time, and the rate and content of thought.

puberty the age at which the secondary sex characteristics appear.

pulmonary pertaining to the lungs.

pulse regular expansion of the artery walls caused by the beating of the heart.

Punnett square a grid system used in computing possible combinations of genes resulting from random fertilization.

pupa the stage in an insect having complete metamorphosis that follows the larva stage.

pupil the opening in the front of the eyeball, the size of which is controlled by the iris.

pyloric caeca pouches extending from the upper end of the intestine in fishes.

pyloric valve a sphincter valve regulating the passing of substances from the stomach to the duodenum.

pyrenoid a small protein body that serves as a center for starch formation in *Spirogyra*.

Q R

quadrate bone the bone in the snake's skull to which the lower jaw is attached.

quarantine isolation of plants or animals to prevent the spread of infection.

radicle embryonic root in a seed.

radioactive refers to an element that spontaneously gives off radiations.

reaction time the elapsed time between the moment when a stimulus is received and that in which a response occurs.

receptacle the end of the flower stalk bearing the reproductive structures.

receptor a cell, or group of cells, that receives a stimulus.

recessive refers to a gene or character that is masked when a dominant allele is present.

rectum the posterior portion of the large intestine, above the anus.

red corpuscles (or *erythrocytes*) disk-shaped blood cells containing hemoglobin.

red marrow found in flat bones and the ends of long bones; forms red corpuscles and certain white corpuscles.

reduction division the reduction of chromosomes during meiosis from the diploid number to the haploid number.

reflex action a nervous reaction in which a stimulus causes the passage of a sensory nerve impulse to the spinal cord or brain, from which, involuntarily, a motor impulse is transmitted to a muscle or gland.

regeneration the ability of organisms to form new parts.

renal relating to the kidneys.

replication self-duplication, or the process whereby a DNA molecule makes an exact duplicate of itself.

reproduction the process through which organisms produce offspring.

resolution the production under a microscope of a visible image in which details can be seen.

respiration the exchange of oxygen and carbon dioxide between cells and their surroundings, accompanied by oxidation and energy release.

response the reaction to a stimulus.

retina the inner layer of the eyeball, formed from the expanded end of the optic nerve.

Rh factor any one of six or more protein substances found on the surface of the red blood cells of most people.

rhizoid a rootlike structure that carries on absorption.

rhizome horizontal underground stem, often enlarged for storage, that can carry on vegetative propagation.

rhythmic regular periodicity in organisms.

ribosomes tiny, dense granules attached to the endoplasmic reticulum and lying between its folds. They contain RNA and protein-synthesizing enzymes.

rickettsiae a group of organisms that cause disease, and are midway between the viruses and bacteria in size.

RNA (ribonucleic acid) a nucleic acid in which the sugar is ribose. A product of DNA, it serves in controlling certain cell activities, including protein synthesis.

rod a cell of the retina of the eye that receives impulses from light rays and that is sensitive to shades but not to colors.

root cap a tissue at the tip of a root that projects the tissues behind it.

root hair a projection of an epidermal cell of a young root.

root pressure that which is built up in roots due to water intake and the resulting turgor.

rostrum a protective area that is an extension of the carapace in crustaceans.

ruminant a cud-chewing ungulate; for example, a cow.

S

saliva a fluid secreted into the mouth by the salivary glands.

salivary gland a group of secretory cells producing saliva.

saprophyte an organism that lives on dead or nonliving organic matter.

savannah a grassland area with a few scattered trees

scales the epidermal plates forming the outer covering in fishes and reptiles.

scavengers animals that feed on dead organisms.

scion the portion of a twig grafted onto a rooted stock.

sclerenchyma a plant-strengthening tissue, including fibers, mechanical tissue, and stone cells.

sclerotic layer the outer layer of the wall of the eyeball.

scolex knob-shaped head with hooks or suckers, as seen on some parasitic flatworms.

scrotum the pouch outside the body that contains the testes.

scutes the broad scales on the lower side of the snake's body.

secondary oocyte a cell that results from reduction division and develops into the ootid.

secondary root a branch root developing from the pericycle of another root.

secondary tissues those produced by the vascular cambium, a lateral secondary meristematic tissue, of a root or stem.

secretion formation of essential chemical substances by cells.

sedative an agent that depresses body activities.

seed a complete embryo plant surrounded by an endosperm and protected by seed coats.

segregation, law of Mendel's first law, based on his third hypothesis, stating that a pair of factors (genes) is segregated, or separated, during the formation of gametes (spores in lower plants).

selectively permeable membrane one that lets substances pass through more readily than other substances, but changes in permeability for a substance continually.

semen fertilizing fluid consisting of sperms and fluids from the seminal vesicle, prostate gland, and Cowper's gland.

semicircular canals the three curved passages in the inner ear that are associated with balance.

semilunar valves cup-shaped valves at the base of the aorta and the pulmonary artery that prevent backflow into the heart ventricles.

seminal receptacles structures that receive sperm cells in certain animals.

seminal vesicles structures that store sperm cells in certain animals.

seminiferous tubules   a mass of coiled tubes in which the sperms are formed within the testes.

sensory neurons   those that carry impulses from a receptor to the spinal cord or brain.

sepal   the outermost part of a flower, usually green and not involved in the reproductive process.

septum   a wall separating two cavities or masses of tissues; as, the nasal or heart septum.

serum   a substance (usually an extract of blood containing antibodies) used in treating disease and to produce immediate passive immunity.

serum albumin   a blood protein necessary for absorption.

serum globulin   a blood protein that contains antibodies.

sessile   a leaf lacking a petiole; an animal such as a sponge, that lives attached to another object.

setae   bristles on the earthworm used in locomotion.

sex chromosomes   the two kinds of chromosomes (X and Y) that determine the sex of an offspring.

sex-influenced character   a trait that is dominant in one sex, recessive in the other.

sex-limited character   a trait that develops only in the presence of sex hormones.

sex-linked character   a recessive trait carried on the X type of sex chromosome.

sexual reproduction   that involving the union of a female gamete, or egg, and a male gamete, or sperm; in some lower organisms, the gametes may be alike.

shell membrane   a double lining around the albumen and beneath the shell of a bird's egg.

shoot apex   a conical mass of meristematic tissue deep within the bud scales.

sieve plate   in the starfish, the opening of the water-vascular system to the outside.

sieve tube   a conducting tube of the phloem.

simple eye   a small, photosensitive organ of many lower animals.

sinoatrial node   a mass of tissue in the right atrium of the heart in which the beat originates.

sinus   a space or cavity.

sinus venosus   a thin-walled sac, formed by an enlargement of the cardinal vein of the fish and the venae cavae of the frog, that lies at the entrance to the heart.

skeletal muscle   that which is striated and voluntary.

slime layer   that which surrounds a bacterium.

small intestine   the digestive tube, about seven meters long in humans, that begins at the pylorus.

smog   a combination of the pollutant smoke with fog.

smooth muscle   that which is involuntary and that is found lining the walls of the intestine, stomach, and arteries.

soft palate   forms the roof of the mouth behind the chewing area.

soil flora   bacteria, molds, and other fungi that live in the soil.

solar plexus   the large nerve ganglion of the sympathetic nervous system, located in the abdomen.

solute   the dissolved substance in a solution.

solution   a homogeneous mixture of two or more substances where one is dissolved in another.

solvent   the dissolving component of a solution.

sori   small clusters of sporangia that appear on fern leaves when mature.

spawn   to discharge gametes directly into water, as fish do; a mass of eggs discharged by a fish or other aquatic animal.

speciation   the development of a species.

sperm   a male reproductive cell.

spermatid   a structure formed from a secondary spermatocyte that matures into a sperm.

spermatocyte   (primary) a structure formed by meiosis from a spermatogonial cell; (secondary) a structure formed by division of a primary spermatocyte.

spermatogenesis   the process of the development of male reproductive cells whereby the diploid chromosome number is reduced to the haploid.

sphincter muscle   a ring of smooth muscle that closes or contracts an opening or a tube.

spicule   the material forming the skeleton of certain sponges.

spinal cord   the main dorsal nerve of the central nervous system in vertebrates, extending down the back from the medulla.

spinal nerves   large nerves connecting the spinal cord with various parts of the body.

spindle   the numerous fine threads formed between the poles of the nucleus during mitosis.

spinnerets   structures on the tip of a spider's abdomen containing numerous silk tubes.

spiracles   external openings of the insect's tracheal tubes on the thorax and abdomen.

spirillum   a spiral-shaped bacterium.

spirochete   a group of spiral-shaped one-celled organisms resembling both protozoans and bacteria.

spongin   fibers composing the skeleton of certain sponges.

spongocoel   the central cavity in sponges.

spongy mesophyll   loosely constructed leaf tissue containing many spaces.

spontaneous generation   a disproved belief that certain nonliving or dead materials could be changed into living organisms.

sporangiophore   in molds, an ascending hypha bearing sporangia.

sporangium   a structure that produces spores.

spore   an asexual reproductive cell.

sporophyte the stage that produces spores in an organism having alternation of generations.

stamen the male reproductive part of the flower bearing an anther at its tip.

statocyst the balancing organ of the crayfish.

sternum breastbone.

stigma the part of the pistil that receives pollen grains.

stimulant an agent that increases or elevates body activity.

stimulus a factor or environmental change capable of producing activity in protoplasm.

stipe the stalk portion of a fruiting body of a mushroom.

stipule a leaflike or scalelike structure at the base of many leaf petioles.

stock the plant on which a scion has been grafted; a line of descent.

stolon a transverse hypha of a mold; also, a horizontal, creeping underground stem.

stomach an organ that receives ingested food, prepares it for digestion, and begins protein digestion.

stomata pores regulating the passage of air and water vapor to and from the leaf.

style the stalk of the pistil.

sublingual gland one of the pair of salivary glands lying under the tongue.

submaxillary gland one of the pair of salivary glands lying in the angle of the lower jaw.

substrate a layer or substance in which an organism takes root or to which it attaches.

succession the changing plant and animal populations of a given area.

successive osmosis the cell-to-cell diffusion of water.

succulent leaf a thick, fleshy leaf.

suspension a mixture formed by particles that are larger than ions or molecules.

sweepstakes dispersal the movement of organisms into new areas despite strong barriers.

swimmerets appendages on the abdomen of a crustacean.

symbiosis the relationship in which two organisms live together in close association.

symmetry the general form of an organism.

sympathetic nervous system a division of the autonomic nervous system.

synapse the space between nerve endings.

synapsis the coming together of homologous pairs of chromosomes during meiosis.

synergid one of two structures formed on either side of the egg in the embryo sac of flowers.

syngamy the fusion of gametes during fertilization.

synovial fluid a secretion of cartilage that lubricates a joint.

syrinx the song box of a bird.

systemic relating to the body.

system a group of organs forming a functional unit.

systole part of the cycle of the heart during which the ventricles contract and force blood into the arteries.

systolic blood pressure arterial pressure produced when the ventricles contract.

T

taproot the main root of a plant, often serving as a food reservoir.

taste buds flask-shaped structures in the tongue containing nerve endings that are stimulated by flavors.

taxonomy the science of classifying living things.

teliospore a two-celled, black winter spore of wheat rust.

telophase the last stage of mitosis, during which two daughter cells are formed.

telson the posterior segment of the abdomen of certain crustaceans.

temperate phage a phage that injects its DNA into a bacterial cell without causing the production of phage particles.

temperature inversion an atmospheric phenomenon in which a layer of cold air moves under a lid of warm air.

template a pattern, such as a specific sequence of bases in the messenger RNA molecule that acts as a pattern for the synthesis of a protein molecule.

tendon a strong band of connective tissue to which the fleshy portion of a muscle attaches.

tendril a part of a plant modified for climbing.

tentacle a long appendage, or "feeler," of certain invertebrates.

terrestrial land-living.

testa the outer seed coat.

testes the male reproductive organs of animals.

tetrad a group of four cells.

tetraploid a term used to indicate that a cell has four sets of homologous chromosomes.

thallus a plant body, such as an alga, that lacks differentiation into stems, leaves, and roots and that does not grow from an apical point.

theory a hypothesis that is continually supported by experimental evidence.

thermal pollution the addition of heat to a body of water.

thigmotropism a response of an organ or an organism to an object; for example, the wrapping of the tendrils of a climbing plant around an object.

thoracic duct a vessel carrying lymph and emptying into the left subclavian vein.

thorax the middle region of the body of an insect between the head and abdomen; the chest region of mammals.

thrombin   a substance formed in blood clotting as a result of the reaction of prothrombin, thromboplastin, and calcium.

thromboplastin   a substance essential to blood clotting formed by disintegration of blood platelets.

thymus   one of the ductless glands, situated in the upper chest cavity.

thyroid   the ductless gland, located in the neck on either side of the larynx, that regulates metabolism.

tissue   a group of cells that are similar in structure and activity.

tissue fluid   that which bathes the cells of the body; called lymph when contained in vessels.

tolerance   an organism's ability to withstand an environmental condition.

tone (muscle)   the condition in which flexor and extensor muscles oppose each other, resulting in a continuous state of slight contraction.

tonsil   a mass of lymphatic tissue in the throat of higher animals.

topography   the physical features of the earth.

toxin   a poisonous substance produced by bacteria and other organisms that acts in the body or on foods.

toxin-antitoxin   a mixture of diphtheria antitoxin and toxin, formerly used to develop active immunity.

toxoid   toxin weakened by mixing with formaldehyde or salt solution, used extensively to develop immunity to diphtheria, scarlet fever, and tetanus.

trachea   an air tube in insects and spiders; the windpipe in air-breathing vertebrates.

trachelds   thick-walled conducting tubes that strengthen woody tissue.

tracheophyte   a plant that has vessels for the conduction of fluids.

transcription   the process whereby a molecule of DNA codes the building of a molecule of RNA.

transfer RNA   a form of RNA thought to deliver amino acids to the template formed by messenger RNA on the ribosomes.

transformation   in pneumococcus, the change from a noncapsulated to a capsulated form, brought about by the transfer of DNA.

transformers   bacteria that change the simpler substances left by the decomposers into nitrogen compounds that are used by plants.

translocation   the movement of water, dissolved foods, and other substances in plants.

transpiration   the loss of water from plants.

transpiration-cohesion theory   an explanation of water translocation based on the loss of water through leaves and an attraction of water molecules for one another.

transpiration pull   one of the forces involved in the rise of water in a stem. As cells lose water to the atmosphere, water enters them from adjacent cells, resulting in upward movement of water.

trichocysts   sensitive protoplasmic threads in the paramecium, concerned with protection.

trisomy   the presence of three homologous chromosomes in all body cells.

trochophore   a larval form of mollusks.

tropism   an involuntary growth response of an organism to a stimulus.

truncus arteriosus   a branch of the conus arteriosus in the frog.

tube feet   movable suction discs on the rays of most echinoderms.

tube nucleus   one of the three nuclei present in a pollen tube.

tuber   an enlarged tip of a rhizome swollen with stored food.

tubule   a tiny collecting tube extending from a Bowman's capsule of a kidney.

turbinate   one of three layers of bones in the nasal passages.

turgor   the stiffness of plant cells due to the presence of water.

tympanic membrane   the eardrum.

tympanum   a membrane in certain anthropods, serving a vibratory function; also used for tympanic membrane.

U

umbilical cord   found in female mammals, leading from the placenta to the embryo.

unit character   principle of Mendel's concept that the various hereditary characteristics are controlled by factors (genes), and that these factors occur in pairs.

urea   a nitrogenous waste substance found chiefly in the urine of mammals, but also formed in the liver from broken-down proteins.

ureter   a tube leading from a kidney to the bladder or cloaca.

urethra   the tube leading from the urinary bladder to an external opening of the body.

uric acid   a nitrogenous waste product of cell activity.

urinary bladder   the sac at the base of the ureters that stores urine.

urine   the liquid waste filtered from the blood in the kidney and voided by the bladder.

uropod   a flipper, or developed swimmeret, at the posterior end of the crayfish.

uterus   the organ in which young mammals are nourished until they are born; egg storage tube in some flukes.

uvula   the extension of the soft palate.

V

vaccination   method of producing immunity by inoculating with a vaccine.

vaccine   a substance used to produce immunity.

vacuolar membrane   a membrane surrounding a vacuole in a cell and regulating the movement of materials in and out of the vacuole.

vacuole   one of the spaces scattered through the cytoplasm of a cell and containing fluid.

vagina   cavity of the female immediately outside and surrounding the cervix of the uterus.

vagus nerve   the principal nerve of the parasympathetic nervous system.

valve   one of the shells of a mollusk; also, a fold or flap of tissue controlling the direction of blood flow, as in the heart or veins of some organisms.

vasa deferentia   ducts that transport sperms from the testes.

vasa efferentia   tiny tubes in the reproductive system of the frog through which sperm pass.

vascular bundles   strands of phloem and xylem found in the roots, stems, and leaves of higher plants.

vascular cylinder   the innermost region of a root, containing the xylem and phloem.

vascular rays   sheets or ribbons of parenchyma cells radiating from the pith through the xylem of a woody stem.

vascular tissue   fluid-conducting tissues characteristic of the tracheophytes.

vector (or *arthropod carrier*)   an insect or other arthropod that carries infectious organisms.

veins   strengthening and conducting structures in leaves; vessels carrying blood to the heart.

vena cava   a large collecting vein found in many vertebrates.

venation   the arrangement of veins through the leaf blade.

venom   the poison secreted by glands of poisonous snakes or other animals.

ventricle   a muscular chamber of the heart; also, a space in the brain.

venules   small branches of veins.

vermiform appendix   a fingerlike outgrowth of the intestinal caecum in humans.

vertebra   a bone of the spinal column of vertebrates.

vertebrate   an animal with a backbone.

vestigial organs   those that are poorly developed and not functioning.

villi   microscopic projections of the wall of the small intestine that increase the absorbing surface.

virulence   the potency of the ability of an organism to cause disease.

virulent phage   a bacteriophage that produces a lytic cycle of destruction.

viruses   particles that are noncellular and have no nucleus, no cytoplasm, and no surrounding membrane. They may reproduce in living tissue.

visual purple   the chemical in the rods of the eye necessary for functioning in reduced light.

vitamin   a organic substance that, though not a food, is essential for normal body activity.

vitreous humor   a transparent substance that fills the interior of the eyeball.

viviparous   refers to animals that bear their young alive, and that nourish them before birth by means of a placenta.

vocal cords   those structures within the larynx that vibrate to produce sound.

voluntary muscle   a striated muscle that can be controlled at will.

vomerine teeth   scalelike teeth in the roof of the frog's mouth that aid in holding prey.

W

water cycle   the continuous movement of water from the atmosphere to the earth and from the earth to the atmosphere.

watershed   a hilly region, usually extending over a large area, that conducts surface water to streams.

water table   the level at which water is standing underground.

water-vascular system   the system of tubes connecting the tube-feet in certain echinoderms.

white corpuscles   colorless, nucleated blood cells

withdrawal symptoms   nervous reactions and hallucinations resulting from the lack of a drug to which the victim is addicted.

X Y Z

X chromosome   a sex chromosome present singly in human males and as a pair in females.

xanthophyll   a yellow pigment, one of the chlorophyll pigments found in certain chromoplasts.

xerophyte   a plant that requires very little water to live.

xylem   the woody tissue of a root or stem that conducts water and dissolved minerals upward.

Y chromosome   a sex chromosome found only in males.

yellow marrow   fills the central cavity of a long bone and is primarily composed of fat cells.

yolk   the part of an egg from which the egg cell and developing embryo obtains its nourishment.

yolk sac   an extraembryonic membrane providing food for the embryo.

zoospores   in *Ulothrix* and certain other algae, the flagellated cells that leave the mother cell and later develop into new organisms.

zygospore   the dormant form of some protists when the zygote forms a thick protective wall.

zygote   a fusion body formed when two gametes unite.

zymase   an enzyme that splits molecules of simple sugars (glucose or fructose).

INDEX

Page references for illustrations are printed in **boldface**.

brain, fish, 431–432, **431**
　frog, 448, **448**
　human, 514–515, **514**, 583–586, **583, 584, 585**
　vertebrate, **507**
brain cavities, 583
brain membranes, 583
brain stem, 586
brazil nut, as energy source, **74**
bread mold, 223–225, **224**
breathing, control of, 572
　defined, 569
　environmental effects of, 576
　mechanics of, 571–572, **572, 573**
　movements of, 572, **572**
　see also respiration
breeding plants and animals, 140
　see also animal breeding, plant breeding
Bridges, C. B., and genetic research, 113, 116–117
bronchi, and respiration, 570–571
　bronchial tubes, 570
bronchioles, 570
Brontosaurus, 455
brown algae, 238, 247, **247**
Brownian movement, 186
Bryophytes, 253–257, **255, 256, 257**
bud(s), plant, 294–296, **295**
　sponge, 344
bud mutant, 144
budding, 90, **90**
　plant, 322–323
bulb, 302, **302**
bulk-feeders, 654
bunchberry, **324**
bundle scars, 294
Burbank, Luther, and plant breeding, 140, **140**
butterfly, metamorphosis in, 401–402, **402**

cactus, 285
　in desert habitat, **650**
　night blooming, **312**
calcium, in bone, 526–527
calorie, defined, 536
calyx, 323
cambium, 269
camels, evolution of, 158, **158**
cancer, and viruses, 180
canine tooth, human, **544**
capillaries, 561
　fish, 430
capillarity, 307, **308**
capillary water, 305
capsule, bacteria, 185–186
carapace, 383, 469
carbohydrates, described, 36–38, 538
　digestion of, **545**
carbon, in organic compounds, 35
carbon dioxide, importance of, 35
　transport of, 575
carbon-dioxide acceptor, in photosynthesis, 68
carbon-dioxide cycle, 639–640, **639**
carbon isotope, 30
carbon molecule, 35–36
carbon-monoxide poisoning, 576–577
Carboniferous Age forest, 257–258, **258**
cardiac muscle cell, **530**, 531
Carnivora, 502–503, **502**
carnivores, 502–503, **502**
carotene(s), 48, **64**

carrot root, **293**
cartilage, 526
"cartilage fish(es)," 423–425, **424, 425**
cat family, 165
catalyst, chlorophyll as, 64
　defined, 64
caterpillar(s), 401, **402**
caudal fin, 428
Caudata, 439
Cecropia moth, metamorphosis of, 400–401, **400, 401**
cedar-apple rust, 229
cell(s), animal, **14, 46,** 58
　bacterial, 185–186
　chromosomes in, 87–88
　as defense against disease, 199
　defined, 14
　discovery of, 42–43
　division of, 86–90
　energy source for, 62
　and environment, **54**
　explained, 42
　limits to growth, 86
　model of, 46
　mouse tumor, **44**
　onion root, **86**
　phagocytic, 199
　plant, 14, **44, 49,** 57–58
　　mitosis in, 90
　and mitosis, 86–88
　processes of, 43–44
　replication in, 87–88
　self-fueling, 62
　specialization in, 341
　spermatogonial, 92
　use by organisms, 14–15
　and viruses, 180–181
　see also blood cells, mitosis
cell energy, uses of, 76–77
cell membrane, 45
　diffusion through, 56–60
　and homeostasis, 54
cell nucleus, structure, 44–45
cell specialization, 50–51
cell theory, 43
cell wall, 49
cellular organization, and taxonomy, 164
cellular respiration, process of, 74–75, **74, 76**
cellulose, 37, 538
Cenozoic Age mammals, **489**
centipede(s), 387, **387**
central nervous system, 581, **587**
centrifuge tubes, **43**
centrioles, 88
centromere, 88
centrosome, 88
cephalization, defined, **353**
Cephalopods, 372
cephalothorax, 383
cerebellum, fish, 431
　human, 585
cerebrum, 417
　fish, 431
　human, 583–585, **585**
cervix, 624
Cetacea, 500–501, **501**
chalaza, 484
chameleon, 465–466, **465**
chelipeds, 383
chemical bonds, see bonds
chemical change in matter, 27
chemical compounds, see compounds
chemical elements, see elements

chemical energy, 28
chemical reactions, inorganic, 72
chemosynthesis, defined, 72
chemotherapy, 206
chemotropism, 318
chicken(s), life span, **16**
　see also bird(s), egg(s)
chicken embryo, development of, 484–485, **485**
chiggers, 389
Chilopoda, 387
chimpanzee, 504, **504**
　skull, 514, **514**
　teeth, 514, **514**
Chiroptera, 496–497, **497**
chloride ions, **33**
chlorine atom, 30
chlorophyll, 48
　absorption spectrum, **72**
　as energy carrier, 68
　and photosynthesis, 63
chlorophyll molecule, formula, **64**
chloroplast, 48, **48,** 63–64
cholesterol, structural formula, **36**
　chlorella, 241
chlorophyta, see green algae
chondrichthyes, 413, 423
Chondrus crispus, **248**
Chordata, 411–412
chordates, 411–412
　characteristics of, 411–412
chorion, 457
chromatid(s), 88, **88**
chromatin, 44
chromatophores, 426
chromoplasts, 48
chromosome(s), 44, 87–88
　and crossing-over, 117–118
　described, 79
　female and male, **91**
　genes in, 112–113
　and nondisjunction, 116–117, 136–138
　sex, 113–114
　sex linkage in, 115–116
chromosome maps, 118, **118**
chromosome mutations, defined, 122
chromosome number, in algae reproduction, 244
　and cell reproduction, 91–92
chromosome replication, **88**
chrysallis, 401, **402**
Chrysophyta, diatoms as, 245–246, **245**
circulatory system, human, 525, 552, 558–563, **559, 560, 562, 563**
　see also blood
cirrhosis, 600
citric acid cycle, in respiration, 75
clam(s), 369–370, **369, 370**
classes, 166
classification, animal, 374–375
　problems in, 167, 170
　science of, 163
　of viruses, 176–177
　see also taxonomy
classification system, groupings in, 166–167
cleavage furrow, 89
climatic barrier, 671
climatic zones, 672
　see also biome(s)
climax species, defined, 667
climbing roots, 293
clitellum, 359
cloaca, frog, 445
clotting, blood, 555–556, **556**

diurnal animal(s), 660
division plate, 90
Domagk, Gerhard, and chemotherapy, 206
dominance and recessiveness, principle of, 101
dominant and recessive genes, 104–105
dominant traits, 101
dormant period, 649
dormant plants, 314
dorsal, defined, 351
dorsal fin, 428
double helix, 79, **79**, **80**
Down's syndrome, 137, **137**
drinking, *see* alcohol
drone, 404, **404**
Drosophila, see fruit fly
droughts, 688
drug(s), and addiction, 604
defined, 603
see also addicts, addiction, individual drugs
duckbilled platypus, 493–494, **494**
duct(s), 542
ductless gland(s), 610
and their secretions (table), 612
see also endocrine gland(s), individual glands
Dujardin, Félix, 43

ear(s), and balance, 592
and hearing, 591–592
structure of, 590–592, **591**
early land plants, time scale, **254**
earth, ages of, **152**
development of life on, **148**
history of, 148–149
life on, time scale, **153**
origin of life on, 149
earthworm(s), 359–362, **360**, **362**
reproduction in, 361–362, **362**
structure of, 359–361, **360**
systems, 359–361, **359**
echinoderm(s), time scale, **367**
Echinodermata, 368, 372–374, **373, 374**
ecology, defined, 635
ecosystem(s), change in, 637
defined, 635
food chains in, 653
food pyramid in, 653–654, **653, 654**
humans in, 637
relationships in, 636
see also environment, environmental factors, population density
ectoderm, hydra, 345
ectoplasm, ameba, 211
Edentata, 500, **500**
eels, spawning of, 433–434
egg, bird, 483–486, **484, 485**
in sexual reproduction, 91
egg cell, 483–484, **484**
egg tooth, 486
Ehrlich, Paul, and chemotherapy, 206
electron, in atom, 29
and electronmicroscope, 10–11
transfer, 31–32
electron microscope, 10–11, **10, 11**
element(s), chemically active, 31
essential to man (table), 34
explained, 28
inert, 31
symbols for, 29
elephant, **501**
elongation region, 289, **290**

embryo, bird, 484–485, **485**
defined, 627
development of, 627–629, **628**
fern, 259–260
embryo sac, 325
empirical formula, 36
endocrine gland(s), 610
balance in, 619–620
see also individual glands
endocrine system, human, 525
endoplasm, ameba, 211
endoplasmic reticulum, 45, **45**
endoskeleton, 416
human, 526
endosperm, seed, 327
endosperm nucleus, 327
endospores, bacterial, 189–190, **189**
endotoxins, 198
energy, activation, 28
bond, 31
cell, 76–77
chemical, 28
defined, 27
food as source, **74**
kinetic, 27–28
and living things, **62**
oxidation, 74
potential, 27–28
radiant, 27
source of for cells, 62
use by organisms, 14
energy carrier, chlorophyll as, 68
energy crisis, 696–697
energy level(s), of atoms, 29
energy transfer, 281
in photosynthesis, 65
entomology, 391
environment, and altering of genetic trait, **119**
defined, 17
effects on breathing and respiration, 576
and evolution, 157–159
and heredity, 97, **97**
and living things, 17–18
environmental factor(s), atmosphere as, 653, **653**
light as, 650–651
soil as, 648–649, **648**
temperature as, 649
water as, 649–650, **650**
enzymes, defined, 38
described, 39–40
synthesis of, 125
work of, **40**
enzyme system, defined, 40
enzyme-substrate complex, 40
Eohippus, 490, **490**
epicotyl, 332
epidermal hairs, 277–278
epidermal tissue, 269
epidermis, human, 565–566
leaf, 276, 277–278, **277**
root, 291
sponge, 343
epinephrine (adrenalin), 616
epithelial tissues, human, 523
Equisetum, 260–261, **261**
era(s), of earth, 149
erythrocytes, 553–554, **554**
erosion, soil, 686–687, **686**
wind, 687–688, **687**
esophagus, earthworm, 360
grasshopper, 396
human, 544

essential elements (table), 34
estivation, 663
frog, 452
estrogen, 617, 624
etiolated leaves and stems, 312
euglena, **167**
described, 215
structure, 215, **215**
Euglena gracilis, 215
euglenoid movement, 215
Eustachian tubes, frog, 444
human, 590
evaporation, defined, 638
evolution, and adaptive radiation, 160
convergent, 161
Darwin's theory of, 155–156
and environment, 157–159
and isolation, 159
Lamarck's theory of, 154–155
and migration, 157–158
mutation theory of, 156
process of, 150–154
and speciation, 159–161
excretion, and cells, 44
defined, 563
excretory system, human, 525, 563–567, **564, 565, 566**
excurrent growth, 296, **296**
excurrent pores, 342
excurrent siphon, 368
exoskeleton, 379, 382
exotoxins, 197
experiment, controlled, 6–7
experimental factor, defined, 6
expiration, defined, 572
external fertilization, 432
external respiration, 569–570, **569**
extraembryonic membrane, 627
eye, compared with camera, **594**
movement of, 595
protection of, 595
structure, 592–593, **593**
and vision, 593–594, **594**
eye color, as genetic trait, 133
inheritance of, **135**

FSH (follicle stimulating hormone), 624
facultative aerobes, bacteria as, 188
fairy ring mushroom, 232, **232**
Fallopian tubes, 624
fallout, 696
families, 166
farm pond, 704
fat(s), 38
body use of, 540
digestion of, **545**
fat bodies, frog, 452
fat molecule, dehydration synthesis, **38**
fatty acid, 38
fatty liver, 600
feathers, 477–478, **477**
feces, 500
feedback, 619–620, **619**
female reproductive system, 624–624, **625**
fermentation, 188
alcoholic, **76**
and bacteria, 183–184
lactic acid, **76**
and respiration, 75–76
of yeast, 227
fern(s), 257–258, **258**
life cycle, 257–260, **259**
fertilization, 93
of egg cell, 483–484

movement of, 394
reproductive organs, 397
respiratory structure, 395–396
response in, 397, **397**
structure of, 394–397, **394, 395, 396, 397**
grasslands, as biome, 677, **677**
green algae, 238, 240–243, **240, 241**
green glands, 384
green plants, *see* plants
Green Revolution, 145
Griffith, Frederick, and DNA, 120–122
groundwater, 638
growth, of organisms, 15–16
growth regulators, 314
grunions, 665–666, **665**
guard cells, 277
guinea pigs, crossing of, 108
dominant and recessive genes in, 104–105
gullet, 213
gully control, **686,** 687
gully erosion, 686
guttation, 310–311, **310**
defined, 310
gymnodinium, 246
Gymnospermae, 262
gymnosperms, 262, 264–266, **264**

habitat, defined, 647
limiting factors in, 648
half-life, 517
halophytes, 306
hands, human and ape compared, 514
514
haploid number, 92
hard palate, 542
Haversian canals, 528
hawk, **660**
head, human, **543**
hearing, 590–592
heart, fish, 429–430
frog, 446–447, **447**
human, and circulatory system, 558–560, **559**
as muscle, **530, 531**
vertebrate, **506**
heart beat, 560
heartwood, 299, **300**
hemoglobin, 553–554
hemophilia, as sex-linked trait, 116, 133–134, **134**
hemotoxin, 465
herbaceous dicotyledonous stems, 300, **300**
herbaceous plants, 271
heredity, and blood type, 131–132
and DNA, 87
and diseases, 135–136
and environment, 97, **97**
and genetic disorders, 136–138
human, 127
and intelligence, 136
hermaphroditic, defined, 353
heterocysts, algae, 239
heterogametes, algae, 237, **237**
heterotrophs, bacteria as, 187
heterozygous organism, 102
hibernation, 662, **663**
in frogs, 452
hilum, 332
hindbrain, 507
hive, bee, 405

homeostasis, and membrane, 54
explained, 53–54
Homo sapiens, 519
homoiothermic animal(s), 649
homologous bones, **151**
homologous chromosomes, 91
homologous organs, 151
homology, 374
homozygous crosses, **108**
homozygous organism, 102
honey, production of, 405
honeybee, 403–406, **403, 404, 405, 406**
Hooke, Robert, and cells, 42–43
microscope of, **42**
hookworm, 358
hormone(s), 610
effects on human body, **610**
in insect metamorphosis, 400–401, **401**
plant, 314–316, **314, 315, 316**
see also individual hormones
horned lizard, 466, **466**
horny outer layer, 369
horse, evolution of, 490, **490**
horsetails, 260–261, **261**
host cell, defined, 175
human(s), characteristics of, 513, 516
communication between, 515
early forms, 518–519
in ecosystems, 637
modern forms, 519–521, **520**
sex-linked traits in, 132–133
similarity with other mammals, 516
tool use by, 513–514
upright posture in, 513–515, **513**
human body, alcohol effects on, 599–600
circulation in, 561–562, **562**
circulatory system, 552, 558–563, **559, 560, 562, 563**
defenses against disease, 198–199
digestive organs, **541**
see also individual organs
digestive system of, 541–546, **541, 542, 543, 544, 545**
excretory system, 563–567, **564, 565, 566**
joints in, 528, **528**
metabolism of, 576
minerals in, 535
muscle system of, 529–531, **529, 530, 531**
nervous system, 581–583
see also individual parts
organs and systems of, 525
regions of, 525
reproductive system, 525, 623–625, **623, 624, 625**
skeletal system, 525–528, **526, 527, 528**
smoking effects on, 598–599, **598**
tissues in, 523–525, **524** (table)
vitamin use by, 535–536
water use in, 533–535
see also Insert between pages 518–519.
human brain, development of, 514–515, **514**
human development, 626–629, **627**
theories about, 516–517
human egg, 111
human hand, 514, **514**
human heredity, nature of, 127
human pelvis, 513, **513**
human populations, growth of, 645, **645**

human skeleton, **416**
human skull, 514, **514**
and primate skull compared, **520**
human virus(es), 179–180
humus, 305
hybrid(s), animal, 145–146, **145**
corn, 142–144
defined, 101
plant, 141–142, **141**
hybrid vigor, 142
hybridization, defined, 141
of plants, 141–142
hydra, 345–347, **345, 346**
food acquisition by, 345–346, **345**
reaction in, 350–351
reproduction in, 346
structure of, 345–346, **345**
hydrochloric acid, as defense against disease, 199
hydrogen acceptor, 68
hydrogen atom, 29
hydrogen transport, in respiration, 75
hydrolysis, defined, 38
hydroscopic water, 305
hydrotropism, 318
hyperthyroidism, 611, 613
hypertonic solution, 58–59, **58, 59**
hyphae, 223
hypothalamus, 618–619
hypothesis, defined, 6
hypothyroidism, 613
hypotonic solution, 57

identical twins, **130,** 131
immune carriers of disease, 197
immune therapy, beginnings of, 203
immunity, defined, 201–203
types of (table), 203
see also vaccination
immunization, natural and artificial, **202**
imperfect fungus, 232
inbreeding, defined, 142
in plants, 142
incomplete dominance, **108,** 109, **109**
incomplete metamorphosis, 398, 400
incubation, egg, 484–486, **485**
incurrent pores, 342
incurrent siphon, 368
independent assortment, law of, 101–102
individual traits, 98
industrial melanism, 159, **159**
inert elements, 31
infection(s), *see* disease(s)
inheritance, chromosome theory of, 111–112
see also heredity
initiator codons, 81
innate behavior, 417–419
inorganic chemical reactions, 72
inorganic compounds, 34–35
inorganic molecules, formation into organic molecules, **150**
insect(s), behavior of, 402–406, **403, 404, 405**
characteristics of, 391, 394–395
with complete metamorphosis (table), 399
described, 391–392, **392**
diversity of, 394
division of labor among, 403–405, **403, 404**
with incomplete metamorphosis (table), 398

physical change in, 27, **27**
solid state of, 27, **27**
see also atom(s), element(s)
maturation region, 289
maxillae, crayfish, 383
grasshopper, 394
maxillipeds, 383
measles virus, cells infected by, **180**
medulla oblongata, fish, 431
human, 586
medusa, 346-347, **347**
megaspores, 325
meiosis, described, 92–93
membrane(s), brain, 583
permeable, 54
Mendel, Gregor, and heredity, **98,** 99–
105, **99, 101, 103, 105**
meninges, 583, **583**
menstruation, defined, 625
meristematic tissue, 269
mesentry, frog, 445
mesoderm, worm, 352
mesoglea, 345
mesophyll, 276, 278
mesothorax, grasshopper, 394
messenger codons, 81–82
messenger RNA, 80
codons for the amino acids (table), 82
metabolic processes, and mutant
genes, 125
metabolism, defined, 276
human, 576
and thyroid gland, 611–614
metamorphosis, 397–402, **400, 401,**
402
adaptive value of, 401–402, **402**
defined, 397
frog, 450–451, **451**
hormone role in, 400–401, **400, 401**
metaphase, of mitosis, 89, **89**
metathorax, grasshopper, 394
methadone maintenance, 608
methane, formation of, 189
structural formula, **35**
microbiologist tools, 182
Micrographia, 43
micronucleus, of paramecia, 214
microorganisms, *see* bacteria, viruses
micropyle, 325
microscope(s), compound, 8–9, **9**
early, **8**
electron, 10–11, **10, 11**
Hooke's, **42**
light, 8–10, **11**
and magnification, 9–10
and resolution, 9–10
scanning electron, **11**
simple, 8
and spontaneous generation, 21–22
microspores, 324
midbrain, 507
middle lamella, 49
migration, 663–665, **663, 664**
and evolution, 157–158
millimicron, defined, 173
millipedes, 387, **387**
milt, 432
mimicry, 657, **657**
mineral(s), absorption by plant roots,
306–307
in human body, 535
mineral compounds, importance of, 35
mites, 389
mitochondria, 47, **47**

mitosis, in animal cell, **87**
phases of, **88, 89**
see also cell(s)
mixture(s), explained, 33–34
modified roots, 292–293
modified stems, 301–302, **302**
mold(s), described, 223–225
mold spore, germination of, 223
mole, 497
molecular compounds, 32
molecular motion, 55
molecule(s), active transport of, 59
carbon, 35–36
defined, 32
diatomic, 32
fat, 38
mollusks, bivalves, 368–370, **369**
cephalopods, 372
described, 366–367
echinoderms, 372–374, **373, 374**
structure of, 368
time scale, 367
molting, 478, **478**
monarch butterfly, migration of, **664**
metamorphosis of, 401–402, **402**
mongolism, *see* Down's syndrome
monocot, 267
flowers of, 324, **324**
seeds of, 333, **333**
monocotyledonous stems, 300, 301
monohybrid crosses (table), 104- 105,
105
monosaccharides, 36, 538
structural formula, **37**
monosomy, 136
Monotremata, 493–494, **494**
monotreme(s), 493–494, **494**
Morgan, Thomas Hunt, and gene linkage, 113–114
moss(es), economic importance of,
256–257
life cycle of, 254–256, **255, 256**
structure of, 253–254
motor neuron, 582
motor unit, 529, **529**
mountain goats, 13
mountain laurel, hybridization of, **141**
mouth, digestion in, 546–547
human, **542**
mouth pore, of paramecia, 213
morel, 227–228, **227**
mucus, 199, 542
mucous membranes, as defense
against disease, 198
Muller, Herman J., and mutation, 123–
124
multicellular organisms, 50–51
multiple alleles, 131
muscle, contraction of, 529, **529**
muscle cells, types of, 529–531, **530**
muscle system, human, 523, 525, 529–
531, **529, 530, 531**
muscle tissue, 50, 523
mushrooms, 221, 230–231, **231**
mutation(s), causes of, 123–124
and evolution, 156–157
nature of, 122–123
and new plant strains, 144
and radiation, 123–124
types of, 122
mutation theory of evolution, 156
mutualism, 655
defined, 248
mycelium, 223

mycoplasma, 180–181, **180**
Myriapodia, 387
myxomycophyta, 233, **233**

NADP, and photosynthesis, 68
"naked" seeds, 264
narcotics, 604–605
nares, 479
nasal passages, 570
nastic movements, of plants, 318, **318**
national parks and forests, 709
natural enemies, 644
natural immunization, 202, **202**
natural selection, 18
Darwin's theory of, 155–156
Neanderthal, 519
Needham, John, and spontaneous generation, 21–22, **22**
nematocysts, 345
Nematoda, 356–359, **357, 358**
nematode, structure of, 375
nephridia, 361
nephron(s), 564–565, **565**
nerve(s), described, 581–582
nerve cell(s), *see* neuron(s)
nerve cord, 411
nerve impulse, 582–583, **582**
nerve net, 346, 350–351
nervous reaction(s), 586, 587–588
nervous system, human, 525
alcohol effect on, 600
parts of, 581–583
nervous tissues, human, 523
neuron(s), 581–582, **581, 582**
neurospora, isolating nutritional
mutant of, **125**
neurotoxin, 465
neutron(s), 30
newts, 440–441
niche, defined, 647
nictitating membrane, 444
nitrification, 641
nitrogen cycle, 640–642, **640**
nitrogen fixation, 641, **641**
nocturnal animal(s), 660
nodes, 294
nondisjunction, 116–117
in human chromosomes, 136–138
nonliving things, defined, 13
nonsense codons, 81
North American climatic zones, 672
Norway maple, 274
nose, in respiration, 570
Nostoc, 239
notochord, 411
nuclear membrane, 44
nucleic acid(s), described, 40–41
in viruses, 174–175
nucleolus, 44, **45**
nucleoplasm, 44
nucleotide, defined, 80
nucleus, atomic, 29
cell, 44–45, **44, 45**
nudibranch, 371
nutrition, and cells, 44
nutritional relationships, 652–656,
652, 653, 654

obligate aerobes, bacteria as, 188
octopus, 372, **372**
Oedogonium, reproduction in, 243–244,
243
oil(s), 38
see also fat(s)

development of, 526, **526**
 and chimpanzee compared, 514, **514**
 and primate compared, **520**
slime layer, of bacteria, 185
slime molds, 233, **233**
slugs, 371–372, **371**
small intestine, 545
 absorption in, 549–550, **550**
 digestion in, 548–549
smallpox vaccine, 203–204
smell, as sense, 589–590, **590**
smog, 694, **694**
smoking, dangers of, 597–599, **598**
 effect on body, 598–599, **598**
smooth muscle, 529, **530**
smuts, 229–230, **230**
snails, 371–372, **371**
snakes, described, 459
 feeding habits of, 460–461
 head of, 459–460, **460**
 internal organs of, 462
 movement of, 461–462
 nonpoisonous, 463
 poisonous, **460,** 461, 463–465, **464**
 reproduction in, 462–463, **463**
 structure of, 459–460, **460**
 swallowing in, 461
 venom, 461, 465
snapping turtle, 468
social insects, 403
 see also honeybee
sodium chloride crystals, 32
sodium ions, 33
soft palate, 542
soft-shelled turtle, 468
soil, composition of, 304–305, **305**
 conservation of, 685–687, **686**
 depletion, 685
 as environmental factor, 648–649, **648**
 erosion, 686–687, **686**
 and water, 304–305
solid, diffusion in liquid, 55
solid state, of matter, 27, **27**
solid wastes, as environmental problem, 691–692
 recycling of, 692–693, **692**
solute, defined, 33
solutions, defined, 33
 hypotonic, 57–59
 isotonic, 59
 saturated, 33
solvent, defined, 33
somatic mutation, defined, 122
sorus, 258
Spallanzani, Lazzaro, and spontaneous generation, 22–23, **22**
spawning, of fish, 432–434, **433, 434**
specialization, cell, 341
 defined, 341
speciation, and adaptive radiation, 160
 and convergent evolution, 161
 defined, 159
species, in classification system, 164, 166
 defined, 159
species immunity, 202
species preservation, 418–419
species traits, 97–98
sperm, in sexual reproduction, 91
sperm cell, human, 624, **624**
sperm nuclei, 326
spermatids, 93
spermatocytes, 92
spermatogenesis, 92
spermatogonial cells, 92

sphagnum moss, 256, **256**
Sphenodon, 458–459, **458**
spicules, 343
spiders, 388–389, **388**
spinal cord, fish, 431–432
 human, 586–587, **586**
spinal nerves, fish, 432
 human, 586–587
spindle, 88
spinneret, 388
spiny anteaters, 493–494
spiracles, grasshopper, 395
spirillum bacteria, 185, **185**
spirochetes, described, 193–194
Spirogyra, 241–242, **241**
 reproduction in, 241–242
sponges, 342–343, **342, 343, 344**
 reproduction in, 344
 structure of, 343–344, **344**
 time scale, **343**
spongy mesophyll, 278
spontaneous generation, 19–24, **19, 20, 21, 22, 23**
sporangiophore, 224
spores, formation of bacterial, 189–190
 production of, **90,** 91
sporophyte generation, 244
squash, genetically manipulated, **140**
squirrels, isolation and evolution of, **159**
stamen, 99, 324
Stanley, Wendell, and viruses, 174
starch(es), 37, 538
starfish, 166, 372–374, **373, 374**
statocyst, 385
Stegosaurus, 455
stem(s), growth of, 296–297, **296**
 herbaceous dicotyledonous, 300, **300**
 modified, 301–302, **302**
 monocotyledonous, **300,** 301
 plant, 294–295, **295**
sterile animal, 145
sternum, bird, 479
stimulant(s), as drugs, 606–607
stimulating drugs, 604
stipules, 274
stolons, 223, 301, **302**
stomach, grasshopper, 396
 human, 544–545
stomata, 277, **277**
 function and work of, 282–283, **282**
strawberry, vegetative reproduction in, **320,** 321
streaming, of cytoplasm, 45
strengthening tissues, of plants, 269
streptomycin, 207
striated muscle tissue, 50
strip cropping, 686, 687
structural formula, defined, 35–36
structural proteins, 38
substrate, defined, 40
succession, 666–668, **667**
 defined, 666
succulent leaves, 284
sucrose, 36–37, 538
sugars, 538
 types of, 36–37
 use by plants, 279
sulfa drugs, 206
supersonic transport (SST), 693
suspension, defined, 34
Sutton, Walter S., and genetic traits, 112–113, **112**
swimmerets, 383
symbiosis, 655, **655**
symbols, for elements, 29

symmetry, bilateral, **352**
 types of, 350–352, **351, 352**
sympathetic nervous system, 587–588
synapses, 92, 582
synovial fluid, 528
synthetic vitamins, 536
syphilis organism, 193
syrinx, 482
systemic circulation, 562
systole, 560

tadpole, 441, 450–451, **451**
 see also frog(s)
taiga, as biome, 675–676, **675**
tapeworms, 355–356, **356**
taproot, 288–289, **289**
taste, 589, **589**
taste buds, 543
Tatum, Edward L., and mutant genes, 125
taxonomy, 163–164
 see also classification
tears, as defense against disease, 199
teeth, human, compared with chimpanzee and baboon, 515, **515**
 in digestion, 543–544, **544**
 mammalian, 492, **492**
telophase, of mitosis, 89, **89**
telson, 383
temperate phage, 179, **180**
temperature, and diffusion, 56
 as environmental factor, 649
 and gene action, 119
 and photosynthesis, 71–72
temperature inversion, 694
template, RNA as, 81
temporary wilting, 310, **310**
tendons, 530–531
tendrils, 284
tentacles, hydra, 345
terracing, 686, 687
terrapins, 468
terrestrial plants, defined, 650
testes(a), 92
 human, 617–618
 in reproduction, 623
testa, seed, 332
testosterone, 617–618
tetracycline antibiotics, 207
tetrad, 92
thallus, 236, 257
theory, defined, 6
thermal pollution, 690
thigmotropism, 317
thoracic cavity, 525
thymine, in DNA, 80
thymus, 618
thyroid gland, 611, **611**
 measuring activity of, 613–614, **613**
 and metabolic processes, 611–614
ticks, 389
tidal pool, 665
tide, 665
time scales, *see* individual time scales
tissue(s), bark, 297–298, **298**
 blood as, 552–553
 defined, 50
 leaf, 276, 279
 muscle, 50, 523
 nervous, 523
 root, 291–292, **291**
  (table), 293
 in seed plants, 268–271, **270**
 vascular, 269, 271
 wood, 298–299